W9-CHW-000

PrincetonReview.com

THE BEST 371 COLLEGES

2010 Edition

**By Robert Franek,
Tom Meltzer, Christopher Maier, Erik Olson,
Julie Doherty, and Eric Owens**

Random House, Inc., New York
2010 Edition

The Princeton Review, Inc.
2315 Broadway
New York, NY 10024
E-mail: bookeditor@review.com

© 2009 by The Princeton Review, Inc.

All rights reserved under International and Pan-American Copyright Conventions. Published in the United States by Random House, Inc., New York, and simultaneously in Canada by Random House of Canada Limited, Toronto. This is a revised edition of a book first published in 1992.

All rankings, ratings, and listings are intellectual property of The Princeton Review, Inc. No rankings, ratings, listings, or other proprietary information in this book may be repurposed, abridged, excerpted, combined with other data, or altered for reproduction in any way without express permission of TPR.

ISBN   978-0-375-42938-5

VP, Publisher: Robert Franek
Editors: Steven Aglione, Seamus Mullarkey, Laura Braswell
Senior Production Editor: M. Tighe Wall
AVP, Production: Scott Harris
AVP, Data Collection: Ben Zelevansky

Printed in the United States of America on partially recycled paper.

9 8 7 6 5 4 3 2 1

2010 Edition

ACKNOWLEDGMENTS

Each year we assemble an awe-inspiringly talented group of colleagues who work together to produce our guidebooks; this year is no exception. Everyone involved in this effort—authors, editors, data collectors, production specialists, and designers—gives so much more than is required to make *The Best 371 Colleges* an exceptional student resource guide. This new edition gives prospective college students what they really want: The most honest, accessible, and pertinent information about the colleges they are considering attending.

My sincere thanks go to the many who contributed to this tremendous project. I know our readers will benefit from our collective efforts to collect the opinions of current students at the outstanding schools we profile. A special thank you goes to our authors, Tom Meltzer, Christopher Maier, Erik Olson, Julie Doherty, and Eric Owens, for their dedication in sifting through tens of thousands of surveys to produce the essence of each school profiled. Very special thanks go to Seamus Mullarkey and Laura Braswell for their editorial commitment and vision. A warm and special thank you goes to our Student Survey Manager Andrea Kornstein, who works exceptionally well with school administrators and students alike. Andrea is in the trenches every day, and her spirit never wavers. My continued thanks go to our data collection pros, Ben Zelevansky and David Soto, for their successful efforts in collecting and accurately representing the statistical data that appear with each college profile. A sincere thank-you goes to Ben Zelevansky for all the detailed work he does with the data for generation and presentation. The enormousness of this project and its deadline constraints could not have been realized without the calm presence of our production team, Scott Harris, AVP, Production; and M. Tighe Wall, Senior Production Editor. Their unconditional dedication, focus, and most important, careful eyes, continue to inspire and impress me. They deserve great thanks for their flexible schedules and uncompromising efficiency. Special thanks also go to Jeanne Krier, our Random House publicist, for the work she has done on this book and the overall series since its inception. Jeanne continues to be my trusted colleague, media advisor, and friend. I would also like to make special mention of Tom Russell and Nicole Benhabib, our Random House publishing team, for their continuous investment and faith in our ideas. Last, I thank John Katzman, Mark Chernis, and Young Shin for their steadfast confidence in this book and our publishing department, and for always being the champions of student opinion. It is a pleasure to work with each of you. Again, to all who contributed so much to this publication, thank you for your efforts; they do not go unnoticed.

Robert Franek
VP—Publisher
Lead Author—*The Best 371 Colleges*

DOONESBURY

By Garry Trudeau

DOONESBURY © 1999 G.B. Trudeau. Reprinted with permission of UNIVERSAL PRESS SYNDICATE. All rights reserved.

Contents

PART 5: **INDEXES** 801

PART I INTRODUCTION

Getting Into College: A Guide For High School Students

What we've put together in this book is a guide to the nation's 371 most academically outstanding institutions so that you can be informed about the unique opportunities these schools offer and what it's really like to be a student at them. As selective as you'll be about choosing the right college for you, know that many of the colleges we profile will be selective in choosing the students right for them. While some of the schools you'll read about here admit upwards of 80% of their applicants, the majority have many more applicants than they have seats to fill and some admit less than 10% of the students who apply. That means—depending on which colleges you're pinning your hopes on attending—you are likely going to have to put quite a bit of effort into getting in. High grades in challenging courses are just the beginning!

If you're like most of the 2 million (and growing!) high school students who apply to college each year, you're probably wondering what college admissions officers are really looking for in an applicant. What exactly does it take to get into college? What can I do to make my application stand out? Once I get accepted, how do I know which college is best for me?

In order to get you started on the road to a successful application, we're going to give you a few goals, suggestions and tips for checkpoints along the way. This brief primer will help you know what you should be doing year by year in high school to prepare yourself for admission to your "Best" college.

6 STEPS TO GETTING INTO COLLEGE

Sure, high school is supposed to be fun, but putting some effort into your schoolwork and extracurricular experiences can make applying to your choice colleges a lot less stressful. Though it might sound like boring advice, the following steps are extremely important!

1. Work hard for good grades.
2. Enroll in challenging courses.
3. Spend time preparing for the SAT or the ACT and SAT Subject Tests.
4. Polish your writing skills.
5. Establish relationships with teachers and advisors who can write strong letters of recommendation for you.
6. Get involved in some activities, community service, or work experiences that will enable you to show your values, talents and skills.

NEED MORE HELP?

For more information on how you can make the most of your high school years and turn those experiences into a successful college application, check out our offering of college admissions books at PrincetonReview.com/bookstore.

Freshman Year

Getting a good start is the best way to get a strong finish! You don't want to have to play catch-up during your junior and senior years when you're supposed to be focusing on bigger things. During your freshman year, make sure you concentrate on your studies and work hard to earn good grades. Get to know your teachers and ask for their help if you are having trouble in a subject—as well as if you just really enjoy it and want to learn more. They'll most certainly want to help you do your best. If there is an honor roll at your school, make it a goal to get on it. And if your grades are so good that you qualify for membership in the National Honor Society, pat yourself on the back and don't think twice about accepting the invitation to join. Make it a point to meet your guidance counselor so you can begin pinpointing colleges you may be interested in and studying for the courses and admission tests they require. The great thing about freshman year is that you have plenty of time to focus on projects that can make your admissions applications during your senior year look the best they can. Make sure you take hold of that opportunity!

> *"During your freshman year, make sure you concentrate on your studies and work hard to earn good grades."*

Read a Good Book! (or two)

Strong vocabulary and reading skills are essential to doing well on the SAT and ACT (and most tests you'll take for that matter — even math tests require good reading skills!). By cracking open a few good books, you can do some early prep for both tests. Here are some books we love by interesting authors. Not only will you learn some stuff by reading them, but we think you'll love them too!

- *The Curious Incident of the Dog in the Night-Time: A Novel* by Mark Haddon
- *A Heartbreaking Work of Staggering Genius* by Dave Eggers
- *Life of Pi* by Yann Martel
- *Reading Lolita in Tehran* by Azar Nafisi
- *White Teeth* by Zadie Smith

Another Good Book

For extra practice building your vocabulary, check out our *Word Smart* books. Our flagship *Word Smart* book has more than 1,500 words including our "SAT Hit Parade": words most frequently on the SAT.

Sophomore Year

As a sophomore, you'll need to stay focused on your studies, If you didn't earn strong grades during your freshman year, start doing so this year. Scope out the Advanced Placement courses that are offered at your school. You'll want to sign up for as many AP courses as you can reasonably take, starting in your junior year. In sophomore year, you'll also want to choose one or more extracurriculars that interest you. Admissions officers tell us they look favorably on involvement in student government, student newspaper, community service, and sports. What you don't want to do is overload your schedule with activities just to rack up a long list of extracurriculars. Colleges would much rather see you focus on a few worthwhile extracurriculars than divide your time among a bunch of different activities that you're not passionate about. Your sophomore year is when you'll have an opportunity to take the PSAT. Given every October, the PSAT is a shortened version of the SAT. It is used to predict how well you will do on the SAT, and it determines eligibility for National Merit Scholarships. While your PSAT scores won't count until you retake the test in your junior year, you should approach this as a test run for the real thing, because the real thing is coming, and it's coming fast. Sophomore year will be over before you know it, and you'll soon have to step it up and be running strong in the critical part of the race to reach the application finish line.

> "Colleges would much rather see you focus on a few worthwhile extracurriculars than divide your time among a bunch of different activities that you're not passionate about."

What Should You Do This Summer?

Ahhh, summer. The possibilities seem endless. You can get a job, intern, travel, study, volunteer, or do nothing at all. Here are a few ideas to get you started:

- Go to college: No, not for real. However, you can participate in summer programs at colleges and universities at home and abroad. Programs can focus on anything from academics (stretch your brain by taking an intensive science or language course) to sports to admissions guidance. This is also a great opportunity to explore college life firsthand, especially if you get to stay in a dorm.
- Prep for the PSAT, SAT, or ACT: So maybe it's not quite as adventurous as trekking around Patagonia for the summer (it's also not as expensive!) or as cool as learning to slam dunk at basketball camp, but hey, there's nothing adventurous or cool about being rejected from your top-choice college because of unimpressive test scores. Plus, you'll be ahead of the game if you can return to school with much of your PSAT, SAT, and ACT preparation behind you.
- Research scholarships: College is expensive. While you should never rule out a school based on cost, the more scholarship money you can secure beforehand, the more college options you will have. You'll find loads of info on financial aid and scholarships (including a scholarship search tool) on our site, PrincetonReview.com.

Get Help

Admissions officers will want to see that you've earned high grades in challenging classes. The Princeton Review's test-prep series, *Cracking the AP*, offers guides to the most popular AP subject tests to help give you a leg up on passing the exams . High AP scores can boost your chances of admission, plus they are used for placement in college courses and for awarding college credit (ka-ching! ka-ching!) saving on tuition costs! We also offer *Cracking the PSAT /NMSQT,* which has two full-length practice tests and tips on how to score your best on the test. And a great vocabulary will help you with both AP classes and the PSAT, so sign up for the Princeton Review's Vocab Minute on PrincetonReview.com.

Junior Year

Your junior year is going to be exciting and challenging and extremely important in your academic career. You'll start the year off by taking the PSAT in October. High PSAT scores in junior year qualify you for the National Merit Scholarship competition. To become a finalist, you also need great grades and a recommendation from your school. It's critical that your junior-year grades are solid.

"When colleges look at your transcripts they put a heavy emphasis on junior-year grades."

When colleges look at your transcripts they put a heavy emphasis on junior-year grades. Decisions are made before admissions officers see your second-semester, senior-year grades and possibly before they see your first-semester, senior-year grades! During your junior year, you'll probably take the SAT or ACT test for the first time. Most colleges require scores from one of these tests for admission and/or scholarship award decisions. Also take time during your junior year to research colleges, and, if possible, visit schools high on your "hopes" list. When researching colleges, you'll want to consider a variety of factors besides whether or not you can get in, including location, school size, majors or programs offered that interest you, and cost and availability of financial aid. It helps to visit schools because it's the best way to learn whether a school may be right for you. If you can schedule an interview with an admissions officer during your visit, it may help him or her discover how right you may be for the school.

ACT or SAT?

Not sure which test to take? First make sure that all the schools to which you're applying accept both tests (nearly all colleges now do so, but it's best to check). Then take the test on which you do better. Visit PrincetonReview.com to take a free assessment test that will help you identify whether the ACT or SAT is better for you. We also have a new book on this very subject: *ACT or SAT? Choosing the Right Exam for You.* More and more students are opting to take the ACT in addition to, or instead of, the SAT. No matter which test you end up taking, you should plan to spend 3 to 12 weeks preparing for the tests.

About the SAT: The SAT is comprised of Math, Critical Reading, and Writing sections. Colleges will see your individual section scores and your composite score, but generally they'll be most concerned with your composite score. Prior to March 2009, if you took the SAT several times, all your scores were sent to the colleges, but effective with the March 2009 SAT and May 2009 SAT Subject

Tests, a new "Score Choice" policy is in place. It allows students to choose which scores (of a complete SAT test, not of one section of a test) will be sent to colleges. However, some colleges are asking to see all of your test scores, so be sure to check this out on a per school basis.

About the ACT: The ACT has an English, Reading, Math, and Science section, plus the optional Writing section. (Some schools require the essay, so be sure to ask before you take the test.) You can take the ACT several times and choose which of your scores will be sent to the colleges.

About SAT Subject Tests: Most highly selective colleges also require you to take three SAT Subject Tests in addition to the SAT or ACT. If you have SAT Subject Tests to take, plan now. You can't take the SAT and SAT Subject Tests on the same day.

Senior Year

It's finally here! Senior year! It's now time to get serious about pulling everything together on your applications. Deadlines will vary from school to school, and you will have a lot to keep track of, so make checklists of what's due when. If you're not happy with your previous SAT scores, you should take the October SAT. If you still need to take any SAT Subject Tests, now's the time.

When you ask teachers to write recommendations for you, give them everything they need. Tell them your application deadline and include a stamped, addressed envelope, or directions on how to submit the recommendation online, and be sure to send them a thank-you note after you know the recommendation was turned in.

Your essay, on the other hand, is the one part of your application you have total control over. Don't repeat information from other parts of your application. And by all means, proofread! You'll find tips from admissions officers on what they look for (and what peeves them the most) about college applicants' essays in our book, *College Essays That Made a Difference.*

If you have found the school of your dreams and you're happy with your grades and test scores, consider filing an early decision application. Many selective colleges commit more than half of their admissions spots to early decision applicants. To take this route, you must file your application in early November. By mid-December, you'll find out whether you got in—but there's a catch. If you're accepted early decision to a college, you must withdraw all applications to other colleges. This means that your financial aid offer might be hard to negotiate, so be prepared to take what you get. Regardless of which route you decide to take, have a backup plan. Make sure you apply to at least one safety school—one that you feel confident you can get into and afford. Another option is to apply early decision at one school, but apply to other colleges during the regular decision period in the event that you are rejected from the early decision college.

We know how exciting but stressful that decision can be. If you're having a difficult time choosing between two colleges, try to visit each of them one more time. Can you imagine yourself walking around that campus, building a life in that community, and establishing friendships with those people? Finally, decide and be happy. Don't forget to thank your recommenders and tell them where you'll be going to school. Some of the best times of your life await!

Our Other "Majorly" Helpful Books

Our *College Navigator* book has hundreds of lists of colleges identifying everything from top schools for 70 different majors to schools that offer free-trade coffee in their dining halls and even schools that let you bring your pets!

Our *K & W Guide to Colleges for Students with Learning Disabilities or Attention Deficit Disorders* profiles more than 300 schools and includes advice from specialists in the field of learning disabilities, and strategies to help students identify and successfully apply to the best programs for their needs.

Our *Gay & Lesbian Guide to College Life* addresses challenges that LGBT students face from finding and applying to colleges to dealing with campus life issues. Appendixes provide lists of LGBT scholarships, support networks, advocacy groups, and academic/career resources.

Our *Guide to College Majors* profiles more than 400 undergraduate majors and covers high school preparation for them, college courses you'll likely take, career options, and salary prospects.

You'll find information about these and our more than 165 guidebooks at PrincetonReview.com/bookstore.

Paying for College: Savvy Strategies for Financial Aid

The Princeton Review's *Paying for College Without Going Broke* is the only annually updated guide to financial aid that has detailed, line-by-line strategies for completing the highly complicated FAFSA for the upcoming school year (as well as the CSS/PROFILE form) to one's best advantage. It explains how the financial aid process works and reveals strategies—all legal—for maximizing your eligibility for aid. Authored by Kal Chany, one of the nation's most widely sourced experts on college funding, it also includes annually updated information on education tax breaks, college savings programs, and student and parent loans.

See page 814 for more information.

Financial Aid 101

All students applying for financial aid (including federal, state, and institutional need-based aid), need to complete the FAFSA (Free Application for Federal Student Aid) form. The FASFA is the need analysis document used to determine your "EFC" (Expected Family Contribution)—the amount of money the family is expected to ante up toward the cost of college. The form is very complex (it has more than 100 questions), and it's revised each year. The FAFSA form for aid applicants for the 2011–12 school year will be available online (and in paper versions in high schools) in December 2010, but you can't submit it until January 2011. You may also need to complete the PROFILE form (required by many private colleges and some state schools and available via The College Board), state aid forms, and forms provided by the colleges.

In March/April, colleges will send you a decision from the admissions office regarding your admission or rejection. If you are admitted (and you applied for financial aid) you'll also receive a decision from the financial aid office detailing your aid award package. The decision from the financial aid office can sometimes be appealed. The decision from the admissions office is almost always final. If you are wait-listed, don't lose hope. Write a letter to the college expressing how much you'd still like to attend the school and include an update on your recent activities. When colleges admit students from wait lists, they almost always give preference to students who have made it clear that they really want to attend. It's important to wait until you've heard from all of the colleges you've applied to before making your final choice. May 1 is when you'll need to commit to the lucky college that will have you in its freshman class.

Flip to the back of this book to the section "Paying for College 101." It explains briefly how the aid application process works and gives you a quick rundown on the various components of aid award packages. It's a helpful starting point to learn basics about grants, scholarships, work study, and parent and student loan opportunities.

Want to Search by Cost?

We say it over and over: Never rule out applying to a college because of its "sticker" price. Many schools are very generous with their financial aid, and it can cost less to attend an expensive private college than an inexpensive public university. Check out our list of "Best Value Colleges" at PrincetonReview.com/best-value-colleges.aspx to see the 100 institutions (50 public, 50 private) we saluted in January 2009 as our recommended "best value" picks in the nation. You'll also find the list in this book on page 50. (Also in that section of the book, check out our list "Financial Aid Great" on p. 37: it names the top 20 schools at which students we surveyed were happiest with their financial aid awards.) In this book, in addition to giving you tons of facts and stats about the schools' financial aid offerings and policies (we even have a Financial Aid Rating) in the school profiles, we also offer an index of colleges in this book sorted by cost. You'll find it on page 810.

There is also an index by location!

Great Schools for 15 of the Most Popular Undergraduate Majors

Worried about having to declare a major on your college application? Relax. Most colleges won't require you to declare a major until the end of your sophomore year, giving you plenty of time to explore your options. However, problems may arise if you are thinking about majoring in a program that limits its enrollment—meaning that if you don't declare that major early on, you might not get into that program at a later date.

On the flip side, some students declare a major on their application because they believe it will boost their chances of gaining admission. This is a slippery slope to climb, however. If you later decide to change your major and it involves switching from one school within the college to another (from the school of arts and sciences to the school of business, for example), it can be tricky.

Never choose a college solely on the perceived prestige of a particular program. College will expose you to new and exciting learning opportunities. To choose a school based on a major before you even know what else is out there would limit you in many ways. (Choosing a school based on program availability is a different story.) You may also want to investigate opportunities to design your own major.

How Did We Compile These Lists?

Each year we collect data from more than a thousand colleges on the subject of—among many other things—undergraduate academic offerings. We ask colleges not only to report which undergraduate majors they offer, but also which of their majors have the highest enrollment. The list below identifies (in alphabetical order) 15 of the 40 "most popular" majors that the schools responding to our survey reported to us. We also conduct our own research on college majors. We look at institutional data, and we consult with our in-house college admissions experts as well as our National College Counselor Advisory Panel (whom we list in our index, page 802) for their input on schools offering great programs in these majors. We thank them and all of the guidance counselors, college admissions counselors, and education experts across the country whose recommendations we considered in developing these lists. Of the roughly 3,500 schools across the United States, those on these lists represent only a snapshot of the many offering great programs in these majors. Use our lists as a starting point for further research. Some schools on these lists may not appear in the *Best 371 Colleges* (these are marked with an asterisk*), but you can find profiles of them in our *Complete Book of Colleges*, 2010 Edition.

Great Schools for Accounting Majors

- Alfred University
- Auburn University
- Babson College
- Baylor University
- Birmingham—Southern College
- Boston College
- Boston University
- Brigham Young University
- Bucknell University
- Calvin College
- Claremont McKenna College
- Clemson University
- College of Charleston
- Cornell University
- DePaul University
- Drexel University
- Duquesne University
- Elon University
- Emory University
- Fordham University
- Georgetown University
- Indiana University—Bloomington
- Iowa State University
- James Madison University
- Lehigh University
- Michigan State University
- New York University
- Northeastern University
- Pennsylvania State University
- Pepperdine University
- Rider University
- Rochester Institute of Technology
- Seton Hall University
- Suffolk University
- Temple University
- Texas A&M University— College Station
- University of Illinois at Urbana-Champaign
- University of Michigan— Ann Arbor
- University of Pennsylvania
- University of Southern California
- The University of Texas at Austin

Great Schools for Biology Majors

- Agnes Scott College
- Albion College
- Austin College
- Baylor University
- Brandeis University
- Carleton College
- Colby College
- Cornell University
- Drexel University
- Duke University
- Guilford College
- Harvard College
- Haverford College
- Howard University
- Illinois Wesleyan University
- Indiana University—Bloomington
- Johns Hopkins University
- Louisiana State University
- Loyola University—Chicago
- Massachusetts Institute of Technology
- Mount Holyoke College
- The Ohio State University— Columbus
- Pomona College
- Reed College
- Rice University
- Siena College
- Swarthmore College
- Temple University
- Texas A&M University— College Station
- University of California—Davis
- The University of Chicago
- University of Dallas
- University of Delaware
- University of Denver
- University of New Mexico
- University of the Pacific
- Wofford College
- Xavier University of Louisiana

Schools marked with an asterisk do not appear in the *Best 371 Colleges*.
You can find those school profiles in *Complete Book of Colleges, 2010 Edition*.

Great Schools for Business/Finance Majors

- Babson College
- Bentley College
- Boston College
- Carnegie Mellon University
- City University of New York—
  Baruch College
- Cornell University
- DePaul University
- Emory University
- Florida State University
- Indiana University—Bloomington
- Iowa State University
- Lehigh University
- Massachusetts Institute of
  Technology
- Miami University
- Michigan State University
- New York University
- Northwestern University
- Ohio University—Athens
- Rice University
- Seattle University
- University of California—Berkeley
- University of California—
  Los Angeles
- University of Chicago
- University of Florida
- University of Illinois at
  Urbana-Champaign
- University of Michigan
- University of Pennsylvania
- University of Southern California
- The University of Texas at Austin
- University of Virginia
- Washington University in St. Louis
- Wharton University of
  Pennsylvania

Great Schools for Communications Majors

- Augsburg College*
- Baylor University
- Boise State University*
- Boston University
- Bradley University
- City University of New York—
  Hunter College
- Clemson University
- College of Charleston
- Cornell University
- Denison University
- DePaul University
- Duquesne University
- Eckerd College
- Emerson College
- Fairfield University
- Fordham University
- Gonzaga University
- Gustavus Adolphus College
- Hollins University
- Indiana University—Bloomington
- Iowa State University
- Ithaca College
- James Madison University
- Lake Forest College
- Loyola University—New Orleans
- Michigan State University
- Muhlenberg College
- New York University
- Northwestern University
- Pepperdine University
- Ripon College
- Salisbury University
- Seton Hall University
- St. John's University (NY)
- Stanford University
- Suffolk University
- Syracuse University
- University of California—San Diego
- University of California—
  Santa Barbara
- University of Iowa
- University of Maryland—
  College Park
- University of Southern California
- The University of Texas at Austin
- University of Utah

Schools marked with an asterisk do not appear in the *Best 371 Colleges*.
You can find those school profiles in *Complete Book of Colleges, 2010 Edition*.

Great Schools for Computer Science/Computer Engineering Majors

- Auburn University
- Boston University
- Bradley University
- Brown University
- California Institute of Technology
- Carnegie Mellon University
- Clemson University
- Drexel University
- Florida State University
- George Mason University
- Georgia Institute of Technology
- Gonzaga University
- Hampton University
- Harvey Mudd College
- Iowa State University
- Johns Hopkins University
- Lehigh University
- Massachusetts Institute of Technology
- Michigan State University
- New Jersey Institute of Technology
- Northeastern University
- Northwestern University
- Princeton University
- Rice University
- Rochester Institute of Technology
- Rose-Hulman Institute of Technology
- Seattle University
- Stanford University
- State University of New York at Binghamton
- State University of New York—University at Buffalo
- Texas A&M University—College Station
- United States Air Force Academy
- University of Arizona
- University of California—Berkeley
- University of California—Los Angeles
- University of California—Riverside
- University of Illinois at Urbana-Champaign
- University of Massachusetts—Amherst
- University of Michigan—Ann Arbor
- University of Washington

Great Schools for Criminology Majors

- American University
- Auburn University
- City University of New York—John Jay College of Criminal Justice*
- North Carolina State University
- The Ohio State University—Columbus
- Ohio University—Athens
- Quinnipiac University
- Sam Houston State University
- Suffolk University
- University of California—Irvine
- University of Delaware
- University of Denver
- University of Maryland—College Park
- University of Miami
- University of New Hampshire
- University of South Florida
- University of Utah
- Valparaiso University

Schools marked with an asterisk do not appear in the *Best 371 Colleges*.
You can find those school profiles in *Complete Book of Colleges, 2010 Edition*.

Great Schools for Education Majors

- Adelphi University*
- Alma College*
- Arcadia University*
- Ashland University*
- Auburn University
- Augsburg College*
- Barnard College
- Bethany College (WV)*
- Bryn Athyn College of the New Church*
- Bucknell University
- California State University— Sacramento*
- Carthage College*
- City University of New York— Brooklyn College
- City University of New York— Hunter College
- Colgate University
- College of William & Mary
- Columbia College (MO)
- Columbia University
- Cornell College
- Cornell University
- Duquesne University
- Elon University
- Franklin Pierce College*
- Gonzaga University
- Goucher College
- Hardin-Simmons University*
- Hillsdale College
- Indiana University—Bloomington
- Jewish Theological Seminary— Albert A. List College*
- LaSalle University*
- Loyola Marymount University
- Marquette University
- McGill University
- Miami University
- Montana State University—Bozeman*
- Nazareth College of Rochester*
- New York Institute of Technology*
- New York University
- Northeastern University
- Northwestern University
- The Ohio State University—Columbus
- San Francisco State University*
- Simmons College
- Skidmore College
- Smith College
- State University of New York— New Paltz*
- Trinity University (Washington, DC)*
- Trinity University (San Antonio, TX)
- University of Maine
- The University of Montana
- University of St. Thomas (TX)
- University of Toledo*
- Vanderbilt University
- Villanova College
- Wagner College
- Wellesley College
- Xavier University (OH)

Great Schools for Engineering Majors

- California Institute of Technology
- California Polytechnic State University
- Carnegie Mellon University
- Columbia University
- Cooper Union
- Cornell University
- Drexel University
- Duke University
- Franklin W. Olin College of Engineering
- Georgia Institute of Technology
- Harvard College
- Harvey Mudd College
- Illinois Institute of Technology
- Johns Hopkins University
- Massachusetts Institute of Technology
- Pennsylvania State University
- Princeton University
- Purdue University—West Lafayette
- Rose-Hulman Institute of Technology
- Stanford University
- Texas A&M University— College Station
- University of California—Berkeley
- University of California—Los Angeles
- The University of Texas at Austin
- University of Wisconsin—Madison
- Worcester Polytechnic Institute

Schools marked with an asterisk do not appear in the *Best 371 Colleges*.
You can find those school profiles in *Complete Book of Colleges, 2010 Edition*.

Great Schools for English Literature and Language Majors

- Amherst College
- Auburn University
- Bard College
- Barnard College
- Bennington College
- Boston College
- Brown University
- City University of New York— Hunter College
- Claremont McKenna College
- Clemson University
- Colby College
- Colgate University
- Columbia University
- Cornell University
- Dartmouth College
- Denison University
- Duke University
- Emory University
- Fordham University
- George Mason University
- Gettysburg College
- Harvard College
- Johns Hopkins University
- Kenyon College
- The New School University
- Pitzer College
- Pomona College
- Princeton University
- Rice University
- Stanford University
- Syracuse University
- Tufts University
- University of California—Berkeley
- The University of Chicago
- University of Michigan—Ann Arbor
- University of Notre Dame
- University of Utah
- Vassar College
- Washington University in St. Louis
- Wellesley College
- Yale University

Great Schools for History Majors

- Bowdoin College
- Brown University
- Centre College
- Colgate University
- College of the Holy Cross
- Columbia University
- Drew University
- Furman University
- Georgetown University
- Grinnell College
- Hampden-Sydney College
- Harvard College
- Haverford College
- Hillsdale College
- Kenyon College
- Oberlin College
- Princeton University
- Trinity College (CT)
- Tulane University
- University of Virginia
- Wabash College
- Washington and Lee University
- Yale University

Schools marked with an asterisk do not appear in the *Best 371 Colleges*.
You can find those school profiles in *Complete Book of Colleges, 2010 Edition*.

Great Schools for Journalism Majors

- American University
- Boston University
- Carleton College
- Columbia University
- Emerson College
- Hampton University
- Howard University
- Indiana University at Bloomington
- Loyola University—New Orleans
- Middle Tennessee State University
- Northwestern University
- Ohio University—Athens
- Pennsylvania State University
- Samford University
- St. Bonaventure University
- Syracuse University
- Temple University
- University of Florida
- University of Maryland—College Park
- University of Missouri—Columbia
- The University of North Carolina at Chapel Hill
- University of Oregon
- University of Southern California
- The University of Texas at Austin
- University of Wisconsin—Madison

Great Schools for Marketing and Sales Majors

- Babson College
- Baylor University
- Bentley College
- Duquesne University
- Fairfield University
- Hofstra University
- Indiana University—Bloomington
- Iowa State University
- James Madison University
- Miami University
- Providence College
- Seattle University
- Siena College
- Syracuse University
- Texas A&M University
- University of Central Florida
- University of Michigan—Ann Arbor
- University of Mississippi
- University of Pennsylvania
- University of South Florida
- The University of Texas at Austin

Great Schools for Mechanical Engineering Majors

- Bradley University
- California Institute of Technology
- Clarkson University
- Colorado School of Mines*
- Drexel University
- Franklin W. Olin College of Engineering
- Georgia Institute of Technology
- Harvey Mudd College
- Iowa State University
- Lehigh University
- Massachusetts Institute of Technology
- New Jersey Institute of Technology
- North Carolina State University
- Purdue University—West Lafayette
- Rose-Hulman Institute of Technology
- Stanford University
- State University of New York— University at Buffalo
- Stevens Institute of Technology
- United States Military Academy
- University of California—Berkeley
- University of Illinois at Urbana-Champaign
- University of Michigan—Ann Arbor
- University of Missouri—Rolla
- Worcester Polytechnic Institute

Schools marked with an asterisk do not appear in the *Best 371 Colleges*.
You can find those school profiles in *Complete Book of Colleges, 2010 Edition*.

Great Schools for Political Science/Government Majors

- American University
- Amherst College
- Bard College
- Bates College
- Bowdoin College
- Brigham Young University
- Bryn Mawr College
- Carleton College
- Claremont McKenna College
- College of the Holy Cross
- Columbia University
- Davidson College
- Dickinson College
- Drew University
- Furman University
- George Mason University
- George Washington University
- Georgetown University
- Gettysburg College
- Gonzaga University
- Harvard College
- Kenyon College
- Macalester College
- Princeton University
- Stanford University
- Swarthmore College
- Syracuse University
- University of Arizona
- University of California—Berkeley
- University of California—Los Angeles
- University of Washington
- Vassar College
- Yale University

Great Schools for Psychology Majors

- Albion College
- Bates College
- Carnegie Mellon University
- Clark University
- Colorado State University
- Columbia University
- Cornell University
- Dartmouth College
- Duke University
- George Mason University
- Gettysburg College
- Harvard College
- James Madison University
- Lewis & Clark College
- Loyola University—Chicago
- New York University
- Pitzer College
- Princeton University
- Smith College
- Stanford University
- University of California—Davis
- University of California—Los Angeles
- University of California—Riverside
- University of California—Santa Barbara
- University of California—Santa Cruz
- University of Michigan—Ann Arbor
- University of Southern California
- The University of Texas at Austin
- University of Utah
- Washington University in St. Louis
- Yale University

Schools marked with an asterisk do not appear in the *Best 371 Colleges*.
You can find those school profiles in *Complete Book of Colleges, 2010 Edition*.

How and Why We Produce This Book

This Year's Edition

In the 17 years since the first edition of this book, our *Best Colleges* guide has grown considerably. We've added more than 100 colleges to the guide and deleted several along the way. How we choose the schools for the book, and how we produce it, however, has not changed significantly over the years (with the exception of how we conduct our student survey—more on this follows).

To determine which schools will be in each edition, we don't use mathematical calculations or formulas. Instead we rely on a wide range of input, both quantitative and qualitative. Every year we collect data from nearly 2,000 colleges that we use for our *Complete Book of Colleges*, this book, and our web-based profiles of schools. We visit dozens of colleges and meet with their admissions officers, deans, presidents and college students. We talk with hundreds of high school counselors, parents, and students. Colleges also submit information to us requesting consideration for inclusion in the book. As a result, we are able to maintain a constantly evolving list of colleges to consider adding to each new edition of the book. Any college we add to the guide, however, must agree to support our efforts to survey its students via our anonymous student survey. (Sometimes a college's administrative protocols will not allow it to participate in our student survey; this has caused some academically outstanding schools to be absent from the guide.) Finally, we work to ensure that our roster of colleges in the book presents a wide representation of institutions by region, character, and type. Here you'll find profiles of public and private schools, historically black colleges and universities, men's and women's colleges, science- and technology-focused institutions, nontraditional colleges, highly selective schools, and some with virtually open-door admissions policies.

For this year's edition we added six schools to the guide: Angelo State University, Green Mountain College, Marywood University, Stonehill College, and the University of Charleston.

Our ranking lists in this edition are based on our surveys of 122,000 students attending the 371 colleges in the book. We surveyed about 330 students per campus on average, though that number varies depending on the size of the student population. We've surveyed anywhere from 20-some students at Deep Springs College (100 percent of the all-male student body) to more than 1,000 collegians at such colleges as Drexel University, Clemson University, and the United States Military Academy.

All of the institutions in this guide are academically terrific in our opinion. The 371 schools featured—our picks of the cream of the crop colleges and universities—comprise only the top 10 percent of all colleges in the nation. Not every college will appeal to every student but that is the beauty of it. These are all very different schools with many different and wonderful things to offer. We hope you will use this book as a starting point (it will certainly give you a snapshot of what life is like at these schools) but not as the final word on any one school. Check out other resources. Visit as many colleges as you can. Talk to students at those colleges—ask what they love and what bothers them most about their schools.

> *"We worked to create a guide that would help people who couldn't always get to the campus nonetheless get in-depth campus feedback to find the schools best for them."*

Finally, form your own opinions about the colleges you are considering. At the end of the day, it's what YOU think about the schools that matters most, and that will enable you to answer that all-important question: "Which college is best for me?"

The History of This Book

When we published the first edition of this book in 1992, there was a void in the world of college guides (hard to believe, but true!). No publication provided college applicants with statistical data from colleges that covered academics, admissions, financial aid, and student demographics along with narrative descriptions of the schools based on comprehensive surveys of students attending them. Of course, academic rankings of colleges had been around for some time. They named the best schools on hierarchical lists, from 1 to 200 and upwards, some in tiers. Their criteria factored in such matters as faculty salaries, alumni giving, and peer reviews (i.e. what college administrators thought of the schools that, in many cases, they competed with for students). But no one was polling students at these terrific colleges about their experiences on campus—both inside and outside the classroom. We created our first *Best Colleges* guide to address that void. It was born out of one very obvious omission in college guide publishing and two very deep convictions we held then and hold even more strongly today:

- One: The key question for students and parents researching colleges shouldn't be "What college is best, academically?" The thing is, it's not hard to find academically great schools in this country. (There are hundreds of them.) The key question—and one that is truly tough to answer—is "What is the best college for me?"

- Two: We believe the best way for students and parents to know if a school is right—and ultimately best—for them is to visit it. Travel to the campus, get inside a dorm, audit a class, browse the town and—most importantly—talk to students attending the school. In the end it's the school's customers—its students—who are the real experts about the college. Only they can give you the most candid and informed feedback on what life is really like on the campus.

Guided by these convictions, we worked to create a resource that would help people who couldn't always get to the campus nonetheless get in-depth campus feedback to find the schools best for them. We culled an initial list of 250 academically great schools, based on our own college knowledge and input from 50 independent college counselors. We gathered institutional data from those schools and surveyed 30,000 students attending them (about 120 per campus on average). We wrote the school profiles, incorporating school data and extensive quotes from surveyed students, and we compiled for the book over 60 ranking lists of top 20 schools in various categories based on our surveys of students at the schools.

With support from nearly a million students who've participated in our student surveys over the years, and administrators at nearly 400 colleges, we're pleased to offer what we continue to believe is the most substantive resource you can find to know which of these 371 schools may be best for you.

About Our Student Survey for our "Best Colleges" Books

Our undergraduate student survey is a mammoth undertaking. In the first few years that we published this book, we formally surveyed students at all of the colleges and universities in the book on an annual basis. By the time we'd gone through a few editions, we found that barring some grand upheaval or administrative change on campus, there's little change in student opinion from one year to the next, but that shifts emerge in a third or fourth year (as surveyed students leave or matriculate). With this in mind, we switched to a three-year cycle for formally resurveying each campus. Thus, each year we target about 125 campuses for resurveying. We resurvey colleges more often than that if colleges request it (and we can accommodate the request) or if we believe it is warranted for one reason or another.

In the early years, our surveys were conducted on campuses and on paper, but the launch in the late 1990s of our online survey (http://survey.review.com), has made it possible for students to complete a survey anytime and anywhere. Now more than 99 percent of our student surveys are now completed online. Some schools prefer the old-fashioned paper survey route; in those instances we work with the administration to hire a campus representative (usually a student) to set up shop in one or more highly-trafficked areas of the campus where students can stop and fill out the survey.

Online surveys submitted by students outside of a school's normal survey cycle and independent of any solicitation on our part are factored into the subsequent year's rankings and ratings calculations. In that respect, our surveying is a continuous process. All colleges and universities whose students we plan to survey are notified about the survey through our administrative contacts at the schools. We depend upon them for assistance either in notifying the student body about the availability of the online survey via email or, if the school opts for a paper version of the survey, in identifying common, high-traffic areas on campus at which to survey.

The survey has more than 80 questions divided into four sections: "About Yourself," "Your School's Academics/Administration," "Students," and "Life at Your School." We ask about all sorts of things, from "How many out-of-class hours do you spend studying each day?" to "How do you rate your campus food?" Most questions offer students a five-point grid on which to indicate their answer choices (headers may range from "Excellent" to "Awful"). Eight questions offer students the opportunity to expand on their answers with narrative comment. These essay-type responses are the sources of the student quotations that appear in the school profiles. Once the surveys have been completed and responses stored in our database, every college is given a score (similar to a grade point average) for its students' answers to each question. This score enables us to compare students' responses to a particular question from one college to the next. We use these scores as an underlying data point in our calculation of the ratings in the profile sidebars and the ranking lists in the section of the book titled "Schools Ranked by Category."

Once we have the student survey information in hand, we write the college profiles. Student quotations in each profile are chosen because they represent the sentiments expressed by the majority of survey respondents from the college; or, they illustrate one side or another of a mixed bag of student opinion, in which case there will also appear a counterpoint within the text. In order to guard against producing a write-up that's off the mark for any particular college, we send our administrative contact at each school a copy of the profile we intend to publish prior to its publication date, with ample opportunity to respond with corrections, comments, and/or outright objections. In every case in which we receive requests for changes, we take careful measures to review the school's suggestions against the student survey data we collected and make appropriate changes when warranted.

HOW THIS BOOK IS ORGANIZED

Each of the colleges and universities in this book has its own two-page profile. To make it easier to find and compare information about the schools, we've used the same profile format for every school. Look at the sample pages below: Each profile has nine major components. First, at the very top of the profile you will see the school's address, telephone, and fax numbers for the admissions office, the telephone number for the financial aid office, and the school's website and/or e-mail address. Second, there are two sidebars (the narrow columns on the outside of each page, which consist mainly of statistics) divided into the categories of Campus Life, Academics, Selectivity, and Financial Facts. Third, there are four headings in the narrative text: Students Say, Admissions, Financial Aid, and From the Admissions Office. Here's what you'll find in each part:

The Sidebars

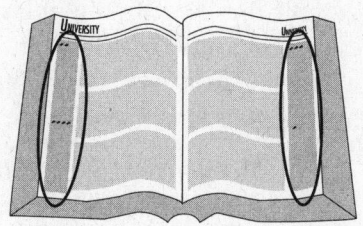

The sidebars contain various statistics culled from our surveys of students attending the school and from questionnaires that school administrators complete at our request in the fall of each year. Keep in mind that not every category will appear for every school—in some cases the information is not reported or not applicable. We compile the eight ratings—Quality of Life, Fire Safety, Green Rating, Academic, Profs Interesting, Profs Accessible, Admissions Selectivity, and Financial Aid—listed in the sidebars based on the results from our student surveys and/or institutional data we collect from school administrators.

These ratings are on a scale of 60–99 If a 60* (60 with an asterisk) appears as any rating for any school, it means that the school reported so few of the rating's underlying data points by our deadline that we were unable to calculate an accurate rating for it. (These measures are outlined in the ratings explanation below.) Be advised that because the Admissions Selectivity Rating is a factor in the computation that produces the Academic Rating, a school that has 60* (60 with an asterisk) as its Admissions Selectivity Rating will have an Academic Rating that is lower than it should be. Also bear in mind that each rating places each college on a continuum for purposes of comparing colleges within this edition only. Since our ratings computations may change from year to year, it is invalid to compare the ratings in this edition to those that appear in any prior or future edition.

Finally, these ratings are quite different from the ranking lists that appear in Part 2 of the book, "Schools Ranked by Category." The ratings are numerical measures that show how a school "sizes up," if you will, on a fixed scale. Our 62 ranking lists report the top 20 (or in some cases bottom 20) schools of the 371 in the book (not of all schools in the nation) in various categories. They are based on our surveys of students at the schools and/or institutional data. We don't rank the schools in the book 1 to 371 hierarchically. Here is what each heading in the sidebar tells you, in order of their appearance:

Quality of Life Rating

On a scale of 60–99, this rating is a measure of how happy students are with their campus experiences outside the classroom. To compile this rating, we weighed several factors, all based on students' answers to questions on our survey. They included the students' assessments of: their overall happiness; the beauty, safety, and location of the campus; comfort of dorms; quality of food; ease of getting around campus and dealing with administrators; friendliness of fellow students; and the interaction of different student types on campus and within the greater community.

> "Ratings are quite different from the ranking lists. The ratings are numerical measures that show how a school "sizes up," if you will, on a fixed scale. Our 62 ranking lists report the top 20 (or in some cases bottom 20) schools of the 371 in the book (not of all schools in the nation) in various categories."

Fire Safety Rating

On a scale of 60–99, this rating measures how well prepared a school is to prevent or respond to campus fires, specifically in residence halls. We asked schools several questions about their efforts to ensure fire safety for campus residents. We developed the questions in consultation with the Center for Campus Fire Safety (www.campusfiresafety.org). Each school's responses to eight questions were considered when calculating its Fire Safety Rating. They cover:

1. The percentage of student housing sleeping rooms protected by an automatic fire sprinkler system with a fire sprinkler head located in the individual sleeping rooms.

2. The percentage of student housing sleeping rooms equipped with a smoke detector connected to a supervised fire alarm system.

3. The number of malicious fire alarms that occur in student housing per year.

4. The number of unwanted fire alarms that occur in student housing per year.

5. The banning of certain hazardous items and activities in residence halls, like candles, smoking, halogen lamps, etc.

6. The percentage of student housing fire alarm systems that, if activated, result in a signal being transmitted to a monitored location, where security investigates before notifying the fire department.

7. The percentage of student housing fire alarm systems that, if activated, result in a signal being transmitted immediately to a continuously monitored location which can then immediately notify the fire department to initiate a response.

8. How often fire safety rules-compliance inspections are conducted each year.

Schools that did not report answers to a sufficient number of questions receive a Fire Safety Rating of 60* (60 with an asterisk). You can also find Fire Safety Ratings for the *Best 371 Colleges* (and several additional schools) in our *Complete Book of Colleges,* 2010 Edition. On page 49 of this book, you'll find a list of the schools with 99 (the highest score) Fire Safety Ratings.

Green Rating

We asked all the schools we collect data from annually to answer a number of questions that evaluate the comprehensive measure of their performance as an environmentally aware and responsible institution. The questions were developed in consultation with ecoAmerica, a research and partnership-based environmental nonprofit that convened an expert committee to design this comprehensive rating system, and cover: 1) whether students have a campus quality of life that is both healthy and sustainable; 2) how well a school is preparing students not only for employment in the clean energy economy of the 21st century, but also for citizenship in a world now defined by environmental challenges; and 3) how environmentally responsible a school's policies are. Each school's responses to ten questions were considered when calculating its Green Rating. They cover:

1. The percentage of food expenditures that go toward local, organic, or otherwise environmentally preferable food.

2. Whether the school offers programs including free bus passes, universal access transit passes, bike sharing/renting, car sharing, carpool parking, vanpooling, or guaranteed rides home to encourage alternatives to single-passenger automobile use for students.

3. Whether the school has a formal committee with participation from students that is devoted to advancing sustainability on campus.

4. Whether new buildings are required to be LEED Silver certified or comparable.

5. The schools overall waste diversion rate.

6. Whether the school has an environmental studies major, minor or concentration.

7. Whether the school has an 'environmental literacy' requirement.

8. Whether a school has produced a publicly available greenhouse gas emissions inventory and adopted a climate action plan consistent with 80% greenhouse gas reductions by 2050 targets.

9. What percentage of the school's energy consumption, including heating/cooling and electrical, is derived from renewable resources (this definition included 'green tags' but not nuclear or large scale hydro power).

10. Whether the school employs a dedicated full-time (or full-time equivalent) sustainability officer.

Colleges that did not supply answers to a sufficient number of the green campus questions for us to fairly compare them to other colleges receive a Green Rating of 60*. On page 49 of this book, you'll find a list of the schools with 99 (the highest score) Green Ratings.

Type of school

Whether the school is public or private.

Affiliation
Any religious order with which the school is affiliated.

Environment
Whether the campus is located in an urban, suburban, or rural setting.

Total undergrad enrollment
The total number of degree-seeking undergraduates who attend the school.

"% male/female" through "# countries represented"
Demographic information about the full-time undergraduate student body, including male to female ratio, ethnicity, and the number of countries represented by the student body. Also included are the percentages of the student body who are from out of state, attended a public high school, live on campus, and belong to Greek organizations.

Survey Says . . .
A snapshot of key results of our student survey. This list shows what the students we surveyed felt unusually strongly about, both positively and negatively, at their schools (see the end of this section for a detailed explanation of items on the list).

Academic Rating
On a scale of 60–99, this rating is a measure of how hard students work at the school and how much they get back for their efforts. The rating is based on results from our surveys of students and data we collect from administrators. Factors weighed included how many hours students reported that they study each day outside of class, students' assessments of their professors' teaching abilities and of their accessibility outside the classroom and the quality of students the school attracts as measured by admissions statistics.

Calendar
The school's schedule of academic terms. A "semester" schedule has two long terms, usually starting in September and January. A "trimester" schedule has three terms, one usually beginning before Christmas and two after. A "quarterly" schedule has four terms, which go by very quickly: the entire term, including exams, usually lasts only nine or ten weeks. A "4-1-4" schedule is like a semester schedule, but with a month-long term in between the fall and spring semesters. (Similarly, a 4-4-1 has a short term following two longer semesters.) When a school's academic calendar doesn't match any of these traditional schedules, we note that by saying "other." For schools that have "other" as their calendar, it is best to call the admissions office for details.

Student/faculty ratio
The ratio of full-time undergraduate instructional faculty members to all undergraduates.

Profs interesting rating
On a scale of 60–99, this rating is based on levels of surveyed students' agreement or disagreement with the statement: "Your instructors are good teachers."

Profs accessible rating
On a scale of 60–99, this rating is based on levels of surveyed students' agreement or disagreement with the statement: "Your instructors are accessible outside the classroom."

% profs teaching UG courses

The percentage of professors who teach undergraduates. This statistic distinguishes between faculty who teach and faculty who focus solely on research.

% classes taught by TAs

The percentage of classes that are taught by TAs (teaching assistants) instead of regular faculty. Many universities that offer graduate programs use graduate students as teaching assistants. They teach undergraduate courses, primarily at the introductory level.

Most common lab size; Most common regular class size

The most commonly occurring class size for regular courses and for labs/discussion sections.

Most Popular Majors

The three majors with the highest enrollments at the school.

Admissions Selectivity Rating

On a scale of 60–99, this rating is a measure of how competitive admission is at the school. This rating is determined by several factors, including the class rank of entering freshmen, test scores, and percentage of applicants accepted.

% of applicants accepted

The percentage of applicants to whom the school offered admission.

% of acceptees attending

The percentage of accepted students who eventually enrolled at the school

accepting a place on wait list

The number of students who decided to take a place on the wait list when offered this option.

% admitted from wait list

The percentage of applicants who opted to take a place on the wait list and were subsequently offered admission. These figures will vary tremendously from college to college, and should be a consideration when deciding whether to accept a place on a college's wait list.

of early decision applicants

The number of students who applied under the college's early decision or early action plan.

% accepted early decision

The percentage of early decision or early action applicants who were admitted under this plan. By the nature of these plans, the vast majority who are admitted ultimately enroll. (See the early decision/action description that follows in the Glossary section for more detail.)

Range/Average SAT Verbal, Range/Average SAT Math, Range/Average SAT Writing

The average and the middle 50 percent range of test scores for entering freshmen.

Don't be discouraged from applying to the school of your choice even if your combined SAT scores are 80 or even 120 points below the average, because you may still have a chance of getting in. Remember that many schools value other aspects of your application (e.g., your grades, how good a match you make with the school) more heavily than test scores.

Minimum TOEFL

The minimum test score necessary for entering freshmen who are required to take the TOEFL (Test of English as a Foreign Language). Most schools will require all international students or non-native English speakers to take the TOEFL in order to be considered for admission.

Average HS GPA

The average grade point average of entering freshman. We report this on a scale of 1.0–4.0 (occasionally colleges report averages on a 100 scale, in which case we report those figures). This is one of the key factors in college admissions.

% graduated top 10%, top 25%, top 50% of class

Of those students for whom class rank was reported, the percentage of entering freshmen who ranked in the top tenth, quarter, and half of their high school classes.

Early decision/action deadlines

The deadline for submission of application materials under the early decision or early action plan.

Early decision, early action, priority, and regular admission deadlines

The dates by which all materials must be postmarked (we'd suggest "received in the office") in order to be considered for admission under each particular admissions option/cycle for matriculation in the fall term.

Early decision, early action, priority, and regular admission notification

The dates by which you can expect a decision on your application under each admissions option/cycle.

Nonfall registration

Some schools will allow incoming students to register and begin attending classes at times other than the fall term, which is the traditional beginning of the academic calendar year. Other schools will allow you to register for classes only if you can begin in the fall term. A simple "yes" or "no" in this category indicates the school's policy on nonfall registration.

Applicants also look at

These lists are based on information we receive directly from the colleges. Admissions officers are annually given the opportunity to review and suggest alterations to these lists for their schools, as most schools track as closely as they can other schools to which applicants they accepted applied, and whether the applicants chose their school over the other schools, or vice versa.

Financial Aid Rating

On a scale of 60–99, this rating is a measure of the financial aid the school awards and how satisfied students are with the aid they receive. It is based on school-reported data on financial aid and students' responses to the survey question, "If you receive financial aid, how satisfied are you with your financial aid package?" On page 49 of this book you'll find a list of the schools with 99 (the highest score) Financial Aid Ratings.

Annual in-state tuition

The tuition at the school, or for public colleges, the cost of tuition for a resident of the school's state. Usually much lower than out-of-state tuition for state-supported public schools.

Annual out-of-state tuition

For public colleges, the tuition for a nonresident of the school's state. This entry appears only for public colleges, since tuition at private colleges is generally the same regardless of state of residence.

Required fees

Any additional costs students must pay beyond tuition in order to attend the school. These often include fitness center fees and the like. A few state schools may not officially charge in-state students tuition, but those students are still responsible for hefty fees.

Tuition and fees

In cases when schools do not report separate figures for tuition and required fees, we offer this total of the two.

Comprehensive fee

A few schools report one overall fee that reflects the total cost of tuition, room and board, and required fees. If you'd like to see how this figure breaks down, we recommend contacting the school.

Room & board

Estimated annual room and board costs.

Books and supplies

Estimated annual cost of necessary textbooks and/or supplies.

% frosh receiving need-based aid

The percentage of all degree-seeking freshmen who applied for financial aid, were determined to have financial need, and received any sort of aid, need-based or otherwise.

% UG receiving need-based aid

The percentage of all degree-seeking undergrads who applied for financial aid, were determined to have financial need, and received any sort of aid, need-based or otherwise.

Avg frosh grant

The average grant or scholarship given to freshmen who receive either or both.

Avg frosh loan

The average amount of loans disbursed to freshmen.

Avg Indebtedness

The average per-borrower cumulative undergraduate indebtedness of those who borrowed at any time through any loan programs (institutional, state, Federal Perkins, Federal Stafford Sub-sidized and Unsubsidized, private loans that were certified by your institution, etc.; exclude parent loans). Include both Federal Direct Student Loans and Federal Family Education Loans.

Nota Bene: The statistical data reported in this book, unless otherwise noted, was collected from the profiled colleges from the fall of 2008 through the spring of 2009. In some cases, we were unable to publish the most recent data because schools did not report the necessary statistics to us in time, despite our repeated outreach efforts. Because the enrollment and financial statistics, as well as application and financial aid deadlines, fluctuate from one year to another, we recommend that you check with the schools to make sure you have the most current information before applying.

Students Say

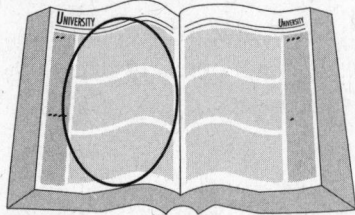

This section shares the straight-from-the-campus feedback we get from the school's most important customers: The students attending them. It summarizes the opinions of freshman through seniors we've surveyed and it includes direct quotes from scores of them. When appropriate, it also incorporates statistics provided by the schools. The Students Say section is divided into three subsections: Academics, Life, and Student Body. The Academics section describes how hard students work and how satisfied they are with the education they are getting. It also often tells you which programs or academic departments students rated most favorably and how professors interact with students. Student opinion regarding administrative departments also works its way into this section. The Life section describes life outside the classroom and addresses questions ranging from "How comfortable are the dorms?" to "How popular are fraternities and sororities?" In this section, students describe what they do for entertainment both on-campus and off, providing a clear picture of the social environment at their particular school. The Student Body section will give you the lowdown on the types of students the school attracts and how the students view the level of interaction among various groups, including those of different ethnic, socioeconomic, and religious backgrounds.

All quotations in these sections are from students' responses to open-ended questions on our survey. We select quotations based on the accuracy with which they reflect overall student opinion about the school as conveyed in the survey results. Entertaining but non-representative student responses about the Academics, Life, and Student Body at a school are featured in a special section in the back of this book titled "Cow Tipping Is Definitely Passé Here." Be sure to check it out for a good laugh.

Admissions

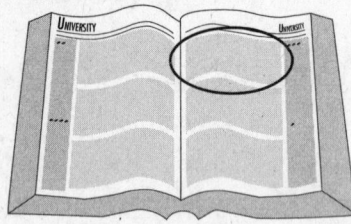

This section lets you know which aspects of your application are most important to the admissions officers at the school. It also lists the high school curricular prerequisites for applicants, which standardized tests (if any) are required, and special information about the school's admissions process (e.g., Do minority students and legacies, for example, receive special consideration? Are there any unusual application requirements for applicants to special programs?).

Financial Aid

Here you'll found out what you need to know about the financial aid process at the school, namely what forms you need and what types of merit-based aid and loans are available. Information about need-based aid is contained in the financial aid sidebar. This section includes specific deadline dates for submission of materials as reported by the colleges. We strongly encourage students seeking financial aid to file all forms—federal, state, and institutional—carefully, fully, and on time.

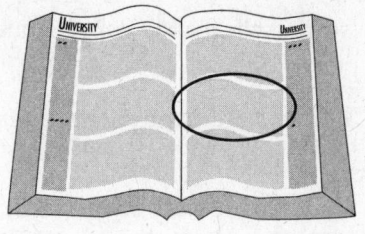

The Inside Word

This section gives you the inside scoop on what it takes to gain admission to the school. It reflects our own insights about each school's admissions process and acceptance trends. (We visit scores of colleges each year and talk with hundreds of admissions officers in order to glean this info.) It also incorporates information from institutional data we collect and our surveys over the years of students at the school.

From the Admissions Office

This section presents the key things the school's admissions office would like you to know about their institution. For schools that did not respond to our invitation to supply text for this space, we excerpted an appropriate passage from the school's catalog, web site, or other admissions literature. For this section, we also invited schools to submit a brief paragraph explaining their admissions policies regarding the SAT (especially the Writing portion of the exam) and the SAT Subject Tests. We are pleased that nearly every school took this opportunity to clarify its policies as we know there has been some student and parent confusion about how these scores are evaluated for admission.

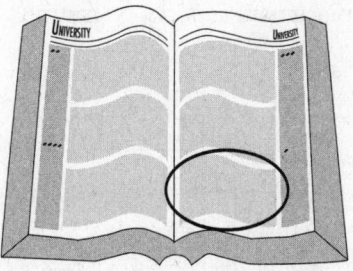

Survey Says

Our Survey Says list, located in the Campus Life sidebar on each school's two-page spread, is based entirely on the results of our student survey. In other words, the items on this list are based on the opinions of the students we surveyed at those schools (*not* on any quantitative analysis of library size, endowment, etc.). These items reveal popular or unpopular trends on campus for the purpose of providing a snapshot of life on *that campus only*. The appearance of a Survey Says item in the sidebar does *not* reflect the popularity of that item relative to its popularity amongst the student bodies at other schools. To ascertain the relative popularity of certain items/trends on campus, see the appropriate ranking (e.g., for the Survey Says item "Library needs improving," see the "This is a Library?" ranking). Some of the terms that appear on the Survey Says list are not entirely self-explanatory; these terms are defined below.

Different types of students interact: We asked students whether students from different class and ethnic backgrounds interacted frequently and easily. When students' collective response is "yes," the heading "Different types of students interact" appears on the list. When the collective student response indicates there are not many interactions between students from different class and ethnic backgrounds, the phrase "Students are cliquish" appears on the list.

No one cheats: We asked students how prevalent cheating is at their school. If students reported cheating to be rare, the term "No one cheats" shows up on the list.

Students are happy: This category reflects student responses to the question "Overall, how happy are you?"

Students are very religious *or* **Students aren't religious:** We asked students how religious students are at their school. Their responses are reflected in this category.

Diverse student types on campus: We asked students whether their student body is made up of a variety of ethnic groups. This category reflects their answers to this question. This heading shows up as "Diversity lacking on campus" or "Diverse student types on campus." It does not reflect any institutional data on this subject.

Students get along with local community: This category reflects student responses to a question concerning how well the student body gets along with residents of the college town or community.

Career services are great: This category reflects student opinion on the quality of career/job placement services on campus. This heading shows up as "Career services are great."

Cow Tipping?

We hope that the student quotes we include in each school's narrative profile give you some insight into the personalities of the student body of each campus. We do not select quotes for their extreme nature, humor, bias, or perspective. Instead, we dedicate a section of this book titled, "Cow Tipping Is Definitely Passé Here," to these kinds of quotes. To find out what else might be passé, flip to page 795 to check them out!

PrincetonReview.com offers:
Podcasts
Sample tests
More information on college admissions

ABOUT THE COLLEGE RANKING LISTS

Finding a college that has terrific academics is easy. There are hundreds of academically great colleges out there. Their campus cultures, student bodies, and school offerings, however, differ widely. Finding the academically great school that is right for you is the tough part. Hence, we compile not one ranking list but 62 unique lists, each one reporting the top 20 (or in some cases bottom 20) schools from our *Best Colleges* book in a specific category.

None of the lists are based on what we think of the schools (though members of the media, the public, and school administrators mistakenly credit or blame us for the results, saying "According to The Princeton Review, X school is the best in the nation for…" or "The Princeton Review ranks Y school the 10th most…."). In fact, the only thing we say is that all of the 371 colleges in this book are outstanding (hence, the "Best" designation). It's what students think of their schools—how they rate various aspects of their colleges' offerings and what they report to us about their campus experiences—that results in a school's appearance on our ranking lists.

Here you won't find the colleges in the book ranked hierarchically, 1 to 371. We think such lists—particularly those driven by and perpetuating a "best academics" mania—are not useful for the people they are supposed to serve (college applicants). More and more college administrators—including several at schools ranked high on these lists—agree. In fact, the primary reason we developed this book was to give applicants and parents better and broader information that will help them winnow a list of colleges right for them.

About 85 percent of the schools in our book end up on one or more of the lists in each edition. The students are the raters—we are simply the folks who compile the ranking lists based on their opinions. To college officials happy about the lists their schools are on, we say don't thank us, we're just the messengers. To college officials unhappy about the lists their schools are on (and unsurprisingly, it is mainly they who say our student survey has no validity whatsoever), we say don't blame us, we're just the messengers.

All of these ranking lists are based entirely on students' answers to questions on our surveys (e.g. our "Best Campus Food" list and inverse list, "Is it Food?" are each based on the single survey question, "How do you rate your campus food?") or students' answers to a combination of survey questions (e.g. our "Party Schools" list and our inverse list, "Stone-cold Sober Schools" are each based on students' answers to survey questions concerning the use of alcohol and drugs on their campuses, the popularity of the frat/sorority scene on their campuses, and the number of hours they say they study each day outside of class time).

Each list, even those with somewhat irreverent titles (such as "Dorms Like Dungeons"), covers one of many aspects of a college's character that can be helpful in deciding if it's the right or wrong place for an individual student. The lists report on a wide range of issues that may be important, either singly or, more likely, in combination. Our ranking lists cover: financial aid, campus facilities and amenities, extracurriculars, town-gown relations, the student body's political leanings, social life, race/class relations, gay-friendly (or not so friendly) atmosphere, career services, athletic facilities, and more.

> *"It's what students think of their schools—how they rate various aspects of their colleges' offerings and what they report to us about their campus experiences—that results in a school's appearance on our ranking lists."*

New in this edition are two ranking list categories: "Easiest Campus to Get Around," and "Most Popular Study Abroad Program"

The ranking list category that media covers the most (though it appears 57th among the lists in our "Schools Ranked by Category" section, and is only referenced briefly in our press materials) is the "Party Schools" list. It's even been the subject of a *Doonesbury* cartoon (which appears on the frontispiece of this book) as well as a *USA Today* editorial in which the paper commended us for reporting the list, calling it "a public service." Our "Party Schools" list draws a wide range of reaction every year. Some students complain that their college didn't make the list, while others are irate because their college did. One reporter from the *Washington Post* whose alma mater was #1 on the list several years back wrote a column in which he argued that the ranking was grossly undeserved: He had recently visited his campus and pronounced the then current student body lame as "partiers" compared to the revelers of *his day*.

Many incorrectly assume that an institution that shows up on the "Party Schools" list is not an advisable college to attend. We recommend all 368 schools in this book as outstanding institutions at which to earn one's college degree. But just as the schools on our "Alternative Lifestyle Not an Alternative" (gay-unfriendly) list may not be ideal campuses for gay students, the schools on our "Party Schools" list may not be ideal for students seeking a campus at which the use of alcohol and drugs and the frat/sorority scene is, well, less exuberant.

On the other hand, no one should make the mistake of assuming that the colleges and universities that don't show up on our "Party Schools" list are in any way insulated from the influences of alcohol and drugs on their campuses. An oft-quoted Harvard University School of Public Health study a few years back found that 44 percent of undergraduates, in general, binge drink (consume five or more alcoholic beverages in one sitting for men, four drinks or more for women).[1] These facts are alarming, as they should be. College administrators face tremendous challenges in creating and enforcing campus alcohol and drug use/abuse policies. Many struggle with problems resulting from the prevalence of bars and liquor stores near their campuses; at some universities that have appeared on our "Party Schools" list there are more than 100 such establishments within a few miles from the campus. "Dry campus" policies often exacerbate the problem, driving drinking off-campus, making it even more dangerous for students.

Despite the claims of some administrators at colleges that have repeatedly made our "Party School" list that our reporting this list promotes drinking on campuses (a group of such administrators receiving funding through the American Medical Association to address their campus alcohol problems made the news several years back with this claim, after which *USA Today* published the editorial praising our ranking as a "public service"), we neither encourage nor discourage students who wish to drink. None of our lists promote behavior: They report on it, plain and simple. What we promote is information.

---

1 Harvard University School of Public Health. "College Student Binge Drinking Rates Remain High Despite Efforts by School Administrations." www.hsph.harvard.edu/news/press-releases/2000-releases/press03142000.html.

What we do say to college students—as we have said in this very section of this book for over 10 years—is this: If you're going to drink, do it safely, smartly, responsibly, and legally. If you're going off campus to drink, don't drive back drunk—get a designated driver. Don't let a peer situation (fraternity rush, etc.) put you in jeopardy—it's simply not worth it. Don't use alcohol or drugs as a badge of your coolness—there's not much of a fine line between someone who's socially engaging and someone who's totally disengaging because he or she has performed a chemical auto-lobotomy. Last, don't simply take responsibility for yourself; remember to keep an eye on your friends, and never leave them passed out and alone.

Finally, we'd like to thank all the college officials, college counselors, advisors, students, and parents, who have made this annual guide possible by supporting us these past fifteen years. Our ranking lists have, collectively, been based on surveys of more than 750,000 students whose input has been vital to our publication of this book. We know that it has helped students find great colleges perfect for them, and it has brought to the colleges in our book many outstanding students who otherwise may not have considered attending their institutions.

To all of our readers, we welcome your feedback on how we can continue to improve this guide. We hope you will share with us your comments, questions, and suggestions. Please contact us at Editorial Department, Princeton Review Books, 2315 Broadway, New York, NY 10024, or e-mail us at bookeditor@review.com. We welcome it.

To college applicants, we wish you all the best in your college search. And when you get to your campuses and settle in to your college life, come back to us online; participate in our survey for this book at http://survey.review.com. Let your honest comments about your schools guide prospective students who want your help answering the $64,000 question (goodness knows, the sticker price at some schools may be that high or even higher!): *"Which is the best college for me?"*

WE WANT TO HEAR FROM YOU

To all of our readers, we welcome your feedback on how we can continue to improve this guide. We hope you will share with us your comments, questions, and suggestions. Please contact us at Editorial Department, Princeton Review Books, 2315 Broadway, New York, NY 10024, or e-mail us at bookeditor@review.com.

To college applicants, we wish you all the best in your college search. And when you get to your campuses and settle in to your college life, come back to us online; participate in our survey for this book at http://survey.review.com. Let your honest comments about your schools guide prospective students who want your help answering the $64,000 question (goodness knows, the sticker price at some schools may be that high or even higher!): "Which is the best college for me?"

PART 2

School Rankings and Lists

We present our 62 "Top 20" ranking lists in eight categories.

Schools by Type

Under each list heading, we tell you the survey question or assessment that we used to tabulate the list. We tally student responses to several questions on our survey for our lists "Best Classroom Experience," "Best Quality of Life," and the six lists in our Schools by Type rankings (including our "Party Schools" and "Stone-cold Sober Schools" lists). Be aware that all of our 62 ranking lists are based entirely on our student surveys. They do not reflect our opinions of the schools. They are entirely the result of what students attending these schools tell us about them: It's how students rate their own schools and what they report to us about their campus experiences at them that make our ranking lists so unusual. After all, what better way is there to judge a school than by what its customers—its students—say about it?

Honor Rolls

ACADEMICS/ADMINISTRATION

Best Classroom Experience

Based on a combination of survey questions concerning teachers, classroom/lab facilities, classes attended, and amount of in-class discussion

1. Pomona College
2. Reed College
3. Wellesley College
4. Stanford University
5. Franklin W. Olin College of Engineering
6. Mount Holyoke College
7. Williams College
8. United States Military Academy
9. Princeton University
10. Middlebury College
11. Whitman College
12. Hamilton College
13. Sarah Lawrence College
14. Colgate University
15. Marlboro College
16. Wesleyan College
17. Bennington College
18. University of Richmond
19. Bowdoin College
20. Emerson College

Students Study the Most

How many out-of-class hours do you spend studying each day?

1. California Institute of Technology
2. Massachusetts Institute of Technology
3. Reed College
4. Franklin W. Olin College of Engineering
5. Havard College
6. Middlebury College
7. Swarthmore College
8. University of Chicago
9. Princeton University
10. Davidson College
11. Williams College
12. United States Coast Guard Academy
13. United States Military Academy
14. The Cooper Union for the Advancement of Science and Art
15. Bryn Mawr College
16. Sweet Briar College
17. Carleton College
18. Harvey Mudd College
19. College of the Holy Cross
20. Grinnell College

Students Study the Least
How many out-of-class hours do you spend studying each day?

1. West Virginia University
2. University of Maryland—College Park
3. State University of New York at Albany
4. University of Mississippi
5. University of North Dakota
6. Louisiana State University—Baton Rouge
7. Florida State University
8. University of Florida
9. Florida Southern College
10. University of Georgia
11. Pennsylvania State University—University Park
12. University of Central Florida
13. City University of New York—Brooklyn College
14. Arizona State University
15. The University of Texas at Austin
16. The University of Alabama—Tuscaloosa
17. Ohio University—Athens
18. University of Louisiana at Lafayette
19. Rutgers, The State University of New Jersey—New Brunswick
20. Salisbury University

Professors Get High Marks
Are your instructors good teachers?

1. Davidson College
2. Wellesley College
3. Sweet Briar College
4. Middlebury College
5. Reed College
6. Kenyon College
7. Franklin W. Olin College of Engineering
8. College of William and Mary
9. Whitman College
10. New College of Florida
11. Hampden-Sydney College
12. Sarah Lawrence College
13. Claremont McKenna College
14. Carleton College
15. Harvey Mudd College
16. Wabash College
17. Marlboro College
18. Swarthmore College
19. Wittenberg University
20. Oglethorpe University

Professors Get Low Marks
Are your instructors good teachers?

1. United States Merchant Marine Academy
2. Stevens Institute of Technology
3. California Institute of Technology

4. University of Illinois at Urbana-Champaign
5. Georgia Institute of Technology
6. University of Connecticut
7. University of California—San Diego
8. New Jersey Institute of Technology
9. Illinois Institute of Technology
10. Rutgers, The State University of New Jersey—New Brunswick
11. Rensselaer Polytechnic Institute
12. Case Western Reserve University
13. University of California—Riverside
14. University of Rhode Island
15. University of Toronto
16. Johns Hopkins University
17. State University of New York—University at Buffalo
18. Iowa State University
19. Washington State University
20. University of Florida

Most Accessible Professors
Are your instructors accessible outside the classroom?

1. United States Military Academy
2. Sweet Briar College
3. Wabash College
4. United States Air Force Academy
5. Hampden-Sydney College
6. Lawrence University
7. Webb Institute
8. Williams College
9. United States Naval Academy
10. Claremont McKenna College
11. Wellesley College
12. Harvey Mudd College
13. Colgate University
14. University of Puget Sound
15. St. John's College (NM)
16. Davidson College
17. Stonehill College
18. St. John's College (MD)
19. Bowdoin College
20. Simon's Rock College of Bard

Least Accessible Professors
Are your instructors accessible outside the classroom?

1. Illinois Institute of Technology
2. Georgia Institute of Technology
3. University of Toronto
4. Rutgers, The State University of New Jersey—New Brunswick
5. Tuskegee University
6. Stevens Institute of Technology
7. University of Kentucky
8. Howard University
9. Auburn University

10. University of Georgia
11. United States Merchant Marine Academy
12. New Jersey Institute of Technology
13. University of Massachusetts—Amherst
14. University of Rhode Island
15. Drexel University
16. State University of New York at Albany
17. Spelman College
18. University of California—Riverside
19. University of Arizona
20. McGill University

Class Discussions Encouraged
How much of your overall class time is devoted to discussion as opposed to lectures?

1. Sarah Lawrence College
2. Bennington College
3. Marlboro College
4. Eugene Lang College
5. Simon's Rock College of Bard
6. Green Mountain College
7. Prescott College
8. Reed College
9. Hampshire College
10. Sweet Briar College
11. College of the Atlantic
12. Colorado College
13. Hanover College
14. Bard College
15. United States Military Academy
16. Wesleyan College
17. Goucher College
18. Emerson College
19. Stanford University
20. Stonehill College

Class Discussions Rare
How much of your overall class time is devoted to discussion as opposed to lectures?

1. McGill University
2. University of Toronto
3. California Institute of Technology
4. Georgia Institute of Technology
5. University of California—San Diego
6. Missouri University of Science and Technology (formerly University of Missouri—Rolla)
7. North Carolina State University
8. Louisiana State University—Baton Rouge
9. Webb Institute
10. Virginia Tech
11. State University of New York— Stony Brook University
12. Rose-Hulman Institute of Technology
13. Rutgers, The State University of New Jersey—New Brunswick

14. University of California—Davis
15. United States Merchant Marine Academy
16. Clarkson University
17. Stevens Institute of Technology
18. Montana Tech of the Univ. of Montana
19. Texas A&M University—College Station
20. Colorado State University

Most Popular Study Abroad Program
How popular is studying abroad at your school?

1. Colby College
2. Middlebury College
3. Bates College
4. Pepperdine University
5. Goucher College
6. Connecticut College
7. Georgetown University
8. Tufts University
9. Trinity College (CT)
10. Pitzer College
11. Claremont McKenna College
12. Lewis & Clark College
13. Stonehill College
14. Loyola University—Maryland
15. Macalester College
16. Colgate University
17. Dickinson College
18. Hobart and William Smith Colleges
19. Colorado College
20. Beloit College

Best Career Services
Based on students' rating of campus career/job placement services

1. University of Florida
2. Barnard College
3. Clemson University
4. Northeastern University
5. University of Texas at Austin
6. Pennsylvania State University— University Park University
7. Claremont McKenna College
8. Sweet Briar College
9. Rose-Hulman Institute of Technology
10. Yale University
11. Connecticut College
12. Bentley University
13. Smith College
14. Middlebury College
15. Cornell University
16. University of Notre Dame
17. Stonehill College
18. Rochester Institute of Technology
19. American University
20. Franklin W. Olin College of Engineering

Best College Library
Based on students' assessment of library facilities

1. Harvard College
2. Princeton University
3. Columbia University
4. Duke University
5. Loyola University—New Orleans
6. Cornell University
7. College of William and Mary
8. Furman University
9. Colgate University
10. Wesleyan University
11. University of Chicago
12. Mount Holyoke College
13. Emory University
14. Hampden-Sydney College
15. The University of Texas at Austin
16. Brigham Young University (UT)
17. The College of New Jersey
18. Case Western Reserve University
19. Whitman College
20. West Virginia University

This is a Library?
Based on students' assessment of library facilities

1. Clarkson University
2. United States Coast Guard Academy
3. Bradley University
4. Spelman College
5. Bard College
6. University of Dallas
7. College of the Atlantic
8. Duquesne University
9. Eugene Lang College
10. Wells College
11. William Jewell College
12. Tuskegee University
13. Centenary College of Louisiana
14. State University of New York—Purchase College
15. Salisbury University
16. Wagner College
17. United States Merchant Marine Academy
18. Catawba College
19. Stevens Institute of Technology
20. Catholic University of America

Great Financial Aid
Based on students' assessments of how satisfied they are with their financial aid package.

1. Swarthmore College
2. Stanford University
3. Harvard College
4. Washington University in St. Louis
5. Pomona College

6. New College of Florida
7. Ohio University—Athens
8. Princeton University
9. University of Virginia
10. California Institute of Technology
11. Beloit College
12. Lake Forest College
13. Claremont McKenna College
14. Wabash College
15. Denison University
16. Williams College
17. Yale University
18. Amherst College
19. Rice University
20. College of the Atlantic

Students Dissatisfied with Financial Aid
Based on students' assessments of how satisfied they are with their financial aid package.

1. New York University
2. Pennsylvania State University—University Park
3. Connecticut College
4. Elon University
5. Sonoma State University
6. Villanova University
7. Washington State University
8. Auburn University
9. Emerson College
10. University of Massachusetts—Amherst
11. Haverford College
12. Quinnipiac University
13. Rutgers, The State University of New Jersey—New Brunswick
14. Colorado State University
15. Bucknell University
16. University of Mary Washington
17. Hampton University
18. State University of New York at Albany
19. University of Arizona
20. Miami University

School Runs Like Butter
Overall, how smoothly is your school run?

1. Stanford University
2. Middlebury College
3. Claremont McKenna College
4. Davidson College
5. Bowdoin College
6. Rose-Hulman Institute of Technology
7. Pomona College
8. Wabash College
9. Washington University in St. Louis
10. Carleton College
11. University of Notre Dame

12. Whitman College
13. Furman University
14. Princeton University
15. Amherst College
16. Elon University
17. Vanderbilt University
18. Yale University
19. Williams College
20. Clemson University

Long Lines and Red Tape
Overall, how smoothly is your school run?

1. Eugene Lang College
2. United States Merchant Marine Academy
3. Tuskegee University
4. Wells College
5. Hampton University
6. State University of New York—
   Purchase College
7. New York University
8. Drexel University
9. State University of New York at Albany
10. Howard University
11. Hampshire College
12. Illinois Institute of Technology
13. The Cooper Union for the Advancement
    of Science and Art
14. State University of New York—
    Stony Brook University
15. Fisk University
16. City University of New York—
    Hunter College
17. University of New Orleans
18. Catholic University of America
19. University of New Mexico
20. Whittier College

QUALITY OF LIFE

Happiest Students
Overall, how happy are you?

1. Brown University
2. Clemson University
3. Claremont McKenna College
4. Stanford University
5. Bowdoin College
6. Yale University
7. Stonehill College
8. Rice University
9. St. Mary's College of Maryland
10. Colorado College
11. University of Alabama at Birmingham
12. Prescott College
13. University of Dayton

14. College of William and Mary
15. Whitman College
16. Franklin W. Olin College of Engineering
17. Colgate University
18. James Madison University
19. Duke University
20. Worcester Polytechnic Institute

Least Happy Students
Overall, how happy are you?

1. United States Merchant Marine Academy
2. United States Coast Guard Academy
3. State University of New York—
   Stony Brook University
4. Fisk University
5. New York University
6. New Jersey Institute of Technology
7. Tuskegee University
8. University of California—Riverside
9. United States Naval Academy
10. State University of New York at Albany
11. Illinois Institute of Technology
12. University of Massachusetts-Amherst
13. Clarkson University
14. Eugene Lang College
15. Hanover College
16. United States Air Force Academy
17. Whittier College
18. United States Military Academy
19. Alfred University
20. Trinity College (CT)

Most Beautiful Campus
Based on students' rating of campus beauty

1. Colgate University
2. Sweet Briar College
3. Mount Holyoke College
4. Scripps College
5. Sewanee—The University of the South
6. University of San Diego
7. Princeton University
8. Wellesley College
9. Lewis & Clark College
10. University of California—Santa Cruz
11. University of Notre Dame
12. St. Mary's College of Maryland
13. Vassar College
14. Stonehill College
15. Pepperdine University
16. Swarthmore College
17. Rollins College
18. Wittenberg University
19. Wagner College
20. University of Richmond

Least Beautiful Campus
Based on students' rating of campus beauty

1. New Jersey Institute of Technology
2. State University of New York at Albany
3. Drexel University
4. State University of New York— Purchase College
5. University of Dallas
6. City University of New York— Hunter College
7. Harvey Mudd College
8. University of Massachusetts—Amherst
9. Clarkson University
10. North Carolina State University
11. Illinois Institute of Technology
12. University of Tennessee
13. Massachusetts Institute of Technology
14. University of New Orleans
15. Rutgers, The State University of New Jersey—New Brunswick
16. Eugene Lang College
17. Xavier University of Louisiana
18. Rochester Institute of Technology
19. State University of New York— University at Buffalo
20. Missouri University of Science and Technology (formerly University of Missouri—Rolla)

Easiest Campus to Get Around
Based on students' assessments of ease of getting around their campus

1. Claremont McKenna College
2. Agnes Scott College
3. Davidson College
4. Susquehanna University
5. Hendrix College
6. Loyola University—New Orleans
7. University of Dayton
8. Grinnell College
9. Illinois Wesleyan University
10. Connecticut College
11. Stanford University
12. Sweet Briar College
13. Stonehill College
14. DePauw University
15. Catawba College
16. Columbia University
17. Southwestern University
18. Bowdoin College
19. Scripps College
20. Smith College

Best Campus Food
Based on students' rating of campus food

1. Virginia Tech
2. Bowdoin College
3. St. Olaf College
4. James Madison University
5. Franklin W. Olin College of Engineering
6. Colby College
7. Bryn Mawr College
8. Gustavus Adolphus College
9. Cornell University
10. Washington University in St. Louis
11. University of Notre Dame
12. University of Georgia
13. Wheaton College (IL)
14. Middlebury College
15. University of California—Los Angeles
16. Claremont McKenna College
17. Bates College
18. College of the Atlantic
19. Purdue University—West Lafayette
20. Gettysburg College

Is It Food?
Based on students' rating of campus food

1. United States Merchant Marine Academy
2. Wells College
3. New College of Florida
4. Fisk University
5. Wesleyan College
6. State University of New York at Albany
7. Eugene Lang College
8. Hampton University
9. United States Air Force Academy
10. Carnegie Mellon University
11. Centenary College of Louisiana
12. Hiram College
13. Fordham University
14. Hollins University
15. Bard College
16. United States Naval Academy
17. Flagler College
18. Whittier College
19. Catawba College
20. Missouri University of Science and Technology (formerly University of Missouri—Rolla)

Dorms Like Palaces
Based on students' rating of dorm comfort

1. Smith College
2. Loyola University Maryland
3. Franklin W. Olin College of Engineering
4. Scripps College
5. Bennington College

6. Bryn Mawr College
7. Bowdoin College
8. The George Washington University
9. Harvard College
10. Washington University in St. Louis
11. Claremont McKenna College
12. Trinity University
13. Mount Holyoke College
14. Pomona College
15. Skidmore College
16. Thomas Aquinas College
17. Wellesley College
18. Pepperdine University
19. Williams College
20. Stanford University

Dorms Like Dungeons
Based on students' rating of dorm comfort

1. Hampton University
2. United States Merchant Marine Academy
3. United States Coast Guard Academy
4. Tuskegee University
5. University of New Orleans
6. University of Louisiana at Lafayette
7. State University of New York at Albany
8. Hanover College
9. University of New Mexico
10. New Jersey Institute of Technology
11. University of Florida
12. The University of Montana
13. University of Idaho
14. Temple University
15. Arizona State University
16. Xavier University of Louisiana
17. University of Mississippi
18. United States Military Academy
19. California State University—Stanislaus
20. The Evergreen State College

Best Quality of Life
Based on The Princeton Review's QUALITY OF LIFE RATING (page 20)

1. Rice University
2. Bowdoin College
3. Claremont McKenna College
4. Washington University in St. Louis
5. Virginia Tech
6. Middlebury College
7. Smith College
8. Barnard College
9. Saint Michael's College
10. Clemson University
11. Bryn Mawr College
12. Westminster College of Salt Lake City
13. Franklin W. Olin College of Engineering

14. St. Olaf College
15. Brown University
16. Davidson College
17. Furman University
18. Stanford University
19. Pomona College
20. Whitman College

POLITICS

Most Conservative Students
Based on students' assessment of their personal political views

1. Texas A&M University—College Station
2. Hillsdale College
3. Grove City College
4. Brigham Young University (UT)
5. Hampden-Sydney College
6. United States Naval Academy
7. College of the Ozarks
8. Wheaton College (IL)
9. University of Dallas
10. United States Merchant Marine Academy
11. United States Air Force Academy
12. Baylor University
13. Samford University
14. Clemson University
15. The University of Alabama—Tuscaloosa
16. Thomas Aquinas College
17. United States Military Academy
18. University of Mississippi
19. Rose-Hulman Institute of Technology
20. United States Coast Guard Academy

Most Liberal Students
Based on students' assessment of their personal political views

1. Warren Wilson College
2. Hampshire College
3. New College of Florida
4. Bennington College
5. Prescott College
6. Bard College
7. Sarah Lawrence College
8. Marlboro College
9. Reed College
10. Occidental College
11. Pitzer College
12. The Evergreen State College
13. Macalester College
14. Wesleyan University
15. Lewis & Clark College
16. Eugene Lang College
17. Vassar College

18. Mills College
19. Swarthmore College
20. Beloit College

Most Politically Active Students
How popular are political/activist groups?

1. The George Washington University
2. American University
3. College of the Atlantic
4. George Mason University
5. New College of Florida
6. United States Military Academy
7. Simon's Rock College of Bard
8. Georgetown University
9. Wesleyan University
10. Claremont McKenna College
11. Harvard College
12. Hampshire College
13. Warren Wilson College
14. Bates College
15. Macalester College
16. Smith College
17. United States Air Force Academy
18. Princeton University
19. United States Naval Academy
20. The University of Texas at Austin

Election? What Election?
How popular are political/activist groups?

1. Salisbury University
2. Sacred Heart University
3. Fisk University
4. University of Scranton
5. Ohio Northern University
6. University of Rhode Island
7. College of the Ozarks
8. Stonehill College
9. Florida Southern College
10. Westminster College (PA)
11. Rose-Hulman Institute of Technology
12. Worcester Polytechnic Institute
13. University of Louisiana at Lafayette
14. Monmouth University (NJ)
15. Birmingham-Southern College
16. University of California—Riverside
17. Pennsylvania State University—
    University Park
18. Stevens Institute of Technology
19. Moravian College
20. Washington State University

Lots of Race/Class Interaction
Do different types of students (Black/White, rich/poor) interact frequently and easily?

1. University of Miami
2. Franklin W. Olin College of Engineering
3. University of Alabama at Birmingham
4. Stanford University
5. St. Mary's College of Maryland
6. Beloit College
7. Pitzer College
8. The College of Idaho
9. Mount Holyoke College
10. Oglethorpe University
11. Rice University
12. Randolph College
13. St. John's College (MD)
14. Yale University
15. Claremont McKenna College
16. Prescott College
17. Brown University
18. Millsaps College
19. Manhattanville College
20. The University of North Carolina
    at Greensboro

Little Race/Class Interaction
Do different types of students (Black/White, rich/poor) interact frequently and easily?

1. Fairfield University
2. Trinity College (CT)
3. University of New Hampshire
4. Miami University
5. Providence College
6. Quinnipiac University
7. Wake Forest University
8. Syracuse University
9. Texas Christian University
10. Rollins College
11. Union College (NY)
12. Gettysburg College
13. Lehigh University
14. University of Mississippi
15. Southern Methodist University
16. University of Richmond
17. Boston College
18. Vanderbilt University
19. College of the Holy Cross
20. Bucknell University

Gay Community Accepted
Is there very little discrimination against homosexuals?

1. New York University
2. Stanford University
3. New College of Florida
4. Swarthmore College
5. Emerson College
6. Simon's Rock College of Bard
7. Prescott College
8. Wellesley College
9. Marlboro College
10. Mount Holyoke College
11. Bennington College
12. Franklin W. Olin College of Engineering
13. Macalester College
14. Hampshire College
15. Grinnell College
16. Warren Wilson College
17. Reed College
18. Smith College
19. Pitzer College
20. Vassar College

Alternative Lifestyles Not an Alternative*
Is there very little discrimination against homosexuals?

1. Wheaton College (IL)
2. Grove City College
3. Thomas Aquinas College
4. Hampden-Sydney College
5. University of Notre Dame
6. Trinity College (CT)
7. Brigham Young University (UT)
8. University of Dallas
9. College of the Ozarks
10. Seton Hall University
11. Baylor University
12. Samford University
13. Calvin College
14. Southern Methodist University
15. Texas A&M University—College Station
16. Providence College
17. Pepperdine University
18. Hillsdale College
19. Auburn University
20. Duquesne University

Most Religious Students
Are students very religious?

1. Thomas Aquinas College
2. Brigham Young University (UT)
3. Wheaton College (IL)
4. Hillsdale College
5. University of Dallas
6. Grove City College
7. College of the Ozarks
8. University of Notre Dame
9. Furman University
10. Samford University
11. Baylor University
12. Calvin College
13. Texas A&M University—College Station
14. United States Air Force Academy
15. Pepperdine University
16. Catholic University of America
17. St. Anselm College
18. Brandeis University
19. Auburn University
20. University of Utah

Least Religious Students
Are students very religious?

1. Bennington College
2. Eugene Lang College
3. Reed College
4. Bard College
5. Emerson College
6. Simon's Rock College of Bard
7. Vassar College
8. Hampshire College
9. Sarah Lawrence College
10. College of the Atlantic
11. Pitzer College
12. Skidmore College
13. Pomona College
14. New College of Florida
15. Macalester College
16. Wesleyan University
17. Lewis & Clark College
18. Beloit College
19. Whitman College
20. University of Puget Sound

TOWN LIFE

Great College Towns
Based on students' assessment of the surrounding city or town

1. Columbia University
2. The George Washington University
3. Barnard College
4. Eugene Lang College
5. University of San Francisco
6. The University of Texas at Austin
7. American University
8. Georgetown University
9. Northeastern University
10. Emerson College

* Each of the five military academies was excluded from this list because of current, "Don't ask, don't tell" policies.

11. DePaul University
12. New York University
13. University of Colorado—Boulder
14. Boston College
15. Suffolk University
16. Stevens Institute of Technology
17. Boston University
18. University of San Diego
19. University of Wisconsin—Madison
20. The Cooper Union for the Advancement of Science and Art

More to Do on Campus
Based on students' assessment of the surrounding city or town

1. Union College (NY)
2. Tuskegee University
3. United States Military Academy
4. Albion College
5. New Jersey Institute of Technology
6. Wheaton College (MA)
7. Hofstra University
8. United States Coast Guard Academy
9. Beloit College
10. Rose-Hulman Institute of Technology
11. Stanford University
12. University of the Pacific
13. Rensselaer Polytechnic Institute
14. Vassar College
15. DePauw University
16. University of Notre Dame
17. Duke University
18. College of the Holy Cross
19. New Mexico Institute of Mining & Technology
20. Clark University

Town-Gown Relations are Great
Do students get along well with members of the local community?

1. Clemson University
2. Saint Michael's College
3. Davidson College
4. Franklin W. Olin College of Engineering
5. Wheaton College (IL)
6. Stonehill College
7. College of the Ozarks
8. St. Olaf College
9. Agnes Scott College
10. Samford University
11. Loyola University—New Orleans
12. William Jewell College
13. University of Louisiana at Lafayette
14. Catawba College
15. Seattle University
16. Kansas State University

17. The University of Tulsa
18. Montana Tech of the Univ. of Montana
19. Westminster College (PA)
20. The University of Texas at Austin

Town-Gown Relations are Strained
Do students get along well with members of the local community?

1. Trinity College (CT)
2. Union College (NY)
3. Lehigh University
4. Sarah Lawrence College
5. Illinois Institute of Technology
6. University of New Hampshire
7. Duke University
8. Colorado College
9. DePauw University
10. Howard University
11. College of the Holy Cross
12. Vassar College
13. United States Merchant Marine Academy
14. Providence College
15. Bates College
16. Northwestern University
17. New Jersey Institute of Technology
18. The College of Wooster
19. Fairfield University
20. Franklin & Marshall College

EXTRACURRICULARS

Best Athletic Facilities
Based on students' rating of campus athletic facilities

1. University of Maryland—College Park
2. University of Florida
3. Pennsylvania State University— University Park
4. Wabash College
5. Georgia Institute of Technology
6. Texas A&M University—College Station
7. The University of Alabama—Tuscaloosa
8. Texas Christian University
9. The Ohio State University—Columbus
10. Loyola University—Maryland
11. West Virginia University
12. University of Georgia
13. Hendrix College
14. University of Alabama at Birmingham
15. University of Richmond
16. Lafayette College
17. Clemson University
18. United States Military Academy
19. Middlebury College
20. The University of Texas at Austin

Students Pack the Stadiums
How popular are intercollegiate sports?

1. Pennsylvania State University— University Park
2. University of Florida
3. University of Michigan—Ann Arbor
4. University of Notre Dame
5. University of Maryland—College Park
6. The University of Texas at Austin
7. Duke University
8. West Virginia University
9. Boston College
10. Wabash College
11. Gonzaga University
12. University of Wisconsin—Madison
13. The University of Alabama—Tuscaloosa
14. Texas A&M University—College Station
15. Virginia Tech
16. University of Nebraska—Lincoln
17. Indiana University—Bloomington
18. University of Kansas
19. Williams College
20. University of Southern California

Intercollegiate Sports Unpopular or Nonexistent
How popular are intercollegiate sports?

1. Eugene Lang College
2. St. John's College (NM)
3. College of the Atlantic
4. New College of Florida
5. Bennington College
6. Thomas Aquinas College
7. Prescott College
8. Marlboro College
9. Reed College
10. Hampshire College
11. Sarah Lawrence College
12. Franklin W. Olin College of Engineering
13. St. John's College (MD)
14. University of Chicago
15. New York University
16. State University of New York— Purchase College
17. Harvey Mudd College
18. The Evergreen State College
19. Simon's Rock College of Bard
20. New Mexico Institute of Mining & Technology

Everyone Plays Intramural Sports
How popular are intramural sports?

1. University of Notre Dame
2. Grove City College
3. Wabash College

4. Whitman College
5. Clemson University
6. Pennsylvania State University— University Park
7. Stonehill College
8. Gonzaga University
9. Colorado College
10. University of Dayton
11. United States Air Force Academy
12. Carleton College
13. St. John's College (MD)
14. United States Naval Academy
15. University of Florida
16. University of Nebraska—Lincoln
17. Wittenberg University
18. United States Coast Guard Academy
19. Providence College
20. Brigham Young University (UT)

Nobody Plays Intramural Sports
How popular are intramural sports?

1. Sarah Lawrence College
2. Eugene Lang College
3. Emerson College
4. New York University
5. Prescott College
6. New College of Florida
7. Bryn Mawr College
8. Bennington College
9. Suffolk University
10. The Evergreen State College
11. College of the Atlantic
12. The Cooper Union for the Advancement of Science and Art
13. Hampshire College
14. Simon's Rock College of Bard
15. Randolph College
16. Marlboro College
17. Spelman College
18. Barnard College
19. Hollins University
20. St. John's College (NM)

Best College Radio Station
How popular is the radio station?

1. Ithaca College
2. St. Bonaventure University
3. Seton Hall University
4. DePauw University
5. Emerson College
6. Brown University
7. Stanford University
8. Guilford College
9. Knox College
10. Howard University
11. University of Puget Sound

12. Carleton College
13. Alfred University
14. Reed College
15. Swarthmore College
16. Whitman College
17. Westminster College (PA)
18. Bates College
19. Skidmore College
20. Manhattanville College

Best College Newspaper
How popular is the newspaper?

1. The University of North Carolina at Chapel Hill
2. Harvard College
3. Yale University
4. University of Maryland—College Park
5. Texas A&M University—College Station
6. Pennsylvania State University—University Park
7. Howard University
8. University of Florida
9. Duke University
10. Louisiana State University—Baton Rouge
11. West Virginia University
12. University of Mississippi
13. The University of Texas at Austin
14. University of California—Los Angeles
15. University of Pennsylvania
16. University of Wisconsin—Madison
17. Purdue University—West Lafayette
18. Syracuse University
19. Indiana University—Bloomington
20. Northwestern University

Best College Theater
How popular are college theater productions?

1. Drew University
2. Yale University
3. Wagner College
4. Muhlenberg College
5. Vassar College
6. Nazareth College
7. Carnegie Mellon University
8. Emerson College
9. Ithaca College
10. Lawrence University
11. College of the Ozarks
12. Whitman College
13. Brown University
14. Simon's Rock College of Bard
15. Knox College
16. Cornell College
17. Oglethorpe University

18. Manhattanville College
19. Hampshire College
20. Trinity University

SOCIAL SCENE

Lots of Beer
How widely used is beer?

1. Pennsylvania State University—University Park
2. University of New Hampshire
3. Providence College
4. University of Florida
5. Claremont McKenna College
6. Ohio University—Athens
7. Hampden-Sydney College
8. West Virginia University
9. Colgate University
10. University of Wisconsin—Madison
11. Lehigh University
12. The University of Texas at Austin
13. Union College (NY)
14. Florida State University
15. DePauw University
16. Trinity College (CT)
17. Eckerd College
18. Gettysburg College
19. Indiana University—Bloomington
20. University of Mississippi

Got Milk?
How widely used is beer?

1. Brigham Young University (UT)
2. Wheaton College (IL)
3. College of the Ozarks
4. Wesleyan College
5. City University of New York—Queens College
6. Grove City College
7. Spelman College
8. City University of New York—Brooklyn College
9. California State University, Stanislaus
10. Xavier University of Louisiana
11. United States Coast Guard Academy
12. City University of New York—Baruch College
13. Howard University
14. Fisk University
15. Mills College
16. St. John's University—Queens
17. City University of New York—Hunter College

18. Calvin College
19. Flagler College
20. Berea College

Lots of Hard Liquor
How widely used is hard liquor?

1. University of Mississippi
2. Providence College
3. Fairfield University
4. The University of Texas at Austin
5. Tulane University
6. University of Wisconsin—Madison
7. Indiana University—Bloomington
8. University of Georgia
9. Pennsylvania State University—University Park
10. Trinity College (CT)
11. University of Colorado—Boulder
12. Sewanee—The University of the South
13. Ohio University—Athens
14. Lehigh University
15. University of North Dakota
16. University of Tennessee
17. University of Iowa
18. University of Florida
19. Loyola University—New Orleans
20. University of California—Santa Barbara

Scotch and Soda, Hold the Scotch
How widely used is hard liquor?

1. Brigham Young University (UT)
2. Wheaton College (IL)
3. College of the Ozarks
4. Wesleyan College
5. Grove City College
6. City University of New York—Queens College
7. California State University—Stanislaus
8. United States Coast Guard Academy
9. City University of New York—Brooklyn College
10. City University of New York—Baruch College
11. City University of New York—Hunter College
12. Calvin College
13. Mills College
14. Simmons College
15. Wellesley College
16. Spelman College
17. Bellarmine University
18. Berea College
19. United States Air Force Academy
20. Xavier University of Louisiana

Reefer Madness
How widely used is marijuana?

1. University of California—Santa Cruz
2. Skidmore College
3. University of Vermont
4. Bard College
5. University of Colorado—Boulder
6. New College of Florida
7. Colorado College
8. Hampshire College
9. University of California—Santa Barbara
10. Eckerd College
11. Ithaca College
12. Sarah Lawrence College
13. Warren Wilson College
14. Pitzer College
15. University of Oregon
16. Guilford College
17. West Virginia University
18. Wesleyan University
19. State University of New York—Purchase College
20. Green Mountain College

Don't Inhale
How widely used is marijuana?

1. Brigham Young University (UT)
2. United States Coast Guard Academy
3. United States Naval Academy
4. United States Air Force Academy
5. United States Military Academy
6. Wheaton College (IL)
7. Thomas Aquinas College
8. United States Merchant Marine Academy
9. Wesleyan College
10. College of the Ozarks
11. Webb Institute
12. University of Notre Dame
13. Hillsdale College
14. Grove City College
15. California State University—Stanislaus
16. Furman University
17. Samford University
18. Valparaiso University
19. University of Dallas
20. City University of New York—Queens College

Major Frat and Sorority Scene
How popular are fraternities/sororities?

1. Wofford College
2. University of Mississippi
3. Pennsylvania State University—University Park
4. Transylvania University

5. Birmingham-Southern College
6. Vanderbilt University
7. Lehigh University
8. Sewanee—The University of the South
9. Wake Forest University
10. University of Iowa
11. DePauw University
12. University of Florida
13. University of Illinois
    at Urbana-Champaign
14. Union College (NY)
15. University of Georgia
16. The University of Alabama—Tuscaloosa
17. Albion College
18. Bucknell University
19. Gettysburg College
20. University of Tennessee

SCHOOLS BY TYPE

Party Schools
Based on a combination of survey questions concerning the use of alcohol and drugs, hours of study each day, and the popularity of the Greek system

1. Pennsylvania State University—
   University Park
2. University of Florida
3. University of Mississippi
4. University of Georgia
5. Ohio University—Athens
6. West Virginia University
7. The University of Texas at Austin
8. University of Wisconsin—Madison
9. Florida State University
10. University of California—Santa Barbara
11. University of Colorado—Boulder
12. University of Iowa
13. Union College (NY)
14. Indiana University—Bloomington
15. DePauw University
16. University of Tennessee
17. Sewanee—The University of the South
18. University of North Dakota
19. Tulane University
20. Arizona State University

Stone-Cold Sober Schools
Based on a combination of survey questions concerning the use of alcohol and drugs, hours of study each day, and the popularity of the Greek system

1. Brigham Young University (UT)
2. Wheaton College (IL)
3. United States Coast Guard Academy
4. College of the Ozarks

5. Wesleyan College
6. United States Air Force Academy
7. United States Naval Academy
8. Wellesley College
9. Thomas Aquinas College
10. Calvin College
11. Grove City College
12. United States Military Academy
13. Franklin W. Olin College of Engineering
14. City University of New York—
    Queens College
15. Marywood University
16. Mills College
17. Berea College
18. California State University—Stanislaus
19. Agnes Scott College
20. Simmons College

Jock Schools
Based on a combination of survey questions concerning intercollegiate and intramural sports, and the popularity of the Greek system

1. Clemson University
2. University of Florida
3. Pennsylvania State University—
   University Park
4. Wabash College
5. The University of North Carolina at
   Chapel Hill
6. University of Nebraska—Lincoln
7. Florida State University
8. University of Notre Dame
9. The Ohio State University—Columbus
10. University of Connecticut
11. Villanova University
12. University of Georgia
13. University of Michigan—Ann Arbor
14. University of Tennessee
15. Purdue University—West Lafayette
16. Texas A&M University—College Station
17. Michigan State University
18. Duke University
19. University of Oklahoma
20. Kansas State University

Dodgeball Targets
Based on a combination of survey questions concerning intercollegiate and intramural sports, and the popularity of the Greek system

1. Sarah Lawrence College
2. New College of Florida
3. St. John's College (NM)
4. Hampshire College
5. Marlboro College
6. Prescott College

7. Eugene Lang College
8. Bennington College
9. Reed College
10. Simon's Rock College of Bard
11. Emerson College
12. College of the Atlantic
13. Bard College
14. Goucher College
15. New York University
16. State University of New York—Purchase College
17. Suffolk University
18. New Mexico Institute of Mining & Technology
19. The Evergreen State College
20. Lewis & Clark College

Future Rotarians and Daughters of the American Revolution

Based on a combination of survey questions concerning the political persuasion, the use of drugs, the popularity of student government, and the level of acceptance of the gay community on campus

1. Brigham Young University (UT)
2. Grove City College
3. Hillsdale College
4. Wheaton College (IL)
5. College of the Ozarks
6. University of Dallas
7. Thomas Aquinas College
8. United States Air Force Academy
9. United States Naval Academy
10. Samford University
11. University of Notre Dame
12. Baylor University
13. United States Military Academy
14. Texas A&M University—College Station
15. Clemson University
16. Furman University
17. United States Coast Guard Academy
18. United States Merchant Marine Academy
19. Calvin College
20. Pepperdine University

Birkenstock-Wearing, Tree-Hugging, Clove-Smoking Vegetarians

Based on a combination of survey questions concerning the political persuasion, the use of drugs, the popularity of student government, and the level of acceptance of the gay community on campus

1. Bard College
2. Hampshire College
3. Eugene Lang College
4. New College of Florida
5. Reed College
6. Clark University
7. Sarah Lawrence College
8. Bennington College
9. Simon's Rock College of Bard
10. Marlboro College
11. Vassar College
12. Pitzer College
13. Wesleyan University
14. University of California—Santa Cruz
15. Lewis & Clark College
16. Macalester College
17. Emerson College
18. Oberlin College
19. Warren Wilson College
20. State University of New York—Purchase College

Deep Springs Honor Roll

Since Deep Springs is a two-year college (and the only one in The Best 371 Colleges), we remove it from our rankings tallies in order to avoid comparing "apples and oranges." Instead we present this list of some ranking categories in which Deep Springs ranks high (or low, as it were) among the best colleges in our book.

Students Study the Most
Class Discussions Encouraged
This is a Library?
School Runs Like Butter
Most Beautiful Campus
Dorms Like Palaces
Best Quality of Life
Most Liberal Students
Lots of Race/Class Interaction
Gay Community Accepted
Least Religious Students
Great College Towns
Intercollegiate Sports Unpopular or Nonexistent
Got Milk?
Scotch and Soda, Hold the Scotch
Don't Inhale
Stone-Cold Sober Schools

PRINCETON REVIEW "FINANCIAL AID RATING," "FIRE SAFETY RATING" AND "GREEN RATING" HONOR ROLLS

We salute theses schools that received a 99 (the highest score) in the tallies for our "Financial Aid," "Fire Safety," and "Green" Ratings—three of eight ratings on some of the school profiles in this book as well as in our *Best Northeastern Colleges* and *Complete Book of Colleges*, 2010 editions, and at www.PrincetonReview.com. Our school ratings are numerical scores (note: they are not ranking lists) that show how a school "sizes up" on a fixed scale. They are comparable to grades and based primarily on institutional data we collect directly from the colleges.

Financial Aid Honor Roll

Schools are listed in alphabetical order See p. 24 for information on how our "Financial Aid Rating" is determined.

American Jewish University*
Beloit College
Bowdoin College
California Institute of Technology
Claremont McKenna College
Gettysburg College
Harvard College
Lake Forest College
Swarthmore College
Thomas Aquinas College
Wabash College
Washington University in St. Louis
Williams College

Fire Safety Honor Roll

Schools are listed in alphabetical order See p. 20 for information on how our "Fire Safety Rating" is determined.

Adelphi University*
Bay Path College*
Bentley University
California State University, Stanislaus
Cazenovia College*
College of Mount St. Joseph*
Dominican University of California*
Edinboro University of Pennsylvania*
Georgian Court University*
Kean University*
Milwaukee School of Engineering *
Mountain State University*
Suffolk University
The College of Saint Rose*
University of South Carolina Aiken*

Green Honor Roll

Schools are listed in alphabetical order See p. 21 for information on how our "Green Rating" is determined.

Arizona State University at the Tempe campus
Bates College
College of the Atlantic
Colorado College
Dickinson College
The Evergreen State College
Georgia Institute of Technology
Harvard College
Middlebury College
Northeastern University
State University of New York at Binghamton
University of California—Berkeley
University of New Hampshire
University of Washington
Yale University

Tuition-Free Schools Honor Roll

The following schools have been excluded from our ranking lists dealing with financial aid:

Berea College
College of the Ozarks
The Cooper Union for the Advancement
    of Science and Art
Franklin W. Olin College of Engineering
United States Air Force Academy
United States Coast Guard Academy
United States Merchant Marine Academy
United States Military Academy
United States Naval Academy
Webb Institute

We commend these schools on their ability to do the seemingly impossible: not charge tuition. While some charge students for room & board and other fees, the overall cost of attendance at these schools is very low, and at some schools: free!   (Note: we do not include these schools in our ranking lists dealing with financial aid, since they would have an unfair advantage over schools that charged even a moderate tuition.)

Schools marked with an asterisk do not appear in the *Best 371 Colleges*.
You can find those school profiles in *Complete Book of Colleges*, 2010 Edition.

The Princeton Review and *USA TODAY* have collaborated to bring you this list of 100 Best Value Colleges. We selected the 100 schools (50 private and 50 public) in January 2009 based on 30 factors covering academics, costs, and financial aid. For information about each school and an exclusive analysis in an interactive database and map, go to www.bestvaluecolleges.usatoday.com

Top 50 Private

Agnes Scott College
Amherst College
Babson College
Barnard College
Bates College
Bowdoin College
Brigham Young University (UT)
Bryn Mawr College
California Institute of Technology
Carleton College
Centre College
Colgate University
Colorado College
The Cooper Union for the Advancement of
    Science and Art
Dartmouth College
Davidson College
Duke University
Elon University
Emory University
Franklin W. Olin College of Engineering
Furman University
Grinnell College
Grove City College
Hamilton College
Harvard College
Harvey Mudd College
Hillsdale College
Lafayette College
Oberlin College
Pomona College
Princeton University
Reed College
Rhodes College
Rice University
Rollins College
Sewanee—The University of the South
Smith College
Stanford University
Swarthmore College
Thomas Aquinas College
Trinity College (CT)
University of Richmond
The University of Tulsa
Vanderbilt University
Vassar College
Webb Institute
Wheaton College (IL)
Whitman College
Williams College
Yale University

Top 50 Public

California State University—Long Beach*
City University of New York—Baruch College
City University of New York—
    Brooklyn College
City University of New York—Hunter College
City University of New York—Queens College
The College of New Jersey
College of William and Mary
Florida State University
George Mason University
Georgia College & State University*
Georgia Institute of Technology
Indiana University—Bloomington
James Madison University
New College of Florida
New Jersey Institute of Technology
North Carolina State University
Purdue University—West Lafayette
St. Mary's College of Maryland
Salisbury University
State University of New York—
    Binghamton University
Texas A&M University—College Station
Towson University*
United States Air Force Academy
United States Coast Guard Academy
United States Merchant Marine Academy
United States Military Academy
United States Naval Academy
University of Arkansas—Fayetteville
The University of Alabama—Tuscaloosa*
University of California—Davis
University of California—Irvine*
University of California—San Diego
University of Central Florida
University of Colorado—Boulder
University of Delaware
University of Georgia
University of Kansas
University of Mary Washington
University of Maryland—Baltimore County
University of Michigan—Ann Arbor
The University of North Carolina at Asheville
The University of North Carolina at Greensboro
University of North Carolina—Wilmington*
University of North Florida*
University of Oklahoma
University of South Florida
University of Tennessee
University of Virginia
University of Wisconsin—Eau Claire*
Virginia Tech

Schools marked with an asterisk do not appear in the *Best 371 Colleges*.

You can find those school profiles in *Complete Book of Colleges, 2010 Edition*.

PART 3

THE BEST
371 COLLEGES

AGNES SCOTT COLLEGE

141 EAST COLLEGE AVENUE, DECATUR, GA 30030-3797 • ADMISSIONS: 404-471-6285 • FAX: 404-471-6414

CAMPUS LIFE

Quality of Life Rating	98
Fire Safety Rating	96
Green Rating	94
Type of school	private
Affiliation	Presbyterian
Environment	metropolis

STUDENTS

Total undergrad enrollment	757
% male/female	0/100
% from out of state	45
% from public high school	80
% live on campus	87
% African American	21
% Asian	4
% Caucasian	54
% Hispanic	3
% international	4
# of countries represented	19

SURVEY SAYS . . .

No one cheats
Lab facilities are great
Students get along with local
community
Students love Atlanta/Decatur, GA
Great off-campus food
Dorms are like palaces
Campus feels safe
Frats and sororities are unpopular or
nonexistent

ACADEMICS

Academic Rating	92
Calendar	semester
Student/faculty ratio	8:1
Profs interesting rating	95
Profs accessible rating	89
Most common reg class size	10–19 students
Most common lab size	10–19 students

MOST POPULAR MAJORS

economics
English language and literature
psychology

STUDENTS SAY "..."

Academics

"Agnes Scott College is about empowering the next generation of strong women in the world," students at this small women's college tell us, and statistics prove that this is more than empty rhetoric. ASC ranks high among undergraduate institutions in the percentage of its alumnae who continue on to advanced degree programs, and women here enjoy a highly personalized educational experience. As one student explains, "It makes me feel good that my professors know my name! Overall, I feel like this school cares about me. There is nothing impersonal about Agnes Scott." That intimacy, coupled with ASC's close proximity to Atlanta where there are "so many internships and jobs," provides ASC with a killer one-two punch. Writing and independent thinking are the focus of the curriculum here; classes "are engaging and encourage students to think critically about the subject, not just memorize a bunch of facts and dates." While the "small size of the school...makes it difficult to offer some courses," ASC "makes up for it with opportunities for reading courses, independent studies," and "wonderful personal interaction with one's professors." Students warn, "There are no cake classes at Agnes," but may also say that "one-on-one relationships with the professors" help undergrads master the ASC's "rigorous" academics. To sum it all up, "Agnes Scott is a very challenging school, but it provides you with more than enough resources to come out on top."

Life

Life at ASC "can be a bubble if you make it a bubble. There are people who never go out, and they suffer socially. There are also people who go out, party too much, and suffer academically. Most people are successful in finding a healthy balance." Fortunately, ASC women have a lot of options to choose from when it comes to finding entertainment. There are "tons of hall activities at the dorms, where the girls all get to know one another really well!" In addition, "There are numerous campus-wide activities like Diversifest—where diversity is celebrated with Chinese calligraphy banners, the showing of *Ringu*, and a Day of the Dead workshop"—not to mention a popular "pre-exam pancake jam." ASC is located in Decatur, an upscale area just outside of the Atlanta city limits that boasts "fabulous restaurants" and great "shopping at Little Five Points," an alternative hotspot nearby. Students head into Atlanta, "an amazing city...ridiculously accessible by MARTA or car," to enjoy "various museums, including the High Art Museum and the Georgia Aquarium," not to mention "tons of great restaurants, shopping, plays, concerts, and nightlife." As for the dating scene, "Georgia Tech isn't far away, so if people are looking for parties that include boys, that's usually the first stop."

Student Body

"There is no typical student per se" at Agnes Scott, as "Everyone kind of goes to the beat of her own drum." The student body runs the gamut "from the radical, left-wing lesbian to the far-right, pearls-wearing, charm school graduate, and any combination after that." Many "were the 'weird girls' from high school...the ones who got good grades but were eccentric." While "People are very different here," students concede that there are identifiable "social circles" on campus. As one student explains, "We definitely have 'groups' on campus, including the religious right...the girls who drink too much and the girls who ask to rewrite their A- papers. The groups might not always get along, but when it comes down to it, Agnes Scott students are devoted to each other and the school." While political perspectives vary, the majority here "lean to the political left," to the point that those who are not "very liberal and idealistic...often have some trouble fitting in." Students also observe that "because of an international focus and location in metro Atlanta, the student body is diverse in ethnicity."

AGNES SCOTT COLLEGE

FINANCIAL AID: 404-471-6395 • E-MAIL: ADMISSION@AGNESSCOTT.EDU • WEBSITE: WWW.AGNESSCOTT.EDU

THE PRINCETON REVIEW SAYS

Admissions

Very important factors considered include: Class rank, application essay, academic GPA, recommendation(s), rigor of secondary school record, standardized test scores, character/personal qualities, talent/ability. *Important factors considered include:* Extracurricular activities, volunteer work, work experience. *Other factors considered include:* Alumni/ae relation, first generation, geographical residence, interview, level of applicant's interest, racial/ethnic status, state residency. SAT or ACT required. ACT with Writing component required. TOEFL required of all international applicants. High school diploma is required and GED is accepted. *Academic units recommended:* 4 English, 3 mathematics, 2 science (2 science labs), 2 foreign language, 2 social studies, 2 history.

Financial Aid

Students should submit: FAFSA, previous year's tax return. Regular filing deadline is 5/1. The Princeton Review suggests that all financial aid forms be submitted as soon as possible after 1/1. *Need-based scholarships/grants offered:* Federal Pell, SEOG, state scholarships/grants, private scholarships, the school's own gift aid. *Loan aid offered:* FFEL Subsidized Stafford, FFEL Unsubsidized Stafford, FFEL PLUS, college/university loans from institutional funds. Applicants will be notified of awards on a rolling basis beginning 3/1. Federal Work-Study Program available. Institutional employment available. Off-campus job opportunities are excellent.

The Inside Word

Are you on the fence about applying to Agnes Scott College? Apply online, and the college will waive the application fee—it will only cost you the time it takes to fill it out. Don't treat this application lightly, though; Agnes Scott is highly selective, and you'll need to submit an impressive application to gain admission. Don't worry about falling through the cracks here—every candidate is assigned her own specific admission counselor who works with the student throughout the application process.

THE SCHOOL SAYS "..."

From The Admissions Office

"Who will you become? If you are looking for a liberal arts college that will help you explore, strive, and surpass what you think is your potential, then consider Agnes Scott College. Our students and alumnae say it best:

"'I find the academic program to be extremely challenging at Agnes Scott; but it's not overwhelming—it's easy to go to your teachers and ask for help because they know who you are and take a personal interest.'—Evan Joslin, Class of 2008, Atlanta, GA.

"'Agnes Scott College didn't teach me what to think. They taught me how to think,' says Jessica Owen Sanfilippo, Class of 1998, who majored in biology at ASC, received a master's degree in cancer biology from Stanford and an MBA from Harvard.

"Students find their passions and their voices through guaranteed internships, international study experiences, and collaborative learning in places like the science center, facilities that were designed expressly to facilitate faculty-student research. Your next 4 years are about you. We invite you to come for a visit and imagine the possibilities for you.

"Students applying for admission are required to submit score results from the SAT or the ACT, with the Writing section recommended."

SELECTIVITY

Admissions Rating	**92**
# of applicants	1,593
% of applicants accepted	48
% of acceptees attending	23
# accepting a place on wait list	25
% admitted from wait list	72

FRESHMAN PROFILE

Range SAT Critical Reading	520–680
Range SAT Math	500–610
Range SAT Writing	520–660
Range ACT Composite	22–28
Minimum paper TOEFL	577
Minimum computer TOEFL	233
Average HS GPA	3.61
% graduated top 10% of class	34
% graduated top 25% of class	68
% graduated top 50% of class	93

DEADLINES

Early action	
Deadline	11/15
Notification	12/15
Regular	
Priority	3/1
Nonfall registration?	yes

APPLICANTS ALSO LOOK AT

AND OFTEN PREFER
Emory University
University of Georgia

AND SOMETIMES PREFER
Mercer University—Macon

AND RARELY PREFER
Wesleyan College

FINANCIAL FACTS

Financial Aid Rating	**92**
Annual tuition	$29,890
Room and board	$9,850
Required fees	$215
Books and supplies	$1,000
% frosh rec. need-based scholarship or grant aid	71
% UG rec. need-based scholarship or grant aid	70
% frosh rec. non-need-based scholarship or grant aid	54
% UG rec. non-need-based scholarship or grant aid	35
% frosh rec. need-based self-help aid	61
% UG rec. need-based self-help aid	61
% UG borrow to pay for school	73
Average cumulative indebtedness	$24,070

ALBION COLLEGE

611 EAST PORTER, ALBION, MI 49224 • ADMISSIONS: 517-629-0321 • FAX: 517-629-0569

CAMPUS LIFE
Quality of Life Rating	**65**
Fire Safety Rating	**70**
Green Rating	**88**
Type of school	private
Affiliation	Methodist
Environment	village

STUDENTS
Total undergrad enrollment	1,845
% male/female	46/54
% from out of state	9
% from public high school	75
% live on campus	90
% in (# of) fraternities	41 (6)
% in (# of) sororities	39 (7)
% African American	3
% Asian	2
% Caucasian	88
% Hispanic	1
% international	1
# of countries represented	20

SURVEY SAYS . . .
No one cheats
Lab facilities are great
Students are friendly
Low cost of living
Frats and sororities dominate social scene
Lots of beer drinking

ACADEMICS
Academic Rating	**87**
Calendar	semester
Student/faculty ratio	12:1
Profs interesting rating	90
Profs accessible rating	94
Most common reg class size	10–19 students
Most common lab size	10–19 students

MOST POPULAR MAJORS
biology/biological sciences
economics
psychology

STUDENTS SAY ". . ."

Academics

Albion College, a small liberal arts school with "a great biology department" and "wonderful programs in the sciences and pre-law," has "an amazing ability to provide the 'small school' intimacy with peers and instructors while delivering world-class education that competes with major universities," according to its students. Albion boasts of "professors that would make many bigger schools drool," and "Since it's strictly an undergraduate institution, Albion's services are all geared toward the students." Indeed, "The entire faculty and staff always make time for students and even acknowledge you by name when you walk past them on campus," and "The professors seem to genuinely envision a greater academic career for all students and strongly encourage further schooling after attaining the four-year degree." Students also enjoy a "number of available opportunities, in class and out of class, for internships and studying abroad, even after the students leave here," thanks to a strong alumni network. As one undergrad explains, "Albion is about connections. Even though it is a small school, everyone knows someone who goes to or has graduated from Albion. Even though it is out of the way, we are very connected to the wider world." A solid selection of study abroad and research opportunities also "puts us on the cutting edge of this shrinking world." The Albion curriculum is flexible enough to "emphasize the freedom of choice for every individual. It allows students to express themselves in various ways and allows students to get hands-on experience of specific areas of work" while completing their studies.

Life

"There isn't a lot to do in the city of Albion itself," but students tell us that "There is always something happening on campus" to compensate. Greek life "is a very large part of Albion, and there are always things going on at the frats"; about one-third of all students join Greek organizations. Other options include "concerts, comedians, and other activities put on by Union Board, an event planning committee sponsored with student activity funds." The school works hard to draw big-name entertainment and in recent years has hosted performances by Dane Cook, Pablo Francisco, OAR, and Less Than Jake. While "A lot of people drink and party because they don't know what else to do," students insist that those who choose not to drink have plenty of options. Hometown Albion "is a small one-horse town where there isn't a whole bunch for the residents to do, let alone the student body." The town's one saving grace is the Bohm movie theatre, "where all students get in for free with ID."

Student Body

"I think one word can describe the Albion student: involved," one student writes, adding that "Nearly every Albion student is involved with multiple organizations that engage in community outreach, philosophical discussions, diversity awareness, hobby enthusiasts, and nearly every other aspect of a social organization you can think of." Most here "seem to come from either wealthy backgrounds or are from the surrounding town and are from low-income families," with the balance tilted firmly toward the former group. "There is not a dominant religion" on campus, "but Albion College was founded as a Christian school," meaning that "many of the students are Christian." Most "are white, and many "have always lived in Michigan" and "could be described as the attractive, popular, smart kid in school" who "came to Albion to be a big fish in a small pond."

FINANCIAL AID: 517-629-0440 • E-MAIL: ADMISSIONS@ALBION.EDU • WEBSITE: WWW.ALBION.EDU

THE PRINCETON REVIEW SAYS

Admissions

Very important factors considered include: Application essay, academic GPA, rigor of secondary school record, character/personal qualities, extracurricular activities, level of applicant's interest, talent/ability. *Important factors considered include:* Recommendation(s), volunteer work, work experience. *Other factors considered include:* Standardized test scores, alumni/ae relation, first generation, geographical residence, interview. SAT or ACT required. SAT and SAT Subject Tests or ACT recommended. TOEFL required of all international applicants. High school diploma is required and GED is accepted. *Academic units required:* 4 English, 3 mathematics, 3 science (2 science labs), 2 foreign language, 3 social studies. *Academic units recommended:* 4 English, 4 mathematics, 4 science, 3 foreign language, 4 social studies.

Financial Aid

Students should submit: FAFSA. The Princeton Review suggests that all financial aid forms be submitted as soon as possible after 1/1. *Need-based scholarships/grants offered:* Federal Pell, SEOG, state scholarships/grants, private scholarships, the school's own gift aid. *Loan aid offered:* Direct Subsidized Stafford, Direct Unsubsidized Stafford, Direct PLUS, FFEL Subsidized Stafford, FFEL Unsubsidized Stafford, FFEL PLUS, Federal Perkins. Applicants will be notified of awards on a rolling basis beginning 3/15. Federal Work-Study Program available. Institutional employment available. Off-campus job opportunities are fair.

The Inside Word

Albion fills each incoming class with solid—if not exceptional high school students. The average GPA for incoming students is about 3.56, and the average SAT score is 1200. Albion applicants are a self-selecting group, which explains the schools 80+ percent acceptance rate. Borderline candidates can improve their chances by presenting an impressive roster of extracurriculars and volunteer work, strong essays, and a strong interview. A campus visit is highly encouraged.

THE SCHOOL SAYS "..."

From The Admissions Office

"Some schools are for jocks and others for geeks and some for average Joes, at Albion, we are for thinkers! No matter how else you describe yourself, if you are a thinker, then Albion could be the perfect college for you. We are thinking about sustainability, mating habits of nurse sharks, and how the time of day affects test performance…we are thinking about grad schools, alternative spring breaks, the ethics of genetic cloning and myriad other topics…so the question is: what are you thinking? Albion is home to six interdisciplinary and experiential institutes for business, public policy and service, environmental studies, pre-medical and health care studies, teacher education and honors. Albion is among the top 85 liberal arts colleges for the number of alumni who are corporate executives. Our graduates are admitted to top-notch medical, dental and law schools at a 95% clip. In a typical year 45% of our graduates go directly to graduate school, attending institutions such as Harvard, Vanderbilt, Northwestern, and Stanford. A full-service, 80-stall equestrian center opened in 2004. Our equestrian teams compete in IHSA events. Our Division III sports teams compete in the Michigan Intercollegiate Athletic Association and field 21 varsity sports. Recent athletic programs to compete in NCAA post-season tournaments include football, men's and women's basketball, women's soccer, both tennis teams, numerous swimmers, and track and field athletes. Albion has more than 120 student organizations that encompass the full array of service, religious, academic and athletic interests."

SELECTIVITY

Admissions Rating	89
# of applicants	1,958
% of applicants accepted	83
% of acceptees attending	30

FRESHMAN PROFILE

Range SAT Critical Reading	560–630
Range SAT Math	500–650
Range SAT Writing	500–630
Range ACT Composite	23–27
Minimum paper TOEFL	550
Minimum computer TOEFL	270
Average HS GPA	3.55
% graduated top 10% of class	27
% graduated top 25% of class	61
% graduated top 50% of class	91

DEADLINES

Early action	
Deadline	12/1
Notification	11/1
Regular	
Priority	12/1
Deadline	5/1
Notification	rolling
Nonfall registration?	yes

APPLICANTS ALSO LOOK AT

AND OFTEN PREFER
University of Michigan—Ann Arbor

AND SOMETIMES PREFER
Hope College
Kalamazoo College
Michigan State University

FINANCIAL FACTS

Financial Aid Rating	89
Annual tuition	$28,380
Room and board	$8,190
Required fees	$500
Books and supplies	$900
% frosh rec. need-based scholarship or grant aid	65
% UG rec. need-based scholarship or grant aid	61
% frosh rec. non-need-based scholarship or grant aid	63
% UG rec. non-need-based scholarship or grant aid	56
% frosh rec. need-based self-help aid	49
% UG rec. need-based self-help aid	50
% frosh rec. any financial aid	98
% UG rec. any financial aid	98

ALFRED UNIVERSITY

ALUMNI HALL, ONE SAXON DRIVE, ALFRED, NY 14802-1205 • ADMISSIONS: 607-871-2115 • FAX: 607-871-2198

CAMPUS LIFE

Quality of Life Rating	78
Fire Safety Rating	60*
Green Rating	60*
Type of school	private
Environment	rural

STUDENTS

Total undergrad enrollment	1,971
% male/female	51/49
% from out of state	35
% live on campus	67
% African American	4
% Asian	2
% Caucasian	64
% Hispanic	2
% international	3

SURVEY SAYS . . .

Students are friendly
Frats and sororities are unpopular or nonexistent
College radio is popular
Lots of beer drinking

ACADEMICS

Academic Rating	80
Calendar	semester
Student/faculty ratio	12:1
Profs interesting rating	85
Profs accessible rating	84
Most common reg class size	10–19 students
Most common lab size	fewer than 10 students

MOST POPULAR MAJORS

business/commerce
ceramic sciences and engineering
fine/studio arts

STUDENTS SAY ". . ."

Academics

Alfred University is best known for its unique and prestigious glass engineering, ceramic arts, and ceramic engineering programs ("the best in the nation," students insist). These programs' reputations are well earned, but they occasionally overshadow AU's many other assets, according to undergrads here; as one student points out, "Alfred offers tons of majors and minors within four different undergraduate schools (Art School, Engineering School, College of Liberal Arts and Sciences, and the College of Business)," and the school does a good job of "integrating the 4 very distinct schools into one cohesive whole, so you can make friends from absolutely every conceivable background while pursuing any course of study." Engineering is among the school's hallmark disciplines, attracting nearly one in seven undergraduates; business studies are nearly as popular. AU offers its breadth of academic options on an intimate scale; explains one undergrad, "The size of the school is a strength. Because the school is so small, students have chances that they might never have had at other schools. Some of the best friends I have made here are upperclassmen whom I probably would not have met had I gone to a larger school. In such a small school, everyone also has the chance to make his or her voice heard in a way that probably cannot happen at larger schools."

Life

Alfred University is located "in the middle of nowhere" in "the one-stoplight town" of Alfred, New York. "If the Student Activities Board does not provide it, it does not happen," warns one student. Undergrads fill their spare time with more than "one hundred clubs and organizations" and "crazy stuff" like "snow sculptures and secret sledding (we have snow more often than not)." Students here "are very forward thinking," so many "try to get internships and co-ops during their undergraduate years." Otherwise, there's always the "multiple events and programs each week, especially on the weekends," sponsored by Student Activities, which are "very well-publicized and have great attendance." Such events include "movies, lectures, comedy acts, music shows, art shows, and plays." Low-key activities such as group dinners, watching DVDs, and video gaming are also quite popular. As one student sums up the situation, "Life is quiet for those who like it quiet, but it also offers something for everybody." Party nights "are pretty popular," and "a lot of students from both schools"—Alfred State College, located across the street, and Alfred University—"go out to a party and drink."

Student Body

"There really is no typical student at Alfred" because the "wide variety of majors and minors…attracts such a wide variety of students." The predominant note is "a mix of engineers and art students" (they make up about 40 percent of the student body) with "a smattering of other majors" across a broad range of disciplines, business and psychology most prominent among them. Students report that the population is "polarized among the art school, the liberal arts school, and the business school. Everybody seems to fit in somewhere, though." Engineers and artists tend toward the outer edges of the bell curve, so it's not surprising that "The school is made up of crazies of every variety. If you're a freak in high school, you will fit right in at Alfred. We have everything from people who will fall over themselves to discuss postmodernism to people who make chain-mail bikinis." Most here "are from small towns, although there is also a proportionally high percentage of study abroad students."

FINANCIAL AID: 607-871-2159 • E-MAIL: ADMISSIONS@ALFRED.EDU • WEBSITE: WWW.ALFRED.EDU

THE PRINCETON REVIEW SAYS

Admissions

Very important factors considered include: Class rank, recommendation(s), rigor of secondary school record, character/personal qualities, extracurricular activities. *Important factors considered include:* Application essay, standardized test scores, volunteer work, work experience. *Other factors considered include:* Interview, racial/ethnic status, talent/ability. SAT or ACT required. TOEFL required of all international applicants. High school diploma is required and GED is accepted. *Academic units required:* 4 English, 2 mathematics, 2 science (2 science labs), 2 social studies. *Academic units recommended:* 4 mathematics, 3 science (3 science labs), 3 social studies.

Financial Aid

Students should submit: FAFSA, institution's own financial aid form, state aid form, noncustodial profile, business/farm supplement. Regular filing deadline is 3/15. The Princeton Review suggests that all financial aid forms be submitted as soon as possible after 1/1. *Need-based scholarships/grants offered:* Federal Pell, SEOG, state scholarships/grants, private scholarships, the school's own gift aid. *Loan aid offered:* FFEL Subsidized Stafford, FFEL Unsubsidized Stafford, FFEL PLUS, Federal Perkins, college/university loans from institutional funds, other private alternative loans. Applicants will be notified of awards on a rolling basis beginning 2/15. Federal Work-Study Program available. Institutional employment available. Off-campus job opportunities are poor.

The Inside Word

Alfred is a fine university with a solid local reputation. The allure for arts students is obvious—Alfred's programs in the arts are especially well regarded—and as a result, competition is fiercest among applicants for these programs. A killer portfolio, even more than great grades and standardized test scores, is your most likely ticket in. Competition for the engineering school is also tight. Applicants will need rigorous high school program.

THE SCHOOL SAYS ". . ."

From The Admissions Office

"The admissions process at Alfred University is the foundation for the personal attention each student can expect during their time at AU. Each applicant is evaluated individually and receives genuine, individual care and consideration.

"The best way to discover all Alfred University has to offer is to come to campus. We truly have something for everyone with more than 60 courses of study, 22 intercollegiate athletic teams, and 100 clubs and organizations. You can tour campus; meet current students, faculty, coaches, and staff; attend a class; and eat in our dining hall—experience first hand what life at AU is like.

"Alfred University is a place where students are free to pursue their dreams and interests—all of them—no matter how varied or different. Academics, athletics, study abroad, special interests—they're all part of what makes you who you are and who you are going to become."

SELECTIVITY

Admissions Rating	77
# of applicants	2,355
% of applicants accepted	74
% of acceptees attending	28
# of early decision applicants	53
% accepted early decision	83

FRESHMAN PROFILE

Range SAT Critical Reading	440–610
Range SAT Math	500–620
Range ACT Composite	22–27
Minimum paper TOEFL	550
Minimum computer TOEFL	213
% graduated top 10% of class	18
% graduated top 25% of class	46
% graduated top 50% of class	85

DEADLINES

Early decision	
Deadline	12/1
Notification	12/15
Regular	
Priority	2/1
Notification	rolling
Nonfall registration?	yes

APPLICANTS ALSO LOOK AT
AND OFTEN PREFER
State University of New York at Geneseo

AND SOMETIMES PREFER
State University of New York—
University at Buffalo
Syracuse University

FINANCIAL FACTS

Financial Aid Rating	86
Annual tuition	$23,428
Room and board	$10,796
Required fees	$850
Books and supplies	$900
% frosh rec. need-based scholarship or grant aid	74
% UG rec. need-based scholarship or grant aid	73
% frosh rec. non-need-based scholarship or grant aid	44
% UG rec. non-need-based scholarship or grant aid	39
% frosh rec. need-based self-help aid	66
% UG rec. need-based self-help aid	66
% frosh rec. any financial aid	92
% UG rec. any financial aid	90
% UG borrow to pay for school	82.5
Average cumulative indebtedness	$23,292

ALLEGHENY COLLEGE

OFFICE OF ADMISSIONS, ALLEGHENY COLLEGE, MEADVILLE, PA 16335 • ADMISSIONS: 814-332-4351 • FAX: 814-337-0431

CAMPUS LIFE
Quality of Life Rating	**75**
Fire Safety Rating	**77**
Green Rating	**98**
Type of school	private
Environment	town

STUDENTS
Total undergrad enrollment	2,099
% male/female	44/56
% from out of state	40
% from public high school	83
% live on campus	78
% in (# of) fraternities	21 (5)
% in (# of) sororities	34 (5)
% African American	3
% Asian	3
% Caucasian	90
% Hispanic	2
% international	1
# of countries represented	33

SURVEY SAYS . . .
Lab facilities are great
Athletic facilities are great
Career services are great
School is well run
Students are friendly
Students are happy
Student government is popular

ACADEMICS
Academic Rating	**91**
Calendar	semester
Student/faculty ratio	13:1
Profs interesting rating	91
Profs accessible rating	89
Most common reg class size	10–19 students
Most common lab size	10–19 students

MOST POPULAR MAJORS
biology/biological sciences
economics
psychology

STUDENTS SAY ". . ."

Academics

Allegheny College "allows students to follow a very unique path by encouraging distribution within majors and minors." Indeed, the school requires students to declare both a major and a minor concentration outside their major division of knowledge (e.g. natural science majors must minor in a humanities or social science discipline), a requirement that undergraduates say "pushes students to achieve more than they ever thought." Likewise, a mandatory research-based senior project in one's major field of study makes for a "challenging" academic experience. One student says the school is so tough that "it over-prepares us for the 'real world,'" and that toughness helps give the school its "amazing reputation for a higher standard of learning." Pre-meds are especially drawn by the school's success in placing graduates in better medical schools; the psychology and English departments also earn students' praise. Allegheny goes the extra mile on service; professors "are always available when you need help or someone to talk to," the college president "is always walking around campus talking to the students," and the career services office "is excellent," offering "all forms of out-of-class learning in a central location. A student can go there to find out about internships, community service, or international services (studying abroad)." All of those combined elements explain why students tell us that "Allegheny College is the perfect place to get a well-rounded education and a jump start on your career after graduation."

Life

Allegheny academics are demanding, so "students are often found in the library studying and/or other various areas on the campus during the weekdays. We take our studies very seriously and spend a lot of time getting our work done." Weekends, however, "are filled with various activities held on campus and usually sponsored by the school or random parties at off-campus houses." Some brag that "There are infinite things to do on campus. There is always an event going on, or a play, or a dance, or many other possibilities." Greek life is fairly big on campus, and the school's alcohol policy "is pretty moderate. The college treats us like adults who can make our own decisions." Students add that "We aren't one of those schools where drinking is the only thing to do. We run around and sled in the snow, go to movies (Tuesday is only $5!), go out to eat in town, see concerts, etc." It's fortunate that campus is so busy because hometown Meadville is a small town that "doesn't offer much" in the way of diversions. The weather isn't so hot either; "The school is located near Lake Erie, so there is a lot of precipitation throughout the year....Slush builds up, and students, faculty, and visiting families must leap across snowdrifts in order to access the sidewalks."

Student Body

The typical student at Allegheny "is white, middle class, and prepared to learn." Many are "extremely devoted to both their schoolwork and involvement in extracurricular activities," and they "'overload' [on] credits every semester while taking on leadership position after leadership position." "Those who go Greek" and the "tree-loving hippie liberals" are among the more conspicuous groups at Allegheny, but "There are all types here. Qualities that most students have are intelligence and openness to new ideas. We do have people that look quite strange sometimes, but people are nice to them. We have so many groups that even the crazy art kids who have colored hair and don't wear shoes find their niche and interact positively with sorority girls who always wear heels."

FINANCIAL AID: 800-835-7780 • E-MAIL: ADMISSIONS@ALLEGHENY.EDU • WEBSITE: WWW.ALLEGHENY.EDU

THE PRINCETON REVIEW SAYS

Admissions

Very important factors considered include: Class rank, academic GPA, rigor of secondary school record. *Important factors considered include:* Recommendation(s), standardized test scores, character/personal qualities, extracurricular activities, interview, level of applicant's interest. *Other factors considered include:* Application essay, alumni/ae relation, first generation, geographical residence, racial/ethnic status, talent/ability, volunteer work, work experience. SAT or ACT required. ACT with Writing component recommended. TOEFL required of all international applicants. High school diploma is required and GED is accepted. *Academic units required:* 4 English, 3 mathematics, 3 science, 2 foreign language, 3 social studies, 1 academic elective.

Financial Aid

Students should submit: FAFSA. The Princeton Review suggests that all financial aid forms be submitted as soon as possible after 1/1. *Need-based scholarships/grants offered:* Federal Pell, SEOG, state scholarships/grants, private scholarships, the school's own gift aid, Federal Academic Competitiveness Grant, National SMART Grant, Veterans Educational Benefits. *Loan aid offered:* Direct Subsidized Stafford, Direct Unsubsidized Stafford, Direct PLUS, Federal Perkins, other private loans from commercial lenders. Applicants will be notified of awards on a rolling basis beginning 3/1. Federal Work-Study Program available. Institutional employment available. Off-campus job opportunities are excellent.

The Inside Word

Not everybody accepted to Allegheny was a stellar high-school student—about one in four undergrads here graduated out of the top 25 percent of their high school class—but the typical admit here has solid high school grades in a demanding curriculum and above-average standardized test scores. Extras count; admissions officers take the time to get to know applicants' full profiles and may find compelling evidence in recommendations or extracurricular experiences to mitigate less-than-optimal grades and/or test scores.

THE SCHOOL SAYS "..."

From The Admissions Office

"We're proud of Allegheny's beautiful campus and cutting-edge technologies, and we know that our professors are leading scholars who pride themselves even more on being among the best teachers in the United States. Yet it's our students who make Allegheny the unique and special place that it is. Allegheny attracts students with unusual combinations of interests, skills, and talents. How do we characterize them? Although it's impossible to label our students, they do share some common characteristics. You'll find an abiding passion for learning and life, a spirit of camaraderie, and shared inquiry that spans across individuals as well as areas of study. You'll see over and over again such a variety of interests and passions and skills that, after a while, those unusual combinations don't seem so unusual at all.

"Allegheny is not for everybody. If you find labels reassuring, if you're looking for a narrow technical training, if you're in search of the shortest distance between point A and point B, then perhaps another college will be better for you.

"But, if you recognize that everything you experience between points A and B will make you appreciate point B that much more; if you've noticed that when life gives you a choice between two things, you're tempted to answer both or simply yes; if you start to get excited because you sense there is a college willing to echo the resounding *yes*, then we look forward to meeting you.

"Applicants are required to take either the SAT or ACT (Writing section is recommended but not required). If both tests are taken, we will use the better score of the two. The Writing score of both the SAT and ACT will be reviewed but will not be a major factor in admission decisions."

SELECTIVITY

Admissions Rating	91
# of applicants	4,243
% of applicants accepted	61
% of acceptees attending	22
# accepting a place on wait list	362
% admitted from wait list	4
# of early decision applicants	86
% accepted early decision	71

FRESHMAN PROFILE

Range SAT Critical Reading	550–660
Range SAT Math	560–650
Range ACT Composite	23–28
Minimum paper TOEFL	550
Minimum computer TOEFL	213
Minimum web-based TOEFL	80
Average HS GPA	3.7
% graduated top 10% of class	46
% graduated top 25% of class	78
% graduated top 50% of class	96

DEADLINES

Early decision	
Deadline	11/15
Notification	12/15
Regular	
Deadline	2/15
Notification	4/1
Nonfall registration?	yes

APPLICANTS ALSO LOOK AT

AND OFTEN PREFER
Kenyon College, Bucknell University, Boston University, University of Rochester

AND SOMETIMES PREFER
The College of Wooster, Denison University, Dickinson College, Gettysburg College

AND RARELY PREFER
Duquesne University, Miami University, Washington & Jefferson College, Penn State—University Park, University of Pittsburgh—Pittsburgh Campus

FINANCIAL FACTS

Financial Aid Rating	87
Annual tuition	$33,240
Room and board	$8,440
Required fees	$320
Books and supplies	$1,000
% frosh rec. need-based scholarship or grant aid	69
% UG rec. need-based scholarship or grant aid	68
% frosh rec. non-need-based scholarship or grant aid	12
% UG rec. non-need-based scholarship or grant aid	10
% frosh rec. need-based self-help aid	59
% UG rec. need-based self-help aid	59
% frosh rec. any financial aid	98
% UG rec. any financial aid	98

AMERICAN UNIVERSITY

4400 Massachusetts Avenue, Northwest, Washington, DC 20016-8001 • Admissions: 202-885-6000 • Fax: 202-885-1025

CAMPUS LIFE

Quality of Life Rating	**95**
Fire Safety Rating	**93**
Green Rating	**88**
Type of school	private
Affiliation	Methodist
Environment	metropolis

STUDENTS

Total undergrad enrollment	6,028
% male/female	38/62
% from out of state	84
% live on campus	64
% in (# of) fraternities	14 (11)
% in (# of) sororities	16 (12)
% African American	4
% Asian	5
% Caucasian	62
% Hispanic	4
% international	6
# of countries represented	137

SURVEY SAYS . . .
Career services are great
Students love Washington, D.C.
Great off-campus food
Low cost of living
Political activism is popular
(Almost) no one smokes

ACADEMICS

Academic Rating	**86**
Calendar	semester
Student/faculty ratio	13.5:1
Profs interesting rating	83
Profs accessible rating	81

MOST POPULAR MAJORS
business/commerce
international relations and affairs
mass communication/media studies

STUDENTS SAY " . . ."

Academics

American University exploits its Washington, D.C. location—that facilitates a strong faculty, prestigious guest lecturers, and "a wealth of internship opportunities"—to offer "incredibly strong programs" in political science and international relations. "The poli-sci kids are all going to be president one day, and the international studies ones are all going to save the world," a student insists. The school of communications also excels, and the school works hard to accommodate "interdisciplinary majors and the opportunities associated with studying them," which include "taking advantage of the resources of the city. The school values learning out of the classroom as much as learning in the classroom." As you might expect from a school with a strong international relations program, "AU's study abroad program is one of the best." Although AU "does not have the automatically recognizable prestige of nearby Georgetown," that's not necessarily a drawback; on the contrary, "The administration and professors go out of their way to ensure a great academic experience," in part because the school is trying to "climb in the rankings and gain recognition as one of the nation's top universities." However, AU is still "not the place for science majors," and some concede that "the university could improve programs in other fields, aside from its specialties in international studies, public affairs, business, and communication."

Life

"The greatest strength of AU is the activity level both politically and in the community," students tell us, noting that during the most recent election the campus "was a proxy holy war...Whether it was signs in windows, talk in the class or in the hallways, T-shirts, or canvassing in Metro-accessible Virginia, students on both sides took November 4 religiously." As one student explains, "Let's put it this way: A politician who comes to campus is likely to draw about 90 percent of the student population [and] an AU basketball game, about nine [percent]." Students get involved in the community through "campus outreach by student-run organizations," which many see as "the school's greatest asset." The typical undergrad is "incredibly engaged and active...Students seek internships in every line of work, becoming actively involved in a field of interest before graduation." When it's time to relax, "Washington, D.C. offers limitless opportunities to explore." Many "enjoy partying and hanging out off-campus and on campus (even though AU is a 'dry campus')," but there are also "a lot of people who don't drink and have a very good time just using what D.C. has to offer: museums, restaurants, parks, cinemas, theaters, and shops." As one student sums it up: "The city is the school's greatest resource. You will never run out of things to do in Washington."

Student Body

AU attracts a "liberal, non-religious" crowd that "tends to be very ideologically driven." "Liberals run the show," most here agree, although they add that "Plenty of students don't fit this mold, and I've never seen anyone rejected for what they believe." The campus "is very friendly to those with alternative lifestyles (GLBT, vegetarian, green-living, etc.)," but students with more socially conservative inclinations note that "while AU boasts about the many religious groups on campus, there is still a general antipathy toward piety, especially Christianity." The perception that some departments outshine others is reflected in the way students perceive each other; one says, "You have the political studies know-it-alls, the international studies student who thinks he is going to save the world, the artsy film/communication students, and the rest [who] are unhappy students who couldn't get into George Washington or Georgetown."

FINANCIAL AID: 202-885-6100 • E-MAIL: AFA@AMERICAN.EDU • WEBSITE: WWW.AMERICAN.EDU

THE PRINCETON REVIEW SAYS

Admissions

Very important factors considered include: Academic GPA, rigor of secondary school record, standardized test scores. *Important factors considered include:* Application essay, recommendation(s), level of applicants interest, extracurricular activities, volunteer work. *Other factors considered include:* Alumni/ae relation, character/personal qualities, first generation, geographical residence, racial/ethnic status, talent/ability, work experience. SAT Subject Tests recommended. SAT or ACT required. ACT with Writing component required. TOEFL required of all international applicants. High school diploma is required and GED is accepted. *Academic units required:* 4 English, 3 mathematics, 3 science (2 science labs), 2 foreign language, 2 social studies, 3 academic electives. *Academic units recommended:* 4 English, 4 mathematics, 4 science, 3 foreign language, 4 social studies, 4 academic electives.

Financial Aid

Students should submit: FAFSA, and CSS profile. Regular filing deadline is 2/15. The Princeton Review suggests that all financial aid forms be submitted as soon as possible after 1/1. *Need-based scholarships/grants offered:* Federal Pell, SEOG, state scholarships/grants, private scholarships, the school's own gift aid. Academic merit scholarships: presidential scholarships, dean's scholarships, Frederick Douglass scholarships, Phi Theta Kappa scholarships (transfers only), tuition exchange scholarships, United Methodist scholarships, and other private/restricted scholarships are awarded by the Undergraduate Admissions Office. Most scholarships do not require a separate application and are renewable for up to three years if certain criteria are met. *Loan aid offered:* Direct Subsidized Stafford, Direct Unsubsidized Stafford, Direct PLUS, FFEL PLUS, Federal Perkins. Applicants will be notified of awards on or about 4/1. Federal Work-Study Program available. Institutional employment available. Off-campus job opportunities are excellent.

The Inside Word

American asks applicants to indicate their intended field of study. Those selecting one of American's hallmark disciplines—e.g. political science, international studies, communications—will have the highest hurdles to clear. No one cruises into American. However, despite strong competition from other area powerhouses, American sees a strong applicant pool that allows it to be very selective.

THE SCHOOL SAYS "..."

From The Admissions Office

"American University is located in the residential "Embassy Row" neighborhood of Washington, D.C. Nestled among embassies and ambassadorial residences, AU's campus offers a safe, suburban environment with easy access to Washington's countless cultural destinations via the Metrorail subway system. AU's faculty includes scholars, journalists, artists, diplomats, authors and scientists in 70 programs across five undergraduate schools. Combining a liberal arts core curriculum with in-depth professional programs, academics at AU provide the necessary balance between theoretical study and hands-on experience. Our Career Center will work with you to enhance this experience with access to unique internship opportunities available only in Washington. Combine this with our diverse national and international student body and our world-class study abroad program, and AU can open up a world of possibilities.

"AU requires all applicants graduating from high school to take the SAT or the ACT with the Writing section."

SELECTIVITY

Admissions Rating	**93**
# of applicants	15,413
% of applicants accepted	53
% of acceptees attending	19
# accepting a place on wait list	201
# of early decision applicants	397
% accepted early decision	75

FRESHMAN PROFILE

Range SAT Critical Reading	580–700
Range SAT Math	570–670
Range SAT Writing	580–680
Range ACT Composite	25–30
Minimum paper TOEFL	610
Minimum computer TOEFL	263
Minimum web-based TOEFL	101
% graduated top 10% of class	46
% graduated top 25% of class	79
% graduated top 50% of class	97

DEADLINES

Early decision	
Deadline	11/15
Notification	12/31
Regular	
Deadline	1/15
Notification	4/1
Nonfall registration?	yes

APPLICANTS ALSO LOOK AT
AND OFTEN PREFER
The George Washington University
New York University
Georgetown University
Boston University

AND SOMETIMES PREFER
Northeastern University
Boston College
Tufts University

AND RARELY PREFER
Fordham University
University of Pennsylvania
Syracuse University

FINANCIAL FACTS

Financial Aid Rating	**86**
Annual tuition	$34,456
Room and board	$12,930
Required fees	$517
Books and supplies	$1,000
% frosh rec. need-based scholarship or grant aid	21
% UG rec. need-based scholarship or grant aid	25
% frosh rec. non-need-based scholarship or grant aid	27
% UG rec. non-need-based scholarship or grant aid	20
% frosh rec. need-based self-help aid	38
% UG rec. need-based self-help aid	42
% frosh rec. athletic scholarships	3
% UG rec. athletic scholarships	3
% frosh rec. any financial aid	82
% UG rec. any financial aid	69

AMHERST COLLEGE

CAMPUS BOX 2231, PO BOX 5000, AMHERST, MA 01002 • ADMISSIONS: 413-542-2328 • FAX: 413-542-2040

CAMPUS LIFE
Quality of Life Rating	91
Fire Safety Rating	60*
Green Rating	60*
Type of school	private
Environment	town

STUDENTS
Total undergrad enrollment	1,697
% male/female	49/51
% from out of state	88
% from public high school	58
% live on campus	98
% African American	10
% Asian	10
% Caucasian	42
% Hispanic	9
% international	7
# of countries represented	39

SURVEY SAYS . . .
No one cheats
School is well run
Dorms are like palaces
Campus feels safe
Low cost of living
Musical organizations are popular

ACADEMICS
Academic Rating	94
Calendar	semester
Student/faculty ratio	8:1
Profs interesting rating	86
Profs accessible rating	90
Most common reg class size	10–19 students
Most common lab size	10–19 students

MOST POPULAR MAJORS
economics
political science and government
psychology

STUDENTS SAY ". . ."

Academics
With just fewer than 1,700 students, Amherst College "has a strong sense of community born of its small size" that goes hand-in-hand with an atmosphere that "encourages discussion and cooperation." Many here are quick to praise the "fantastic" professors and "supportive" administration. "Professors come here to teach," says one undergrad, "not just to do research." The "enriching" academics are bolstered by the "dedicated" faculty, but slackers be warned: You must be "willing to sit down and read a text forward and backward and firmly grasp it" as "skimming will do you no good." Besides having "easily accessible" professors, some students also appreciate that "registration is done by paper" as "it forces you to talk to your advisor." Another student notes that "I'm amazed at how easy it is to sit down for a casual lunch with anyone in the administration without there having to be a problem that needs to be discussed." Indeed, most here agree that "the support for students is as good as anyone could expect." However, some mention that despite the "administration, staff, and faculty" being "accessible and receptive to student input on every level," the "realities of running a small school in this economic climate mean a lot of suggestions won't be acted upon any time soon." Nevertheless, Amherst's alumni have a solid track record when it comes to obtaining postgraduate degrees—so much so that some think of the college "as prep school for grad school."

Life
While students at Amherst are "focused first and foremost on academics, nearly every student is active and enjoys life outside of the library." "There's a club or organization for every interest" here, and students assure us that if there isn't one that you're interested in, "the school will find the money for it." Students also praise the "awesome" dorms (some say they're "as spacious, well-maintained, and luxurious as many five-star hotels"), for being "designed to facilitate social interaction." Coincidentally, the dorms tend to serve as the school's social hub, particularly since Greek organizations were banned back in 1985. Amherst makes up for the lack of frat houses with "a number of socials put on by student government and I-Club (International Club) that are held throughout the year at bars downtown." And don't worry if you don't have a car since these events "have free buses that transport students to and from the bars." Some bemoan that the town of Amherst is "incredibly small" and doesn't feature much in the way of fun. Others take solace in "the many eateries in town that feature lots of ethnically diverse foods" and "go to sporting events." And since Amherst is part of the Five Colleges consortium, there's "an extended social life to be had," however "not that many people go out of their way to experience it." For those who like liquor with their extracurricular activities, most "drink on-campus instead of off-campus" thanks to some "huge apartment parties."

Student Body
Traditionally, the student body at Amherst has been known by the "stereotype of the preppy, upper middle class, white student," but many here note that the school is "at least as racially diverse as the country and more economically diverse than people think." That's not to say that the college doesn't have "a sizeable preppy population fresh from East Coast boarding schools," but overall students here report that "Diversity—racial, ethnic, geographic, socioeconomic—is more than a buzzword here." The campus is also "a politically and environmentally conscious" place, as well as a "highly athletic one." The school's small size "means that no group is isolated and everyone interacts and more or less gets along." Others, however, aren't as convinced about the student body's unity. "There is definitely a divide in the student body," says one undergrad. "The typical Amherst student is either an extremely quiet, bookish nerd or a lumbering, backward-baseball-cap-wearing jock." That said, the school is filled with "open-minded, intellectually passionate, and socially-conscious critical thinkers." As one student puts it, "Most students—even our most drunken athletes and wild party-goers—are concerned about learning and academics."

FINANCIAL AID: 413-542-2296 • E-MAIL: ADMISSION@AMHERST.EDU • WEBSITE: WWW.AMHERST.EDU

THE PRINCETON REVIEW SAYS

Admissions

Very important factors considered include: Application essay, academic GPA, recommendation(s), rigor of secondary school record, standardized test scores, character/personal qualities, extracurricular activities, first generation, talent/ability. *Important factors considered include:* Class rank, alumni/ae relation, volunteer work. *Other factors considered include:* Geographical residence, state residency, work experience. SAT and SAT Subject Tests or ACT required. ACT with Writing component recommended. TOEFL required of all international applicants. High school diploma or equivalent is not required. *Academic units recommended:* 4 English, 4 mathematics, 3 science (1 science lab), 4 foreign language, 2 social studies, 2 history.

Financial Aid

Students should submit: FAFSA, CSS/financial aid profile, noncustodial profile, business/farm supplement. Income documentation submitted through College. The Princeton Review suggests that all financial aid forms be submitted as soon as possible after 1/1. *Need-based scholarships/grants offered:* Federal Pell, SEOG, state scholarships/grants, private scholarships, the school's own gift aid. *Loan aid offered:* Direct Subsidized Stafford, Direct Unsubsidized Stafford, Direct PLUS, Federal Perkins, college/university loans from institutional funds. Applicants will be notified of awards on or about 4/5. Federal Work-Study Program available. Institutional employment available. Off-campus job opportunities are excellent.

The Inside Word

Membership certainly has its benefits at Amherst College. For the price of entry to this school students also gain entrance to the prestigious Five Colleges consortium, which allows enrolled students to take courses for credit at no additional cost at any of the four participating consortium members (Hampshire College, Mount Holyoke College, Smith College, and the University of Massachusetts—Amherst). And this deal isn't just confined to the classroom: Students can use other schools' libraries, eat meals at the other cafeterias, and participate in extracurricular activities offerred at the other schools. And don't worry about how you'll get there—your bus fare is covered, too.

THE SCHOOL SAYS " . . ."

From The Admissions Office

"Amherst College looks, above all, for men and women of intellectual promise who have demonstrated qualities of mind and character that will enable them to take full advantage of the college's curriculum....Admission decisions aim to select from among the many qualified applicants those possessing the intellectual talent, mental discipline, and imagination that will allow them most fully to benefit from the curriculum and contribute to the life of the college and of society. Whatever the form of academic experience—lecture course, seminar, conference, studio, laboratory, independent study at various levels—intellectual competence and awareness of problems and methods are the goals of the Amherst program, rather than the direct preparation for a profession.

"Applicants must submit scores from the SAT plus two SAT Subject Tests. Students may substitute the ACT with the Writing component."

SELECTIVITY

Admissions Rating	98
# of applicants	7,745
% of applicants accepted	15
% of acceptees attending	38
# accepting a place on wait list	806
% admitted from wait list	5
# of early decision applicants	404
% accepted early decision	34

FRESHMAN PROFILE

Range SAT Critical Reading	660–760
Range SAT Math	660–760
Range SAT Writing	660–760
Range ACT Composite	29–33
Minimum paper TOEFL	600
Minimum computer TOEFL	250
Minimum web-based TOEFL	100
% graduated top 10% of class	79
% graduated top 25% of class	35
% graduated top 50% of class	99

DEADLINES

Early decision	
Deadline	11/15
Notification	12/15
Regular	
Deadline	1/1
Notification	4/5
Nonfall registration?	no

APPLICANTS ALSO LOOK AT

AND OFTEN PREFER
Harvard College
Yale University
Princeton University

AND SOMETIMES PREFER
Dartmouth College
Stanford University
Williams College
Brown University

FINANCIAL FACTS

Financial Aid Rating	93
Annual tuition	$36,970
Room and board	$9,790
Required fees	$670
Books and supplies	$1,000
% frosh rec. need-based scholarship or grant aid	50
% UG rec. need-based scholarship or grant aid	53
% UG rec. non-need-based scholarship or grant aid	13
% UG rec. need-based self-help aid	44
% UG borrow to pay for school	46
Average cumulative indebtedness	$12,603

ANGELO STATE UNIVERSITY

2601 WEST AVENUE N, SAN ANGELO, TX 76909 • ADMISSIONS: 325-942-2041 • FAX: 325-942-2078

CAMPUS LIFE

Quality of Life Rating	73
Fire Safety Rating	90
Green Rating	67
Type of school	public
Environment	city

STUDENTS

Total undergrad enrollment	5,570
% male/female	45/55
% from out of state	2
% from public high school	96
% live on campus	31
% in (# of) fraternities	3 (4)
% in (# of) sororities	4 (2)
% African American	8
% Asian	1
% Caucasian	65
% Hispanic	25
% Native American	1
# of countries represented	21

SURVEY SAYS . . .

Low cost of living
(Almost) no one smokes
Very little drug use

ACADEMICS

Academic Rating	65
Calendar	semester
Student/faculty ratio	19:1
Profs interesting rating	75
Profs accessible rating	71
% classes taught by TAs	2
Most common reg class size	20–29 students
Most common lab size	20–29 students

MOST POPULAR MAJORS

business administration and management
health and physical education
multi-/interdisciplinary studies

STUDENTS SAY ". . ."

Academics

Angelo State University, a member of the Texas Tech University System, is "a small school with big opportunities." "Bang for your buck" is reportedly ample. In addition to a "relatively cheap tuition price compared to other public universities in Texas," ASU offers tremendous financial aid and "excellent scholarship opportunities." Academically, this place is a "science haven." "The technology here is great." The on-campus planetarium is one of the biggest and best at any school, anywhere. Students also praise the education, agriculture, and nursing programs. "Classes are generally small." Professors "are on a first-name basis with their students" and "get to know you personally." As far as teaching, some profs are "pretty much awesome" while others are merely "subject matter experts, not teachers." The administration is "relatively well organized." On the whole, students tell us that they feel "supported and encouraged." "I'm uber-happy to be at Angelo State and can't imagine being anywhere else," gloats an accounting major.

Life

ASU's campus is "very small and easy to navigate." Students note "it can be really hard to find a parking space on campus" and note the need for "more student parking around certain buildings." Some facilities are "not big enough." Students also warn, "Be cautious of the cafeteria food." "Campus life is very active." "ASU does an excellent job of trying to involve its students." "Many people play intramural sports." The University Center is popular for "killing time." Activities on offer include ping pong, a wealth of videogames, and "Texas hold 'em tournaments." For nature lovers, there is a state park nearby with biking and hiking trails. By the time the weekend rolls around, some people "go to the bars and clubs." "House parties" are also frequent. On the other hand, Greek life is paltry. One student describes the surrounding city of San Angelo as "a very 'old person' town." Another student says that "people coming from small towns to San Angelo are able to keep entertained outside of school fairly easily," observes a shrewd first-year student. "Conversely, people coming from larger cities find it hard to have fun because, out here, you do need some creativity in finding things to do." For serious leisure, "you have to drive three hours to Austin."

Student Body

While drawing students from throughout Texas, including the major metropolitan areas, the typical student at ASU attended "a very small high school" in "a tiny west Texas town." Most come from "lower- to middle-class" families. Almost three quarters receive financial aid. Students describe themselves as "friendly, hardworking," and "career oriented." They tend to be "conservative." "There aren't a whole lot of cowboy hats, but it's relatively traditional," explains a junior. "There is nothing too radical around here." There are some "dullards," but "academics are pretty important" to most students. It's not uncommon for students to "use ASU as a bridge or a stepping stone and transfer to a larger university after one or two years to finish their degrees." Nontraditional students are quite common as well. "There are all different types of people and all different ages," notes a junior. "This makes it easier to fit in."

FINANCIAL AID: 325-942-2246 • E-MAIL: ADMISSIONS@ANGELO.EDU • WEBSITE: WWW.ANGELO.EDU

THE PRINCETON REVIEW SAYS

Admissions

Very important factors considered include: Class rank, rigor of secondary school record, standardized test scores. *Other factors considered include:* Academic GPA, first generation, SAT or ACT required. TOEFL required of all international applicants. High school diploma is required and GED is accepted. *Academic units recommended:* 4 English, 3 mathematics, 3 science, 2 foreign language, 3 social studies, 1 academic elective.

Financial Aid

Students should submit: FAFSA. The Princeton Review suggests that all financial aid forms be submitted as soon as possible after 1/1. *Need-based scholarships/grants offered:* Federal Pell, SEOG, state scholarships/grants, private scholarships, the school's own gift aid, federal nursing scholarships. *Loan aid offered:* FFEL Subsidized Stafford, FFEL Unsubsidized Stafford, FFEL PLUS, Federal Perkins, federal nursing, state loans, college/university loans from institutional funds. Applicants will be notified of awards on a rolling basis beginning 4/1. Federal Work-Study Program available. Institutional employment available. Off-campus job opportunities are good.

The Inside Word

The admissions process at Angelo State embodies an inclusive attitude that encourages students who may not have established their full academic potential in high school to invest in attaining a higher degree. Students in the top ten percent of their class are granted automatic admission. Those applicants who do not meet general admission requirements may apply for alternative admission. In this case, leadership activities, community service, talents and awards, extenuating circumstances, and employment history play a large role.

THE SCHOOL SAYS " . . ."

From The Admissions Office

"Angelo State University provides an education in value, both in the quality for the cost and in the low average debt burden students accrue in securing an Angelo State degree. ASU remains an affordable institution with a superb record of sending graduates on to medical, law, and professional school. ASU maintains strong academic programs in traditional fields such as physics, biology, mathematics, education, business, agriculture, and nursing while developing such innovative offerings as the computer gaming design sequence through computer science.

"Graduates leave ASU with an average debt burden that is 31 percent below the state of Texas average and lower than every state average but one nationally. This is possible because of the university's strong gift aid program, including the Carr Scholarship Program, which annually awards more than $3 million in scholarships, benefiting one in every six ASU students. Additionally, ASU offers its Blue and Gold Guarantee program for students from low income families as well as the Graduation Incentive Program, which pays students to graduate in four years. ASU also offers special scholarships to students with 900–1100 SAT and 21–24 ACT scores.

"Because of its low 19:1 student-faculty ratio and individualized instruction, ASU attracts many first-generation students, who benefit from special programs and scholarships. Almost a quarter of the student body is Hispanic, enhancing the university's overall diversity. A strong honors program and numerous opportunities for international study enhance the college experience on the 268-acre Angelo State campus known for its safety and modern academic and recreational facilities."

SELECTIVITY

Admissions Rating	**72**
# of applicants	3,010
% of applicants accepted	97
% of acceptees attending	50

FRESHMAN PROFILE

Range SAT Critical Reading	410–520
Range SAT Math	430–540
Range SAT Writing	400–510
Range ACT Composite	17–23
Minimum paper TOEFL	550
Minimum computer TOEFL	213
% graduated top 10% of class	14
% graduated top 25% of class	28
% graduated top 50% of class	73

DEADLINES

Regular	
Priority	8/15
Deadline	8/15
Notification	rolling
Nonfall registration?	yes

FINANCIAL FACTS

Financial Aid Rating	**86**
Annual in-state tuition	$3,968
Annual out-of-state tuition	$12,398
Room and board	$6,612
Required fees	$1,443
Books and supplies	$1,000
% frosh rec. need-based scholarship or grant aid	45
% UG rec. need-based scholarship or grant aid	49
% frosh rec. non-need-based scholarship or grant aid	49
% UG rec. non-need-based scholarship or grant aid	31
% frosh rec. need-based self-help aid	43
% UG rec. need-based self-help aid	44
% frosh rec. any financial aid	76
% UG rec. any financial aid	72
Average cumulative indebtedness	$11,400

ARIZONA STATE UNIVERSITY

PO Box 870112, Tempe, AZ 85287-0112 • Admissions: 480-965-7788 • Fax: 480-965-3610

CAMPUS LIFE

Quality of Life Rating	71
Fire Safety Rating	86
Green Rating	99
Type of school	public
Environment	metropolis

STUDENTS

Total undergrad enrollment	52,883
% male/female	48/52
% from out of state	22
% live on campus	14
% in (# of) fraternities	5 (31)
% in (# of) sororities	6 (23)
% African American	5
% Asian	6
% Caucasian	65
% Hispanic	15
% Native American	2
% international	2
# of countries represented	129

SURVEY SAYS . . .

Great off-campus food
Everyone loves the Sun Devils
Student publications are popular
Lots of beer drinking
Hard liquor is popular

ACADEMICS

Academic Rating	70
Calendar	semester
Profs interesting rating	63
Profs accessible rating	68
Most common reg class size	10–19 students
Most common lab size	20–29 students

MOST POPULAR MAJORS

psychology
interdisciplinary
nursing (RN, ASN, BSN, MSN)

STUDENTS SAY " . . ."

Academics

"Arizona State University is energetic, exciting, an up-and-coming university, and the place to be" according to students at this large public university near sunny Phoenix, Arizona. With almost 53,000 undergraduates, "the opportunities are endless," but "you get exactly what you put into it." "The professors at ASU are typically approachable and care about their students' success." Class size ranges from small seminars of 10 students to lecture classes with hundreds, but "even though there are thousands of students here I've never had a professor that made me feel like a number." The Barrett Honors College in particular gets high marks from students: "Having access to the resources of a large university, combined with the individual access of outstanding honors college professors made [ASU] too great of a deal to pass up." ASU also has "all the research opportunities that a student could want." The business, architecture, construction management, journalism, and child psychology programs are all well-regarded, but with 250 undergraduate programs and majors to choose from, there is "something for everyone to get excited about." While the professors and academic programs have students' near-universal acclaim, ASU's administration gets mixed reviews. "The administration always seems to try to do what's best for the students," says one student; but, although it "handles issues well," "most of the decisions and policies are not favored by the students," says another. This year, a lot of students are worried about the economy and how the recession could affect their university. "ASU has a ton of potential," sums up one student, "the only thing that may stop any progress is the state's current financial crisis and the proposed budget cuts."

Life

"Life at ASU is about doing your work during the week to have fun on weekends," says one student. While ASU has earned its reputation as a party school, there are a wealth of options for students looking for more low-key recreation. "There is a lot to do in the city of Phoenix. It's always booming. You have to try real hard to be bored while going to ASU. " Intercollegiate sports—especially football—are very popular, and students can also "drive into Phoenix or Glendale for Cardinals games, Coyotes games, Suns games, or Diamondbacks games." In addition to sporting events, the university "is conveniently located if you're looking for down time." The Tempe campus is "walking distance from Tempe Town Lake, just a short drive to the mountain for hiking, and best of all—it's right off of Mill Avenue," the thoroughfare that runs along one side of Tempe campus and has "tons of shops, restaurants, and an awesome night life." And the weather's great too: "ASU is one of the few places where you can study by the pool all year long."

Student Body

"ASU is the melting pot of the West Coast," says a student. "There are people from everywhere you can imagine, in and out of the U.S. The university reflects people's diverse backgrounds." "Whether you [are] a bookworm or a party animal or somewhere in between, there is something for everyone at ASU." Another student says: "I wouldn't know how to describe the typical student. We're such a large school with a diverse population that it would be like trying to describe the typical American." "The upside to this is that everyone can find a niche, whether it be with a group of friends or one of the hundreds of student organizations on campus." Many agree that "the students at ASU love to party!" However, "that is not the entire population. There are many dedicated students—such as those involved in different types of clubs and outlets on campus." Some students aren't quite so positive: "The typical student is by all accounts average: average grades, average ambition, average goals, average wants in a university." "Most students seem to be unaware of the world outside of the one they were raised in," complains another. All in all, though, "the typical ASU student is friendly and outgoing" and "seems intent on reaching the goals that they have set for themselves."

FINANCIAL AID: 480-965-3355 • E-MAIL: ADMISSIONS@ASU.EDU • WEBSITE: WWW.ASU.EDU

THE PRINCETON REVIEW SAYS

Admissions

Important factors considered include: Class rank, academic GPA, standardized test scores. Nonresident students have higher admission requirements. SAT or ACT required (test scores are also used for merit scholarship consideration and class placement). ACT with writing component recommended. TOEFL required of all international applicants. High school diploma is required and GED is accepted. *Academic units required:* 4 English, 4 mathematics, 3 science (3 science labs), 2 foreign language, 1 social studies, 1 history, 1 fine arts.

Financial Aid

Students should submit: FAFSA. The Princeton Review suggests that all financial aid forms be submitted as soon as possible after 1/1. *Need-based scholarships/grants offered:* Federal Pell, SEOG, state scholarships/grants, private scholarships, the school's own gift aid, federal nursing scholarships. *Loan aid offered:* Direct Subsidized Stafford, Direct Unsubsidized Stafford, Direct PLUS, FFEL PLUS. Federal Perkins Federal Work-Study Program available. Institutional employment available. Off-campus job opportunities are good.

The Inside Word

ASU is a large public school, with thousands of applicants every year, so numbers count for a lot when you're applying. That being said, you have excellent odds of acceptance if you meet the minimum requirements on your GPA, curriculum, and standardized test scores. It's a state school, so you have an even better shot if you're an Arizona resident. The business, engineering, and journalism schools have additional requirements, as does Barrett, the Honors College. ASU awards a lot of merit-based scholarships, particularly for the honors program.

THE SCHOOL SAYS "..."

From The Admissions Office

"Arizona State University is creating a new model for higher education, an unprecedented combination of academic excellence, entrepreneurial energy, and broad access. This New American University positively impacts the economic, social, cultural and environmental well-being of the communities we serve. Our research is inspired by real world application, blurring the boundaries that traditionally separate academic disciplines.

"ASU serves more than 67,000 undergraduate and graduate students across four unique campuses in metropolitan Phoenix. At the Tempe campus, ASU focuses on research-based education that is analytic and preparatory for employment or graduate or professional school. At the Polytechnic campus, ASU focuses on hands-on, team-based learning with an interdisciplinary approach to professional and technological programs that meet industry and societal needs. With a focus on arts and sciences as well as education and business programs at the West campus, ASU brings unique approaches to learning and a breadth of education in an interdisciplinary arts and sciences environment. Through the Downtown Phoenix campus, ASU focuses on programs with a direct urban and public connection.

"With 250+ undergraduate majors, ASU is a learning environment where personal expression is valued as much as research and discovery. ASU champions intellectual and cultural diversity, and welcomes students from all 50 states and more than 100 nations across the globe. Our distinguished faculty receives prestigious national and international honors including the Nobel Prize and Scientist of the Year awards and membership in the National Academies. Student achievements include Goldwater, Rhodes, Marshall and Fulbright scholars."

SELECTIVITY
Admissions Rating	88
# of applicants	27,089
% of applicants accepted	90
% of acceptees attending	40

FRESHMAN PROFILE
Range SAT Critical Reading	470–600
Range SAT Math	480–610
Range ACT Composite	20–26
Minimum paper TOEFL	500
Minimum computer TOEFL	173
Minimum web-based TOEFL	61
Average HS GPA	3.41
% graduated top 10% of class	31.4
% graduated top 25% of class	58
% graduated top 50% of class	84.8

DEADLINES
Nonfall registration?	yes

FINANCIAL FACTS
Financial Aid Rating	72
Annual in-state tuition	$5,679
Annual out-of-state tuition	$18,582
Room and board	$8,790
Required fees	$255
Books and supplies	$1,130
% frosh rec. need-based scholarship or grant aid	37
% UG rec. need-based scholarship or grant aid	36
% frosh rec. non-need-based scholarship or grant aid	5
% UG rec. non-need-based scholarship or grant aid	2
% frosh rec. need-based self-help aid	22
% UG rec. need-based self-help aid	29
% frosh rec. athletic scholarships	1
% UG rec. athletic scholarships	1
% frosh rec. any financial aid	74.7
% UG rec. any financial aid	66.6
% UG borrow to pay for school	43
Average cumulative indebtedness	$17,732

AUBURN UNIVERSITY

202 MARY MARTIN HALL, AUBURN, AL 36849-5149 • ADMISSIONS: 334-844-4080 • FAX: 334-844-6179

CAMPUS LIFE

Quality of Life Rating	87
Fire Safety Rating	60*
Green Rating	60*
Type of school	public
Environment	town

STUDENTS

Total undergrad enrollment	20,031
% male/female	51/49
% from out of state	35
% from public high school	86
% live on campus	13
% in (# of) fraternities	21 (30)
% in (# of) sororities	31 (19)
% African American	8
% Asian	2
% Caucasian	86
% Hispanic	2
% Native American	1
% international	1
# of countries represented	39

SURVEY SAYS . . .

Great library
School is well run
Students are friendly
Students get along with local community
Students are happy
Everyone loves the Tigers
Student publications are popular
Student government is popular

ACADEMICS

Academic Rating	70
Calendar	semester
Student/faculty ratio	18:1
Profs interesting rating	64
Profs accessible rating	64
Most common reg class size	20–29 students
Most common lab size	10–19 students

MOST POPULAR MAJORS

business administration and management
education
engineering

STUDENTS SAY ". . ."

Academics

Auburn University, a school that "is about family, traditions, and education," is the sort of place that inspires "a strong sense of pride in the past and future of [the school]." In fact, Auburn's "traditions and sense of family continue even after graduation." These traditions are numerous, beloved, and often involve football. The education offerings are strong also; Auburn numbers among its many academic assets "a good business school, one of the best vet schools, and one of the best architecture schools in the nation." The school also excels in engineering, education, and communications. Students enrolled in Auburn's honors program enjoy "priority registration [and] smaller classes" that are almost always taught by professors—not TAs. Speaking of Auburn's professors, students appreciate that they are "readily available," "super friendly," and "always willing to help no matter what size the class." They are "concerned with each student's progress," and "always willing to work with [students] to teach the curriculum and how it applies to [their] life." Academically, "As with any school, you get out of it what you put into it. You can put in the bare minimum and be happy with your C, or you can go to class every day, study hard, and make an A. No one here is going to baby you. You won't get reminders not to miss class, and teachers won't hunt you down for make-ups."

Life

Auburn is "an ideal college town" with "enough bars and such to keep one occupied but small enough to where there is a definite sense of community." The town also offers "movies, bowling, a park," and the attractions of nearby Birmingham, which "isn't that far away." Auburn might not be a good fit for the sort of big-city types who "lament about how few options we have for entertainment, and how food consists [solely] of pizza, chicken tenders (on every corner), and subs," but everyone else seems to love it. They love that the campus is "beautiful" and "life is slow paced—full of sweet tea and southern food." Be warned, though: Auburn "is a drinking town with a football problem." "Football seems to dominate the Fall semester here. It's a huge deal, and it's when most big parties and events [take place]. If you hate football, this might not be the place for you." When they are not cheering on the AU Tigers, students take advantage of Auburn's "very popular" outdoor activities, and when they want to head off-campus, nearby Birmingham or Atlanta, Ga., is a "great stop for city life and entertainment."

Student Body

Auburn students share "an incredible sense of pride" that "most who have never been here will never comprehend. Ask any Auburn student or alumn[us], and they'll generally tell you that Auburn ranks among God, country, family, and the South as things most beloved." Many students "love how Auburn is deeply Republican when most colleges are quite banal in their liberalism," and "prides itself in not being politically correct, and this is not due to ignorance." Not everyone at this large university fits the same mold. "At a school this large, there are people from all walks of life," but a significant number of students do, and they set the tone for the campus. While "slightly conservative," Southern, "white, Protestants" may dominate the student body here, there are also "black, Asian, and a lot of foreign exchange students [at Auburn]." Whatever their background, Auburn students across the board "are very open-minded, and accept everyone for who they are."

FINANCIAL AID: 334-844-4367 • E-MAIL: ADMISSIONS@AUBURN.EDU • WEBSITE: WWW.AUBURN.EDU

THE PRINCETON REVIEW SAYS

Admissions

Very important factors considered include: Application essay, academic GPA, standardized test scores. *Other factors considered include:* Class rank, recommendation(s), rigor of secondary school record, alumni/ae relation, character/personal qualities, extracurricular activities, first generation, geographical residence, state residency, talent/ability, volunteer work, work experience. SAT or ACT required. TOEFL required of all international applicants. High school diploma is required and GED is accepted. *Academic units required:* 4 English, 3 mathematics, 2 science (1 science lab), 3 social studies. *Academic units recommended:* 4 English, 3 mathematics, 3 science, 1 foreign language, 4 social studies.

Financial Aid

Students should submit: FAFSA. The Princeton Review suggests that all financial aid forms be submitted as soon as possible after 1/1. *Need-based scholarships/grants offered:* Federal Pell, SEOG, state scholarships/grants, private scholarships, the school's own gift aid. *Loan aid offered:* FFEL Subsidized Stafford, FFEL Unsubsidized Stafford, FFEL PLUS, Federal Perkins, federal nursing scholarships, college/university loans from institutional funds. Applicants will be notified of awards on a rolling basis beginning 10/2. Off-campus job opportunities are excellent.

The Inside Word

Auburn Admissions officers crunch the numbers, sorting students according to high school GPA and standardized test scores, then offering admission to all who qualify from the top of the list down. The school also looks at "fit" meaning the student's potential to make contributions to the Auburn community. With a 69 percent admitance rate, it's safe to say that these factors only come into play for marginal candidates to mitigate poor grades or test scores.

THE SCHOOL SAYS "..."

From The Admissions Office

"Auburn University is a comprehensive land-grant university serving Alabama and the nation. The university is especially charged with the responsibility of enhancing the economic, social, and cultural development of the state through its instruction, research, and extension programs. In all of these programs, the university is committed to the pursuit of excellence. The university assumes an obligation to provide an environment of learning in which the individual and society are enriched by the discovery, preservation, transmission, and application of knowledge; in which students grow intellectually as they study and do research under the guidance of competent faculty, and in which the faculty develop professionally and contribute fully to the intellectual life of the institution, community, and state. This obligation unites Auburn University's continuing commitment to its land-grant traditions and the institution's role as a dynamic and complex, comprehensive university.

"Applicants for Fall 2009 must submit scores from the SAT or ACT (with the Writing components from either test)."

SELECTIVITY

Admissions Rating	89
# of applicants	17,068
% of applicants accepted	71
% of acceptees attending	33

FRESHMAN PROFILE

Range SAT Critical Reading	520–620
Range SAT Math	550–650
Range SAT Writing	520–620
Range ACT Composite	23–28
Minimum paper TOEFL	550
Minimum computer TOEFL	213
Minimum web-based TOEFL	79
Average HS GPA	3.69
% graduated top 10% of class	31
% graduated top 25% of class	60
% graduated top 50% of class	91

DEADLINES

Regular	
Priority	2/1
Notification	rolling
Nonfall registration?	yes

APPLICANTS ALSO LOOK AT
AND SOMETIMES PREFER

University of Tennessee—Knoxville
Clemson University
Georgia Institute of Technology
University of Alabama—Tuscaloosa
University of Florida
University of Georgia

FINANCIAL FACTS

Financial Aid Rating	64
Annual in-state tuition	$5,880
Annual out-of-state tuition	$17,640
Room and board	$8,260
Required fees	$620
Books and supplies	$1,100
% frosh rec. need-based scholarship or grant aid	22
% UG rec. need-based scholarship or grant aid	20
% frosh rec. non-need-based scholarship or grant aid	4
% UG rec. non-need-based scholarship or grant aid	3
% frosh rec. need-based self-help aid	21
% UG rec. need-based self-help aid	25
% frosh rec. athletic scholarships	2
% UG rec. athletic scholarships	2
% frosh rec. any financial aid	63
% UG rec. any financial aid	54
% UG borrow to pay for school	39
Average cumulative indebtedness	$34,398

BABSON COLLEGE

LUNDER UNDERGRADUATE ADMISSION CENTER, BABSON PARK, MA 02457 • ADMISSIONS: 781-239-5522 • FAX: 781-239-4135

CAMPUS LIFE
Quality of Life Rating	85
Fire Safety Rating	84
Green Rating	60*
Type of school	private
Environment	village

STUDENTS
Total undergrad enrollment	1,851
% male/female	58/42
% from out of state	70
% from public high school	50
% live on campus	84
% in (# of) fraternities	13 (4)
% in (# of) sororities	15 (3)
% African American	4
% Asian	13
% Caucasian	42
% Hispanic	9
% international	20
# of countries represented	64

SURVEY SAYS . . .
School is well run
Diverse student types on campus
Campus feels safe
Low cost of living
(Almost) no one smokes

ACADEMICS
Academic Rating	88
Calendar	semester
Student/faculty ratio	16:1
Profs interesting rating	88
Profs accessible rating	87
Most common reg class size	30–39 students

MOST POPULAR MAJORS
accounting
entrepreneurial and small business operations
finance

STUDENTS SAY ". . ."

Academics

Babson is a school well suited to the age of specialization. Its business is business; if you're looking for a well-regarded undergraduate degree in business, Babson can serve your needs because the school "offers multiple opportunities for students to gear their own educations" to develop "a complete set of management skills." As one student puts it, "When I took a quick look at the curriculum, I was positive whatever I wanted to study in business could be found" at Babson. The school is best known for its emphasis on entrepreneurship; all freshmen must undertake the school's Foundations in Management and Entrepreneurship immersion course, during which undergrads create their own startups. Those who choose to pursue the field further can jockey for space in E-Tower, a "community of 21 highly motivated entrepreneurs chosen to live together" and immerse themselves in all things entrepreneurial (similar housing options are available for students in, among others, finance and green business). Internship opportunities are abundant thanks to the school's reputation and proximity to Boston, providing students "a hands-on experience of how things work in the real world." Professors "want nothing more than to see their students learn and do well. Many…refer to themselves as 'pracademics' because they have had such amazing real-world experience from which they can draw on in the classroom. From executives of Fortune 500 companies to entrepreneurs who own multi-million dollar companies, the knowledge of professors at Babson is only rivaled by their desire to see students do well." Career placement services here "are really strong."

Life

Babson is in the "perfect location," "near Boston but not in it." One student explains: "We are not in the busy city life on a daily basis, but we are able to get into Boston very easily, whether it's driving, taking the T, or the Babson Shuttle that drops you off right in the center of Fanueil Hall." (The shuttle runs only on weekends.) Campus life, once considered subpar, "is definitely a lot better. [Student government] sponsors and hosts many events throughout the months to keep students entertained and involved," including "Knight Parties, where there are monthly dance parties in one of our large auditoriums" and "spring, winter, and fall weekend, where they have entertainment and bands come to the school. This year we even had Jimmy Fallon come for a comedy concert in the fall—the show was packed; it was standing room only." Students report that "A favorite hangout on a Thursday night is the pub, where there is entertainment and food. Babson [provides] supervised drinking for those of legal drinking age." The school's numerous student-run clubs "are very motivated, providing diverse and educating events" such as mixers and symposia.

Students

"It is hard to pin-point a typical student, as Babson is so diverse," but the common thread is that "we all view business as a primary, shared strand that can link our interests and passions in order to help us make a difference in the world." Babson "is an international college. Outside of our library, there is a flag tree where the flags of different students represented on our campus are flown to show our diversity. We have students from about 64 different countries," and students "learn from each others' differences. It is one of the great pieces of knowledge we are able to pick up at Babson." The "dominant domestic students will be the preppy white boy and girl who treat their designer clothes like aprons," while "international students are mostly of Indian and Hispanic descent who do not refrain from displaying their wealth," all supplemented by "a small population of students that are swimming in personal debt to attend Babson or could never place a foot on the campus if it weren't for their financial aid."

BABSON COLLEGE

FINANCIAL AID: 781-239-4219 • E-MAIL: UGRADADMISSION@BABSON.EDU • WEBSITE: WWW.BABSON.EDU

THE PRINCETON REVIEW SAYS

Admissions

Very important factors considered include: Application essay, academic GPA, recommendation(s), rigor of secondary school record, standardized test scores, character/personal qualities. *Important factors considered include:* Class rank, extracurricular activities. *Other factors considered include:* Alumni/ae relation, first generation, geographical residence, interview, level of applicant's interest, racial/ethnic status, state residency, talent/ability, volunteer work, work experience. SAT or ACT required. SAT and SAT Subject Tests or ACT recommended. ACT with Writing component required. TOEFL required of all international applicants. High school diploma is required and GED is accepted. *Academic units recommended:* 4 English, 4 mathematics, 4 science (3 science labs), 4 foreign language, 2 social studies, 2 history, 1 pre-calculus.

Financial Aid

Students should submit: FAFSA, CSS/financial aid profile, noncustodial profile, business/farm supplement, federal tax returns, W-2s, and verification worksheet. Regular filing deadline is 2/15. The Princeton Review suggests that all financial aid forms be submitted as soon as possible after 1/1. *Need-based scholarships/grants offered:* Federal Pell, SEOG, state scholarships/grants, the school's own gift aid. *Loan aid offered:* FFEL Subsidized Stafford, FFEL Unsubsidized Stafford, FFEL PLUS, Federal Perkins, state loans. Applicants will be notified of awards on or about 4/1. Federal Work-Study Program available. Institutional employment available. Off-campus job opportunities are good.

The Inside Word

Babson's national profile is ascending quickly, resulting in a substantial uptick in the number of applications received each year. Expect admissions standards to rise in accordance. The school considers writing ability a strong indicator of preparedness for college; proceed accordingly.

THE SCHOOL SAYS "..."

From The Admissions Office

"In addition to theoretical knowledge, Babson College is dedicated to providing its students with hands-on business experience. The Foundations of Management and Entrepreneurship (FME) and Management Consulting Field Experience (MCFE) are two prime examples of this commitment. During the FME, all freshmen are placed into groups of 30 and actually create their own businesses that they operate until the end of the academic year. The profits of each FME business are then donated to the charity of each group's choice.

"MCFE offers upperclassmen the unique and exciting opportunity to work as actual consultants for private companies and/or nonprofit organizations in small groups of three to five. Students receive academic credit for their work as well as invaluable experience in the field of consulting. FME and MCFE are just two of the ways Babson strives to produce business leaders with both theoretical knowledge and practical experience.

"Babson College requires freshmen applicants to submit scores from either the new SAT or the ACT with Writing component. The school recommends that students also submit results from SAT Subject Tests."

SELECTIVITY
Admissions Rating	93
# of applicants	4,318
% of applicants accepted	35
% of acceptees attending	33
# accepting a place on wait list	262
% admitted from wait list	4
# of early decision applicants	180
% accepted early decision	50

FRESHMAN PROFILE
Range SAT Critical Reading	555–650
Range SAT Math	610–690
Range SAT Writing	580–660
Range ACT Composite	25–29
Minimum paper TOEFL	600
Minimum computer TOEFL	250
Minimum web-based TOEFL	100
% graduated top 10% of class	22
% graduated top 25% of class	61
% graduated top 50% of class	91

DEADLINES
Early decision	
Deadline	11/1
Notification	12/15
Early action	
Deadline	11/15
Notification	11/1
Regular	
Priority	11/1
Deadline	1/15
Notification	4/1
Nonfall registration?	no

FINANCIAL FACTS
Financial Aid Rating	90
Annual tuition	$37,824
% frosh rec. need-based scholarship or grant aid	40
% UG rec. need-based scholarship or grant aid	38
% frosh rec. non-need-based scholarship or grant aid	6
% UG rec. non-need-based scholarship or grant aid	6
% frosh rec. need-based self-help aid	44
% UG rec. need-based self-help aid	41
% frosh rec. any financial aid	44
% UG rec. any financial aid	42
% UG borrow to pay for school	51
Average cumulative indebtedness	$27,598

BARD COLLEGE

OFFICE OF ADMISSIONS, ANNANDALE-ON-HUDSON, NY 12504 • ADMISSIONS: 845-758-7472 • FAX: 845-758-5208

CAMPUS LIFE
Quality of Life Rating	**66**
Fire Safety Rating	**77**
Green Rating	**90**
Type of school	private
Environment	rural

STUDENTS
Total undergrad enrollment	1,826
% male/female	43/57
% from out of state	76
% from public high school	64
% live on campus	75
% African American	2
% Asian	3
% Caucasian	71
% Hispanic	3
% Native American	1
% international	10
# of countries represented	49

SURVEY SAYS . . .
Lots of liberal students
No one cheats
Students aren't religious
Campus feels safe
Frats and sororities are unpopular or nonexistent
Political activism is popular
(Almost) everyone smokes

ACADEMICS
Academic Rating	**92**
Calendar	semester
Student/faculty ratio	9:1
Profs interesting rating	88
Profs accessible rating	86
Most common	
reg class size	10–19 students

MOST POPULAR MAJORS
English language and literature
social sciences
visual and performing arts

STUDENTS SAY ". . ."
Academics
Students come to Bard seeking "a liberal arts college with a left-leaning student body of creative thinkers who are all actively interested in political and social activism and learning/academia for its own sake," and "we find it," they tell us. Those yearning for "an atmosphere of curious individuals striving for knowledge," a place where "there are intelligent discussions both inside and outside the classroom" will find a home at this small liberal arts school in the scenic Hudson Valley. All students start their educations here building a solid grounding, starting with a three-week orientation and intensive communication and research workshop, followed by the year-long freshman seminar that is a survey of history's "great ideas." As one student observes, "The curriculum at Bard is set up to give students a broad foundation of knowledge," a foundation they get to test when completing their senior project in their final year. As at many elite small schools, "The administration and professors are amazingly accessible. A simple e-mail can get you an appointment with the dean of students, and the professors encourage students to ask for help or to discuss any ideas they may have." Students aren't coddled, however; writes one, "One reason that the school doesn't run as 'smoothly' [as other schools] is that this place isn't about handing life's jewels to everyone. All the students must put some effort into their work to get the real payoff. It's a bit like real life in that manner." As one student puts it, "Bard, more than any other school, is what you make of it. If you wish to make a big splash, the school will provide you with the proper equipment (large boulders, diving boards etc.). It is up to you, though, to take advantage of it."

Life
Bard "has a gorgeous campus," and undergrads "take full advantage of that when the weather is warm. Blithewood, our Spanish-style gardens, is often full of students picnicking and playing Frisbee, and elsewhere on campus most trees have at least one student reading, or perhaps playing an instrument, in the shade. Other popular pastimes/attractions include the on-campus art museum, the waterfall, and many winding, hilly hiking trails that snake around Blithewood and along the Hudson River." The campus hosts a rich cultural life; the "student-run entertainment space—a converted auto garage known as SMOG—holds many fantastic music shows (both student bands and musical guests), as well as the very popular themed dance parties," and "Art is everywhere. Students frequently have the opportunities to see world-class performances by the American Symphony Orchestra for free or for a mere $5." All this activity makes up for the fact that "the campus is a little isolated," as does the fact that "shuttles run to nearby towns rather frequently." Undergrads tell us that "This is not a beer-pong school. Rather than the norm being the stereotypical frat-style college party, many 'parties' are just friends sitting together; drinking boxed wine; listening to jazz or indie rock; and discussing philosophy, art, current events, etc." When they need to get away, "Many kids go to New York City for the weekends."

Student Body
"Bard is a safe haven for all hipsters, serious intellectuals, artists, and dreamers," so it should come as no surprise that "Everyone at Bard was atypical in high school, and consequently it's difficult to classify anyone as either typical or atypical. Students here are brilliant, enthusiastic, passionate, and genuinely different." They tend to be "very passionate about their specific interests and work hard to manifest them in the community," with "an unbelievable sensitivity to the subtleties of, and a passion for, language." "It's 'cool' to be intellectual, artistic, and well-read" here, and "'hipster' fashion is in style." Occasionally some "do try to be a little too philosophical, and some kids can border on pretentious or self-righteous, but most are absolutely amazing people with fascinating backgrounds."

FINANCIAL AID: 845-758-7526 • E-MAIL: ADMISSION@BARD.EDU • WEBSITE: WWW.BARD.EDU

THE PRINCETON REVIEW SAYS

Admissions

Very important factors considered include: Application essay, academic GPA, recommendation(s), rigor of secondary school record, character/personal qualities, extracurricular activities, talent/ability. *Important factors considered include:* Volunteer work, work experience. *Other factors considered include:* Class rank, standardized test scores, alumni/ae relation, first generation, geographical residence, interview, level of applicant's interest, racial/ethnic status, religious affiliation/commitment, state residency, TOEFL required of all international applicants. High school diploma is required and GED is accepted. *Academic units recommended:* 4 English, 4 mathematics, 4 science (3 science labs), 4 foreign language, 4 social studies, 4 history.

Financial Aid

Students should submit: FAFSA, CSS/financial aid profile, state aid form, noncustodial profile, business/farm supplement. Regular filing deadline is 2/15. The Princeton Review suggests that all financial aid forms be submitted as soon as possible after 1/1. *Need-based scholarships/grants offered:* Federal Pell, SEOG, state scholarships/grants, private scholarships, the school's own gift aid. *Loan aid offered:* FFEL Subsidized Stafford, FFEL Unsubsidized Stafford, FFEL PLUS, Federal Perkins, loans from institutional funds (for international students only). Applicants will be notified of awards on or about 4/1. Federal Work-Study Program available. Institutional employment available. Off-campus job opportunities are good.

The Inside Word

Bard receives more than enough applications from students with the academic credentials to gain admission, so the school has the luxury of focusing on matchmaking. The goal is to find students who can handle the independence allowed here and who will thrive in an intellectually intensive environment. The school requires two application essays; expect both to be very carefully scrutinized by the admissions office.

THE SCHOOL SAYS " . . ."

From The Admissions Office

"An alliance with Rockefeller University, the renowned graduate scientific research institution, gives Bardians access to Rockefeller's professors and laboratories and to places in Rockefeller's Summer Research Fellows Program. Almost all our math and science graduates pursue graduate or professional studies; 90 percent of our applicants to medical and health professional schools are accepted.

"The Globalization and International Affairs (BGIA) Program is a residential program in the heart of New York City that offers undergraduates a unique opportunity to undertake specialized study with leading practitioners and scholars in international affairs and to gain internship experience with international-affairs organizations. Topics in the curriculum include human rights, international economics, global environmental issues, international justice, managing international risk, and writing on international affairs, among others. Internships/tutorials are tailored to students' particular fields of study.

"Student dormitory and classroom facilities are in Bard Hall, 410 West Fifty-eighth Street, a newly renovated 11-story building near the Lincoln Center District in New York City.

"Bard College does not require SAT scores to be submitted for admissions consideration. Students may choose to submit scores, and, if submitted, we will consider them in the context of the overall application. "

SELECTIVITY
Admissions Rating	96
# of applicants	5,459
% of applicants accepted	25
% of acceptees attending	38
# accepting a place on wait list	250

FRESHMAN PROFILE
Range SAT Critical Reading	680–740
Range SAT Math	650–690
Minimum paper TOEFL	600
Minimum computer TOEFL	250
Average HS GPA	3.5
% graduated top 10% of class	63
% graduated top 25% of class	95
% graduated top 50% of class	100

DEADLINES
Early action	
Deadline	11/1
Notification	1/1
Regular	
Deadline	1/15
Notification	4/1
Nonfall registration?	no

APPLICANTS ALSO LOOK AT
AND OFTEN PREFER
Brown University
AND SOMETIMES PREFER
Oberlin College
New York University
Reed College
Vassar College

FINANCIAL FACTS
Financial Aid Rating	88
Annual tuition	$35,784
Books and supplies	$850
% frosh rec. need-based scholarship or grant aid	55
% UG rec. need-based scholarship or grant aid	53
% frosh rec. need-based self-help aid	48
% UG rec. need-based self-help aid	45
% frosh rec. any financial aid	65
% UG rec. any financial aid	62
% UG borrow to pay for school	58
Average cumulative indebtedness	$20,201

BARNARD COLLEGE

3009 BROADWAY, NEW YORK, NY 10027 • ADMISSIONS: 212-854-2014 • FAX: 212-854-6220

CAMPUS LIFE

Quality of Life Rating	98
Fire Safety Rating	68
Green Rating	85
Type of school	private
Environment	metropolis

STUDENTS

Total undergrad enrollment	2,359
% male/female	0/100
% from out of state	68
% from public high school	58
% live on campus	90
% African American	5
% Asian	16
% Caucasian	67
% Hispanic	9
% international	4
# of countries represented	37

SURVEY SAYS . . .

No one cheats
Career services are great
Students love New York, NY
Great off-campus food
Campus feels safe
Political activism is popular

ACADEMICS

Academic Rating	95
Calendar	semester
Student/faculty ratio	9:1
Profs interesting rating	94
Profs accessible rating	89
Most common reg class size	10–19 students
Most common lab size	fewer than 10 students

MOST POPULAR MAJORS

psychology
English
political science
economics
history

STUDENTS SAY ". . ."

Academics

Life is lived in the fast lane at Barnard, an all-women's liberal arts college partnered with Columbia University that incorporates "a small school feel with big school resources and incorporates both campus and city life." Nestled in the Morningside Heights neighborhood of Manhattan on a gated (main) campus, the school maintains an "independent spirit" while providing a "nurturing environment," and its partnership with a larger research university gives it the "best of both worlds" and affords its students the opportunities, course options, and resources that many colleges don't have.

The academic experience at Barnard is simply "wonderful," according to the students. Teachers here are "experts in their field" and "value their positions as both teachers and mentors," to the extent "they make you want to stay on Barnard's campus for class and not take classes at Columbia." "I've never been in an environment where there is such a reciprocal relationship between students wanting to learn and be challenged and professors wanting to teach and help," says a junior. Though underclassmen typically aren't able to get into as many of the small classes (the process of which "is a nightmare"), one student claims that "some of the best classes I've had have been in large lecture halls." The administration gets thumbs up nearly across the board for their accessibility and compassion for students. Deans are always available to students wanting to meet, and the alumni network and career services are singled out for their efficacy. "Every time there is an issue on campus that students care about or an event that has happened, we get e-mails and town-hall style meetings devoted to discussing the issues." "Barnard is New York—busy, exciting, full of opportunity," says one student.

Life

Not much goes on around campus, to the chagrin of a few, but as one freshman puts it, "Why stay on campus when you're in New York?" Students take advantage of the resources available to them in New York City, from Broadway shows and Central Park to museums and restaurants; "the possibilities are endless," and "make it impossible to stick to a budget." Theater and a capella are also very big here, and many students are involved with clubs and organizations at Columbia, sometimes even dominating them. There are some complaints that facilities and dorms are "crumbling," but the new student activities building (called the Nexus) should help alleviate building woes when it's completed in January of 2010. According to one junior, "Life at Barnard is probably 60–75% academic, and around 25–40% free."

Student Body

Even though it's all women here, Barnard is "the anti-women's college," as "very, very few students are here for the single-sex education"—they're here for the academics and New York. There's a definite liberal slant on campus, and these "usually politically savvy," "very cultured," "energetic and motivated" women are "ambitious and opinionated," with career and leadership goals at the top of their agenda. "Barnard students are not lazy" and have no problems booking their days full of study and activities. Most here learn to "fit into the mad rush" very quickly and take advantage of their four short years. Although quite a few students are from the tri-state area and the majority are white, "there is still a sense of diversity" thanks to a variety of different backgrounds, both cultural and geographical; there's also a "tiny gay community" that seems easily accepted.

FINANCIAL AID: 212-854-2154 • E-MAIL: ADMISSIONS@BARNARD.EDU • WEBSITE: WWW.BARNARD.EDU

THE PRINCETON REVIEW SAYS

Admissions

Very important factors considered include: Application essay, academic GPA, recommendation(s), rigor of secondary school record, character/personal qualities, extracurricular activities. *Important factors considered include:* Class rank, standardized test scores, talent/ability, volunteer work. *Other factors considered include:* Alumni/ae relation, first generation, geographical residence, interview, level of applicant's interest, racial/ethnic status, work experience. SAT and SAT Subject Tests or ACT required. ACT with Writing component required. TOEFL required of all international applicants. High school diploma or equivalent is not required. *Academic units recommended:* 4 English, 3 mathematics, 3 science (2 science labs), 3 foreign language.

Financial Aid

Students should submit: FAFSA, institution's own financial aid form, CSS/financial aid profile, state aid form, noncustodial profile, business/farm supplement. federal income tax returns. Regular filing deadline is 2/1. The Princeton Review suggests that all financial aid forms be submitted as soon as possible after 1/1. *Need-based scholarships/grants offered:* Federal Pell, SEOG, state scholarships/grants, private scholarships, the school's own gift aid. *Loan aid offered:* FFEL Subsidized Stafford, FFEL Unsubsidized Stafford, FFEL PLUS, Federal Perkins, state loans, college/university loans from institutional funds. Applicants will be notified of awards on or about 3/31. Federal Work-Study Program available. Institutional employment available. Off-campus job opportunities are excellent.

The Inside Word

As at many top colleges, early decision applications have increased at Barnard—although the admissions standards are virtually the same as for their regular admissions cycle. The college's admissions staff is suprisingly open and accessible for such a highly selective college with as long and impressive a tradition of excellence. The admissions committee's expectations are high, but their attitude reflects a true interest in who potential students are and what's on their minds. Students have a much better experience throughout the admissions process when treated with sincerity and respect—perhaps this is why Barnard continues to attract and enroll some of the best students in the country.

THE SCHOOL SAYS "..."

From The Admissions Office

"Barnard College is a small, distinguished liberal arts college for women that is partnered with Columbia University and located in the heart of New York City. The college enrolls women from all over the United States, Puerto Rico, and the Caribbean. More than 30 countries, including France, England, Hong Kong, and Greece, are also represented in the student body. Students pursue their academic studies in over 40 majors and are able to cross register at Columbia University.

"Applicants for the entering class must submit scores from the SAT Reasoning Test and two SAT Subject Tests of their choice or the ACT with the Writing component."

SELECTIVITY

Admissions Rating	98
# of applicants	4,274
% of applicants accepted	28
% of acceptees attending	47
# accepting a place on wait list	457
% admitted from wait list	3
# of early decision applicants	432
% accepted early decision	48

FRESHMAN PROFILE

Range SAT Critical Reading	640–740
Range SAT Math	610–700
Range SAT Writing	650–750
Range ACT Composite	29–31
Minimum paper TOEFL	600
Minimum computer TOEFL	250
Average HS GPA	3.88
% graduated top 10% of class	74
% graduated top 25% of class	90
% graduated top 50% of class	100

DEADLINES

Early decision	
Deadline	11/15
Notification	12/15
Regular	
Deadline	1/1
Notification	4/1
Nonfall registration?	no

APPLICANTS ALSO LOOK AT
AND OFTEN PREFER
Harvard College, Columbia University, Yale University, Brown University
AND SOMETIMES PREFER
University of Chicago, Stanford University Wellesley College, Wesleyan University Tufts University, University of Pennsylvania
AND RARELY PREFER
Fordham University, University of California—Berkeley, Cornell University Vassar College, Bryn Mawr College, Boston College

FINANCIAL FACTS

Financial Aid Rating	95
Annual tuition	$37,052
% frosh rec. need-based scholarship or grant aid	41
% UG rec. need-based scholarship or grant aid	42
% frosh rec. need-based self-help aid	44
% UG rec. need-based self-help aid	44
% frosh rec. any financial aid	57
% UG rec. any financial aid	52
% UG borrow to pay for school	44
Average cumulative indebtedness	$17,630

BATES COLLEGE

23 CAMPUS AVENUE, LINDHOLM HOUSE, LEWISTON, ME 04240 • ADMISSIONS: 207-786-6000 • FAX: 207-786-6025

CAMPUS LIFE
Quality of Life Rating	**86**
Fire Safety Rating	**91**
Green Rating	**99**
Type of school	private
Environment	town

STUDENTS
Total undergrad enrollment	1,660
% male/female	48/52
% from out of state	89
% from public high school	57
% live on campus	92
% African American	3
% Asian	6
% Caucasian	81
% Hispanic	2
% international	5
# of countries represented	65

SURVEY SAYS . . .
Students are friendly
Great food on campus
Frats and sororities are unpopular or nonexistent
Student publications are popular

ACADEMICS
Academic Rating	**94**
Calendar	4/1/4
Student/faculty ratio	10:1
Profs interesting rating	89
Profs accessible rating	94
Most common reg class size	10–19 students
Most common lab size	10–19 students

MOST POPULAR MAJORS
economics
political science and government
psychology

STUDENTS SAY ". . ."

Academics

"You will not find it hard to gain access to resources" at Bates College, a small school in Maine that "tries to be unique in the homogeneous world of New England's small liberal arts colleges by weaving together academics with real world experience." First-year seminars, mandatory senior theses, service-learning, and a range of interdisciplinary majors are part of the academic experience. About two-thirds of the students here study abroad at some point before graduation. "Research and internship opportunities" are absurdly abundant. A fairly unusual 4-4-1 calendar includes two traditional semesters and an "incredible" five-week spring term that provides really cool opportunities. Examples include studying marine biology on the Maine coast, Shakespearean drama in England, or economics in China and Taiwan. The "brilliant, accessible, and friendly" faculty does "whatever it takes to actually teach you the material instead of just lecturing and leaving." "The professors at Bates are here because they are passionate about their field and want to be teaching," explains a politics major. "I have never met so many professors who are willing to dedicate endless time outside of class to their students," gushes a psychology major. Course selection can be sparse but the "regularly available" administration is "responsive to student concerns" as well.

Life

"The library is the place to be during the week because everyone is there." The academic workload is reportedly substantial, but "it is entirely manageable and does not restrict you from participating in athletics, clubs, or just having some down time." Parties are common on the weekends, and students "stand mashed up against everyone else in the keg line." There's a great college radio station—91.5 on your FM dial—and many students get involved. "Bates also has a lot of traditions that students get excited about." In the winter during Puddle Jump, just for instance, Batesies who feel especially courageous can take the plunge into the frigid water of Lake Andrews. Otherwise, "dances, comedians, and trivia challenges are shockingly well attended because there's not a whole lot else to do." The biggest social complaint here centers on the surrounding area. It's the kind of place where "you wouldn't want to be walking alone at 3 in the morning." Also, relations between Batesies and local residents are reportedly strained. "The interaction between the town and college is relatively minimal," relates a junior. When students feel they just have to get away, they can "hit up the nearby ski slopes." The great outdoors is another option. Bates rents "tents, sleeping bags, kayaks, climbing gear, stoves, vans—really anything you want for outdoor fun." Also, Boston and some smaller cities such as Freeport and Portland are easily accessible.

Student Body

Students tell us that "Bates needs to improve its ethnic diversity." Most of the students here are white. "Your typical Batesie owns at least two flannel shirts" and "likes to have fun on the weekends." There are "a lot of jocks," and some "take the sports teams here way too seriously." Students here call themselves "down to earth" yet "intellectually driven." They enjoy "participating in academics, sports, and clubs." They "love the outdoors." However, this campus is "eclectic," and "Bates students are by no means monolithic in character." "We have everyone from the prep-school spoiled brat to the hippie environmentalist, from people with all different gender and sexual preferences and orientations to the former or current goth," observes a junior. "There are dorks, brains, goof-offs, and class clowns." There are "plenty of kids who apparently haven't found the dorm showers," too. "There are few, if any, cliques on campus." "Crossing boundaries" is quite common. "There are different groups but none of them are exclusive in any way." "Even those who do not fit into any specific social group are widely accepted" (with the possible exception of the people who "plain suck").

FINANCIAL AID: 207-786-6096 • E-MAIL: ADMISSIONS@BATES.EDU • WEBSITE: WWW.BATES.EDU

THE PRINCETON REVIEW SAYS

Admissions

Very important factors considered include: Class rank, application essay, academic GPA, recommendation(s), rigor of secondary school record, character/personal qualities, extracurricular activities, interview, level of applicant's interest, talent/ability. *Other factors considered include:* Standardized test scores, alumni/ae relation, first generation, geographical residence, racial/ethnic status, state residency, volunteer work, work experience. TOEFL required of all international applicants. High school diploma is required and GED is not accepted. *Academic units required:* 4 English, 3 mathematics, 3 science (2 science labs), 2 foreign language, 3 social studies. *Academic units recommended:* 4 English, 4 mathematics, 4 science (3 science labs), 4 foreign language, 4 social studies.

Financial Aid

Students should submit: FAFSA, CSS/financial aid profile, noncustodial profile, business/farm supplement. Regular filing deadline is 2/1. The Princeton Review suggests that all financial aid forms be submitted as soon as possible after 1/1. *Need-based scholarships/grants offered:* Federal Pell, SEOG, state scholarships/grants, private scholarships, the school's own gift aid. *Loan aid offered:* FFEL Subsidized Stafford, FFEL Unsubsidized Stafford, FFEL PLUS, Federal Perkins, state loans. Applicants will be notified of awards on or about 4/1. Federal Work-Study Program available. Institutional employment available. Off-campus job opportunities are good.

The Inside Word

While holding its applicants to lofty standards, Bates strives to adopt a personal approach to the admissions process. Officers favor qualitative information and focus more on academic rigor, essays, and recommendations than GPA and test scores. The school seeks students who look for challenges and take advantage of opportunities in the classroom and beyond. Interviews are strongly encouraged—candidates who opt out may place themselves at a disadvantage.

THE SCHOOL SAYS "..."

From The Admissions Office

"Bates College is widely recognized as one of the finest liberal arts colleges in the nation. The curriculum and faculty challenge students to develop the essential skills of critical assessment, analysis, expression, aesthetic sensibility, and independent thought. Founded by abolitionists in 1855, Bates graduates have always included men and women from diverse ethnic and religious backgrounds. Bates highly values its study-abroad programs, unique calendar (4-4-1), and the many opportunities available for one-on-one collaboration with faculty through seminars, research, service-learning, and the capstone experience of senior thesis. Co-curricular life at Bates is rich; most students participate in club or varsity sports; many participate in performing arts; and almost all students participate in one of more than 100 student-run clubs and organizations. More than two-thirds of alumni enroll in graduate study within 10 years.

"The Bates College Admissions Staff reads applications very carefully; the high school record and the quality of writing are of particular importance. Applicants are strongly encouraged to have a personal interview, either on campus or with an alumni representative. Students who choose not to interview may place themselves at a disadvantage in the selection process. Bates offers tours, interviews, and information sessions throughout the summer and fall. Drop-ins are welcome for tours and information sessions. Please call ahead to schedule an interview.

"At Bates, the submission of standardized testing (the SAT, SAT Subject Tests, and the ACT) is not required for admission. After two decades of optional testing, our research shows no differences in academic performance and graduation rates between submitters and nonsubmitters."

SELECTIVITY

Admissions Rating	**95**
# of applicants	4,434
% of applicants accepted	30
% of acceptees attending	34

FRESHMAN PROFILE

Range SAT Critical Reading	635–710
Range SAT Math	630–700
% graduated top 10% of class	55
% graduated top 25% of class	86
% graduated top 50% of class	99

DEADLINES

Early decision	
Deadline	11/15
Notification	12/20
Regular	
Deadline	1/1
Notification	3/31
Nonfall registration?	yes

APPLICANTS ALSO LOOK AT

AND OFTEN PREFER
Dartmouth College
Williams College
Brown University

AND SOMETIMES PREFER
Middlebury College
Colby College
Bowdoin College

AND RARELY PREFER
Connecticut College
Bucknell University
Trinity College (CT)

FINANCIAL FACTS

Financial Aid Rating	**94**
Comprehensive fee	$46,800
Books and supplies	$1,150
% frosh rec. need-based scholarship or grant aid	41
% UG rec. need-based scholarship or grant aid	38
% frosh rec. need-based self-help aid	39
% UG rec. need-based self-help aid	38
% frosh rec. any financial aid	44
% UG rec. any financial aid	41
% UG borrow to pay for school	48.1
Average cumulative indebtedness	$13,947

BAYLOR UNIVERSITY

ONE BEAR PLACE #97056, WACO, TX 76798-7056 • ADMISSIONS: 254-710-3435 • FAX: 254-710-3436

CAMPUS LIFE

Quality of Life Rating	77
Fire Safety Rating	87
Green Rating	78
Type of school	private
Affiliation	Baptist
Environment	city

STUDENTS

Total undergrad enrollment	12,105
% male/female	42/58
% from out of state	18
% live on campus	39
% in (# of) fraternities	13 (24)
% in (# of) sororities	18 (18)
% African American	7
% Asian	7
% Caucasian	71
% Hispanic	11
% Native American	1
% international	2
# of countries represented	70

SURVEY SAYS . . .

Lab facilities are great
Athletic facilities are great
Students are friendly
Students are very religious
Students are happy
Intramural sports are popular
Student publications are popular

ACADEMICS

Academic Rating	79
Calendar	semester
Student/faculty ratio	15:1
Profs interesting rating	76
Profs accessible rating	78
Most common reg class size	10–19 students
Most common lab size	10–19 students

MOST POPULAR MAJORS

biology/biological sciences
nursing/registered nurse (RN, ASN, BSN, MSN)
psychology

STUDENTS SAY ". . ."

Academics

Baylor University, the largest Baptist school on the planet, "provides a great education and a wholesome Christian atmosphere where the professors seem to genuinely care about their students." "There is quite a bit of studying" for everyone, and "most professors are very involved with the students," exudes a nursing major. "I cannot say enough good things about my professors and about my academic experience at Baylor." Other students are more moderate in their praise. "There are some great professors and some not-so-great ones," sagely counsels a senior. "You just have to pick the right ones." Also, freshmen and sophomore classes can be sizeable, and "all the tests are multiple-choice" in these larger courses. There is a "fantastic" Honors College. Other outstanding programs here include engineering, the entrepreneurship program, and "strong science programs." The rather conservative administration receives mixed reviews. There is "what can only be described as a profound disconnect between the student population and the administrative personnel," says one student. Others say that management "keeps things running smoothly most of the time."

Life

The surrounding town of Waco offers "absolutely nothing to do." Consequently, life at Baylor is centered on campus. Students call it "the Baylor Bubble." "Baylor is not small and lonely, but it is also not overwhelming like most public universities." Intramural sports are big, and the student recreation center is an athletic paradise. School spirit is "outrageous." Here, "you become a Baylor Bear, and you are really part of the family." "Traditions are crazy." Homecoming is a huge deal and features a tremendous parade. On Diadeloso in the spring, classes are cancelled and students are treated to athletic events, live shows, and a campus-wide party. Given Baylor's Baptist affiliation, it's not surprising that "rules are very strict." It's a gravely dry campus, and you can't have anyone of the opposite sex in your dorm room after midnight. "Required chapel sessions" for freshmen involve "lectures about how people found Christ" as well as discussion about time management and study techniques. "There is a large sect of students who do not do anything besides church and religious activities." These students also participate in mission trips around the world and go forth to "serve the city of Waco"—mentoring disadvantaged kids, taking care of the elderly, and building houses. "There is a party scene at Baylor" too, and it's dominated by a large Greek system. "Most people think of Baylor as an innocent Baptist school, which is semi-correct, but it for sure has its wild partiers," explains a sophomore. Still, "it is not the normal thing to go get drunk every night."

Student Body

Baylor's undergrads are overwhelmingly female, and "the bounty of beautiful Baptist babes is unmatched." Sadly though, at least according to one female, "Baylor boys aren't the greatest." Ethnic diversity isn't bad, and students swear it's getting better. "Gays or lesbians are almost nonexistent or do not identify themselves." Baylor is generally "conservative" and "very Christian." "It is an expensive private university, so you have plenty of students here that are very financially well off." While some students are "preppy, rich types who drive a Lexus and have a 2.0 GPA," "the vast majority of students seek out Baylor for the Christian environment and strong academic reputation." "The stereotype of Bobby and Betty Baylor...actually does not fit nearly as many students as I thought," reckons a freshman. "Many of us work hard to get the money to come here through scholarships and jobs." "There are good people at Baylor, and there are many of them." Virtually everyone is "super nice." There are "radical Pentecostals" and "the kids who have never committed a sin in their lives and are somewhat naïve." There are others "who become obsessed with Greek Life" or "who party and drink all night." If you don't embrace religion, chances are you'll fit in fine. "As an atheist at a Christian school it might be expected that I would find myself isolated from the broader population, but this simply wasn't the case," reflects a senior.

FINANCIAL AID: 254-710-2611 • E-MAIL: ADMISSIONS_SERV_OFFICE@BAYLOR.EDU • WEBSITE: WWW.BAYLOR.EDU

THE PRINCETON REVIEW SAYS

Admissions

Very important factors considered include: Class rank, rigor of secondary school record, standardized test scores. *Important factors considered include:* Academic GPA, recommendation(s). *Other factors considered include:* alumni/ae relation, character/personal qualities, extracurricular activities, first generation, geographical residence, interview, level of applicant's interest, religious affiliation/commitment, talent/ability, volunteer work. SAT or ACT required. ACT with Writing component required. TOEFL required of all international applicants. High school diploma is required and GED is accepted. *Academic units required:* 4 English, 3 mathematics, 3 science (2 science labs), 2 foreign language, 1 social studies, 1 history, 3 academic electives.

Financial Aid

Students should submit: FAFSA, state residency affirmation. Regular filing deadline is 8/1. The Princeton Review suggests that all financial aid forms be submitted as soon as possible after 1/1. *Need-based scholarships/grants offered:* Federal Pell, SEOG, state scholarships/grants, the school's own gift aid. *Loan aid offered:* FFEL Subsidized Stafford, FFEL Unsubsidized Stafford, FFEL PLUS, Federal Perkins. Applicants will be notified of awards on a rolling basis beginning 3/1. Federal Work-Study Program available. Institutional employment available. Off-campus job opportunities are good.

The Inside Word

Baylor's pool of largely self-selected applicants faces a straightforward admissions process. If your values reflect those of the community here and you have good grades in a solidly college-prep high school curriculum and decently high standardized test scores, you'll be admitted.

THE SCHOOL SAYS ". . ."

From The Admissions Office

"Baylor University is a Christian university in the Baptist tradition and is affiliated with the Baptist General Convention of Texas. As the oldest institution of higher learning in the state, Baylor's founders sought to establish a college dedicated to Christian principles, superior academics, and a shared sense of community. Students come from all 50 states and some 90 foreign countries. Baylor's nationally recognized academic divisions offer 146 undergraduate degree programs, 71 master's degree programs, and 20 doctoral degree programs. Baylor ranks in the top 15 percent of colleges and universities participating in the National Merit Scholarship program. Baylor is one of the select 11 percent of U.S. colleges and universities with a Phi Beta Kappa chapter. The Templeton Foundation repeatedly names Baylor as one of America's top character-building colleges. Baylor's undergraduate programs emphasize the central importance of vocation (calling) and service in students' lives, helping them explore their value and role in society. Baylor is a charter member of the Independent 529 Tuition Plan, a prepaid college tuition plan. Baylor's tuition is one of the lowest of any major private university in the Southwest and one of the least expensive in the nation. Approximately 84 percent of Baylor students receive student financial assistance. The 508-acre main campus adjoins the Brazos River near downtown Waco, a Central Texas city of 110,000 people. By 2012, Baylor intends to enter the top tier of American universities while reaffirming its distinctive Christian mission. This bold 10-year vision, Baylor 2012, is well underway, benefiting students entering Baylor now.

"Baylor University requires applicants for admission to take the SAT or the ACT with the Writing section."

SELECTIVITY

Admissions Rating	88
# of applicants	25,501
% of applicants accepted	51
% of acceptees attending	23
# accepting a place on wait list	122
% admitted from wait list	20

FRESHMAN PROFILE

Range SAT Critical Reading	540–650
Range SAT Math	560–660
Range SAT Writing	530–630
Range ACT Composite	23–28
Minimum paper TOEFL	540
Minimum computer TOEFL	207
Minimum web-based TOEFL	76
% graduated top 10% of class	41
% graduated top 25% of class	72
% graduated top 50% of class	95

DEADLINES

Early action	
Deadline	11/1
Notification	1/15
Nonfall registration?	yes

FINANCIAL FACTS

Financial Aid Rating	71
Annual tuition	$25,320
Room and board	$8,569
Required fees	$2,590
Books and supplies	$1,398
% frosh rec. need-based scholarship or grant aid	54
% UG rec. need-based scholarship or grant aid	48
% frosh rec. non-need-based scholarship or grant aid	53
% UG rec. non-need-based scholarship or grant aid	40
% frosh rec. need-based self-help aid	46
% UG rec. need-based self-help aid	40
% frosh rec. athletic scholarships	2
% UG rec. athletic scholarships	3
% frosh rec. any financial aid	93
% UG rec. any financial aid	85

BELLARMINE UNIVERSITY

2001 NEWBURG ROAD, LOUISVILLE, KY 40205 • ADMISSIONS: 502-452-8131 • FAX: 502-452-8002

CAMPUS LIFE

Quality of Life Rating	**84**
Fire Safety Rating	**90**
Green Rating	**60***
Type of school	private
Affiliation	Roman Catholic
Environment	metropolis

STUDENTS

Total undergrad enrollment	2,068
% male/female	36/64
% from out of state	30
% from public high school	64
% live on campus	43
% in (# of) fraternities	1 (1)
% in (# of) sororities	1 (1)
% African American	3
% Asian	3
% Caucasian	82
% Hispanic	2
% international	2
# of countries represented	29

SURVEY SAYS . . .

Students get along with local
community
Students love Louisville, KY
Great off-campus food
Low cost of living
(Almost) no one smokes
Very little drug use

ACADEMICS

Academic Rating	**82**
Calendar	semester
Student/faculty ratio	12:1
Profs interesting rating	87
Profs accessible rating	87
Most common reg class size	10–19 students
Most common lab size	10–19 students

MOST POPULAR MAJORS

biology/biological sciences
business/commerce
nursing/registered nurse
(RN, ASN, BSN, MSN)

STUDENTS SAY ". . ."

Academics

A "small, private, Catholic university," in the heart of vibrant Louisville, Kentucky, Bellarmine University has a curriculum that casts an eye toward the future and provides a "well-rounded education" that is not only "demanding in academic excellence" but also "prepares students for the real world, both mentally and socially." Bellarmine's unique combination of "service, academics, and learning" ensures that "each student is fully prepared to excel in their job opportunities, as well as in life." A "premier college" with an academic lens that merges rigorous education and spiritual awareness toward practical ends, students note the curriculum's "real-world" focus on "teaching students to become professional adults." Professors are "friendly and approachable," with "a genuine love of their craft" and an investment in "ensuring an enriching experience for students beyond the classroom." Bellarmine is "a small school with big-school quality and ambitions," and students benefit from "small classes" and "personalized attention" and are often drawn to Bellarmine for its "great reputation" and "generous scholarships." With an academic mission that focuses on "exploration, discovery, and growth in yourself and your understanding of the world," Bellarmine encourages its students to continue their educations outside the university setting. Its "study-abroad programs are fantastic." The university also has "a great physical therapy and nursing program," according to students.

Life

A "tight-knit community" with "a beautiful campus," Bellarmine balances big city sophistication with an active, conscientious student body. As one student aptly summarizes, "Bellarmine is all about creating the small school atmosphere on an academically strong campus in the heart of a big city." Students are quick to note the campus's proximity to Louisville's Bardstown Road where there is a plethora of "restaurants, stores, and coffee shops" "within walking distance from campus." On the weekends, students "frequent [Louisville's] opera and theater productions and visit museums." On campus, "life at Bellarmine is very upbeat." The university sponsors "a large variety of sports and extracurricular events." "Students are extremely interested in getting involved," and "intramurals are very popular." For many, due to its small size, Bellarmine embodies "a home away from home." Though students note that Bellarmine has a somewhat "homogeneous population," "the part of the city of Louisville where Bellarmine is located is a very liberal/art oriented. Bellarmine champions a commitment to "community; how you are involved in it, how you can change it for the better, and what it can do for you."

Student Body

Like the academic curriculum itself, Bellarmine students are "willing to broaden the mind and be introduced to new experiences." The typical Bellarmine student is "friendly, helpful, and intellectual." With an eye toward advancement and applying education in a real-world setting, students describe themselves as "hardworking" and "dedicated to making good grades, graduating, and starting a career." However, Bellarmine's students acknowledge that it's not all nose in the book at Bellarmine. In the words of one student, "Bellarmine students like to relax AND achieve." Students are "extremely motivated," "take pride in their work," and still "can enjoy good times outside of school." A typical Bellarmine student might be found "sitting on the grass in the quad, playing Frisbee, in the library, or in their studio working on their next big project." By and large, students describe the population at Bellarmine as "upper-middle-class Caucasian" with "lots of athletes." Due to the school's religious foundation, many students come from "private Catholic schools" in the Louisville vicinity. Though students remark that there are "not a lot of atypical students," those who march to the beat of a different drummer "do find a place to fit in." "Open-minded and personable," "most students who attend Bellarmine are there for a reason—to succeed."

FINANCIAL AID: 502-452-8124 • E-MAIL: ADMISSIONS@BELLARMINE.EDU • WEBSITE: WWW.BELLARMINE.EDU

THE PRINCETON REVIEW SAYS

Admissions

Very important factors considered include: Academic GPA, recommendation(s), rigor of secondary school record, standardized test scores, character/personal qualities, level of applicant's interest. *Important factors considered include:* Class rank, extracurricular activities. *Other factors considered include:* Application essay, alumni/ae relation, first generation, geographical residence, interview, racial/ethnic status, state residency, talent/ability, volunteer work, work experience. SAT or ACT required. TOEFL required of all international applicants. High school diploma is required and GED is accepted. *Academic units required:* 4 English, 3 mathematics, 3 science (2 science labs), 2 foreign language, 2 social studies, 1 history, 5 academic electives. *Academic units recommended:* 4 English, 4 mathematics, 4 science (2 science labs), 2 foreign language, 3 social studies, 2 history, 7 academic electives.

Financial Aid

Students should submit: FAFSA. The Princeton Review suggests that all financial aid forms be submitted as soon as possible after 1/1. *Need-based scholarships/grants offered:* Federal Pell, SEOG, state scholarships/grants, private scholarships, the school's own gift aid. *Loan aid offered:* FFEL Subsidized Stafford, FFEL Unsubsidized Stafford, FFEL PLUS, Federal Perkins, state loans, college/university loans from institutional funds. Applicants will be notified of awards on a rolling basis beginning 4/1. Federal Work-Study Program available. Institutional employment available. Off-campus job opportunities are excellent.

The Inside Word

With an 80 percent selectivity rating, admissions at Bellarmine University is competitive. However, much like their mission statement, Bellarmine's admissions committee views applicants' profiles from a composite perspective and is looking for a well-rounded candidate whose qualifications reflect more than the sum total of a GPA and test scores. Recommendations and personal statements—which present a stronger picture of the students' educational goals—volunteer experiences, and extracurricular commitments, hold significant weight. Candidates with strong grades and diverse interests are likely to earn acceptance.

THE SCHOOL SAYS "..."

From The Admissions Office

"Bellarmine University is known for providing students with outstanding personal attention in the classroom. For many out-of-town students, however, Bellarmine's location makes the difference. Just 5 miles from downtown Louisville, Bellarmine is at the heart of the cultural and recreational offerings of the nation's sixteenth-largest city. The 135-acre campus is set in a safe, historic neighborhood that features an executive golf course, indoor and outdoor tennis courts, a fitness center, a sand volleyball court, and athletic fields. Recent additions to the campus reflect the university's academic emphasis on a liberal arts core curriculum surrounded by competitive graduate and professional schools. The state-of-the-art Norton Health Sciences Center and a Service Learning Clinic offer real-life, hands-on experience for nursing and physical therapy students, while the campus library houses the largest collection of works by and about internationally renowned author and Trappist monk Thomas Merton. With more than 50 clubs and organizations on campus and 18 NCAA Division II athletic teams, and Division I men's lacrosse, Bellarmine offers a variety of recreational opportunities for all students. Countless internships and study-abroad programs offer additional opportunities for students to expand their horizons outside the classroom. Students who live on campus will also find a Bellarmine difference, namely the living arrangements. From the traditional college residence hall layout to apartment-style and suite living arrangements, students have many housing options. All residence halls offer amenities such as laundry facilities, computer labs, study rooms, and air conditioning."

SELECTIVITY

Admissions Rating	80
# of applicants	4,336
% of applicants accepted	58
% of acceptees attending	23

FRESHMAN PROFILE

Range SAT Critical Reading	500–600
Range SAT Math	500–600
Range ACT Composite	22–26
Minimum paper TOEFL	550
Minimum computer TOEFL	213
Minimum web-based TOEFL	80
Average HS GPA	3.47
% graduated top 10% of class	22
% graduated top 25% of class	55
% graduated top 50% of class	83

DEADLINES

Early action	
Deadline	11/1
Notification	12/1
Regular	
Priority	2/1
Deadline	8/15
Notification	rolling
Nonfall registration?	yes

FINANCIAL FACTS

Financial Aid Rating	78
Annual tuition	$27,800
Room and board	$8,410
Required fees	$1,100
Books and supplies	$744
% frosh rec. need-based scholarship or grant aid	75
% UG rec. need-based scholarship or grant aid	69
% frosh rec. non-need-based scholarship or grant aid	30
% UG rec. non-need-based scholarship or grant aid	27
% frosh rec. need-based self-help aid	50
% UG rec. need-based self-help aid	49
% frosh rec. athletic scholarships	8
% UG rec. athletic scholarships	9
% frosh rec. any financial aid	100
% UG rec. any financial aid	97
% UG borrow to pay for school	66
Average cumulative indebtedness	$19,055

BELOIT COLLEGE

700 College Street, Beloit, WI 53511 • Admissions: 608-363-2500 • Fax: 608-363-2075

CAMPUS LIFE
Quality of Life Rating	80
Fire Safety Rating	69
Green Rating	77
Type of school	private
Environment	town

STUDENTS
Total undergrad enrollment	1,297
% male/female	43/57
% from out of state	78
% from public high school	78
% live on campus	96
% in (# of) fraternities	8 (3)
% in (# of) sororities	6 (3)
% African American	4
% Asian	3
% Caucasian	78
% Hispanic	3
% international	5
# of countries represented	32

SURVEY SAYS . . .
No one cheats
Students are friendly
Students aren't religious
Low cost of living
Political activism is popular

ACADEMICS
Academic Rating	93
Calendar	semester
Student/faculty ratio	11:1
Profs interesting rating	90
Profs accessible rating	94
Most common reg class size	10–19 students

MOST POPULAR MAJORS
anthropology
international relations and affairs
psychology

STUDENTS SAY ". . ."

Academics

"Professors and the general administration are always very open to students" at Beloit College, a school whose community "feels like a big family." Professors, in fact, "often prefer to be thought of as friends and advisors (for example, all of my professors insist on being called by their first names rather than by honorifics)." One student's experiences are typical: "My Chinese professor requires a 15-minute private conference with each student weekly to practice conversation. My First Year Initiative leader conferences with us about every draft of every paper and tells us how to improve. My psych teacher gives us essay tests and specific comments on how to improve." These touches make "the academic experience at Beloit is very personal and friendly," placing the emphasis "on cooperating while at the same time developing each unique individual however his/her potential/interest leads." Even though professors have a range of teaching styles, "Classes are very interdisciplinary and often unintentionally work well in conjunction with other courses." Standout disciplines include political science, international relations (bolstered by "a great study-abroad program to match a great language arts department"), anthropology, and chemistry; "What sets these departments apart from most schools is that there are research-related classes that provide interesting extracurricular experiences" and give students the opportunity "to explore social, academic, and occupational aspects of life in an experiential, hands-on manner."

Life

Life at Beloit is fairly low-key; it's "generally about going to classes that you appreciate, hanging out with friends, playing some type of sport and doing homework." Low-key doesn't mean boring, though; on the contrary, "Weekends are a lot of fun, partly because you can drink wherever, whenever, and whatever you like" thanks to an "extremely lenient" drinking policy (students hasten to add that "Beloit students are rarely irresponsible or obnoxious and usually look out for each other"). Those uninterested in the party scene will find "some substance-free housing and a lot of fun and crazy stuff to do (ranging from Friday night movies to sledding on cafeteria trays)." Weeknights are generally given over to "all sorts of presentations [and] lectures by guests," that capture the interest of many undergrads or to hanging at "the Java Joint, the campus coffee shop, [where students] play chess, board games, or do a puzzle." When they need a change of scenery, students take the bus or find a friend with a car and road trip to Madison, Milwaukee, or Chicago to go out on the town. When they're not relaxing, "People are very politically active; they encourage voting and the signing of a ridiculous amount of petitions."

Student Body

"Everybody has a niche at Beloit, whether you're interested in Greek life or LARPing on Saturday nights, and everything in between," and students "are really friendly, even (if not especially) with others who have wildly different interests" because "Beloit students are generally very curious about and accepting of the unfamiliar, with the single exception of religion. Christians at Beloit sometimes feel they need to hide their faith or risk being judged as conservative, judgmental, or uptight." Indeed, most here are "very liberal," which can make "discussion hard sometimes because so many people have the same ideas. Those with more conservative ideas either don't talk about their political views or are very bad at it." As far as diversity in its traditional sense is concerned, "There are lots of rich kids, but the school does a good job recruiting (and financing) students from lower socioeconomic classes."

FINANCIAL AID: 608-363-2500 • E-MAIL: ADMISS@BELOIT.EDU • WEBSITE: WWW.BELOIT.EDU

THE PRINCETON REVIEW SAYS

Admissions

Very important factors considered include: Application essay, academic GPA, recommendation(s), rigor of secondary school record. *Important factors considered include:* Class rank, standardized test scores, interview. *Other factors considered include:* Alumni/ae relation, character/personal qualities, extracurricular activities, first generation, level of applicant's interest, talent/ability, volunteer work, work experience. SAT or ACT required. TOEFL required of all international applicants. High school diploma is required and GED is accepted. *Academic units recommended:* 4 English, 4 mathematics, 3 science, 2 foreign language, 4 social studies.

Financial Aid

Students should submit: FAFSA, institution's own financial aid form, state aid form. Regular filing deadline is 3/1. The Princeton Review suggests that all financial aid forms be submitted as soon as possible after 1/1. *Need-based scholarships/grants offered:* Federal Pell, SEOG, state scholarships/grants, private scholarships, the school's own gift aid. *Loan aid offered:* FFEL Subsidized Stafford, FFEL Unsubsidized Stafford, FFEL PLUS, Federal Perkins, college/university loans from institutional funds. Applicants will be notified of awards on a rolling basis beginning 4/1. Federal Work-Study Program available. Institutional employment available. Off-campus job opportunities are good.

The Inside Word

Beloit takes a well-rounded approach to the admissions game. Realizing that applicants are more than statistics on a page, the college works diligently to assess the total package. While most weight is given to a candidate's secondary school transcript, which is evaluated not only for grades but also for academic rigor, significant attention is also paid to essays and recommendations. Counselors strive to find students who not only demonstrate success in the classroom but also display strong character and leadership skills.

THE SCHOOL SAYS "..."

From The Admissions Office

"While Beloit students clearly understand the connection between college and career, they are more apt to value learning for its own sake than for the competitive advantage that it will afford them in the workplace. As a result, Beloit students adhere strongly to the concept that an educational institution, in order to be true to its own nature, must imply and provide a context in which a free exchange of ideas can take place. This precept is embodied in the mentoring relationship that takes place between professor and student and the dynamic, participatory nature of the classroom experience.

"Beloit College requires that students applying submit scores from the ACT or SAT. The writing exam from either test is not evaluated for purposes of admission. Beloit offers a nonbinding early action plan with a December 1 deadline. The preferred deadline for regular decision applicants is January 15."

SELECTIVITY

Admissions Rating	**92**
# of applicants	2,248
% of applicants accepted	63
% of acceptees attending	24
# accepting a place on wait list	80
% admitted from wait list	41

FRESHMAN PROFILE

Range SAT Critical Reading	570–700
Range SAT Math	560–690
Range ACT Composite	25–30
Minimum paper TOEFL	550
Minimum computer TOEFL	213
Average HS GPA	3.41
% graduated top 10% of class	40
% graduated top 25% of class	71
% graduated top 50% of class	95

DEADLINES

Early action	
Deadline	12/1
Notification	1/1
Regular	
Priority	1/15
Notification	rolling
Nonfall registration?	yes

APPLICANTS ALSO LOOK AT

AND OFTEN PREFER
Carleton College

AND SOMETIMES PREFER
Lawrence University
Macalester College
Grinnell College

FINANCIAL FACTS

Financial Aid Rating	**99**
Annual tuition	$33,188
Books and supplies	$600
% frosh rec. need-based scholarship or grant aid	66
% UG rec. need-based scholarship or grant aid	62
% frosh rec. need-based self-help aid	64
% UG rec. need-based self-help aid	61
% frosh rec. any financial aid	93
% UG rec. any financial aid	90
% UG borrow to pay for school	68
Average cumulative indebtedness	$26,014

BENNINGTON COLLEGE

OFFICE OF ADMISSIONS, BENNINGTON, VT 05201 • ADMISSIONS: 800-833-6845 • FAX: 802-440-4320

CAMPUS LIFE

Quality of Life Rating	81
Fire Safety Rating	81
Green Rating	88
Type of school	private
Environment	town

STUDENTS

Total undergrad enrollment	618
% male/female	34/66
% from out of state	96
% from public high school	59
% live on campus	98
% African American	2
% Asian	2
% Caucasian	83
% Hispanic	3
% international	4
# of countries represented	12

SURVEY SAYS . . .

Lots of liberal students
Class discussions encouraged
Students aren't religious
Dorms are like palaces
Low cost of living
Intercollegiate sports are unpopular
or nonexistent
Frats and sororities are unpopular or
nonexistent
Theater is popular
(Almost) no one smokes

ACADEMICS

Academic Rating	98
Calendar	15 week Fall–Spring; 7 week Winter Work Term
Student/faculty ratio	9:1
Profs interesting rating	94
Profs accessible rating	93
Most common reg class size	10–19 students
Most common lab size	fewer than 10 students

MOST POPULAR MAJORS

English language and literature
foreign languages and literatures
visual and performing arts

STUDENTS SAY "..."

Academics

Bennington caters to students who want maximum control over their academic endeavors; all students here participate in the Plan Process, "which allows students to create their own course of study." Here's how it works: "Either a student devises his own personalized set of requirements, or [the requirements] are recommended by a 'plan committee' of usually three faculty members personally assigned to each student." The idea is to "leave up to the student the chance to connect ideas and classes that would normally be left out of a core curriculum," and unsurprisingly, students here love it—for many it is the primary reason they choose to attend Bennington. The Field Work Term internship program is another compelling factor. This "seven-week internship term in the winter" gives students "the ideal opportunity to connect with professionals in our areas of interest and learn what you are (and what you aren't) interested in pursuing" while also building a resume. The social sciences, humanities, and performing/creative arts are strongest here, but students insist that the hard sciences are also "strong...and more popular than one might think for a small 'alternative' liberal arts school." Bennington professors "range from being very available to ridiculously available," and "most are extremely active and respected in their fields, and all are willing to meet outside of class and help a motivated student find professional connections."

Life

Bennington undergrads are "very focused on work. All students share a passion for what they are doing," to the extent that "The class doesn't end when we leave the classroom. Discussions often continue, and people are always talking about their classes and their work." Because Bennington is a small school "people are generally friendly and very interested in one another and their work," and because the campus "is a little isolated" "there isn't much to do off-campus," so students must be "good at entertaining themselves." Fortunately, "There is always plenty to do on campus. Sometimes there are too many events to choose from: dance concerts, plays, readings, themed parties, art openings, and many more events, on campus and off." Some party intensely "to blow off some steam" because "we all work so exceedingly hard," but most here agree the situation is under control; students can't ignore academics for too long because "with the way our academic system works, you can be kicked out for getting too many C's." When they need to get away, undergrads "are most likely to take day trips to nearby Brattleboro and Williamstown, each of which are very close and offer all sorts of diversions."

Student Body

"Self-motivated, voraciously curious, and open to growth," the typical Bennington student "is very devoted to his work and personally invested in creating something meaningful with [his] time. A stereotype for the general student body could be 'indie kid,' but that doesn't quite fit because the students here have a broader awareness of disciplines and interests outside of their own due to the cross-disciplinary nature of [the] studies." To some, it seems that "Everyone here is a total nerd: art nerd, science nerd, lit nerd, language nerd, math nerd, drama nerd, dance nerd. Nerds of all shapes, types, and aesthetic genres." They are "the type of people who would rather dance in polyester or read a book than go to a basketball game." There are "probably fewer than a handful of republicans on campus, and there are definitely no Abercrombie & Fitch sweatshirts around."

FINANCIAL AID: 802-440-4325 • E-MAIL: ADMISSIONS@BENNINGTON.EDU • WEBSITE: WWW.BENNINGTON.EDU

THE PRINCETON REVIEW SAYS

Admissions

Very important factors considered include: Application essay, academic GPA, recommendation(s), rigor of secondary school record, character/personal qualities, extracurricular activities, interview, talent/ability. *Other factors considered include:* Standardized test scores, class rank, alumni/ae relation, first generation, geographical residence, level of applicant's interest, racial/ethnic status, volunteer work, work experience. TOEFL required of all international applicants. High school diploma is required and GED is accepted. *Academic units recommended:* 4 English, 4 mathematics, 3 science, 2 foreign language, 4 social studies, 4 history.

Financial Aid

Students should submit: FAFSA, institution's own financial aid form, CSS/financial aid profile, noncustodial profile, student and parent federal tax returns and W-2s. The Princeton Review suggests that all financial aid forms be submitted as soon as possible after 1/1. *Need-based scholarships/grants offered:* Federal Pell, SEOG, state scholarships/grants, private scholarships, the school's own gift aid. *Loan aid offered:* FFEL Subsidized Stafford, FFEL Unsubsidized Stafford, FFEL PLUS, college/university loans from institutional funds. NOTE: College/university loans from institutional funds for International students only. Applicants will be notified of awards on or about 4/1. Federal Work-Study Program available. Institutional employment available. Off-campus job opportunities are good.

The Inside Word

Bennington students need to be academically accomplished, driven, and self-directed in order to handle the academic freedom granted by the curriculum. The admissions office seeks all these qualities in applicants and, because of the school's prestige, typically finds them in all admitted students. A campus visit isn't required but is strongly recommended as an excellent way to demonstrate your interest in the school, and provide admissions officers with the personal contact they prefer in evaluating candidates.

THE SCHOOL SAYS " . . ."

From The Admissions Office

"The educational philosophy of Bennington is rooted in an abiding faith in the talent, imagination, and responsibility of the individual; thus, the principle of learning by practice underlies every major feature of a Bennington education. We believe that a college education should not merely provide preparation for graduate school or a career, but should be an experience valuable in itself and the model for lifelong learning. Faculty, staff, and students at Bennington work together in a collaborative environment based upon respect for each other and the power of ideas to make a difference in the world. We are looking for intellectually curious students who have a passion for learning, are willing to take risks, and are open to making connections.

"Submission of standardized test scores (the SAT, SAT Subject Tests, or the ACT) is optional."

SELECTIVITY

Admissions Rating	95
# of applicants	1,056
% of applicants accepted	62
% of acceptees attending	29
# accepting a place on wait list	25
% admitted from wait list	84
# of early decision applicants	75
% accepted early decision	60

FRESHMAN PROFILE

Range SAT Critical Reading	620–720
Range SAT Math	560–660
Range SAT Writing	590–690
Range ACT Composite	24–28
Minimum paper TOEFL	577
Minimum computer TOEFL	233
Average HS GPA	3.43
% graduated top 10% of class	31
% graduated top 25% of class	80
% graduated top 50% of class	97

DEADLINES

Early decision	
Deadline	11/15
Notification	12/15
Regular	
Deadline	1/5
Notification	4/1
Nonfall registration?	yes

APPLICANTS ALSO LOOK AT

AND OFTEN PREFER

New York University, Bard College

AND SOMETIMES PREFER

Eugene Lang College The New School for Liberal Arts, Vassar College, University of Vermont, Sarah Lawrence College

AND RARELY PREFER

Hampshire College, Marlboro College, Skidmore College

FINANCIAL FACTS

Financial Aid Rating	75
Annual tuition	$37,280
Room and board	$10,680
Required fees	$990
Books and supplies	$800
% frosh rec. need-based scholarship or grant aid	59
% UG rec. need-based scholarship or grant aid	64
% frosh rec. non-need-based scholarship or grant aid	8
% UG rec. non-need-based scholarship or grant aid	4
% frosh rec. need-based self-help aid	52
% UG rec. need-based self-help aid	60
% frosh rec. any financial aid	74
% UG rec. any financial aid	77
% UG borrow to pay for school	68
Average cumulative indebtedness	$25,957

BENTLEY UNIVERSITY

175 FOREST STREET, WALTHAM, MA 02452-4705 • ADMISSIONS: 781-891-2244 • FAX: 781-891-3414

CAMPUS LIFE
Quality of Life Rating	88
Fire Safety Rating	99
Green Rating	95
Type of school	private
Environment	town

STUDENTS
Total undergrad enrollment	4,187
% male/female	60/40
% from out of state	50
% from public high school	73
% live on campus	82
% in (# of) fraternities	12 (7)
% in (# of) sororities	12 (4)
% African American	3
% Asian	8
% Caucasian	62
% Hispanic	5
% international	8
# of countries represented	78

SURVEY SAYS . . .
Great library
Athletic facilities are great
Career services are great
School is well run
Dorms are like palaces
Campus feels safe

ACADEMICS
Academic Rating	82
Calendar	semester
Student/faculty ratio	12:1
Profs interesting rating	82
Profs accessible rating	85
Most common reg class size	20–29 students

MOST POPULAR MAJORS
accounting and related services
finance
marketing/marketing management

STUDENTS SAY ". . ."

Academics
Bentley University, an institution dedicated to creating "business and business-technical leaders," combines a winning location with an intense focus on technology to produce "the business moguls of tomorrow." Students say that the "Resources here are second to none, if you need help scheduling classes, choosing a major, creating a resume…anything at all, then there is an entire office of people ready and willing to help you in any way possible." Some of Bentley's perks include "a state-of-the-art trading room, a "superbly wired campus," and a brand-new library that "has all the resources a student could need, with quite a few significant, (not so necessary) extras" (such as a "large flat-panel TV monitors in each of its 20-some odd study rooms"). Bentley doesn't just flash the hardware, though; it also teaches students how to "integrate the newest technological resources into the business environment" by "embedding them into [your] courses. This is important, because technology "is key to success in the business world, whatever profession you are interested in." Bentley's proximity to Boston "makes this a very special place," helping students find meaningful internships and, after graduation, meaningful jobs. Academics here "are challenging but not overwhelming," and most of the classes "weigh class participation in the overall grade, which motivates [you] to complete the readings and assignments in a timely manner." Professors typically have "previous real-life experience in the business world. They like to incorporate that in the classroom."

Life
Life is "very hectic" at Bentley, where "Students tend to crack down during the weekdays and really get their work done. By Thursday [we're] ready for the weekend to start." Bentley's "beautiful campus" has "tons to offer" when it comes to finding activities outside of class, including "Greek life, sports organizations," and "tons of bars, restaurants, sports events, and concerts" so that "it's hard to be bored." Intramural sports "are also very popular, as is exercising in general. Being fit and working out are definitely the 'in' things to do." There are also plenty of parties; "Registered parties are allowed (with regulations) where of-age students can have keg parties in their room," but "There is also substance-free housing available if that's not your fancy." Students across the board agree that "Boston is Bentley's main attraction." Fortunately the city "is easily accessible via the school's shuttle service." Students love to head for Cambridge, the North End, Quincy Market, and other city destinations on the weekend "just to see a show, eat at a restaurant, shop, or just walk around," although some prefer to hang out on campus because the city can be "pretty expensive."

Students
The typical Bentley undergrad is "rich, foreign, and smart." Check that, they're "usually two out of the three: rich and foreign, rich and smart, or smart and foreign." Internationals make up a conspicuous subpopulation, "which is interesting" because you get to "learn from other cultures." One student writes, "Venture through any apartment complex to be greeted to the smells of Indian, Creole, Chinese, South American, and European foods. Diversity is greatly appreciated, as is evidenced by the fact that one of the events with the largest attendance each year is the Festival of Colors, an international extravaganza." The exception to the rule, we're told, is that students from Europe "hail from very big money" and "very rarely interact with domestic students." Most here, unsurprisingly, "are typical business students, usually quite driven and business-oriented. They are fairly fun loving as well," the sort who are "studious during the week, rowdy on weekends." Overall, students tend to be "preppy collar-poppin' kids" who can "talk the talk" and "take pride [in] attending Bentley."

FINANCIAL AID: 781-891-3441 • E-MAIL: UGADMISSION@BENTLEY.EDU • WEBSITE: WWW.BENTLEY.EDU

THE PRINCETON REVIEW SAYS

Admissions

Very important factors considered include: Academic GPA, rigor of secondary school record, standardized test scores. *Important factors considered include:* Class rank, application essay, recommendation(s), character/personal qualities, extracurricular activities, volunteer work, work experience. *Other factors considered include:* Alumni/ae relation, first generation, geographical residence, interview, level of applicant's interest, racial/ethnic status, state residency, talent/ability. SAT or ACT required. ACT with Writing component required. TOEFL required of all international applicants. High school diploma is required and GED is accepted. *Academic units recommended:* 4 English, 4 mathematics, 3 science (3 science labs), 3 foreign language, 3 social studies, 2 additional English, mathematics, social or lab science, or foreign language.

Financial Aid

Students should submit: FAFSA, CSS/financial aid profile, noncustodial profile, business/farm supplement, federal tax returns, including all schedules for parents and student. Regular filing deadline is 2/1. The Princeton Review suggests that all financial aid forms be submitted as soon as possible after 1/1. *Need-based scholarships/grants offered:* Federal Pell, SEOG, state scholarships/grants, private scholarships, the school's own gift aid. *Loan aid offered:* FFEL Subsidized Stafford, FFEL Unsubsidized Stafford, FFEL PLUS, Federal Perkins, state loans. Applicants will be notified of awards on a rolling basis beginning 3/25. Federal Work-Study Program available. Institutional employment available. Off-campus job opportunities are good.

The Inside Word

If you've got a bunch of electives available to you senior year, you may think that choosing business classes is the best way to impress the Bentley Admissions Office. Not so; the school would prefer you take a broad range of challenging classes—preferably at the AP level—in English, history/social sciences, math, lab sciences, and foreign language. The school enjoys a sizable applicant pool, so you'll need solid grades and test scores to gain admission.

THE SCHOOL SAYS " . . ."

From The Admissions Office

"Bentley University, a leader in business education, is dedicated to preparing a new kind of business leader, one with the deep technical skills, broad global perspective and the high ethical standards required to make a difference in an ever-changing world. Bentley infuses its advanced business curriculum with the richness of a liberal arts education, providing students with relevant, practical, and transferable skills—precisely what they need to succeed and pursue their passions in life. Bentley also offers a double major in business and liberal studies, allowing students to graduate with a well-rounded skill set that makes them stand out to future employers. Concepts and theories learned in the classroom come alive in hands-on, high-tech learning laboratories such as the Financial Trading Room, Center for Marketing Technology, and Media & Culture Labs and Studio. Ethics and social responsibility are woven throughout the school's curriculum, making the Bentley Service-Learning Program one of the top-ranked in the U.S. Students choose from numerous athletic, social, and cultural opportunities, including 27 countries for study abroad. Students develop skills and build their resume through internships with leading companies. State-of-the-art athletic and recreation facilities complement 23 varsity teams in Division I & II, plus extensive intramural and recreational sports programs. Boston and Cambridge are minutes from campus and are rich resources for internships, job opportunities, cultural events, and social life."

SELECTIVITY

Admissions Rating	91
# of applicants	7,238
% of applicants accepted	38
% of acceptees attending	36
# accepting a place on wait list	475
% admitted from wait list	3
# of early decision applicants	187
% accepted early decision	54

FRESHMAN PROFILE

Range SAT Critical Reading	550–630
Range SAT Math	610–680
Range SAT Writing	550–650
Range ACT Composite	25–29
Minimum paper TOEFL	550
Minimum computer TOEFL	213
Minimum web-based TOEFL	80
% graduated top 10% of class	45.2
% graduated top 25% of class	84.8
% graduated top 50% of class	98.4

DEADLINES

Early decision	
Deadline	11/15
Notification	12/19
Early action	
Deadline	11/15
Notification	1/23
Regular	
Deadline	1/15
Notification	4/1
Nonfall registration?	yes

APPLICANTS ALSO LOOK AT
AND SOMETIMES PREFER
Northeastern University
Villanova University
Boston College
Boston University
Babson College

FINANCIAL FACTS

Financial Aid Rating	83
Annual tuition	$33,030
Room and board	$11,320
Required fees	$1,458
Books and supplies	$1,030
% frosh rec. need-based scholarship or grant aid	39
% UG rec. need-based scholarship or grant aid	41
% frosh rec. non-need-based scholarship or grant aid	24
% UG rec. non-need-based scholarship or grant aid	12
% frosh rec. need-based self-help aid	42
% UG rec. need-based self-help aid	45
% frosh rec. athletic scholarships	1
% UG rec. athletic scholarships	1
% frosh rec. any financial aid	78
% UG rec. any financial aid	73
% UG borrow to pay for school	65
Average cumulative indebtedness	$30,577

BEREA COLLEGE

CPO 2220, BEREA, KY 40404 • ADMISSIONS: 859-985-3500 • FAX: 859-985-3512

CAMPUS LIFE

Quality of Life Rating	75
Fire Safety Rating	84
Green Rating	89
Type of school	private
Environment	village

STUDENTS

Total undergrad enrollment	1,491
% male/female	40/60
% from out of state	56
% live on campus	87
% African American	17
% Asian	1
% Caucasian	68
% Hispanic	2
% Native American	1
% international	7
# of countries represented	64

SURVEY SAYS . . .

Athletic facilities are great
Diverse student types on campus
Low cost of living
Frats and sororities are unpopular or nonexistent
Musical organizations are popular

ACADEMICS

Academic Rating	86
Calendar	4/1/4
Student/faculty ratio	10:1
Profs interesting rating	82
Profs accessible rating	80
Most common reg class size	10–19 students

MOST POPULAR MAJORS

biology/biological sciences
business/commerce
family and consumer
sciences/human sciences

STUDENTS SAY ". . ."

Academics

Berea College in central Kentucky is "about bringing underprivileged high school graduates from the Appalachian region and beyond together for a chance at a higher education, a career, and a better life." Thanks to a labor program that requires all students to work 10 to 15 hours each week and a ton of donated cash, tuition here is "free." "Each student receives a laptop to use while in school" as well. "No tuition does not mean a full ride," though. "Extra costs such as technology fees, insurance, food plans, etc. add up quickly," advises a business major. About two-thirds of the students receive additional financial aid. Berea's administration is efficient, but it "tends to be too parental in nature" can be overly concerned with image. "Donors hear a story of poor kids who are getting help from a school that sometimes styles itself as a charity," explains a junior. In addition to a decent range of liberal arts and sciences majors, there are several career-oriented programs. The academic atmosphere is "rigorous." Class attendance is mandatory. A few "hardcore" professors "abuse the idea of homework." Others "need refresher courses on how to deal with people." On the whole, though, faculty members are "witty," and they "have a strong passion for what they are teaching." "Everyone who I've had has been completely accessible outside of class," describes a nursing major. "Students are able to get so much more one-on-one time than at larger colleges."

Life

"Buildings, facilities, and technology are not always the newest, nicest, or most expensive" on this "tiny campus." There's no cable television in the dorm rooms, and the "crazy" visitation policy for members of the opposite sex is "borderline 19th century." Academics take up a lot of time, and "every student is required to have an on-campus job." Some students make stoneware pottery. Others "feed sheep and goats" on the college farm. However, "janitorial work," computer support, and similarly mundane jobs are more typical. "With work, classes, and studying, there's not much time left for anything else." "There are many clubs" and several religious groups. "Movie marathons" and "dances" are common. "Pick-up games" and intramurals are popular. "Some of us go camping when it's nice out, that kind of thing," says a first-year student. Otherwise, "life at Berea is generally regarded as boring." "If it weren't for videogames, I'd go nuts," speculates a junior. The surrounding town is "very small." "There is not even a movie theater." "Someone from a big city would be in for a shock." Freshmen can't bring cars at all and, generally, only students who live far away can ever have vehicles. The county is dry, and there are no bars. Berea's alcohol polices are theoretically harsh but more lenient in practice. "If you can hide it, you can drink it." However, alcohol and drug usage is "very low." "We're not a party school," says a junior. "Basically, our weekends consist of walking down to Wal-Mart," explains a sophomore," and that's if we're really ready for a crazy night."

Student Body

"The typical student at Berea College is broke" but "has big dreams." "Most people are from working-class families." They were "raised in backwoods hollows" around "the Appalachian area." "We are all here because we have no money but are equipped with the hope for a bright future and a desire to learn," declares a senior. Students at Berea are "sleep deprived" and "too busy to really have the time to slack off (though there are some that still manage it)." They're "bright, hardworking," and "studious." "Most of us are nerds," admits a senior. There are "quite a few Bible thumpers." At the same time, Berea is "probably more liberal than conservative," and this is something of "a hippie school." "People are really big about recycling, sustainability, and the environment." Students tell us that Berea has "more diversity than most schools." "There is a very large homeschool population." There are quite a few "young married students." There's also a noticeable contingent of international students and "a large population of African Americans." Some students claim that minorities "blend in well." Others say the campus is "widely segregated."

FINANCIAL AID: 859-985-3310 • E-MAIL: ADMISSIONS@BEREA.EDU • WEBSITE: WWW.BEREA.EDU

THE PRINCETON REVIEW SAYS

Admissions

Very important factors considered include: Class rank, academic GPA, rigor of secondary school record, standardized test scores, geographical residence. *Important factors considered include:* Application essay, character/personal qualities, extracurricular activities, interview, racial/ethnic status, talent/ability, volunteer work. *Other factors considered include:* Recommendation(s), first generation, level of applicant's interest, state residency, work experience. SAT or ACT required. TOEFL required of all international applicants. High school diploma is required and GED is accepted. *Academic units recommended:* 4 English, 3 mathematics, 2 science (2 science labs), 2 foreign language, 1 social studies, 1 history.

Financial Aid

Students should submit: FAFSA. The Princeton Review suggests that all financial aid forms be submitted as soon as possible after 1/1. *Need-based scholarships/grants offered:* Federal Pell, SEOG, state scholarships/grants, private scholarships, the school's own gift aid. *Loan aid offered:* FFEL Subsidized Stafford, FFEL Unsubsidized Stafford, FFEL PLUS, Federal Perkins, college/university loans from institutional funds. Applicants will be notified of awards on or about 4/15.

Inside Word

The full-tuition scholarship that every student receives understandably attracts a lot of applicants. Competition among candidates is intense. To make matters worse, you may be too wealthy to get admitted here. Berea won't admit students whose parents can afford to send them elsewhere. Financially qualified applicants should apply as early as possible.

THE SCHOOL SAYS "..."

From The Admissions Office

"Founded in 1855 by ardent abolitionists, Berea College was the first racially integrated coeducational college in the South. Over the past 150 years, Berea's has evolved into one of the most distinctive colleges in the United States. Serving students primarily from the Appalachian region, Berea College seeks to serve students who possess great academic promise but have access to limited financial resources. Berea provides an inviting and personal educational experience, evidenced in part by an 11:1 student/faculty ratio and extensive, faculty-led advising and orientation programs.

"In support of students with limited financial resources, every enrolling student receives a full-tuition scholarship, a laptop computer, as well as a paid on-campus job. Students pay room, board, and fee charges to the extent that they are able as determined by their FAFSA results. Any remaining room, board, and fee charges are covered through scholarships and grant-based aid. Students may use earnings from their jobs to assist with their portion of room, board, and fee charges; books and supplies; and other personal expenses.

"As a result of this combination of academic reputation and generous financial assistance, Berea attracts many more applicants than are able to be accepted, so admission is competitive. The best means of improving the chances for admission is to complete the application process as early as possible, preferably by November 30 of the senior year.

"Applicants must submit scores from the SAT or ACT (with or without the Writing components from either test)."

SELECTIVITY

Admissions Rating	92
# of applicants	2,468
% of applicants accepted	22
% of acceptees attending	78

FRESHMAN PROFILE

Range SAT Critical Reading	490–620
Range SAT Math	480–590
Range SAT Writing	480–610
Range ACT Composite	21–25
Minimum paper TOEFL	500
Minimum computer TOEFL	173
Average HS GPA	3.4
% graduated top 10% of class	24.6
% graduated top 25% of class	63.5
% graduated top 50% of class	95.5

DEADLINES

Regular	
Priority	11/30
Deadline	4/30
Notification	rolling
Nonfall registration?	yes

FINANCIAL FACTS

Financial Aid Rating	85
Annual tuition	$24,500
% frosh rec. need-based scholarship or grant aid	100
% UG rec. need-based scholarship or grant aid	100
% frosh rec. need-based self-help aid	100
% UG rec. need-based self-help aid	100
% frosh rec. any financial aid	100
% UG rec. any financial aid	100
% UG borrow to pay for school	78
Average cumulative indebtedness	$8,505

BIRMINGHAM-SOUTHERN COLLEGE

900 ARKADELPHIA ROAD, BIRMINGHAM, AL 35254 • ADMISSIONS: 205-226-4696 • FAX: 205-226-3074

CAMPUS LIFE

Quality of Life Rating	91
Fire Safety Rating	98
Green Rating	84
Type of school	private
Affiliation	Methodist
Environment	metropolis

STUDENTS

Total undergrad enrollment	1,412
% male/female	49/51
% from out of state	34
% from public high school	65
% live on campus	70
% in (# of) fraternities	41 (6)
% in (# of) sororities	49 (6)
% African American	8
% Asian	3
% Caucasian	84
% Hispanic	1
# of countries represented	9

SURVEY SAYS . . .

No one cheats
Lab facilities are great
Great off-campus food
Campus feels safe
Frats and sororities dominate social
scene

ACADEMICS

Academic Rating	89
Calendar	4/1/4
Student/faculty ratio	12:1
Profs interesting rating	95
Profs accessible rating	88
Most common	
reg class size	10–19 students
Most common	
lab size	10–19 students

MOST POPULAR MAJORS
business/commerce
English language and literature
psychology

STUDENTS SAY ". . ."

Academics

"Birmingham-Southern college is the best school in Alabama" students at this small, academically intense college in the state's largest city insist. Undergrads praise how the school achieves a "happy medium between well-rounded education and focused concentration on one's major," reporting that "BSC does a great job of preparing students for graduate, law, and medical school." It also has "a good education program…and an excellent dance department that offers a top-notch dance faculty with a focus on ballet." Students tell us that "the overall academic experience is challenging, yet very rewarding," and that "classroom discussion is not only encouraged, but is a necessity, since many of the grades are derived from participation." Experiential learning is paramount; one student reports, "I have not had a class yet that didn't provide some sort of hands-on experience. I have participated in everything from labs at the Cahaba River in my population ecosystem course to observations at a local Montessori school in my human growth and development class." The small classes mean "Teachers get to know you by name, and many are willing to spend countless hours working with you individually on school matters and helping you plan [your] future. They take an interest in you as a person, not just as a student." Some here point out that "while being small is a benefit, it is also sometimes a downfall. Most classes are available every year, but you must be careful to schedule courses that only occur every other year or once a year carefully in order to graduate on time."

Life

"Most people live on campus because BSC is a smaller college," students here tell us, and "This allows for an attractive community-like atmosphere." Campus life includes "many student organizations, a very strong Greek system, [and] many different shows throughout the year, from dance to theater to music to art, all produced by the performing arts departments." Youth groups and religious organizations "are also big at the school. Many people attend chapel services." There's fun to be had off campus as well, as "Birmingham is a rockin' city. There is always a concert or something off campus." Exploring Birmingham "is very easy [because] the school is located downtown, although it doesn't feel that way. You can go out to the middle of the academic quad at 11:00 P.M. and feel safe." There's "plenty to do off campus, including shopping, visiting the zoo, or going to see a show at one of the many theaters in town." One student sums up, "Fun is either a night out in Birmingham—that's what you do if you have money: You go out to eat, then to the bars, a movie, or a small off-campus party at someone's apartment—or, if you're broke and you want to have fun, you usually end up on fraternity row. At least one of the fraternities is usually having a party, and there are always people down there."

Student Body

BSC undergrads "typically come from the Alabama, Mississippi, Tennessee, and Georgia areas," although "there are some students here from elsewhere." Many "are involved in Greek life, probably about 50 percent. Many more girls go Greek than guys, and the independents are still like their own Greek group," as they "find their own groups in which to socialize, such as the ultimate Frisbee team or service clubs such as Students Offering Support." Most here agree that "the school could do better at attracting minorities and people of color" but point out that "with the size of our school you can only expect so much."

FINANCIAL AID: 205-226-4688 • E-MAIL: ADMISSION@BSC.EDU • WEBSITE: WWW.BSC.EDU

THE PRINCETON REVIEW SAYS
Admissions
Very important factors considered include: Application essay, academic GPA, recommendation(s), rigor of secondary school record, standardized test scores. *Important factors considered include:* Character/personal qualities. *Other factors considered include:* Extracurricular activities, interview, level of applicant's interest, talent/ability, work experience. SAT or ACT required. ACT with Writing component recommended. TOEFL required of all international applicants. High school diploma is required and GED is accepted. *Academic units required:* 4 English. *Academic units recommended:* 4 mathematics, 4 science (2 science labs), 2 foreign language, 2 social studies, 2 history, 10 academic electives.

Financial Aid
Students should submit: FAFSA. The Princeton Review suggests that all financial aid forms be submitted as soon as possible after 1/1. *Need-based scholarships/grants offered:* Federal Pell, SEOG, state scholarships/grants, private scholarships, the school's own gift aid, United Negro College Fund. *Loan aid offered:* FFEL Subsidized Stafford, FFEL Unsubsidized Stafford, FFEL PLUS, Federal Perkins. Applicants will be notified of awards on a rolling basis beginning 3/1. Federal Work-Study Program available. Institutional employment available. Off-campus job opportunities are excellent.

The Inside Word
Birmingham-Southern's lack of widespread national recognition by students and parents results in a small applicant pool, the majority of whom are admitted. Most of the admits are looking for a quality Southern college, recognize a good situation here and decide to enroll. Few, however, regret their decision. In a reflection of the entire administration, the admissions staff is truly personal and very helpful to prospective students.

THE SCHOOL SAYS "..."
From The Admissions Office
"Respected publishers continue to recognize Birmingham-Southern College as one of the top-ranked liberal arts colleges in the nation. One guide highlights our small classes and the fact that we still assign each student a 'faculty-mentor,' to assure individualized attention to our students. One notable aspect of our academic calendar is our January interim term, a 4-week period in which students can participate in special projects in close collaboration with faculty members, either on or off campus. One dimension of Birmingham-Southern's civic focus is the commitment to volunteerism. The Center for Leadership Studies assists students in realizing their leadership potential by combining the academic study of leadership with significant community service.

"Freshman applicants must present acceptable scores on the SAT or the ACT; they must also submit an original essay and a satisfactory recommendation from the high school."

SELECTIVITY
Admissions Rating	86
# of applicants	2,101
% of applicants accepted	69
% of acceptees attending	31

FRESHMAN PROFILE
Range SAT Critical Reading	520–540
Range SAT Math	510–630
Range ACT Composite	23–28
Minimum paper TOEFL	500
Minimum computer TOEFL	173
Minimum web-based TOEFL	61
Average HS GPA	3.4
% graduated top 10% of class	32
% graduated top 25% of class	53
% graduated top 50% of class	82

DEADLINES
Regular	
Priority	1/1
Notification	rolling
Nonfall registration?	yes

APPLICANTS ALSO LOOK AT
AND OFTEN PREFER
Rhodes College
Vanderbilt University
AND SOMETIMES PREFER
University of Alabama—Tuscaloosa
Auburn University

FINANCIAL FACTS
Financial Aid Rating	85
Annual tuition	$12,900
% frosh rec. need-based scholarship or grant aid	44
% UG rec. need-based scholarship or grant aid	38
% frosh rec. non-need-based scholarship or grant aid	53
% UG rec. non-need-based scholarship or grant aid	48
% frosh rec. need-based self-help aid	41
% UG rec. need-based self-help aid	38
% UG rec. athletic scholarships	4
% frosh rec. any financial aid	99
% UG rec. any financial aid	98
% UG borrow to pay for school	79
Average cumulative indebtedness	$27,798

BOSTON COLLEGE

140 COMMONWEALTH AVENUE, DEVLIN HALL 208, CHESTNUT HILL, MA 02467-3809 • ADMISSIONS: 617-552-3100

CAMPUS LIFE
Quality of Life Rating	**93**
Fire Safety Rating	**91**
Green Rating	**88**
Type of school	private
Affiliation	Roman Catholic
Environment	city

STUDENTS
Total undergrad enrollment	9,060
% male/female	48/52
% from out of state	71
% from public high school	50
% live on campus	82
% African American	6
% Asian	9
% Caucasian	71
% Hispanic	8
% international	3
# of countries represented	81

SURVEY SAYS . . .
Students love Chestnut Hill, MA
Campus feels safe
Everyone loves the Eagles
Frats and sororities are unpopular or nonexistent
Student publications are popular

ACADEMICS
Academic Rating	**87**
Calendar	semester
Student/faculty ratio	13:1
Profs interesting rating	83
Profs accessible rating	82
Most common reg class size	10–19 students

MOST POPULAR MAJORS
communication and media studies
English language and literature
finance

STUDENTS SAY ". . ."

Academics

Students praise the strong academics, the competitive athletic teams, the lively social scene, and the premium location that all combine to create a remarkable all-around college experience at Boston College. For many, though, BC's greatest asset is the "strong spiritual presence [that] shows how positive an influence religion can have on one's life." Don't worry; "They don't try to make anybody be Catholic" here. Rather, the school "simply reflects the Jesuit ideals of community, spirituality, and social justice," and these ideals pervade both the curriculum and the academic community. True to the Jesuit ideal of "educating the entire person," BC requires a thorough core curriculum "including philosophy, theology, and language requirements," rounded out by "strong [but optional] programs, such as internships and studying abroad." Beyond the core curriculum, "BC offers something for everyone. If you go here, you are with business students, nursing students, education majors, and arts and science majors." Even though this is a fairly large school, students insist that "you never feel like a number here. Yes, you have to be independent and seek out your professors. But when you do seek them out, you get incredible individualized attention." One undergrad sums it up like this: "BC's strength is a mix of everything. It may not be an Ivy League school in academics or win national championships everywhere in NCAA athletics, but it is a 'jack of all trades' when it comes to academics, athletics, art, and social activity."

Life

There is a "real spirit of volunteerism and giving back to the community [that] is one of BC's greatest strengths," many students here tell us, reporting that "there are about a million volunteer groups on campus, as well as a bunch of immersion trips to different places, the most renowned of which is the Appalachia group trip." Students here "really care about the world outside of Chestnut Hill. In a way, even the notion of studying abroad has turned into a question of 'How can I help people while there?' BC's Jesuit mission is contagious." Not all extracurricular life at BC is so altruistic, however; students here love to have fun in "the greatest location of any college ever! We are on the T [train], so we can get into the city of Boston whenever we like, but we are in suburbia, so we can relax without all of the gimmicks of city life." Undergrads love to explore Boston, a city with "tons of great museums, historical sights, restaurants, and a lot of great concerts," that also happens to be "such a big college town. It's easy to meet kids that go to BU, Harvard, Emerson, Northeastern, or any of the other universities in the area." Closer to campus, BC has "great sports. The ice hockey team is consistently ranked high nationally," and students turn out to support their Eagles in both men's and women's athletics.

Student Body

Boston Magazine once described the BC student body as "a J. Crew catalog with a slight hangover," and while students protest that "there are a number of students who do not conform to such a vision of the student body," they also admit that "there are a lot of preppy people at our school. Girls usually wear skirts and Uggs (unless it's freezing out, but it has to be very, very cold), and boys usually wear jeans and T-shirts or collared cotton shirts." And yes, "the typical BC student is white, Catholic, usually from the Northeast, [and] probably had family who went to BC," but with 9,000 undergrads, "We have students from all sorts of backgrounds, religions, sexual orientations." BC students tend to be extremely ambitious; they are "those super-involved people in high school who were three-season team captains, class presidents, and straight-A students. [They] have carried over that focus and determination into college."

FAX: 617-552-0798 • FINANCIAL AID: 800-294-0294 • E-MAIL: UGADMIS@BC.EDU • WEBSITE: WWW.BC.EDU

THE PRINCETON REVIEW SAYS

Admissions
Very important factors considered include: Academic GPA, rigor of secondary school record, standardized test scores. *Important factors considered include:* Class rank, application essay, recommendation(s), alumni/ae relation, character/personal qualities, religious affiliation/commitment, talent/ability, volunteer work. *Other factors considered include:* Extracurricular activities, first generation, racial/ethnic status, work experience. SAT and SAT Subject Tests or ACT required. ACT with Writing component required. TOEFL required of all international applicants. High school diploma is required and GED is accepted. *Academic units recommended:* 4 English, 4 mathematics, 4 science (4 science labs), 4 foreign language, 4 social studies.

Financial Aid
Students should submit: FAFSA, CSS/financial aid profile, noncustodial profile, business/farm supplement. The Princeton Review suggests that all financial aid forms be submitted as soon as possible after 1/1. *Need-based scholarships/grants offered:* Federal Pell, SEOG, state scholarships/grants, private scholarships, the school's own gift aid. *Loan aid offered:* FFEL Subsidized Stafford, FFEL Unsubsidized Stafford, FFEL PLUS, Federal Perkins, federal nursing scholarships, state loans. Applicants will be notified of awards on or about 4/1. Federal Work-Study Program available. Institutional employment available. Off-campus job opportunities are good.

The Inside Word
BC is one of many selective schools that eschew set admissions formulae. While a challenging high school curriculum and strong test scores are essential for any serious candidate, the college seeks students who are passionate and make connections between academic pursuits and extracurricular activities. The application process should reveal a distinct, mature voice and a student whose interest in education goes beyond the simple desire to earn an A.

THE SCHOOL SAYS ". . ."

From The Admissions Office
"Boston College students achieve at the highest levels with honors including two Rhodes scholarship winners, nine Fulbrights, and one each for Marshall, Goldwater, Madison, and Truman Postgraduate Fellowship Programs. Junior Year Abroad and Scholar of the College Program offer students flexibility within the curriculum. Facilities opened in the past 10 years include: the Merkert Chemistry Center, Higgins Hall (housing the Biology and Physics departments), three new residence halls, the Yawkey Athletics Center, the Vanderslice Commons Dining Hall, the Hillside Cafe, and a state-of-the-art library. Students enjoy the vibrant location in Chestnut Hill with easy access to the cultural and historical richness of Boston.

"Boston College requires freshman applicants to take the SAT with writing (or the ACT with the writing exam required). Two SAT Subject Tests are required; students are encouraged to take Subject Tests in fields in which they excel."

SELECTIVITY
Admissions Rating	97
# of applicants	30,845
% of applicants accepted	26
% of acceptees attending	27
# accepting a place on wait list	2,300
% admitted from wait list	14

FRESHMAN PROFILE
Range SAT Critical Reading	610–700
Range SAT Math	640–730
Range SAT Writing	620–710
Range ACT Composite	28–32
Minimum paper TOEFL	600
Minimum computer TOEFL	250
Minimum web-based TOEFL	100
% graduated top 10% of class	80
% graduated top 25% of class	95
% graduated top 50% of class	99

DEADLINES
Early action	
Deadline	11/1
Notification	12/25
Regular	
Deadline	1/1
Notification	4/15
Nonfall registration?	yes

APPLICANTS ALSO LOOK AT
AND OFTEN PREFER
University of Notre Dame, Harvard College, Cornell University, Georgetown University, University of Pennsylvania
AND SOMETIMES PREFER
New York University, Tufts University
AND RARELY PREFER
Villanova University, Boston University

FINANCIAL FACTS
Financial Aid Rating	94
Annual tuition	$37,410
Room and board	$12,395
Required fees	$540
Books and supplies	$750
% frosh rec. need-based scholarship or grant aid	35
% UG rec. need-based scholarship or grant aid	35
% frosh rec. non-need-based scholarship or grant aid	1
% UG rec. non-need-based scholarship or grant aid	1
% frosh rec. need-based self-help aid	38
% UG rec. need-based self-help aid	39
% frosh rec. athletic scholarships	3
% UG rec. athletic scholarships	3
% frosh rec. any financial aid	64
% UG rec. any financial aid	70
% UG borrow to pay for school	53
Average cumulative indebtedness	$18,799

BOSTON UNIVERSITY

121 BAY STATE ROAD, BOSTON, MA 02215 • ADMISSIONS: 617-353-2300 • FAX: 617-353-9695

CAMPUS LIFE

Quality of Life Rating	82
Fire Safety Rating	60*
Green Rating	88
Type of school	private
Environment	metropolis

STUDENTS

Total undergrad enrollment	18,534
% male/female	41/59
% from out of state	77
% from public high school	70
% live on campus	65
% in (# of) fraternities	3 (9)
% in (# of) sororities	5 (9)
% African American	4
% Asian	15
% Caucasian	61
% Hispanic	8
% international	12
# of countries represented	100

SURVEY SAYS . . .

Athletic facilities are great
Students love Boston, MA
Great food on campus
Great off-campus food
Student publications are popular

ACADEMICS

Academic Rating	84
Calendar	semester
Student/faculty ratio	15:1
Profs interesting rating	78
Profs accessible rating	78
% classes taught by TAs	6
Most common reg class size	10–19 students
Most common lab size	20–29 students

MOST POPULAR MAJORS

business/commerce
international relations and affairs
psychology

STUDENTS SAY ". . ."

Academics

Boston University's greatest strengths, students tell us, lie in "the choices students are granted. Do you want to be an alterna-teen or a jock? Do you want to drink or go to shows? Do you want to study ballet, bio, or film? Do you want a scenic riverside location or an energetic urban one? You can have all of the above at BU, which is both overwhelming and exciting." A "top-notch educational institution in the middle of one of the best college cities in the world," BU is the perfect place for independent students anxious to explore all options. As one student puts it, "BU not only allowed me access to more than 65 majors in my school, the College of Arts and Sciences (I tried out astronomy, international relations, psychology, and anthropology before deciding on anthro/religion and French), but also majors in other schools (I took two drama classes in the College of Fine Arts)." Many are drawn here by the "top-notch pre-professional programs" that include "an excellent communications program," a "great management program," and "a great biology program." Students note that "BU fosters independence: Students can do whatever they want; they just have to have the motivation." Academics "are very, very rigorous," with more than a few students hypothesizing the existence of an unwritten "grade deflation" policy, which, understandably, they regard as unfair.

Life

BU "doesn't have a campus in a traditional sense, and that takes some getting used to. It also means that most of your social life isn't centered on the university," but more on the city itself. To many here, "Boston is the perfect city. Easy to walk around; not as big and crazy as NYC; and plenty to do on the weekends besides party," such as "walking all the way downtown, passing through all the big entertainment areas, or walking over to Cambridge and Central Square or down the river and over the footbridge to Harvard Square…A short T-ride puts you in the North End with its Italian food heaven. If you can't find what you're looking for within 20 minutes of campus, you just haven't looked hard enough." Parties typically occur off campus "since the university has a fairly strict alcohol and drug policy which, RAs monitor closely. The off-campus parties are typically big (100-plus) and, of course, have beer and cheap liquor more than accessible. The bar and club scene is also big, with Lansdowne Street only a few blocks away, so going out to drink and dance on the weekends is also pretty common." Cabs are easy to snag so getting around the city is "pretty simple." For those who prefer to stick with school activities, "The school makes a real effort to get students involved and to provide activities for us, albeit through our yearly undergraduate student fee. They have comedy clubs, student concerts, and several interesting lectures for every interest imaginable, etc."

Student Body

The undergraduate student body at BU is more than 18,000 strong, so "there is no 'typical' BU student." Students here "tend to be liberal and politically aware, but other than that, one of the most desirable aspects of BU is that there are no "types." Because BU has strong athletics, as well as strong programs in the arts, "there is a nice mix" and "everyone seems to get along well enough." This diversity adds an amazing dynamic to class discussions. This is one of the most valuable aspects of a BU education." That said, many here tell us that "a solid majority of people are very rich, well dressed, and reasonably snobby." New England prep-school grads are well represented, but so, too, are a broad array of states and nations.

FINANCIAL AID: 617-353-2965 • E-MAIL: ADMISSIONS@BU.EDU • WEBSITE: WWW.BU.EDU

THE PRINCETON REVIEW SAYS

Admissions

Very important factors considered include: Rigor of secondary school record. *Important factors considered include:* Class rank, application essay, academic GPA, recommendation(s), standardized test scores. *Other factors considered include:* Alumni/ae relation, character/personal qualities, extracurricular activities, first generation, geographical residence, level of applicant's interest, racial/ethnic status, state residency, volunteer work, work experience. SAT and SAT Subject Tests or ACT required. ACT with Writing component required. TOEFL required of all international applicants. High school diploma is required and GED is accepted. *Academic units recommended:* 4 English, 3 mathematics, 3 science (4 laboratory), 2 foreign language, 3 social studies.

Financial Aid

Students should submit: FAFSA, CSS/financial aid profile, state aid form, non-custodial profile, business/farm supplement. Regular filing deadline is 2/15. The Princeton Review suggests that all financial aid forms be submitted as soon as possible after 1/1. *Need-based scholarships/grants offered:* Federal Pell, SEOG, state scholarships/grants, private scholarships, the school's own gift aid. *Loan aid offered:* Direct Subsidized Stafford, Direct Unsubsidized Stafford, Direct PLUS, Federal Perkins, state loans. Applicants will be notified of awards on a rolling basis beginning 3/15.

The Inside Word

BU has grown more selective over the years. Requirements and admissions standards are somewhat more lenient for the College of General Studies, a 2-year program that takes students right up to the point at which they declare a major and enter one of the university's 8 other undergraduate schools. Students in the College of General Studies are admitted as four-year degree candidates and continue as juniors in one of the other schools or colleges, with no new application required.

THE SCHOOL SAYS ". . ."

From The Admissions Office

"Boston University (BU) is a private teaching and research institution with a strong emphasis on undergraduate education. We are committed to providing the highest level of teaching excellence, and fulfillment of this pledge is our highest priority. Boston University has 10 undergraduate schools and colleges offering more than 250 major and minor areas of concentration. Students may choose from programs of study in areas as diverse as biochemistry, theater, physical therapy, elementary education, broadcast journalism, international relations, business, and computer engineering. BU has an international student body, with students from every state and 100 countries. In addition, opportunities to study abroad exist through over 70 semester-long programs, spanning more than 22 countries on six continents.

"BU requires freshman applicants to take the SAT and two SAT Subject Tests. Students are encouraged to take subject tests in fields in which they excel. Students may submit the results of the ACT (with the Writing section) in lieu of the SAT and SAT Subject Tests."

SELECTIVITY

Admissions Rating	96
# of applicants	38,010
% of applicants accepted	54
% of acceptees attending	20
# accepting a place on wait list	1,467
% admitted from wait list	38
# of early decision applicants	836
% accepted early decision	41

FRESHMAN PROFILE

Range SAT Critical Reading	580–670
Range SAT Math	600–690
Range SAT Writing	590–680
Range ACT Composite	25–30
Minimum paper TOEFL	550
Minimum computer TOEFL	215
Average HS GPA	3.5
% graduated top 10% of class	55
% graduated top 25% of class	87
% graduated top 50% of class	99

DEADLINES

Early decision	
Deadline	11/1
Notification	12/15
Regular	
Deadline	1/1
Nonfall registration?	yes

APPLICANTS ALSO LOOK AT

AND OFTEN PREFER
The George Washington U., NYU, U. of Southern California

AND SOMETIMES PREFER
Cornell University, Boston College, Tufts University, Syracuse University

AND RARELY PREFER
Northeastern University, University of Massachusetts Amherst, Brown University

FINANCIAL FACTS

Financial Aid Rating	84
Annual tuition	$37,910
Room and board	$18,848
Required fees	$530
Books and supplies	$940
% frosh rec. need-based scholarship or grant aid	44
% UG rec. need-based scholarship or grant aid	40
% frosh rec. non-need-based scholarship or grant aid	17
% UG rec. non-need-based scholarship or grant aid	10
% frosh rec. need-based self-help aid	40
% UG rec. need-based self-help aid	38
% frosh rec. athletic scholarships	1
% UG rec. athletic scholarships	2
% frosh rec. any financial aid	65
% UG rec. any financial aid	64
% UG borrow to pay for school	58
Average cumulative indebtedness	$26,586

BOWDOIN COLLEGE

5000 COLLEGE STATION, BOWDOIN COLLEGE, BRUNSWICK, ME 04011-8441 • ADMISSIONS: 207-725-3100 • FAX: 207-725-3101

CAMPUS LIFE
Quality of Life Rating	99
Fire Safety Rating	96
Green Rating	94
Type of school	private
Environment	village

STUDENTS
Total undergrad enrollment	1,716
% male/female	49/51
% from out of state	87
% from public high school	55
% live on campus	94
% African American	6
% Asian	12
% Caucasian	68
% Hispanic	9
% Native American	1
% international	3
# of countries represented	26

SURVEY SAYS . . .
School is well run
Great food on campus
Dorms are like palaces
Frats and sororities are unpopular or nonexistent

ACADEMICS
Academic Rating	97
Calendar	semester
Student/faculty ratio	9:1
Profs interesting rating	95
Profs accessible rating	97
Most common reg class size	10–19 students
Most common lab size	10–19 students

MOST POPULAR MAJORS
economics
history
political science and government

STUDENTS SAY ". . ."

Academics

Highly selective Bowdoin College is all about providing an "excellent liberal arts education in a supportive, small community" in "a beautiful part of the country." Undergrads cite Bowdoin's "intelligent" and "diverse" student body, "absolutely top-notch" professors, and "challenging, fascinating academic program that allows you to explore all your areas of interest" as particularly deserving of praise. Students here reap the benefits of "a close-knit community of learners, teachers, and leaders pursuing academics, athletics, music, art, clubs, and fun with relentless, positive enthusiasm" in "a very nurturing and safe environment." Standout programs include environmental studies, neuroscience, foreign languages, and the English and education departments which students described as "excellent, bar none." The workload at Bowdoin "is just a few steps shy from unmanageable, which is good" because it forces students to "not only do your work," but "to do it carefully." Students also appreciate a faculty that is "truly interested in learning everyone's name," and "will stay hours after review sessions" until students grasp the concepts. "Professors challenge you, and push you to go beyond just the books." Great facilities include the Career Planning Center, Writing Center, Baldwin Center for Academic Development, Counseling Center, and administrative offices. The cherry on the sundae? "Excellent alumni networking."

Life

Students love how Bowdoin "embraces the intellectual experience in a balanced, healthy way, so that students are generally very happy. There is an awareness, learning comes from everywhere, so there is a real effort by the Bowdoin administration as well as Bowdoin students to bring speakers, events, and entertainment to the campus so students can learn in every way possible." Extracurriculars are part of the constant learning; students here "are always doing at least one if not 10 things at a time." Physical activity is part of the mix as many students participate in Outing Club events like hiking, whitewater kayaking, and rafting at nearby parks. "It seems like almost everyone is on a sports team, so during the week most people find a release there," students tell us that "on the weekends, there is a lot of partying (and with that comes a lot of alcohol)," but "It's not excessive." Plus, the "alcohol policies are also pretty sweet—as long as everyone can be responsible and things are not out of control, security does not want to get anyone in trouble," and "a safe ride system" provides free rides home to intoxicated students for free. Those who don't drink tell us "There is plenty of music at night" and "Brunswick is great for a concert, coffee shop, or bowling." Gourmands, take note: "Bowdoin food is the best!"

Student Body

While "a fair amount of preppy kids" congregate on Bowdoin's campus, "There are all types of people here, providing an interesting mix of personalities, backgrounds, and interactions." Personality types "range from typical straight-out-of-prep-school to crusty hippies to jocks to artsy kids." "Bowdoin students either wear Chacos or Polos with their collars popped. Some even alternate between these two personalities." They also tend to be "multifaceted and multilayered; they are great intellectuals, as well as athletes, political activists, dancers, and community leaders. No one here is involved in just academic activities." Students say everyone is "down to earth and very passionate about something— the environment, politics, science, the welfare of goats in Chile, etc." Despite being "extremely intelligent" and "highly motivated," Bowdoin undergrads "are not fiercely competitive or grade-grubby," and "Everyone gets along well."

FINANCIAL AID: 207-725-3273 • E-MAIL: ADMISSIONS@BOWDOIN.EDU • WEBSITE: WWW.BOWDOIN.EDU

THE PRINCETON REVIEW SAYS

Admissions

Very important factors considered include: Class rank, application essay, academic GPA, recommendation(s), rigor of secondary school record, character/personal qualities, extracurricular activities, talent/ability. *Important factors considered include:* Standardized test scores, alumni/ae relation, first generation. *Other factors considered include:* Geographical residence, interview, racial/ethnic status, state residency, TOEFL required of all international applicants. High school diploma is required and GED is not accepted. *Academic units recommended:* 4 English, 4 mathematics, 4 science (3 science labs), 4 foreign language, 4 social studies.

Financial Aid

Students should submit: FAFSA, CSS/financial aid profile, noncustodial profile, business/farm supplement. Regular filing deadline is 2/15. The Princeton Review suggests that all financial aid forms be submitted as soon as possible after 1/1. *Need-based scholarships/grants offered:* Federal Pell, SEOG, state scholarships/grants, private scholarships, the school's own gift aid. *Loan aid offered:* FFEL Subsidized Stafford, FFEL Unsubsidized Stafford, FFEL PLUS, Federal Perkins, state loans, college/university loans from institutional funds. Applicants will be notified of awards on or about 4/5. Federal Work-Study Program available. Institutional employment available. Off-campus job opportunities are good.

The Inside Word

Standardized test scores are optional at Bowdoin, but if you aced the SAT or ACT you should definitely report your scores. The school will almost certainly look at them; in the spring of 2006, the Dean of Admissions at Bowdoin said as much to *The New York Times*, explaining that he considers test scores helpful. He noted that high school transcripts are difficult to compare, especially in light of grade inflation at many schools.

THE SCHOOL SAYS "..."

From The Admissions Office

"A liberal arts education at Bowdoin isn't about being small and safe—it's about having the support to take surprising risks. That means caring more about the questions than giving the right answers. Discovering you're good at something you didn't think was your strength. Making connections where none appears to exist. Bowdoin's curriculum offers a bold blueprint for liberal education designed to inspire students to become world citizens with acute sensitivity to the social and natural worlds. Its interdisciplinary focus encourages students to make connections among subjects, to discover disciplines that excite their imaginations, and to develop keen skills for addressing the challenges of a changing world.

"A Bowdoin education is best summed up by 'The Offer of The College':"

> To be at home in all lands and all ages;
> To count Nature a familiar acquaintance,
> And Art an intimate friend;
> To gain a standard for the appreciation of others' work
> And the criticism of your own;
> To carry the keys of the world's library in your pocket,
> And feel its resources behind you in whatever task you undertake;
> To make hosts of friends...
> Who are to be leaders in all walks of life;
> To lose yourself in generous enthusiasms
> And cooperate with others for common ends—
> This is the offer of the college for the best four years of your life."

Adapted from the original 'Offer of the College'
by William DeWitt Hyde
President of Bowdoin College 1885–1917"

SELECTIVITY

Admissions Rating	99
# of applicants	6,033
% of applicants accepted	19
% of acceptees attending	44
# of early decision applicants	690
% accepted early decision	30

FRESHMAN PROFILE

Range SAT Critical Reading	650–760
Range SAT Math	650–750
Range SAT Writing	660–730
Range ACT Composite	29–33
Minimum paper TOEFL	600
Minimum computer TOEFL	250
Minimum web-based TOEFL	100
Average HS GPA	3.8
% graduated top 10% of class	82
% graduated top 25% of class	98
% graduated top 50% of class	100

DEADLINES

Early decision	
Deadline	11/15
Notification	12/31
Regular	
Deadline	1/1
Notification	4/5
Nonfall registration?	no

APPLICANTS ALSO LOOK AT

AND OFTEN PREFER
Harvard College
Yale University
Princeton University

AND SOMETIMES PREFER
Dartmouth College
Williams College
Brown University
Amherst College

AND RARELY PREFER
Middlebury College
Colby College
Tufts University

FINANCIAL FACTS

Financial Aid Rating	99
Annual tuition	$37,790
Room and board	$10,380
Required fees	$400
Books and supplies	$800
% frosh rec. need-based scholarship or grant aid	41
% UG rec. need-based scholarship or grant aid	43
% frosh rec. need-based self-help aid	36
% UG rec. need-based self-help aid	39
% frosh rec. any financial aid	45
% UG rec. any financial aid	47
% UG borrow to pay for school	51
Average cumulative indebtedness	$17,530

BRADLEY UNIVERSITY

1501 West Bradley Avenue, Peoria, IL 61625 • Admissions: 309-677-1000 • Fax: 309-677-2797

CAMPUS LIFE

Quality of Life Rating	**70**
Fire Safety Rating	**73**
Green Rating	**60***
Type of school	private
Environment	city

STUDENTS

Total undergrad enrollment	5,064
% male/female	46/54
% from out of state	11
% live on campus	68
% in (# of) fraternities	33 (16)
% in (# of) sororities	27 (11)
% African American	7
% Asian	4
% Caucasian	83
% Hispanic	3
% international	1
# of countries represented	30

SURVEY SAYS . . .

Athletic facilities are great
Students are friendly
Low cost of living
Frats and sororities dominate social scene
(Almost) no one smokes
Very little drug use

ACADEMICS

Academic Rating	**69**
Calendar	semester
Student/faculty ratio	13:1
Profs interesting rating	69
Profs accessible rating	77
Most common reg class size	20–29 students

MOST POPULAR MAJORS

mechanical engineering
nursing/registered nurse (RN, ASN, BSN, MSN)
organizational communication

STUDENTS SAY ". . ."

Academics

"A medium-sized school with the personality of a large "state" Division I school" for many students, Bradley boasts the affordability of an in-state education with "the prestige and community" of a small-school atmosphere due to its "intimate class settings" and "devoted professors." Often noted for its "great nursing program," Bradley and its academic offerings are united by "passion, tradition, and a striving for consistent improvement and excellence." With a focus on providing students with "everything they need to be successful out in the 'real world,'" Bradley is "great at making students feel welcome" while providing alums with "lessons to build upon for a lifetime." "Bradley is all about teaching the individual student" and "developing one's intellect for what comes next." Students are often drawn to Bradley for its "job placement, good facilities, diverse areas of study, student/teacher relationships, and class sizes." Professors are "very knowledgeable and have a vested interest in every student's learning." Many students champion the school's new president and administration for the scope of their vision as well as their renewed commitment to soliciting student opinion. President Glasser "makes an excellent role model for young women." She is "very in tune" and "makes [students] her number 1 priority."

Life

Life at Bradley provides "the resources of a large university with the familiarity that comes from a small liberal arts school." With a student body of approximately 5,000, "Bradley has a wide variety of students. If you need study partners we have those; if you want to party on Friday night, we have those students; if you want to stay in and watch a movie, we have plenty of those. You can easily find someone with the same interests." "Bradley is all about community." As one student says, Bradley provides a "'salad bowl' environment because people from all backgrounds generally get along." Due to "the variety of campus clubs, activities, and organizations," "everyone finds a niche." "Almost everyone on campus is associated with some sort of Greek organization or athletic team. Spending time with the group of friends that each person develops is the most common idea of fun." When it comes to facilities, though students remark that "the library needs to be updated with more and better computers," the recreation center is the "beauty of the campus" and "offers hundreds of activities to join." "The new Markin Fitness Center is very popular."

Student Body

When it comes to describing the typical Bradley student, one shoe does not fit all. Benefiting from its size and diversity, there is a "huge variety in student types at Bradley," including "some students from big city suburbs [and] some from small farm towns, with the income base varying greatly no matter where they came from." The "typical student is intelligent, but yet very sociable and easy to get along with," and "involved in at least one outside organization." Though variety seems to be the norm, others note that in general "there are two types [of students]: The suburban type—usually from St. Louis or Chicago. This type is more trendy and into the latest fads and such. Then there is the small-town type. These tend to be very interesting people who are laid-back yet conservative."

FINANCIAL AID: 309-677-3089 • E-MAIL: ADMISSIONS@BRADLEY.EDU • WEBSITE: WWW.BRADLEY.EDU

THE PRINCETON REVIEW SAYS

Admissions

Very important factors considered include: Academic GPA, rigor of secondary school record. *Important factors considered include:* Class rank, standardized test scores. *Other factors considered include:* Application essay, recommendation(s), alumni/ae relation, character/personal qualities, extracurricular activities, geographical residence, interview, level of applicant's interest, racial/ethnic status, talent/ability, volunteer work, work experience. SAT or ACT required. TOEFL required of all international applicants. High school diploma is required and GED is accepted. *Academic units required:* 4 English, 3 mathematics, 2 science (2 science labs), 2 social studies. *Academic units recommended:* 5 English, 4 mathematics, 3 science (3 science labs), 2 foreign language, 3 social studies, 2 history.

Financial Aid

Students should submit: FAFSA. The Princeton Review suggests that all financial aid forms be submitted as soon as possible after 1/1. *Need-based scholarships/grants offered:* Federal Pell, SEOG, state scholarships/grants, private scholarships, the school's own gift aid. *Loan aid offered:* Direct Subsidized Stafford, Direct Unsubsidized Stafford, Direct PLUS, FFEL PLUS, Federal Perkins, federal nursing scholarships. Federal Work-Study Program available.

The Inside Word

With much regional appeal, the vast majority of students at Bradley originate from Illinois. With an active eye toward broadening the student body's geographic demographics, the school presents an opportunity for out-of-staters seeking to attend an excellent university without having to endure the grueling admissions process of many private universities. Above-average students should find that gaining admission here is a relatively painless experience.

THE SCHOOL SAYS "..."

From The Admissions Office

"Unlike many smaller private colleges, Bradley offers the academic variety of more than 100 undergraduate and 30 graduate programs of study. In addition to the traditional liberal arts and sciences, academic programs include business, communications, education, engineering, fine and performing arts, and health sciences. Unique programs include entrepreneurship, multimedia, and a doctorate program in physical therapy. While students have the academic choices of a larger university, they also have the guidance and mentoring of faculty. Unlike many larger institutions, the Bradley academic experience happens in faculty-taught classes that average just 23 students. One-on-one interaction with professionals is the expectation at Bradley.

"Beyond a great academic experience, what really makes Bradley exceptional is campus life. Bradley students are involved in more than 220 student organizations, including more than 50 dedicated to student leadership and community service. Integration of career development is central to the Bradley experience. One measurable outcome of this career development integration is that 96 percent of graduates begin work, graduate school, or other postgraduate experiences within 6 months of graduation.

"The Peoria area is the largest metropolitan region in Illinois south of Chicago and is home to more than 360,000 residents. The sizeable city provides ample opportunities for internships, practicums, cooperative education, and volunteer experiences.

"In summary, the Bradley experience is unlike most other universities. A Bradley student will experience a blend of quality academics, focused career preparation, extensive activities, and leadership opportunities.

"Bradley requires freshman applicants to submit scores from the SAT or the ACT, with or without the Writing component."

SELECTIVITY
Admissions Rating	79
# of applicants	5,932
% of applicants accepted	64
% of acceptees attending	27
# accepting a place on wait list	42
% admitted from wait list	50

FRESHMAN PROFILE
Range SAT Critical Reading	500–630
Range SAT Math	520–650
Range ACT Composite	22–27
Minimum paper TOEFL	530
Minimum computer TOEFL	197
% graduated top 10% of class	29
% graduated top 25% of class	65
% graduated top 50% of class	92

DEADLINES
Regular	
Priority	3/1
Notification	rolling
Nonfall registration?	yes

APPLICANTS ALSO LOOK AT
AND OFTEN PREFER
Purdue University—West Lafayette
University of Illinois at Urbana-Champaign
Loyola University of Chicago

AND SOMETIMES PREFER
Marquette University
DePaul University
University of Illinois at Chicago

AND RARELY PREFER
Southern Illinois University—Edwardsville
Illinois State University
Northern Illinois University

FINANCIAL FACTS
Financial Aid Rating	72
Annual tuition	$22,600
Room and board	$7,350
% frosh rec. need-based scholarship or grant aid	64
% UG rec. need-based scholarship or grant aid	68
% frosh rec. non-need-based scholarship or grant aid	11
% UG rec. non-need-based scholarship or grant aid	8
% frosh rec. need-based self-help aid	51
% UG rec. need-based self-help aid	55
% frosh rec. athletic scholarships	2
% UG rec. athletic scholarships	2
% frosh rec. any financial aid	98
% UG rec. any financial aid	93
Average cumulative indebtedness	$18,398

BRANDEIS UNIVERSITY

415 SOUTH STREET, MS003, WALTHAM, MA 02454 • ADMISSIONS: 781-736-3500 • FAX: 781-736-3536

CAMPUS LIFE

Quality of Life Rating	**80**
Fire Safety Rating	**60***
Green Rating	**60***
Type of school	private
Environment	city

STUDENTS

Total undergrad enrollment	3,169
% male/female	44/56
% from out of state	74
% from public high school	72
% live on campus	77
% African American	4
% Asian	10
% Caucasian	53
% Hispanic	5
% international	8
# of countries represented	97

SURVEY SAYS . . .

No one cheats
Students are friendly
Campus feels safe
Musical organizations are popular
Student publications are popular
Political activism is popular

ACADEMICS

Academic Rating	**88**
Calendar	semester
Profs interesting rating	82
Profs accessible rating	82
Most common	
reg class size	10–19 students

MOST POPULAR MAJORS

biology/biological sciences
economics
psychology

STUDENTS SAY "..."

Academics

Home to "lots of 'pre-somethings' trying to figure out if that 'something' is right for them," Brandeis University is "a good jumping-off point for those looking to go into medicine or law." Boasting "a very good liberal arts education," Brandeis also provides plenty of alternatives to those who start down the "pre-something" path only to find that it's not for them. Even those who stay the course appreciate the "large variety of options"; as one student explains, "Brandeis is very academically stimulating and has many interesting courses, professors who make themselves available outside of class, and teaching assistants who are very helpful." Aspiring doctors are drawn here by a "stellar" neuroscience department that gives undergraduates "the experience of graduate students as far as research is concerned," in addition to "a very high acceptance rate at medical schools." Other strong programs include psychology, music, economics, political science, and history. Students agree that most professors are "passionate about what they teach." Classes "are generally small, which puts pressure on you to come prepared," and there is "a fair amount of class discussion, which can be great or awful." Students are ready to be engaged in class, as they are typically "friendly and talkative. An intense philosophical discussion is more common at Brandeis than drunken boorishness."

Life

Brandeis boasts "plenty of performance-based clubs (theater, musical, improv comedy, sketch comedy, dance), community-service organizations, activist clubs, ethnic clubs, religious clubs, political clubs, independent sports clubs, and also clubs just for fun, like the hookah club. There are so many opportunities to be involved here," and students "take [their] extracurriculars just as seriously as [their] studies, and tend to excel in both." Students also love their access to Boston, noting that "a free shuttle runs us to and from the city Thursdays through Sundays, and the commuter rail stop on campus." The proximity of Boston helps offset the fact that "there is really nothing to do in Waltham. There is a movie theater, and some restaurants, and bars, but that is about it. Proximity to [Boston College] and Bentley is nice, however." Students say the social scene at Brandeis "is somewhat lacking. If you are looking for big sporting events with lots of spirit or parties with lots of people, you won't like Brandeis." Parties "don't ever fall into your lap at Brandeis; you have to look for them." For some, this is a plus; as one student writes, "I like the school because if you want a quiet Friday night with board games and old movies, it's very easy to do. People won't judge you or pressure you into drinking. But on Saturday when you're ready for some fun, you have to do a little digging."

Student Body

Brandeis has long been a popular destination for Jewish students. About 40 percent of the student population (undergrad and grad) is Jewish, and undergrads tell us that "there are a lot of orthodox Jews here, more than at your average college. Yet, there are also a lot of non-religious students, observant Muslims, and Christians. So the school just teaches us to recognize each others' religions," and "You never feel like your fellow students are judging you." A "nice-sized international community" also "helps diversify the school." Many here tend to be "pretty socially awkward, and kind of an overachiever, but generally well-intentioned and sweet." One student told us that students tend to be "quirky, prone to traditionally nerdy pursuits, and very friendly. At Brandeis, weird is normal." Everyone works hard here "because they want to do well," and students "spend most of their time studying."

FINANCIAL AID: 781-736-3700 • E-MAIL: SENDINFO@BRANDEIS.EDU • WEBSITE: WWW.BRANDEIS.EDU

THE PRINCETON REVIEW SAYS

Admissions

Very important factors considered include: Class rank, academic GPA, rigor of secondary school record, standardized test scores, character/personal qualities, level of applicant's interest. *Important factors considered include:* Application essay, recommendation(s), extracurricular activities, first generation, talent/ability, volunteer work, work experience. *Other factors considered include:* Alumni/ae relation, geographical residence, interview, racial/ethnic status. SAT or ACT required. ACT with Writing component required. TOEFL required of applicants. Requirement waived if score 600+ on critical reading for whom English is a second language. High school diploma is required and GED is accepted. *Academic units recommended:* 4 English, 3 mathematics, 1 science (1 science lab), 3 foreign language, 1 history, 4 academic electives.

Financial Aid

Students should submit: FAFSA, CSS/financial aid profile, noncustodial profile, business/farm supplement. The Princeton Review suggests that all financial aid forms be submitted as soon as possible after 1/1. *Need-based scholarships/grants offered:* Federal Pell, SEOG, state scholarships/grants, private scholarships, the school's own gift aid. *Loan aid offered:* Direct Subsidized Stafford, Direct Unsubsidized Stafford, Direct PLUS, Federal Perkins, state loans, college/university loans from institutional funds. Federal Work-Study Program available. Institutional employment available. Off-campus job opportunities are fair.

The Inside Word

Brandeis requires one of two combinations of standardized test scores: the SAT or the ACT with Writing component. Most students choose the SAT. Brandeis is often looked at as a safety school for students applying to Ivies; as the Ivies now routinely reject many highly qualified applicants, admission to Brandeis is extremely competitive despite its safety school reputation.

THE SCHOOL SAYS "..."

From The Admissions Office

"Education at Brandeis is personal, combining the intimacy of a small liberal arts college and the intellectual power of a large research university. Classes are small and are taught by professors, 98 percent of whom hold the highest degree in their fields. They give students personal attention in state-of-the-art resources, giving them the tools to succeed in a variety of postgraduate endeavors.

"This vibrant, freethinking, intellectual university was founded in 1948. Brandeis University reflects the values of the first Jewish Supreme Court Justice Louis Brandeis, which are passion for learning, commitment to social justice, respect for creativity and diversity, and concern for the world.

"Brandeis has an ideal location on the commuter rail nine miles west of Boston; state-of-the-art sports facilities; and internships that complement interests in law, medicine, government, finance, business, and the arts. Brandeis offers generous university scholarships and need-based financial aid that can be renewed for 4 years.

"Brandeis requires that students send official scores for the SAT or ACT with Writing. Students for whom English is not their first language should take the TOEFL (Test of English as a Foreign Language)."

SELECTIVITY
Admissions Rating	99
# of applicants	7,724
% of applicants accepted	32
% of acceptees attending	30
# accepting a place on wait list	404
% admitted from wait list	19
# of early decision applicants	458
% accepted early decision	53

FRESHMAN PROFILE
Range SAT Critical Reading	640–720
Range SAT Math	650–730
Range SAT Writing	640–730
Range ACT Composite	29–32
Minimum paper TOEFL	600
Minimum computer TOEFL	250
Minimum web-based TOEFL	100
Average HS GPA	3.85
% graduated top 10% of class	82
% graduated top 25% of class	94
% graduated top 50% of class	100

DEADLINES
Early decision	
Deadline	11/15
Notification	12/15
Early action	
Deadline	12/15
Notification	2/15
Regular	
Deadline	1/15
Notification	4/1
Nonfall registration?	yes

FINANCIAL FACTS
Financial Aid Rating	79
Annual tuition	$36,122
Room and board	$10,354
Required fees	$1,172
% frosh rec. need-based scholarship or grant aid	50
% UG rec. need-based scholarship or grant aid	46
% frosh rec. non-need-based scholarship or grant aid	6
% UG rec. non-need-based scholarship or grant aid	5
% frosh rec. need-based self-help aid	46
% UG rec. need-based self-help aid	42
% frosh rec. any financial aid	53
% UG rec. any financial aid	48
% UG borrow to pay for school	77
Average cumulative indebtedness	$20,095

BRIGHAM YOUNG UNIVERSITY (UT)

A-153 ASB, PROVO, UT 84602-1110 • ADMISSIONS: 801-422-2507 • FAX: 801-422-0005

CAMPUS LIFE
Quality of Life Rating	**98**
Fire Safety Rating	**63**
Green Rating	**60***
Type of school	private
Affiliation	Church of Jesus Christ of Latter Day Saints
Environment	city

STUDENTS
Total undergrad enrollment	30,912
% male/female	51/49
% from out of state	62
% live on campus	5
% Asian	4
% Caucasian	87
% Hispanic	4
% Native American	1
% international	2
# of countries represented	121

SURVEY SAYS . . .
Students are very religious
Musical organizations are popular
Very little beer drinking
Very little hard liquor
(Almost) no one smokes
Very little drug use

ACADEMICS
Academic Rating	**88**
Calendar	semester
Student/faculty ratio	20:1
Profs interesting rating	83
Profs accessible rating	76
Most common reg class size	10–19 students

MOST POPULAR MAJORS
business/commerce
elementary education and teaching
exercise physiology

STUDENTS SAY ". . ."

Academics

Brigham Young University—perhaps you've heard of it? This "largely religious" Utah school gathers a lot of "like-minded individuals" in a beautiful setting, providing them with a "high level of education in which LDS themes may be incorporated" and "high moral standards" all rolled into one. Students here are exceptionally bright and motivated, matching up perfectly with "accessible" professors that "genuinely care about their students and are passionate about what [professors] teach," even if it can be a bit lecture-heavy. "Even in classes of several hundred they would memorize everyone's name," says one biochemistry major. Classes are "challenging, but not impossible," and those students who are motivated have plenty of hands-on opportunities to work with professors in order to prepare them for the work force. Though intro classes can be large, there is plenty of flexibility offered in honors courses and electives that "allows students to shape their course of study." All in all, BYU is a "great place to learn in an environment that is not cluttered with drinking and other such things that fill other college campuses." Much like the teachers, the administration at BYU is similarly high-regarded by most, and these "righteous individuals" are always trying to help and "listening to students about what they want." It doesn't stop there—every aspect of the BYU machine prepares graduates "mentally, emotionally, and spiritually to go forth and serve the world in many different capacities." The academics here place a heavy emphasis on book smarts and on how a graduate can contribute to the community and "build relationships [that] will help him fulfill a lifelong commitment to returning service to mankind." Most students express a commitment to using their education to give to others, and the school encourages students to achieve "greatness academically, morally, and spiritually." One sophomore sums it up by saying, "BYU—where your best hasn't been good enough since 1875."

Student Body

Unsurprisingly, the typical BYU student is "culturally LDS" and therefore "does not smoke, drink alcohol, coffee or tea, does not swear, and is generally trustworthy and honest." Beyond this, all who actively follow the school's behavioral and honor codes are well-accepted regardless of race or religion; those who don't "do not remain students here for long." This relative homogeneity allows for plenty of niches, and "there are lots of different students with wide varieties of interests." With such a large student body, most atypical students can still find large groups of supportive friends: "The BYU Democrats club now claims more members than the BYU Republicans." However, some students feel BYU "could improve its awareness on social issues such as gay rights." Hard work and service abound at BYU, and not very many students come to class claiming that the dog ate their homework. Most students "are very well accomplished and have high standards" and do a great deal of community service. Because of the LDS church's emphasis on missionary experience, the majority of the student body "speaks a foreign language fluently and commands an impressive depth of knowledge on the country they served in." 21% of undergrads at BYU are married.

Campus Life

Without the influences of some of the more popular college vices, BYU students "mainly think about making a difference in the world, serving missions, and getting married." There are lots of dances and activities on campus, and students "get creative" in amusing themselves—social games such as Apples to Apples and Guitar Hero are all the rage. "We'll make huge snowmen when it snows, carol in the streets, or make cookies to Christmas music in the winter," says a senior. Many amusements "revolve around the school's strong athletic programs in football and basketball. Studies are never neglected, and the library is a popular place to be found, which means "there is plenty of library romance going on." Because Utah is very close to Provo Canyon and the mountains, hiking and skiing are popular, and "Provo City has art festivals and other things that go on in the summer and early autumn."

Brigham Young University (UT)

Financial Aid: 801-422-4104 • E-mail: admissions@byu.edu • Website: www.byu.edu

THE PRINCETON REVIEW SAYS

Admissions

Very important factors considered include: Academic GPA, rigor of secondary school record, standardized test scores, character/personal qualities, interview, religious affiliation/commitment. *Important factors considered include:* Application essay, recommendation(s), extracurricular activities, racial/ethnic status, volunteer work. *Other factors considered include:* Talent/ability, work experience. ACT with Writing component require. TOEFL required of all international applicants. High school diploma is required and GED is accepted. *Academic units required:* 4 English, 3 mathematics, 2 science (2 science labs), 2 foreign language, 2 history, 2 literature or writing. *Academic units recommended:* 4 English, 4 mathematics, 3 science (3 science labs), 4 foreign language.

Financial Aid

Students should submit: FAFSA. The Princeton Review suggests that all financial aid forms be submitted as soon as possible after 1/1. *Need-based scholarships/grants offered:* Federal Pell, state scholarships/grants, private scholarships, the school's own gift aid. *Loan aid offered:* FFEL Subsidized Stafford, FFEL Unsubsidized Stafford, FFEL PLUS, college/university loans from institutional funds. Applicants will be notified of awards on a rolling basis beginning 4/1.

The Inside Word

An applicant pool of 9,000 necessitates a reliance on numbers, especially during the first round of cuts. Much of the matchmaking done at other schools isn't necessary here, as a highly self-selecting applicant pool typically precludes those who'd make a poor fit. Still, admissions officers want to see at least respect (if not reverence) for LDS principles, without which survival here would be difficult indeed.

THE SCHOOL SAYS "..."

From The Admissions Office

"The mission of Brigham Young University—founded, supported, and guided by the Church of Jesus Christ of Latter-day Saints—is to assist individuals in their quest for perfection and eternal life. That assistance should provide a period of intensive learning in a stimulating setting where a commitment to excellence is expected and the full realization of human potential is pursued. All instruction, programs, and services at BYU, including a wide variety of extracurricular experiences, should make their own contribution toward the balanced development of the total person. Such a broadly prepared individual will not only be capable of meeting personal challenge and change but will also bring strength to others in the tasks of home and family life, social relationships, civic duty, and service to mankind.

"Freshman applicants are required to take either the ACT (with the optional Writing section) or the SAT. The highest composite score will be used in admissions decisions."

SELECTIVITY

Admissions Rating	96
# of applicants	10,081
% of applicants accepted	69
% of acceptees attending	78

FRESHMAN PROFILE

Range SAT Critical Reading	550–660
Range SAT Math	570–680
Range ACT Composite	25–30
Minimum paper TOEFL	500
Minimum computer TOEFL	173
Average HS GPA	3.76
% graduated top 10% of class	49
% graduated top 25% of class	83
% graduated top 50% of class	98

DEADLINES

Regular	
Deadline	2/1
Nonfall registration?	yes

APPLICANTS ALSO LOOK AT AND SOMETIMES PREFER
University of Utah

FINANCIAL FACTS

Financial Aid Rating	77
Out-of-state tuition	$4,290
Room and board	$6,840
Books and supplies	$1,000
% frosh rec. need-based scholarship or grant aid	10
% UG rec. need-based scholarship or grant aid	26
% frosh rec. non-need-based scholarship or grant aid	10
% UG rec. non-need-based scholarship or grant aid	16
% frosh rec. need-based self-help aid	6
% UG rec. need-based self-help aid	14
% frosh rec. athletic scholarships	1
% UG rec. athletic scholarships	1
% frosh rec. any financial aid	53
% UG rec. any financial aid	64
% UG borrow to pay for school	35
Average cumulative indebtedness	$13,926

BROWN UNIVERSITY

PO BOX 1876, 45 PROSPECT STREET, PROVIDENCE, RI 02912 • ADMISSIONS: 401-863-2378 • FAX: 401-863-9300

CAMPUS LIFE

Quality of Life Rating	**97**
Fire Safety Rating	**86**
Green Rating	**93**
Type of school	private
Environment	city

STUDENTS

Total undergrad enrollment	5,874
% male/female	48/52
% from out of state	95
% from public high school	60
% live on campus	79
% in (# of) fraternities	12 (8)
% in (# of) sororities	4 (2)
% African American	7
% Asian	16
% Caucasian	45
% Hispanic	9
% Native American	1
% international	8
# of countries represented	104

SURVEY SAYS . . .
No one cheats
Students are friendly
Great off-campus food
Students are happy
College radio is popular
Student publications are popular
Political activism is popular

ACADEMICS

Academic Rating	**91**
Calendar	semester
Student/faculty ratio	8:1
Profs interesting rating	88
Profs accessible rating	89
Most common reg class size	10–19 students

MOST POPULAR MAJORS
biology/biological sciences
economics
international relations and affairs

STUDENTS SAY " . . ."

Academics
Known for its somewhat unconventional (but still highly-regarded) approaches to life and learning, Brown University remains the slightly odd man out of the Ivy League, and the school wouldn't have it any other way. The school's willingness to employ and support different, untested methods such as the shopping period, the first two weeks of the semester where anyone can drop into any class in order to "find out if it's something they're interested in enrolling in," or the *Critical Review*, a student publication that produces reviews of courses based on evaluations from students who have completed the course, is designed to treat students "like an adult" through "freedom and choice." This open-minded environment allows them "to practice passion without shame or fear of judgment," the hallmark of a Brown education. Even if students do find themselves exploring the wrong off-the-beaten path, "there are multitudes of built-in support measures to help you succeed despite any odds." Even grades are a non-issue here, "except amongst paranoid premeds."

Professors are mostly hits with a few misses, but there are "amazing professors in every department, and they're not hard to find;" it's just "up to students to find the teaching styles that work for them." "Academics at Brown are what you make of them," and even though students are diligent in their academic pursuits and feel assured they're "getting a wonderful education with the professors," most agree that their education is "really more about the unique student body and learning through active participation in other activities." The administration gets cautiously decent reviews for their accessibility and general running of the school, but it also gets scolded for getting "distracted by the long term." The president, however, is absolutely loved by students for being "an incredible person with a great vision for the school."

Life
Thinking—yes, thinking—and discussing take up a great deal of time of time at Brown. "People think about life, politics, society at large, global affairs, the state of the economy, developing countries, animals, plants, rocket science, math, poker, each other, sex, sexuality, the human experience, gender studies, what to do with our lives, etc.," says a senior anthropology major. "Most people here don't go home that often," and like any school, "there are people who go out 5 nights a week and people who go out 5 nights a semester." "Alcohol and weed are pretty embedded in campus life," and most parties are dorm room events, even though partying "never gets in the way of academics or friendship. If you don't drink/smoke, that's totally cool." There's also plenty of cultural activities, such as indie bands, student performances, jazz, swing dancing, and speakers. Themed housing (art house, tech house, interfaith house) and co-ops are also popular social mediators.

Student Body
It's a pretty unique crowd here, where "athletes, preps, nerds, and everyone in between come together" because they "love learning for the sake of learning, and love Brown equally as much." "The 'mainstream' is full of people who are atypical in sense of fashion, taste in music, and academic interests," says a junior. Unsurprisingly, everyone here's "very smart," as well as "very quirky and often funny," and "a great amount are brilliant and passionate about their interests"; "most have interesting stories to tell." People here are "curious and open about many things," which is perhaps why sexual diversity is a "strong theme" among Brown interactions and events. The overall culture "is pretty laid-back and casual," and "most of the students are friendly and mesh well with everyone."

FINANCIAL AID: 401-863-2721 • E-MAIL: ADMISSION_UNDERGRADUATE@BROWN.EDU • WEBSITE: WWW.BROWN.EDU

THE PRINCETON REVIEW SAYS

Admissions

Very important factors considered include: Rigor of secondary school record, character/personal qualities, level of applicant's interest, talent/ability. *Important factors considered include:* Class rank, application essay, academic GPA, recommendation(s), standardized test scores, extracurricular activities. *Other factors considered include:* Alumni/ae relation, first generation, geographical residence, interview, racial/ethnic status, state residency, volunteer work, work experience. SAT and SAT Subject Tests or ACT required. ACT with Writing component required. TOEFL required of all international applicants. High school diploma is required and GED is not accepted. *Academic units required:* 4 English, 3 mathematics, 3 science (2 science labs), 3 foreign language, 2 history, 1 academic elective. *Academic units recommended:* 4 English, 4 mathematics, 4 science (3 science labs), 4 foreign language, 2 history, 1 visual/performing arts, 1 academic elective.

Financial Aid

Students should submit: FAFSA, CSS/financial aid profile, noncustodial profile, business/farm supplement. Regular filing deadline is 2/1. The Princeton Review suggests that all financial aid forms be submitted as soon as possible after 1/1. *Need-based scholarships/grants offered:* Federal Pell, SEOG, state scholarships/grants, private scholarships, the school's own gift aid. *Loan aid offered:* Direct Subsidized Stafford, Direct Unsubsidized Stafford, Direct PLUS, Federal Perkins, college/university loans from institutional funds. Applicants will be notified of awards on or about 4/1. Federal Work-Study Program available. Institutional employment available. Off-campus job opportunities are excellent.

The Inside Word

The cream of just about every crop applies to Brown. Gaining admission requires more than just a superior academic profile from high school. Some candidates, such as the sons and daughters of Brown graduates (who are admitted at virtually double the usual acceptance rate), have a better chance for admission than most others. Minority students benefit from some courtship, particularly once admitted. Ivies like to share the wealth and distribute offers of admission across a wide range of constituencies. Candidates from states that are overrepresented in the applicant pool, such as New York, have to be particularly distinguished in order to have the best chance at admission. So do those who attend high schools with many seniors applying to Brown, as it is rare for several students from any one school to be offered admission.

THE SCHOOL SAYS "..."

From The Admissions Office

"Founded in 1764, Brown is a private, coeducational, Ivy League university in which the intellectual development of undergraduate students is fostered by a dedicated faculty on a traditional New England campus.

"Applicants will be required to submit results of the SAT Reasoning Test and any two SAT Subject Tests (except for the SAT Subject Test Writing). Students may substitute any SAT tests with the ACT with the Writing component."

SELECTIVITY

Admissions Rating	99
# of applicants	20,633
% of applicants accepted	14
% of acceptees attending	55
# accepting a place on wait list	450
% admitted from wait list	15
# of early decision applicants	2,453
% accepted early decision	23

FRESHMAN PROFILE

Range SAT Critical Reading	650–760
Range SAT Math	670–780
Range SAT Writing	660–770
Range ACT Composite	28–33
Minimum paper TOEFL	600
Minimum computer TOEFL	250
Minimum web-based TOEFL	100
% graduated top 10% of class	93
% graduated top 25% of class	99
% graduated top 50% of class	100

DEADLINES

Early decision	
Deadline	11/1
Notification	12/15
Regular	
Deadline	1/1
Notification	4/1
Nonfall registration?	no

APPLICANTS ALSO LOOK AT AND OFTEN PREFER

Harvard College
Stanford University
Yale University
Princeton University

FINANCIAL FACTS

Financial Aid Rating	96
Annual tuition	$36,928
Room and board	$10,812
% frosh rec. need-based scholarship or grant aid	41
% UG rec. need-based scholarship or grant aid	41
% frosh rec. need-based self-help aid	35
% UG rec. need-based self-help aid	39
% frosh rec. any financial aid	44
% UG rec. any financial aid	44
% UG borrow to pay for school	44
Average cumulative indebtedness	$19,390

BRYANT UNIVERSITY

1150 Douglas Pike, Smithfield, RI 02917 • Admissions: 401-232-6100 • Fax: 401-232-6741

CAMPUS LIFE

Quality of Life Rating	83
Fire Safety Rating	90
Green Rating	83
Type of school	private
Environment	town

STUDENTS

Total undergrad enrollment	3,474
% male/female	57/43
% from out of state	85
% live on campus	82
% in (# of) fraternities	5 (6)
% in (# of) sororities	3 (3)
% African American	3
% Asian	3
% Caucasian	84
% Hispanic	4
% international	4
# of countries represented	50

SURVEY SAYS . . .

Great library
Athletic facilities are great
Career services are great
School is well run
Campus feels safe
Lots of beer drinking
Hard liquor is popular

ACADEMICS

Academic Rating	78
Calendar	semester
Student/faculty ratio	17:1
Profs interesting rating	78
Profs accessible rating	82
Most common reg class size	30–39 students
Most common lab size	20–29 students

MOST POPULAR MAJORS

accounting
finance
marketing/marketing management

STUDENTS SAY ". . ."

Academics

There are liberal arts programs at Bryant University, but business is the top draw here. A wealth of programs in accounting, finance, marketing, and management has earned Bryant a reputation far and wide as "a business-driven institution that blends the academic and the real world." The placement rate for internships and meaningful jobs after graduation is "very high," thanks to a loyal alumni base and an "excellent" career center that offers a ton of personalized services. "During interview season, I had interviews every day, which led to second interviews, which led to multiple job offers," boasts an accounting major. Students also rave about their cutting-edge campus technology. Academically, we hear students complain about "too many PowerPoint presentations" and "an excessive amount of group work," but "classes are always small" and professors are "always available." Many professors are "obsessed with their jobs" and "pride themselves on seeing their students succeed." They are "good at teaching but even better at providing real working knowledge and examples." Others, however, could definitely improve "when it comes to the fundamentals of teaching and being able to effectively communicate the subject matter." The part-time faculty is especially "hit-or-miss." Despite some complaints about registration and limited course offerings, Bryant's "very friendly" and "approachable" administration generally ensures that things "flow smoothly." Red tape is rare.

Life

"Life at Bryant is the typical college experience." Most undergrads choose to live on this clean, "beautiful," and modern campus "all four years," and there's "a great sense of community." The "intense" academic workload means that weekdays can be "stressful." Nevertheless, students at Bryant are "very involved" in "massive amounts of extracurriculars." "The athletic facilities are great," and many students participate in both intramurals and varsity sports. Students are in charge of most of the activities on campus, and they put on a lot of events. The "fun social scene" typically begins on Thursday. "Parties are generally all on campus," and "most people get really drunk on the weekends." An assortment of harder stimulants is also popular. "If you want to do drugs, you will be able to find them," suggests one student. "At the same time, if you want nothing to do with drugs, you will never see them." The surrounding town of Smithfield "has nothing to do," but "a short drive into Providence" leads to "great food, bars, clubs, and shopping." For more serious urban life, students can always head up to Boston as well.

Student Body

"Students at Bryant are very similar, with similar goals and objectives in mind." There's kind of a "common mold" here of "health-conscious" suburbanites "from the Northeast" who have "aspirations to make good sums of money after entering the job market." "The administrators and teachers are pretty much the most liberal people on campus," explains a senior. "We are a relatively conservative school." During the week, these "competitive" (occasionally "cutthroat") "business leaders of tomorrow" are "hardworking and diligent." Preppy attire dominates, and "clothes often seem to be a big deal." "It is not unusual to see students in suits," but only "when they have presentations or interviews, not just for the hell of it." On the weekends, students tend to be "typical party kids." "There definitely are students who deviate" from the norm but there aren't many and they "don't fit in as well." Some students contend that this place is "diverse economically." Others tell us that "the typical student is white, middle-to upper-middle-class." Ethnic diversity is "rather low," and minority students "tend to stick together." International students do, too. In fact, the whole campus is "very cliquey." With more than 56% of students involved in more than 80 clubs and organizations on campus, there is something for everyone at Bryant. It's important to be involved, as some students note, "If you're not involved in a sport, or Greek life, or another group, then your social life will be limited to your small group of friends."

FINANCIAL AID: 401-232-6020 • E-MAIL: ADMISSION@BRYANT.EDU • WEBSITE: ADMISSION.BRYANT.EDU

THE PRINCETON REVIEW SAYS

Admissions

Very important factors considered include: Academic GPA, rigor of secondary school record. *Important factors considered include:* Class rank, application essay, recommendation(s), standardized test scores. *Other factors considered include:* Alumni/ae relation, character/personal qualities, extracurricular activities, first generation, geographical residence, interview, level of applicant's interest, racial/ethnic status, state residency, talent/ability, volunteer work, work experience. SAT or ACT required. TOEFL required of all international applicants. High school diploma is required and GED is accepted. *Academic units required:* 4 English, 4 mathematics, 2 science (2 science labs), 2 foreign language, 2 history. *Academic units recommended:* 4 English, 4 mathematics, 3 science (2 science labs), 3 foreign language, 3 history.

Financial Aid

Students should submit: FAFSA. Regular filing deadline is 2/15. The Princeton Review suggests that all financial aid forms be submitted as soon as possible after 1/1. *Need-based scholarships/grants offered:* Federal Pell, SEOG, state scholarships/grants, private scholarships, the school's own gift aid. *Loan aid offered:* Direct Subsidized Stafford, Direct Unsubsidized Stafford, FFEL PLUS, Federal Perkins, privately funded education loans. Applicants will be notified of awards on or about 3/24. Federal Work-Study Program available. Institutional employment available. Off-campus job opportunities are fair.

The Inside Word

If you're a solid student you should meet little trouble getting into Bryant. The university's admissions effort has brought in qualified applicants from across the country, but the heaviest draw remains from New England. Students attending Bryant will receive a strong education that integrates business and the arts and sciences. You will benefit from the precious connections in the corporate world offered through Bryant's career services.

THE SCHOOL SAYS ". . ."

From The Admissions Office

"Bryant is a four-year, private university in New England where students build knowledge, develop character, and achieve success—as they define it. In addition to a first-class faculty, state-of-the-art facilities, and advanced technology, Bryant offers stimulating classroom dynamics; internship opportunities at more than 350 companies; 70-plus student clubs and organizations; varsity, intramural, and club sports for men and women; and many opportunities for community service and leadership development. Bryant is the choice for individuals seeking the best integration of business and liberal arts, utilizing state-of-the-art technology. Bryant offers degrees in actuarial mathematics, applied mathematics and statistics, applied economics, applied psychology, business administration, communication, global studies, history, information technology, international business, literary and cultural studies, politics and law, and sociology.

"A cross-disciplinary academic approach teaches students the skills they need to successfully compete in a complex, global environment. Students can pursue one of 27 minors in business and liberal arts, and 80 areas of study. Bryant's rigorous academic standards have been recognized and accredited by NEASC and AACSB International. Bryant's international business program is a member of CUIBE, the Consortium for Undergraduate International Business Education. Technology is a fundamental component of the learning process at Bryant. Every entering freshman is provided with a Thinkpad® laptop for personal use. Students exchange their laptop for a new one in their junior year, which they will own upon graduation.

"Bryant University is situated on a beautiful 420-acre campus in Smithfield, Rhode Island. The campus is only 15 minutes away from the state capital, Providence; 45 minutes from Boston; and 3 hours from New York City.

"Bryant requires that enrolling students take the SAT, or the ACT (Writing section not required)."

SELECTIVITY

Admissions Rating	**90**
# of applicants	6,253
% of applicants accepted	45
% of acceptees attending	32
# accepting a place on wait list	720
% admitted from wait list	23
# of early decision applicants	239
% accepted early decision	59

FRESHMAN PROFILE

Range SAT Critical Reading	510–600
Range SAT Math	560–630
Range SAT Writing	520–600
Range ACT Composite	23–26
Minimum paper TOEFL	550
Minimum computer TOEFL	213
Minimum web-based TOEFL	80
Average HS GPA	3.41
% graduated top 10% of class	25
% graduated top 25% of class	63
% graduated top 50% of class	93

DEADLINES

Early decision	
Deadline	11/15
Notification	12/15
Regular	
Deadline	2/1
Notification	3/21
Nonfall registration?	yes

APPLICANTS ALSO LOOK AT

AND OFTEN PREFER
U. of Massachusetts—Amherst, Boston U., Providence College, Bentley University

AND SOMETIMES PREFER
U. of New Hampshire, Fairfield U., Northeastern U., U. of Connecticut, Quinnipiac U., Stonehill College

AND RARELY PREFER
Assumption College

FINANCIAL FACTS

Financial Aid Rating	**93**
Annual tuition	$31,974
Room and board	$11,757
Books and supplies	$1,200
% frosh rec. need-based scholarship or grant aid	56
% UG rec. need-based scholarship or grant aid	54
% frosh rec. non-need-based scholarship or grant aid	42
% UG rec. non-need-based scholarship or grant aid	43
% frosh rec. need-based self-help aid	58
% UG rec. need-based self-help aid	58
% frosh rec. athletic scholarships	8
% UG rec. athletic scholarships	8
% frosh rec. any financial aid	67
% UG rec. any financial aid	68
% UG borrow to pay for school	80
Average cumulative indebtedness	$34,268

BRYN MAWR COLLEGE

101 NORTH MERION AVENUE, BRYN MAWR, PA 19010-2859 • ADMISSIONS: 610-526-5152 • FAX: 610-526-7471

CAMPUS LIFE
Quality of Life Rating	96
Fire Safety Rating	73
Green Rating	85
Type of school	private
Environment	metropolis

STUDENTS
Total undergrad enrollment	1,274
% male/female	0/100
% from out of state	84
% from public high school	62
% live on campus	95
% African American	6
% Asian	12
% Caucasian	46
% Hispanic	4
% international	7
# of countries represented	58

SURVEY SAYS . . .
Great food on campus
Dorms are like palaces
Low cost of living
Frats and sororities are unpopular or nonexistent
Student government is popular

ACADEMICS
Academic Rating	98
Calendar	semester
Student/faculty ratio	8:1
Profs interesting rating	91
Profs accessible rating	94
Most common reg class size	10–19 students

MOST POPULAR MAJORS
English language and literature
mathematics
psychology

STUDENTS SAY ". . ."

Academics

Bryn Mawr College is "a community of women scholars" that offers "an amazing, intense, multifaceted," and "pretty tough" academic experience. Coursework "can be stressful, especially around midterms and final times, but in the end it's worth it." The faculty is mostly stellar. "One of the main things I love about Bryn Mawr is the personal relationships formed over the years with the professors," boasts a chemistry major. "Anywhere you go to school you will have some bad teachers and some boring classes, and Bryn Mawr is no exception," relates a junior, "but overall I have been extremely impressed with and challenged by the classes I have taken at my college." The highly popular administration is "here for the students' success." "Bryn Mawr is an extremely autonomous place where students are given a lot of freedom to do as they please." "If you need something and you go to the right people, you can pretty much make it happen." Additionally, students can take courses at nearby Haverford, Swarthmore, and Penn. And upon graduation, Mawrters can take advantage of a loyal network of alumnae who "are doing amazing things and have a really strong connection to the school."

Life

Bryn Mawr's "absolutely beautiful" campus is "ensconced in collegiate Gothic arches." The dorms are gorgeous, and the food is "delicious." It's all a little slice of heaven—except for the "bleak" athletic facilities. Neat traditions at Bryn Mawr include Hell Week, which allows first-year students to bond with everyone else, and May Day, an entire day of catered picnics, live music, and hanging out on the greens, which always involves a Maypole dance, a Robin Hood play, and a late-night screening of *The Philadelphia Story* (starring BMC alum Katherine Hepburn). "These traditions are unique, intimate experiences that bring the whole school together and make you feel proud to be a Mawrter," explains a junior. When students aren't basking in the warm glow of ritual, they "love to study, study, study," but other activities are plentiful. "There is always something to do on campus, whether it's a student theatre production, an a cappella concert, an improv group show, movies being shown, outside groups coming to perform, speakers coming to campus, you name it," says a senior. Sports and dance are big extracurricular activities, too. Mawrters drink "more than you'd think for an allegedly quiet, nerdy women's college," but "Bryn Mawr's party scene is more of an intimate-friends-over-to-your-room type of deal." Trips to Swarthmore, Villanova, or Haverford provide "plenty of chances to interact with the opposite sex, if that's what you're after." "There are tons of great restaurants, music venues, galleries, and shopping all within minutes of campus" as well, and nearby Philadelphia offers more urban recreation.

Student Body

Many students say that diversity "is one of the things that makes Bryn Mawr stand out." Others say that students looking for diversity "may not find it here." Whatever the case, "Bryn Mawr is a bunch of brilliant women." They are "nerdy, ambitious, driven, talented" people who "can occasionally be over-competitive" and are "swamped with work yet thriving on it." "We all came into Bryn Mawr with a background in leadership, and all intend to leave Bryn Mawr as future leaders in our respective fields," asserts a junior. It's definitely a left-leaning crowd. "A lot of students at Bryn Mawr are adamant about being politically correct to the point that it begins to become annoying." "Contrary to popular belief, Bryn Mawr isn't a haven for lesbians," though "homosexuality is common and visible." Socially, there is a variety of types of people at the school—from awkward, socially uncomfortable people to very outgoing, social butterflies" to "mud-splattered" rugby players. "Some of us fly that freak flag high and proud," declares a senior. However, "there are plenty of average girls who look at *Cosmo*," too.

FINANCIAL AID: 610-526-5245 • E-MAIL: ADMISSIONS@BRYNMAWR.EDU • WEBSITE: WWW.BRYNMAWR.EDU

THE PRINCETON REVIEW SAYS

Admissions

Very important factors considered include: Recommendation(s), rigor of secondary school record. *Important factors considered include:* Application essay, academic GPA, character/personal qualities, extracurricular activities. *Other factors considered include:* Class rank, standardized test scores, alumni/ae relation, first generation, geographical residence, interview, racial/ethnic status, talent/ability, volunteer work, work experience. SAT and two (2) SAT Subject Tests or ACT (We recommend also taking the optional ACT Writing test). TOEFL required of all international applicants. High school diploma and GED is accepted. *Academic units recommended:* 4 English, 3 mathematics, 2 science (1 science lab), 3 foreign language, 2 social studies, 2 history.

Financial Aid

Students should submit: FAFSA, CSS Profile, and federal tax returns submitted through the College Board's Imaging Documentation Service (IDOC). Regular filing deadline is 3/1. Financial aid forms should be submitted as soon as possible after 1/1. *Need-based scholarships/grants offered:* Federal Pell, SEOG, state scholarships/grants, the school's own gift aid, Federal Academic Competitiveness Grant (ACG), Federal National Science and Mathematics to Retain Talent Grant (SMART). *Loan aid offered:* FFEL Subsidized Stafford, FFEL Unsubsidized Stafford, FFEL PLUS, Federal Perkins. Applicants will be notified of awards on or about 3/23.

The Inside Word

Bryn Mawr's student body is among the academically best in the nation. Outstanding preparation for graduate study draws an applicant pool that is well prepared and intellectually curious.

THE SCHOOL SAYS "..."

From The Admissions Office

"Bryn Mawr is one of the nation's most distinctive, distinguished colleges. Every year 1,300 women from around the world gather on the College's historic campus to study with leading scholars, conduct advanced research, and expand the boundaries of what's possible. A Bryn Mawr woman is defined by a rare combination of personal characteristics: an intense intellectual commitment; a purposeful vision of her life; and a desire to make a meaningful contribution to the world. Consistently producing outstanding scholars, Bryn Mawr is ranked among the top ten of all colleges and universities in percentage of graduates who go on to earn a Ph.D., and is considered excellent preparation for the nation's top law, medical and business schools. More than 500 students collaborate with faculty on independent projects every year; and to augment an already strong curriculum, students may choose from more than 5,000 courses offered through nearby Haverford and Swarthmore Colleges, as well as the University of Pennsylvania. Committed to recruiting a diverse student body, more than a third of Bryn Mawr students are women of color and international students. Furthermore, more than 40% of all students opt to study overseas. Minutes outside of Philadelphia and only two hours by train from New York City and Washington, D.C., Bryn Mawr is recognized by many as one of the most stunning college campuses in the United States. Its mixture of collegiate Gothic architecture and post-modern buildings owe much of their beauty to the original campus plan that was created and executed by Fredrick Law Olmsted and Calvert Vaux, landscape architects and the designers of New York's Central Park."

SELECTIVITY

Admissions Rating	97
# of applicants	2,150
% of applicants accepted	49
% of acceptees attending	35
# accepting a place on wait list	174
% admitted from wait list	4
# of early decision applicants	130
% accepted early decision	53

FRESHMAN PROFILE

Range SAT Critical Reading	620–730
Range SAT Math	580–680
Range SAT Writing	620–720
Range ACT Composite	27–31
Minimum paper TOEFL	600
Minimum computer TOEFL	250
Minimum web-based TOEFL	90
% graduated top 10% of class	65
% graduated top 25% of class	96
% graduated top 50% of class	99

DEADLINES

Early decision	
Deadline	11/15
Notification	12/15
Regular	
Deadline	1/15
Notification	4/1
Nonfall registration?	no

APPLICANTS ALSO LOOK AT

AND OFTEN PREFER
Brown University, University of Pennsylvania

AND SOMETIMES PREFER
Haverford College, Mount Holyoke College, Wellesley College
Smith College, Swarthmore College

AND RARELY PREFER
Vassar College

FINANCIAL FACTS

Financial Aid Rating	94
Annual tuition	$37,120
Room and board	$12,000
Required fees	$914
Books and supplies	$1,000
% frosh rec. need-based scholarship or grant aid	48
% UG rec. need-based scholarship or grant aid	50
% frosh rec. non-need-based scholarship or grant aid	4
% UG rec. non-need-based scholarship or grant aid	2
% frosh rec. need-based self-help aid	44
% UG rec. need-based self-help aid	48
% frosh rec. any financial aid	62
% UG rec. any financial aid	62
% UG borrow to pay for school	54
Average cumulative indebtedness	$20,019

BUCKNELL UNIVERSITY

FREAS HALL, BUCKNELL UNIVERSITY, LEWISBURG, PA 17837 • ADMISSIONS: 570-577-1101 • FAX: 570-577-3538

CAMPUS LIFE

Quality of Life Rating	81
Fire Safety Rating	89
Green Rating	86
Type of school	private
Environment	village

STUDENTS

Total undergrad enrollment	3,560
% male/female	47/53
% from out of state	75
% from public high school	63
% live on campus	86
% in (# of) fraternities	39 (13)
% in (# of) sororities	40 (6)
% African American	3
% Asian	6
% Caucasian	81
% Hispanic	4
% international	3
# of countries represented	53

SURVEY SAYS . . .

Athletic facilities are great
Low cost of living
Frats and sororities dominate social scene
(Almost) no one smokes

ACADEMICS

Academic Rating	89
Calendar	semester
Student/faculty ratio	11:1
Profs interesting rating	88
Profs accessible rating	86
Most common reg class size	10–19 students
Most common lab size	10–19 students

MOST POPULAR MAJORS

biology/biological sciences
business administration and management
economics

STUDENTS SAY "..."

Academics

A "medium-sized liberal arts college in a great setting in central Pennsylvania with an outstanding business program," Bucknell offers a "top-notch education with an intense focus on extracurricular activities, whether they be sports, student government, or otherwise." In addition to "a great reputation for excellent academics," Bucknell's "study-abroad opportunities, alumni presence, professor/faculty relationship with students, and small school/class size" also attract students. A "friendly atmosphere and picturesque campus" provide the backdrop for "small class sizes and caring professors." "Professors are generally very passionate about their subject matter" and "inspire enthusiasm," which makes for "a phenomenal education." Professors are "always available for help outside of class" and "are always willing to go the extra mile for students." Legendary for its "excellent engineering program and Division 1 athletics," Bucknell succeeds in nearly every arena. And with an "amazing" alumni network, Bucknellians are quick to remember one of their own. School spirit and networking opportunities extend far beyond a student's four-year tenure. "The connections you make as an undergraduate will serve you for the rest of your life. Job opportunities open up just because you went to Bucknell." Due to its rigorous academic program and vigorous alumni support, "Bucknell is great at preparing students for life after graduation."

Life

Set in on a sprawling 450-acre estate in rural Pennsylvania, Bucknell features a "breath-taking" campus and "a small, close-knit environment," where students "feel a part of a unified community." Due to the campus' physical remove, some students remark that the university may appear as though it is "in the middle of nowhere." However, with "over 100 interest clubs," "there is always something to do." "Bucknell is all about community and balancing an active social and academic lifestyle." Though students are quick to apply the "work hard, play hard" slogan to life at Bucknell, one student notes the adage might be better re-written: "work hard, THEN play hard." "People are generally involved in many clubs or do lots of community service." When it comes to letting off steam on the weekends, "Greek life is the foundation of Bucknell's social life." However, "everyone is very accomplished," and "the population is unique and interesting in its talents, personalities, and abilities."

Student Body

The majority of students at Bucknell are "fun-loving, but they know when to crack the whip and get work done and study." With a zest for social activities that rival the school's rigorous academic program, the typical students at Bucknell are "spirited, athletic Greeks who care tremendously about their academic and co-curricular experiences." "Athletic and hardworking" "on the surface, Bucknellians may seem homogeneous," but "everyone finds a niche on campus." "People are all extremely smart;" however, due to the "friendly atmosphere" and "school spirit" fostered by this tight-knit community, "it is not an incredibly competitive environment." Though the typical student is described as "wealthy, preppy, and Caucasian," students say "there is very little racial discrimination." Despite the school's efforts to increase diversity, "minority students tend to stick together," though "they are generally accepted and supported." As one student remarks, Bucknell is "truly an undefinable place" and "a great microcosm of the world as it combines a great education" while having the jocks interacting with the hippies."

FINANCIAL AID: 570-577-1331 • E-MAIL: ADMISSIONS@BUCKNELL.EDU • WEBSITE: WWW.BUCKNELL.EDU

THE PRINCETON REVIEW SAYS

Admissions

Very important factors considered include: Class rank, application essay, academic GPA, rigor of secondary school record, standardized test scores, character/personal qualities, talent/ability. *Important factors considered include:* Recommendation(s), extracurricular activities, level of applicant's interest, volunteer work, work experience. *Other factors considered include:* Alumni/ae relation, first generation, geographical residence, racial/ethnic status, religious affiliation/commitment. SAT or ACT required. ACT with Writing component required. TOEFL required of all international applicants. High school diploma is required and GED is accepted. *Academic units required:* 4 English, 3 mathematics, 2 science, 2 foreign language, 2 social studies, 2 history, 1 academic elective. *Academic units recommended:* 4 English, 4 mathematics, 3 science, 4 foreign language, 2 social studies, 2 history, 1 academic elective.

Financial Aid

Students should submit: FAFSA, CSS/financial aid profile, noncustodial profile. Regular filing deadline is 1/1. The Princeton Review suggests that all financial aid forms be submitted as soon as possible after 1/1. *Need-based scholarships/grants offered:* Federal Pell, SEOG, state scholarships/grants, private scholarships, the school's own gift aid, Federal ACG Grant, Federal SMART. *Loan aid offered:* FFEL Subsidized Stafford, FFEL Unsubsidized Stafford, FFEL PLUS, Federal Perkins. Applicants will be notified of awards on or about 4/1. Federal Work-Study Program available. Institutional employment available. Off-campus job opportunities are poor.

The Inside Word

Due to the popularity of certain majors, admissions rates vary at Bucknell. With business representing the most competitive application pool, only about a quarter of applicants are admitted. Admit rates are higher among populations that tend to be self-selecting, including science majors, computer science majors, and engineers. Those listing undecided as their prospective major made up about 17 percent of applicants; 33 percent of such applicants were admitted. Though prospective business majors should not shy away from stating their intended course of study, if you have doubts about your intended major, you certainly don't hurt yourself by listing undecided.

THE SCHOOL SAYS "..."

From The Admissions Office

"Bucknell combines the personal experience of a small liberal arts college with the breadth and opportunity typically found at larger research universities. With a low student/faculty ratio, students gain exceptional hands-on experience, working closely with faculty in an environment enhanced by first-class academic, residential, and athletic facilities. Together, the College of Arts and Sciences and the College of Engineering offer 53 majors and 64 minors. Learning opportunities permeate campus life in and out of the classroom and across the disciplines. For example, engineering students participate in music ensembles, theater productions, and poetry readings, while arts and sciences students take engineering courses, conduct scientific research in the field, and produce distinctive creative works. Students also pursue their interests in more than 150 organizations and through athletic competition in the prestigious Division I Patriot League. These activities constitute a comprehensive approach to learning that teaches students how to think critically and develop their leadership skills so that they are prepared to make a difference locally, nationally, and globally."

SELECTIVITY

Admissions Rating	96
# of applicants	8,024
% of applicants accepted	30
% of acceptees attending	40
# accepting a place on wait list	875
% admitted from wait list	1
# of early decision applicants	567
% accepted early decision	65

FRESHMAN PROFILE

Range SAT Critical Reading	600–680
Range SAT Math	630–710
Range SAT Writing	610–700
Range ACT Composite	27–31
Minimum paper TOEFL	550
Minimum computer TOEFL	213
Minimum web-based TOEFL	106
Average HS GPA	3.51
% graduated top 10% of class	69
% graduated top 25% of class	90
% graduated top 50% of class	99

DEADLINES

Early decision	
Deadline	11/15
Notification	12/15
Regular	
Deadline	1/15
Notification	4/1
Nonfall registration?	no

APPLICANTS ALSO LOOK AT

AND OFTEN PREFER
U. of Virginia, Cornell U.

AND SOMETIMES PREFER
Wake Forest U.

AND RARELY PREFER
U. of Richmond, College of William and Mary, Gettysburg College

FINANCIAL FACTS

Financial Aid Rating	93
Annual tuition	$39,434
Room and board	$9,504
Required fees	$218
Books and supplies	$870
% frosh rec. need-based scholarship or grant aid	42
% UG rec. need-based scholarship or grant aid	44
% frosh rec. non-need-based scholarship or grant aid	5
% UG rec. non-need-based scholarship or grant aid	5
% frosh rec. need-based self-help aid	42
% UG rec. need-based self-help aid	44
% frosh rec. athletic scholarships	2
% UG rec. athletic scholarships	1
% frosh rec. any financial aid	62
% UG rec. any financial aid	58
% UG borrow to pay for school	61
Average cumulative indebtedness	$18,500

CALIFORNIA INSTITUTE OF TECHNOLOGY

1200 East California Boulevard, Mail Code 328-87, Pasadena, CA 91125 • Admissions: 626-395-6341 • Fax: 626-683-3026

CAMPUS LIFE

Quality of Life Rating	82
Fire Safety Rating	60*
Green Rating	60*
Type of school	private
Environment	metropolis

STUDENTS

Total undergrad enrollment	913
% male/female	69/31
% from out of state	65
% from public high school	70
% live on campus	90
% African American	1
% Asian	38
% Caucasian	43
% Hispanic	5
% international	9
# of countries represented	32

SURVEY SAYS . . .

Class discussions are rare
No one cheats
Lab facilities are great
Students are friendly
Campus feels safe
Frats and sororities are unpopular or nonexistent

ACADEMICS

Academic Rating	88
Calendar	quarter
Student/faculty ratio	3:1
Profs interesting rating	61
Profs accessible rating	67
Most common reg class size	fewer than 10 students
Most common lab size	20–29 students

MOST POPULAR MAJORS
mathematics
mechanical engineering
physics

STUDENTS SAY "..."

Academics

According to students at the California Institute of Technology, their tiny school is "the greatest research university out there." "Caltech's math, science, and engineering programs are indisputably first-rate," gloats a senior. "If you like science and know that you want some sort of career in research, engineering, or academia, this is one of the best places to come in the world." The mandatory core curriculum is heavy on math, physics, and chemistry. It also includes a humanities requirement. Beyond that, students can choose from a host of majors and minors. Whatever path you choose, "the resources are incredible," and "lab facilities are top-notch." There are fabulous opportunities "for students to conduct research at every class level," too. Be prepared for "a crippling workload," though. The academic atmosphere here is "probably the most intense you could hope to find." It's "like trying to drink from a fire hose" ("even if this is an overused cliché"). "There is no grade inflation." "Caltech has the ability to crush your own opinion of how smart you are." "If you were the top student all your life, prepare to experience a big dose of humility because you'll have to work hard just to stay in the middle of the pack." "Introductory classes are often taught by Nobel laureates" and world renowned scientists. "The quality of professors as teachers, rather than brilliant researchers, however, is often hit-or-miss," explains an applied physics major. Professors "tend to be very passionate about their subjects," but "only a select few professors teach well."

Life

Life at Caltech "involves doing a lot of homework." "A sizable population of the school does not come out of their rooms much." Clubs and extracurricular activities run the gamut, though, and it's very easy to get involved "no matter your experience." "Computer games, card games, role-playing games," and the like are popular. Otherwise, social life relies heavily on Caltech's unique housing system. First-year students are required to live on campus, in one of 8 houses. "The houses combine the feel and purpose of a dorm with the pride and spirit of a fraternity." "Each house plans social events" and "provides the main social community" for students. When Caltech students throw a party, "it's a major operation." "Most parties here involve two weeks of prior planning and construction," and the end result is "usually pretty epic." Off campus, Caltech's location in sunny Pasadena provides ample opportunities for outdoor activities. There are "beaches, mountains, and desert all within a 2-hour drive." The proximity of Los Angeles provides a ready escape as well. "Once in a while we'll all pile in a car and go to L.A. for a concert or something," notes a senior, "and that's a lot of fun." "Plotting pranks" is another common pastime here. Techers have a notorious reputation for "amusing" and generally harmless mischief. Students once altered the famous Hollywood Sign to read "Caltech". In another instance, they adjusted the scoreboard at the Rose Bowl to show Caltech leading hated MIT by an impressive score of 38-9.

Student Body

Caltech is home to "lots of whites and Asians," and the student population is overwhelmingly male. "The ratio sucks," laments a lonely senior. "Your typical student here was the math team/science team/quiz bowl type in high school." "This is nerd heaven." "Everyone's a scientist," and "every student is brilliant." Students also describe themselves as "hard-working," "quirky," and "slightly eccentric." You'll find a wide variety, though, "from cool party types, to scary hard-core nerds, to cool party types who build massive railguns in their spare time." Some students are "terribly creative." Some are "socially inept" and "very strange." Ultimately, it's a hard group to pigeonhole. "You will meet someone who you might think is a total jock if you saw him or her on the street, but [he or she] works late at night on homework and aces exams," promises one student. "If you come here with stereotypes in mind, they will be broken."

FINANCIAL AID: 626-395-6280 • E-MAIL: UGADMISSIONS@CALTECH.EDU • WEBSITE: ADMISSIONS.CALTECH.EDU

THE PRINCETON REVIEW SAYS

Admissions

Very important factors considered include: Rigor of secondary school record. *Important factors considered include:* Class rank, application essay, recommendation(s), standardized test scores, character/personal qualities, extracurricular activities. *Other factors considered include:* Alumni/ae relation, first generation, racial/ethnic status, talent/ability, volunteer work, work experience. SAT Subject Tests required. SAT or ACT required. High school diploma or equivalent is not required. *Academic units required:* 3 English, 4 mathematics, 2 science (1 science lab), 1 social studies, 1 history. *Academic units recommended:* 4 English, 4 science, 3 foreign language, 3 social studies, 1 history.

Financial Aid

Students should submit: FAFSA, CSS/financial aid profile, state aid form, noncustodial profile, business/farm supplement. Noncustodial Parent's Statement and Business/Farm Supplement forms are required only when applicable. Regular filing deadline is 1/15. The Princeton Review suggests that all financial aid forms be submitted as soon as possible after 1/1. *Need-based scholarships/grants offered:* Federal Pell, SEOG, state scholarships/grants, private scholarships, the school's own gift aid. *Loan aid offered:* Direct Subsidized Stafford, Direct Unsubsidized Stafford, Direct PLUS, Federal Perkins, college/university loans from institutional funds. Applicants will be notified of awards on or about 4/15. Federal Work-Study Program available. Institutional employment available.

The Inside Word

Each Caltech application receives three independent reads before it is presented to the admissions committee. This ensures that all candidates receive a thorough evaluation. The school values the unique drive and energy of its current students and desires applicants who display a similar combination of creativity and intellect. Stellar academic credentials are a must, and prospective students must display an aptitude for math and science.

THE SCHOOL SAYS "..."

From The Admissions Office

"Admission to the freshman class is based on many factors—some quantifiable, some not. What you say in your application is important! Because we don't interview students for admission, your letters of recommendation are weighed heavily. High school academic performance is very important, as is a demonstrated interest in math, science, and/or engineering. We are also interested in your character, maturity, and motivation. We are very proud of the process we use to select each freshman class. It's very individual, it has great integrity, and we believe it serves all the students who apply. If you have any questions about the process or about Caltech in general, write us a letter or give us a call. We'd like to hear from you!

"Freshman applicants must submit scores from either the SAT or ACT. In addition, students must submit the results of two SAT Subject Tests: Mathematics IIC and one of the following: biology (ecological or molecular), chemistry, or physics. "

SELECTIVITY

Admissions Rating	99
# of applicants	3,597
% of applicants accepted	17
% of acceptees attending	52
# accepting a place on wait list	164
% admitted from wait list	18

FRESHMAN PROFILE

Range SAT Critical Reading	700–780
Range SAT Math	770–800
Range SAT Writing	680–770
Range ACT Composite	32–35
% graduated top 10% of class	99
% graduated top 25% of class	100
% graduated top 50% of class	100

DEADLINES

Early action	
Deadline	11/1
Notification	12/15
Regular	
Deadline	1/1
Notification	4/1
Nonfall registration?	no

APPLICANTS ALSO LOOK AT
AND OFTEN PREFER
Harvard College
Stanford University
Princeton University

AND SOMETIMES PREFER
Massachusetts Institute of Technology

FINANCIAL FACTS

Financial Aid Rating	99
Annual tuition	$31,437
Room and board	$10,146
Required fees	$3,000
Books and supplies	$1,194
% frosh rec. need-based scholarship or grant aid	60
% UG rec. need-based scholarship or grant aid	53
% frosh rec. non-need-based scholarship or grant aid	2
% UG rec. non-need-based scholarship or grant aid	4
% frosh rec. need-based self-help aid	41
% UG rec. need-based self-help aid	41
% frosh rec. any financial aid	60
% UG rec. any financial aid	60
% UG borrow to pay for school	56
Average cumulative indebtedness	$6,268

CALIFORNIA STATE UNIVERSITY—STANISLAUS

ONE UNIVERSITY CIRCLE, TURLOCK, CA 95382 • ADMISSIONS: 209-667-3070 OR 800-300-7420 (CA ONLY) • FAX: 209-667-3394

CAMPUS LIFE
Quality of Life Rating	**77**
Fire Safety Rating	**99**
Green Rating	**93**
Type of school	public
Environment	town

STUDENTS
Total undergrad enrollment	6,906
% male/female	36/64
% from out of state	2
% from public high school	93
% live on campus	9
% in (# of) fraternities	(7)
% in (# of) sororities	(9)
# of countries represented	32

SURVEY SAYS . . .
Diverse student types on campus
Different types of students interact
Low cost of living
(Almost) no one smokes
Very little drug use

ACADEMICS
Academic Rating	**76**
Calendar	4/1/4
Profs interesting rating	75
Profs accessible rating	69
Most common reg class size	20–29 students
Most common lab size	20–29 students

MOST POPULAR MAJORS
business/commerce
liberal arts and sciences/liberal studies
psychology/criminal justice and corrections

STUDENTS SAY ". . ."

Academics

"Best known for its nursing, criminal justice, and psychology programs" as well as what many students believe is "one of the best teacher credential programs in California," California State University—Stanislaus provides to its 7,000 undergraduates "a very practical education" in "a friendly environment." Small in comparison to many state universities, CSU—Stanislaus can offer "small class sizes that allow better communication with both professors and fellow classmates," which is a huge plus. A "friendly, accessible faculty" is another; professors are "well educated, well written, and have the experience to back up what they teach. When students stop in to ask a question, the professors stop what they are doing and give their full attention to the student." Programs are designed with the goal of accommodating a wide variety of students; the school "has a main campus and two satellite campuses and offers both day and night classes" so that part-time students can access the same educational opportunities as traditional full-timers. As at many state schools, budgetary problems occasionally impose hardships, such as course cancellations that result in "a lack of classes [required] to graduate. Budget cuts have made this tough for a lot of students, and many of my friends will now have to attend the college for an additional year in order to graduate."

Life

CSU—Stanislaus students who live on-campus tell us that "the dorms and the school provide students with tons of activities and fun events to attend. Stanislaus really makes an effort to get their students involved and become well-rounded individuals" by offering "lots of activities put on by the Student Union and lots more put on by the Residential Life people or by specific floors in the dorms. Intramural sports are very popular. Students add that "There are also lots of clubs and organizations to get involved with on campus." Hometown Turlock is "a small town" with "not a ton of things to do" other than "a decent movie theatre," but "it's only a short drive to Modesto where there really are tons of things to do," including "some great restaurants." Commuters have a rougher time integrating into campus life; "It's hard to build friendships with people because more often [than] not they live pretty far away," one explains. Currently, less than 10 percent of all students live in on-campus housing.

Student Body

"A CSU Stanislaus poster student would be a white female in her 20s"—two in three students here are women—but "there is a wide range of diversity on this campus," including a substantial Hispanic population. Undergrads "all seem to fit in well with each other." "The are two types of students at CSU—Stanislaus: the commuter and the one who's incredible involved." Commuters tend to focus on get[ting] their degree and get[ting] into their career," and can be a "bit disconnected from the social life on campus." However, other students are "involved in almost everything," are "in clubs and are active in student government." The prevailing attitude here is low-key and business-like; "everyone is down-to-earth relaxed and chill" but also "more focused and driven than the average 20-year-old."

FINANCIAL AID: 209-667-3336 • E-MAIL: OUTREACH_HELP_DESK@CSUSTAN.EDU • WEBSITE: WWW.CSUSTAN.EDU

THE PRINCETON REVIEW SAYS

Admissions

Very important factors considered include: Academic GPA, rigor of secondary school record, standardized test scores. *Important factors considered include:* Class rank, TOEFL required of all international applicants. High school diploma is required and GED is accepted. *Academic units required:* 4 English, 3 mathematics, 2 science (2 science labs), 2 foreign language, 1 social studies, 1 history, 1 visual/performing arts, 1 academic elective.

Financial Aid

Students should submit: FAFSA. The Princeton Review suggests that all financial aid forms be submitted as soon as possible after 1/1. *Need-based scholarships/grants offered:* Federal Pell, SEOG, state scholarships/grants, private scholarships, the school's own gift aid, federal nursing scholarships. *Loan aid offered:* FFEL Subsidized Stafford, FFEL Unsubsidized Stafford, FFEL PLUS, Federal Perkins, college/university loans from institutional funds. Applicants will be notified of awards on a rolling basis beginning 3/15. Federal Work-Study Program available. Institutional employment available. Off-campus job opportunities are good.

The Inside Word

Like most state schools, CSU—Stanislaus admissions practices are fairly straightforward. The university adheres to the eligibility index as defined by the California state system, so applicants who meet GPA and standardized test score minimums are automatically granted admission. Out-of-state candidates face more stringent requirements, as do those applying for highly competitive majors and programs, such as the Pre-Licensure Nursing Program.

THE SCHOOL SAYS "..."

From The Admissions Office

"CSU—Stanislaus was recognized by the American Association of State Colleges and Universities as one of 12 public universities nationwide that demonstrate exceptional performance in retention and graduation rates. Student success is facilitated by a dense network of on-campus resources including consistent advising, a strong first-year program, frequent and meaningful contact with professors, and supportive staff and administrators.

"CSU—Stanislaus has 13 nationally accredited programs and is widely recognized for its quality academics. A new state-of-the-art science building opened in 2007 along with a new bookstore in 2008 and student recreation complex in 2007. The campus is widely known as the most beautiful and friendly of the CSU campuses, blending modern facilities with the pastoral charm of the countryside. The campus enjoys an ideal location in the heart of California's Central Valley, a short distance from the San Francisco Bay Area, Monterey, the Sierra Nevada mountains, and Yosemite National Park. The proximity allows for hiking, skiing, snowboarding, kayaking, surfing, and other outdoors sports and activities.

"CSU—Stanislaus awarded more than $24.5 million in merit- and need-based grants and scholarships for the 2008–2009 school year. Approximately 68 percent of freshmen received need-based aid and the average gift aid for the group was $5,190. Scholarships range from full tuition, board, and books through the President's Scholarship to hundreds of other scholarships ranging from $100 to $5,000 per school year. The CSU—Stanislaus experience can be summed up as providing a small private school atmosphere at a public school price."

SELECTIVITY

Admissions Rating	71
# of applicants	4,751
% of applicants accepted	66
% of acceptees attending	31

FRESHMAN PROFILE

Range SAT Critical Reading	420–530
Range SAT Math	420–540
Range ACT Composite	17–22
Minimum paper TOEFL	500
Minimum computer TOEFL	173
Minimum web-based TOEFL	61
Average HS GPA	3.2

DEADLINES

Regular	
Priority	11/30
Deadline	3/1
Notification	rolling
Nonfall registration?	yes

FINANCIAL FACTS

Financial Aid Rating	61
Annual out-of-state tuition	$10,170
Room and board	$7,936
Required fees	$3,819
Books and supplies	$1,566
% frosh rec. need-based scholarship or grant aid	36
% UG rec. need-based scholarship or grant aid	50
% frosh rec. non-need-based scholarship or grant aid	3
% UG rec. non-need-based scholarship or grant aid	4
% frosh rec. need-based self-help aid	32
% UG rec. need-based self-help aid	40
% frosh rec. athletic scholarships	2
% UG rec. athletic scholarships	1
% frosh rec. any financial aid	48
% UG rec. any financial aid	67
% UG borrow to pay for school	23
Average cumulative indebtedness	$17,000

CALVIN COLLEGE

3201 BURTON STREET SOUTHEAST, GRAND RAPIDS, MI 49546 • ADMISSIONS: 616-526-6106 • FAX: 616-526-6777

CAMPUS LIFE
Quality of Life Rating	84
Fire Safety Rating	67
Green Rating	78
Type of school	private
Affiliation	Christian Reformed
Environment	metropolis

STUDENTS
Total undergrad enrollment	4,021
% male/female	46/54
% from out of state	44
% from public high school	43
% live on campus	57
% African American	2
% Asian	3
% Caucasian	83
% Hispanic	1
% international	7
# of countries represented	54

SURVEY SAYS . . .
Students get along with local community
Great off-campus food
Low cost of living
Frats and sororities are unpopular or nonexistent
Musical organizations are popular
Very little drug use

ACADEMICS
Academic Rating	85
Calendar	4/1/4
Student/faculty ratio	11:1
Profs interesting rating	85
Profs accessible rating	87
Most common reg class size	20–29 students
Most common lab size	20–29 students

MOST POPULAR MAJORS
business/commerce
engineering
nursing/registered nurse
(RN, ASN, BSN, MSN)

STUDENTS SAY ". . ."

Academics

Calvin College, a small, liberal arts school affiliated with the Christian Reformed Church, is "not just a college with a Christian label, it is a Christian community that challenges academically as well as spiritually." Indeed, while Calvin "integrates faith with learning" throughout its curriculum, students are adamant that they are not simply being spoon fed dogma here; on the contrary, they "are encouraged to have open discussions about the hard issues. One cannot come to Calvin and not be challenged." The result is "serious academics from a Christian perspective" capable of "training students to engage thoughtfully with the world around them and examine what it means to be a reformed Christian living in a secular world." Despite the school's relatively small size, "the resources available to students at Calvin are phenomenal. We have spectacular research facilities as well as a career development office that is very willing to engage with students." Biotech labs feature "many types of instrumentation that even bigger schools lack." Study-abroad opportunities are "'sweet' and accessible," as are internships. Best of all, Calvin students receive all these perks without forfeiting the personal attention students understandably expect at a small private school. "Professors actually care about their students and want them to learn" and "are so willing to give help outside the classroom. They are very approachable." No wonder one student sums up: "I think many students come to Calvin with only moderate excitement about the school, but almost everyone leaves the school a proud Knight."

Life

The Calvin community "is incredibly strong. There are always people studying together and living life together. Support is easy to find from dorm leadership or just the people on your floor. It's easy to get involved in a club or within the dorm." Students "are very focused on faith, so many of them go to church, LOFT (evening worship on Sundays), and many of the weekday chapel breaks." In addition, "many of the students are extremely involved in sports," and "evening lectures are well attended. Student-run talent showcases like Dance Guild, Airband, and Rangeela performances are extremely popular. The Improv and Calvin Theater Company are top-notch. Hockey games attract hundreds of students. And, the library is always full." In short, "If you think college should be more than drinking and partying, come here. If that idea scares the hell out of you, then avoid this place at all cost." That's not to say a party scene doesn't exist; however, "Nearly all parties are 5 to 10 minutes away (where most off-campus students live)." One student points out that "there is a lot to do at Calvin, but most of it requires a drive off campus." "Restaurants are either on several major streets 5 minutes away or downtown (10 to 15 minutes)." Downtown Grand Rapids provides "a number of things to do," including ice skating, shopping, and eatin at restaurants."

Student Body

"Many of the students here are from a Christian Reformed Church background, and many are Dutch," but "there are exceptions. The atypical students fit in well." "Tall, blond, and blue-eyed" is the standard look here; "moderate to conservative" is the mainstream political perspective. "It is a strange dynamic to be at a college where the professors are more liberal than the student body as a whole," one student explains. However, the times are changing here, as one student reports: "The typical Calvin student is not the typical Calvin student from 20 years ago." The student body is "becoming increasingly diverse." Students "represent many faith backgrounds and ethnicities," and they are very open to people of differing backgrounds and beliefs.

FINANCIAL AID: 616-957-6134 • E-MAIL: ADMISSIONS@CALVIN.EDU • WEBSITE: WWW.CALVIN.EDU

THE PRINCETON REVIEW SAYS

Admissions

Very important factors considered include: Academic GPA, rigor of secondary school record, standardized test scores, religious affiliation/commitment. *Important factors considered include:* Application essay, recommendation(s), character/personal qualities, extracurricular activities. *Other factors considered include:* Class rank, level of applicant's interest, volunteer work, work experience. SAT or ACT required. TOEFL required of all international applicants. High school diploma is required and GED is accepted. *Academic units required:* 3 English, 3 mathematics, 2 science, 2 social studies, 3 academic electives. *Academic units recommended:* 4 English, 3 mathematics, 2 science (1 science lab), 2 foreign language, 3 social studies, 3 academic electives.

Financial Aid

Students should submit: FAFSA. The Princeton Review suggests that all financial aid forms be submitted as soon as possible after 1/1. *Need-based scholarships/grants offered:* Federal Pell, SEOG, state scholarships/grants, private scholarships, the school's own gift aid. *Loan aid offered:* Direct Subsidized Stafford, Direct Unsubsidized Stafford, Direct PLUS, Federal Perkins, state loans, college/university loans from institutional funds, alternative educational loans. Applicants will be notified of awards on a rolling basis beginning 3/15. Federal Work-Study Program available. Institutional employment available. Off-campus job opportunities are excellent.

The Inside Word

Calvin's applicant pool is highly self-selected and small. Nearly all candidates get in, and nearly half choose to enroll. The freshman academic profile is fairly solid, but making a good match with the college philosophically, is by far the most important factor for gaining admission.

THE SCHOOL SAYS " . . ."

From The Admissions Office

"Calvin's well-respected faculty, innovative core curriculum, and inquiring student body come together in an environment that links intellectual freedom with a heart for service. Calvin's 400-acre campus is home to 4,200 students and 400 professors who chose Calvin because of its national reputation for academic excellence and faith-shaped thinking. Calvin encourages students to explore all things and offers more than 100 academic options to choose from, including accredited professional programs.

"Quality teaching and accessibility to students are considered top priorities by faculty members. More than 80 percent of Calvin professors hold the highest degree in their field, the student/faculty ratio is 11:1, and the average class size is 22. The college's 4-1-4 calendar offers opportunities for off-campus and international study, while service-learning projects draw Calvin students into the local community. Internships allow students to try their individual gifts in the workplace while gaining professional experience. In a recent survey, 96 percent of Calvin graduates reported that they had either secured a job or begun graduate school within 6 months of graduation. Calvin is among the top 3 percent of 4-year private colleges in the number of graduates who go on to earn a PhD.

"Students applying for admission are required to submit scores from either the SAT or the ACT college entrance exam. Calvin does not require the Writing section of either test."

SELECTIVITY
Admissions Rating	91
# of applicants	2,169
% of applicants accepted	94
% of acceptees attending	46

FRESHMAN PROFILE
Range SAT Critical Reading	530–660
Range SAT Math	545–665
Range ACT Composite	23–28
Minimum paper TOEFL	550
Minimum computer TOEFL	213
Average HS GPA	3.58
% graduated top 10% of class	26.7
% graduated top 25% of class	52.6
% graduated top 50% of class	81.7

DEADLINES
Regular	
Deadline	8/15
Notification	rolling
Nonfall registration?	yes

APPLICANTS ALSO LOOK AT

AND OFTEN PREFER
Hope College

AND SOMETIMES PREFER
Wheaton College (IL)
Grand Valley State University
University of Michigan—Ann Arbor

AND RARELY PREFER
Michigan State University

FINANCIAL FACTS
Financial Aid Rating	77
Annual tuition	$22,940
Room and board	$7,970
Required fees	$225
Books and supplies	$860
% frosh rec. need-based scholarship or grant aid	64
% UG rec. need-based scholarship or grant aid	61
% frosh rec. non-need-based scholarship or grant aid	16
% UG rec. non-need-based scholarship or grant aid	13
% frosh rec. need-based self-help aid	53
% UG rec. need-based self-help aid	55
% frosh rec. any financial aid	95
% UG rec. any financial aid	93
% UG borrow to pay for school	64
Average cumulative indebtedness	$27,400

CARLETON COLLEGE

100 SOUTH COLLEGE STREET, NORTHFIELD, MN 55057 • ADMISSIONS: 507-222-4190 AND 800-995-2275 • FAX: 507-222-4526

CAMPUS LIFE

Quality of Life Rating	93
Fire Safety Rating	60*
Green Rating	60*
Type of school	private
Environment	village

STUDENTS

Total undergrad enrollment	1,975
% male/female	48/52
% from out of state	76
% from public high school	73
% live on campus	90
% African American	5
% Asian	10
% Caucasian	73
% Hispanic	5
% Native American	1
% international	6
# of countries represented	42

SURVEY SAYS . . .

No one cheats
School is well run
Campus feels safe
Frats and sororities are unpopular or nonexistent

ACADEMICS

Academic Rating	97
Calendar	trimester
Student/faculty ratio	9:1
Profs interesting rating	98
Profs accessible rating	96
Most common reg class size	10–19 students
Most common lab size	10–19 students

MOST POPULAR MAJORS

biology/biological sciences
economics
political science and government
international relations

STUDENTS SAY "..."

Academics

Students interested in "discovering what it is you want to learn and then learning it within a wide context" are drawn to Carleton College, a small and extremely rigorous school that is "strongly liberal arts-oriented" but also boasts "serious science departments." One freshman explains the reasoning behind choosing Carleton: "I could truly explore what I wanted to do without feeling as though I would have to have a sub-par education in science, if that was what I chose to major in." The "intensely passionate" undergrads of Carleton enjoy "a sense of community that's hard to find elsewhere." One undergraduate says, "You'll find yourself striking up conversations with complete strangers at the post office, in town, and along sidewalks in the middle of a snowy night. New friends are found everywhere." This is true even among the faculty; "Carleton is not a research college, so while professors do some research, they are much more focused on students." Carleton operates on a trimester calendar, which students endorse. "It's nice to be only taking three classes, though more intensely, rather than spreading yourself over four or five." Students also love the "great study-abroad office," which has provided students here with "opportunities to travel to China, Thailand, Spain, and, Africa."

Life

"Small and quaint" are two words Carleton students frequently use to describe their school's hometown. "Northfield is not that exciting," cedes a freshman, "but I'm not sure anyone wants to change that." Most students are content simply to find "nice restaurants" and "locals [who] are darn helpful in about any situation" in town. This might be because things are much livelier on campus. "An evening doesn't go by without some kind of event, whether it be musical, artistic, theatrical, or political," a sophomore writes. The notoriously heavy workload means "people study most of the time on weekdays" and occasionally "lose it. This comes more in the form of weird, creative outlets than it does self-destructive behavior, though. There are a lot of naked Winter Olympics, pranks, traditions, and general goofing off." Students are proud of this "little bit of eccentricity [that] makes everything fun." Intramurals "are really hot at Carleton; the people who aren't playing them are much fewer and [farther] between than the people who are." Ultimate Frisbee and broomball are the games of choice. There are also "plenty of parties," and while a portion "of the student body will be drunk on a typical weekend," there is "absolutely no pressure to drink if you don't want to." One freshman tells us that for fun she "makes a smoothie run to the Sayles-Hill Student Center," then later stops by "Dacie Moses House, a place where students gather to bake cookies." Students are even upbeat about the harsh winters here, describing them as "a uniting element in the fact that it's negative 50 degrees outside."

Student Body

The "creative, warm, compassionate, and helpful" undergrads of Carleton are "quirky," but "everyone is accepting of these little eccentricities." "Everyone's surprising," writes one student, "and that can be a little exhausting at times," but mostly students embrace the challenges their peers present. They "don't form cliques based on [conventional] criteria" such as "socioeconomic background, race, gender, [or] sexual orientation." An upbeat-studio-art major writes, "We have a wonderful mix of people that reaches from nerds to jocks, people who dye their hair to [those] who swear by Abercrombie, people who are Republican to those who are Democrat to those who are Independent to those who don't care; we have vegetarians, and we have people who would live on steak if you let them. We have a truly rich mix of all sorts of people, and we all enjoy each other and end up with the most amazing groups of friends."

THE PRINCETON REVIEW SAYS

Admissions

Very important factors considered include: Class rank, academic GPA, rigor of secondary school record. *Important factors considered include:* Application essay, recommendation(s), standardized test scores, alumni/ae relation, character/personal qualities, extracurricular activities, racial/ethnic status, talent/ability, volunteer work, work experience. *Other factors considered include:* First generation, geographical residence, interview, state residency. SAT Subject Tests recommended. SAT or ACT required. ACT with Writing component required. TOEFL required of all international applicants. High school diploma is required and GED is accepted. *Academic units recommended:* 4 English, 3 mathematics, 3 science (1 science lab), 3 foreign language, 3 social studies and history.

Financial Aid

Students should submit: FAFSA, CSS/financial aid profile, noncustodial profile, business/farm supplement. Prior year tax forms. Regular filing deadline is 2/15. The Princeton Review suggests that all financial aid forms be submitted as soon as possible after 1/1. *Need-based scholarships/grants offered:* Federal Pell, SEOG, state scholarships/grants, private scholarships, the school's own gift aid. *Loan aid offered:* FFEL Subsidized Stafford, FFEL Unsubsidized Stafford, FFEL PLUS, Federal Perkins, state loans, college/university loans from institutional funds, Minnesota SELF loan program. Applicants will be notified of awards on or about 4/1. Federal Work-Study Program available.

The Inside Word

Carleton admissions are highly competitive. It's possible to get in without stellar high-school grades and test scores if you have some exceptional talent or show tremendous promise, but most successful applicants have all of these qualities. High school record is most important here; standardized test scores weigh heavily, as does your personal essay. Interviews are not required but they are recommended. Sit for one, even if you can't schedule a campus visit; a local rep should be able to interview you in or near your hometown.

THE SCHOOL SAYS "..."

From The Admissions Office

"In an annual college freshmen survey, Carleton students identify themselves as everything from conservatives to liberals, with a majority of them falling in the moderate to liberal range. Although individualistic and energetic Carls take their academics seriously, they don't take themselves seriously. Participation in athletics, theater or music, religious events, or dining hall discussions over fare marks the Carleton experience. The College broke ground recently on two new residence halls, on track to house students for the upcoming academic year. With nearly three-fifths of the student body receiving need-based grant aid, there is a broad socioeconomic representation across the student body. Seven percent of all students are international, and 21 percent come from traditionally underrepresented groups, and about eight percent are first-generation students. A look at majors in the past decade shows that graduates cover all areas, with about one-third of them in each of the following: math/science, humanities and arts, and social sciences. More than two-thirds of all students will spend time earning class credits off campus; Carleton participates in programs worldwide from Asia to Africa. You can scuba dive off the Great Barrier Reef or walk the Great Wall of China. Five years after graduating, between 65 percent and 75 percent of alumni pursue graduate or professional degrees. More Carleton graduates have pursued their doctorates in the sciences in the past 20 years than have graduates of other small, comparable liberal arts colleges. Applicants must take the SAT or ACT with Writing component. SAT Subject Tests are not required though it is recommended that a student submit these if they have taken any."

SELECTIVITY

Admissions Rating	97
# of applicants	4,956
% of applicants accepted	27
% of acceptees attending	36
# accepting a place on wait list	363
% admitted from wait list	2
# of early decision applicants	375
% accepted early decision	55

FRESHMAN PROFILE

Range SAT Critical Reading	660–750
Range SAT Math	650–740
Range SAT Writing	650–750
Range ACT Composite	29–33
Minimum paper TOEFL	600
Minimum computer TOEFL	250
% graduated top 10% of class	74
% graduated top 25% of class	96
% graduated top 50% of class	100

DEADLINES

Early decision	
Deadline	11/15
Notification	12/15
Regular	
Deadline	1/15
Notification	4/15
Nonfall registration?	no

APPLICANTS ALSO LOOK AT

AND OFTEN PREFER
Williams College
Yale University

AND SOMETIMES PREFER
Washington University in St. Louis

AND RARELY PREFER
Macalester College

FINANCIAL FACTS

Financial Aid Rating	98
Annual tuition	$39,546
Room and board	$10,428
Required fees	$231
Books and supplies	$728
% frosh rec. need-based scholarship or grant aid	54
% UG rec. need-based scholarship or grant aid	55
% frosh rec. non-need-based scholarship or grant aid	10
% UG rec. non-need-based scholarship or grant aid	10
% frosh rec. need-based self-help aid	50
% UG rec. need-based self-help aid	53
% frosh rec. any financial aid	54
% UG rec. any financial aid	56
% UG borrow to pay for school	52
Average cumulative indebtedness	$20,083

CARNEGIE MELLON UNIVERSITY

5000 FORBES AVENUE, PITTSBURGH, PA 15213 • ADMISSIONS: 412-268-2082 • FAX: 412-268-7838

CAMPUS LIFE
Quality of Life Rating	**70**
Fire Safety Rating	**76**
Green Rating	**95**
Type of school	private
Environment	metropolis

STUDENTS
Total undergrad enrollment	5,892
% male/female	60/40
% from out of state	77
% live on campus	64
% in (# of) fraternities	13 (18)
% in (# of) sororities	9 (8)
% African American	5
% Asian	24
% Caucasian	39
% Hispanic	5
% international	15
# of countries represented	100

SURVEY SAYS . . .
Lab facilities are great
Diverse student types on campus
Campus feels safe
Theater is popular

ACADEMICS
Academic Rating	**99**
Calendar	semester
Student/faculty ratio	11:1
Profs interesting rating	70
Profs accessible rating	76
Most common reg class size	fewer than 10 students
Most common lab size	20–29 students

MOST POPULAR MAJORS
liberal arts
engineering
fine arts and sciences

STUDENTS SAY ". . ."

Academics
CMU is an academic powerhouse that "pushes [students] to a much greater level of understanding." Undergrads are quick to reason that this is due to "outstanding faculty who are extremely passionate about their fields of study." Of course, this passion "transfers to rigorous and interesting courses." Indeed, "one definitely develops an excellent work ethic by attending this institution." A bio and psych double-major concurs stating, "Every student works hard: It is unavoidable." Fortunately, he goes on to say, "I have never had any trouble accessing any of my professors. They are quick to answer e-mails and are more than willing to meet with you outside of class and office hours." The university "offers a huge variety of top-ranked programs, such as the business school, the engineering school, the computer science school, and the music and drama departments." Naturally this "makes it easy to take a variety of classes but still get a quality education." And as one student puts it, "At the end of the day knowledge is oozing from my pores. I love it!" One senior did reveal that signing up for class can be a hassle because "the registration system is pretty much from the '80s." However, he did assure us that the administration is aware of the issues and "working on it." Overall, students are fairly happy with the "accessible" administration. One happy sophomore shares that those on the faculty "listen to students' requests and move to make changes on campus accordingly." And a computer science major sums up by stating, "The administration is helpful when you need it and never too intrusive."

Life
Though undergrads at Carnegie Mellon are "very focused on their education and their [future] careers" many students are still able to strike "a balance." Indeed, one senior assures us that he and his peers "know how to have fun too." Students in need of a study break can find distraction in a myriad of campus events. The residential staff (residential assistants and faculty advisors) often host activities like "movie nights, stressball crafting, and snowball fights." Additionally, undergrads can participate in anything from "intramural sports teams, to building racing vehicles [and] designing computer games." Performances from the many "a capella and drama groups" are also well attended. Though one junior admits that "we're not big partiers comparatively," plenty of students "do go to frat parties on the weekend." And many undergrads revel in CMU traditions, such as carnival when "classes are cancelled for two days, and week-long parties occur." Impressively, "public transportation is free for Carnegie Mellon students" making Pittsburgh highly accessible. The city offers a number "of museums to visit," and "the Waterfront, where there's great shopping, a movie theater, and various restaurants are only a bus ride away." Finally, those who are 21 can take advantage of "the vast number of bars, lounges, and clubs in the area."

Student Body
Carnegie Mellon seems to attract "focused, intelligent" students who are "ambitious, goal-oriented" and "maybe a little too smart for [their] own good." In short, the university is "a utopia for nerds." And while this might mean you'll encounter a few "socially awkward" peers, one sophomore assures us that it's "a very comfortable, friendly environment." Though a number of undergrads proclaim that there's "no typical student," there are "two common types—the artsy student and the total computer geek." Don't be misled however, these kids can't easily be pigeon-holed. Indeed, quick to praise their "quirky" and "well-rounded" fellow students, many undergrads here greatly appreciate the fact that people "are passionate about a variety of subjects." Impressively, "Students are not only ethnically and religiously diverse, but every person here has some unique or interesting characteristic." Moreover, "everyone is really accepting of students that are different than them." And as a content chemical engineering major shares, "everyone finds their place."

FINANCIAL AID: 412-268-2068 • E-MAIL: UNDERGRADUATE-ADMISSIONS@ANDREW.CMU.EDU • WEBSITE: WWW.CMU.EDU

THE PRINCETON REVIEW SAYS

Admissions

Very important factors considered include: Class rank, academic GPA, rigor of secondary school record, standardized test scores. *Important factors considered include:* Application essay, recommendation(s), alumni/ae relation, character/personal qualities, extracurricular activities, first generation, interview, level of applicant's interest, racial/ethnic status, talent/ability, volunteer work, work experience. SAT Subject Tests required. SAT or ACT required. SAT and SAT Subject Tests or ACT required. ACT with Writing component required. TOEFL required of all international applicants who scored below 600 on their SAT Critical Reading. High school diploma is required and GED is accepted. *Academic units required:* 4 English, 3 mathematics, 3 science (3 science labs), 2 foreign language, 3 academic electives. *Academic units recommended:* 4 English, 3 mathematics, 3 science (3 science labs), 2 foreign language, 4 academic electives.

Financial Aid

Students should submit: FAFSA; institution's own financial aid form; U.S. Federal Income Tax Return, if you were required to complete a Schedule C, and/or Partnership Schedule K-1, and/or IRS Form 2555 (Foreign Earned Income Exclusion); Parental W-2 Wage and Tax Statements for dependent, undergraduate students only; Foreign Tax Documents, if necessary. Regular filing deadline is 5/1. The Princeton Review suggests that all financial aid forms be submitted as soon as possible after 1/1. *Need-based scholarships/grants offered:* Federal Pell, Federal ACG, SEOG, state scholarships/grants, private scholarships, the school's own gift aid. *Loan aid offered:* FFEL Subsidized Stafford, FFEL Unsubsidized Stafford, FFEL PLUS, Federal Perkins, Gate student loan, Private Loans. Applicants will be notified of awards on or about 3/15. Federal Work-Study Program available. Institutional employment available. Off-campus job opportunities are good.

The Inside Word

Don't be misled by Carnegie Mellon's acceptance rate. Although relatively high for a university of this caliber, the applicant pool is fairly self-selecting. If you haven't loaded up on demanding courses in high school, you are not likely to be a serious contender. The admissions office explicitly states that it doesn't use formulas when making decisions. That said, a record of strong academic performance in the area of your intended major is key.

THE SCHOOL SAYS "..."

From The Admissions Office

"Carnegie Mellon is a private, coeducational university with approximately 5,892 undergraduates; 5,066 graduate students; and 1,237 full-time faculty members. The university's 144-acre campus is located in the Oakland area of Pittsburgh, five miles from downtown. The university is composed of 7 colleges: the Carnegie Institute of Technology (engineering), the College of Fine Arts, the College of Humanities and Social Sciences (combining liberal arts education with professional specializations), the Tepper School of Business (undergraduate business and industrial management), the Mellon College of Science, the School of Computer Science, and the H. John Heinz III College (graduate programm).

"Freshman applicants must take the SAT plus two SAT Subject Tests, depending on their major interest. Students may take the ACT with Writing in lieu of the SAT. An applicant's best scores will be used in admissions decision-making.

"Carnegie Mellon has campuses in the Silicon Valley, California, and Qatar in the Arabian Gulf."

SELECTIVITY

Admissions Rating	98
# of applicants	23,090
% of applicants accepted	28
% of acceptees attending	23
# accepting a place on wait list	320
# of early decision applicants	1109
% accepted early decision	24

FRESHMAN PROFILE

Range SAT Critical Reading	620–720
Range SAT Math	670–780
Range SAT Writing	620–710
Range ACT Composite	29–33
Minimum paper TOEFL	600
Minimum computer TOEFL	250
Average HS GPA	3.61
% graduated top 10% of class	73
% graduated top 25% of class	93
% graduated top 50% of class	98

DEADLINES

Early decision	
Deadline	11/1
Notification	12/15
Regular	
Deadline	1/1
Notification	4/15
Nonfall registration?	no

FINANCIAL FACTS

Financial Aid Rating	79
Annual tuition	$40,300
Room and board	$10,340
Required fees	$620
Books	$1,000
% frosh rec. need-based scholarship or grant aid	49
% UG rec. need-based scholarship or grant aid	46
% frosh rec. non-need-based scholarship or grant aid	8
% UG rec. non-need-based scholarship or grant aid	14
% frosh rec. need-based self-help aid	49
% UG rec. need-based self-help aid	45
% frosh rec. any financial aid	56
% UG rec. any financial aid	64
% UG borrow to pay for school	50
Average cumulative indebtedness	$30,533

CASE WESTERN RESERVE UNIVERSITY

103 TOMLINSON HALL, 10900 EUCLID AVENUE, CLEVELAND, OH 44106-7055 • ADMISSIONS: 216-368-4450 • FAX: 216-368-5111

CAMPUS LIFE

Quality of Life Rating	**66**
Fire Safety Rating	**66**
Green Rating	**83**
Type of school	private
Environment	metropolis

STUDENTS

Total undergrad enrollment	4,267
% male/female	57/43
% from out of state	46
% from public high school	70
% live on campus	78
% in (# of) fraternities	29 (14)
% in (# of) sororities	28 (7)
% African American	6
% Asian	17
% Caucasian	57
% Hispanic	2
% international	3
# of countries represented	22

SURVEY SAYS . . .

Lab facilities are great
Great library
Great off-campus food
Low cost of living
Student publications are popular
Student government is popular

ACADEMICS

Academic Rating	**83**
Calendar	semester
Student/faculty ratio	9.7:1
Profs interesting rating	65
Profs accessible rating	71
% classes taught by TAs	5
Most common reg class size	10–19 students
Most common lab size	10–19 students

MOST POPULAR MAJORS

biology/biological sciences
biomedical/medical engineering
business administration and
management

STUDENTS SAY ". . ."

Academics

With more than half its students in the labor-intensive disciplines of engineering and the sciences, it's no wonder students tell us that "Case is about hard work." Undergrads here tell us that "a 9-to-5 job will be exceptionally easy after a Case undergraduate education (which is 9-to-5 classes, then 5-to-2 homework)." While some complain that Case Western "is designed to beat students down [and they] attempt to compete with better schools by giving more homework," others counter that "you can choose to complain about it all the time or you can take advantage of everything that's offered here—enjoy yourself and get a great education." For those who know where to look, Case offers "great means for student development outside of the classroom. The Emerging Leaders Program for first-year students…holds leadership conferences—largely planned and organized by students for students—every semester." It's also "incredibly easy to get involved" in the "ground-breaking research" that occurs on this campus daily. Some here acknowledge that Case "could improve on diversifying its non-engineering and non-science offerings," a matter of significance to all since the school introduced mandatory interdisciplinary seminars (called the SAGE program, which students tell us "is still a work in progress"). Most agree that while the administration "has done a better job at getting to know the students," most would like to see an increase in "their willingness to cater to students' interests, especially when these differ from the beaten path."

Life

"Many students feel that Case Western students do much more work than a typical student and thus miss out on more chances for socializing, even during the weekend," but others tell us that despite the "ton of hard work," there is "still plenty of time in the day for extracurricular activities." "Actually, that's part of the reason why people are so busy in the first place," says one student. Case offers "a wide range of on- and off-campus activities to choose from. Events such as Drag Ball, a local sorority's Mr. CWRU, and our university program board's major concerts pull hundreds of students out to bond and have a great time. Smaller events are always going on through one of our officially recognized student organizations, be they guest lecturers brought in by the Case Democrats, choral showcases featuring one or many of our a cappella groups, or simply smaller events." Cleveland provides further diversion; the school is located in University Circle, home to "a number of museums, the Cleveland Orchestra, the Botanical Gardens, and much more. This is a great resource of our school, which we are encouraged to take advantage of." The party scene here is "more mellow" than other colleges. "If you want to party, you can." If you'd rather stay away from that scene, you can. "There's no pressure."

Student Body

A typical Case student is "heartily dedicated to classes and tries to figure out what else can fit into his/her schedule." Because the school is "so academically focused, there are plenty of the overstressing pre-medical students" along with similarly disposed engineers ("mostly male") and nursing students ("mostly female"). While "many Case students are primarily gamers" who "may not leave their rooms," very often, students "who are incredibly involved and busy joining and leading numerous organizations" are "increasingly more common" on campus. There is also "a vibrant musical community" as well as an active group of intramural sports enthusiasts. One student sums it up, "The greatest strengths of Case are the diversity of the student body, the studious character of the student body, the professors, and the tolerance students have toward different students."

CASE WESTERN RESERVE UNIVERSITY

FINANCIAL AID: 216-368-4530 • E-MAIL: ADMISSION@CASE.EDU • WEBSITE: WWW.CASE.EDU

THE PRINCETON REVIEW SAYS

Admissions

Very important factors considered include: Class rank, academic GPA, rigor of secondary school record, standardized test scores, extracurricular activities. *Important factors considered include:* Application essay, recommendation(s), character/personal qualities, interview, talent/ability, volunteer work, work experience. *Other factors considered include:* Alumni/ae relation, first generation, level of applicant's interest, racial/ethnic status. SAT or ACT required. ACT with Writing component required. TOEFL required of all international applicants. High school diploma is required and GED is accepted. *Academic units required:* 4 English, 3 mathematics, 3 science (2 science labs), 2 foreign language, 3 social studies. *Academic units recommended:* 4 mathematics (3 science labs), 3 foreign language, 4 social studies.

Financial Aid

Students should submit: FAFSA, institution's own financial aid form, business/farm supplement. Parent and student income tax returns and W-2 forms. The Princeton Review suggests that all financial aid forms be submitted as soon as possible after 1/1. *Need-based scholarships/grants offered:* Federal Pell, SEOG, state scholarships/grants, private scholarships, the school's own gift aid. *Loan aid offered:* FFEL Subsidized Stafford, FFEL Unsubsidized Stafford, FFEL PLUS, Federal Perkins, federal nursing scholarships, state loans, college/university loans from institutional funds. Applicants will be notified of awards on a rolling basis beginning 2/15. Federal Work-Study Program available. Institutional employment available. Off-campus job opportunities are excellent.

The Inside Word

Case faces tough competition from similar schools and handles it well as both the number of overall applications and out-of-state applications has increased substantially over the past decade, indicating an improving national profile. As a result, Case grows ever more selective. Case uses a 'single door' admissions policy, meaning that once you are admitted you can change your intended major without having to reapply, even if it means switching schools (e.g. switching from the School of Engineering to the School of Management).

THE SCHOOL SAYS "..."

From The Admissions Office

"Challenging and innovative academic programs, next-level technology, experiential learning, real-world environments, and faculty mentors are at the core of the Case Western Reserve University experience. Case's faculty challenges and supports motivated students, and its partnerships with world-class cultural, educational, and scientific institutions ensure that your education extends beyond the classroom. Case offers more than 75 majors and minors and a single-door admission policy; once admitted to Case, you can major in any of our programs, or double and even triple major in several of them. Our student/faculty ratio, among the best in the nation, allows students to have close interaction with professors. Co-ops, internships, study abroad and other opportunities bring theory to life in amazing settings, and 66 percent of students participate in research and independent study. SAGES, Case's 4-year undergraduate core curriculum, connects students with faculty, peers and the community through small seminars that explore effective communication and analytical skills, and culminates in a Senior Capstone project.

"With 85 percent of students living on campus, Case has a residential feel unique to urban universities. First-year students live together in one of three themed residential colleges that involve resources from across Northeast Ohio: Cedar (arts), Juniper (world culture) and Mistletoe (leadership through service).

"Admission Counselors consider all sections of the SAT, taking the best score for each section from multiple dates. The SAT (or ACT with writing) is used for evaluating applications for admission (and not used for course placement purposes)."

SELECTIVITY
Admissions Rating	98
# of applicants	7,351
% of applicants accepted	73
% of acceptees attending	19
# accepting a place on wait list	254
% admitted from wait list	30

FRESHMAN PROFILE
Range SAT Critical Reading	590–690
Range SAT Math	620–720
Range SAT Writing	580–680
Range ACT Composite	26–32
Minimum paper TOEFL	550
Minimum computer TOEFL	213
Minimum web-based TOEFL	80
% graduated top 10% of class	62.7
% graduated top 25% of class	87.2
% graduated top 50% of class	99

DEADLINES
Early action	
Deadline	11/1
Notification	12/15
Regular	
Deadline	1/15
Notification	4/1
Nonfall registration?	yes

APPLICANTS ALSO LOOK AT
AND OFTEN PREFER
Johns Hopkins University
Cornell University
Northwestern University

AND SOMETIMES PREFER
Carnegie Mellon University
The Ohio State University—Columbus

FINANCIAL FACTS
Financial Aid Rating	94
Annual tuition	35,900
Room and board	$10,890
Books and supplies	$1,833
% frosh rec. need-based scholarship or grant aid	71
% UG rec. need-based scholarship or grant aid	63
% frosh rec. non-need-based scholarship or grant aid	59
% UG rec. non-need-based scholarship or grant aid	52
% frosh rec. need-based self-help aid	58
% UG rec. need-based self-help aid	58
% frosh rec. any financial aid	90
% UG rec. any financial aid	84
% UG borrow to pay for school	65
Average cumulative indebtedness	$37,892

CATAWBA COLLEGE

2300 WEST INNES STREET, SALISBURY, NC 28144 • ADMISSIONS: 704-637-4402 • FAX: 704-637-4222

CAMPUS LIFE
Quality of Life Rating	86
Fire Safety Rating	78
Green Rating	79
Type of school	private
Affiliation	United Church of Christ
Environment	town

STUDENTS
Total undergrad enrollment	1,225
% male/female	47/53
% from out of state	23
% from public high school	80
% live on campus	72
% African American	15
% Caucasian	80
% Hispanic	1
% international	2
# of countries represented	14

SURVEY SAYS . . .
Students are friendly
Students are happy
Everyone loves the Catawba Indians
Theater is popular
Student government is popular

ACADEMICS
Academic Rating	79
Calendar	semester
Student/faculty ratio	15:1
Profs interesting rating	91
Profs accessible rating	86
Most common reg class size	10–19 students
Most common lab size	fewer than 10 students

MOST POPULAR MAJORS
business/commerce
drama and dramatics/theatre arts
elementary education and teaching

STUDENTS SAY "..."

Academics

Catawba College, a "small school with a student body of fewer than two thousand" "known for its environmental science and theater programs," is the sort of place where students meet "people who make a big difference in your life, whether it be your caring admissions counselor, easily accessible professor, friendly department head, or large group of friends," all of whom boast a "diverse range of interests. At Catawba, it's the people who define the school." An "atmosphere of creativity and curiosity" envelops a "learning community focused on involvement in academics, athletics, campus clubs, and volunteer work." This is abetted by faculty who "are generally very willing to work with and help you if you are confused," not to mention "a good tutoring system." An honors program "is top-notch, but underappreciated," providing participants with courses specifically designed to facilitate "discussion and interaction." The theater department "comprises one-fifth of the student population" and "puts a lot of effort into productions and regularly wins awards." The school is undergoing a growth spurt these days, and the administration "is continuing to change and update the buildings." Although "construction could go faster," students love the direction in which their school is headed, telling us that the college is "constantly improving and growing."

Life

Catawba's administration imposes some moderately strict regulations—students must be 23 years old in order to live off campus, for example—leading some to complain that the school "runs on a high school mindset." "It's as if the administration didn't get the memo that Catawba is a college, not a boarding school." Not all students mind the restrictions; some happily report that "for the most part people love Catawba" and that "there is almost always something going on around campus that you can get into. Everyone goes to the same places—movies, dinner, bars, clubs, on-campus events—and hangs out and has fun." As one student puts it, "life at school is dependent upon how many activities you are involved with. The more activities that you participate in, the more fun you will have on campus. We have outdoor movies, casino nights, late-night campus-sponsored events, intramurals, athletics, and much more." Some undergrads demur, reporting that "there are very few activities or facilities for us to enjoy on campus. After dark, there is nothing to do." All agree that sports are extremely popular. "People come from all over to see the Indians play. Tailgate parties are a regular thing." "There's not much to do as far as social events" in hometown Salisbury. "The music scene in Salisbury is nonexistent, which is frustrating, so parties tend to be kind of exclusive (theater majors tend to stick together, etc.). There is a lot drinking on Saturday nights." It's possible some drink to forget the school dining service. Student reviews range from "getting better but still not great" to "needs some help" to "really dreadful."

Student Body

Catawba "is a very diverse school with all different people and majors, but it's very divided into sects: the theater kids, the e-sci kids, the sports kids, etc. Catawba's nickname—Catawba High—sums us up." The theater group is further divided into "the more 'bohemian' set and the musical theater set." While these groups don't actively socialize with one another, the campus is hardly Balkanized. "The athletes go to the plays and music events, and the theater people support the athletes in their events." Catawba undergrads "tend to be from within 200 miles of the school. This is reflected in the 'Southern values' mindset of the school. Being from New York, I find it to be a refreshing change." Students' activities tend not to be "limited to the classroom; instead, they are athletes, actors, and club presidents. You would be hard-pressed to find anyone on campus who isn't involved in something else other than just going to class. This involvement in school really makes Catawba as great as it is."

FINANCIAL AID: 704-637-4416 • E-MAIL: ADMISSION@CATAWBA.EDU • WEBSITE: WWW.CATAWBA.EDU

THE PRINCETON REVIEW SAYS

Admissions

Very important factors considered include: Class rank, application essay, academic GPA, recommendation(s), standardized test scores. *Important factors considered include:* Rigor of secondary school record, character/personal qualities, extracurricular activities, interview, level of applicant's interest, talent/ability. *Other factors considered include:* Volunteer work. SAT or ACT required. ACT with Writing component recommended. TOEFL required of all international applicants. High school diploma is required and GED is accepted. *Academic units required:* 4 English, 3 mathematics, 3 science, 2 social studies, 4 academic electives. *Academic units recommended:* 4 English, 3 mathematics, 3 science (3 science labs), 2 foreign language, 3 social studies, 3 academic electives.

Financial Aid

Students should submit: FAFSA, state aid form. The Princeton Review suggests that all financial aid forms be submitted as soon as possible after 1/1. *Need-based scholarships/grants offered:* Federal Pell, SEOG, state scholarships/grants, private scholarships, the school's own gift aid. *Loan aid offered:* FFEL Unsubsidized Stafford, FFEL PLUS, Federal Perkins, college/university loans from institutional funds, TERI loans, Nellie Mae loans, advantage loans, alternative loans. Applicants will be notified of awards on a rolling basis beginning 2/15. Off-campus job opportunities are good.

The Inside Word

Because it competes with so many top schools for regional students, Catawba is willing to take a chance on some applicants who may not make the cut at Davidson, Duke, or Chapel Hill. High school underachievers who are ready to excel at the college level will find a great opportunity to do just that at Catawba. Such students may well benefit from the close attention administrators and professors lavish on Catawba undergrads.

THE SCHOOL SAYS "..."

From The Admissions Office

"Catawba College prepares students for rewarding lives and careers in the liberal arts tradition. This attractive campus is centrally located in Salisbury, North Carolina, a short drive away from the mountains and Atlantic beaches. The community possesses a rich past and commitment to preserving its cultural and historic charm. In contrast, just 45 minutes away is the much faster pace of Charlotte, North Carolina where shopping, transportation, and entertainment of all kinds are readily available.

"On campus, students study and socialize in a small college setting that offers strong traditions, excellent facilities, and beautiful surroundings. The high standards of quality set by Catawba's academic programs are matched by equally demanding sports and co-curricular programs. Students describe the community as caring and personable. They also exhibit a high rate of involvement in campus activities ranging form the performing arts to homecoming and travel abroad. Faculty and staff are described by students as being important mentors. Whether in a state-of-the-art environmental science facility, attractive music and theatrical performance center, classroom, or one of the college's first-class athletic facilities, students report they feel as if they are among family when on campus.

"Perhaps the most important testimony to the attractiveness of Catawba is found in the words of its graduates who report numerous successful careers and rich memories of their time at school.

"Students applying for admissions to Catawba College are required submit to scores from the SAT, including the Writing portion of the test. In lieu of SAT scores, Catawba will accept student scores on the ACT when they include scores on the ACT Writing portion of the test. Catawba will use the student's best scores from either test in making admissions decisions."

SELECTIVITY

Admissions Rating	78
# of applicants	992
% of applicants accepted	61
% of acceptees attending	41

FRESHMAN PROFILE

Range SAT Critical Reading	450–580
Range SAT Math	480–590
Range ACT Composite	19–25
Minimum paper TOEFL	525
Minimum computer TOEFL	197
Average HS GPA	3.5
% graduated top 10% of class	21
% graduated top 25% of class	50
% graduated top 50% of class	86

DEADLINES

Regular	
Notification	rolling
Nonfall registration?	yes

APPLICANTS ALSO LOOK AT
AND SOMETIMES PREFER
Appalachian State University
University of North Carolina at Charlotte

AND RARELY PREFER
University of North Carolina at Greensboro

FINANCIAL FACTS

Financial Aid Rating	86
Annual tuition	$23,740
Room and board	$8,200
Books and supplies	$800
% frosh rec. need-based scholarship or grant aid	48
% UG rec. need-based scholarship or grant aid	44
% frosh rec. non-need-based scholarship or grant aid	75
% UG rec. non-need-based scholarship or grant aid	70
% frosh rec. need-based self-help aid	55
% UG rec. need-based self-help aid	53
% frosh rec. athletic scholarships	30
% UG rec. athletic scholarships	25
% frosh rec. any financial aid	96
% UG rec. any financial aid	96
% UG borrow to pay for school	76
Average cumulative indebtedness	$21,892

THE CATHOLIC UNIVERSITY OF AMERICA

OFFICE OF ENROLLMENT SERVICES, WASHINGTON, DC 20064 • ADMISSIONS: 202-319-5305 • FAX: 202-319-6533

CAMPUS LIFE

Quality of Life Rating	**67**
Fire Safety Rating	**85**
Green Rating	**88**
Type of school	private
Affiliation	Roman Catholic
Environment	metropolis

STUDENTS

Total undergrad enrollment	3,431
% male/female	45/55
% from out of state	95
% from public high school	48
% live on campus	68
% in (# of) fraternities	1 (1)
% in (# of) sororities	0.3 (1)
% African American	5
% Asian	3
% Caucasian	66
% Hispanic	7
% international	3
# of countries represented	79

SURVEY SAYS . . .

Students are friendly
Great off-campus food
Frats and sororities are unpopular or
nonexistent
Musical organizations are popular
Student government is popular
Political activism is popular
Lots of beer drinking
Hard liquor is popular

ACADEMICS

Academic Rating	**78**
Calendar	semester
Student/faculty ratio	11:1
Profs interesting rating	73
Profs accessible rating	75
% classes taught by TAs	9
Most common	
reg class size	10–19 students
Most common	
lab size	10–19 students

MOST POPULAR MAJORS
architecture (barch, ba/bs, march,
ma/ms, phd)
engineering (biomedical, civil,
electrical and computer science,
mechanical)
nursing/registered nurse (rn, asn,
bsn, msn)
political science and government

STUDENTS SAY ". . ."

Academics

You'll receive "an education heavy in philosophy and theology" at The Catholic University of America on "a beautiful college campus located in the heart of our nation's capital." Every student at CUA completes a core curriculum with an "emphasis on philosophy and religion, and students are required to take a series of both. Unless you are planning on making a career out of either, when else in life will you study these in depth than college?" For a school of just more than 6,500 students, CUA has a remarkable number of strong disciplines. Undergrads laud the "incredibly strong" nursing program, a "wonderful music program" that's ideal for students who "don't want conservatory straight out of high school but still want a challenging program," "the best education in architecture in the D.C. area," and a "very strong" drama department. While liberal arts and science programs aren't as highly regarded, students appreciate that "professors are helpful and always available," and point out that political studies are greatly abetted by the school's location. Of the school's location in the nation's captial, one student says it provides, "easy access to internships, government, and seemingly endless other political opportunities." The school also offers an honors program that "challenges students to push [to] the edge of their abilities."

Life

CUA's Washington, D.C. address "is absolutely one of the great strengths of the school. A student can get on the Metro and go basically wherever they want, and get whatever it is they need." Indeed, students "have D.C., a storied and cosmopolitan city," at their fingertips, "with plenty of concert venues, movie theaters, play houses, shopping districts, landmarks, and museums to visit on the weekends." Undergrads "go to Starbucks and have study sessions…on Sundays, or go and visit friends at George Washington University or Georgetown on the weekends." "Chinatown, Dupont Circle, and Union Station" are also popular destinations for "fun times." As one student sums up,"We are in the nation's capital, we have plenty to do." Some students tell us that "almost everyone on this campus likes to drink." However, other students note, "the school tries really hard to offer nonalcoholic alternatives on the weekends." Drinking generally takes place in the bars, as "house parties are almost nonexistent" on campus. However, students also tell us that "there is always some option for you" including campus ministry events which provide "students [with] a healthy environment and people to be around as an alternative to drinking."

Student Body

The typical student at CUA "is from the Mid-Atlantic states, white, went to a Catholic high school," "is fairly conservative," and looks like a "page out of an Abercrombie & Fitch ad." "Everyone wears flip-flops, polo shirts, and khakis. People only wear jeans during the wintertime." Exceptions to the rule include "the very vocal minority groups" who work to make sure "diversity is highlighted" on campus, "people of other religious backgrounds," and the many "musical theater students" including a large number of "gay men, which is pretty surprising at a Catholic university." Many students are devout and "very open about their faith," but "very few people will force religion down your throat." Atypical students are "generally welcomed and accepted by these 'typical' students with little or no friction due to religion, sexual orientation, race or socioeconomic class."

FINANCIAL AID: 202-319-5307 • E-MAIL: CUA-ADMISSIONS@CUA.EDU • WEBSITE: WWW.CUA.EDU

THE PRINCETON REVIEW SAYS

Admissions

Very important factors considered include: academic GPA, recommendation(s), rigor of secondary school record, standardized test scores, character/personal qualities, level of applicant's interest, volunteer work. *Important factors considered include:* Application essay, extracurricular activities, first generation, interview, talent/ability. *Other factors considered include:* alumni/ae relation, racial/ethnic status, work experience. SAT Subject Tests recommended; SAT or ACT required; ACT with Writing component required. TOEFL required of all international applicants. High school diploma is required and GED is accepted. *Academic units recommended:* 4 English, 3 mathematics, 3 science, (1 science labs), 2 foreign language, 4 social studies, 1 Fine arts or humanities.

Financial Aid

Students should submit: FAFSA. Alumni and Parish Scholarship Applications if appropriate. The Princeton Review suggests that all financial aid forms be submitted as soon as possible after 1/1. Need-based scholarships/grants offered: Federal Pell, SEOG, state scholarships/grants, private scholarships, the school's own gift aid, Federal Nursing Scholarships. *Loan aid offered:* FFEL Subsidized Stafford, FFEL Unsubsidized Stafford, FFEL PLUS, Federal Perkins, Federal Nursing, college/university loans from institutional funds, commericial loans. Federal Work-Study Program available. Institutional employment available. Off-campus job opportunities are good.

The Inside Word

The Catholic University of America is a conservative school that adopts a very traditional approach to higher education. Your application should demonstrate an appreciation for the school's unique qualities and educational philosophy. Present your strongest case by showing solid grades in a demanding curriculum, backed by above average test scores, and you should have little trouble gaining admission. CUA now accepts the common application.

THE SCHOOL SAYS " . . . "

From The Admissions Office

"The Catholic University of America's friendly atmosphere, rigorous academic programs, and emphasis on time-honored values attract students from all 50 states and more than 95 foreign countries. Its 193-acre, tree-lined campus is only 10 minutes from the nation's capital. Distinguished as the national university of the Catholic Church in the United States, CUA is the only institution of higher education established by the U.S. Catholic bishops; however, students from all religious traditions are welcome.

"CUA offers undergraduate degrees in more than 80 major areas in seven schools of study. Students enroll into the School of Arts and Sciences, Architecture, Nursing, Engineering, Metropolitan School, Music, or Philosophy. Additionally, CUA students can concentrate in areas of preprofessional study including law, dentistry, medicine, or veterinary studies.

"With Capitol Hill, the Smithsonian Institution, NASA, the Kennedy Center, and the National Institutes of Health among the places students obtain internships, firsthand experience is a valuable piece of the experience that CUA offers. Numerous students also take the opportunity in their junior year to study abroad at one of Catholic's 17 country program sites. Political science majors even have the opportunity to do a Parliamentary Internship in either England or Ireland. With the campus just minutes away from downtown via the Metrorail rapid transit system, students enjoy a residential campus in an exciting city of historical monuments, theaters, festivals, ethnic restaurants, and parks.

"Matriculating students should submit the SAT Subject Test: Foreign Language exam if they plan to continue studying that language at CUA."

SELECTIVITY
Admissions Rating	88
# of applicants	5,180
% of applicants accepted	81
% of acceptees attending	22

FRESHMAN PROFILE
Range SAT Critical Reading	510–610
Range SAT Math	500–610
Range ACT Composite	21–27
Minimum paper TOEFL	550
Minimum computer TOEFL	213
Minimum web-based TOEFL	80
Average HS GPA	3.24
% graduated top 10% of class	23.78
% graduated top 25% of class	50.35
% graduated top 50% of class	81.82

DEADLINES
Early action	
Deadline	11/15
Notification	12/15
Regular	
Deadline	2/15
Notification	rolling
Nonfall registration?	yes

APPLICANTS ALSO LOOK AT
AND OFTEN PREFER
University of Maryland—University College
Boston College
AND RARELY PREFER
The George Washington University
American University

FINANCIAL FACTS
Financial Aid Rating	84
Annual tuition	$31,740
% frosh rec. need-based scholarship or grant aid	62
% UG rec. need-based scholarship or grant aid	54
% frosh rec. need-based self-help aid	57
% UG rec. need-based self-help aid	50
% frosh rec. any financial aid	91
% UG rec. any financial aid	88

CENTENARY COLLEGE OF LOUISIANA

2911 CENTENARY BOULEVARD, SHREVEPORT, LA 71104 • ADMISSIONS: 318-869-5131 • FAX: 318-869-5005

CAMPUS LIFE

Quality of Life Rating	**75**
Fire Safety Rating	**78**
Green Rating	**60***
Type of school	private
Affiliation	Methodist
Environment	metropolis

STUDENTS

Total undergrad enrollment	891
% male/female	41/59
% from out of state	43
% from public high school	72
% live on campus	66
% in (# of) fraternities	28 (5)
% in (# of) sororities	35 (2)
% African American	8
% Asian	2
% Caucasian	82
% Hispanic	4
% international	2
# of countries represented	12

SURVEY SAYS . . .
Registration is a breeze
Students are friendly
Musical organizations are popular
Student publications are popular
Student government is popular

ACADEMICS

Academic Rating	**85**
Calendar	semester
Student/faculty ratio	12:1
Profs interesting rating	88
Profs accessible rating	87
Most common	
reg class size	10–19 students

MOST POPULAR MAJORS
biology/biological sciences
business/commerce
mass communication/media studies

STUDENTS SAY ". . ."

Academics

With fewer than 1,000 undergraduates, Centenary College of Louisiana certainly qualifies as a small school. In fact, there are only a handful of elite undergraduate institutions smaller. That said, smallness has its virtues. As one student notes, "The small size of the student body gives students the opportunity to receive individual attention in class, be involved in many organizations and hold leadership positions outside of class." It also fosters "a community atmosphere" in which "professors really care about you emotionally and academically," along with providing "a lot of one-on-one help and projects." Premedical sciences are said to be excellent (nearly 20 percent of all students major in life sciences), as are business studies, music, and communications. Academics are "extremely rigorous and thorough," so much so that "no one graduates without expanding their knowledge base." As at many small schools, "the professors are absolutely wonderful. They're engaging, knowledgeable, and really care about what they're teaching and about their students." The school places a premium on such high-caliber teaching skill. "Bad teachers do not last long around here," one undergrad assures us. The downside of a small school, of course, is that certain limitations are an unavoidable fact of life. Some "miss the perks a bigger school [has to offer] like more classes and a better cafeteria."

Life

"Campus life centers around athletics, clubs, and Greek life" at Centenary, where "the real trick is finding that one thing that you love (be it sororities, radio, theatre, whatever) and excelling at it. The school has a lot of opportunities for responsible individuals." There's the "awesome" radio station, for one, and lots of lectures, internships, and mentoring opportunities. And while "There are occasional events on weekdays, including sports games," when it comes time for fun "life at Centenary revolves around the weekend" and "includes going to some of the local attractions, to a movie, to dinner, or to either one of the sport teams' house or a fraternity house." Because the campus is officially dry, "those unwilling to hide their contraband alcohol...normally just hang out in residence hall lobbies and watch movies" or they "go down to the fraternity houses (which allow alcohol)." Hometown Shreveport "doesn't offer many options for students, especially students under 21. It's definitely not a 'college town.'" Another student explains, "There is not a lot to do in Shreveport besides shopping, but there are many opportunities to do so in the surrounding area. There are not too many local music shows, but the Shreveport Opera and community theaters are worth the time."

Student Body

For such a small school, Centenary does a good job of drawing a diverse mix of interests and backgrounds. Here "You can find everything from far right-wing ministry majors to highly liberal individuals actively involved in campus organizations promoting gay rights" as well as "a large and diverse number of international students, most notably from Europe and Hong Kong." What you won't find is a lot of minority students; "There are very few minorities on this campus," one student observes. Most students here "are overachievers or hard workers, whether it is in an academic sense or in an extracurricular sense." Though many note that the student body is "generally white, middle-class, and religious," they are also quick to point out that it also accommodates "a lot of gay and lesbian students, and overall, the campus is very accepting and supportive of these students."

CENTENARY COLLEGE OF LOUISIANA

FINANCIAL AID: 318-869-5137 • E-MAIL: ADMISSIONS@CENTENARY.EDU • WEBSITE: WWW.CENTENARY.EDU

THE PRINCETON REVIEW SAYS

Admissions

Very important factors considered include: Academic GPA, rigor of secondary school record. *Important factors considered include:* Class rank, application essay, recommendation(s), standardized test scores, alumni/ae relation, character/personal qualities, extracurricular activities, interview, level of applicant's interest, talent/ability, volunteer work, work experience. *Other factors considered include:* Geographical residence, racial/ethnic status, religious affiliation/commitment. SAT or ACT required. TOEFL required of all international applicants. High school diploma is required and GED is accepted. *Academic units recommended:* 4 English, 3 mathematics, 3 science (2 science labs), 2 foreign language, 3 social studies.

Financial Aid

Students should submit: FAFSA, institution's own financial aid form. The Princeton Review suggests that all financial aid forms be submitted as soon as possible after 1/1. *Need-based scholarships/grants offered:* Federal Pell, SEOG, state scholarships/grants, private scholarships, the school's own gift aid. *Loan aid offered:* FFEL Subsidized Stafford, FFEL Unsubsidized Stafford, FFEL PLUS, Federal Perkins. Applicants will be notified of awards on or about 3/15. Federal Work-Study Program available. Institutional employment available. Off-campus job opportunities are good.

The Inside Word

Centenary's applicant pool has grown substantially over the past decade, allowing the school to become more selective in its admissions process. The school's reputation, though regional, is quite solid, and the college does a good job of enrolling those it admits—a sign that the school is tops on more than a few applicants' lists. No doubt a very friendly and efficient admissions office also contributes to this success.

THE SCHOOL SAYS "..."

From The Admissions Office

"Just as a student's 4-year experience at Centenary will be very personalized, so too is the application process. We pride ourselves on treating each applicant as an individual. We encourage all interested students to visit us—not only so they can see our campus and get a sense of the atmosphere, but also to provide us the opportunity to meet and get to know them.

"Consider Centenary for a life-changing experience. Our professors value your ideas and contributions and are passionate about teaching.We consider the Centenary Experience to be more than just a degree. You will live in a comprehensive learning environment that features connections to your academic, social, personal, and residential lives.

"Our students work and live within a strong community to create personalized, distinctive experiences, and enjoy a vibrant college life and graduate from Centenary prepared for their professional and personal lives.

"First-year applicants must submit either ACT or SAT scores. We recommend, but do not require, the ACT Writing component."

SELECTIVITY
Admissions Rating	85
# of applicants	1,069
% of applicants accepted	65
% of acceptees attending	34

FRESHMAN PROFILE
Range SAT Critical Reading	500–620
Range SAT Math	510–620
Range ACT Composite	23–28
Minimum paper TOEFL	550
Minimum computer TOEFL	213
% graduated top 10% of class	35
% graduated top 25% of class	62
% graduated top 50% of class	83

DEADLINES
Early action Deadline	12/15
Regular Priority	2/15
Deadline	8/1
Notification	rolling
Nonfall registration?	yes

FINANCIAL FACTS
Financial Aid Rating	86
Annual tuition	$20,940
Room and board	$7,600
Required fees	$1,140
Books and supplies	$1,200
% frosh rec. need-based scholarship or grant aid	67
% UG rec. need-based scholarship or grant aid	58
% frosh rec. non-need-based scholarship or grant aid	15
% UG rec. non-need-based scholarship or grant aid	16
% frosh rec. need-based self-help aid	46
% UG rec. need-based self-help aid	35
% frosh rec. athletic scholarships	13
% UG rec. athletic scholarships	14
% frosh rec. any financial aid	98
% UG rec. any financial aid	93
% UG borrow to pay for school	52
Average cumulative indebtedness	$20,640

CENTRE COLLEGE

600 WEST WALNUT STREET, DANVILLE, KY 40422 • ADMISSIONS: 800-423-6236 • FAX: 859-238-5373

CAMPUS LIFE

Quality of Life Rating	**83**
Fire Safety Rating	**60***
Green Rating	**85**
Type of school	private
Affiliation	Presbyterian
Environment	village

STUDENTS

Total undergrad enrollment	1,193
% male/female	46/54
% from out of state	38
% from public high school	79
% live on campus	98
% in (# of) fraternities	34 (4)
% in (# of) sororities	40 (4)
% African American	4
% Asian	2
% Caucasian	90
% Hispanic	2
% international	2
# of countries represented	12

SURVEY SAYS . . .

No one cheats
Athletic facilities are great
School is well run
Campus feels safe
Low cost of living
(Almost) no one smokes
Very little drug use

ACADEMICS

Academic Rating	**95**
Calendar	4/1/4
Student/faculty ratio	11:1
Profs interesting rating	99
Profs accessible rating	94
Most common reg class size	10–19 students
Most common lab size	10–19 students

MOST POPULAR MAJORS
economics
English language and literature
history

STUDENTS SAY ". . ."

Academics

The idea that education should be "personal" is at the core of Centre's ethos. The school makes a concerted effort to hire professors who are "first and foremost dedicated to teaching." And their hard work clearly seems to have paid off. Centre is chock full of "amazing" professors who "really care about you and [want to] help you succeed with whatever your final goal is." Make no mistake though; undergrads at this college can't simply kick back for four years. According to one knowledgeable senior, "The curriculum is hard, and no class is easy." Fortunately, any overwhelmed student can take solace in the fact that teachers always have "their doors open." And the rigorous courseload guarantees a "truly enriching academic experience." As one junior boasts, "All aspects of my academic abilities have improved including studying habits, critical thinking, problem solving, laboratory familiarity, writing ability, and public speaking/oral presentation ability." Though there's the occasional gripe about policy, by and large undergrads are quite pleased with Centre's administration. They are fairly "responsive" and "make a point to become familiar with many of the students." This accessibility extends even to the president who "does everything from eat in the campus dining hall to go sledding with students in the winter time."

Life

Undergrads at Centre typically "fit the mold of students who both work hard and play hard." Students admit that while "the all-night study rooms and all-night computer labs" are frequently occupied during the week, students readily embrace the weekend as a "time for relaxation and as a way to escape [academic] stresses." Greek life is extremely popular, and "sororities and fraternities definitely dominate the college social [life]." Luckily, it's a pretty welcoming scene "where everyone is invited [and] all the houses are always open." Additionally the "student council is good about organizing other activities." These range from "movie nights [and] Carnival" to "study breaks" and "camping trips." While some describe hometown Danville as "small" and "hick," a number of students enjoy eating at some "great [local] restaurants" and taking advantage of "free midnight movies at the Danville Theater." As one sophomore admits, "Wal-mart is always a hot spot to go browsing around." Those looking for a little more action should take heart in knowing that both Lexington and Louisville are within driving distance. It's not uncommon for students to take a road trip to either city to attend a concert or to indulge in a little shopping.

Student Body

Despite a small student body, Centre College is a place where every undergrad is fortunate to "be able to find their niche." While groups of students can easily be categorized as "Greeks" or "non-Greeks," "athletes" or "artists," everyone "interacts well." One sophomore attributes this to the fact that the college "encourages students to express their own ideas, faith, and orientations while also being open and considerate to other people's views and beliefs." Regardless of interests and affiliations, Centre students can easily find common ground. Indeed, by and large, undergrads are "here to get a really great education and to have fun." The vast majority of students are "committed to its coursework" and "dedicated to learning as much as possible." Additionally, it's an outgoing and active community where "almost everyone is involved in something outside of academics." However, though the student body is comprised of people who have "a wide range of interests," Centre "does not provide a wide range of ethnic diversity." As one senior reveals, "The typical student is white, and from the south." Rest assured, however, that the college "is aware of its diversity problem and is working consciously to help eliminate it."

FINANCIAL AID: 859-238-5365 • E-MAIL: ADMISSION@CENTRE.EDU • WEBSITE: WWW.CENTRE.EDU

THE PRINCETON REVIEW SAYS

Admissions

Very important factors considered include: Academic GPA, rigor of secondary school record. *Important factors considered include:* Class rank, application essay, recommendation(s), standardized test scores. *Other factors considered include:* Alumni/ae relation, character/personal qualities, extracurricular activities, first generation, geographical residence, interview, level of applicant's interest, racial/ethnic status, talent/ability, volunteer work, work experience. SAT or ACT required. ACT with Writing component recommended. TOEFL required of all international applicants. High school diploma or equivalent is not required. *Academic units required:* 4 English, 4 mathematics, 2 science (2 science labs), 2 foreign language, 2 history. *Academic units recommended:* 4 English, 4 mathematics, 4 science (3 science labs), 4 foreign language, 2 social studies, 2 history, 1 visual/performing arts.

Financial Aid

Students should submit: FAFSA, institution's own financial aid form. Regular filing deadline is 3/1. The Princeton Review suggests that all financial aid forms be submitted as soon as possible after 1/1. *Need-based scholarships/grants offered:* Federal Pell, SEOG, state scholarships/grants, private scholarships, the school's own gift aid, Federal ACG Federal SMART + Federal TEACH. *Loan aid offered:* FFEL Subsidized Stafford, FFEL Unsubsidized Stafford, FFEL PLUS, Federal Perkins, college/university loans from institutional funds. Applicants will be notified of awards on or about 3/25. Federal Work-Study Program available. Institutional employment available. Off-campus job opportunities are fair.

The Inside Word

Centre's small but very capable student body reflects solid academic preparation from high school. If you're ranked in the top quarter of your graduating class and have taken challenging courses throughout your high school career, you should have smooth sailing through the admissions process. Those who rank below the top quarter or who have inconsistent academic transcripts will find entrance here more difficult and may benefit from an interview.

THE SCHOOL SAYS "..."

From The Admissions Office

"Centre provides its students with a personal education that enables them to achieve extraordinary success in advanced study and their careers. Centre professors, virtually all of whom hold the highest degree available in their fields, challenge their students and give them the individual attention and support they need to meet those challenges. The end result is highly capable graduates with a can-do attitude and the ability to accomplish their goals.

"Centre offers a multitude of advantages, such as a national top-50 academic reputation, majors options, and exposure to the internationally known Artists and Scholars; benefits like these produce extraordinary success. For example, entrance to top graduate and professional schools; the most prestigious post-graduate scholarships (Rhodes, Fulbright, Goldwater); interesting, rewarding jobs (97 percent of graduates are either employed or engaged in advance study within ten months of graduation).

"How do alumni respond? They have expressed their customer satisfaction by leading the United States in their percentage of annual financial support over the past 25 years. How much does all this cost? Because of our nation-leading alumni support, Centre is the most affordable of America's top 50 national liberal arts colleges and has been ranked as the No.1 value among all U.S. colleges.

SELECTIVITY
Admissions Rating	95
# of applicants	2,176
% of applicants accepted	63
% of acceptees attending	25
# accepting a place on wait list	38

FRESHMAN PROFILE
Range SAT Critical Reading	560–700
Range SAT Math	570–670
Range SAT Writing	550–680
Range ACT Composite	26–30
Minimum paper TOEFL	580
Average HS GPA	3.54
% graduated top 10% of class	53
% graduated top 25% of class	81
% graduated top 50% of class	97

DEADLINES
Early action	
Deadline	12/1
Notification	1/15
Regular	
Deadline	2/1
Notification	3/15
Nonfall registration?	no

APPLICANTS ALSO LOOK AT
AND SOMETIMES PREFER
Rhodes College
Furman University

AND RARELY PREFER
University of Kentucky
Transylvania University

FINANCIAL FACTS
Financial Aid Rating	82
Comprehensive fee	$37,000
Books and supplies	$1,100
% frosh rec. need-based scholarship or grant aid	60
% UG rec. need-based scholarship or grant aid	57
% frosh rec. need-based self-help aid	40
% UG rec. need-based self-help aid	40
% UG borrow to pay for school	56
Average cumulative indebtedness	$17,600

CHAPMAN UNIVERSITY

One University Drive, Orange, CA 92866 • Admissions: 714-997-6711 • Fax: 714-997-6713

CAMPUS LIFE
Quality of Life Rating	**81**
Fire Safety Rating	**60***
Green Rating	**60***
Type of school	private
Affiliation	Disciples of Christ
Environment	metropolis

STUDENTS
Total undergrad enrollment	4,264
% male/female	42/58
% from out of state	26
% from public high school	70
% live on campus	37
% in (# of) fraternities	26 (6)
% in (# of) sororities	30 (6)
% African American	3
% Asian	9
% Caucasian	68
% Hispanic	10
% Native American	1
% international	2
# of countries represented	58

SURVEY SAYS . . .
(Almost) no one smokes

ACADEMICS
Academic Rating	**81**
Calendar	4/1/4
Student/faculty ratio	14:1
Profs interesting rating	80
Profs accessible rating	81
Most common	
reg class size	20–29 students
Most common	
lab size	10–19 students

MOST POPULAR MAJORS
public relations and advertising
business administration
film & television production
theater, music, and dance

STUDENTS SAY ". . ."

Academics

Chapman University is "a wealthy private institution" "in the heart of Orange County" that is "just the right size." There are "a lot of great facilities" here. Film production is "Chapman's most celebrated department." Resources are "totally state of the art." Students have access to "equipment that even the best studios will never have." The music conservatory is world class. Other notable majors include accounting, business administration, theater, dance, and public relations and advertising. Chapman offers a bevy of opportunities to study abroad in the summer and between semesters. "The travel courses are awesome," rejoices a political science major. International internships are also available. "Small class sizes" (typically about 20 students) are a plus. A broad yet flexible set of general education requirements ensures that everybody gets a firm grounding in the liberal arts. The administration isn't very popular. The top brass is "very ambitious" but "more focused on the school's image than its students." The registration process, which "can be a nightmare sometimes for everyone except for freshmen," "could be better," and higher-ups are "insanely difficult to contact," particularly for a smaller school. The faculty is generally "outstanding," though. "There is the occasional bad seed" who "should be avoided at all costs." "On the whole, though, the professors are very good and very accommodating," relates a computer science major. "They will always work with you for whatever you need, and you don't have to deal with any teaching assistants, period." You can talk to professors "about anything," adds a public relations major.

Life

Students here enjoy an "immaculate" and "truly beautiful campus." "The amenities are wonderful." "Chapman spends a ridiculous amount of money keeping the grounds nice." "We love sitting around the fountains in the sun between classes," says a sophomore. "It is such a nice place to spend four years," reflects a wistful senior. The food is "overpriced," though, and the cafeteria hours aren't long enough. "Get me some chain restaurants!" demands a ravenous first-year student. The social atmosphere is "lively." "It's not a hardcore party school," explains a sophomore, "but there [are] definitely parties every weekend if that's your scene." Many students participate in an intercollegiate sport. There is "a good variety of awesome clubs." "Greek life is huge" as well, and students who pledge tend to get "very, very involved" in their fraternities and sororities. Off campus, the town of Orange is "cute and historic" but "sleepy" and "sort of boring." However, "the beach is super close, like 15 minutes," and Disneyland is "just up the street." Annual passes are reportedly "a good investment." "It's fun to go on random weekdays when it's not crowded." For more urban fare, Los Angeles is only about 30 miles north. Students often "go there for weekend visits and such."

Student Body

"If you're looking for a big, diverse school, keep looking," advises a junior. At Chapman, "the typical student would be an upper-class white kid from a relatively sheltered background." To be sure, there is a healthy percentage of "down-to-earth kids" "on loans" and scholarships. "I know I wouldn't be able to attend this school if I didn't have such an awesome financial aid package," notes a senior. There are also plenty of "rich Orange County children." "Three-outfits-a-day sorority types" who "wear Uggs with shorts" and "look like they've just walked out of a reality TV show" are not unusual. Students predominantly come from Southern California, and they describe themselves as "tan," "athletic," and "attractive." "I would say 98 percent of students are ridiculously good looking," estimates a captivated first-year student. The campus is also "very cliquey." However, "there are plenty of sub-groups," giving Chapman "a very distinct, melting-pot sort of flair." There are the "liberal, tree-hugging vegans." There are the "surfers," the "stoners," the "crazy frat boys," the "oblivious pleasure-seekers," "the quiet types, the rockers, and the preppy people." "There are also a lot of creative types," primarily "eccentric" "film geeks" who "love movies and enjoy watching, making, and talking about movies."

FINANCIAL AID: 714-997-6741 • E-MAIL: ADMIT@CHAPMAN.EDU • WEBSITE: WWW.CHAPMAN.EDU

THE PRINCETON REVIEW SAYS

Admissions

Very important factors considered include: Class rank, application essay, academic GPA, rigor of secondary school record, standardized test scores, character/personal qualities. *Important factors considered include:* Extracurricular activities, talent/ability, volunteer work. *Other factors considered include:* Recommendation(s), alumni/ae relation, first generation, geographical residence, racial/ethnic status, state residency, work experience. SAT Subject Tests recommended. SAT or ACT required. ACT with Writing component required. TOEFL required of all international applicants. High school diploma is required and GED is accepted. *Academic units required:* 2 English, 2 mathematics, 2 science (1 science lab), 2 foreign language, 3 social studies. *Academic units recommended:* 4 English, 3 mathematics, 3 science (1 science lab), 3 foreign language, 4 social studies.

Financial Aid

Students should submit: FAFSA, state aid form. The Princeton Review suggests that all financial aid forms be submitted as soon as possible after 1/1. *Need-based scholarships/grants offered:* Federal Pell, SEOG, state scholarships/grants, private scholarships, the school's own gift aid, Academic Competitiveness Grants. *Loan aid offered:* FFEL Subsidized Stafford, FFEL Unsubsidized Stafford, FFEL PLUS, Federal Perkins. Applicants will be notified of awards on a rolling basis beginning 3/15. Federal Work-Study Program available. Institutional employment available. Off-campus job opportunities are excellent.

Inside Word

Despite a plethora of California schools, Chapman continues to receive a steady stream of applications. Rather than work with formulas or cut-offs, admissions officers here prefer to take many factors into account. Well-rounded students are likely to make the most impact. Applicants who are service-oriented are also apt to do well, particularly given Chapman's "global responsibility" program.

THE SCHOOL SAYS "..."

From The Admissions Office

"During our 144-year history, Chapman has evolved from a small, church-related liberal arts college into a vibrant and comprehensive midsized liberal arts and sciences university distinguished for an eclectic group of nationally recognized programs including athletic training, film and television production, business and economics, dance, music, theater, writing, and teacher education. Our Orange County, California location was recently rated by *Places Rated Almanac* as "the number-one place to live in North America" citing superior climate, cultural, recreational, educational, and career entry opportunities.

"Chapman's environment is involving, and we seek students who are willing to enter an atmosphere of healthy competition where their talents will be nurtured and manifest to the fullest—whether in the classroom, on the stage, or on the athletic field. We challenge prospective students to thoroughly investigate our fine balance of liberal and professional learning so they may make a fully informed decision about 'fit' with regard to their personalities and that of the university.

"Chapman is a member of the Common Application group. Applicants for freshman admission to Chapman University will be required to submit scores from either the SAT or the ACT including the ACT Writing section."

SELECTIVITY

Admissions Rating	94
# of applicants	5,356
% of applicants accepted	50
% of acceptees attending	36
# accepting a place on wait list	134
% admitted from wait list	34

FRESHMAN PROFILE

Range SAT Critical Reading	548–666
Range SAT Math	561–674
Range SAT Writing	559–672
Range ACT Composite	25–29
Minimum paper TOEFL	550
Minimum computer TOEFL	213
Average HS GPA	3.65
% graduated top 10% of class	51
% graduated top 25% of class	92
% graduated top 50% of class	98

DEADLINES

Early action	
Deadline	11/15
Notification	1/10
Regular	
Deadline	1/15
Notification	rolling
Nonfall registration?	yes

APPLICANTS ALSO LOOK AT

AND OFTEN PREFER
New York University
University of Southern California
University of San Diego
Loyola Marymount University

AND SOMETIMES PREFER
Pepperdine University

FINANCIAL FACTS

Financial Aid Rating	96
Annual tuition	$35,790
Room and board	$12,832
Required fees	$974
Books and supplies	$1,200
% frosh rec. need-based scholarship or grant aid	60
% UG rec. need-based scholarship or grant aid	57
% frosh rec. need-based self-help aid	49
% UG rec. need-based self-help aid	49
% frosh rec. any financial aid	79
% UG rec. any financial aid	76
% UG borrow to pay for school	67
Average cumulative indebtedness	$22,955

CITY UNIVERSITY OF NEW YORK—BARUCH COLLEGE

ONE BERNARD BARUCH WAY, NEW YORK, NY 10010 • ADMISSIONS: 646-312-1400 • FAX: 646-312-1361

CAMPUS LIFE

Quality of Life Rating	74
Fire Safety Rating	60*
Green Rating	66
Type of school	public
Environment	metropolis

STUDENTS

Total undergrad enrollment	12,473
% male/female	48/52
% from out of state	4
% from public high school	72
% in (# of) fraternities	10 (9)
% in (# of) sororities	10 (7)
% African American	10
% Asian	31
% Caucasian	30
% Hispanic	17
% international	12
# of countries represented	151

SURVEY SAYS . . .
Great library
Diverse student types on campus
Students love New York, NY
Student publications are popular
Very little drug use

ACADEMICS

Academic Rating	73
Calendar	semester
Student/faculty ratio	18:1
Profs interesting rating	64
Profs accessible rating	64
% classes taught by TAs	1
Most common reg class size	20–29 students
Most common lab size	20–29 students

MOST POPULAR MAJORS
accounting
finance

STUDENTS SAY ". . ."

Academics

Baruch College consists of three schools, and although its School of Arts and Sciences and School of Public Affairs are both fine, it's the Zicklin School of Business that garners nearly all the attention here (as well over three-quarters of the student body). Zicklin offers a "very demanding business-oriented program that provides a great education in an overcrowded environment" where "it's very easy to get lost," but just as easy for go-getters to access "unparalleled internships, career, and networking opportunities to major global companies' headquarters." Because New York City is a worldwide finance capital, Baruch's connections and internships provide "a gateway to the world of finance," and it is for this reason—as well as for the fact that "tuition is about one-fourth what it is at NYU," making it "the best college value in New York City"—that students flock to Baruch. Students warn that you must be willing to "put 110 percent into your studies and take advantage of the NYC network and Starr Career Development Center" to reap all available benefits here. Those who make the effort will discover a career office that "works tirelessly to prepare its students for the working world. Not only do they offer workshops on how to make yourself an attractive candidate, they also offer counseling and even resume reviews to make sure your resume is perfect, as well as mock interviews that help you analyze your strengths and weaknesses as an interviewer."

Life

Baruch has no campus, just a collection of six buildings scattered over four city blocks. Most of the action centers around the 17-story Newman Vertical Campus facility, which is "beautiful" but "does not offer a lot of things to do" between classes. Furthermore, the mostly residential area surrounding the school offers "few places you can hang out at, especially when you have huge breaks between classes." Although the building is fairly new, "the escalators almost never work" and the elevators "are always as packed as the commute on the train." Many here grumpily opt for the stairway. School-related extracurriculars are hampered by the lack of a "real campus" and by the fact that many students are commuters who work part-time. Some get involved in community service and/or major-related clubs and organizations, but anyone coming here for a traditional college experience will be sorely disappointed. However access to New York City, for most, more than compensates for this drawback.

Student Body

The "hard-working" student body at Baruch could well be "the most diverse university in the country." It's the sort of place where "You can eat samosas on Tuesday, mooncakes on Wednesday, and falafel on Thursdays for free because of all the cultural events that are held." Students brag that "hundreds of countries are represented in our student body" and note that "The one common thread would be we are mostly business-oriented and have jobs/internships outside of school." While students get along well in class, outside the classroom they can be "very cliquey." One student explains, "If you know people from your high school, you stick with them; if you're a foreign student you stick with others from your home country. Otherwise you get the cold shoulder." Because "the school puts tremendous pressure on grades," most students are "extremely stressed."

CITY UNIVERSITY OF NEW YORK—BARUCH COLLEGE

FINANCIAL AID: 646-312-1360 • E-MAIL: ADMISSIONS@BARUCH.CUNY.EDU • WEBSITE: WWW.BARUCH.CUNY.EDU

THE PRINCETON REVIEW SAYS

Admissions

Very important factors considered include: Academic GPA, rigor of secondary school record, standardized test scores. *Important factors considered include:* Application essay, recommendation(s). *Other factors considered include:* Class rank, alumni/ae relation, character/personal qualities, extracurricular activities, interview, talent/ability, work experience. SAT or ACT required. TOEFL required of all international applicants. High school diploma is required and GED is accepted. *Academic units required:* 4 English, 3 mathematics, 2 science (2 science labs), 2 foreign language, 4 social studies. *Academic units recommended:* 4 mathematics, 3 foreign language, 1 academic elective.

Financial Aid

Students should submit: FAFSA, state aid form. Regular filing deadline is 4/30. The Princeton Review suggests that all financial aid forms be submitted as soon as possible after 1/1. *Need-based scholarships/grants offered:* Federal Pell, SEOG, state scholarships/grants, the school's own gift aid, City merit scholarships. *Loan aid offered:* Direct Subsidized Stafford, Direct Unsubsidized Stafford, Direct PLUS, Federal Perkins. Applicants will be notified of awards on a rolling basis beginning 4/1. Federal Work-Study Program available. Institutional employment available. Off-campus job opportunities are excellent.

The Inside Word

Baruchs business school greatly upgrades the school's profile in its hallmark academic field. Admissions have grown steadily more competitive since, especially for students seeking undergraduate business degrees. Today, Baruch receives nearly 10 applications for every slot in its freshman class. Your math scores on standardized tests count more heavily here than verbal scores.

THE SCHOOL SAYS " . . ."

From The Admissions Office

"Baruch College is in the heart of New York City. As an undergraduate, you will join a vibrant learning community of students and scholars in the middle of an exhilarating city full of possibilities. Baruch is a place where theory meets practice. You can network with city leaders; secure business, cultural, and non-profit internships; access the music, art, and business scene; and meet experts who visit our campus. You will take classes that bridge business, arts, science, and social policy, learning from professors who are among the best in their fields.

"Baruch offers 23 majors and 62 minors in three schools: the School of Public Affairs, the Weissman School of Arts and Science, and the Zicklin School of Business. Highly qualified undergraduates may apply to the Baruch College Honors program, which offers scholarships, small seminars and honors courses. Students may also study abroad through programs in 100 countries.

"Our seventeen-floor Newman Vertical Campus serves as the college's hub. Here you will find the atmosphere and resources of a traditional college campus, but in a lively urban setting. Our classrooms have state-of-the-art technology, and our library was named the top college library in the nation. Baruch also has a simulated trading floor for students who are interested in Wall Street. You can also enjoy a three-level athletics and recreation complex, which features a 25-meter indoor pool as well as a performing arts complex.

"Baruch's selective admission standards, strong academic programs, and top national honors make it an exceptional educational value."

SELECTIVITY

Admissions Rating	88
# of applicants	18,834
% of applicants accepted	24
% of acceptees attending	34

FRESHMAN PROFILE

Range SAT Critical Reading	480–590
Range SAT Math	550–660
Minimum paper TOEFL	620
Minimum computer TOEFL	260
Average HS GPA	3.15
% graduated top 10% of class	37
% graduated top 25% of class	66
% graduated top 50% of class	90

DEADLINES

Early decision	
Deadline	12/13
Notification	1/7
Regular	
Priority	3/15
Notification	rolling
Nonfall registration?	yes

APPLICANTS ALSO LOOK AT AND SOMETIMES PREFER

City University of New York—Hunter College

FINANCIAL FACTS

Financial Aid Rating	71
Annual in-state tuition	$4,000
Annual out-of-state tuition	$8,640
Required fees	$320
% frosh rec. need-based scholarship or grant aid	50
% UG rec. need-based scholarship or grant aid	59
% frosh rec. non-need-based scholarship or grant aid	69
% UG rec. non-need-based scholarship or grant aid	18
% frosh rec. need-based self-help aid	21
% UG rec. need-based self-help aid	20
% frosh rec. any financial aid	72
% UG rec. any financial aid	57
% UG borrow to pay for school	19
Average cumulative indebtedness	$14,159

CITY UNIVERSITY OF NEW YORK—BROOKLYN COLLEGE

2900 BEDFORD AVENUE, BROOKLYN, NY 11210-2889 • ADMISSIONS: 718-951-5001 • FAX: 718-951-4506

CAMPUS LIFE

Quality of Life Rating	64
Fire Safety Rating	60*
Green Rating	84
Type of school	public
Environment	metropolis

STUDENTS

Total undergrad enrollment	12,160
% male/female	40/60
% from out of state	2
% in (# of) fraternities	2 (8)
% in (# of) sororities	2 (8)
% African American	26
% Asian	14
% Caucasian	41
% Hispanic	12
% international	6

SURVEY SAYS . . .

Great library
Diverse student types on campus
(Almost) everyone smokes
Very little drug use

ACADEMICS

Academic Rating	64
Calendar	semester
Student/faculty ratio	15:1
Profs interesting rating	63
Profs accessible rating	63
Most common reg class size	20–29 students
Most common lab size	20–29 students

STUDENTS SAY ". . ."

Academics

Brooklyn College "is the perfect representative of Brooklyn as a borough and [of] success in the community," an institution that, like its home borough, "educates its students in an environment that reflects diversity, opportunity (study abroad, research, athletics, employment), and support." "Lauded as one of the best senior colleges in CUNY" and boasting "a beautiful campus," Brooklyn College entices a lot of bright students looking for an affordable, quality, undergraduate experience as well as some attracted by the school's relatively charitable admissions standards. It's easier to get in here than to stay in; Brooklyn College is "an academically challenging and rigorous school" that "feels a lot more competitive than one would anticipate." Professors "are fabulous" and "really passionate about the subjects that they teach and their students' career paths," although there are some "grumpy and nasty professors" that might best be avoided. Students are especially sanguine about special programs here, such as the various honors programs, in which "you will meet tons of highly intelligent people. Honors classes boast very good in-class discussions and highly vibrant, enthusiastic students. Non-honors classes are more run-of-the-mill but still very good academically." The school also works hard to provide "constant and innumerable job opportunities available to students and the Magner Center, which helps students find jobs and internships, and [to] help them prepare for the real world through resume writing workshops [and] job interview workshops." There are also "many financial awards available."

Life

"Apart from all the clubs and athletics on campus, most people come for class and then leave" at Brooklyn College because "we are a commuter school with no dorms, so it has to be this way. All social activities happen off campus." There are "pretty nice places to hang out around campus for the occasional coffee," and "there are a lot of student organization and a lot of activities done to help enhance student life on campus," but the "immediate surroundings of the Brooklyn College campus are generally not where you would want to stay for hours," and "on weekends the campus usually is dead." That said, "The campus is quite beautiful, and the quad during spring time is usually a nice place to sit and relax." Furthermore, "New York City hotspots are a 20- to 40-minute [subway] ride away," and Brooklyn itself is "a great place to live" where "there are always fun things happening."

Student Body

"The typical student at Brooklyn College is hard-working, from the NY metro area, and a commuter" (the last because there are no residence halls here). Many "hold part-time jobs and pay at least part of their own tuition, so they are usually in a rush because they have a lot more responsibility on their shoulders than the average college student." Like Brooklyn itself, "The student body is very diversified," with everyone from "an aspiring opera singer to quirky film majors to single mothers looking for a better life for their children," and so "no student can be described as being typical. Everyone blends in as normal, and little segregation is noticed (if it exists)." Students here represent more than 100 nations and speak nearly as many languages. There are even students "that come from Long Island to North Carolina, from Connecticut to even Hong Kong."

FINANCIAL AID: 718-951-5051 • E-MAIL: ADMINQRY@BROOKLYN.CUNY.EDU • WEBSITE: WWW.BROOKLYN.CUNY.EDU

THE PRINCETON REVIEW SAYS

Admissions

Very important factors considered include: Academic GPA, rigor of secondary school record, standardized test scores. *Other factors considered include:* Recommendation(s). SAT or ACT required. TOEFL required of all international applicants. High school diploma is required and GED is accepted. *Academic units recommended:* 4 English, 3 mathematics, 3 science, 3 foreign language, 4 social studies, 4 academic electives.

Financial Aid

Students should submit: FAFSA, state aid form. The Princeton Review suggests that all financial aid forms be submitted as soon as possible after 1/1. *Need-based scholarships/grants offered:* Federal Pell, SEOG, state scholarships/grants, private scholarships, the school's own gift aid. *Loan aid offered:* Direct Subsidized Stafford, Direct Unsubsidized Stafford, Direct PLUS, Federal Perkins. Applicants will be notified of awards on a rolling basis beginning 5/1. Federal Work-Study Program available. Institutional employment available. Off-campus job opportunities are excellent.

The Inside Word

Brooklyn College does not set the bar inordinately high; students with less-than-stellar high school records can receive a chance to prove themselves here. Once they get in, though, they'd better be prepared to work; Brooklyn College typically loses about 20 percent of its freshman class each year, and 6-year graduation rates rarely exceed 50 percent. Getting into Brooklyn College is one thing; surviving its academic challenges is a whole other thing entirely.

THE SCHOOL SAYS "..."

From The Admissions Office

"Brooklyn College, a premier public liberal arts college founded in 1930. For the last five years it has been designated as one of "America's Best Value Colleges" by the Princeton Review and, in 2009, was cited as one of the top 50 Best-Value Public Colleges in the nation.

"Respected nationally for its rigorous academic standards, the college has increased both the size and academic quality of its student body. It takes pride in such innovative programs as its award-winning Freshman Year College; the Honors Academy, which houses six programs for high achievers; and the core curriculum. Its School of Education is ranked among the top twenty in the country. Brooklyn College's strong academic reputation has attracted an outstanding faculty of nationally renowned teachers and scholars. Among the awards they have won are Pulitzers, Guggenheims, Fulbrights, and National Institutes of Health grants.

"The student body consists of more than 16,000 undergraduate and graduate students who represent the ethnic and cultural diversity of the borough. The College's accessibility by subway or bus allows students to further enrich their educational experience through New York City's many cultural events and institutions. In recent years, student achievements have been acknowledged with Rhodes, Fulbright, and Truman Scholarships and an Emmy Award.

"The Brooklyn College campus, considered to be among the most beautiful in the nation, is in the midst of an ambitious program of expansion and renewal. The dazzling new library is the most technologically advanced educational and research facility in the CUNY system and we are building a student residence hall off-campus and expects to open for the fall 2009 semester. The West Quad Building, a state-of-the-art student services and physical education facility, will also open in fall 2009. Ground will be broken soon for a new performing arts center, followed in the coming years with a new science complex."

SELECTIVITY

Admissions Rating	**80**
# of applicants	16,190
% of applicants accepted	35
% of acceptees attending	24

FRESHMAN PROFILE

Range SAT Critical Reading	450–570
Range SAT Math	480–590
Minimum paper TOEFL	500
Minimum computer TOEFL	173
Average HS GPA	3.3
% graduated top 10% of class	14
% graduated top 25% of class	49
% graduated top 50% of class	79

DEADLINES

Regular	
Priority	3/1
Notification	rolling
Nonfall registration?	yes

FINANCIAL FACTS

Financial Aid Rating	**96**
Annual in-state tuition	$4,000
Annual out-of-state tuition	$10,800
Required fees	$431
% frosh rec. need-based scholarship or grant aid	74
% UG rec. need-based scholarship or grant aid	66
% frosh rec. non-need-based scholarship or grant aid	24
% UG rec. non-need-based scholarship or grant aid	20
% frosh rec. need-based self-help aid	72
% UG rec. need-based self-help aid	69
% frosh rec. any financial aid	80
% UG rec. any financial aid	64
% UG borrow to pay for school	45
Average cumulative indebtedness	$16,000

CITY UNIVERSITY OF NEW YORK—HUNTER COLLEGE

695 PARK AVENUE, NEW YORK, NY 10021 • ADMISSIONS: 212-772-4490 • FAX: 212-650-3336

CAMPUS LIFE
Quality of Life Rating	**67**
Fire Safety Rating	**93**
Green Rating	**86**
Type of school	public
Environment	metropolis

STUDENTS
Total undergrad enrollment	14,700
% male/female	33/67
% from out of state	4.1
% from public high school	70
% in (# of) fraternities	1 (2)
% in (# of) sororities	(2)
% African American	12
% Asian	20
% Caucasian	39
% Hispanic	20
% international	10

SURVEY SAYS . . .
Diverse student types on campus
Different types of students interact
Students get along with local community
Students love New York, NY
Political activism is popular
Very little drug use

ACADEMICS
Academic Rating	**70**
Calendar	semester
Student/faculty ratio	15:1
Profs interesting rating	66
Profs accessible rating	62
Most common reg class size	20–29 students

MOST POPULAR MAJORS
accounting
English literature (British and commonwealth)
psychology

STUDENTS SAY ". . ."

Academics

Prospective students for looking for an academic "bang for the buck" in New York City should take a long look at Hunter College, the largest (in terms of enrollment) and most selective of the CUNY colleges. Physically, Hunter is a reflection of its hometown; more than 14,000 undergraduates attending classes in four buildings on three blocks of the Upper East Side, the "halls of Hunter College are extremely crowded." There are figurative similarities to the city, too. Like the Big Apple itself, Hunter has a ton to offer academically, but it's not just handed to you: "The academic experience can be inspiring or painfully dull, depending on one's interests, motivation, and desire to be challenged intellectually, as well as luck." Take professors, for example: "Many professors are accomplished and respected," are "often winners of the highest awards in their chosen profession[s], work as professionals in New York City, and are excellent contacts for further academic pursuits or for work after college." Others are "graduate students with limited experience or time" for students. Moreover, "dealing with administrative matters at this school is not for the faint of heart," and "run-of-the mill transactions (processing of financial aid paperwork, registering for classes)" can "devour hours of your life." But students assure us that "if you are self-motivated you'll be fine." Registration is tough "because everyone is competing against each other for classes," but on the upside, "Hunter's class schedule is very accommodating to people who work either part or full time," and "evening classes are abundant."

Life

As a commuter school, "There isn't as much campus life as you would find in other schools." Only about 600 of Hunter's 14,700 undergraduates live in the college's lone residence hall, and of the vast majority of students who are commuters, many simply "have too much going on outside of school to try to experience all that college life has to offer." But that's not to say that school unity is totally lacking. In lieu of residence life bonding experiences, "clubs are very good at connecting people with similar interests." Plus, during the school day, "There are plenty of places [around campus] to just lounge with friends." Off campus—the question is, what *isn't* there? For those who like to unwind outside, "the school is close to Central Park." For the more urban-minded, "there are concerts, Broadway plays, and comedy shows." There are "movies," "great restaurants, bars, nightclubs, and shopping." And let's not forget that this is New York City; "just walking down the street can be a very entertaining experience."

Student Body

The typical Hunter student "is from one of the five boroughs and commutes to school every day." That's pretty much where generalizations of the student body end. Hunter College has made repeated appearances on this publication's "Diverse Student Population" top 20 ranking list, and for good reason. "In terms of socioeconomic status, immigrants, languages, cultures, religion, race, ethnicity, age…Hunter has it all." "Students range in age from newly graduated high schoolers to retirees." And "There really doesn't seem to be [a] dominant ethnic group." It's the kind of place where "nothing seems too out of the ordinary," "everyone fits in fine," and where it won't surprise you to see a "white punk-rock girl having a friendly conversation with a Muslim girl in the full head-to-toe [garb]." If you must generalize, it's easier to say what most Hunter students are not. This list is short: "out-of-state students" who are "not liberal."

City University of New York—Hunter College

Financial Aid: 212-772-4820 • E-mail: admissions@hunter.cuny.edu • Website: www.hunter.cuny.edu

THE PRINCETON REVIEW SAYS

Admissions

Very important factors considered include: Application essay, academic GPA, rigor of secondary school record, standardized test scores. SAT or ACT required. TOEFL required of all international applicants. High school diploma is required and GED is accepted. *Academic units required:* 2 English, 2 mathematics, 1 science (1 science lab). *Academic units recommended:* 4 English, 3 mathematics, 2 science, 2 foreign language, 4 social studies, 1 visual/performing arts, 1 academic elective.

Financial Aid

Students should submit: FAFSA, state aid form. The Princeton Review suggests that all financial aid forms be submitted as soon as possible after 1/1. *Need-based scholarships/grants offered:* Federal Pell, state scholarships/grants, the school's own gift aid. *Loan aid offered:* Direct Subsidized Stafford, Direct Unsubsidized Stafford, Direct PLUS, Federal Perkins, state loans, college/university loans from institutional funds, CUNY Student Assistance Program (CUSTA), Aide for Part-Time-Study (APTS), SEEK. Applicants will be notified of awards on a rolling basis beginning 5/15. Federal Work-Study Program available. Institutional employment available. Off-campus job opportunities are fair.

The Inside Word

In terms of statistics, Hunter College is the most selective of the CUNY undergraduate colleges, but this doesn't mean that you have to be an academic superstar in high school to be admitted. Hunter is, after all, first and foremost a CUNY, dedicated to educating the citizens of New York City. But given an applicant pool comprised mainly of New York City residents, high school grades and test scores are the main factors separating those admitted from those who are not. If you are planning to apply to Hunter's Honors College, note that applications are due December 15, rather than on the regular application deadline of March 15.

THE SCHOOL SAYS "..."

From The Admissions Office

"Located in the heart of Manhattan, Hunter offers students the stimulating learning environment and career-building opportunities you might expect from a college that's been a part of the world's most exciting city since 1870. The largest college in the City University of New York, Hunter pulses with energy. Hunter's vitality stems from a large, highly diverse faculty and student body. Its schools—Arts and Sciences, Education, the Health Professions, and Social Work—provide an affordable first-rate education. Undergraduates have extraordinary opportunities to conduct high-level research under renowned faculty, and many opt for credit-bearing internships in such exciting fields as media, the arts, and government. The college's high standards and special programs ensure a challenging education. The Block Program for first-year students keeps classmates together as they pursue courses in the liberal arts, pre-health science, pre-nursing, premed, or honors. A range of honors programs is available for students with strong academic records, including the highly competitive tuition-free Hunter CUNY Honors College for entering freshmen and the Thomas Hunter Honors Program, which emphasizes small classes with personalized mentoring by outstanding faculty. Qualified students also benefit from Hunter's participation in minority science research and training programs, the prestigious Andrew W. Mellon Minority Undergraduate Program, and many other passports to professional success.

"Applicants for the entering class are required to take either the SAT or the ACT."

SELECTIVITY

Admissions Rating	85
# of applicants	27,866
% of applicants accepted	28
% of acceptees attending	26

FRESHMAN PROFILE

Range SAT Critical Reading	490–580
Range SAT Math	510–610
Minimum paper TOEFL	500
Minimum computer TOEFL	173

DEADLINES

Regular	
Deadline	3/15
Notification	rolling
Nonfall registration?	yes

FINANCIAL FACTS

Financial Aid Rating	84
Annual in-state tuition	$4,000
Annual out-of-state tuition	$10,800
Room and board	$3,500
Required fees	$399
% frosh rec. need-based scholarship or grant aid	54
% UG rec. need-based scholarship or grant aid	38
% frosh rec. non-need-based scholarship or grant aid	42
% UG rec. non-need-based scholarship or grant aid	14
% frosh rec. need-based self-help aid	10
% UG rec. need-based self-help aid	16
% frosh rec. any financial aid	91
% UG rec. any financial aid	94
% UG borrow to pay for school	41
Average cumulative indebtedness	$7,125

City University of New York—Queens College

65-30 Kissena Boulevard, Flushing, NY 11367 • Admissions: 718-997-5000 • Fax: 718-997-5617

CAMPUS LIFE

Quality of Life Rating	**67**
Fire Safety Rating	**60***
Green Rating	**60***
Type of school	public
Environment	metropolis

STUDENTS

Total undergrad enrollment	14,497
% male/female	40/60
% from out of state	1
% in (# of) fraternities	1 (4)
% in (# of) sororities	1 (3)
% African American	9
% Asian	22
% Caucasian	45
% Hispanic	18
% international	6
# of countries represented	140

SURVEY SAYS . . .

Diverse student types on campus
Students get along with local
community
Students love Flushing, NY
Students are happy
Musical organizations are popular
Very little beer drinking
Very little drug use

ACADEMICS

Academic Rating	**72**
Calendar	semester
Student/faculty ratio	15:1
Profs interesting rating	65
Profs accessible rating	63
% classes taught by TAs	1
Most common	
reg class size	20–29 students

MOST POPULAR MAJORS

accounting
psychology
sociology

STUDENTS SAY ". . ."

Academics

New York state residents can get "a great education for a cheap price" at Queens College, one of the premier campuses of the City University of New York system. The school's affordable tuition "gives many students a chance to get a higher education." Some here go so far as to call QC "the Harvard of the CUNY system," although students at Baruch, Hunter, City College, and Brooklyn College would probably beg to differ. Regardless of its relative status in the CUNY system, QC undoubtedly provides "great and challenging programs" that are "unique and comprehensive, and are compatible [with one's objectives]." QC serves primarily a commuter population focused on "building career opportunities" by "getting an education in service of your future profession (and maybe having some fun)." Accounting, psychology, and sociology are among the most popular majors, and is also home to a competitive school of music. Students tell us that "the administration is okay—comparable to any other out there," and teachers here are surprisingly "easy to talk to and very helpful, not at all intimidating." "You're not afraid to express yourself in class." Students also say smaller classes and "more students in campus involvement" would be nice, but overall they are satisfied with the college's "multicultural feast sprinkled with a quasi-intellectual environment."

Life

Queens College "is [primarily] a commuter school, so campus life is not very lively." However this may be changing. As of August '09, the school plans to open a residence hall. Its students are "education- and career-oriented." Many "Students work part-time jobs so they really do not have much time left for other activities." Even so, "Queens has a strong community that is diverse and conducive to positive social interactions and communication." The campus is home to tons of "clubs and organizations," and those with the time to do so report that "joining a club helps make the experience at Queens College worthwhile." One student writes, "Political clubs are pretty popular. A lot of times there are club fairs on the grass. Also, anyone can play club sports. The girls could join the soccer club with the boys if they wanted to." While few students stick around campus once their final classes for the day are done, "between classes students lounge around in the cafeterias or Student Union to talk with friends." Undergrads tell us that there are events to go to "almost every day of the week," in part because the school's New York City location allows it to attract some prominent speakers. The QC campus is large and sports a surprising expanse of green space for an urban campus. Queens is a truly international borough and the area surrounding QC is no exception; right outside the campus gates students will find restaurants serving everything from Kosher to Korean, from cannolis to Cantonese.

Student Body

"There is no 'typical' student at Queens College, and that's what's great about the student body," say the students who belong to this "diverse and dedicated community." "Every racial background imaginable is represented and has a group [on campus], and every religious background is apparent." QC is a place where "everywhere you turn people are able to speak more than one language." There is also plenty of diversity in personality types. "Most students are very different and that makes it easy for everybody to fit in." Although all students tend to be "very focused," expect "some very religious students" and some nonbelievers as well. In short, "Everyone is unique" here, but students across the board "work hard, and are eager to learn," and "this is something that bonds people together."

CITY UNIVERSITY OF NEW YORK—QUEENS COLLEGE

FINANCIAL AID: 718-997-5101 • E-MAIL: ADMISSIONS@QC.EDU • WEBSITE: WWW.QC.EDU

THE PRINCETON REVIEW SAYS

Admissions

Very important factors considered include: Academic GPA, rigor of secondary school record, standardized test scores. SAT Subject Tests recommended; SAT or ACT required; TOEFL required of all international applicants. High school diploma is required and GED is accepted. *Academic units required:* 4 English, 3 mathematics, 2 science, (2 science labs), 3 foreign language, 4 social studies. *Academic units recommended:* 3 science, (3 science labs).

Financial Aid

Students should submit: FAFSA, institution's own financial aid form, state aid form. The Princeton Review suggests that all financial aid forms be submitted as soon as possible after 1/1. *Need-based scholarships/grants offered:* Federal Pell, SEOG, state scholarships/grants, private scholarships, the school's own gift aid. *Loan aid offered:* Direct Subsidized Stafford, Direct Unsubsidized Stafford, Direct PLUS, Federal Perkins. Applicants will be notified of awards on a rolling basis beginning 3/1. Federal Work-Study Program available. Institutional employment available. Off-campus job opportunities are good.

The Inside Word

Minority enrollment has declined at CUNY in the past 7 years, partially as a result of changes to admissions criteria and stiffer competition for minority applicants. The school would love to boost its numbers, meaning that qualified minority students could be able to finagle a pretty nice financial aid package here, making an already economical education even more affordable.

THE SCHOOL SAYS "..."

From The Admissions Office

"At Queens College, you will engage the world of ideas with faculty and students from the world over, prepare for your career, and enjoy the many activities our beautiful, 77-acre campus has to offer. And with the August 2009 opening of The Summit—our new residence hall—you'll find a place to enjoy everything that comes with a college residential experience.

"Since 1937, we've provided a premier liberal arts education to talented students. From graduate and undergraduate degrees, a variety of honors and pre-professional programs to research and real-work internship opportunities, you'll find countless ways to realize your potential under the guidance of our award-winning, dedicated faculty. We offer nationally recognized programs—such as our Aaron Copland School of Music—in many fields. And we're also the ideal choice for aspiring teachers, preparing more future educators than any college in the tri-state area.

"Located only minutes from Manhattan, our campus boasts a traditional quad overlooking the skyline. You'll find a stimulating and welcoming environment here, with a bustling student union, an impressive arts center, and opportunities to participate in dozens of clubs and sports. (We're the only City University of New York college to participate in Division II.) Campus-wide wi-fi, computer kiosks, and cybercafes keep you informed and in touch. And best of all, as part of CUNY, we can offer all this at an affordable cost. To apply for Fall 2010, submit your application online along with your SATs comprising Critical Reading, Writing, and Math."

SELECTIVITY

Admissions Rating	60*
# of applicants	15,724
% of applicants accepted	38
% of acceptees attending	28

FRESHMAN PROFILE

Range SAT Critical Reading	450–550
Range SAT Math	480–580
Range SAT Writing	490–550
Minimum paper TOEFL	500
Minimum computer TOEFL	173
Minimum web-based TOEFL	62

DEADLINES

Regular	
Priority	1/1
Notification	rolling
Nonfall registration?	yes

FINANCIAL FACTS

Financial Aid Rating	63
Annual in-state tuition	$4,000
Annual out-of-state tuition	$8,640
Required fees	$447
% frosh rec. need-based scholarship or grant aid	36
% UG rec. need-based scholarship or grant aid	46
% frosh rec. non-need-based scholarship or grant aid	27
% UG rec. non-need-based scholarship or grant aid	10
% frosh rec. need-based self-help aid	22
% UG rec. need-based self-help aid	15
% frosh rec. athletic scholarships	2
% UG rec. athletic scholarships	1
% frosh rec. any financial aid	50
% UG rec. any financial aid	50
% UG borrow to pay for school	41
Average cumulative indebtedness	$14,000

CLAREMONT McKENNA COLLEGE

890 COLUMBIA AVENUE, CLAREMONT, CA 91711 • ADMISSIONS: 909-621-8088 • FAX: 909-621-8516

CAMPUS LIFE

Quality of Life Rating	99
Fire Safety Rating	89
Green Rating	93
Type of school	private
Environment	town

STUDENTS

Total undergrad enrollment	1,212
% male/female	54/46
% from out of state	54
% from public high school	70
% live on campus	98
% African American	4
% Asian	12
% Caucasian	50
% Hispanic	11
% international	6
# of countries represented	24

SURVEY SAYS . . .

School is well run
Great food on campus
Dorms are like palaces
Frats and sororities are unpopular or
nonexistent
Student government is popular
Political activism is popular

ACADEMICS

Academic Rating	97
Calendar	semester
Student/faculty ratio	8:1
Profs interesting rating	96
Profs accessible rating	98
Most common reg class size	10–19 students

MOST POPULAR MAJORS
economics
international relations and affairs
political science and government

STUDENTS SAY ". . ."

Academics

It's almost awkward the way students at Claremont McKenna College gush about their "pragmatic" little liberal arts school. "There is no better place to come to college," promises a sophomore. CMC offers small classes and a "challenging academic environment." "Classes kick my butt, but I keep coming back for more," admits a biology major. Courses also tend toward discussion, and CMCers report that "your beliefs and ideologies will be challenged whether you like it or not." There are "super boring" profs but, generally, "professors are here because they want to teach and their enthusiasm is palpable." The faculty is "on a completely different level of accessibility" as well. Administratively, CMC is among "the best-run" anywhere. Even the folks in financial aid are "amazing." The broad core curriculum includes a mandatory senior thesis. Resources are "vast." "Students have the opportunity to get involved with nearly anything they can think of, and mostly with the college footing the bill." A wealth of institutes allows undergrads to participate in research. Internships and study abroad (and internships abroad) are readily available. The Claremont Colleges Consortium allows students to supplement their curricula with classes at four other schools. The Athenaeum brings a slew of "prominent speakers" to campus (e.g., Bill Clinton, Antonin Scalia, and Bono). Great programs here include many in the hard sciences and some students loathe the notion that CMC is purely based on economics and government. However, the fact is that "the school is incredibly focused on those fields."

Life

CMC's campus is "constantly abuzz with activity." There are so many events around the Claremont campuses "that you constantly have to sacrifice one for another." Intramural and varsity sports enjoy tremendous popularity even though CMC's athletics facilities *really* need improvement." "Food is good and healthy, dorms are big and spacious, and the campus is always green and sunny." "People are always outside." There's also a "vibrant" political atmosphere. These students "debate politics 24/7." "It's common to overhear very complex political discussion as you walk by people who appear to be casually conversing." The level of debauchery is solid if not outstanding. If you don't drink, "it doesn't make you uncool." On the whole, though, "people at CMC party." They also "know how to manage their time well" because, in addition to all the diversions, there are "bundles of work." "Learn to balance them," warns one student, "or you will be screwed." "The school is very academic from Sunday till Thursday. Then everyone parties Thursday, Friday, and Saturday." The festivities "are open to everyone, as there are no frats." There are many "big, school-sponsored outdoor parties that are generally themed." "The student government buys us alcohol and that's important," notes a junior. The other Five C's throw a lot of bashes, too. "There will always be a big party somewhere, and there will usually be free drinks."

Student Body

"People here are smart, and they have a pretty good idea of what they want to do in their life and what has to get done in order for them to be able to do it." CMCers are "driven," "extremely career oriented," and "incredibly ambitious." More than two-thirds end up with advanced degrees. The typical student "drinks a lot but studies like a slave." Some "would trade their soul for a keg or an internship." "CMC students are all closet nerds," reflects a senior. "They look like normal people, work out a lot, love to go outside on sunny days and throw footballs around, play some video games, and drink a lot of beer. On the other hand, they talk about politics, investment strategy and economics, philosophy, and science while doing all those things." Many students are "relatively rich" but others come "from less affluent backgrounds" thanks to generous financial aid packages. "Very few students can be described as reclusive." "You won't see too many students with dyed hair," either. Politically, CMC has a conservative reputation but liberalism flourishes just fine here. "I think the number of Democrats outweighs the number of Republicans, but only slightly," estimates a junior.

FINANCIAL AID: 909-621-8356 • E-MAIL: ADMISSION@CLAREMONTMCKENNA.EDU • WEBSITE: WWW.CLAREMONTMCKENNA.EDU

THE PRINCETON REVIEW SAYS

Admissions

Very important factors considered include: Rigor of secondary school record, standardized test scores, extracurricular activities. *Important factors considered include:* Application essay, recommendation(s), volunteer work. *Other factors considered include:* Academic GPA, alumni/ae relation, first generation, geographical residence, interview, racial/ethnic status, talent/ability, work experience. SAT or ACT required. ACT with Writing component required. TOEFL required of all international applicants. High school diploma is required and GED is accepted. *Academic units required:* 4 English, 3 mathematics, 2 science (2 science labs), 3 foreign language, 1 social studies, 1 history. *Academic units recommended:* 4 mathematics, 3 science.

Financial Aid

Students should submit: FAFSA, CSS/financial aid profile. Regular filing deadline is 2/1. The Princeton Review suggests that all financial aid forms be submitted as soon as possible after 1/1. *Need-based scholarships/grants offered:* Federal Pell, SEOG, state scholarships/grants, private scholarships, the school's own gift aid. *Loan aid offered:* FFEL Subsidized Stafford, FFEL Unsubsidized Stafford, FFEL PLUS, Federal Perkins. Applicants will be notified of awards on or about 4/1. Federal Work-Study Program available. Institutional employment available. Off-campus job opportunities are excellent.

The Inside Word

Although applicants have to possess exemplary academic qualifications to gain admission to Claremont McKenna, the importance of making a good match should not be underestimated. Colleges of such small size and selectivity devote much more energy to determining whether the candidate as an individual fits instead of whether a candidate has the appropriate test scores.

THE SCHOOL SAYS "..."

From The Admissions Office

"CMC's mission is clear: To educate students for meaningful lives and responsible leadership in business, government, and many other professions. While many other colleges champion either a traditional liberal arts education with emphasis on intellectual breadth or training that stresses acquisition of technical skills, CMC offers a clear alternative. Instead of dividing the liberal arts and working world into separate realms, education at CMC is rooted in the interplay between the world of ideas and the world of events. By combining the intellectual breadth of liberal arts with the more pragmatic concerns of public affairs, CMC students gain the vision, skills, and values necessary for leadership in all sectors of society.

"Applicants must take the SAT Reasoning Test or ACT with Writing. We will use the highest scores from the SAT or ACT. SAT Subject Tests are recommended but not required."

SELECTIVITY

Admissions Rating	98
# of applicants	3,670
% of applicants accepted	22
% of acceptees attending	40
# accepting a place on wait list	222
# of early decision applicants	316
% accepted early decision	28

FRESHMAN PROFILE

Range SAT Critical Reading	630–740
Range SAT Math	660–750
Minimum paper TOEFL	600
Minimum computer TOEFL	250
Minimum web-based TOEFL	100
% graduated top 10% of class	85
% graduated top 25% of class	98
% graduated top 50% of class	100

DEADLINES

Early decision	
Deadline	11/15
Notification	12/15
Regular	
Deadline	1/2
Notification	4/1
Nonfall registration?	no

APPLICANTS ALSO LOOK AT

AND OFTEN PREFER
Harvard College
Stanford University
Princeton University

AND SOMETIMES PREFER
Washington University in St. Louis
Pomona College
Georgetown University
Williams College
University of Pennsylvania

AND RARELY PREFER
Pitzer College
University of Southern California
Tufts University

FINANCIAL FACTS

Financial Aid Rating	99
Annual tuition	$34,980
Books and supplies	$1,850
% frosh rec. need-based scholarship or grant aid	45
% UG rec. need-based scholarship or grant aid	44
% frosh rec. non-need-based scholarship or grant aid	7
% UG rec. non-need-based scholarship or grant aid	7
% frosh rec. need-based self-help aid	30
% UG rec. need-based self-help aid	27
% frosh rec. any financial aid	45
% UG rec. any financial aid	51
% UG borrow to pay for school	35
Average cumulative indebtedness	$11,164

CLARK UNIVERSITY

950 MAIN STREET, WORCESTER, MA 01610-1477 • ADMISSIONS: 508-793-7431 • FAX: 508-793-8821

CAMPUS LIFE

Quality of Life Rating	72
Fire Safety Rating	96
Green Rating	87
Type of school	private
Environment	city

STUDENTS

Total undergrad enrollment	2,293
% male/female	40/60
% from out of state	64
% from public high school	70
% live on campus	76
% African American	2
% Asian	4
% Caucasian	68
% Hispanic	2
% international	8
# of countries represented	63

SURVEY SAYS . . .

Lots of liberal students
No one cheats
Students are friendly
Frats and sororities are unpopular or
nonexistent
Political activism is popular

ACADEMICS

Academic Rating	84
Calendar	semester
Student/faculty ratio	10:1
Profs interesting rating	83
Profs accessible rating	84
Most common reg class size	10–19 students
Most common lab size	10–19 students

MOST POPULAR MAJORS

biology/biological sciences
political science and government
psychology

STUDENTS SAY ". . ."

Academics

Clark University is a "vibrant," "left-wing" liberal arts school in Worcester, Massachusetts. There are "good research opportunities" and standout offerings in psychology, geography, and the hard sciences. Clark also offers an accelerated, one-year Master's program in several majors at no extra charge. Coursework is "hard but doable." "I am challenged but not burned out," reports an English major. "Overall, you'll get a lot out of Clark if you're willing to work for it." "The small size is very comfortable and welcoming" and "Class discussions are often interesting and enlightening." Professors are generally "committed to facilitating their students' education." "Most get very enthusiastic when teaching." "I've never had a class here with a sage on a stage who just stands behind a lectern and reads from their lecture notes without making eye contact," reports a government major. "My professors have always been available outside of class for help," adds a business major. However, there are also some "utter bores" who "really don't seem to know what they are teaching." The range of classes is "limited" as well. "There is not much variety" and popular courses "fill up fast." Views of the administration are very mixed. Some students call management "nondescript." Others contend that Clark's bureaucracy "rivals some small countries." Still others insist that the brass is "very visible and accessible" and "tries to listen to what the students want."

Life

Some buildings on Clark's "pretty compact" campus are "falling apart." Some classrooms are "kind of crappy." "The food leaves something to be desired," too. "Please send frozen dinners," begs a sophomore. Socially, there's a community feel. Many students are involved in community service and various kinds of activism. "Politics play a huge role." "Every student here believes strongly in something, which makes for an interesting campus." "There aren't big turnouts" at athletic events. "Students are actually more likely to attend a lecture on refugees from Rwanda than a basketball game," predicts a senior. "Many students hang out in small groups in their dorms, suites, or apartments." "There's a substance-free scene." There's also "plenty of weed and alcohol with dabbles here and there into harder drugs." "Clark isn't a major party school," though. "People here like to be mellow." "The area around the school isn't the greatest" but some students tell us that Worcester is "a perfectly good place to go to school." "Nightlife off campus is fun," they say, and "there are so many restaurants, it's ridiculous." Also, the "extremely active" Colleges of Worcester Consortium allows students to attend classes and events at several nearby schools. Others students complain that "the city of Worcester is depressing and gloomy at best." "It's unfortunate that Clark is where it is," laments one Clarkie. When students want to escape, Boston isn't too far.

Student Body

"If you couldn't find your niche in high school, you will probably find it at Clark," advises a junior. "It is kind of a haven for the awkward and slightly awkward." Clarkies are an "eclectic" "collection of independent minds." "There's a little of everything." "You can carve your own path here without being a loner." Conservatives are "accepted with curiosity" but most students are "socially conscious" types who "scream their bleeding liberal hearts out at any given cause of the week." Clark also "has an artsy feel." "Hipsteresque" "groovy people" who "dress sloppily in expensive clothes" are numerous. Jocks are here but they are "in the vast minority." "The closet-rich hippie" is not uncommon. However, many students tell us that Clark's flower-power reputation is unwarranted. "Sure, there are maybe a token five students who don't wear shoes, don't shower as often as most people would like, and own bongos," asserts a sophomore, "but three of them are posers anyway." You'll find "various sexual orientations" at Clark but ethnic diversity is pretty limited. There is a strong contingent of Jewish students and a large population of "filthy rich" international students but little in the way of traditionally underrepresented minorities.

CLARK UNIVERSITY

FINANCIAL AID: 508-793-7478 • E-MAIL: ADMISSIONS@CLARKU.EDU • WEBSITE: WWW.CLARKU.EDU

THE PRINCETON REVIEW SAYS

Admissions

Very important factors considered include: Academic GPA, recommendation(s), rigor of secondary school record, standardized test scores, character/personal qualities. *Important factors considered include:* Application essay, extracurricular activities, talent/ability, volunteer work. *Other factors considered include:* Class rank, alumni/ae relation, first generation, geographical residence, interview, level of applicant's interest, racial/ethnic status, work experience. SAT or ACT required. TOEFL required of all international applicants. High school diploma is required and GED is accepted. *Academic units recommended:* 4 English, 3 mathematics, 3 science (2 science labs), 2 foreign language, 2 social studies, 2 history.

Financial Aid

Students should submit: FAFSA, CSS/financial aid profile. Regular filing deadline is 2/1. The Princeton Review suggests that all financial aid forms be submitted as soon as possible after 1/1. *Need-based scholarships/grants offered:* Federal Pell, SEOG, state scholarships/grants, the school's own gift aid. *Loan aid offered:* FFEL Subsidized Stafford, FFEL Unsubsidized Stafford, FFEL PLUS, Federal Perkins, state loans. Applicants will be notified of awards on or about 3/31. Federal Work-Study Program available. Institutional employment available. Off-campus job opportunities are good.

The Inside Word

Clark is surrounded by formidable competitors, and its selectivity suffers because of it. Most B students will encounter little difficulty gaining admission. Given the university's solid academic environment and access to other member colleges in the Worcester Consortium, it can be a terrific choice for students who are not up to the ultra-competitive admission expectations of "top-tier" universities.

THE SCHOOL SAYS "..."

From The Admissions Office

"Clark University prepares students to make a meaningful difference in a world hungry for change.

"Our vibrant intellectual life is an outgrowth of a dedicated faculty who are as passionate about teaching and mentoring as they are about generating new knowledge. As undergraduates, Clark students have an array of opportunities to not only study with award-winning researchers but also to work at their side in pursuit of solutions to pressing global problems.

"This approach to education—learning through inquiry—is just one of the three distinguishing features of a Clark education. The other two are making a difference and experiencing diverse cultures. Each permeates campus life in many ways: through rigorous academic courses, independent projects, internships and other educational experiences; through research and social action, both locally and globally; and through interactions with the dynamic members of the Clark community and study-abroad experiences. Students also have the possibility of earning a bachelor's and master's degree in five years, with the fifth year is tuition free.

"Clark's status as a small research university grounded in the liberal arts, its urban location, and its tradition of community partnerships place Clark students in an ideal position to breathe life into the University's motto, "Challenge convention, change our world."

"Clark requires that students submit scores from the SAT. Students will be judged by their performance in Critical Reading and Math; Clark does not look at the results of the Writing section."

SELECTIVITY
Admissions Rating	90
# of applicants	5,201
% of applicants accepted	56
% of acceptees attending	20
# accepting a place on wait list	28
% admitted from wait list	25
# of early decision applicants	90
% accepted early decision	84

FRESHMAN PROFILE
Range SAT Critical Reading	553–660
Range SAT Math	543–650
Range ACT Composite	24–28
Minimum paper TOEFL	550
Minimum computer TOEFL	213
Average HS GPA	3.47
% graduated top 10% of class	32
% graduated top 25% of class	74
% graduated top 50% of class	98

DEADLINES
Early decision	
Deadline	11/15
Notification	12/15
Regular	
Deadline	1/15
Notification	4/1
Nonfall registration?	yes

APPLICANTS ALSO LOOK AT
AND OFTEN PREFER
Brandeis University
Boston College
Boston University
AND SOMETIMES PREFER
Northeastern University
Skidmore College
AND RARELY PREFER
University of Massachusetts—Amherst
Wheaton College (MA)

FINANCIAL FACTS
Financial Aid Rating	92
Annual tuition	$33,900
Room and board	$6,650
Required fees	$320
Books and supplies	$800
% frosh rec. need-based scholarship or grant aid	52
% UG rec. need-based scholarship or grant aid	52
% frosh rec. non-need-based scholarship or grant aid	31
% UG rec. non-need-based scholarship or grant aid	31
% frosh rec. need-based self-help aid	45
% UG rec. need-based self-help aid	45
% frosh rec. any financial aid	78
% UG rec. any financial aid	81
% UG borrow to pay for school	99
Average cumulative indebtedness	$21,100

CLARKSON UNIVERSITY

PO Box 5605, Potsdam, NY 13699 • Admissions: 315-268-6479 • Fax: 315-268-7647

CAMPUS LIFE

Quality of Life Rating	62
Fire Safety Rating	74
Green Rating	95
Type of school	private
Environment	village

STUDENTS

Total undergrad enrollment	2,584
% male/female	73/27
% from out of state	27
% from public high school	84
% live on campus	82
% in (# of) fraternities	12 (10)
% in (# of) sororities	13 (3)
% African American	3
% Asian	3
% Caucasian	88
% Hispanic	3
% international	3
# of countries represented	39

SURVEY SAYS . . .

Class discussions are rare
Career services are great
Students are friendly
Students aren't religious
Low cost of living
Everyone loves the Golden Knights
Lots of beer drinking
Hard liquor is popular

ACADEMICS

Academic Rating	68
Calendar	semester
Student/faculty ratio	15.3:1
Profs interesting rating	64
Profs accessible rating	72
% classes taught by TAs	1
Most common reg class size	10–19 students
Most common lab size	10–19 students

MOST POPULAR MAJORS
biology/biological sciences
business/commerce
engineering

STUDENTS SAY "..."

Academics

A "demanding," "hands-on," and "absolutely innovative" academic environment is the big draw at tech-heavy Clarkson University in the "frozen wasteland" of northern New York. The hard sciences and other fields "are growing," but Clarkson basically remains an "engineering school with some business classes." For engineers, "Clarkson is all about preparing you for the ridiculous amount of work you will get in the real world by giving you an even more ridiculous amount of work." Outstanding programs for business majors include entrepreneurship and supply-chain management. Classroom discussion is generally rare here and the faculty gets wildly mixed reviews, which is pretty normal wherever techies congregate. Some professors are "super friendly" and "willing to meet outside of their office hours." "Others couldn't teach at elementary schools" and are "more interested in their own research than their classes." Opinions concerning the administration also vary. Some students call management "very visible" and "truly concerned about student life," others strongly disagree." "I feel like they market to get students in," vents a senior, "and then really drop the ball." We would be remiss if we did not also add that a few students consider Clarkson's library to be "worthless." Opportunities "for co-ops, internships, and jobs" are a great feature. "Companies love to hire future employees" here.

Life

"There's nothing to do" in "extremely rural" Potsdam. "Don't come here if you like the city," advises a senior. "There is a bittersweet relationship between the students and Clarkson," adds a freshman. The "dreary" campus is full of "atrocious" "concrete buildings," the food is "horrible," the "overcrowded" dorms "could use some updating," and winters are "cold and desolate." On the plus side, the students here are "fairly tight knit." "It's a small campus with small classes in a small town" explains a junior, "so people get a chance to develop meaningful relationships." Also, the Adirondack Mountains are "very close" and "a lot of the students" enjoy the outdoors. If you like ice hockey, it's "the most popular thing on campus." The team here is a Division I powerhouse and home games "bring the whole school together" "We show so much school spirit it's like the other team's fans aren't there," vaunts a first-year student. Business majors (and others) reportedly have "copious amounts of free time." For the engineers, though, grading can be "merciless" and "downtime is a luxury." It's "very hard to achieve good grades but rewarding when you do." Weekend life at Clarkson ranges from a popular Greek life to students who "just stay in their dorms all day and night" playing videogames.

Student Body

Overall, Clarkson students are "something of a nerdy crowd." "The typical student is a nerdy white guy," observes a senior. "It's mostly white males and Asians" "looking to get managerial and high-end engineering jobs" here. "There are many athletes" and plenty of business majors with "gelled hair." "The only people I have my nerdy classes with are other nerdy white guys." "Pretty much everyone looks the same from an outsider's view," agrees a sophomore. "Diversity has a different meaning at Clarkson," adds a junior. "What type of a techie are you?" Students describe themselves as "very smart," "hardworking," and "generally ambitious." A large contingent is "friendly" and outgoing. The "socially awkward" "quiet kid in high school" who "doesn't understand hygiene" is also here in spades. Clarkson's "horrible ratio of men to women" makes for a "miserable sausage fest," at least according to many males. Meanwhile, women have their own complaints. "It's hard to find a good looking guy," laments a senior. "There is a saying: 'although the odds are good, the goods are odd.'" "If you take out most of the antisocial engineering boys, the ratio becomes closer to 50:50." Other students claim that the ratio is "improving" and note that "SUNY Potsdam isn't far."

FINANCIAL AID: 315-268-7699 • E-MAIL: ADMISSION@CLARKSON.EDU • WEBSITE: WWW.CLARKSON.EDU

THE PRINCETON REVIEW SAYS

Admissions

Very important factors considered include: Academic GPA, rigor of secondary school record, interview. *Important factors considered include:* Class rank, recommendation(s), standardized test scores, extracurricular activities, volunteer work. *Other factors considered include:* Application essay, alumni/ae relation, character/personal qualities, first generation, level of applicant's interest, talent/ability, work experience. SAT Subject Tests recommended. SAT or ACT required. TOEFL required of all international applicants. High school diploma is required and GED is accepted. *Academic units required:* 4 English, 3 mathematics, 2 science. *Academic units recommended:* 4 mathematics, 3 science.

Financial Aid

Students should submit: FAFSA, institution's own financial aid form, state aid form. The Princeton Review suggests that all financial aid forms be submitted as soon as possible after 1/1. *Need-based scholarships/grants offered:* Federal Pell, SEOG, state scholarships/grants, private scholarships, the school's own gift aid, HEOP. *Loan aid offered:* Direct Subsidized Stafford, Direct Unsubsidized Stafford, Direct PLUS, FFEL Subsidized Stafford, FFEL Unsubsidized Stafford, FFEL PLUS, Federal Perkins, college/university loans from institutional funds, private/alternative loans. Applicants will be notified of awards on or about 3/19. Federal Work-Study Program available. Institutional employment available. Off-campus job opportunities are excellent.

The Inside Word

Clarkson's acceptance rate is too high for solid applicants to lose much sleep about gaining admission. Serious candidates should interview anyway. If you are particularly solid and really want to come here, it could help you get some scholarship money. Women and minorities will encounter an especially friendly admissions committee.

THE SCHOOL SAYS "..."

From The Admissions Office

"Clarkson University, a private, nationally ranked research university located in Potsdam, New York, is the institution of choice for 3,000 enterprising, high-ability scholars from diverse backgrounds who embrace challenge and thrive in a rigorous, highly collaborative learning environment.

"Clarkson's programs in engineering, business, the sciences, liberal arts, and health sciences emphasize team-based learning as well as creative problem solving and leadership skills. Clarkson is also on the leading edge of today's emerging technologies and fields of study offering innovative, boundary-spanning degree programs in engineering and management, digital arts and sciences, and environmental science and policy, among others.

"At Clarkson, students and faculty work closely together in a supportive, friendly environment. Students are encouraged to participate in faculty-mentored research projects from their first year, and to take advantage of co-ops and study abroad programs. Our collaborative approach to education translates into graduates in high demand; our placement rates are among the highest in the country. Alumni experience accelerated career growth. One in seven alumni are already a CEO, president, or vice president of a company.

"Applicants are required to take the ACT with Writing section optional or the SAT. We will use the student's best scores from either test. SAT Subject Tests are recommended but not required."

SELECTIVITY

Admissions Rating	91
# of applicants	3,204
% of applicants accepted	79
% of acceptees attending	29
# accepting a place on wait list	21
% admitted from wait list	67
# of early decision applicants	113
% accepted early decision	94

FRESHMAN PROFILE

Range SAT Critical Reading	500–560
Range SAT Math	610–660
Range SAT Writing	480–590
Range ACT Composite	24–28
Minimum paper TOEFL	550
Minimum computer TOEFL	213
Average HS GPA	3.48
% graduated top 10% of class	38
% graduated top 25% of class	70
% graduated top 50% of class	91

DEADLINES

Early decision	
Deadline	12/1
Notification	1/1
Regular	
Deadline	1/15
Notification	rolling
Nonfall registration?	yes

APPLICANTS ALSO LOOK AT

AND OFTEN PREFER
Rensselaer Polytechnic Institute
Rochester Institute of Technology

AND SOMETIMES PREFER
Lehigh University
Worcester Polytechnic Institute
University of Rochester

AND RARELY PREFER
Syracuse University

FINANCIAL FACTS

Financial Aid Rating	66
Annual tuition	$32,220
Room and board	$11,118
Required fees	$690
Books and supplies	$1,100
% frosh rec. need-based scholarship or grant aid	61
% UG rec. need-based scholarship or grant aid	64
% frosh rec. non-need-based scholarship or grant aid	14
% UG rec. non-need-based scholarship or grant aid	9
% frosh rec. need-based self-help aid	53
% UG rec. need-based self-help aid	70
% frosh rec. athletic scholarships	2
% UG rec. athletic scholarships	1
% frosh rec. any financial aid	100
% UG rec. any financial aid	98
% UG borrow to pay for school	84
Average cumulative indebtedness	$33,625

CLEMSON UNIVERSITY

106 SIKES HALL, BOX 345124, CLEMSON, SC 29634-5124 • ADMISSIONS: 864-656-2287 • FAX: 864-656-2464

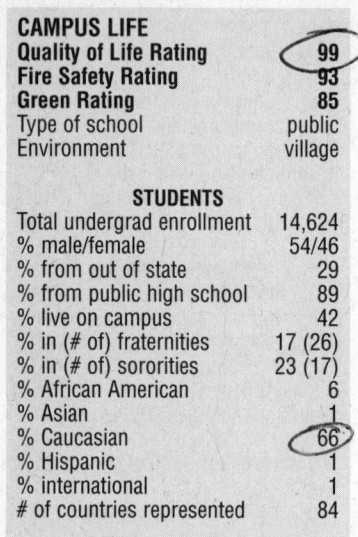

CAMPUS LIFE
Quality of Life Rating	**99**
Fire Safety Rating	**93**
Green Rating	**85**
Type of school	public
Environment	village

STUDENTS
Total undergrad enrollment	14,624
% male/female	54/46
% from out of state	29
% from public high school	89
% live on campus	42
% in (# of) fraternities	17 (26)
% in (# of) sororities	23 (17)
% African American	6
% Asian	1
% Caucasian	66
% Hispanic	1
% international	1
# of countries represented	84

SURVEY SAYS . . .
Athletic facilities are great
Students get along with local
community
Low cost of living
Everyone loves the Tigers
Intramural sports are popular
(Almost) no one smokes

ACADEMICS
Academic Rating	**83**
Calendar	semester
Student/faculty ratio	14:1
Profs interesting rating	81
Profs accessible rating	87
% classes taught by TAs	7
Most common reg class size	10–19 students
Most common lab size	10–19 students

MOST POPULAR MAJORS
biology/biological sciences
business/commerce
engineering

STUDENTS SAY ". . ."

Academics

Widely known to have one of the most beautiful campuses in the south, Clemson University also boasts a "family atmosphere" that students "fall in love with." Indeed, while most students here heap praise on the "challenging" and "outstanding" academics, "what really sets it apart is the entire campus's commitment to getting involved, bettering the community, and ostentatiously sporting some 'solid orange' Tiger pride." As one undergrad explains, "Clemson is about pride: pride in its athletics, academics, current students, and alumni." (That said, such pride can lead some to comment that the "school spirit [here] is insane.") By and large though, nearly everyone agrees that "Clemson is the whole package" thanks to its "great professors, athletics, cultural events, and student life," all of which is "packed into a small town that supports the school and students 100 percent." The "diverse" curriculum is backed up by "amazing" professors who, besides being "experts in their fields," are "interesting and willing to work with students to make sure the material is understood." This supportive environment extends to the administration as well. "The administrators actually care about the students," says one student, adding that "We're their first and foremost priority." "Like all bureaucracies," dealing with the administration "can be challenging at times," but nearly everyone here appreciates its "transparent" and "accessible" nature. "The administration has always been open and willing to meet with students," notes one undergrad.

Life

According to those in know, "A typical day for a Clemson student is never the same." However, you can count on a few certainties: "fun, friends, service, and academics." "The campus is beautiful, the opportunities are amazing, and the people are so friendly," says one undergrad. "There is never a shortage of things to do here." This rings particularly true for sporting types. Many note that nearly all students are "avid sports fans." Clemson is an "intensely athletic-focused school," and students "cheer on the Tigers at every opportunity." But sports aren't just for spectators here as "Clemson students are physically active," and you'll always find them "at the gym or walking around campus." Greek life is also very popular on-campus, and "most people that are of age drink on weekends" at parties or in bars downtown. The town of Clemson gets mixed reviews with some students finding that "there isn't much to do" while others say it's filled "with neat shops and restaurants." Regardless of your take, there's usually plenty going on, including "rodeos, concerts, plays, and other shows at the Brooks Center." Ultimately, this tight-knit campus "is a place where everyone comes together for a common cause, whether it happens to be academics, community service, sports, or anything else—everyone here contributes."

Student Body

The typical student at Clemson is "very southern," "loves football, goes to class the majority of the time, and is concerned with passing while also taking time out to have fun." "Girls wear pearls and Uggs," while gents "wear collared shirts, slacks, and sunglasses around their necks." "We are a walking advertisement," says one undergrad. "The campus is right out of a postcard, and there is designer everything everywhere you turn—but the students here are also very motivated and very smart." Most agree that "the student body is not very diverse" and that "students are not always understanding of each other because there is so little diversity." That said, there are "numerous atypical students" who "fit in by either hanging out with people like themselves or by creating their own path." Some would like to see the school take steps toward making "the fraternities and sororities less influential on campus." Overall, despite a "conservative" majority of students, most find everyone to be "very friendly" and full of "school spirit."

FINANCIAL AID: 864-656-2280 • E-MAIL: CUADMISSIONS@CLEMSON.EDU • WEBSITE: WWW.CLEMSON.EDU

THE PRINCETON REVIEW SAYS

Admissions

Very important factors considered include: Class rank, academic GPA, rigor of secondary school record, standardized test scores, state residency. *Important factors considered include:* Alumni/ae relation. *Other factors considered include:* Application essay, recommendation(s), extracurricular activities, talent/ability. SAT or ACT required. ACT with Writing component required. TOEFL required of all international applicants. High school diploma is required and GED is accepted. *Academic units required:* 4 English, 3 mathematics, 3 science (3 science labs), 3 foreign language, 3 social studies, 1 history, 2 academic electives, 1 PE or ROTC. *Academic units recommended:* 4 mathematics (4 science labs).

Financial Aid

Students should submit: FAFSA. The Princeton Review suggests that all financial aid forms be submitted as soon as possible after 1/1. *Need-based scholarships/grants offered:* Federal Pell, SEOG, state scholarships/grants, private scholarships, the school's own gift aid, federal nursing scholarships. *Loan aid offered:* Direct Subsidized Stafford, Direct Unsubsidized Stafford, Direct PLUS, FFEL Subsidized Stafford, FFEL Unsubsidized Stafford, FFEL PLUS, Federal Perkins, state loans, college/university loans from institutional funds. Applicants will be notified of awards on a rolling basis beginning 4/1. Federal Work-Study Program available. Institutional employment available. Off-campus job opportunities are fair.

The Inside Word

Clemson's admissions decisions are based largely on academic credentials, meaning, as you'd expect, that if your grades fit the bill, you're in. However, keep in mind that a straightforward admissions philosophy doesn't come with any guarantees. The university has seen its popularity grow steadily as its national profile has increased thanks to a combination of solid academics and passionate athletics. As a result, the school has become increasingly competitive.

THE SCHOOL SAYS "..."

From The Admissions Office

"One of the country's most selective public research universities, Clemson University was founded with a mission to be a high seminary of learning dedicated to teaching, research, and service. Nearly 120 years later, these three concepts remain at the heart of this university and provide the framework for an exceptional educational experience for Clemson students.

"At Clemson, professors take the time to get to know students and to explore innovative ways of teaching. Exceptional teaching is one reason Clemson's retention and graduation rates rank among the highest in the country among public universities. Exceptional teaching is also why Clemson continues to attract an increasingly talented student body. The class rank and SAT scores of Clemson's incoming freshman are among the highest of the nation's public research universities.

"Clemson offers over 250 student clubs and organizations; the spirit that students show for this university is unparalleled.

"Midway between Charlotte, North Carolina, and Atlanta, Georgia, Clemson University is located on 1,400 acres of beautiful rolling hills within the foothills of the Blue Ridge Mountains and along the shores of Lake Hartwell.

"Applicants are required to take the SAT or the ACT with the Writing section. The best combined scores from SAT test will be used in the admissions process. We do not however, combine sub scores from the ACT in order to create a new composite score."

SELECTIVITY

Admissions Rating	96
# accepting a place on wait list	162
% admitted from wait list	22

FRESHMAN PROFILE

Range SAT Critical Reading	550–640
Range SAT Math	587–680
Range ACT Composite	25–30
Minimum paper TOEFL	550
Minimum computer TOEFL	213
Average HS GPA	4.13
% graduated top 10% of class	52
% graduated top 25% of class	75
% graduated top 50% of class	97

DEADLINES

Regular	
Priority	12/1
Deadline	5/1
Notification	rolling
Nonfall registration?	yes

APPLICANTS ALSO LOOK AT

AND OFTEN PREFER
University of North Carolina at Chapel Hill

AND SOMETIMES PREFER
University of Virginia
Georgia Institute of Technology
University of Georgia

AND RARELY PREFER
University of South Carolina—Columbia
North Carolina State University
University of Maryland—College Park
Auburn University
Florida State University

FINANCIAL FACTS

Financial Aid Rating	67
Annual in-state tuition	$9,886
Annual out-of-state tuition	$22,908
Room and board	$5,874
Required fees	$823
Books and supplies	$900
% frosh rec. need-based scholarship or grant aid	15
% UG rec. need-based scholarship or grant aid	18
% frosh rec. non-need-based scholarship or grant aid	38
% UG rec. non-need-based scholarship or grant aid	22
% frosh rec. need-based self-help aid	24
% UG rec. need-based self-help aid	28
% frosh rec. athletic scholarships	3
% UG rec. athletic scholarships	3
% frosh rec. any financial aid	87
% UG rec. any financial aid	71
% UG borrow to pay for school	44
Average cumulative indebtedness	$17,882

COE COLLEGE

1220 FIRST AVENUE NORTHEAST, CEDAR RAPIDS, IA 52402 • ADMISSIONS: 319-399-8500 • FAX: 319-399-8816

CAMPUS LIFE

Quality of Life Rating	85
Fire Safety Rating	60*
Green Rating	60*
Type of school	private
Affiliation	Presbyterian
Environment	city

STUDENTS

Total undergrad enrollment	1,310
% male/female	44/55
% from out of state	39
% from public high school	90
% live on campus	84
% in (# of) fraternities	23 (5)
% in (# of) sororities	19 (3)
% African American	2
% Asian	1
% Caucasian	85
% Hispanic	2
% international	4
# of countries represented	18

SURVEY SAYS . . .

Career services are great
Students are friendly
Student government is popular

ACADEMICS

Academic Rating	87
Calendar	semester
Student/faculty ratio	11:1
Profs interesting rating	86
Profs accessible rating	91
Most common reg class size	10–19 students
Most common lab size	fewer than 10 students

MOST POPULAR MAJORS

biology/biological sciences
business administration and management
psychology

STUDENTS SAY ". . ."

Academics

Coe College, a small liberal arts school in Iowa's second-largest city, is "an institution that fosters community, political awareness, active student involvement, and the broadening of minds through multiple venues not expressed at other colleges and especially universities." Coe's distinctiveness results in part from the Coe Plan, with integrated curricular and experiential components, including service learning requirements, campus engagement activities, opportunities to participate in job-search workshops, and an academic practicum, completed in their junior or senior year. The school also offers "fantastic research opportunities for undergraduate students" that "allow them to interact with professors on more of a colleague level" and provide "experiences that most students don't get until graduate school." Academic offerings here feature "special attention to the natural sciences" as well as strengths in nursing, fine arts, and math. The school's Writing Center is one of the only writing centers in the country to allow freshmen to become consultants; students call it "a great strength" of the school. As at most small schools, "The availability of the professors is astounding. Many professors provide students with their home phone numbers, allowing students to become more comfortable with conversing and asking questions rather than trying to interpret the assignment on their own."

Life

Life on the Coe campus "is very relaxing but at the same time involved." Students tell us that "there always seems to be something going on at Coe: late night movies on Fridays, musicians in the pub, Bible study groups, Blindspot [an open mic/experimental theater event], visiting speakers, and the list goes on. People are always welcoming to a new person joining the group." Greek organizations "are very popular for men and women," and "athletics are important, including intramural sports and general fitness in our two fitness centers." Coe "still has a wet campus," so while students hit the books hard during the week, "on the weekends we do make up for our good behavior" and "party hard." Students add that "while there is a heavy drinking culture at Coe, it is very possible to have fun and find things to do if you choose not to drink." Hometown Cedar Rapids offers "lots of restaurants, bars, and shopping venues for students to go to" and "also hosts environmental or cultural events that students can walk to and participate in."

Student Body

Coe students "know they are here for an education and study accordingly, but they also know that there is a time and place to get involved, have fun, and interact with faculty, students, and the surrounding community." They are "able to balance athletics, class, and free time" and, "have time to be social and time to study." Coe students "cannot be pinned down as being a jock, or a geek, or any other stereotype. The vast majority of students at Coe are involved in multiple activities on a very diverse scale." While "most students at Coe are from small towns in Iowa" and "many of us may be Caucasian, there are also plenty of foreign exchange students who really add to the mix. We embrace cultural differences through multiple clubs, as well as our Annual Cultural Show."

FINANCIAL AID: 319-399-8540 • E-MAIL: ADMISSION@COE.EDU • WEBSITE: WWW.COE.EDU

THE PRINCETON REVIEW SAYS

Admissions

Very important factors considered include: Rigor of secondary school record, standardized test scores. *Important factors considered include:* Class rank, application essay, recommendation(s). *Other factors considered include:* Alumni/ae relation, character/personal qualities, extracurricular activities, interview, racial/ethnic status, talent/ability, volunteer work. SAT or ACT required. TOEFL required of all international applicants. High school diploma is required and GED is accepted. *Academic units recommended:* 4 English, 3 mathematics, 3 science (1 science lab), 2 foreign language, 3 social studies, 2 academic electives.

Financial Aid

Students should submit: FAFSA. The Princeton Review suggests that all financial aid forms be submitted as soon as possible after 1/1. *Need-based scholarships/grants offered:* Federal Pell, SEOG, state scholarships/grants, private scholarships, the school's own gift aid. *Loan aid offered:* Direct Subsidized Stafford, Direct Unsubsidized Stafford, Direct PLUS, Federal Perkins, college/university loans from institutional funds. Applicants will be notified of awards on a rolling basis beginning 3/15. Federal Work-Study Program available. Institutional employment available. Off-campus job opportunities are excellent.

The Inside Word

Coe's small incoming classes allow the school to be extremely selective in admissions. Your application will get a very close review here, so take the time to make it distinctive. Don't be afraid to contact the school and plead your case; a firm commitment to attending Coe may tip the balance for marginal applicants. Even so, no one gets in here without at least decent academic credentials; most admitted students, in fact, excelled at the high school level.

THE SCHOOL SAYS "..."

From The Admissions Office

"A Coe education begins to pay off right away. In fact, 98 percent of last year's graduating class was either working or in graduate school within 6 months of graduation. One reason our graduates do so well is the Coe Plan—a step-by-step sequence of activities designed to prepare our students for life after Coe. This required sequence stretches from the first-year seminar to community service, issue dinners, career planning seminars, and the required hands-on experience. The hands-on component may be satisfied through an internship, research, practicum, or study abroad. One student lived with a Costa Rican family while she studied the effects of selective logging on rain forest organisms. Others have interned at places like Warner Brothers in Los Angeles and the Chicago Board of Trade. Still others combine travel with an internship or student teaching for an unforgettable off-campus experience. Coe College is one of the few liberal arts institutions in the country to require hands-on learning for graduation."

SELECTIVITY

Admissions Rating	86
# of applicants	1,943
% of applicants accepted	63
% of acceptees attending	28

FRESHMAN PROFILE

Range SAT Critical Reading	560–680
Range SAT Math	550–670
Range ACT Composite	23–28
Minimum paper TOEFL	500
Minimum computer TOEFL	173
Average HS GPA	3.66
% graduated top 10% of class	25
% graduated top 25% of class	66
% graduated top 50% of class	94

DEADLINES

Early action	
Deadline	12/10
Notification	1/20
Regular	
Priority	12/10
Deadline	3/1
Notification	3/15
Nonfall registration?	yes

APPLICANTS ALSO LOOK AT AND SOMETIMES PREFER

University of Iowa
Cornell College

FINANCIAL FACTS

Financial Aid Rating	84
Annual tuition	$28,950
Room and board	$7,150
Required fees	$320
Books and supplies	$1,000
% frosh rec. need-based scholarship or grant aid	73
% UG rec. need-based scholarship or grant aid	72
% frosh rec. non-need-based scholarship or grant aid	26
% UG rec. non-need-based scholarship or grant aid	24
% frosh rec. need-based self-help aid	58
% UG rec. need-based self-help aid	62
% frosh rec. any financial aid	98
% UG rec. any financial aid	96
% UG borrow to pay for school	83
Average cumulative indebtedness	$29,710

COLBY COLLEGE

4000 MAYFLOWER HILL, WATERVILLE, ME 04901-8848 • ADMISSIONS: 800-723-3032 • FAX: 207-859-4828

CAMPUS LIFE

Quality of Life Rating	83
Fire Safety Rating	95
Green Rating	95
Type of school	private
Environment	city

STUDENTS

Total undergrad enrollment	1,846
% male/female	46/54
% from out of state	88
% from public high school	54
% live on campus	94
% African American	2
% Asian	8
% Caucasian	65
% Hispanic	3
% international	5
# of countries represented	63

SURVEY SAYS . . .

Great food on campus
Dorms are like palaces
Frats and sororities are unpopular or nonexistent

ACADEMICS

Academic Rating	89
Calendar	4/1/4
Student/faculty ratio	10:1
Profs interesting rating	91
Profs accessible rating	87
Most common reg class size	10–19 students
Most common lab size	10–19 students

MOST POPULAR MAJORS

biology/biological sciences
economics
political science and government

STUDENTS SAY ". . ."

Academics

This small, close-knit liberal arts college draws praise from students for its rigorous but caring approach to academics. It's a place where devoted professors "invite students to dinner" and learning happens "for learning's sake." Small classes are one of Colby's biggest draws. "Professors are always willing to go the extra mile," one student says. A senior adds, "Over the course of my time at Colby I've been to at least six different professors' houses for departmental events, class dinners, and group discussions." Professors get high grades for their teaching and accessibility, which together foster a "love for learning" in undergraduates. As one student dryly notes, "Waterville, Maine is not the country's academic capital, so the professors that choose to be at Colby are here to teach, not to use the facilities." This dedication to academics can make Colby an intense place to go to school, and students here aren't "afraid to work hard and study." In addition, students must not only complete their major requirements but also fulfill a hefty load of distribution requirements to graduate. The popular "Jan Plan" allows students to pursue focused course work, independent study or internships during an intensive 4- week term in January. While the administration "works hard to keep students happy and entertained," some feel that their needs are "occasionally ignored in favor of the everlasting quest to turn Colby into a small Ivy."

Life

"Friends and a sense of community drive life at Colby," one senior writes. Students live together in coed, mixed-class dorms. Everything centers around the campus, which is "constructed on a gorgeous wooded hill near the Kennebec River in Central Maine." Since "there isn't a ridiculous amount to do" in these self-contained environs, "Colby works hard to fill the day with countless events, lectures, discussions, and concerts. People can study hard, party, take advantage of the beautiful outdoors, and most do all three." A student notes that "the size of the school is perfect: On any given day, I could see five friends or acquaintances (and countless familiar faces!) on my way to class." This makes for a friendly atmosphere as "it's easy to start up a conversation with pretty much anyone. When the great outdoors beckons, students answer the call by hiking in autumn and spring, skiing in winter, and participating in traditional outdoor sports like football. A senior explains, "People like to unwind after our incredibly stressful weeks with movies, skiing, and partying." The "alcohol-centered social scene" usually takes place at small dorm parties or at the few local pubs.

Student Body

While the prototypical Colby student may be "white and from 20 minutes outside of Boston," undergrads are quick to point out that their "campus is very open to diversity and ready to embrace it." Students single out the administration for "doing a great job of bringing in a more diverse student population." One student explains that "more and more international students and urban kids are coming through programs like the Posse Scholarship." A junior adds, "We have students here that dress in business suits and bow ties while others walk around in capes." Most students, however, settle for the more general description of "preppy students who enjoy the outdoors and enjoy having a good time." That said, students report that "there's pretty much a place for everyone somewhere at Colby; chances are you'll find people both very similar to you in interests, background, etc. and people who are completely the opposite." One student elaborates, explaining that despite all differences, "the one word I'd use to describe a Colby student is friendly."

FINANCIAL AID: 800-723-3032 • E-MAIL: ADMISSIONS@COLBY.EDU • WEBSITE: WWW.COLBY.EDU

THE PRINCETON REVIEW SAYS

Admissions

Very important factors considered include: Rigor of secondary school record, character/personal qualities. *Important factors considered include:* Class rank, application essay, academic GPA, recommendation(s), standardized test scores, extracurricular activities, racial/ethnic status, talent/ability. *Other factors considered include:* Alumni/ae relation, first generation, geographical residence, interview, level of applicant's interest, state residency, volunteer work, work experience. TOEFL or IELTS required of all international applicants. High school diploma or equivalent is not required. *Academic units recommended:* 4 English, 3 mathematics, 2 science (2 science labs), 3 foreign language, 2 social studies, 2 academic electives.

Financial Aid

Students should submit: FAFSA and the CSS Profile. The Business/farm supplement may be required. Regular filing deadline is 2/1. The Princeton Review suggests that all financial aid forms be submitted as soon as possible after 1/1. *Need-based scholarships/grants offered:* Federal Pell, SEOG, state scholarships/grants, private scholarships, the school's own gift aid. *Loan aid offered:* Direct Subsidized Stafford, Direct Unsubsidized Stafford, Direct PLUS, FFEL Subsidized Stafford, FFEL Unsubsidized Stafford, FFEL PLUS, Federal Perkins, state loans, alternative loans. Applicants will be notified of awards on or about 4/1. Federal Work-Study Program available. Institutional employment available. Off-campus job opportunities are poor. Calculated need is met with grant and work; loans available to reduce family contribution.

The Inside Word

Colby continues to be both very selective and successful in converting admits to enrollees, which makes for a perpetually challenging admissions process. Currently, only 33 percent of applicants are accepted, so hit those books and ace those exams to stand a fighting chance. One thing that could set you apart from the pack? An interest in travel. Two-thirds of Colby students study abroad—in fact, for some degrees it's required.

THE SCHOOL SAYS "..."

From The Admissions Office

"Colby is one of only a handful of liberal arts colleges that offer world-class academic programs, leadership in internationalism, an active community life, and rich opportunities after graduation. Set in Maine on one of the nation's most beautiful campuses, Colby provides students a host of opportunities for active engagement, in Waterville or around the world. The Goldfarb Center for Public Affairs and Civic Engagement connects teaching and research with current political, economic, and social issues at home and abroad. Recently Colby replaced loans in its financial aid packages with grants, which don't have to be repaid, making it possible for students to graduate without college-loan debt.

"Students' access to Colby's outstanding faculty is extraordinary, and the college is a leader in undergraduate research and project-based learning. The college has won awards for sustainable environmental practices as well as one of the first Senator Paul Simon Awards for Internationalizing the Campus.

"The challenging academic experience at the heart of Colby's programs is complemented by a vibrant community life and campus atmosphere featuring more than 100 student-run organizations, more than 50 athletic and recreational choices, and numerous leadership and volunteer opportunities.

"Colby graduates succeed, finding their places at the finest medical and other graduate schools, top Wall Street firms, and in the arts, government service, social service, education, and nonprofit organizations.

"Applicants must submit scores from the SAT, or SAT Subject Tests in three different subject areas. The choice of which test(s) to take is entirely up to each applicant. The optional ACT Writing Test is recommended."

SELECTIVITY
Admissions Rating	96
# of applicants	4,835
% of applicants accepted	31
% of acceptees attending	32
# accepting a place on wait list	431
% admitted from wait list	4
# of early decision applicants	455
% accepted early decision	47

FRESHMAN PROFILE
Range SAT Critical Reading	640–720
Range SAT Math	640–710
Range SAT Writing	630–710
Range ACT Composite	28–31
Minimum paper TOEFL	600
Minimum computer TOEFL	240
Minimum web-based TOEFL	100
% graduated top 10% of class	61
% graduated top 25% of class	90
% graduated top 50% of class	98

DEADLINES
Early decision	
Deadline	1/1
Notification	2/1
Regular	
Deadline	1/1
Notification	4/1
Nonfall registration?	yes

APPLICANTS ALSO LOOK AT
AND OFTEN PREFER
Dartmouth College
Middlebury College
Williams College
Bowdoin College
Amherst College

AND SOMETIMES PREFER
Colgate University
Boston College
Bates College

AND RARELY PREFER
Hamilton College
University of Vermont
Skidmore College

FINANCIAL FACTS
Financial Aid Rating	95
Comprehensive fee	$48,520
Books and supplies	$700
% frosh rec. need-based scholarship or grant aid	39
% UG rec. need-based scholarship or grant aid	4
% frosh rec. need-based self-help aid	32
% UG rec. need-based self-help aid	3
% frosh rec. any financial aid	41
% UG rec. any financial aid	43
% UG borrow to pay for school	41
Average cumulative indebtedness	$24,900

COLGATE UNIVERSITY

13 OAK DRIVE, HAMILTON, NY 13346 • ADMISSIONS: 315-228-7401 • FAX: 315-228-7544

CAMPUS LIFE
Quality of Life Rating	89
Fire Safety Rating	85
Green Rating	87
Type of school	private
Environment	rural

STUDENTS
Total undergrad enrollment	2,836
% male/female	48/52
% from out of state	72
% from public high school	65
% live on campus	91
% in (# of) fraternities	24 (6)
% in (# of) sororities	35 (3)
% African American	6
% Asian	6
% Caucasian	73
% Hispanic	6
% Native American	1
% international	5
# of countries represented	36

SURVEY SAYS . . .
Lab facilities are great
Great library
School is well run
Dorms are like palaces
Students are happy
Lots of beer drinking
Hard liquor is popular

ACADEMICS
Academic Rating	96
Calendar	semester
Student/faculty ratio	10:1
Profs interesting rating	94
Profs accessible rating	97
Most common reg class size	10–19 students
Most common lab size	10–19 students

MOST POPULAR MAJORS
economics
English language and literature
history

STUDENTS SAY ". . ."

Academics

Colgate University, "the epitome of a work hard, play hard school," provides "a rigorous academic environment, an outstanding student and faculty population, and an abundance of social opportunities" to its "preppy," "intelligent-but-not-nerdy" student body. Students report that "Colgate is academically strong in the humanities, such as political science, English, psychology, and economics" and "also has good natural sciences programs that are enhanced by the new science building," a $56.3 million structure that houses 40 research labs, 13 teaching labs, and a teaching/research greenhouse. All students here must complete a set of general education requirements that "force you to look beyond your major work," sometimes leading to discovery of new, unanticipated areas of interest. "It is not uncommon for students to double major in two vastly different departments" as a result of their gen-ed experiences, students tell us. Colgate's size and location foster community-building; the "administration and faculty don't just work at Colgate, but live Colgate. In this way, they are dedicated to your education and create a passionate, hands-on, and inspiring place to learn," translating into "great opportunities to research with great professors and be in leadership positions." The workload is tough here; "at the end of a semester you may have four final exams and 80 pages of writing to do, but that absolutely won't stop you from going out on Friday night. (Saturday night too. And Wednesday night. Maybe Monday also.)"

Life

Colgate students take pride in the fact that they can handle both demanding academics and a bustling party scene. "The daytime is for work, nighttime (except Tuesday) is for fun," explains one student. "If you know where to look, you can find a party five days a week, and definitely on weekends." Some warn that "The social/party scene around here can get a bit frustrating for some girls at times. If you like to be in serious relationships, Colgate is going to be a whole different ballgame for you…mostly the students here are interested in hook-ups," but by and large student feedback on the party scene is positive. Greek life "makes up a lot of the social scene, but the school itself provides many opportunities open to the entire campus that are generally very well attended," including "banquets, sports events, movies, etc." Colgate football and hockey are "extremely popular;" the school is "Division I in athletics, which is unique for a small liberal arts school. This aspect brings a lot of school spirit and adds to the sense of community here." There's "not much to do in Hamilton" other than "three main bars and The Jug," the latter being a "legendary" "bar/mosh pit that underclassmen go to after making the long trek from the dorms up on campus into town."

Student Body

"When looking from the surface, Colgate students don't appear diverse" because of the "undeniable majority of white students all in Uggs and Oxfords," but "although most students dress alike, there are great discussions in and out of the classroom because each Colgate student is actually very different from the next once you have the opportunity to talk to them." Even so, just about everyone here concedes that "this is a very preppy campus." Students tend to be "very laid-back, but in that perfectly groomed, 'I just rolled out of bed looking this good' kind of way." They are also "passionate about something. Everyone has her own thing to enjoy. It could be a recreational club, a dance group, a community service group, an academic or research project, a student club, etc. You find that a lot of Colgate students are active members in one way or another."

FINANCIAL AID: 315-228-7431 • E-MAIL: ADMISSION@MAIL.COLGATE.EDU • WEBSITE: WWW.COLGATE.EDU

THE PRINCETON REVIEW SAYS

Admissions

Very important factors considered include: Class rank, academic GPA, rigor of secondary school record. *Important factors considered include:* Application essay, recommendation(s), standardized test scores, character/personal qualities, extracurricular activities, talent/ability. *Other factors considered include:* Alumni/ae relation, first generation, geographical residence, racial/ethnic status, volunteer work, work experience. SAT or ACT required. TOEFL required of all international applicants. High school diploma is required and GED is accepted. *Academic units required:* 4 English, 3 mathematics, 3 science (2 science labs), 3 foreign language, 3 social studies. *Academic units recommended:* 4 English, 4 mathematics, 4 science (3 science labs), 4 foreign language, 4 social studies.

Financial Aid

Students should submit: CSS/financial aid profile, noncustodial profile, business/farm supplement. Regular filing deadline is 1/15. The Princeton Review suggests that all financial aid forms be submitted as soon as possible after 1/1. *Need-based scholarships/grants offered:* Federal Pell, SEOG, state scholarships/grants, private scholarships, the school's own gift aid. *Loan aid offered:* FFEL Subsidized Stafford, FFEL Unsubsidized Stafford, FFEL PLUS, Federal Perkins. Applicants will be notified of awards on or about 4/1. Federal Work-Study Program available. Institutional employment available. Off-campus job opportunities are fair.

The Inside Word

As at many colleges, Colgate admissions caters to some long-established special interests. Athletes, minorities, and legacies (children of alumni) are among those who benefit from more favorable review. Wait-listed students, take note—less than two percent of students on the waitlist wind up admitted to the school.

THE SCHOOL SAYS "..."

From The Admissions Office

"Students and faculty alike are drawn to Colgate by the quality of its academic programs. Faculty initiative has given the university a rich mix of learning opportunities that includes a liberal arts core, 51 academic concentrations, and a wealth of Colgate faculty-led, off-campus study programs in the United States and abroad. But there is more to Colgate than academic life, including more than 180 student organizations, athletics and recreation at all levels, and a full complement of living options set within a campus described as one of the most beautiful in the country. A new center for community service builds upon the tradition of Colgate students interacting with the surrounding community in meaningful ways. Colgate students become extraordinarily devoted alumni, contributing significantly to career networking and exploration programs on and off campus. For students in search of a busy and varied campus life, Colgate is a place to learn and grow."

SELECTIVITY

Admissions Rating	96
# of applicants	9,416
% of applicants accepted	24
% of acceptees attending	33
# accepting a place on wait list	515
% admitted from wait list	2
# of early decision applicants	741
% accepted early decision	51

FRESHMAN PROFILE

Range SAT Critical Reading	630–730
Range SAT Math	640–730
Range ACT Composite	29–32
Average HS GPA	3.7
% graduated top 10% of class	65
% graduated top 25% of class	89
% graduated top 50% of class	99

DEADLINES

Early decision	
Deadline	11/15
Notification	12/15
Regular	
Deadline	1/15
Notification	4/1
Nonfall registration?	no

APPLICANTS ALSO LOOK AT

AND OFTEN PREFER
Dartmouth College
Cornell University
Middlebury College
Tufts University

AND SOMETIMES PREFER
Boston College

FINANCIAL FACTS

Financial Aid Rating	98
Annual tuition	$39,545
Room and board	$9,625
Required fees	$270
% frosh rec. need-based scholarship or grant aid	32
% UG rec. need-based scholarship or grant aid	33
% frosh rec. need-based self-help aid	24
% UG rec. need-based self-help aid	25
% frosh rec. athletic scholarships	5
% UG rec. athletic scholarships	6
% frosh rec. any financial aid	35
% UG rec. any financial aid	46
% UG borrow to pay for school	34
Average cumulative indebtedness	$20,164

COLLEGE OF THE ATLANTIC

105 EDEN STREET, BAR HARBOR, ME 04609 • ADMISSIONS: 207-288-5015 • FAX: 207-288-4126

CAMPUS LIFE

Quality of Life Rating	**90**
Fire Safety Rating	**93**
Green Rating	**99**
Type of school	private
Environment	rural

STUDENTS

Total undergrad enrollment	312
% male/female	37/63
% from out of state	80
% from public high school	71
% live on campus	43
% Asian	1
% Caucasian	29
% Hispanic	1
% international	13
# of countries represented	37

SURVEY SAYS . . .

No one cheats
Students are friendly
Students aren't religious
Great food on campus
Low cost of living
Intercollegiate sports are unpopular
or nonexistent
Frats and sororities are unpopular or
nonexistent
(Almost) no one smokes

ACADEMICS

Academic Rating	**94**
Calendar	trimester
Student/faculty ratio	11:1
Profs interesting rating	92
Profs accessible rating	95
Most common	
reg class size	10–19 students
Most common	
lab size	10–19 students

MOST POPULAR MAJORS

biology/biological sciences
ecology
education

STUDENTS SAY ". . ."

Academics

The College of the Atlantic takes a unique approach to academics. All undergrads "major in Human Ecology," an interdisciplinary philosophy that addresses environmental and social issues. While there are distribution requirements, a sophomore ensures us that "those are easy to fulfill" and asserts that "all other classes are elective." Unfortunately, due to COA's small size, "most classes are [only] offered every other year." Therefore, if a particular course sparks your interest, you "need to jump on the [opportunity]." The intimate size does have plenty of advantages however. Undergrads here seem to unanimously agree that "COA is a very close-knit community" where "inter-personal relationships with staff, faculty, and administration" flourish. Students eagerly sing the praises of their professors: "an eclectic and brilliant group of people" who are "extremely accessible." And this availability isn't limited to normal workday hours. One junior told us that it's quite common for professors "to give out their home phone numbers." Though friendly and supportive, professors don't let their students slack off. While the workload "varies from class to class" it's most definitely "not light." Luckily, these "self-motivated" undergrads happily embrace their assignments. As one impressed freshman sums up, "For students in search of a school that will challenge them, [COA] is an excellent place."

Life

Though COA students are frequently "swamped with reading and homework" there is always "time to have fun." Hometown Bar Harbor is a place "that is booming with tourists in the summer and pretty much dead in the winter." While undergrads frequent a few local hangouts, they mostly "make our own fun." Students can often be found playing "hockey on the pond" or "pickup games of soccer," hosting "spontaneous midnight poetry readings," "tobogganing at the golf course," or throwing "dance parties in the art gallery." There's even the occasional "sword fight in the library." COA's location is an outdoor enthusiast's dream, and students are quick to take advantage of the school's proximity to Acadia National Park. Opportunities abound to "hike, bike [and] go out on the ocean" and "snowshoe/ski in the winter." The small population helps to ensure a "strong sense of community," and undergrads are always content with attending a potluck and simply enjoying "philosophical conversations that last until early morning." There is a party scene, but "alcohol does not dominate social life at all." Finally, the school also hosts a variety of activities "such as concerts, open mics, and hiking trips."

Student Body

Undergrads at the College of the Atlantic readily acknowledge that many people assume they're "all tree-hugging hippies" who always wear "Birkenstocks and tie dye." And while there are plenty of "outdoorsy" types, students are quick to assert that many of their peers shatter this stereotype. Though the majority might categorize themselves as "atypical," most everyone is "compassionate, kind, and aware." Passion is another common attribute, and one freshman gushes, "Everyone is incredibly cool and into something, whether it be poetry, fighting climate change, dance, whales [or] organic farming...everyone wants to improve the lives of others." With such a politically aware student body, COA is a bastion for liberal, left-leaning undergrads. Indeed, this sentiment is punctuated by a sophomore who exclaims, "I think there are about two Republicans in the whole school." That being said, "The college [has] a very egalitarian outlook, [and] everyone is equal and equally valued." While the majority of COA undergrads are "white [and] middle-class," the college manages to attract "a lot of international students through the Davis Scholarship Program," ensuring a diversity of experience and opinion.

FINANCIAL AID: 207-288-5015 • E-MAIL: INQUIRY@ECOLOGY.COA.EDU • WEBSITE: WWW.COA.EDU

THE PRINCETON REVIEW SAYS

Admissions

Very important factors considered include: Application essay, recommendation(s), rigor of secondary school record. *Important factors considered include:* Class rank, academic GPA, character/personal qualities, extracurricular activities, interview, talent/ability, volunteer work, work experience. *Other factors considered include:* Standardized test scores, alumni/ae relation, first generation, geographical residence, level of applicant's interest, racial/ethnic status, state residency, TOEFL required of all international applicants. High school diploma is required and GED is accepted. *Academic units required:* 4 English, 3 mathematics, 2 science (2 science labs), 2 social studies. *Academic units recommended:* 4 mathematics, 3 science, 2 foreign language, 2 history, 1 academic elective.

Financial Aid

Students should submit: FAFSA, institution's own financial aid form, noncustodial profile, business/farm supplement. Regular filing deadline is 2/15. The Princeton Review suggests that all financial aid forms be submitted as soon as possible after 1/1. *Need-based scholarships/grants offered:* Federal Pell, SEOG, state scholarships/grants, private scholarships, the school's own gift aid. *Loan aid offered:* FFEL Subsidized Stafford, FFEL Unsubsidized Stafford, FFEL PLUS, Federal Perkins. Applicants will be notified of awards on or about 4/1. Federal Work-Study Program available. Off-campus job opportunities are good.

The Inside Word

As applicants might expect, admissions standards at College of the Atlantic are somewhat atypical. The school covets students who carve their own intellectual courses rather than follow a conventional academic path. Students at COA are expected to bring strong ideas and values to the classroom, and applicants are assessed accordingly. Essays and interviews are where you can make your mark. Of course, the college's integrated approach also means you should have a well-rounded secondary school record. Candidates should also demonstrate a kinship with the philosophy of human ecology.

THE SCHOOL SAYS "..."

From The Admissions Office

"College of the Atlantic is a small, intellectually challenging college on Mount Desert Island, Maine. We look for students seeking a rigorous, hands-on, self-directed academic experience. Come for a visit, and you will begin to understand that COA's unique approach to education, governance and community life extends throughout its structure. Resolutely value centered and interdisciplinary—there are no departments and no majors, COA sees its mission as preparing people to become independent thinkers, to challenge conventional wisdom, to deal with pressing global change—both environmental and social—and to be passionately engaged in transforming the world around them into a better place.

"College of the Atlantic does not require standardized testing as part of the application process. Learning and intelligence can be gauged in many ways; standardized test scores are just one of many measures. If an applicant chooses to submit standardized test scores for consideration, the SAT, SAT Subject Tests, or ACT scores are all acceptable."

SELECTIVITY
Admissions Rating	91
# of applicants	314
% of applicants accepted	69
% of acceptees attending	32
# of early decision applicants	39
% accepted early decision	79

FRESHMAN PROFILE
Range SAT Critical Reading	600–690
Range SAT Math	500–650
Range SAT Writing	550–680
Range ACT Composite	25–29
Minimum paper TOEFL	567
Minimum computer TOEFL	227
Minimum web-based TOEFL	86
Average HS GPA	3.49
% graduated top 10% of class	31
% graduated top 25% of class	62
% graduated top 50% of class	96

DEADLINES
Early decision	
Deadline	12/1
Notification	12/15
Regular	
Deadline	2/15
Notification	4/1
Nonfall registration?	yes

APPLICANTS ALSO LOOK AT
AND OFTEN PREFER
Colby College
Bowdoin College
AND SOMETIMES PREFER
Hampshire College
Bard College
AND RARELY PREFER
Warren Wilson College
Green Mountain College
University of Maine

FINANCIAL FACTS
Financial Aid Rating	87
Annual tuition	$32,580
Room and board	$8,490
Required fees	$480
Books and supplies	$600
% frosh rec. need-based scholarship or grant aid	80
% UG rec. need-based scholarship or grant aid	82
% frosh rec. need-based self-help aid	80
% UG rec. need-based self-help aid	79
% frosh rec. any financial aid	80
% UG rec. any financial aid	82
% UG borrow to pay for school	56
Average cumulative indebtedness	$23,762

COLLEGE OF CHARLESTON

66 GEORGE STREET, CHARLESTON, SC 29424 • ADMISSIONS: 843-953-5670 • FAX: 843-953-6322

CAMPUS LIFE

Quality of Life Rating	**91**
Fire Safety Rating	**92**
Green Rating	**81**
Type of school	public
Environment	city

STUDENTS

Total undergrad enrollment	9,415
% male/female	36/64
% from out of state	36
% from public high school	81.3
% in (# of) fraternities	11 (12)
% in (# of) sororities	16 (11)
% African American	5
% Asian	2
% Caucasian	84
% Hispanic	2
% international	1
# of countries represented	67

SURVEY SAYS . . .

Great library
Students love Charleston, SC
Great off-campus food
Students are happy
Lots of beer drinking
Hard liquor is popular
(Almost) everyone smokes

ACADEMICS

Academic Rating	**77**
Calendar	semester
Student/faculty ratio	16.06:1
Profs interesting rating	80
Profs accessible rating	82
% classes taught by TAs	4.1
Most common reg class size	20–29 students
Most common lab size	20–29 students

MOST POPULAR MAJORS

biology/biological sciences
business administration and management
communication studies/speech communication and rhetoric

STUDENTS SAY " . . ."

Academics

It's satisfaction guaranteed at the College of Charleston, where one enters "the gateway to Southern charm, grace, and hospitality" and gets "a private school atmosphere with a public school cost." Though the almost Siren-like appeal of the South Carolina location seems to have been the deciding factor for a fair number of students, the great value of the education (particularly for in-state residents) is cited by many as a definite perk to an already-perky school.

As for the learning part of the easy living, the "very high faculty to student ratio makes it easy to get help when you need it," and the class sizes "are just a little bigger than in high school," which is "conducive to learning." Science and pre-med programs are singled out as being particularly solid, and strong academics also abound in the "challenging courses, especially upper-level classes." Some lament that it can be "sort of hard as an underclassman to get into the classes and sections you want". Registration can be hit or miss, but professors are "totally available and oftentimes brilliant," offering "many opportunities to help, whether it be office hours, meetings or review sessions." Those enrolled here are satisfied with the "enthusiastic" administration as well, who are trying to counteract the school's homogeneity by "really trying to expand the school."

Life

Students just love, love, love Charleston, and it's not often you find most students using the phrase "Elysian backdrop" outside of a term paper. "When I tell people that I go to school in Charleston, they say, 'You are not going to school, you are going on vacation!'" says one. "The water is a five-minute walk; the beach is a five minute drive," says another. "You read on the greenest grass in a scene from a movie. You walk around in 70-degree weather with smiling friends and class-mates during November and December," says yet another starry-eyed student. The campus is located in the center of the city, so campus housing options can be somewhat limited. The food has been universally panned, but a new cafeteria, opened in August 2007, will likely improve the culinary quality. Most students walk rather than drive, and having a car "is actually a hindrance," which comes in handy for resisting the temptation on the weekends, since the school "has great parties and an atmosphere to support them." Not that this means students shirk their work, they just learn to allocate their time (upperclassmen usually manage this better than the party-happy freshmen). "The real issue at hand is deciding: bar or library?" The arts are also big here—"theatre and music mostly"—and the historic sites even get a fair amount of patronage, such as the popular walk along the "battery where the Civil War started."

Student Body

The almost sickeningly happy student body is "upbeat and positive about being at C of C," and this collective group of "Southern belles, hard-core Northerners, surfers, nerds and party animals" are "all united by the beach." The simpler split is between preppy or the "the artsy/hippy type." It's inter-esting to note that there's a significantly larger number of women than men, and though the diversity is pretty low, students note that it is growing. Right now C of C has "mostly your typical sorority and frat type students." Politically, "it's definitely the most liberal school in South Carolina," and "most people are very open to other cultures and lifestyles." "For example, I had pink hair one time and everybody loved it!" says a sophomore. "It is highly implau-sible that you won't find your niche within the first weeks of school."

FINANCIAL AID: 843-953-5540 • E-MAIL: ADMISSIONS@COFC.EDU • WEBSITE: WWW.COFC.EDU

THE PRINCETON REVIEW SAYS

Admissions

Very important factors considered include: Academic GPA, rigor of secondary school record, standardized test scores, state residency. *Important factors considered include:* Class rank, character/personal qualities, first generation, talent/ability. *Other factors considered include:* Application essay, recommendation(s), extracurricular activities, racial/ethnic status, volunteer work, work experience. SAT or ACT required. TOEFL required of all international applicants. High school diploma is required and GED is accepted. *Academic units required:* 4 English, 3 mathematics, 3 science (3 science labs), 3 foreign language, 3 social studies, 4 academic electives. *Academic units recommended:* 4 English, 4 mathematics, 2 history.

Financial Aid

Students should submit: FAFSA. The Princeton Review suggests that all financial aid forms be submitted as soon as possible after 1/1. *Need-based scholarships/grants offered:* Federal Pell, SEOG, state scholarships/grants, private scholarships, the school's own gift aid. *Loan aid offered:* Direct Subsidized Stafford, Direct Unsubsidized Stafford, Direct PLUS, Federal Perkins. Applicants will be notified of awards on a rolling basis beginning 4/10. Federal Work-Study Program available. Institutional employment available. Off-campus job opportunities are fair.

The Inside Word

Prime location and relatively low tuition make admissions at College of Charleston quite competitive, and standards are a bit higher still for out-of-state applicants. High school grades and standardized test scores play a significant role in admissions decisions, but the school also takes the time to consider the "complete" student. Expect more personalized treatment here than you would receive from Clemson or the University of South Carolina.

THE SCHOOL SAYS "..."

From The Admissions Office

"To succeed in our increasingly complex world, college graduates must be able to think creatively, explore new ideas, compete, collaborate, and meet the challenges of our global society. At the College of Charleston, students find out about themselves, their lives and the lives of others. They discover how to shape their future, and they prepare to create change and opportunity.

"Founded in 1770, the College of Charleston's mission is to provide students with a first-class education in the arts and sciences, education and business. Students have 128 majors and minors from which to choose—and they often choose to combine several—and complement their academic courses with overseas study, research and internships for a truly customized education.

"Nearly 10,000 undergraduates choose the College for its small-college feel blended with the advantages and diversity of an urban, mid-sized university. The College, home to students from 18 states and 27 countries, provides a creative and intellectually stimulating environment where students are challenged and guided by a committed and caring faculty of 500 distinguished teacher-scholars, all in an incomparable historic setting.

"The city of Charleston serves as a living and learning laboratory for student experiences in business, science, teaching, the humanities, languages and the arts. At the same time, students and faculty are engaged with the community in partnerships to improve education, enhance the business community and enrich the overall quality of life in the region.

"In the great liberal arts tradition, a College of Charleston education focuses on discovery and personal growth, as well as preparation for life, work and service to our society."

SELECTIVITY

Admissions Rating	86
# of applicants	9,964
% of applicants accepted	64
% of acceptees attending	31
# accepting a place on wait list	203
% admitted from wait list	62

FRESHMAN PROFILE

Range SAT Critical Reading	570–650
Range SAT Math	570–650
Range ACT Composite	23–26
Minimum paper TOEFL	550
Minimum computer TOEFL	213
Minimum web-based TOEFL	80
Average HS GPA	3.85
% graduated top 10% of class	26.11
% graduated top 25% of class	61.86
% graduated top 50% of class	92.59

DEADLINES

Early action	
Deadline	11/1
Notification	12/15
Regular	
Priority	11/1
Deadline	4/1
Nonfall registration?	yes

APPLICANTS ALSO LOOK AT

AND OFTEN PREFER
Clemson U., U. of Georgia, U. of North Carolina at Chapel Hill

AND SOMETIMES PREFER
U. of South Carolina—Columbia, Furman U., James Madison U., Elon U.

AND RARELY PREFER
Coastal Carolina U., Winthrop U., Wofford College, Appalachian State U.

FINANCIAL FACTS

Financial Aid Rating	75
Annual in-state tuition	$8,400
Annual out-of-state tuition	$20,418
Room and board	$8,999
Books and supplies	$1,123
% frosh rec. need-based scholarship or grant aid	29
% UG rec. need-based scholarship or grant aid	24
% frosh rec. non-need-based scholarship or grant aid	30
% UG rec. non-need-based scholarship or grant aid	17
% frosh rec. need-based self-help aid	28
% UG rec. need-based self-help aid	30
% frosh rec. athletic scholarships	2
% UG rec. athletic scholarships	2
% frosh rec. any financial aid	39
% UG rec. any financial aid	36
% UG borrow to pay for school	45.8
Average cumulative indebtedness	$17,118

COLLEGE OF THE HOLY CROSS

ADMISSIONS OFFICE, ONE COLLEGE STREET, WORCESTER, MA 01610-2395 • ADMISSIONS: 508-793-2443 • FAX: 508-793-3888

CAMPUS LIFE
Quality of Life Rating	70
Fire Safety Rating	98
Green Rating	94
Type of school	private
Affiliation	Roman Catholic
Environment	city

STUDENTS
Total undergrad enrollment	2,866
% male/female	44/56
% from out of state	62
% from public high school	44
% live on campus	89
% African American	4
% Asian	6
% Caucasian	68
% Hispanic	6
% international	1
# of countries represented	15

SURVEY SAYS . . .
Frats and sororities are unpopular or nonexistent
Student government is popular
Lots of beer drinking
Hard liquor is popular

ACADEMICS
Academic Rating	98
Calendar	semester
Student/faculty ratio	10:1
Profs interesting rating	92
Profs accessible rating	92
Most common reg class size	10–19 students
Most common lab size	fewer than 10 students

MOST POPULAR MAJORS
economics
English language and literature
political science and government

STUDENTS SAY ". . ."

Academics
The College of the Holy Cross is a smallish, "rigorous" Jesuit school "that does an incredible job of giving its students a very broad education [and] preparing them with the tools for the real world." Every student must complete a broad liberal arts curriculum. Regardless of your major, you'll take courses in history, literature, religion, philosophy, foreign language, math, science, and art. In additional, all first-year students take part in full-year seminars that are heavy on intellectual development. There's an array of exciting and often exotic study abroad options. The semester in Washington, D.C. receives a lot of praise. Internship programs are also abundant, and students also have access to a "large and strong alumni network." "Holy Cross alums are insane" about their old alma mater, and they love to hire the latest batch of graduates. "The emphasis here is on teaching and learning, not research," and the academic atmosphere is intense. "At Holy Cross, the professors will keep you busy throughout the week." "Classes are hard," warns a biology major. Good grades are hard to come by. "You have to work your tail off to just get an A–." At the same time, students love their "caring" and "amazing" professors, and they point out that small class sizes provide opportunities for meaningful faculty-student interaction. Profs are "very accessible outside the classroom," too. In fact, they "almost force you to get to know them." "If you show interest and work hard, you will do well," concludes an English major.

Life
There's "a lively social scene" on this "beautiful" hilltop campus. There are more than 80 clubs and organizations, and virtually everyone is "active in something, whether it be a varsity team, intramurals, student government, clubs, the newspaper, theater, or music." Studying is also an exceedingly common pastime. "The libraries and study rooms are often packed with students at night." On the weekends, however, "Holy Cross is a very big party school." "Although I would not consider Holy Cross to be the most outrageously fun school," relates a senior, "the student body at Holy Cross likes to drink." "People work hard during the week, and they like to let loose and have fun." Parties generally occur "in dorm rooms or at nearby off-campus housing." "Bars are popular," too, and usually "cheap." Students are also quick to call our attention to the fact that there is plenty to do on the weekends besides drinking. "If that's not your scene, there are so many other things to do," reports one student. There is everything "from going to plays, to sporting events, dances, karaoke, and stand-up comedians—all right here on campus." The food is probably the biggest complaint we hear. "Stick to the pasta," recommends a senior. The surrounding city of Worcester is home to "great" grub, but it's kind of sketchy otherwise. Luckily, "trips to Boston and Providence are extremely feasible, and the school has free buses to these locations on the weekends."

Student Body
Holy Cross is a "remarkably" welcoming campus. "This is the most friendly campus you will ever step foot on," claims a senior. You can find students from just about every state, but the majority tends to come from New England and the mid-Atlantic states. Students tend to be Catholic, though there are certainly plenty of people with different religions and with no religion at all. "Religion is not a major issue" here, really. Atypical students exist, and they "fit in just fine," but most of the undergraduate population at HC does kind of fit a certain mold. "The typical student is upper-middle-class, white, somewhat preppy, and athletic." That student is "smart," "hardworking," and probably "from the suburbs." "If you dress really preppy all the time, party hard on the weekends, and study in the rest of your remaining time, this is the school for you."

FINANCIAL AID: 508-793-2265 • E-MAIL: ADMISSIONS@HOLYCROSS.EDU • WEBSITE: WWW.HOLYCROSS.EDU

THE PRINCETON REVIEW SAYS

Admissions

Very important factors considered include: Class rank, academic GPA, rigor of secondary school record. *Important factors considered include:* Application essay, recommendation(s), alumni/ae relation, character/personal qualities, extracurricular activities, interview. *Other factors considered include:* Standardized test scores, first generation, geographical residence, level of applicant's interest, racial/ethnic status, talent/ability, volunteer work, work experience. TOEFL required of all international applicants. High school diploma is required and GED is accepted. *Academic units recommended:* 4 English, 4 mathematics, 4 science, 3 foreign language, 2 social studies, 2 history, 1 academic elective.

Financial Aid

Students should submit: FAFSA, CSS/financial aid profile, noncustodial profile, business/farm supplement. Parent and student federal tax returns. Regular filing deadline is 2/1. The Princeton Review suggests that all financial aid forms be submitted as soon as possible after 1/1. *Need-based scholarships/grants offered:* Federal Pell, SEOG, state scholarships/grants, private scholarships, the school's own gift aid. *Loan aid offered:* Direct Subsidized Stafford, Direct Unsubsidized Stafford, Direct PLUS, Federal Perkins, MEFA. Applicants will be notified of awards on or about 4/1. Federal Work-Study Program available. Institutional employment available. Off-campus job opportunities are fair.

The Inside Word

Admission to Holy Cross is competitive; therefore, a demanding high school course load is required to be a viable candidate. The college values effective communication skills—it thoroughly evaluates each applicant's personal statement and short essay responses. Interviews are important, especially for those applying early decision. Students who graduate from a Catholic high school might find themselves at a slight advantage.

THE SCHOOL SAYS ". . ."

From The Admissions Office

"When applying to Holy Cross, two areas deserve particular attention. First, the essay should be developed thoughtfully, with correct language and syntax in mind. That essay reflects for the Board of Admissions how you think and how you can express yourself. Second, activity beyond the classroom should be clearly defined. Since Holy Cross [has only] 2,800 students, the chance for involvement/participation is exceptional. The board reviews many applications for academically qualified students. A key difference in being accepted is the extent to which a candidate participates in-depth beyond the classroom—don't be modest; define who you are.

"Standardized test scores (i.e., SAT, SAT Subject Tests, and ACT) are optional. Students may submit their scores if they believe the results paint a fuller picture of their achievements and potential, but those students who don't submit scores will not be at a disadvantage in admissions decisions."

SELECTIVITY

Admissions Rating	96
# of applicants	7,227
% of applicants accepted	34
% of acceptees attending	30
# accepting a place on wait list	382
% admitted from wait list	9
# of early decision applicants	522
% accepted early decision	56

FRESHMAN PROFILE

Range SAT Critical Reading	580–670
Range SAT Math	600–680
Minimum paper TOEFL	550
Minimum computer TOEFL	213
Minimum web-based TOEFL	79
% graduated top 10% of class	61
% graduated top 25% of class	90
% graduated top 50% of class	99

DEADLINES

Early decision	
Deadline	12/15
Notification	1/15
Regular	
Deadline	1/15
Notification	4/1
Nonfall registration?	yes

APPLICANTS ALSO LOOK AT
AND OFTEN PREFER

University of Notre Dame
Georgetown University
Boston College
Tufts University

AND SOMETIMES PREFER

Fairfield University
Fordham University
Loyola University Maryland
Villanova University
Boston University
Providence College

FINANCIAL FACTS

Financial Aid Rating	93
Annual tuition	$38,180
Room and board	$10,620
Required fees	$542
Books and supplies	$700
% frosh rec. need-based scholarship or grant aid	42
% UG rec. need-based scholarship or grant aid	45
% frosh rec. non-need-based scholarship or grant aid	2
% UG rec. non-need-based scholarship or grant aid	2
% frosh rec. need-based self-help aid	39
% UG rec. need-based self-help aid	44
% frosh rec. athletic scholarships	1
% UG rec. athletic scholarships	1
% frosh rec. any financial aid	60
% UG rec. any financial aid	59

THE COLLEGE OF IDAHO

2112 CLEVELAND BOULEVARD, CALDWELL, ID 83605 • ADMISSIONS: 208-459-5305 • FAX: 208-459-5757

CAMPUS LIFE
Quality of Life Rating	**82**
Fire Safety Rating	**67**
Green Rating	**81**
Type of school	private
Environment	town

STUDENTS
Total undergrad enrollment	928
% male/female	40/60
% from out of state	25
% live on campus	62
% in (# of) fraternities	21 (3)
% in (# of) sororities	20 (4)
% African American	1
% Asian	2
% Caucasian	62
% Hispanic	8
% international	6
# of countries represented	28

SURVEY SAYS . . .
Students are friendly
Different types of students interact
Campus feels safe
Low cost of living
(Almost) no one smokes

ACADEMICS
Academic Rating	**86**
Calendar	13/6/13
Student/faculty ratio	11:1
Profs interesting rating	92
Profs accessible rating	89
Most common reg class size	fewer than 10 students

MOST POPULAR MAJORS
biology/biological sciences
business/commerce
psychology

STUDENTS SAY " . . . "

Academics

A small liberal arts school, The College of Idaho is "like a diamond in the rough." Students tell us, "You'd be surprised at the very high quality this little school offers!" The small class sizes and low student-to-teacher ratio promote the school's emphasis on "individual learning" and a "personalized education plan." The academic experience at The College of Idaho is "incredibly rigorous but also very rewarding." Though the school has a "well developed" liberal arts core, students also describe the biology and pre-med programs as "fantastic." Courses are "challenging," "fascinating," and "great preparation for both graduate school and the professional world." The small school environment provides a "sense of community" and allows students to develop "strong working relationships" with their professors. Students tell us their professors are "attentive," "very accessible," and "passionate about what they teach." One graduating senior described the school as "an academic gold mine of some of the most published and highly regarded professors and researchers in the field." The "personal teaching" approach the professors at the C of I take makes them "consistently recognized nationally and internationally for their contributions to the academic community and to their students." The administration is "involved with the students" and "effective" though "the professors are what make The College of Idaho great." Also great is the fact that the school is "cost competitive" and offers "generous scholarships." As one freshman tells us, "My school is way more than a place for me to learn. My teachers have become more like guardians for my education, and my peers...my second family."

Life

Life in Caldwell can be "pretty quiet" but Boise, the capital, is only about a 30-minute drive away, and the school regularly hosts trips into the city. However, the campus "strives" and "mostly succeeds" in making up for the town by sponsoring many activities on campus. A student tells us, "On campus there is always something going on...I rarely have a night where there isn't something that I could do for fun." The College of Idaho offers a variety of extracurricular activities. The school's Program Council "puts on great events all year long." Such events as movie and bowling nights are open to all students and are often offered free of charge. Students at The College of Idaho also tend to be very interested in clubs and club-sponsored events. With a multitude of clubs to join, there is a club "for all personality types." One student tells us, "Whether it is attending a theater or band concert, an athletic event, or a club meeting, there are plenty of ways to get involved." Students describe their school life as "great overall," and because the school is so small, "any major campus-sponsored activity brings us all together as one, giant, friendly social club."

Student Body

Students tell us, The College of Idaho has "students from many walks of life" and a "student body full of individuals." While a majority of the student body is "white, middle class, and right out of high school," students at The College of Idaho promote an "atmosphere of learning from others no matter their background." Many students tell us that there really isn't a "typical student," which isn't so surprising given its large international student population. Each student at The College of Idaho is "an active participant in the campus community." One junior tells us students are, "overly involved," and "extremely busy with clubs, campus activities, athletics, and academics."

Students are "hard working but social," "intelligent," and "well-rounded." According to one sophomore, "though [we are all] different, the commonality of going to C of I brings us together."

FINANCIAL AID: 208-459-5308 • E-MAIL: ADMISSION@COLLEGEOFIDAHO.EDU • WEBSITE: WWW.COLLEGEOFIDAHO.EDU

THE PRINCETON REVIEW SAYS

Admissions

Very important factors considered include: Application essay, academic GPA, recommendation(s), rigor of secondary school record, standardized test scores, character/personal qualities, extracurricular activities, level of applicant's interest, *Important factors considered include:* Class rank, interview. *Other factors considered include:* alumni/ae relation, first generation, geographical residence, talent/ability, volunteer work, SAT or ACT required; ACT with Writing component required. TOEFL required of all international applicants. High school diploma is required and GED is accepted. *Academic units required:* 3 English, 2 mathematics, 3 social studies, 3 history, 3 academic electives. *Academic units recommended:* 4 English, 4 mathematics, 3 science, (3 science labs), 3 foreign language, 3 social studies, 3 history, 3 academic electives.

Financial Aid

Students should submit: FAFSA, institution's own financial aid form. The Princeton Review suggests that all financial aid forms be submitted as soon as possible after 1/1. Need-based scholarships/grants offered: Federal Pell, SEOG, state scholarships/grants, private scholarships, the school's own gift aid. *Loan aid offered:* FFEL Subsidized Stafford, FFEL Unsubsidized Stafford, FFEL PLUS, Federal Perkins, Alternative Education Loans. Applicants will be notified of awards on a rolling basis beginning 2/1. Federal Work-Study Program available. Off-campus job opportunities are good.

The Inside Word

Despite its high acceptance rate, the admissions committee at The College of Idaho is looking for students who have taken high school seriously. Candidates who demonstrate reasonable academic success and a variety of extracurricular activities will be handed the keys to a quality academic program and a unique college experience, one that stresses self-confidence and social responsibility.

THE SCHOOL SAYS "..."

From The Admissions Office

"While the mission of The College of Idaho is traditional in that it remains committed to the teaching of the liberal arts, many of the approaches to accomplishing this goal are unique. Within the campus community is the opportunity to create classroom opportunities for students that span the globe—both technologically and geographically. Here, students are just as apt to attend a biology class on campus as they are to hike in the nearby Owyhee or Sawtooth Mountains to carry out field research. During the college's 6-week winter term, more than 30 percent of the students are emailing friends and family from such locales as Australia, Israel, France, Ireland, England, Peru, and or Mexico while taking part in faculty-led, multidisciplinary trips. Students are invited to visit the campus and the admissions counselors, either in person or online.

"C of I requires all admission candidates (who have not reached sophomore status in college) to submit either the SAT or the ACT with the Writing component. ACI will consider all scores. There is no SAT Subject Test requirement, but scores will be considered as part of a holistic evaluation."

SELECTIVITY
Admissions Rating	86
# of applicants	1,275
% of applicants accepted	59
% of acceptees attending	37

FRESHMAN PROFILE
Range SAT Critical Reading	470–623
Range SAT Math	490–630
Range SAT Writing	460–570
Range ACT Composite	22–27
Minimum paper TOEFL	550
Minimum computer TOEFL	213
Minimum web-based TOEFL	79
Average HS GPA	3.63
% graduated top 10% of class	29
% graduated top 25% of class	68
% graduated top 50% of class	91

DEADLINES
Early action	
Deadline	12/15
Notification	ongoing
Regular	
Priority	6/1
Deadline	8/1
Notification	rolling
Nonfall registration?	yes

APPLICANTS ALSO LOOK AT
AND OFTEN PREFER
Boise State University
Idaho State University
University of Oregon
University of Idaho
University of Utah

FINANCIAL FACTS
Financial Aid Rating	80
Annual tuition	$19,300
Room and board	$7,478
Required fees	$735
Books and supplies	$900
% frosh rec. need-based scholarship or grant aid	45
% UG rec. need-based scholarship or grant aid	39
% frosh rec. non-need-based scholarship or grant aid	66
% UG rec. non-need-based scholarship or grant aid	59
% frosh rec. need-based self-help aid	49
% UG rec. need-based self-help aid	44
% frosh rec. athletic scholarships	21
% UG rec. athletic scholarships	26
% frosh rec. any financial aid	99
% UG rec. any financial aid	98
% UG borrow to pay for school	76
Average cumulative indebtedness	$24,919

THE COLLEGE OF NEW JERSEY

PO Box 7718, Ewing, NJ 08628-0718 • Admissions: 609-771-2131 • Fax: 609-637-5174

CAMPUS LIFE

Quality of Life Rating	**94**
Fire Safety Rating	**95**
Green Rating	**90**
Type of school	public
Environment	village

STUDENTS

Total undergrad enrollment	6,194
% male/female	41/59
% from out of state	5
% from public high school	65
% live on campus	58
% in (# of) fraternities	13 (11)
% in (# of) sororities	13 (15)
% African American	7
% Asian	6
% Caucasian	68
% Hispanic	9
# of countries represented	11

SURVEY SAYS . . .

Lab facilities are great
Great library
School is well run
Students are friendly
Low cost of living
Students are happy
Student publications are popular
(Almost) no one smokes

ACADEMICS

Academic Rating	**86**
Calendar	semester
Student/faculty ratio	13:1
Profs interesting rating	89
Profs accessible rating	86
Most common reg class size	20–29 students
Most common lab size	10–19 students

MOST POPULAR MAJORS

biology/biological sciences
elementary education and teaching
psychology

STUDENTS SAY ". . ."

Academics

The College of New Jersey, "a small, liberal arts, state school that offers, to the best of its abilities, everything that a private school offers," earns plaudits from a student body that understands just what a great deal the school represents. "Many of my friends had well above 1300 SAT scores and got into very prestigious schools such as Georgetown, NYU, Columbia, and Villanova, but chose TCNJ because of its unbeatable cost," explains one student, who warns that the school is "no joke" academically and notes that even those aforementioned friends "are constantly studying and find no cake-walk when it comes to classes." Students benefit from "up-to-date facilities" including "an amazing library" and solid career services. Most impressive, however, is the small-school service students here receive; professors "clearly have their students' best interests in mind," and the administration is not only "amazingly helpful" but also solicitous of student opinion; "Whenever a position opens up in a department, the students are encouraged to attend lectures by prospective candidates and offer their input," one student writes. No wonder undergrads insist that TCNJ is "a smaller school that is a bargain for its quality of education."

Life

With "a beautiful campus, great location, top-notch faculty, the newest technology, an interested student body, and competitive sports teams," TCNJ really "is the total package." There "are a lot of things going on on-campus for people to get involved in," including "clubs and intramural sports that people commonly do for fun." The student center "offers games, and there are always performances going on," and "there are tons of student organizations and club teams." Although "People are generally the Abercrombie or Hollister type" here, "you don't have to be athletic or involved at all to be popular at TCNJ. It's completely acceptable to just hang out with people doing nothing constructive." The off-campus party scene "is fine," and "many people "attend the fraternity parties offered on Tuesdays, Fridays, and Saturdays," but "There is not much to do once you leave campus unless you have a car," and one student notes "some of the surrounding areas are a little sketchy." Further afield things get better, as "our school is a 15-minute drive from Princeton and 45 minutes outside of Philly."

Student Body

"You can find any personality type at TCNJ," students tell us, from "your typical jocks who love to party" to "extremely conservative kids who haven't missed a Sunday mass since getting here" and "a few hippie types and everything in between. Whatever your social circle, you're bound to fit in." What they share in common is that most are "smart, dedicated people who care about their education very much," "were in the top 15 percent of their high school class," and "are willing to push themselves to do better in school." While "everyone has different interests, inside the classroom there is never an intellectual differentiation between those in the Medieval Club and those in Greek life. I think everyone is atypical in his own way, and this is a great place for everyone to be able to find a niche." And while "the typical student at TCNJ is white and middle-upper class to upper class," the school also hosts a solid population of students of "different faiths and ethnicities."

FINANCIAL AID: 609-771-2211 • E-MAIL: ADMISS@VM.TCNJ.EDU • WEBSITE: WWW.TCNJ.EDU

THE PRINCETON REVIEW SAYS

Admissions

Very important factors considered include: Class rank, rigor of secondary school record, standardized test scores, extracurricular activities, volunteer work, *Important factors considered include:* Application essay, recommendation(s), character/personal qualities, geographical residence, state residency, talent/ability. *Other factors considered include:* academic GPA, alumni/ae relation, first generation, level of applicant's interest, racial/ethnic status, work experience. SAT or ACT required; TOEFL required of all international applicants. High school diploma is required and GED is accepted. *Academic units required:* 4 English, 3 mathematics, 3 science, (2 science labs), 2 foreign language, 2 social studies. *Academic units recommended:* 4 English, 3 mathematics, 3 science, (3 science labs), 3 foreign language, 3 social studies.

Financial Aid

Students should submit: FAFSA Regular filing deadline is 10/1. The Princeton Review suggests that all financial aid forms be submitted as soon as possible after 1/1. Need-based scholarships/grants offered: Federal Pell, SEOG, state scholarships/grants, private scholarships, the school's own gift aid. *Loan aid offered:* FFEL Subsidized Stafford, FFEL Unsubsidized Stafford, FFEL PLUS, Federal Perkins, Federal Nursing. Applicants will be notified of awards on a rolling basis beginning 6/1. Federal Work-Study Program available. Institutional employment available. Off-campus job opportunities are excellent.

The Inside Word

The College of New Jersey accepts nearly half of all applicants, but that figure is deceiving; this is a self-selecting applicant pool; those with no chance of acceptance simply don't bother. Admissions are as competitive as you'd expect at a school that offers state residents a small-college experience and a highly respected degree for bargain-basement prices. Competition among biology majors has grown especially fierce; applications must be in by January 1 rather than February 15, and biology majors' applications are not processed on a rolling basis.

THE SCHOOL SAYS "..."

From The Admissions Office

"The College of New Jersey is one of the United States' great higher education success stories. With a long history as New Jersey's preeminent teacher of teachers, the college has grown into a new role as educator of the state's best students in a wide range of fields. The College of New Jersey has created a culture of constant questioning—a place where knowledge is not merely received but reconfigured. In small classes, students and faculty members collaborate in a rewarding process: As they seek to understand fundamental principles, apply key concepts, reveal new problems, and pursue new lines of inquiry, students gain a fluency of thought in their disciplines. The college's 289-acre tree-lined campus is a union of vision, engineering, beauty, and functionality. Neoclassical Georgian Colonial architecture, meticulous landscaping, and thoughtful design merge in a dynamic system, constantly evolving to meet the needs of TCNJ students. About half percent of TCNJ's entering class will be academic scholars, with large numbers of National Merit finalists and semifinalists. More than 400 students in the class received awards from New Jersey's Outstanding Student Recruitment Program. The College of New Jersey is bringing together the best ideas from around the nation and building a new model for public undergraduate education on one campus...in New Jersey!

"The College of New Jersey will accept the SAT as well as the ACT with or without the Writing component."

SELECTIVITY

Admissions Rating	93
# of applicants	9,692
% of applicants accepted	42
% of acceptees attending	31
# accepting a place on wait list	405
% admitted from wait list	19
# of early decision applicants	450
% accepted early decision	57

FRESHMAN PROFILE

Range SAT Critical Reading	560–660
Range SAT Math	590–690
Range SAT Writing	570–670
Minimum paper TOEFL	550
Minimum computer TOEFL	213
% graduated top 10% of class	66
% graduated top 25% of class	90
% graduated top 50% of class	99

DEADLINES

Early Decision	
Deadline	11/15
Notification	12/15
Regular	
Deadline	2/15
Notification	rolling
Nonfall registration?	yes

APPLICANTS ALSO LOOK AT
AND OFTEN PREFER

Rutgers, The State University of New Jersey—New Brunswick
University of Delaware
New York University
Drexel University
Villanova University

AND SOMETIMES PREFER

University of Maryland—College Park
Rowan University
Lehigh University
Boston University

FINANCIAL FACTS

Financial Aid Rating	71
Annual in-state tuition	$8,718
Annual out-of-state tuition	$16,825
Room and board	$9,612
Required fees	$3,590
Books and supplies	$1,000
% frosh rec. need-based scholarship or grant aid	16
% UG rec. need-based scholarship or grant aid	16
% frosh rec. non-need-based scholarship or grant aid	21
% UG rec. non-need-based scholarship or grant aid	16
% frosh rec. need-based self-help aid	28
% UG rec. need-based self-help aid	31
% frosh rec. any financial aid	88
% UG rec. any financial aid	68
% UG borrow to pay for school	58
Average cumulative indebtedness	$22,088

COLLEGE OF THE OZARKS

OFFICE OF ADMISSIONS, POINT LOOKOUT, MO 65726 • ADMISSIONS: 417-334-6411 • FAX: 417-335-2618

CAMPUS LIFE

Quality of Life Rating	92
Fire Safety Rating	64
Green Rating	73
Type of school	private
Environment	rural

STUDENTS

Total undergrad enrollment	1,320
% male/female	43/57
% from out of state	33
% from public high school	82
% live on campus	84
% African American	1
% Asian	1
% Caucasian	94
% Hispanic	1
% Native American	1
% international	2
# of countries represented	15

SURVEY SAYS . . .

Students are very religious
Students get along with local
community
Frats and sororities are unpopular or
nonexistent
Theater is popular
Very little beer drinking
Very little drug use

ACADEMICS

Academic Rating	80
Calendar	semester
Student/faculty ratio	13:1
Profs interesting rating	78
Profs accessible rating	80
Most common	
reg class size	10–19 students
Most common	
lab size	10–19 students

MOST POPULAR MAJORS

agriculture
business administration and
management
elementary education and teaching

STUDENTS SAY ". . ."

Academics

Tiny College of the Ozarks provides a very pre-professional liberal arts education and allows many students to graduate "debt-free" through four years of "honest, old-fashioned, hard work." You still need to cover books, room and board, and some fees but there are no tuition costs. Instead of paying tuition, students here are required to work 15 hours a week during school and two 40-hour weeks each year during breaks. "Students work in all offices and areas of the college." There are pedestrian jobs such as computer support and custodial work but there are cooler jobs, too. You might work for the campus fire department, or at the hog farm, or as a jelly cook in the jelly kitchen. Academically, the nursing and business programs are reportedly "excellent." There are "extraordinary, passionate" professors here and there are others who "just stand up there and read from PowerPoint." "The teachers aren't Einsteins," reflects an English major, "but most are very good teachers and are there for their students if needed." Without question, the administration at C of O is very good at soliciting all the donated money that is required to keep tuition free and it "seems to genuinely care about the students." However, campus rules are very, very strict.

Life

Some dorms and academic buildings at C of O "are in need of repair." ("Hello mold!") "Because the college runs on donations, some renovations simply can't be done until someone wants their name on a building," notes a junior. There is "a surplus" of spiritual events and a "Christian atmosphere" is pervasive. Men's and women's basketball and intramural sports in general are favorite pastimes. "We have movie nights and dances that are pretty cool," comments a sophomore. Mudfest is a campus-wide tug of war. "If you participate, the only part of your body left clean would be your eyes and teeth." "Outdoorsy activities are highly popular" and the Ozark area offers virtually everything. Just down the road, the "big tourist trap" of Branson offers "a lot of entertainment resources." In many ways, though, "life down here is pretty quiet" and "not necessarily a real world experience." Attendance at Chapel is required a few times each semester. "Most C of O students are not interested in partying" but there is "a zero-tolerance policy" just in case. Caffeine is the stimulant of choice. Drugs and alcohol are "strictly prohibited." You can't smoke cigarettes, either. Other rules include a 1:00 A.M. curfew and restricted dorm visits by members of the opposite sex. "Weekly room checks" thwart clutter. Students "aren't allowed to dress outrageously." Everyone must maintain "natural-looking hair color." Pretty clearly, this environment is not for everyone. It's really a question of priorities. "What's more important," asks one student, "being able to look trashy or getting out of college without huge amounts of debt?"

Student Body

Ethnic diversity and diversity in general are paltry at College of the Ozarks. "The typical student here is a white, middle to lower class, conservative Christian," and almost certainly "from the Midwest." "There are a lot of home-school students." "For the most part, we come from families who could not afford a 'normal' school and so we are here," asserts one student. "Stuck." "At C of O, you have the Crispies (those who are so Christian and religious that it's bad), the normal Christians who enjoy life but aren't hung up on reciting Bible verses to each other, and the partiers," describes a senior. "That's about all there is to it." The population overwhelmingly falls into the first two groups, though; partiers are a rare and exotic species. These "well-rounded, good Christian kids" are "extremely helpful," "friendly," "down to earth," and "used to earning every penny they have." They typically are involved in extracurricular activities and they enjoy each other's company. "At C of O, most students are personable and enjoy community. Students who seem to be loners or who don't enjoy a close-knit community would probably not enjoy things here."

FINANCIAL AID: 417-334-6411 • E-MAIL: ADMISS4@COFO.EDU • WEBSITE: WWW.COFO.EDU

THE PRINCETON REVIEW SAYS

Admissions

Very important factors considered include: Class rank, rigor of secondary school record, character/personal qualities, interview. *Important factors considered include:* Academic GPA, recommendation(s), standardized test scores, geographical residence, level of applicant's interest, volunteer work, work experience. *Other factors considered include:* Alumni/ae relation, extracurricular activities, first generation, religious affiliation/commitment, state residency, talent/ability. SAT or ACT required. ACT recommended. TOEFL required of all international applicants. High school diploma is required and GED is accepted. *Academic units recommended:* 4 English, 3 mathematics, 2 science (1 science lab), 2 foreign language, 3 social studies, 1 visual/peforming arts/public speaking.

Financial Aid

Students should submit: FAFSA. The Princeton Review suggests that all financial aid forms be submitted as soon as possible after 1/1. *Need-based scholarships/grants offered:* Federal Pell, SEOG, state scholarships/grants, private scholarships, the school's own gift aid. Applicants will be notified of awards on a rolling basis beginning 3/1. Federal Work-Study Program available. Off-campus job opportunities are excellent.

The Inside Word

The highly unusual nature of the College of the Ozarks translates directly into its admissions process. Because of the school's very purpose, providing educational opportunities to those with great financial need, one of the main qualifiers for admission is exactly that—demonstrated financial need. Despite not being a household name, Ozarks attracts enough interest to keep its admit rate consistently low from year to year. To be sure, the admissions process is competitive, but it's more important to be a good fit for the college philosophically and financially than it is to be an academic wizard. If you're a hard worker all around, you're just what they're looking for.

THE SCHOOL SAYS "..."

From The Admissions Office

"College of the Ozarks is unique because of its no-tuition, work-study program, but also because it strives to educate the head, the heart, and the hands. At C of O, there are high expectations of students—the college stresses character development as well as study and work. An education from 'Hard Work U.' offers many opportunities, not the least of which is the chance to graduate debt-free. Life at C of O isn't all hard work and no play, however. There are many opportunities for fun. The nearby resort town of Branson, Missouri, offers ample opportunities for recreation and summer employment, and Table Rock Lake, only a few miles away, is a terrific spot to swim, sun, and relax. Numerous on-campus activities such as Mudfest, Luau Night, dances, and holiday parties give students lots of chances for fun without leaving the college. At 'Hard Work U.,' we work hard, but we know how to have fun, too.

"Applicants are required to submit scores from the ACT or the SAT. We will use the student's best scores from either test. Writing scores are not required."

SELECTIVITY
Admissions Rating	**89**
# of applicants	2,698
% of applicants accepted	12
% of acceptees attending	87
# accepting a place on wait list	420
% admitted from wait list	4

FRESHMAN PROFILE
Range SAT Critical Reading	530–590
Range SAT Math	440–620
Range SAT Writing	460–620
Range ACT Composite	20–25
Minimum paper TOEFL	550
Minimum computer TOEFL	213
Minimum web-based TOEFL	79
Average HS GPA	3.53
% graduated top 10% of class	20
% graduated top 25% of class	55
% graduated top 50% of class	91

DEADLINES
Regular	
Priority	2/15
Deadline	2/15
Notification	rolling
Nonfall registration?	yes

APPLICANTS ALSO LOOK AT
AND OFTEN PREFER
Missouri State University
AND SOMETIMES PREFER
Southwest Baptist University

FINANCIAL FACTS
Financial Aid Rating	**89**
Annual tuition	$0
Room and board	$5,000
Required fees	$390
Books and supplies	$800
% frosh rec. need-based scholarship or grant aid	89
% UG rec. need-based scholarship or grant aid	91
% frosh rec. non-need-based scholarship or grant aid	12
% UG rec. non-need-based scholarship or grant aid	17
% frosh rec. need-based self-help aid	77
% UG rec. need-based self-help aid	73
% frosh rec. athletic scholarships	1
% UG rec. athletic scholarships	3
% frosh rec. any financial aid	100
% UG rec. any financial aid	100
% UG borrow to pay for school	15
Average cumulative indebtedness	$4,878

THE COLLEGE OF WILLIAM & MARY

PO BOX 8795, WILLIAMSBURG, VA 23187-8795 • ADMISSIONS: 757-221-4223 • FAX: 757-221-1242

CAMPUS LIFE

Quality of Life Rating	**90**
Fire Safety Rating	**75**
Green Rating	**90**
Type of school	public
Environment	village

STUDENTS

Total undergrad enrollment	5,850
% male/female	45/55
% from out of state	32
% live on campus	74
% in (# of) fraternities	25 (18)
% in (# of) sororities	27 (12)
% African American	7
% Asian	8
% Caucasian	59
% Hispanic	6
% Native American	1
% international	2
# of countries represented	54

SURVEY SAYS . . .
No one cheats
Great library
Athletic facilities are great
Students are friendly
Campus feels safe
Students are happy
Student publications are popular
Student government is popular

ACADEMICS

Academic Rating	**92**
Calendar	semester
Student/faculty ratio	11:1
Profs interesting rating	96
Profs accessible rating	90
% classes taught by TAs	1

STUDENTS SAY "..."

Academics
The College of William & Mary is "the second oldest school in the country," and it has an honor code "that was started by Thomas Jefferson." "Registration can be a lesson in disappointment" but the administration "is very in touch with the student body" and "openly asks for and is responsive to criticism." The faculty is generally tremendous. "Professors are better than I could have imagined," reflects a geology major. "They are the best teachers I have ever had. They are passionate about what they teach." "I am in classes that range from a large lecture of 300 people to a small seminar of 15," adds a first-year student. "I find that all of the teachers teach in the exact same manner, so it seems like all of my classes are in an intimate setting." "Professors are always available outside of class" as well. Be warned, though, that "the academic scene is definitely intense" at W&M. "The amount of work is often unbearable." "You're not going to get a 4.0," cautions an international relations major. "It's absolutely unheard of." Instead, professor "will give you a 'B–,' smiling." "This school is incredibly challenging," concludes a public policy major, "but at the end of the semester, when you reflect back on just how much you've learned, you realize that the sleepless nights of study and stressful weekends spent cramming instead of relaxing were worth it."

Life
William & Mary is "small enough where you don't feel like you're swallowed up into a crowd of 30,000 people, but it's also large enough to allow you some anonymity." Food is "greasy and not very good," and parking is really bad, but "the sheer number and variety of organizations is a huge strength." "Most students juggle numerous activities in addition to their school work." "I write for the newspaper, sing, and volunteer with a food kitchen," illustrates a sophomore. "That's pretty representative of the student body." "Fun at William & Mary is not completely orthodox." "A capella groups are more popular on campus than sports teams." "Big traditions" include a campus-wide convocation ceremony in the fall; Yule Log in December, when the school president reads *The Grinch Who Stole Christmas*; and the well-attended King & Queens Ball in the spring. W&M "can be draconian toward drinking" but there's "a pretty decent nightlife." "If you want to drink, you won't have a problem finding alcohol and, if you don't drink, the parties are still social and lively, without any pressure." "The Greek scene is visible, but is not huge." Fraternities have dance parties every weekend, "and no one is turned away." "Off-campus parties are popular, but they get busted a lot." Students also hang out a lot at a few nearby delis. They're "pretty much bars, but since Williamsburg doesn't allow the title 'bars,' they call them delis." Surrounding Williamsburg is "a town full of people who are old or like to dress up as colonial people." It's "a historical haven," though, and "a pleasant detour from life's stresses" "after tourist season is over."

Student Body
There are certainly rich kids here but William & Mary is a state school, and "a lot of people come from more modest backgrounds." Many students come from northern Virginia, "but it's not an epidemic." Students tell us that ethnic diversity could improve. "Minorities feel outnumbered," they say. "Dumb people stand out," too. This is a pretty "intelligent and well read" crowd. "It's not unheard of to get into a theoretical discussion of politics or history or literature while drunk at a party." "The typical student is dorky and slightly awkward but nonetheless very friendly," though there are "never-come-out-of-the-library people" and a few "complete social rejects." On the whole, students at W&M are "crazy perfectionists" who are "involved in different things." They're "eclectic and quirky." "They're warm and welcoming." "Everyone at William and Mary is in touch with their inner nerd and happy with it." "It's mainly people being themselves, unabashed and proud." "That guy who sits next to you in your 300-level science class is a starting linebacker on the football team."

FINANCIAL AID: 757-221-2420 • E-MAIL: ADMISS@WM.EDU • WEBSITE: WWW.WM.EDU

THE PRINCETON REVIEW SAYS

Admissions

Very important factors considered include: Class rank, application essay, academic GPA, recommendation(s), rigor of secondary school record, standardized test scores, character/personal qualities, extracurricular activities, state residency, talent/ability. *Other factors considered include:* Alumni/ae relation, first generation, geographical residence, interview, racial/ethnic status, volunteer work, work experience. SAT or ACT required. TOEFL required of all international applicants. High school diploma or equivalent is not required. *Academic units recommended:* 4 English, 4 mathematics, 4 science (3 science labs), 4 foreign language, 4 social studies.

Financial Aid

Students should submit: FAFSA. The Princeton Review suggests that all financial aid forms be submitted as soon as possible after 1/1. *Need-based scholarships/grants offered:* Federal Pell, SEOG, state scholarships/grants, private scholarships, the school's own gift aid. *Loan aid offered:* FFEL Subsidized Stafford, FFEL Unsubsidized Stafford, FFEL PLUS, Federal Perkins. Applicants will be notified of awards on a rolling basis beginning 3/15. Federal Work-Study Program available. Institutional employment available. Off-campus job opportunities are excellent.

The Inside Word

The volume of applications at William & Mary is extremely high; thus admission is ultra-competitive. Only very strong students from out of state should apply. The large applicant pool necessitates a rapid-fire candidate evaluation process; each admissions officer reads roughly 100 application folders per day during the peak review season. But this is one admissions committee that moves fast without sacrificing a thorough review. There probably isn't a tougher public college admissions committee in the country.

THE SCHOOL SAYS "..."

From The Admissions Office

"William & Mary is the nation's second-oldest college and preeminent small public university. Yes, we have one of the lowest student/faculty ratio (11:1) of any public university. We're also known for having one of the most successful undergraduate business programs in the United States, a model United Nations team that perennially vies for the world championship, and extensive opportunities for undergraduate research. Students at William & Mary follow in the footsteps of alumni ranging from Thomas Jefferson, James Monroe, and John Tyler to Comedy Central's Jon Stewart, President Obama's Chair of the Council of Economic Advisers Christina Romer, and Super-Bowl-winning Pittsburg Steeler's coach Mike Tomlin. In short, William & Mary offers a top-rated educational experience at a comparatively low cost and in the company of interesting people from a broad variety of backgrounds. If you are an academically strong, involved student looking for a challenge in a great campus community, William & Mary may well be the place for you."

SELECTIVITY

Admissions Rating	98
# of applicants	11,636
% of applicants accepted	34
% of acceptees attending	35
# accepting a place on wait list	1,368
% admitted from wait list	12
# of early decision applicants	900
% accepted early decision	52

FRESHMAN PROFILE

Range SAT Critical Reading	630–730
Range SAT Math	620–710
Range SAT Writing	610–720
Range ACT Composite	27–32
Minimum paper TOEFL	600
Minimum computer TOEFL	250
Minimum web-based TOEFL	100
Average HS GPA	4
% graduated top 10% of class	79
% graduated top 25% of class	96.5
% graduated top 50% of class	99.8

DEADLINES

Early decision	
Deadline	11/1
Notification	12/1
Regular	
Deadline	1/1
Notification	4/1
Nonfall registration?	no

APPLICANTS ALSO LOOK AT
AND OFTEN PREFER
University of Virginia
Duke University
Georgetown University

FINANCIAL FACTS

Financial Aid Rating	84
Annual in-state tuition	$10,800
Annual out-of-state tuition	$30,964
% frosh rec. need-based scholarship or grant aid	21
% UG rec. need-based scholarship or grant aid	23
% frosh rec. non-need-based scholarship or grant aid	13
% UG rec. non-need-based scholarship or grant aid	10
% frosh rec. need-based self-help aid	23
% UG rec. need-based self-help aid	24
% frosh rec. athletic scholarships	4
% UG rec. athletic scholarships	5
% frosh rec. any financial aid	67
% UG rec. any financial aid	58
% UG borrow to pay for school	39
Average cumulative indebtedness	$12,859

THE COLLEGE OF WOOSTER

847 COLLEGE AVENUE, WOOSTER, OH 44691 • ADMISSIONS: 330-263-2322 • FAX: 330-263-2621

CAMPUS LIFE

Quality of Life Rating	76
Fire Safety Rating	70
Green Rating	74
Type of school	private
Environment	town

STUDENTS

Total undergrad enrollment	1,884
% male/female	47/53
% from out of state	54
% from public high school	65
% live on campus	98
% in (# of) fraternities	13 (5)
% in (# of) sororities	17 (6)
% African American	5
% Asian	2
% Caucasian	73
% Hispanic	2
% international	5
# of countries represented	30

SURVEY SAYS . . .
No one cheats
Lab facilities are great
Great library
Students are friendly
Low cost of living
Students are happy
Musical organizations are popular
Lots of beer drinking

ACADEMICS

Academic Rating	90
Calendar	semester
Student/faculty ratio	11.48:1
Profs interesting rating	90
Profs accessible rating	87
Most common reg class size	10–19 students
Most common lab size	10–19 students

MOST POPULAR MAJORS
English language and literature
history
psychology

STUDENTS SAY ". . ."

Academics

Undergrads here maintain that The College of Wooster "is about developing the autonomy of its students in all areas" from "their academic achievement and extracurricular activities to their self-awareness and ability to help others." Nowhere is this more evident than in the curriculum's "nationally renowned senior Independent Study (IS) project," which is where, students say, the "gold of Wooster lies." One student explains, "The Independent Study allowed me to customize and focus my interests into a thoroughly challenging, yet enjoyable, year-long project. Being able to organize and approach my own selected topic was an invaluable experience that has prepared me for the prospect of graduate school." A junior states that she chose Wooster "because it seemed to me that if students were expected to create such an intensive project then the classes must also be at a high caliber. I have certainly found this to be the case." Physics, chemistry, business and management, music, and history are among the standout disciplines here. Like most top-notch liberal arts schools, Wooster features "a small, closely-knit campus and accessible, genuinely interested professors, making it the ideal setting to branch out, both in and out of the classroom." Academics here involve "a lot of homework and reading," but students tell us that they get a good overall experience, one that "incorporat[es] relatively healthy doses of student activities, good dining halls, and a beautiful campus populated by (in general) great people."

Life

Wooster "is a tradition-based school with awesome activities, from the kilt-wearing marching band to the many sports teams, varsity and intramural," and students embrace these traditions with gusto. "The school is good at providing activities on weekends," students say, which include "bands and outside entertainment" as well as showcases of "students' talents." This is a good thing given that the town of Wooster "is very small [and] has little to offer in terms of activities besides restaurants and movies." Big-city entertainment can be found in Cleveland and Columbus, but both are an hour's drive away, so they're only an option if you have a car or are chummy with someone who has wheels. The on-campus party scene is robust; on "Wooster Wednesday" "people drink like it's Friday" (on actual Fridays "Many students go to the college bar/club called the Underground") and the "fraternity and sorority houses" are known for their "themed parties (Beach Party, Funk Party, Heaven and Hell, Stop and Go)." For students in search of other weekend options, the school "sponsors events to substitute [for] partying for those of us who do not participate." Have we mentioned that Wooster also has "lots of student organizations"? Word on campus is that the average student "participates in a vast array" of them.

Student Body

"There are a lot of different types of students" at Wooster, including "people who seem to be at school just to have a good time," and many more people who "seem to be here to get as much as possible out of the[ir] education." Many are "from Ohio or the Midwest," but there are also "many international students on campus, and they fit in with the rest of the student population as much as anyone else." The typical undergrad is "liberal, but rather apathetic to politics and religion." Socially, the school "is divided into countless little social groups," many of which form "based on first-year experiences, athletic involvement, or extracurricular interests." Indeed, you'll find "a lot of athletes" among the student population, and many who "are involved in a wide array of extracurricular activities"; these activities prompt "students from different backgrounds and social groups [to] interact and work together."

FINANCIAL AID: 800-877-3688 • E-MAIL: ADMISSIONS@WOOSTER.EDU • WEBSITE: WWW.WOOSTER.EDU

THE PRINCETON REVIEW SAYS

Admissions

Very important factors considered include: Class rank, academic GPA, rigor of secondary school record, *Important factors considered include:* Application essay, recommendation(s), standardized test scores, character/personal qualities, talent/ability. *Other factors considered include:* alumni/ae relation, extracurricular activities, geographical residence, interview, racial/ethnic status, state residency, volunteer work, work experience. SAT or ACT required; ACT with Writing component required. TOEFL required of all international applicants. High school diploma is required and GED is accepted. *Academic units required:* 4 English, 3 mathematics, 3 science, 2 foreign language, 3 social studies, 2 academic electives. *Academic units recommended:* 4 mathematics, 4 science, 3 foreign language, 4 social studies.

Financial Aid

Students should submit: FAFSA, institution's own financial aid form, CSS/Financial Aid PROFILE Regular filing deadline is 9/1. The Princeton Review suggests that all financial aid forms be submitted as soon as possible after 1/1. Need-based scholarships/grants offered: Federal Pell, SEOG, state scholarships/grants, private scholarships, the school's own gift aid. *Loan aid offered:* Direct Subsidized Stafford, Direct Unsubsidized Stafford, Direct PLUS, Federal Perkins, college/university loans from institutional funds. Applicants will be notified of awards on or about 4/1. Federal Work-Study Program available. Institutional employment available. Off-campus job opportunities are good.

The Inside Word

The College of Wooster is a small, selective liberal arts school. Stiff competition from similarly situated institutions means the school occasionally admits students who may not be up to the challenges of the curriculum, but, by and large, only solid students get past the gatekeepers here. Expect a thorough review of your entire application.

THE SCHOOL SAYS "..."

From The Admissions Office

"At The College of Wooster, our mission is to graduate educated, not merely trained, people; to produce responsible, independent thinkers, rather than specialists in any given field. Our commitment to independence is especially evident in IS, the college's distinctive program in which every senior works one-to-one with a faculty mentor to complete a project in the major. IS comes from 'independent study,' but, in reality, it is an intellectual collaboration of the highest order and permits every student the freedom to pursue something in which he or she is passionately interested. IS is the centerpiece of an innovative curriculum. More than just the project itself, the culture that sustains IS—and, in turn, is sustained by IS—is an extraordinary college culture. The same attitudes of student initiative, openness, flexibility, and individual support enrich every aspect of Wooster's vital residential college life.

"College of Wooster requires freshman applicants to submit scores from the SAT. Students may also choose to submit scores from the ACT (with the Writing component) in lieu of the SAT."

SELECTIVITY

Admissions Rating	90
# of applicants	3,445
% of applicants accepted	81
% of acceptees attending	19
# accepting a place on wait list	25
% admitted from wait list	100
# of early decision applicants	87
% accepted early decision	87

FRESHMAN PROFILE

Range SAT Critical Reading	540–670
Range SAT Math	540–660
Range SAT Writing	540–660
Range ACT Composite	23–29
Minimum paper TOEFL	550
Minimum computer TOEFL	213
Minimum web-based TOEFL	80
Average HS GPA	3.51
% graduated top 10% of class	25
% graduated top 25% of class	63
% graduated top 50% of class	89

DEADLINES

Early Decision	
Deadline	12/1
Notification	12/15
Regular	
Deadline	2/15
Notification	4/1
Nonfall registration?	yes

FINANCIAL FACTS

Financial Aid Rating	93
Comprehensive fee	$43,900
% frosh rec. need-based scholarship or grant aid	62
% UG rec. need-based scholarship or grant aid	55
% frosh rec. non-need-based scholarship or grant aid	11
% UG rec. non-need-based scholarship or grant aid	7
% frosh rec. need-based self-help aid	46
% UG rec. need-based self-help aid	42
% frosh rec. any financial aid	100
% UG rec. any financial aid	100
% UG borrow to pay for school	63
Average cumulative indebtedness	$29,815

COLORADO COLLEGE

14 EAST CACHE LA POUDRE STREET, COLORADO SPRINGS, CO 80903 • ADMISSIONS: 719-389-6344 • FAX: 719-389-6816

CAMPUS LIFE

Quality of Life Rating	82
Fire Safety Rating	60*
Green Rating	99
Type of school	private
Environment	metropolis

STUDENTS

Total undergrad enrollment	1,972
% male/female	46/54
% from out of state	74
% from public high school	60
% live on campus	77
% in (# of) fraternities	6 (2)
% in (# of) sororities	13 (3)
% African American	2
% Asian	6
% Caucasian	77
% Hispanic	7
% Native American	1
% international	3
# of countries represented	26

SURVEY SAYS . . .

Lab facilities are great
School is well run
Students are friendly
Students are happy
Intramural sports are popular
Lots of beer drinking
Hard liquor is popular

ACADEMICS

Academic Rating	95
Calendar	8 sessions each 3.5 weeks long, 1 class
Student/faculty ratio	9.6:1
Profs interesting rating	97
Profs accessible rating	95
Most common reg class size	10–19 students

MOST POPULAR MAJORS

biology/biological sciences
economics
English language and literature

STUDENTS SAY ". . ."

Academics

The unique thing about small, "intimate" and "intensive" Colorado College is the Block Plan. The school year here is broken into eight three-and-a-half-week chunks. Students take just one course during each block. "Taking one class at a time allows you to devote all of your time to it," explains an English major. Classes average about 15 students and typically last for 3 hours each morning, though "there are some classes with labs in the afternoon." Students love the "personalized" nature of the program and the flexibility it offers. Double majors are frequent, almost normal. Internships are profuse. Studying abroad is very easy. "Many students" spend time abroad for a single block or for consecutive blocks in places such as China, Costa Rica, India, and Russia. There are also semesters in Washington, D.C. and Chicago. However, the Block Plan is also a pressure-packed situation. Work piles up quickly in every class. "Sciences are very tough." "Forget about getting sick, even for a day." The "super-duper" administration at CC is "very interested in student input." The full-time faculty is generally stellar. "Your professors know you by name and remember you." They "genuinely care about each of their students," and they are "always available" outside of class. Visiting professors can be another story, though. They often "don't seem to understand how the system works and tend to either give way too much work or hardly any at all."

Life

Colorado College is located in "a cute little town." The beautiful campus "makes life feel like a resort." Social life is bountiful. "My favorite thing about CC is that there is always something going on," declares a happy junior, "from readings by famous poets to porn debates, internationally known advocates to lacrosse games, protests to plays, music festivals to dances, techno raves to campus political debates, and fencing club to midnight pancake breakfasts." "There is a drug and alcohol scene," and students who participate "party pretty hard." Intramural and intercollegiate sports are also popular, especially hockey. The fabled men's team here is a "perennial contender" at the Division I level. The Block Plan gives life an unusual tempo. "The beginning of the block is really fun," explains one student. "You're not bogged down with tons of work yet, so we go out and party a lot." Toward the end of each block, papers come due, finals loom, and life becomes very hectic. Then, after "cramming a semester's work in three and a half weeks," students get a four-day vacation. Some students take advantage of the countless outdoor activities in the area. "skiing is very popular." Others students take part in activities sponsored by the school. You can take a bicycle trip to Aspen, just for example, or raft the Colorado River. Still other students "fill breaks with crazy adventures" or just enjoy "hardcore relaxation before being violently thrown into an entirely new and different world for the next block."

Student Body

"The population is not so diverse" at Colorado College according to some students. "Most students are white" and "from affluent families." The "trustafarian" is a pretty common creature. Otherwise, students describe themselves as "intellectual, easygoing, and active." They are "environmentally aware," "idealistic," and "enthusiastic about trying new things." They have "many creative interests." They are "very liberal," too. "It is rare to find a conservative on campus." Other students tell us that Colorado College is "eclectic" and filled with every sort of student. There are two main groups: "hippies and preps." There are also plenty of "outdoor enthusiasts" "dressed in fancy outdoor gear." However, CC is small enough and students are open enough that there is quite a bit of overlap among cliques. "You can have an athlete who is the president of her sorority or a really outdoorsy person who plays in the school orchestra."

COLORADO COLLEGE

FINANCIAL AID: 719-389-6651 • E-MAIL: ADMISSION@COLORADOCOLLEGE.EDU • WEBSITE: WWW.COLORADOCOLLEGE.EDU

THE PRINCETON REVIEW SAYS

Admissions

Very important factors considered include: Rigor of secondary school record. *Important factors considered include:* Class rank, application essay, academic GPA, recommendation(s), standardized test scores, extracurricular activities, interview. *Other factors considered include:* Alumni/ae relation, character/personal qualities, first generation, level of applicant's interest, racial/ethnic status, religious affiliation/commitment, talent/ability, volunteer work, work experience. SAT or ACT required. TOEFL required of all international applicants. High school diploma or equivalent is not required. *Academic units required:* 4 English. *Academic units recommended:* 4 English.

Financial Aid

Students should submit: FAFSA, CSS/financial aid profile, noncustodial profile, federal 1040 parent and student tax returns and parent W-2 forms. Regular filing deadline is 2/15. The Princeton Review suggests that all financial aid forms be submitted as soon as possible after 1/1. *Need-based scholarships/grants offered:* Federal Pell, SEOG, state scholarships/grants, private scholarships, the school's own gift aid, Federal ACG and SMART grants. *Loan aid offered:* FFEL Subsidized Stafford, FFEL Unsubsidized Stafford, FFEL PLUS, Federal Perkins. Applicants will be notified of awards on or about 3/20. Federal Work-Study Program available. Institutional employment available. Off-campus job opportunities are good.

The Inside Word

Colorado College works to identify those students who will most benefit from its distinct academic environment. Because the Block Program requires focus and demands that students become active participants in their education, admissions officers value applicants who take on a rigorous course load in high school and engage in activities that complement their intellectual achievements. All candidates should take the application essay seriously—strong writing skills are seen as critical to success at CC.

THE SCHOOL SAYS "..."

From The Admissions Office

"Students enter Colorado College for the opportunity to study intensely in small learning communities. Groups of students work closely with one another and faculty in discussion-based classes and hands-on labs. CC encourages a well-rounded education, combining the academic rigor of an honors college with rich programs in athletics, community service, student government, the arts, and more. The college encourages students to push themselves academically, and many continue their studies at the best graduate and professional schools in the nation. CC is a great choice for field study and for international study (CC ranks fourth nationally in the number of students studying abroad). CC also takes advantage of its location, using its Baca campus in the San Luis Valley and the mountain cabin for a variety of classes. Its location at the base of the Rockies makes CC a great choice for students who enjoy backpacking, hiking, climbing, and skiing.

"Colorado College requires students to submit either the SAT or ACT. Scores are accepted for both. CC uses the highest sub score on the SAT and the highest ACT composite. SAT Subject Tests are accepted for review."

SELECTIVITY
Admissions Rating	**95**
# of applicants	5,338
% of applicants accepted	26
% of acceptees attending	40
# accepting a place on wait list	321
# of early decision applicants	414
% accepted early decision	41

FRESHMAN PROFILE
Range SAT Critical Reading	620–700
Range SAT Math	610–700
Range SAT Writing	620–700
Range ACT Composite	28–32
Minimum paper TOEFL	550
Minimum computer TOEFL	213
Minimum web-based TOEFL	79
% graduated top 10% of class	66
% graduated top 25% of class	87
% graduated top 50% of class	98

DEADLINES
Early decision	
Deadline	11/15
Notification	12/20
Early action	
Deadline	11/15
Notification	1/15
Regular	
Priority	1/15
Deadline	1/15
Notification	4/1
Nonfall registration?	yes

FINANCIAL FACTS
Financial Aid Rating	**89**
Annual tuition	$35,844
Room and board	$9,096
Required fees	$200
Books and supplies	$988
% frosh rec. need-based scholarship or grant aid	35
% UG rec. need-based scholarship or grant aid	38
% frosh rec. non-need-based scholarship or grant aid	8
% UG rec. non-need-based scholarship or grant aid	7
% frosh rec. need-based self-help aid	31
% UG rec. need-based self-help aid	33
% frosh rec. athletic scholarships	1
% UG rec. athletic scholarships	2
% frosh rec. any financial aid	43
% UG rec. any financial aid	39
% UG borrow to pay for school	9
Average cumulative indebtedness	$16,503

COLORADO STATE UNIVERSITY

SPRUCE HALL, FORT COLLINS, CO 80523 • ADMISSIONS: 970-491-6909 • FAX: 970-491-7799

CAMPUS LIFE
Quality of Life Rating	**82**
Fire Safety Rating	**71**
Green Rating	**91**
Type of school	public
Environment	city

STUDENTS
Total undergrad enrollment	20,829
% male/female	48/52
% from out of state	16
% live on campus	25
% in (# of) fraternities	6 (21)
% in (# of) sororities	7 (14)
% African American	2
% Asian	3
% Caucasian	80
% Hispanic	6
% Native American	2
% international	2
# of countries represented	85

SURVEY SAYS . . .
Students love Fort Collins, CO
Great off-campus food
Low cost of living
Student publications are popular
(Almost) no one smokes

ACADEMICS
Academic Rating	**71**
Calendar	semester
Student/faculty ratio	17:1
Profs interesting rating	72
Profs accessible rating	72
% classes taught by TAs	9.7
Most common reg class size	10–19 students
Most common lab size	20–29 students

MOST POPULAR MAJORS
business administration and management
construction engineering technology/technician
psychology

STUDENTS SAY "..."

Academics
Colorado State University offers a breadth and depth of quality academics, especially in career-specific disciplines. Students here heap praise on the university's programs in such diverse fields as engineering, social work, math, business, interior design, health and exercise science, and music therapy. Topping many students' lists are agricultural and other natural sciences; one student explains, "Science-oriented classes are definitely quite challenging and a huge strength of our school, considering we have the second-highest-ranked veterinary college in the nation." Given its size and research mission, CSU surprisingly satisfies many students with the level of one-on-one service; many here insist that CSU "is big enough that people have heard of it but small enough that you don't get lost in the numbers" and that it "has a small-school feel because professors are always available and not everything is taught by TAs." This sense strengthens considerably once students clear the hurdles of underclassman requirements. Students warn that "entry-level courses have very large class sizes and not many opportunities for personal interactions academically in class or out of it," but add that "as you progress through your field of study, class size becomes a lot smaller and more intimate."

Life
The CSU campus and surrounding area offer a lot of distractions, so "Life at Colorado State can be challenging. It can be difficult to keep your focus on school when the mountains are right there" to tantalize students with snowboarding, skiing, hiking, and mountain biking. There's also Horsetooth Reservoir, a popular spot for swimming and hanging out during the warm season, and road trips to Laramie, Boulder, and Denver. Closer to home, "there is always something fun going on at campus like free movie showings, dance recitals, and choir concerts. CSU does a good job of bringing in guests like Barack Obama, Eva Longoria, Zach Braff, Matt Roloff, and Holocaust survivors." College football draws a raucous and devoted crowd; "Students usually come about an hour early to tailgate and enjoy one another's company. People wear crazy outfits and scream at the top of their lungs, cheering on their favorite players." CSU also offers "intramural and club sports," "plenty of organizations," and, of course, the requisite party scene. "People around here love beer," and with "four microbreweries serving world-class beer" nearby students can indulge in quality brew when the mood strikes. Hometown Fort Collins "is also a great place" that's "very safe with lots of places to eat and a good downtown. It has everything you need, but it still has somewhat of a small-town atmosphere," making it "a great college town" in the eyes of many.

Student Body
"The typical student at CSU is a Colorado resident, although there are plenty of people from outside the state," with students representing every state and 85 foreign nations. Undergrads are generally "committed to academics but also enjoy having fun when they aren't studying. Outdoor recreation is really important on this campus," and for many the school's access to the mountains is one of its chief allures. The school "does not draw huge minority populations...despite its efforts to increase diversity," but "there is a great focus on making minority students feel welcome and a part of the campus," so those who do come should find a solid support network. The typical undergrad is "very down-to-earth and environmentally friendly" and "politically conservative," although "the campus has shifted somewhat," and "there aren't as many conservative students here as there once were."

COLORADO STATE UNIVERSITY

FINANCIAL AID: 970-491-6321 • E-MAIL: ADMISSIONS@COLOSTATE.EDU • WEBSITE: WWW.COLOSTATE.EDU

THE PRINCETON REVIEW SAYS

Admissions

Very important factors considered include: Class rank, academic GPA, rigor of secondary school record, standardized test scores. *Important factors considered include:* Application essay, recommendation(s), character/personal qualities, extracurricular activities, talent/ability, volunteer work. *Other factors considered include:* Alumni/ae relation, first generation, geographical residence, interview, level of applicant's interest, state residency, work experience. SAT or ACT required. TOEFL required of all international applicants. High school diploma is required and GED is accepted. *Academic units required:* 4 English, 3 mathematics, 3 science (2 science labs), 2 social studies, 1 history, 2 academic electives. *Academic units recommended:* 4 English, 4 mathematics, 3 science (2 science labs), 2 foreign language, 2 social studies, 1 history, 2 academic electives.

Financial Aid

Students should submit: FAFSA. The Princeton Review suggests that all financial aid forms be submitted as soon as possible after 1/1. *Need-based scholarships/grants offered:* Federal Pell, SEOG, state scholarships/grants, private scholarships, the school's own gift aid. *Loan aid offered:* Direct Subsidized Stafford, Direct Unsubsidized Stafford, Direct PLUS, Federal Perkins, college/university loans from institutional funds, alternative loans. Applicants will be notified of awards on a rolling basis beginning 3/1. Federal Work-Study Program available. Institutional employment available. Off-campus job opportunities are excellent.

The Inside Word

CSU admits nearly 9 in 10 applicants; the primary task of its admissions office is to determine who not to admit. Certain majors and programs are more competitive and impose additional admissions qualifications. Art and design programs, for example, require a portfolio review; programs in art, biomedical sciences, business, computer science, engineering, and technical journalism impose higher GPA and standardized test score floors than the school's other programs.

THE SCHOOL SAYS "..."

From The Admissions Office

"As one of the nation's premier research universities, Colorado State offers more than 150 undergraduate programs of study in eight colleges. Students come here from 50 states and 85 countries, and they appreciate the quality and breadth of the university's academic offerings. But Colorado State is more than just a place where students can take their scholarship to the highest level. It's also a place where they can gain invaluable experience in the fields of their choice, whether they're immersing themselves in professional internships, studying on the other side of the globe or teaming up with faculty on groundbreaking research projects. In addition to an outstanding experiential learning environment, Colorado State students enjoy a sense of community that's unusual for a large university. They develop meaningful relationships with faculty members who bring out their best work, and they live and learn with diverse peers who value their ideas and expand their perspectives. These types of connections lead to countless opportunities for social networking and professional accomplishments. By the time our students graduate from Colorado State, they have the knowledge, practical experience, and interpersonal skills they need to make a significant contribution to their world.

"Although academic performance is a primary factor in admissions decisions, Colorado State's holistic review process also recognizes personal qualities and experiences that have the potential to enrich the university and the Fort Collins community. To apply, students may submit the Common Application or the Colorado State University application for admission."

SELECTIVITY

Admissions Rating	86
# of applicants	12,494
% of applicants accepted	86
% of acceptees attending	41

FRESHMAN PROFILE

Range SAT Critical Reading	500–610
Range SAT Math	510–620
Range SAT Writing	480–590
Range ACT Composite	22–26
Minimum paper TOEFL	450
Minimum computer TOEFL	130
Minimum web-based TOEFL	45
Average HS GPA	3.53
% graduated top 10% of class	19.57
% graduated top 25% of class	49
% graduated top 50% of class	86.88

DEADLINES

Regular	
Priority	2/1
Deadline	7/1
Notification	rolling
Nonfall registration?	yes

APPLICANTS ALSO LOOK AT
AND OFTEN PREFER

University of Colorado—Boulder
Arizona State University
Cornell University
University of Denver
Colorado School of Mines

FINANCIAL FACTS

Financial Aid Rating	77
Annual in-state tuition	$4,424
Annual out-of-state tuition	$20,140
Room and board	$8,134
Required fees	$1,450
Books and supplies	$1,126
% frosh rec. need-based scholarship or grant aid	29
% UG rec. need-based scholarship or grant aid	35
% frosh rec. need-based self-help aid	21
% UG rec. need-based self-help aid	31
% frosh rec. athletic scholarships	1
% UG rec. athletic scholarships	1
% frosh rec. any financial aid	52
% UG rec. any financial aid	62
% UG borrow to pay for school	61
Average cumulative indebtedness	$18,607

COLUMBIA UNIVERSITY

212 HAMILTON HALL MC 2807, 1130 AMSTERDAM AVENUE, NY, NY 10027 • ADMISSIONS: 212-854-2522 • FAX: 212-894-1209

CAMPUS LIFE

Quality of Life Rating	93
Fire Safety Rating	60*
Green Rating	60*
Type of school	private
Environment	metropolis

STUDENTS

Total undergrad enrollment	5,677
% male/female	53/47
% from out of state	71
% from public high school	59
% live on campus	95
% in (# of) fraternities	10 (17)
% in (# of) sororities	10 (11)
% African American	10
% Asian	18
% Caucasian	39
% Hispanic	11
% Native American	1
% international	10
# of countries represented	87

SURVEY SAYS . . .
Great library
Diverse student types on campus
Students love New York, NY
Great off-campus food
Campus feels safe
Students are happy
Student publications are popular
Political activism is popular

ACADEMICS

Academic Rating	96
Calendar	semester
Student/faculty ratio	6:1
Profs interesting rating	77
Profs accessible rating	74
Most common reg class size	10–19 students

MOST POPULAR MAJORS
engineering
English language and literature
political science and government

STUDENTS SAY ". . ."

Academics

Nestled in Manhattan's upper west side neighborhood and "at the crossroads of the world," Columbia's campus "itself is an inspiration and a motivation to push and to excel academically." While being "one of the world's great research universities," the school still manages to feel "closer to a liberal arts college than a gigantic mega-school." Students are drawn to this "first rate intellectual oasis" for its "holistic education" and "rich, historic Columbia core curriculum," which "surveys the humanities and the sciences" and "serves as a knowledge base as well as the connecting thread to all Columbia students." Another boon is the "high quality" of "thought-provoking" and "brilliant and successful" professors who are "truly invested in teaching the things they love to their students" but who "will not hold your hand or check up on you." "It is very, very difficult to get an A here, but it's difficult to do too much worse as well." Using a "tough love" approach, Columbia "believes in treating its students like adults" and pushes them toward "independence and self sufficiency" while providing "amazing resources in fields of networking, research, and internships" that will make everyone "a better citizen of the world." Although students acknowledge that Columbia's administration "truly cares about its students and the health of the school," many wish to improve the school's bureaucracy, which is "notoriously difficult to deal with."

Life

"Columbia is as cosmopolitan and entertaining as New York City," sums up one satisfied student. Provided with "the best of both worlds," students often take advantage of their "secluded and idyllic green" campus' prime location, which gives them "unparalleled access to all the resources of the greatest city in the world." Another student boasts that attending Columbia gives you an "easy pass to the city, whether you are visiting museums for free with a flash of your ID or seeing your application pushed to the front when applying for amazing internships." The majority of students "venture downtown at least once a week to see a Broadway show, go to a concert or museum, or just explore." For those who are not tempted by the "free admission to over 30 museums in New York" or "a meal or dessert in Chinatown or Little Italy," there are plenty of "campus clubs and activities, including the fraternity and sorority scenes or on-campus parties." With a campus that "caters to every single person that comes through its doors," Columbia is "like being in a really rich agar" where students can pursue whatever they are interested in from "engaging in intellectual conversation" to "getting involved in politics through student groups on campus to continuing (or discovering) a love for the arts by being a part of a musical ensemble."

Student Body

A "diverse community of serious thinkers who also know how to have fun," Columbia students describe themselves as "bookworms" who are "cynical but enthusiastic" as well as "very politically active and liberal." With "driven" people "from distinct backgrounds, distinct ideologies, distinct everything," Columbia students list the school's diversity as one of its strengths, but one student cautions that "the diversity could use less of a leftist bias." "Extremely smart and interested in learning for its own sake," a "typical" Columbia student "has strong views but is willing to discuss and change them." Columbia students are also "more intense than those you might find at other schools," points out one student. Indeed, during exam season it's not uncommon to see students "bring sleeping bags and cases of Red Bull to the library." Despite this intensity, there is "a minimal amount of ill-intended competition," and "nobody is scrutinized for being different or pressured to be anything they are not."

FINANCIAL AID: 212-854-3711 • WEBSITE: WWW.STUDENTAFFAIRS.COLUMBIA.EDU/ADMISSIONS

THE PRINCETON REVIEW SAYS

Admissions

Very important factors considered include: Class rank, application essay, academic GPA, recommendation(s), rigor of secondary school record, standardized test scores, character/personal qualities. *Important factors considered include:* Extracurricular activities, talent/ability. *Other factors considered include:* Alumni/ae relation, geographical residence, interview, racial/ethnic status, volunteer work, work experience. SAT and 2 SAT Subject Tests or ACT and 2 SAT Subject Tests required. ACT with Writing component required. TOEFL required of all international applicants. High school diploma is required and GED is accepted. *Academic units recommended:* 4 English, 4 mathematics, 4 science (4 science labs), 4 foreign language, 4 history, 4 academic electives.

Financial Aid

Students should submit: FAFSA, CSS/financial aid profile, noncustodial profileParent and student income tax forms. Regular filing deadline is 3/1. The Princeton Review suggests that all financial aid forms be submitted as soon as possible after 1/1. *Need-based scholarships/grants offered:* Federal Pell, SEOG, state scholarships/grants, private scholarships, the school's own gift aid. *Loan aid offered:* FFEL Subsidized Stafford, FFEL Unsubsidized Stafford, FFEL PLUS, Federal Perkins, alternative loans. Applicants will be notified of awards on or about 4/1. Federal Work-Study Program available. Institutional employment available. Off-campus job opportunities are excellent.

The Inside Word

Earning an acceptance letter from Columbia is no easy feat. Applications to the university continue to rise, and many great candidates are rejected each year. Admissions officers take a holistic approach to evaluating applications; there's no magic formula or pattern to guide students seeking admission. One common denominator among applicants is stellar grades in rigorous classes and personal accomplishments in non-academic activities. Admissions officers are looking to build a diverse class that will greatly contribute to the university.

THE SCHOOL SAYS "..."

From The Admissions Office

"Columbia maintains an intimate college campus within one of the world's most vibrant cities. After a day exploring New York City you come home to a traditional college campus within an intimate neighborhood. Nobel Prize–winning professors will challenge you in class discussions and meet one-on-one afterward. The core curriculum attracts intensely free-minded scholars, and connects all undergraduates. Science and engineering students pursue cutting-edge research in world-class laboratories with faculty members at the forefront of scientific discovery. Classroom discussions are only the beginning of your education. Ideas spill out from the classrooms, electrifying the campus and Morningside Heights. Friendships formed in the residence halls solidify during a game of Frisbee on the South Lawn or over bagels on the steps of Low Library. From your first day on campus, you will be part of our diverse community.

"Columbia offers extensive need-based financial aid and meets the full need of every student admitted as a first-year with grants instead of loans. Parents with calculated incomes below $60,000 are not expected to contribute any income or assets to tuition, room, board and mandatory fees and families with calculated incomes between $60,000 and $100,000 and with typical assets have a significantly reduced contribution. To support students pursuing study abroad, research, internships and community service opportunities, Columbia offers additional funding and exemptions from academic year and summer work expectations. A commitment to diversity—of every kind—is a long-standing Columbia hallmark. We believe cost should not be a barrier to pursuing your educational dreams."

SELECTIVITY	
Admissions Rating	99
# of applicants	22,584
% of applicants accepted	10
% of acceptees attending	64
# of early decision applicants	2,509
% accepted early decision	25

FRESHMAN PROFILE	
Range SAT Critical Reading	680–770
Range SAT Math	680–780
Range SAT Writing	690–770
Range ACT Composite	29–34
Minimum paper TOEFL	600
Minimum computer TOEFL	250
Average HS GPA	3.9
% graduated top 10% of class	94
% graduated top 25% of class	99
% graduated top 50% of class	100

DEADLINES	
Early decision	
Deadline	11/1
Notification	12/15
Regular	
Deadline	1/2
Notification	4/1
Nonfall registration?	no

APPLICANTS ALSO LOOK AT

AND OFTEN PREFER
Harvard College
Stanford University
Massachusetts Institute of Technology
Yale University

AND SOMETIMES PREFER
University of Pennsylvania
Princeton University

AND RARELY PREFER
New York University
Dartmouth College
Cornell University
Brown University

FINANCIAL FACTS	
Financial Aid Rating	97
Annual tuition	$37,470
% frosh rec. need-based scholarship or grant aid	48
% UG rec. need-based scholarship or grant aid	47
% frosh rec. need-based self-help aid	36
% UG rec. need-based self-help aid	36
% frosh rec. any financial aid	57
% UG rec. any financial aid	54

CONNECTICUT COLLEGE

270 MOHEGAN AVENUE, NEW LONDON, CT 06320 • ADMISSIONS: 860-439-2200 • FAX: 860-439-4301

CAMPUS LIFE

Quality of Life Rating	81
Fire Safety Rating	80
Green Rating	80
Type of school	private
Environment	town

STUDENTS

Total undergrad enrollment	1,741
% male/female	40/60
% from out of state	81
% from public high school	55
% live on campus	99
% African American	4
% Asian	5
% Caucasian	74
% Hispanic	6
% international	4
# of countries represented	74

SURVEY SAYS . . .

Career services are great
Low cost of living
Frats and sororities are unpopular or nonexistent
Student government is popular
(Almost) no one smokes

ACADEMICS

Academic Rating	94
Calendar	semester
Student/faculty ratio	9:1
Profs interesting rating	90
Profs accessible rating	90
Most common reg class size	10–19 students
Most common lab size	10–19 students

MOST POPULAR MAJORS

English language and literature
political science and government
psychology

STUDENTS SAY "..."

Academics

"Warm environment" doesn't always refer to the weather at Connecticut College, a close-knit school in eastern Connecticut. It refers to an environment that encourages students "to get out and experience the world," and "prepares them for life in the 'real world' as a grad." The school's relatively small size allows students to get to know one another well and affords "a large variety of academic opportunities" to each one—a far cry from the waiting-list mentality that often overtakes larger universities. Numerous resources are provided to help with academics, such as a writing center, language lab, a career services office, internship and study abroad programs, and the school's unique certificate programs, though most students agree that physical facilities could use some updating. Students also all adhere to the school's Honor Code, which "instills a sense of self-awareness and self-governance among the student body." The student government garners a high level of respect from the body at large, and there is a feeling that it "really enacts change on campus and in the New London community."

Classes are "engaging and interesting," which makes for a smooth transition from high school to college, and "professors are available inside and outside of the classroom." Indeed, professors' personal touches are the most highly-sung aspect of Conn College life, and students rave over having "more than just a teacher-student relationship, but rather a person-person relationship" with their teachers. Most professors go by their first name, and are "down-to-earth people who place themselves at the same level as their students." "I am constantly learning and enthralled in class," says a senior art history major.

Life

Students without cars have trouble getting off campus, which doesn't matter as "there is basically nothing to do in New London." However, the city does have a few distractions like museums and restaurants and happens to be "perfectly located right in between New York City and Boston," with a train station conveniently located downtown. The vast majority of people live on campus, so dorms are "great social houses" in which people leave their doors open and are interested in getting to know their neighbors. When the weather is nice, going to the beach and hanging out on the green is very popular, and when it's not, students are given free-rein to start their own clubs and to volunteer with local organizations. People work hard during the week, but Thursdays and Saturdays are the big days to let loose. Everyone stays on campus on the weekends, and the school organizes plenty of things to do, such as theme dances, movies, a capella shows, and "Friday Night Lives" where up-and-coming bands come and play a concert for students.

Student Body

"People are just nice" at Conn College, and friends aren't hard to come by." Most people here are highly involved in the social and academic atmosphere of the school, play a sport, and are "open-minded and involved in a variety of activities." "For better or worse, people are unapologetically themselves...it is a unique quality about Conn that makes it both wonderful and unbearable at times," says one student. The typical student is from "right outside of Boston, New York, Connecticut, or any other New England state." There "is not a particularly diverse student body at Conn," though life experiences and interests of the students make it so that the perceived diversity is "truly immense." "Generally, students are wealthy" and "uncommonly good-looking." There "are a few academic superstars but, for the most part, students are on the same page academically." The school has many international students and study-abroad options to promote academic and personal diversity.

CONNECTICUT COLLEGE

FINANCIAL AID: 860-439-2200 • E-MAIL: ADMISSION@CONNCOLL.EDU • WEBSITE: WWW.CONNCOLL.EDU

THE PRINCETON REVIEW SAYS

Admissions

The submission of standardized tests (SAT Reasoning, SAT II, or ACT) is optional, although students whose primary language is not English are required to submit TOEFL scores. High school diploma is required and GED is accepted.

Financial Aid

Students should submit: FAFSA, CSS/financial aid profile, noncustodial profile, business/farm supplement, federal tax returns, personal, partnership, federal W-2 statements. Regular filing deadline is 2/1. The Princeton Review suggests that all financial aid forms be submitted as soon as possible after 1/1. *Need-based scholarships/grants offered:* Federal Pell, SEOG, state scholarships/grants, the school's own gift aid. *Loan aid offered:* Direct Subsidized Stafford, Direct Unsubsidized Stafford, Direct PLUS, FFEL Subsidized Stafford, FFEL Unsubsidized Stafford, FFEL PLUS, Federal Perkins Federal Work-Study Program available. Institutional employment available. Off-campus job opportunities are good.

The Inside Word

Connecticut College is the archetypal selective New England college, and admissions officers are judicious in their decisions. Competitive applicants will have pursued a demanding course load in high school. Admissions officers look for students who are curious and who thrive in challenging academic environments. Since Connecticut College has a close-knit community, personal qualities are also closely evaluated, and interviews are important.

THE SCHOOL SAYS "..."

From The Admissions Office

"Chartered in 1911, Connecticut College was founded in the spirit of political and social equality, self-determination, and shared governance. The college seeks students who are not only smart and intellectually curious, but who also bring a wide range of life experiences and perspectives that enable this spirit to endure within the College community. The College's near century-old Honor Code defines campus life and is observed by all students, faculty, and staff. The Honor Code inspires students to challenge themselves and their peers to see the world from diverse perspectives, to remain receptive to new ideas and experiences, and, by instilling a sense of mutual respect, to consider how their actions and education may ultimately better the common good. Ninety-nine percent of students live on campus. There is no Greek system. Dozens of clubs represent the students' numerous activist, volunteer, spiritual, creative, or athletic interests.

"The College offers more than 50 majors and minors and a series of interdisciplinary learning centers. All classes and labs are taught by professors. Students participate in the NCAA Division III New England Small College Athletic Conference (NESCAC.) The College is nationally known for pioneering environmental initiatives, including commitments to renewable energy, and career and internship placement. The College has been called a "college with a conscience" by the Princeton Review for fostering social responsibility and public service and is one of the top sending schools for both Teach for America and The Peace Corps. In the past two years, ten Connecticut College students have been awarded Fulbright Scholarships."

SELECTIVITY
Admissions Rating	95
# of applicants	4,716
% of applicants accepted	37
% of acceptees attending	29
# accepting a place on wait list	360
% admitted from wait list	17
# of early decision applicants	301
% accepted early decision	65

FRESHMAN PROFILE
Range SAT Critical Reading	600–700
Range SAT Math	600–690
Range SAT Writing	620–710
Range ACT Composite	25–30
Minimum paper TOEFL	600
Minimum computer TOEFL	250
Minimum web-based TOEFL	100
% graduated top 10% of class	60
% graduated top 25% of class	93
% graduated top 50% of class	99

DEADLINES
Early decision	
Deadline	11/15
Notification	12/15
Regular	
Deadline	1/1
Notification	3/31
Nonfall registration?	no

APPLICANTS ALSO LOOK AT
AND OFTEN PREFER
Hamilton College
Vassar College
Wesleyan University
Middlebury College
Colby College
Boston College
Tufts University
Bates College
Bowdoin College
AND SOMETIMES PREFER
Trinity College (CT)
AND RARELY PREFER
Brown University
Skidmore College

FINANCIAL FACTS
Financial Aid Rating	92
Comprehensive fee	$51,115
Books and supplies	$1,000
% frosh rec. need-based scholarship or grant aid	38
% UG rec. need-based scholarship or grant aid	38
% frosh rec. need-based self-help aid	34
% UG rec. need-based self-help aid	36
% frosh rec. any financial aid	41
% UG borrow to pay for school	41
Average cumulative indebtedness	$21,283

THE COOPER UNION FOR THE ADVANCEMENT OF SCIENCE AND ART

30 COOPER SQUARE, NEW YORK, NY 10003 • ADMISSIONS: 212-353-4120 • FAX: 212-353-4342

CAMPUS LIFE

Quality of Life Rating	79
Fire Safety Rating	97
Green Rating	80
Type of school	private
Environment	metropolis

STUDENTS

Total undergrad enrollment	898
% male/female	63/37
% from out of state	40
% from public high school	65
% live on campus	20
% in (# of) fraternities	10 (2)
% in (# of) sororities	5 (1)
% African American	6
% Asian	23
% Caucasian	45
% Hispanic	9
% Native American	1
% international	14

SURVEY SAYS . . .

No one cheats
Athletic facilities need improving
Diverse student types on campus
Students get along with local community
Students love New York, NY
Great off-campus food
Frats and sororities are unpopular or nonexistent
(Almost) everyone smokes

ACADEMICS

Academic Rating	88
Calendar	semester
Student/faculty ratio	8.5:1
Profs interesting rating	64
Profs accessible rating	64
Most common reg class size	10–19 students
Most common lab size	20 students

MOST POPULAR MAJORS

electrical, electronics and communications engineering
fine arts and art studies
mechanical engineering

STUDENTS SAY ". . ."

Academics

One of the coolest things about The Cooper Union is that there is no tuition. The school "offers a full-tuition scholarship to everyone who is accepted." We hasten to add, though, that room and board (in New York City), books and supplies, and various fees add up to quite a bit each year. There is a mandatory core curriculum here in the humanities and social sciences but, so far as majors go, programs in engineering, art, and architecture are the only options on the menu. Cooper is "one of the best schools for what it does in the country." "It is a school where the students can really go crazy and learn a lot." "Classes are small" and "professors are more than willing to give extra help outside of class." However, it's "not for the weak of heart." The "very visceral and involving" academic experience is "hell." The pace is "exhaustive and murderous." "Cooper Union: where your best just isn't good enough," muses a civil engineering major. Cooper is about "hours of study, neglect of personal life," and generally "working your ass off." And "the work you put in does not necessarily reflect in your grades." "I have never worked so hard in my life and probably never will," speculates a junior, but "as long as you can get through it, you're set for life." Complaints among students here include "worthless" adjunct professors, lab equipment "could be upgraded," "the administration is sometimes difficult to approach" and "scheduling is always weird." Nonetheless, management "mostly meets the students' needs, with minor mishaps."

Life

"There is no meal plan" at Cooper and the lodging situation is harsh. "There is only housing guaranteed for first-year students and since Manhattan is a very expensive place to live, it becomes a problem after that." "Everyone is extraordinarily busy," comments a fine-arts major. "School is life and there's no way around it." For the architecture students, life is "nothing except architecture in radical explorations and expressions." For engineers, "Cooper is about selling your soul for four years." Art students sometimes "take time off because it's hard to be creative every minute." "The intense workload gives little break for fun." There are "many extracurricular programs" but the urban fare of New York City consumes most free time. The surrounding East Village is full of funky shops, cheap eateries, theaters, bars, and live music venues; subways can whisk students throughout the five boroughs at any time of day. "Drinking with friends is a great and sometimes necessary way to decompress" but for most students, "ruthlessly sucking on booze" is a very occasional thing. "We are not a party school," says a sophomore. "We get to campus in the morning, and leave late at night." "Cooper isn't for everybody," advises a senior. "If you need excessive guidance, or prefer an exclusive, well-defined campus structure, you won't be happy here."

Student Body

Diversity here is simply dreamy. Cooper's overwhelming male population is exceptionally ethnically diverse and "everyone is very different from everyone else." "The student body is teeming with sensitive and excitable minds, which caters to an unbridled sense of adventure and exploration." These "really ridiculously smart" students have "incredible, raw talent." Personalities "range from your seemingly typical frat jock to your genius who knows everything but how to socialize." Cooper students are very often "hardcore" and come in three stereotypes. "The art kids all wear the same 'unique' clothing and smoke a lot," and they're "definitely more free-spirit, social people." "The engineers are either playing video games or saying sad jokes that only other engineers would understand." And "the architecture students can be a mixture of both, or anywhere in between, but they are hard to catch because all they do is work all the time." These three groups of students "don't mix so much" and sometimes there are rivalries. "The battle is like the Cold War, mostly sent in written messages on bathroom walls but no direct actions. It's benign in nature and just for amusement."

THE COOPER UNION FOR THE ADVANCEMENT OF SCIENCE AND ART

FINANCIAL AID: 212-353-4130 • E-MAIL: ADMISSIONS@COOPER.EDU • WEBSITE: WWW.COOPER.EDU

THE PRINCETON REVIEW SAYS

Admissions

Very important factors considered include: academic GPA, rigor of secondary school record, standardized test scores, level of applicant's interest, talent/ability, *Important factors considered include:* Application essay, character/personal qualities, extracurricular activities. *Other factors considered include:* Class rank, recommendation(s), first generation, interview, racial/ethnic status, volunteer work, work experience. SAT or ACT required; ACT with Writing component recommended. TOEFL required of all international applicants. High school diploma is required and GED is accepted. *Academic units required:* 4 English, 1 mathematics, 1 science, 1 social studies, 1 history, 8 academic electives. *Academic units recommended:* 4 English, 4 mathematics, 4 science, (3 science labs), 2 foreign language, 4 social studies.

Financial Aid

Students should submit: FAFSA, CSS/Financial Aid PROFILE Regular filing deadline is 6/1. The Princeton Review suggests that all financial aid forms be submitted as soon as possible after 1/1. Need-based scholarships/grants offered: Federal Pell, SEOG, state scholarships/grants, private scholarships, the school's own gift aid. *Loan aid offered:* FFEL Subsidized Stafford, FFEL Unsubsidized Stafford, FFEL PLUS, Federal Perkins, college/university loans from institutional funds. Applicants will be notified of awards on or about 6/1. Federal Work-Study Program available. Institutional employment available. Off-campus job opportunities are excellent.

The Inside Word

It's ultra-tough to get into The Cooper Union. There are typically more than 3,000 applicants vying for fewer than 300 slots. Not only do students need to have top academic accomplishments, but they also need to be a good fit for Cooper's offbeat milieu.

THE SCHOOL SAYS "..."

From The Admissions Office

"Each of Cooper Union's three schools, architecture, art, and engineering, adheres strongly to preparation for its profession and is committed to a problem-solving philosophy of education in a unique, scholarly environment. A rigorous curriculum and group projects reinforce this unique atmosphere in higher education and contribute to a strong sense of community and identity in each school. With McSorley's Ale House and the Joseph Papp Public Theatre nearby, Cooper Union remains at the heart of the city's tradition of free speech, enlightenment, and entertainment. Cooper's Great Hall has hosted national leaders, from Abraham Lincoln to Booker T. Washington, from Mark Twain to Samuel Gompers, from Susan B. Anthony to Betty Friedan, and more recently, President Bill Clinton and Senator Barack Obama.

"In addition, we eagerly await the arrival of our new academic building slated to open in 2009. Designed by Pritzker Prize–winning architect, Thom Mayne, the new building is expected to enhance and encourage more interaction between students in all three schools.

"We're seeking students who have a passion to study our professional programs. Cooper Union students are independent thinkers, following the beat of their own drum. Many of our graduates become world-class leaders in the disciplines of architecture, fine arts, design, and engineering.

"For art and architecture applicants, SAT scores are considered after the home test and portfolio work. For engineering applicants, high school grades and the SAT and SAT Subject Test scores are the most important factors considered in admissions decisions. Currently, we do not use the Writing section of the SAT to assist in making admissions decisions. We expect to reconsider that policy as more data is available in the near future."

SELECTIVITY

Admissions Rating	98
# of applicants	3,055
% of applicants accepted	9
% of acceptees attending	73
# accepting a place on wait list	59
% admitted from wait list	14
# of early decision applicants	449
% accepted early decision	16

FRESHMAN PROFILE

Range SAT Critical Reading	620–710
Range SAT Math	640–780
Range ACT Composite	29–33
Minimum paper TOEFL	600
Minimum computer TOEFL	250
Minimum web-based TOEFL	100
Average HS GPA	3.6
% graduated top 10% of class	93
% graduated top 25% of class	98
% graduated top 50% of class	99

DEADLINES

Early Decision	
Deadline	12/1
Notification	12/23
Regular	
Priority	12/1
Deadline	1/1
Notification	4/1
Nonfall registration?	no

APPLICANTS ALSO LOOK AT

AND OFTEN PREFER
Cornell University
Massachusetts Institute of Technology

AND SOMETIMES PREFER
Carnegie Mellon University

FINANCIAL FACTS

Financial Aid Rating	92
Annual tuition	$35,000
Room and board	$13,700
Required fees	$1,600
Books and supplies	$1,800
% frosh rec. need-based scholarship or grant aid	30
% UG rec. need-based scholarship or grant aid	28
% frosh rec. non-need-based scholarship or grant aid	30
% UG rec. non-need-based scholarship or grant aid	30
% frosh rec. need-based self-help aid	20
% UG rec. need-based self-help aid	21
% frosh rec. any financial aid	100
% UG rec. any financial aid	100
% UG borrow to pay for school	29
Average cumulative indebtedness	$9,900

CORNELL COLLEGE

600 FIRST STREET WEST, MOUNT VERNON, IA 52314-1098 • ADMISSIONS: 319-895-4477 • FAX: 319-895-4451

CAMPUS LIFE

Quality of Life Rating	**80**
Fire Safety Rating	**62**
Green Rating	**78**
Type of school	private
Affiliation	Methodist
Environment	rural

STUDENTS

Total undergrad enrollment	1,106
% male/female	50/50
% from out of state	75
% from public high school	79
% live on campus	90
% in (# of) fraternities	20 (8)
% in (# of) sororities	21 (7)
% African American	3
% Asian	2
% Caucasian	80
% Hispanic	3
% Native American	1
% international	4
# of countries represented	19

SURVEY SAYS . . .
No one cheats
Students are friendly
Students get along with local community
Low cost of living
Theater is popular

ACADEMICS

Academic Rating	**87**
Calendar	semester
Student/faculty ratio	11:1
Profs interesting rating	94
Profs accessible rating	94
Most common reg class size	20–29 students

MOST POPULAR MAJORS
economics
English language and literature
psychology

STUDENTS SAY ". . ."

Academics

Welcome to Cornell College, a small liberal arts school in Iowa that employs a unique one-course-at-a-time program, allowing students to focus on just one course (or "block") each month and providing an "intense, thorough, complete immersion." Though students agree that this "series of experiences" makes for "three crazy weeks," it also increases the quality and amount of knowledge gained and gives them a better chance to throw themselves into their extracurriculars. "You either are overloaded or underloaded with your class; there's no mixing," says a freshman. Some classes may not be thr most challenging, but "upper-level courses are very engaging and fulfilling." The block plan also makes it very easy to gain off-campus field experience or do international study, and "it's really nice that they can bring in professionals and outside experts to teach class for a block." Administration is generally well-liked here for their accessibility and their devotion to the institution though some note that, "there is not much transparency at the administrative level," which can be "out of touch" at times. The registrar is "the most dreaded office on campus," with residence life a close second. On the classroom side, professors "are incredibly helpful and really want students to succeed," and though "you may get a bad apple maybe once a year," they are "very supportive of students in their academic endeavors." "I could not possibly imagine being closer to my profs. Not a single one has asked us to call him/her by anything other than her/his first name, and generally by the end of a block I feel I know my prof as a person," says a student. All in all, students love the block structure and the sense of community it creates, as "no matter what it is you may want to do, you can find someone to do it with you." One student claims he "cannot imagine learning any other way."

Life

Since Cornell is very campus-focused ("there is very little to do in the surrounding area"), the school makes sure there is "a large variety of campus organizations to fit everyone's personality and interest." Cedar Rapids and Iowa City are both only a 20 minute drive away for those seeking shopping, bowling, and movies, and "ice climbing, rock climbing, paddling, and hiking" are popular outdoor pastimes. In addition, the school provides seven "block breaks, which last 4.5 days and give students the opportunity to travel or go skiing or camping, etc. The cold weather can cause problems here, in both a locked-in feel and the possibility for accidents, and a few students wish the school did a better job of clearing the snow and ice on the sidewalks. Many here tend to have a love-hate relationship with sports; some claim that the athletics are a huge boon, while others think there is an "unfortunately high number of jocks." Much like the curriculum, lunchtimes are pretty unique, and students all eat in a common cafeteria, naturally falling into a somewhat "high school" habit of eating at the same tables every day. The meals themselves are another matter. One student sums up the feelings of all: "Cornell needs to work on the food. There, I said it." Parties do take place on weekends, as do long, cold walks to the bars, but "it is entirely possible to not be involved with substance use at Cornell."

Student Body

There is "a great spectrum" of people that attend Cornell, and students have a hard time defining a more common characteristic than the fact that almost all are driven and involved. Some division into typical groups does occur—the "jocks, nerds, and the 'artsy' students"—but "even group to group there is always mingling because you never know who will be in your next class." Since the classes are so small and "you see the same people 4 hours a day for 3.5 weeks," students "get to know the people under the stereotypes, and most everyone is very accepting." As one freshman says, "The only intolerance I've seen is toward the consistently indolent."

FINANCIAL AID: 319-895-4216 • E-MAIL: ADMISSIONS@CORNELLCOLLEGE.EDU • WEBSITE: WWW.CORNELLCOLLEGE.EDU

THE PRINCETON REVIEW SAYS

Admissions

Very important factors considered include: Application essay, academic GPA, recommendation(s), rigor of secondary school record. *Important factors considered include:* Class rank, standardized test scores, character/personal qualities, extracurricular activities, first generation, interview, level of applicant's interest, talent/ability, volunteer work, work experience. *Other factors considered include:* Alumni/ae relation, geographical residence, racial/ethnic status, state residency. SAT or ACT required. TOEFL required of all international applicants. High school diploma is required and GED is accepted. *Academic units recommended:* 4 English, 3 mathematics, 3 science, 2 foreign language, 3 social studies.

Financial Aid

Students should submit: FAFSA, institution's own financial aid formNoncustodial (Divorced/Separated) Parent's Statement. Regular filing deadline is 3/1. The Princeton Review suggests that all financial aid forms be submitted as soon as possible after 1/1. *Need-based scholarships/grants offered:* Federal Pell, SEOG, state scholarships/grants, private scholarships, the school's own gift aid, AC, SMART, and TEACH Grants. *Loan aid offered:* Direct Subsidized Stafford, Direct Unsubsidized Stafford, Direct PLUS, Federal Perkins, McElroy loan, Sherman loan, United Methodist loan. Applicants will be notified of awards on a rolling basis beginning 3/1. Federal Work-Study Program available. Institutional employment available. Off-campus job opportunities are fair.

The Inside Word

Given Cornell's relatively unique approach to study, it's no surprise that the admissions committee here focuses attention on both academic and personal strengths. Cornell's small, highly self-selected applicant pool is chock-full of students with solid self-awareness, motivation, and discipline. Pay particular attention to offering evidence of challenging academic course work and solid achievement on your high school record. Strong writers can do much for themselves under admissions circumstances such as these.

THE SCHOOL SAYS "..."

From The Admissions Office

"Very few colleges are truly distinctive like Cornell College. Founded in 1853, Cornell is recognized as one of the nation's finest colleges of the liberal arts and sciences. It is Cornell's combination of special features, however, that distinguishes it. An attractively diverse, caring residential college, Cornell places special emphasis on service and leadership. Foremost, it is a place where theory and practice are brought together in exciting ways through the college's one-course-at-a-time academic calendar. Here, students enjoy learning as they immerse themselves in a single subject for a 3.5-week term. They and their professor devote all of their efforts to that course in an engagingly interactive learning environment. This academic system also offers wonderful enrichment experiences through field-based-study, travel abroad, student research, and meaningful internship opportunities. Nine terms are offered each year; 32 course credits are required for graduation with each course equal to 4 credit hours. Since all classes are on a standard schedule, students are able to pursue their extracurricular interests, whether in the performing arts, athletics, or interest groups, with the same passion with which they pursue their course work. Typically, each year applicants from all 50 states and more than 40 countries apply for admission. Cornell graduates are in demand, with more than two-thirds eventually earning advanced degrees. The college's beautiful hilltop campus is one of only two campuses nationwide listed on the National Register of Historic Places. Located in the charming town of Mount Vernon, Cornell is also within commuting distance of Iowa City (home of the University of Iowa) and Cedar Rapids (the second largest city in the state). Freshman applicants are required to submit their SAT Reasoning or ACT results (the Writing component is optional for the ACT, as students are required to submit an essay as part of the application for admission). In addition, for students submitting multiple score reports their best scores from either exam will be used in the application review process. SAT Subject Tests are not required."

SELECTIVITY

Admissions Rating	87
# of applicants	2,916
% of applicants accepted	44
% of acceptees attending	27
# accepting a place on wait list	55
% admitted from wait list	76

FRESHMAN PROFILE

Range SAT Critical Reading	550–660
Range SAT Math	570–660
Range ACT Composite	24–29
Minimum paper TOEFL	550
Minimum computer TOEFL	213
Average HS GPA	3.44
% graduated top 10% of class	24
% graduated top 25% of class	50
% graduated top 50% of class	85

DEADLINES

Early action	
Deadline	12/1
Notification	2/1
Regular	
Priority	2/1
Deadline	2/1
Notification	3/20
Nonfall registration?	yes

APPLICANTS ALSO LOOK AT AND SOMETIMES PREFER
Coe College
Beloit College
Knox College
Colorado College

FINANCIAL FACTS

Financial Aid Rating	87
Annual tuition	$27,670
Room and board	$7,220
Required fees	$180
Books and supplies	$810
% frosh rec. need-based scholarship or grant aid	69
% UG rec. need-based scholarship or grant aid	68
% frosh rec. non-need-based scholarship or grant aid	58
% UG rec. non-need-based scholarship or grant aid	58
% frosh rec. need-based self-help aid	69
% UG rec. need-based self-help aid	68
% frosh rec. any financial aid	96
% UG rec. any financial aid	96
% UG borrow to pay for school	73
Average cumulative indebtedness	$29,825

CORNELL UNIVERSITY

UNDERGRADUATE ADMISSIONS, 410 THURSTON AVENUE, ITHACA, NY 14850 • ADMISSIONS: 607-255-5241 • FAX: 607-255-0659

CAMPUS LIFE

Quality of Life Rating	88
Fire Safety Rating	71
Green Rating	96
Type of school	private
Environment	town

STUDENTS

Total undergrad enrollment	13,846
% male/female	51/49
% from out of state	63
% from public high school	69
% live on campus	57
% in (# of) fraternities	32 (50)
% in (# of) sororities	23 (20)
% African American	5
% Asian	17
% Caucasian	49
% Hispanic	6
% international	8
# of countries represented	77

SURVEY SAYS . . .
Great library
Great food on campus
Student publications are popular

ACADEMICS

Academic Rating	88
Calendar	semester
Student/faculty ratio	9:1
Profs interesting rating	74
Profs accessible rating	78
Most common reg class size	10–19 students
Most common lab size	10–19 students

MOST POPULAR MAJORS
agriculture
biological/life sciences
engineering
social sciences
business

STUDENTS SAY ". . ."

Academics

"A large, diverse university offering a huge variety of courses and majors," Cornell University seems intent on putting the "universe" in "university." Students tell us that "all the academic programs are strong, so no matter what you want to study, Cornell has the resources." But just in case Cornell's standout undergraduate departments in engineering, business, biology, industrial and labor relations, hotel administration, food science, animal science, and natural resources don't get you going, "You can [always] design your own major." Cornell offers "a mix of anything and everything, with more opportunities than you could ever want." Undergrads point out that "Cornell is a great place for people who know what they want to do in life and want to get things done sooner rather than later, because each major program is very focused and concentrated right from the beginning." Academics here "are hard, extremely tough." "We don't all have 4.0s, but we work harder than students at the other Ivy League schools. Cornell is the easiest Ivy to get into, and the hardest to graduate from. Grade inflation doesn't exist here." The school does its best to help students navigate the academic challenges, offering "enough help so that even the most lost student can find his/her way to a good, deserving grade." Professors "are available anytime you need them and are more than happy to lend you a helping hand," while both your "peer advisor and faculty advisor" are "easily accessible." The administration does a great job "running the school smoothly" and "makes the effort to keep lines of communication open." Students tell us that "undergraduates are offered unbelievable research opportunities and instruction from those who are at the top of their respective fields." And when it's time to find a job, "Cornell has a really good alumni network" and a "helpful Career Services" Office.

Life

Cornell is located in remote Ithaca, "on the top of a hill in the middle of a beautiful and cold nowhere." "Beautiful gorges" and "unrivaled" outdoor activities—"everything from kayaking to pumpkin picking is just a small trip away either by foot or by bus." "There really isn't anything you can't do when it comes to nature at Cornell," but there is not much in the way of urban diversion. As a result, many "students exist strictly within the Cornell bubble." They "have no escape from the stress of school and everything they do revolves around school." For many, weekend options consist of "bars in Collegetown and house parties," along with some on-campus "concerts, activities, and student-led initiatives." Lots of students "participate in intramural sports or one of the many clubs." One student observes, "being in a small town like Ithaca means that most people do one thing for fun: drink. At the same time, some of the dorms—i.e. the ones with fewer drinkers—are still up on the weekends playing poker or something like that. Nevertheless, the lack of a big city around you means that sometimes you can get pretty bored"—but then, there is always schoolwork to attend to.

Student Body

Cornell's student body "is diverse, and not just in the racial or ethnic sense. There are so many different courses of study at Cornell that a wide range of personalities and interests are represented. Every day, architects, engineers, hotel school students, and dairy farm majors sit down to lunch together." Furthermore, "because Cornell is half private and half public, the students come from diverse economic backgrounds." Pressed to provide a general description of their peers, students tell us that "the student body is divided into about three groups: the well-off, stylish-if-conservatively dressed 'practical majors' (most frat members, premeds, pre-laws, sorority girls, hoteleys, aggies); the study-a-holics (engineers, applied sciences, some of the premeds); and the Euro-acting, blazer-and-hoodie wearing, always-thin hipsters (English, comparative literature, philosophy, film, theater, etc.)."

FINANCIAL AID: 607-255-5145 • E-MAIL: ADMISSIONS@CORNELL.EDU • WEBSITE: WWW.CORNELL.EDU

THE PRINCETON REVIEW SAYS

Admissions

Very important factors considered include: Application essay, academic GPA, recommendation(s), rigor of secondary school record, standardized test scores, extracurricular activities, talent/ability. *Important factors considered include:* Class rank. *Other factors considered include:* Alumni/ae relation, character/personal qualities, first generation, geographical residence, interview, racial/ethnic status, state residency, volunteer work, work experience. SAT or ACT required. ACT with Writing component required. TOEFL required of all international applicants. High school diploma or equivalent is not required. *Academic units required:* 4 English, 3 mathematics. *Academic units recommended:* 3 science (3 science labs), 3 foreign language, 3 social studies, 3 history.

Financial Aid

Students should submit: FAFSA, institution's own financial aid form, CSS/financial aid profile, noncustodial profile, business/farm supplement, prior year tax forms. Regular filing deadline is 1/2. The Princeton Review suggests that all financial aid forms be submitted as soon as possible after 1/1. *Need-based scholarships/grants offered:* Federal Pell, SEOG, state scholarships/grants, private scholarships, the school's own gift aid. *Loan aid offered:* Direct Subsidized Stafford, Direct Unsubsidized Stafford, Direct PLUS, FFEL Subsidized Stafford, FFEL Unsubsidized Stafford, FFEL PLUS, Federal Perkins, college/university loans from institutional funds. Applicants will be notified of awards on or about 4/1. Federal Work-Study Program available. Institutional employment available. Off-campus job opportunities are fair.

The Inside Word

Gaining admission to Cornell is a tough coup regardless of your intended field of study, but some of the university's seven schools are more competitive than others. If you're thinking of trying to 'backdoor' your way into one of the most competitive schools—by gaining admission to one, then transferring after one year—be aware that you will have to resubmit the entire application and provide a statement outlining your academic plans. It's not impossible to accomplish, but Cornell works hard to discourage this sort of maneuvering.

THE SCHOOL SAYS "..."

From The Admissions Office

"Cornell University, an Ivy League school and land-grant college located in the scenic Finger Lakes region of central New York, provides an outstanding education to students in seven small to midsize undergraduate colleges: Agriculture and Life Sciences; Architecture, Art, and Planning; Arts and Sciences; Engineering; Hotel Administration; Human Ecology; and Industrial and Labor Relations. Cornellians come from all 50 states and more than 100 countries, and they pursue their academic goals in more than 100 departments. The College of Arts and Sciences, one of the smallest liberal arts schools in the Ivy League, offers more than 40 majors, most of which rank near the top nationwide. Applied programs in the other six colleges also rank among the best in the world. "Other special features of the university include a world-renowned faculty; 4,000 courses available to all students; an extensive undergraduate research program; superb research, teaching, and library facilities; a large, diverse study-abroad program; and more than 800 student organizations and 36 varsity sports. Cornell's campus is one of the most beautiful in the country; students pass streams, rocky gorges, and waterfalls on their way to class. First-year students make their home on North Campus, a living-learning community that features a special advising center, faculty-in-residence, a fitness center, and traditional residence halls as well as theme-centered buildings such as Ecology House. Cornell University invites applications from all interested students and uses the Common Application exclusively with a short required Cornell Supplement. Students applying for admissions will submit scores from the SAT or ACT (with writing). We also require SAT Subject Tests. Subject test requirements are college-specific."

SELECTIVITY

Admissions Rating	98
# of applicants	33,073
% of applicants accepted	21
% of acceptees attending	46
# accepting a place on wait list	2,163
% admitted from wait list	2
# of early decision applicants	3,064
% accepted early decision	37

FRESHMAN PROFILE

Range SAT Critical Reading	630–730
Range SAT Math	670–770
Range ACT Composite	29–33
Minimum paper TOEFL	550
Minimum computer TOEFL	250
% graduated top 10% of class	88
% graduated top 25% of class	98
% graduated top 50% of class	100

DEADLINES

Early decision	
Deadline	11/1
Notification	12/15
Regular	
Deadline	1/2
Notification	4/1
Nonfall registration?	no

FINANCIAL FACTS

Financial Aid Rating	97
Annual tuition	$36,300
Room and board	$11,640
Required fees	$204
Books and supplies	$740
% frosh rec. need-based scholarship or grant aid	37
% UG rec. need-based scholarship or grant aid	38
% frosh rec. need-based self-help aid	34
% UG rec. need-based self-help aid	37
% frosh rec. any financial aid	40
% UG rec. any financial aid	41
% UG borrow to pay for school	52
Average cumulative indebtedness	$23,485

CREIGHTON UNIVERSITY

2500 CALIFORNIA PLAZA, OMAHA, NE 68178 • ADMISSIONS: 402-280-2703 • FAX: 402-280-2685

CAMPUS LIFE
Quality of Life Rating	**82**
Fire Safety Rating	**86**
Green Rating	**89**
Type of school	private
Affiliation	Roman Catholic
Environment	metropolis

STUDENTS
Total undergrad enrollment	4,087
% male/female	41/59
% from out of state	61
% from public high school	53
% live on campus	62
% in (# of) fraternities	23 (5)
% in (# of) sororities	21 (7)
% African American	4
% Asian	9
% Caucasian	78
% Hispanic	4
% Native American	1
% international	1
# of countries represented	40

SURVEY SAYS . . .
Lab facilities are great
School is well run
Students are friendly
Students get along with local community
Intramural sports are popular

ACADEMICS
Academic Rating	**87**
Calendar	semester
Student/faculty ratio	11:1
Profs interesting rating	83
Profs accessible rating	83
Most common reg class size	10–19 students
Most common lab size	10–19 students

MOST POPULAR MAJORS
business/commerce
health/medical preparatory programs
psychology

STUDENTS SAY " . . ."

Academics

The voices echoing from this Omaha school are resoundingly pleased with their choice to attend "a great Jesuit university focused on academics and creating well-rounded students." Students are also active outside the classroom, getting "involved" in the campus and local community, and the school makes sure it churns a student out as a complete package: "academically, socially, culturally, faith-filled, and service-oriented." Creighton wants to form students who are driven inside the classroom but "want to find deeper meanings in all that they do to enact change in the world." Though classes are tough, the typical class size is small, which "makes discussion possible in nearly every class." Likewise, professors are extraordinarily helpful and "know how to present material in an interesting manner for the most part." Professors are all "exceptional" and really run the gamut "from quirky nerds to outspoken rebels to hilarious Jesuit priests." Many students come here for medical school, allied health, or business school. There are also a variety of services offered, such as a tutoring program called "The Study," where students get help from other students on a one-on-one basis. "Students at Creighton learn to enjoy the process, rather than just the product," says one. Both the teaching staff and administration are highly accessible; office hours don't seem to stop, and every Wednesday morning the much-loved president has breakfast with a different group of students to listen to their concerns and to talk about how life at Creighton is going. "At Creighton students come first, and it is as simple as that!" chirps a happy junior.

Life

"While academics are a huge part of our schooling, they are not all-encompassing," says a student. Community service happily takes up a lot of students' time, and there are fall break and spring break service trips all over the United States. Sports, both intercollegiate and intramural, are huge on and off campus; Omaha and the Old Market have plenty of music venues, bowling, shopping, and restaurants (a good thing, because the food at Creighton is universally despised and "needs to be improved drastically"). Students would like to see some more options for getting off campus, though; the difficulty and cost of living off campus means on-campus housing is in high demand. The Greek community at Creighton "is not as intense as at state schools," but students in sorority or fraternities hold many leadership positions on campus. Weeknights are mainly for studying, but house parties are available on weekends, and "the bar scene is where many students spend their nights off." The school and student government do an excellent job of providing plenty of activities that are enjoyed by all, such as ice skating, weekly movies, and "mock TV shows like the 'Price is Right,'" and no one has any problem with peer pressure. "It is very easy to be productive and involved but still be able to find time for fun," says a biology and Spanish major.

Student Body

The typical student is white and from the Midwest, and most are "outgoing and friendly," which is probably why atypical students have no problems fitting in. And the "old brick road that runs down the middle of campus (called the mall) provides excellent opportunities to meet new people." "It doesn't matter where you came from or why you're here" as "most students have the same values, which allows the community to feel connected." "Everyone is interconnected through someone; there are very few degrees of separation between individuals," says one student, though others claim that there is no shortage of cliques. Creighton students are incredibly balanced in their work and play, and are "over-the-top involved" with activities and community service while maintaining full academic loads. The school is very involved in study-abroad programs, so there are a fair number of international students in each class. "I've never been in a place where so many people will hold the door open for me to walk through, if that gives any indication of the type of student here," says a student.

FINANCIAL AID: 402-280-2731 • E-MAIL: ADMISSIONS@CREIGHTON.EDU • WEBSITE: WWW.ADMISSION.CREIGHTON.EDU

THE PRINCETON REVIEW SAYS

Admissions

Very important factors considered include: Academic GPA, rigor of secondary school record. *Important factors considered include:* Application essay, standardized test scores. *Other factors considered include:* Class rank, recommendation(s), character/personal qualities, extracurricular activities, first generation, level of applicant's interest, racial/ethnic status, talent/ability, volunteer work. SAT or ACT required. TOEFL required of all international applicants. High school diploma is required and GED is accepted. *Academic units required:* 4 English, 3 mathematics, 2 science, 2 foreign language, 2 social studies, 3 academic electives. *Academic units recommended:* 4 English, 4 mathematics, 3 science, 3 foreign language, 3 social studies, 1 history, 3 academic electives.

Financial Aid

Students should submit: FAFSA, institution's own financial aid form The Princeton Review suggests that all financial aid forms be submitted as soon as possible after 1/1. *Need-based scholarships/grants offered:* Federal Pell, SEOG, state scholarships/grants, private scholarships, the school's own gift aid. *Loan aid offered:* FFEL Subsidized Stafford, FFEL Unsubsidized Stafford, FFEL PLUS, Federal Perkins. Federal nursing applicants will be notified of awards on a rolling basis beginning 3/15. Federal Work-Study Program available. Institutional employment available. Off-campus job opportunities are excellent.

The Inside Word

Creighton's lack of name recognition and its location can handicap its search for quality students, occasionally forcing the school to lower the bar to fill its incoming classes, so the school's loss could well be your gain. For those comfortable in a Jesuit school, Creighton offers bright, hardworking students a great opportunity at a quality education.

THE SCHOOL SAYS "..."

From The Admissions Office

"Creighton University, a Midwestern gem with a national reputation, is committed to being a leading Catholic, Jesuit University in the United States, helping students achieve academic and personal goals with a compassionate, faith-filled view of the world. Creighton's complex and sophisticated academic offerings draw students from across the nation and around the globe. Students find great balance within rigorous academics, abundant opportunities for undergraduate research and life-changing community service experiences. Creighton is steamrolling into the future, with more than $285 million in new construction and renovations, including: a state-of-the-art integrated science building, technology-rich junior/senior town homes, a nationally recognized soccer stadium and campus mall, and a signature student life and learning center. With about 7,000 students (approximately 4,000 undergraduates), more than 50 undergraduate majors and more than 20 graduate and professional programs. Creighton is the complete package—small, personal classes, accomplished faculty mentors, a wealth of internship opportunities and a 96 percent job placement rate within eight months of graduation. With recognition from prestigious organizations such as the Fulbright Fellows and Goldwater Scholars programs and extraordinary synergy among undergraduate, graduate and professional faculty, it's not surprising that Creighton launches about half of arts and sciences graduates into medical, dental, pharmacy, physical or occupational therapy, graduate or law school—one of the highest rates nationally for a university our size. At Creighton, teaching matters, students matter and values matter; and our students are not only prepared to succeed in their careers, but challenged to go out and shape a more just world."

SELECTIVITY
Admissions Rating	96
# of applicants	4,740
% of applicants accepted	82
% of acceptees attending	25
# accepting a place on wait list	110
% admitted from wait list	40

FRESHMAN PROFILE
Range SAT Critical Reading	500–610
Range SAT Math	540–650
Range SAT Writing	510–620
Range ACT Composite	24–29
Minimum paper TOEFL	550
Minimum computer TOEFL	213
Average HS GPA	3.75
% graduated top 10% of class	42
% graduated top 25% of class	73
% graduated top 50% of class	93

DEADLINES
Regular	
Priority	12/1
Deadline	2/15
Notification	rolling
Nonfall registration?	yes

APPLICANTS ALSO LOOK AT
AND OFTEN PREFER
University of Missouri—Columbia
University of Notre Dame
AND SOMETIMES PREFER
Saint Louis University
University of Colorado—Boulder
Marquette University
University of Kansas
University of Nebraska at Omaha
Gonzaga University
AND RARELY PREFER
University of Saint Thomas (MN)
University of Iowa
Iowa State University
Drake University
University of Nebraska—Lincoln

FINANCIAL FACTS
Financial Aid Rating	83
Annual tuition	$28,238
% frosh rec. need-based scholarship or grant aid	60
% UG rec. need-based scholarship or grant aid	51
% frosh rec. non-need-based scholarship or grant aid	51
% UG rec. non-need-based scholarship or grant aid	44
% frosh rec. need-based self-help aid	47
% UG rec. need-based self-help aid	41
% frosh rec. athletic scholarships	4
% UG rec. athletic scholarships	5
% frosh rec. any financial aid	97
% UG rec. any financial aid	89
% UG borrow to pay for school	61
Average cumulative indebtedness	$32,560

DARTMOUTH COLLEGE

6016 McNUTT HALL, HANOVER, NH 03755 • ADMISSIONS: 603-646-2875 • FAX: 603-646-1216

CAMPUS LIFE
Quality of Life Rating	88
Fire Safety Rating	60*
Green Rating	96
Type of school	private
Environment	village

STUDENTS
Total undergrad enrollment	4,147
% male/female	50/50
% from out of state	97
% live on campus	85
% in (# of) fraternities	43 (14)
% in (# of) sororities	42 (6)
% African American	8
% Asian	14
% Caucasian	55
% Hispanic	7
% Native American	4
% international	7

SURVEY SAYS . . .
School is well run
Campus feels safe
Frats and sororities dominate social scene
Student publications are popular
Lots of beer drinking

ACADEMICS
Academic Rating	96
Calendar	quarter
Student/faculty ratio	8:1
Profs interesting rating	78
Profs accessible rating	82
Most common reg class size	10–19 students

MOST POPULAR MAJORS
economics
government
psychology
history
English

STUDENTS SAY ". . ."

Academics

Dartmouth College "has a reputation of being like summer camp, and it's true: Students take their academic work very seriously, but they're also all extremely happy to be here, and they have a lot of fun, no matter what their idea of fun is." A school that is small "without being suffocating or lacking opportunities, challenging but not too competitive, has good academics and access to professors, and has its own ski hill" obviously has a lot to offer; how else could it entice "artists, athletes, musicians, and future leaders to all gather together in the middle of nowhere?" Students love that Dartmouth is "very undergraduate-focused, unlike the other Ivies that neglect their undergrads to only concentrate on research." They also love the D-Plan, which divides the academic year into four 10-week terms in order to provide maximum flexibility and study-abroad opportunities ("many students use the D-Plan to study abroad up to three times"). Dartmouth professors "are some of the greatest minds in the country, and they're almost all willing to just sit and chat if you feel like it. I've had at least one professor each year who's invited the whole class to her/his house for dinner and discussion (sometimes with famous guests). It's a great way to learn information that is above and beyond what you're learning in the classroom." No wonder "everyone is happy here."

Life

Dartmouth's greatest strength, students tell us, "is its incredible sense of community and tradition," traditions that include "singing the alma mater, dancing the Salty Dog Rag, and running 100-plus laps around a 40-foot bonfire." One undergrad notes, "[Students] have a ton of school spirit," and "from the first day on campus, students are learning all about what it means to be a Dartmouth student." Situated in the Upper Connecticut River Valley, Dartmouth has "a great location for skiing and outdoor activities," and it's a place "where the student body is very active, both outdoors (i.e., hiking, biking, rock climbing, ice climbing, and skiing) as well as indoors partying. Whatever you want to do, you can find it here." That is, unless what you want is constant big-city entertainment; hometown Hanover is a "very small town," and "Boston and Montreal, though available, are rarely sought." Students are more likely to flock to the campus' popular Greek scene: "Most people like to go drink at frats on weekends and attend parties. I think like 20 percent of the student population abstains from drinking, but everyone else is pretty into it." Students are also "very involved in on-campus organizations and sports teams." As one junior explains, "There's always more to do than can ever be done, and the hardest thing is making time for sleep along with classes, clubs, and friends."

Student Body

The typical Dartmouth student "is hard to define. If I mashed them all up into one person, it'd be a kid from Jersey driving a Lexus with a kayak on the top. His collar popped but his pants torn. In his bag there'd be the works of Marx next to those of Friedman. We're all so different, but at the same time, we're just all here to learn, to love, and to live." Dartmouth "strives to create a world of very different people," and its reputation allows it to cherry-pick top students from all around the globe. The school has a reputation for political conservatism that some argue is overblown: "There are very liberal students at Dartmouth, and there are very conservative students...but most tend to fall in between." Also, while the school "has a stereotype of being a big party school full of jocks," it's "not really that way," and "That should be more recognized." Across the board students tend to be "well-balanced" and "outgoing," and everyone from the "sweet frat dude to the library dweller all find a place to fit in."

FINANCIAL AID: 603-646-2451 • E-MAIL: ADMISSIONS.OFFICE@DARTMOUTH.EDU • WEBSITE: WWW.DARTMOUTH.EDU

THE PRINCETON REVIEW SAYS

Admissions

Very important factors considered include: Class rank, application essay, academic GPA, recommendation(s), rigor of secondary school record, standardized test scores, character/personal qualities, extracurricular activities. *Important factors considered include:* Talent/ability, volunteer work. *Other factors considered include:* Alumni/ae relation, first generation, geographical residence, interview, racial/ethnic status. SAT or ACT (SAT subjects tests are required with both ACT or SAT scores and includes writing) Subject Tests with writing required. ACT with Writing component required. TOEFL required of all international applicants. High school diploma or equivalent is not required. *Academic units recommended:* 4 English, 4 mathematics, 3 science, 3 social studies, 3 history.

Financial Aid

Students should submit: FAFSA, CSS/financial aid profile, noncustodial profile, business/farm supplement, current W-2 or federal tax returns. Regular filing deadline is 2/1. The Princeton Review suggests that all financial aid forms be submitted as soon as possible after 1/1. *Need-based scholarships/grants offered:* Federal Pell, SEOG, state scholarships/grants, private scholarships, the school's own gift aid. *Loan aid offered:* FFEL Subsidized Stafford, FFEL Unsubsidized Stafford, FFEL PLUS, Federal Perkins, state loans, college/university loans from institutional funds. Applicants will be notified of awards on or about 4/2. Federal Work-Study Program available. Institutional employment available. Off-campus job opportunities are excellent.

The Inside Word

Like other elite schools, Dartmouth is swamped with more applications from qualified students than it can accommodate. More kids are applying to Dartmouth every year. So give this your best shot, and don't take it personally if you don't get in; unfortunately, many great candidates don't.

THE SCHOOL SAYS "..."

From The Admissions Office

"Dartmouth's mission is to endow students with the knowledge and wisdom needed to make creative and positive contributions to society. The College brings together a breadth of cultures, traditions, and ideas to create a campus that is alive with ongoing debate and exploration. From student-initiated round-table discussions that attempt to make sense of world events to the late-night exchanges in a dormitory lounge, Dartmouth students take advantage of their opportunities to learn from each other. The unique benefits of this interchange are accompanied by a great sense of responsibility. Each individual's commitment to the College's 'Principles of Community' ensures the vitality of this learning environment, and Dartmouth's size enhances the quality of the experience for all involved.

"To help all Dartmouth students take full advantage of the 'Dartmouth Experience,' the College has eliminated loans from its financial aid packages. Students from families with incomes less than $75,000 receive free tuition to the College.

"All applicants, including those who apply from foreign countries, are required to take the SAT (or ACT) and any two SAT Subject Tests. All testing must be completed by January of the senior year in high school. If standardized testing is repeated, the admissions committee only considers highest scores."

SELECTIVITY

Admissions Rating	98
# of applicants	16,538
% of applicants accepted	13
% of acceptees attending	49
# accepting a place on wait list	797
# of early decision applicants	1,428
% accepted early decision	28

FRESHMAN PROFILE

Range SAT Critical Reading	660–770
Range SAT Math	670–780
Range SAT Writing	660–770
Range ACT Composite	29–34
% graduated top 10% of class	91
% graduated top 50% of class	100

DEADLINES

Early decision	
Deadline	11/1
Notification	12/15
Regular	
Deadline	1/1
Notification	4/1
Nonfall registration?	no

FINANCIAL FACTS

Financial Aid Rating	93
Annual tuition	$36,915
Room and board	$10,930
Required fees	$213
Books and supplies	$1,412
% frosh rec. need-based scholarship or grant aid	50
% UG rec. need-based scholarship or grant aid	49
% frosh rec. need-based self-help aid	44
% UG rec. need-based self-help aid	48
% frosh rec. any financial aid	51
% UG rec. any financial aid	51
% UG borrow to pay for school	52
Average cumulative indebtedness	$20,126

DAVIDSON COLLEGE

PO Box 7156, Davidson, NC 28035-7156 • Admissions: 704-894-2230 • Fax: 704-894-2016

CAMPUS LIFE
Quality of Life Rating	97
Fire Safety Rating	60*
Green Rating	60*
Type of school	private
Affiliation	Presbyterian
Environment	village

STUDENTS
Total undergrad enrollment	1,661
% male/female	49/51
% from out of state	80
% from public high school	51
% live on campus	94
% in (# of) fraternities	40 (8)
% African American	6
% Asian	4
% Caucasian	74
% Hispanic	4
% Native American	1
% international	4
# of countries represented	36

SURVEY SAYS . . .
No one cheats
Lab facilities are great
School is well run
Students are friendly
Students get along with local
community
Campus feels safe

ACADEMICS
Academic Rating	97
Calendar	semester
Student/faculty ratio	10:1
Profs interesting rating	98
Profs accessible rating	98
Most common reg class size	10–19 students
Most common lab size	10–19 students

MOST POPULAR MAJORS
biology/biological sciences
English language and literature
history

STUDENTS SAY ". . ."

Academics

This small school north of Charlotte, North Carolina, cultivates an environment "that is very open to change and improvement" and empowers students to "be better people and make a difference in the world." The administration works hard to create an on-campus community and constantly makes efforts "to support and improve Davidson," all while keeping students happy and minds full. "I have never witnessed people so eager to come do their job every day. [Professors] are almost too willing to help," says a student. There is also a trickle-down effect because even the student body is supportive and "eager to watch you succeed." The school offers a classic liberal arts education, encouraging students to take classes in all areas, and "all of these people come out smarter than they came in." "If I could spend 20 years being educated by this administration and these professors, I would," says a very happy junior. School is the number one priority for all of the students here, and while academics are all-consuming, time-wise, they are also "fascinating and rewarding." Without a doubt, Davidson is a tough school— "99 percent of us left our 4.0 GPA's back in high school," claims a student—and professors don't believe in grade inflation or curving grades, but they do readily make themselves available outside of class for help or discussion. There is a lot of work, but it "is accompanied by even more resources with which it can be successfully managed." One student testimonial: "My calculus teacher last semester has office hours in the student union, and invited the whole class over to his house for chicken dinner—twice!" The dedication of the staff is contagious, and "though the work is rigorous, time spent in school never feels wasted."

Life

Davidson "possesses an intense study culture, and people hit the books regularly; it's cool to be smart." One of the many wonderful things about Davidson "is that academics voluntarily leave the classroom." "It's not uncommon to hear people discussing their current academic topics at lunch or in the gym." Basketball is a huge common ground for the student body at large; "Everyone enjoys being a part of the underdog/Cinderella story." Weeks are devoted to study, as well as extracurricular activities—"you see your friends because you are doing homework together or eating meals together, not because you're vegging out." Of course, even Davidson students need to kick back and there are always plenty of parties to be found on the weekends. Fraternities and eating houses (the Davidson version of sororities) are popular. Fortunately, "There really is no pressure to drink. You can go out and dance and have a great time or have movie nights with friends," says a student. The combination of the idyllic atmosphere and the workload "can make it hard to stay up-to-date on current events, yet most students remain well-informed."

Student Body

Davidson is "an amalgamation of all types of people, religiously, ethnically, politically, economically, etc.," all "united under the umbrella of intellectual curiosity" and their devotion to the school as a community. The typical Davidson student is "probably white," but in the past few years, admissions has been making progress in racially diversifying the campus, which students agree upon as necessary. Though there are plenty of southern, preppy, athletic types to fit the brochure examples, there are many niches for every type of "atypical" student. "There are enough people that one can find a similar group to connect with, and there are few enough people that one ends up connecting with dissimilar [prople] anyway," says a student. Everyone here is smart and well-rounded; admissions "does a good job...so if you're in you'll probably make the cut all the way through the four years." Most students have several extracurriculars to round out their free time, and they have a healthy desire to enjoy themselves when the books shut. "During the week we work hard. On the weekends we play hard. We don't do anything halfway," says a senior. Though the majority of students lean to the left, there's a strong conservative contingent, and there are no real problems between the two.

FINANCIAL AID: 704-894-2232 • E-MAIL: ADMISSION@DAVIDSON.EDU • WEBSITE: WWW.DAVIDSON.EDU

THE PRINCETON REVIEW SAYS

Admissions

Very important factors considered include: Rigor of secondary school record, grade performance, application essay, character/personal qualities. *Important factors considered include:* recommendations, co-curricular activities, talent/ability. *Other factors considered include:* Class rank, standardized test scores. SAT or ACT required. SAT and SAT Subject Tests or ACT recommended. TOEFL required of all international applicants. High school diploma is required and GED is not accepted. *Academic units required:* 4 English, 3 mathematics, 2 science, 2 foreign language, 2 social studies or history. *Academic units recommended:* 4 mathematics, 4 science, 4 foreign language, 4 social studies or history.

Financial Aid

Students should submit: FAFSA, CSS/financial aid profile, noncustodial profile, business/farm supplement, noncustodial (divorced/separated) parent's statement; corporate tax return and/or noncustodial parent tax return(if applicable); parent and student tax returns and W-2 forms. Regular filing deadline is 2/15. The Princeton Review suggests that all financial aid forms be submitted as soon as possible after 1/1. *Need-based scholarships/grants offered:* Federal Pell, SEOG, state scholarships/grants, private scholarships, the school's own gift aid. Applicants will be notified of awards on or about 4/1. Federal Work-Study Program available. Institutional employment available. Off-campus job opportunities are excellent.

The Inside Word

The combination of Davidson's low acceptance rate and high yield really packs a punch. Prospective applicants beware: Securing admission at this prestigious school is no easy feat. Admitted students are typically at the top of their high school classes and have strong standardized test scores. Candidates with leadership experience generally garner the favor of admissions officers. The college takes its honor code seriously and, as a result, seeks out students of demonstrated reputable character.

THE SCHOOL SAYS "..."

From The Admissions Office

"Davidson College is one of the nation's premier academic institutions, a college of the liberal arts and sciences respected for its intellectual vigor, the high quality of its faculty and students, and the achievements of its alumni. Davidson is distinguished by its strong honor code, close collaboration between professors and students, an environment that encourages both intellectual growth and community service, and a commitment to international education. Davidson places great value on student participation in extracurricular activities, intercollegiate athletics, and intramural sports. The college has a strong regional identity, grounded in traditions of civility and mutual respect, and has historic ties to the Presbyterian Church. The college has a strong commitment to making a Davidson education affordable. Beginning with the 2007–2008 academic year, the college no longer includes student loans in its financial aid packages. Through the Davidson Trust, 100% of demonstrated financial need will be met with a combination of grants and student employment.

"Applicants are required to complete and submit scores from the SAT and/or the ACT. SAT Subject Tests (mathematics and one of your choice) are recommended. Davidson will utilize the scores that place the student in the greatest possible light."

SELECTIVITY
Admissions Rating	98
# of applicants	4,412
% of applicants accepted	26
% of acceptees attending	43
# of early decision applicants	549
% accepted early decision	40

FRESHMAN PROFILE
Range SAT Critical Reading	630–730
Range SAT Math	640–730
Range SAT Writing	630–730
Range ACT Composite	28–32
Minimum paper TOEFL	600
Minimum computer TOEFL	250
Average HS GPA	3.85
% graduated top 10% of class	81
% graduated top 25% of class	97
% graduated top 50% of class	100

DEADLINES
Early decision	
Deadline	11/15
Notification	12/15
Regular	
Deadline	1/2
Notification	4/1
Nonfall registration?	no

FINANCIAL FACTS
Financial Aid Rating	98
Annual tuition	$34,776
Room and board	$9,906
Required fees	$348
Books and supplies	$1,000
% frosh rec. need-based scholarship or grant aid	33
% UG rec. need-based scholarship or grant aid	33
% frosh rec. non-need-based scholarship or grant aid	12
% UG rec. non-need-based scholarship or grant aid	13
% frosh rec. need-based self-help aid	19
% UG rec. need-based self-help aid	22
% frosh rec. athletic scholarships	11
% UG rec. athletic scholarships	11
% frosh rec. any financial aid	35
% UG rec. any financial aid	35
% UG borrow to pay for school	33.1
Average cumulative indebtedness	$25,025

DEEP SPRINGS COLLEGE

HC 72 BOX 45001, DEEP SPRINGS, CA VIA DYER, NV 89010-9803 • ADMISSIONS: 760-872-2000 • FAX: 760-872-4466

CAMPUS LIFE

Quality of Life Rating	96
Fire Safety Rating	81
Green Rating	60*
Type of school	private
Environment	rural

STUDENTS

Total undergrad enrollment	26
% male/female	100/0
% from out of state	80
% from public high school	50
% live on campus	100
# of countries represented	3

SURVEY SAYS . . .

Lots of liberal students
Class discussions encouraged
Great food on campus
Dorms are like palaces
Low cost of living
Intercollegiate sports are unpopular
or nonexistent
Frats and sororities are unpopular or
nonexistent
Very little beer drinking
Very little hard liquor
(Almost) no one smokes
Very little drug use

ACADEMICS

Academic Rating	97
Calendar	Semester
Student/faculty ratio	4:1
Profs interesting rating	90
Profs accessible rating	96
Most common reg	
class size fewer than 10 students	

MOST POPULAR MAJORS

liberal arts and sciences studies and
humanities

STUDENTS SAY ". . ."

Academics

The "three pillars" of a Deep Springs education—"labor, academics, and self-governance"—combine to produce "unparalleled challenges" that run the gamut "from fixing a hay baler in the middle of the night to puzzling over a particularly difficult passage of Hegel." That's what the 26 men who attend Deep Springs tell us. These unique undergraduates basically run their own school, work the ranch where it is located, and complete a rigorous curriculum, an itinerary that "creates an environment of intense growth and responsibility." Class work occurs in a seminar format in which "the distinction between teacher and student becomes fuzzy [because] everyone is equally invested, thoughtful, and engaged." Composition and public speaking are the only required courses; all others are chosen by the student body and taught by a faculty of three long-term professors (one each in the humanities, social sciences, and natural sciences) and three visiting scholars or artists. The system relies on a commitment to self-determination, which means "the smoothness with which many programs run depends largely on the kind of responsibility students take. Sometimes students do a good job taking care of administrative tasks, sometimes a worse job. It's all part of the educational experience." While the size of the school inevitably means that "lab and library facilities are not what they might be," students tell us that the overall Deep Springs experience compensates for any shortcomings. As one student explains, "through intense academics and running the college administratively and practically, we receive an unprecedented education in citizenship of a conscious human being."

Life

Deep Springs is totally unlike other colleges in terms of the everyday life of a student," because "no one drinks, everyone helps run the ranch in some way, and no one can be totally self-absorbed (unless he's out hiking in the desert)." Instead, students immerse themselves in the Deep Springs way. As one student explains, "The Deep Springs program is our whole life. The intellectual questions we're asking and the labor we're doing is all bound up with our identity." Students spend their free time "thinking about intellectual things: moral issues, politics, and the community. 'Fun' is hard to come by, and one has to learn how to enjoy people, work, and engagement." Students do occasionally take a break, however; "On weekends in the rumpus room of the dorm, you can find a group of motley adventurers engaged in a Dungeons & Dragon's quest or a pack of students watching 'Gossip Girl.' You'll find even more people scoffing at such pedantry and watching arty French movies," and "communal soccer is excellent…we even play in the snow." Also, occasionally "We have dance parties called 'boojies,'" and "We do some other strange things for fun, like sledding naked down 800-foot-tall sand dunes in neighboring Eureka Valley." Undergrads concede that Deep Springs "life can be intense. Students usually are utterly exhausted. But most of the time we know that something good is coming out of this," and that keeps undergrads energized and motivated.

Student Body

"Having only 26 students makes it even harder to characterize the 'typical' Deep Springer," students understandably warn, but they add that "we're all very able and driven, but in our own ways, not in the way that most Ivy League students are. Deep Springs isn't a stepping stone to the world of white-collar work but an end in itself that we all pursue with all our hearts. So I guess the typical student has a healthy disgust for the pedagogy of most other universities." Undergrads are also predictably "intelligent, motivated, and responsible," as they "must demonstrate depth of thought to be accepted" to the school. As one student puts it, "The typical student at Deep Springs is committed to the life of the intellect and committed to finding education in our labor program. Most of the students here believe that a life of service, informed by discourse and labor, is a necessary notion to understand in today's world."

FINANCIAL AID: 760-872-2000 • E-MAIL: APCOM@DEEPSPRING.EDU • WEBSITE: WWW.DEEPSPRINGS.EDU

THE PRINCETON REVIEW SAYS

Admissions

Very important factors considered include: Application essay, character/personal qualities, interview, level of applicant's interest. *Important factors considered include:* Academic GPA, rigor of secondary school record, extracurricular activities, volunteer work, work experience. *Other factors considered include:* Class rank, recommendation(s), standardized test scores, racial/ethnic status, talent/ability. SAT or ACT required. High school diploma or equivalent is not required. *Academic units required:* None.

Financial Aid

The Princeton Review suggests that all financial aid forms be submitted as soon as possible after 1/1. Applicants will be notified of awards on or about 4/15.

The Inside Word

Students will be hard-pressed to find a school with a more personal or thorough application process than Deep Springs. Given the intimate and collegial atmosphere of the school, matchmaking is the top priority. Candidates are evaluated by a body composed of students, faculty, and staff members. The application is writing intensive; finalists are expected to spend several days on campus, during which they will undergo a lengthy interview.

THE SCHOOL SAYS "..."

From The Admissions Office

"Founded in 1917, Deep Springs College lies isolated in a high desert valley of eastern California, 30 miles from the nearest town. Its enrollment is limited to 26 students, each of whom receives a full scholarship that covers tuition, room and board and is valued at more than $50,000 per year. Students engage in rigorous academics, govern themselves, and participate in the operation of our cattle and alfalfa ranch. After 2 years, students generally transfer to other schools to complete their studies. Students regularly transfer to Harvard, The University of Chicago, and Brown, but also choose Cornell, Columbia, Stanford, Swarthmore, University of California—Berkeley, and Yale.

In the past five years Deep Springers have won the following national scholarship competitions:

• The Jack Kent Cooke Scholarship (2)

• The Barry M. Goldwater Scholarship (1)

• The Rhodes Scholarship (1)

• The Harry S. Truman Scholarship (5)

• The Morris Udall Scholarship (1)"

SELECTIVITY

Admissions Rating	99
# of applicants	170
% of applicants accepted	7
% of acceptees attending	92
# accepting a place on wait list	3

FRESHMAN PROFILE

Range SAT Critical Reading	750–800
Range SAT Math	700–800
% graduated top 10% of class	86
% graduated top 25% of class	93
% graduated top 50% of class	100

DEADLINES

Regular	
Deadline	11/15
Notification	4/15
Nonfall registration?	no

APPLICANTS ALSO LOOK AT AND RARELY PREFER

Harvard College
University of Chicago
Swarthmore College

FINANCIAL FACTS

Financial Aid Rating	60*
Books and supplies	$1,200
% frosh rec. any financial aid	100
% UG rec. any financial aid	100

*All students receive scholarships.

DENISON UNIVERSITY

Box 740, Granville, OH 43023 • Admissions: 740-587-6276 • Fax: 740-587-6306

CAMPUS LIFE
Quality of Life Rating	**83**
Fire Safety Rating	**88**
Green Rating	**87**
Type of school	private
Environment	village

STUDENTS
Total undergrad enrollment	2,180
% male/female	44/56
% from out of state	65
% from public high school	71
% live on campus	99
% in (# of) fraternities	20 (8)
% in (# of) sororities	29 (6)
% African American	5
% Asian	2
% Caucasian	82
% Hispanic	3
% international	5
# of countries represented	25

SURVEY SAYS . . .
Lab facilities are great
School is well run
Campus feels safe
Lots of beer drinking

ACADEMICS
Academic Rating	**88**
Calendar	semester
Student/faculty ratio	10:1
Profs interesting rating	86
Profs accessible rating	89
Most common	
reg class size	10–19 students

MOST POPULAR MAJORS
economics
English language and literature

STUDENTS SAY ". . ."

Academics

Students describe Denison University as "a mecca of top-notch academics" located "in the seclusion of rural Ohio." By necessity Denison University may be "huge on community," but regardless of the impetus, students, faculty, and administrators here "become like a big family where everyone takes care of one another." Students agree that that's a good thing, as this environment provides "academically motivated students a chance to excel in their respective studies through a supportive student population and dedicated faculty, while also providing many social opportunities." Denison is "all about educating the whole student, whether it be through classes, speakers, sports, clubs, or even Greek life." Academically, Denison can be "challenging." "It is possible to spend an entire semester stressed out to the extreme with 20-plus academic credits and no time to do the readings for every class. But it is also very possible to manage your time well and get everything done in a mannerly fashion, without overexerting yourself, but still having a successful and productive semester." Students who find themselves in over their heads can count on "professors who are willing to go the extra mile with their students." Professors "have organized study groups before exams and extend their office hours so that you can meet with them about a paper or project." As one student observes, "It's your own fault if you do poorly, because there are so many ways for you to get help through teachers, study groups, tutoring, etc."

Life

"What is nice about Denison is that most people stay on campus during the weekends, so there is always something to do," students here report. The school and the Student Activities Committee "always sponsor concerts, speakers, and events around campus," and, of course, there is always a party or two available on the weekends. "There is so much to do all week, every week," which "is somewhat necessary, as the town of Granville is quite small and offers few diversions." A party scene "is available if that's what you want," and quite a few students do, telling us that "go-out-and-party nights" are Fridays and Saturdays and "Mondays and Wednesdays also, since some students have fewer classes on Tuesdays and Thursdays." There's a lot of partying on campus (Greek life encompasses about 21 percent of the student body) in the student residences. Denison has "a number of sports teams that are nationally ranked," but students are just as likely to follow OSU as Denison. While hometown Granville is "small" and "very quiet," Columbus "is only 30 minutes away which allows [students] to visit other restaurants, bars, concerts, and, of course, big sister OSU." Easton "is just 25 minutes away and has a huge shopping center."

Student Body

While "There are not a lot of atypical students on the extreme ends of 'different'" at Denison, students hasten to point out that "Denison does not solely consist of popped collars and Uggs. Those students just like to make themselves known." Though some students note that the population tends towards the generally affluent, they are quick to add. There are "a lot of athletes on campus, and fraternities and sororities are pretty big." "Kids are hardworking and usually friendly." Also, Denison is not without its "internationals, artsy types, and [even] the socially awkward." There's "even a small counterculture made up of environmentalists and hippies who live at the Homestead and hang out at Bandersnatch." These people "are the minority, but there's a niche for them." As one student explains, "It's pretty easy to find a core group of friends."

FINANCIAL AID: 740-587-6279 • E-MAIL: ADMISSIONS@DENISON.EDU • WEBSITE: WWW.DENISON.EDU

THE PRINCETON REVIEW SAYS

Admissions

Very important factors considered include: Academic GPA, rigor of secondary school record, application essay, recommendation(s). *Important factors considered include:* Extracurricular activities, interview, level of applicant's interest, talent/ability. *Other factors considered include:* Class rank, standardized test scores, alumni/ae relation, character/personal qualities, first generation, geographical residence, racial/ethnic status, state residency, volunteer work, work experience. SAT or SAT Subject Tests or ACT are optional. TOEFL required of all international applicants. High school diploma is required and GED is accepted. *Academic units required:* 4 English, 4 mathematics, 4 science, 3 foreign language, 2 social studies, 1 history, 1 academic elective.

Financial Aid

Students should submit: FAFSA. The Princeton Review suggests that all financial aid forms be submitted as soon as possible after 1/1. *Need-based scholarships/grants offered:* Federal Pell, SEOG, state scholarships/grants, private scholarships, the school's own gift aid. *Loan aid offered:* Direct Subsidized Stafford, Direct Unsubsidized Stafford, Direct PLUS, Federal Perkins, college/university loans from institutional funds. Applicants will be notified of awards on or about 3/30. Federal Work-Study Program available. Institutional employment available. Off-campus job opportunities are fair.

The Inside Word

Admission to Denison is pretty straightforward. The school "suggests" an interview, meaning you should do one if at all possible. It's a great way to demonstrate your interest in the school, which improves your chances of admission, especially if your grades, test scores, and overall profile put you on the admit/reject borderline.

THE SCHOOL SAYS "..."

From The Admissions Office

"Denison is a college that can point with pride to its success in enrolling and retaining intellectually motivated, diverse, and well-balanced students who are being taught to become effective leaders in the twenty-first century. This year, over 50 percent of our first-year students were in the top 10 percent of their high school graduating class; their SAT scores average 1300, 25 percent of the in coming class is students of color or internaional; and a large percentage of our student body is receiving some type of financial assistance. Our First-Year Program focuses on helping students make a successful transition from high school to college, and the small classes and accessibility of faculty assure students the opportunity to interact closely with their professors and fellow students. We care about our students, and the loyalty of our 28,000 alumni proves that the Denison experience is one that lasts for a lifetime.

"Denison operates under a 'test optional' admissions policy."

SELECTIVITY

Admissions Rating	91
# of applicants	5,305
% of applicants accepted	38
% of acceptees attending	30
# accepting a place on wait list	511
# of early decision applicants	153
% accepted early decision	78

FRESHMAN PROFILE

Range SAT Critical Reading	580–690
Range SAT Math	570–680
Range ACT Composite	25–30
Minimum paper TOEFL	550
Minimum computer TOEFL	213
Average HS GPA	3.6
% graduated top 10% of class	50
% graduated top 25% of class	34
% graduated top 50% of class	16

DEADLINES

Early decision	
Deadline	12/1
Notification	1/1
Regular	
Priority	12/1
Deadline	1/15
Notification	4/1
Nonfall registration?	no

APPLICANTS ALSO LOOK AT AND OFTEN PREFER

Wake Forest University
Vanderbilt University
University of Richmond
University of Michigan—Ann Arbor

AND SOMETIMES PREFER

Oberlin College
College of Wooster
Gettysburg College
Kenyon College

AND RARELY PREFER

Xavier University (OH)
Wittenberg University
Ohio Wesleyan University

FINANCIAL FACTS

Financial Aid Rating	94
Annual tuition	$35,650
Activity fee	$500
Health Center Fee	$200
Room (multiple)	$5,040
Board	$4,120
% frosh rec. need-based scholarship or grant aid	48
% UG rec. need-based scholarship or grant aid	43
% frosh rec. non-need-based scholarship or grant aid	43
% UG rec. non-need-based scholarship or grant aid	38
% frosh rec. need-based self-help aid	33
% UG rec. need-based self-help aid	29
% frosh rec. any financial aid	94
% UG rec. any financial aid	94

DePaul University

ONE EAST JACKSON BOULEVARD, CHICAGO, IL 60604-2287 • ADMISSIONS: 312-362-8300 • FAX: 312-362-5749

CAMPUS LIFE

Quality of Life Rating	88
Fire Safety Rating	84
Green Rating	86
Type of school	private
Affiliation	Roman Catholic
Environment	metropolis

STUDENTS

Total undergrad enrollment	14,661
% male/female	44/56
% from out of state	19
% from public high school	71.1
% live on campus	13
% in (# of) fraternities	3 (11)
% in (# of) sororities	5 (14)
% African American	8
% Asian	9
% Caucasian	60
% Hispanic	12
% international	1
# of countries represented	99

SURVEY SAYS . . .

Athletic facilities are great
Diverse student types on campus
Students love Chicago, IL
Great off-campus food
Low cost of living
(Almost) no one smokes

ACADEMICS

Academic Rating	77
Calendar	quarter
Student/faculty ratio	17:1
Profs interesting rating	79
Profs accessible rating	79
% classes taught by TAs	1
Most common reg class size	20–29 students
Most common lab size	fewer than 10 students

MOST POPULAR MAJORS
accounting
communication studies/speech
communication and rhetoric
psychology

STUDENTS SAY "..."

Academics

The mission at this "very city-school structured" university located in Chicago is about Vincentian values in an urban setting. Whether encouraging its students to help those less fortunate (there's a strong "commitment to social justice and community service") or cheering on its always-solid basketball team, DePaul University is "about diversity and real-world experience" instead of books and tests. This message is even further carried out by the leanings of the teachers, the majority of whom "are not strictly academics—they have a great deal of applicable experience." Though students report a few bad apples in the teaching lot, most students enjoy their classes (many account for student discussion as part of the grade) and teachers on the whole and say it "is easy to get in touch with professors outside of the classroom." "Professors not only have open-door policies but do everything but make candy trails into their offices," says a student.

There are multiple colleges within the university, so there are plenty of opportunities for student leadership for studies within your field, but students do cite red tape issues when trying to maneuver between colleges. The administration here is "sometimes annoying," and it is "very slow to solve problems and not empathetic when registration errors are made." Still, "the study spectrum is huge," so "you'll find what you want to do here." "All of my classes are challenging and force me to work harder than I may want to, but they are never overbearing to the point where I give up," says a sophomore. Music education and the honors programs are some of the school's stronger programs.

Life

Just like the school itself, the students embrace Chicago for all it's worth and actively try to both help and patronize the community. "There are so many plays, galleries, museums, restaurants, clubs, bars, and stores that life is always interesting," says a student, adding to a list that already includes "improv/comedy shows, Broadway in Chicago, Jerry Springer, the beach, and Wrigley & Lakeside." Life at DePaul can differ depending on what campus you use—The Loop or Lincoln Park. The LPC provides "a more classical college environment and sense of community," while The Loop gives more of "a city-school feel." DePaul itself hosts many events for students, and though students are pleased overall with the variety of extracurriculars offered, they say that "more advertising for clubs, sports, organizations, etc., would be helpful," especially for the commuters. The food on campus may be "atrocious," but the nightlife is "great" at DePaul; many students go out to the bars in Lincoln Park, but are careful to avoid the school's feared "three-strike rule." There are also many students who choose" to just hang out and watch movies, go for dinner, and don't drink." "There is always something happening in this city," says a student. Depaul also offers a good chance to get a job on campus, which not only allows students to make money, but "you can often find something that relates to your major and would look good on your resume."

Student Body

Students here "know how to balance a social life with their academic life," which is generally a difficult thing to do in a big city. Beyond that commonality, students really span the spectrum of personal and ethnic diversity. "There are your frat boys who live to party and your book worms who never leave the dorm," but everyone eventually settles into their own and "seems to be able to find at least one other person they can start a conversation with." The school is "definitely very open-minded and liberal, despite being religiously-affiliated." Many students live off campus; a fair number are from the suburbs, so a lot of them go home each weekend. There is a large LBGT population at DePaul, which is very well accepted, and people are "very aware of domestic and foreign affairs."

DePaul University

FINANCIAL AID: 312-362-8091 • E-MAIL: ADMITDPU@DEPAUL.EDU • WEBSITE: WWW.DEPAUL.EDU

THE PRINCETON REVIEW SAYS

Admissions

Very important factors considered include: Rigor of secondary school record. *Important factors considered include:* Class rank, application essay, academic GPA, recommendation(s), standardized test scores, character/personal qualities, extracurricular activities, level of applicant's interest, talent/ability, volunteer work, work experience. *Other factors considered include:* Alumni/ae relation, first generation, geographical residence, interview, racial/ethnic status, religious affiliation/commitment, state residency. SAT or ACT required. TOEFL required of all international applicants. High school diploma is required and GED is accepted. *Academic units required:* 4 English, 3 mathematics, 3 science (2 science labs), 2 social studies, 4 academic electives.

Financial Aid

Students should submit: FAFSA. Regular filing deadline is 5/1. The Princeton Review suggests that all financial aid forms be submitted as soon as possible after 1/1. *Need-based scholarships/grants offered:* Federal Pell, SEOG, state scholarships/grants, private scholarships, the school's own gift aid, Federal Academic Competitiveness Grant and Federal SMART Grant. *Loan aid offered:* Direct Subsidized Stafford, Direct Unsubsidized Stafford, Direct PLUS, Federal Perkins, private loans. Applicants will be notified of awards on a rolling basis beginning 3/15. Federal Work-Study Program available. Institutional employment available. Off-campus job opportunities are excellent.

The Inside Word

DePaul has earned its reputation as one of the most diverse campuses in the United States. The school courts minority students not only as freshmen but also as transfers. It recognizes that its tuition is beyond the means of many (even with financial aid), so it works with area community colleges to allow students to fulfill requirements at a lower cost before completing their degrees at DePaul.

THE SCHOOL SAYS "..."

From The Admissions Office

"The nation's largest Catholic university, DePaul University is nationally recognized for its innovative academic programs that embrace a comprehensive learn-by-doing approach. DePaul has two residential campuses and four commuter campuses in the suburbs. The Lincoln Park campus is located in one of Chicago's most exciting neighborhoods, filled with theaters, cafés, clubs, and shops. It is home to DePaul's College of Liberal Arts and Sciences, the School of Education, the Theater School, and the School of Music. New buildings on the 36-acre campus include residence halls, a science building, a student recreational facility, and the student center, which features a café where students can gather with friends. The Loop campus, located in Chicago's downtown—a world-class center for business, government, law, and culture—is home to DePaul's College of Commerce; College of Law; School of Computer Science, Telecommunications, and Information Systems; School for New Learning; and School of Accountancy and Management Information Systems.

"Applicants are required to take either the ACT or the SAT. The Writing Test on the ACT and the Writing section on the SAT are not required for admission consideration."

SELECTIVITY

Admissions Rating	82
# of applicants	12,450
% of applicants accepted	63
% of acceptees attending	32

FRESHMAN PROFILE

Range SAT Critical Reading	520–630
Range SAT Math	510–620
Range SAT Writing	530–620
Range ACT Composite	22–27
Minimum paper TOEFL	550
Minimum computer TOEFL	213
Minimum web-based TOEFL	80
Average HS GPA	3.4
% graduated top 10% of class	20
% graduated top 25% of class	48.3
% graduated top 50% of class	82.5

DEADLINES

Early action	
Deadline	11/15
Notification	1/15
Regular	
Priority	2/1
Notification	rolling
Nonfall registration?	yes

FINANCIAL FACTS

Financial Aid Rating	67
Annual tuition	$23,820
Room and board	$9,955
Required fees	$574
Books and supplies	$900
% frosh rec. need-based scholarship or grant aid	45
% UG rec. need-based scholarship or grant aid	45
% frosh rec. non-need-based scholarship or grant aid	27
% UG rec. non-need-based scholarship or grant aid	19
% frosh rec. need-based self-help aid	48
% UG rec. need-based self-help aid	50
% frosh rec. athletic scholarships	2
% UG rec. athletic scholarships	2
% frosh rec. any financial aid	79
% UG rec. any financial aid	68
% UG borrow to pay for school	65
Average cumulative indebtedness	$22,569

DePauw University

101 East Seminary, Greencastle, IN 46135 • Admissions: 765-658-4006 • Fax: 765-658-4007

CAMPUS LIFE

Quality of Life Rating	74
Fire Safety Rating	60*
Green Rating	70
Type of school	private
Affiliation	Methodist
Environment	village

STUDENTS

Total undergrad enrollment	2,241
% male/female	43/57
% from out of state	55
% from public high school	83
% live on campus	95
% in (# of) fraternities	78 (13)
% in (# of) sororities	68 (11)
% African American	6
% Asian	3
% Caucasian	80
% Hispanic	4
% international	5
# of countries represented	32

SURVEY SAYS . . .

Lab facilities are great
Frats and sororities dominate social scene
College radio is popular
Student publications are popular
Lots of beer drinking
Hard liquor is popular

ACADEMICS

Academic Rating	95
Calendar	4/1/4
Student/faculty ratio	10:1
Profs interesting rating	88
Profs accessible rating	96
Most common reg class size	10–19 students
Most common lab size	10–19 students

MOST POPULAR MAJORS
economics
English composition
mass communication/media studies

STUDENTS SAY ". . ."

Academics

Serious-minded students are drawn to DePauw University for its "small classes," "encouraging" professors, and the "individual academic attention" they can expect to receive. Academically, DePauw is "demanding but rewarding," and "requires a lot of outside studying and discipline" in order to keep up. Professors' "expectations are very high," which means "you can't slack off and get good grades." Be prepared to pull your "fair share of all-nighters." Fortunately, DePauw professors are more than just stern taskmasters. Though they pile on the work, they "are always helpful and available" to students in need. When things get overwhelming, "They are very understanding and will cut you a break if you really deserve" it. As a result, students come to know their professors "on a personal level," making DePauw the kind of school where it is "common [for students] to have dinner at a professor's house." Beyond stellar professors, DePauw's other academic draws include "extraordinary" study-abroad opportunities and a "wonderful" alumni network great for "connections and networking opportunities." Alums also "keep our endowment pretty high, making it easy for the school to give out merit scholarships," which undergraduates appreciate. Student opinion regarding the administration ranges from ambivalent to slightly negative. One especially thorny issue is class registration; you "rarely" get into all the classes you want.

Life

Few schools are as Greek as DePauw, but students are quick to point out that "it is by no means *Animal House*." The Greek system here is more holistic than that. It "promotes not only social activities but also philanthropic events." That's not to say there aren't lots of frat parties here. There are. But "the administration has cracked down big time" on the larger frat parties, and "now there are just small parties in apartments and dorms." One recently issued rule is that freshmen "will not be allowed on Greek property until after rush, which is the first week of second semester." In addition to administrative regulation, students exercise their own self-restraint; for the typical undergraduate, "the week is mostly reserved for studying." Beyond the frats and sororities, "there is always a theater production, athletic event, or organization-sponsored event going on," and popular bands occasionally perform on campus. It's a good thing so much is happening at the school because off-campus entertainment options are scarce: "If there is really any fun to be had, it's not in Greencastle." The situation could be greatly improved if there were just a few "more restaurants and stores in the town or a nearby town." As things stand, however, students "have to go to Indianapolis (45 miles) to go shopping, watch a good movie, eat at a good restaurant, etc."

Student Body

The typical DePauw student is "upper-middle class," "a little preppy, a little athletic," and "hardworking;" "parties hard on weekend," and "usually become involved with the Greek system." Students describe their peers as "driven" "polos and pearls." They "have all had multiple internships, international experience, and [held] some type of leadership position." Though these folks may seem "overcommitted," they "always get their work done." For those who don't fit this mold, don't fret; most students seem to be "accepting of the different types" of people on campus. Diversity on campus is augmented through the school's partnership with the Posse Foundation, which brings in urban (though not necessarily minority) "students from Chicago and NYC every year." These students are described as "leaders on campus" and "take real initiative to hold their communities together."

FINANCIAL AID: 765-658-4030 • E-MAIL: ADMISSION@DEPAUW.EDU • WEBSITE: WWW.DEPAUW.EDU

THE PRINCETON REVIEW SAYS

Admissions

Very important factors considered include: Academic GPA, rigor of secondary school record, standardized test scores. *Important factors considered include:* Class rank, application essay, recommendation(s). *Other factors considered include:* Alumni/ae relation, character/personal qualities, extracurricular activities, first generation, geographical residence, interview, level of applicant's interest, state residency, talent/ability, volunteer work, work experience. SAT or ACT required. TOEFL required of all international applicants. High school diploma is required and GED is accepted. *Academic units recommended:* 4 English, 4 mathematics.

Financial Aid

Students should submit: FAFSA, institution's own financial aid form The Princeton Review suggests that all financial aid forms be submitted as soon as possible after 1/1. *Need-based scholarships/grants offered:* Federal Pell, SEOG, state scholarships/grants, private scholarships, the school's own gift aid. *Loan aid offered:* FFEL Subsidized Stafford, FFEL Unsubsidized Stafford, FFEL PLUS, Federal Perkins, college/university loans from institutional funds. Applicants will be notified of awards on or about 3/27. Federal Work-Study Program available. Institutional employment available. Off-campus job opportunities are fair.

The Inside Word

Prospective applicants should not be deceived by DePauw's high acceptance rate. The students who are accepted and choose to enroll here have the academic goods to justify their admission. Many of them are accepted by more "competitive" schools and still choose DePauw. DePauw's generous merit scholarships have a lot to do with students' choice to enroll.

THE SCHOOL SAYS "..."

From The Admissions Office

"DePauw University is nationally recognized for intellectual and experiential challenge that links liberal arts education with life's work, preparing graduates for uncommon professional success, service to others, and personal fulfillment. DePauw graduates count among their ranks a Nobel Laureate, a vice president and U.S. congressman, Pulitzer Prize winning and Newbery Award winning authors, and a number of CEOs and humanitarian leaders. Our students demonstrate a love for learning, a willingness to serve others, the reason and judgment to lead, an interest in engaging worlds and cultures unknown to them, the courage to question their assumptions, and a strong commitment to community. Pre-professional and career exploration are encouraged through winter term, when more than 700 students pursue their own off-campus internships. This represents more students in experiential learning opportunities than at any other liberal arts college in the nation. Other innovative programs include Honor Scholars, Information Technology Associates Program, Management Fellows, Media Fellows, and Science Research Fellows, affording selected students additional seminar and internship opportunities.

"Freshman applicants are required to submit scores of the Writing section of the SAT or the ACT."

SELECTIVITY

Admissions Rating	94
# of applicants	4,064
% of applicants accepted	65
% of acceptees attending	23
# of early decision applicants	50
% accepted early decision	82

FRESHMAN PROFILE

Range SAT Critical Reading	540–640
Range SAT Math	570–670
Range SAT Writing	540–650
Range ACT Composite	25–29
Minimum paper TOEFL	560
Minimum computer TOEFL	225
Average HS GPA	3.6
% graduated top 10% of class	51
% graduated top 25% of class	83
% graduated top 50% of class	98

DEADLINES

Early decision	
Deadline	11/1
Notification	1/1
Early action	
Deadline	12/1
Notification	2/15
Regular	
Deadline	2/1
Notification	4/1
Nonfall registration?	yes

APPLICANTS ALSO LOOK AT

AND OFTEN PREFER
University of Notre Dame
Vanderbilt University
Indiana University at Bloomington

AND SOMETIMES PREFER
Washington University in St. Louis
Purdue University—West Lafayette
Denison University
University of Illinois at Urbana-Champaign
Miami University

AND RARELY PREFER
Hanover College

FINANCIAL FACTS

Financial Aid Rating	98
Annual tuition	$31,400
Room and board	$8,400
Required fees	$400
Books and supplies	$750
% frosh rec. any financial aid	97
% UG rec. any financial aid	96

DICKINSON COLLEGE

PO BOX 1773, CARLISLE, PA 17013-2896 • ADMISSIONS: 717-245-1231 • FAX: 717-245-1442

CAMPUS LIFE

Quality of Life Rating	79
Fire Safety Rating	75
Green Rating	99
Type of school	private
Environment	city

STUDENTS

Total undergrad enrollment	2,364
% male/female	45/55
% from out of state	73
% from public high school	60
% live on campus	91
% in (# of) fraternities	21 (8)
% in (# of) sororities	24 (6)
% African American	4
% Asian	5
% Caucasian	77
% Hispanic	5
% international	6
# of countries represented	40

SURVEY SAYS . . .

Lab facilities are great
Great library
School is well run
Low cost of living
Lots of beer drinking
Hard liquor is popular

ACADEMICS

Academic Rating	89
Calendar	semester
Student/faculty ratio	10:1
Profs interesting rating	86
Profs accessible rating	89
Most common	
reg class size	10–19 students

MOST POPULAR MAJORS

English language and literature
international business/trade/
commerce
political science and government

STUDENTS SAY ". . ."

Academics

Dickinson College is a "quintessential small liberal arts school" in a "small town in central Pennsylvania." The big draw here is an "aggressive" global focus. "Dickinson has completely followed through on all of their promises of a campus that supports international experiences," says a sociology major. Courses "have a strong focus on international issues." Studying abroad "fits seamlessly into the curriculum" and is "a huge deal." "Dickinson has exceptional study-abroad programs everywhere in the world." The administration is sometimes "preoccupied with rising in the ranks and improving superficial perceptions" of the school but Dickinson's president is insanely popular. He "has weekly office hours." "From the president down, the faculty and administrators make themselves available." "Any complaint is heard and listened to, not just brushed off." The academic atmosphere here is "difficult but doable." Classes are small. "Students do not often skip, as professors do take note." The "completely accommodating" faculty receives high marks. "They are good teachers, passionate about their subjects, and it is very easy for students to develop strong out-of-the-classroom relationships with their professors," says an international business major. "I can honestly say I've only had one professor who I didn't consider high quality," adds one junior.

Life

"The campus is beautiful," observes a senior at Dickinson. "On a nice day, it can take your breath away." It's also "overloaded with clubs and organizations." During the week, "there is a lot to do if you're willing to do it, and a lot of it is college sponsored." There is a "consistently full schedule of lectures." There are plenty of arts-related events. "All the different cultural clubs have a dinner every semester." "Intramural sports are a big deal." "The gym is in constant use." "Greek life is really big at Dickinson" as well. "On the weekends, the majority of people get nice and drunk." Drugs are not uncommon, either. Students who don't party are here too, "trying desperately to make their own fun." There's also "a lot of drama" on campus. "We like to call it Dickinson High," one student admits. The "dull" surrounding town is "not a social mecca." "I love art museums, live music, and cultural diversity," says a senior. "Carlisle does not have any of that." "There is nothing to do in Carlisle unless you are 21 and can get into the bars, where the most exciting thing to do is drink and maybe dance with a nice townie." "If you don't mind small towns, you'll be fine," advises a junior, "but big city people should look elsewhere for their college experience unless they're tired of the rat race."

Student Body

"The most glaring trait of the student body is that it is mostly white," says one student though others claim that "there are tons of international students," and the "growing" Posse program brings minority kids to campus. Still, as a first-year student relates, "the school is not as diverse as some of us would want it to be." Overall, "there is a lot of homogeneity." Most students here are "socially oriented" and come from somewhere on the East Coast or in the mid-atlantic states. "Many students are very rich and have no problem spending copious amounts of money." "The parking lots are filled with Jeep Grand Cherokees, Saabs, and BMWs." Other students receive "sweet financial aid deals," though. Academically, Dickinsonians "range anywhere from overzealous to apathetic," but the vast majority "can usually balance a full academic load with an active and rich social life." "The typical student at Dickinson is very preppy. The girls are gorgeous, and the guys look like they are straight out of a J. Crew catalog, and everyone is also really athletic." "Finding the oddballs can be difficult." Cliques are common, and "the campus is quite split between Greek life and non-Greek life."

FINANCIAL AID: 717-245-1308 • E-MAIL: ADMIT@DICKINSON.EDU • WEBSITE: WWW.DICKINSON.EDU

THE PRINCETON REVIEW SAYS

Admissions

Very important factors considered include: Academic GPA, rigor of secondary school record, extracurricular activities, talent/ability, volunteer work. *Important factors considered include:* Class rank, recommendation(s), standardized test scores, alumni/ae relation, work experience. *Other factors considered include:* Application essay, character/personal qualities, first generation, geographical residence, interview, level of applicant's interest, racial/ethnic status, state residency. SAT or ACT recommended. TOEFL required of all international applicants. High school diploma is required and GED is accepted. *Academic units required:* 4 English, 3 mathematics, 3 science (2 science labs), 2 foreign language, 2 social studies, 2 academic electives. *Academic units recommended:* 3 foreign language.

Financial Aid

Students should submit: FAFSA, CSS/financial aid profile, state aid form, non-custodial profile, business/farm supplement. Regular filing deadline is 2/1. The Princeton Review suggests that all financial aid forms be submitted as soon as possible after 1/1. *Need-based scholarships/grants offered:* Federal Pell, SEOG, state scholarships/grants, private scholarships, the school's own gift aid. *Loan aid offered:* FFEL Subsidized Stafford, FFEL Unsubsidized Stafford, FFEL PLUS, Federal Perkins, college/university loans from institutional funds. Applicants will be notified of awards on or about 3/31. Federal Work-Study Program available. Institutional employment available. Off-campus job opportunities are good.

The Inside Word

Dickinson's admissions process is typical of most small liberal arts colleges. The best candidates for such a place are those with solid grades and broad extracurricular involvement—the stereotypical "well-rounded student." Admissions selectivity is kept in check by a strong group of competitor colleges that fight tooth and nail for their cross-applicants.

THE SCHOOL SAYS "..."

From The Admissions Office

"College is more than a collection of courses. It is about crossing traditional boundaries, about seeing the interrelationships among different subjects, about learning a paradigm for solving problems, about developing critical thinking and communication skills, and about speaking out on issues that matter. Dickinson was intended as an alternative to the 15 colleges that existed in the U.S. at the time of its founding; its aim, then as now, was to provide a "useful" education whereby students would 'learn by doing' through hands-on experience and engagement with the community, the region, the nation, and the world. And this is truer today than ever, with workshop science courses replacing traditional lectures, fieldwork experiences in community studies in which students take oral histories, and 13 study centers abroad in nontourist cities where students, under the guidance of a Dickinson faculty director, experience a true international culture. Almost 53 percent of the student body study abroad, and a total of 58 percent study off campus, preparing them to compete and succeed in a complex global world.

"Applicants wishing to be considered for academic scholarships are required to submit scores from either the SAT or ACT, but Dickinson does not require results from either test for admission."

SELECTIVITY

Admissions Rating	93
# of applicants	5,282
% of applicants accepted	44
% of acceptees attending	26
# accepting a place on wait list	422
% admitted from wait list	5
# of early decision applicants	348
% accepted early decision	84

FRESHMAN PROFILE

Range SAT Critical Reading	600–700
Range SAT Math	590–690
Range ACT Composite	26–31
Minimum paper TOEFL	600
Minimum computer TOEFL	250
Minimum web-based TOEFL	100
% graduated top 10% of class	50
% graduated top 25% of class	87
% graduated top 50% of class	98

DEADLINES

Early decision	
Deadline	11/15
Notification	12/15
Early action	
Deadline	12/1
Notification	2/1
Regular	
Deadline	2/1
Notification	3/31
Nonfall registration?	no

APPLICANTS ALSO LOOK AT

AND OFTEN PREFER
Middlebury College, Colgate University, Brown University, Tufts University

AND SOMETIMES PREFER
Hamilton College, Gettysburg College, Lafayette College, Bucknell University, Franklin & Marshall College

AND RARELY PREFER
College of William and Mary

FINANCIAL FACTS

Financial Aid Rating	92
Annual tuition	$39,780
Room and board	$10,080
Required fees	$334
Books and supplies	$1,000
% frosh rec. need-based scholarship or grant aid	48
% UG rec. need-based scholarship or grant aid	45
% frosh rec. non-need-based scholarship or grant aid	7
% UG rec. non-need-based scholarship or grant aid	4
% frosh rec. need-based self-help aid	42
% UG rec. need-based self-help aid	43
% frosh rec. any financial aid	50
% UG rec. any financial aid	48
% UG borrow to pay for school	53
Average cumulative indebtedness	$21,924

DREW UNIVERSITY

OFFICE OF COLLEGE ADMISSIONS, MADISON, NJ 07940-1493 • ADMISSIONS: 973-408-3739 • FAX: 973-408-3068

CAMPUS LIFE
Quality of Life Rating	**77**
Fire Safety Rating	**97**
Green Rating	**85**
Type of school	private
Affiliation	Methodist
Environment	village

STUDENTS
Total undergrad enrollment	1,575
% male/female	38/62
% from out of state	41
% from public high school	65
% live on campus	86
% African American	7
% Asian	5
% Caucasian	61
% Hispanic	9
% international	2
# of countries represented	19

SURVEY SAYS . . .
Frats and sororities are unpopular or nonexistent
Theater is popular
Student publications are popular
Political activism is popular

ACADEMICS
Academic Rating	**87**
Calendar	semester
Student/faculty ratio	11:1
Profs interesting rating	87
Profs accessible rating	85
Most common reg class size	10–19 students
Most common lab size	10–19 students

MOST POPULAR MAJORS
economics
political science and government
psychology

STUDENTS SAY ". . ."

Academics

For fifteen years, Drew University was practically synonymous with Tom Kean, the popular university president who had previously served as Governor of New Jersey. Kean's prominence brought lots of regional and national attention to this small school, to the great benefit of students and the university alike. His departure ruffled some feathers, but Drew seems to have weathered the transition. The plans for expansion (which were started under Kean) have resulted in new majors in Business Studies and Environmental Studies and Sustainability. New scholarships for students who volunteer in their communities for high school are in the works as well. The vast majority of students here continue to extol this "small school with a beautiful campus and prime location" near New York City. The school's location allows students to take advantage of "programs such as Wall Street Semester and United Nations Semester, as well as field trips to theaters on Broadway and Art museums." They also tell us that location affords "awesome job opportunities in the surrounding areas." Students praise the curriculum's liberal arts focus that ensures "that everyone gets exposed to at least a little bit of every other subject before they leave." Drew's "small class sizes allow for the difficulty of the classes to be manageable" and students say "every professor wants to know your name by the end of the semester." While students acknowledge that "Drew is a school that's in the midst of finding and creating its unique identity," they also don't feel any imperative to rush the process. In fact, they tell us that Drew is "one of the best schools in New Jersey when it comes to education," just as it is.

Life

Drew's small size, coupled with the fact that "there are so many clubs, organizations, and sports teams to join" encourages student participation in extracurricular activities. One student opines: "With a school so small, I doubt that anyone who graduates does not have a leadership position in something." An active performing arts program means that there is "lots of involvement in the arts," among students including theater, musical performances, a capella, and student art exhibits." Drew "is not a party school per se" but "for people who do like to party, it's very easy because the alcohol policy is like the world's most un-enforced thing." More often, when students want a wild night they "simply hop on the train a block away and head for Morristown or New York for an evening or weekend" or "when the weather is conducive" they might "take a trip with a few friends down to the beach." Hometown Madison is "adorable" with "a small-town atmosphere." On the downside, "there isn't much to do in town," but with New York City "right around the corner," that's hardly a make-or-break problem.

Student Body

Drew "caters to a lot of wealthy kids from Dirty Jerz (New Jersey)," students who "live within a few hours of campus and have the opportunity to travel home if they choose to, although it does not at all feel like a 'suitcase school.'" Despite this trend, "There is a very wide variety of students at Drew—all different races, ethnicities, and backgrounds." The student body includes "tons of theatre kids" as well as "your typical jocks." (One student observes that "there is definitely a division between jocks and everyone else at this school—not that our sports teams are even good.") Students tell us that "Drew is a reach school for some and a safety for others, so there are very, very brilliant students here, while others…not so much." Women outnumber men by a healthy 3-to-2 ratio.

FINANCIAL AID: 973-408-3112 • E-MAIL: CADM@DREW.EDU • WEBSITE: WWW.DREW.EDU

THE PRINCETON REVIEW SAYS

Admissions

Very important factors considered include: Academic GPA, rigor of secondary school record, talent/ability. *Important factors considered include:* Application essay, recommendation(s), extracurricular activities, interview, level of applicant's interest. *Other factors considered include:* Class rank, standardized test scores, alumni/ae relation, character/personal qualities, first generation, geographical residence, racial/ethnic status, volunteer work, work experience. ACT with Writing component recommended. TOEFL required of all international applicants. High school diploma or equivalent is not required. *Academic units recommended:* 4 English, 3 mathematics, 2 science, 2 foreign language, 2 social studies, 2 history, 3 academic electives.

Financial Aid

Students should submit: FAFSA, CSS/financial aid profile. Regular filing deadline is 2/15. The Princeton Review suggests that all financial aid forms be submitted as soon as possible after 1/1. *Need-based scholarships/grants offered:* Federal Pell, SEOG, state scholarships/grants, private scholarships, the school's own gift aid. *Loan aid offered:* FFEL Subsidized Stafford, FFEL Unsubsidized Stafford, FFEL PLUS, Federal Perkins, state loans. Applicants will be notified of awards on or about 4/1. Federal Work-Study Program available. Institutional employment available. Off-campus job opportunities are fair.

The Inside Word

Drew University gives applicants the option of submitting a graded writing sample in place of standardized test scores. If the goal was to attract more applicants, all we can say is: mission accomplished. Drew now draws more than 5,200 applicants. The profile of the average admitted student, oddly, hasn't changed; instead, Drew seems to be attracting more applications from those who see the school as a safety.

THE SCHOOL SAYS "..."

From The Admissions Office

"At Drew, great teachers are transforming the undergraduate learning experience. With a commitment to teaching, Drew professors have made educating undergraduates their top priority. With a spirit of innovation, they have brought the most advanced technology and distinctive modes of experiential learning into the Drew classroom. The result is a stimulating and challenging education that connects the traditional liberal arts and sciences to the workplace and to the world.

"Drew University will require applicants to take either the SAT or the ACT or, in lieu of standardized test scores, submit a graded paper from one of their high school classes. The Selection Committee will consider the highest Verbal, Math, and Writing scores individually in its evaluation of candidates for admission."

SELECTIVITY	
Admissions Rating	**90**
# of applicants	5,219
% of applicants accepted	68
% of acceptees attending	11
# of early decision applicants	28
% accepted early decision	75

FRESHMAN PROFILE	
Range SAT Critical Reading	520–650
Range SAT Math	510–620
Range SAT Writing	510–640
Range ACT Composite	23–28
Minimum paper TOEFL	550
Minimum computer TOEFL	213
Average HS GPA	3.33
% graduated top 10% of class	36
% graduated top 25% of class	68
% graduated top 50% of class	90

DEADLINES	
Early decision	
Deadline	12/1
Notification	12/24
Regular	
Deadline	2/15
Notification	3/21
Nonfall registration?	yes

FINANCIAL FACTS	
Financial Aid Rating	**80**
Annual tuition	$35,910
Room and board	$9,978
Required fees	$560
% UG rec. need-based	
scholarship or grant aid	53
% UG rec. non-need-based	
scholarship or grant aid	8
% UG rec. need-based	
self-help aid	44
% frosh rec. any financial aid	97
% UG rec. any financial aid	88
% UG borrow to pay for school	61.3
Average cumulative	
indebtedness	$16,640

DREXEL UNIVERSITY

3141 CHESTNUT STREET, PHILADELPHIA, PA 19104 • ADMISSIONS: 215-895-2400 • FAX: 215-895-5939

CAMPUS LIFE
Quality of Life Rating	**65**
Fire Safety Rating	**76**
Green Rating	**95**
Type of school	private
Environment	metropolis

STUDENTS
Total undergrad enrollment	13,139
% male/female	55/45
% from out of state	48
% from public high school	70
% live on campus	25
% in (# of) fraternities	3 (12)
% in (# of) sororities	3 (11)
% African American	8
% Asian	12
% Caucasian	63
% Hispanic	3
% international	6
# of countries represented	104

SURVEY SAYS . . .
Career services are great
Diverse student types on campus
Students love Philadelphia, PA
Great off-campus food
Student publications are popular
Lots of beer drinking
Hard liquor is popular

ACADEMICS
Academic Rating	**71**
Calendar	quarter for most; semester for College of Medicine
Student/faculty ratio	9:1
Profs interesting rating	62
Profs accessible rating	62
Most common reg class size	10–19 students

MOST POPULAR MAJORS
biology/biological sciences
information science/studies
mechanical engineering

STUDENTS SAY ". . ."

Academics

Drexel University "is a lot of work squarely aimed at integration into the professional world," whether that world involves the school's popular majors in engineering, technology, and business, or less-known offerings like the school's programs in the music industry or hospitality management. Drexel has a growing digital media program, making it "one of the only schools in the area with a developed program" in the field. Central to the Drexel experience is the "extremely beneficial" co-op program, which many agree is "the best thing about Drexel." Co-op provides 18 months of professional experience during the 5-year undergraduate program. One student writes, "You will learn as much in the first couple of months of working in the real world as you did in any college. Drexel gives you all of that knowledge before you're even out of school and gives you the preparation necessary to succeed in the real world." The school's location in Philadelphia, "a source of endless fun and opportunity," helps a co-op program considerably. "Engineering dominates" at Drexel, but the school "has a variety of programs fit for almost anyone," with "a lot of classes run with Web-based resources. Lectures are posted online in WebCT, as well as course syllabi and assignments. This makes it easy to access information. Teachers are easy to get in touch with via e-mail and are very accessible to meet with as needed." Administrative tasks are not so convenient; students warn of "lots of red tape," adding that "most issues require visits to at least three different offices, sometimes on opposite ends of campus." Fortunately, the campus isn't that large.

Life

Campus life at Drexel must compete with the temptations offered by Philadelphia, one of the nation's largest cities. Philly provides "so many things to do (if you have the money) that it can be hard to know where to begin." Students tell us that "museums are great. Lots of kids go to concerts, and there are all sorts, all the time. First Fridays in Center City is also popular." The area immediately surrounding the school has plenty of "great bars, food, and dancing." Drexel is close to the UPenn campus, "and students often go into their parties, which are extraordinary." On campus, "There are numerous fraternities and societies you can join." Intercollegiate sports "aren't incredibly popular here," but "the basketball team is really taking off and is always sold out." Drexel's grounds, once an unbroken sea of brick and concrete, have been renovated; today "there are plenty of green grassy areas for students to hang out and relax," as well as "a new beautiful amphitheater and some nice tree-lined walkways with benches and tables."

Student Body

There "are no real typical students at Drexel. [It's] is a pretty diverse school, with students involved in different kinds of activities, dressing differently, and motivated differently." The school "is a melting pot" with "many, many international and minority students." One student notes, "Drexel's common factor seems to be not race or economic background, but a sense of personal drive. Drexel students work hard—it's a requirement to keep afloat—and that self-propulsion seems to be the tie that binds the student body together." If undergrads "seem to fit in well together," that may be because "students here are very casual and easygoing." Some have quirky senses of humor; take the one who reports that "the students tend to be of the human variety, with genders varying from male to female. Everyone has a clique, and it takes quite a bit of effort to be excluded from them all."

FINANCIAL AID: 215-895-2535 • E-MAIL: ENROLL@DREXEL.EDU • WEBSITE: WWW.DREXEL.EDU

THE PRINCETON REVIEW SAYS

Admissions

Very important factors considered include: Class rank, academic GPA, rigor of secondary school record, standardized test scores. *Important factors considered include:* Application essay, recommendation(s), character/personal qualities. *Other factors considered include:* Alumni/ae relation, extracurricular activities, first generation, interview, level of applicant's interest, talent/ability, volunteer work, work experience. SAT or ACT required. TOEFL required of all international applicants. High school diploma is required and GED is accepted. *Academic units required:* 3 mathematics, 1 science (1 science lab). *Academic units recommended:* 1 foreign language.

Financial Aid

Students should submit: FAFSA. The Princeton Review suggests that all financial aid forms be submitted as soon as possible after 1/1. *Need-based scholarships/grants offered:* Federal Pell, SEOG, state scholarships/grants, private scholarships, the school's own gift aid, United Negro College Fund. *Loan aid offered:* FFEL Subsidized Stafford, FFEL Unsubsidized Stafford, FFEL PLUS, Federal Perkins, federal nursing scholarships, college/university loans from institutional funds. Applicants will be notified of awards on a rolling basis beginning 3/15. Federal Work-Study Program available.

The Inside Word

Drexel operates on a rolling admissions basis, meaning that admissions decisions are made relatively quickly after all application materials reach the school. Rolling admissions tend to favor those who apply early in the process, when schools are still worried about whether they will be able to fill their incoming classes. Regardless of when you apply, you shouldn't have too much trouble here if your application establishes you as firmly above average.

THE SCHOOL SAYS "..."

From The Admissions Office

"Drexel has gained a reputation for academic excellence since its founding in 1891. In 2006, Drexel became the first top-ranked doctoral university in more than 25 years to open a law school. Its main campus is a 10-minute walk from Center City Philadelphia. Students prepare for successful careers through Drexel's prestigious experiential education program—The Drexel Co-op. Alternating periods of full-time, professional employment with periods of classroom study, students can earn an average of $14,000 per 6-month co-op. At any one time, about 2,000 full-time undergraduates are on co-op assignments. Drexel integrates science and technology into all 70 undergraduate majors. Students looking for a special challenge can apply to one of 14 accelerated degree programs including the BS/MBA in business; BA/BS/MD in medicine; BA/BS/JD in law; BS/MS or BS/PhD in engineering; BS/MS in information technology; and BS/DPT in physical therapy.

"Pennoni Honors College offers high achievers unique opportunities. Students Tackling Advanced Research (STAR) allows qualified undergraduates to participate in a paid summer research project, and the Center for Civic Engagement matches students with community service opportunities. Students in any major can take dance, music, and theater classes offered through Drexel's performing arts programs.

"Drexel's study-abroad program allows students to spend a term or more earning credits while gaining international experience. Adventurous students can also enjoy co-op abroad. Locations include London, Costa Rica, Prague, Rome, and Paris. The admissions office invites prospective students to schedule a campus visit for a first-hand look at all Drexel offers."

SELECTIVITY

Admissions Rating	88
# of applicants	16,867
% of applicants accepted	72
% of acceptees attending	20

FRESHMAN PROFILE

Range SAT Critical Reading	530–630
Range SAT Math	560–670
Range ACT Composite	23–28
Minimum paper TOEFL	550
Minimum computer TOEFL	213
Average HS GPA	3.47
% graduated top 10% of class	30
% graduated top 25% of class	60
% graduated top 50% of class	86

DEADLINES

Regular	
Deadline	3/1
Nonfall registration?	yes

FINANCIAL FACTS

Financial Aid Rating	61
Annual tuition	$29,800
Room and board	$12,680
Required fees	$2,035
Books and supplies	$1,800
% UG rec. need-based scholarship or grant aid	38
% UG rec. need-based self-help aid	40
% frosh rec. any financial aid	94
% UG rec. any financial aid	89
% UG borrow to pay for school	75
Average cumulative indebtedness	$31,333

DUKE UNIVERSITY

2138 CAMPUS DRIVE, DURHAM, NC 27708 • ADMISSIONS: 919-684-3214 • FAX: 919-681-8941

CAMPUS LIFE

Quality of Life Rating	**75**
Fire Safety Rating	**60***
Green Rating	**96**
Type of school	private
Affiliation	Methodist
Environment	city

STUDENTS

Total undergrad enrollment	6,259
% male/female	52/48
% from out of state	85
% from public high school	65
% live on campus	82
% in (# of) fraternities	29 (21)
% in (# of) sororities	42 (14)
% African American	10
% Asian	14
% Caucasian	56
% Hispanic	7
% international	5
# of countries represented	89

SURVEY SAYS . . .

Lab facilities are great
Great library
Athletic facilities are great
Students are happy
Everyone loves the Blue Devils
Student publications are popular
Student government is popular

ACADEMICS

Academic Rating	**91**
Calendar	semester
Student/faculty ratio	11:1
Profs interesting rating	80
Profs accessible rating	82
% classes taught by TAs	4
Most common	
reg class size	10–19 students
Most common	
lab size	10–19 students

MOST POPULAR MAJORS
economics
psychology
public policy analysis

STUDENTS SAY "..."

Academics

Duke University "is the complete package: great academics, fun students, exciting athletics, and school spirit," all enjoyed in "an almost Mediterranean climate." Undergraduates choose Duke because they "are passionate about a wide range of things, including academics, sports, community service, research, and fun," and because the school seems equally committed to accommodating all of those pursuits; as one student puts it, "Duke is for the Ivy League candidate who is a little bit more laid back about school and overachieving (but just a bit) and a lot more into the party scene." Academics "are very difficult in the quantitative majors (engineering, math, statistics, economics, pre-med)" and "much easier in the non-quantitative majors, but [it] still take a lot of work not to fall behind." In all areas, "the laid-back atmosphere makes competition practically nonexistent. It's the norm to have large study groups, and the review sessions, peer tutoring system, writing center, and academic support center are always helpful when students are struggling with anything from math homework to creating a resume." Professors' "number one priority is teaching undergraduates," a situation made more remarkable by the fact that many are engaged in "ground-breaking" research. Because "the school has a lot of confidence in its students," it offers them "many research opportunities," one of many manifestations of Duke's "commitment to the undergraduate experience. Duke doesn't ignore its undergrads in favor of its graduate programs."

Life

Life at Duke "is very relaxed," with "a great balance between academics and fun. People typically work Monday through Thursday and then go out and enjoy themselves Thursday, Friday, and Saturday." Because "The student union and other organizations provide entertainment all the time, from movies to shows to campus wide parties," there "is always something to do on campus." Indeed, "people usually stay on campus for fun," as hometown Durham "has a few quirky streets and squares with restaurants, shops, clubs, etc., but to really do much you have to go to Raleigh or Chapel Hill," each 20 to 30 minutes away by car. The perception that "Durham is pretty dangerous" further dampens students' enthusiasm for the city. Undergrads' fervor for Blue Devils sports, on the other hand, can be boundless; sports, "especially basketball, are a huge deal here," and undergrads "will paint themselves completely blue and wait in line on the sidewalk in K-ville for three days to jump up and down in Cameron Indoor Stadium." Greek life "essentially runs the party scene, but almost all the parties are open so it definitely isn't hard to get into a party." A solid contingent abjures the Greek scene; some turn to the "several very active selective living groups on campus, which are like a watered-down version of a fraternity or sorority. Several are co-ed, and some have special themes like service and foreign language, but many are just social groups to join."

Student Body

The typical Duke student "is someone who cares a lot about his or her education but at the same time won't sacrifice a social life for it. To go to school here is to find the perfect balance, even if that means some late-night cram sessions or last-minute papers. Everyone's focused on success, but that includes social success as well." They tend to be "perfectionists, very involved in seeking out a 'type A' career (read: investment banking or consulting), and go out two to three times a week, always looking polished, even when wasted." An "overwhelming number" are athletes, "not just varsity athletes…but athletes in high school or generally active people. Duke's athletic pride attracts this kind of person." The student body "is surprisingly ethnically diverse, with a number of students of Asian, African, and Hispanic descent."

FINANCIAL AID: 919-684-6225 • E-MAIL: UNDERGRAD-ADMISSIONS@DUKE.EDU • WEBSITE: WWW.DUKE.EDU

THE PRINCETON REVIEW SAYS

Admissions

Very important factors considered include: Application essay, recommendation(s), rigor of secondary school record, standardized test scores, extracurricular activities, talent/ability. *Important factors considered include:* Character/personal qualities. *Other factors considered include:* Class rank, academic GPA, alumni/ae relation, geographical residence, interview, racial/ethnic status, state residency, volunteer work, work experience. SAT and SAT Subject Tests or ACT required. High school diploma is required and GED is not accepted. *Academic units recommended:* 4 English, 4 mathematics, 4 science, 4 foreign language, 4 social studies.

Financial Aid

Students should submit: FAFSA, CSS/financial aid profile, noncustodial profile, business/farm supplement, parent and student income tax returns. Regular filing deadline is 3/1. The Princeton Review suggests that all financial aid forms be submitted as soon as possible after 1/1. *Need-based scholarships/grants offered:* Federal Pell, SEOG, state scholarships/grants, private scholarships, the school's own gift aid, ROTC. *Loan aid offered:* FFEL Subsidized Stafford, FFEL Unsubsidized Stafford, FFEL PLUS, Federal Perkins, college/university loans from institutional funds, private loans. Applicants will be notified of awards on or about 4/1. Federal Work-Study Program available. Institutional employment available. Off-campus job opportunities are good.

The Inside Word

Duke is an extremely selective undergraduate institution, which affords the school the luxury of rejecting many qualified applicants. You'll have to present an exceptional record just to be considered; to make the cut, you'll have to impress the admissions office that you can contribute something unique and valuable to the incoming class. Being one of the best basketball players in the nation (male or female) helps a lot, but even athletes have to show academic excellence in order to get in the door here.

THE SCHOOL SAYS ". . ."

From The Admissions Office

"Duke University offers an interesting mix of tradition and innovation, undergraduate college and major research university, Southern hospitality and international presence, and athletic prowess and academic excellence. Students come to Duke from all over the United States and the world and from a range of racial, ethnic, and socioeconomic backgrounds. They enjoy contact with a world-class faculty through small classes and independent study. More than 40 majors are available in the arts and sciences and engineering; arts and sciences students may also design their own curriculum through Program II. Certificate programs are available in a number of interdisciplinary areas. Special academic opportunities include the Focus Program and seminars for first-year students, study abroad, study at the Duke Marine Laboratory and Duke Primate Center, the Duke in New York and Duke in Los Angeles arts programs, and several international exchange programs. While admission to Duke is highly selective, applications of U.S. citizens and permanent residents are evaluated without regard to financial need and the university pledges to meet 100 percent of the demonstrated need of all admitted U.S. students and permanent residents. A limited amount of financial aid is also available for foreign citizens, and the university will meet the full demonstrated financial need for those admitted students as well.

"Applicants must take either the ACT with the Writing exam, or the SAT plus two SAT Subject Tests (Mathematics Subject Test required for applicants to the Pratt School of Engineering)."

SELECTIVITY

Admissions Rating	99
# of applicants	18,090
% of applicants accepted	22
% of acceptees attending	43
# accepting a place on wait list	1,026
% admitted from wait list	10
# of early decision applicants	1,482
% accepted early decision	32

FRESHMAN PROFILE

Range SAT Critical Reading	690–770
Range SAT Math	690–800
Range ACT Composite	29–34
% graduated top 10% of class	90
% graduated top 25% of class	98
% graduated top 50% of class	100

DEADLINES

Early decision	
Deadline	11/1
Notification	12/15
Regular	
Deadline	1/2
Notification	4/1
Nonfall registration?	no

APPLICANTS ALSO LOOK AT
AND OFTEN PREFER
Harvard College
Stanford University
Yale University
Princeton University
AND SOMETIMES PREFER
Dartmouth College
Cornell University
Brown University
University of Pennsylvania
AND RARELY PREFER
University of Virginia
Georgetown University
University of North Carolina at Chapel Hill
Northwestern University

FINANCIAL FACTS

Financial Aid Rating	95
Annual tuition	$31,420
Room and board	$8,950
Required fees	$1,180
Books and supplies	$970
% frosh rec. need-based scholarship or grant aid	38
% UG rec. need-based scholarship or grant aid	37
% frosh rec. non-need-based scholarship or grant aid	1
% UG rec. non-need-based scholarship or grant aid	1
% frosh rec. need-based self-help aid	35
% UG rec. need-based self-help aid	35
% UG borrow to pay for school	40
Average cumulative indebtedness	$16,502

DUQUESNE UNIVERSITY

600 FORBES AVENUE, PITTSBURGH, PA 15282 • ADMISSIONS: 412-396-2222 • FAX: 412-396-5644

CAMPUS LIFE

Quality of Life Rating	79
Fire Safety Rating	88
Green Rating	84
Type of school	private
Affiliation	Roman Catholic
Environment	metropolis

STUDENTS

Total undergrad enrollment	5,616
% male/female	42/58
% from out of state	20
% live on campus	59
% in (# of) fraternities	12 (8)
% in (# of) sororities	9 (7)
% African American	4
% Asian	2
% Caucasian	83
% Hispanic	1
% international	2
# of countries represented	80

SURVEY SAYS . . .

Students love Pittsburgh, PA
Great off-campus food
Campus feels safe
Lots of beer drinking
(Almost) everyone smokes

ACADEMICS

Academic Rating	77
Calendar	semester
Student/faculty ratio	15.5:1
Profs interesting rating	72
Profs accessible rating	76
Most common reg class size	10–19 students
Most common lab size	20–29 students

MOST POPULAR MAJORS

accounting
nursing/registered nurse
(RN, ASN, BSN, MSN)
pharmacy (PHARMD [USA],
PHARMD, or BS/BPHARM [Canada])

STUDENTS SAY ". . ."

Academics

Located in a great town for both career networking and college fun, Pittsburgh's Duquesne University offers a prestigious private-school education to a "smart, ambitious, and very goal-oriented" student body that "prides itself on its 'Catholic' tradition." DU is perhaps best known for its health sciences programs. Students laud the "rigorous pharmacy curriculum;" the "wonderful" physical therapy program; and "great" nursing, occupational, and athletic training programs, all of which benefit from "great access to all the hospitals in the area." The music program at Duquesne is "amazing," and students say "the employment rate of students that have graduated from the music education program is phenomenal. I'm almost positive every senior that graduated was placed at a job already." Students in many of these areas pursue DUs accelerated bachelor's/graduate degree programs. Regardless of what they study, all DU students must complete a core curriculum that stresses broad general knowledge; students have mixed feelings about the core, warning that these classes are "harder than other courses" and are especially labor-intensive. Throughout the school, "Most classes are lecture-driven courses" with relatively large class sizes at the lower levels. The majority of professors are "excellent teachers and very knowledgeable of their respective fields," although, as anywhere, "There are a few awful ones." Nearly all "make themselves available to help you anytime you need," and if you are not good at a particular subject, they…have tutors available to help you."

Life

Student life at Duquesne "is lots of fun," although students say that has more to do with hometown Pittsburgh than with the DU campus. True, the campus offers numerous diversions, including "movies and crafts and sports and tons of organizations," in addition to weekend frat parties, which are quite popular with the Greek crowd and underclassmen. However, most students find city life more tempting, reporting that they "like to go downtown to shop, or to the South Side, or to the Waterfront." Oakland is really close by, with "lots of bars, restaurants," and "other colleges." One student explains, "There's always something going on in Pittsburgh, whether it's free concerts, cultural events, or art exhibits, many of which you are admitted into for free or reduced price with a Duquesne ID." The only downside is the weather: "if you're looking for fun, be prepared to bundle up in the winter and to travel by bus or taxi," one student warns. The "beautiful" DU campus features "lots of fountains and grassy areas and stuff." Location is another plus, as the campus is in the middle of Pittsburgh but still has a very private feel. "We have the opportunities of the city but we are secluded on the bluff."

Student Body

Typical Duquesne undergrad are either "well put together" or they "care too much about the way they look"—it's all a matter of perspective. Since most here are the "dress for success" type, the former viewpoint is more popular than the latter, although the "wearing-sweats-and-being-comfortable crowd" make up "about a third" of the campus, so they're hardly a tiny minority. Because "many students at Duquesne went to high school together," the school tends to be quite clique-y. Undergrads also tend to self-segregate by major. As one music student writes, "the typical music major is completely different from the typical student. The majority of music majors have somewhat eclectic taste in fashion, clothing, hobbies…which reflects in our personalities. We also talk about stuff we're doing in class outside of school, which isn't very common among other majors." While most students here are Catholic, "there are also people of different religions," and the school "doesn't impose religion" on anyone.

DUQUESNE UNIVERSITY

FINANCIAL AID: 412-396-6607 • E-MAIL: ADMISSIONS@DUQ.EDU • WEBSITE: WWW.DUQ.EDU

THE PRINCETON REVIEW SAYS

Admissions

Very important factors considered include: Application essay, academic GPA, recommendation(s), rigor of secondary school record, standardized test scores. *Important factors considered include:* Class rank, character/personal qualities, extracurricular activities, interview, talent/ability, volunteer work. *Other factors considered include:* Alumni/ae relation, first generation, level of applicant's interest, racial/ethnic status, work experience. SAT or ACT required. ACT with Writing component required. High school diploma is required and GED is accepted. *Academic units recommended:* 4 English, 2 mathematics, 2 science, 2 foreign language, 2 social studies, 4 academic electives.

Financial Aid

Students should submit: FAFSA, institution's own financial aid form. Regular filing deadline is 5/1. The Princeton Review suggests that all financial aid forms be submitted as soon as possible after 1/1. *Need-based scholarships/grants offered:* Federal Pell, SEOG, state scholarships/grants, private scholarships, the school's own gift aid, United Negro College Fund. *Loan aid offered:* FFEL Subsidized Stafford, FFEL Unsubsidized Stafford, FFEL PLUS, Federal Perkins, federal nursing scholarships, private alternative loans. Applicants will be notified of awards on a rolling basis beginning 3/1. Federal Work-Study Program available. Institutional employment available. Off-campus job opportunities are good.

The Inside Word

Duquesne's overall high admit rate masks the competitiveness of its top programs. Applicants seeking admission to programs in pharmacy, physical therapy, physician's assistant, and forensic science should expect a rigorous review. Others should have little difficulty getting through the door provided they present a respectable complement of transcripts and test scores.

THE SCHOOL SAYS "..."

From The Admissions Office

"Duquesne University was founded in 1878 by the Holy Ghost Fathers. Although it is a private, Roman Catholic institution, Duquesne is proud of its ecumenical reputation. Duquesne University's attractive and secluded campus is set on a 48-acre hilltop ('the bluff') overlooking the large corporate metropolis of Pittsburgh's Golden Triangle. It offers a wide variety of educational opportunities, from the liberal arts to modern professional training. Duquesne is a medium-sized university striving to offer personal attention to its students in addition to the versatility and opportunities of a true university. A deep sense of tradition is combined with innovation and flexibility to make the Duquesne experience both challenging and rewarding. The Palumbo Convocation/Recreation Complex features a 6,300-seat arena, home court to the university's Division I basketball team; racquetball and handball courts; weight rooms; and saunas. Extracurricular activities are recognized as an essential part of college life, complementing academics in the process of total student development. Students are involved in nearly 100 university-sponsored activities, and Duquesne's location gives students the opportunity to enjoy sports and cultural events both on campus and in the city. There are six residence halls with the capacity to house 3,511 students."

SELECTIVITY

Admissions Rating	89
# of applicants	5,715
% of applicants accepted	76
% of acceptees attending	33
# of early decision applicants	294
% accepted early decision	72

FRESHMAN PROFILE

Range SAT Critical Reading	510–600
Range SAT Math	520–610
Range SAT Writing	510–600
Range ACT Composite	22–26
Average HS GPA	3.59
% graduated top 10% of class	23
% graduated top 25% of class	55
% graduated top 50% of class	87

DEADLINES

Early decision	
Deadline	11/1
Notification	12/15
Early action	
Deadline	12/1
Notification	1/15
Regular	
Priority	11/1
Deadline	7/1
Notification	rolling
Nonfall registration?	yes

APPLICANTS ALSO LOOK AT
AND OFTEN PREFER
Washington & Jefferson College
Penn State—University Park
University of Pittsburgh

AND SOMETIMES PREFER
West Virginia University
Gannon University
Saint Vincent College

FINANCIAL FACTS

Financial Aid Rating	87
Annual tuition	$23,470
Room and board	$8,888
Required fees	$2,005
Books and supplies	$600
% frosh rec. need-based scholarship or grant aid	71
% UG rec. need-based scholarship or grant aid	67
% frosh rec. non-need-based scholarship or grant aid	68
% UG rec. non-need-based scholarship or grant aid	59
% frosh rec. need-based self-help aid	64
% UG rec. need-based self-help aid	61
% frosh rec. athletic scholarships	7
% UG rec. athletic scholarships	7
% frosh rec. any financial aid	98
% UG rec. any financial aid	95
% UG borrow to pay for school	80
Average cumulative indebtedness	$29,616

ECKERD COLLEGE

4200 FIFTY-FOURTH AVENUE SOUTH, ST. PETERSBURG, FL 33711 • ADMISSIONS: 727-864-8331 • FAX: 727-866-2304

CAMPUS LIFE
Quality of Life Rating	**80**
Fire Safety Rating	**60***
Green Rating	**89**
Type of school	private
Affiliation	Presbyterian
Environment	city

STUDENTS
Total undergrad enrollment	1,807
% male/female	42/58
% from out of state	74
% live on campus	78
% African American	3
% Asian	2
% Caucasian	75
% Hispanic	5
% international	3
# of countries represented	28

SURVEY SAYS . . .
Great library
Career services are great
Frats and sororities are unpopular or nonexistent
Lots of beer drinking
Hard liquor is popular

ACADEMICS
Academic Rating	**85**
Calendar	4/1/4
Student/faculty ratio	13:1
Profs interesting rating	85
Profs accessible rating	92
Most common reg class size	20–29 students
Most common lab size	10–19 students

MOST POPULAR MAJORS
business administration and management
environmental studies
marine biology and biological oceanography

STUDENTS SAY ". . ."

Academics

Florida's Eckerd College may be small, but it only seems small "where it matters, like class size[s] and relationships with professors." It also offers many "big-school opportunities that make it seem bigger than it is." Among the school's most distinguished offerings are an "amazing" marine science program—"if it's not your passion," students say, "it will eat you alive"—and a "great international relations program." The latter benefits from a school-wide commitment to undergraduate international travel. One student writes: "International education is great. I spent last January (winter term) in Vietnam, Thailand, Laos, and Cambodia, and next semester I'll be in Sweden on an exchange program." Students tell us that academic programs other than the sciences and international relations "aren't nearly as demanding, and professors don't seem to expect as much out of the students." As one student puts it, "There are two kinds of Eckerd students: Those with easy majors and those [who] watch everyone else party on Tuesdays and skip class to go the beach." Eckerd offers "much flexibility for designing your own concentration or for independent studies" as well as many opportunities "to do research with your professors and advance in ways you couldn't imagine at larger schools." How accessible are professors here? "Pitchers with Professors"—where students and professors can discuss class lectures or [have] general conversation over a pitcher of beer or a soda"—"is a common occurrence each month."

Life

"It's Florida," explains one student. "Life at school is laid-back." The warm weather "definitely has an effect on the attitude of most people who live on campus." Eckerd's environs include various sports grounds, including beach volleyball courts and a private waterfront where students can take sailing and windsurfing classes. If that's not enough, two gorgeous beaches are less than 10 minutes away, downtown Tampa is only a half-hour away, and Busch Gardens and Disney World are 45 and 90 minutes away, respectively. One student sums up, "the location is amazing. Waking up on the Tampa Bay each morning energizes you." The only drawback is that "Eckerd is somewhat separated from St. Petersburg at large. It's [on] the southern tip of the city and you're really out of luck if you don't have a car or don't know someone who does, since mostly everything worth doing is far away." On campus "The most random of events happen...We've got drum circles on the beach, Saturday Morning Market, Kappa Karnival, Pitchers with Professors, Saturday boat trips to Shell Island, Ybor City, and lots of other things to explore."

Student Body

The Eckerd student body includes "science majors (geeks, if you will)" along with "a small dosage of preppy students," "a lot of surfers, sailors, and tanners," "athletes," "church people," and "trustafarians." Athletes "stick together within their groups," and "the marine science majors sort of are a collective," but students report that "it's easy to make friends and know people in every group." "Overall my friends are a varied crowd," a junior declares. While Eckerd's student body is "mostly white and from a middle- to upper-class background" this "is not a typical college," especially by Florida standards. "Don't expect sorority girls and football players," students warn. It's worth noting that Eckerd "is a very liberal campus, with many Democrats, hippies, marijuana, parties, pets, environmental concern, and a basic openness to new things. If you're close-minded and don't want to see others' views, don't come here."

FINANCIAL AID: 727-864-8334 • E-MAIL: ADMISSIONS@ECKERD.EDU • WEBSITE: WWW.ECKERD.EDU

THE PRINCETON REVIEW SAYS

Admissions

Very important factors considered include: Academic GPA, rigor of secondary school record. *Important factors considered include:* Application essay, recommendation(s), standardized test scores, character/personal qualities, extracurricular activities, interview, talent/ability. *Other factors considered include:* Class rank, alumni/ae relation, first generation, level of applicant's interest, volunteer work, work experience. SAT or ACT required. TOEFL required of all international applicants. High school diploma is required and GED is accepted. *Academic units required:* 4 English, 3 mathematics, 3 science (2 science labs), 2 foreign language, 2 social studies, 1 history, 3 academic electives. *Academic units recommended:* 4 mathematics, 4 science (3 science labs), 3 foreign language, 2 history, 3 academic electives.

Financial Aid

Students should submit: FAFSA. The Princeton Review suggests that all financial aid forms be submitted as soon as possible after 1/1. *Need-based scholarships/grants offered:* Federal Pell, SEOG, state scholarships/grants, private scholarships, the school's own gift aid. *Loan aid offered:* FFEL Subsidized Stafford, FFEL Unsubsidized Stafford, FFEL PLUS, Federal Perkins, college/university loans from institutional funds. Applicants will be notified of awards on a rolling basis beginning 2/15. Federal Work-Study Program available. Institutional employment available. Off-campus job opportunities are excellent.

The Inside Word

Eckerd is looking to upgrade its student body, but competition from other small liberal arts schools is stiff; the school is still a relatively easy admit for B-plus students with decent standardized test scores. The school practices rolling admissions, so apply early to improve your chances—Eckerd can afford to be more selective later in the admissions process, especially with candidates who appear to be headed for its most competitive programs (i.e., marine science and international relations).

THE SCHOOL SAYS " . . . "

From The Admissions Office

"Eckerd's diverse student body comes from 49 states and 49 countries. In this international setting, the majors of international relations and international business are very popular. Close to 70 percent of our graduates spend at least one term studying abroad. The beautiful waterfront campus is a perfect location for the study of marine science and environmental studies. We characterize Eckerd students as competent givers because of their extensive involvement in the life of the campus and their many volunteer service contributions to the local environment and the St. Petersburg community. The Academy of Senior Professionals draws to campus distinguished persons who have retired from fields our students aspire to enter. Academy members, such as the late novelist James Michener, Nobel Prize–winner Elie Wiesel, and noted black historian John Hope Franklin, enrich classes and offer valuable counsel for career and life planning.

"Students applying for admission are allowed to submit SAT or ACT examination results, and Eckerd will use the best scores from either test."

SELECTIVITY
Admissions Rating	83
# of applicants	3,398
% of applicants accepted	66
% of acceptees attending	22

FRESHMAN PROFILE
Range SAT Critical Reading	510–615
Range SAT Math	510–610
Range SAT Writing	500–600
Range ACT Composite	22–27
Minimum paper TOEFL	550
Minimum computer TOEFL	213
Minimum web-based TOEFL	79
Average HS GPA	3.31
% graduated top 10% of class	16
% graduated top 25% of class	48
% graduated top 50% of class	85

DEADLINES
Regular	
Notification	rolling
Nonfall registration?	yes

FINANCIAL FACTS
Financial Aid Rating	83
Annual tuition	$30,304
Room and board	$8,754
Required fees	$286
Books and supplies	$1,000
% frosh rec. need-based scholarship or grant aid	56
% UG rec. need-based scholarship or grant aid	56
% frosh rec. need-based self-help aid	57
% UG rec. need-based self-help aid	56
% frosh rec. athletic scholarships	2
% UG rec. athletic scholarships	2
% frosh rec. any financial aid	96.7
% UG rec. any financial aid	94.4
% UG borrow to pay for school	65
Average cumulative indebtedness	$28,219

ELON UNIVERSITY

2700 CAMPUS BOX, ELON, NC 27244-2010 • ADMISSIONS: 336-278-3566 • FAX: 336-278-7699

CAMPUS LIFE

Quality of Life Rating	85
Fire Safety Rating	78
Green Rating	94
Type of school	private
Affiliation	United Church of Christ
Environment	town

STUDENTS

Total undergrad enrollment	4,992
% male/female	41/59
% from out of state	71
% from public high school	68
% live on campus	59
% in (# of) fraternities	19 (11)
% in (# of) sororities	34 (12)
% African American	6
% Asian	1
% Caucasian	81
% Hispanic	2
% international	2
# of countries represented	51

SURVEY SAYS . . .

School is well run
Low cost of living
Frats and sororities dominate social scene
(Almost) no one smokes

ACADEMICS

Academic Rating	86
Calendar	4/1/4
Student/faculty ratio	14:1
Profs interesting rating	85
Profs accessible rating	89
Most common reg class size	10–19 students
Most common lab size	10–19 students

MOST POPULAR MAJORS

business
communications
biology
psychology
elementary education

STUDENTS SAY ". . ."

Academics

Elon University works hard to "broaden students' horizons in all aspects of life, both in and out of the classroom" by "embracing the idea that student involvement is a key tool to developing a strong future." Central to this mission is the school's emphasis on experiential learning. "You will work your butt off in the classroom," students assure us, "but that is not where your day ends—you get involved outside the classroom and gain more knowledge" through "extensive undergraduate research, service learning, study-abroad, and internship opportunities." Of these, students are most vocal about the "amazing study-abroad program," through which Elon seeks to transform a student into a "world citizen rather than just another American with a college degree." Undergrads report approvingly that the school "fully prepares you for your [study-abroad] experience and tries to ensure that every student gets to go somewhere." The school's strengths trend toward the professions—business, communications, education, and biology are all considered among the best departments here—but Elon also boasts "one of the very best performing arts schools with a liberal arts education," including "a great dance department." In all departments, "The class sizes are small, and professors take an interest in student achievement both inside and outside of academics." "The class size and teacher-student ratio, I'm convinced, are the main reasons I am succeeding at this school," one student believes. "If it weren't for the teachers knowing me personally, I probably wouldn't care at all."

Life

"Any individual can fit in at Elon, so long as they take the time to find what they are interested in," because "Elon offers a wide variety in its student population and activities. Going to sporting events, attending schools plays, and getting involved in community service organizations are all major factors of Elon life," and "if Elon does not have exactly what you want, you can start it up." That said, students who love the Greek scene will have an easier time fitting in than those who don't; Even though "there are a ton of other things to get involved with so long as students try to get involved," many here still believe "in order to have fun at Elon, students should get involved in Greek life." Students report "the campus is absolutely gorgeous," contributing to "a definite aspect of southern comfort." Burlington, the nearest town, "is the fast food capital of North Carolina, so there is always somewhere to go out and eat, but in terms of entertainment we have a bowling alley, parks, the mall, and a movie theater—which isn't much. But, we're also 30 minutes from Chapel Hill and 15 minutes from Greensboro, so we're within traveling distance of other areas with a more varied choice of activities."

Student Body

The Elon student body is sometimes criticized "for being too preppy or not diverse enough, but these are just generalizations," students tell us. "Sure, there are a lot of preppy people here, but there are a lot of different types of people as well. Not everyone here is rich, Southern, and dresses like an Easter egg." They are hardly your stereotypical selfish, rich kids, as "the majority of students at Elon simply want to make a difference in one way or another. We are a very community-service based school and constantly have fundraisers and drives for a variety of causes." "The typical student is in a sorority of fraternity, and the Greeks have a very large presence on campus. There is a lack of 'atypical' students as most people tend to fit the Elon 'mold.' If you are interested in Greek life, this is a great place to be, but if you aren't, don't bother."

FINANCIAL AID: 800-334-8448 • E-MAIL: ADMISSIONS@ELON.EDU • WEBSITE: WWW.ELON.EDU

THE PRINCETON REVIEW SAYS

Admissions

Very important factors considered include: Academic GPA, rigor of secondary school record, standardized test scores. *Important factors considered include:* Application essay, recommendation(s), alumni/ae relation, extracurricular activities, talent/ability. *Other factors considered include:* Class rank, character/personal qualities, first generation, geographical residence, level of applicant's interest, racial/ethnic status, state residency, volunteer work, work experience. SAT or ACT required. ACT with Writing component required. TOEFL required of all international applicants. High school diploma is required and GED is accepted. *Academic units required:* 4 English, 3 mathematics, 3 science (1 science lab), 2 foreign language, 1 social studies, 2 history. *Academic units recommended:* 4 mathematics, 3 foreign language, 3 history.

Financial Aid

Students should submit: FAFSA, institution's own financial aid form, CSS/financial aid profile. The Princeton Review suggests that all financial aid forms be submitted as soon as possible after 1/1. *Need-based scholarships/grants offered:* Federal Pell, SEOG, state scholarships/grants, private scholarships, the school's own gift aid. *Loan aid offered:* FFEL Subsidized Stafford, FFEL Unsubsidized Stafford, FFEL PLUS, Federal Perkins, state loans, privately funded alternative loans. Applicants will be notified of awards on a rolling basis beginning 3/30. Federal Work-Study Program available. Institutional employment available. Off-campus job opportunities are good.

The Inside Word

Elon has worked hard to elevate its national profile, and admissions standards have risen with the school's reputation. Today, Elon has more than enough solid performers to fill its incoming class with accomplished, capable students; there are no seats left over for slackers. That said, Elon considers the entire application and will use evidence of academic promise (e.g. excellent writing and glowing recommendations) to mitigate weaknesses in test scores or, occasionally, even high school grades.

THE SCHOOL SAYS ". . ."

From The Admissions Office

"Elon offers the comprehensive resources of a university in a close-knit community atmosphere. The university's 4,992 undergraduates choose from 51 majors in the arts and sciences, business, communications, and education. Graduate programs are offered in business administration, law, education, interactive media and physical therapy. The National Survey of Student Engagement recognizes Elon among the nation's most effective universities in promoting hands-on learning. Academic and co-curricular activities are seamlessly blended, especially in the Elon Experiences: study abroad, internships, service, leadership, and undergraduate research. Participation is among the highest in the nation. Seventy-one percent of graduating seniors have studied abroad, 80 percent have internship experiences and 89 percent have participated in service. Elon's 4-1-4 academic calendar allows students to devote January to international study or to explore innovative on-campus courses. Elon's historic 575-acre campus is recognized as one of the most beautiful in the country. New additions include the $10-million Ernest A. Koury, Sr. Business Center, featuring a digital theater and finance trading room; Lindner Hall, the "greenest" building on campus and anchor for the Academic Village, a quad dedicated to the arts and sciences; and The Colonnades Dining Hall, a two-story dining facility featuring a full-service restaurant, an organic market, and a fire stone oven for pizzas. Elon's NCAA Division I Phoenix athletics programs compete in the Southern Conference.

"Freshman applicants are required to take the SAT (or the ACT with the writing section). The best critical reading, math and writing scores from either test will be used."

SELECTIVITY

Admissions Rating	92
# of applicants	9.434
% of applicants accepted	42
% of acceptees attending	32
# accepting a place on wait list	1,215
% admitted from wait list	1
# of early decision applicants	422
% accepted early decision	75

FRESHMAN PROFILE

Range SAT Critical Reading	560–650
Range SAT Math	570–660
Range SAT Writing	570–660
Range ACT Composite	25–29
Minimum paper TOEFL	550
Minimum computer TOEFL	213
Minimum web-based TOEFL	79
Average HS GPA	3.90
% graduated top 10% of class	33
% graduated top 25% of class	68
% graduated top 50% of class	94

DEADLINES

Early decision	
Deadline	11/1
Notification	12/1
Early action	
Deadline	11/10
Notification	12/20
Regular	
Priority	11/1
Deadline	1/10
Notification	12/20
Nonfall registration?	no

APPLICANTS ALSO LOOK AT AND OFTEN PREFER

University of North Carolina at Chapel Hill

FINANCIAL FACTS

Financial Aid Rating	84
Annual tuition	$25,746
Room and board	$7,770
Required fees	$330
Books and supplies	$900
% frosh rec. need-based scholarship or grant aid	29
% UG rec. need-based scholarship or grant aid	28
% frosh rec. non-need-based scholarship or grant aid	5
% UG rec. non-need-based scholarship or grant aid	4
% frosh rec. need-based self-help aid	24
% UG rec. need-based self-help aid	25
% frosh rec. athletic scholarships	5
% UG rec. athletic scholarships	6
% frosh rec. any financial aid	77
% UG rec. any financial aid	71
% UG borrow to pay for school	45
Average cumulative indebtedness	$23,392

EMERSON COLLEGE

120 BOYLSTON STREET, BOSTON, MA 02116-4624 • ADMISSIONS: 617-824-8600 • FAX: 617-824-8609

CAMPUS LIFE
Quality of Life Rating	**90**
Fire Safety Rating	**73**
Green Rating	**76**
Type of school	private
Environment	metropolis

STUDENTS
Total undergrad enrollment	3,418
% male/female	43/57
% from out of state	75
% from public high school	70
% live on campus	48
% in (# of) fraternities	3 (4)
% in (# of) sororities	3 (3)
% African American	3
% Asian	5
% Caucasian	69
% Hispanic	7
% Native American	1
% international	3
# of countries represented	48

SURVEY SAYS . . .
Students aren't religious
Students love Boston, MA
Great off-campus food
College radio is popular
Theater is popular
Student publications are popular
(Almost) everyone smokes

ACADEMICS
Academic Rating	**82**
Calendar	semester
Student/faculty ratio	14:1
Profs interesting rating	80
Profs accessible rating	77
% classes taught by TAs	3
Most common reg class size	10–19 students
Most common lab size	10–19 students

MOST POPULAR MAJORS
cinematography and film/video
production
creative writing
theatre/theater

STUDENTS SAY "..."

Academics
God help the future Wall Streeters who somehow find themselves members of the student body at Emerson, a big happy group of "creative people" who come together to share their passions ("whether it be on the stage, the page, the big screen or the small"), and learn more about their own mediums of self-expressions via collaboration with diverse individuals. The focus on the more creative side of communication and the arts, provides "a community that (usually) understands what an artist needs to thrive and grow." "People come to Emerson knowing exactly what they want to do, and then [they] do that thing all out for four years," says a sophomore. According to its students, Emerson "brings creativity and ingenuity to the arts and communication unlike any other school in the country." Although those who attend the school are more than aware that most of their fellow students might be "part of the next generation of America's starving artists (unless you're a marketing or CSD major)," the school does a tremendous job of offering each student a "specialized career-oriented experience," no matter how non-traditional the career path.

The excellent student-teacher ratio means personal attention that goes beyond just office hours, which translates into a lot of time spent with people who are "practicing professionals in their respective fields." The largest classroom at Emerson can accommodate only about 70 students, so lectures (if a student even has any) "are only about 50 students large," and one must "be prepared to do most of your learning outside of the classroom in projects." Design and technology majors in particular get a good deal of hands-on experience. While there can be "a little too much red tape around some of the administrative aspects of Emerson," one student claims that "there is no other school I have encountered where one would feel more easily acknowledged and listened to by their professors."

Life
The drive to succeed in such competitive industries means "a majority of students are busier than the average professional" and "don't really sleep," which is not surprising, considering all of the rehearsals, film shoots, concerts, and organization meetings seemingly required of Emerson life. The school is located right in the heart of downtown Boston, and many admit that it can be hard to concentrate with Boston Common right across the street and the realization that "you live in a city, not a campus bubble." After sophomore year "most people live offcampus," which is where most parties are also hosted; although there's a fair share of partying for those who are interested, "students are more inclined to have an 80s costume and dance party than a frat bash." For those who resist the lure of the cafés, theaters, bars, and performances, plain old-fashioned silliness in the dorms seems equally as exciting, "like coloring or old video games or children's books—everyone just wants to have fun."

Student Body
Around Boston, "an Emerson student can be spotted from a mile away," not because they all look alike, but because they all look so different (although "if you wanted to peg Emerson students as the artsy young adults with an offbeat fashion-forward style and a cigarette in one hand and Starbucks in the other, it wouldn't be horribly inaccurate"). Almost all students find a common thread in a love of the arts, which often results in a unifying ambition amongst "people wanting to 'make it' in their field." One film student remarks that Emerson is filled with what she refers to as "my 'type' of people." This "friendly, eclectic, and fun" group of students leans pretty far to the left politically, and there is a large gay community at Emerson. There seems to be one student in every class that "can be pretentious and annoying," but these souls are in the minority. Overall, Emersonians are a "very accepting community" of driven individuals.

FINANCIAL AID: 617-824-8655 • E-MAIL: ADMISSION@EMERSON.EDU • WEBSITE: WWW.EMERSON.EDU

THE PRINCETON REVIEW SAYS

Admissions

Very important factors considered include: Academic GPA, standardized test scores. *Important factors considered include:* Class rank, application essay, recommendation(s), rigor of secondary school record, character/personal qualities, extracurricular activities, talent/ability. *Other factors considered include:* Alumni/ae relation, first generation, geographical residence, racial/ethnic status, volunteer work, work experience. SAT or ACT required. ACT with Writing component required. TOEFL required of all international applicants. High school diploma is required and GED is accepted. *Academic units required:* 4 English, 3 mathematics, 3 science, 3 foreign language, 3 social studies. *Academic units recommended:* 4 English, 3 mathematics, 3 science, 3 foreign language, 3 social studies, 4 academic electives.

Financial Aid

Students should submit: FAFSA, CSS/financial aid profile, noncustodial profile, business/farm supplement, tax returns. The Princeton Review suggests that all financial aid forms be submitted as soon as possible after 1/1. *Need-based scholarships/grants offered:* Federal Pell, SEOG, state scholarships/grants, private scholarships, the school's own gift aid. *Loan aid offered:* FFEL Subsidized Stafford, FFEL Unsubsidized Stafford, FFEL PLUS, Federal Perkins, state loans. Applicants will be notified of awards on or about 4/1. Federal Work-Study Program available. Institutional employment available. Off-campus job opportunities are excellent.

The Inside Word

Expect your living situation to be made easier by recent developments on Emerson's campus. The Max Mutchnick Campus Center, named in recognition of the substantial gift made by the Emerson alumnus and co-creator/executive producer of *Will & Grace*, is an 185,000-square-foot building that features a gym, offices, and residence hall. This facility, combined with the recent acquisition of the Colonial Theatre (which will also feature dorm rooms), means nearly three quarters of the students will be able to live on campus and indulge in affordable rent.

THE SCHOOL SAYS "..."

From The Admissions Office

"Founded in 1880, Emerson is one of the premier colleges in the country for communication and the arts. Students may choose from more than two-dozen undergraduate and graduate programs supported by state-of-the-art facilities and a nationally renowned faculty. The campus is home to WERS-FM, the oldest noncommercial radio station in Boston; the historic 1,200-seat Cutler Majestic Theatre; and *Ploughshares*, the award winning literary journal for new writing.

"Located on Boston Common in the heart of the city's Theatre District, the campus is walking distance from the Massachusetts State House, Chinatown, and historic Freedom Trail. More than half the students reside on-campus, some in special learning communities such as the Writers' Block and Digital Culture Floor. There is also a fitness center, athletic field, and new gymnasium and campus center.

"Emerson has nearly 70 student organizations and performance groups as well as 15 NCAA teams, student publications, and honor societies. The College also sponsors programs in Los Angeles and Washington, D.C.; study abroad in the Netherlands, Taiwan, and Czech Republic; and course cross-registration with the six-member Boston ProArts Consortium.

"Students have access to outstanding facilities, including sound treated television studios, digital editing and audio post-production suites. An 11-story performance and production center houses a theatre design/technology center, makeup lab, and costume shop. There are seven programs to observe speech and hearing therapy, a professional marketing focus group room, and digital newsroom. In 2010, a 9-story performance development center will open with a sound stage, scene shop, and film screening room."

SELECTIVITY

Admissions Rating	92
# of applicants	6,944
% of applicants accepted	37
% of acceptees attending	30
# accepting a place on wait list	560
% admitted from wait list	41

FRESHMAN PROFILE

Range SAT Critical Reading	580–680
Range SAT Math	550–640
Range SAT Writing	580–670
Range ACT Composite	25–29
Minimum paper TOEFL	550
Minimum computer TOEFL	213
Minimum web-based TOEFL	80
Average HS GPA	3.6
% graduated top 10% of class	39.1
% graduated top 25% of class	81
% graduated top 50% of class	97.8

DEADLINES

Early action	
Deadline	11/1
Notification	12/15
Regular	
Deadline	1/5
Notification	4/1
Nonfall registration?	yes

APPLICANTS ALSO LOOK AT

AND OFTEN PREFER
New York University

AND SOMETIMES PREFER
University of Southern California
Ithaca College

AND RARELY PREFER
Boston University
Syracuse University

FINANCIAL FACTS

Financial Aid Rating	86
Annual tuition	$28,352
Room and board	$11,832
Required fees	$532
Books and supplies	$720
% frosh rec. need-based scholarship or grant aid	50
% UG rec. need-based scholarship or grant aid	43
% frosh rec. non-need-based scholarship or grant aid	3
% UG rec. non-need-based scholarship or grant aid	2
% frosh rec. need-based self-help aid	57
% UG rec. need-based self-help aid	52
% frosh rec. any financial aid	85.3
% UG rec. any financial aid	70.6
% UG borrow to pay for school	65
Average cumulative indebtedness	$15,701

EMORY UNIVERSITY

BOISFEUILLET JONES CENTER, ATLANTA, GA 30322 • ADMISSIONS: 404-727-6036 • FAX: 404-727-4303

CAMPUS LIFE

Quality of Life Rating	87
Fire Safety Rating	68
Green Rating	95
Type of school	private
Affiliation	Methodist
Environment	town

STUDENTS

Total undergrad enrollment	6,787
% male/female	45/55
% from out of state	70
% live on campus	66
% in (# of) fraternities	28 (14)
% in (# of) sororities	30 (12)
% African American	10
% Asian	20
% Caucasian	52
% Hispanic	4
% international	7
# of countries represented	40

SURVEY SAYS . . .

Lab facilities are great
Great library
Students love Atlanta, GA
Great off-campus food
Campus feels safe
Student publications are popular

ACADEMICS

Academic Rating	89
Calendar	semester
Student/faculty ratio	7:1
Profs interesting rating	86
Profs accessible rating	82
% classes taught by TAs	10
Most common reg class size	10–19 students
Most common lab size	10–19 students

MOST POPULAR MAJORS
business/commerce
economics
English language and literature

STUDENTS SAY ". . ."

Academics

Students rise to the challenge at Emory University, an academically impressive school that supports its students in their individual endeavors in and out of the classroom. Though academics can be difficult, students prove more than capable, and the in-it-togetherness helps things sail even more smoothly. Students "get together for study sessions regularly and are always cooperative and helpful to one another," and the "FirstClass system," a social networking application that allows students to post questions online so that other students or professors can answer, helps further discussions. Many who attend Emory are career-oriented from the start, and business and pre-med are popular tracks. The school also stresses the development of students on a cultural and social front, providing "a multitude of enriching speakers, environments, and unique opportunities" designed to do just that. The "forward-driven" administration is "extremely accessible," particularly the well-liked president, who holds regular office hours to discuss anything and everything on students' minds (and whose wife regularly dispenses homemade cookies). Many of the teachers also follow suit. "Office hours aren't a chore for professors; they enjoy getting to know the students on a more personal level." Small classes make the professors "very approachable," and they receive high marks for their compassion and accessibility, not to mention knowledge and experience. "It's pretty cool to be taught by experts in your field," says one political science major. Professors do "expect you to live up to their expectations," but the workload at Emory is "very manageable," and there are countless outside tutoring and paper-editing resources available to students in times of need. "My professors have always been incredibly interested in what I'm getting out of my classes," says a student. While a few students do just enough to get by, "many try very hard and do go above and beyond" what is required of the classes.

Life

Life at the "safe, separate, suburban campus" is just as exciting as life in nearby Atlanta, which provides the standard theater, concert, bar, and restaurant distractions. The student government association sponsors shuttles to various things including a weekly shuttle to the mall, and "there are always all sorts of events going on around campus—and actually interesting events, not just hippie drum circles and the like." Greek life and events are fairly popular but not overwhelming. People tend to be preoccupied with grades and academics Sunday through Thursday, but come Thursday night, campus tends to ease up a bit. While there "is certainly a contingent of Emory that drinks, and/or drinks heavily," many people do not, and "there's a great social life regardless of what side of the 'drinking spectrum' you are on." Students at Emory are "intellectually engaged," and lounges and dorm rooms are rife with discussions of politics and sustainability. Most students "find an organization to be highly involved with that keeps them busy most of the time," and if they aren't a part of some organization, then students will spend more time studying or seeking out Atlanta's entertainment scene.

Student Body

This "diverse and tolerant campus" has all sorts of unique characters; as one sophomore puts it, "I'm not saying there are large numbers of people who wear capes to class. There's a few, obviously, but not half of the student body." From an ethnic standpoint, Emory's financial aid department "truly provides for many students," and all races and backgrounds are represented, though there are a fair number of Jewish students. "I learn a lot more from class discussions that involve people from other backgrounds," says a student. Students at Emory tend to be very involved in extracurricular activities and community service, and they often don't require additional encouragement from the faculty—these activities are also where students tend to make most of their friends. Hard workers though they may be, "the typical student also enjoys going out. The atypical student simply doesn't go out as much."

FINANCIAL AID: 800-727-6039 • E-MAIL: ADMISS@EMORY.EDU • WEBSITE: WWW.EMORY.EDU

THE PRINCETON REVIEW SAYS
Admissions
Very important factors considered include: Application essay, academic GPA, recommendation(s), rigor of secondary school record, standardized test scores, character/personal qualities, extracurricular activities, level of applicant's interest. *Important factors considered include:* Talent/ability. *Other factors considered include:* Class rank, alumni/ae relation, first generation, geographical residence, interview, racial/ethnic status, state residency, volunteer work, work experience. SAT or ACT required. ACT with Writing component required. TOEFL required of all international applicants. High school diploma is required and GED is not accepted. *Academic units required:* 4 English, 3 mathematics, 2 science (2 science labs), 2 foreign language, 2 social studies, 2 history, 1 visual/performing arts, 2 academic electives. *Academic units recommended:* 4 mathematics, 3 science, 3 foreign language.

Financial Aid
Students should submit: FAFSA, CSS/financial aid profile, noncustodial profile. Regular filing deadline is 3/1. The Princeton Review suggests that all financial aid forms be submitted as soon as possible after 1/1. *Need-based scholarships/grants offered:* Federal Pell, SEOG, state scholarships/grants, private scholarships, the school's own gift aid. *Loan aid offered:* FFEL Subsidized Stafford, FFEL Unsubsidized Stafford, FFEL PLUS, Federal Perkins, federal nursing scholarships, state loans, college/university loans from institutional funds. Applicants will be notified of awards on or about 4/1.

The Inside Word
Early decision applications to Emory have risen drastically over the past few years, creating a quandary for aspiring Emory students: Do they join the growing crowd of early applicants and presumably increase the likelihood of admission, or do they take their chances with the regular admission date? Locking into one school early in the process can be a blessing or a curse; what if the aid package (which doesn't arrive until mid-April) isn't sufficient? Here's the good news: Emory financial aid has traditionally met 100 percent of applicants' demonstrated need.

THE SCHOOL SAYS "..."
From The Admissions Office
"As a destination for path-breaking researchers, renowned teachers, superb students, and dedicated staff, Emory University strives to help its community members fulfill their highest aspirations. Our vision is to discover truth, share it, and ignite in others a passion for its pursuit. The newly adopted Emory Strategic Plan provides a map to guide our growth and development over the next decade, focusing on strengthening faculty distinction, preparing engaged scholars, creating community, confronting the human condition and experience, and exploring new frontiers in science and technology. Similarly, our revised Campus Master Plan outlines a bold proposal for reshaping Emory's presence in Atlanta. Critical to that presence are programs in the arts, university-community partnerships, and the global reach of our initiatives through such Emory entities as the Carter Center.

"Emory remains more than the sum of its parts—a strong intellectual community that seeks excellence, not to compete with other institutions, but to contribute to the shaping of a better world.

"All applicants are required to submit scores from the SAT or the ACT."

SELECTIVITY
Admissions Rating	99
# of applicants	17,446
% of applicants accepted	27
% of acceptees attending	28
# accepting a place on wait list	800
% admitted from wait list	18
# of early decision applicants	1,904
% accepted early decision	26

FRESHMAN PROFILE
Range SAT Critical Reading	640–740
Range SAT Math	670–760
Range SAT Writing	650–740
Range ACT Composite	30–33
Minimum paper TOEFL	600
Minimum computer TOEFL	250
Average HS GPA	3.82
% graduated top 10% of class	90
% graduated top 25% of class	90
% graduated top 50% of class	100

DEADLINES
Early decision	
Deadline	11/1
Notification	12/15
Regular	
Deadline	1/15
Notification	4/1
Nonfall registration?	no

FINANCIAL FACTS
Financial Aid Rating	95
Annual tuition	$35,800
Room and board	$10,572
Required fees	$536
Books and supplies	$1,000
% frosh rec. need-based scholarship or grant aid	37
% UG rec. need-based scholarship or grant aid	37
% frosh rec. non-need-based scholarship or grant aid	2
% UG rec. non-need-based scholarship or grant aid	2
% frosh rec. need-based self-help aid	34
% UG rec. need-based self-help aid	33
% frosh rec. any financial aid	78
% UG rec. any financial aid	42
% UG borrow to pay for school	42
Average cumulative indebtedness	$23,181

EUGENE LANG COLLEGE THE NEW SCHOOL FOR LIBERAL ARTS

65 WEST ELEVENTH STREET, OFFICE OF ADMISSION, NEW YORK, NY 10011 • ADMISSIONS: 212-229-5665 • FAX: 212-229-5166

CAMPUS LIFE
Quality of Life Rating	71
Fire Safety Rating	60*
Green Rating	94
Type of school	private
Environment	metropolis

STUDENTS
Total undergrad enrollment	1,347
% male/female	32/68
% from out of state	71
% live on campus	31
% African American	4
% Asian	6
% Caucasian	58
% Hispanic	7
% Native American	1
% international	4
# of countries represented	34

SURVEY SAYS . . .
Class discussions encouraged
Athletic facilities need improving
Students aren't religious
Students love New York, NY
Great off-campus food
Intercollegiate sports are unpopular
or nonexistent
Intramural sports are unpopular or
nonexistent
Frats and sororities are unpopular or
nonexistent
(Almost) everyone smokes

ACADEMICS
Academic Rating	85
Calendar	semester
Student/faculty ratio	14:1
Profs interesting rating	81
Profs accessible rating	78
Most common	
reg class size	10–19 students
Most common	
lab size	10–19 students

STUDENTS SAY ". . ."

Academics

Eugene Lang College is an "unconventional," highly urban school with few academic requirements where courses have "really long poetic titles" and professors "go by their first names." "Lang is about small classes in a big city," summarizes a writing major. There's a "rich intellectual tradition" and, no matter what your major, an "interdisciplinary curriculum." "At Eugene Lang, you have the freedom to pursue your artistic or intellectual direction with absolute freedom," says a philosophy major. However, "students who are uncomfortable in a city and who are not excited about learning for learning's sake should not come to this school." Lang's "clueless," "incredibly bureaucratic" administration is hugely unpopular. The "approachable" and monolithically "radical" faculty is a mixed bag. "seventy-five percent of the professors are pure gold, but the 25 percent who are not really are awful." "Lang's greatest strength (other than location) is its seminar style of teaching," explains a first-year student. "I've yet to be in a class with more then 15 people." Students say their class discussions are phenomenal. "The students, however, at times can be somewhat draining." "All the teachers are highly susceptible to being led off on long tangents" and some "are too gentle and not comfortable shutting down wandering or irrelevant conversation." Juniors and seniors can take classes at several schools within the larger university (including Parsons The New School for Design and Mannes College The New School for Music). "So if Lang's ultra-liberal, writing-intensive seminars are too much," notes an urban studies major, "you can always take a break." Internships all over Manhattan are common, too.

Life

There are "great talks given on campus every week by a wide variety of academics on almost every social issue imaginable." Otherwise, "Lang is the anti-college experience." "There is very little community" on this speck of a campus on the northern end of Greenwich Village. "Space and facilities are limited." "There is no safe haven in the form of a communal student space" except for "a courtyard of a million cigarette butts." Certainly, "you aren't going to have the traditional college fun" here. On the other hand, few students anywhere else enjoy this glorious level of independence. "Life at Eugene Lang is integrated completely with living in New York City," and "you have the entire city at your fingertips." When you walk out of class, "you walk out into a city of 9 million people." There are dorms here, but "most students have apartments," especially after freshman year. For fun, Lang students sometimes "hang around other students' apartments and smoke pot." Many "thoroughly enjoy the club scene." Mostly though, "people band into small groups and then go out adventuring in the city" where "there is always something to do that you've never done, or even heard of, before."

Student Body

"Lang offers the kids with dreadlocks and piercings an alternative place to gather, smoke, and write pretentious essays." It's "overrun with rabid hipsters." "Cool hair" and "avant-garde" attitudes proliferate. So do "tight pants." "Every student at Lang thinks they are an atypical student." "There is a running joke that all Lang students were 'that kid' in high school," says a senior. "Shock is very popular around here," and "everyone fits in as long as they are not too mainstream." "It's the normal ones who have the trouble," suggests a sophomore. "But once they take up smoking and embrace their inner hipster, everything's cool." "There are a lot of queer students, who seem to be comfortable." "We're really not all that ethnically diverse," admits a first-year student. There are "less affluent kids due to great financial aid," and there is a strong contingent of "trust-fund babies" and "over-privileged communists from Connecticut." "Most students are wealthy but won't admit it," says a senior. "To be from a rich family and have it be apparent is a cardinal sin." "Most students are extremely liberal and on the same wavelength politically." "Conservative kids are the freaks at our school. Left is in. But having a Republican in class is so exciting," suggest a senior. "We can finally have a debate."

EUGENE LANG COLLEGE THE NEW SCHOOL FOR LIBERAL ARTS

FINANCIAL AID: 212-229-8930 • E-MAIL: LANG@NEWSCHOOL.EDU • WEBSITE: WWW.LANG.EDU

THE PRINCETON REVIEW SAYS

Admissions

Very important factors considered include: Application essay, academic GPA, recommendation(s), rigor of secondary school record. *Important factors considered include:* Standardized test scores, character/personal qualities, interview, level of applicant's interest, volunteer work. *Other factors considered include:* Class rank, alumni/ae relation, extracurricular activities, first generation, geographical residence, work experience. SAT or ACT required. TOEFL required of all international applicants. High school diploma is required and GED is accepted. *Academic units required:* 4 English. *Academic units recommended:* 3 mathematics, 3 science, 2 foreign language, 3 social studies, 2 history.

Financial Aid

Students should submit: FAFSA. The Princeton Review suggests that all financial aid forms be submitted as soon as possible after 1/1. *Need-based scholarships/grants offered:* Federal Pell, SEOG, state scholarships/grants, private scholarships, the school's own gift aid. *Loan aid offered:* FFEL Subsidized Stafford, FFEL Unsubsidized Stafford, FFEL PLUS, Federal Perkins, college/university loans from institutional funds. Applicants will be notified of awards on a rolling basis beginning 3/1. Federal Work-Study Program available. Institutional employment available.

The Inside Word

The college draws a very self-selected and intellectually curious pool. Those who demonstrate little self-motivation will find themselves denied. It would be a terrible idea to blow off the interview here.

THE SCHOOL SAYS ". . ."

From The Admissions Office

"Eugene Lang College offers students of diverse backgrounds an innovative and creative approach to a liberal arts education, combining the stimulating classroom activity of a small, intimate college with the rich resources of a dynamic, urban university—The New School. The curriculum at Lang is challenging and flexible. Small classes, limited in size to 18 students, promote energetic and thoughtful discussions, and writing is an essential component of all classes. Students can earn a bachelor's degree in Liberal Arts by designing their own program of study within one of 14 interdisciplinary areas in the arts, social sciences, and humanities. Lang also offers bachelor's degrees in the Arts (pending New York State approval), Culture and Media, Economics, Education Studies, Environmental Studies (pending New York State approval), History (pending New York State approval), Philosophy, and Psychology. Students have the opportunity to pursue a five-year BA/BFA or BA/MA with other programs offered at the university. Lang's Greenwich Village location puts many of the city's cultural treasures—museums, libraries, music venues, theaters, and more—at your doorstep."

SELECTIVITY
Admissions Rating	88
# of applicants	1,984
% of applicants accepted	55
% of acceptees attending	27

FRESHMAN PROFILE
Range SAT Critical Reading	550–660
Range SAT Math	500–610
Range SAT Writing	560–670
Range ACT Composite	23–27
Minimum paper TOEFL	550
Minimum web-based TOEFL	92
Average HS GPA	3.3
% graduated top 10% of class	29
% graduated top 25% of class	73
% graduated top 50% of class	91

DEADLINES
Early decision	
Deadline	11/15
Notification	12/15
Regular	
Deadline	2/1
Notification	rolling
Nonfall registration?	yes

FINANCIAL FACTS
Financial Aid Rating	74
Annual tuition	$32,350
Room and board	$15,260
Required fees	$710
Books and supplies	$2,050
% frosh rec. need-based scholarship or grant aid	56
% UG rec. need-based scholarship or grant aid	51
% frosh rec. non-need-based scholarship or grant aid	7
% UG rec. non-need-based scholarship or grant aid	6
% frosh rec. need-based self-help aid	57
% UG rec. need-based self-help aid	52
% UG borrow to pay for school	68
Average cumulative indebtedness	$21,511

THE EVERGREEN STATE COLLEGE

2700 EVERGREEN PARKWAY, NORTHWEST, OFFICE OF ADMISSIONS, OLYMPIA, WA 98505 • ADMISSIONS: 360-867-6170 • FAX: 360-867-5114

CAMPUS LIFE
Quality of Life Rating	**72**
Fire Safety Rating	**83**
Green Rating	**99**
Type of school	public
Environment	city

STUDENTS
Total undergrad enrollment	4,228
% male/female	45/55
% from out of state	28
% live on campus	22
% African American	5
% Asian	5
% Caucasian	70
% Hispanic	5
% Native American	3
% international	1
# of countries represented	13

SURVEY SAYS . . .
Lots of liberal students
Low cost of living
Frats and sororities are unpopular or nonexistent
Political activism is popular
(Almost) no one smokes

ACADEMICS
Academic Rating	**77**
Calendar	quarter
Student/faculty ratio	22:1
Profs interesting rating	86
Profs accessible rating	74
Most common reg class size	20–29 students

STUDENTS SAY ". . ."

Academics

The Evergreen State College takes a decidedly different approach to higher education. At this small public school, there are no grades. Collaboration is encouraged, and coursework is entirely interdisciplinary. Each term, Evergreen students sign up for one course or "program," through which a single topic is explored by a team of teachers from a variety of different subject areas. Many students choose Evergreen precisely for this type of academic freedom, saying it's the right school for "students who want to engineer their education instead of being handed a list of requirements and sent on their way." A current student elaborates, "the interdisciplinary programs have allowed me to learn things I would never have expected—like microscopy in an art class or critical theory in a history class. It's allowed me to find what I'm truly passionate about and pursue it." On this "green" campus, the environmental studies program is very strong, and the "forest land is often utilized for learning experiences." In fact, "field trips are common" in many programs, and there is an "emphasis on group projects and on hands-on work here. At Evergreen you learn by doing, not just by reading about it." Usually addressed by their first name, "the professors at Evergreen are more than teachers; they are your partner in education and dedicate themselves to facilitating the students' learning." By the same token, students say it's important to do a little research before signing up for courses because "a personal dispute with a professor can be a big problem."

Life

There is no Greek system and no football team, but that doesn't mean the Evergreen campus lacks spirit, pride, or culture. On the contrary, "there is always something going on" at Evergreen, and, for those living on campus, "social life is very vivid." With acres of pristine forest surrounding the school grounds, "many students go walking in the woods to socialize, unwind, and appreciate its almost natural state." In addition, outdoorsy activities like "hiking, kayaking, biking, and snowboarding" are popular pastimes. On campus, "there are clubs and student organizations for pretty much anything you can imagine, from the 'Evergreen Jesus Folk' to the local SDS chapter." A student enthuses, "I've also started trying tons of new activities since I got here. Now I go to yoga twice a week; I go rock climbing all the time; I go swimming a bunch and to the sauna; I go down to the beach and into the woods pretty frequently; [and] I do a lot more bike riding and reading." There is a modest party scene on and off campus, yet Evergreen students tend toward mellower activities. In their free time, "most people take the bus or ride their bikes downtown to see a show or have a meal at a café," and potluck dinner parties are "one of the main social outlets in Olympia." For those who like to boogie, "there are a lot of musicians on campus, and there is a thriving music scene in Olympia."

Student Life

Evergreen is a "quirky" college and, as such, it tends to attract students looking for something other than the classic undergraduate experience. There is "no typical student" at Evergreen, but you'll definitely meet your share of "hipster, coffee-shop types" and "Earth-friendly, artsy types" at this alternative school. A sophomore jokes, "I'm not sure what you would have to wear to not fit in at Evergreen—maybe a suit and tie?" Politically and socially, "the student body definitely swings left, with a large portion of students interested in environmental conservation, organic farming, LGBT rights, and Eastern philosophy and religion." While "hiking boots, sweaters, and bicycles are everywhere," students say there is more diversity at Evergreen than meets the eye. A current student shares, "I have had classes with any type of student one can imagine. I've had seminar with WWII Navy veterans sitting next to radical freshman activists." On that note, Evergreen attracts many returning students, and undergraduates "range from young to old, experienced in life to just out of high school, living with parents to having children of their own."

THE EVERGREEN STATE COLLEGE

FINANCIAL AID: 360-867-6205 • E-MAIL: ADMISSIONS@EVERGREEN.EDU • WEBSITE: WWW.EVERGREEN.EDU

THE PRINCETON REVIEW SAYS

Admissions

Very important factors considered include: Application essay, academic GPA, rigor of secondary school record, *Important factors considered include:* standardized test scores, first generation, level of applicant's interest. *Other factors considered include:* recommendation(s), extracurricular activities, interview, volunteer work, work experience. SAT or ACT required; TOEFL required of all international applicants. High school diploma is required and GED is accepted. *Academic units required:* 4 English, 3 mathematics, 2 science, (1 science labs), 2 foreign language, 3 social studies, 1 academic electives, 1 Fine, visual or performing arts elective or other college prep elective from the areas above.

Financial Aid

Students should submit: FAFSA, institution's own financial aid form. The Princeton Review suggests that all financial aid forms be submitted as soon as possible after 1/1. Need-based scholarships/grants offered: Federal Pell, SEOG, state scholarships/grants, private scholarships, the school's own gift aid, Federal Academic Competitiveness Grant (ACG); National Science and Mathematics Access to Retain Talent Grant (SMART Grant). *Loan aid offered:* FFEL Subsidized Stafford, FFEL Unsubsidized Stafford, FFEL PLUS, Federal Perkins, private alternative loans. Applicants will be notified of awards on a rolling basis beginning 4/1. Federal Work-Study Program available. Institutional employment available. Off-campus job opportunities are good.

The Inside Word

While admissions are not particularly selective, many students enter Evergreen with a strong academic record. Evergreen places a lot of credence in character and personal qualities when making admissions decisions. The school's atypical academic program calls for a curious and independent spirit, and admissions officers want to ensure that applicants will have the maturity to direct their own educational development.

THE SCHOOL SAYS "..."

From The Admissions Office

"Evergreen, a public college of arts and sciences, is a national leader in developing full-time interdisciplinary studies programs. Students work closely with faculty (there are no teaching assistants) to study an issue or theme from the perspective of several academic disciplines. They apply what's learned to real world issues, complete projects in groups, and discuss concepts in seminars that typically involve a faculty member and 22 students. The emphasis on seminars, interdisciplinary problem solving, and collaboration means students are well prepared for graduate school and the world of work. Our students tend to be politically active, environmentally savvy, and more concerned about social justice than competition and personal gain.

"All applicants are encouraged to complete a Free Application for Federal Student Aid (FAFSA). Evergreen's priority financial aid deadline is March 15, though applicants may submit the form later and may be awarded aid if funds are still available.

"Freshman applicants are required to submit test scores from either the SAT or ACT tests. The student's best composite score will be used in the admissions process."

SELECTIVITY

Admissions Rating	79
# of applicants	1,989
% of applicants accepted	94
% of acceptees attending	35

FRESHMAN PROFILE

Range SAT Critical Reading	530–660
Range SAT Math	470–600
Range ACT Composite	22–27
Minimum paper TOEFL	550
Minimum computer TOEFL	213
Minimum web-based TOEFL	79
Average HS GPA	3.05
% graduated top 10% of class	9
% graduated top 25% of class	22
% graduated top 50% of class	61

DEADLINES

Regular	
Priority	3/1
Notification	rolling
Nonfall registration?	yes

APPLICANTS ALSO LOOK AT
AND OFTEN PREFER
Western Washington University
University of California—Santa Cruz
University of Washington

AND SOMETIMES PREFER
Hampshire College
Central Washington University
Washington State University

AND RARELY PREFER
Pacific Lutheran University
Lewis & Clark College
University of Oregon

FINANCIAL FACTS

Financial Aid Rating	69
Annual in-state tuition	$4,797
Annual out-of-state tuition	$15,657
Room and board	$8,052
Required fees	$546
Books and supplies	$924
% frosh rec. need-based scholarship or grant aid	28
% UG rec. need-based scholarship or grant aid	46
% frosh rec. non-need-based scholarship or grant aid	22
% UG rec. non-need-based scholarship or grant aid	9
% frosh rec. need-based self-help aid	25
% UG rec. need-based self-help aid	43
% frosh rec. athletic scholarships	1
% UG rec. athletic scholarships	1
% frosh rec. any financial aid	40
% UG rec. any financial aid	54
% UG borrow to pay for school	51
Average cumulative indebtedness	$15,597

FAIRFIELD UNIVERSITY

1073 NORTH BENSON ROAD, FAIRFIELD, CT 06824 • ADMISSIONS: 203-254-4100 • FAX: 203-254-4199

CAMPUS LIFE

Quality of Life Rating	**75**
Fire Safety Rating	**91**
Green Rating	**88**
Type of school	private
Affiliation	Roman Catholic-Jesuit
Environment	town

STUDENTS

Total undergrad enrollment	3,948
% male/female	42/58
% from out of state	76
% from public high school	54
% live on campus	79
% African American	3
% Asian	3
% Caucasian	61
% Hispanic	7
% international	1
# of countries represented	47

SURVEY SAYS . . .
Great library
Diversity lacking on campus
Great off-campus food
Frats and sororities are unpopular or nonexistent
Student publications are popular
Lots of beer drinking
Hard liquor is popular

ACADEMICS

Academic Rating	**81**
Calendar	semester
Student/faculty ratio	12:1
Profs interesting rating	85
Profs accessible rating	82
Most common reg class size	20–29 students

MOST POPULAR MAJORS
communication studies/speech
communication and rhetoric
finance
nursing/registered nurse
(RN, ASN, BSN, MSN)

STUDENTS SAY ". . ."

Academics

Study amongst the trees of the "breathtaking campus" at Fairfield University, a competitive mid-sized school with a Division I basketball team and Jesuit ideals. A stalwart of the preppy New England college scene, the school has wealth and is definitely "image conscious," but financial aid packages are said to be super for students in need." Fairfield's extremely rigorous and time-consuming core courses ensure that students receive a well-rounded education, and the small enrollment assures students small class sizes once they move beyond the mandatory curriculum. The school's Connecticut location is just an hour away from New York City, which provides a plethora of work study and internship possibilities for the students. This is especially convenient for students in Fairfield's notably strong nursing and business programs, the latter of which is taught by a faculty mostly comprised of current and ex-professionals.

Though students are generally happy here, thanks to an involved student government and a high quality of life, many wish that there was "more school spirit" amongst the student body. The "Leviathan" administration has not curried much favor with students, with the Registrar, Career Planning and the Division of Student Affairs receiving singular complaints. Complaints of inefficacy and bureaucracy abound, and the various offices "act in distinct bubbles, with one hand not knowing what the other is doing." Opinions of professors are at the opposite end of the spectrum, as most find almost all their teachers "extremely engaging" and "wonderful people." "They actually read your essays and provide constructive criticism," says a student. "Professors have been amazing, inspiring, accessible, and have defined my time at Fairfield," says another.

Life

Not surprising for a school with an "ideal party location on the beaches of the Long Island Sound, only an hour north of New York City by train," students here like to drink. Although all go to "most of the classes," they know that they "must leave time for going out on Tuesdays, Thursdays, and the weekend," making Fairfield "the opposite of a suitcase school." "Weekends are usually for partying, whether it's a townhouse party or a party down at the beach."There are some great bars in town, too. This isn't to say that hedonism completely rules the school; many students remain very active in student activities and service organizations, and for those who don't want to party, the late-night programming "offers tons of activities and trips almost every Thursday, Friday, and Saturday night." The student government organizes many of these events, as well as trips into the city for Broadway performances, comedy shows, and sporting events.

Student Body

Almost everyone hails from the Northeast at this "homogenous, preppy school" with "generally very intelligent" students. Pockets run pretty deep amongst students, which leads some of this "Ugg wearing, blond haired, Seven for All Mankind-wearing" crowd to "think they're God's gift to mankind." There are plenty of "more mellow, normal folks" here, and even though "it doesn't take much" to be considered an atypical student, those who are usually "find their own niche and have no problems living their lives the way they wish." The school is attempting to increase this diversity—minority enrollment has increased in the past years, and there's a "growing gay and lesbian population."

FINANCIAL AID: 203-254-4125 • E-MAIL: ADMIS@MAIL.FAIRFIELD.EDU • WEBSITE: WWW.FAIRFIELD.EDU

THE PRINCETON REVIEW SAYS

Admissions

Very important factors considered include: Application essay, academic GPA, recommendation(s), rigor of secondary school record, standardized test scores. *Important factors considered include:* Character/personal qualities, extracurricular activities, first generation, talent/ability, volunteer work, work experience. *Other factors considered include:* Class rank, alumni/ae relation, geographical residence, interview, racial/ethnic status. SAT or ACT optional. TOEFL required of all international applicants. High school diploma is required and GED is not accepted. *Academic units required:* 4 English, 3 mathematics, 2 science (2 science labs), 2 foreign language, 2 social studies, 2 history, 1 academic elective. *Academic units recommended:* 4 English, 4 mathematics, 3 science (2 science labs), 4 foreign language, 2 social studies, 2 history, 1 academic elective.

Financial Aid

Students should submit: FAFSA, CSS/financial aid profile, noncustodial profile, business/farm supplement. Regular filing deadline is 2/15. The Princeton Review suggests that all financial aid forms be submitted as soon as possible after 1/1. *Need-based scholarships/grants offered:* Federal Pell, SEOG, state scholarships/grants, private scholarships, the school's own gift aid, United Negro College Fund. *Loan aid offered:* FFEL Subsidized Stafford, FFEL Unsubsidized Stafford, FFEL PLUS, Federal Perkins, alternative loans. Applicants will be notified of awards on or about 4/1. Federal Work-Study Program available. Institutional employment available. Off-campus job opportunities are good.

The Inside Word

Steady increases in the number of admission applications has nicely increased selectivity in recent years. Fairfield's campus and central location, combined with improvements to the library, campus center, classrooms, athletic facilities, and campus residences, make this a campus worth seeing.

THE SCHOOL SAYS ". . ."

From The Admissions Office

"Fairfield University welcomes students of unique promise into a learning and living community that will give them a solid intellectual foundation and the confidence they need to reach their individual goals. Students at Fairfield benefit from the deep-rooted Jesuit commitment to education of the whole person—mind, body, and spirit, and our admission policies are consistent with that mission. When considering an applicant, Fairfield looks at measures of academic achievement, students' curricular and extracurricular activities, their life skills and accomplishments, and the degree to which they have an appreciation for Fairfield's mission and outlook. In keeping with its holistic review process, Fairfield is test optional for undergraduate students seeking admission for the fall of 2010 and beyond. Students who decide not to submit SAT or ACT scores will be required to write an additional essay and are encouraged to participate in an admission interview.

"Fairfield University students are challenged to be creative and active members of a community in which diversity is encouraged and honored. With its commitment to education for an inspired life, Fairfield has developed a unique educational model to ensure that students receive the guidance they need to reach their fullest potential. The integration of living and learning is at the heart of a Fairfield education through students' participation in living and learning communities, vocational exploration, civic engagement, and finally, discernment of how they want to put their gifts and education to work in the world. As a result of this holistic model of education, Fairfield graduates are highly successful in gaining admission to selective graduate schools, while others achieve satisfying careers. A signification achievement for the university is that 52 Fairfield graduates have been tapped as Fulbright scholars since 1993."

SELECTIVITY

Admissions Rating	90
# of applicants	8,732
% of applicants accepted	59
% of acceptees attending	17
# accepting a place on wait list	946
% admitted from wait list	13

FRESHMAN PROFILE

Range SAT Critical Reading	520–610
Range SAT Math	540–630
Range SAT Writing	540–630
Range ACT Composite	23–27
Minimum paper TOEFL	550
Minimum computer TOEFL	213
Minimum web-based TOEFL	80
Average HS GPA	3.41
% graduated top 10% of class	38
% graduated top 25% of class	76
% graduated top 50% of class	98

DEADLINES

Early action	
Deadline	11/15
Notification	1/1
Regular	
Deadline	1/15
Notification	4/1
Nonfall registration?	no

APPLICANTS ALSO LOOK AT
AND OFTEN PREFER
Boston College
AND SOMETIMES PREFER
Fordham University
College of the Holy Cross
Villanova University
Providence College

FINANCIAL FACTS

Financial Aid Rating	77
Annual tuition	$36,900
Room and board	$11,270
Required fees	$590
Books and supplies	$900
% frosh rec. need-based scholarship or grant aid	48
% UG rec. need-based scholarship or grant aid	45
% frosh rec. non-need-based scholarship or grant aid	19
% UG rec. non-need-based scholarship or grant aid	14
% frosh rec. need-based self-help aid	47
% UG rec. need-based self-help aid	43
% frosh rec. athletic scholarships	9
% UG rec. athletic scholarships	7
% frosh rec. any financial aid	68
% UG rec. any financial aid	63
% UG borrow to pay for school	59
Average cumulative indebtedness	$32,857

FISK UNIVERSITY

1000 SEVENTEENTH AVENUE NORTH, NASHVILLE, TN 37208-3051 • ADMISSIONS: 615-329-8665 • FAX: 615-329-8774

CAMPUS LIFE
Quality of Life Rating	**62**
Fire Safety Rating	**60***
Green Rating	**60***
Type of school	private
Environment	metropolis

STUDENTS
Total undergrad enrollment	812
% from out of state	71
% from public high school	85
% live on campus	65
% in (# of) fraternities	15 (4)
% in (# of) sororities	20 (4)
% African American	98
% international	2
# of countries represented	5

SURVEY SAYS . . .
Athletic facilities need improving
Students are friendly
Lousy food on campus
Great off-campus food
Low cost of living
Frats and sororities dominate social
scene
Musical organizations are popular
Student government is popular
Very little drug use

ACADEMICS
Academic Rating	**76**
Calendar	semester
Student/faculty ratio	12:1
Profs interesting rating	70
Profs accessible rating	65
%·profs teaching	
UG courses	100
% classes taught by TAs	0

STUDENTS SAY ". . ."

Academics

With its rich past and impressive list of alumni, Historically Black College/University Fisk University is "about history and continuing a legacy." But history and legacy alone wouldn't be enough to attract top students to this small Nashville school. To do that, Fisk has to deliver the goods, and it does: Fisk graduates more than three-quarters of its enrollees, more than 70 percent of whom go on to graduate and professional schools. Indeed, for every student who mentioned Fisk's illustrious history as a reason for choosing the school, at least two cite Fisk's reputation for "graduating African Americans to become wonderful professionals" as a reason to attend. As one student puts it, "Fisk University is all about nurturing young black people with the goal of preparing them to thrive" in the world while remaining committed to "community involvement." With fewer than 1,000 undergraduates and limited finances, Fisk must focus its efforts on a few key disciplines. Departments that track to health care careers—biology, physics, chemistry, nursing, and psychology—fare well, as do computer science and business administration. A core curriculum encompassing humanities, mathematics, and science ensures that everyone leaves with a well-rounded education. The school's size results in "wonderful" relationships with professors who "actually care about your matriculation through the school." The faculty "is generally very approachable" and they "take the time to work with you when you request help." Academics are "rigorous," and the mantra on campus is "Success is in the details (by which we mean diversity, excellence, teamwork, accountability, integrity, leadership, service)." Fisk also excels at procuring "internships and study-abroad" opportunities.

Life

At a school as small as Fisk, "campus life can be boring," and many students say they are "sheltered and separated from the real world." For some (especially freshmen, who are not yet fully integrated into campus life and often lack automobiles), free time consists of little more than "going out to the yard to throw the football around or hanging in the lounge playing spades, pool, or watching TV. Just enjoying one another's company is making our own fun." The campus sponsors a number of activities, including "step shows, organizational meetings, choir, sports, clubs, dances, yard gatherings, etc." Social life centers on Fisk's Greek organizations and the Jubilee Singers, the school's world-renowned singing group, famous for its repertoire of slave spirituals. On the weekends, "Students go to clubs or Greek-hosted parties," but are just as likely to head out to Nashville for fun. Nashville is a great music town, and as a tourist destination, boasts many attractions, including great restaurants, amusement parks, and plenty of shopping. Fisk fields 15 NAIA athletic teams, seven for men (basketball, baseball, soccer, tennis, cross-country, track, and golf) and eight for women (basketball, softball, volleyball, cross-country, tennis, track, soccer, and golf).

Student Body

Fisk is a "small school" with a "family environment," even though "the only thing most students share in common is that we are all black. There are, however, many different types of students," from those who "are first-generation college students to others who are fourth- and fifth-generation Fiskites." Undergraduates come from "various regions of the country" and all across the world, and range in personality types from "the really wild kids who are always partying to the students in really hard majors who no one ever sees to the different cliques of rich girls, international students, etc." With many students hailing from Tennessee and nearby states, "southern hospitality" and "sociable" natures are the norm among students at Fisk.

FINANCIAL AID: 615-329-8735 • E-MAIL: ADMISSIONS@FISK.EDU • WEBSITE: WWW.FISK.EDU

THE PRINCETON REVIEW SAYS

Admissions

Very important factors considered include: Rigor of secondary school record. *Important factors considered include:* Class rank, application essay, academic GPA, standardized test scores, character/personal qualities, extracurricular activities, interview. *Other factors considered include:* Recommendation(s), alumni/ae relation, geographical residence, level of applicant's interest, talent/ability, volunteer work. SAT or ACT required. ACT with Writing component recommended. TOEFL required of all international applicants. High school diploma is required and GED is accepted. *Academic units required:* 4 English, 3 mathematics, 3 science (2 science labs), 1 foreign language, 1 history. *Academic units recommended:* 4 English, 4 mathematics, 3 science (2 science labs), 2 foreign language, 1 history.

Financial Aid

Students should submit: FAFSA. The Princeton Review suggests that all financial aid forms be submitted as soon as possible after January 1. *Need-based scholarships/grants offered:* Pell Grant, SEOG, state scholarships/grants, private scholarships, the school's own gift aid, United Negro College Fund. *Loan aid offered:* Direct Subsidized Stafford, Direct Unsubsidized Stafford, Direct PLUS, FFEL PLUS, Federal Perkins Loan. Applicants will be notified of awards on a rolling basis beginning or about April 1. Federal Work-Study Program available. Off-campus job opportunities are excellent.

The Inside Word

Intangibles can play a big part in the admissions decision at Fisk, especially for borderline candidates. A marked improvement in high school grades during junior and senior years, a demonstrated high level of determination, and commitment to school, community, and/or church can all help create a successful application.

THE SCHOOL SAYS "..."

From The Admissions Office

"Founded in 1866, the university is coeducational, private, and one of America's premier Historically Black Universities. The first black college to be granted a chapter of Phi Beta Kappa Honor Society, Fisk serves a diverse student body with students from 40 states and 6 foreign countries. There are residence halls for men and women. The focal point of the 40-acre campus and architectural symbol of the university is Jubilee Hall, the first permanent building for the education of blacks in the South, named for the internationally renowned Fisk Jubilee Singers, who continue their tradition of singing and sharing classic Negro spirituals along with other genres of music from African, Brazilian, African American and other diverse cultures. From its earliest days, Fisk faculty and alumni have been among America's intellectual leaders providing leadership in several fields including medicine, science, art, humanities, religion, literature, sociology and philosophy. Fisk Alumni include W. E. B. Du Bois, the first black Ph.D. from Harvard, and co-founder of the NAACP, Nikki Giovanni, poet/writer; Dr. John Hope Franklin, historian/scholar; David Lewis, professor/recipient of the prestigious Pulitzer Prize; Hazel O'Leary, Fisk President and former U.S. Secretary of Energy; John Lewis, U.S. Representative (GA); Judith Jamison, director of the Alvin Ailey Dance Company; and Johnetta B. Cole, former President of Spelman College. In proportion to its size, Fisk continues to contribute a higher percentage of African American alumni to the ranks of scholars pursuing doctoral degrees than any other institution in the United States."

SELECTIVITY

Admissions Rating	83
# of applicants	2,700
% of applicants accepted	45
% of acceptees attending	51

FRESHMAN PROFILE

Range SAT Critical Reading	467–546
Range SAT Math	455–540
Range SAT Writing	447–547
Range ACT Composite	18–23
Minimum paper TOEFL	550
Average HS GPA	3.33
% graduated top 10% of class	10
% graduated top 25% of class	30
% graduated top 50% of class	75

DEADLINES

Early action	
Deadline	12/1
Notification	12/20
Regular	
Priority	3/1
Deadline	3/1
Notification	rolling

FINANCIAL FACTS

Financial Aid Rating	72
Comprehensive fee	$15,140
Room and board	$7,730
Required fees	$1,100
Books and supplies	$1,500

FLAGLER COLLEGE

74 KING STREET, PO BOX 1027, ST. AUGUSTINE, FL 32085-1027 • ADMISSIONS: 800-304-4208 • FAX: 904-826-0094

CAMPUS LIFE
Quality of Life Rating	**76**
Fire Safety Rating	**89**
Green Rating	**65**
Type of school	private
Environment	town

STUDENTS
Total undergrad enrollment	2,651
% male/female	41/59
% from out of state	39
% from public high school	78
% live on campus	40
% African American	2
% Asian	1
% Caucasian	88
% Hispanic	4
% international	1
# of countries represented	34

SURVEY SAYS . . .
Low cost of living
Frats and sororities are unpopular or nonexistent
(Almost) no one smokes

ACADEMICS
Academic Rating	**76**
Calendar	semester
Student/faculty ratio	21:1
Profs interesting rating	85
Profs accessible rating	80
Most common reg class size	20–29 students

MOST POPULAR MAJORS
business/commerce
communication, journalism,
elementary education and teaching

STUDENTS SAY ". . ."

Academics

Students "like the small-school feel" of Flagler College, an intimate liberal arts school with "an excellent education program" (including "one of the best deaf education programs in the country") and a "sound business department." Programs in communication, English, and graphic design also earn students' praises. No matter what they study, Flagler undergrads "actually get the chance to have a personal relationship with professors" who "are always there to help. They take a genuine interest and concern in the students. Most have their doctorates and are very knowledgeable about the classes they teach." The faculty also boasts some impressive real-world credentials; writes one business major, "I have professors who work for the FBI teaching us about criminal justice, major CEO's giving business lessons, and a retired judge teaching me about law and society. I have the best of all worlds. I really enjoy the curriculum and the small classrooms that make learning much more accessible." On the downside, the school's administration is widely regarded as "extremely conservative. It is like living with your parents when you are on campus if they were staunch Pat Robertson supporters." The most prominent example of this paternalism is a relatively strict class attendance policy, which many regard as "repressive and demeaning to students. We are adults, and if we have not learned to manage our time appropriately by now, we have much bigger problems than missing classes." Some, however, appreciate how the policy "keeps us in check."

Life

The conservatism of Flagler's administration is most evident in the way it governs campus life. Students report that "there is a no-tolerance rule on-campus for alcohol (it is not allowed in the dorms, and you cannot be on-campus drunk)" and "there is a no inter-dorm visitation policy (no guys/girls allowed in each other's halls)," restrictions that many find "Draconian and unnecessary." Fortunately there's a simple work-around; "We mostly just hang off-campus at other students' houses." More than half of all students, including a large majority of non-freshmen, live off-campus. Hometown St. Augustine is "a tourist town" that "does not cater to the college but rather the tourist. Shops and places close at 8 P.M.," and town police tend to act quickly to discourage off-campus rowdiness, so Flagler parties tend to be "smaller get-togethers" rather than raging Bacchanalias. But here again students find acceptable alternatives; "Jacksonville is only a 30-minute drive, and we are also very close to Daytona. And there is always the beach," one explains. Intramural sports "are really popular on-campus," and "there are a ton of clubs on-campus for every kind of interest." All in all, "life at Flagler is pretty easygoing." a situation that fits most students' temperaments.

Student Body

Flagler draws a lot of "artsy types with a unique style and attitude...many of whom are environmentally conscious," as well as a solid contingent of "religious types—intervarsity members and students that join local churches." Finally, "there are the surfers, who probably make up one-third of the campus. They chose to come here because they knew the school was near the beach." Most are "laid-back, easy-going individuals, although not in a lazy way." Flagler is academically rigorous, after all, so students must "work hard to achieve our goals and help each other achieve our goals," and many "have multiple majors and are academically inclined." Women substantially outnumber men here. While the majority of students are white Floridians, "the recruiters are doing excellent job of trying to diversify the student population."

FINANCIAL AID: 904-819-6225 • E-MAIL: ADMISS@FLAGLER.EDU • WEBSITE: WWW.FLAGLER.EDU

THE PRINCETON REVIEW SAYS

Admissions

Very important factors considered include: Rigor of secondary school record. *Important factors considered include:* Application essay, academic GPA, standardized test scores, alumni/ae relation, extracurricular activities. *Other factors considered include:* Class rank, recommendation(s), character/personal qualities, first generation, interview, level of applicant's interest, talent/ability, volunteer work. SAT or ACT required. TOEFL required of all international applicants. High school diploma is required and GED is accepted. *Academic units required:* 4 English, 3 mathematics, 2 science (1 science lab), 3 social studies, 1 history, 2 academic electives. *Academic units recommended:* 4 English, 4 mathematics, 3 science (2 science labs), 2 foreign language, 3 social studies, 2 history, 1 visual/performing arts, 1 computer science, 2 academic electives.

Financial Aid

Students should submit: FAFSA, institution's own financial aid form, state aid form. The Princeton Review suggests that all financial aid forms be submitted as soon as possible after 1/1. *Need-based scholarships/grants offered:* Federal Pell, SEOG, state scholarships/grants, private scholarships, the school's own gift aid. *Loan aid offered:* Direct Subsidized Stafford, Direct Unsubsidized Stafford, Direct PLUS, Federal Perkins, private alternative loans. Applicants will be notified of awards on a rolling basis beginning 4/1. Federal Work-Study Program available. Institutional employment available. Off-campus job opportunities are excellent.

The Inside Word

Several high-profile programs, a desirable location, and a small, incoming freshman class all conspire to drive down Flagler's admissions rate. Still, Flagler is not top-tier when it comes to selectivity, and strong candidates should meet little resistance from the admissions office. Admission as a prospective education major requires a minimum 1010 combined SAT score; admission to the department itself occurs by the end of sophomore year and is dependent on the student's performance at Flagler during the first two years.

THE SCHOOL SAYS "..."

From The Admissions Office

"Flagler College is an independent, 4-year, coeducational, residential institution located in picturesque St. Augustine. A famous historic tourist center in northeast Florida, it is located to the south of Jacksonville and north of Daytona Beach. Flagler students have ample opportunity to explore the rich cultural heritage and international flavor of St. Augustine, and there's always time for a relaxing day at the beach, about four miles from campus. The annual cost for tuition, room, and board at Flagler is about the same as state universities. The small student body helps to keep one from becoming 'just a number.' Flagler serves a predominately full-time student body and seeks to enroll students who can benefit from the type of educational experience the college offers. Because of the college's unique mission and distinctive characteristics, some students may benefit more from an educational experience at Flagler than others. The college's admission standards and procedures are designed to select from among the applicants those students most likely to succeed academically, to contribute significantly to the student life program at Flagler, and to become graduates of the college. Flagler College provides an exceptional opportunity for a private education at an extremely affordable cost.

"All applicants to Flager College must submit either their SAT or ACT scores."

SELECTIVITY

Admissions Rating	88
# of applicants	2,368
% of applicants accepted	45
% of acceptees attending	58
# accepting a place on wait list	131
% admitted from wait list	17
# of early decision applicants	571
% accepted early decision	72

FRESHMAN PROFILE

Range SAT Critical Reading	520–580
Range SAT Math	510–580
Range SAT Writing	500–580
Range ACT Composite	21–25
Minimum paper TOEFL	550
Minimum computer TOEFL	213
Average HS GPA	3.29
% graduated top 10% of class	18
% graduated top 25% of class	49
% graduated top 50% of class	90

DEADLINES

Early decision	
Deadline	12/1
Notification	12/15
Regular	
Priority	1/15
Deadline	3/1
Notification	3/30
Nonfall registration?	yes

APPLICANTS ALSO LOOK AT
AND RARELY PREFER
Florida Southern College

FINANCIAL FACTS

Financial Aid Rating	75
Annual tuition	$13,300
Room and board	$7,190
Books and supplies	$1,100
% frosh rec. need-based scholarship or grant aid	25
% UG rec. need-based scholarship or grant aid	32
% frosh rec. non-need-based scholarship or grant aid	24
% UG rec. non-need-based scholarship or grant aid	30
% frosh rec. need-based self-help aid	25
% UG rec. need-based self-help aid	33
% frosh rec. athletic scholarships	3
% UG rec. athletic scholarships	4
% frosh rec. any financial aid	69
% UG rec. any financial aid	86
% UG borrow to pay for school	60.6
Average cumulative indebtedness	$18,415

FLORIDA SOUTHERN COLLEGE

OFFICE OF ADMISSIONS, 111 LAKE HOLLINGSWORTH DRIVE, LAKELAND, FL 33801 • ADMISSIONS: 800-274-4131 • FAX: 863-680-4120

CAMPUS LIFE
Quality of Life Rating	**76**
Fire Safety Rating	**79**
Green Rating	**72**
Type of school	private
Affiliation	Methodist
Environment	city

STUDENTS
Total undergrad enrollment	1,736
% male/female	41/59
% from out of state	24
% from public high school	79
% live on campus	70
% in (# of) fraternities	29 (5)
% in (# of) sororities	23 (6)
% African American	6
% Asian	2
% Caucasian	81
% Hispanic	7
% international	4
# of countries represented	31

SURVEY SAYS . . .
Athletic facilities are great
Great off-campus food
Intramural sports are popular
Musical organizations are popular
Student government is popular

ACADEMICS
Academic Rating	**78**
Calendar	semester
Student/faculty ratio	12:1
Profs interesting rating	76
Profs accessible rating	79
Most common reg class size	10–19 students
Most common lab size	10–19 students

MOST POPULAR MAJORS
biology/biological sciences
marketing/marketing management
psychology

STUDENTS SAY ". . ."

Academics
Florida Southern College offers "a fairly strong liberal arts core," a total community atmosphere," and a throng of degrees and majors. Standout programs include business, music, and the sciences. There is "an incredible education program," too. "Extremely exciting" study-abroad programs will take you to England, China, Australia, and many other places all across the globe. Class sizes are "small." FSC's "hands-on" administration "is very open to student ideas and easy to contact." The faculty is "a big mix." "Most of the professors are deeply committed to the students and will go to great lengths to help." "Teachers care when you miss class," says one student who appreciates the extra attention. "We don't have teaching assistants so the relationships are directly with the professors." "It is very uncommon" to have professors who don't "know you by name" "even if you only had them one time." Some professors "aren't so good," though. "A lot of professors are the only one teaching a particular subject, especially when you get to the upper-level classes in your major," one student told us.

Life
Florida Southern's lakefront campus is home to the largest single-site collection of Frank Lloyd Wright architecture on earth. As such, it's no wonder that students describe it as "very beautiful." Life here is "interactive" and "comfortable." The Greek system is somewhat big. The Wellness Center, the campus pool, and activities on Lake Hollingsworth are popular hang-out spots for students. There are fairly strict rules regarding when males and females can be "in each others' dorms." Also, FSC is "supposed to be a dry campus" but "everybody drinks, anyway." While it's theoretically possible to "go out every night and party," "It's not your typical *Animal House* scene" here. "It's more laid-back." The surrounding city of Lakeland "isn't too thrilling." A few "hole-in-the-wall bars" are the big draw on "Thursday nights" ("which makes Friday the most interesting class day"). For real off-campus fun, "Students often go to Tampa or Orlando," both just "short" rides away.

Students
"Everyone knows each other and gets along," notes one student. It's "one big community." "You can really be yourself here," says a sophomore, so just "being silly with [your] friends" isn't looked down on. "The majority of the campus is female," and from Florida, though about one-third of the students come from out of state. FSC students are "hardworking" and "energetic." Many are "rich" or, at least, "from a decently well-off family." Many others "act rich." Most students are "very friendly," though you will find a few "snotty" types. One student noted that "nearly the entire population is preppy." With a 15% ethnic diversity Florida Southern has one of the highest minority enrollments of any private institution of its size in the state. However students say that the presence of minority and international students remains an area in which the school could continue to grow. There are many "very religious" people on campus. "A lot of students" are "involved in Christian ministries." Politically, you can find "both conservative and liberal extremes" on campus.

FINANCIAL AID: 800-205-1600 • E-MAIL: FSCADM@FLSOUTHERN.EDU • WEBSITE: WWW.FLSOUTHERN.EDU

THE PRINCETON REVIEW SAYS

Admissions

Very important factors considered include: Academic GPA, rigor of secondary school record. *Important factors considered include:* Application essay, recommendation(s), standardized test scores, character/personal qualities, extracurricular activities, talent/ability. *Other factors considered include:* Class rank, alumni/ae relation, interview, level of applicant's interest, volunteer work, work experience. SAT or ACT required. TOEFL or IELTS required of all international applicants. High school diploma is required and GED is accepted. *Academic units required:* 4 English, 3 mathematics, 2 science (2 science labs), 3 social studies, 3 history, 2 academic electives. *Academic units recommended:* 2 foreign language.

Financial Aid

Students should submit: FAFSA, institution's own financial aid form. The Princeton Review suggests that all financial aid forms be submitted as soon as possible after 1/1. *Need-based scholarships/grants offered:* Federal Pell, SEOG, state scholarships/grants, private scholarships, the school's own gift aid. *Loan aid offered:* FFEL Subsidized Stafford, FFEL Unsubsidized Stafford, FFEL PLUS, Federal Perkins. Applicants will be notified of awards on a rolling basis beginning 3/1. Federal Work-Study Program available. Institutional employment available. Off-campus job opportunities are good.

The Inside Word

Individual attention is the cornerstone of a Florida Southern education and this sentiment extends to the admissions process. A close-knit community, admissions officers seek out applicants who best embody FSC's spirit and are likely to contribute to the campus' vitality. Focus is therefore paid not only on grades and test scores, but personal attributes and experiences that reveal involvement beyond the classroom. Candidates are encouraged to employ creative measures throughout their application and are welcome to submit additional academic materials and portfolio samples.

THE SCHOOL SAYS "..."

From The Admissions Office

"Florida Southern is friendly and dynamic, offering terrific engaged learning opportunities including student-faculty collaborative research and performance, study-abroad, service learning, and guaranteed internships. The College offers an unusually wide choice of undergraduate majors—50—such as art, business, communication, nursing, psychology, education, music performance, and biology, and a new self-designed major. Pre-professional programs include pre-med, pre-dental and pre-law. FSC is known for great professors and faculty mentors with a student-faculty ratio of 12:1. A new technology plan is being implemented to support dynamic instruction. Students have won national competitions in biology, advertising, and psychology. Forty percent of graduating seniors have studied abroad, 52 percent have completed formal internships, and 94 percent go on to professional or graduate school or land jobs in their chosen fields. Overlooking beautiful Lake Hollingsworth, Florida Southern is home to the world's largest collection of Frank Lloyd Wright architecture, which provides a stunning setting for living and learning. New campus additions include a Residential Life Center with bedroom views to the lake; the phenomenal Nina B. Hollis Wellness Center and adjacent Lakefront Program with kayaks, canoes, and sailboats; a cyber café serving Starbuck's products in the library; and an upcoming humanities building featuring a modern language lab and film studies center."

SELECTIVITY

Admissions Rating	83
# of applicants	2,110
% of applicants accepted	67
% of acceptees attending	35
# of early decision applicants	77
% accepted early decision	83

FRESHMAN PROFILE

Range SAT Critical Reading	470–580
Range SAT Math	490–580
Range SAT Writing	460–570
Range ACT Composite	20–25
Minimum paper TOEFL	550
Minimum IBT	79–80
Average HS GPA	3.4
% graduated top 10% of class	25
% graduated top 25% of class	53
% graduated top 50% of class	87

DEADLINES

Early decision	
Deadline	12/1
Notification	12/15
Regular	
Deadline	3/1
Notification	rolling
Nonfall registration?	yes

FINANCIAL FACTS

Financial Aid Rating	77
Annual tuition	$22,270
Required Fees	$525
Room and board	$8,242
Books	$1,150
% frosh rec. need-based scholarship or grant aid	51
% UG rec. need-based scholarship or grant aid	43
% frosh rec. non-need-based scholarship or grant aid	65
% UG rec. non-need-based scholarship or grant aid	55
% frosh rec. need-based self-help aid	43
% UG rec. need-based self-help aid	43
% frosh rec. athletic scholarships	10
% UG rec. athletic scholarships	13
% frosh rec. any financial aid	98
% UG rec. any financial aid	96
% UG borrow to pay for school	66
Average cumulative indebtedness	$19,864

FLORIDA STATE UNIVERSITY

2500 UNIVERSITY CENTER, TALLAHASSEE, FL 32306-2400 • ADMISSIONS: 850-644-6200 • FAX: 850-644-0197

CAMPUS LIFE

Quality of Life Rating	85
Fire Safety Rating	83
Green Rating	82
Type of school	public
Environment	city

STUDENTS

Total undergrad enrollment	29,405
% male/female	45/55
% from out of state	10.1
% from public high school	84
% in (# of) fraternities	18.1 (28)
% in (# of) sororities	18.3 (23)
% African American	10
% Asian	3
% Caucasian	72
% Hispanic	12
% Native American	1
# of countries represented	133

SURVEY SAYS . . .

Athletic facilities are great
Everyone loves the Seminoles

ACADEMICS

Academic Rating	72
Calendar	semester
Student/faculty ratio	20.5:1
Profs interesting rating	74
Profs accessible rating	74
% classes taught by TAs	28
Most common	
reg class size	20–29 students

MOST POPULAR MAJORS

criminal justice/safety studies
English language and literature
finance

STUDENTS SAY "..."

Academics

Florida State University, "a major research university in Florida's capital city," provides students "with lots of opportunities for experimentation" while "making pivotal career decisions." Indeed, it's difficult to imagine a school that provides more options; FSU offers excellent programs in everything from business, psychology, and education to music, graphic art, and creative writing to meteorology, professional golf management, and exercise science. The school even has a circus program! As at most big state schools, "Lecture classes are large and can be intimidating," but "teachers are always willing to help outside of class," and "taking advantage of this help can make or break your grade." Professors "are hit-or-miss," although "in general they are very nice and helpful and try to learn everyone's name, even when the class is fairly large." Those seeking a more personal experience should shoot for the honors program, "where class sizes are small" and "they really encourage research." FSU works hard to stay up to date, building "state-of-the-art facilities" and embracing technologies that make it "as convenient as possible for students and professors to communicate and achieve success." Partner campuses "in London, Valencia, Florence, and Panama with a variety of other programs across the world" facilitate wonderful study-abroad opportunities. As one student sums up, "Overall, if you're looking for a school with endless possibilities and opportunities, FSU is the place to be."

Life

FSU is "known for our house parties, kegs, and bonfires," and students readily admit that there's "a lot of drinking and partying" both on campus and throughout the city of Tallahassee. They also insist that "people are able to stay out of that scene and still have a lot of fun." Just about everyone loves football, telling us that "There's nothing better than Tallahassee in the fall on game day! A stadium full of fans doing the chop will give you chills every time." The Greek scene "is big here," but "there are lots of different scenes, from Greek to Black Student Union to Catholic Student Union to the film school kids. There are all sorts of clubs and groups to get involved with, especially if you're interested in getting out there and doing community service." There's even "a surprisingly big arts community, so there are always concerts, art exhibits, and independent coffee shops to check out if you don't mind digging a little to find them." And students can also enjoy "hookah lounges, a great cinema" and "a Chili's on campus (always busy, but delicious!)." In short, "The amount of student activities, sports clubs, and organizations are endless due to FSU's size." And for an added bonus: "The beach is only an hour away."

Student Body

"There's a bit of everything for everyone, and there's nothing that you don't see on campus" at FSU, where a student population of just less than 30,000 ensures a place for people of all types. Expect "a lot of southern hospitality," which basically centers on "making others feel welcome." The southern accent is also found in a vocal minority of conservative Christian students who "are into furthering their religious views within the school bounds" (one such student complained that the school had "a bias toward science and evolutionary thinking"). At the other end of the spectrum, "There are also a lot of vegetarian activists and recycling activists on campus." Lots of folks here "are in some sort of organization, probably multiple organizations. If they're not in a fraternity or sorority, they're probably in a religious group or something else."

FINANCIAL AID: 850-644-5871 • E-MAIL: ADMISSIONS@ADMIN.FSU.EDU • WEBSITE: WWW.FSU.EDU

THE PRINCETON REVIEW SAYS

Admissions

Very important factors considered include: Academic GPA, rigor of secondary school record. *Important factors considered include:* Standardized test scores, state residency, talent/ability. *Other factors considered include:* Class rank, application essay, recommendation(s), alumni/ae relation, character/personal qualities, extracurricular activities, first generation, geographical residence, volunteer work, work experience. SAT or ACT required. ACT with Writing component required. TOEFL required of all international applicants. High school diploma is required and GED is accepted. *Academic units required:* 4 English, 4 mathematics, 3 science (2 science labs), 2 foreign language, 1 social studies, 2 history, 3 academic electives. *Academic units recommended:* 4 English, 4 mathematics, 4 science (2 science labs), 4 foreign language, 2 social studies, 2 history, 3 academic electives.

Financial Aid

Students should submit: FAFSA. The Princeton Review suggests that all financial aid forms be submitted as soon as possible after 1/1. *Need-based scholarships/grants offered:* Federal Pell, SEOG, state scholarships/grants, private scholarships, the school's own gift aid. *Loan aid offered:* FFEL Subsidized Stafford, FFEL Unsubsidized Stafford, FFEL PLUS, Federal Perkins. Applicants will be notified of awards on a rolling basis beginning 3/15. Federal Work-Study Program available. Institutional employment available. Off-campus job opportunities are good.

The Inside Word

With 25,000 applications to process annually, FSU must rely on a formula-driven approach to triage its applicant pool. With the exception of applicants to special programs, only borderline candidates receive a truly thorough review; all others are either clearly in or clearly out based on grades, curriculum, and test scores. Candidates for programs in fine arts, creative arts, and performing arts must undergo a more rigorous review that includes a portfolio or audition.

THE SCHOOL SAYS "..."

From The Admissions Office

"Established in 1851, Florida State University is one of the nation's premier research universities, known for attracting leading scholars from all over the world and providing students with some of the best academic mentors of any university in the U.S. Sixteen colleges and schools offer nearly 200 undergraduate majors, 214 graduate degrees, and professional degrees in law and medicine. Florida State enjoys an excellent reputation for groundbreaking academic achievements, including establishing the first new medical college in the nation in 20 years. Technologically enhanced classrooms and wireless networking allow state-of-the-art teaching techniques in every discipline. Through the University Honors Program, faculty and undergraduate students who share academic interests can work on-on-one to design and conduct original research projects. Our innovative student services include an internationally renowned career center, a comprehensive campus-wide leadership learning program, and a center for community-based learning through service. World-class cultural events, championship athletics, extensive recreation facilities, and a friendly, close-knit university community enrich student life and extend learning well beyond the classroom. Our diverse student body hails from all 50 states and more than 130 countries, and our many international programs throughout the world include year-round programs in Florence, Italy; London, England; Panama City, Panama; and Valencia, Spain.

"Students applying to the university are required to submit the Writing section of the SAT or take the optional Writing test of the ACT. We will continue to use the highest subscores on the ACT and SAT for admission purposes."

SELECTIVITY

Admissions Rating	88
# of applicants	25,485
% of applicants accepted	47
% of acceptees attending	42
# accepting a place on wait list	667
% admitted from wait list	42

FRESHMAN PROFILE

Range SAT Critical Reading	550–640
Range SAT Math	560–650
Range ACT Composite	24–28
Minimum paper TOEFL	550
Minimum computer TOEFL	213
Average HS GPA	3.72
% graduated top 10% of class	31
% graduated top 25% of class	71
% graduated top 50% of class	96

DEADLINES

Regular	
Deadline	1/21
Nonfall registration?	yes

FINANCIAL FACTS

Financial Aid Rating	91
Annual in-state tuition	$4,007
Annual out-of-state tuition	$18,452
% frosh rec. need-based scholarship or grant aid	20
% UG rec. need-based scholarship or grant aid	21
% frosh rec. non-need-based scholarship or grant aid	32
% UG rec. non-need-based scholarship or grant aid	26
% frosh rec. need-based self-help aid	22
% UG rec. need-based self-help aid	27
% frosh rec. athletic scholarships	1
% UG rec. athletic scholarships	1
% frosh rec. any financial aid	98
% UG rec. any financial aid	88
% UG borrow to pay for school	48
Average cumulative indebtedness	$16,927

FORDHAM UNIVERSITY

441 EAST FORDHAM ROAD, THEBAUD HALL, NEW YORK, NY 10458 • ADMISSIONS: 718-817-4000 • FAX: 718-367-9404

CAMPUS LIFE

Quality of Life Rating	**75**
Fire Safety Rating	**60***
Green Rating	**60***
Type of school	private
Affiliation	Roman Catholic
Environment	metropolis

STUDENTS

Total undergrad enrollment	7,994
% male/female	45/55
% from out of state	46
% from public high school	47
% live on campus	56
% African American	6
% Asian	7
% Caucasian	58
% Hispanic	13
% international	2
# of countries represented	58

SURVEY SAYS . . .

Great library
Great off-campus food
Campus feels safe
Students are happy
Frats and sororities are unpopular or nonexistent
Student publications are popular
Hard liquor is popular
(Almost) everyone smokes

ACADEMICS

Academic Rating	**79**
Calendar	semester
Student/faculty ratio	12:1
Profs interesting rating	71
Profs accessible rating	73
Most common reg class size	20–29 students
Most common lab size	10–19 students

MOST POPULAR MAJORS
business/commerce
communication and media studies
social sciences

STUDENTS SAY ". . ."

Academics

Fordham University is two schools in one. First, there's the school's long-established campus in the Rose Hill section of the Bronx, which might best be regarded as Fordham's 'conventional' undergraduate site. Then there's the newer campus at Manhattan's Lincoln Center, which is "very small and geared toward theater and dance students [though the school says the largest number of majors is liberal arts]." Students are adamant that "they are two different schools going in different directions with different student bodies and different academic focuses." The campuses do share a number of common traits, however. Each is a Jesuit school "with really big core requirements" that provide undergrads with "a strong background in a broad area of academics before actually specializing in one area, thereby educating the whole mind." The Jesuit influence is also seen in the way each school "promotes social awareness, caring for others, and expanding one's knowledge of the world and helping find one's contribution to it." Each school, of course, benefits from a city location that provides near limitless opportunities for networking, internships, and enriching extracurricular experiences. Rose Hill's students praise Fordham's College of Business ("the school for business professionals,"), its pre-law and pre-medical programs, and its psychology program; undergrads at Lincoln Center boast of "one of the best theater departments in the country" and "a great dance program."

Life

Fordham's Rose Hill Campus "is truly beautiful, and the location is pretty much the best of both worlds—the city as well as plenty of green." Here, "life centers around the weekends. Most people go out to local bars, leaving no one on campus on a Tuesday, Friday, or Saturday night...There are numerous events going on on campus all the time, although many of these events are based in religion or politics." Students are also "very involved...in intramural sports teams as well as performing arts groups." There's also the city, of course; you can reach it in 15 minutes by Metro North train, or you can save a few bucks and ride the subway. Expect the trip downtown to take about 30 minutes. Closer by is Arthur Avenue, the Bronx's own (and, many say, much better) version of Manhattan's Little Italy. Life at Lincoln Center is understandably less campus-centric; no campus can compete with all that downtown New York City has to offer. One student explains, "The bar and restaurant scene at Lincoln Center is very popular because of the variety of places to go in Manhattan. Dorm parties are not as usual as I would imagine them to be at other colleges. Students from all...of Fordham come to Lincoln Center to set out for their various night activities because of the campus's proximity to everything...I try to take advantage of the incredible amount of things to do here that one isn't able to do in most other places, but things are very expensive." Lincoln Center dorms "are like apartments, which I know is a definite attraction for many students."

Student Body

Students on the Rose Hill campus tend to be "from an upper-class home in New Jersey, Connecticut, or Long Island[and] wear sandals and jeans and polos, with some popped collars sprinkled in...Off campus (in the Bronx) they stick out like a sore thumb." Many are business and communications majors who favor conservative politics and a businesslike approach to academics. Students at Lincoln Center are more diverse; one writes, "there is no such thing as a typical student at Lincoln Center. Most students who choose to go here are liberal and artsy (writers, dancers, actors). Students tend to be very creative in their clothing choices." The majority of students here are women, and "most of the boys are gay."

FORDHAM UNIVERSITY

FINANCIAL AID: 718-817-3800 • E-MAIL: ENROLL@FORDHAM.EDU • WEBSITE: WWW.FORDHAM.EDU

THE PRINCETON REVIEW SAYS

Admissions

Very important factors considered include: Class rank, rigor of secondary school record, standardized test scores. *Important factors considered include:* Application essay, recommendation(s), character/personal qualities, extracurricular activities, talent/ability. *Other factors considered include:* Alumni/ae relation, first generation, geographical residence, racial/ethnic status, volunteer work, work experience. SAT Subject Tests recommended. SAT or ACT required. ACT with Writing component recommended. TOEFL required of all international applicants. High school diploma is required and GED is accepted. *Academic units required:* 4 English, 3 mathematics, 3 science, 2 foreign language, 2 social studies, 2 history, 6 academic electives. *Academic units recommended:* 4 English, 4 mathematics, 4 science, 3 foreign language, 2 social studies, 2 history, 6 academic electives.

Financial Aid

Students should submit: FAFSA, CSS/financial aid profile, noncustodial profile, business/farm supplement. Regular filing deadline is 2/1. The Princeton Review suggests that all financial aid forms be submitted as soon as possible after 1/1. *Need-based scholarships/grants offered:* Federal Pell, SEOG, state scholarships/grants, private scholarships, the school's own gift aid. *Loan aid offered:* FFEL Subsidized Stafford, FFEL Unsubsidized Stafford, FFEL PLUS, Federal Perkins. Applicants will be notified of awards on or about 4/1.

The Inside Word

Applicants to Fordham are required to indicate whether they are applying to Fordham College—Rose Hill, Fordham College—Lincoln Center, or the College of Business Administration. Admissions criteria vary by school, but all are very competitive. Graduation from one of the area's many prestigious Catholic high schools is certainly a plus.

THE SCHOOL SAYS "..."

From The Admissions Office

"Fordham University offers a distinctive, values-centered educational experience that is rooted in the Jesuit tradition of intellectual rigor and personal attention. Located in New York City, Fordham offers to students the unparalleled educational, cultural, and recreational advantages of one of the world's greatest cities. Fordham has two residential campuses in New York—the tree-lined, 85-acre Rose Hill in the Bronx, and the cosmopolitan Lincoln Center campus in the heart of Manhattan's performing arts center. The university's state-of-the-art facilities and buildings include one of the most technologically advanced libraries in the country. Fordham offers a variety of majors, concentrations, and programs that can be combined with an extensive career planning and placement program. More than 2,600 organizations in the New York metropolitan area offer students internships that provide hands-on experience and valuable networking opportunities in fields such as business, communications, medicine, law, and education.

"Applicants are required to take SAT or the ACT with the Writing section. SAT Subject Tests are recommended but not required."

SELECTIVITY
Admissions Rating	92
# of applicants	18,161
% of applicants accepted	47
% of acceptees attending	20
# accepting a place on wait list	1,189
% admitted from wait list	10

FRESHMAN PROFILE
Range SAT Critical Reading	570–670
Range SAT Math	560–660
Range SAT Writing	560–660
Range ACT Composite	25–29
Minimum paper TOEFL	575
Minimum computer TOEFL	231
Average HS GPA	3.7
% graduated top 10% of class	42.5
% graduated top 25% of class	73
% graduated top 50% of class	96

DEADLINES
Early action	
Deadline	11/1
Notification	12/25
Regular	
Priority	1/15
Deadline	1/15
Notification	4/1
Nonfall registration?	yes

APPLICANTS ALSO LOOK AT
AND OFTEN PREFER
The George Washington University
New York University
Boston College

AND SOMETIMES PREFER
Rutgers, The State University of New Jersey—Camden
Loyola College in Maryland
College of the Holy Cross

AND RARELY PREFER
Hofstra University
Marist College

FINANCIAL FACTS
Financial Aid Rating	73
Annual tuition	$34,200
Room and board	$12,980
Required fees	$1,057
Books and supplies	$800
% frosh rec. need-based scholarship or grant aid	66
% UG rec. need-based scholarship or grant aid	62
% frosh rec. non-need-based scholarship or grant aid	8
% UG rec. non-need-based scholarship or grant aid	5
% frosh rec. need-based self-help aid	51
% UG rec. need-based self-help aid	52
% frosh rec. athletic scholarships	2
% UG rec. athletic scholarships	2
% frosh rec. any financial aid	67
% UG rec. any financial aid	62

FRANKLIN & MARSHALL COLLEGE

PO BOX 3003, LANCASTER, PA 17604-3003 • ADMISSIONS: 717-291-3953 • FAX: 717-291-4381

CAMPUS LIFE
Quality of Life Rating	**72**
Fire Safety Rating	**60***
Green Rating	**93**
Type of school	private
Environment	town

STUDENTS
Total undergrad enrollment	2,118
% male/female	48/52
% from out of state	67
% from public high school	58
% live on campus	80
% in (# of) fraternities	26 (7)
% in (# of) sororities	12 (2)
% African American	4
% Asian	4
% Caucasian	69
% Hispanic	4
% international	9
# of countries represented	64

SURVEY SAYS . . .
No one cheats
Lab facilities are great
Great library
School is well run
Lots of beer drinking
Hard liquor is popular

ACADEMICS
Academic Rating	**93**
Calendar	semester
Student/faculty ratio	10:1
Profs interesting rating	89
Profs accessible rating	94
Most common reg class size	10–19 students
Most common lab size	10–19 students

MOST POPULAR MAJORS
business/commerce
economics
political science and government
English
psychology
biology

STUDENTS SAY "..."

Academics

Franklin & Marshall is widely regarded as a school that "prepares students well for law school and medical school," along with retaining "a stellar reputation in graduate school admissions departments," but there's more to F&M than a bunch of high-strung future doctors and lawyers. True, the school has earned a reputation as a pre-professional powerhouse through its "intense workload" and "very difficult grading structure," conditions that some see as necessary in order to provide "an environment for intense personal and academic growth and development of the skills necessary to achieve well-rounded success in life." However, students deem the workload "far too academically demanding for an average liberal arts college." But F&M also boasts "amazing departments in German, economics, history, government...and geology/environmental science," among others. And in all areas—not just in the high-profile sciences and business—the school ensures that "independent research, especially for upperclassmen, is a vital part of the academic experience" and that "there are enough resources that can be accessed to make good grades more easily attainable," the "demanding" workload notwithstanding. Close student-teacher relationships help make the experience; professors here "are by far the greatest thing about this school. If you're interested in doing something, you can always find a professor or other staff member who would love to help you."

Life

"There is a grind at F&M" during the week, "not a bad one, but you have to be ready for it. Everyone takes his role as a student here very seriously: class, library, meetings, more class, more library, extracurriculars. Most students follow this itinerary during the week." Weeknight respites come in the form of "concerts, movies, amazing lectures, and other things to break up the schedule." For most, weekends "are a good time to relax and drink and forget about all of the work that has been done and still needs to be done in the week to come," so "most students like to go to one or more of the numerous fraternity parties or they may go to a party in someone's room or apartment." And "If you aren't into the drinking scene or the partying scene on campus"—and contrary to the school's reputation, some students here aren't—"you can go to Ben's Underground, which is an alcohol-free, student-run club. Students can go to play pool or see comedians. It's really a nice facility to use and open all week." Also, "athletics are fairly popular for a division three school, and the orchestra draws as well." Hometown Lancaster offers "a bunch of art galleries, really good cafés, an old opera house that has great plays, and a concert venue that has pretty big-name bands play." However, by the time most students are juniors, "Lancaster and the frat scene get old, so older students take to the local bars and sometimes take road trips to...Philadelphia or Washington, D.C."

Student Body

F&M is "an extremely preppy school, and many designers are flashed all around campus. Students are not afraid to show that they have money, but they are never in your face about it." Not everyone here is a slave to fashion. "You have students that do not get all dressed up for class that just wear sweats and sweatshirt," says a student. Along with those students "from boarding schools or expensive private schools," you'll find "a handful of international students, a smaller handful of minority students, and a few 'townies.' Everyone finds a niche, though." The small campus sometimes feels smaller because students can be cliquish; undergrads here "can be broken into many groups: frats, sororities, specific athletic groups, similar interests (arts, music, etc.)."

FRANKLIN & MARSHALL COLLEGE

FINANCIAL AID: 717-291-3991 • E-MAIL: ADMISSION@FANDM.EDU • WEBSITE: WWW.FANDM.EDU

THE PRINCETON REVIEW SAYS

Admissions

Very important factors considered include: Class rank, academic GPA, rigor of secondary school record, character/personal qualities. *Important factors considered include:* Application essay, recommendation(s), standardized test scores, extracurricular activities, interview, talent/ability, volunteer work. *Other factors considered include:* Alumni/ae relation, geographical residence, level of applicant's interest, racial/ethnic status, work experience. TOEFL required of all international applicants. High school diploma is required and GED is accepted. *Academic units required:* 4 English, 3 mathematics, 2 science (2 science labs), 2 foreign language, 1 social studies, 2 history, 1 visual/performing arts. *Academic units recommended:* 4 mathematics, 4 science (3 science labs), 4 foreign language, 4 social studies, 3 history.

Financial Aid

Students should submit: FAFSA, CSS/financial aid profile, noncustodial profile, business/farm supplement. Regular filing deadline is 2/15. The Princeton Review suggests that all financial aid forms be submitted as soon as possible after 1/1. *Need-based scholarships/grants offered:* Federal Pell, SEOG, state scholarships/grants, private scholarships, the school's own gift aid. *Loan aid offered:* FFEL Subsidized Stafford, FFEL Unsubsidized Stafford, FFEL PLUS, Federal Perkins, college/university loans from institutional funds. Applicants will be notified of awards on or about 3/25. Federal Work-Study Program available.

The Inside Word

Applicants who feel that their standardized test scores do not accurately reflect their abilities may opt to omit them from their applications, in which case they must instead include two recent (junior or senior year) graded papers, preferably from a humanities or social science course. Since F&M is a school that requires a significant amount of writing from its students, there could hardly be a better way to demonstrate your qualifications to attend than with the written word.

THE SCHOOL SAYS "..."

From The Admissions Office

"Franklin & Marshall students choose from a variety of fields of study, traditional and interdisciplinary, that typify liberal learning. Professors in all of these fields are committed to a common purpose, which is to teach students to think, speak, and write with clarity and confidence. Whether the course is in theater or in physics, the class will be small, engagement will be high, and discussion will dominate over lecture. Thus, throughout their 4 years, beginning with the First-Year Seminar, students at Franklin & Marshall are repeatedly invited to active participation in intellectual play at high levels. Our graduates consistently testify to the high quality of an F&M education as a mental preparation for life."

SELECTIVITY

Admissions Rating	95
# of applicants	5,632
% of applicants accepted	36
% of acceptees attending	29
# accepting a place on wait list	670
% admitted from wait list	12
# of early decision applicants	582
% accepted early decision	70

FRESHMAN PROFILE

Range SAT Critical Reading	630–700
Range SAT Math	610–690
Minimum paper TOEFL	600
Minimum computer TOEFL	250
Average HS GPA	3.57
% graduated top 10% of class	61
% graduated top 25% of class	87
% graduated top 50% of class	99

DEADLINES

Early decision	
Deadline	11/15
Notification	12/15
Regular	
Deadline	2/1
Notification	4/1
Nonfall registration?	yes

APPLICANTS ALSO LOOK AT
AND SOMETIMES PREFER

Dickinson College
Lafayette College
Bucknell University

FINANCIAL FACTS

Financial Aid Rating	83
Annual tuition	$38,580
Room and board	$9,870
Required fees	$50
Books and supplies	$650
% frosh rec. need-based scholarship or grant aid	36
% UG rec. need-based scholarship or grant aid	38
% frosh rec. non-need-based scholarship or grant aid	12
% UG rec. non-need-based scholarship or grant aid	15
% frosh rec. need-based self-help aid	37
% UG rec. need-based self-help aid	40
% frosh rec. any financial aid	49
% UG rec. any financial aid	58
% UG borrow to pay for school	54
Average cumulative indebtedness	$30,657

FRANKLIN W. OLIN COLLEGE OF ENGINEERING

OLIN WAY, NEEDHAM, MA 02492-1200 • ADMISSIONS: 781-292-2222 • FAX: 781-292-2210

CAMPUS LIFE

Quality of Life Rating	**97**
Fire Safety Rating	**98**
Green Rating	**70**
Type of school	private
Environment	town

STUDENTS

Total undergrad enrollment	308
% male/female	60/40
% from out of state	90
% African American	1
% Asian	11
% Caucasian	43
% Hispanic	4
% international	5
# of countries represented	10

SURVEY SAYS . . .
No one cheats
Lab facilities are great
Students are friendly
Different types of students interact
Students get along with local community
Great food on campus
Dorms are like palaces
Campus feels safe
Students are happy
Student government is popular

ACADEMICS

Academic Rating	**99**
Calendar	semester
Student/faculty ratio	8:1
Profs interesting rating	99
Profs accessible rating	98
Most common reg class size	20–29 students

MOST POPULAR MAJORS
electrical, electronics and communications engineering
engineering
mechanical engineering

STUDENTS SAY " . . ."

Academics
An "innovative," "exceptional" "project-based" curriculum attracts the country's math and science whiz kids to Franklin W. Olin College of Engineering. The school's "small size" and "open atmosphere that's supportive of everyone" are very appealing to the approximately 300 undergraduates on campus. But the piece de resistance—the thing that has students choosing this place over schools like MIT and Cal Tech—has got to be the "free tuition." "Academics-wise, the school kicks people's [butts] right and left. It takes the best and the brightest and breaks them, pushing them when they likely have never had to work hard before. Around here, everyone is smart, and professors assume that, so the classes are taken to that level; there is no such thing as an easy class." One might describe professors here as "grown-up Olin kids" insofar as they "are geniuses," but they also "young" and just "generally awesome people." "They love teaching," and are "mostly on [a] first-name basis" with undergrads; professors bend over backwards to make themselves accessible, either in person or over e-mail, which means "that they always seem to be available." In terms of how smoothly things run, keep in mind that Olin is "an experiment, so you never really know what's going to happen," which "tends to lead to some chaos." That doesn't mean that the administration isn't trying—it's actually trying all the time. There is a "constant dialogue of feedback between the students, staff, and faculty," and the administration "always has open doors to everyone." "You can sit down and eat lunch [in the dining hall] with the president if you want to." Feedback drives a "continual reassessment" of the institution with the aim of constant "improvement in all departments."

Life
A popular saying used to describe student life at Olin goes like this: "Choose two: work, sleep, fun." The majority of students choose the first and the last because "An Oliner at rest is an unhappy Oliner." The "entrepreneurial spirit is strong" here, leading many people to choose to spend what little free time they have "working on cool projects" like "hacking the thermostat in their room" and "playing with lasers and circuits." Not everyone engages in genius science "geek" endeavors in their free time. Instead many do plain-Jane, run-of-the-mill, vanilla geek activities like "playing DDR" and "video gaming." Still, normal college student stuff happens here, too. "There are definitely typical college parties with drinking games," and "clubs and student organizations put on a lot of activities." Plenty of students also get heavily involved "with local service groups (FIRST Robotics and Habitat for Humanity are particularly active)." And as it is at every one of the gazillion colleges in the greater Beantown area, "going into Boston for events" is a popular pastime here too. Concerning the more mundane details of day-to-day life on campus, students are pleased. The dorms are "nice and warm," and "the food is amazing."

Student Body
Picture this: "engineers with social skills." Yes, they really do exist, and about 300 of them live and learn happily together at this small college on the outskirts of Boston. These folks "are all extremely intelligent and very high-achieving." "There are students here that have held patents since high school, [and others] who have worked for NASA." Perhaps because people like this—people who have "already made incredible, insane contributions to the world"—are not in short supply, "The majority [of students] don't seem to feel like they're especially smart." So there's little threat of being smothered by peers' egos if one enrolls here. "Olin has a very diverse student body with regard to everything except race." "The full-tuition scholarship allows for students from less wealthy backgrounds" to attend, and a "strong group of very religious students" coexists peacefully with a "decent number of people who express alternative sexualities." In sum, a live-and-let-live philosophy is pervasive. "People are allowed to have their own passions and opinions so long as they have passions and opinions."

FRANKLIN W. OLIN COLLEGE OF ENGINEERING

FINANCIAL AID: 781-292-2222 • E-MAIL: INFO@OLIN.EDU • WEBSITE: WWW.OLIN.EDU

THE PRINCETON REVIEW SAYS

Admissions

Very important factors considered include: Application essay, academic GPA, recommendation(s), rigor of secondary school record, character/personal qualities, extracurricular activities, level of applicant's interest, talent/ability. *Important factors considered include:* Class rank, standardized test scores, racial/ethnic status, volunteer work. *Other factors considered include:* First generation, geographical residence, interview, state residency, work experience. SAT or ACT required. SAT and SAT Subject Tests or ACT required. High school diploma is required and GED is accepted. *Academic units required:* 4 English, 4 mathematics, 3 science (3 science labs), 2 foreign language, 2 social studies, 2 history. *Academic units recommended:* 1 calculus, 1 physics.

Financial Aid

Students should submit: FAFSA. Regular filing deadline is 2/15. The Princeton Review suggests that all financial aid forms be submitted as soon as possible after 1/1. *Need-based scholarships/grants offered:* Federal Pell, SEOG, private scholarships, the school's own gift aid. *Loan aid offered:* FFEL Subsidized Stafford, FFEL Unsubsidized Stafford, FFEL PLUS. Applicants will be notified of awards on a rolling basis beginning 4/1. Institutional employment available.

The Inside Word

Not many colleges can boast that they are filled with students who turned down offers from the likes of MIT, Cal Tech, and Carnegie Mellon, but Olin can. Olin is unique among engineering schools in that the Admissions Office really looks for more than just brains. Things like social skills and eloquence are taken extremely seriously here, so reclusive geniuses seeking 4 years of technical monasticism will be at a disadvantage in the application process.

THE SCHOOL SAYS "..."

From The Admissions Office

"Every admitted student receives a merit scholarship for 4 years. In addition to a merit scholarship, Olin will meet the full demonstrated need, determined by the FAFSA, primarily with grants.

"The selection process at Olin College is unique to college admission. Each year a highly self-selecting pool of approximately 900 applications is reviewed on traditional selection criteria. Approximately 190 finalists are invited to one of two Candidates' Weekends in February and March. These candidates are group into five-person teams for a weekend of design-and-build exercises, group discussions, and interviews with Olin students, faculty, and alumni. Written evaluations and recommendations for each candidate are prepared by all Olin participants and submitted to the faculty admission committee. The committee admits about 140 candidates to yield a freshman class of 85. The result is that the freshman class is ultimately chosen on the strength of personal attributes such as leadership, cooperation, creativity, communication, and their enthusiasm for Olin College.

"A waiting list of approximately 20 is also established. Some wait-list candidates who are not offered a spot in the class may defer enrollment for 1 year—with the guarantee of the Olin Scholarship. Wait list students are strongly encouraged to do something unusual, exciting, and productive during their sabbatical year.

"Student applying for admission are required to take the SAT (or the ACT with the writing section). Olin College also require scores from two SAT Subject Tests: math (level 1 or 2), and a Science of the student's choice."

SELECTIVITY

Admissions Rating	99
# of applicants	969
% of applicants accepted	14
% of acceptees attending	57
# accepting a place on wait list	12
% admitted from wait list	58

FRESHMAN PROFILE

Range SAT Critical Reading	700–790
Range SAT Math	740–800
Range SAT Writing	670–770
Range ACT Composite	32–35
Average HS GPA	3.9
% graduated top 10% of class	95
% graduated top 25% of class	100

DEADLINES

Regular	
Deadline	1/1
Notification	3/21
Nonfall registration?	no

FINANCIAL FACTS

Financial Aid Rating	96
Annual tuition	$36,400
Room and board	$13,230
Required fees	$395
Books and supplies	$750
% frosh rec. need-based scholarship or grant aid	11
% UG rec. need-based scholarship or grant aid	12
% frosh rec. non-need-based scholarship or grant aid	100
% UG rec. non-need-based scholarship or grant aid	100
% frosh rec. any financial aid	100
% UG rec. any financial aid	100

FURMAN UNIVERSITY

3300 POINSETT HIGHWAY, GREENVILLE, SC 29613 • ADMISSIONS: 864-294-2034 • FAX: 864-294-3127

CAMPUS LIFE
Quality of Life Rating	**96**
Fire Safety Rating	**83**
Green Rating	**98**
Type of school	private
Environment	city

STUDENTS
Total undergrad enrollment	2,771
% male/female	43/57
% from out of state	70
% from public high school	63
% live on campus	91
% in (# of) fraternities	33 (7)
% in (# of) sororities	44 (7)
% African American	7
% Asian	3
% Caucasian	81
% Hispanic	2
% international	2
# of countries represented	47

SURVEY SAYS . . .
Students are friendly
Musical organizations are popular

ACADEMICS
Academic Rating	**93**
Calendar	semester
Student/faculty ratio	11:1
Profs interesting rating	92
Profs accessible rating	95
Most common	
reg class size	10–19 students

MOST POPULAR MAJORS
communication studies/speech
communication and rhetoric
history
political science and government

STUDENTS SAY " . . ."

Academics

Furman University, "a small, private, liberal arts school with a gorgeous campus," has "a great reputation, especially in the Southeast." These are just some of the reasons students choose the school. Undergraduates also love the "great collegiate atmosphere," "generous scholarships, plenty of undergraduate research opportunities, and personal attention from professors," and the "sweet downtown scene" in hometown Greenville. In short, they come because they feel that "Furman offers a great overall experience." Students warn that "Furman is hard. There are no 'gimmes' here. You work for what you get and oftentimes the result shocks freshmen who grew accustomed to cruising in high school." As one student writes, "Furman places a great deal of emphasis on class discussion and active participation. This is often quite fun, but it usually is a pretty effective test of whether you read the deconstruction article last night or whether you truly have the Greek aorist passive down." Students' efforts to keep up are abetted by "small class sizes and a good faculty" that provides "the feeling that your professors not only know you as a person, but care about you. Even when classes are kicking your butt, Furman still provides a very enjoyable academic experience, and you're left thinking of the good over the bad."

Life

Furman University is a good fit for "students who have truly come to get an education but also find an abundance of other activities that they love." Even walking to class offers a pleasant diversion "because of how picturesque the campus is." For some, "life at Furman is definitely centered around Furman itself. Students call it "the bubble." Students are generally "very active in at least one activity on campus other than their academic responsibilities." Major events include homecoming, which is "one of the most fun weeks all year, with competitions and…gathering on the mall Friday night for float building, carnival rides, funnel cakes, and for many students, alcohol intake." Others leave campus fairly frequently to take advantage of downtown Greenville ("one of the coolest places") and the many "outdoor opportunities in the surrounding area." Students occasionally venture farther a-field: "We're only 2 hours from Atlanta, Charlotte, and Columbia, so we go to concerts there. We're right in the mountains, so we go hiking and camping, and sometimes we make the 4-hour drive to the beach." Just about everyone enjoys the frequent and popular Greek parties; although "only about one-third of the student body is involved in Greek organizations, at least two-thirds go to the parties and other Greek events." A large jock population drives an active athletic scene; music groups and religious organizations are also "very popular."

Student Body

"Furman kids are often viewed as being rich, White, and preppy (sororadorable and frat-tastic are two common terms)." "While the majority may fit into those categories," there are also "plenty that are outside that spectrum." True, the typical student may be "a southern (probably from Tennessee, Georgia, or South Carolina) Protestant Christian of a conservative denomination, athletic, snappily dressed, and hard-studying, but not possessing deep intellectual interest in more than a couple of subjects;" but the University is working hard to overcome its reputation as a "a school only for conservative, rich, white kids" by "opening up its doors to many different types of people. Last year, for example, the student body president was a Muslim of Pakistani descent." Most here "are religious to some degree," and many "can quote any and every line of the Bible, making those who are less religious feel a little out of place." Rich or not, religious or agnostic, southern or otherwise, "The one unifying factor here is the desire for Furman to retain a spirit of southern hospitality no matter the diversity of its student body."

FINANCIAL AID: 864-294-2204 • E-MAIL: ADMISSIONS@FURMAN.EDU • WEBSITE: WWW.FURMAN.EDU

THE PRINCETON REVIEW SAYS

Admissions

Very important factors considered include: Rigor of secondary school record. *Important factors considered include:* Class rank, application essay, academic GPA, standardized test scores, character/personal qualities, extracurricular activities. *Other factors considered include:* Recommendation(s), alumni/ae relation, first generation, level of applicant's interest, racial/ethnic status, talent/ability, volunteer work, work experience. SAT or ACT recommended. ACT with Writing component recommended. TOEFL required of all international applicants. High school diploma is required and GED is accepted. *Academic units required:* 4 English, 3 mathematics, 2 science (2 science labs), 2 foreign language, 3 social studies. *Academic units recommended:* 4 English, 4 mathematics, 3 science (2 science labs), 3 foreign language, 4 social studies.

Financial Aid

Students should submit: FAFSA, institution's own financial aid form, CSS/financial aid profile, state aid formSouth Carolina residents must complete required state forms for South Carolina. Regular filing deadline is 1/15. The Princeton Review suggests that all financial aid forms be submitted as soon as possible after 1/1. *Need-based scholarships/grants offered:* Federal Pell, SEOG, state scholarships/grants, private scholarships, the school's own gift aid, Federal SMART and ACG grants. *Loan aid offered:* FFEL Subsidized Stafford, FFEL Unsubsidized Stafford, FFEL PLUS, Federal Perkins, state loans, donor-sponsored loans for study abroad. Applicants will be notified of awards on or about 3/15. Federal Work-Study Program available. Institutional employment available. Off-campus job opportunities are excellent.

The Inside Word

Furman's high acceptance rate is deceptive; the applicant pool here is highly self-selected, meaning that most who apply have pretty strong credentials. The following stats are more telling: the average applicant has completed five AP courses, earned an unweighted high school GPA of 3.5, and scored pretty well on standardized tests. In the absence of similarly strong credentials, you'll need to find some way to sell yourself to the admissions committee. A demonstrated ability to contribute to the school community—perhaps through athletics, the arts, or community service—will help.

THE SCHOOL SAYS "..."

From The Admissions Office

"From its position as a nationally ranked independent, coeducational liberal arts college of 2,600 students, Furman takes great pride in its beautiful campus, its gifted student body, its distinguished and active faculty, and the many notable accomplishments of its alumni. Furman emphasizes engaged learning, a hands-on, problem-solving, and collaborative educational philosophy that encourages students to put into practice the theories and methods learned from texts and lectures. Using the latest in wired and wireless technology, students have multiple opportunities to become engaged in their academic pursuits through an array of internships, service-learning programs, faculty/student creative projects and significant undergraduate research. Furman offers an unusual combination of a top-tier liberal arts college, 17 Division I men's and women's athletic teams, and a nationally competitive music program that features 26 performing ensembles. Students are involved in hundreds of organizations and clubs on campus ranging from professional organizations to fraternities and sororities. In sum, Furman is a diverse learning community that celebrates its differences and is committed to the development of the whole student. Furman applicants can meet our standardized test requirement but submitting scores choosing from one of the following options: SAT; ACT and optional writing test; two SAT Subject Tests—one in English, one in Math; two AP exams, one from English (Language and Composition or Literature and Composition) and one from Math (Calculus AB or BC); two IB exams, one in English Language (A1) and one in Mathematics; or the TOEFL (for international students ONLY)."

SELECTIVITY

Admissions Rating	97
# of applicants	4,414
% of applicants accepted	57
% of acceptees attending	30
# accepting a place on wait list	181
# of early decision applicants	639
% accepted early decision	66

FRESHMAN PROFILE

Range SAT Critical Reading	590–690
Range SAT Math	590–680
Range SAT Writing	580–680
Range ACT Composite	26–30
Minimum paper TOEFL	570
Minimum computer TOEFL	230
Average HS GPA	3.52
% graduated top 10% of class	59
% graduated top 25% of class	87
% graduated top 50% of class	99

DEADLINES

Early decision	
Deadline	11/15
Notification	12/15
Regular	
Deadline	1/15
Notification	3/15
Nonfall registration?	no

APPLICANTS ALSO LOOK AT

AND OFTEN PREFER
Vanderbilt University
Wake Forest University
Duke University

AND SOMETIMES PREFER
University of South Carolina—Columbia
Clemson University
Emory University
Davidson College

FINANCIAL FACTS

Financial Aid Rating	87
Annual tuition	$34,048
Room and board	$8,966
Required fees	$540
Books and supplies	$850
% frosh rec. need-based scholarship or grant aid	42
% UG rec. need-based scholarship or grant aid	39
% frosh rec. non-need-based scholarship or grant aid	35
% UG rec. non-need-based scholarship or grant aid	32
% frosh rec. need-based self-help aid	31
% UG rec. need-based self-help aid	29
% frosh rec. athletic scholarships	9
% UG rec. athletic scholarships	10
% frosh rec. any financial aid	85
% UG rec. any financial aid	83
% UG borrow to pay for school	45
Average cumulative indebtedness	$24,325

GEORGE MASON UNIVERSITY

4400 UNIVERSITY DRIVE MSN 3A4, FAIRFAX, VA 22030-4444 • ADMISSIONS: 703-993-2400 • FAX: 703-993-2392

CAMPUS LIFE

Quality of Life Rating	**73**
Fire Safety Rating	**74**
Green Rating	**91**
Type of school	public
Environment	city

STUDENTS

Total undergrad enrollment	18,240
% male/female	47/53
% from out of state	10
% from public high school	86
% live on campus	25
% in (# of) fraternities	1 (22)
% in (# of) sororities	1 (13)
% African American	7
% Asian	16
% Caucasian	43
% Hispanic	6
% international	3
# of countries represented	129

SURVEY SAYS . . .

Athletic facilities are great
Diverse student types on campus

ACADEMICS

Academic Rating	**71**
Calendar	semester
Student/faculty ratio	15:1
Profs interesting rating	70
Profs accessible rating	73
% classes taught by TAs	9.9
Most common reg class size	20–29 students
Most common lab size	20–29 students

MOST POPULAR MAJORS

biology/biological sciences
political science and government
psychology

STUDENTS SAY "..."

Academics

George Mason University, a school in the Virginia suburbs just outside of D.C., has spent the past few years trying to get beyond its reputation as a commuter school, and it looks like it has been doing a good job of it. This innovative spirit and focus on "finding a new way to do what every other older school does" is one of Mason's greatest attributes, and though complaints about construction may pop up from time to time, the school is pushing through "the developmental stage" on its way to becoming a top university. Well-known for having one of the best nursing programs in northern Virginia, as well as a similarly strong school of management and economics department, the location of the school means that "students take their own initiative in finding internships and jobs to better their career prospects."

Students are happy with many of their professors, but quite a few people complain that the number of adjuncts teaching make classes too easy, especially for the required courses. "I feel like I'm taking the same classes I took in high school again, just with more homework," says a freshman. However, "once you get into your major courses the classes as well as professors improve." There are many tutoring service and other programs available for students who need help, and due to the close proximity to the nation's capital, the school has the opportunity "to host a large number of guest speakers/special lectures including politicians, CEOs and other professionals from major defense contractors in the area, and non-governmental representatives." At times "it may seem that the administrators are out of touch with reality," but they "generally receive student input well."

Life

While the school has undertaken massive efforts to drop the commuter label by providing more residence halls and events (on-campus housing availability is now completely caught up to demand), most agree that both the quality and the advertising of the weekend activities could use some work. "There is always something going on every weekend, but it may not be exactly what every student wants to do," says a senior. Many of those who do stay on campus for the weekend think the school should "make a better effort to acknowledge that people actually do live on campus during the weekends…we are all capable of making our own fun, but when the food hours and locations are so restricted we don't feel like we're even supposed to be there, that's taking it a little bit far." Still, the school is doing its best to amuse its students, and programs like Every Freakin' Friday ensure there's an event, well, every Friday, and more than 200 organizations keep students occupied. Trips to the city for eating, shopping, and nightlife are frequent, and from November through March, basketball games are also popular. The school is almost legendary for its "serious parking problem," which can be a very real concern for the commuter majority here, and people "party pretty hard to relieve the stress accrued from parking on-campus."

Student Body

There is a "wide variety" of students found at this big school, with commuters and non-commuters representing "a mix of traditional and non-traditional students," most of who are "moderately preppy" and come from in-state. There are a fair number of international and Muslim students, and "simply walking through the student center you will hear at least three different languages being spoken." Mason has "very little if any discrimination," and in general most students are very aware of global issues and different cultures. With this physical diversity also comes academic diversity, "where some students like to study a lot and some students like to party a lot."

FINANCIAL AID: 703-993-2353 • E-MAIL: ADMISSIONS@GMU.EDU • WEBSITE: WWW.MASONMETRO.EDU

THE PRINCETON REVIEW SAYS

Admissions

Very important factors considered include: Academic GPA, rigor of secondary school record. *Important factors considered include:* Class rank, application essay, recommendation(s), alumni/ae relation, character/personal qualities, talent/ability. *Other factors considered include:* Standardized test scores, extracurricular activities, first generation, level of applicant's interest, volunteer work, work experience. SAT and SAT Subject Tests or ACT recommended. TOEFL required of all international applicants. High school diploma is required and GED is accepted. *Academic units required:* 4 English, 3 mathematics, 3 science (3 science labs), 2 foreign language, 3 social studies, 3 academic electives. *Academic units recommended:* 4 English, 4 mathematics, 4 science (4 science labs), 3 foreign language, 4 social studies, 5 academic electives.

Financial Aid

Students should submit: FAFSA. The Princeton Review suggests that all financial aid forms be submitted as soon as possible after 1/1. *Need-based scholarships/grants offered:* Federal Pell, SEOG, state scholarships/grants, private scholarships, the school's own gift aid, Federal ACG and SMART Grants. *Loan aid offered:* FFEL Subsidized Stafford, FFEL Unsubsidized Stafford, FFEL PLUS, Federal Perkins, federal nursing scholarships. Applicants will be notified of awards on a rolling basis beginning 4/1. Federal Work-Study Program available. Institutional employment available. Off-campus job opportunities are excellent.

The Inside Word

George Mason is a popular destination for college for two key reasons: Its proximity to Washington, D.C. and the fact that it is not nearly as difficult to gain admission at Mason as it is at University of Virginia or William & Mary, the two flagships of the Virginia state system. The university's quality faculty and impressive facilities make it worth taking a look if low-cost, solid programs in the D.C. area are high on your list.

THE SCHOOL SAYS "..."

From The Admissions Office

"George Mason University enjoys the best location in the world. Our connections to the DC area result in faculty members who are engaged in the top research in their fields. We have professors who are regular contributors on all of the major news networks, and you can hardly listen to a program on National Public Radio without hearing from one of our scholars. This connectivity extends to our students, who take internships and get jobs at some of the best organizations and companies in the world. We have students at AOL/Time Warner, the National Institutes of Health, the Kennedy Center, the World Bank, the White House, and the National Zoo. We have all the advantages of the excitement of our nation's Capital combined with the comfort and security of this beautiful suburban campus. At Mason, we pride ourselves on being among the most innovative universities in the world. Many of our degree programs are the first of their kinds, including the first PhD program in biodefense, the first DC-based undergraduate program in conflict resolution, the first integrated school of information technology and engineering based on computer related programs, and one of the most innovative performing arts management programs in the United States. As a result, George Mason University is at the forefront of the emerging field of biotechnology, is a natural leader in the performing arts, and holds a preeminent position in the fields of economics, electronic journalism, and history, just to name a few. George Mason University will accept the ACT, and the SAT. Scores from the Writing section will not be considered in our admission decisions, as our faculty does not feel the Writing section reflects quality or methodology of our award-winning writing across the curriculum program. Mason has the largest score-optional program in the U.S."

SELECTIVITY

Admissions Rating	83
# of applicants	12,943
% of applicants accepted	63
% of acceptees attending	32
# accepting a place on wait list	597
% admitted from wait list	35

FRESHMAN PROFILE

Range SAT Critical Reading	500–600
Range SAT Math	520–610
Range ACT Composite	22–26
Minimum paper TOEFL	570
Minimum computer TOEFL	230
Minimum web-based TOEFL	88
Average HS GPA	3.48
% graduated top 10% of class	18
% graduated top 25% of class	52
% graduated top 50% of class	93

DEADLINES

Early action	
Deadline	11/1
Notification	12/19
Regular	
Priority	12/1
Deadline	1/15
Notification	4/1
Nonfall registration?	yes

APPLICANTS ALSO LOOK AT AND SOMETIMES PREFER

The George Washington University
Virginia Tech
University of Virginia
James Madison University

FINANCIAL FACTS

Financial Aid Rating	71
Annual in-state tuition	$5,526
Annual out-of-state tuition	$19,662
Room and board	$7,360
Required fees	$1,986
Books and supplies	$900
% frosh rec. need-based scholarship or grant aid	32
% UG rec. need-based scholarship or grant aid	29
% frosh rec. non-need-based scholarship or grant aid	12
% UG rec. non-need-based scholarship or grant aid	6
% frosh rec. need-based self-help aid	32
% UG rec. need-based self-help aid	31
% frosh rec. athletic scholarships	2
% UG rec. athletic scholarships	2
% frosh rec. any financial aid	63.9
% UG rec. any financial aid	51.6
% UG borrow to pay for school	54
Average cumulative indebtedness	$18,547

THE GEORGE WASHINGTON UNIVERSITY

2121 I STREET NORTHWEST, SUITE 201, WASHINGTON, D.C. 20052 • ADMISSIONS: 202-994-6040 • FAX: 202-994-0325

CAMPUS LIFE

Quality of Life Rating	94
Fire Safety Rating	60*
Green Rating	60*
Type of school	private
Environment	metropolis

STUDENTS

Total undergrad enrollment	10,370
% male/female	45/55
% from out of state	98
% from public high school	70
% live on campus	64
% in (# of) fraternities	19 (12)
% in (# of) sororities	18 (9)
% African American	6
% Asian	10
% Caucasian	62
% Hispanic	6
% international	4
# of countries represented	101

SURVEY SAYS . . .

Athletic facilities are great
Students love Washington, D.C.
Great off-campus food
Dorms are like palaces
Campus feels safe
Students are happy
Student publications are popular
Student government is popular
Political activism is popular

ACADEMICS

Academic Rating	86
Calendar	semester
Student/faculty ratio	13:1
Profs interesting rating	77
Profs accessible rating	75
% classes taught by TAs	3
Most common reg class size	10–19 students
Most common lab size	20–29 students

STUDENTS SAY "..."

Academics

At George Washington University, it's all about "being in the center of the most powerful city in the world and deciding where to make your mark," where students can tap "the nation's capital, whether [for] sports, science and medicine, politics, or psychology." Politics are the primary drawing card; the stellar Elliot School of International Affairs trains tomorrow's diplomats, while solid programs in political science and political communication benefit from heavyweight guest speakers (one student writes, "DeeDee Myers came to my Washington Reporters class, and I got to go interview Bob Siegel of NPR—it's experiences like that that make GW special"), and access to incredible internships; as one student puts it, "GW is government's largest source of slave labor. It isn't uncommon [to] see people from your different classes in the halls of Capital Hill." GW doesn't begin and end with government though; the school also has "a wonderful business program with an abundance of internship opportunities," a "computer security and information assurance" program "that's one of the best in the world and is actually one of only a handful accredited by the National Security Agency," and numerous other strengths. GW's administration seems geared toward training future government workers; students describe it as very "bureaucratic." The school maintains a large adjunct faculty; while some love that the adjuncts "have other projects or jobs on the side that can give students firsthand experience with real issues," others complain that "we lose many great adjunct professors every year" and that the large turnover "would be avoided if we just shelled out a little more money [to take on more full-time faculty]."

Life

"Whether it's going to the Kennedy Center, [to] the 9:30 Club, or [for] a midnight monument tour...D.C. is at the center of a GW student's experience." Undergrads boast that "of all D.C. universities, GW is the best situated. Where else can you party, get drunk, stumble your way to the steps of the Lincoln [Memorial], and attempt to hurry back to get enough sleep to function at your internship on the Hill?" Being in D.C. "makes it easy to always have something to do, from the monuments to the museums...from just hanging out on campus [to] going to sporting events." Speaking of sports, GW basketball "is huge. [Other] than that, we're not much of a sports school. Students are much more interested in joining the College Democrats or the College Republicans." Many are also interested in partying, but a junior stresses that she'd "never call GW a 'party school.' It's definitely there if you want it, but it's not pressured on you at all. Same thing with frats and sororities: Those who want to be in Greek life can be, and those who don't, don't have to [be] in order to have a fulfilling college experience."

Student Body

GW attracts "a lot of wealthy students" (its tuition is among the nation's highest), but there is also "a sense of diversity on campus." Jewish students make up about one-quarter of the undergraduate population; there are also "a lot of international students," "students from each of the 50 states," and, sprinkled among the wealthy, "plenty of middle-class students." At GW, undergrads say, you'll find "people that have disabilities and people from every race, religion, sexual orientation, and ideology." (While all ideologies are represented, it should be noted that "most students characterize themselves as Democrats.") Students tell us that GW isn't as much "a melting pot as a tossed salad, where people from different backgrounds, frats, and student org[anizations] all blend together." Undergrads here tend to be "very driven, constantly thinking about what their next internship is going to be and how they're going to get out into Washington more and things like that."

FINANCIAL AID: 202-994-6620 • E-MAIL: GWADM@GWU.EDU • WEBSITE: WWW.GWU.EDU

THE PRINCETON REVIEW SAYS

Admissions

Very important factors considered include: academic GPA, rigor of secondary school record, *Important factors considered include:* Class rank, application essay, recommendation(s), standardized test scores, extracurricular activities, interview, talent/ability, volunteer work. *Other factors considered include:* alumni/ae relation, character/personal qualities, first generation, geographical residence, level of applicant's interest, racial/ethnic status, work experience. SAT or ACT required; TOEFL required of all international applicants. High school diploma is required and GED is not accepted. *Academic units required:* 4 English, 2 mathematics, 2 science, (1 science labs), 2 foreign language, 2 social studies, *Academic units recommended:* 4 English, 4 mathematics, 4 science, 4 foreign language, 4 social studies.

Financial Aid

Students should submit: FAFSA, CSS/Financial Aid PROFILE Regular filing deadline is 2/1. The Princeton Review suggests that all financial aid forms be submitted as soon as possible after 1/1. Need-based scholarships/grants offered: Federal Pell, SEOG, state scholarships/grants, the school's own gift aid. *Loan aid offered:* FFEL Subsidized Stafford, FFEL Unsubsidized Stafford, FFEL PLUS, Federal Perkins Federal Work-Study Program available. Institutional employment available. Off-campus job opportunities are excellent.

The Inside Word

With almost 20,000 applications to process annually, GW would be forgiven if it gave student essays only a perfunctory glance. However, the school considers essays carefully; a school admissions officer recently told the *Washington Times* that student essays represent "the student's voice in the application," adding that the school's low admit rate means that "everything (in the application) takes on significance."

THE SCHOOL SAYS " . . ."

From The Admissions Office

"At GW, we welcome students who show a measure of impatience with the limitations of traditional education. At many universities, the edge of campus is the real world, but not at GW, where our campus and Washington, DC are seamless. We look for bold, bright students who are ambitious, energetic, and self-motivated. Here, where we are so close to the centers of thought and action in every field we offer, we easily integrate our outstanding academic tradition and faculty connections with the best internship and job opportunities of Washington, DC. A generous scholarship and financial assistance program attracts top students from all parts of the country and the world.

"Students applying should send SAT or ACT scores. We will use those scores that best work to the student's advantage. Applicants to the BA/MD, IEMP, and BA/JD programs are required to submit scores for SAT Subject Tests. "

SELECTIVITY

Admissions Rating	96
# of applicants	19,606
% of applicants accepted	37
% of acceptees attending	30
# accepting a place on wait list	702
% admitted from wait list	22

FRESHMAN PROFILE

Range SAT Critical Reading	600–690
Range SAT Math	600–690
Range SAT Writing	600–690
Range ACT Composite	26–29
Minimum paper TOEFL	550
Minimum computer TOEFL	300
% graduated top 10% of class	66
% graduated top 25% of class	90
% graduated top 50% of class	100

DEADLINES

Early Decision	
Deadline	11/10
Notification	12/15
Regular	
Priority	12/1
Deadline	1/10
Notification	4/1
Nonfall registration?	yes

APPLICANTS ALSO LOOK AT

AND OFTEN PREFER
University of Virginia
New York University
Emory University—Oxford College
Georgetown University
Boston University

AND SOMETIMES PREFER
The Catholic University of America
University of Maryland—College Park
University of Vermont
Tufts University
American University

FINANCIAL FACTS

Financial Aid Rating	88
Annual tuition	$38,500
Room and board	$12,155
Required fees	$30
Books and supplies	$1,000
% frosh rec. need-based scholarship or grant aid	35
% UG rec. need-based scholarship or grant aid	39
% frosh rec. non-need-based scholarship or grant aid	11
% UG rec. non-need-based scholarship or grant aid	11
% frosh rec. need-based self-help aid	31
% UG rec. need-based self-help aid	34
% frosh rec. athletic scholarships	1
% UG rec. athletic scholarships	2
% UG borrow to pay for school	49
Average cumulative indebtedness	$30,817

GEORGETOWN UNIVERSITY

THIRTY-SEVENTH AND P STREETS, NORTHWEST, WASHINGTON, D.C. 20057 • ADMISSIONS: 202-687-3600 • FAX: 202-687-5084

CAMPUS LIFE

Quality of Life Rating	84
Fire Safety Rating	91
Green Rating	95
Type of school	private
Affiliation	Roman Catholic
Environment	metropolis

STUDENTS

Total undergrad enrollment	6,692
% male/female	46/54
% from out of state	97
% from public high school	45.5
% live on campus	69
% African American	7
% Asian	10
% Caucasian	68
% Hispanic	7
% international	5
# of countries represented	138

SURVEY SAYS . . .

Students love Washington, D.C.
Great off-campus food
Students are happy
Frats and sororities are unpopular or nonexistent
Student publications are popular
Political activism is popular
Lots of beer drinking

ACADEMICS

Academic Rating	92
Calendar	semester
Student/faculty ratio	11:1
Profs interesting rating	82
Profs accessible rating	80
% classes taught by TAs	8

MOST POPULAR MAJORS
English language and literature
international relations and affairs
political science and government

STUDENTS SAY ". . ."

Academics

This moderately-sized elite academic establishment stays true to its Jesuit foundations by educating its students with the idea of "cura personalis," or "care for the whole person." The "well-informed" student body perpetuates upon itself, creating an atmosphere full of vibrant intellectual life, that is "also balanced with extra-curricular learning and development." "Georgetown is...a place where people work very, very hard without feeling like they are in direct competition," says an international politics major. Located in Washington, D.C., there's a noted School of Foreign Service here, and the access to internships is a huge perk for those in political or government programs. In addition, the proximity to the nation's capital fetches "high-profile guest speakers," with many of the most powerful people in global politics speaking regularly, as well as a large number of adjunct professors who, either are currently working in government, or have retired from high level positions.

Georgetown offers a "great selection of very knowledgeable professors, split with a good proportion of those who are experienced in realms outside of academia (such as former government officials) and career academics," though there are a few superstars who might be "somewhat less than totally collegial." Professors tend to be "fantastic scholars and teachers" and are "generally available to students," as well as often being "interested in getting to know you as a person (if you put forth the effort to talk to them and go to office hours)." Though Georgetown has a policy of grade deflation, meaning "A's are hard to come by," there are "a ton of interesting courses available" and TAs are used only for optional discussion sessions and help with grading. The academics "can be challenging or they can be not so much (not that they are ever really easy, just easier);" it all depends on the courses you choose and how much you actually do the work. The school administration is well-meaning and "usually willing to talk and compromise with students," but the process of planning activities can be full of headaches and bureaucracy, and the administration itself "sometimes is overstretched or has trouble transmitting its message." Nevertheless, "a motivated student can get done what he or she wants."

Life

Students are "extremely well aware of the world around them," from government to environment, social to economic, and "Georgetown is the only place where an argument over politics, history, or philosophy is preceded by a keg stand." Hoyas like to have a good time on weekends, and parties at campus and off-campus apartments and townhouses "are generally open to all comers and tend to have a somewhat networking atmosphere; meeting people you don't know is a constant theme." With such a motivated group on such a high-energy campus, "people are always headed somewhere, it seems—to rehearsal, athletic practice, a guest speaker, [or] the gym." Community service and political activism are particularly popular, as is basketball. Everything near Georgetown is in walking distance, including the world of D.C.'s museums, restaurants, and stores, and "grabbing or ordering late night food is a popular option."

Student Body

There are "a lot of wealthy students on campus," and preppy-casual is the fashion de rigueur; this is "definitely not a 'granola' school," but students from diverse backgrounds are typically welcomed by people wanting to learn about different experiences. Indeed, everyone here is well-traveled and well-educated, and there are "a ton of international students." "You better have at least some interest in politics or you will feel out-of-place," says a student. The school can also be "a bit cliquish, with athletes at the top," but there are "plenty of groups for everybody to fit into and find their niche," and "there is much crossover between groups."

GEORGETOWN UNIVERSITY

THE PRINCETON REVIEW SAYS

Admissions

Very important factors considered include: Class rank, application essay, academic GPA, recommendation(s), rigor of secondary school record, standardized test scores, character/personal qualities, talent/ability. *Important factors considered include:* Extracurricular activities, interview, volunteer work. *Other factors considered include:* Alumni/ae relation, geographical residence, racial/ethnic status, state residency, work experience. SAT Subject Tests recommended. SAT or ACT required. TOEFL required of all international applicants. High school diploma is required and GED is accepted. *Academic units recommended:* 4 English, 2 mathematics, 1 science, 2 foreign language, 2 social studies, 2 history.

Financial Aid

Students should submit: FAFSA, CSS/financial aid profile, noncustodial profile, business/farm supplement, tax returns. Regular filing deadline is 2/1. The Princeton Review suggests that all financial aid forms be submitted as soon as possible after 1/1. *Need-based scholarships/grants offered:* Federal Pell, SEOG, state scholarships/grants, private scholarships, the school's own gift aid. *Loan aid offered:* FFEL Subsidized Stafford, FFEL Unsubsidized Stafford, FFEL PLUS, Federal Perkins, federal nursing scholarships, alternative loans. Applicants will be notified of awards on or about 4/1. Federal Work-Study Program available. Institutional employment available. Off-campus job opportunities are excellent.

The Inside Word

It was always tough to get admitted to Georgetown, but in the early 1980s Patrick Ewing and the Hoyas created a basketball sensation that catapulted the place into position as one of the most selective universities in the nation. There has been no turning back since. GU gets almost 10 applications for every space in the entering class, and the academic strength of the pool is impressive. Virtually 50 percent of the entire student body took AP courses in high school. Candidates who are waitlisted should hold little hope for an offer of admission; over the past several years Georgetown has taken very few off their lists.

THE SCHOOL SAYS "..."

From The Admissions Office

"Georgetown was founded in 1789 by John Carroll, who concurred with his contemporaries Benjamin Franklin and Thomas Jefferson in believing that the success of the young democracy depended upon an educated and virtuous citizenry. Carroll founded the school with the dynamic Jesuit tradition of education, characterized by humanism and committed to the assumption of responsibility and action. Georgetown is a national and international university, enrolling students from all 50 states and over 100 foreign countries. Undergraduate students are enrolled in one of four undergraduate schools: the College of Arts and Sciences, School of Foreign Service, Georgetown School of Business, and Georgetown School of Nursing and Health Studies. All students share a common liberal arts core and have access to the entire university curriculum.

"Applicants must submit scores from SAT or the ACT. SAT Subject Tests can also be recommended."

SELECTIVITY
Admissions Rating	98
# of applicants	18,696
% of applicants accepted	19
% of acceptees attending	45
# accepting a place on wait list	1,307
% admitted from wait list	11

FRESHMAN PROFILE
Range SAT Critical Reading	650–740
Range SAT Math	660–750
Range ACT Composite	26–33
Minimum paper TOEFL	200

DEADLINES
Early action	
Deadline	11/1
Notification	12/15
Regular	
Deadline	1/10
Notification	4/1
Nonfall registration?	no

APPLICANTS ALSO LOOK AT
AND OFTEN PREFER
Duke University
University of Pennsylvania
AND SOMETIMES PREFER
University of Notre Dame
University of Virginia
Cornell University
Northwestern University
AND RARELY PREFER
The George Washington University
New York University
Boston College
Tufts University

FINANCIAL FACTS
Financial Aid Rating	95
Annual tuition	$37,536
Room and board	$12,753
Required fees	$411
Books and supplies	$1,125
% frosh rec. need-based scholarship or grant aid	40
% UG rec. need-based scholarship or grant aid	37
% frosh rec. non-need-based scholarship or grant aid	8
% UG rec. non-need-based scholarship or grant aid	7
% frosh rec. need-based self-help aid	38
% UG rec. need-based self-help aid	36
% frosh rec. athletic scholarships	5
% UG rec. athletic scholarships	4
% frosh rec. any financial aid	40.22
% UG rec. any financial aid	38.55
% UG borrow to pay for school	44
Average cumulative indebtedness	$23,333

GEORGIA INSTITUTE OF TECHNOLOGY

219 UNCLE HEINE WAY, ATLANTA, GA 30332-0320 • ADMISSIONS: 404-894-4154 • FAX: 404-894-9511

CAMPUS LIFE
Quality of Life Rating	**85**
Fire Safety Rating	**88**
Green Rating	**99**
Type of school	public
Environment	metropolis

STUDENTS
Total undergrad enrollment	12,533
% male/female	70/30
% from out of state	27
% from public high school	87
% live on campus	60
% in (# of) fraternities	24 (34)
% in (# of) sororities	32 (14)
% African American	7
% Asian	17
% Caucasian	65
% Hispanic	5
% international	5
# of countries represented	74

SURVEY SAYS . . .
Athletic facilities are great
Diverse student types on campus
Students love Atlanta, GA
Great off-campus food
Everyone loves the Yellow Jackets
Student publications are popular

ACADEMICS
Academic Rating	**74**
Calendar	semester
Student/faculty ratio	14:1
Profs interesting rating	61
Profs accessible rating	61
% classes taught by TAs	3
Most common reg class size	20–29 students
Most common lab size	20–29 students

MOST POPULAR MAJORS
business administration and management
industrial engineering
mechanical engineering

STUDENTS SAY ". . ."

Academics

The Georgia Institute of Technology—Georgia Tech for short— "challenges its students academically while providing a culturally diverse environment, all culminating in preparation for life after college." Students warn that the school "is extremely challenging, academically. If you don't like learning it's probably not for you." They also point out that "since Georgia Tech is a research school, most professors are more concerned about their own research than the quality of their teaching. You're basically teaching yourself the entire subject in order to prepare for an almost impossible exam," although students also add that "while many of the professors at GT are focused on their research, there are teachers who truly care about their students and the learning process." As one student advises, "a lot of classes seem to be more about getting the right professor: some are bad teachers, some are inaccessible, but some are so good that their classes fill up seconds after registration opens." And while "classes are challenging," they're also "interesting" so all of that hard work is "not too bad. If you're organized and get help when you need it, you'll be okay, because we have tons of free tutoring on campus…If you need help with anything, there are countless different places that offer tutoring. The best resource is usually fellow students. Because everyone knows how tough of a school it is, there is a spirit of camaraderie here that you don't find anywhere else." Students also appreciate that Tech "is one of the only schools in the country that offers the B.S. distinction for liberal arts majors because we [get] such a rigorous grounding in math and science." Finally, students note that "career services are outstanding."

Life

One GT engineer sums up the typical student itinerary this way: "Study, study, drink. Repeat." As another student puts it, "there is a saying here that between good grades, a social life, and sleep, you can only have two." That's why "basically people bust their [butts] during the week, and when the weekends arrive they're prepared to let loose a bit." Fortunately, "Georgia Tech has a little something for everyone. Salsa club on weekends, musical groups, intramural sports— even a skydiving club!" Other options include "a 'good enough' NCAA Division I sports program, a good social scene," a welcoming Greek community, "and for everyone else, there's the city of Atlanta right at your doorstep. You're just a short ride away from movies, shopping, the Fox Theatre, the High Museum of Art, Piedmont Park, and one of the best club and bar scenes in the South," centered mainly in the neighborhoods of Buckhead and Midtown. For those without cars in this driving city, transportation comes in the form of "a 'Tech Trolley' that takes a route around midtown, and a 'Stinger Shuttle' that goes to the MARTA [Atlanta's subway] station, giving students access to the airport, downtown (although that is walkable), and Lenox Mall." With more than "300 organizations already on campus," students seeking leadership experience can most likely find it, and they can find other students with like-minded interests.

Student Body

"The greatest strength of Georgia Tech is its diversity," undergrads report. "Students, activities, opportunities, teachers—all are diverse." One observes that the school hosts "the full range of stereotypes, from the fraternity boys with their croackies and boat shoes to the socially challenged nerds who stay in their rooms 24/7 programming computers. But no matter what, you know everyone is highly intelligent. Many times it is the students who have the best grades who are the drunkest." One student explains, "unlike at high school, no one looks down upon you if you know the entire periodic table, if you can do differential equations, or you can speak three languages; rather, you are respected." One sore spot: Men outnumber women here by greater than a 2:1 ratio. The situation is most pronounced in engineering (3:1) and computer (more than 4:1) disciplines. Women actually outnumber men in the liberal arts and science colleges.

GEORGIA INSTITUTE OF TECHNOLOGY

FINANCIAL AID: 404-894-4160 • E-MAIL: ADMISSION@GATECH.EDU • WEBSITE: WWW.GATECH.EDU

THE PRINCETON REVIEW SAYS

Admissions

Very important factors considered include: Academic GPA. *Important factors considered include:* Application essay, rigor of secondary school record, standardized test scores, extracurricular activities, geographical residence, state residency, talent/ability, volunteer work, work experience. SAT or ACT required. ACT with Writing component required. High school diploma is required and GED is accepted. *Academic units required:* 4 English, 4 mathematics, 3 science (2 science labs), 2 foreign language, 3 social studies.

Financial Aid

Students should submit: FAFSA, institution's own financial aid form. Regular filing deadline is 3/1. The Princeton Review suggests that all financial aid forms be submitted as soon as possible after 1/1. *Need-based scholarships/grants offered:* Federal Pell, SEOG, state scholarships/grants, private scholarships, the school's own gift aid, G. Wayne Clough Georgia Tech Promise Scholarship; president's scholarships; Federal ACG and SMART. *Loan aid offered:* FFEL Subsidized Stafford, FFEL Unsubsidized Stafford, FFEL PLUS, Federal Perkins, college/university loans from institutional funds. Applicants will be notified of awards on a rolling basis beginning 4/1. Federal Work-Study Program available. Institutional employment available. Off-campus job opportunities are excellent.

The Inside Word

Students considering Georgia Tech should not be deceived by the relatively high acceptance rate. GT is a demanding school, and its applicant pool is largely self-selecting. While admissions counselors have begun to implement a more well-rounded approach to the admissions process, grades and test scores are still where candidates make their mark. Requirements vary depending on the school one applies to at GT—applicants are advised to inquire in advance.

THE SCHOOL SAYS "..."

From The Admissions Office

"Georgia Tech consistently ranks among the nation's top public universities producing leaders in engineering, computing, management, architecture, and the sciences while remaining one of the best college buys in the country. The 330-acre campus is nestled in the heart of the fun, dynamic and progressive city of Atlanta. During the past decade, over $400 million invested in campus improvements has yielded new state-of-the-art academic and research buildings, apartment-style housing, phenomenal social and recreational facilities, and the most extension fiber-optic cable system on any college campus.

"A fundamental part of Georgia Tech's mission is to provide a student-focused education. Georgia Tech's Office of Success Programs provides students such initiatives as a freshman seminar course taught by current faculty and staff. The course teaches new students useful strategies that promote their academic, professional, and social success.

"With a Division I ACC sports program and access to Atlanta's music, theater, and other cultural venues, Georgia Tech offers its diverse and passionate student body a unique combination of top academics in a thriving and vibrant setting. We encourage you to come visit campus and see why Georgia Tech continues to attract the nation's most motivated, interesting, and creative students."

SELECTIVITY

Admissions Rating	97
# of applicants	10,258
% of applicants accepted	61
% of acceptees attending	42
# accepting a place on wait list	98
% admitted from wait list	94

FRESHMAN PROFILE

Range SAT Critical Reading	600–690
Range SAT Math	650–730
Range SAT Writing	590–680
Range ACT Composite	27–31
Average HS GPA	3.75
% graduated top 10% of class	58
% graduated top 25% of class	87
% graduated top 50% of class	98

DEADLINES

Regular	
Deadline	1/15
Notification	3/15
Nonfall registration?	yes

APPLICANTS ALSO LOOK AT

AND OFTEN PREFER

Emory University
Virginia Tech
University of Michigan—Ann Arbor
Duke University
University of Florida
University of Georgia

AND SOMETIMES PREFER

University of Virginia
University of Maryland—College Park
University of Illinois at Urbana-Champaign
Cornell University
Carnegie Mellon University

AND RARELY PREFER

Purdue University—West Lafayette
Rice University
Rensselaer Polytechnic Institute

FINANCIAL FACTS

Financial Aid Rating	79
Annual in-state tuition	$6,070
Annual out-of-state tuition	$24,280
% frosh rec. need-based scholarship or grant aid	28
% UG rec. need-based scholarship or grant aid	27
% frosh rec. non-need-based scholarship or grant aid	1
% UG rec. non-need-based scholarship or grant aid	3
% frosh rec. need-based self-help aid	17
% UG rec. need-based self-help aid	22
% frosh rec. athletic scholarships	2
% UG rec. athletic scholarships	2
% frosh rec. any financial aid	81
% UG rec. any financial aid	70
% UG borrow to pay for school	48
Average cumulative indebtedness	$20,881

GETTYSBURG COLLEGE

ADMISSIONS OFFICE, EISENHOWER HOUSE, GETTYSBURG, PA 17325-1484 • ADMISSIONS: 717-337-6100 • FAX: 717-337-6145

CAMPUS LIFE

Quality of Life Rating	**86**
Fire Safety Rating	**87**
Green Rating	**87**
Type of school	private
Affiliation	Lutheran
Environment	village

STUDENTS

Total undergrad enrollment	2,457
% male/female	47/53
% from out of state	75
% from public high school	70
% live on campus	94
% in (# of) fraternities	38 (10)
% in (# of) sororities	26 (6)
% African American	5
% Asian	2
% Caucasian	83
% Hispanic	3
% international	2
# of countries represented	27

SURVEY SAYS . . .

Lab facilities are great
Great food on campus
Dorms are like palaces
Campus feels safe
Students are happy
Frats and sororities dominate social scene
Lots of beer drinking

ACADEMICS

Academic Rating	**91**
Calendar	semester
Student/faculty ratio	11:1
Profs interesting rating	85
Profs accessible rating	88
Most common reg class size	10–19 students

MOST POPULAR MAJORS

business/commerce
political science and government
psychology

STUDENTS SAY ". . ."

Academics

Gettysburg College is a quintessential small liberal arts college, a place where "you can be challenged academically in an intimate environment of smaller class sizes and a smaller student-to-faculty ratio," enabling "students to develop a close rapport with peers and professors." Students here speak glowingly of the "welcoming community with limitless opportunities" to get involved and "grow in and out of the classroom." Those opportunities include "strong study abroad programs, community service activities, internships, and externships." Academically, "Gettysburg isn't a walk in the park. Your professors have expectations of you whether you are a first-year in a 101 class or a senior looking into a research proposal." Help is available to those in danger of falling behind; one student writes, "the offices are there to help you from calc-aid [tutors], biology [reviews], and the writing center…There is so much available; you just need to go take advantage of it." The school's strongest disciplines include political science, music, biology, environmental studies, and (unsurprisingly) Civil War–era studies. Gettysburg also "has a great management department for a small liberal arts school."

Life

"Greek life is where the majority of social life is centered" at Gettysburg, with a strong percentage of all male students joining a fraternity, "But that's not to say that there are not options beyond that." True, "Greek life is huge at Gettysburg, and for a male who chooses not to 'go Greek' life can be hard socially." It's not as big a deal for females, because "Gettysburg does not have sorority houses." The Greek scene as a whole is "not exclusive"—everyone "goes to the frats." Moreover, "The college doesn't allow rush to take place until second year, so hopefully students have made friends before making the choice to branch out into other social groups such as the frats." "Most everyone makes a conscious effort to get involved on campus in lots of different activities," so the Greeks, while big, aren't the only game in town. The school "does a lot of extras for the students, such as themed dinners, concerts, and special events," and "the activity board also brings bands and movies on weekends so there are other things to do." College sports teams "are very strong, both men's and women's," and "lots of students play intramurals or work out." Hometown Gettysburg, with its battlefield and "ghost tours," is a great for history buffs and has a lot of "small town charm"; others may prefer to "take day trips" to D.C. and Baltimore for fun, although each requires a 90-minute drive.

Student Body

Gettysburg students tend to be "smart, outgoing, preppy, and determined," the kind of folks who "work really hard during the week and then have fun on the weekend," but also find time to "volunteer and [get] involved in extracurriculars, clubs, and athletics." Students admit that "there is very little diversity on campus, but the majority of the students come from high schools with the same situation," so many "don't notice the lack of diversity, though this can make you stand out if you're different." Students who don't fit the mold tell us they are comfortable here; one writes, "Gettysburg students tend to come from families who are mid- to upper-class, [and] there is a high percentage of legacy students on campus." Quite frequently, students show their wealth "in the form of clothing or cars," but "money isn't the only thing that matters here." While it may be plentiful, "Even if you don't wear Lily Pulitzer or Burberry you will be just fine as long as flip-flops are your favorite footwear!" Students tend to be politically conservative, although the "the Frisbee team is one niche of politically liberal people" on campus.

FINANCIAL AID: 717-337-6611 • E-MAIL: ADMISS@GETTYSBURG.EDU • WEBSITE: WWW.GETTYSBURG.EDU

THE PRINCETON REVIEW SAYS

Admissions

Very important factors considered include: Class rank, academic GPA, recommendation(s), rigor of secondary school record. *Important factors considered include:* Application essay, standardized test scores, character/personal qualities, extracurricular activities, interview, talent/ability, volunteer work. *Other factors considered include:* Alumni/ae relation, first generation, geographical residence, level of applicant's interest, racial/ethnic status, work experience. SAT or ACT strongly recommended. TOEFL required of all international applicants. High school diploma is required and GED is accepted. *Academic units required:* 4 English, 3 mathematics, 3 science (3 science labs), 3 foreign language, 3 social studies, 3 history. *Academic units recommended:* 4 English, 4 mathematics, 4 science (4 science labs), 4 foreign language, 4 social studies, 4 history.

Financial Aid

Students should submit: FAFSA, CSS/financial aid profile, business/farm supplement. Regular filing deadline is 2/15. The Princeton Review suggests that all financial aid forms be submitted as soon as possible after 1/1. *Need-based scholarships/grants offered:* Federal Pell, SEOG, state scholarships/grants, private scholarships, the school's own gift aid. *Loan aid offered:* FFEL Subsidized Stafford, FFEL Unsubsidized Stafford, FFEL PLUS, Federal Perkins, college/university loans from institutional funds. Applicants will be notified of awards on or about 3/26. Federal Work-Study Program available. Institutional employment available. Off-campus job opportunities are excellent.

The Inside Word

Expect a thorough and highly personalized review of your application at Gettysburg College. Excellent students with relatively weak standardized test scores, take note: Gettysburg no longer requires test scores as part of its application package. The goal of this new policy is to "enrich the classroom environment by encouraging students with a high secondary school grade point average (GPA) and other creative talents who do not perform well on standardized tests to apply for admission." The effect should be to open Gettysburg's doors to capable students who might otherwise not have been previously admitted.

THE SCHOOL SAYS "..."

From The Admissions Office

"Four major goals of Gettysburg College to best prepare students to enter the real world, include: first, to accelerate the intellectual development of our first-year students by integrating them more quickly into the intellectual life of the campus; second, to use interdisciplinary courses combining the intellectual approaches of various fields; third, to encourage students to develop an international perspective through course work, study abroad, association with international faculty, and a variety of extracurricular activities; and fourth, to encourage students to develop (1) a capacity for independent study by ensuring that all students work closely with individual faculty members on an extensive project during their undergraduate years and (2) the ability to work with their peers by making the small group a central feature in college life.

"Gettysburg College strongly recommends that freshman applicants submit scores from the SAT. Students may also choose to submit scores from the ACT (with or without the Writing component) in lieu of the SAT."

SELECTIVITY	
Admissions Rating	95
# of applicants	5,790
% of applicants accepted	38
% of acceptees attending	33
# accepting a place on wait list	846
# of early decision applicants	472
% accepted early decision	65

FRESHMAN PROFILE	
Range SAT Critical Reading	610–690
Range SAT Math	610–670
Minimum paper TOEFL	570
Minimum computer TOEFL	230
% graduated top 10% of class	66
% graduated top 25% of class	89
% graduated top 50% of class	99

DEADLINES	
Early decision	
Deadline	11/15
Notification	12/15
Regular	
Priority	2/1
Deadline	2/1
Notification	4/1
Nonfall registration?	yes

APPLICANTS ALSO LOOK AT
AND OFTEN PREFER
Colgate University
AND SOMETIMES PREFER
Bucknell University
AND RARELY PREFER
Muhlenberg College

FINANCIAL FACTS	
Financial Aid Rating	99
Annual tuition	$37,600
Room and board	$9,100
Required fees	$410
Books and supplies	$500
% frosh rec. need-based scholarship or grant aid	52
% UG rec. need-based scholarship or grant aid	53
% frosh rec. non-need-based scholarship or grant aid	25
% UG rec. non-need-based scholarship or grant aid	23
% frosh rec. need-based self-help aid	43
% UG rec. need-based self-help aid	44
% frosh rec. any financial aid	70
% UG rec. any financial aid	70
% UG borrow to pay for school	66
Average cumulative indebtedness	$23,992

GONZAGA UNIVERSITY

502 EAST BOONE AVENUE, SPOKANE, WA 99258 • ADMISSIONS: 509-323-6572 • FAX: 509-323-5780

CAMPUS LIFE
Quality of Life Rating	**84**
Fire Safety Rating	**89**
Green Rating	**60***
Type of school	private
Affiliation	Roman Catholic
Environment	city

STUDENTS
Total undergrad enrollment	4,442
% male/female	47/53
% from out of state	50
% from public high school	72
% live on campus	57
% African American	1
% Asian	5
% Caucasian	77
% Hispanic	4
% Native American	1
% international	2
# of countries represented	36

SURVEY SAYS . . .
Athletic facilities are great
Students are friendly
Everyone loves the Bulldogs
Intramural sports are popular
Frats and sororities are unpopular or nonexistent

ACADEMICS
Academic Rating	**83**
Calendar	semester
Student/faculty ratio	10.91:1
Profs interesting rating	80
Profs accessible rating	86
Most common reg class size	20–29 students
Most common lab size	10–19 students

MOST POPULAR MAJORS
political science and government
psychology

STUDENTS SAY "..."

Academics

Students tell us that Jesuit-run Gonzaga University is "one big family comprised of Catholics and non-Catholics alike" who "all work together in achieving success. We embrace the Jesuit traditions of service, spirituality, social justice, and leadership." The Jesuit influence is indeed pervasive. It can be seen in the effort to "educate the entire person" through a broad liberal arts curriculum, though Gonzaga requires four semesters of philosophy and three of religious studies. "They are classes that open your eyes to many harsh realities out in the world and ways that we can contribute with our careers to change [them]," one undergrad observes. It is also seen in the school's commitment to social service; "Almost everyone here is involved in some kind of community service, whether as a class requirement or just for fun," one student explains. "GU also requires a social justice class as part of the core curriculum [in the College of Arts and Sciences]." The school is "big enough to have good programs, small enough that you feel cared about." Academic standouts here include engineering, nursing, and business. The fine arts, on the other hand, "could use some more attention" and "need better facilities." The school also "has great support programs. There are endless offices where people can go to get help that include great counselors' offices and homework help." Those same services are "also very good about helping you figure out what you really want to do with your life."

Life

Gonzaga students "love to go to basketball games," even though "it takes a lot of time out of your week between waiting in line on Sundays to get tickets and waiting in line on game days to get seats. However, when you are in the stands among all those red Kennel Club t-shirts, it is totally worth it." Beyond the hardwood floor, GU's campus "is extremely active, which results in a lot of fun, active ways to entertain oneself," including "extremely popular" intramural and club sports and extracurricular clubs ("everyone is involved in a few"). While "The majority of people do go out and party on the weekends, and most parties take place at off campus houses in the Logan neighborhood surrounding campus," students may also choose from among "lots of things to do here that don't involve drinking. Every other week, the Gonzaga University Theater Sports (GUTS) club puts on an improv comedy show which is hilarious without fail. There are also outdoor programs and trips, a myriad of clubs, and service-learning opportunities." Students also take "a very active role in the surrounding community (the Logan neighborhood, which is the poorest neighborhood in all of Spokane). Gonzaga puts on and sponsors a lot of after-school programs for the kids of the local elementary schools and junior highs." Hometown Spokane "has a lot to offer if you know where to look," including "concert venues, cafes, great food, movie theaters showing both mainstream and independent films, and shopping."

Student Body

"There is not a lot of diversity at GU," where "a majority of students are white, upper-middle class." They "are active and generally good students, but they don't take school too seriously" and "like to go out." While they may not love learning for its own sake, they are "intelligent go-getters" who are "eager to grow and eager to explore the world." Most "are or have been involved in sports, either intramural or varsity level. Also, most students are involved with the communities around them, either through services like 'Campus Kitchen,' which serves food to those in the community, or 'Campus Kids' or 'SMILE,' which bring elementary to middle-school kids on campus as an after-school activity to play with and be mentored by the students on campus." Undergrads tend to be "at least moderately religious."

FINANCIAL AID: 800-793-1716 • E-MAIL: ADMISSIONS@GONZAGA.EDU • WEBSITE: WWW.GONZAGA.EDU

THE PRINCETON REVIEW SAYS

Admissions

Very important factors considered include: Academic GPA, rigor of secondary school record, character/personal qualities, first generation. *Important factors considered include:* Application essay, recommendation(s), standardized test scores, extracurricular activities, talent/ability. *Other factors considered include:* Class rank, alumni/ae relation, interview, level of applicant's interest, racial/ethnic status, volunteer work, work experience. SAT or ACT required. TOEFL required of all international applicants. High school diploma is required and GED is not accepted. *Academic units required:* 4 English, 3 mathematics, 3 science (3 science labs), 2 world language (ASL accepted), 2 social studies, 2 history, 2 academic electives. *Academic units recommended:* 4 English, 4 mathematics, 4 science (4 science labs), 4 foreign language, 3 social studies, 3 history, 3 academic electives.

Financial Aid

Students should submit: FAFSA. The Princeton Review suggests that all financial aid forms be submitted as soon as possible after 1/1. *Need-based scholarships/grants offered:* Federal Pell, SEOG, state scholarships/grants, private scholarships, the school's own gift aid, United Negro College Fund, federal nursing scholarships. *Loan aid offered:* FFEL Subsidized Stafford, FFEL Unsubsidized Stafford, FFEL PLUS, Federal Perkins, federal nursing scholarships, state loans, college/university loans from institutional funds. Applicants will be notified of awards on a rolling basis beginning 3/1. Federal Work-Study Program available. Institutional employment available. Off-campus job opportunities are excellent.

The Inside Word

Gonzaga is a great example of how a high-profile athletic program can transform a competitive school into a highly competitive one. During the past decade, Gonzaga's admit rate has decreased substantially while class rank, standardized test scores, and high school GPA have all increased measurably. Perhaps the only substandard students admitted here these days are those who can consistently drain three pointers.

THE SCHOOL SAYS "..."

From The Admissions Office

"Education at Gonzaga is not comparable to an academic 'assembly line'; rather, it is person-to-person and face-to-face. This personal quality is also true of our admission and financial aid processes. Therefore, allow us to know you beyond the boundaries of your college application. Visit campus, phone us, e-mail us—let us see the person behind the data. Good luck with your college search and your applications. Go Zags!

"All sections of the SAT will be accepted, but the Written portion will not receive universal consideration. The Written score will be considered in cases where more information specific to writing ability would be helpful in decision making."

SELECTIVITY

Admissions Rating	93
# of applicants	5,026
% of applicants accepted	78
% of acceptees attending	28
# accepting a place on wait list	58
% admitted from wait list	43

FRESHMAN PROFILE

Range SAT Critical Reading	540–630
Range SAT Math	550–650
Range ACT Composite	24–29
Minimum paper TOEFL	550
Minimum computer TOEFL	213
Average HS GPA	3.66
% graduated top 10% of class	36.3
% graduated top 25% of class	69.38
% graduated top 50% of class	91.73

DEADLINES

Early action	
Deadline	11/15
Notification	1/15
Regular	
Priority	2/1
Deadline	2/1
Notification	3/15
Nonfall registration?	yes

APPLICANTS ALSO LOOK AT
AND SOMETIMES PREFER
University of Washington
Santa Clara University
AND RARELY PREFER
Washington State University

FINANCIAL FACTS

Financial Aid Rating	85
Annual tuition	$26,120
Room and board	$7,520
Required fees	$438
Books and supplies	$900
% frosh rec. need-based scholarship or grant aid	55
% UG rec. need-based scholarship or grant aid	56
% frosh rec. non-need-based scholarship or grant aid	23
% UG rec. non-need-based scholarship or grant aid	21
% frosh rec. need-based self-help aid	31
% UG rec. need-based self-help aid	41
% frosh rec. athletic scholarships	3
% UG rec. athletic scholarships	4
% frosh rec. any financial aid	97
% UG rec. any financial aid	95
% UG borrow to pay for school	75
Average cumulative indebtedness	$24,094

GOUCHER COLLEGE

1021 DULANEY VALLEY ROAD, BALTIMORE, MD 21204-2794 • ADMISSIONS: 410-337-6100 • FAX: 410-337-6354

CAMPUS LIFE

Quality of Life Rating	**78**
Fire Safety Rating	**85**
Green Rating	**98**
Type of school	private
Environment	suburban

STUDENTS

Total undergrad enrollment	1,434
% male/female	32/68
% from out of state	72
% from public high school	63
% live on campus	84
% African American	6
% Asian	3
% Caucasian	68
% Hispanic	4
% international	1
# of countries represented	29

SURVEY SAYS . . .

Lots of liberal students
No one cheats
Students are friendly
Frats and sororities are unpopular or
nonexistent
Political activism is popular
(Almost) everyone smokes

ACADEMICS

Academic Rating	**87**
Calendar	semester
Student/faculty ratio	10:1
Profs interesting rating	87
Profs accessible rating	82
Most common reg class size	10–19 students

MOST POPULAR MAJORS

English language and literature
mass communication/media studies
psychology

STUDENTS SAY ". . ."

Academics

Goucher College, a "delightfully odd" school at which "Everybody is quirky in some way," offers a surprising number of first-rate programs for a school of its size. The performing and creative arts are big here, and students tout the dance program as "the best non-conservatory program in the country." Goucher's broad "liberal arts education" ensures that all students get to experience "a little bit of everything" academically. Students praise a "great science/premed program," "good writing and theater programs," and a riding program bolstered by "stables right on campus." Goucher's growing international relations program reflects the school's "education without boundaries" philosophy, and includes an "innovative and exciting" study abroad requirement. Most students love this requirement, citing it as a primary reason for choosing Goucher; a few naysayers complain that the program "can add up financially" (despite the $1,200 voucher students receive to help offset costs). There's no disagreement about Goucher's professors, however, whom students describe as "amazing people and great mentors." They expect a lot from you, "but in the end [you] accomplish more than [you] ever thought possible, and they are willing to help you every step of the way." Goucher also offers "very good academic support services for students with learning disabilities."

Life

"Goucher students spend lots of time in class and studying hard," but when it's time to take a break, there is always something to do on campus, including painting, horseback riding, and dancing," while others participate in "various clubs and organizations." Students "often travel into downtown Baltimore on the weekends, and like to hang out at the local cafes and farmer's markets, and see shows." Inner Harbor is "also a frequent destination for fun." Goucher runs "a free college shuttle that picks students up and drops them off at other area universities (Johns Hopkins, Loyola, College of Notre Dame, Towson University) as well as at Penn Station," from which students can easily access downtown Washington, D.C., and the Inner Harbor. Hometown Towson, a satellite of Baltimore, provides "cute restaurants and stores," but little in the way of collegiate nightlife. On campus, undergrads can choose from "100 student clubs and activities, and "Anyone can start a new club (it is really easy)." Many here feel that "the lack of Greek societies [on campus] limits a lot of social life," which "isn't to say that drinking doesn't go on here. It does, but it happens quietly and [is] low-key in dorms." Dating "is pretty difficult" due to the lopsided male-female ratio. "The few straight boys are usually taken or they are extremely awkward. It's not uncommon to walk into any boys' dorm and find Magic cards and posters of *Lord of the Rings* all over."

Student Body

Goucher has "many of the staple groups, such as jocks," but also "a lot of atypical students" including "pirates [there is a Goucher Pirate Alliance], people who play zombies [regular combatants in Humans vs. Zombies, a game played with Nerf guns]," and "lots of aspiring artists and writers who think they are the cream of the crop." In fact, many here tell us that the atypical student in high school is the typical Goucher undergrad, the kid "who was not very popular in high school but rather the creative type, often existing on the periphery." The "only thing that makes Goucher students similar is their acceptance of other students' weirdness." Students also tend to be "laid-back people who enjoy getting an education rather than competing for one." Undergrads report that "there is a strong Jewish community here, but Christian groups are also present." "The student body is very friendly as a whole."

FINANCIAL AID: 410-337-6141 • E-MAIL: ADMISSION@GOUCHER.EDU • WEBSITE: WWW.GOUCHER.EDU

THE PRINCETON REVIEW SAYS

Admissions

Very important factors considered include: Academic GPA, rigor of secondary school record. *Important factors considered include:* Application essay, recommendation(s), talent/ability. *Other factors considered include:* Class rank, standardized test scores, alumni/ae relation, character/personal qualities, extracurricular activities, first generation, geographical residence, interview, level of applicant's interest, racial/ethnic status, state residency, volunteer work, TOEFL required of all international applicants. High school diploma is required and GED is accepted. *Academic units required:* 4 English, 3 mathematics, 2 science, 2 foreign language, 3 social studies, 2 academic electives. *Academic units recommended:* 4 English, 4 mathematics, 3 science, 4 foreign language, 3 social studies, 2 academic electives.

Financial Aid

Students should submit: FAFSA, CSS/financial aid profile, noncustodial profile, business/farm supplement. Regular filing deadline is 2/1. The Princeton Review suggests that all financial aid forms be submitted as soon as possible after 1/1. *Need-based scholarships/grants offered:* Federal Pell, SEOG, state scholarships/grants, private scholarships, the school's own gift aid. *Loan aid offered:* FFEL Subsidized Stafford, FFEL Unsubsidized Stafford, FFEL PLUS, Federal Perkins, college/university loans from institutional funds. Applicants will be notified of awards on a rolling basis beginning 4/1. Federal Work-Study Program available. Institutional employment available. Off-campus job opportunities are excellent.

The Inside Word

Although there is a test-optional admissions policy, Goucher accepts the ACT with Writing in lieu of the new SAT and SAT Subject Tests to be considered for merit funding. Goucher's high admit rate masks a self-selecting applicant pool; you cannot gain acceptance here without a solid high school transcript and test scores.

THE SCHOOL SAYS "..."

From The Admissions Office

"Through a broad-based arts and sciences curriculum and a groundbreaking approach to study abroad, Goucher College gives students a sweeping view of the world. Goucher is an independent, coeducational institution dedicated to both the interdisciplinary traditions of the liberal arts and a truly international perspective on education. The first college in the nation to pair required study abroad with a special travel stipend of $1,200 for every undergraduate, Goucher believes in complementing its strong majors and rigorous curriculum with abundant opportunities for hands-on experience. In addition to participating in the college's many study abroad programs (including innovative 3-week intensive courses abroad alongside traditional semester and academic year offerings), many students also complete internships and service-learning projects that further enhance their learning.

"The college's almost 1,500 undergraduate students live and learn on a tree-lined campus of 287 acres just north of Baltimore, Maryland. Goucher boasts a student/faculty ratio of just 10:1, and professors routinely collaborate with students on major research projects—often for publication, and sometimes as early as students' first or second years. The curriculum emphasizes international and intercultural awareness throughout, and students are encouraged to explore their academic interests from a variety of perspectives beyond their major disciplines.

"A Goucher College education encompasses a multitude of experiences that ultimately converge into one cohesive academic program that can truly change lives. Students grow in dramatic and surprising ways here. They graduate with a strong sense of direction and self-confidence, ready to engage the world—and succeed—as true global citizens.

"Goucher College has a test-optional admissions policy."

SELECTIVITY

Admissions Rating	**85**
# of applicants	4,077
% of applicants accepted	64
% of acceptees attending	14
# accepting a place on wait list	82
% admitted from wait list	70

FRESHMAN PROFILE

Range SAT Critical Reading	530–660
Range SAT Math	490–620
Range SAT Writing	530–650
Minimum paper TOEFL	550
Minimum computer TOEFL	213
Average HS GPA	3.17

DEADLINES

Early action	
Deadline	12/1
Notification	2/15
Regular	
Priority	2/1
Deadline	2/1
Notification	4/1
Nonfall registration?	yes

APPLICANTS ALSO LOOK AT
AND OFTEN PREFER
Mount Holyoke College
Skidmore College

AND SOMETIMES PREFER
Loyola University–Maryland
American University

FINANCIAL FACTS

Financial Aid Rating	**79**
Annual Tuition	$33,294
Required Fees	$492
Room and Board	$10,008
% frosh rec. need-based scholarship or grant aid	50
% UG rec. need-based scholarship or grant aid	50
% frosh rec. non-need-based scholarship or grant aid	5
% UG rec. non-need-based scholarship or grant aid	5
% frosh rec. need-based self-help aid	48
% UG rec. need-based self-help aid	47
% frosh rec. any financial aid	80.8
% UG rec. any financial aid	80.1
% UG borrow to pay for school	39
Average cumulative indebtedness	$16,729

GREEN MOUNTAIN COLLEGE

One College Circle, Poultney, VT 05764-1199 • Admissions: 802-287-8000 • Fax: 802-287-8099

CAMPUS LIFE

Quality of Life Rating	76
Fire Safety Rating	60*
Green Rating	60*
Type of school	private
Affiliation	Methodist
Environment	rural

STUDENTS

Total undergrad enrollment	780
% male/female	48/50
% from out of state	86
% from public high school	86
% live on campus	81
% African American	3
% Asian	1
% Caucasian	67
% Hispanic	2
% Native American	1
# of countries represented	18

SURVEY SAYS . . .

Students are friendly
Low cost of living
Frats and sororities are unpopular or
nonexistent
(Almost) no one smokes

ACADEMICS

Academic Rating	81
Calendar	semester
Student/faculty ratio	14:1
Profs interesting rating	86
Profs accessible rating	83
Most common reg class size	10–19 students
Most common lab size	10–19 students

MOST POPULAR MAJORS

environmental studies
adventure education
psychology

STUDENTS SAY ". . ."

Academics

"Small," "incredibly progressive" Green Mountain College in rural Vermont "does the environmental, green thing" throughout its curriculum. "A strong liberal arts program" includes four mandatory core courses that relate in way or another to the environment. Interdisciplinary block courses allow students to focus on one ecological topic. GMC gets more than half of its electricity from Vermont dairy farms. The pride and joy of the campus is a "fossil fuel-free" and generally "kick-ass" farm that "gives students firsthand experience in agriculture and subsistent farming." There's a barn "packed with animals." "We grow delicious, organic produce," notes an environmental studies major. Some courses "aren't as challenging as they could be," but reviews of the academic experience here are generally positive. There is a wealth of opportunities for "hands-on learning," internships, and studying abroad. Unique majors include adventure recreation and resort management. There's also the progressive program, which allows students to chart their own academic course. "Professors go by their first names." A few are "absolutely awful," but most are "a joy to have in class." They are "very approachable" and active in the larger community. "I love going to a bluegrass concert and seeing my stats professor playing banjo," gushes a happy first-year student.

Life

"Green Mountain is all about environmentalism, skiing, the outdoors, and the Grateful Dead." Maple trees "cover the campus." There are several "very pretty buildings," too. In keeping with its environmentally sustainable ethos, a LEED Gold Certified residence hall is scheduled to be completed in fall of 2009. Socially, "life is laid-back" "Everybody pretty much knows everybody." "During the winter, the weather is harsh," but both fall and spring are pleasant. "It is amazing to go outside when it is nice out to see rugby, Frisbee, volleyball, music circles, and music coming from all different dorms," observes a junior. "There is a river right behind the college, and it's a popular hangout spot," adds a senior. "People swim during the day and have bonfires at night." "There is a lot of partying" as well. Campus activities include "concerts, contra-dances, dinners, parties, and much more." The "isolated" hamlet of Poultney has "little to offer beyond small-town New England charm." "The closest city, Rutland, isn't that big and is a half hour away." The area is "scenic," though, and it's a nature lover's paradise. "There are ski hills in every direction," and the College "runs trips almost every weekend to do outdoor activities such as kayaking, rock climbing, hiking, etc."

Student Body

"The typical student is white and from New England." That student is also a "tree-loving" "outdoors type" who "has long hair." Individuality is "deeply embraced" here. "Our school population consists mainly of people who would be atypical at other schools," explains a senior. However, most students are "left-wing liberals" who are "environmentally aware." "If you have a different point of view, it can be overwhelming." "Future activists" proliferate. There are "many vegetarians and vegans." On the whole, Green Mountain's student population is "a conglomeration of hippies and ski bums." Students are "sixties-oriented in fashion, lifestyle, food choices, and personality." Even the rare preppy students "seem to be able to embrace their inner hippie." "At times, it's like a time warp."

FINANCIAL AID: 802-287-8210 • E-MAIL: ADMISS@GREENMTN.EDU • WEBSITE: WWW.GREENMTN.EDU

THE PRINCETON REVIEW SAYS

Admissions

Very important factors considered include: Application essay, academic GPA, rigor of secondary school record, character/personal qualities. *Important factors considered include:* Class rank, recommendation(s), extracurricular activities, interview, volunteer work. *Other factors considered include:* Standardized test scores, level of applicant's interest, talent/ability, work experience. SAT or ACT recommended. TOEFL required of all international applicants. High school diploma is required and GED is accepted. *Academic units required:* 4 English, 3 mathematics, 3 science (2 science labs), 2 foreign language, 3 social studies, 1 history, 5 academic electives. *Academic units recommended:* 4 mathematics, 4 science, 3 foreign language, 3 social studies, 2 history.

Financial Aid

Students should submit: FAFSA, CSS/financial aid profile, noncustodial profile The Princeton Review suggests that all financial aid forms be submitted as soon as possible after 1/1. *Need-based scholarships/grants offered:* Federal Pell, SEOG, state scholarships/grants, private scholarships, the school's own gift aid. *Loan aid offered:* FFEL Subsidized Stafford, FFEL Unsubsidized Stafford, FFEL PLUS, state loans, alternative loans. Applicants will be notified of awards on a rolling basis beginning 1/1.

The Inside Word

It's a holistic process here, which is fabulous news if your academic record thus far is less than stellar. Standardized test scores are optional. Only send yours if they are good. Don't miss the interview. Pay meticulous attention to the essay. Take advantage of the opportunity to supplement your application with additional materials. Also, note that financial aid is ample.

THE SCHOOL SAYS "..."

From The Admissions Office

"Green Mountain College is a liberal arts college that's been on the forefront of sustainability education since 1995, when we introduced our Environmental Liberal Arts general education program. We have received a 2007 sustainability leadership award from the Association for the Advancement of Sustainability in Higher Education (AASHE) and other national accolades for the field-based, interdisciplinary and service-oriented approach to education in our 21 majors. A LEED-certified residence hall and a new biomass heating plant complement our historic New England campus.

"GMC is a close-knit community of students from around the world who share a passion for social action. We pride ourselves on being a place where diversity thrives and where the artist, the athlete, the environmentalist, and the scholar live and learn in harmony.

"At GMC, applicants may elect not to submit test scores if they feel those scores don't accurately reflect their ability. Instead they may submit an "Insight Portfolio" (three short essays) for consideration, along with their GPA and other academic credentials.

"We award scholarships for service, leadership, visual and performing arts, and environmental advancement at the time of admission, so students should include evidence of their involvement in these areas. The College is consistently striving to enhance affordability and has initiated a four-year graduation guarantee. Students who maintain a minimum 2.0 GPA, choose a major in a timely manner, and meet regularly with an academic advisor are guaranteed to graduate in four years or additional tuition will be waived."

SELECTIVITY

Admissions Rating	75
# of applicants	1,579
% of applicants accepted	70
% of acceptees attending	25

FRESHMAN PROFILE

Range SAT Critical Reading	470–600
Range SAT Math	450–560
Range SAT Writing	460–580
Range ACT Composite	20–26
Minimum paper TOEFL	500
Minimum computer TOEFL	173
Average HS GPA	3.1
% graduated top 10% of class	10.6
% graduated top 25% of class	24.7
% graduated top 50% of class	57.6

DEADLINES

Regular	
Priority	4/1
Notification	rolling
Nonfall registration?	yes

FINANCIAL FACTS

Financial Aid Rating	78
Annual tuition	$24,938
Room and board	$9,522
Required fees	$900
Books and supplies	$1,100
% frosh rec. need-based scholarship or grant aid	68
% UG rec. need-based scholarship or grant aid	73
% frosh rec. non-need-based scholarship or grant aid	11
% UG rec. non-need-based scholarship or grant aid	11
% frosh rec. need-based self-help aid	61
% UG rec. need-based self-help aid	68
% frosh rec. any financial aid	80
% UG rec. any financial aid	84
% UG borrow to pay for school	78

GRINNELL COLLEGE

OFFICE OF ADMISSION, 1103 PARK STREET, 2ND FLOOR, GRINNELL, IA 50112-1690 • ADMISSIONS: 641-269-3600 • FAX: 641-269-4800

CAMPUS LIFE
Quality of Life Rating	79
Fire Safety Rating	86
Green Rating	82
Type of school	private
Environment	village

STUDENTS
Total undergrad enrollment	1,639
% male/female	46/54
% from out of state	88
% from public high school	65
% live on campus	87
% African American	5
% Asian	8
% Caucasian	62
% Hispanic	6
% international	11
# of countries represented	54

SURVEY SAYS . . .
No one cheats
Frats and sororities are unpopular or nonexistent
Student government is popular
Political activism is popular

ACADEMICS
Academic Rating	98
Calendar	semester
Student/faculty ratio	9:1
Profs interesting rating	91
Profs accessible rating	94
Most common reg class size	10–19 students
Most common lab size	fewer than 10 students

MOST POPULAR MAJORS
economics
history
sociology

STUDENTS SAY "..."

Academics

Offering "a great mix of serious academics and a fun community," Grinnell College "is a crazy, unique, busy, caffeinated cornfield of geniuses" whose "hard work, critical thinking, and social consciousness" define the Grinnell experience. The school "is challenging academically," so "you have to work very hard, and it's not always easy. It can be stressful at times, but the pressure all comes from yourself. It's not a competitive atmosphere. And the academics here are extremely effective." An open curriculum ("no requirements other than the freshman tutorial") and a self-governance policy mean that "students feel at home here because we are independent," operating "without stringent rules about how to live our lives and what choices to make." A low teacher-student ratio allows for close relationships, meaning students aren't entirely without guidance. "I have never heard of an inaccessible professor," one student reports. "They are very willing to help and genuinely care about us and our performance in class. In addition, I have never heard of a class with more than 30 people in it: They just don't exist." That commitment to having small classes "ensures group discussion and personal attention: There are no straight lecture classes." Thanks to a "huge endowment," students have tremendous latitude in plotting their studies. One undergrad observes, "Money never really seems to be an issue here. If you can dream it, Grinnell can pay for it." The school is "full of resources! Students needing to do research in museums, archives, and libraries for thesis-level research projects can easily get funding from the college. Also, the arts and science facilities are top-of-the-line."

Life

The academic rigors at Grinnell are substantial. You "won't have to worry about surviving the Midwest winter" here, because "being buried in books and papers and paper revisions and articles and essays and book reviews and to-do lists keeps you surprisingly warm." The environment can be stressful, and many are inclined toward traditional collegiate stress-relieving activities. "That being said, there is no pressure to try things if one is not interested," and there are in fact "many substance-free students, some of whom choose to live in sub-free housing." "The administration, as part of self governance, does not police drinking/drugs," but it does encourage students to act responsibly. "Student security is present at school-sponsored parties." Students agree that "extracurricular activities are highly popular," running the gamut from "artists the college brings in" to "lectures, movies, concerts, even therapy dogs during mid-semester exams" to "just hanging out with some cards or 'How I Met Your Mother' DVDs." Hometown Grinnell is "isolated," but not without its charms. One student explains, "I love the town of Grinnell and think Midwest-nice is a great asset, but that's my personal taste. I like recognizing the lady who walks her dog by our house every day and the kid who bags our groceries. And I love going to the farmer's market and things like the 4-H tractor show that took place this summer."

Student Body

Grinnell undergrads describe themselves and their classmates as "students interested in social justice and having a good time." They tend to be "highly intelligent, motivated, and inquisitive" students who constantly challenge one another "to examine topics from different perspectives. This constant thinking outside of the box is a primary aspect of a true liberal arts education." Grinnellians "are frequently left-leaning, but there's not a typical Grinnell student. All the students are different, so there are few issues with fitting in." Intellect and intensity are the most frequent common denominators; as one student explains, "I've heard that every single student is a nerd about something. Perhaps that is what unites us—our passion, whether that be for a sport, academic subject, Joss Whedon, foam-sword fighting, or politics. We all respect that we have different interests but bond because we are interested rather than apathetic, therefore interesting and unique."

FINANCIAL AID: 641-269-3250 • E-MAIL: ASKGRIN@GRINNELL.EDU • WEBSITE: WWW.GRINNELL.EDU

THE PRINCETON REVIEW SAYS

Admissions

Very important factors considered include: Class rank, academic GPA, recommendation(s), rigor of secondary school record, standardized test scores, extracurricular activities, talent/ability. *Important factors considered include:* Application essay, interview, racial/ethnic status. *Other factors considered include:* Alumni/ae relation, character/personal qualities, first generation, geographical residence, level of applicant's interest, state residency, volunteer work, work experience. SAT or ACT required. TOEFL required of all international applicants. High school diploma is required and GED is accepted. *Academic units recommended:* 4 English, 4 mathematics, 4 science (3 science labs), 4 foreign language, 4 social studies.

Financial Aid

Students should submit: FAFSA, institution's own financial aid form, noncustodial profile. Regular filing deadline is 2/1. The Princeton Review suggests that all financial aid forms be submitted as soon as possible after 1/1. *Need-based scholarships/grants offered:* Federal Pell, SEOG, state scholarships/grants, private scholarships, the school's own gift aid. *Loan aid offered:* FFEL Subsidized Stafford, FFEL Unsubsidized Stafford, FFEL PLUS, Federal Perkins, college/university loans from institutional funds. Applicants will be notified of awards on or about 4/1. Federal Work-Study Program available. Institutional employment available. Off-campus job opportunities are excellent.

The Inside Word

Grinnell's admissions process is refreshingly straightforward. According to the school's website, the school bases 50 percent of its decision on high school performance, including quality of curriculum, and 25 percent depends on standardized test scores. The remaining 25 percent is based on the school's assessment of each candidate's potential contributions in the classroom and to the Grinnell campus community. Grinnell is extremely selective, so you'll have to give it your all. An interview isn't required here, but do it anyway.

THE SCHOOL SAYS "..."

From The Admissions Office

"Grinnell College is a place where independence of thought and social conscience are instilled. It is a wide-open space of resources, professors, and students in search of truth, understanding, and shared endeavors. Grinnell is a college with the resources of a school 10 times its size, a faculty that reads like a Who's Who of Teaching, and a learning environment where debate does not end in the classroom and often begins in the Campus Center.

"Grinnellians are committed to learning, respect for themselves and others, contributing to global social good, willing collaboration, and the courage to try. Grinnell College is a place of endless possibilities, a place where there are no limits on what you can accomplish.

"We look for students who show strong potential, have the courage to try new things, demonstrate a willingness to speak out and share their opinions, and bring different perspectives to our international campus in the middle of Iowa. Grinnell College is filled with students who are serious about learning but are not always serious."

SELECTIVITY
Admissions Rating	**95**
# of applicants	3,217
% of applicants accepted	43
% of acceptees attending	34
# accepting a place on wait list	402
% admitted from wait list	1
# of early decision applicants	200
% accepted early decision	69

FRESHMAN PROFILE
Range SAT Critical Reading	615–740
Range SAT Math	620–710
Range ACT Composite	28–32
Minimum paper TOEFL	550
Minimum computer TOEFL	220
Minimum web-based TOEFL	80
% graduated top 10% of class	64
% graduated top 25% of class	90
% graduated top 50% of class	99

DEADLINES
Early decision	
Deadline	11/15
Notification	12/15
Regular	
Deadline	1/2
Notification	4/1
Nonfall registration?	no

**APPLICANTS ALSO LOOK AT
AND SOMETIMES PREFER**
Carleton College

AND RARELY PREFER
Macalester College
Kenyon College

FINANCIAL FACTS
Financial Aid Rating	**98**
Annual tuition	$35,428
Room and board	$8,272
Books and supplies	$900
% frosh rec. need-based scholarship or grant aid	68
% UG rec. need-based scholarship or grant aid	60
% frosh rec. non-need-based scholarship or grant aid	10
% UG rec. non-need-based scholarship or grant aid	6
% frosh rec. need-based self-help aid	57
% UG rec. need-based self-help aid	52
% frosh rec. any financial aid	89
% UG rec. any financial aid	86
% UG borrow to pay for school	53
Average cumulative indebtedness	$19,526

GROVE CITY COLLEGE

100 CAMPUS DRIVE, GROVE CITY, PA 16127-2104 • ADMISSIONS: 724-458-2100 • FAX: 724-458-3395

CAMPUS LIFE

Quality of Life Rating	**75**
Fire Safety Rating	**86**
Green Rating	**64**
Type of school	private
Affiliation	Presbyterian
Environment	rural

STUDENTS

Total undergrad enrollment	2,490
% male/female	51/49
% from out of state	53
% from public high school	75
% live on campus	93
% in (# of) fraternities	17 (8)
% in (# of) sororities	28 (8)
% African American	1
% Asian	2
% Caucasian	94
% Hispanic	1
% international	1
# of countries represented	8

SURVEY SAYS . . .

Career services are great
Diversity lacking on campus
Students are very religious
Low cost of living
Intramural sports are popular
(Almost) no one smokes
Very little drug use

ACADEMICS

Academic Rating	**83**
Calendar	semester
Student/faculty ratio	15:1
Profs interesting rating	77
Profs accessible rating	88
Most common reg class size	10–19 students
Most common lab size	10–19 students

MOST POPULAR MAJORS

elementary education and teaching
English language and literature
mechanical engineering

STUDENTS SAY ". . ."

Academics

Students see the world from a "Christian viewpoint in a safe atmosphere" at Grove City, a college in Pennsylvania that offers "conservative libertarian Christianity applied to a serious Western liberal arts curriculum." As one student puts it, "we are a school that celebrates the trinity of Jesus, C.S. Lewis, and Ronald Reagan." Students here "serve God while working their butts off" in academically rigorous classes designed to give "a good education based on biblical values" through the integration of faith in both the curriculum and college life. Administration makes it a point to be available to the students; the president of the college has weekly time set apart when students can personally talk with him. Still, campus living can sometimes get complicated, as "rules at Grove City are not always enforced as they say, and some rules exist that are not written anywhere." Class registration is "one of the most stressful things EVER!" The campus itself is beautiful, and the school "does a great job with keeping it up," but parking is both expensive and far away. Since the average class size at GCC is relatively small, the classroom is "definitely a student-friendly setting." Though many have a couple of teachers they've been unhappy with, all are very satisfied with both what the professors give them and ask of them. Professors have extremely high expectations for their students and "have challenging tests and a lot of work," but they "truly care about you and are open to students asking questions and talking to them about work or anything else outside of class." "They are committed to learning and mastering all areas of human endeavor for the glory of God," says a student. The school's excellent job placement rate and "reasonable price" are just a few more of the many reasons students choose to come here.

Life

Activities abound at Grove City, with "excellent" intramurals topping the popularity list, and "a million and one" clubs. "I am involved in Clowns for Christ, Life Advocates (a pro-life group), and the Grove City Democrats," says a busy student. A favorite activity on campus is Warriors, which is an hour of worship once a week. This dry campus is "not exactly a party school or one where weekend life is traditionally 'hopping.'" On weekends, students typically hang out in their friends' rooms and watch movies or go to dances. The rules here are quite strict—there are "inter-visitation rules proscribing which hours males and females may be on male and female halls"—so students do "fun but non-illegal things" in their spare time. Many agree that the school could stand to "[rein] in campus safety." No one is a big fan of the town itself, but Pittsburgh is only an hour or so away. There are also, thankfully, "good restaurants within 15 or 20 minutes," since the school "could improve drastically in quality of food provided." All students live on campus and must have meal plans. "I'd have to say that the most fun is making up your own fun," says a student. One "could stop and have a deep conversation with a perfect stranger, and it would be normal," and indeed, "you hear many conversations about religious issues."

Student Body

No doubt about it—the typical student here is "white, middle- to upper-class, and very religious." Many of these "Grovers" were home-schooled. As for atypical students and minorities, well, "there aren't a lot," but they do manage to find each other. Diversity here could definitely use some TLC—a large number of students wish that the school would "[bring] in people who are not all the same." Students of different sexual orientation are not allowed to attend Grove City College, and those who are not religious to some (relatively strong) degree can be uncomfortable here. Still, most people are "friendly and helpful," and "there is rarely an interpersonal conflict." Studies tend to be a center of focus here, and the "library is constantly crowded with students working hard to keep up." They all "work together in order to achieve a diploma instead of believing they have to compete with each other." "Everyone on campus is over-committed. Coming to Grove City, you basically admit to and crave being stressed beyond belief," says an elementary education major.

FINANCIAL AID: 724-458-2163 • E-MAIL: ADMISSIONS@GCC.EDU • WEBSITE: WWW.GCC.EDU/PR

THE PRINCETON REVIEW SAYS

Admissions

Very important factors considered include: Application essay, rigor of secondary school record, standardized test scores, character/personal qualities, extracurricular activities, interview, religious affiliation/commitment. *Important factors considered include:* Recommendation(s), talent/ability. *Other factors considered include:* Class rank, alumni/ae relation, geographical residence, racial/ethnic status, state residency, volunteer work, work experience. SAT or ACT required. TOEFL required of all international applicants. High school diploma is required and GED is accepted. *Academic units recommended:* 4 English, 3 mathematics, 3 science (2 science labs), 3 foreign language, 2 social studies, 2 history.

Financial Aid

Students should submit: institution's own financial aid form. Regular filing deadline is 4/15. The Princeton Review suggests that all financial aid forms be submitted as soon as possible after 1/1. *Need-based scholarships/grants offered:* state scholarships/grants, private scholarships, the school's own gift aid. *Loan aid offered:* Other, Private, alternative loans. Applicants will be notified of awards on a rolling basis beginning 3/20. Institutional employment available. Off-campus job opportunities are good.

The Inside Word

Admission to Grove City has become very competitive, and any serious contender will need to hit the books. While a rigorous class schedule is a given, admissions officers also closely assess character and personal qualities. GCC is steeped in Christian values, and the school seeks students who will be comfortable in such an environment. As such, interviews and recommendations hold significant weight.

THE SCHOOL SAYS "..."

From The Admissions Office

"A good college education doesn't have to cost a fortune. For decades, Grove City College has offered a quality education at costs among the lowest nationally. Since the 1990s, increased national academic acclaim has come to Grove City College. Grove City College is a place where professors teach; you will not see graduate assistants or teacher's aides in the classroom. Our professors are also active in the total life of the campus. More than 100 student organizations on campus afford opportunity for a wide variety of cocurricular activities. Outstanding scholars and leaders in education, science, and international affairs visit the campus each year. The environment at GCC is friendly, secure, and dedicated to high standards. Character-building is emphasized and traditional Christian values are supported.

"There is a fresh spiritual vitality on campus that touches every aspect of your college life. In the classroom we don't shy away from discussing all points of view, however we adhere to Christ's teaching as relevant guidance for living. Come and visit and learn more."

SELECTIVITY

Admissions Rating	**94**
# of applicants	1,916
% of applicants accepted	55
% of acceptees attending	62
# accepting a place on wait list	236
% admitted from wait list	7
# of early decision applicants	630
% accepted early decision	51

FRESHMAN PROFILE

Range SAT Critical Reading	566–702
Range SAT Math	574–691
Range ACT Composite	25–30
Minimum paper TOEFL	550
Minimum computer TOEFL	213
Average HS GPA	3.71
% graduated top 10% of class	52
% graduated top 25% of class	83
% graduated top 50% of class	97

DEADLINES

Early decision	
Deadline	11/15
Notification	12/15
Regular	
Deadline	2/1
Notification	3/15
Nonfall registration?	yes

APPLICANTS ALSO LOOK AT
AND OFTEN PREFER
Wheaton College (IL)
Hillsdale College
Penn State—University Park

AND SOMETIMES PREFER
Houghton College

FINANCIAL FACTS

Financial Aid Rating	**62**
Annual tuition	$12,074
Room and board	$6,440
Books and supplies	$900
% frosh rec. need-based scholarship or grant aid	41
% UG rec. need-based scholarship or grant aid	33
% frosh rec. non-need-based scholarship or grant aid	7
% UG rec. non-need-based scholarship or grant aid	4
% frosh rec. need-based self-help aid	18
% UG rec. need-based self-help aid	19
% frosh rec. any financial aid	40
% UG rec. any financial aid	35
% UG borrow to pay for school	62
Average cumulative indebtedness	$24,721

GUILFORD COLLEGE

5800 WEST FRIENDLY AVENUE, GREENSBORO, NC 27410 • ADMISSIONS: 336-316-2100 • FAX: 336-316-2954

CAMPUS LIFE
Quality of Life Rating	**74**
Fire Safety Rating	**72**
Green Rating	**95**
Type of school	private
Affiliation	Quaker
Environment	city

STUDENTS
Total undergrad enrollment	2,641
% male/female	40/60
% from out of state	64
% from public high school	71
% live on campus	72
% African American	23
% Asian	2
% Caucasian	66
% Hispanic	3
% Native American	1
% international	1
# of countries represented	10

SURVEY SAYS . . .
No one cheats
Students are friendly
Frats and sororities are unpopular or nonexistent
College radio is popular
Political activism is popular
(Almost) everyone smokes

ACADEMICS
Academic Rating	**87**
Calendar	semester
Student/faculty ratio	16:1
Profs interesting rating	86
Profs accessible rating	81
Most common reg class size	10–19 students
Most common lab size	10–19 students

MOST POPULAR MAJORS
business/commerce
criminal justice/safety studies
psychology

STUDENTS SAY " . . ."

Academics

Guilford College, "promotes academic excellence, social and cultural awareness, critical analysis, and community involvement" while "incorporating Quaker ideals and traditions." Undergrads here warn that this small liberal arts school requires "a lot of work," and that the program "is very reading-and-writing intensive." As one student explains, "I've had to write papers for every class except chemistry, and in one class I've written around 10 papers." Support for students is strong, both from "incredible" professors who "are where they say they are going to be when they say they are going to be there, which makes it incredibly easy to get help." Guilford also offers "many resources" to help students handle the workload, such as "the Academic Skills Center." The school promotes autonomy, providing undergrads "the ability to design their own programs," without sacrificing "personal and positive relationships with most teachers and many members of the administration. They are always open to hear from students on any issue." Especially strong areas of study at Guilford include the criminal justice program (it "rocks"), as well as "great programs for theater and adult studies."

Life

As at most small, rigorous, liberal arts schools, "classes take up a good deal of time" at Guilford, and students keep themselves busy during their few off-hours with "extracurricular activities, hanging out with friends, and going off campus." One student writes, "considering the relatively small size of the campus, there is a constant list of social, political, and spiritual activities going on for seemingly every preference or belief one might have." Another student concurs: "Whether for class or socially, the campus is always active." The "great Quaker heritage here makes for an open and personal environment" in which "people leave their doors open all the time." Students are "very social...I've never heard of someone just sitting alone in their room if that wasn't what they wanted." Guilford's Quaker heritage also attracts a lot of politically active students, who share an "environmental concern." There are also "lots of sports and club activities." Hometown Greensboro is a small city but big enough to support a decent club scene. Students say Guilford "is unique because it is within a fairly cosmopolitan area, yet has many natural alcoves and secrets to explore. The lake, the woods, and the meadows on campus are beautiful and fun treasures for students to enjoy. Guilford is also beautifully landscaped and decorated with student-created art, but it isn't pretentious."

Student Body

"Guilford sometimes seems like it attracts the atypical student. People here aren't afraid to express their personal point of view, either vocally or through their activities or style." The population includes a lot of "liberal, granola people," although some here notice a trend toward greater diversity on campus. Recently the school has increased diversity in "ethnic backgrounds and spiritual, political, and socio-cultural beliefs," and has also added to its continuing education population, meaning students here "range from 17 to 60-plus years old." As one student observes, "Because Guilford College promotes a global view of the world, the diverse student body is simply an extension of this academic principle and is nurtured as such." Some students note that "almost everyone who bridges these gaps bonds over a case or keg."

GUILFORD COLLEGE

FINANCIAL AID: 336-316-2354 • E-MAIL: ADMISSION@GUILFORD.EDU • WEBSITE: WWW.GUILFORD.EDU

THE PRINCETON REVIEW SAYS

Admissions

Very important factors considered include: Rigor of secondary school record. *Important factors considered include:* Application essay, academic GPA, standardized test scores, character/personal qualities, extracurricular activities, level of applicant's interest, talent/ability. *Other factors considered include:* Class rank, recommendation(s), alumni/ae relation, first generation, geographical residence, interview, racial/ethnic status, religious affiliation/commitment, state residency, volunteer work, work experience. SAT or ACT recommended. TOEFL required of all international applicants. High school diploma is required and GED is accepted. *Academic units recommended:* 4 English, 3 mathematics, 3 science, 2 foreign language.

Financial Aid

Students should submit: FAFSA. Regular filing deadline is 3/1. The Princeton Review suggests that all financial aid forms be submitted as soon as possible after 1/1. *Need-based scholarships/grants offered:* Federal Pell, SEOG, state scholarships/grants, private scholarships, the school's own gift aid. *Loan aid offered:* FFEL Subsidized Stafford, FFEL Unsubsidized Stafford, FFEL PLUS, Federal Perkins, college/university loans from institutional funds. Applicants will be notified of awards on a rolling basis beginning 2/1. Federal Work-Study Program available. Institutional employment available. Off-campus job opportunities are good.

The Inside Word

Guilford has traditionally drawn its students primarily from the Mid-Atlantic and Southern states; the school has recently begun to recruit more aggressively outside these areas, and now employs a full-time regional recruiter based in Boston. Additional recruiting should yield additional applications, increasing competition for classroom seats. The upside in terms of admissions is that this effort to build a more national student body creates opportunities for students from outside the school's traditional target zones. If you're willing to travel a long way to attend Guilford, you may find yourself handsomely rewarded.

THE SCHOOL SAYS " . . ."

From The Admissions Office

"Guilford is proud to be included for the 18th consecutive year in The Princeton Review's 'Best College' edition. Guilford can best be described by its academic rigor, preparation for graduate school, and its commitment to service in a caring, socially aware and supportive community.

"Comments from a small sample of Guilford students do not adequately convey the richness of the campus experience. Guilford is building a community that honors traditional as well as alternative lifestyles and viewpoints. No one lifestyle or thought predominates the campus. Regardless of your background, if you are open-minded and willing to interact with others, the Guilford experience can be transformational. If you enroll at Guilford, there will be others like you.

"There is no stereotypical Guilford student. Our students have many passions including athletics and intramurals, community service, social justice and multiculturalism. However the bond that ties them together is the academic curriculum that prepares them for life and a career."

SELECTIVITY

Admissions Rating	89
# of applicants	3,610
% of applicants accepted	60
% of acceptees attending	20
# accepting a place on wait list	68
% admitted from wait list	134

FRESHMAN PROFILE

Range SAT Critical Reading	500–620
Range SAT Math	500–600
Range SAT Writing	480–610
Range ACT Composite	21–26
Minimum paper TOEFL	550
Minimum computer TOEFL	213
Average HS GPA	3.12
% graduated top 10% of class	76
% graduated top 25% of class	45
% graduated top 50% of class	83

DEADLINES

Early action	
Deadline	1/15
Notification	2/15
Regular	
Priority	1/15
Deadline	2/15
Notification	rolling
Nonfall registration?	yes

APPLICANTS ALSO LOOK AT
AND OFTEN PREFER
Oberlin College
AND SOMETIMES PREFER
Earlham College
University of North Carolina at Chapel Hill
Goucher College
Elon University

FINANCIAL FACTS

Financial Aid Rating	90
Annual tuition	$25,700
Required fees	$330
Books and supplies	$1,050
% frosh rec. need-based scholarship or grant aid	60
% UG rec. need-based scholarship or grant aid	67
% frosh rec. need-based self-help aid	53
% UG rec. need-based self-help aid	62
% frosh rec. any financial aid	88
% UG rec. any financial aid	92
% UG borrow to pay for school	66
Average cumulative indebtedness	$22,780

GUSTAVUS ADOLPHUS COLLEGE

800 WEST COLLEGE AVENUE, SAINT PETER, MN 56082 • ADMISSIONS: 507-933-7676 • FAX: 507-933-7474

CAMPUS LIFE

Quality of Life Rating	**83**
Fire Safety Rating	**89**
Green Rating	**89**
Type of school	private
Affiliation	Lutheran
Environment	village

STUDENTS

Total undergrad enrollment	2,515
% male/female	43/57
% from out of state	18
% from public high school	92
% live on campus	81
% in (# of) fraternities	11 (5)
% in (# of) sororities	12 (5)
# of countries represented	15

SURVEY SAYS . . .

Athletic facilities are great
Great food on campus
Musical organizations are popular

ACADEMICS

Academic Rating	**87**
Calendar	4/1/4
Student/faculty ratio	12:1
Profs interesting rating	82
Profs accessible rating	85
Most common reg class size	10–19 students
Most common lab size	10–19 students

MOST POPULAR MAJORS

biology/biological sciences
business/commerce
psychology

STUDENTS SAY ". . ."

Academics

Gustavus Adolphus College, "a school that fosters a close community between the students, staff, and faculty and strives to prepare the students academically and vocationally for the post-college world," gets high marks from undergrads for its "demanding, yet encouraging" professors who are "there to help you learn, not just to give you a grade." As one student explains, "each year I become more and more impressed with how devoted members of the faculty and administration are devoted to the students. My professors always bend over backward to meet with students who have questions and work with them on problems related and unrelated to course material." Although professors have "high expectations," the "extra guidance" that is offered helps students achieve "far beyond graduation." Expect to be challenged by classes that are "rigorous and discussion-based." Small class sizes allow for "great interaction with professors" but will leave your "empty chair sticking out like a neon sign" if you are absent. Unique opportunities here include the Curriculum II general-education program, an integrated series of courses that, together, provide a survey of Western civilization, with supplemental study of non-Western cultures for context and comparison. Enrollment is limited to 60 students and typically attracts some of the college's brightest undergrads.

Life

Gustavus boasts "a very academically strong student body" that is also "known for our athletics, specifically tennis, hockey, and soccer." Students "attend a lot of sporting events" as well as "parties and social events on campus and off" over the weekends, when campus is "a great place to be…because very few people go home. We are certainly not a suitcase college." Besides the aforementioned activities, "shows, concerts, and basketball games" are "especially popular," as are the "free movies on Fridays and Saturdays" and the "on-campus student dance club 'The Dive.'" Most students choose to unwind with "a good amount of partying and drinking," but while alcohol and parties are easy to find on campus, abstaining students "never feel any pressure to do either." Being located in a small town is no problem for most; students tell us that "the town is supportive of Gustavus and thankful to have the college in town" and explain that "there are always things going on at school," so the lack of big-city fun isn't that much of a drawback. Students who get cabin fever can head to nearby Mankato and its "excellent mall and restaurants" for entertainment. Although the Minnesotan winter may be long, things heat up in January during "J-term" when a light course load gives students a "chance to take a class outside their major" or just "hang out with friends." When students really want a thrill, they'll "borrow a tray from the cafeteria and sled down the many hills behind the dorms" in a Gustavus tradition called "traying."

Student Body

Gustavus "is known to have a very close community consisting of students who not only achieve academically but are [also] very involved in their community and school. There are more than 140 student organizations on campus. For a student population [of] approximately 2,600, that is a lot." "Virtually everyone here is white and of Scandinavian descent," and "of these, roughly half seem to come from small rural towns in Minnesota or surrounding Midwest states (Iowa, Wisconsin, North and South Dakota, etc.), and the other half from well-off suburbs of Minneapolis-St. Paul…Most tend to have some Christian affiliation, but not necessarily a strong one, and there are a fair amount of non-religious students, which is refreshing." Students are polite in a way that seems unusual on the coasts but less so in the Midwest; it has been said that if students visit the campus, "they don't have to hold any doors because the students are so friendly and welcoming," one student reports.

FINANCIAL AID: 507-933-7527 • E-MAIL: ADMISSION@GUSTAVUS.EDU • WEBSITE: WWW.GUSTAVUS.EDU

THE PRINCETON REVIEW SAYS

Admissions

Very important factors considered include: Rigor of secondary school record. *Important factors considered include:* Application essay, academic GPA, recommendation(s), standardized test scores. *Other factors considered include:* Alumni/ae relation, extracurricular activities, first generation, geographical residence, interview, level of applicant's interest, racial/ethnic status, religious affiliation/commitment, state residency, talent/ability, volunteer work, work experience. SAT or ACT recommended. TOEFL required of all international applicants. High school diploma is required and GED is accepted. *Academic units required:* 4 English, 3 mathematics, 2 science (2 science labs), 2 foreign language, 2 social studies, 2 history. *Academic units recommended:* 4 mathematics, 3 science (3 science labs), 3 foreign language, 2 academic electives.

Financial Aid

Students should submit: FAFSA, CSS/financial aid profile. CSS profile required of all students applying for need-based assistance. Regular filing deadline is 4/15. The Princeton Review suggests that all financial aid forms be submitted as soon as possible after 1/1. *Need-based scholarships/grants offered:* Federal Pell, SEOG, state scholarships/grants, private scholarships, the school's own gift aid. *Loan aid offered:* Direct Subsidized Stafford, Direct Unsubsidized Stafford, Direct PLUS, Federal Perkins, state loans, alternative loans from private lenders. Applicants will be notified of awards on a rolling basis beginning 1/20. Federal Work-Study Program available. Institutional employment available. Off-campus job opportunities are good.

The Inside Word

Gustavus Adolphus considers a variety of factors when making admissions decisions. Students should display motivation for tackling challenging courses and a desire to be active participants in their community. The majority of applicants are from local areas—those who can provide some geographic diversity are welcome. The school has a rolling admissions policy, so interested students should think about sending in their applications early. All available slots are usually filled by early spring.

THE SCHOOL SAYS "..."

From The Admissions Office

"To better serve students and their families, there is no application fee.

"Applications completed by November 1 will be notified of an admission decision by November 20. Applications completed after November 1 will be reviewed on a competitive rolling basis beginning December 20.

"Early financial aid awards will be available to admitted students who submit the CSS/Financial Aid PROFILE prior to February 15. Students who submit the FAFSA will continue to receive a financial aid award in a timely fashion.

"The college is committed to excellence, community, justice, service, and faith. These values are pervasive in the college community and can be seen throughout campus activities and events like the 'Our Story' workshop on African American culture, Nobel Conference, Building Bridges Diversity Conference, MAYDAY! Peace Conference, and NYSP summer sports camp. Campus facilities support student life and development. Recent projects include a 200-bed apartment and suite configuration residence hall (also houses an additional 200-bed youth hostel), cardiovascular exercise area, Nobel Hall of Science equipment additions of a DNA sequencer, mass spectrometer microscope, cell growth culture labs, Old Main classroom renovation, International Center for residential living and international education, and, the Jackson Campus Center, which houses student services such as Diversity Center, Market Place cafeteria and Courtyard Café, Ticket Center, student activities offices and work space, Hillstrom Museum, bookstore, and much more. Gustavus Adolphus College requires freshman applicants to submit scores from SAT. Students may also choose to submit scores from the ACT (with or without the Writing component) in lieu of the SAT."

SELECTIVITY

Admissions Rating	90
# of applicants	3,128
% of applicants accepted	75
% of acceptees attending	27

FRESHMAN PROFILE

Range SAT Math	580–690
Range ACT Composite	24–29
Minimum paper TOEFL	550
Minimum computer TOEFL	213
Minimum web-based TOEFL	80
Average HS GPA	3.64
% graduated top 10% of class	34
% graduated top 25% of class	69
% graduated top 50% of class	97

DEADLINES

Early action	
Deadline	11/1
Notification	11/20
Regular	
Notification	rolling
Nonfall registration?	yes

FINANCIAL FACTS

Financial Aid Rating	87
Annual tuition	$29,990
Room and board	$7,460
Required fees	$140
Books and supplies	$750
% frosh rec. need-based scholarship or grant aid	70
% UG rec. need-based scholarship or grant aid	65
% frosh rec. non-need-based scholarship or grant aid	35
% UG rec. non-need-based scholarship or grant aid	39
% frosh rec. need-based self-help aid	70
% UG rec. need-based self-help aid	65
% frosh rec. any financial aid	96
% UG rec. any financial aid	95
% UG borrow to pay for school	70
Average cumulative indebtedness	$24,297

HAMILTON COLLEGE

198 COLLEGE HILL ROAD, CLINTON, NY 13323 • ADMISSIONS: 315-859-4421 • FAX: 315-859-4457

CAMPUS LIFE

Quality of Life Rating	83
Fire Safety Rating	82
Green Rating	96
Type of school	private
Environment	rural

STUDENTS

Total undergrad enrollment	1,834
% male/female	48/52
% from out of state	70
% from public high school	59
% live on campus	98
% in (# of) fraternities	34 (10)
% in (# of) sororities	18 (7)
% African American	4
% Asian	7
% Caucasian	70
% Hispanic	5
% Native American	1
% international	5
# of countries represented	44

SURVEY SAYS . . .
Lab facilities are great
Athletic facilities are great
School is well run
Low cost of living
(Almost) no one smokes

ACADEMICS

Academic Rating	95
Calendar	semester
Student/faculty ratio	10:1
Profs interesting rating	96
Profs accessible rating	94
Most common reg class size	10–19 students
Most common lab size	10–19 students

MOST POPULAR MAJORS
economics
political science and government
psychology

STUDENTS SAY ". . ."

Academics

A small, liberal arts school, Hamilton College "runs smoothly" with "top-notch" professors who are "very committed, passionate, and genuinely caring." The close student-faculty relationships are a distinguishing characteristic of Hamilton. One junior who chose Hamilton for its "small class size and opportunity to really establish a relationship with the professors" described the accessibility of the professors as "AMAZING." A graduating senior tells us, "My professors have inspired me to take on my education as a truly personal and important aspect of my life, even after I complete my formal education." One student comments on how Hamilton is a leader in teaching effective writing and persuasive speaking: "Hamilton challenges me to improve my writing each and every day, regardless of the class…writing is a central aspect." Though the "extraordinary focus on writing" is paramount at Hamilton, the school also offers a "strong science program." The science curriculum emphasizes "undergraduate research" and a recently built, state-of-the-art science facility provides students with ample "research opportunities." Students also love Hamilton's distinct open curriculum. The "lack of distribution requirements" gives students the freedom to make their own educational choices and to select classes that reflect their unique interests. With "no required curriculum…it's nice to know that you're not wasting any time and are taking the classes that you really want [and] need to."

Life

A "picturesque oasis of academia" Hamilton makes students feel like the fact that they are "isolated away from city noise and bustle, but close enough to an urban area to be connected." The closest major city is Syracuse, located about an hour's drive from campus, and the school "organizes trips to New York City regularly." Hamilton is a "small town," but students agree that though Hamilton "is in the middle of nowhere" it does not mean it is lacking in things to do. In fact, says one student, "that's far from the truth." During the week, "the pressure is on," and life at Hamilton is "academically oriented" with everyone working hard and "little time to play." At week's end, students are ready to "have as much fun as possible," and the focus turns to "various fraternity or sorority parties and any athletic events going on." Students tell us, "Greek life is popular but not threatening" and "provides much of the party life on-campus." Most Greek events are "open to the campus" but foster a "very inclusive social environment." The campus "accommodates students so that everyone is able to get together and have fun." Students agree that there is "something to do for everyone." Hamilton boasts a long list of student-run clubs and teams, active intramural leagues, "incredible athletic and workout facilities," a "pretty decent" 9-hole golf course, and "miles of trails for skiing, snow-shoeing, and jogging." Winters tend to be quite long, "so curling up with a blanket and a movie in a dorm room is always popular."

Student Body

If you are looking for a school "where you hold doors for people" and "greet friends, acquaintances, and even professors" while walking around campus, Hamilton may be just the place for you. Students are enthusiastic about the "tight-knit community" of students and professors on campus. One student tells us, "There's such a great sense of community. Everyone is friendly, intelligent, and driven without being overly competitive." Students find that Hamilton provides a great opportunity to attend an "elite liberal arts school" where "students will want to help you instead of compete against you." One freshman tells us that the student body at Hamilton was "frighteningly friendly." While Hamilton "doesn't exactly have a wealth of diversity," the "student body is very inclusive." The majority of Hamilton students are "very preppy, white, and upperclass," but "everyone and anyone can find their niche" and still be "respected as an individual by the community at large." Overall, students at Hamilton have "diverse interests" and are often involved on campus in a variety of ways. When it comes to the environment, politics, or any other current events, students tell us, "It's the most aware group of people I've ever met."

HAMILTON COLLEGE

FINANCIAL AID: 800-859-4413 • E-MAIL: ADMISSION@HAMILTON.EDU • WEBSITE: WWW.HAMILTON.EDU

THE PRINCETON REVIEW SAYS

Admissions

Very important factors considered include: Class rank, academic GPA, rigor of secondary school record. *Important factors considered include:* Application essay, recommendation(s), standardized test scores, character/personal qualities, extracurricular activities, interview. *Other factors considered include:* Alumni/ae relation, first generation, geographical residence, level of applicant's interest, racial/ethnic status, talent/ability, volunteer work, work experience. SAT and SAT Subject Tests or ACT required. TOEFL required of all international applicants. High school diploma is required and GED is accepted. *Academic units recommended:* 4 English, 3 mathematics, 3 science, 3 foreign language, 3 social studies.

Financial Aid

Students should submit: FAFSA, institution's own financial aid form, CSS/financial aid profile, state aid form, noncustodial profile, business/farm supplement. Regular filing deadline is 2/8. The Princeton Review suggests that all financial aid forms be submitted as soon as possible after 1/1. *Need-based scholarships/grants offered:* Federal Pell, SEOG, state scholarships/grants, private scholarships, the school's own gift aid. *Loan aid offered:* FFEL Subsidized Stafford, FFEL Unsubsidized Stafford, FFEL PLUS, Federal Perkins, college/university loans from institutional funds. Applicants will be notified of awards on or about 4/1. Federal Work-Study Program available. Institutional employment available.

The Inside Word

Similar to any prestigious liberal arts schools, Hamilton takes a well-rounded, personal approach to admissions. They rely heavily on academic achievement and intellectual promise, but in a mission to create a talented and diverse incoming class, admissions officers also strive to attain a complete, accurate profile of each candidate. The admissions team at Hamilton is adamant about interviews either on or off campus with alumni volunteers. Serious applicants may want to polish up their interview skills as students who decline to interview put themselves at a competitive disadvantage.

THE SCHOOL SAYS "..."

From The Admissions Office

"As a national leader for teaching students to write effectively, learn from one another, and think for themselves, Hamilton produces graduates who have the knowledge, skills, and confidence to make their own voices heard on issues of importance to them and their communities.

"A key component of the Hamilton experience is the college's open, yet rigorous, liberal arts curriculum. In place of distribution requirements that are common at most colleges, Hamilton gives its students freedom to choose the courses that reflect their unique interests and plans. Faculty advisors assist students in planning a coherent and highly individualized academic program. In fact, close student-faculty relationships at Hamilton are a distinguishing characteristic of the college, but ultimately students at Hamilton take responsibility for their own future. Part of that future includes a lifelong relationship with the college. Hamilton alumni are exceptionally loyal and passionate supporters of their alma mater. That support manifests itself through internships, speaking engagements, job-shadowing opportunities, and financial donations.

"The intellectual maturity that distinguishes a Hamilton education extends to the application process. Students are free to choose which standardized tests to submit, based on a specified set of options, so that those who do not test well on the SAT or ACT may decide to submit the results of their AP or SAT Subject Tests. The approach allows students the freedom to decide how to present themselves best to the Committee on Admission."

SELECTIVITY

Admissions Rating	96
# of applicants	5,073
% of applicants accepted	28
% of acceptees attending	32
# accepting a place on wait list	275
% admitted from wait list	19
# of early decision applicants	612
% accepted early decision	36

FRESHMAN PROFILE

Range SAT Critical Reading	650–730
Range SAT Math	650–720
% graduated top 10% of class	76
% graduated top 25% of class	95
% graduated top 50% of class	99

DEADLINES

Early decision	
Deadline	11/15
Notification	12/15
Regular	
Deadline	1/1
Notification	4/1
Nonfall registration?	yes

APPLICANTS ALSO LOOK AT

AND OFTEN PREFER
Dartmouth College
Williams College
Bowdoin College

AND SOMETIMES PREFER
Colby College
Colgate University
Bates College

FINANCIAL FACTS

Financial Aid Rating	95
Annual tuition	$38,220
Room and board	$9,810
Required fees	$380
Books and supplies	$1,300
% frosh rec. need-based scholarship or grant aid	41
% UG rec. need-based scholarship or grant aid	41
% frosh rec. non-need-based scholarship or grant aid	2
% UG rec. non-need-based scholarship or grant aid	3
% frosh rec. need-based self-help aid	35
% UG rec. need-based self-help aid	36
% frosh rec. any financial aid	49.1
% UG rec. any financial aid	66.9
% UG borrow to pay for school	43
Average cumulative indebtedness	$18,259

THE BEST 371 COLLEGES ■ 265

HAMPDEN-SYDNEY COLLEGE

PO BOX 667, HAMPDEN-SYDNEY, VA 23943 • ADMISSIONS: 434-223-6120 • FAX: 434-223-6346

CAMPUS LIFE

Quality of Life Rating	83
Fire Safety Rating	75
Green Rating	75
Type of school	private
Affiliation	Presbyterian
Environment	rural

STUDENTS

Total undergrad enrollment	1,120
% male/female	100/0
% from out of state	34
% from public high school	57
% in (# of) fraternities	34 (11)
% African American	3
% Asian	1
% Caucasian	63
% Hispanic	1
% international	1
# of countries represented	17

SURVEY SAYS . . .

No one cheats
Career services are great
Students are friendly
Students are happy
Student government is popular
Lots of beer drinking

ACADEMICS

Academic Rating	87
Calendar	semester
Student/faculty ratio	11:1
Profs interesting rating	98
Profs accessible rating	99
Most common reg class size	10–19 students

MOST POPULAR MAJORS

economics
history
political science and government

STUDENTS SAY "..."

Academics

Highlights at tiny, all-male Hampden-Sydney College in Virginia include "insane" study abroad programs, a "very approachable" administration, and "an alumni network that will take care of you." HSC is mostly known for its hardcore liberal arts focus, though. The demanding core curriculum includes foreign language, literature, science, math, fine arts, and a boatload of Western civilization. Students also must "take two semesters of rhetoric, which consists of an intensive study and application of the principles of good writing." "Academically, this school is an orgy of ideas waiting for the next enthusiastic participant." Professors are "absolutely great," and personal attention is "unrivaled." Courses are "very tough," though. "We don't grade-inflate around here," warns a junior. A strict, student-enforced honor code "is taken extremely seriously" as well. "At Sydney, I can leave my laptop unattended in the library for hours, maybe even days, and nobody will touch it," maintains a history major. "I think that's pretty cool." Students say that HSC is "a place where honor lives and boys enter so that they may leave as gentlemen." The word "brotherhood" is omnipresent. There is much talk of "moral integrity." If all that sounds kind of hokey, then, obviously, HSC isn't for you. "It takes a certain kind of man to come to Hampden-Sydney College, and if you want to be here, then you will love it. If you don't want to be here, you will hate it."

Life

"The school is its own little city," and Hamden-Sydney students spend most of their time on campus. "The dorm rooms are huge," and "laundry is free," but the food is "not very good." Clubs and organizations include "a prestigious debating society." "A majority of the student body is involved in some type of sport." Football weekends are "a great time to be on campus." (Students dress "in formal coat and tie.") "Most students work and study hard from Monday to Thursday." "With no females at school, it is easier to focus during the week," claims one student. "During the week, every night is a guys' night," explains a sophomore. "When we aren't studying, we are playing video games or cards, watching a sporting event, and basically just hanging out." Weekends are usually spent "partying incredibly hard" with "females from Sweet Briar, Longwood, Randolph College, and Hollins." "Frat boys run the social scene," but "the fraternities are very open and almost everyone is welcome at parties." Off campus, Farmville lives up to its name. The rural surrounding area offers "breathtaking scenery" and some of the best hunting and outdoor activity anywhere, though. "Shooting guns," i.e., hunting, is generally popular. "No one looks at you twice for walking through your dorm to the parking lot with your deer rifle over your shoulder."

Student Body

Ethnic diversity is negligible. This is a "very homogeneous" school. The small homosexual population is "tolerated" at best. "Gay students probably won't feel too comfortable," suggests a junior. "They typical Hampden-Sydney student comes from the south, enjoys outdoor activities such as hunting and fishing, and is likely conservative and preppy." He "wears polos and khakis." He "can tie a bowtie" and probably has "a ragged, old baseball cap snugly fit over lip-length curly brown hair." "Our reputation for being made up of white middle- to upper-class conservatives who dress preppy most of the time and in camouflage during the winter is unavoidable," concedes one student. Politically, a kind of conservative snobbery reigns supreme. "Overall, they seem invested in the notion of preserving the ideas of the old South," relates a junior. "They're also geographic elitists and somewhat skeptical of outsiders." "Hampden-Sydney has been educating men since before the United States was founded," rejoins a proud sophomore, "and 35 congressmen, 12 senators, 12 governors, one U.S. president, and countless other prominent Americans later, we feel we're doing a fine job."

FINANCIAL AID: 804-223-6119 • E-MAIL: ADMISSIONS@HSC.EDU • WEBSITE: WWW.HSC.EDU

THE PRINCETON REVIEW SAYS

Admissions

Very important factors considered include: Application essay, academic GPA, recommendation(s), rigor of secondary school record, standardized test scores, character/personal qualities. *Important factors considered include:* Class rank, extracurricular activities. *Other factors considered include:* First generation, interview, level of applicant's interest, talent/ability, volunteer work, work experience. SAT or ACT required. SAT and SAT Subject Tests or ACT recommended. ACT with Writing component recommended. TOEFL required of all international applicants. High school diploma is required and GED is accepted. *Academic units required:* 4 English, 3 mathematics, 2 science (1 science lab), 2 foreign language, 1 social studies, 1 history, 3 academic electives. *Academic units recommended:* 4 mathematics, 3 science, 3 foreign language.

Financial Aid

Students should submit: FAFSA, CSS/financial aid profile, state aid form. Regular filing deadline is 5/1. The Princeton Review suggests that all financial aid forms be submitted as soon as possible after 1/1. *Need-based scholarships/grants offered:* Federal Pell, SEOG, state scholarships/grants, private scholarships, the school's own gift aid. *Loan aid offered:* FFEL Subsidized Stafford, FFEL Unsubsidized Stafford, FFEL PLUS, Federal Perkins, college/university loans from institutional funds, private loans. Applicants will be notified of awards on a rolling basis beginning 12/15. Federal Work-Study Program available. Institutional employment available. Off-campus job opportunities are fair.

The Inside Word

Hampden-Sydney is one of the last of its kind. Understandably, the applicant pool is heavily self-selected, and a fairly significant percentage of those who are admitted choose to enroll. This enables the admissions committee to be more selective, which in turn requires candidates to take the process more seriously than might otherwise be necessary. Students with consistently sound academic records should have little to worry about nonetheless.

THE SCHOOL SAYS ". . ."

From The Admissions Office

"The spirit of Hampden-Sydney is its sense of community. As one of only 1,120 students, you will be in small classes and find it easy to get extra help or inspiration from professors when you want it. Many of our professors live on campus and enjoy being with students in the snack bar as well as in the classroom. They give you the best, most personal education as possible. A big bonus of small-college life is that everybody is invited to go out for everything, and you can be as much of a leader as you want to be. From athletics to debating to publications to fraternity life, this is part of the process that produces a well-rounded Hampden-Sydney graduate.

"Hampden-Sydney College requires either the SAT or ACT standardized test with essay."

SELECTIVITY

Admissions Rating	79
# of applicants	1,553
% of applicants accepted	64
% of acceptees attending	32
# of early decision applicants	103
% accepted early decision	74

FRESHMAN PROFILE

Range SAT Critical Reading	500–610
Range SAT Math	515–610
Range SAT Writing	480–590
Range ACT Composite	20–26
Minimum paper TOEFL	570
Minimum computer TOEFL	230
Average HS GPA	3.2
% graduated top 10% of class	15
% graduated top 25% of class	31
% graduated top 50% of class	66

DEADLINES

Early decision	
Deadline	11/15
Notification	12/15
Early action	
Deadline	1/15
Notification	2/15
Regular	
Deadline	3/1
Notification	4/15
Nonfall registration?	yes

APPLICANTS ALSO LOOK AT

AND OFTEN PREFER
Virginia Tech
University of Virginia

AND SOMETIMES PREFER
University of North Carolina at Chapel Hill
James Madison University

AND RARELY PREFER
Randolph—Macon College

FINANCIAL FACTS

Financial Aid Rating	82
Annual tuition	$28,250
Room and board	$9,228
Required fees	$1,261
Books and supplies	$1,100
% frosh rec. need-based scholarship or grant aid	53
% UG rec. need-based scholarship or grant aid	47
% frosh rec. non-need-based scholarship or grant aid	12
% UG rec. non-need-based scholarship or grant aid	9
% frosh rec. need-based self-help aid	41
% UG rec. need-based self-help aid	38
% frosh rec. any financial aid	99
% UG rec. any financial aid	98
% UG borrow to pay for school	67
Average cumulative indebtedness	$17,277

HAMPSHIRE COLLEGE

ADMISSIONS OFFICE, 893 WEST STREET, AMHERST, MA 01002 • ADMISSIONS: 413-559-5471 • FAX: 413-559-5631

CAMPUS LIFE

Quality of Life Rating	**84**
Fire Safety Rating	**60***
Green Rating	**84**
Type of school	private
Environment	town

STUDENTS

Total undergrad enrollment	1,402
% male/female	42/58
% from out of state	82
% from public high school	48
% live on campus	90
% African American	4
% Asian	4
% Caucasian	74
% Hispanic	6
% Native American	1
% international	4
# of countries represented	31

SURVEY SAYS . . .

Lots of liberal students
Class discussions encouraged
No one cheats
Students aren't religious
Great off-campus food
Frats and sororities are unpopular or
nonexistent
Political activism is popular
(Almost) everyone smokes

ACADEMICS

Academic Rating	**91**
Calendar	4/1/4
Student/faculty ratio	11:1
Profs interesting rating	86
Profs accessible rating	81
Most common reg class size	10–19 students
Most common lab size	10–19 students

MOST POPULAR MAJORS
English language and literature
film/video and photographic arts,
fine arts and art studies

STUDENTS SAY ". . ."

Academics

Undergrads come to Hampshire College "seduced by the prospect of designing [their] own program of study." The school offers students "a self-designed curriculum" facilitated by "close relationships with professors, small classes, and the great combination of communal living and individualism that a true Hampshire student embodies." A "divisional system," with a student's academic career consisting of three divisions, imposes some sense of order. Division I "is first-year requirements and such," while "Divisions II and III constitute the core of your time. That's when you focus down upon the areas that interest you more than the rest of the school." Undergrads explain that "in class, students learn as a group in discussions or hands-on activities (few lectures, no tests), while outside of class one focuses on independent projects (research, reading, writing, art-making)." The experience culminates in a 'Division III,' an all-consuming year-long senior thesis project "that allows students to become excited and completely invested" while "producing a unique product at the end of the year." Students "receive evaluations instead of grades, which we feel is a much more productive system." While Hampshire "is very small," which might limit students' choices, "it belongs to the Five Colleges consortium," a group that includes the massive University of Massachusetts—Amherst. With the course offerings of 5 colleges available to them, Hampshire students can "take any course we could dream of."

Life

"Life at Hampshire seems extremely spontaneous," so "while one minute we may be complaining of boredom, the next we may start doing something fun and exciting. We are normally very good at entertaining ourselves." "Usually what people do is just hang out with a small group of friends," and "there is partying on the weekends," although "parties here consist generally of 50 people or less, never the roaring, dangerously wild parties that are often found at colleges." Parties often take place in the "mods," apartment-style housing favored by upperclassmen, where students "throw a lot of sweaty dance parties where hippies, scenesters, and geeks all grind up against each other." Also, "live music is very common" on and around campus, "drum circles and random games of Frisbee are unavoidable," and "going to the nearby towns of Amherst or Northampton isn't bad." Students can also choose from "tons of clubs, from Spinsters Unite! to the Red Scare Ultimate Frisbee Team, [or] Students for a Free Tibet to Excalibur, which is the sci-fi and fantasy club. You can even take yoga, karate, or tai chi classes. There are parties all the time for those who like that kind of thing, and movies, video games, clubs, and playing in the forest or on the farm for those who don't." There are also "five colleges in the area to hang out at. Enough said."

Student Body

"Picture all the various groups of misfits in high school" and you'll have a picture of the students at Hampshire, a place where "Nonconformity is so normal it's almost conformist to be nonconformist. You can't say 'the kid with the dreadlocks' because the person would reply with 'Which one?'" Undergrads assure us that "Hampshire is really open to any type of student. There may be some discrimination against the preppiest of individuals, and they will have to endure the occasional 'Shouldn't you be going to Amherst?' comment, but that is really as bad as it gets." The common threads among students: "They are all interesting. They all have talents, stories, and are just plain interesting to be around. They are full of creativity and life and seem to really enjoy where they are." They also tend to be "socially conscious, left-wing, and artistic. We are fond of do-it-yourself philosophies, from [magazines] to music and film production to designing ecologically sustainable communities." One student warns, "this is not a good school for fundamentalist Christians."

FINANCIAL AID: 413-559-5484 • E-MAIL: ADMISSIONS@HAMPSHIRE.EDU • WEBSITE: WWW.HAMPSHIRE.EDU

THE PRINCETON REVIEW SAYS

Admissions

Very important factors considered include: Application essay, character/personal qualities. *Important factors considered include:* Recommendation(s), rigor of secondary school record, extracurricular activities, level of applicant's interest, talent/ability. *Other factors considered include:* Class rank, academic GPA, standardized test scores, alumni/ae relation, interview, racial/ethnic status, volunteer work, work experience. TOEFL required of all international applicants. High school diploma is required and GED is accepted. *Academic units required:* 4 English, 3 mathematics, 3 science (2 science labs), 3 foreign language, 3 history. *Academic units recommended:* 4 English, 4 mathematics, 4 science (2 science labs), 4 foreign language, 4 history.

Financial Aid

Students should submit: FAFSA, CSS/financial aid profile, noncustodial profile. The Princeton Review suggests that all financial aid forms be submitted as soon as possible after 1/1. *Need-based scholarships/grants offered:* Federal Pell, SEOG, state scholarships/grants, private scholarships, the school's own gift aid. *Loan aid offered:* Direct Subsidized Stafford, Direct Unsubsidized Stafford, FFEL PLUS, Federal Perkins. Applicants will be notified of awards on a rolling basis beginning 4/1. Federal Work-Study Program available.

The Inside Word

Hampshire's admissions policies are the antithesis of formula-based practices. Officers want to know the individual behind the transcript, and personal characteristics hold substantial weight in the admissions decision. Demonstrating discipline and an independent and inquisitive spirit may just carry more weight than a perfect 4.0. Writing is pivotal to a Hampshire education, and applicants must put considerable thought into their personal statements. They will be read carefully.

THE SCHOOL SAYS "..."

From The Admissions Office

"Students tell us they like our application. It is less derivative and more open-ended than most. Rather than assigning an essay topic, we ask to learn more about you as an individual and invite your ideas. Instead of just asking for lists of activities, we ask you how those activities (and academic or other endeavors) have shown some of the traits that lead to success at Hampshire (initiative, independence, persistence, for example). This approach parallels the work you will do at Hampshire, defining the questions you will ask and the courses and experiences that will help you to answer them, and integrating your interests.

"Hampshire College requires freshman applicants to submit scores from the SAT. Students may also choose to submit scores from the ACT (with or without the Writing component) in lieu of the SAT."

SELECTIVITY

Admissions Rating	87
# of applicants	2,842
% of applicants accepted	53
% of acceptees attending	27
# accepting a place on wait list	94
% admitted from wait list	28
# of early decision applicants	98
% accepted early decision	71

FRESHMAN PROFILE

Range SAT Critical Reading	610–710
Range SAT Math	540–660
Range SAT Writing	590–700
Range ACT Composite	26–29
Minimum paper TOEFL	577
Minimum computer TOEFL	233
Average HS GPA	3.45
% graduated top 10% of class	25
% graduated top 25% of class	56
% graduated top 50% of class	81

DEADLINES

Early decision	
Deadline	11/15
Notification	12/15
Early action	
Deadline	12/1
Notification	2/15
Regular	
Priority	11/15
Deadline	1/15
Notification	4/1
Nonfall registration?	yes

APPLICANTS ALSO LOOK AT

AND OFTEN PREFER
Bard College

AND SOMETIMES PREFER
Sarah Lawrence College

AND RARELY PREFER
University of Vermont

FINANCIAL FACTS

Financial Aid Rating	93
Annual tuition	$37,789
Books and supplies	$500
% frosh rec. need-based scholarship or grant aid	55
% UG rec. need-based scholarship or grant aid	54
% frosh rec. non-need-based scholarship or grant aid	40
% UG rec. non-need-based scholarship or grant aid	31
% frosh rec. need-based self-help aid	55
% UG rec. need-based self-help aid	54
% frosh rec. any financial aid	87
% UG rec. any financial aid	74
% UG borrow to pay for school	63
Average cumulative indebtedness	$21,300

HAMPTON UNIVERSITY

OFFICE OF ADMISSIONS, HAMPTON UNIVERSITY, HAMPTON, VA 23668 • ADMISSIONS: 757-727-5328 • FAX: 757-727-5095

CAMPUS LIFE

Quality of Life Rating	63
Fire Safety Rating	60*
Green Rating	60*
Type of school	private
Environment	city

STUDENTS

Total undergrad enrollment	5,056
% male/female	36/64
% from out of state	69
% from public high school	90
% live on campus	59
% in (# of) fraternities	5 (6)
% in (# of) sororities	4 (3)
% African American	96
% Asian	1
% Caucasian	12
% Hispanic	1
# of countries represented	33

SURVEY SAYS . . .

Great library
Campus feels safe
Everyone loves the Pirates
Frats and sororities dominate social
scene
Musical organizations are popular
Student publications are popular
Student government is popular

ACADEMICS

Academic Rating	74
Calendar	semester
Student/faculty ratio	16:1
Profs interesting rating	68
Profs accessible rating	66
Most common reg class size	20–29 students
Most common lab size	10–19 students

MOST POPULAR MAJORS

business/commerce
journalism
psychology

STUDENTS SAY ". . ."

Academics

Hampton University, "one of the premier historically black colleges and universities in the country," is "perfect for students who desire to be around other intelligent and focused black students who have a future and are making plans to achieve their goals. Our students are making changes in this world and will always continue to." With popular programs in business and management, psychology, pharmacy, nursing, sociology, the hard sciences, and communications, Hampton "is about producing successful, bright, and talented professionals." The school has made a special commitment to journalism and communications, opening a state-of-the-art facility afew years back that includes a full working studio with editing facilities, a student-run radio station, and five computer labs. Throughout its many departments, Hampton stresses the importance of experiential learning, "presenting a host of opportunities for students to get internships and jobs." One student reports, "I have had three internships and have been on the campus radio station for my entire career at HU." Professors here earn good marks for dedication and teaching skills; the administration, on the other hand, is notorious for 'the Hampton Run-Around,' in which "a student spends their day running around campus trying to get a simple form signed or for a person to help them in whatever way, and in the end find out that the initial person they met with could have dealt with the problem." Most agree the inconvenience is worth it for "the connections and networking" Hampton provides. As one student notes, "everyone here is important, related to, or knows someone important, and everyone will become successful and important."

Life

"Hampton is not the typical party school," students agree. One student writes, "life at Hampton is pretty boring compared to where I'm from." Undergrads report that "most events take place off campus, so you really have to find your own fun." Fortunately the area provides some diversion, including "malls, fine dining, and parties…Also, Hampton is surrounded by cities that are no more than 15 to 20 minutes away," including Norfolk, Newport News, and Virginia Beach. "Nearby amusement parks are also great attractions for the spring and summer." On campus, "there is a really nice student center that turns into a virtual party every day from noon to 2:00 P.M. The student center is tri-level and has everything from a theater to [a] bowling ally and a fitness center." Hampton's Greek system is very popular; the most popular ones "are highly competitive and selective, and the whole process is crazy and oh-so-hard to get into." Some here complain that restrictive regulations dampen campus life. One student writes, "Rules and regulations prevent us from body painting at sporting events. Students are not allowed to have refrigerators apparently due to outdated wiring in the dorms…Administration, faculty, and staff do not respect students as adults."

Student Body

Hampton "is a historically black [college and] university, but the range of black students here is amazing. There is a niche for everyone, and I mean everyone, and most are universally accepted." Many are "very outgoing and professional," and "are well off and come from a nice home." Some "tend to be very materialistic and…care a lot about social matters. They all dress well, spend plenty of money on clothes, and drive very nice cars (even better cars than teachers)," but "there are many different types of students." Atypical students here "mesh well with the others," because Hampton students are a part of a family. "We are called Hamptonians, symbolizing our unity. Here we have a bond that is very strong—we all fit in—and it is not to be broken."

270 ■ THE BEST 371 COLLEGES

FINANCIAL AID: 800-624-3341 • E-MAIL: ADMIT@HAMPTONU.EDU • WEBSITE: WWW.HAMPTONU.EDU

THE PRINCETON REVIEW SAYS

Admissions

Very important factors considered include: Application essay, rigor of secondary school record, standardized test scores, character/personal qualities. *Important factors considered include:* Class rank, recommendation(s). *Other factors considered include:* Alumni/ae relation, extracurricular activities, talent/ability, volunteer work. SAT or ACT required. TOEFL required of all international applicants. High school diploma is required and GED is accepted. *Academic units required:* 4 English, 3 mathematics, 2 science (2 science labs), 2 social studies, 6 academic electives. *Academic units recommended:* 2 foreign language.

Financial Aid

Students should submit: FAFSA. The Princeton Review suggests that all financial aid forms be submitted as soon as possible after 1/1. *Need-based scholarships/grants offered:* Federal Pell, SEOG, state scholarships/grants, private scholarships, the school's own gift aid, federal nursing scholarships. *Loan aid offered:* Direct Subsidized Stafford, Direct Unsubsidized Stafford, Direct PLUS, FFEL Subsidized Stafford, FFEL Unsubsidized Stafford, FFEL PLUS, Federal Perkins, alternative loans. Applicants will be notified of awards on a rolling basis beginning 4/15. Federal Work-Study Program available. Off-campus job opportunities are excellent.

The Inside Word

Hampton University allows for early action admissions, meaning that students can receive an early decision without having to commit to attending the school. Well more than half of HU's applicant pool pursues this option. You would be wise to follow suit; the school is bound to be more lenient early in the process than later, when it has already admitted many qualified students. Don't be fooled by the fact that the number of applicants to HU has dropped in recent years; that is the result of more stringent admission standards, not a drop in the school's cachet.

THE SCHOOL SAYS ". . ."

From The Admissions Office

"Hampton attempts to provide the environment and structures most conducive to the intellectual, emotional, and aesthetic enlargement of the lives of its members. The university gives priority to effective teaching and scholarly research while placing the student at the center of its planning. Hampton will ask you to look inwardly at your own history and culture and examine your relationship to the aspirations and development of the world."

SELECTIVITY
Admissions Rating	87
# of applicants	7,120
% of applicants accepted	37
% of acceptees attending	43

FRESHMAN PROFILE
Range SAT Critical Reading	481–552
Range SAT Math	464–606
Range ACT Composite	17–26
Minimum paper TOEFL	550
Minimum computer TOEFL	214
Average HS GPA	3.2
% graduated top 10% of class	20
% graduated top 25% of class	45
% graduated top 50% of class	90

DEADLINES
Early action	
Deadline	12/1
Notification	12/15
Regular	
Priority	3/1
Nonfall registration?	yes

APPLICANTS ALSO LOOK AT
AND OFTEN PREFER
Spelman College
Morehouse College
Florida A&M University
AND SOMETIMES PREFER
Virginia Tech
University of Maryland—College Park
Howard University

FINANCIAL FACTS
Financial Aid Rating	62
Annual tuition	$13,358
Room and board	$6,746
Required fees	$1,460
Books and supplies	$750
% frosh rec. need-based scholarship or grant aid	96
% UG rec. need-based scholarship or grant aid	44
% frosh rec. non-need-based scholarship or grant aid	23
% UG rec. non-need-based scholarship or grant aid	13
% frosh rec. need-based self-help aid	79
% UG rec. need-based self-help aid	44
% frosh rec. any financial aid	44
% UG rec. any financial aid	100
% UG borrow to pay for school	51
Average cumulative indebtedness	$17,125

HANOVER COLLEGE

PO BOX 108, HANOVER, IN 47243-0108 • ADMISSIONS: 812-866-7021 • FAX: 812-866-7098

CAMPUS LIFE

Quality of Life Rating	64
Fire Safety Rating	74
Green Rating	78
Type of school	private
Affiliation	Presbyterian
Environment	rural

STUDENTS

Total undergrad enrollment	921
% male/female	45/55
% from out of state	35
% from public high school	82
% live on campus	95
% in (# of) fraternities	32 (4)
% in (# of) sororities	34 (4)
% African American	1
% Asian	2
% Caucasian	86
% Hispanic	1
% Native American	1
% international	3
# of countries represented	13

SURVEY SAYS . . .
Lab facilities are great
Athletic facilities are great
Students are friendly
Campus feels safe
Low cost of living
Frats and sororities dominate social
scene
Lots of beer drinking
Hard liquor is popular

ACADEMICS

Academic Rating	92
Calendar	semester
Student/faculty ratio	10:1
Profs interesting rating	88
Profs accessible rating	88
Most common	
reg class size	10–19 students

MOST POPULAR MAJORS
biology/biological sciences
history
psychology

STUDENTS SAY ". . ."

Academics

"Demanding course work" and a "small-school atmosphere" pervade the "picturesque" Georgian-style campus of Hanover College, an "excellent" bastion of the liberal arts and sciences in southeastern Indiana. Hanover operates on a fairly unique 4-4-1 calendar, in which there are two traditional semesters followed by a spring term during which students concentrate on a single class, participate in an array of off-campus internships, or study abroad. Classes are very small, and there is a strong focus on "teaching students to think and write critically." Students must complete a wide range of distribution requirements and agree that the curriculum is "intense." Sometimes "the workload is barely manageable." While the "amazing" and "very intelligent" professors at Hanover may "require a lot from the students," they are "very attentive." "Personal attention from professors" is commonplace, and professors "spend a lot of time out of class with the students." "Teachers are tough" but in the end, "you really learn." "The professors here are some of the best teachers, mentors, and friends that one could hope to find anywhere," beams a classical studies major. More than 90 percent of all students receive at least some financial assistance and more than a few say they chose Hanover because they got "a lot of scholarship money." Students say the Career Services staff is "really good," although registration can be "a hassle." While the "distant" administration is almost uniformly unpopular, students are happy with the president. One student tells us "she is a breath of fresh air, and I believe she will make a difference."

Life

"Hanover's campus is one of the most beautiful places I have ever been," swears a junior. "This place is beautiful the whole year round," "even in the soggy dreariness of late March." A "family-like" environment "allows people to really get to know each other and have connections." "Academics are very important," but "there are also many opportunities to get involved in extracurricular activities." Greek life is an exceptionally big deal here ("most students on campus are strongly Greek affiliated" and fraternities and sororities dominate the social scene. During the week, "most students are doing homework and studying," and they "just hang out casually"—except for Wednesday. "Wednesday nights and the weekends are when people party." Students say most people on campus "at least talk about partying a lot" and that "parties are pretty much just at the fraternities." "Though the rules about alcohol are rather strict, they are not necessarily heavily enforced (in the fraternities anyway). It is much harder to drink in residence halls." Some students complain that there is little to do "outside of fraternity parties or bars." To be sure, "the surrounding towns of Hanover and Madison" are "not very exciting" and may be a little "too rural" for some tastes. "This is the worst place a college town could be," laments one junior. Students with cars can avail themselves of more urban pursuits available in nearby "Cincinnati, Louisville, and Indianapolis."

Student Body

There are just fewer than 1,000 students here from more than 35 states and 13 countries, though "most tend to be from Indiana, Kentucky, or Ohio." "The typical student is an upper-middle-class white athlete" and very likely "Christian." A lot of students come from "suburbia," while others come from small Midwestern towns. "There are a few blacks, a few gays, and a lot of Nepalese and Hawaiian students." "The little ethnic diversity here is from the international students, not diverse Americans," though. "There are not a lot of atypical students" and those who are "tend to stick together." The generally homogenous nature of the student population creates a good deal of cohesion. "We pretty much all get along," reports one first-year student. Students describe themselves as "friendly," "easygoing," and "pretty casual." "There's a little bit of everything as far as goals, interests, and ambitions." There are "quite a few [students who] like to party frequently;" "However, most study and work hard." More than 60 percent of Hanover's newly minted graduates eventually go on to graduate and professional schools.

FINANCIAL AID: 812-866-7030 • E-MAIL: ADMISSION@HANOVER.EDU • WEBSITE: WWW.HANOVER.EDU

THE PRINCETON REVIEW SAYS

Admissions

Very important factors considered include: Class rank, academic GPA, rigor of secondary school record. *Important factors considered include:* Recommendation(s), standardized test scores, talent/ability. *Other factors considered include:* Application essay, alumni/ae relation, character/personal qualities, extracurricular activities, first generation, geographical residence, interview, level of applicant's interest, racial/ethnic status, state residency, volunteer work, work experience. SAT or ACT required. ACT with Writing component recommended. TOEFL required of all international applicants. High school diploma is required and GED is not accepted. *Academic units required:* 4 English, 3 mathematics, 3 science (2 science labs), 2 foreign language, 2 social studies, 2 history, 2 academic electives. *Academic units recommended:* 4 English, 4 mathematics, 4 science (3 science labs), 4 foreign language, 3 social studies, 3 history, 3 academic electives.

Financial Aid

Students should submit: FAFSA. The Princeton Review suggests that all financial aid forms be submitted as soon as possible after 1/1. *Need-based scholarships/grants offered:* Federal Pell, state scholarships/grants, private scholarships, the school's own gift aid. *Loan aid offered:* FFEL Subsidized Stafford, FFEL Unsubsidized Stafford, FFEL PLUS, college/university loans from institutional funds. Applicants will be notified of awards on a rolling basis beginning 3/1. Institutional employment available. Off-campus job opportunities are fair.

The Inside Word

Admission is competitive, but the applicant pool is not huge, and Hanover accepts a relatively high percentage of its applicants. High school grades (especially during your junior and senior years) and class rank are the most important determining factors for the admissions committee. If you are vying for an academic scholarship—and many, many applicants will be—it pays to invest some serious thought and time into Hanover's application process.

THE SCHOOL SAYS "..."

From The Admissions Office

"Since our founding in 1827, we have been committed to providing students with a personal, rigorous, and well-rounded liberal arts education. Part of the college search process is finding that school that proves to be a good match. For those who see the value in an education that demands engagement and who see college as a time for exploration and involvement, they will find that Hanover is all they could hope for and more.

"The admission process serves as an introduction to the personal education that students receive at Hanover College. Every application is considered individually with emphasis being placed on a student's high school curriculum and the student's academic performance in that curriculum. While we realize that not every high school has the same course offerings, we expect students to have selected a college preparatory curriculum as challenging as possible within his or her particular high school or academic setting.

"Hanover College accepts both the SAT and ACT. Students taking the ACT are required to take the optional Writing section. For students who have taken one or both of the tests multiple times, we will use the highest sub scores when calculating a student's score on either test for admission and scholarship purposes."

SELECTIVITY

Admissions Rating	89
# of applicants	2,233
% of applicants accepted	66
% of acceptees attending	23

FRESHMAN PROFILE

Range SAT Critical Reading	500–630
Range SAT Math	510–610
Range SAT Writing	480–590
Range ACT Composite	22–28
Minimum paper TOEFL	550
Minimum computer TOEFL	213
Minimum web-based TOEFL	120
Average HS GPA	3.61
% graduated top 10% of class	31
% graduated top 25% of class	66
% graduated top 50% of class	95

DEADLINES

Early action	
Deadline	12/1
Notification	12/20
Regular	
Deadline	3/1
Notification	rolling
Nonfall registration?	yes

APPLICANTS ALSO LOOK AT

AND OFTEN PREFER
DePauw University
Butler University

AND SOMETIMES PREFER
Wabash College
Centre College
University of Evansville
Miami University
Indiana University at Bloomington

FINANCIAL FACTS

Financial Aid Rating	87
Annual tuition	$25,800
Room and board	$7,900
Required fees	$550
Books and supplies	$900
% frosh rec. need-based scholarship or grant aid	72
% UG rec. need-based scholarship or grant aid	67
% frosh rec. non-need-based scholarship or grant aid	16
% UG rec. non-need-based scholarship or grant aid	13
% frosh rec. need-based self-help aid	55
% UG rec. need-based self-help aid	53
% frosh rec. any financial aid	99
% UG rec. any financial aid	98
% UG borrow to pay for school	67
Average cumulative indebtedness	$21,296

HARVARD COLLEGE

BYERLY HALL, EIGHT GARDEN STREET, CAMBRIDGE, MA 02138 • ADMISSIONS: 617-495-1551 • FAX: 617-495-8821

CAMPUS LIFE
Quality of Life Rating	85
Fire Safety Rating	60*
Green Rating	99
Type of school	private
Environment	city

STUDENTS
Total undergrad enrollment	6,678
% male/female	50/50
% from out of state	84
% African American	8
% Asian	17
% Caucasian	44
% Hispanic	7
% Native American	1
% international	10
# of countries represented	108

SURVEY SAYS . . .
Lab facilities are great
Great library
Diverse student types on campus
Musical organizations are popular
Student publications are popular
Political activism is popular

ACADEMICS
Academic Rating	99
Calendar	semester
Student/faculty ratio	6.8:1
Profs interesting rating	71
Profs accessible rating	66
Most common reg class size	fewer than 10 students

MOST POPULAR MAJORS
economics
political science and government
psychology

STUDENTS SAY " . . . "

Academics
Those who are lucky enough to attend this legendarily "beautiful, fun, historic and academically alive place" in Cambridge, Massachusetts, find a "dynamic universe" that has the ability to both inspire and intimidate, and to open up a portal to an "amazing irresistible hell," plus about a billion opportunities beyond that. Needless to say, it's "very difficult, academically," but the school "does a good job of watching over its freshmen through extensive advising programs." Those that are not willing to go after what they want—classes, positions in extracurriculars, jobs, etc,—do not gain access to the vast resources of the university. With such a definitive grouping of intelligent people, there does tend to be "latent competition." Nobody is cut-throat in classes, but "people find ways to make everything (especially clubs and even partying) competitive." Still, this is a good thing, and one student claims his experience to be "rewarding beyond anything else I've ever done." "It is impossible to 'get the most out of Harvard' because Harvard offers so much," says another. As at any school, "some professors are better than others," but for the most part, the "the brightest minds in the world" here are "incredible" and "every so often, fantastic," and "the level of achievement is unbelievable." says a student. Harvard employs a lot of Teaching Fellows (TFs) for the larger lecture classes, so "you do have to go to office hours to get to know your big lecture class professors on a personal level," but "this is not a deterrent." The administration can be "waaaaay out of touch with students" and "reticent to change," and there are more than a few claims of bureaucracy, but many agree it has the students' best interests at heart.

Life
Most students have resolved their study habits by the time they get to Harvard, so "studying becomes routine and there is a vibrant social atmosphere on campus, and between students and the local community." In Cambridge and Boston, there's always something to do, whether it's "go see a play, a concert, hit up a party, go to the movies, or dine out." The new pub on campus is an excellent place to hang out and see people, "especially if you want to play a game of pool or have a reasonably priced drink," drinking also occurs on weekends at parties or at Harvard's finals clubs, though it is by no means a prevalent part of social life here. In addition to school-sponsored events such as panels and film screenings, the number of student organizations is staggering. "Basically, if you want to do it, Harvard either has it or has the money to give to you so you can start it," says a student. "Boredom does not exist here. There are endless opportunities and endless passionate people to do them with." During freshman year, the school organizes a lot of holiday/special event parties for people to get to know one another, and conversations are rarely surface-level and "often incorporate some sort of debate or interesting/important topic."

Student Body
Everyone is here to achieve, and this makes for a very common, and broad mold of a typical student. As one junior computer science major succinctly puts it: "Works really hard. Doesn't sleep. Involved in a million extracurriculars." People here have nothing but the highest opinion of their fellow students, and when it comes to finding the lowest common denominator, it's that "everyone is great for one reason or another." However, all of these virtuosos are down-to-earth, and there are also a lot of well-rounded kids "who aren't geniuses but are pretty good at most things." Admitting the best of the best makes for quite a diverse campus, and "there is a lot of tolerance and acceptance at Harvard for individuals of all races, religions, socio-economic backgrounds, life styles, etc."

FINANCIAL AID: 617-495-1581 • E-MAIL: COLLEGE@FAS.HARVARD.EDU • WEBSITE: WWW.FAS.HARVARD.EDU

THE PRINCETON REVIEW SAYS

Admissions

Factors considered include: Application essay, academic GPA, recommendation(s), rigor of secondary school record, standardized test scores, alumni/ae relation, character/personal qualities, extracurricular activities, first generation, geographical residence, interview, racial/ethnic background. SAT Subject Tests required. SAT or ACT required. ACT with Writing component required. High school diploma or equivalent is not required. *Academic units recommended:* 4 English, 4 mathematics, 4 science, 4 foreign language, 3 social studies, 2 history.

Financial Aid

Students should submit: FAFSA, CSS/financial aid profile, noncustodial profile, business/farm supplement, tax forms through IDOC. Regular filing deadline is 2/1. The Princeton Review suggests that all financial aid forms be submitted as soon as possible after 1/1. *Need-based scholarships/grants offered:* Federal Pell, SEOG, state scholarships/grants, private scholarships, the school's own gift aid. *Loan aid offered:* Direct Subsidized Stafford, Direct Unsubsidized Stafford, Direct PLUS, Federal Perkins, college/university loans from institutional funds. Applicants will be notified of awards on or about 4/1. Federal Work-Study Program available. Institutional employment available. Off-campus job opportunities are excellent.

The Inside Word

It just doesn't get any tougher than this. Candidates to Harvard face dual obstacles—an awe-inspiring applicant pool and, as a result, admissions standards that defy explanation in quantifiable terms. Harvard denies admission to the vast majority, and virtually all of them are top students. It all boils down to splitting hairs, which is quite hard to explain and even harder for candidates to understand. Rather than being as detailed and direct as possible about the selection process and criteria, Harvard keeps things close to the vest—before, during, and after. They even refuse to admit that being from lesser populated states like South Dakota is an advantage. Thus the admissions process does more to intimidate candidates than to empower them. Moving to a common application seemed to be a small step in the right direction, but with the current explosion of early-decision applicants and a super-high yield of enrollees, things are not likely to change dramatically.

THE SCHOOL SAYS "..."

From The Admissions Office

"The admissions committee looks for energy, ambition, and the capacity to make the most of opportunities. Academic ability and preparation are important, and so is intellectual curiosity—but many of the strongest applicants have significant, non-academic interests and accomplishments, as well. There is no formula for admission, and applicants are considered carefully, with attention to future promise.

"Freshman applicants may submit the SAT. The ACT with Writing component is also accepted. All students must also submit three SAT Subject Tests of their choosing."

SELECTIVITY
Admissions Rating	99
# of applicants	27,462
% of applicants accepted	8
% of acceptees attending	76

FRESHMAN PROFILE
Range SAT Critical Reading	690–800
Range SAT Math	700–780
Range SAT Writing	690–790
Range ACT Composite	31–35
% graduated top 10% of class	95
% graduated top 25% of class	100
% graduated top 50% of class	100

DEADLINES
Regular	
Priority	12/1
Deadline	1/1
Notification	4/1
Nonfall registration?	no

FINANCIAL FACTS
Financial Aid Rating	99
Annual tuition	$33,696
% frosh rec. need-based scholarship or grant aid	60
% UG rec. need-based scholarship or grant aid	57
% frosh rec. need-based self-help aid	37
% UG rec. need-based self-help aid	46
% frosh rec. any financial aid	70
% UG rec. any financial aid	70
% UG borrow to pay for school	39
Average cumulative indebtedness	$10,813

HARVEY MUDD COLLEGE

301 PLATT BOULEVARD, CLAREMONT, CA 91711-5990 • ADMISSIONS: 909-621-8011 • FAX: 909-607-7046

CAMPUS LIFE

Quality of Life Rating	**88**
Fire Safety Rating	**72**
Green Rating	**86**
Type of school	private
Environment	town

STUDENTS

Total undergrad enrollment	738
% male/female	64/36
% from out of state	50
% from public high school	71.3
% live on campus	99
% African American	2
% Asian	21
% Caucasian	57
% Hispanic	8
% Native American	1
% international	3
# of countries represented	15

SURVEY SAYS . . .

No one cheats
Lab facilities are great
School is well run
Students are friendly
Dorms are like palaces
Low cost of living
Frats and sororities are unpopular or nonexistent

ACADEMICS

Academic Rating	**99**
Calendar	semester
Student/faculty ratio	8.5:1
Profs interesting rating	99
Profs accessible rating	98
Most common reg class size	fewer than 10 students
Most common lab size	10–19 students

MOST POPULAR MAJORS

computer and information sciences
engineering
mathematics

STUDENTS SAY "..."

Academics

Harvey Mudd, the math, science, and engineering centerpiece of the five Claremont Colleges, "is a vortex of challenges and opportunities where you work until you drop, but it doesn't bother you because everyone else is in the same, exact situation you are." A curriculum that teaches "way more math and science than you knew existed, then adds one-third humanities on top of it" means students here leave with "a broad education" that "prepares undergraduates (and undergraduates only) for both industry and grad school." Opportunities are further enhanced by "limitless undergraduate research opportunities." One engineering major reports "Mudd is extremely good at offering research experience for undergraduates. Engineering majors participate in 'Clinic' where they collaborate with other Mudders to satisfy the requests of an actual company." Best of all, Mudd manages to accomplish all this without creating the high-stress environment common at other tech schools. Many students attribute this to the honor code, "a very strong driving force" providing students with "many freedoms." For example, students can "work collaboratively on the vast majority of their assignments, where people contribute what they know and the group as a whole can find a solution." Moreover, "take-home closed-book tests are the norm. We also have full access via our ID cards to all the academic buildings 24/7. Theft is also essentially a non-issue. It's hard to imagine a better setup." Indeed, a school where undergrads are "given all the freedom and resources to explore all the brilliant, not so brilliant, and downright foolish ideas we conceive" can accurately be described as "pretty much as good as it gets. As long as students are serious about learning math and science, you will be happy here."

Life

Even though "Mudd schedules are extremely busy," most students here "know how to lighten up so we aren't completely crushed." "Sports like ultimate Frisbee are very popular, and each dorm occasionally hosts study breaks where students can watch a movie or relax from work. Art clubs like the sewing club or crafts club are available for people who like working on artistic things in groups, and there are many political or environmentally-oriented activist groups." Students report the incidence of pranking—the perpetration of elaborate yet harmless pranks, such as completely filling a classmate's dorm room with inflated garbage bags—is down from past years. However, Mudd remains "known for pretty good parties" among all the Claremont colleges, in part because of "a loose alcohol policy" on the Mudd campus. Even so, the workload is simply too great for partying to ever get out of hand. As one undergrad explains, "People are pretty busy, so a lot of socializing is done over homework." Dorm communities are "very strong, so people will generally hang out in their own dorms, although there's always crossover between dorms." Hometown Claremont "can be a little lackluster" and pricey as well, but fortunately greater Los Angeles isn't too far off.

Student Body

Mudd undergrads are "intelligent yet social—at least within their own social groups. There are some who don't get out much or at all, but that's going to happen at a nerd school like Mudd." While students readily concede "there are some odd students" on campus, depending on the exact nature of their eccentricity, "people either leave them alone or they do well socially." As one student observes, "Swordfights in dorm courtyards are not uncommon, but neither are more typical college parties." Unsurprisingly, students "are all really into science and technology, but there is quite a bit of variation within that." Though "a bit heavy on the white, upper-class males," there has been "a strong effort to recruit talented underrepresented groups and some success recently in recruiting more women." Most students here are "fairly sleep-deprived."

FINANCIAL AID: 909-621-8055 • E-MAIL: ADMISSION@HMC.EDU • WEBSITE: WWW.HMC.EDU

THE PRINCETON REVIEW SAYS

Admissions

Very important factors considered include: Application essay, academic GPA, recommendation(s), rigor of secondary school record, character/personal qualities, talent/ability. *Important factors considered include:* Class rank, standardized test scores, extracurricular activities, first generation, racial/ethnic status. *Other factors considered include:* Alumni/ae relation, geographical residence, interview, level of applicant's interest, state residency, volunteer work, work experience. SAT or ACT required. SAT and SAT Subject Tests or ACT required. ACT with Writing component required. TOEFL required of all international applicants. High school diploma is required and GED is accepted. *Academic units required:* 4 English, 3 mathematics, 3 science, 1 history. *Academic units recommended:* 4 mathematics (2 science labs), 2 foreign language, 2 social studies, 2 history.

Financial Aid

Students should submit: FAFSA, CSS/financial aid profile, state aid form, noncustodial profile, business/farm supplement. Regular filing deadline is 2/1. The Princeton Review suggests that all financial aid forms be submitted as soon as possible after 1/1. *Need-based scholarships/grants offered:* Federal Pell, SEOG, state scholarships/grants, private scholarships, the school's own gift aid Federal ACG and SMART Grants. *Loan aid offered:* FFEL Subsidized Stafford, FFEL Unsubsidized Stafford, FFEL PLUS, Federal Perkins, college/university loans from institutional funds, alternative loans. Applicants will be notified of awards on or about 4/1. Federal Work-Study Program available. Institutional employment available. Off-campus job opportunities are excellent.

The Inside Word

There's little mystery to the admissions process at Harvey Mudd College. Like most top-tier science, math, and engineering schools, Harvey Mudd considers far more qualified applicants than it can accommodate in its incoming class. Give the application your all and accept the fact that being perfectly qualified to attend this school is no guarantee of admission.

THE SCHOOL SAYS "..."

From The Admissions Office

"HMC is a wonderfully unusual combination of a liberal arts college and research institute. Our students love math and science, want to live and learn deeply in an intimate climate of cooperation and trust, thrive on innovation and discovery, and enjoy rigorous coursework in arts, humanities, and social sciences in addition to a technical curriculum. At least a year of research or our innovative Clinic program is required (or guaranteed, if you prefer). The resources at HMC are astounding, and all are accessible to undergraduates: labs, shops, work areas, and most importantly, faculty. You'll find the professors and student body stimulating and supportive—they'll challenge you inside and outside the classroom, and share your love of learning and collaboration. They'll also share your love of fun and sense of humor (math jokes and all). In addition, we benefit from the unique consortium that is the Claremont Colleges.

"While we may not take ourselves too seriously, employers and graduate schools do. We enjoy a powerful reputation for preparing our graduates for all kinds of career paths. A wide range of companies are eager to hire our seniors, and HMC sends the highest proportion of graduates to PhD programs of any undergraduate college in the country."

SELECTIVITY

Admissions Rating	99
# of applicants	2,190
% of applicants accepted	36
% of acceptees attending	26
# accepting a place on wait list	197
# of early decision applicants	103
% accepted early decision	34

FRESHMAN PROFILE

Range SAT Critical Reading	670–770
Range SAT Math	750–800
Range SAT Writing	680–760
Range ACT Composite	33–35
Minimum paper TOEFL	600
Minimum computer TOEFL	250
Minimum web-based TOEFL	100
% graduated top 10% of class	94.9
% graduated top 25% of class	99.4
% graduated top 50% of class	100

DEADLINES

Early decision	
Deadline	11/15
Notification	12/15
Regular	
Deadline	1/2
Notification	4/1
Nonfall registration?	no

APPLICANTS ALSO LOOK AT

AND OFTEN PREFER
University of California—Berkeley
Stanford University
California Institute of Technology
Massachusetts Institute of Technology

AND SOMETIMES PREFER
Cornell University
Rice University
Carnegie Mellon University

AND RARELY PREFER
Virginia Tech
Worcester Polytechnic Institute

FINANCIAL FACTS

Financial Aid Rating	97
Annual tuition	$36,402
Room and board	$11,971
Required fees	$233
Books and supplies	$800
% frosh rec. need-based scholarship or grant aid	55
% UG rec. need-based scholarship or grant aid	53
% frosh rec. non-need-based scholarship or grant aid	29
% UG rec. non-need-based scholarship or grant aid	27
% frosh rec. need-based self-help aid	31
% UG rec. need-based self-help aid	40
% frosh rec. any financial aid	86
% UG rec. any financial aid	83
% UG borrow to pay for school	52.63
Average cumulative indebtedness	$21,018

HAVERFORD COLLEGE

370 WEST LANCASTER AVENUE, HAVERFORD, PA 19041 • ADMISSIONS: 610-896-1350 • FAX: 610-896-1338

CAMPUS LIFE

Quality of Life Rating	93
Fire Safety Rating	74
Green Rating	88
Type of school	private
Environment	town

STUDENTS

Total undergrad enrollment	1,169
% male/female	47/53
% from out of state	86
% from public high school	61
% live on campus	99
% African American	8
% Asian	10
% Caucasian	67
% Hispanic	9
% Native American	1
% international	3
# of countries represented	38

SURVEY SAYS . . .
No one cheats
School is well run
Low cost of living
Frats and sororities are unpopular or nonexistent
(Almost) no one smokes

ACADEMICS

Academic Rating	97
Calendar	semester
Student/faculty ratio	8:1
Profs interesting rating	88
Profs accessible rating	92
Most common reg class size	fewer than 10 students
Most common lab size	fewer than 10 students

MOST POPULAR MAJORS
biology/biological sciences
economics
English language and literature

STUDENTS SAY ". . ."

Academics

"The academic experience is nothing less than stellar" at Haverford. "The classroom is an incredible place where I have been intellectually pushed beyond what I believed possible." The work load can be "intense," but "professors are always available and willing to help," and there is "a support system to help you...composed of students and faculty." Everyone raves about the accessibility of professors. "I have the cell phone number or house number of all my professors. An incredible number of professors live on or within a block of campus and regularly invite students over for tea or dinner." Some students note the lack of research opportunities, but most "love how we have access to Bryn Mawr, Penn, and Swarthmore. The schools really work together to provide a wide range of courses." Haverford is known for its honor code, which "really works, and we actually do have things like closed-book, timed, take-home tests. I honestly don't know of anyone that who ever cheated." The administration also receives high marks. "There is a lot of discourse between the administration and the students," and "the deans...are pretty receptive to student opinions." Though a few students feel "the degree of transparency between the administration and students has dropped in recent years," the "administration does a good job of keeping us informed about important news," and the president holds weekly office hours.

Life

The academic demands of Haverford keep its students focused. "In general, students go to class, participate in extracurriculars, and do homework all day Monday through Thursday." "Students are very active on campus," "with classes, work, on-campus jobs, volunteering, running clubs, and acting on administrative committees." "People are very oriented toward social justice, and overall, our student body is very aware." "Conversations at meals consist of discussions on political issues, scientific breakthroughs, etc." "But that doesn't mean people don't know how to have fun," students assure us. "There are a ton of concerts, a capella shows, student theater, movies, dinners, dances, sponsored events in Philly." "While students here do party," many note and there's no pressure to drink, and plenty of students don't. There is easy access to public transportation, and students say "it's nice to have Philadelphia so close—the music scene is amazing." At the same time, "a lot of people never leave campus because there is so much to do there." Thursday and Saturday are the nights to party, owing to the athletic teams' schedules, and there's not much of a bar scene. Most socializing is on campus, and school-sponsored events are well-attended. "Every weekend night there are at least three options—a music show, an improv show, a movie, or games." It seems Haverford students never really disengage from the classroom, though "Don't be surprised if you witness a discussion about someone's senior thesis next to a keg-stand."

Student Body

Many students describe themselves as a little "nerdy" or "quirky," but in the best possible way. "For the most part, Haverfordians are socially awkward, open to new friends, and looking for moral, political, [or] scholarly debate." The honor code draws a particular type of student—"don't choose to go here if you're not dedicated to the ideas of trust, concern, and respect and to making sure we are a well-run community." Most are "liberal-minded" and "intellectual" and "want to save the world after they graduate."

FINANCIAL AID: 610-896-1350 • E-MAIL: ADMITME@HAVERFORD.EDU • WEBSITE: WWW.HAVERFORD.EDU

THE PRINCETON REVIEW SAYS

Admissions

Very important factors considered include: Application essay, academic GPA, recommendation(s), rigor of secondary school record, character/personal qualities, extracurricular activities. *Important factors considered include:* Class rank, standardized test scores, talent/ability, volunteer work, work experience. *Other factors considered include:* Alumni/ae relation, first generation, geographical residence, interview, level of applicant's interest, racial/ethnic status. SAT Subject Tests required. SAT or ACT required. ACT with Writing component recommended. TOEFL required of all international applicants. High school diploma or equivalent is not required.

Financial Aid

Students should submit: FAFSA, CSS/financial aid profile, noncustodial profile, business/farm supplement. CSS College Board Noncustodial Parents' Statement is required-not the noncustodial supplement. Regular filing deadline is 1/31. The Princeton Review suggests that all financial aid forms be submitted as soon as possible after 1/1. *Need-based scholarships/grants offered:* Federal Pell, SEOG, state scholarships/grants, the school's own gift aid. *Loan aid offered:* FFEL Subsidized Stafford, FFEL Unsubsidized Stafford, FFEL PLUS, Federal Perkins. Applicants will be notified of awards on or about 4/1. Federal Work-Study Program available. Institutional employment available. Off-campus job opportunities are good.

The Inside Word

Haverford's applicant pool is an impressive and competitive lot. Intellectual curiosity is paramount, and applicants are expected to keep a demanding academic schedule in high school. Additionally, the college places a high value on ethics, as evidenced by its honor code. The admissions office seeks students who will reflect and promote Haverford's ideals.

THE SCHOOL SAYS " . . ."

From The Admissions Office

"Haverford strives to be a college in which integrity, honesty, and concern for others are dominant forces. The college does not have many formal rules; rather, it offers an opportunity for students to govern their affairs and conduct themselves with respect and concern for others. Each student is expected to adhere to the honor code as it is adopted each year by the Students' Association. Haverford's Quaker roots show most clearly in the relationship of faculty and students, in the emphasis on integrity, in the interaction of the individual and the community, and through the college's concern for the uses to which its students put their expanding knowledge. Haverford's 1,100 students represent a wide diversity of interests, backgrounds, and talents. They come from public, parochial, and independent schools across the United States, Puerto Rico, and 38 foreign countries. Students of color are an important part of the Haverford community.

"Haverford College requires that all applicants submit the results of the SAT exam or the ACT with the optional Writing test. Two SAT Subject Tests are required."

SELECTIVITY

Admissions Rating	98
# of applicants	3,311
% of applicants accepted	27
% of acceptees attending	37
# accepting a place on wait list	333
% admitted from wait list	1
# of early decision applicants	215
% accepted early decision	51

FRESHMAN PROFILE

Range SAT Critical Reading	650–740
Range SAT Math	640–740
Range SAT Writing	660–750
Minimum paper TOEFL	600
Minimum computer TOEFL	250
% graduated top 10% of class	91
% graduated top 25% of class	97
% graduated top 50% of class	100

DEADLINES

Early decision	
Deadline	11/15
Notification	12/15
Regular	
Deadline	1/15
Notification	4/15
Nonfall registration?	no

FINANCIAL FACTS

Financial Aid Rating	93
Annual tuition	$37,175
Room and board	$11,450
Required fees	$350
Books and supplies	$1,194
% frosh rec. need-based scholarship or grant aid	48
% UG rec. need-based scholarship or grant aid	45
% frosh rec. need-based self-help aid	46
% UG rec. need-based self-help aid	42
% frosh rec. any financial aid	46
% UG rec. any financial aid	44
% UG borrow to pay for school	41
Average cumulative indebtedness	$17,125

HENDRIX COLLEGE

1600 WASHINGTON AVENUE, CONWAY, AR 72032 • ADMISSIONS: 501-450-1362 • FAX: 501-450-3843

CAMPUS LIFE

Quality of Life Rating	88
Fire Safety Rating	64
Green Rating	78
Type of school	private
Affiliation	Methodist
Environment	town

STUDENTS

Total undergrad enrollment	1,341
% male/female	45/55
% from out of state	51
% from public high school	71
% live on campus	84
% African American	4
% Asian	3
% Caucasian	83
% Hispanic	4
% Native American	1
% international	2
# of countries represented	13

SURVEY SAYS . . .

Lab facilities are great
Athletic facilities are great
Frats and sororities are unpopular or nonexistent

ACADEMICS

Academic Rating	94
Calendar	semester
Student/faculty ratio	12:1
Profs interesting rating	94
Profs accessible rating	95
Most common reg class size	10–19 students
Most common lab size	10–19 students

MOST POPULAR MAJORS

biology/biological sciences
English language and literature
psychology

STUDENTS SAY "..."

Academics

Hendrix College in Arkansas is strong in the humanities as well as the hard sciences. "The biggest and nicest buildings on campus are definitely the science buildings," notes one student. "The study abroad program is amazing." Internships and research opportunities are readily available. Scholarships are profuse. Many students receive "phenomenal aid that would be ridiculous to turn down." "Academically, Hendrix is not a walk in the park." "Some mandatory classes are pointless," but "dull or otherwise bad classes seem uncommon." "Class sizes are small, which allows for enriching, intimate discussion." The "courageously friendly" professors are "some of the best and most challenging around." "Ninety percent of the professors are amazingly top-notch," estimates an American studies major. "Generally, they all push you to do well." "One of Hendrix's selling points is the personal relationships that students build with their professors," adds a political science major. Be forewarned: "they know when you're missing class or when you're really struggling with the material or when you're not even trying." The administration here is "the same as anywhere you will go." It's "competent and keep the school running smoothly" but sometimes "out of touch with the desires of the students." Decisions "seem uninformed or just plain random" now and then.

Life

"Hendrix is one of those schools where you have to really study and work hard." Nevertheless, social life is very active. "On warm days, the pecan grove in the center of campus is bustling with people just hanging out." "There are always activities going on which students can attend for free." Virtually everyone is "active in at least one organization." Many are "very involved" in theater productions. Ultimate Frisbee is pretty big. A decent percentage of students plays intercollegiate sports, but "those who don't couldn't care less." There's no frat or sorority scene, and students here say that's "a good thing." "On the weekends there is a pretty strong drinking culture," and there are occasionally "big" campus-wide parties and "some awesome theme parties." "The food is very good." However, the residence halls are "a universal source of concern." "Housing is a difficult process here" and the dorms are "cramped." However, the college recently acquired several more apartment buildings that have added space for more than 300 students. Also, the Internet connection can be "truly abysmal." Though hometown Conway is one of the fastest growing cities in Arkansas, students still complain that, "There's not much to do" and "there aren't really any bars except the VFW." As a result, "most people hardly ever leave" the "breathtaking" campus. When they do depart, they usually head "a mere" 30 minutes away to the somewhat urban environs of Little Rock. "Outdoorsy" activities are also available. "There is a lot of nature in the surrounding area, but no one seems to want to go there."

Student Body

"Hendrix is a cross between a hippie school and a nerd college." It's mostly "off-the-wall and very creative" "southern kids." "I don't think there really is a typical Hendrix student," a junior tells us. "What unites us is our strong sense of individuality and our unerring desire to learn about each other." "If you are different or have little quirks, you fit right in," guarantees a senior. Most students say "it's easy to float from group to group" but "cliques at Hendrix are very obvious." There are "whiny upper-middle-class trustafarians." There are "socially awkward people." There are "granola kids" and "stoners." "Most students lie somewhere on the spectrum from studious to party animal." Gay students are "very out." "The athletes sequester themselves." "Race-wise, you have your choice of 12 flavors of vanilla." "Despite what the administration wants prospective students to think, there are not a lot of minority students at Hendrix," discloses a freshman. Though diversity is increasing and "Minorities seemed to be accepted into the social crowd." Politically, the atmosphere is "heavily liberal." "Hendrix is kind of like being in a time warp harkening back to the '60s and '70s." Some students note a "slight dislike of conservatives." "Their political beliefs are given little to no respect by a majority of the student body," says a sophomore. Other students don't see the problem. "I myself am a conservative Republican, and I have many friends and have never felt unaccepted," asserts a sophomore. "We just agree to disagree."

FINANCIAL AID: 501-450-1368 • E-MAIL: ADM@HENDRIX.EDU • WEBSITE: WWW.HENDRIX.EDU

THE PRINCETON REVIEW SAYS

Admissions

Very important factors considered include: Application essay, academic GPA, rigor of secondary school record, standardized test scores. *Important factors considered include:* Class rank, recommendation(s), character/personal qualities, extracurricular activities, interview. *Other factors considered include:* talent/ability, volunteer work. SAT or ACT required. TOEFL or IELTS required of all international applicants. High school diploma is required and GED is accepted. *Academic units recommended:* 4 English, 3 mathematics, 2 science, 2 foreign language, 3 social studies.

Financial Aid

Students should submit: FAFSA. The Princeton Review suggests that all financial aid forms be submitted as soon as possible after 1/1. *Need-based scholarships/grants offered:* Federal Pell, SEOG, ACG, SMART, TEACH, state scholarships/grants, private scholarships, the school's own gift aid. *Loan aid offered:* FFEL and FDSL Subsidized Stafford, FFEL and FDSL Unsubsidized Stafford, FFEL PLUS and FDSL , Federal Perkins, Methodist loan. Applicants will be notified of awards on a rolling basis beginning 2/15. Federal Work-Study Program available. Institutional employment available. Off-campus job opportunities are good.

The Inside Word

Hendrix is something of a sleeper school. The acceptance rate is high but the applicant pool is small and well-qualified. Hendrix is an especially good bet for students with strong grades who lack the test scores usually necessary for admission to colleges on a higher level of selectivity. Also, financial aid abounds, so don't let the cost of tuition be a deterrent.

THE SCHOOL SAYS "..."

From The Admissions Office

"Hendrix students are participants, not spectators. They like to be involved, and they like to know that what they do makes a difference. Hendrix students are voting members of almost every campus committee, which gives them an important voice in college governance. They are very hands-on about their education as well. Internships, study abroad, research projects, service projects, expressive arts projects, and leadership development—these are all areas that Hendrix students find attractive. A few years ago, Hendrix introduced a new program that guarantees every Hendrix student will have at least three hands-on experiences selected from six categories. The program is called *Your Hendrix Odyssey: Engaging in Active Learning.* Students receive transcript credit for their Odyssey projects. The benefits of this hands-on approach to learning are so obvious that we believe every Hendrix student should have the opportunity to participate. The college is raising money to provide grants and fellowships that will help remove the economic barriers to participation in out-of-class experiences. It is an exciting time to be a Hendrix student! The Hendrix curriculum is demanding, but the environment is one of support and cooperation—not competition. Hendrix students form a close-knit, inclusive community. They build lifetime connections and close friendships, the kind of relationships that grow in a residential college where learning is a 24/7 kind of thing. It doesn't hurt that the campus is beautifully maintained and that Hendrix graduates are admitted to top graduate schools and recruited for good jobs around the world.

"Hendrix College has no preference on which standardized test (SAT/ACT) is taken, but we strongly encourage all applicants to take one of the tests during their senior year. While the Writing scores will be considered, at this point weight will only be given to the Critical Reading and Math sections of the SAT and the required sections of the ACT."

SELECTIVITY

Admissions Rating	99
# of applicants	1,420
% of applicants accepted	94
% of acceptees attending	32

FRESHMAN PROFILE

Range SAT Critical Reading	580–690
Range SAT Math	550–660
Range ACT Composite	25–31
Minimum paper TOEFL	550
Minimum computer TOEFL	213
Minimum web-based TOEFL	79
Minimum IELTS	6.0
Average HS GPA	3.76
% graduated top 10% of class	41
% graduated top 25% of class	75
% graduated top 50% of class	95

DEADLINES

Regular	
Priority	2/1
Deadline	8/1
Notification	rolling
Nonfall registration?	yes

APPLICANTS ALSO LOOK AT

AND OFTEN PREFER
Rhodes College
University of Central Arkansas
Millsaps College
Trinity University
The University of Tulsa
University of Arkansas—Fayetteville

AND SOMETIMES PREFER
Washington University in St. Louis
Centenary College of Louisiana
Tulane University
Louisiana State University
Austin College
Southwestern University

FINANCIAL FACTS

Financial Aid Rating	87
Annual tuition	$25,780
Room and board	$7,950
Required fees	$300
Books and supplies	$900
% frosh rec. need-based scholarship or grant aid	57
% UG rec. need-based scholarship or grant aid	58
% frosh rec. non-need-based scholarship or grant aid	19
% UG rec. non-need-based scholarship or grant aid	15
% frosh rec. need-based self-help aid	41
% UG rec. need-based self-help aid	44
% frosh rec. any financial aid	100
% UG rec. any financial aid	100
% UG borrow to pay for school	81.05
Average cumulative indebtedness	$17,484

HILLSDALE COLLEGE

33 EAST COLLEGE STREET, HILLSDALE, MI 49242 • ADMISSIONS: 517-607-2327 • FAX: 517-607-2223

CAMPUS LIFE

Quality of Life Rating	**81**
Fire Safety Rating	**87**
Green Rating	**63**
Type of school	private
Environment	village

STUDENTS

Total undergrad enrollment	1,326
% male/female	48/52
% from out of state	59
% from public high school	48
% live on campus	86
% in (# of) fraternities	35 (3)
% in (# of) sororities	45 (3)
% international	2
# of countries represented	13

SURVEY SAYS . . .

No one cheats
Students are friendly
Students are very religious
Campus feels safe
Low cost of living
Students are happy
Musical organizations are popular
Student publications are popular
Political activism is popular
Very little drug use

ACADEMICS

Academic Rating	**96**
Calendar	semester
Student/faculty ratio	10:1
Profs interesting rating	98
Profs accessible rating	95
Most common reg class size	fewer than 10 students
Most common lab size	20–29 students

MOST POPULAR MAJORS
biology/biological sciences
business administration and management
education

STUDENTS SAY ". . ."

Academics

"Tiny" Hillsdale College "provides a classic liberal arts education" "grounded in the great traditions of Western civilization." Students spend their time "reading dead guys," grappling with "timeless ideas," and "constantly fighting change." A "strong core curriculum" includes the standard liberal arts and sciences requirements as well as mandatory courses on the Constitution, Western civilization, and the "great books" (stuff like *The Odyssey* and Dante's *Inferno*). "Writing skills are heavily addressed" and "academics are very rigorous." There is "no grade inflation" whatsoever, cautions a Spanish major. "Here, the 'C' reigns." While professors "demand a lot," "lectures are engaging" and most students have nothing but praise for the academic experience. The faculty is reportedly full of "profoundly enlightening, deep thinkers" who are "always available" outside of class. The administration is "well organized" despite "periodic quirks." The single biggest complaint on this campus involves the "awkward" and "archaic" way in which students sign up for classes. "Hillsdale students are begging for an easier and more efficient registration process." Many rules are severe, too. Management has "no qualms about keeping a close eye on the students." Also, you should be aware that "Hillsdale refuses to accept government money." Every scholarship and financial aid dime is privately funded. Don't worry, though, the average aid package is more than $12,000.

Life

Hillsdale's "rural" and "boring" location "almost makes it seem like a secret intellectual getaway," but mostly there's a lot to be desired. Consequently, the "beautiful" campus here "is the hub of social life." Residence halls are "spacious" but there are no co-ed dorms and visitation hours are "strict." During the week, students "don't have copious amounts of free time." "Virtually everyone is studying like mad." Nevertheless, students are "involved in many organizations." "The Greek system is strong." Religious groups are "prominent" as well. Varsity athletics "don't get much support" but "intramural sports are always popular." There are "frequent" concerts and recitals. There's "sledding" and "organized snowball fights." "Everyone loves ideas and good debate" and everything from theology and philosophy to sports and popular culture is fair game. "It is not uncommon to walk to the bathroom, only to get sucked into a three-hour debate on the political ramifications of World War II with someone you have barely ever spoken to," swears a sophomore. "We are not one of those evangelical schools that forbids alcohol," declares a junior. "Kegs and drinking games" are occasionally available. Smaller get-togethers "where people have a few drinks" are more common. For road trips, student often head about 70 miles northeast to the "real college town" of Ann Arbor.

Student Body

"Hillsdale prides itself on being one of the first colleges to openly accept anyone irrespective of nation, color, or sex." All the same, the population here is almost entirely composed of "white, upper-middle-class" students. "There certainly isn't a lot of ethnic diversity." There are "leftish students" and plenty of people who don't go to church. "There's a good libertarian crowd," too. However, Christianity and right-wing politics dominate. "The typical student is religious and conservative," relates a sophomore. "That's the nature of the college." Students describe themselves as "ambitious" and "clean cut." They are "very sweet, very friendly, and good people" who "love learning and willingly participate in intellectual discussions." There's a large contingent of "homeschooled" students and there are definitely "Bible-beating people." You'll find the "little Christian ray of sunshine who studies all the time and goes to bed early." "It's not uncommon to see a long-skirted female posse longing for a beau to court them à la chivalry love," observes a senior. Greeks, athletes, and thespians people constitute the other main cliques. "Overall, people get along and mesh well" but "there tends to be a large rift between the group of overly conservative students and the group consisting of the partying athletes and fraternity and sorority members."

FINANCIAL AID: 517-437-7341 • E-MAIL: ADMISSIONS@HILLSDALE.EDU/ADMISSIONS • WEBSITE: WWW.HILLSDALE.EDU

THE PRINCETON REVIEW SAYS

Admissions

Very important factors considered include: Academic GPA, rigor of secondary school record, standardized test scores, character/personal qualities, interview. *Important factors considered include:* Class rank, application essay, recommendation(s), extracurricular activities, level of applicant's interest, volunteer work, work experience. *Other factors considered include:* Alumni/ae relation, talent/ability. SAT or ACT required. ACT with Writing component recommended. TOEFL required of all international applicants. High school diploma is required and GED is accepted. *Academic units recommended:* 4 English, 4 mathematics, 3 science (1 science lab), 2 foreign language, 1 social studies, 2 history.

Financial Aid

Students should submit: institution's own financial aid form, noncustodial profile, business/farm supplement. Regular filing deadline is 3/15. The Princeton Review suggests that all financial aid forms be submitted as soon as possible after 1/1. *Need-based scholarships/grants offered:* private scholarships, the school's own gift aid. *Loan aid offered:* college/university loans from institutional funds. Applicants will be notified of awards on a rolling basis beginning 2/15. Institutional employment available. Off-campus job opportunities are good.

Inside Word

Don't be fooled by Hillsdale's high acceptance rate. Only serious, solid candidates bother applying here and the academic profile of incoming freshmen is tremendous. While you don't have to be politically conservative to get in, a passionate and well-reasoned essay defending traditional values or singing the praises of free-market economics certainly can't hurt you.

THE SCHOOL SAYS "..."

From The Admissions Office

"Personal attention is a hallmark at Hillsdale. Small classes are combined with teaching professors who make their students a priority. The academic environment at Hillsdale will actively engage you as a student. Extracurricular activities abound at Hillsdale with the more than 50 clubs and organizations that offer excellent leadership opportunities. From athletics and the fine arts, to Greek life and community volunteer programs, you will find it difficult not to be involved in our thriving campus community. In addition, numerous study-abroad programs, a conservation research venture in South Africa, a professional sales internship program with national placements and the Washington-Hillsdale Internship Program (WHIP) are just a few of the unique off-campus opportunities available to you at Hillsdale.

"Our strength as a college is found in our mission and in our curriculum. The core curriculum at Hillsdale contains the essence of the classical liberal arts education. Through it you are introduced to the history, the philosophical and theological ideas, the works of literature, and the scientific discoveries that set Western Civilization apart. As explained in our mission statement, 'the college considers itself a trustee of modern man's intellectual and spiritual inheritance from the Judeo-Christian faith and Greco-Roman culture, a heritage finding its clearest expression in the American experiment of self-government under law.'

"We seek students who are ambitious, intellectually curious and who are ready to become leaders worthy of this heritage in their personal as well as professional lives.

"Applicants can meet admissions requirements by submitting the results of the SAT, or the ACT (Writing section optional). We will use the student's best composite/combined score in the evaluation process. The SAT Subject Tests in Literature and U.S. History are also recommended."

SELECTIVITY

Admissions Rating	96
# of applicants	1,401
% of applicants accepted	64
% of acceptees attending	42
# accepting a place on wait list	35
% admitted from wait list	14
# of early decision applicants	80
% accepted early decision	85

FRESHMAN PROFILE

Range SAT Critical Reading	640–720
Range SAT Math	570–660
Range SAT Writing	610–690
Range ACT Composite	25–30
Minimum paper TOEFL	570
Minimum computer TOEFL	210
Average HS GPA	3.72
% graduated top 10% of class	47
% graduated top 25% of class	75
% graduated top 50% of class	98

DEADLINES

Early decision	
Deadline	11/15
Notification	12/1
Early action	
Deadline	1/1
Notification	1/20
Regular	
Priority	1/1
Deadline	2/15
Nonfall registration?	yes

APPLICANTS ALSO LOOK AT

AND OFTEN PREFER
University of Dallas, Wheaton College (IL), Hope College

AND SOMETIMES PREFER
Taylor U., Purdue U.—West Lafayette, Albion College, Pepperdine U.

FINANCIAL FACTS

Financial Aid Rating	84
Annual tuition	$18,650
Room and board	$7,340
Required fees	$490
Books and supplies	$850
% frosh rec. need-based scholarship or grant aid	47
% UG rec. need-based scholarship or grant aid	41
% frosh rec. non-need-based scholarship or grant aid	32
% UG rec. non-need-based scholarship or grant aid	26
% frosh rec. need-based self-help aid	47
% UG rec. need-based self-help aid	41
% frosh rec. athletic scholarships	17
% UG rec. athletic scholarships	16
% frosh rec. any financial aid	83
% UG rec. any financial aid	86
% UG borrow to pay for school	62
Average cumulative indebtedness	$14,500

HIRAM COLLEGE

PO Box 67, Hiram, OH 44234 • Admissions: 800-362-5280 • Fax: 330-569-5944

CAMPUS LIFE
Quality of Life Rating	72
Fire Safety Rating	60*
Green Rating	60*
Type of school	private
Affiliation	Disciples of Christ
Environment	rural

STUDENTS
Total undergrad enrollment	1,173
% male/female	44/56
% from out of state	16
% from public high school	86
% live on campus	91
% in (# of) fraternities	NR (3)
% in (# of) sororities	NR (3)
% African American	10
% Asian	1
% Caucasian	68
% Hispanic	2
% international	5
# of countries represented	17

SURVEY SAYS . . .
Athletic facilities are great
Students are friendly
Different types of students interact
Students get along with local community
Campus feels safe
Low cost of living

ACADEMICS
Academic Rating	80
Calendar	semester
Student/faculty ratio	14:1
Profs interesting rating	84
Profs accessible rating	84

MOST POPULAR MAJORS
education

STUDENTS SAY ". . ."

Academics

Students come to Hiram College seeking "a very community-based environment" that provides "not only a feeling of immediate comfort but also the appeal of being in close relationship with my professors," and few leave disappointed. Undergrads here "love how involved all of the professors are into guiding the students through not just classes and majors, but future plans and career paths" and praise the "big-school opportunities in a small-school environment." As one student points out, "Undergrads can work in research with professors here, which is an invaluable skill and great for resumes." Students tell us Hiram boasts "a great biology program that does well getting its students into veterinary and medical school," a "great education program," and strong offerings in environmental science. Throughout the school "small classes of no more than 30 students and the intimate nature of the learning [environment] keep us from feeling lost in a sea of students." A "unique semester system splits terms into a 12-week main session followed by a three-week intensive class. It gives you fewer classes to have to take all at once, and the three-week is a great opportunity for electives or study-abroad trips that I couldn't do for a whole semester for financial reasons or because I can't spare that time away from my major."

Life

Most students concede that Hiram is "in the middle of nowhere," but not all see this as an insurmountable negative. On the contrary, many appreciate how the location "allows for us to meet together and create our own fun, make new friends, and enjoy the simplest pleasures in life. Hiram is especially fun in the winter, as we get tons of snow and have so many hills you [can] sled off. Everyone goes out at night and sleds together." Others "find unique things to do—stargazing, making our own apple cider, going to local square dances…we learn lots of cool things." Furthermore, "the school is excellent for providing the students with gatherings multiple times a week. Each club on campus is required to sponsor a campus-wide event each semester, and the student-run club, KCPB, is devoted to organizing as many on-campus and off-campus events as possible. Examples include movie nights in town, Destressfests before mid-terms and finals," Bowler First Fridays, talent shows, and game shows. While "drinking is prohibited in rooms where the resident is not 21, and [the rule] is enforced," those looking to party usually can find the opportunity. Undergrads report "for the most part everyone is respectful. The students usually regulate each other and take care of issues when someone gets out of control."

Student Body

Hiram is "a gentle mix of athletes, artists, and scientists, and…Everyone gets along and respects what the others are capable of doing." The school "gets the rap of having 'weird' kids," which most here wear as a badge of honor. As one puts it, "The jocks can be philosophy majors, and the band geeks can be THE people to hang out with on a Friday night…This place doesn't respect stereotypes." Though proud "each individual brings something unique and interesting to the community here," students are also quick to point out their commonalities. "All students do have a dedication to serving others, in varying degrees and…attempt to include themselves in the community in a variety of different ways (social groups, athletics, community service or social activism groups, student government, etc.)."

FINANCIAL AID: 330-569-5107 • E-MAIL: ADMISSION@HIRAM.EDU • WEBSITE: ADMISSION.HIRAM.EDU

THE PRINCETON REVIEW SAYS

Admissions

Very important factors considered include: Academic GPA. *Important factors considered include:* Application essay, rigor of secondary school record, standardized test scores, character/personal qualities, extracurricular activities. *Other factors considered include:* Class rank, recommendation(s), alumni/ae relation, first generation, geographical residence, interview, level of applicant's interest, state residency, talent/ability, volunteer work, work experience. SAT or ACT required. TOEFL required of all international applicants. High school diploma is required and GED is accepted. *Academic units required:* 4 English, 3 mathematics, 3 science (2 science labs), 2 foreign language, 3 social studies, 1 history, 2 academic electives. *Academic units recommended:* 3 foreign language.

Financial Aid

The Princeton Review suggests that all financial aid forms be submitted as soon as possible after 1/1.

The Inside Word

The typical Hiram admit performed solidly but not spectacularly in a college preparatory high school curriculum and earned above average but not stellar standardized test scores. Applicants seem to know whether they fit the Hiram profile, explaining the school's high admissions rate as few who don't stand a decent chance of getting in bother to apply. A thorough application review process allows hopefuls to make up for academic deficiencies with solid essays and/or strong recommendations. Admissions are rolling, a process that favors early applicants.

THE SCHOOL SAYS " . . ."

From The Admissions Office

"Hiram College offers distinctive programs that set us apart from other small, private liberal arts colleges. About half of Hiram's students study abroad at some point during their four years. In 2007–2008, a group of 17 students led by two faculty members traveled around the world to study climate change, stopping in nine different locations. Common study-abroad destinations include France, China, Mexico, Guatemala, Costa Rica, the Galapagos Islands, and several African countries. Because Hiram students receive credits for the courses taught by Hiram faculty on these trips, studying abroad will not impede progress in their majors or delay graduation.

"Another unique aspect of a Hiram education is our academic calendar, known as the Hiram Plan. Our semesters are divided into 12-week and three-week periods. Students usually enroll in three courses during each 12-week, and one intensive course during the three-week. Many students spend the three-week on study abroad trips or taking unusual courses not typically offered during the 12-week. Our small classes encourage interaction between students and their professors. Students can work with professors on original research projects and often participate in musical groups and intramural sports teams alongside faculty members.

"The Hiram College Tuition Guarantee ensures that the annual cost for tuition will not increase between the first year a student is enrolled and the student's senior year."

SELECTIVITY

Admissions Rating	79
# of applicants	1,551
% of applicants accepted	77
% of acceptees attending	28

FRESHMAN PROFILE

Range SAT Critical Reading	480–610
Range SAT Math	470–600
Range ACT Composite	20–25
Minimum paper TOEFL	550
Average HS GPA	3.34
% graduated top 10% of class	20
% graduated top 25% of class	48
% graduated top 50% of class	79

DEADLINES

Regular	
Priority	2/15
Deadline	4/15
Notification	rolling
Nonfall registration?	yes

APPLICANTS ALSO LOOK AT
AND SOMETIMES PREFER
The College of Wooster
John Carroll University
AND RARELY PREFER
Kent State University—Kent Campus

FINANCIAL FACTS

Financial Aid Rating	60*
Annual tuition	$26,435
Room and Board	$9,010
Required fees	$700
Books and supplies	$700

HOBART AND WILLIAM SMITH COLLEGES

629 SOUTH MAIN STREET, GENEVA, NY 14456 • ADMISSIONS: 315-781-3472 • FAX: 315-781-3471

CAMPUS LIFE
Quality of Life Rating	70
Fire Safety Rating	60*
Green Rating	60*
Type of school	private
Environment	village

STUDENTS
Total undergrad enrollment	1,855
% male/female	46/54
% from out of state	55
% from public high school	65
% live on campus	90
% in (# of) fraternities	15 (5)
% African American	4
% Asian	2
% Caucasian	88
% Hispanic	4
% international	2
# of countries represented	18

SURVEY SAYS . . .
No one cheats
Career services are great
Dorms are like palaces
Students are happy
Everyone loves the Statesmen
Lots of beer drinking
Hard liquor is popular

ACADEMICS
Academic Rating	90
Calendar	semester
Student/faculty ratio	11:1
Profs interesting rating	87
Profs accessible rating	90
Most common	
reg class size	10–19 students

MOST POPULAR MAJORS
economics
English language and literature
history

STUDENTS SAY ". . ."

Academics

"Students come before all else" at tiny, upstate Hobart and William Smith, a pair of associated single-sex colleges that share a campus, faculty, and administration, yet remain very distinct in their identities, combining to make the academic and social lives of the students as varied and interesting as possible. While "there aren't always tons of options" for classes, "there are lots of interesting choices offered for such a small school." This "liberal arts education with a flair" also places a strong emphasis on studying abroad as a part of a student's education. Tuition can be a workout for some however there are many grants offered. Students are enthralled with the school, from the "beautiful, green campus" offering "a small slice of New England stuck in upstate New York" to the "unrivalled experience."

The "vibrant" professors have "diverse viewpoints," and though "you have to learn to adapt to different teaching styles," they treat students with complete respect, so "the academic experience is more in the vein of colleagues." Everyone here is happy with their academic experience, and even though there's an occasional dud, "for every professor who seems mediocre, there's two more who are absolute gems of teaching ability." "I have had professors invite me to office hours, send me internship opportunities, discuss my career goals, and even invite me to their houses for dinner," says another. As for higher up, the raves are similar. The administration works very hard to accommodate everyone on campus and "is usually successful at it." This success is partly due to the coordinate system, which allows for separate deans for both Hobart and William Smith, granting "more individual attention to the students." They will "get to know you and will stop on the sidewalk and have a chat whenever they see you." However, students do wish the administration was a little less strict in its policies and enforcement.

Life

Life in general is pretty hectic, but students are "very good at balancing school and socializing." Most kids always stay busy with their school work, but "really let loose on the weekends." Bars, frat parties, and campus parties can all occur in the same night, and the school offers "a very positive program" called Safe Rides, which provides late-night van rides. Geneva is a beautiful town, but it's no NYC. The cold winter months can be endless, and the rural location means students "make their own fun here," whether through tray-sledding, barbequing, or skinny-dipping, and it "kind of works out better." On nice days, the quad acts as a hub of student life, when students "bring horse shoes, Frisbees, footballs, baseballs, and blankets and just spend the day together." There's also skiing, malls and outlets for shopping, and a wildlife refuge not too far away. Without a nearby big urban center, students are "continuously immersed in campus life and happenings," and most are very happy with the offerings from the school and campus groups. Community service is very popular here, as well.

Student Body

"Preppy white person" seems to encapsulate most everyone's perception of the student body, with "Polo, L.L.Bean, Lily Pulitzer & Lacoste everywhere." A lot of students come from affluent backgrounds, but in recent years, thanks to scholarships and opportunity programs, there's a significant number of international students and minority students and "they blend in seamlessly." there are "rich kids and alternative types melting all together in a pretty good harmony," sums up a student. People "usually get along with each other regardless of being typical or not," partially due to the rampant involvement in student organizations and groups. With fewer than 2,000 people in the student body, there's not much mystery left after a couple of years, when "you can walk to class and recognize at 90 percent of the people you see," but the general pervading friendliness of the school as a whole means that "there is a happy niche here for everyone."

FINANCIAL AID: 315-781-3315 • E-MAIL: ADMISSIONS@HWS.EDU • WEBSITE: WWW.HWS.EDU

THE PRINCETON REVIEW SAYS

Admissions

Very important factors considered include: Rigor of secondary school record. *Important factors considered include:* Class rank, application essay, academic GPA, recommendation(s), standardized test scores, character/personal qualities, extracurricular activities, volunteer work, work experience. *Other factors considered include:* Alumni/ae relation, first generation, geographical residence, interview, level of applicant's interest, racial/ethnic status, talent/ability. SAT or ACT required. ACT with Writing component required. TOEFL required of all international applicants. High school diploma is required and GED is accepted. *Academic units required:* 4 English, 3 mathematics, 3 science (2 science labs), 2 foreign language, 2 social studies, 2 history, 2 academic electives. *Academic units recommended:* 3 foreign language, 3 social studies, 4 academic electives.

Financial Aid

Students should submit: FAFSA, CSS/financial aid profile, state aid form, non-custodial profile, parents' and student's tax returns. Regular filing deadline is 2/1. The Princeton Review suggests that all financial aid forms be submitted as soon as possible after 1/1. *Need-based scholarships/grants offered:* Federal Pell, SEOG, state scholarships/grants, private scholarships, the school's own gift aid. *Loan aid offered:* FFEL Subsidized Stafford, FFEL Unsubsidized Stafford, FFEL PLUS, Federal Perkins. Applicants will be notified of awards on or about 4/1. Federal Work-Study Program available. Institutional employment available. Off-campus job opportunities are good.

The Inside Word

Applicants to the academic side of Seneca Lake's scenic shore should know that HSW likes to see a student who embraces a challenge. They recommend that hopefuls prepare themselves for a rigorous college curriculum by taking at least two years of a foreign language and a couple of AP courses for good measure.

THE SCHOOL SAYS "..."

From The Admissions Office

"Hobart and William Smith Colleges seek students with a sense of adventure and a commitment to the life of the mind. Inside the classroom, students find the academic climate to be rigorous, with a faculty that is deeply involved in teaching and working with them. Outside, they discover a supportive community that helps to cultivate a balance and hopes to foster an integration among academics, extracurricular activities, and social life. Hobart and William Smith, as coordinate colleges, have an awareness of gender differences and equality and are committed to respect and a celebration of diversity.

"Freshman applicants are required to take either the ACT with or without the optional Writing portion or the SAT. Their highest composite score will be used in admissions decisions. Students are encouraged to submit results of any SAT Subject Test they have taken."

SELECTIVITY

Admissions Rating	88
# of applicants	3,410
% of applicants accepted	65
% of acceptees attending	25
# accepting a place on wait list	194
% admitted from wait list	16

FRESHMAN PROFILE

Range SAT Critical Reading	530–640
Range SAT Math	540–630
Range ACT Composite	24–27
Minimum paper TOEFL	550
Minimum computer TOEFL	220
Average HS GPA	3.22
% graduated top 10% of class	33
% graduated top 25% of class	67
% graduated top 50% of class	95

DEADLINES

Early decision	
Deadline	11/15
Notification	12/15
Regular	
Deadline	2/1
Notification	4/1
Nonfall registration?	no

APPLICANTS ALSO LOOK AT

AND OFTEN PREFER
Connecticut College
Colgate University
Trinity College (CT)

AND SOMETIMES PREFER
Dickinson College
Gettysburg College
Kenyon College
Skidmore College

AND RARELY PREFER
Ithaca College
University of Vermont
State University of New York at Geneseo

FINANCIAL FACTS

Financial Aid Rating	92
Annual tuition	$31,850
Room and board	$8,386
Required fees	$887
Books and supplies	$850
% frosh rec. need-based scholarship or grant aid	58
% UG rec. need-based scholarship or grant aid	60
% frosh rec. non-need-based scholarship or grant aid	10
% UG rec. non-need-based scholarship or grant aid	7
% frosh rec. need-based self-help aid	48
% UG rec. need-based self-help aid	53
% frosh rec. any financial aid	74
% UG rec. any financial aid	64
% UG borrow to pay for school	65
Average cumulative indebtedness	$21,545

HOFSTRA UNIVERSITY

ADMISSIONS CENTER, BERNON HALL, HEMPSTEAD, NY 11549 • ADMISSIONS: 516-463-6700 • FAX: 516-463-5100

CAMPUS LIFE

Quality of Life Rating	62
Fire Safety Rating	94
Green Rating	83
Type of school	private
Environment	city

STUDENTS

Total undergrad enrollment	8,179
% male/female	48/52
% from out of state	49
% live on campus	79
% in (# of) fraternities	10 (19)
% in (# of) sororities	9 (15)
% African American	9
% Asian	5
% Caucasian	63
% Hispanic	8
% international	1
# of countries represented	73

SURVEY SAYS . . .

Great library
Frats and sororities dominate social
scene
College radio is popular
Student publications are popular
Lots of beer drinking
Hard liquor is popular
(Almost) everyone smokes

ACADEMICS

Academic Rating	75
Calendar	4/1/4
Student/faculty ratio	14:1
Profs interesting rating	72
Profs accessible rating	69
Most common reg class size	10–19 students
Most common lab size	10–19 students

MOST POPULAR MAJORS

business administration and
management
marketing/marketing management
psychology

STUDENTS SAY ". . ."

Academics

To experience "Long Island in a nutshell," consider Hofstra University, a school that "is dedicated to preparing its students for successful careers." Nearly one-third of the student body is business majors. Hofstra's "great finance program" benefits from "the number-one college Financial Trading Room in the country," while the marketing program supports the Hofstra American Marketing Cub, "which won 'Business Club of the Year.'" Hofstra is also "a great place for accounting majors." Students tell us the communications department is "amazing," with "a state-of-the-art radio station" that "offers a large variety of ways to get involved, whether it's having a show or being behind the scenes." The school also plays "a large variety of music," from "rap to rock to Irish." Hofstra's education program is also highly regarded, boasting "one of the best music education programs in the country." In all areas, students laud "real-world experience on real-world equipment" and great opportunities for internships. In fact, "there are more internships available than there are people, so we are always informed of new opportunities in our majors as they emerge. Our location [relative] to the city presents many summer and winter internships in Manhattan, especially for communications and business majors." Hofstra students can't sit around and wait for someone to tell them what to do. One student writes, "If you want to get something done, you definitely can't wait for it to happen. You have to put yourself out there and meet with teachers and join clubs."

Life

Those who live on or near campus tell us " plenty to do here, but you have to have a car to really do it, [because] walking in the area isn't that safe." There are a "ton of malls, movie theaters, and restaurants right around campus." Hofstra "is known as a bar school," and students have many venues to choose from in Hempstead and "cute little surrounding towns" like Mineola and Garden City. On campus, "interest in [intercollegiate] athletics has grown dramatically"; even so, "Many students don't advantage of the free or discounted activities offered at the campus," but enthusiasts say this just forces students "to be more creative" when it comes to finding fun. "With Manhattan only 45 minutes away via the Long Island Railroad," lots of "people also go into New York City for fun, whether it is to shop, see shows, or go to nightclubs." Hofstra makes it easy for students to take regular trips into the city, offering a "free bus from campus that takes students to the train station."

Student Body

Long Island is a pretty diverse place, and Hofstra University reflects that diversity reasonably well. One student writes, "My first roommate was a white Orthodox Jew, [who was] very serious about school. My second set of roommates were white Greek and Italian Christians, loud partiers who played beer pong every night," and "my third roommate is white, Catholic, and gay," and "is the nicest person I know." Undergrads tell us "there are two types of students at Hofstra University: The kind who work hard, study and succeed, and the other kind who carelessly roll into class 25 minutes late (if they even go at all) with their Chanel sunglasses and Ugg boots, talking on their cell phones to their friends about their fabulous night out." The latter group is sometimes referred to derisively as "the Long Island kids," and some students describe them as "materialistic" and "apathetic" about school. While there might be lot of "stereotypical Long Island kids" on campus, the school also has "a large minority population," and "It's not hard to find someone here who is interested in the same things you are."

FINANCIAL AID: 516-463-6680 • E-MAIL: ADMITME@HOFSTRA.EDU • WEBSITE: WWW.HOFSTRA.EDU

THE PRINCETON REVIEW SAYS

Admissions

Very important factors considered include: Class rank, application essay, academic GPA, recommendation(s), rigor of secondary school record, standardized test scores. *Important factors considered include:* Character/personal qualities, extracurricular activities, interview, talent/ability. *Other factors considered include:* Alumni/ae relation, geographical residence, level of applicant's interest, racial/ethnic status, volunteer work, work experience. SAT Subject Tests recommended. ACT with Writing component required. TOEFL required of all international applicants. High school diploma is required and GED is accepted. *Academic units required:* 4 English, 3 mathematics, 3 science (1 science lab), 2 foreign language, 3 social studies. *Academic units recommended:* 4 mathematics, 4 science (2 science labs), 3 foreign language, 4 social studies.

Financial Aid

Students should submit: FAFSA, state aid form. The Princeton Review suggests that all financial aid forms be submitted as soon as possible after 1/1. *Need-based scholarships/grants offered:* Federal Pell, SEOG, state scholarships/grants, private scholarships, the school's own gift aid, ACG & SMART. *Loan aid offered:* FFEL Subsidized Stafford, FFEL Unsubsidized Stafford, FFEL PLUS, Federal Perkins, college/university loans from institutional funds. Applicants will be notified of awards on a rolling basis beginning 3/1. Federal Work-Study Program available. Institutional employment available. Off-campus job opportunities are excellent.

The Inside Word

This is not your father's Hofstra. The school reports that admission requirements have grown tougher during the years. Average GPAs and standardized test scores of admitted students have gone up, and this has been accompanied by a rise in rejection rates among applicants. Expect an especially thorough review if you indicate communications as your intended field of study.

THE SCHOOL SAYS ". . ."

From The Admissions Office

"Hofstra is a university on the rise. When you step onto campus you feel the energy and sense the momentum of a university building a national reputation as a center for academic excellence.

"At Hofstra, you'll find an outstanding faculty dedicated to teaching, and small classes, averaging just 22 students. Outside the classroom, you'll find a multitude of study abroad options, a vibrant extracurricular life, and amazing internship opportunities and cultural experiences in nearby New York City.

"The Hofstra campus—so beautiful it is recognized as an arboretum—features new and cutting-edge teaching facilities. At Hofstra, you will share your classrooms and residence halls with students from nearly every U.S. state and more than 70 countries.

"Students applying for admission may submit either SAT or ACT scores, and an essay is required. The admission team at Hofstra realizes that each applicant is unique and gives each one individual attention."

SELECTIVITY

Admissions Rating	85
# of applicants	20,071
% of applicants accepted	53
% of acceptees attending	16
# accepting a place on wait list	934
% admitted from wait list	89

FRESHMAN PROFILE

Range SAT Critical Reading	540–630
Range SAT Math	550–630
Range ACT Composite	23–27
Minimum paper TOEFL	550
Minimum computer TOEFL	213
Minimum web-based TOEFL	80
Average HS GPA	3.35
% graduated top 10% of class	26
% graduated top 25% of class	52
% graduated top 50% of class	83

DEADLINES

Early action	
Deadline	12/15
Notification	1/15
Regular	
Notification	rolling
Nonfall registration?	yes

APPLICANTS ALSO LOOK AT

AND OFTEN PREFER
New York University
Fordham University
Syracuse University

AND SOMETIMES PREFER
State University of New York—
Stony Brook
Penn State—University Park

AND RARELY PREFER
Rutgers, The State University of New
Jersey—New Brunswick
Quinnipiac University

FINANCIAL FACTS

Financial Aid Rating	66
Annual tuition	$27,600
Room and board	$10,825
Required fees	$1,030
Books and supplies	$1,000
% frosh rec. need-based scholarship or grant aid	51
% UG rec. need-based scholarship or grant aid	49
% frosh rec. non-need-based scholarship or grant aid	7
% UG rec. non-need-based scholarship or grant aid	4
% frosh rec. need-based self-help aid	49
% UG rec. need-based self-help aid	48
% frosh rec. athletic scholarships	1
% UG rec. athletic scholarships	1
% frosh rec. any financial aid	89
% UG rec. any financial aid	82
% UG borrow to pay for school	52

HOLLINS UNIVERSITY

PO Box 9707, Roanoke, VA 24020-1707 • Admissions: 540-362-6401 • Fax: 540-362-6218

CAMPUS LIFE

Quality of Life Rating	**79**
Fire Safety Rating	**70**
Green Rating	**79**
Type of school	private
Environment	city

STUDENTS

Total undergrad enrollment	785
% male/female	0/100
% from public high school	77
% live on campus	85
% African American	8
% Asian	2
% Caucasian	82
% Hispanic	3
% Native American	1
% international	4
# of countries represented	15

SURVEY SAYS . . .

No one cheats
Great library
Low cost of living
Frats and sororities are unpopular or nonexistent
Student government is popular

ACADEMICS

Academic Rating	**90**
Calendar	4/1/4
Student/faculty ratio	10:1
Profs interesting rating	93
Profs accessible rating	90
Most common reg class size	10–19 students
Most common lab size	fewer than 10 students

MOST POPULAR MAJORS

communication and media studies
English language and literature
psychology

STUDENTS SAY ". . ."

Academics

You're "not just a number" at Hollins University, a liberal arts school that creates "strong female leaders ready to face the world." Founded in 1842, this all-girls school is steeped in tradition while being "about individuality and free speech" and leaving "enough room and attention for you to grow." Basically, if you don't like something at Hollins, you have the power to change it, and pretty easily at that. As the motto states, "Women Who Are Going Places Start at Hollins."

As one can imagine, alumni connections remain strong, and the extensive network is often called upon to help Hollins graduates in the working world. The school provides excellent opportunities for study abroad, internships, and "building sisterhood." The highly individualized classes are challenging, "without being completely overwhelming or impossible," and the small size makes it "easy to make your voice heard and [to] connect with the material that you are learning." Professors "are so incredibly open with us; it is very flattering and gives me a sense of trust and responsibility that I was not allowed to have in high school," says a freshman. Indeed, the amount of credence given to making sure students' needs are met borders on overwhelming. The administration "always listens to us, and they all have their doors open at all times," and professors make themselves available at almost all hours, many "checking e-mails at midnight and giving you personal contact info for extra assistance." "Every teacher I have had has been 100% committed to making me feel comfortable with the subject matter they are teaching," says a junior English major. Classes often have an interesting twist, whether it is "the quirky teacher or the crazy science experiments, or both."

Life

Life is "very laid-back and comfortable" at Hollins, where "watching movies over bowls of popcorn" is just as popular as going to parties. The activities board tries to keep the nights filled with options such as productions, parties, and dances, and students are very active in political and environmental causes. A key to the Hollins community is the plethora of specialty housing, which lets people with similar interests live together. This option helps people to be "very dedicated to campus life and [to] embrace the strong sense of sisterhood that exists on campus and within the extended Hollins community." Long-held traditions such as Ring Night, Tinker Day, and First Step "allow for bonding between the classes and promote sisterhood." During the week there are "fun and educational lectures that are optional, such as self-defense and environmental lectures," and the school also has a great outdoors program that has trips every weekend to go hiking, canoeing, rock climbing, etc. Downtown Roanoke can be charming, if not a little dull, and students often go to other nearby schools (like Virginia Tech and UVA) on the weekends to seek fun, or go to the monthly mixers. "We ship in guys," one student says.

Student Body

With "everything from geeks and punks to the equestrians," the student body at Hollins is as diverse as it is driven, meaning it's pretty hard to qualify as "atypical." Almost everyone on campus is involved in multiple clubs and organizations, making it so "there's a little something for everyone," and this creates a tremendous sense of community among the Hollins girls. Many break themselves and their fellow students into three loose types of students: "the NEFA (Near East Fine Arts dorm) artsy types, the 'pearl girls' or 'Holly dollies' (who ride horses and wear pearls and pink with everything, even their sweatpants); and everyone else." Still, no one group is exclusive or snobby, and everyone "is more than willing to interact with everyone they meet, regardless of their style." "For all the girls who are tired of high school drama, this is the school for you," says a freshman. There is a "very strong" GLBT community here, and "everyone is very accepting of differences, especially regarding minority and sexual orientation, so it causes the population to be very aware." Most students tend to lean to the left politically, although "there is a strong conservative voice, as well."

FINANCIAL AID: 540-362-6332 • E-MAIL: HUADM@HOLLINS.EDU • WEBSITE: WWW.HOLLINS.EDU

THE PRINCETON REVIEW SAYS

Admissions

Very important factors considered include: Academic GPA, standardized test scores. *Important factors considered include:* Application essay, recommendation(s), talent/ability. *Other factors considered include:* Class rank, rigor of secondary school record, alumni relation, character/personal qualities, extracurricular activities, first generation, interview, level of applicant's interest, racial/ethnic status, volunteer work, work experience. SAT or ACT required. TOEFL required of all international applicants. High school diploma is required and GED is accepted. *Academic units required:* 4 English, 3 mathematics, 3 science, 3 foreign language, 3 social studies.

Financial Aid

Students should submit: FAFSA, state aid form. The Princeton Review suggests that all financial aid forms be submitted as soon as possible after 1/1. *Need-based scholarships/grants offered:* Federal Pell, SEOG, state scholarships/grants, private scholarships, the school's own gift aid. *Loan aid offered:* Direct Subsidized Stafford, Direct Unsubsidized Stafford, Direct PLUS, Federal Perkins, college/university loans from institutional funds, PLATO, CitiAssist, SallieMae, Nelnet, Campus Door. Applicants will be notified of awards on a rolling basis beginning 3/1. Federal Work-Study Program available. Institutional employment available. Off-campus job opportunities are good.

The Inside Word

Only candidates who overtly display their lack of compatibility with the Hollins milieu are likely to encounter difficulty in gaining admission. A high level of self-selection and its weak-but-improving freshman profile allow most candidates to relax.

THE SCHOOL SAYS "..."

From The Admissions Office

"Hollins University's slogan, 'Women who are going places start at Hollins,' endures because it captures what this independent liberal arts institution means to its students. Hollins has been a motivating force for women to go places creatively, intellectually, and geographically since it was founded over 165 years ago. As Hollins graduate and Pulitzer Prize–winner Annie Dillard said, Hollins is a place 'where friendships thrive, minds catch fire, careers begin, and hearts open to a world of possibility.'

"Hollins offers majors in 27 fields. While perhaps best known for its creative writing discipline, the university features strong programs in the visual and performing arts (especially dance) and the social and physical sciences. Hollins also has an innovative general education program called Education Through Skills and Perspectives (ESP). In ESP, students acquire knowledge across the curriculum. One of the most sought-after programs at Hollins is the Batten Leadership Institute, a comprehensive curricular program designed to maximize each student's leadership style and potential and teach her skills she will use both now and in the future. It is the only program of its kind in the nation.

"Hollins was among the first colleges in the nation to offer an international study abroad program. Today, almost half of Hollins' students—many times the national average—study abroad. Internship opportunities are another of Hollins' distinctions. Thanks to an active, dedicated network of alumnae and friends of the university, more than 80 percent of Hollins students put their education to work with a diverse group of organizations.

"Hollins' slogan underscores the most important question each student is asked from the moment she arrives until the day she leaves, and it is asked by her professors, her peers, and especially by herself: 'Where do you want to go?'"

SELECTIVITY

Admissions Rating	89
# of applicants	658
% of applicants accepted	87
% of acceptees attending	36
# accepting a place on wait list	20
% admitted from wait list	5
# of early decision applicants	50
% accepted early decision	90

FRESHMAN PROFILE

Range SAT Critical Reading	540–650
Range SAT Math	490–590
Minimum paper TOEFL	550
Minimum computer TOEFL	213
Average HS GPA	3.52
% graduated top 10% of class	30
% graduated top 25% of class	59
% graduated top 50% of class	84

DEADLINES

Early decision	
Deadline	12/1
Notification	12/15
Regular	
Priority	2/1
Notification	rolling
Nonfall registration?	yes

FINANCIAL FACTS

Financial Aid Rating	77
Annual tuition	$27,550
Room and board	$10,040
% frosh rec. need-based scholarship or grant aid	67
% UG rec. need-based scholarship or grant aid	80
% frosh rec. non-need-based scholarship or grant aid	33
% UG rec. non-need-based scholarship or grant aid	34
% frosh rec. need-based self-help aid	55
% UG rec. need-based self-help aid	63
% frosh rec. any financial aid	97
% UG rec. any financial aid	93
% UG borrow to pay for school	85
Average cumulative indebtedness	$15,227

THE BEST 371 COLLEGES ■ 291

HOWARD UNIVERSITY

2400 SIXTH STREET NORTHWEST, WASHINGTON, DC 20059 • ADMISSIONS: 202-806-2700 • FAX: 202-806-4462

CAMPUS LIFE

Quality of Life Rating	65
Fire Safety Rating	97
Green Rating	60*
Type of school	private
Environment	metropolis

STUDENTS

Total undergrad enrollment	6,963
% male/female	33/67
% from out of state	77
% from public high school	80
% live on campus	55
% in (# of) fraternities	2 (10)
% in (# of) sororities	1 (8)
% African American	67
% Asian	1
% international	5
# of countries represented	86

SURVEY SAYS . . .

Students are happy
Musical organizations are popular
College radio is popular
Student publications are popular
Student government is popular
Political activism is popular

ACADEMICS

Academic Rating	78
Calendar	semester
Student/faculty ratio	8:1
Profs interesting rating	65
Profs accessible rating	63
Most common reg class size	fewer than 10 students
Most common lab size	10–19 students

MOST POPULAR MAJORS

biology/biological sciences
journalism
radio and television

STUDENTS SAY " . . ."

Academics

Howard University, which students proclaim as "the Mecca of black education," parlays a storied history and an excellent location (ideal for students seeking internships and post-graduation job placements) to "prepare students for the future through academic integrity and social enterprise." Recruiters flock to the Howard campus, in part because "academically, Howard is very strong," and in part because "the university has connections all across the country. Howard does a great job of bringing those connections to campus," in part because of the perception that "organizations are forced to come here to employ their minority quotas." Undergrads here report that "The academic experience largely depends on what you major in. If you're going for African-American studies, business or dentistry you'll get what you've paid for." The presence of a college of medicine (and its affiliated hospital) bolsters offerings in life sciences and premedical studies as well. Other disciplines can present "a challenging and somewhat unfulfilling college experience," students warn. They also caution that "facilities are outdated and need a major technological and physical update" and "the administration needs some work. There are great, qualified people in places of high authority. However, the people you have to go through to get to the people who actually care are usually horrible. They never move with a sense of urgency. If it's not their problem, its not a problem, and they usually talk to you like you are 12."

Life

"We always, always, always have something going on" on the "very active" Howard campus. There are "hundreds of organizations that tailor to any needs you can think of," and students are "very active politically and socially, so there are rallies and there are parties. Each and every extreme is met with its opposite here." There's "always somewhere to go" on campus, "whether it be the Punchout Cafe to hang with your friends, Power Hall to relax, study and work with your friends, to 'the yard' to chill and people watch, [or] to the gym to work out. If you are isolated on Howard's campus it is because you choose to be." The world awaiting off campus is even more active. As one student explains, "There is so much to do in the Washington, D.C. area that there is rarely any room for boredom. Georgetown, Chinatown, and Pentagon City are just a few of the places that students go." Adams Morgan is another popular destination. No need to bring a car here. "Everything we would want to go to is Metro-accessible so there's no problem moving about D.C. as if we've lived here our whole lives." Fun is typically confined to weekends, as "Many of us work very hard during the week. Sunday through Thursday, we stay on campus and focus on getting school-work done and attending any organizational meetings or events."

Student Body

The typical Howard student "is African American with a deep desire toward success." Undergrads are "extremely serious about their career goals and their academic achievement," and "very involved in political activism, campus organizations, and community." They also tend to be "very fashion-conscious and dwell a lot on others, perceptions of us, although many of us profess to be strong individuals." Although nearly all black, the student population "is extremely diverse. I sit in classes with people from Spain, England, Trinidad and Tobago, South Africa, Nigeria, Alaska, etc." Students "come from all walks of life. You can find people with different religious beliefs, ethnic origins, and sexual preferences. There are students with interests in every field imaginable. Howard represents the black world."

HOWARD UNIVERSITY

FINANCIAL AID: 202-806-2800 • E-MAIL: ADMISSION@HOWARD.EDU • WEBSITE: WWW.HOWARD.EDU

THE PRINCETON REVIEW SAYS

Admissions

Very important factors considered include: Class rank, rigor of secondary school record, standardized test scores. *Important factors considered include:* Recommendation(s), character/personal qualities. *Other factors considered include:* Application essay, alumni/ae relation, extracurricular activities, talent/ability, volunteer work, work experience. SAT or ACT required. ACT with Writing component required. TOEFL required of all international applicants. High school diploma is required and GED is accepted. *Academic units required:* 4 English, 2 mathematics, 2 science, 2 foreign language, 2 social studies, 2 history. *Academic units recommended:* 4 English, 3 mathematics, 4 science (2 science labs), 2 foreign language, 2 social studies, 2 history, 4 any other academic courses counted toward graduation.

Financial Aid

Students should submit: FAFSA. Regular filing deadline is 8/15. The Princeton Review suggests that all financial aid forms be submitted as soon as possible after 1/1. *Need-based scholarships/grants offered:* Federal Pell, SEOG, state scholarships/grants, private scholarships, the school's own gift aid, federal nursing scholarships. *Loan aid offered:* Direct Subsidized Stafford, Direct Unsubsidized Stafford, Direct PLUS, Federal Perkins. Federal nursing applicants will be notified of awards on a rolling basis beginning 4/1. Federal Work-Study Program available. Institutional employment available. Off-campus job opportunities are excellent.

The Inside Word

A large applicant pool and graduation rate of those who enroll is a combination that adds up to selectivity at Howard. The school is willing to give applicants a pass on standardized test scores if their high school records indicate seriousness about, and the ability to handle, advanced study.

THE SCHOOL SAYS "..."

From The Admissions Office

"Since its founding, Howard has stood among the few institutions of higher learning where blacks and other minorities have participated freely in a truly comprehensive university experience. Thus, Howard has assumed a special responsibility in preparing its students to exercise leadership wherever their interests and commitments take them. Howard has issued approximately 99,318 degrees, diplomas, and certificates to men and women in the professions, the arts and sciences, and the humanities. The university has produced and continues to produce a high percentage of the nation's African American professionals in the fields of medicine, dentistry, pharmacy, engineering, nursing, architecture, religion, law, music, social work, education, and business. There are more than 8,906 students from across the nation and approximately 85 countries and territories attending the university. Their varied customs, cultures, ideas, and interests contribute to Howard's international character and vitality. More than 1,598 faculty members represent the largest concentration of black scholars in any single institution of higher education.

"All applicants who have never been to college are required to submit scores from either the SAT or the ACT (with the Writing component)."

SELECTIVITY
Admissions Rating	87
# of applicants	7,603
% of applicants accepted	54
% of acceptees attending	36

FRESHMAN PROFILE
Range SAT Critical Reading	460–660
Range SAT Math	440–650
Range SAT Writing	410–650
Range ACT Composite	20–28
Minimum paper TOEFL	550
Minimum computer TOEFL	213
Average HS GPA	3.2
% graduated top 10% of class	23
% graduated top 25% of class	49
% graduated top 50% of class	82

DEADLINES
Early decision	
Deadline	11/1
Notification	12/24
Early action	
Deadline	11/1
Notification	12/24
Regular	
Priority	11/1
Deadline	2/15
Nonfall registration?	yes

APPLICANTS ALSO LOOK AT
AND OFTEN PREFER
Spelman College
Morehouse College
Hampton University

AND SOMETIMES PREFER
The George Washington University
University of Maryland—College Park
Florida A&M University

AND RARELY PREFER
Morgan State University

FINANCIAL FACTS
Financial Aid Rating	64
Annual tuition	$13,215
Room and board	$6,976
Required fees	$805
Books and supplies	$1,300
% frosh rec. need-based scholarship or grant aid	35
% UG rec. need-based scholarship or grant aid	35
% frosh rec. non-need-based scholarship or grant aid	63
% UG rec. non-need-based scholarship or grant aid	63
% frosh rec. need-based self-help aid	18
% UG rec. need-based self-help aid	25
% frosh rec. athletic scholarships	40
% UG rec. athletic scholarships	33
% frosh rec. any financial aid	96
% UG rec. any financial aid	96
% UG borrow to pay for school	80
Average cumulative indebtedness	$16,473

ILLINOIS INSTITUTE OF TECHNOLOGY

10 WEST THIRTY-THIRD STREET, CHICAGO, IL 60616 • ADMISSIONS: 312-567-3025 • FAX: 312-567-6939

CAMPUS LIFE

Quality of Life Rating	65
Fire Safety Rating	71
Green Rating	92
Type of school	private
Environment	metropolis

STUDENTS

Total undergrad enrollment	2,590
% male/female	72/28
% from out of state	32
% from public high school	85
% live on campus	46
% in (# of) fraternities	12 (7)
% in (# of) sororities	17 (3)
% African American	4
% Asian	13
% Caucasian	46
% Hispanic	7
% Native American	1
% international	17
# of countries represented	92

SURVEY SAYS . . .

Class discussions are rare
Diverse student types on campus
Students love Chicago, IL
Great off-campus food
Very little drug use

ACADEMICS

Academic Rating	75
Calendar	semester
Student/faculty ratio	9:1
Profs interesting rating	61
Profs accessible rating	61
Most common reg class size	10–19 students
Most common lab size	10–19 students

MOST POPULAR MAJORS

architecture (BARCH, BA/BS, MARCH, MA/MS, PHD)
mechanical engineering

STUDENTS SAY "..."

Academics

Illinois Institute of Technology "is all about the demanding work and promised payoffs" students report, warning "the IIT experience is focused on the career afterwards. There is very little pizzazz about the atmosphere and virtually no social life, unless you can relate to all of the other geeks who either stare at their computers in their rooms or just sit and chat about academics." Not that you'd have time for much of a social life here anyway, since "classes are difficult, and lots of studying is required. If you got straight A's in high school, expect to work hard to get B's and C's." The various engineering departments are, of course, a major strength here. Civil engineering "is definitely one of the best departments in the school," while the biomedical, electrical, and mechanical engineering programs also earn students' accolades, with "an emphasis on practicality" across the board. The computer science program "is run like a well-oiled machine." IIT is also renowned for its architecture program, which students tell us is "incredible, and quite influential on the Chicago scene." Students in all disciplines benefit from "a small-school environment" that promotes "personal attention" and allows the professors to "get to know you." "For instance, I can walk into my department chair's office or my professor's office whenever and they know me personally." Professors "are really accommodating" and explain the material to you "when you have a problem," although whether you'll understand them is another question entirely. "Professors in certain classes may barely speak English, or may be awesome teachers, it varies greatly,"—and sometimes, they're both.

Life

In the past, IIT has earned a reputation for having a dreary extracurricular life. The situation has improved somewhat, as "the school has put forth a great effort and a vast amount of money to create a school-sponsored program every single weekend. This practice started in 2007, and the school has kept up with it. Whether it's a movie night, a dance, or a comedy act we have at least one thing every weekend, [and] this has improved IIT." Of course, some students "would rather sit in their room and play computer games than socialize" in their free time, but at least the options are expanding, and more students are taking advantage of them. IIT's frat scene "offers numerous chances for social activities from sports to parties and community service." We're told for many, joining "makes life a lot more enjoyable." Others leave campus whenever they can spare the time away. ITT is only "five miles south of downtown Chicago," a city that "provides a good playground" with "a lot of things to do." For good cheap eats, "Chinatown is just one stop down" on the El.

Student Body

IIT has "plenty of typical math and science students," meaning "many nerds" and more than a few "students who like their computers more than seems humanly possible and whose only human contact occurs when they make a weekly trip to the cafeteria or their bi-weekly trip to the shower." There are also "many atypical students, enough so that they can form or join a club or group that fits their own personality." Numbers appear to be growing as a result of "significant outreach by students groups and more social incoming classes." The international population is substantial, with many students from "India, China, and Korea." While "not everyone talks to each other, when they do talk, they learn a lot about [each] other's culture." Undergrads tend to be stressed out, and are "the kind of people who feel guilty when they have no work to do for a day." A lopsided male to female ratio means there are "barely any women on campus."

FINANCIAL AID: 312-567-7219 • E-MAIL: ADMISSION@IIT.EDU • WEBSITE: WWW.IIT.EDU

THE PRINCETON REVIEW SAYS

Admissions

Very important factors considered include: Academic GPA, rigor of secondary school record. *Important factors considered include:* Class rank, application essay, recommendation(s), standardized test scores. *Other factors considered include:* character/personal qualities, leadership experience, extracurricular activities, first generation, talent/ability, volunteer work, work experience. ACT with Writing component recommended. TOEFL required of all international applicants. High school diploma is required and GED is accepted. *Academic units required:* 4 English, 4 mathematics, 3 science (2 science labs), 2 foreign language, 2 social studies. *Academic units recommended:* 4 English, 4 mathematics, 3 science (2 science labs), 2 foreign language, 2 social studies, 2 history, 1 1 computer science.

Financial Aid

Students should submit: FAFSA. The Princeton Review suggests that all financial aid forms be submitted as soon as possible after 1/1. *Need-based scholarships/grants offered:* Federal Pell, SEOG, state scholarships/grants, private scholarships, the school's own gift aid. *Loan aid offered:* FFEL Subsidized Stafford, FFEL Unsubsidized Stafford, FFEL PLUS, Federal Perkins, college/university loans from institutional funds. Applicants will be notified of awards on a rolling basis beginning 3/1. Federal Work-Study Program available. Institutional employment available. Off-campus job opportunities are good.

The Inside Word

Students at IIT say it's "easy to get in, tough to get out," but the term "easy" is relative in this case. Easy in comparison to MIT or CalTech, perhaps, but not in comparison to the vast majority of undergraduate institutions. IIT's high acceptance rate is deceptive; few bother to apply here unless they suspect they can handle the demanding curriculum, meaning only the extremely bright and/or extremely ambitious actually do.

THE SCHOOL SAYS " . . ."

From The Admissions Office

"IIT is committed to providing students a distinctive and relevant education through hands-on learning, dedicated teachers, small class sizes, and undergraduate research opportunities. Classes are taught by senior faculty—not teaching assistants—who foster our culture of innovation with their own first-hand research experience.

"Students are immersed in our interdisciplinary approach to learning through the team-based, creative problem solving experience of the Interprofessional Projects Program (IPROs). The Office of Undergraduate Research provides mentored collaborative research experiences for undergraduates. Our entrepreneurship program challenges students to develop start-up technology companies. University Technology Park at IIT, a business incubator located on campus, supports this challenge by providing numerous opportunities to work with companies at every stage of growth, from conception to sophistication. The Leadership Academy teaches leadership skills that advance students in their personal and professional development.

"IIT's location in the world class city of Chicago gives students priceless access to the professional world through internships and employment. The university's own diverse student population mirrors the global work environment faced by all graduates.

"'First year students applying for admission into the entering class are required to submit an SAT or ACT score. We will use the student's best scores from either test. Subject tests are accepted, but not required.'

"It is highly recommended that transfer applicants have completed 30 credit hours and have taken calculus and/or physics. Both first year and transfer students are evaluated for significant merit based scholarships upon admission."

SELECTIVITY

Admissions Rating	92
# of applicants	3,092
% of applicants accepted	57
% of acceptees attending	30

FRESHMAN PROFILE

Range SAT Critical Reading	520–640
Range SAT Math	610–700
Range SAT Writing	520–630
Range ACT Composite	25–30
Minimum paper TOEFL	550
Minimum computer TOEFL	213
Minimum web-based TOEFL	80
Average HS GPA	3.84
% graduated top 10% of class	42
% graduated top 25% of class	76
% graduated top 50% of class	98

DEADLINES

Early decision	
Deadline	11/4
Notification	12/4
Early action	
Deadline	12/9
Notification	1/8
Regular	
Priority	2/3
Notification	rolling
Nonfall registration?	yes

APPLICANTS ALSO LOOK AT

AND OFTEN PREFER
Washington University in St. Louis,
University of Michigan—Ann Arbor

AND SOMETIMES PREFER
Marquette University, Milwaukee School
of Engineering, Iowa State University

AND RARELY PREFER
Purdue University—West Lafayette
University of Minnesota—Twin Cities

FINANCIAL FACTS

Financial Aid Rating	79
Annual tuition	$28,512
Room and board	$11,219
Required fees	$850
Books and supplies	$1,000
% frosh rec. need-based scholarship or grant aid	64
% UG rec. need-based scholarship or grant aid	59
% frosh rec. non-need-based scholarship or grant aid	16
% UG rec. non-need-based scholarship or grant aid	9
% frosh rec. need-based self-help aid	39
% UG rec. need-based self-help aid	45
% frosh rec. athletic scholarships	4
% UG rec. athletic scholarships	5
% frosh rec. any financial aid	99.85
% UG rec. any financial aid	94.76
% UG borrow to pay for school	60
Average cumulative indebtedness	$20,308

ILLINOIS WESLEYAN UNIVERSITY

PO Box 2900, Bloomington, IL 61702-2900 • Admissions: 309-556-3031 • Fax: 309-556-3820

CAMPUS LIFE

Quality of Life Rating	**82**
Fire Safety Rating	**81**
Green Rating	**77**
Type of school	private
Environment	city

STUDENTS

Total undergrad enrollment	2,115
% male/female	42/58
% from out of state	13
% from public high school	84
% live on campus	76
% in (# of) fraternities	35 (6)
% in (# of) sororities	32 (5)
% African American	6
% Asian	4
% Caucasian	78
% Hispanic	3
% international	4
# of countries represented	22

SURVEY SAYS . . .

Lab facilities are great
Great library
Athletic facilities are great
Low cost of living
Musical organizations are popular

ACADEMICS

Academic Rating	**88**
Calendar	4/4/1
Student/faculty ratio	11:1
Profs interesting rating	79
Profs accessible rating	84
Most common reg class size	10–19 students
Most common lab size	10–19 students

MOST POPULAR MAJORS

biology/biological sciences
business/commerce
psychology

STUDENTS SAY ". . ."

Academics

Illinois Wesleyan University, "a small liberal arts school that will give you lots of personal attention," is "the right size, small enough that you feel comfortable walking around because you always see familiar faces wherever you go, but also big enough where you don't know everybody and you can find your own niche." The school strives to "create a personal educational experience with professors, classmates, and staff." The school is the kind of place where professors "make themselves available to read essay drafts, offer career advice, and write letters of recommendation on top of giving great lectures." IWU excels in such diverse areas as biology (the school "has a great reputation in the sciences"), nursing, English, psychology, theater, and music ("extremely competitive," but much more liberal arts-oriented than "conservatory-like"). "The school encourages exploring multiple interests, and double majors and dual degrees are pursued by many students." One student writes, "Right now, I'm a business major with a philosophy minor, and I'm making up my own minor between the music and physics department in electroacoustic music, and I'm still going to graduate in 4 years." You can really "make your degree yours" here. Students on track for graduate study love "the high acceptance rates into grad school" that IWU enjoys in many programs, and everyone appreciates the school's May term, which "gives you a really great option to take inventive, unique classes or travel abroad."

Life

IWU is located in Bloomington-Normal, which "certainly isn't Chicago" but is still a "great place to live with so much to do." While some kids from the Chicago area complain about the location, telling us that "it's not very exciting," those from elsewhere are more generous in their assessments, observing that "it's better than a suburb. Both Bloomington and Normal have downtown areas with quaint boutiques next to new bars and eateries, and the recent boom in the Latino and East Asian populations have provided excellent cuisine options!" With well more than one-quarter of the student body involved in Greek life, "Frats and sororities play a large part in social activities" of the campus. Illinois State University is "just down the street," offering another party alternative "to those who want to escape the IWU bubble." The Student Activities Office "brings awesome entertainment to our campus on the weekends like concerts, movies, [and] comedians," and since the activities are covered by the student activity fee, there is "no charge to the student," though they are usually "over pretty early." IWU has numerous intercollegiate teams, but "Basketball is the only main sports attraction. Very few students actually attend football games or other sporting events." Wesleyan dormitories "are amazing. The majority of students live on campus all 4 years because of all the great living options."

Student Body

IWU draws heavily from the affluent suburbs of Chicago, attracting a student body that is largely white and "somewhat wealthy." That said, there are many who do not fit this mold; including a significant number who receive need-based aid. Most "have very diverse interests, sometimes even majors that you never thought would be possible: music and science, foreign language and pre-professional science, and so on. Furthermore, they are usually involved in a diverse number of extracurricular activities: sports, clubs, organizations, etc." Students tell us that everyone here is "pretty easy-going, though if one is a bio or chem major, studying is constantly on the mind due to the amount needed to be memorized," though for many, "a long week of paper-writing and test taking is rewarded with a few long nights of debauchery." IWU also has a fair number of international students; one student writes, "My floor alone has girls from Nigeria, Germany, and Bangladesh, and there are other girls of Asian, Indian, and African descent as well."

FINANCIAL AID: 309-556-3096 • E-MAIL: IWUADMIT@TITAN.IWU.EDU • WEBSITE: WWW.IWU.EDU

THE PRINCETON REVIEW SAYS

Admissions

Very important factors considered include: Academic GPA, rigor of secondary school record, interview. *Important factors considered include:* Class rank, application essay, standardized test scores, character/personal qualities, extracurricular activities, talent/ability. *Other factors considered include:* Recommendation(s), alumni/ae relation, first generation, geographical residence, level of applicant's interest, racial/ethnic status, state residency, volunteer work, work experience. SAT or ACT required; TOEFL required of all international applicants. High school diploma is required and GED is accepted. *Academic units recommended:* 4 English, 3 mathematics, 3 science, (2 science labs), 3 foreign language, 2 social studies.

Financial Aid

Students should submit: FAFSA, institution's own financial aid form, CSS/Financial Aid PROFILE. Regular filing deadline is 3/1. The Princeton Review suggests that all financial aid forms be submitted as soon as possible after 1/1. *Need-based scholarships/grants offered:* Federal Pell, SEOG, state scholarships/grants, private scholarships, the school's own gift aid. *Loan aid offered:* FFEL Subsidized Stafford, FFEL Unsubsidized Stafford, FFEL PLUS, Federal Perkins, Federal Nursing, college/university loans from institutional funds. Applicants will be notified of awards on a rolling basis beginning 2/15. Federal Work-Study Program available. Institutional employment available. Off-campus job opportunities are good.

The Inside Word

There's no application fee at IWU, and the school accepts the Common Application (with the IWU Common Application Supplement, which asks for your intended major and an essay explaining your reasons for wanting to attend IWU), so there are few reasons not to apply to IWU if you're at all interested in the school. Don't expect to breeze through, though; you won't get in here without a solid academic profile or a compelling story.

THE SCHOOL SAYS "..."

From The Admissions Office

""Illinois Wesleyan University attracts a wide variety of students who are interested in pursuing diverse fields such as vocal performance, biology, psychology, German, physics, or business administration. At IWU, students are not forced into either/or choices. Rather, they are encouraged to pursue multiple interests simultaneously—a philosophy that is in keeping with the spirit and value of a liberal arts education. The distinctive 4-4-1 calendar allows students to follow their interests each school year in two semesters followed by an optional month-long class in May. May term opportunities include classes on campus; research collaboration with faculty; travel and study in such places as Australia, China, South Africa, and Europe; as well as local, national, and international internships. Study abroad is very popular, with one out of every two students enjoying a travel experience.

"The IWU mission statement reads in part: 'A liberal education at Illinois Wesleyan fosters creativity, critical thinking, effective communication, strength of character, and a spirit of inquiry; it deepens the specialized knowledge of a discipline with a comprehensive world view. It affords the greatest possibilities for realizing individual potential while preparing students for democratic citizen-ship and life in a global society...The university, through its policies, programs, and practices, is committed to diversity, social justice, and environmental sustainability. A tightly knit, supportive university community, together with a variety of opportunities for close interaction with excellent faculty, both challenges and supports students in their personal and intellectual development."

SELECTIVITY

Admissions Rating	90
# of applicants	3,136
% of applicants accepted	52
% of acceptees attending	34
# accepting a place on wait list	79
% admitted from wait list	29

FRESHMAN PROFILE

Range SAT Critical Reading	550–690
Range SAT Math	590–710
Range ACT Composite	26–30
Minimum paper TOEFL	550
Minimum computer TOEFL	213
Average HS GPA	3.7
% graduated top 10% of class	45
% graduated top 25% of class	80
% graduated top 50% of class	98

DEADLINES

Regular	
Priority	11/1
Notification	rolling
Nonfall registration?	yes

APPLICANTS ALSO LOOK AT

AND OFTEN PREFER
University of Notre Dame
Northwestern University

AND SOMETIMES PREFER
Washington University in St. Louis
University of Illinois at Urbana-Champaign

AND RARELY PREFER
Marquette University
Augustana College (IL)

FINANCIAL FACTS

Financial Aid Rating	87
Annual tuition	$33,808
% frosh rec. need-based scholarship or grant aid	64
% UG rec. need-based scholarship or grant aid	56
% frosh rec. non-need-based scholarship or grant aid	7
% UG rec. non-need-based scholarship or grant aid	4
% frosh rec. need-based self-help aid	51
% UG rec. need-based self-help aid	41
% frosh rec. any financial aid	95
% UG rec. any financial aid	91
% UG borrow to pay for school	62
Average cumulative indebtedness	$26,555

INDIANA UNIVERSITY—BLOOMINGTON

300 NORTH JORDAN AVENUE, BLOOMINGTON, IN 47405-1106 • ADMISSIONS: 812-855-0661 • FAX: 812-855-5102

CAMPUS LIFE
Quality of Life Rating	91
Fire Safety Rating	78
Green Rating	60*
Type of school	public
Environment	city

STUDENTS
Total undergrad enrollment	31,087
% male/female	50/50
% from out of state	34
% live on campus	36
% in (# of) fraternities	16 (22)
% in (# of) sororities	18 (23)
% African American	5
% Asian	4
% Caucasian	82
% Hispanic	2
% international	5
# of countries represented	136

SURVEY SAYS . . .
Great off-campus food
Students are happy
Everyone loves the Hoosiers
Student publications are popular
Hard liquor is popular

ACADEMICS
Academic Rating	78
Calendar	semester
Student/faculty ratio	18:1
Profs interesting rating	77
Profs accessible rating	81
Most common reg class size	20–29 students
Most common lab size	20–29 students

MOST POPULAR MAJORS
business/commerce
communication, journalism
education

STUDENTS SAY ". . ."

Academics

Although many think of Indiana University as "a party school with an active Greek population"—an image students reinforce when they insist that IU is "about going to massive parties...and getting the job done, but not being defined by schoolwork"—the school is "in actuality a Big Ten research university that offers a huge variety of classes and majors (even allowing students to create their own) with a surprisingly diverse student body that allows anybody to fit in regardless of whether they enjoy partying or are interested in the Greek system." Most students appreciate both the academic and social aspects of the school, telling us that IU offers "the best combination of academics and extracurriculars one could ask for in a school." IU's "world renowned" business school is taught by professors who "are at the top of their respective fields of expertise. They have a lot to teach us, and they are almost universally excellent at doing so." An equally acclaimed music school and a language department that "has everything from the romance languages to Urdu, Haitian Creole, and Tibetan" also draw students' attention. Many majors require students to hold an internship before graduating, so "you really have to be self-motivated, since IUB is one hour away from a metropolitan area. Although being in this town has its social benefits, it definitely makes it tougher as you prepare for life after college."

Life

"Every day is a new and exciting experience at Indiana University," where "there is too much going on all of the time." The campus is alive with lectures, art exhibits, theatrical and musical shows, and the school's beloved intercollegiate athletics. "We spend a lot of time thinking about basketball and football, depending obviously on the season," students tell us. You don't have to look hard to find a party here, and "a lot of people tend to get drunk as entertainment," but that's hardly the only option, and many pass four happy years here outside the party scene. Undergrads love hometown Bloomington, "a great city to live in" with "amazing cultural events, such as the Lotus World Music Festival and Chocolate Fest" along with "lots of little stores demonstrating their own niches and a wide range of different authentic-ish ethnic restaurants." Campus-wide traditions such as Little 500, a party "at the end of the year when the whole campus stops what they're doing to attend concerts, parties, and the men's and women's bike races," help cement a strong sense of school spirit.

Student Body

While "most IU students are white and come from a middle-class background," the school's "international and minority student populations are growing, and there are a lot of services available to help minority students feel comfortable on campus." Those who aren't native Hoosiers are most often Chicagoans or East Coasters from New York and New Jersey, although IU attracts students from all 50 states and 136 countries. The school is big enough to accommodate many personality types: "some Greeks, some who are academically oriented, some who enjoy and actively pursue the arts, and others who enjoy sports such as IU basketball...small cultures exist within the larger IU culture." There are "a lot of students who come to IU with the intention of partying all the time, and rarely studying," but most don't last long; those who "work hard all week and worship the weekends," on the other hand, can and often do thrive here.

FINANCIAL AID: 812-855-0321 • E-MAIL: IUADMIT@INDIANA.EDU • WEBSITE: WWW.IUB.EDU

THE PRINCETON REVIEW SAYS

Admissions

Very important factors considered include: Class rank, academic GPA, rigor of secondary school record, and standardized test scores. *Other factors considered include:* Application essay, recommendation(s), alumni/ae relation, character/personal qualities, extracurricular activities, first generation, geographical residence, interview, level of applicant's interest, racial/ethnic status, state residency, talent/ability. SAT Subject Tests recommended; SAT or ACT required; ACT with Writing component required. High school diploma is required and GED is accepted. *Academic units required:* 4 English, 3 mathematics, 1 science, (1 science lab), 2 social studies, 4 academic electives. *Academic units recommended:* 4 mathematics, 3 science, 3 foreign language, 3 social studies.

Financial Aid

Students should submit: FAFSA. The Princeton Review suggests that all financial aid forms be submitted as soon as possible after 1/1. *Need-based scholarships/grants offered:* Federal Pell, SEOG, state scholarships/grants, private scholarships, the school's own gift aid. *Loan aid offered:* Direct Subsidized Stafford, Direct Unsubsidized Stafford, Direct PLUS, Federal Perkins, college/university loans from institutional funds. Applicants will be notified of awards on a rolling basis beginning 4/1. Federal Work-Study Program available. Institutional employment available. Off-campus job opportunities are good.

The Inside Word

Above-average high school performers should meet little resistance from the IU admissions office. Others may be able to improve their chances by attending IU recruiting events (the school visits many locations throughout the state) and visiting the campus. Rolling admissions favor those who apply early in the process. IU's music program is highly competitive; admission hinges upon a successful audition.

THE SCHOOL SAYS "..."

From The Admissions Office

"Indiana University—Bloomington, one of America's great teaching and research universities, extends learning and teaching beyond the walls of the traditional classroom. When visiting campus, students and parents typically describe IU as 'what a college should look and feel like.' Students bring their diverse experiences, beliefs, and backgrounds from all 50 states and 136 countries, which adds a richness and diversity to life at IU—a campus often cited as one of the most beautiful in the nation. Indiana University—Bloomington truly offers a quintessential college town, campus, and overall experience. Students enjoy all of the advantages, opportunities, and resources that a larger school can offer, while still receiving personal attention and support. Because of the variety of outstanding academic and cultural resources, students at IU have the best of both worlds.

"Indiana offers more than 5,000 courses and 183 undergraduate majors, of which many are known nationally and internationally. IU Bloomington is known worldwide for outstanding programs in the arts, sciences, humanities, and social sciences as well as for highly rated Schools of Business, Music, Education, Journalism, Optometry; Public and Environmental Affairs; and Health, Physical Education, and Recreation. Students can customize academic programs with double and individualized majors, internships, and research opportunities, while utilizing state-of-the-art technology. Representatives from more than 1,000 businesses, government agencies, and not-for-profit organizations come to campus each year to recruit IU students.

"IUB requires the SAT the ACT with Writing component. The university will use the writing sections to determine possible credit, placement or exemption from writing requirements. We encourage, but do not require, SAT Subject Tests."

SELECTIVITY

Admissions Rating	89
# of applicants	31,160
% of applicants accepted	71
% of acceptees attending	34

FRESHMAN PROFILE

Range SAT Critical Reading	510–620
Range SAT Math	530–640
Range ACT Composite	23–29
Average HS GPA	3.57
% graduated top 10% of class	31
% graduated top 25% of class	69
% graduated top 50% of class	97

DEADLINES

Regular	
Priority	4/1
Nonfall registration?	yes

APPLICANTS ALSO LOOK AT
AND OFTEN PREFER
University of Illinois at Urbana-Champaign
AND SOMETIMES PREFER
Purdue University—West Lafayette
Miami University

FINANCIAL FACTS

Financial Aid Rating	76
Annual in-state tuition	$6,096
Annual out-of-state tuition	$22,483
Room and board	$7,138
Required fees	$863
Books and supplies	$790
% frosh rec. need-based scholarship or grant aid	33
% UG rec. need-based scholarship or grant aid	28
% frosh rec. non-need-based scholarship or grant aid	6
% UG rec. non-need-based scholarship or grant aid	4
% frosh rec. need-based self-help aid	26
% UG rec. need-based self-help aid	29
% frosh rec. athletic scholarships	1
% UG rec. athletic scholarships	1
% frosh rec. any financial aid	79
% UG rec. any financial aid	71
% UG borrow to pay for school	56
Average cumulative indebtedness	$22,015

INDIANA UNIVERSITY OF PENNSYLVANIA

117 SUTTON HALL, INDIANA, PA 15705 • ADMISSIONS: 724-357-2230 • FAX: 724-357-6281

CAMPUS LIFE
Quality of Life Rating	66
Fire Safety Rating	94
Green Rating	60*
Type of school	public
Environment	village

STUDENTS
Total undergrad enrollment	11,928
% male/female	45/55
% from out of state	5
% from public high school	95
% in (# of) fraternities	9 (19)
% in (# of) sororities	7 (14)
% African American	11
% Asian	1
% Caucasian	77
% Hispanic	2
% international	2
# of countries represented	58

SURVEY SAYS . . .
Frats and sororities dominate social scene
Student publications are popular
Lots of beer drinking
Hard liquor is popular
(Almost) everyone smokes

ACADEMICS
Academic Rating	70
Calendar	semester
Student/faculty ratio	16:1
Profs interesting rating	75
Profs accessible rating	76
Most common reg class size	20–29 students
Most common lab size	10–19 students

MOST POPULAR MAJORS
criminology
management information systems
nursing/registered nurse
(rn, asn, bsn, msn)

STUDENTS SAY

Academics

"An affordable school that has something to offer everyone," Indiana University of Pennsylvania (IUP) serves up "excellent academic programs" that are "academically challenging but not impossible if you make an honest effort." "Music, nursing, and education are the school's greatest strengths," one student says. Others laud the "fantastic fine arts program;" IUP's "very good College of Business;" and solid programs in theater, mathematics, chemistry, criminology, and English. Students here enjoy "awesome professors" who are "concerned with [students'] welfare and academic growth," and the students find their teachers "ridiculously easy to get into contact with—no need to make an appointment." The vast majority of students here are firmly focused on their post-graduation earning potential; they tell us that the school "is about learning to be the best at your career in the future." Students with higher intellectual and academic ambitions usually find their way into the Robert E. Cook Honors College, which "teaches students to think critically, participate in cultural events, and take active roles in the global community." The program has "fewer than 100 students in the freshman class, which means that we can have very small classes. Our professors know who we are and are able to give us more individual attention than would be possible with a larger group."

Life

Indiana, Pennsylvania, is the kind of town John Mellencamp would sing about— small, working-class, but not without its charms or bars. In fact, some claim the town "has a lot to offer kids to do. Malls, skating rinks, restaurants, movie theaters, ice hockey rinks, sports events, and campus events keep most of the students busy." Others aren't so sure; one writes, "Indiana is a small town with little to do, especially in the winter, when we get a lot of snow," which is why "people drink," and "when we aren't drinking, we think about the next time we will be drinking." Students concede that "Sometimes IUP gets a bad rap being known as a party school," but they point out that "college is all what you make it. The academic programs are exceptional," and those students "who want no alcohol/drugs involved in their college life whatsoever" will find options available to them, including trips to town, "movies and games," and "outdoor activities when the weather is nice." The school also boasts a "good selection of clubs" that provide a quick way "to meet people." If you need a taste of city life, "Pittsburgh is an hour away by car" and has "lots to do."

Student Body

Most IUP undergrads "are from the surrounding small towns," which are "predominantly white," but the school remains "more diverse" than the region (although "less diverse than U.S. Census percentage numbers") by drawing from other areas, including the city of Pittsburgh. Students describe the population as "very mixed," affording "the opportunity to interact with more people" than they would at "many other colleges." "No matter what your interest is, it wouldn't be too hard to find someone that you can share this interest with," one student tells us. Students view themselves as "down-to-earth" and pragmatic; as one explains, "This is the kind of school where intellectual growth is not the primary concern; it seems as if people are interested in getting a degree to get a better job...The few that are here for intellectual growth and enlightenment suffer from an apathetic community."

FINANCIAL AID: 724-357-2218 • E-MAIL: ADMISSIONS-INQUIRY@IUP.EDU • WEBSITE: WWW.IUP.EDU

THE PRINCETON REVIEW SAYS

Admissions

Very important factors considered include: Academic GPA, standardized test scores. *Important factors considered include:* Rigor of secondary school record. *Other factors considered include:* Class rank, application essay, recommendation(s), extracurricular activities. SAT or ACT required; TOEFL required of all international applicants. High school diploma is required and GED is accepted. *Academic units recommended:* 3 English, 3 mathematics, 3 science, 2 foreign language, 3 social studies.

Financial Aid

Students should submit: FAFSA. The Princeton Review suggests that all financial aid forms be submitted as soon as possible after 1/1. *Need-based scholarships/grants offered:* Federal Pell, SEOG, state scholarships/grants, private scholarships, the school's own gift aid, United Negro College Fund. *Loan aid offered:* FFEL Subsidized Stafford, FFEL Unsubsidized Stafford, FFEL PLUS, Federal Perkins, Private Alternative Loans. Applicants will be notified of awards on a rolling basis beginning 3/15. Federal Work-Study Program available. Institutional employment available. Off-campus job opportunities are good.

The Inside Word

IUP serves a dual mission: to provide low-cost higher education to as broad a range of students as possible and to maintain rigorous academic standards. Accordingly, admissions aren't as competitive here as they are at other top schools; students with above-average secondary school records and average or better standardized test scores are likely admits here. Once in, middling students better be prepared to step up their game, or they will soon find themselves on their way out the door.

THE SCHOOL SAYS ". . ."

From The Admissions Office

"At IUP, we look at each applicant as an individual, not as a number. That means we'll review your application materials very carefully. When reviewing applications, the admissions committee's primary focus is on the student's high school record and SAT scores. In addition, the committee often reviews the optional personal essay and letters of recommendations submitted by the student to help aid in the decision-making process. We're always happy to speak with prospective students. Call us toll-free at 800-422-6830 or 724-357-2230 or e-mail us at admissions-inquiry@iup.edu.

"Students applying for admission are required to take the SAT or ACT."

SELECTIVITY

Admissions Rating	64
# of applicants	11,030
% of applicants accepted	64
% of acceptees attending	44

FRESHMAN PROFILE

Range SAT Critical Reading	440–540
Range SAT Math	440–540
Range SAT Writing	430–520
Minimum paper TOEFL	500
Minimum computer TOEFL	173
% graduated top 10% of class	8
% graduated top 25% of class	26
% graduated top 50% of class	59

DEADLINES

Regular	
Notification	rolling
Nonfall registration?	yes

APPLICANTS ALSO LOOK AT

AND OFTEN PREFER
Duquesne University
Westminster College
Millersville University of Pennsylvania
Clarion University of PA
Shippensburg University of Pennsylvania
Penn State—University Park

AND SOMETIMES PREFER
University of Delaware
West Virginia University
Kutztown University of Pennsylvania
James Madison University
Slippery Rock University of Pennsylvania

AND RARELY PREFER
Lock Haven University of Pennsylvania
Ohio University—Athens
Mansfield University
Bloomsburg University of Pennsylvania

FINANCIAL FACTS

Financial Aid Rating	71
Annual in-state tuition	$5,358
Annual out-of-state tuition	$13,396
Room and board	$8,224
Required fees	$1,601
Books and supplies	$1,100
% frosh rec. need-based scholarship or grant aid	50
% UG rec. need-based scholarship or grant aid	47
% frosh rec. non-need-based scholarship or grant aid	25
% UG rec. non-need-based scholarship or grant aid	15
% frosh rec. need-based self-help aid	65
% UG rec. need-based self-help aid	59
% frosh rec. athletic scholarships	2
% UG rec. athletic scholarships	2
% frosh rec. any financial aid	81
% UG rec. any financial aid	81
% UG borrow to pay for school	82
Average cumulative indebtedness	$23,265

IOWA STATE UNIVERSITY

100 ENROLLMENT SERVICES, AMES, IA 50011-2011 • ADMISSIONS: 515-294-5836 • FAX: 515-294-2592

CAMPUS LIFE

Quality of Life Rating	89
Fire Safety Rating	73
Green Rating	60*
Type of school	public
Environment	town

STUDENTS

Total undergrad enrollment	21,607
% male/female	56/44
% from out of state	23
% from public high school	91
% live on campus	40
% in (# of) fraternities	10.6 (28)
% in (# of) sororities	12.2 (15)
% African American	3
% Asian	3
% Caucasian	84
% Hispanic	3
% international	4
# of countries represented	106

SURVEY SAYS . . .

Low cost of living
Student publications are popular
(Almost) no one smokes

ACADEMICS

Academic Rating	72
Calendar	semester
Student/faculty ratio	15.6:1
Profs interesting rating	62
Profs accessible rating	68
% classes taught by TAs	14
Most common reg class size	20–29 students
Most common lab size	20–29 students

MOST POPULAR MAJORS

management science
marketing/marketing management
mechanical engineering

STUDENTS SAY ". . ."

Academics

Iowa State University holds true to its initial mission of providing affordable, practical education with a special focus on agriculture. Today, the school remains "a great agriculture school" with "a great food science program" and a strong pre-veterinary program. Students also proudly tout its status as "one of the top engineering schools" in the region (offering noteworthy support for women engineers) and the home to a "strong architecture program." Students praise this "large university with a small-town feel," telling us that "I felt like I could find a home here and be exposed to almost limitless opportunities." Throughout the curriculum, "There are a lot of opportunities for student research and 'hands on' learning"; so many, in fact, that some students claim ISU is "the best 'outside of class' university in the nation." Undergrads also appreciate a strong support network; one explains, "There are so many services on campus to help students, it is almost unreal. From tutoring to study sessions and counseling to mock interviews and resume building, ISU offers a wide variety of services to students." The faculty "is one of ISU's strengths. If students take a chance and get to know their professors and other staff members, they make a great professional connection [with someone who] will bend over backwards, whether it be as a professional reference or helping fund a trip. The faculty really is here for students." Likewise, career services "are excellent" and offer such pluses as "one of the largest engineering career fairs."

Life

"Life at Iowa State can be as great as you want to make it," with more than "600 clubs and organizations" plus "a large intramural program, great crowds at athletic events, various free events, and many ways to get involved in leadership positions." Intercollegiate athletics are quite popular; "There's always a great turnout for big events," and "0ftentimes the discussions around campus are [about] football or other sports. Very rarely do you find a group of people discussing world issues." Just for fun students enjoy recreational and surrounding community activities."Hometown Ames is no bustling metropolis; the population "doubles with students around, and the city has adapted to this increase. That said, there is always plenty to do throughout the year. Many students take advantage of the dollar theater (which is actually $1.50) or attend events on campus." Ames also has some "unique restaurants," and Cyride (the bus system that is operated by the city and university) offers students free transportation to mostly everywhere in Ames." Students agree that "the campus is really beautiful."

Student Body

As at many big schools, "It is hard to describe a typical student at Iowa State because there are many styles of students." "Every stereotype is here; sorority girl/frat boy, farmer kid, international student, nerd, computer geek, socially awkward, [and] goth. Iowa State has every kind of person." Iowa is a conservative state, and ISU has a large agricultural student population. The "population of out-of-state students seems to be growing," and "there is a diversity of international students" filling out the ranks as well, so most students can find a niche at ISU, and fortunately "Everyone here is laid-back and easygoing," so the overall vibe is live-and-let-live.

FINANCIAL AID: 515-294-2223 • E-MAIL: ADMISSIONS@IASTATE.EDU • WEBSITE: WWW.IASTATE.EDU

THE PRINCETON REVIEW SAYS

Admissions

Very important factors considered include: Class rank, academic GPA, rigor of secondary school record, standardized test scores. *Other factors considered include:* Application essay, recommendation(s), character/personal qualities, extracurricular activities, geographical residence, interview, state residency, talent/ability, volunteer work, work experience. SAT or ACT required; TOEFL required of all international applicants. High school diploma is required and GED is accepted. *Academic units required:* 4 English, 3 mathematics, 3 science, (2 science labs), 2 foreign language, 2 social studies. *Academic units recommended:* 4 English, 4 mathematics, 4 science, (3 science labs), 3 foreign language, 4 social studies.

Financial Aid

Students should submit: FAFSA. The Princeton Review suggests that all financial aid forms be submitted as soon as possible after 1/1. *Need-based scholarships/grants offered:* Federal Pell, SEOG, state scholarships/grants, the school's own gift aid. *Loan aid offered:* Direct Subsidized Stafford, Direct Unsubsidized Stafford, Direct PLUS, Federal Perkins, state loans, college/university loans from institutional funds, Private alternative loans. Applicants will be notified of awards on a rolling basis beginning 4/1. Federal Work-Study Program available. Institutional employment available. Off-campus job opportunities are excellent.

The Inside Word

Admission to ISU is formula-driven and based on: ACT composite score; high school GPA; high school percentile rank; and number of high school courses completed in the core subject areas. The formula, known as the Regent Admission Index (RAI), is as follows: RAI = (2 x ACT composite score) + (1 x percentile high school rank) + (20 x high school grade point average) + (5 x number of years of high school courses completed in the core subject areas). Anyone earning an RAI score of at least 245 is automatically admitted; the admissions office reviews applicants scoring below 245 individually to determine which will also be admitted.

THE SCHOOL SAYS "..."

From The Admissions Office

"Iowa State University offers all the advantages of a major university along with the friendliness and warmth of a residential campus. There are more than 100 undergraduate programs of study in the Colleges of Agriculture, Business, Design, Human Sciences, Engineering, Liberal Arts and Sciences, and Veterinary Medicine. Our 1,700 faculty members include Rhodes Scholars, Fulbright Scholars, and National Academy of Sciences and National Academy of Engineering members. Recognized for its high quality of life, Iowa State has taken practical steps to make the university a place where students feel like they belong. Iowa State has been recognized for the high quality of campus life and the exemplary out-of-class experiences offered to its students. Along with a strong academic experience, students also have opportunities for further developing their leadership skills and interpersonal relationships through any of the more than 700 student organizations, 60 intramural sports, and a multitude of arts and recreational activities.."

SELECTIVITY

Admissions Rating	88
# of applicants	12,549
% of applicants accepted	87
% of acceptees attending	42

FRESHMAN PROFILE

Range SAT Critical Reading	490–650
Range SAT Math	550–680
Range ACT Composite	22–27
Minimum paper TOEFL	530
Minimum web-based TOEFL	71
Average HS GPA	3.49
% graduated top 10% of class	27
% graduated top 25% of class	60
% graduated top 50% of class	92

DEADLINES

Regular	
Deadline	7/1
Notification	rolling
Nonfall registration?	yes

APPLICANTS ALSO LOOK AT AND OFTEN PREFER

Purdue University—West Lafayette
University of Wisconsin—Madison
University of Illinois at Urbana-Champaign
University of Minnesota—Twin Cities

FINANCIAL FACTS

Financial Aid Rating	79
Annual in-state tuition	$5,756
Annual out-of-state tuition	$16,976
Room and board	$7,277
Required fees	$895
Books and supplies	$1,000
% frosh rec. need-based scholarship or grant aid	53
% UG rec. need-based scholarship or grant aid	53
% frosh rec. non-need-based scholarship or grant aid	25
% UG rec. non-need-based scholarship or grant aid	26
% frosh rec. need-based self-help aid	42
% UG rec. need-based self-help aid	45
% frosh rec. athletic scholarships	2
% UG rec. athletic scholarships	2
% frosh rec. any financial aid	85.6
% UG rec. any financial aid	79.2
% UG borrow to pay for school	71.1
Average cumulative indebtedness	$31,616

ITHACA COLLEGE

100 Job Hall, Ithaca, NY 14850-7020 • Admissions: 607-274-3124 • Fax: 607-274-1900

CAMPUS LIFE

Quality of Life Rating	79
Fire Safety Rating	74
Green Rating	98
Type of school	private
Environment	town

STUDENTS

Total undergrad enrollment	5,968
% male/female	44/56
% from out of state	55.4
% from public high school	73
% live on campus	70
% in (# of) fraternities	1 (3)
% in (# of) sororities	1 (1)
% African American	3
% Asian	4
% Caucasian	75
% Hispanic	4
% international	2
# of countries represented	78

SURVEY SAYS . . .

Great off-campus food
Frats and sororities are unpopular or nonexistent
Musical organizations are popular
College radio is popular
Theater is popular
Student publications are popular
Lots of beer drinking
Hard liquor is popular

ACADEMICS

Academic Rating	80
Calendar	semester
Student/faculty ratio	12:1
Profs interesting rating	81
Profs accessible rating	80
% classes taught by TAs	1
Most common reg class size	10–19 students

MOST POPULAR MAJORS

business/commerce
music
radio and television

STUDENTS SAY ". . ."

Academics

If you don't know whether you'd be happier at a small school or a large university, Ithaca College offers the best of both worlds. With just more than 6,000 undergraduates, Ithaca College is "not so big that you get lost, but not so small that you have a lack of opportunities." The school offers 100 major programs, with instructors who "are enthusiastic and genuinely interested in the subject matter and the students." A senior tells us, "In the end they become more mentors or friends than professors. We call them by their first names, and they take note of what's happening in our lives outside the classroom." Ithaca College was originally founded as a Music Conservatory, and their music programs continue to have an excellent reputation, as does the Park School of Communications. More than 1,000 Ithaca undergraduates are pursuing majors within the communications field, doling out praises for their strong and practical education. A senior enthuses, "We run radio and television stations, newspapers, [and] ad campaigns. We make films! We try to make a mini-real world so that we are super prepared for real life." Not everyone has contact with the school's administration; those who do say that they are "more than willing to work with you and give you respect." A junior attests, "I am a member of Student Government, and thus far the administration has really valued the opinions and ideas of the students." While the town of Ithaca's natural beauty is universally touted, on campus "some buildings are a little dated," and the university Internet system is slow.

Students

Getting involved in the community is second nature to most Ithaca students. A junior explains, "The typical student has a cause: some issue that they are passionate about and will devote much of their in-class study and extracurricular activities to—from gender issues, to LGBT issues, to race, to sustainability and the environment." Of particular note, "many students here are concerned about their environmental impact. There are a lot of clubs and classes centered around environmental awareness and education." Nearly 45 percent of the student population comes from the state of New York, and "the general student population is similar in background." However, students repeatedly reassure us that, "while Ithaca College is not the most diverse school, it prides itself on making everyone feel welcome and accepted. We are a community, and no one gets left out." Students acknowledge the existence of cliques, but they reassure us that, "unlike high school, you are not limited to being friends with the ones who are just like you. Everyone interacts and gets to know each other."

Life

Ithaca is a great place to get the full college experience. Residential life helps to forge a strong bond between undergraduates, as "all students live on campus for the first three years." In their free time, almost every student takes part in extracurricular clubs, sports teams, or campus activities. Off campus, Ithaca is a bustling college town with plenty of student-oriented attractions. In their free time, "a lot of people enjoy what is offered in the town of Ithaca. The commons has a large variety of restaurants and shops, and the farmers market is amazing!" Due to the natural beauty of the region, "going hiking in the gorges is also very popular, especially in the warmer months." At the same time, students warn us that, "the weather here is usually very gloomy; sun is very rare past November." When the snow begins to fall, "a good amount of the population enjoys skiing and snowboarding" and, students admit, partying becomes a more popular activity. In general, however, partying is just one of the many options available to IC students; life at Ithaca is well rounded, multifaceted, and fulfilling. A senior agrees, "People here focus on everything from school work to parties to political issues. There really is a good balance."

FINANCIAL AID: 607-274-3131 • E-MAIL: ADMISSION@ITHACA.EDU • WEBSITE: WWW.ITHACA.EDU

THE PRINCETON REVIEW SAYS

Admissions

Very important factors considered include: Academic GPA, rigor of secondary school record, standardized test scores. *Important factors considered include:* Class rank, application essay, recommendation(s), character/personal qualities, extracurricular activities, talent/ability. *Other factors considered include:* Alumni/ae relation, first generation, level of applicant's interest, volunteer work, work experience. SAT or ACT required; ACT with Writing component required; TOEFL required of all international applicants. High school diploma is required and GED is accepted. *Academic units required:* 4 English, 3 mathematics, 3 science, 2 foreign language, 4 social studies, 1 academic elective.

Financial Aid

Students should submit: FAFSA. The Princeton Review suggests that all financial aid forms be submitted as soon as possible after 1/1. *Need-based scholarships/grants offered:* Federal Pell, SEOG, state scholarships/grants, private scholarships, the school's own gift aid. *Loan aid offered:* FFEL Subsidized Stafford, FFEL Unsubsidized Stafford, FFEL PLUS, Federal Perkins, Alternative Loans. Applicants will be notified of awards on a rolling basis beginning 2/15. Federal Work-Study Program available. Institutional employment available. Off-campus job opportunities are good.

The Inside Word

Ithaca College brings the personal touch to the admissions process, offering one-on-one admissions counseling to prospective students during the application process or after acceptance to the college. Admissions is selective, with roughly 12,000 applicants for just 1,600 first-year spots, and 49 percent of incoming freshman held a spot in the top 15 percent of their high school class.

THE SCHOOL SAYS " . . ."

From The Admissions Office

"Ithaca College was founded in 1892 as a music conservatory, and it continues that commitment to performance and excellence. Its modern, residential 750-acre campus, equipped with state-of-the-art facilities, is home to the Schools of Business, Communications, Health Sciences and Human Performance, Humanities and Sciences, and Music and our new Division of Interdisciplinary and International Studies. With more than 100 majors—from biochemistry to business administration, journalism to jazz, philosophy to physical therapy, and special programs in Washington, D.C.; Los Angeles; London; and Australia—students enjoy the curricular choices of a large campus in a personalized, smaller school environment. And Ithaca's students benefit from an education that emphasizes active learning, small classes, collaborative student-faculty research, and development of the whole student. Located in central New York's spectacular Finger Lakes region in what many consider the classic college town, the college has 25 highly competitive varsity teams, more than 130 campus clubs, two radio stations, and a television station, as well as hundreds of concerts, recitals, and theater performances annually.

"Students applying for admission must have official scores from either the SAT or the ACT with the Writing section sent to Ithaca College by the testing agency. The college will also consider results of SAT Subject Tests, if submitted."

SELECTIVITY

Admissions Rating	87
# of applicants	12,233
% of applicants accepted	66
% of acceptees attending	18

FRESHMAN PROFILE

Range SAT Critical Reading	540–640
Range SAT Math	550–640
Range SAT Writing	540–640
Minimum paper TOEFL	550
Minimum computer TOEFL	213
Minimum web-based TOEFL	80
% graduated top 10% of class	34.6
% graduated top 25% of class	72.9
% graduated top 50% of class	96.3

DEADLINES

Early decision	
Deadline	11/1
Notification	12/15
Regular	
Deadline	2/1
Notification	rolling
Nonfall registration?	yes

APPLICANTS ALSO LOOK AT

AND OFTEN PREFER
New York University
Northeastern University
Boston University
Syracuse University

AND SOMETIMES PREFER
Cornell University
University of Vermont
Penn State—University Park

AND RARELY PREFER
Rutgers, The State University of New Jersey—New Brunswick
Marist College
University of Rhode Island

FINANCIAL FACTS

Financial Aid Rating	85
Annual tuition	$30,606
Room and board	$11,162
Books and supplies	$1,130
% frosh rec. need-based scholarship or grant aid	68
% UG rec. need-based scholarship or grant aid	63
% frosh rec. non-need-based scholarship or grant aid	24
% UG rec. non-need-based scholarship or grant aid	16
% frosh rec. need-based self-help aid	62
% UG rec. need-based self-help aid	60
% frosh rec. any financial aid	93
% UG rec. any financial aid	87

JAMES MADISON UNIVERSITY

SONNER HALL, MSC 0101, HARRISONBURG, VA 22807 • ADMISSIONS: 540-568-5681 • FAX: 540-568-3332

CAMPUS LIFE

Quality of Life Rating	93
Fire Safety Rating	70
Green Rating	93
Type of school	public
Environment	town

STUDENTS

Total undergrad enrollment	16,648
% male/female	40/60
% from out of state	29
% live on campus	36
% in (# of) fraternities	10 (15)
% in (# of) sororities	12 (9)
% African American	4
% Asian	5
% Caucasian	82
% Hispanic	2
% international	1
# of countries represented	70

SURVEY SAYS . . .

Athletic facilities are great
School is well run
Students are friendly
Great food on campus
Students are happy
Student publications are popular
Lots of beer drinking

ACADEMICS

Academic Rating	76
Calendar	semester
Student/faculty ratio	16:1
Profs interesting rating	82
Profs accessible rating	82
% classes taught by TAs	1
Most common reg class size	20–29 students
Most common lab size	20–29 students

MOST POPULAR MAJORS

community health
services/liaison/counseling
liberal arts and sciences/
liberal studies
marketing/marketing management

STUDENTS SAY ". . ."

Academics

Offering "great facilities and great prospects for the future" through "tons of valuable experiences such as a great study abroad program and internships," Virginia's James Madison University "prepares students for the future" with a mix of broad-ranging, general education requirements and career-oriented majors. Students grumble about the "gen eds," which require classes in the arts, humanities, and sciences and consume about one-third of all undergraduate credits. But students also admire the school's commitment to "educating students in all areas, not just a major concentration" and concede that the classes provide "foundation knowledge every graduating student should have." Standout offerings here include undergraduate business, education, and music programs; the School of Media Arts and Design; and the School of Communications. Students also tell us that "The study-abroad program at JMU is fabulous" and that "A large number of students study abroad" thanks to an "absolutely flawless" office of International Programs. JMU's "very good and unique" Integrated Science and Technology (ISAT) program emphasizes cross-disciplinary problem solving and innovation that are "applicable to the real world." All students here benefit from "great recruitment fairs and internship opportunities, small classes," professors who "go out of their way to help you understand a concept," and administrators who "strive to meet the demands of students. Many on the faculty have undertaken projects around campus to help with the overwhelming expansion of the student body."

Life

"There are tons to keep people occupied on campus" at JMU including the campus hangout Taylor Down Under (a place "to catch up with one another, grab a smoothie or some coffee, attend events like open mic night or watch the comedy club, etc."), the Grafton Stovall Theater ("which shows two different movies each week" at a $2.50 admission price), "sports, bands, frats, a cappella shows, interest groups, everything that a huge university offers"). In addition, there is "a significant amount happening off campus." "A bus line takes you to all the different apartments day and night" as well as "to the different restaurants, the close Wal-Mart, tanning salons, and local mall." In warm weather, "students flock to the quad to sunbathe, play guitar, and play Frisbee" or "go on day trips to go kayaking, rafting, horseback riding etc., through UREC…or swimming in Blue Hole." Off-campus apartments are home to a robust party scene; reports one undergrad, "For fun, people party. Sunday though Wednesday people are involved in school and their clubs and study. Then Thursday through Saturday it's house parties. The beer is free…just with the understanding that when you get a house and you are 21 you flip the bill once or twice." Hometown Harrisonburg "is a great town" with "lots of excellent restaurants, outdoor opportunities, and a great music scene," but "the Harrisonburg community conflicts with the students due to the weekend partying."

Student Body

The face of JMU may well be the "Ugg-Northface-pearls-sweatpants-wearing sorority girl" (one student observes it is difficult to get past with the 60:40 ratio of females to males"), but those who dig deeper discover "different crowds" clustered about campus. "A lot of students at JMU are prep kids from up north, but…there is also a great downtown crowd made up of very creative and artistic people. There is a group for everyone." Undergrads tend to be "involved in multiple organizations and clubs while balancing a substantial course load. We tend to be go-getters; we're very motivated to succeed, and we love any and everything JMU." And while the campus "is not known for being as politically involved as larger institutions, JMU finds its niche in community service. Service organizations are extremely popular at JMU, especially the Alternative Spring Break trips (these are so popular, a raffle system has been implemented to cope with the demand)." The student body is "pretty white," and "Although the Center for Multicultural Student Services has a definite voice on campus, whites seem to significantly outnumber other races. In recent years, an effort seems to have been made to diversify campus."

FINANCIAL AID: 540-568-7820 • E-MAIL: GOTOJMU@JMU.EDU • WEBSITE: WWW.JMU.EDU

THE PRINCETON REVIEW SAYS

Admissions

Very important factors considered include: Academic GPA, rigor of secondary school record. *Important factors considered include:* Standardized test scores. *Other factors considered include:* Class rank, application essay, recommendation(s), alumni/ae relation, character/personal qualities, extracurricular activities, geographical residence, state residency, talent/ability, volunteer work, work experience. SAT or ACT required; TOEFL required of all international applicants. High school diploma is required and GED is accepted. *Academic units required:* 4 English, 4 mathematics, 3 science, (3 science labs), 3 social studies. *Academic units recommended:* 4 English, 4 mathematics, 4 science, (4 science labs), 3 foreign language, 4 social studies.

Financial Aid

Students should submit: FAFSA. The Princeton Review suggests that all financial aid forms be submitted as soon as possible after 1/1. *Need-based scholarships/grants offered:* Federal Pell, SEOG, ACG, SMART Grant, state scholarships/grants, private scholarships, the school's own gift aid. *Loan aid offered:* Subsidized Direct Loan, Unsubsidized Direct Loan, Parent PLUS Direct Loan, Federal Perkins. Applicants will be notified of awards on a rolling basis beginning 4/1. Federal Work-Study Program available. Institutional Employment available. Off-campus job opportunities are good.

The Inside Word

Virginia boasts one of the most robust university public undergraduate education systems in the nation. James Madison ranks third in most students' preference behind University of Virginia and the College of William and Mary, but third place in that company is far from shabby. The school is large enough to accommodate all those who weren't quite solid enough to gain entry to choices one and two. Virginia students are competitive enough that you still need solidly above-average grades and test scores to sail through JMU's admissions process.

THE SCHOOL SAYS ". . ."

From The Admissions Office

"James Madison University's philosophy of inclusiveness—known as 'all together one'—means that students become a part of a real community that nurtures its own to learn, grow, and succeed. Our professors, many of whom have a wealth of real-world experience, pride themselves on making teaching their top priority. We take seriously the responsibility to maintain an environment that fosters learning and encourages students to excel in and out of the classroom. Our rich variety of educational, social, and extracurricular activities include more than 100 innovative and traditional undergraduate majors and programs, a well-established study abroad program, a cutting-edge information security program, more than 280 student clubs and organizations, and a 147,000-square-foot, state-of-the-art recreation center. The university's picturesque, self-contained campus is located in the heart of the Shenandoah Valley, a four-season area that's easy to call home. Great food, fun times, exciting intercollegiate athletics, and rigorous academics all combine to create the unique James Madison experience. From the library to the residence halls and from our outstanding honors program to our highly successful career placement program, the university is committed to equipping our students with the tools they need to achieve their dreams."

SELECTIVITY

Admissions Rating	**89**
# of applicants	19,245
% of applicants accepted	65
% of acceptees attending	32
# accepting a place on wait list	765
% admitted from wait list	18

FRESHMAN PROFILE

Range SAT Critical Reading	520–620
Range SAT Math	540–630
Range SAT Writing	520–620
Range ACT Composite	22–26
Minimum paper TOEFL	550
Minimum computer TOEFL	213
Average HS GPA	3.7
% graduated top 10% of class	29
% graduated top 25% of class	73
% graduated top 50% of class	97

DEADLINES

Early action	
Deadline	11/1
Notification	1/15
Regular	
Priority	11/1
Deadline	1/15
Notification	4/1
Nonfall registration?	no

APPLICANTS ALSO LOOK AT

AND OFTEN PREFER
Virginia Tech
University of Virginia

AND SOMETIMES PREFER
University of Delaware
College of William and Mary
George Mason University

FINANCIAL FACTS

Financial Aid Rating	**67**
Annual tuition in-state	$6,964
Out of State	$18,458
Room and board	$7,172
% frosh rec. need-based scholarship or grant aid	15
% UG rec. need-based scholarship or grant aid	13
% frosh rec. non-need-based scholarship or grant aid	11
% UG rec. non-need-based scholarship or grant aid	7
% frosh rec. need-based self-help aid	30
% UG rec. need-based self-help aid	24
% frosh rec. athletic scholarships	2
% UG rec. athletic scholarships	2
% frosh rec. any financial aid	56
% UG rec. any financial aid	53
% UG borrow to pay for school	46
Average cumulative indebtedness	$17,395

JOHNS HOPKINS UNIVERSITY

3400 NORTH CHARLES STREET/140 GARLAND, BALTIMORE, MD 21218 • ADMISSIONS: 410-516-8171 • FAX: 410-516-6025

CAMPUS LIFE

Quality of Life Rating	**68**
Fire Safety Rating	**75**
Green Rating	**96**
Type of school	private
Environment	metropolis

STUDENTS

Total undergrad enrollment	4,725
% male/female	52/48
% from out of state	85
% from public high school	69
% live on campus	56
% in (# of) fraternities	24 (12)
% in (# of) sororities	23 (7)
% African American	7
% Asian	24
% Caucasian	48
% Hispanic	7
% Native American	1
% international	6
# of countries represented	71

SURVEY SAYS . . .
Lab facilities are great
Great library
Athletic facilities are great

ACADEMICS

Academic Rating	**86**
Calendar	4/1/4
Profs interesting rating	61
Profs accessible rating	68
Most common reg class size	10–19 students
Most common lab size	20–29 students

MOST POPULAR MAJORS
international relations and affairs
neuroscience
public health

STUDENTS SAY ". . ."

Academics

Johns Hopkins University is a pre-med powerhouse and one of the nation's great producers of tomorrow's prominent doctors and medical researchers. Boasting one of the "top research [hospitals] in the country," the country's "number-one undergraduate biomedical engineering program," and "the number-one school for public health studies," it's no wonder JHU draws so many aspiring doctors. Students sometimes think, "almost everyone is premed." Such a misconception is one of the reasons JHU's many other strengths are often overlooked. Those other strengths are many, including "a fantastic international studies program," a highly respected writing seminar that "is paving the way for liberal arts on this science-dominated campus," a school of engineering that offers students "amazing research experience," and "a wonderful relationship with the Peabody Conservatory for those seriously interested in music." No matter what they study, students at JHU inhabit "an intense academic environment that works hard to make us the best applicants we can be for grad school while teaching us how to be a part of a global community." Research is "a big highlight here." As one student explains, "JHU was the first research university in the U.S.A.," and you'll find "a lot of [research] opportunities" from freshman year on. What you won't find is a lot of hand-holding, since "Hopkins is an institution where students are given a wide range of freedom with their classes and with their social life. More importantly, [such freedom] it teaches students to be responsible for their own actions and decisions, both academically and socially."

Life

"Johns Hopkins has a reputation for being a living hell, however, it is actually quite nice," students assure us. One explains, "It is true that we have a very rigorous academic program, but that does not prevent us from having fun and enjoying the many activities offered by the school and the neighborhood. The frats and sororities are quite active but not ridiculous. there are many trendy areas in Baltimore with good bars, restaurants, and clubs. On campus and there are many events ranging from a cappella concerts to lectures from prominent political figures to concerts by artists like Guster and Talib Kweli." Hometown Baltimore "gets a bad rep" (if you watch HBO's *The Wire*, you know what that rep is), "but there is a lot to do in and around campus. There is tons of shopping, and lots of really good restaurants to eat at in the city." There's also "a good band scene, as well as really cheap baseball tickets." All in all, "it's a very fun city." For fun on campus, "students normally go to frat parties." JHU has some "great Division I sports teams"—men's lacrosse and soccer are always highly ranked—and the student body regularly rallies to their support. The "beautiful" campus is a short walk from the Baltimore Museum of Art, a great place to blow off steam when the pressures of school start to build, and "is free for students."

Student Body

JHU students aren't sure "whether there is such a thing as one typical student, because there is a strong division between engineering and arts and science students." That said, "most students work hard and play hard." There are "lots of complaints about the workload, but people are secretly proud of the work they do." Many here "are intensely competitive," which is a "reflection of the pressure they feel on campus." But "it is a myth that Hopkins is filled with cut-throat nerds." Though "it is a stressful atmosphere at times because students want to get ahead, most of the students are very helpful and nice." Demographically speaking, "there are all kinds of people here, which means everyone can fit in. No matter what kind of person someone may appear to be on the outside, you know that if they're at Hopkins they must be pretty nerdy on the inside, so there's a kind of camaraderie there." Most students "are a little of everything, and it seems like everyone here is exceptional at something."

FINANCIAL AID: 410-516-8028 • E-MAIL: GOTOJHU@JHU.EDU • WEBSITE: WWW.JHU.EDU

THE PRINCETON REVIEW SAYS

Admissions

Very important factors considered include: Academic GPA, recommendation(s), rigor of secondary school record, character/personal qualities. *Important factors considered include:* Class rank, application essay, standardized test scores, extracurricular activities, talent/ability, volunteer work, work experience. *Other factors considered include:* Alumni/ae relation, first generation, geographical residence, interview, racial/ethnic status, state residency. SAT or ACT required; SAT and SAT Subject Tests or ACT recommended; ACT with Writing component required; TOEFL required of all international applicants. High school diploma or equivalent is not required. *Academic units recommended:* 4 English, 4 mathematics, 4 science, 4 foreign language, 2 social studies, 2 history.

Financial Aid

Students should submit: FAFSA, CSS/Financial Aid PROFILE, noncustodial PROFILE, business/farm supplement, current year federal tax returns. Regular filing deadline is 3/1. The Princeton Review suggests that all financial aid forms be submitted as soon as possible after 1/1. *Need-based scholarships/grants offered:* Federal Pell, SEOG, state scholarships/grants, private scholarships, the school's own gift aid. *Loan aid offered:* Direct Subsidized Stafford, Direct Unsubsidized Stafford, Direct PLUS, Federal Perkins, college/university loans from institutional funds. Applicants will be notified of awards on or about 4/1. Federal Work-Study Program available. Institutional employment available.

The Inside Word

Top schools like Hopkins receive more and more applications every year and, as a result, grow harder and harder to get into. With nearly 16,000 applicants, Hopkins has to reject numerous applicants who are thoroughly qualified. Give your application everything you've got, and don't take it personally if you don't get a fat envelope in the mail.

THE SCHOOL SAYS ". . ."

From The Admissions Office

"The Hopkins tradition of preeminent academic excellence naturally attracts the very best students in the nation and from around the world. The admissions committee carefully examines each application for evidence of compelling intellectual interest and academic performance as well as strong personal recommendations and meaningful extracurricular contributions. Every applicant who matriculates to Johns Hopkins University was found qualified by the admissions committee through a 'whole person' assessment, and every applicant accepted for admission is fully expected to graduate. The admissions committee determines whom they believe will take full advantage of the exceptional opportunities offered at Hopkins, contribute the most to the educational process of the institution, and be the most successful in using what they have learned and experienced for the benefit of society.

"Freshman applicants may take either the SAT or the ACT with Writing component. For those submitting SAT scores, submitting scores from three SAT Subject Tests is recommended."

SELECTIVITY

Admissions Rating	**99**
# of applicants	16,011
% of applicants accepted	25
% of acceptees attending	30
# accepting a place on wait list	3,474
% admitted from wait list	1
# of early decision applicants	1,049
% accepted early decision	48

FRESHMAN PROFILE

Range SAT Critical Reading	630–740
Range SAT Math	660–770
Range SAT Writing	640–740
Range ACT Composite	29–33
Minimum paper TOEFL	600
Minimum computer TOEFL	250
Average HS GPA	3.71
% graduated top 10% of class	84
% graduated top 25% of class	98
% graduated top 50% of class	99

DEADLINES

Early decision	
Deadline	11/1
Notification	12/15
Regular	
Deadline	1/1
Notification	4/1
Nonfall registration?	no

APPLICANTS ALSO LOOK AT

AND OFTEN PREFER
Harvard College, Yale University
University of Pennsylvania
Princeton University

AND SOMETIMES PREFER
Cornell University
Northwestern University

AND RARELY PREFER
Washington University in St. Louis

FINANCIAL FACTS

Financial Aid Rating	**90**
Annual tuition	$37,700
Room and board	$11,578
Books and supplies	$1,200
% frosh rec. need-based scholarship or grant aid	38
% UG rec. need-based scholarship or grant aid	39
% frosh rec. non-need-based scholarship or grant aid	6
% UG rec. non-need-based scholarship or grant aid	6
% frosh rec. need-based self-help aid	38
% UG rec. need-based self-help aid	39
% frosh rec. athletic scholarships	1
% UG rec. athletic scholarships	1
% frosh rec. any financial aid	47
% UG rec. any financial aid	45
% UG borrow to pay for school	50
Average cumulative indebtedness	$21,984

JUNIATA COLLEGE

1700 MOORE STREET, HUNTINGDON, PA 16652 • ADMISSIONS: 814-641-3420 • FAX: 814-641-3100

CAMPUS LIFE
Quality of Life Rating	**83**
Fire Safety Rating	**75**
Green Rating	**72**
Type of school	private
Environment	village

STUDENTS
Total undergrad enrollment	1,402
% male/female	44/56
% from out of state	28
% from public high school	87
% live on campus	82
% African American	1
% Asian	2
% Caucasian	89
% Hispanic	2
% international	4
# of countries represented	34

SURVEY SAYS . . .
Lab facilities are great
Students are friendly
Campus feels safe
Low cost of living
Frats and sororities are unpopular or nonexistent

ACADEMICS
Academic Rating	**88**
Calendar	semester
Student/faculty ratio	12:1
Profs interesting rating	84
Profs accessible rating	88
Most common reg class size	10–19 students
Most common lab size	10–19 students

MOST POPULAR MAJORS
biology/biological sciences
business/commerce
education

STUDENTS SAY "..."

Academics

Juniata College has catapulted from regional to national status in the past decade on the strength of its great natural science programs, housed in the 88,000-square-foot, state-of-the-art Von Liebig Center for Science (VLCS). Students tell us while Juniata "is centered around a very tough but rewarding science program," science is hardly the only game in town. The "business, theatre, and education departments are strong, too." Another student explains, "Other departments are beginning to receive support from trustees and alumni now that VLCS is complete. Several buildings will be undergoing renovations to allow for the expansion of the humanities and social sciences." Business, in particular, seems likely to receive a lot of attention as it is among the school's most popular disciplines. Undergrads tout JC's "great entrepreneurial program...where all students are encouraged to start their own businesses and some are given start-up cash." Education is also popular. Students appreciate they are "given a practicum their first semester freshman year," meaning "if they don't like being in the classroom, they can change their major right away." "At most other schools, you have to wait until your junior year to get some classroom experience, [in your major]" says a student. Other perks of a Juniata education include the prominence of the study-abroad program and the (Program of Emphasis) where, "students are afforded the option to create their own major which allows us to explore many possibilities that would otherwise be restricted by a designated major."

Life

Juniata "is located in Huntingdon, PA, which is a tiny town in the middle of nowhere, 30 minutes south of State," so "needless to say, there is not a lot to do off campus." Fortunately, "the Juniata Activities Board (JAB) brings numerous acts to campus including comedians, musicians, hypnotists, magicians." The campus also hosts "various weekend parties, but they normally don't happen until Saturday nights because a large population of the student body is active in athletics with games either Friday night or Saturday afternoon." Since Juniata "doesn't have any Greek societies," students compensate by being "active in many clubs, including the Agriculture Club, Health Occupations Students of America, student government, the Equine club, and the Student Alumni Association." Otherwise, quiet fun ("video games and movie-watching are very popular") dominates. One student explains, "The people who are dissatisfied with Juniata were definitely expecting something else, usually something more along the lines of Penn State."

Student Body

Juniata "is notoriously middle-class and Caucasian" with "very few minority students." Diversity arrives in the form of "a vast number of international students, both in semester and year-long exchange programs. The international presence at Juniata does a lot for class debate, and often opens the eyes of otherwise typically American students to the perspectives of those from other nations." Undergrads here "work hard for their grades. They want to excel. Basically, they're motivated and determined to succeed in the real world," to the point they often "choose to do homework and study above most other activities." Ultimately, "a typical student is really studious and really cares about their education. Everyone is able to find their own clique in which they fit into and feel comfortable."

FINANCIAL AID: 814-641-3142 • E-MAIL: INFO@JUNIATA.EDU • WEBSITE: WWW.JUNIATA.EDU

THE PRINCETON REVIEW SAYS

Admissions

Very important factors considered include: Application essay, academic GPA, recommendation(s), rigor of secondary school record, standardized test scores, character/personal qualities. *Important factors considered include:* Extracurricular activities, first generation, interview, talent/ability, volunteer work. *Other factors considered include:* Alumni/ae relation, geographical residence, level of applicant's interest, state residency. SAT or ACT recommended; TOEFL required of all international applicants. High school diploma is required and GED is accepted. *Academic units required:* 4 English, 3 mathematics, 3 science, (2 science labs), 2 foreign language, 1 social studies, 3 history. *Academic units recommended:* 4 English, 4 mathematics, 4 science, 2 foreign language, 1 social studies, 3 history.

Financial Aid

Students should submit: FAFSA. Regular filing deadline is 3/1. The Princeton Review suggests that all financial aid forms be submitted as soon as possible after 1/1. *Need-based scholarships/grants offered:* Federal Pell, SEOG, state scholarships/grants, private scholarships, the school's own gift aid. *Loan aid offered:* FFEL Subsidized Stafford, FFEL Unsubsidized Stafford, FFEL PLUS, Federal Perkins, college/university loans from institutional funds. Applicants will be notified of awards on a rolling basis beginning 2/21. Federal Work-Study Program available. Institutional employment available. Off-campus job opportunities are good.

The Inside Word

As at many traditional liberal arts schools, the admissions process at Juniata is a personal one. Applications are scoured for evidence the student is committed to attending Juniata and to remaining there for the full four years. The school is best known for its premedical programs, meaning applicants to these programs will have the highest hurdles to clear.

THE SCHOOL SAYS ". . ."

From The Admissions Office

"Juniata's unique approach to learning has a flexible, student-centered focus. With the help of two advisors, more than half of Juniata's students design their own majors (called the "Program of Emphasis" or "POE"). Those who choose a more traditional academic journey still benefit from the assistance of two faculty advisors and interdisciplinary collaboration between multiple academic departments.

"In addition, all students benefit from the recent, significant investments in academic facilities that help students actively learn by doing. For example, the new Halbritter Performing Arts Center houses an innovative theater program where theater professionals work side-by-side with students. The Sill Business Incubator provides $5,000 in seed capital to students with a desire to start their own business. The LEEDS-certified Shuster Environmental Studies Field Station, located on nearby Raystown Lake, gives unparalleled, hands-on study opportunities to students. And the von Liebig Center for Science provides opportunities for student/faculty research surpassing those available at even large universities.

"As the 2003 Middle States Accreditation Team noted, 'Juniata is truly a student-centered college. There is a remarkable cohesiveness in this commitment—faculty, students, trustees, staff, and alumni, each from their own vantage point, describe a community in which the growth of the student is central.' This cohesiveness creates a dynamic learning environment that enables students to think and grow intellectually, to evolve in their academic careers, and to graduate as active, successful participants in the global community.

"Freshman applicants may submit the SAT (or the ACT with the Writing component). We will use their best scores from either test."

SELECTIVITY
Admissions Rating	94
# of applicants	2,349
% of applicants accepted	69
% of acceptees attending	28
# of early decision applicants	92
% accepted early decision	88

FRESHMAN PROFILE
Range SAT Critical Reading	545–650
Range SAT Math	550–640
Minimum paper TOEFL	550
Minimum computer TOEFL	213
Average HS GPA	3.75
% graduated top 10% of class	44
% graduated top 25% of class	79
% graduated top 50% of class	97

DEADLINES
Early decision	
Deadline	12/1
Notification	12/31
Early action	
Deadline	1/1
Notification	1/30
Regular	
Priority	12/1
Deadline	3/15
Notification	rolling
Nonfall registration?	yes

APPLICANTS ALSO LOOK AT
AND OFTEN PREFER
Gettysburg College
AND SOMETIMES PREFER
Franklin & Marshall College
Susquehanna University
Allegheny College
AND RARELY PREFER
Dickinson College, Ursinus College
Penn State—University Park

FINANCIAL FACTS
Financial Aid Rating	82
Annual tuition	$29,610
Room and board	$8,420
Required fees	$670
Books and supplies	$600
% frosh rec. need-based scholarship or grant aid	71
% UG rec. need-based scholarship or grant aid	70
% frosh rec. non-need-based scholarship or grant aid	14
% UG rec. non-need-based scholarship or grant aid	11
% frosh rec. need-based self-help aid	57
% UG rec. need-based self-help aid	58
% frosh rec. any financial aid	99
% UG rec. any financial aid	99
% UG borrow to pay for school	85
Average cumulative indebtedness	$21,343

KALAMAZOO COLLEGE

1200 ACADEMY STREET, KALAMAZOO, MI 49006 • ADMISSIONS: 269-337-7166 • FAX: 269-337-7390

CAMPUS LIFE

Quality of Life Rating	80
Fire Safety Rating	60*
Green Rating	84
Type of school	private
Environment	city

STUDENTS

Total undergrad enrollment	1,361
% male/female	44/56
% from out of state	31
% from public high school	85
% live on campus	78
% African American	4
% Asian	6
% Caucasian	73
% Hispanic	3
% international	2
# of countries represented	20

SURVEY SAYS . . .

No one cheats
Great library
Frats and sororities are unpopular or nonexistent
Political activism is popular

ACADEMICS

Academic Rating	95
Calendar	quarter
Student/faculty ratio	14:1
Profs interesting rating	95
Profs accessible rating	89
Most common reg class size	10–19 students
Most common lab size	fewer than 10 students

MOST POPULAR MAJORS
economics
English language and literature
psychology

STUDENTS SAY "..."

Academics

Kalamazoo College "is all about the K-Plan and giving students the best liberal arts education possible." The K-Plan consists of two mandatory components (a core liberal arts curriculum and a Senior Individualized Project) and two voluntary components (externships/internships and study abroad). Students say the K-Plan makes Kalamazoo "the epitome of experiential education," starting with the optional Land/Sea first-year orientation experience, (a team-building exercise involving hiking, canoeing, climbing, and rappelling), and continuing with an "off-campus internship sophomore year, study-abroad junior year, and a senior project before you graduate!" From beginning to end, it's a "very hands-on education." As at many selective, small schools rigorous academics are delivered by "a faculty who shares in the interests of the student" amid "an awesome collection of competitive but supportive peers." The intensity is ratcheted up somewhat by Kalamazoo's accelerated academic calendar. Operating on a quarter system means that "courses last only 10 weeks" and "everything moves extremely quickly. There's a lot of work involved." In other words, this place "is not a playground." Some feel the workload is a bit too much and feel a reduction would mean "less reading but more thinking," and even those who appreciate the challenge concede "B's at K are like A's at other schools."

Life

Life at Kalamazoo is, "at the most basic level, heavily focused around academics. Everything else is just gravy." Not to say there aren't "a great many opportunities in which to take part," but rather "before [you do any of that], you have to finish your homework" which is usually substantial. When the books are finally closed, "there are always events going on either here or at Western Michigan University [also in Kalamazoo], and nearly everyone at K is part of some club or organization. Political organizations like Campus Republicans and Campus Democrats are very popular, as is our gay and lesbian group, Kaleidoscope." Students say, "Choir and sports like tennis are also popular here. Our theater department is small but dedicated." And let's not forget the CGC, "the Childish Games Commission, where students play red rover, dodgeball, zombie tag, and jump in leaf piles. It gives us an excuse to goof around for an hour or two and break from school work." Many tell us "Kalamazoo is a great town to live in. We are lucky to be a part of a real, thriving community, with which we can interact through service-learning, jobs, or shopping and entertainment. There are theater productions, concerts, and festivals year-round." When students want a more conventional undergrad party scene, they head to the "keggers" happening "any day of the week" at WMU.

Student Body

Kalamazoo students tend to be extremely bright and a little high-strung, to the point many are at least one standard deviation from the norm. As one undergrad puts it, "My friend has this theory: There is a secret question on the application that no one remembers answering. The question is 'On a scale of 1 to 10, 10 being the oddest, how odd are you?' If you don't score at least a 5, you don't get in." Mostly, "Students here are very smart and nice, but a little on the awkward antisocial side." Other, smaller demographics on campus include "the rich, party types who take blow-off classes and get all C's." Mostly, the school is full of the type of "people who can balance work and play but tend to be the type of people who enjoy a game of 'zombie tag'," the fervent feminists, and "the gay community, [which is] very strong, active, and supportive."

FINANCIAL AID: 269-337-7192 • E-MAIL: ADMISSION@KZOO.EDU • WEBSITE: WWW.KZOO.EDU

THE PRINCETON REVIEW SAYS

Admissions

Very important factors considered include: Academic GPA, rigor of secondary school record, extracurricular activities, volunteer work, work experience. *Important factors considered include:* Application essay, recommendation(s), standardized test scores, character/personal qualities, interview, talent/ability. *Other factors considered include:* Alumni/ae relation, first generation, geographical residence, level of applicant's interest, racial/ethnic status. SAT or ACT required; ACT with Writing component required; TOEFL required of all international applicants. High school diploma is required and GED is accepted. *Academic units required:* 4 English, 3 mathematics, 3 science, 3 foreign language, 2 social studies, 2 history. *Academic units recommended:* 4 English, 4 mathematics, 4 science, 4 foreign language, 2 social studies, 2 history.

Financial Aid

Students should submit: FAFSA, CSS/Financial Aid PROFILE. The Princeton Review suggests that all financial aid forms be submitted as soon as possible after 1/1. *Need-based scholarships/grants offered:* Federal Pell, SEOG, state scholarships/grants, private scholarships, the school's own gift aid. *Loan aid offered:* Direct Subsidized Stafford, Direct Unsubsidized Stafford, Direct PLUS, Federal Perkins. Applicants will be notified of awards on a rolling basis beginning 3/21. Federal Work-Study Program available. Institutional employment available. Off-campus job opportunities are good.

The Inside Word

Kalamazoo offers early decision and one round of early action, indicating the school works aggressively to fill its incoming class as early in the admissions process as possible. If you are dead certain you want to attend Kalamazoo, apply early decision. If the school is among your top choices, consider applying early action; your application will probably receive a slightly more generous review than will those that arrive later in the admission process.

THE SCHOOL SAYS " . . ."

From The Admissions Office

"Anyone can pursue any component of the K-Plan at any college, but it is rare to see the purposeful integration and high participation rate found at Kalamazoo. During the past 50 years, 85 percent of our graduates have formally studied in another country while 80 percent have completed an internship or externship, and 100 percent complete a senior project. Our students often pursue international internships and senior project experiences, in addition to their planned study abroad terms. Also, Kalamazoo is one of the few selective liberal arts colleges to be found in a city—the Kalamazoo metro area has a population of approximately 240,000 with the advantage of being near a university of nearly 30,000 students. It is a diverse and vibrant community with wonderful access to the arts, athletics, service-learning, and community-service opportunities. We are a small and personal college with bigger opportunities.

"An SAT or ACT score is required for admission; SAT Subject Tests are not. Students taking only the ACT must take the writing portion."

SELECTIVITY

Admissions Rating	**95**
# of applicants	2,059
% of applicants accepted	70
% of acceptees attending	25
# accepting a place on wait list	60
% admitted from wait list	62
# of early decision applicants	22
% accepted early decision	77

FRESHMAN PROFILE

Range SAT Critical Reading	600–710
Range SAT Math	590–670
Range SAT Writing	580–680
Range ACT Composite	26–30
Minimum paper TOEFL	550
Minimum computer TOEFL	213
Minimum web-based TOEFL	80
Average HS GPA	3.63
% graduated top 10% of class	42
% graduated top 25% of class	78
% graduated top 50% of class	99

DEADLINES

Early decision	
Deadline	11/10
Notification	11/20
Early action	
Deadline	11/20
Notification	12/20
Regular	
Deadline	2/1
Notification	4/1
Nonfall registration?	no

APPLICANTS ALSO LOOK AT

AND OFTEN PREFER
University of Michigan—Ann Arbor

AND SOMETIMES PREFER
Oberlin College
Macalester College

AND RARELY PREFER
Hope College
Alma College
Albion College

FINANCIAL FACTS

Financial Aid Rating	**73**
Annual tuition	$32,643
Room and board	$7,776
% frosh rec. need-based scholarship or grant aid	50
% UG rec. need-based scholarship or grant aid	52
% frosh rec. non-need-based scholarship or grant aid	50
% UG rec. non-need-based scholarship or grant aid	50
% frosh rec. need-based self-help aid	41
% UG rec. need-based self-help aid	42
% frosh rec. any financial aid	98
% UG rec. any financial aid	98

KANSAS STATE UNIVERSITY

119 ANDERSON HALL, MANHATTAN, KS 66506 • ADMISSIONS: 800-432-8270 OR 785-532-6250 • FAX: 785-532-6393

CAMPUS LIFE

Quality of Life Rating	95
Fire Safety Rating	64
Green Rating	84
Type of school	public
Environment	village

STUDENTS

Total undergrad enrollment	18,114
% male/female	52/48
% from out of state	13
% from public high school	81
% in (# of) fraternities	14 (28)
% in (# of) sororities	14 (16)
% African American	4
% Asian	1
% Caucasian	85
% Hispanic	3
% Native American	1
% international	3
# of countries represented	105

SURVEY SAYS . . .

Students are friendly
Students get along with local community
Everyone loves the Wildcats

ACADEMICS

Academic Rating	73
Calendar	semester
Student/faculty ratio	20:1
Profs interesting rating	73
Profs accessible rating	76
% classes taught by TAs	17
Most common reg class size	10–19 students

MOST POPULAR MAJORS

animal sciences
business administration and management
elementary education and teaching

STUDENTS SAY ". . ."

Academics

"Underrated" and tremendously affordable Kansas State University is "a big school with a small-school feel." Agriculture will always be prevalent here, but there are nine colleges and "more 250 majors and options." Other "marquee programs" include engineering, the hard sciences, and a "grueling" architecture program. The library is "amazing." The faculty is "a mixed bag." "Some instructors you'll love and some you won't be able to stand," says a microbiology major. Intro and general education courses can be on the large side. They're "awkward and usually just rehash information from the textbook." "We struggle with graduate teaching assistants, especially those whose first language is not English," notes a political science major. In upper level courses, "it becomes easier to cultivate a relationship with your professor." Administratively, "the school is a pretty well-oiled machine." Management is full of "gifted people who genuinely love K-State" and "students have a large say in everything the university does." Also, the top brass is ultra-accessible for such a large institution. The president frequently rides his bike around campus "in his purple sweat suit." In some areas, though, red tape is unavoidable. "If you change your major here," cautions a junior, "you're pretty much screwed as far as trying to graduate on time."

Life

The residence halls could use some sprucing up and some buildings "are about to crumble" but this "very compact" campus is "easy to navigate" and "beautiful in every season." KSU offers a "laid-back atmosphere" and "an extensive variety of clubs." "Movies on the lawn are fun." "Greek life is also huge and is responsible for a multitude of events." Hordes of students are "sports crazy." Intramurals are popular and "cheering on the 'Cats is a must.' In the fall, "people are obsessed with K-State football." "During game day weekends, the whole town is dressed in purple." "I do get tired of hearing about the football team 24/7," admits a senior, "but whatever." Beyond campus, Manhattan is a "great college town." It's "just big enough and everything you need for college life is available" including "a decent party scene." House parties and frat parties are common but most students head to Aggieville, the Little Apple's "famous" bar district. K-Staters call it "four square blocks of fun" and "one of the greatest places on Earth." Watering holes are "usually full on the weekends" and, "a lot of times, a weeknight at the bars can be even more fun." "Every college student should experience Aggieville," recommends one proud junior.

Student Body

The "hardworking and honest" students at K-State tell us they bask in "country hospitality." "The students are the friendliest in the country," asserts a senior. "You cannot walk through campus without people smiling or acknowledging you"—"not in that creepy, stalker way, but the way that makes you feel warm and fuzzy inside." The "typical Midwestern" population here mostly comes in two varieties. There are the "yokels" and "farm boys from small towns in Kansas." There are also the kids from "suburban white neighborhoods" in Kansas City and Wichita. You'll see "punk rock kids," "cowboys in Wranglers," and "the occasional hippie," but "they form their own weird groups." For the most part, the vibe is "very homogeneous" and "hopelessly vanilla." "The vast majority of the students look, dresse, and act the same." Politically, K-State "tends towards conservatism." On the whole, though, these students "generally represent the middle of the road in nearly every American way of thought." As for minority enrollment, it's pretty low, and many K-Staters lament "the lack of diversity." On the other hand, what can you do? "I understand why certain ethnicities would not choose a school in the middle of nowhere," admits one student.

KANSAS STATE UNIVERSITY

FINANCIAL AID: 877-817-2287 OR 785-532-6420 • E-MAIL: K-STATE@K-STATE.EDU • WEBSITE: CONSIDER.K-STATE.EDU

THE PRINCETON REVIEW SAYS

Admissions

Very important factors considered include: Class rank, academic GPA, rigor of secondary school record, standardized test scores. *Other factors considered include:* Recommendation(s). SAT or ACT recommended. High school diploma is required and GED is accepted. *Academic units recommended:* 4 English, 3 mathematics, 3 science, 2 social studies, 1 history, 1 Computer Technology.

Financial Aid

Students should submit: FAFSA. The Princeton Review suggests that all financial aid forms be submitted as soon as possible after 1/1. *Need-based scholarships/grants offered:* Federal Pell, SEOG, state scholarships/grants, private scholarships, the school's own gift aid. *Loan aid offered:* Direct Subsidized Stafford, Direct Unsubsidized Stafford, Direct PLUS, FFEL Subsidized Stafford, FFEL Unsubsidized Stafford, FFEL PLUS, Federal Perkins, college/university loans from institutional funds, Alternative Student Loans. Applicants will be notified of awards on a rolling basis beginning 4/1. Federal Work-Study Program available. Institutional employment available.

The Inside Word

Though K-State is chock full of strong students, admission is very undemanding. The process here is also refreshingly straightforward. Basically, get a 21 on the ACT or graduate in the top third of your high school class, and you're in. If you are a Kansas resident, a third way to get accepted is to complete a college-bound curriculum with a 2.0 GPA. Non-residents need at least a 2.5.

THE SCHOOL SAYS "..."

From The Admissions Office

"Kansas State University offers strong academic programs, a lively intellectual atmosphere, a friendly campus community, and an environment where students achieve: K-State's total of Rhodes, Marshall, Truman, Goldwater, and Udall scholars since 1986 ranks first in the nation among state universities. In the Goldwater competition, only Princeton, Harvard, and Duke have produced more winners. K-State's student government was named best in the nation in 1997 and 1995. The forensics squad finished seventh in the 2005 national tournament. A K-State team finished in the top eight at the national debate tournament in 2003. Research facilities include the Konza Prairie, the world's largest tall grass prairie preserve, and the Macdonald Lab, the only university accelerator devoted primarily to atomic physics. Open House, held each spring, is a great way to explore K-State's more than 250 majors and options and 400 student organizations.

"Kansas State University requires ACT or SAT scores to complete a freshman applicant file. The SAT or ACT Writing score is not considered for admission to the university. Students may submit scores from any or all test dates. The best score from any one test date is used."

SELECTIVITY
Admissions Rating	77
# of applicants	9,453
% of applicants accepted	84
% of acceptees attending	47

FRESHMAN PROFILE
Range ACT Composite	20–27
% graduated top 25% of class	62
% graduated top 50% of class	90

DEADLINES
Nonfall registration?	yes

FINANCIAL FACTS
Financial Aid Rating	71
Annual tuition in-state	$5,557
Annual tuition- out-of-state	$15,175
Required fees	$673
% frosh rec. need-based scholarship or grant aid	34
% UG rec. need-based scholarship or grant aid	13
% frosh rec. non-need-based scholarship or grant aid	34
% UG rec. non-need-based scholarship or grant aid	21
% frosh rec. need-based self-help aid	39
% UG rec. need-based self-help aid	43
% frosh rec. athletic scholarships	3
% UG rec. athletic scholarships	2
% UG rec. any financial aid	53
% UG borrow to pay for school	57

KENYON COLLEGE

ADMISSIONS OFFICE, RANSOM HALL, GAMBIER, OH 43022-9623 • ADMISSIONS: 740-427-5776 • FAX: 740-427-5770

CAMPUS LIFE

Quality of Life Rating	85
Fire Safety Rating	64
Green Rating	83
Type of school	private
Environment	rural

STUDENTS

Total undergrad enrollment	1,653
% male/female	48/52
% from out of state	80
% from public high school	51
% live on campus	98
% in (# of) fraternities	25 (8)
% in (# of) sororities	10 (4)
% African American	4
% Asian	5
% Caucasian	81
% Hispanic	3
% Native American	1
% international	3
# of countries represented	35

SURVEY SAYS . . .
No one cheats
Lab facilities are great
Athletic facilities are great
Students are friendly
Campus feels safe
Students are happy
Musical organizations are popular
Lots of beer drinking

ACADEMICS

Academic Rating	96
Calendar	semester
Student/faculty ratio	10:1
Profs interesting rating	99
Profs accessible rating	96
Most common reg class size	10–19 students

MOST POPULAR MAJORS
English language and literature
political science and government
psychology

STUDENTS SAY " . . ."

Academics

At Kenyon College, an "entrancingly pretty" campus and "personal, small, and intimate" classes combine to create "a low-stress setting" for a "liberal arts experience that allows you to make profound changes in your approach to life." Kenyon is primarily "known as a writers' college." It seems fitting, then, that the English department draws the lion's share of students' praise. The school's reputation, however, seems to derive more from the fact that written communication skills are valued and emphasized "in all departments, ranging from history to math," rather than from a course catalogue only filled with fascinating fiction and poetry courses. In terms of academic workload, it "is large but manageable, and students in general never seem overly worried about it." They seem to know they can count on their "brilliant, incredible" professors who "know their stuff" and "are capable of making it accessible and interesting." Professors give students "as much individual time as [they] need" to digest the material. Administratively the school has experienced "a lot of turnover in the last year," leading many students to feel administrators are "still getting their bearings." While they don't "always follow the student body's opinion," they are at least aware of it and "willing to listen" to students' input. Both "professors and administrators love to take an active experience in the lives of Kenyon students outside of the classroom" by doing things like attending student "art shows, sporting events, [and] musical performances." Such beyond-the-books interaction leads many students to feel "the school is more of a family than a business."

Life

Student life at Kenyon is a unique riff on the typical college social experience. For example, "there are a lot of parties in apartments and fraternity lodges and lounges." Although "frats throw most of the parties," they are "almost always open to anyone," and Greeks are "incorporated into the same housing as everyone else," so it "doesn't feel exclusive." What's more, "people have academic conversations even while out at parties," which is certainly not the case at your typical college bash. Basically, Kenyon undergrads "know how to let go and have a good time, but there's always a slightly intellectual edge to it." Parties aren't the only social options on campus. Considering its small size, Kenyon may "have too much programming rather than too little." "There are movies shown at the KAC [Kenyon Athletic Center]," and regularly scheduled "concerts, theatrical and dance productions, and lectures." For "casual fun," students "go to Middle Ground Cafe or the Gambier Grill for coffee or food." Also, "people go to the bar on campus if [they're] of legal age." "In nice weather, Kenyon students are very outdoorsy." Students enjoy "[going] out to the nature preserve (the BFEC) and play[ing] Frisbee or go[ing] for walks." Off-campus entertainment options are pretty scarce, as hometown Gambier is "in the middle of nowhere." Luckily, "Columbus is under an hour away," so "when people need to go somewhere a little more exciting, they drive [there]."

Student Body

A stereotypical Kenyonian is "generally very smart but not pretentious." Most students are "rich, white, and Democratic," which might explain why they "spend lots of money trying to look like they don't have that much money." Kenyon students "love to party, and [are] generally involved in music, sports, or theater." On this "liberal," "laid-back" campus, students are "not competitive" and describe each other as "seriously friendly." People here "take academics very seriously, but also enjoy social lives." They have a "wide variety of interests. It's not unusual to see a neuroscience major paired with a dance minor." As one student sums up, "the 'Kenyon Quirk' is something you hear of often—in that way, everyone is atypical, as it is typical to be different. Hippies, collar-poppers, girlie-girls, goths, nerds, and introverts all find their place at Kenyon."

FINANCIAL AID: 740-427-5430 • E-MAIL: ADMISSIONS@KENYON.EDU • WEBSITE: WWW.KENYON.EDU

THE PRINCETON REVIEW SAYS

Admissions

Very important factors considered include: Application essay, academic GPA, recommendation(s), rigor of secondary school record, character/personal qualities. *Important factors considered include:* Class rank, standardized test scores, extracurricular activities, interview, level of applicant's interest, racial/ethnic status, talent/ability. *Other factors considered include:* Alumni/ae relation, first generation, geographical residence, state residency, volunteer work, work experience. SAT or ACT required; TOEFL required of all international applicants. High school diploma is required and GED is accepted. *Academic units required:* 4 English, 3 mathematics, 3 science, (3 science labs), 3 foreign language, 1 social studies, 2 history, 3 academic electives. *Academic units recommended:* 4 English, 4 mathematics, 4 science, (3 science labs), 4 foreign language, 1 social studies, 3 history, 3 academic electives.

Financial Aid

Students should submit: FAFSA, CSS/Financial Aid PROFILE, noncustodial PROFILE. Regular filing deadline is 2/15. The Princeton Review suggests that all financial aid forms be submitted as soon as possible after 1/1. *Need-based scholarships/grants offered:* Federal Pell, SEOG, state scholarships/grants, private scholarships, the school's own gift aid. *Loan aid offered:* FFEL Subsidized Stafford, FFEL Unsubsidized Stafford, FFEL PLUS, Federal Perkins, college/university loans from institutional funds. Applicants will be notified of awards on or about 4/1. Federal Work-Study Program available. Institutional employment available. Off-campus job opportunities are poor.

The Inside Word

In terms of admissions selectivity, Kenyon is of the first order of selective, small Midwestern, liberal arts schools. Kenyon shares a lot of application and admit overlap with other schools in this niche, and the choice for many students comes down to "best fit." As Kenyon is a writing-intensive institution, applicants should expect that all written material submitted to the school in the admissions process will be scrutinized. Revise and proofread accordingly.

THE SCHOOL SAYS "..."

From The Admissions Office

"Students and alumni alike think of Kenyon as a place that fosters 'learning in the company of friends.' While faculty expectations are rigorous and the work challenging, the academic atmosphere is cooperative, not competitive. Indications of intellectual curiosity and passion for learning, more than just high grades and test scores, are what we look for in applications. Important as well are demonstrated interests in non-academic pursuits, whether in athletics, the arts, writing, or another passion. Life in this small college community is fueled by the talents and enthusiasm of our students, so the admission staff seeks students who have a range of talents and interests.

"The high school transcript, recommendations, the personal statement, and answers on the supplement are of primary importance in reviewing preparedness and fit. Standardized tests (SAT or ACT) are of secondary importance."

SELECTIVITY

Admissions Rating	97
# of applicants	4,626
% of applicants accepted	29
% of acceptees attending	34
# accepting a place on wait list	378
% admitted from wait list	3
# of early decision applicants	359
% accepted early decision	60

FRESHMAN PROFILE

Range SAT Critical Reading	630–730
Range SAT Math	630–690
Range SAT Writing	630–710
Range ACT Composite	28–32
Minimum paper TOEFL	600
Minimum web-based TOEFL	100
Average HS GPA	3.86
% graduated top 10% of class	73
% graduated top 25% of class	94
% graduated top 50% of class	99

DEADLINES

Early decision	
Deadline	11/15
Notification	12/15
Regular	
Deadline	1/15
Notification	4/1
Nonfall registration?	no

APPLICANTS ALSO LOOK AT
AND OFTEN PREFER
Oberlin College
Carleton University
Middlebury College

AND SOMETIMES PREFER
Denison University
Grinnell College

FINANCIAL FACTS

Financial Aid Rating	89
Annual tuition	$39,080
Room and board	$6,590
Required fees	$1,160
Books and supplies	$1,300
% frosh rec. need-based scholarship or grant aid	39
% UG rec. need-based scholarship or grant aid	43
% frosh rec. non-need-based scholarship or grant aid	13
% UG rec. non-need-based scholarship or grant aid	11
% frosh rec. need-based self-help aid	31
% UG rec. need-based self-help aid	38
% frosh rec. any financial aid	57
% UG rec. any financial aid	66
% UG borrow to pay for school	62
Average cumulative indebtedness	$19,489

KNOX COLLEGE

BOX K-148, GALESBURG, IL 61401 • ADMISSIONS: 309-341-7100 • FAX: 309-341-7070

CAMPUS LIFE

Quality of Life Rating	**73**
Fire Safety Rating	**70**
Green Rating	**77**
Type of school	private
Environment	town

STUDENTS

Total undergrad enrollment	1,360
% male/female	42/58
% from out of state	47
% from public high school	79
% live on campus	87
% in (# of) fraternities	30 (5)
% in (# of) sororities	17 (3)
% African American	5
% Asian	7
% Caucasian	72
% Hispanic	5
% Native American	1
% international	7
# of countries represented	35

SURVEY SAYS . . .
No one cheats
Students are friendly
College radio is popular
Theater is popular
Political activism is popular

ACADEMICS

Academic Rating	**94**
Calendar	trimester
Student/faculty ratio	12:1
Profs interesting rating	94
Profs accessible rating	89
Most common reg class size	10–19 students
Most common lab size	10–19 students

MOST POPULAR MAJORS
creative writing
political science and government
psychology

STUDENTS SAY " . . ."

Academics

You can choose your own educational adventure at Knox College, a small school that offers the resources, support, and creative atmosphere students need to get the most out of their college experience. Many students come to Knox for its lauded creative writing major, as well as its "strong pre-medical program." For those still looking for their calling, the good thing about Knox is there are "very minimal requirements for graduation," and students are encouraged to explore a variety of fields. A freshman says, "Even as a science major preparing for medical school, I'm able to take a ton of electives." In this and every way, students can take an active role in planning and executing their educations. At Knox, "if you have an idea or the inkling of an idea, advisers are quick to help your dreams come true," and 80 percent of undergraduates work on independent study projects during college. In a classroom setting, "professors are incredibly informed and enthusiastic about their subject matter," and coursework is rigorous. Of particular note, the academic calendar is divided into three 10-week terms so, in challenging classes like organic chemistry, you may end up "locking yourself in your room and only emerging for food, showers, and class." The upshot is that, "although most classes are pretty challenging academically, it is very easy, and encouraged, to just drop in and ask questions" of your professors. Administrators are likewise available and ready to attend to student concerns. When you've got a question or problem, "there's no shortage of help and making an appointment with anyone in any office is a breeze."

Students

Individuality is valued at Knox. On this small campus, you'll find an "entertaining and diverse" student body, represented by a range of styles, pastimes, and interests, as well as "great socio-economic diversity." It isn't uncommon for students to lovingly describe their classmates as "Knox Awkward," and most undergraduates appreciate the fact that their classmates aren't "overly concerned with appearance or name brands." A sophomore agrees, "It is easy to make friends at Knox, because nobody is pretentious. That's something I really valued when I visited, and what continues to make me happy [now] I am here." If your politics lean to the left, you'll feel right at home at Knox, where students "are very politically and socially liberal." A student tells us, "Conservative students can have a hard time fitting in here when political tensions are high, but I have friends on both ends of the spectrum, and they get along fine when not talking politics." Aside from political predilections, "students tend to be very open-minded and accepting of all things—religion, gender, race, sexuality." In fact, "the running joke about Knox is that LGBT students are out and proud, and conservatives are in the closet."

Life

Academics are top priority for most Knox undergraduates, but there is much more to life than holing up in the library. A junior explains, "While the academics are very demanding and the expectations are high, it is the life outside of the classroom that truly defines the challenges of a Knox education." With more than 100 student clubs and plenty of administrative support, Knox gives students "the opportunity to create their own atmosphere—everything from creating new clubs and courses to doing independent research and putting up art exhibits." Hometown Galesburg gets a universal thumbs down, so "students usually don't go far outside of the college borders." On the weekends, "most fun consists of attending parties and hanging out with friends on campus." In general, "parties tend to revolve around the frats (sororities don't have their own houses)," and drinking is a popular pastime, though certainly not the only one. A student shares, "As a person who chooses not to drink at Knox, I very rarely feel excluded from activities. I can easily go to a party and refuse alcohol without pressure." For a mellow evening, "Knox is always bringing in political speakers, comedians, performing groups, or individuals to present seminars." To add to the charms, living facilities are top-notch, and "the dorms and suite-style living do wonders for comfort and residential satisfaction."

FINANCIAL AID: 309-341-7149 • E-MAIL: ADMISSION@KNOX.EDU • WEBSITE: WWW.KNOX.EDU

THE PRINCETON REVIEW SAYS

Admissions

Very important factors considered include: Academic GPA, rigor of secondary school record. *Important factors considered include:* Class rank, application essay, recommendation(s), character/personal qualities. *Other factors considered include:* Standardized test scores, alumni/ae relation, extracurricular activities, first generation, geographical residence, interview, level of applicant's interest, racial/ethnic status, state residency, talent/ability, volunteer work. TOEFL required of all international applicants. High school diploma is required and GED is accepted. *Academic units recommended:* 4 English, 4 mathematics, 4 science, (3 science labs), 3 foreign language, 2 social studies, 2 history.

Financial Aid

Students should submit: FAFSA, institution's own financial aid form. The Princeton Review suggests that all financial aid forms be submitted as soon as possible after 1/1. *Need-based scholarships/grants offered:* Federal Pell, SEOG, state scholarships/grants, private scholarships, the school's own gift aid. *Loan aid offered:* Direct Subsidized Stafford, Direct Unsubsidized Stafford, Direct PLUS, Federal Perkins, college/university loans from institutional funds. Applicants will be notified of awards on a rolling basis beginning 3/15. Federal Work-Study Program available. Institutional employment available. Off-campus job opportunities are fair.

The Inside Word

With just fewer than 1,400 students, Knox makes diversity a priority, attracting students from 47 states and 48 countries. Both qualitative and quantitative factors are important to Knox, and admissions are competitive. Seventy-six percent of incoming freshman rank in the top quarter of their high school class.

THE SCHOOL SAYS "..."

From The Admissions Office

"Knox was founded on the idea that education has the power to confer a kind of freedom—what we've come to call 'freedom to flourish.' On the surface, 'freedom to flourish' is a simple and powerful concept—it is the knowledge and skills one needs to live a rewarding personal, professional, and civic life. But 'freedom to flourish' also has more subtle meaning that touches on how education happens at Knox.

"Most schools ask what you want to study and give you a checklist of courses needed for that degree. Knox asks, 'What do you want to know, and what do you want to do with that knowledge?' Within the context of the goals and milestones of one of our many majors, you and your advisor will develop a personalized educational plan of classes, internships, off-campus study, and independent research projects that meet the agenda you set for yourself. In this sense, a Knox education is an act of imagination, an act of entrepreneurship, an act of freedom.'

"That self-direction doesn't end in advising sessions and course selection. You'll be encouraged to bring your own interests and perspective to every class you take, and you'll be challenged to apply what you learn to the world around you. In the end you will learn how to set goals, how to figure out what you need to know to achieve those goals, and how to identify and collaborate with mentors who can help you along the way. That is 'freedom to flourish.'

"At Knox, you'll never be a number. Knox reviews each application holistically, fully considering a student's academic record, course selection, and performance (grades), as well as essays, recommendations, interviews, and other accomplishments. As a result, the submission of SAT or ACT scores is optional for most applicants."

SELECTIVITY

Admissions Rating	93
# of applicants	2,750
% of applicants accepted	66
% of acceptees attending	20
# accepting a place on wait list	85
% admitted from wait list	8

FRESHMAN PROFILE

Range SAT Critical Reading	590–700
Range SAT Math	580–660
Range SAT Writing	560–670
Range ACT Composite	26–31
Minimum paper TOEFL	550
Minimum computer TOEFL	213
Minimum web-based TOEFL	80
Average HS GPA	3.43
% graduated top 10% of class	44
% graduated top 25% of class	76
% graduated top 50% of class	98

DEADLINES

Early action	
Deadline	12/1
Notification	12/31
Regular	
Priority	12/1
Deadline	2/1
Notification	3/31
Nonfall registration?	no

APPLICANTS ALSO LOOK AT

AND SOMETIMES PREFER
Beloit College
Earlham College
Illinois Wesleyan University

AND RARELY PREFER
Washington University in St. Louis
Lawrence University
Macalester College
Augustana College (IL)

FINANCIAL FACTS

Financial Aid Rating	88
Annual tuition	$31,575
Room and board	$7,146
Required fees	$336
Books and supplies	$900
% frosh rec. need-based scholarship or grant aid	75
% UG rec. need-based scholarship or grant aid	67
% frosh rec. non-need-based scholarship or grant aid	8
% UG rec. non-need-based scholarship or grant aid	6
% frosh rec. need-based self-help aid	51
% UG rec. need-based self-help aid	61
% frosh rec. any financial aid	97
% UG rec. any financial aid	98
% UG borrow to pay for school	70
Average cumulative indebtedness	$22,749

LAFAYETTE COLLEGE

118 MARKLE HALL, EASTON, PA 18042 • ADMISSIONS: 610-330-5100 • FAX: 610-330-5355

CAMPUS LIFE
Quality of Life Rating	81
Fire Safety Rating	60*
Green Rating	98
Type of school	private
Affiliation	Presbyterian
Environment	village

STUDENTS
Total undergrad enrollment	2,352
% male/female	54/46
% from out of state	75
% from public high school	68
% live on campus	94
% in (# of) fraternities	27 (7)
% in (# of) sororities	39 (6)
% African American	5
% Asian	4
% Caucasian	71
% Hispanic	5
% international	7
# of countries represented	46

SURVEY SAYS . . .
Lab facilities are great
Athletic facilities are great
Career services are great
School is well run
Campus feels safe

ACADEMICS
Academic Rating	92
Calendar	semester
Student/faculty ratio	11:1
Profs interesting rating	87
Profs accessible rating	88
Most common reg class size	10–19 students
Most common lab size	10–19 students

STUDENTS SAY ". . ."

Academics

Lafayette College is "a small liberal arts college" that is "especially strong in engineering and physical sciences." There are "very cool" undergraduate research opportunities. Career services "are also phenomenal" and "an excellent alumni network" provides abundant career and internship opportunities. The "efficient, helpful, and very accessible" administration "generally listens to the comments of the students" and does "a great job of keeping the school running smoothly." The biggest academic complaint at Lafayette is that the range of courses offered in a typical semester is too narrow. The classes offered tend to be "small" and "difficult." "You must study," reports an economics major. "Not every professor is the greatest." "There is the occasional professor who makes you want to tear your hair out." On the whole, though, Lafayette's professors are "really knowledgeable and really do care about how you do and what you take out of the class." "I feel like I get a lot of individual attention," says a chemical engineering major. "Professors will explain difficult material until you understand," relates a math major, " and not just say it once and look at you like you're stupid if you still don't understand." Outside of class, faculty members typically remain "extremely available" and "beg you to talk to them and meet with them."

Life

Lafayette is located on a hill above Easton, PA. The "gorgeous," "scenic" campus is full of "picturesque North Eastern college-like buildings." A few dorms "are in desperate need of renovation," though, and the "repetitive" food is "not that great tasting." Socially, Lafayette is reportedly "very homey." "At almost any social gathering, there will be people you know." The "amazing" sports center is "a very popular spot." "Lafayette is a very athletic school and most students participate in either varsity athletics or in a club or intramural sport," explains a sophomore. In the fall, "football games are extremely spirited." The annual contest against rival Lehigh "is attended by basically the whole student body." Beyond sports, many students tell us "there is always something to do on campus." "Everyone is really involved," they say. There are "a capella concerts, comedians, movies, and club-sponsored activities." A "multitude of speakers" visit campus. There's "a broad range" of religious groups. Lafayette also has a "huge" Greek system. Other students contend "there should be more to do." "I have not experienced the outpouring of entertainment at the school," grumbles a freshman. Whatever the case, "the party scene is really fun." The frats and various sports teams throw parties "Wednesday through Saturday nights" and many students participate. However, many others don't. "Half the campus considers Lafayette a party school and the other half doesn't know what school the first half is talking about," suggests a junior.

Student Body

Lafayette is a haven for "well-rounded," "preppy," "smart jocks," and "your classic white rich kid" "from New York, New Jersey, or Pennsylvania." "There is certainly a mold," admits a senior. "Everyone is pretty similar." "Collar-popping" suburbanites are everywhere. "Crazy-colored hair and facial piercings are not really something you see," observes a first-year student. "You will see a lot of smiling and door-holding," though. Students take pride in the "incredibly friendly" vibe at Lafayette. Many students are "hard-partying" types. There are also "the kids who live in the library 20 hours a day." Most students fall somewhere in the middle. "People like to have a good time but they are also serious about their work and are genuinely interested in their area of study." "Both conservatives and liberals" will find soul mates at Lafayette but many students are "almost completely apathetic" when it comes to politics. Some students "have a snobby attitude," but others either don't flaunt their wealth or don't come from money at all. "We're not all running around with iPhones and Fendi bags," says a sophomore. Ethnic diversity is pretty minimal. "There are a few minority and foreign students but they hang out with each other in their own little cliques."

FINANCIAL AID: 610-330-5055 • E-MAIL: ADMISSIONS@LAFAYETTE.EDU • WEBSITE: WWW.LAFAYETTE.EDU

THE PRINCETON REVIEW SAYS

Admissions

Very important factors considered include: Academic GPA, rigor of secondary school record. *Important factors considered include:* Class rank, application essay, recommendation(s), standardized test scores, character/personal qualities, extracurricular activities, talent/ability. *Other factors considered include:* Alumni/ae relation, first generation, geographical residence, interview, level of applicant's interest, racial/ethnic status, volunteer work, work experience. SAT Subject Tests recommended; SAT or ACT required; ACT with Writing component required; TOEFL required of all international applicants. High school diploma or equivalent is not required. *Academic units recommended:* 4 English, 3 mathematics, 2 science, (2 science labs), 2 foreign language, 5 academic electives.

Financial Aid

Students should submit: FAFSA, CSS/Financial Aid PROFILE, noncustodial PROFILE, business/farm supplement. Regular filing deadline is 3/15. The Princeton Review suggests that all financial aid forms be submitted as soon as possible after 1/1. *Need-based scholarships/grants offered:* Federal Pell, SEOG, state scholarships/grants, private scholarships, the school's own gift aid. *Loan aid offered:* FFEL Subsidized Stafford, FFEL Unsubsidized Stafford, FFEL PLUS, Federal Perkins, college/university loans from institutional funds, HELP loan to parents (Lafayette Loan Program). Applicants will be notified of awards on or about 4/1. Federal Work-Study Program available. Institutional employment available. Off-campus job opportunities are good.

The Inside Word

Applications are reviewed three to five times and evaluated by as many as nine different committee members. In all cases, students who continually seek challenges and are willing to take risks academically win out over those who play it safe to maintain a high GPA.

THE SCHOOL SAYS ". . ."

From The Admissions Office

"We choose students individually, one by one, and we hope that the ones we choose will approach their education the same way, as a highly individual enterprise. Our first-year seminars have enrollments limited to 15 or 16 students each in order to introduce the concept of learning not as passive receipt of information but as an active, participatory process. Our low average class size and 11:1 student/teacher ratio reflect that same philosophy. We also devote substantial resources to our Marquis Scholars Program, to one-on-one faculty-student mentoring relationships, and to other programs in engineering within a liberal arts context, giving Lafayette its distinctive character, articulated in our second-year seminars exploring values in science and technology. Lafayette provides an environment in which its students can discover their own personal capacity for learning, personal growth, and leadership.

"Submission of scores from either the SAT Reasoning Test or American College Testing Program (ACT) is required. If taking the ACT, the optional Writing Section is required. SAT Subject Test results are recommended but not required. Scores must be submitted directly from the testing agency or via your college counselor on an 'official' high school transcript or testing summary sheet."

SELECTIVITY

Admissions Rating	96
# of applicants	6,357
% of applicants accepted	37
% of acceptees attending	25
# accepting a place on wait list	459
% admitted from wait list	10
# of early decision applicants	436
% accepted early decision	56

FRESHMAN PROFILE

Range SAT Critical Reading	580–670
Range SAT Math	610–700
Range SAT Writing	590–680
Range ACT Composite	26–30
Minimum paper TOEFL	550
Average HS GPA	3.53
% graduated top 10% of class	65
% graduated top 25% of class	93
% graduated top 50% of class	99

DEADLINES

Early decision	
Deadline	2/15
Regular	
Deadline	1/1
Notification	4/1
Nonfall registration?	yes

APPLICANTS ALSO LOOK AT

AND OFTEN PREFER
Cornell University

AND SOMETIMES PREFER
Lehigh University
Bucknell University
Colgate University

FINANCIAL FACTS

Financial Aid Rating	94
Annual tuition	$37,520
Room and board	$11,799
Books and supplies	$1,000
Required fees	$970
% frosh rec. need-based scholarship or grant aid	49
% UG rec. need-based scholarship or grant aid	47
% frosh rec. non-need-based scholarship or grant aid	7
% UG rec. non-need-based scholarship or grant aid	5
% frosh rec. need-based self-help aid	39
% UG rec. need-based self-help aid	37
% frosh rec. athletic scholarships	3
% UG rec. athletic scholarships	1
% UG borrow to pay for school	54
Average cumulative indebtedness	$18,747

LAKE FOREST COLLEGE

555 NORTH SHERIDAN ROAD, LAKE FOREST, IL 60045 • ADMISSIONS: 847-735-5000 • FAX: 847-735-6291

CAMPUS LIFE

Quality of Life Rating	73
Fire Safety Rating	69
Green Rating	60*
Type of school	private
Environment	village

STUDENTS

Total undergrad enrollment	1,350
% male/female	41/59
% from out of state	60
% from public high school	61
% live on campus	80
% in (# of) fraternities	3 (2)
% in (# of) sororities	17 (5)
% African American	5
% Asian	4
% Caucasian	75
% Hispanic	6
% international	10
# of countries represented	69

SURVEY SAYS . . .

Great food on campus
Campus feels safe
Lots of beer drinking
Hard liquor is popular

ACADEMICS

Academic Rating	91
Calendar	semester
Student/faculty ratio	12:1
Profs interesting rating	89
Profs accessible rating	93
Most common reg class size	10–19 students
Most common lab size	10–19 students

MOST POPULAR MAJORS

business/commerce
communication studies/speech
communication and rhetoric
economics

STUDENTS SAY ". . ."

Academics

Students at Lake Forest College rave about "an extraordinary educational environment where students share a close bond with their professors while living and studying in an intimate college community amongst an enriching Chicago background." A broad ranging general education curriculum "emphasizes giving each student an individual and well-rounded education in the liberal arts," one that many pursue in their majors; nearly one-in-10 here majors in English, and departments in psychology, history, the social sciences, and communication are all substantial (as are programs in business and in economics). The curriculum also "emphasizes diversity and global activism a lot, which gives many students a broadened worldview," while the entire Lake Forest experience, academic and extracurricular, "does a good job at incorporating Chicago into the academics and social lives of students." The school differs from similar-sized school in one way; students tell us that "Lake Forest is really what you make it for yourself. The opportunities are there for the taking, but no one is going to hold your hand for four years and tell you what to do." The school is not as well known as it might be if it were located in the Northeast, leading some to describe it as "an undercover gem" and explaining why many regard it as "a safety school for those who can't quite make it into the big-name liberal arts, and a decent compromise for geniuses who could get into Harvard but can't afford the tuition."

Life

The area surrounding Lake Forest College "is an extremely wealthy community, so many of the businesses that are there are too expensive for the average student. There is just one bar, and everything shuts down very early," so "there isn't a lot to do in town" for LFC undergraduates. Students do avail themselves of "the basics: a couple of good restaurants (The Lantern, Burger King, Egg Harbor), a grocery store and pharmacy, and a post office," but "students really have to leave the city to have fun." Vernon Hills, "with a large mall and lots of restaurants, "is about 20 minutes away," but "the best thing to do for fun is go to Chicago! It is only an hour away and only costs $5 for the round trip on the weekends." The train ride delivers "a welcome escape from what can eventually get claustrophobic in Lake Forest College/City. A lot of students seem to get bored of Chicago quickly after they've hit downtown and the museums...as a lifelong Chicagoan I find this silly! There's a reason it's called a 'city of neighborhoods,' and the Loop is probably the least exciting one when it comes to finding your niche." In the past students have noted, lack of activities" outside of movies, athletic events, occasional performances, and "a few parties thrown by different student organizations." However Lake Forest is set to break ground in 2009 with a 63,000 square foot Recreation, Sport and Fitness center. Saturday is the big on-campus party night, "especially in Gregory and Harlan Hall."

Student Body

The typical Lake Forest student "is an intelligent kid who doesn't want to completely devote his life to studying, [and] likes to party," but even though students have the impression that "most of the students in this school come from wealthy families," this doesn't mean there's some kind of class war going on, as everyone is generally quite friendly, and if they aren't, they are at least civil." Minorities are most often represented among the large population of international students, who "give the campus a more diverse feeling." These students "are a great asset to learn about the world outside of the U.S.! There is a special international residence hall, but all of the international students get along really well with everyone else."

FINANCIAL AID: 847-735-5103 • E-MAIL: ADMISSIONS@LAKEFOREST.EDU • WEBSITE: WWW.LAKEFOREST.EDU

THE PRINCETON REVIEW SAYS

Admissions

Very important factors considered include: Academic GPA, recommendation(s), rigor of secondary school record, interview. *Important factors considered include:* Application essay, character/personal qualities, extracurricular activities, level of applicant's interest, talent/ability. *Other factors considered include:* Class rank, standardized test scores, alumni/ae relation, first generation, geographical residence, volunteer work, work experience. TOEFL required of all international applicants. High school diploma is required and GED is accepted. *Academic units required:* 4 English, 3 mathematics, 3 science, (3 science labs), 2 foreign language, 2 social studies, 2 history, 3 academic electives. *Academic units recommended:* 4 English, 4 mathematics, 4 science, (4 science labs), 4 foreign language, 2 social studies, 2 history, 3 academic electives, 1 Honors or AP course.

Financial Aid

Students should submit: FAFSA, institution's own financial aid form, Federal Income Tax return. The Princeton Review suggests that all financial aid forms be submitted as soon as possible after 1/1. *Need-based scholarships/grants offered:* Federal Pell, SEOG, state scholarships/grants, private scholarships, the school's own gift aid. *Loan aid offered:* FFEL Subsidized Stafford, FFEL Unsubsidized Stafford, FFEL PLUS, Federal Perkins, Private loans. Applicants will be notified of awards on a rolling basis beginning 3/15. Federal Work-Study Program available. Institutional employment available. Off-campus job opportunities are good.

The Inside Word

Lake Forest is small enough to give each application it receives close and careful consideration. Solid high school performers should have little difficulty gaining admission, but keep in mind that Lake Forest has a prep-school-at-the-college-level feel and likes to assess the whole candidate, not just grades and test scores. In fact, test scores are optional. The school will look closely at the graded essay you submit with your application, so choose carefully.

THE SCHOOL SAYS "..."

From The Admissions Office

"Lake Forest College's beautiful 107-acre campus is located 30 miles north of downtown Chicago along the shore of Lake Michigan. Abundant internship and research opportunities, close interaction with highly skilled professors, and innovative programs in nearby Chicago set Lake Forest College apart.

"The 1,400 students represent 69 countries and 45 states. With small class sizes and a large on-campus residential community, Lake Forest fosters interaction and shared experiences that are essential to success in a global world. The faculty is dedicated teachers and accomplished scholars and they do all the teaching; you will not find teaching assistants at Lake Forest.

"The College's proximity to Chicago offers students unique experiential learning opportunities, and professors regularly use the city's resources to complement coursework. The College's Center for Chicago Programs facilitates study and internships at Chicago institutions as well as trips to the city's dozens of ethnic neighborhoods.

"With more than 80 student-run organizations and clubs, 17 varsity NCAA Division III teams, and a variety of intramural and club sports, students find many opportunities outside the classroom.

"Lake Forest has a test-optional admission process permitting students to choose whether or not to have their ACT or SAT scores considered for admission. International students and students applying for certain academic scholarships will still be required to submit scores. Lake Forest evaluates each student based on qualities that determine success in college: strong academic performance in a challenging high-school curriculum, leadership experience, and extracurricular involvement and individual talent."

SELECTIVITY	
Admissions Rating	86
# of applicants	2,551
% of applicants accepted	59
% of acceptees attending	25

FRESHMAN PROFILE	
Range SAT Critical Reading	520–640
Range SAT Math	530–630
Range SAT Writing	530–630
Range ACT Composite	23–28
Minimum paper TOEFL	550
Minimum computer TOEFL	220
Average HS GPA	3.51
% graduated top 10% of class	36
% graduated top 25% of class	63
% graduated top 50% of class	88

DEADLINES	
Early decision	
Deadline	12/1
Notification	12/20
Early action	
Deadline	12/1
Notification	1/20
Regular	
Priority	2/15
Notification	3/20
Nonfall registration?	yes

FINANCIAL FACTS	
Financial Aid Rating	99
Annual tuition	$32,130
Room and board	$7,724
Required fees	$390
Books and supplies	$800
% frosh rec. need-based scholarship or grant aid	75
% UG rec. need-based scholarship or grant aid	73
% frosh rec. non-need-based scholarship or grant aid	9
% UG rec. non-need-based scholarship or grant aid	9
% frosh rec. need-based self-help aid	64
% UG rec. need-based self-help aid	60
% frosh rec. any financial aid	90
% UG rec. any financial aid	90
% UG borrow to pay for school	74
Average cumulative indebtedness	$23,962

LAWRENCE UNIVERSITY

PO Box 599, Appleton, WI 54912-0599 • Admissions: 920-832-6500 • Fax: 920-832-6782

CAMPUS LIFE

Quality of Life Rating	92
Fire Safety Rating	71
Green Rating	83
Type of school	private
Environment	city

STUDENTS

Total undergrad enrollment	1,452
% male/female	46/54
% from out of state	62
% from public high school	76
% live on campus	98
% in (# of) fraternities	22 (5)
% in (# of) sororities	12 (3)
% African American	2
% Asian	3
% Caucasian	72
% Hispanic	2
% international	8
# of countries represented	51

SURVEY SAYS . . .
No one cheats
Lab facilities are great
Students are friendly
Campus feels safe
Low cost of living
Students are happy
Musical organizations are popular
Theater is popular

ACADEMICS

Academic Rating	96
Calendar	trimester
Student/faculty ratio	9:1
Profs interesting rating	91
Profs accessible rating	99
Most common	
reg class size	10–19 students

MOST POPULAR MAJORS
biology/biological sciences

STUDENTS SAY ". . ."

Academics

The Lawrence University experience is defined by "intense academics, extreme involvement in extracurricular activities, and a near-obsession with music." Also, located between Oshkosh and Green Bay, LU is a place where "You will freeze your butt off walking to class, have a professor say the most profound thing ever, and then not notice that its 20 below as you walk to the library to study your ass off." A prestigious music conservatory and "great science programs" are the top attractions, but the school also excels in the humanities and social sciences. As one student puts it, "Lawrence doesn't have just one strength, it has many unique and diverse strengths, and I think this quality is reflected in the students." Those students help make LU "an intellectual place, as any good college should be. People are all brilliant in their own ways here, and it's fantastic to find out how." A trimester academic calendar means "classes condense a lot of information (and often a lot of work!) in a shorter period of time" so students "are busy from the first week until the end of the finals week. Stress levels never go down." Fortunately, the student body "is really friendly" and cooperative, resulting in "an intellectually stimulating—not academically cutthroat—environment that fosters both academic and personal growth." LU is a small school where "professors are really willing to work one-on-one with students" but "lacks some technologies and resources that larger schools might have."

Life

People at Lawrence "are generally very busy. Even though each student has only three classes (music students have more), the terms are only 10 weeks long and there is a lot to study." When they can get a break, students are "at a group meeting (Habitat for Humanity, Lambda Sigma, Health and Wellness, etc.), at practice (varsity sports and club sports), or spending some time with other people." Social life on campus "is very strong. People with a wide variety of interests come together and form diverse groups of friends. Athletes, artists, musicians, and academics can usually all be found at one party, and on any given weekend there is a party catering to each distinct social group." Undergrads "are big into the arts and nerdy things," and because "lots of students are musical and artistic...there are interesting outlets on campus" for their creativity. "There are always different concerts, recitals, and performances to go to. Our symphony is very good and popular guest artists visit and perform." All the action on campus helps compensate for the fact that "Appleton is a very small, boring town" with "basically nothing to do" specifically, "no good concert venues, no strong local music scene, and no independent theater or art galleries."

Student Body

The typical Lawrentian "cannot be better described than as a 'cool nerd.'" They seem to be the types of kids who started realizing being smart and artsy was cool some time late in high school, so they have no false delusions about how cool they are. They have strong senses of culture and also have strong senses of satire against conventional norms." They "are interested in learning for the sake of learning, not studying for the sake of receiving the highest grade. Students often study in public areas or in small groups, and always become very involved in the course material. Lawrence is a cooperative, rather than a competitive, learning environment." Students are "probably from Wisconsin, the Twin Cities, Colorado or Portland." Some here detect "a bit of a Sharks-and-Jets division between conservatory and college students at times as they compete for the title of Busiest Student," but the competition is generally friendly and benign.

FINANCIAL AID: 920-832-6583 • E-MAIL: EXCEL@LAWRENCE.EDU • WEBSITE: WWW.LAWRENCE.EDU

THE PRINCETON REVIEW SAYS

Admissions

Very important factors considered include: Class rank, academic GPA, rigor of secondary school record. *Important factors considered include:* Application essay, recommendation(s), character/personal qualities, extracurricular activities, talent/ability. *Other factors considered include:* Standardized test scores, alumni/ae relation, first generation, interview, racial/ethnic status, volunteer work, work experience. TOEFL required of all international applicants. High school diploma is required and GED is not accepted. *Academic units required:* 4 English. *Academic units recommended:* 3 mathematics, 3 science, 2 foreign language, 2 social studies, 2 history.

Financial Aid

Students should submit: FAFSA, institution's own financial aid form, copies of 2007 Federal Tax Returns & W-2 forms for parent and student, noncustodial parent form. The Princeton Review suggests that all financial aid forms be submitted as soon as possible after 1/1. *Need-based scholarships/grants offered:* Federal Pell, SEOG, state scholarships/grants, private scholarships, the school's own gift aid. *Loan aid offered:* Direct Subsidized Stafford, Direct Unsubsidized Stafford, Direct PLUS, FFEL PLUS, Federal Perkins. Applicants will be notified of awards on a rolling basis beginning 3/1. Federal Work-Study Program available. Institutional employment available. Off-campus job opportunities are good.

The Inside Word

Lawrence attracts an accomplished applicant pool, so don't let the high admit rate fool you. You'll need solid high school credentials to get in here. The traditional route is the best way to ensure success: a consistently challenging high school curriculum, good standardized-test scores, well considered and constructed application essays, and an impressive on-campus interview. Of these, standardized test scores are least important. Lawrence will even ignore the scores if you ask the school do so. Lawrence accepts the common application.

THE SCHOOL SAYS "..."

From The Admissions Office

"Lawrence believes college should not be a one-size-fits-all experience, and that you'll learn best when you're educated as a unique individual. Within our college of liberal arts and sciences and our conservatory of music—both devoted exclusively to undergraduate education—you'll have unparalleled opportunities to collaborate closely with your professors in small classes (90 percent have fewer than 20 students in them; 65 percent have total enrollments of one). Our 1,450 students come from nearly every state and more than 50 countries to enjoy the distinctive benefits of this engaged—and engaging—community. It's a close-knit, residential, 24/7 campus filled with smart and talented people who are pursuing an astonishing variety of academic and extracurricular interests. Our picturesque, residential campus is nestled on the banks of the Fox River in Appleton, Wisconsin, (metro population: 200,000), one of the fastest growing metropolitan areas in the Midwest. Björklunden, our 425-acre estate on more than one mile of pristine Lake Michigan shoreline (two hours north of campus), provides educational and recreational opportunities for students to enhance their on-campus learning experiences.

"We seek students who are intellectual, imaginative, and innovative: qualities best quantified from a thorough review of your curriculum, academic performance, essay, activities, and recommendations. Accordingly, Lawrence considers—but does not require—the ACT and the SAT in our review of applications for admission and scholarship."

SELECTIVITY

Admissions Rating	94
# of applicants	2,618
% of applicants accepted	59
% of acceptees attending	25
# accepting a place on wait list	54
% admitted from wait list	63
# of early decision applicants	37
% accepted early decision	95

FRESHMAN PROFILE

Range SAT Critical Reading	590–720
Range SAT Math	610–720
Range SAT Writing	610–690
Range ACT Composite	27–31
Minimum paper TOEFL	575
Minimum computer TOEFL	233
Minimum web-based TOEFL	90
Average HS GPA	3.67
% graduated top 10% of class	41
% graduated top 25% of class	73
% graduated top 50% of class	97

DEADLINES

Early decision	
Deadline	11/15
Notification	12/1
Early action	
Deadline	12/1
Notification	1/15
Regular	
Deadline	1/15
Notification	4/1
Nonfall registration?	no

APPLICANTS ALSO LOOK AT

AND OFTEN PREFER
Saint Olaf College, Macalester College
University of Wisconsin—Madison
Beloit College, Carleton University

AND SOMETIMES PREFER
Oberlin College
Illinois Wesleyan University
Grinnell College, Knox College
Northwestern University

FINANCIAL FACTS

Financial Aid Rating	95
Annual tuition	$34,326
Room and board	$7,053
Fees	$270
Books and supplies	$750
% frosh rec. need-based scholarship or grant aid	67
% UG rec. need-based scholarship or grant aid	66
% frosh rec. need-based self-help aid	48
% UG rec. need-based self-help aid	51
% frosh rec. any financial aid	92
% UG rec. any financial aid	91
% UG borrow to pay for school	69
Average cumulative indebtedness	$26,054

LEHIGH UNIVERSITY

27 MEMORIAL DRIVE WEST, BETHLEHEM, PA 18015 • ADMISSIONS: 610-758-3100 • FAX: 610-758-4361

CAMPUS LIFE

Quality of Life Rating	**71**
Fire Safety Rating	**91**
Green Rating	**84**
Type of school	private
Environment	city

STUDENTS

Total undergrad enrollment	4,856
% male/female	58/42
% from out of state	75
% live on campus	69
% in (# of) fraternities	30 (17)
% in (# of) sororities	34 (8)
% African American	3
% Asian	6
% Caucasian	74
% Hispanic	5
% international	3
# of countries represented	49

SURVEY SAYS . . .

Great library
Low cost of living
Students are happy
Frats and sororities dominate social scene
Student publications are popular
Lots of beer drinking
Hard liquor is popular

ACADEMICS

Academic Rating	**86**
Calendar	semester
Student/faculty ratio	9:1
Profs interesting rating	78
Profs accessible rating	85
Most common reg class size	10–19 students
Most common lab size	20–29 students

MOST POPULAR MAJORS

accounting
finance
mechanical engineering
psychology

STUDENTS SAY ". . ."

Academics

The main thing students at Lehigh University in Bethelehem, Pennsylvania seem to share is a general love for the school and its entire way of life, as evidenced by the "amazing" alumni base that returns to the school frequently (and provides for good networking). Despite rigorous academics, Lehigh "maintains a substantial social scene," and "work hard, play hard is not just a saying here—it's the lifestyle." Students have "to work for grades, they are not just given out," and outside of the classroom, there's a strong emphasis on experimental learning and real-world applications. The engineering and business programs are particularly strong here, as are the international relations and biology departments. Though tuition is dear, new financial aid policies have been put into place and "the school lives up to its academic reputation...You definitely get your money's worth at the end of the day." The level of instruction here is "top-notch," and "the classes aren't necessarily a drag to go to." Teaching becomes better" as students begin to take more and more upper level classes. Instructors "are always available and want to help you out," and they "really try to have a positive relationship with all of the students." Still a few professors seem to be more interested in their research than their teachings. "For my Folktales and Fairytales class, we were invited to the professor's house to tell stories around her fireplace," says a senior. The administration "does not take into account student opinion as well as it could," and many students wish it was more transparent in its reasoning for changes (especially concerning the recent crackdown on partying, the surest way to get a Lehigh student up in arms), but most students are satisfied with the level of accessibility.

Life

Unless you have a car, there really isn't much to do in the immediate surrounding area. The school does provide a shuttle to some common off-campus destinations and the town is home to many festivals throughout the year. On campus, studying takes up most weeknights, and though there are events "here and there," "drinking is king at Lehigh" and "Greek life is everything." "It's party hard, work hard. We have all the Ivy League rejects who are crazy competitive combined with crazy parties. What's better?" asks a sophomore. Though the jury is out as to how crucial drinking is to Lehigh social life, "the school provides a lot of alcohol-free activities such as game night, comedians, movie nights, etc.," and there is "plenty of socializing" through sports, student organizations, and plain old hanging out. "Even kids who are obsessed with video games won't just sit and play alone in their rooms. They'll find others with the same interest and do so together," says a student. "There are tons of ways to get involved on campus and have a good time, you just have to get creative," says another.

Student Body

It's a "white and preppy" world at Lehigh, where most students come from the Northeast and the typical student's economic background can be described as "appreciates the finer things in life." People here "like to look good" and "tend to dress up for classes very often," and the popped collar has a home at Lehigh. There are still "a few splashes of ethnicity" here, and while there used to be a lot of pressure to fit that specific mold, now "there are a lot of different types of students. It's a friendlier campus." The school has actually seen a rise in enrollment by students from underrepresented backgrounds in recent years, and continues to try and build diversity. Socially, there are three types of students at Lehigh: "those who are Greek, those whose friends are Greek, and those who have no friends." The final group is in the extreme minority, as "it isn't hard to find a friend at Lehigh," and even the atypical students "usually just connect with each other." Ever the balanced bunch, Lehigh students "recognize the scholastic opportunity that Lehigh provides but also thrive on the party scene."

FINANCIAL AID: 610-758-3181 • E-MAIL: ADMISSIONS@LEHIGH.EDU • WEBSITE: WWW.LEHIGH.EDU

THE PRINCETON REVIEW SAYS

Admissions

Very important factors considered include: Recommendation(s), Academic GPA, rigor of secondary school record. *Important factors considered include:* Application essay, standardized test scores, character/personal qualities, extracurricular activities, level of applicant's interest, recommendations. *Other factors considered include:* Volunteer work, alumni/ae relation, first generation, geographical residence, racial/ethnic status, work experience. SAT or ACT required; ACT with Writing component required; TOEFL required of all international applicants. High school diploma or equivalent is not required. *Academic units required:* 4 English, 3 mathematics, 2 science, (2 science labs), 2 foreign language, 2 social studies, 3 academic electives.

Financial Aid

Students should submit: FAFSA, CSS/Financial Aid PROFILE, noncustodial PROFILE, business/farm supplement. Regular filing deadline is 2/15. The Princeton Review suggests that all financial aid forms be submitted as soon as possible after 1/1. *Need-based scholarships/grants offered:* Federal Pell, SEOG, state scholarships/grants, private scholarships, the school's own gift aid, United Negro College Fund. *Loan aid offered:* FFEL Subsidized Stafford, FFEL Unsubsidized Stafford, FFEL PLUS, Federal Perkins, college/university loans from institutional funds, Private Educational Alternative Loans. Applicants will be notified of awards on or about 3/30. Federal Work-Study Program available. Institutional employment available. Off-campus job opportunities are good.

The Inside Word

Lots of work at bolstering Lehigh's public recognition for overall academic quality has paid off. Liberal arts candidates will now find the admissions process to be highly selective. Students without solidly impressive academic credentials will have a rough time getting in regardless of their choice of programs, as will unenthusiastic, but academically strong candidates who have clearly chosen Lehigh as a safety.

THE SCHOOL SAYS "..."

From The Admissions Office

"Lehigh University is located 50 miles north of Philadelphia and 75 miles southwest of New York City in Bethlehem, Pennsylvania, where a cultural renaissance has taken place with the opening of more than a dozen ethnic restaurants, the addition of several boutiques and galleries, and Lehigh's Campus Square residential/retail complex. Lehigh combines learning opportunities of a large research university with the personal attention of a small, private college, by offering an education that integrates courses from four colleges and dozens of fields of study. Students customize their experience to their interests by tailoring majors and academic programs from more than 2,000 courses, carrying a double major, or taking courses outside their college or major field of study. Lehigh offers unique learning opportunities through interdisciplinary programs such as the Integrated Degree in Engineering, Arts, and Sciences and Computer Science and Business. You'll learn from and work alongside faculty who are leaders in their field and bring the latest knowledge and newest discoveries to classrooms, laboratories, and workshops to enhance your educational experience and give you real-world exposure. Investigation, innovation, and global exploration will drive your educational experience at Lehigh. Here, we share a common set of core values: integrity and honesty, equitable community, academic freedom, intellectual curiosity, and leadership. Lehigh's vibrant campus life offers many social and extracurricular activities. Choose from 150 and 40 intramural and club sports, in which over 60 percent of undergraduates participate.

"Lehigh requires students to submit scores from the SAT. Students may also take the ACT with the Writing portion in lieu of the SAT. SAT Subject Tests are recommended but not required."

SELECTIVITY

Admissions Rating	97
# of applicants	12,941
% of applicants accepted	28
% of acceptees attending	33
# accepting a place on wait list	1,388
% admitted from wait list	1
# of early decision applicants	939
% accepted early decision	58

FRESHMAN PROFILE

Range SAT Critical Reading	590–680
Range SAT Math	640–720
Minimum paper TOEFL	570
Minimum computer TOEFL	230
Minimum web-based TOEFL	90
% graduated top 10% of class	93
% graduated top 25% of class	99
% graduated top 50% of class	100

DEADLINES

Early decision	
Deadline	11/15
Notification	12/15
Regular	
Deadline	1/1
Notification	4/1
Nonfall registration?	yes

APPLICANTS ALSO LOOK AT

AND OFTEN PREFER
Cornell University, Carnegie Mellon University, Boston College
Tufts University
University of Pennsylvania

AND RARELY PREFER
Lafayette College
Bucknell University
Villanova University
Boston University
Penn State—University Park

FINANCIAL FACTS

Financial Aid Rating	90
Annual tuition	$38,330
Room and board	$10,220
% frosh rec. need-based scholarship or grant aid	42
% UG rec. need-based scholarship or grant aid	42
% frosh rec. non-need-based scholarship or grant aid	3
% UG rec. non-need-based scholarship or grant aid	5
% frosh rec. need-based self-help aid	39
% UG rec. need-based self-help aid	39
% frosh rec. athletic scholarships	1
% UG rec. athletic scholarships	1
% frosh rec. any financial aid	56
% UG rec. any financial aid	59
% UG borrow to pay for school	58
Average cumulative indebtedness	$29,756

LEWIS & CLARK COLLEGE

0615 SOUTHWEST PALATINE HILL ROAD, PORTLAND, OR 97219-7899 • ADMISSIONS: 503-768-7040 • FAX: 503-768-7055

CAMPUS LIFE
Quality of Life Rating	85
Fire Safety Rating	77
Green Rating	80
Type of school	private
Environment	city

STUDENTS
Total undergrad enrollment	1,999
% male/female	39/61
% from out of state	81
% from public high school	74
% live on campus	67
% African American	2
% Asian	6
% Caucasian	66
% Hispanic	5
% Native American	1
% international	8
# of countries represented	58

SURVEY SAYS . . .
Lots of liberal students
Students aren't religious
Students love Portland, OR
Frats and sororities are unpopular or nonexistent
Political activism is popular

ACADEMICS
Academic Rating	91
Calendar	semester
Student/faculty ratio	12:1
Profs interesting rating	86
Profs accessible rating	87
Most common reg class size	10–19 students
Most common lab size	20–29 students

MOST POPULAR MAJORS
biology/biological sciences
international relations and affairs
psychology

STUDENTS SAY ". . ."

Academics

If you want to learn to think for yourself (and meet other people doing the same), try the beautiful environs of Lewis & Clark College in Portland, a school that "makes a community of its anti-community, and is proud of it." The definitively liberal arts curriculum and "self-directed attitude" toward courses of study cultivate "critical thinking and social awareness," and "even lectures tend to include discussions." The academics here are what you make of them, and the course load "can be incredibly simple or very rigorous or challenging" depending on your choices.

The school has been placing "an increasing level of importance on multiculturalism and ethnicity," which is reflected in its "wonderful study-abroad programs," but the administration gets a few complaints from students who "don't think that the administration is totally in sync with what the student body believes or wants." The professors, by and large, "are wonderful." They are passionate in both their teaching and their desire to shape students into independent thinkers, which "really shows in the critical feedback they give and the lengths they go to be accessible to students." Says one familial freshman: "I feel like each one is an aunt or uncle." Availability is not an issue for any aspect of the faculty or staff, as "personal appointments are very easy to get with practically anyone." Facilities also get top marks for their environmental-friendliness and overall degree of pleasantness, as does the number of grants for students looking to do research (often with professors, for those looking to bulk up their grad school resume). Rising tuition costs (without corresponding financial aid) are a main concern at LC.

Life

Those looking to get away for a few hours take a school-chartered shuttle to downtown Portland where bookstores, markets, and coffeeshops offer some respite. A lot of upperclassmen move off-campus, taking them out of "the LC Bubble," and these apartments are where most parties occur on weekends, for those that are interested (and many here are not). "No frats means no one is exclusive. Every party is usually open to everyone!" says a student. Pot usage is pretty prevalent at Lewis & Clark, which leads to a lot of "evenings [spent high out of your mind while watching YouTube videos."] The school provides plenty of sponsored events such as seminars and lectures, though these are usually attended by the underclassmen, and most people take advantage of their location and participate in trips with College Outdoors, such as "hikes on the Oregon coast, kayaking, snowshoeing, or rafting." Between the school and the environment, activities are plentiful, and with such a friendly and "chill" student body, "one cannot get left behind at this school."

Student Body

People here are generous and colorful with their adjectives when describing the gestalt of the student body, ranging from "an eclectic explosion of quirky intelligence, green green green, dreadlocks, vintage stores, hipsters" to "extremely atheist, wannabe hippies, that view clothing as optional and knowledge as power!" Perhaps this says it all—it's a diverse group of individuals at LC (at least as far as personalities go, as the ethnic makeup is quite "vanilla"), with very few students not finding a way to fit in (they "either accept that everyone here is different, or transfer"). There's also a large international and gay/lesbian student quotient. One student sums up the LC population: "As the Cheshire Cat said to Alice, 'We're all mad here.'"

Everyone here is politically active and "open to new experiences and challenging assumptions, with a strong vein of idealism running throughout." Students "constantly engage in academic discussion and debate outside of the classroom," but this is more for rhetoric's sake, as there is an "absence of unhealthily competitive attitudes" at Lewis & Clark.

FINANCIAL AID: 503-768-7090 • E-MAIL: ADMISSIONS@LCLARK.EDU • WEBSITE: WWW.LCLARK.EDU

THE PRINCETON REVIEW SAYS

Admissions

Very important factors considered include: Academic GPA, rigor of secondary school record, racial/ethnic status. *Important factors considered include:* Class rank, application essay, recommendation(s), standardized test scores, alumni/ae relation, character/personal qualities, extracurricular activities, first generation, talent/ability, volunteer work. *Other factors considered include:* Geographical residence, interview, level of applicant's interest, state residency, work experience. TOEFL required of all international applicants. High school diploma is required and GED is accepted. *Academic units recommended:* 4 English, 4 mathematics, 3 science, (2 science labs), 3 foreign language, 4 social studies, 1 visual/performing arts.

Financial Aid

Students should submit: FAFSA, CSS/Financial Aid PROFILE. The Princeton Review suggests that all financial aid forms be submitted as soon as possible after 1/1. *Need-based scholarships/grants offered:* Federal Pell, SEOG, state scholarships/grants, private scholarships, the school's own gift aid. *Loan aid offered:* Direct Subsidized Stafford, Direct Unsubsidized Stafford, Direct PLUS, FFEL Subsidized Stafford, FFEL Unsubsidized Stafford, FFEL PLUS, Federal Perkins. Applicants will be notified of awards on a rolling basis beginning 3/1. Federal Work-Study Program available. Institutional employment available. Off-campus job opportunities are fair.

The Inside Word

Admissions evaluations are thorough, and the Portfolio Path is an intriguing option that guarantees a purely personal evaluation. The Portfolio path to admission is an alternative application option for students who would like to provide additional materials in lieu of standardized testing. Few colleges of Lewis & Clark's quality are as accommodating to students. Interviews may be more helpful for students who have a circumstance but explained in personal communication.

THE SCHOOL SAYS "..."

From The Admissions Office

"The record number of applicants in recent years cited a variety of reasons they were drawn to Lewis & Clark. Many had to do with the multiple environments experienced by our students, including a small arts and sciences college with a 13:1 student/faculty ratio; a location only six miles from downtown Portland (metropolitan population 1.9 million); a setting in the heart of the Pacific Northwest, making more than 80 trips per year possible for our College Outdoors Program; and the rest of the world—almost 60 percent of our graduates included an overseas program in their curriculum. Since 1962, more than 9,600 students and 212 faculty members have participated in 598 programs in 66 countries on 6 continents. Our international curriculum has undergone a total review to better prepare graduates going into the twenty-first century.

"At Lewis & Clark College, SAT Subject Test scores are not required."

SELECTIVITY

Admissions Rating	96
# of applicants	5,551
% of applicants accepted	58
% of acceptees attending	17
# accepting a place on wait list	238
% admitted from wait list	7

FRESHMAN PROFILE

Range SAT Critical Reading	630–720
Range SAT Math	590–680
Range SAT Writing	590–680
Range ACT Composite	27–31
Minimum paper TOEFL	550
Minimum computer TOEFL	213
Average HS GPA	3.7
% graduated top 10% of class	43
% graduated top 25% of class	83
% graduated top 50% of class	99

DEADLINES

Early action	
Deadline	11/1
Notification	1/1
Regular	
Priority	2/1
Deadline	2/1
Notification	4/1
Nonfall registration?	yes

APPLICANTS ALSO LOOK AT
AND OFTEN PREFER
University of California—Santa Cruz
AND SOMETIMES PREFER
University of Puget Sound
Willamette University
Whitman College
AND RARELY PREFER
University of Oregon

FINANCIAL FACTS

Financial Aid Rating	83
Annual tuition	$35,283
% frosh rec. need-based scholarship or grant aid	53
% UG rec. need-based scholarship or grant aid	56
% frosh rec. non-need-based scholarship or grant aid	3
% UG rec. non-need-based scholarship or grant aid	2
% frosh rec. need-based self-help aid	36
% UG rec. need-based self-help aid	38
% frosh rec. any financial aid	78
% UG rec. any financial aid	80
% UG borrow to pay for school	58
Average cumulative indebtedness	$20,127

LOUISIANA STATE UNIVERSITY

110 Thomas Boyd Hall, Baton Rouge, LA 70803 • Admissions: 225-578-1175 • Fax: 225-575-4433

CAMPUS LIFE

Quality of Life Rating	**79**
Fire Safety Rating	**78**
Green Rating	**87**
Type of school	public
Environment	metropolis

STUDENTS

Total undergrad enrollment	23,063
% male/female	49/51
% from out of state	14
% from public high school	57
% live on campus	23
% in (# of) fraternities	12 (22)
% in (# of) sororities	18 (15)
% African American	9
% Asian	3
% Caucasian	81
% Hispanic	3
% international	2
# of countries represented	111

SURVEY SAYS . . .

Athletic facilities are great
Great off-campus food
Everyone loves the Tigers
Frats and sororities dominate social
scene
Student publications are popular
Lots of beer drinking
Hard liquor is popular

ACADEMICS

Academic Rating	**68**
Calendar	semester
Student/faculty ratio	20:1
Profs interesting rating	65
Profs accessible rating	68
% classes taught by TAs	10.5
Most common	
reg class size	10–19 students
Most common	
lab size	20–29 students

MOST POPULAR MAJORS

biology/biological sciences
general studies
psychology

STUDENTS SAY ". . ."

Academics

At Louisiana State University's flagship campus, you'll find "outstanding academics combined with a great college life." Some students here opt for only the latter as for many, "LSU is about football and partying." "Those who wish to apply themselves," however, "have ample opportunity and resources," and they can learn almost anything, since "the greatest strength of LSU by far is its diversity. [You] can come to LSU for sports, music... science, economics, or nearly any sort of humanities discipline you are interested in." Areas of strength include programs in premedical science, engineering, agriculture, and mass communications. The school is huge, which means "somewhere within that huge number is someone that you can get along with," but also it is easy to "get lost in the crowd." "You are just a number to the administration and a good amount of your professors," especially in intro-level classes. However, "once you get into classes that are smaller and more geared toward your chosen major, you are able to develop more of a one-on-one relationship with your professors." Fortunately "many administrative tasks" (such as "bills and registration") "can be completed online, and computers are available all across campus for students who don't have personal computers," making the bureaucracy somewhat easier to navigate. The school also offers academic lifelines such as "free tutoring all day long. The tutors are students who have already taken [the] courses."

Life

LSU is a big enough school to offer something for everyone, and undergrads here enjoy countless activities within a variety of subcultures. Most divisions, however, dissolve on game day, when tailgating is raised to the level of "an art form." A freshman reports, "On Saturdays during football season everyone is on campus before the game with friends, beer, and barbeque." Fans "come from all over and stay out all day. It's the one day when it doesn't matter who you are, as long as you're wearing purple and gold." Other LSU traditions include Thursday nights at the bars of Tigerland, "a street with three popular college bars right next to each other," and parties wherever and whenever possible. The Greek system here is "highly influential," but, students note, "this isn't the kind of school where a student doesn't have a social life if he or she isn't Greek." For the more aesthetically inclined, "LSU has an amazing art center—The Shaw Center—complete with a theater and fancy sushi bar on the top floor, which looks over the Mississippi River." Undergrads report "the beauty of our campus is amazing. The 100-plus-year-old oaks and the Italian Renaissance architecture wow any visitor to LSU's campus."

Student Body

The typical student at LSU "studies moderately—enough to get the grade he or she desires in a class"—and "frequently spends time with friends, possibly going to parties or places that serve alcohol." Mixed in is "a good number of atypical students who study more and do not go partying over the weekends. These students find fulfillment in their own interests regardless of what others think." While "conservative frat boys and sorority girls dominate the campus," the school is home to a diverse population including "many from foreign countries and other ethnic group[s]" and "a huge subculture of indie-rock nerds, skateboarders, hippies, and liberals." There are even a few who "don't give a damn about LSU football"—hey, at a school this big, anything's possible. The student body also includes a substantial population of legacies.

FINANCIAL AID: 225-578-3103 • E-MAIL: ADMISSIONS@LSU.EDU • WEBSITE: WWW.LSU.EDU

THE PRINCETON REVIEW SAYS

Admissions

Very important factors considered include: Academic GPA, rigor of secondary school record, standardized test scores. *Important factors considered include:* Class rank, talent/ability. *Other factors considered include:* Application essay, recommendation(s), extracurricular activities, first generation. SAT or ACT required; ACT with Writing component required; TOEFL required of all international applicants. High school diploma is required and GED is accepted. *Academic units required:* 4 English, 3 mathematics, 3 science, 2 foreign language, 1 social studies, 2 history, 3 academic electives, 1 half credit of Computer Studies.

Financial Aid

Students should submit: FAFSA, institution's own financial aid form. The Princeton Review suggests that all financial aid forms be submitted as soon as possible after 1/1. *Need-based scholarships/grants offered:* Federal Pell, SEOG, state scholarships/grants, private scholarships, the school's own gift aid, ACG/SMART. *Loan aid offered:* FFEL Subsidized Stafford, FFEL Unsubsidized Stafford, FFEL PLUS, Federal Perkins, Alternative/Grad Plus. Applicants will be notified of awards on or about 3/1. Federal Work-Study Program available. Institutional employment available. Off-campus job opportunities are excellent.

The Inside Word

Good students and great athletes are welcome at LSU, where the annual avalanche of applications necessitates a formula-driven approach to admissions. Check LSU's website to see which combinations of GPA, class rank, and test scores qualify students for admission.

THE SCHOOL SAYS "..."

From The Admissions Office

"LSU holds a prominent position in U.S. higher education and is committed to meeting the challenge of pursuing intellectual development for its students, expanding the bounds of knowledge through research, and creating economic opportunities for Louisiana. LSU, one of only 25 universities nationwide designated as both a land-grant and sea-grant institution, also holds the Carnegie Foundation's doctoral research, extensive designation.

"LSU's instructional programs include 198 undergraduate and graduate or professional degrees. Outside of the classroom, residential colleges, service-learning opportunites, and more than 350 registered student organizations contribute to an exciting and meaningful college experience.

"Louisiana State University offers the Southern hospitality of a small community while providing the benefits of a large, technologically advanced institution.

"Freshman applicants are required to take the SAT (or the ACT with the Writing component). LSU will use the best scores from either SAT or ACT, when making admission decisions."

SELECTIVITY

Admissions Rating	85
# of applicants	11,452
% of applicants accepted	73
% of acceptees attending	55

FRESHMAN PROFILE

Range SAT Critical Reading	520–640
Range SAT Math	550–650
Range SAT Writing	490–620
Range ACT Composite	23–28
Minimum paper TOEFL	550
Minimum computer TOEFL	213
Minimum web-based TOEFL	79
Average HS GPA	3.52
% graduated top 10% of class	27
% graduated top 25% of class	55
% graduated top 50% of class	84

DEADLINES

Regular	
Priority	11/15
Deadline	4/15
Nonfall registration?	yes

FINANCIAL FACTS

Financial Aid Rating	69
Annual in-state tuition	$2,981
Annual out-of-state tuition	$11,281
Room and board	$6,852
Required fees	$1,562
Books and supplies	$1,500
% frosh rec. need-based scholarship or grant aid	33
% UG rec. need-based scholarship or grant aid	29
% frosh rec. non-need-based scholarship or grant aid	2
% UG rec. non-need-based scholarship or grant aid	1
% frosh rec. need-based self-help aid	19
% UG rec. need-based self-help aid	25
% frosh rec. athletic scholarships	2
% UG rec. athletic scholarships	2
% frosh rec. any financial aid	95
% UG rec. any financial aid	76
% UG borrow to pay for school	46
Average cumulative indebtedness	$17,057

LOYOLA MARYMOUNT UNIVERSITY

ONE LMU DRIVE, SUITE 100, LOS ANGELES, CA 90045 • ADMISSIONS: 310-338-2750 • FAX: 310-338-2797

CAMPUS LIFE

Quality of Life Rating	94
Fire Safety Rating	60*
Green Rating	78
Type of school	private
Affiliation	Roman Catholic/Jesuit
Environment	metropolis

STUDENTS

Total undergrad enrollment	5,590
% male/female	41/59
% from out of state	23
% from public high school	47
% live on campus	60
% in (# of) fraternities	19 (6)
% in (# of) sororities	30 (8)
% African American	7
% Asian	13
% Caucasian	56
% Hispanic	19
% Native American	1
% international	1
# of countries represented	50

SURVEY SAYS . . .

Athletic facilities are great
Students are friendly
Students love Los Angeles, CA
Great off-campus food
Students are happy
Frats and sororities dominate social
scene

ACADEMICS

Academic Rating	81
Calendar	semester
Student/faculty ratio	13:1
Profs interesting rating	86
Profs accessible rating	96
Most common reg class size	20–29 students
Most common lab size	10–19 students

MOST POPULAR MAJORS

business administration and
management
communication studies/speech
communication and rhetoric
psychology

STUDENTS SAY ". . ."

Academics

You may be technically going to school in the midst of bustling Los Angeles, but attending Loyola Marymount University is more like having "a little family on the bluff." Offering a "well-rounded Jesuit education" on an "absolutely beautiful and modern campus" as well as "many activities and service opportunities." Students here are dedicated to becoming aware of "the pertinent social issues of today's world and how they relate to each student's chosen field(s) of study." LMU is often referred to as a "hidden gem," but those who go here wouldn't mind seeing a bit more publicity for their school.

A small enrollment means small class sizes, and students report having no trouble getting into the courses they desire. Professor quality "varies." Basically, "the professors that teach because they love to teach are amazing. The professors that care more about their research than their students are disappointing." There aren't many gripes about availability, though, as most are "more than willing to assist with any questions or problems." As for the higher ups, there is "some resistance and hiding on the part of the administration when students try to stir things up." But overall those in charge primarily do a good job, remaining active with student life. Several administrators and deans "show their commitment to the students by serving as club moderators" in addition to their day jobs. Many students complain the cost of attending LMU "is a bit ridiculous," and wish financial aid and scholarships were more available to them, rather than the money being spent on ever-present construction.

Life

Students claim to "feel very comfortable living on campus and walking around late at night due to the security on campus." As with many things located in LA, "parking is an issue that needs to be improved." The small size of the student body creates a "bubble" effect, giving the school a "high school" flavor, but the city and neighboring schools provide plenty of options to any student that feels as though the LMU walls are closing. A lot of freshmen choose to go home on the weekends, but most upperclassmen hang around and go to the beach, Santa Monica, or shopping malls, all located within 15 minutes of the campus. "People do party and drink, but it is nothing compared to most other colleges," says one junior. Greek life is popular but not central to the party scene here, and most parties occur off campus. For students wishing to remain close to their dorms, the campus has an excellent sit-down restaurant that provides "almost anything that you can find at a classy off-campus restaurant," and the D-1 sports teams "are entertaining and encourage a great deal of campus spirit."

Student Body

"There is quite a bit of money at LMU," enough that "two students brought 49-inch plasma TVs to their freshman dorm this year." Perhaps they are friends with the "skinny, rich-beyond-belief blonde girls whose version of 'scrubbing it' is wearing their Juicy Couture sweatshirts with their Manolo Blahniks." But "not everyone is rich. The school isn't overly snobby, and there is a niche for everyone." The "most visible" LMU archetype is "the vaguely wholesome, *Saved By the Bell: The College Years* jocky frat/sorority type." But, there are also plenty of "serious student types who are always in the library and no one else ever really gets to know them," as well as "the artsy, theater/coffee-shop types who wear whatever expresses their feelings" as part of the "chill underground." Many in this last group "participate in the film department and the radio station and form their own close community." While "some students here are very LA, others are more focused politically and spiritually and are committed to social justice, service, and participation in student life." At LMU, it may be "easy to feel like you belong" but some say there still "needs to be a stronger sense of the differences in people, races, sexual orientations, and cultures."

LOYOLA MARYMOUNT UNIVERSITY

FINANCIAL AID: 310-338-2753 • E-MAIL: ADMISSIONS@LMU.EDU • WEBSITE: WWW.LMU.EDU

THE PRINCETON REVIEW SAYS

Admissions

Very important factors considered include: Academic GPA, rigor of secondary school record. *Important factors considered include:* Class rank, application essay, standardized test scores, character/personal qualities, talent/ability. *Other factors considered include:* Recommendation(s), alumni/ae relation, extracurricular activities, first generation, geographical residence, interview, volunteer work, work experience. SAT or ACT required; TOEFL required of all international applicants. High school diploma is required and GED is accepted. *Academic units recommended:* 4 English, 3 mathematics, 2 science, (2 science labs), 3 foreign language, 3 social studies, 1 academic elective.

Financial Aid

Students should submit: FAFSA, CSS/Financial Aid PROFILE, business/farm supplement. Regular filing deadline is 4/1. The Princeton Review suggests that all financial aid forms be submitted as soon as possible after 1/1. *Need-based scholarships/grants offered:* Federal Pell, SEOG, state scholarships/grants, private scholarships, the school's own gift aid. *Loan aid offered:* FFEL Subsidized Stafford, FFEL Unsubsidized Stafford, FFEL PLUS, Federal Perkins, college/university loans from institutional funds. Applicants will be notified of awards on a rolling basis beginning 3/15. Federal Work-Study Program available. Institutional employment available. Off-campus job opportunities are excellent.

The Inside Word

Loyola Marymount's admissions committee is particular about candidate evaluation, but a large applicant pool has more to do with the university's moderate acceptance rate than does academic selectivity. Even so, underachievers will have difficulty getting in.

THE SCHOOL SAYS " . . ."

From The Admissions Office

"Loyola Marymount University is a dynamic, student-centered university. We are medium-sized (5,500 undergraduates), and we are the only Jesuit university in the southwestern United States.

"Our campus is located in Westchester, a friendly, residential neighborhood that is removed from the hustle and bustle of Los Angeles, yet offers easy access to all the richnesss of our most cosmopolitan environment. One mile from the ocean, our students enjoy ocean and mountain vistas as well as the moderate climate and crisp breezes characteristic of a coastal location.

"Loyola Marymount is committed to the ideals of Jesuit and Marymount education. We are a student-centered university, dedicated to the education of the whole person and to the preparation of our students for lives of service to their families, communities, and professions. Breadth and rigor are the hallmarks of the curriculum.

"Taken together, our academic program, our Jesuit and Marymount heritage, and our terrific campus environment afford our students unparalleled opportunity to prepare for life and leadership in the 21st century.

"Applicants must submit results from either the SAT the ACT with the Writing section. We will use the student's best scores from either test."

SELECTIVITY

Admissions Rating	88
# of applicants	8,533
% of applicants accepted	51
% of acceptees attending	28

FRESHMAN PROFILE

Range SAT Critical Reading	530–630
Range SAT Math	540–640
Minimum paper TOEFL	550
Minimum computer TOEFL	213
Average HS GPA	3.6
% graduated top 10% of class	30
% graduated top 25% of class	66
% graduated top 50% of class	99

DEADLINES

Regular	
Priority	1/15
Notification	rolling
Nonfall registration?	yes

APPLICANTS ALSO LOOK AT

AND OFTEN PREFER
University of Southern California
University of California—Berkeley
University of California—Los Angeles

AND SOMETIMES PREFER
University of California—San Diego
Santa Clara University
University of California—Santa Barbara

AND RARELY PREFER
Pepperdine University
University of San Diego
University of California—Irvine
Chapman University

FINANCIAL FACTS

Financial Aid Rating	78
Annual tuition	$33,901
Room and board	$11,808
Required fees	$636
Books and supplies	$3,465
% frosh rec. need-based scholarship or grant aid	46
% UG rec. need-based scholarship or grant aid	47
% frosh rec. non-need-based scholarship or grant aid	6
% UG rec. non-need-based scholarship or grant aid	8
% frosh rec. need-based self-help aid	42
% UG rec. need-based self-help aid	44
% frosh rec. athletic scholarships	7
% UG rec. athletic scholarships	4
% UG borrow to pay for school	66
Average cumulative indebtedness	$28,548

LOYOLA UNIVERSITY—CHICAGO

820 NORTH MICHIGAN AVENUE, CHICAGO, IL 60611 • ADMISSIONS: 312-915-6500 • FAX: 312-915-7216

CAMPUS LIFE

Quality of Life Rating	**77**
Fire Safety Rating	**78**
Green Rating	**89**
Type of school	private
Affiliation	Roman Catholic/Jesuit
Environment	metropolis

STUDENTS

Total undergrad enrollment	9,586
% male/female	35/65
% from out of state	34.6
% from public high school	65.3
% live on campus	40
% in (# of) fraternities	3.08 (7)
% in (# of) sororities	5.9 (8)
% African American	4
% Asian	12
% Caucasian	63
% Hispanic	10
% international	1
# of countries represented	96

SURVEY SAYS . . .
Lab facilities are great
Students love Chicago, IL
Great off-campus food
(Almost) everyone smokes

ACADEMICS

Academic Rating	**77**
Calendar	semester
Profs interesting rating	74
Profs accessible rating	76
Most common reg class size	20–29 students
Most common lab size	20–29 students

MOST POPULAR MAJORS
biology/biological sciences
nursing/registered nurse
(rn, asn, bsn, msn)
psychology

STUDENTS SAY ". . ."

Academics

Standing tall alongside the shore of Lake Michigan eight miles north of Chicago, Loyola University benefits from an optimal location (so long as you don't mind cold winters). "The location, Chicago, is key in providing a unique educational experience," one student explains. "The neighborhoods, restaurants, parks, and museums of Chicago provide just as much information as a classroom setting would." A "strong Jesuit tradition" "encourages creative thinking and allows students to explore the complexities of the world in and out of the classroom," which, of course, includes its closest city. Students also appreciate the school's "really strong emphasis on preparing the individual to leave college and start a career. There are plenty of internship opportunities," and the school makes "it relatively easy to get in touch with employers. We have many career fairs." Professors are "amazing overall." Students say they are "very approachable and really care about their students in terms of their academic performance as well as their mental and physical health. They treat students with respect and are passionate about their subjects." "Small class sizes" further help students "feel comfortable asking questions," and professors' "expertise" and "passion" make it "much easier to learn." Students brag of the nursing program's "great reputation," and add that "the history and philosophy departments are really good." Many, however, express disappointment with the administration citing "red tape" and "layers of bureaucracy," which make many offices "a bit inaccessible."

Life

Loyola "has the aspects of a 'normal' campus," but "it has a different twist because it is located in Chicago. Students frequently use the city's attractions as opposed to college activities" for extracurricular diversion. Living in Chicago, "students tend to have plenty of options in terms of what to do for fun." There's an active "local bar scene," as well as "concerts, museums, plays, and almost anything else one can think of doing." Getting around town is really easy: "There is a [CTA] station dedicated to the campus, which makes it extremely easy to travel anywhere within the city. Each student is also given a U-pass, which provides unlimited rides on any Chicago public transportation." Getting from campus to campus is another matter; students complain that "the school needs better transportation from the two campuses. They have one shuttle run every 15 to 20 minutes, but time is of the essence, and if you miss one, it is hard to get from one to the other quickly. This affects classes, meetings, and jobs." Students who prefer to stay on campus for fun will find "plenty of other activities" to capture their attention, including "intramural sports, clubs, and Division I basketball games." "If you're not a drinker, there is still plenty to do" on campus "such as concerts, comedians, or even smaller venues like drag shows or improv." Serious sports fans should be warned, however, as "Sports teams do not rule this school," even though the city itself is pretty well known for its enthusiasm for athletics.

Student Body

"When first coming to a Jesuit school, I feared a conservative rule that would be in order," writes one student. "To my surprise, quite the opposite was here in Chicago. The school is very liberal, and the body is incredibly diverse." Indeed, while many undergrads here are "white and from the Chicago suburbs," many others are "of all different races, ethnicities, religions, and sexual orientations." "There is a very high gay population on campus, and very little discrimination," one undergrad observes. The university supports diversity through its on-campus "ethnic and cultural groups" so that students "rarely feel alone or ostracized." As one student explains, Loyola is a "good place to be surrounded by such a diverse student body" as "there's definitely room for different people." Many here "have a service-oriented mindset and tend to be aware of current events and global issues that need to be dealt with."

FINANCIAL AID: 773-508-3155 • E-MAIL: ADMISSION@LUC.EDU • WEBSITE: WWW.LUC.EDU

THE PRINCETON REVIEW SAYS

Admissions

Very important factors considered include: Academic GPA, rigor of secondary school record, standardized test scores. *Important factors considered include:* Application essay, recommendation(s), character/personal qualities, extracurricular activities, level of applicant's interest, volunteer work. *Other factors considered include:* Class rank, alumni/ae relation, first generation, geographical residence, interview, state residency, talent/ability, work experience. SAT or ACT required; TOEFL required of all international applicants. High school diploma is required and GED is accepted. *Academic units required:* 4 English, 3 mathematics, 3 science, 2 foreign language, 2 social studies, 1 history. *Academic units recommended:* 4 English, 4 mathematics, 3 science, 2 foreign language, 2 social studies, 2 history, 3 academic electives.

Financial Aid

Students should submit: FAFSA. The Princeton Review suggests that all financial aid forms be submitted as soon as possible after 1/1. *Need-based scholarships/grants offered:* Federal Pell, SEOG, state scholarships/grants, private scholarships, the school's own gift aid. *Loan aid offered:* FFEL Subsidized Stafford, FFEL Unsubsidized Stafford, FFEL PLUS, Federal Perkins, Federal Nursing. Applicants will be notified of awards on a rolling basis beginning 2/15. Federal Work-Study Program available. Institutional employment available. Off-campus job opportunities are good.

The Inside Word

Loyola is fairly conventional when it comes to admissions policies. Successful candidates usually have a combination of strong grades, success in a tough college preparatory curriculum, and solid extracurricular activities. The school adheres to Jesuit teaching, so applicants with significant volunteer work should impress admissions officers.

THE SCHOOL SAYS "..."

From The Admissions Office

"To accommodate recent record-breaking freshman classes, Loyola University—Chicago continues to open new facilities and renovate existing buildings, including the state-of-the-art Quinlan Life Sciences Education and Research Center, new residence halls at both the Lake Shore and Water Tower Campuses, and the Sullivan Center for Student Services, a one-stop center that consolidates more than a dozen campus offices. The Information Commons, which opened in 2008 is a high-tech lakefront library featuring large group study spaces, more than 250 computers; wireless Internet connections and a lakefront café. Loyola frequently enhances its undergraduate academic programs and adds new majors in emerging fields. The core curriculum enhances student credentials, by emphasizing lifelong skills and values, and giving students the opportunity to more easily complete a second major or additional minor. Nationally recognized researchers and scholars continue to teach freshman-level as well as advanced courses. These new developments build on Loyola's rich Jesuit tradition, which fosters academic excellence, instills service to others, and educates the whole person. Loyola's Lake Shore and Water Tower Campuses enable students to experience both traditional residential campus life and a vibrant urban environment. With more than 175 campus organizations offering numerous activities and events, as well as cultural, recreational, and internship opportunities throughout the world-class city of Chicago, undergraduate student education at Loyola extends well beyond the classroom. For more information about undergraduate academics, housing, student life, financial assistance, and more, please visit: www.luc.edu/undergrad. All applicants are required to submit a writing sample with their application materials. International students are required to submit TOEFL or IELTS scores."

SELECTIVITY

Admissions Rating	91
# of applicants	17,287
% of applicants accepted	74
% of acceptees attending	17

FRESHMAN PROFILE

Range SAT Critical Reading	540–648
Range SAT Math	530–640
Range SAT Writing	540–630
Range ACT Composite	24–29
Minimum paper TOEFL	550
Minimum web-based TOEFL	79
Average HS GPA	3.57
% graduated top 10% of class	34
% graduated top 25% of class	70
% graduated top 50% of class	97

DEADLINES

Regular	
Priority	4/1
Notification	rolling
Nonfall registration?	yes

APPLICANTS ALSO LOOK AT

AND OFTEN PREFER
Saint Louis University
Michigan State University
University of Wisconsin—Madison
University of Illinois at Urbana-Champaign
Northwestern University

AND SOMETIMES PREFER
Purdue University—West Lafayette
Marquette University
University of Chicago
DePaul University

AND RARELY PREFER
University of Iowa
Bradley University
Illinois Wesleyan University

FINANCIAL FACTS

Financial Aid Rating	74
Annual tuition	$29,850
Room and board	$10,885
Required fees	$806
Books and supplies	$1,200
% frosh rec. need-based scholarship or grant aid	71
% UG rec. need-based scholarship or grant aid	67
% frosh rec. non-need-based scholarship or grant aid	6
% UG rec. non-need-based scholarship or grant aid	5
% frosh rec. need-based self-help aid	67
% UG rec. need-based self-help aid	66
% frosh rec. athletic scholarships	1
% UG rec. athletic scholarships	1
% frosh rec. any financial aid	92.8
% UG rec. any financial aid	91
% UG borrow to pay for school	69.4
Average cumulative indebtedness	$26,874

LOYOLA UNIVERSITY IN MARYLAND

4501 NORTH CHARLES STREET, BALTIMORE, MD 21210 • ADMISSIONS: 410-617-5012 • FAX: 410-617-2176

CAMPUS LIFE

Quality of Life Rating	**94**
Fire Safety Rating	**87**
Green Rating	**74**
Type of school	private
Affiliation	Roman Catholic/Jesuit
Environment	village

STUDENTS

Total undergrad enrollment	3,716
% male/female	42/58
% from out of state	81
% from public high school	60
% live on campus	79
% African American	4
% Asian	3
% Caucasian	85
% Hispanic	4
% international	1
# of countries represented	40

SURVEY SAYS . . .

Athletic facilities are great
School is well run
Dorms are like palaces
Frats and sororities are unpopular or
nonexistent
Student government is popular

ACADEMICS

Academic Rating	**90**
Calendar	semester
Student/faculty ratio	12:1
Profs interesting rating	96
Profs accessible rating	93
Most common reg class size	10–19 students
Most common lab size	10–19 students

MOST POPULAR MAJORS

biology/biological sciences
business/commerce
psychology

STUDENTS SAY ". . ."

Academics

A Jesuit school in suburban Baltimore, Loyola University in Maryland "seeks to develop the whole person—intellectually, emotionally, socially, and spiritually." Jesuit values are stressed through the school's "well-rounded curriculum, encouraging participation in community service, and teaching values in diversity both on and off campus." Across the board, students say the Loyola faculty is comprised of accomplished scholars and talented teachers. A senior shares, "Professors are the best part about Loyola. They love their subjects and their students, and make class interesting with their enthusiasm." When it comes to academic or personal matters, "the professors at Loyola are so caring it almost seems unnatural. They will go out of their way to make sure you understand material and always have their door open after class discussions." What's more, the academic experience is characterized by small class sizes and ample discussion. A sophomore offers, "I could not be happier with my academic experience at Loyola. Even the biggest classes are small enough to facilitate close interaction with the professors." Outside the classroom, academic opportunities abound, and "professors encourage us to become part of the department through research or work-study programs." Likewise, the "administration cares deeply about fostering growth outside of the classroom." A senior attests, "As a three-year member of the student government association at Loyola I have always been impressed with the openness of the administration and their willingness to work for the best interests of the students."

Life

Despite the demands of coursework, you'll get the full college experience at Loyola University in Maryland. Outgoing and social, most Loyola undergraduates are "motivated to achieve a balance between academic success and the social benefits of college." In the admiring words of one junior, "The typical student at Loyola is genius at time management. They find a way to get to the gym at least three times a week, go out at least three times week, and pull off above a 3.0 GPA every semester." However, Loyola students never lose track of their educational priorities, telling us, "The social life is very important here, but in all honesty, academics come first." In addition to hitting the off-campus bars, there are many attractions in the surrounding city of Baltimore. A sophomore reports, "For fun, my friends and I go out to eat in Baltimore, head to Towson mall, and go to the movies or concerts. Baltimore has a lot to offer to the college student." There are also plenty of extracurricular activities, clubs, and organizations at school, and "Loyola goes to great lengths to develop a sense of community across the campus." On that note, day-to-day life is easygoing and pleasant on Loyola's pretty campus. Happily, campus housing is top-notch, and "many students live in suites or apartments, and can thus cook their own food in their own kitchens."

Student Body

Loyola tends to admit outgoing and well-rounded students who want to benefit from all the academic, extracurricular, and social aspects of college life. On the whole, students "care deeply about their education and realize they are here to learn. But they also enjoy themselves and are not too uptight." Considering the fact that Loyola is a private, Jesuit college on the East Coast, it's not surprising that "the average student comes from the greater Philadelphia, New Jersey, and New York area (although that seems to be changing) and ranges in economic background from middle-to upper-class." You'll find a shared affinity for Ugg boots and The North Face apparel on the Loyola campus, and "the majority of students are preppy." Even so, you can't judge a book by its cover. A sophomore tells us, "Everyone seems like they may be a typical 'Loyola Girl' but when you look deeper you find that these people are unique and diverse." No matter what your background or interests, "there are enough clubs and a wonderful student life on-campus that atypical students find their place and become as much a part of Loyola as typical students."

LOYOLA UNIVERSITY IN MARYLAND

FINANCIAL AID: 410-617-2576 • WEBSITE: WWW.LOYOLA.EDU

THE PRINCETON REVIEW SAYS

Admissions

Very important factors considered include: Class rank, academic GPA, rigor of secondary school record, standardized test scores, character/personal qualities. *Important factors considered include:* Application essay, recommendation(s), alumni/ae relation, extracurricular activities, first generation, talent/ability, volunteer work. *Other factors considered include:* Racial/ethnic status, work experience. SAT or ACT required; TOEFL required of all international applicants. High school diploma is required and GED is accepted. *Academic units recommended:* 4 English, 4 mathematics, 4 science, 4 foreign language, 4 social studies, 4 history.

Financial Aid

Students should submit: FAFSA, CSS/Financial Aid PROFILE, noncustodial PROFILE, business/farm supplement. Regular filing deadline is 2/1. The Princeton Review suggests that all financial aid forms be submitted as soon as possible after 1/1. *Need-based scholarships/grants offered:* Federal Pell, SEOG, state scholarships/grants, private scholarships, the school's own gift aid. *Loan aid offered:* Direct Subsidized Stafford, Direct Unsubsidized Stafford, Direct PLUS, Federal Perkins, college/university loans from institutional funds. Applicants will be notified of awards on or about 4/1. Federal Work-Study Program available. Institutional employment available. Off-campus job opportunities are good.

The Inside Word

Grades are more important than standardized test scores in the admissions process at Loyola. Your junior and senior grades are particularly critical. The content of the courses you've taken weighs fairly heavily, too. Obviously, harder courses look better. If your standardized test scores aren't awful and your high school GPA is the equivalent of a "B+" or better, it is extremely likely you will get admitted here. If your GPA is more like a "B," your odds are still pretty good. If your academic profile is a little thin, definitely take advantage of the opportunity to interview.

THE SCHOOL SAYS " . . ."

From The Admissions Office

"To make a wise choice about your college plans, you will need to find out more. We extend to you these invitations. Question-and-answer periods with an admissions counselor are helpful to prospective students. An appointment should be made in advance. Admission office hours are 9:00 A.M. to 5:00 P.M., Monday through Friday. College day programs and Saturday information programs are scheduled during the academic year. These programs include a video about Loyola, a general information session, a discussion of various majors, a campus tour, and lunch. Summer information programs can help high school juniors to get a head start on investigating colleges. These programs feature an introductory presentation about the college and a campus tour."

SELECTIVITY

Admissions Rating	92
# of applicants	7,623
% of applicants accepted	69
% of acceptees attending	20
# accepting a place on wait list	614
% admitted from wait list	2

FRESHMAN PROFILE

Range SAT Critical Reading	540–630
Range SAT Math	560–650
Range SAT Writing	550–650
Range ACT Composite	24–28
Minimum paper TOEFL	550
Minimum computer TOEFL	213
Average HS GPA	3.46
% graduated top 10% of class	30
% graduated top 25% of class	71
% graduated top 50% of class	96

DEADLINES

Early action	
Deadline	11/15
Notification	1/15
Regular	
Priority	11/15
Deadline	1/15
Notification	4/1
Nonfall registration?	no

APPLICANTS ALSO LOOK AT

AND OFTEN PREFER
Boston College

AND SOMETIMES PREFER
College of the Holy Cross
Villanova University

AND RARELY PREFER
Fairfield University
Fordham University
Providence College

FINANCIAL FACTS

Financial Aid Rating	97
Annual tuition	$36,510
Room and board	$10,680
Fees	$1,310
% frosh rec. need-based scholarship or grant aid	40
% UG rec. need-based scholarship or grant aid	36
% frosh rec. non-need-based scholarship or grant aid	20
% UG rec. non-need-based scholarship or grant aid	18
% frosh rec. need-based self-help aid	47
% UG rec. need-based self-help aid	41
% frosh rec. athletic scholarships	3
% UG rec. athletic scholarships	4
% frosh rec. any financial aid	69
% UG rec. any financial aid	70
% UG borrow to pay for school	71
Average cumulative indebtedness	$26,340

LOYOLA UNIVERSITY—NEW ORLEANS

6363 St. Charles Avenue, Box 18, New Orleans, LA 70118 • Admissions: 504-865-3240 • Fax: 504-865-3383

CAMPUS LIFE
Quality of Life Rating	95
Fire Safety Rating	96
Green Rating	75
Type of school	private
Affiliation	Roman Catholic/Jesuit
Environment	city

STUDENTS
Total undergrad enrollment	2,658
% male/female	43/57
% from out of state	49
% from public high school	43.4
% live on campus	37
% in (# of) fraternities	19 (7)
% in (# of) sororities	13 (7)
% African American	13
% Asian	4
% Caucasian	61
% Hispanic	11
% Native American	1
% international	3
# of countries represented	43

SURVEY SAYS . . .
Great library
Students get along with local community
Great off-campus food
Musical organizations are popular
Student publications are popular
Hard liquor is popular
(Almost) everyone smokes

ACADEMICS
Academic Rating	82
Calendar	semester
Student/faculty ratio	11:1
Profs interesting rating	86
Profs accessible rating	83
Most common reg class size	10–19 students
Most common lab size	10–19 students

MOST POPULAR MAJORS
marketing/marketing management
mass communication/media studies
psychology

STUDENTS SAY ". . ."

Academics
Loyola University—New Orleans provides students with "an excellent Jesuit education," that emphasizes a "commitment to the community" in "an intimate college setting," all capped with life in New Orleans, "a great place to go to school." Small by university standards, Loyola has a wonderful "community feeling." "You feel it when you first walk on campus." Professors "know you by name and it's not uncommon to stop by their office hours just to chat. They truly care about their students and how we are doing academically and otherwise." Among Loyola's top offerings is its music industry studies program, "the second-best in the nation," right up there with Berklee College of Music in Boston (but with much better weather!). The communications program is "great," as is the "awesome" College of Business (nearly one in four students here pursues a business major). Loyola also boasts a "strong program in criminal justice, with great internship opportunities in New Orleans," and an "outstanding" music program that "produces many successful musicians." One music student notes, "The greatest thing about the music school here is you are never second to a graduate student. Undergraduates are the priority." All undergraduates must complete a common curriculum covering English, math, natural science, history, philosophy, and religious studies; the common curriculum consumes most of freshman year. Hurricane Katrina robbed Loyola of much-needed tuition funds; cost-cutting measures to deal with subsequent budget shortfalls are still being felt, and have resulted in some "discontent" on campus in recent years. However, many feel that under the circumstances, "The university is doing the very best that it can to function under the same ideals that it represented pre-Katrina."

Life
Though New Orlenas is still rebuilding, Loyola's campus, fortunately, was spared the substantial damage so much of the city endured. Students report that "going to school in New Orleans is so much fun. There's salsa dancing on Friday nights at Cafe Brazil, live music every night of the week at Snug Harbor, D.B.A., Maple Leaf, or the Howlin' Wolf (just to name a few!). There's great food everywhere in the city: Cajun, Creole, or ethnic." Audubon Park is right "up the street," and is "a great place to hang out, feed the ducks, relax, and maybe even do homework." Another distinguishing characteristic of the town is that "drinking is a way of life in New Orleans, and it's a way of life for kids on campus. You only have to be 18 to get into the bars." Most Loyola students get involved in service, and, "Post-Katrina, there's a ridiculous amount of community service that's easily accessible through the university." Loyola's frats provide plenty of on-campus diversion, as do "a wide variety of campus organizations."

Student Body
Loyola undergrads "want a real college life, not just an education. They want to have experiences and take advantage of the city and truly care about impacting their community." All students "go out and do service." "So many people mentor kids at area schools. Social justice is a theme you can't escape at Loyola." "People are very keenly aware of what's going on in the world at large," and students report feeling "more camaraderie and oneness since the hurricane." The school is home to "a wide range of different ethnicities, interests, and so forth. People mostly tend to stick to their own circles, even though people are almost always nice to each other." Prominent subpopulations include the many "sorority and frat people," sometimes "annoying," but "nice people in the end," and the "bohemians and free spirits" drawn here by the music school. "They don't really clash with the more preppy students here." It's New Orleans, so it should come as no surprise that "most students like to drink." "So-called 'straight-edge' students are a minority, but exist."

LOYOLA UNIVERSITY—NEW ORLEANS

FINANCIAL AID: 504-865-3231 • E-MAIL: ADMIT@LOYNO.EDU • WEBSITE: WWW.LOYNO.EDU

THE PRINCETON REVIEW SAYS

Admissions

Very important factors considered include: Academic GPA, rigor of secondary school record, standardized test scores. *Important factors considered include:* Application essay, recommendation(s), extracurricular activities, talent/ability. *Other factors considered include:* Class rank, alumni/ae relation, character/personal qualities, geographical residence, interview, level of applicant's interest, state residency, volunteer work, work experience. SAT or ACT required; TOEFL required of all international applicants. High school diploma is required and GED is accepted. *Academic units required:* 4 English, 2 mathematics, 2 science, 2 social studies. *Academic units recommended:* 4 English, 3 mathematics, 3 science, (1 science lab), 2 foreign language, 2 social studies.

Financial Aid

Students should submit: FAFSA. Regular filing deadline is 6/1. The Princeton Review suggests that all financial aid forms be submitted as soon as possible after 1/1. *Need-based scholarships/grants offered:* Federal Pell, SEOG, private scholarships, the school's own gift aid. *Loan aid offered:* FFEL Subsidized Stafford, FFEL Unsubsidized Stafford, FFEL PLUS, Federal Perkins. Applicants will be notified of awards on a rolling basis beginning 3/1. Federal Work-Study Program available. Institutional employment available. Off-campus job opportunities are excellent.

The Inside Word

Volunteer work and community service will serve your application to any school well, but they're especially helpful at this Jesuit institution. Post-Katrina New Orleans has spooked some prospective applicants, but the school has made great strides in rebuilding undergraduate enrollment, attracting new faculty members, and keeping alive the spirit of the school.

THE SCHOOL SAYS "..."

From The Admissions Office

"Chartered in 1912, Loyola University New Orleans is one of America's 28 Jesuit institutions of higher learning. Its rich history dates back to the early eighteenth century when the Jesuits first arrived in New Orleans. As a Catholic university, Loyola has continued to emphasize the valuable Jesuit tradition of educating the whole person. Our more than 37,000 graduates have excelled in innumerable areas for 97 years; their influence is felt around the world.

"Loyola's growth has increased the diversity of education available, all delivered within the educational values traditionally associated with our Jesuit heritage. This unique, nationally acclaimed institution—the crown jewel for a Jesuit education in the Southern United States—offers a welcoming and festive campus atmosphere and an emphasis on a liberal arts and sciences education, emphasizing self-discovery, exploration of values, while fostering personal initiative and critical thinking. Undergraduates enjoy individual attention in a university that strives to educate not only intellectually, but also spiritually, socially, and athletically. Undergraduate experience is broadened through special programs such as the First Year Experience, learning communities, research, service learning, study abroad and internships.

"Students applying for 2010 admission are required to take the SAT (or the ACT with the Writing section). The highest composite scores will be used in admissions decisions."

SELECTIVITY

Admissions Rating	88
# of applicants	3,651
% of applicants accepted	63
% of acceptees attending	31

FRESHMAN PROFILE

Range SAT Critical Reading	560–660
Range SAT Math	520–630
Range ACT Composite	23–28
Minimum paper TOEFL	550
Minimum computer TOEFL	213
Average HS GPA	3.74
% graduated top 10% of class	30
% graduated top 25% of class	60
% graduated top 50% of class	85

DEADLINES

Regular	
Priority	12/1
Notification	rolling
Nonfall registration?	yes

APPLICANTS ALSO LOOK AT

AND OFTEN PREFER
Saint Louis University
Fordham University
University of Miami
Boston University

AND SOMETIMES PREFER
Tulane University
Louisiana State University
Xavier University of Louisiana
Loyola University of Chicago

FINANCIAL FACTS

Financial Aid Rating	85
Annual tuition	$28,770
Room and board	$6,814
Required fees	$936
Books and supplies	$1,000
% frosh rec. need-based scholarship or grant aid	64
% UG rec. need-based scholarship or grant aid	57
% frosh rec. non-need-based scholarship or grant aid	63
% UG rec. non-need-based scholarship or grant aid	56
% frosh rec. need-based self-help aid	45
% UG rec. need-based self-help aid	44
% frosh rec. any financial aid	98
% UG rec. any financial aid	97
% UG borrow to pay for school	59
Average cumulative indebtedness	$21,401

LYNCHBURG COLLEGE

1501 LAKESIDE DRIVE, LYNCHBURG, VA 24501 • ADMISSIONS: 434-544-8300 • FAX: 434-544-8653

CAMPUS LIFE
Quality of Life Rating	**85**
Fire Safety Rating	**74**
Green Rating	**79**
Type of school	private
Affiliation	Disciples of Christ
Environment	city

STUDENTS
Total undergrad enrollment	2,091
% male/female	41/59
% from out of state	37
% from public high school	78
% live on campus	80
% in (# of) fraternities	10 (4)
% in (# of) sororities	15 (6)
% African American	7
% Asian	1
% Caucasian	77
% Hispanic	3
% Native American	1
% international	1
# of countries represented	17

SURVEY SAYS . . .
No one cheats
School is well run
Students are friendly

ACADEMICS
Academic Rating	**80**
Calendar	semester
Student/faculty ratio	12:1
Profs interesting rating	83
Profs accessible rating	85
Most common	
reg class size	10–19 students
Most common	
lab size	10–19 students

MOST POPULAR MAJORS
business administration and
management
athletic training
communication studies
teacher education and professional
development, specific levels
and methods

STUDENTS SAY " . . ."

Academics
The "tight-knit" sense of community of Lynchburg College in Lynchburg, Virginia is one of the main draws of this liberal arts school. Offering a "pretty little campus and a (pretty) good academic setting," the school provides its students with a solid liberal arts education that also helps "to prepare them for life."

Being a small school, classes are typically not very big and are normally geared toward discussion, and attendance counts towards grading. The quality of teaching here is "above average," with "some truly magnificent professors, but then some really bad ones too." There "are places where students can go for help if they need it," but this isn't really necessary for the more academic minded/honors students, who say that "academic rigor can be lacking," and "classroom discussions can leave the intellectual somewhat disappointed." However, if students are having trouble, "the students have to make a case for themselves—the school doesn't do it for them without effort from the students (a good thing)." Though a few students claim the school has some money management issues, most find the administration here to be "open and accessible," and they really set the course for the school, which "strives to be one of the best private colleges." Freshman orientation does a fantastic job of helping transition students into their new lives; the study abroad programs do a great job of taking them out of it for a bit if they so choose.

Life
There is "not a whole lot to do in Lynchburg" other than "go to Walmart, the dollar theater, and eat," a state that the school attempts to counteract by sponsoring weekend events such as comedians, speakers, concerts, and hypnotists. Outdoor events such as skiing, biking, and rock climbing add to the already well-stocked list of sporty opportunities. "Fridays and Saturdays are crazy" once students stop studying, and partying takes a prominent place in everyone's "loud social life," though "if you want to find somewhere to just chill, you can find that also." Activities that go about on-campus can be anything "from a night in playing *Scene It!* or *Shout About* in a dorm room with a group of friends to a late night out …perusing the frat houses and townhouses." All housing is on-campus, which has its downsides in the myriad complaints about the lack of selection of food in the dining halls.

Student Body
Students use the age-old descriptors of "white" and "middle-class" to portray the typical Lynchburg student, with most hailing from the mid-atlantic region; there is also a noticeably higher percentage of females enrolled. "Kindness is an epidemic at this college," so it shouldn't be surprising that everyone is friendly, and the few atypical students seem to get along well with everyone, or at least find their own niche. Athletics are popular here, and most students keep active with either a sport (club, intramural, or Division III varsity) and/or Greek life. "Everyone always says hi to each other, it is a very friendly environment overall," says a freshman.

FINANCIAL AID: 434-544-8228 • E-MAIL: ADMISSIONS@LYNCHBURG.EDU • WEBSITE: WWW.LYNCHBURG.EDU

THE PRINCETON REVIEW SAYS

Admissions

Very important factors considered include: Academic GPA, rigor of secondary school record, standardized test scores. *Important factors considered include:* Class rank, interview. *Other factors considered include:* Application essay, recommendation(s), extracurricular activities, level of applicant's interest, talent/ability, volunteer work. SAT or ACT required; TOEFL required of all international applicants. High school diploma is required and GED is accepted. *Academic units required:* 4 English, 3 mathematics, 3 science, (2 science labs), 2 foreign language, 2 social studies, 2 history. *Academic units recommended:* 4 mathematics, 4 science, 3 foreign language, 1 academic elective.

Financial Aid

Students should submit: FAFSA, state aid form. The Princeton Review suggests that all financial aid forms be submitted as soon as possible after 1/1. *Need-based scholarships/grants offered:* Federal Pell, SEOG, state scholarships/grants, private scholarships, the school's own gift aid. *Loan aid offered:* FFEL Subsidized Stafford, FFEL Unsubsidized Stafford, FFEL PLUS, Federal Perkins. Applicants will be notified of awards on a rolling basis beginning 3/1. Federal Work-Study Program available. Institutional employment available. Off-campus job opportunities are good.

Inside Word

The admissions process at Lynchburg is about as typical as they come. The school expects that you will have completed a college preparatory curriculum in high school with a B average and have scored near the national mean on the SAT and/or ACT. Two somewhat unique attributes of the process is that letters of recommendation are not required and applications are reviewed on a rolling basis. For those who know that Lynchburg is their first choice, the school has an early decision option.

THE SCHOOL SAYS "..."

From The Admissions Office

"Lynchburg College is Virginia's most comprehensive private college, nationally recognized for going above and beyond in its commitment to student success. From the moment that prospective students step onto the spectacular campus, they are aware that LC is a place where they will have opportunities to grow intellectually, morally, and spiritually, and that there are faculty, staff, and peer mentors waiting to support them in their quest to achieve their personal goals.

"The emphasis at Lynchburg College is on the development of the whole person, as evidenced by the low student/faculty ratio and an abundance of student organizations, athletic teams, intramural and club sports, and experiential learning opportunities, including service learning, internships, study abroad, and faculty-student collaborative research.

"Lynchburg College seeks to enroll students who wish to take advantage of all that the school has to offer and who want to be part of a caring community. LC welcomes and encourages interested high school students to visit the campus to see for themselves why the college has received record numbers of applications and multiple national honors in recent years. The Admissions Office sponsors open houses and other events for prospective students throughout the year. For more information visit our website.

"We allow students to submit scores from either the SAT or the ACT, and we will use the student's best score from these tests. In regard to the SAT, the Critical Reading and Math scores will be the primary SAT scores used for admission decisions."

SELECTIVITY
Admissions Rating	77
# of applicants	4,501
% of applicants accepted	68
% of acceptees attending	19
# of early decision applicants	205
% accepted early decision	52

FRESHMAN PROFILE
Range SAT Critical Reading	460–560
Range SAT Math	450–570
Range SAT Writing	460–560
Range ACT Composite	18–23
Minimum paper TOEFL	525
Minimum computer TOEFL	197
Average HS GPA	3.13
% graduated top 10% of class	11
% graduated top 25% of class	33
% graduated top 50% of class	75

DEADLINES
Early decision	
Deadline	11/15
Notification	12/15
Regular	
Notification	rolling
Nonfall registration?	yes

FINANCIAL FACTS
Financial Aid Rating	84
Annual tuition	$27,980
Room and board	$6,970
Books and supplies	$750
% frosh rec. need-based scholarship or grant aid	64
% UG rec. need-based scholarship or grant aid	62
% frosh rec. non-need-based scholarship or grant aid	11
% UG rec. non-need-based scholarship or grant aid	9
% frosh rec. need-based self-help aid	51
% UG rec. need-based self-help aid	51
% frosh rec. any financial aid	93
% UG rec. any financial aid	91
% UG borrow to pay for school	69
Average cumulative indebtedness	$26,915

MACALESTER COLLEGE

1600 GRAND AVENUE, ST. PAUL, MN 55105 • ADMISSIONS: 651-696-6357 • FAX: 651-696-6724

CAMPUS LIFE

Quality of Life Rating	99
Fire Safety Rating	87
Green Rating	84
Type of school	private
Affiliation	Presbyterian
Environment	metropolis

STUDENTS

Total undergrad enrollment	1,912
% male/female	42/58
% from out of state	78
% from public high school	76
% live on campus	67
% African American	5
% Asian	9
% Caucasian	69
% Hispanic	4
% Native American	1
% international	12
# of countries represented	87

SURVEY SAYS . . .

Lots of liberal students
Students aren't religious
Students love St. Paul, MN
Great food on campus
Frats and sororities are unpopular or nonexistent
Political activism is popular

ACADEMICS

Academic Rating	96
Calendar	semester
Student/faculty ratio	10:1
Profs interesting rating	89
Profs accessible rating	89
Most common reg class size	10–19 students
Most common lab size	fewer than 10 students

MOST POPULAR MAJORS

economics
English language and literature
political science and government

STUDENTS SAY ". . ."

Academics

"Globalism, liberalism, social justice and environmentalism rule the day" at Macalester College, a small, Minnesota liberal arts school where "academics are taken very seriously and students are expected to perform." Academic offerings "are top-notch" here, "particularly chemistry, economics, and international studies," the last of which benefits from "the new Institute for Global Citizenship, study abroad, and the diversity of international students" which together make Macalester "a very worldly place." Departments of psychology, sociology, and political science also have their champions. Students warn that because of Macalester's small size, some other departments "are extremely understaffed, and in combination with small class sizes, that leads to a lot of people being turned away from courses they need." Students report, "In true liberal arts style, every department is somehow interconnected to seemingly opposite departments, numerous interdisciplinary majors exist, and even within individual classes, professors approach teaching their given subject from numerous angles. "While this may make choosing a specific major somewhat difficult, it absolutely enriches everyone's thoughts and sparks discussion across campus about a variety of issues." This can lead to "The 'Macalester Dilemma,' the oh-so-common problem of so many interests and so little time. With so many ways to involve oneself, Mac students, with their wide-ranging interests and their desire to explore them, often find themselves over committed."

Life

"Everything is pretty low key" on the Macalester campus, where "there are rarely large parties. Instead, people will drink and hang out in the dorms (if underclassmen) or friends' houses (if juniors or seniors)" where they tend to discuss 'big ideas.' In this way, "life at Mac is an extension of classes. We talk about gender, sexuality, multiculturalism, politics, etc. I always learn something new in a conversation with my friends because Mac students love analyzing things." As one student notes, "A joke here at Mac is how often the phrase 'social construct' and the word 'hegemony' are used, both in classes and even in social settings." Mac life is not all hanging out and deconstructing. On the contrary, "there's a really strong campus community. There are always events going on on the weekends, both campus-sponsored dances and parties in dorm rooms, etc." as well as "plays, musicals, and other things on campus." And, "when Mac lets us down, there are two cities (Minneapolis and St. Paul) for us to go play in. Everyone should go to the Gay '90s at least once before they graduate." Other urban options include "football or basketball games…some people go clubbing or out to eat. Lots go to the museums or just out shopping." "Getting around on the bus system is easy, although sometimes slow."

Student Body

Macalester "has a very diverse population as far as ethnicity and origin goes, but as a whole is very politically liberal." The typical student "is either a liberal Democrat and environmentalist who wants to make the world a better place, or an international student (who generally doesn't approve of any U.S. politics) who seeks to work in industry in his home country." Undergrads tend to be "fairly relaxed and easy going," "intelligent, high-achieving, hard-working, and unpretentious but conscientious and on top of the news." Many describe themselves as "awkward," adding "we are nerds and proud of it." Jocks that are "only interested in playing football and partying" are atypical, "but they seem to have fun among themselves, too."

FINANCIAL AID: 651-696-6214 • E-MAIL: ADMISSIONS@MACALESTER.EDU • WEBSITE: WWW.MACALESTER.EDU

THE PRINCETON REVIEW SAYS

Admissions

Very important factors considered include: Academic GPA, rigor of secondary school record. *Important factors considered include:* Application essay, recommendation(s), standardized test scores, character/personal qualities, extracurricular activities. *Other factors considered include:* Class rank, alumni/ae relation, first generation, interview, racial/ethnic status, talent/ability, volunteer work, work experience. SAT or ACT required; TOEFL required of all international applicants. High school diploma or equivalent is not required. *Academic units recommended:* 4 English, 3 mathematics, 3 science, (3 science labs), 3 foreign language, 3 social studies.

Financial Aid

Students should submit: FAFSA, CSS/Financial Aid PROFILE, noncustodial PROFILE. Regular filing deadline is 3/1. The Princeton Review suggests that all financial aid forms be submitted as soon as possible after 1/1. *Need-based scholarships/grants offered:* Federal Pell, SEOG, state scholarships/grants, private scholarships. *Loan aid offered:* FFEL Subsidized Stafford, FFEL Unsubsidized Stafford, FFEL PLUS, Federal Perkins, state loans. Applicants will be notified of awards on or about 4/1. Federal Work-Study Program available. Institutional employment available. Off-campus job opportunities are excellent.

The Inside Word

To say that Macalester's star is on the rise is to put it very mildly. The number of applicants to the school continues to increase. The freshman class has grown slightly in that time but not at anything approaching the growth rate of the applicant pool. Accordingly, it has grown substantially more difficult to gain admission here within a very short period of time. Candidates need to put their best foot forward in their applications; expressing a commitment to attending the school if admitted can only help.

THE SCHOOL SAYS "..."

From The Admissions Office

"Macalester has been preparing students for world citizenship and providing an integrated international education for over six decades. The United Nations flag has flown on campus since 1950 and 16 percent of the students are citizens of another country, with 87 countries represented on campus. Over 60% of Mac students study abroad, going to nearly 50 countries all over the world each year. Graduates enter the work force or graduate school with respected scholarship and real experience in a global community, prepared to succeed in their chosen fields. Mac students thrive in a rigorous academic environment, supported by accomplished faculty who love to teach. Located in a friendly residential neighborhood in the heart of a vibrant metropolitan area, Macalester offers unusually broad, easily accessible internship opportunities to add valuable experience, connections and practice at getting things done, often leading to job opportunities after graduation. Two out of three Mac students complete an internship at a Twin Cities business, law firm, hospital, financial institution, museum, theater, state government, research lab, environmental agency or non-profit group (and more), all within a few miles of campus. Students rave about the food at Mac, which includes vegetarian fare, food for meat lovers, plenty of variety and entrées from around the world. A new athletic and recreation center opened in the fall of 2009, including a large fitness center, indoor track, gymnasium, natatorium, field house, gathering spaces, juice bar, atrium and more. Athletic teams frequently earn the highest cumulative GPA in the nation. Macalester meets the full demonstrated need for every admitted student, providing broad socioeconomic representation in the student body."

SELECTIVITY

Admissions Rating	96
# of applicants	4,967
% of applicants accepted	41
% of acceptees attending	24
# accepting a place on wait list	177
% admitted from wait list	19
# of early decision applicants	250
% accepted early decision	46

FRESHMAN PROFILE

Range SAT Critical Reading	630–730
Range SAT Math	620–710
Range SAT Writing	620–720
Range ACT Composite	28–32
Minimum paper TOEFL	573
Minimum computer TOEFL	230
% graduated top 10% of class	68
% graduated top 25% of class	90
% graduated top 50% of class	100

DEADLINES

Early decision	
Deadline	11/15
Notification	12/15
Regular	
Deadline	1/15
Notification	3/30
Nonfall registration?	no

APPLICANTS ALSO LOOK AT

AND OFTEN PREFER
Brown University

AND SOMETIMES PREFER
Oberlin College
University of Minnesota—Twin Cities

AND RARELY PREFER
Colorado College

FINANCIAL FACTS

Financial Aid Rating	98
Annual tuition	$33,494
Room and board	$8,220
Required fees	$200
Books and supplies	$850
% frosh rec. need-based scholarship or grant aid	45
% UG rec. need-based scholarship or grant aid	67
% frosh rec. non-need-based scholarship or grant aid	1
% UG rec. non-need-based scholarship or grant aid	1
% frosh rec. need-based self-help aid	65
% UG rec. need-based self-help aid	67
% frosh rec. any financial aid	71.5
% UG rec. any financial aid	73
% UG borrow to pay for school	70.1
Average cumulative indebtedness	$18,849

MANHATTANVILLE COLLEGE

2900 PURCHASE STREET, ADMISSIONS OFFICE, PURCHASE, NY 10577 • ADMISSIONS: 914-323-5124 • FAX: 914-694-1732

CAMPUS LIFE

Quality of Life Rating	**94**
Fire Safety Rating	**60***
Green Rating	**88**
Type of school	private
Environment	town

STUDENTS

Total undergrad enrollment	1,677
% male/female	33/67
% from out of state	36
% live on campus	80
% African American	5
% Asian	1
% Caucasian	27
% Hispanic	11
% international	8
# of countries represented	60

SURVEY SAYS . . .

*Diverse student types on campus
Different types of students interact
Frats and sororities are unpopular or
nonexistent*

ACADEMICS

Academic Rating	**82**
Calendar	semester
Student/faculty ratio	11:1
Profs interesting rating	83
Profs accessible rating	86
Most common reg class size	10–19 students

MOST POPULAR MAJORS
business/commerce
psychology
visual and performing arts

STUDENTS SAY ". . ."

Academics

"Helpful and easy-to-reach" professors, "very involved" administrators, and "close proximity to New York City" (although still far enough from its "pollution and distractions") all contribute to the "close and supportive community" that is Manhattanville College. Students here have the "unbelievable" opportunity to "exchange ideas" with professors who have "studied in the best universities in the world. There are so many distinguished professors here, ranging from experts in world religions, to former ambassadors in the United Nations. Almost all of them are well-known in their areas of study." Better still, nearly all "are approachable" and "offer office hours and are always there when they are supposed to be." Further help is available through "the Supplemental Instructor Program, which provides free extra help in math, history, and science courses." Mville (as it is affectionately called by its students) places a lot of emphasis on experiential learning, and the school's location is an asset in that regard. Not only is Mville close to the myriad internship opportunities of the megalopolis next door, but "We [also] have tons of corporations literally in our neighborhood, like MasterCard, IBM, MBIA, [and] JPMorgan" that bring "plenty of internships." A "good education program" and "strong programs in psychology and marketing" are among the standouts here. Many undergrads appreciate the fact that "Manhattanville College reaches out to people with no money to pay for school," although they acknowledge the drawbacks. "The school doesn't accept enough people who can pay for school and, therefore, the school does not make money. And then we the students pay for that" through service shortages and class cancellations.

Life

"There is not too much to do on campus" at Manhattanville, "and the school's campus is pretty small so you cannot really explore the grounds too much," students warn. "Many people commute, so the campus is basically dead at night and on weekends," and what socializing might occur is at least in some instances hampered by "the very strict residence assistants and residence directors" who battle on-campus partying. As a result, most students seek fun "in nearby White Plains, a small city filled with different restaurants, malls, Wal-Mart-type places, and a huge movie theater. People also go into New York City for fun, as our Valiant Express bus takes people into the city every weekend, and shuttles go to and from White Plains every day." On-campus options include "lots of interest groups and activities that one can join," and "a game room with different things like billiards and ping-pong." Finally, "the students here have a lot of school spirit, so there is always a great turnout for games." Men's and women's basketball and men's hockey are among the popular draws.

Student Body

"The diversity at Manhattanville is enormous," students report. "Although the school is fairly small, there are people from all over the world." One student observes, "Sometimes I feel like I'm in the minority as a non-Spanish speaker, which is interesting." Undergrads tend to hang with their own; "Dominicans sit with Dominicans, Puerto Ricans with Puerto Ricans, misfits with misfits, artists with artists, jocks with jocks. At Manhattanville the stereotypical personalities are clumped together by habit and for the most part tend to gravitate toward one another, with minor glimpses of interaction with other groups." Regardless of any cliques, "all of the students at the school are extremely cordial. Since it is such a small school, you get to know everyone's face." Undergrads here generally "are not the type of people who are very academically competitive with one another, want to change the world, or have super-high goals for their future. What they may lack in ambition they make up for in kindness. There are a few students here who work very hard and want to go to a great graduate school, or have a great job, and do everything they can to get all A's. They fit in just as well as everyone else because almost all the students here are very accepting and good-natured."

FINANCIAL AID: 914-323-5357 • E-MAIL: ADMISSIONS@MVILLE.EDU • WEBSITE: WWW.MVILLE.EDU

THE PRINCETON REVIEW SAYS

Admissions

Very important factors considered include: Rigor of secondary school record, standardized test scores. *Important factors considered include:* Application essay, recommendation(s), extracurricular activities, interview. *Other factors considered include:* Alumni/ae relation, character/personal qualities, geographical residence, talent/ability, volunteer work, work experience. SAT or ACT required; TOEFL required of all international applicants. High school diploma is required and GED is accepted. *Academic units required:* 4 English, 3 mathematics, 2 science, 2 social studies, 5 academic electives.

Financial Aid

Students should submit: FAFSA, state aid form. The Princeton Review suggests that all financial aid forms be submitted as soon as possible after 1/1. *Need-based scholarships/grants offered:* Federal Pell, SEOG, state scholarships/grants, private scholarships, the school's own gift aid. *Loan aid offered:* FFEL Subsidized Stafford, FFEL Unsubsidized Stafford, FFEL PLUS, Federal Perkins. Applicants will be notified of awards on a rolling basis beginning 3/1. Federal Work-Study Program available. Institutional employment available. Off-campus job opportunities are excellent.

The Inside Word

Applicants demonstrating middle-of-the-road academic achievement will most likely find themselves with an acceptance letter from Manhattanville. The school does seek 'good fits,' however and frequently attempts to assess compatibility with a candidate interview. The college still seeks to achieve greater gender balance, so male candidates enjoy a slightly higher admission rate than female candidates. In addition to meeting regular admissions requirements, students who wish to pursue a degree in fine arts or performing arts must present a portfolio or audition, respectively.

THE SCHOOL SAYS " . . ."

From The Admissions Office

"Manhattanville's mission—to educate ethically and socially responsible leaders for the global community—is evident throughout the college, from academics to athletics to social and extracurricular activities. With 1,600 undergraduates from 59 nations and 39 states, our diversity spans geographic, cultural, ethnic, religious, socioeconomic, and academic backgrounds. Students are free to express their views in this tight-knit community, where we value the personal as well as the global. Any six students with similar interest can start a club, and most participate in a variety of campus wide programs. Last year, students engaged in more than 23,380 hours of community service and social justice activity. Study-abroad opportunities include not only the most desirable international locations, but also a semester-long immersion for living, studying, and working in New York City. In the true liberal arts tradition, students are encouraged to think for themselves and develop new skills—in music, the studio arts, on stage, in the sciences, or on the playing field. With more than 50 areas of study and a popular self-designed major, there is no limit to our academic scope. Our Westchester County location, just 35 miles north of New York City, gives students an edge for jobs and internships. Last year, the men's and women's ice hockey teams were ranked #1 in the nation for Division III."

SELECTIVITY
Admissions Rating	80
# of applicants	4,556
% of applicants accepted	52
% of acceptees attending	24

FRESHMAN PROFILE
Range SAT Critical Reading	500–620
Range SAT Math	500–610
Range ACT Composite	21–24
Minimum paper TOEFL	550
Minimum computer TOEFL	217
% graduated top 10% of class	22
% graduated top 25% of class	47
% graduated top 50% of class	80

DEADLINES
Early decision	
Deadline	12/1
Notification	12/31
Regular	
Priority	3/1
Deadline	3/1
Notification	rolling
Nonfall registration?	yes

APPLICANTS ALSO LOOK AT

AND OFTEN PREFER
New York University

AND SOMETIMES PREFER
Fordham University

AND RARELY PREFER
Pace University—White Plains

FINANCIAL FACTS
Financial Aid Rating	79
Annual tuition	$31,490
Room and board	$13,500
Required fees	$1,270
Books and supplies	$800
% frosh rec. need-based scholarship or grant aid	62
% UG rec. need-based scholarship or grant aid	57
% frosh rec. non-need-based scholarship or grant aid	59
% UG rec. non-need-based scholarship or grant aid	57
% frosh rec. need-based self-help aid	58
% UG rec. need-based self-help aid	54
% frosh rec. any financial aid	75
% UG rec. any financial aid	70
% UG borrow to pay for school	67
Average cumulative indebtedness	$23,253

MARIST COLLEGE

3399 NORTH ROAD, POUGHKEEPSIE, NY 12601-1387 • ADMISSIONS: 845-575-3226 • FAX: 845-575-3215

CAMPUS LIFE
Quality of Life Rating	**75**
Fire Safety Rating	**79**
Green Rating	**81**
Type of school	private
Environment	town

STUDENTS
Total undergrad enrollment	4,796
% male/female	41/59
% from out of state	41
% from public high school	72
% live on campus	75
% in (# of) fraternities	1 (3)
% in (# of) sororities	3 (4)
% African American	3
% Asian	2
% Caucasian	75
% Hispanic	6
# of countries represented	11

SURVEY SAYS . . .
Low cost of living
(Almost) no one smokes

ACADEMICS
Academic Rating	**77**
Calendar	semester
Student/faculty ratio	15:1
Profs interesting rating	75
Profs accessible rating	76
Most common	
reg class size	20–29 students
Most common	
lab size	20–29 students

MOST POPULAR MAJORS
business
communication
education
psychology
fashion

STUDENTS SAY ". . ."

Academics

Marist College, "a smaller private school in a nice area with a great campus life," offers a surprising range of options to its largely career-minded student population. The school is home to "a very good business school;" "a good criminal justice department;" "a reputable teacher education program;" and "great concentrations in teaching, communications, and fashion." All departments benefit from the school's "unique partnership with IBM," which translates into "very advanced computer technology and Web services. Our online library is very extensive and extremely helpful for research papers and projects." Similarly, students appreciate the school's vigorous efforts to place them in meaningful internships. One student explains: "The internship departments have directors in each major, and a great many opportunities are made available to students for internships during both the academic year and the summer months. There is even staff on campus to go over your resume with you and make sure it is properly formatted and has all of the necessary information in it for potential employers to review when you apply for an internship." The school's location, "about an hour and a half from New York City," is key to the success of the internship program. Students also love the "intensive study-abroad program," through which they "can go almost anywhere in the world for the same price as a semester at Marist."

Life

With "breathtaking views of the Hudson River" and "a great campus complete with nature trails and a riverfront park," Marist College offers an idyllic setting in which to pursue a college degree. Students tell us that campus life "pretty much has something for everyone: campus organizations based around race/heritage, Greek organizations, service, sports, performing arts, and co-curricular organizations. Students have many opportunities to build their social network." Many here "are extremely concerned with life after college, and therefore many engage in activities and internships that will give them more experience in their career." They still find time for fun, though. Campus-based diversions include "comedians, bands, hypnotists, singers, and speakers [who] come every week to give performances for the students," while off-campus life includes forays into hometown Poughkeepsie ("the school is about seven minutes from the Galleria Mall, which has a big selection of stores") or nearby historic Hyde Park; trips to New York City are most likely to occur on the weekend, since the city is about 90 minutes away (the trip, however, only requires "an extremely easy train ride to the middle of the city"). Poughkeepsie has an active nightclub and bar scene, students tell us.

Student Body

"A typical Marist student is from New York, New Jersey, or Connecticut;" is "middle- to upper-middle class;" and has "a good background education and social skills." Undergrads here "display a hard work ethic in class while taking the initiative to become involved with student-run clubs, activities, and sports," but students aren't especially driven by academics for their own sake; they simply want to "get their work done and have a good time while getting great grades." Many here "tend to be politically conservative, but a lot of students just don't have an interest in politics. Also, Marist does not have the hipster crowd." The school was once a Catholic school, and although it is now officially nondenominational, vestiges of its old identity are evident in the student body; "most students are Catholic," one student reports, "but religious diversity is increasing bit by bit" as the years pass.

FINANCIAL AID: 845-575-3230 • E-MAIL: ADMISSIONS@MARIST.EDU • WEBSITE: WWW.MARIST.EDU

THE PRINCETON REVIEW SAYS

Admissions

Very important factors considered include: Academic GPA, rigor of secondary school record, standardized test scores. *Important factors considered include:* Class rank, application essay, recommendation(s), extracurricular activities, geographical residence, state residency, talent/ability, volunteer work, work experience. *Other factors considered include:* Alumni/ae relation, level of applicant's interest, racial/ethnic status. SAT or ACT required; ACT with Writing component required; TOEFL required of all international applicants. High school diploma is required and GED is accepted. *Academic units required:* 4 English, 3 mathematics, 3 science, (2 science labs), 2 foreign language, 2 social studies, 1 history, 2 academic electives. *Academic units recommended:* 4 mathematics, 4 science, (3 science labs), 3 foreign language.

Financial Aid

Students should submit: FAFSA. The Princeton Review suggests that all financial aid forms be submitted as soon as possible after 1/1. *Need-based scholarships/grants offered:* Federal Pell, SEOG, state scholarships/grants, private scholarships, the school's own gift aid. *Loan aid offered:* FFEL Subsidized Stafford, FFEL Unsubsidized Stafford, FFEL PLUS, Federal Perkins, Alternative Loans. Applicants will be notified of awards on a rolling basis beginning 3/15. Federal Work-Study Program available. Institutional employment available. Off-campus job opportunities are excellent.

The Inside Word

You don't have to be a stellar high-school student to attend Marist; about one-quarter of its most recent incoming class graduated outside the top 25 percent of their high school class. Those lacking academic bona fides will have to make it up in other areas, however; evidence of leadership, ability to contribute to the life of the campus (e.g. artistic or athletic skill), an interesting background that will add diversity to classroom discussion, or a similar distinguishing trait will be needed to make up for a middling academic record.

THE SCHOOL SAYS "..."

From The Admissions Office

"Marist is a 'hot school' among prospective students. We are seeing a record number of applications each year. But the number of seats available for the freshman class remains the same, about 950. Therefore, becoming an accepted applicant is an increasingly competitive process. Our recommendations: keep your grades up, score well on the SAT/ACT, participate in community service both in and out of school, and exercise leadership in the classroom, athletics, extracurricular activities, and your place of worship. We encourage a campus visit. When prospective students see Marist—our beautiful location on a scenic stretch of the Hudson River, the quality of our facilities, the interaction between students and faculty, and the fact that everyone really enjoys their time here—they want to become a part of the Marist College community. We'll help you in the transition from high school to college through an innovative first-year program that provides mentors for every student. You'll also learn how to use technology in whatever field you choose. We emphasize three aspects of a true Marist experience: excellence in education, community, and service to others. At Marist, you'll get a premium education, develop your skills, have fun and make lifelong friends, be given the opportunity to gain valuable experience through our great internship and study abroad programs, and be ahead of the competition for graduate school or work.

"Marist requires the SAT with the Writing component. We recommend all students take the test at least twice and the ACT once. Marist will use the best Verbal, Math, and Writing scores from the SAT or the highest composite ACT score."

SELECTIVITY

Admissions Rating	89
# of applicants	9,198
% of applicants accepted	37
% of acceptees attending	30
# accepting a place on wait list	465
% admitted from wait list	8
# of early decision applicants	161
% accepted early decision	77

FRESHMAN PROFILE

Range SAT Critical Reading	530–620
Range SAT Math	540–630
Range SAT Writing	540–630
Range ACT Composite	23–27
Minimum paper TOEFL	550
Minimum computer TOEFL	213
Minimum web-based TOEFL	79
Average HS GPA	3.3
% graduated top 10% of class	32
% graduated top 25% of class	73
% graduated top 50% of class	92

DEADLINES

Early decision	
Deadline	11/15
Notification	12/15
Early action	
Deadline	12/1
Notification	1/30
Regular	
Deadline	2/15
Notification	3/30
Nonfall registration?	yes

APPLICANTS ALSO LOOK AT

AND OFTEN PREFER
Providence, Fairfield, SUNY Geneseo
Boston College, Villnova

AND SOMETIMES PREFER
Loyola—Maryland, SUNY—Binghampton

FINANCIAL FACTS

Financial Aid Rating	70
Annual tuition	$25,100
Room and board	$10,730
Required fees	$496
Books and supplies	$1,300
% frosh rec. need-based scholarship or grant aid	60
% UG rec. need-based scholarship or grant aid	57
% frosh rec. non-need-based scholarship or grant aid	35
% UG rec. non-need-based scholarship or grant aid	29
% frosh rec. need-based self-help aid	46
% UG rec. need-based self-help aid	50
% frosh rec. athletic scholarships	8
% UG rec. athletic scholarships	6
% frosh rec. any financial aid	92
% UG rec. any financial aid	86
% UG borrow to pay for school	67
Average cumulative indebtedness	$23,588

MARLBORO COLLEGE

PO Box A, South Road, Marlboro, VT 05344-0300 • Admissions: 802-258-9236 • Fax: 802-451-7555

CAMPUS LIFE
Quality of Life Rating	81
Fire Safety Rating	68
Green Rating	73
Type of school	private
Environment	rural

STUDENTS
Total undergrad enrollment	324
% male/female	47/53
% from out of state	88
% from public high school	70
% live on campus	80
% African American	1
% Asian	3
% Caucasian	82
% Hispanic	3
% Native American	1
% international	1
# of countries represented	2

SURVEY SAYS . . .
Lots of liberal students
Class discussions encouraged
No one cheats
Campus feels safe
Frats and sororities are unpopular or nonexistent
Student government is popular

ACADEMICS
Academic Rating	99
Calendar	semester
Student/faculty ratio	8:1
Profs interesting rating	97
Profs accessible rating	91
Most common reg class size	fewer than 10 students
Most common lab size	fewer than 10 students

MOST POPULAR MAJORS
English language and literature
social sciences
visual and performing arts

STUDENTS SAY "..."

Academics

Marlboro College is all about giving students "the freedom to pursue their own interests and study what they want." Here, undergrads design their own junior and senior curricula, then pursue them in one-on-one tutorials with professors. The process, known here simply as 'The Plan,' culminates in a substantial senior thesis. The goal is to "learn how to think critically and find the resources you need in the course of completing a dissertation-level project," and undergrads here "wouldn't settle for anything less in their academic pursuits." Freshmen and sophomores complete more traditional-style courses, albeit in smaller classrooms and with a greater-than-usual focus on writing and discussion. The size of the school—just more than 300 undergraduates attend—is sometimes a hindrance. One student observes that, "Since there is generally only one professor per field, it is a bit disappointing to realize that there can only be a limited number of classes offered per semester." "Too often a student will reach the final year when his/her Plan sponsor goes on sabbatical and a replacement is not hired in time or hired at all. This presents a problem: Does the student leave the college until their professor returns, or does the student switch Plan sponsors, potentially altering the focus of their work so much they dislike what they're doing?" Despite these issues, "professors are very receptive and try to accommodate individual interests as best they can." Most here feel these are reasonable costs to bear in order to pursue "independent, difficult, intellectually-stimulating work inside a student-centered and directed curriculum."

Life

Marlboro is "a little school on top of a hill" with Brattleboro, the closest town, "about a half hour away," so "life is pretty intensely focused on the campus." "While we do make the trip to Brattleboro fairly often, most of our time is spent 'on the hill,'" says one student. Students "study a lot, but there is also a lot of hanging out, mainly in small impromptu ways." They "like to debate about philosophy, politics, and religion." Fun "is found in the 300 acres that surround the college: skiing, hiking, long walks in an apple orchard, broomball (a hippie version of hockey), soccer, etc." Trips to Brattleboro are pleasant because it's "an arts town." Students occasionally travel to Massachusetts college towns Amherst and Northampton for concerts or shopping and "frequently classes take field trips to NYC or Boston." Many get involved in grassroots political organization, both on campus and off.

Students

The typical Marlboro student "wouldn't fit quite right anywhere else: academically driven, maybe a little nerdy, politically vocal, and looking for a laid-back environment. There is no atypical student at Marlboro, because we all would have been atypical someplace else." Personality types run the gamut, including "hippie environmentalists, geeks and gamers, theater kids, artists, and so on and so forth and every combination thereof. We're underrepresented in the jock and beauty queen categories, but that doesn't seem to bother anybody." Everyone here, we're told, "is extremely passionate about their own little academic niche, and furthermore each person is one of the smartest people you will ever meet." The school is home to "a large gay population and a few transgender students," but "there are a lack of minority students, [and] Republicans."

FINANCIAL AID: 800-343-0049 • E-MAIL: ADMISSIONS@MARLBORO.EDU • WEBSITE: WWW.MARLBORO.EDU

THE PRINCETON REVIEW SAYS

Admissions

Very important factors considered include: Application essay, academic GPA, rigor of secondary school record, character/personal qualities. *Important factors considered include:* Extracurricular activities, interview, talent/ability. *Other factors considered include:* Class rank, recommendation(s), standardized test scores (only if submitted), alumni/ae relation, first generation, geographical residence, level of applicant's interest, state residency, volunteer work, work experience. Submission of SAT or ACT is optional. TOEFL required of all international applicants. High school diploma is required and GED is accepted. *Academic units recommended:* 4 English, 3 mathematics, 3 science, (1 science lab), 3 foreign language, 3 social studies, 3 history, 3 academic electives.

Financial Aid

Students should submit: FAFSA. Regular filing deadline is 3/1. The Princeton Review suggests that all financial aid forms be submitted as soon as possible after 1/1. *Need-based scholarships/grants offered:* Federal Pell, SEOG, state scholarships/grants, private scholarships, the school's own gift aid. *Loan aid offered:* FFEL Subsidized Stafford, FFEL Unsubsidized Stafford, FFEL PLUS. Applicants will be notified of awards on a rolling basis beginning 3/15. Federal Work-Study Program available. Institutional employment available. Off-campus job opportunities are fair.

The Inside Word

Don't be misled by Marlboro's acceptance rate—this is not the type of school that attracts many applications from students unsure of whether they belong at Marlboro. Most applicants are qualified both in terms of academic achievement and sincere intellectual curiosity. The school seeks candidates "with intellectual promise, a high degree of self-motivation, self-discipline, personal stability, social concern, and the ability and desire to contribute to the College community." These are the qualities you should stress on your application.

THE SCHOOL SAYS ". . ."

From The Admissions Office

"Marlboro College is distinguished by its curriculum, praised in higher education circles as unique; it is known for its self-governing philosophy, in which each student, faculty, and staff has an equal vote on many issues affecting the community; and it is recognized for its 60-year history of offering a rigorous, exciting, self-designed course of study taught in very small classes and individualized study with faculty. Marlboro's size also distinguishes it from most other schools. With 300 students and a student/faculty ratio of 8:1, it is one of the nation's smallest liberal arts colleges. Few other schools offer a program where students have such close interaction with faculty, and where community life is inseparable from academic life. The result, the self-designed, self-directed Plan of Concentration, allows students to develop their own unique academic work by defining a problem, setting clear limits on an area of inquiry, and analyzing, evaluating, and reporting on the outcome of a significant project. A Marlboro education teaches you to think for yourself, articulate your thoughts, express your ideas, believe in yourself, and do it all with the clarity, confidence, and self-reliance necessary for later success, no matter what postgraduate path you take."

SELECTIVITY

Admissions Rating	91
# of applicants	447
% of applicants accepted	64
% of acceptees attending	36
# of early decision applicants	12
% accepted early decision	83

FRESHMAN PROFILE

Range SAT Critical Reading	590–690
Range SAT Math	510–650
Range SAT Writing	640–720
Range ACT Composite	24–32
Minimum paper TOEFL	550
Minimum computer TOEFL	213
Minimum web-based TOEFL	80
Average HS GPA	3.2
% graduated top 10% of class	40
% graduated top 25% of class	60
% graduated top 50% of class	95

DEADLINES

Early decision	
Deadline	12/1
Notification	12/15
Early action	
Deadline	2/1
Notification	2/15
Regular	
Deadline	3/1
Notification	rolling
Nonfall registration?	yes

APPLICANTS ALSO LOOK AT
AND OFTEN PREFER
Reed College
AND SOMETIMES PREFER
The Evergreen State College
Bard College
College of the Atlantic
AND RARELY PREFER
Hampshire College
Green Mountain College

FINANCIAL FACTS

Financial Aid Rating	89
Annual tuition	$32,550
Room and board	$9,220
Required fees	$1,110
Books and supplies	$1,000
% frosh rec. need-based scholarship or grant aid	58
% UG rec. need-based scholarship or grant aid	50
% frosh rec. non-need-based scholarship or grant aid	31
% UG rec. non-need-based scholarship or grant aid	47
% frosh rec. need-based self-help aid	78
% UG rec. need-based self-help aid	83
% frosh rec. any financial aid	90
% UG rec. any financial aid	90
% UG borrow to pay for school	85
Average cumulative indebtedness	$19,990

MARQUETTE UNIVERSITY

PO Box 1881, Milwaukee, WI 53201-1881 • Admissions: 414-288-7302 • Fax: 414-288-3764

CAMPUS LIFE

Quality of Life Rating	76
Fire Safety Rating	71
Green Rating	96
Type of school	private
Affiliation	Roman Catholic/Jesuit
Environment	metropolis

STUDENTS

Total undergrad enrollment	7,742
% male/female	46/54
% from out of state	53
% from public high school	54
% live on campus	51
% in (# of) fraternities	2 (11)
% in (# of) sororities	4 (11)
% African American	5
% Asian	5
% Caucasian	83
% Hispanic	5
% international	1
# of countries represented	77

SURVEY SAYS . . .
Great library
Low cost of living
Everyone loves the Golden Eagles
(Almost) no one smokes
Very little drug use

ACADEMICS

Academic Rating	80
Calendar	semester
Student/faculty ratio	15:1
Profs interesting rating	74
Profs accessible rating	81
Most common reg class size	10–19 students
Most common lab size	10–19 students

MOST POPULAR MAJORS
nursing/registered nurse
(rn, asn, bsn, msn)

STUDENTS SAY ". . ."

Academics

Looking for a school with a "dedication to academic excellence," and an "involved and intelligent" student body an "open-minded attitude"? Then the Jesuit ideals at Marquette where "people are dedicated to helping others, are incredibly motivated to do well, and hopefully one day, change the world," may be for you. This medium-sized Milwaukee school manages to be "pretty well-run," and students rave about their professors. One junior tells us, "The professors strive to know you personally and to help you achieve your goals," while one communications major "LOVES, LOVES, LOVES every professor" in her college. One student goes as far as to say, "I haven't had much of an experience with the administration, but it is clear that professors here work because they are committed to the Jesuit way of education and are truly willing to help students in any way possible." However, great professors will only get you so far, "the education you receive at Marquette is what you put into it. The resources are available to you…You just have to reach out and take personal responsibility." Though the school seems to run fairly smoothly, "if you do not get a decent registration slot, prepare for extra years of college." But barring a few minor complaints, students seem to agree "the teachers and administrators work to challenge you so that accomplishment is truly your own and learning is at its highest standard."

Life

As you might expect from a school located in a major city, Marquette students' social lives tend to lead them downtown where they "usually head out to eat and hang out. The city is so big people can actually do anything and are rarely restricted to some activities." Students do know how to let loose. "The lifestyle at Marquette is drinking alcohol on the weekends," and "Milwaukee is known for making good beer, and thus students take advantage of the city." For those who prefer to stay on campus "in the evening, there is almost always something going on or to do with friends. To a program sponsored by the university or a campus organization or a pick-up game of Frisbee." But keep in mind the bright students at Marquette like to exercise their intellect with "discussions ranging from a variety of topics, from politics, religion, issues of social justice, or the economy classes." "Our men's basketball program is a pretty big deal on campus," and students are psyched about new head coach Buzz Williams and the team's three straight NCAA tournament appearances. Some students also participate in Greek life, "intramural sports, student organizations," and "the school's radio station."

Student Body

The majority of Marquette students are "white, upper-middle" and "from the Chicago suburbs," but "it seems as if everyone fits in." Says another, "I haven't seen one single person not fit in; doesn't matter what race, gender, or sexual orientation, everyone hangs out with everyone." "The motto of Marquette is Curas Personalis, which means 'care for the whole person.' This is a saying by which our students live." One student says, "The typical student wears jeans, a Marquette T-shirt, and gym shoes." Sounds about right—school spirit definitely thrives here. Many student's cite the athletics as their favorite part of attending Marquette, and "everyone comes together to support our sports teams." Many others enjoy the school's Jesuit values and its focus on "emphasizing community service, and many are involved in making the city a better place." "Marquette lives up to its promise in promoting Jesuit values in and outside of the classroom."

FINANCIAL AID: 414-288-7390 • E-MAIL: ADMISSIONS@MARQUETTE.EDU • WEBSITE: WWW.MARQUETTE.EDU

THE PRINCETON REVIEW SAYS

Admissions

Very important factors considered include: Academic GPA, rigor of secondary school record. *Important factors considered include:* Class rank, application essay, recommendation(s), standardized test scores. *Other factors considered include:* Alumni/ae relation, character/personal qualities, extracurricular activities, first generation, geographical residence, religious affiliation/commitment, state residency, talent/ability. SAT or ACT required; ACT with Writing component recommended. High school diploma is required and GED is accepted. *Academic units required:* 4 English, 2 mathematics, 2 science, (2 science labs), 2 social studies, 2 academic electives. *Academic units recommended:* 4 English, 4 mathematics, 3 science, (3 science labs), 2 foreign language, 3 social studies, 5 academic electives.

Financial Aid

Students should submit: FAFSA, MU Admissions Application. The Princeton Review suggests that all financial aid forms be submitted as soon as possible after 1/1. *Need-based scholarships/grants offered:* Federal Pell, SEOG, state scholarships/grants, private scholarships, the school's own gift aid. *Loan aid offered:* Direct Subsidized Stafford, Direct Unsubsidized Stafford, Direct PLUS, Federal Perkins, Federal Nursing, state loans, college/university loans from institutional funds, Private educational/alternative loans. Applicants will be notified of awards on a rolling basis beginning 3/20. Off-campus job opportunities are excellent.

The Inside Word

Despite the number of applications Marquette receives, at least two admissions counselors look at each one. Admissions are increasingly selective, and applicants should have solid grades and a respectable course record. Nearly all Marquette students finished in the top half of their graduating class. The admissions department pays close attention to student essays and values writing skills in its candidates.

THE SCHOOL SAYS "..."

From The Admissions Office

"Since 1881, Marquette has been noted for its commitment to educational excellence in the 450-year-old Catholic/Jesuit tradition. Marquette embraces the philosophy that true education should be more than an acquisition of knowledge; it should develop your intellect as well as your moral and spiritual character. This all-encompassing education will challenge you to develop the goals and values that will shape the rest of your life. Each of Marquette's 7,500 undergraduates are admitted as freshman to one of six colleges: Arts and Sciences, Business Administration, Communication, Engineering, Health Sciences, or Nursing. Many co-enroll in the School of Education. The faculty within these colleges are prolific writers and researchers, but more importantly, they all teach and advise students.

"Marquette is nestled in the financial center of Milwaukee, the nation's eighteenth-largest city, allowing you to take full advantage of the city's cultural, professional, and governmental opportunities. Marquette's urban experience is unique; an 80-acre campus, an outdoor athletic complex, and an internationally diverse student body (90 percent of which live on or near campus) all make Marquette a close-knit community in which you can learn and live.

"Marquette applicants must submit scores from either the SAT or the ACT with Writing component. The highest composite score will be used in admissions decisions."

SELECTIVITY

Admissions Rating	85
# of applicants	13,375
% of applicants accepted	67
% of acceptees attending	20
# accepting a place on wait list	687
% admitted from wait list	83

FRESHMAN PROFILE

Range SAT Critical Reading	540–630
Range SAT Math	550–660
Range SAT Writing	530–640
Range ACT Composite	24–29
Minimum paper TOEFL	520
Minimum computer TOEFL	190
% graduated top 10% of class	34
% graduated top 25% of class	65
% graduated top 50% of class	93

DEADLINES

Regular	
Priority	12/1
Deadline	12/1
Notification	1/31
Nonfall registration?	yes

APPLICANTS ALSO LOOK AT
AND OFTEN PREFER
University of Notre Dame
University of Michigan—Ann Arbor
Case Western Reserve University
AND SOMETIMES PREFER
University of Wisconsin—Madison
Augustana College (IL)
AND RARELY PREFER
St. Norbert College

FINANCIAL FACTS

Financial Aid Rating	76
Annual tuition	$26,270
Room and board	$9,280
Required fees	$408
Books and supplies	$900
% frosh rec. need-based scholarship or grant aid	57
% UG rec. need-based scholarship or grant aid	54
% frosh rec. non-need-based scholarship or grant aid	6
% UG rec. non-need-based scholarship or grant aid	4
% frosh rec. need-based self-help aid	48
% UG rec. need-based self-help aid	48
% frosh rec. athletic scholarships	1
% UG rec. athletic scholarships	1
% frosh rec. any financial aid	88
% UG rec. any financial aid	85
% UG borrow to pay for school	88
Average cumulative indebtedness	$32,231

MARYWOOD UNIVERSITY

OFFICE OF ADMISSIONS, 2300 ADAMS AVENU, SCRANTON, PA 18509 • ADMISSIONS: 570-348-6234 • FAX: 570-961-4763

CAMPUS LIFE

Quality of Life Rating	69
Fire Safety Rating	92
Green Rating	70
Type of school	private
Affiliation	Roman Catholic
Environment	city

STUDENTS

Total undergrad enrollment	2,039
% male/female	30/70
% from out of state	27
% from public high school	78
% live on campus	49
% in (# of) sororities	NR (1)
% African American	1
% Asian	2
% Caucasian	84
% Hispanic	3
% international	2
# of countries represented	20

SURVEY SAYS . . .
Athletic facilities are great
Low cost of living
Musical organizations are popular
(Almost) no one smokes
Very little drug use

ACADEMICS

Academic Rating	69
Calendar	semester
Student/faculty ratio	11:1
Profs interesting rating	68
Profs accessible rating	66
Most common reg class size	20–29 students
Most common lab size	10–19 students

MOST POPULAR MAJORS
design and visual communications
psychology
teacher education and professional
development, specific subject areas

STUDENTS SAY "..."

Academics
Marywood University is a small Catholic school that offers a wide range of undergraduate majors and pre-professional programs, from art therapy and music performance to hysician assistant and interior design. No matter what you choose to study, the intimate classroom environment is the strength of a Marywood education. A freshman explains, "Through class discussions, I feel that I am truly learning and absorbing the material, as opposed to other schools where teachers dictate or lecture for hours." Academic programs are "challenging but not overwhelming," and "the professors do everything in their power to help their students learn and be able to apply that knowledge to real life." At the same time, personal accountability is vital. Teachers know you by name, and "small class sizes get you extra attention but also make it obvious if you skip class." If you are looking to take a wide range of classes, Marywood is not the best option, as most majors have extensive course requirements, and it can be difficult to get a spot in classes outside your declared department. On the other hand, "Marywood is awesome if you know exactly what you want to do. It has some excellent programs and combines them with general humanities classes."

Life
When they aren't in the library, Marywood students enjoy college life through "on-campus events, movies, bowling, house parties, and just hanging out in the lounges." School spirit surges during the school's sporting events, and "students get excited about the basketball games as well as the women's soccer games." Even though Marywood is a dry campus, you can always take "a trip down to Scranton University for party life (if that's what you're into)." When it comes to the surrounding city, "a lot of people complain that there is nothing to do around Scranton, but you just have to know where to look." In fact, "there is a lot of good shopping, movie theatres, restaurants, bars and clubs" in Scranton, and some nightclubs permit entry to age 18 and up. If you are willing to take a trip outside the city, "the spring and fall are a great time to go on hikes or enjoy the outdoor attractions" and, in the winter, "there is a ski resort close by."

Student Body
Well-rounded, friendly, and studious, the typical Marywood undergraduate "does well in class, works out at the gym, is involved with clubs, and is surrounded by many friends." Most undergraduates at Marywood are "young, white, middle-class" students from New York, New Jersey, and Pennsylvania, though the campus also attracts "students from all over the world, all different religions." Within the college community, you'll find "art lovers in our art field and sport lovers in our new gym, movie watchers in the Madonna Hall Movie Theater and dancers in our new dance studio. There are sorority girls always looking to add new girls to the Zeta Phi Delta and coffee drinkers at the many coffee spots on campus." Fortunately, all students "fit in as one big friendly community." A freshman shares, "Life at college is very safe and relaxing. People are free to make their own choices and encouraged to have their own opinions."

FINANCIAL AID: 866-279-9663 • E-MAIL: YOURFUTURE@MARYWOOD.EDU • WEBSITE: WWW.MARYWOOD.EDU

THE PRINCETON REVIEW SAYS

Admissions

Very important factors considered include: Class rank, rigor of secondary school record, standardized test scores, character/personal qualities. *Important factors considered include:* Academic GPA, interview, talent/ability. *Other factors considered include:* Application essay, recommendation(s), extracurricular activities, level of applicant's interest, volunteer work. SAT or ACT required; TOEFL required of all international applicants. High school diploma is required and GED is accepted. *Academic units required:* 4 English, 2 mathematics, 1 science, (1 science lab), 3 social studies, 6 academic electives.

Financial Aid

Students should submit: FAFSA. The Princeton Review suggests that all financial aid forms be submitted as soon as possible after 1/1. *Need-based scholarships/grants offered:* Federal Pell, SEOG, state scholarships/grants, private scholarships, the school's own gift aid, Federal Nursing Scholarships. *Loan aid offered:* FFEL Subsidized Stafford, FFEL Unsubsidized Stafford, FFEL PLUS, Federal Perkins, state loans. Applicants will be notified of awards on a rolling basis beginning 2/15. Federal Work-Study Program available.

The Inside Word

After you have applied to Marywood, you can participate in their "College for a Day" program, which gives prospective students an inside look at university life, from the classroom to the cafeteria. Marywood reviews applications on a rolling basis, and therefore, you should apply as early as possible. Once a prospective student has submitted all of the application materials, the admissions department will usually make a decision within two or three weeks.

THE SCHOOL SAYS "..."

From The Admissions Office

Marywood University is a comprehensive, Catholic university with just over 2,000 full-time and part-time men and women undergraduates and 1,300 graduate students on campus. There are over 90 undergraduate programs to choose from, many offering graduate components or even doctoral degree programs, if desired. Established in 1915, the university today houses 1,000 undergraduate resident students on a national award-winning campus considered one of the most beautiful in the northeast. In recent years, the university has made $100 million in improvements to campus, including new athletics, residence hall and dining facilities, and one of the finest studio arts facilities in the northeast. Marywood offered the first doctoral degree programs in the Northeastern Pennsylvania region. Of our full-time faculty members, 84% hold the most advanced degrees in their field. Our faculty members are grounded in professional practice and skilled in the art of teaching, and are highly respected practitioners, industry professionals, and visionary educators.

"Marywood operates on a rolling admissions basis. High school seniors are encouraged to submit their application for admission before March 1. Students applying for federal and state financial aid should submit the Free Application for Federal Student Aid (FAFSA) by February 15. At Marywood, you will discover that a top-notch private college experience is more affordable than you ever dreamed. In fact, 98 percent of our first-time students receive financial assistance in the form of scholarships, grants, loans, and work-study programs."

SELECTIVITY

Admissions Rating	80
# of applicants	1,774
% of applicants accepted	78
% of acceptees attending	31

FRESHMAN PROFILE

Range SAT Critical Reading	480–560
Range SAT Math	470–570
Range SAT Writing	460–550
Minimum paper TOEFL	530
Minimum computer TOEFL	197
Minimum web-based TOEFL	71
Average HS GPA	3.05
% graduated top 10% of class	15
% graduated top 25% of class	49
% graduated top 50% of class	83

DEADLINES

Regular	
Notification	rolling
Nonfall registration?	yes

FINANCIAL FACTS

Financial Aid Rating	76
Annual tuition	$5,150
General fee	$920
Student activities fee	$200
Room	$6,656
Board	$4,842
Books and supplies	$900
% frosh rec. need-based scholarship or grant aid	81
% UG rec. need-based scholarship or grant aid	80
% frosh rec. non-need-based scholarship or grant aid	13
% UG rec. non-need-based scholarship or grant aid	8
% frosh rec. need-based self-help aid	69
% UG rec. need-based self-help aid	68
% frosh rec. any financial aid	100
% UG rec. any financial aid	97
% UG borrow to pay for school	98
Average cumulative indebtedness	$35,900

MASSACHUSETTS INSTITUTE OF TECHNOLOGY

MIT ADMISSIONS OFFICE, ROOM 3-108, 77 MASSACHUSETTS AVENUE, CAMBRIDGE, MA 02139 • ADMISSIONS: 617-253-3400

CAMPUS LIFE

Quality of Life Rating	**87**
Fire Safety Rating	**78**
Green Rating	**90**
Type of school	private
Environment	city

STUDENTS

Total undergrad enrollment	4,163
% male/female	55/45
% from out of state	90
% from public high school	69
% live on campus	90
% in (# of) fraternities	49 (27)
% in (# of) sororities	26 (5)
% African American	7
% Asian	26
% Caucasian	37
% Hispanic	12
% Native American	1
% international	8
# of countries represented	89

SURVEY SAYS . . .

Registration is a breeze
Lab facilities are great
Athletic facilities are great
School is well run
Diverse student types on campus
Students love Cambridge, MA

ACADEMICS

Academic Rating	**97**
Calendar	4/1/4
Student/faculty ratio	6:1
Profs interesting rating	70
Profs accessible rating	76
Most common reg class size	fewer than 10 students
Most common lab size	10–19 students

MOST POPULAR MAJORS

chemical engineering
computer science
mechanical engineering

STUDENTS SAY ". . ."

Academics

Massachusetts Institute of Technology, the East Coast mecca of engineering, science, and mathematics, "is the ultimate place for information overload, endless possibilities, and expanding your horizons." The "amazing collection of creative minds" includes enough Nobel laureates to fill a jury box as well as brilliant students who are given substantial control of their educations; one explains, "The administration's attitude towards students is one of respect. As soon as you come on campus, you are bombarded with choices." Students need to be able to manage a workload that "definitely push[es you] beyond your comfort level." A chemical engineering major elaborates: "MIT is different from many schools in that its goal is not to teach you specific facts in each subject. MIT teaches you how to think, not about opinions but about problem solving. Facts and memorization are useless unless you know how to approach a tough problem." Professors here range from "excellent teachers who make lectures fun and exciting" to "dull and soporific" ones, but most "make a serious effort to make the material they teach interesting by throwing in jokes and cool demonstrations." "Access to an amazing number of resources, both academic and recreational," "research opportunities for undergrads with some of the nation's leading professors," and a rock-solid alumni network complete the picture. If you ask "MIT alumni where they went to college, most will immediately stick out their hand and show you their 'brass rat' (the MIT ring, the second most recognized ring in the world)."

Life

At MIT "It may seem…like there's no life outside problem sets and studying for exams," but "there's always time for extracurricular activities or just relaxing" for those "with good time-management skills" or the "ability to survive on [a] lack of sleep." Options range from "building rides" (recent projects have included a motorized couch and a human-sized hamster wheel) "to partying at fraternities to enjoying the largest collection of science fiction novels in the U.S. at the MIT Science Fiction Library." Students occasionally find time to "pull a hack," which is an ethical prank, "like the life-size Wright brothers' plane that appeared on top of the Great Dome for the one-hundredth anniversary of flight." Undergrads tell us that "MIT has great parties—a lot of Wellesley, Harvard, and BU students come to them," but also that "there are tons of things to do other than party" here. "Movies, shopping, museums, and plays are all possible with our location near Boston. There are great restaurants only [blocks] away from campus, too…From what I can tell, MIT students have way more fun on the weekends then their Cambridge counterparts [at] Harvard."

Student Body

"There actually isn't one typical student at MIT," students here assure us, explaining that "hobbies range from building robots and hacking to getting wasted and partying every weekend. The one thing students all have in common is that they are insanely smart and love to learn. Pretty much anyone can find the perfect group of friends to hang out with at MIT." "Most students do have some form of 'nerdiness'" (like telling nerdy jokes, being an avid fan of *Star Wars*, etc.), but "contrary to MIT's stereotype, most MIT students are not geeks who study all the time and have no social skills. The majority of the students here are actually quite 'normal.'" The "stereotypical student [who] looks techy and unkempt…only represents about 25 percent of the school." The rest include "multiple-sport standouts, political activists, fraternity and sorority members, hippies, clean-cut business types, LARPers, hackers, musicians, and artisans. There are people who look like they stepped out of an Abercrombie & Fitch catalog and people who dress in all black and carry flashlights and multi-tools. Not everyone relates to everyone else, but most people get along, and it's almost a guarantee that you'll fit in somewhere."

FINANCIAL AID: 617-258-8600 • WEBSITE: WEB.MIT.EDU

THE PRINCETON REVIEW SAYS

Admissions

Very important factors considered include: Character/personal qualities. *Important factors considered include:* Class rank, academic GPA, recommendation(s), rigor of secondary school record, standardized test scores, extracurricular activities, interview, talent/ability. *Other factors considered include:* Application essay, alumni/ae relation, first generation, geographical residence, level of applicant's interest, racial/ethnic status, volunteer work, work experience. ACT with Writing component required. High school diploma or equivalent is not required. *Academic units recommended:* 4 English, 4 mathematics, 4 science, 2 foreign language, 2 social studies.

Financial Aid

Students should submit: FAFSA, CSS/Financial Aid PROFILE, noncustodial PROFILE (if applicable), business/farm supplement. Parent's complete federal income tax returns from prior year and W-2s. Regular filing deadline is 2/15. The Princeton Review suggests that all financial aid forms be submitted as soon as possible after 1/1. *Need-based scholarships/grants offered:* Federal Pell, SEOG, state scholarships/grants, private scholarships, the school's own gift aid. *Loan aid offered:* Direct Subsidized Stafford, Direct Unsubsidized Stafford, Direct PLUS, Federal Perkins, college/university loans from institutional funds. Applicants will be notified of awards on or about 4/1. Federal Work-Study Program available. Institutional employment available. Off-campus job opportunities are excellent.

The Inside Word

MIT has one of the nation's most competitive admissions processes. The school's applicant pool is so rich it turns away numerous qualified candidates each year. Put your best foot forward and take consolation in the fact that rejection doesn't necessarily mean that you don't belong at MIT, but only that there wasn't enough room for you the year you applied. Your best chance to get an edge: Find ways to stress your creativity, a quality that MIT's admissions director told *USA Today* is lacking in many prospective college students.

THE SCHOOL SAYS " . . ."

From The Admissions Office

"The students who come to the Massachusetts Institute of Technology are some of America's—and the world's—best and most creative. As graduates, they leave here to make real contributions—in science, technology, business, education, politics, architecture, and the arts. From any class, many will go on to do work that is historically significant. These young men and women are leaders, achievers, and producers. Helping such students make the most of their talents and dreams would challenge any educational institution. MIT gives them its best advantages: a world-class faculty, unparalleled facilities, and remarkable opportunities. In turn, these students help to make the institute the vital place it is. They bring fresh viewpoints to faculty research: More than three-quarters participate in the Undergraduate Research Opportunities Program, developing solutions for the world's problems in areas such as energy, the environment, cancer, and poverty. They play on MIT's 41 intercollegiate teams as well as in its 50+ music, theatre, and dance groups. To their classes and to their out-of-class activities, they bring enthusiasm, energy, and individual style."

SELECTIVITY

Admissions Rating	99
# of applicants	12,445
% of applicants accepted	12
% of acceptees attending	69
# accepting a place on wait list	443
% admitted from wait list	5

FRESHMAN PROFILE

Range SAT Critical Reading	660–760
Range SAT Math	720–800
Range SAT Writing	660–750
Range ACT Composite	31–34
Minimum paper TOEFL	577
Minimum computer TOEFL	233
Minimum web-based TOEFL	90
% graduated top 10% of class	97
% graduated top 25% of class	100
% graduated top 50% of class	100

DEADLINES

Early action	
Deadline	11/1
Notification	12/15
Regular	
Deadline	1/1
Notification	3/20
Nonfall registration?	no

APPLICANTS ALSO LOOK AT

AND OFTEN PREFER
Harvard College

AND SOMETIMES PREFER
Stanford University
Yale University
Princeton University

AND RARELY PREFER
Duke University
Columbia University—Columbia College
Cornell University
California Institute of Technology
University of Pennsylvania

FINANCIAL FACTS

Financial Aid Rating	96
Annual tuition	$34,750
Room and board	$10,400
Required fees	$236
Books and supplies	$1,114
% frosh rec. need-based scholarship or grant aid	63
% UG rec. need-based scholarship or grant aid	60
% frosh rec. need-based self-help aid	51
% UG rec. need-based self-help aid	53
% frosh rec. any financial aid	79
% UG rec. any financial aid	71
% UG borrow to pay for school	41
Average cumulative indebtedness	$15,051

McGill University

845 Sherbrooke Street West, Montreal, QC H3A 2T5, Canada • Admissions: 514-398-3910 • Fax: 514-398-3683

CAMPUS LIFE
Quality of Life Rating 85
Fire Safety Rating 67
Green Rating 85
Type of school public
Environment metropolis

STUDENTS
Total undergrad enrollment 20,831
% male/female 41/59
% from out of state 37
% live on campus 12
% in (# of) fraternities NR (8)
% in (# of) sororities NR (4)
% international 17
# of countries represented 136

SURVEY SAYS . . .
Class discussions are rare
Students love Montreal, QC
Great off-campus food
Student publications are popular

ACADEMICS
Academic Rating 77
Calendar semester
Student/faculty ratio 16:1
Profs interesting rating 64
Profs accessible rating 63
Most common
reg class size 10–19 students
Most common
lab size 20–29 students

MOST POPULAR MAJORS
business/commerce
political science and government
psychology

STUDENTS SAY "..."

Academics

McGill University in Montreal, Quebec, enjoys "international name recognition," and it's "unapologetically a top-notch, high-powered research university." Many resources rival the best anywhere in the world. "The libraries are amazing." Other facilities are "rather shabby," though, and "McGill is unique in that the administration tends to go against the students' society (SSMU)." The administration is "extremely tedious" and "difficult to navigate." "The sheer amount of red tape, inefficiency, and incompetence is astounding." Also, while registration is "fantastically easy," some students "would have appreciated better academic guidance." "McGill forces you to take responsibility for yourself," cautions a biology major. "Nobody's going to be coddling you, but "once you figure out how to make the school work for you, things are mostly smooth sailing." " There are more than 300 areas of study, and "there does not seem to be a lot of integration between disciplines." Some classes have "more than 500 students." Other classes "are not nearly as large." The faculty is a seriously mixed bag. Some professors are "amazingly passionate, talented, dedicated, and interesting" and they "genuinely care about students." Many others are "very disinterested in teaching" or "barely fluent in English." For many students, the workload is "exhausting." "A 'B+' deserves a pat on the back" here and the struggle for good grades can be "cutthroat." Other students aren't as competitive, though, and McGill offers an "easy life for those who just want to pass." "The academic seriousness of each individual student largely correlates to their chosen major."

Life

McGill has a "gorgeous campus," "located in the heart of one of the world's best cities." Students can participate in hundreds of extracurricular clubs and organizations. Intramural sports are reasonably popular. Intercollegiate sports aren't, though, and "school spirit is pretty low." "It's a DIY social experience but there's something for everyone," says a sophomore. Students say they "know when to buckle down and work hard." When the time is right, many students "drink a lot," "but it's done with the same vigor that students give their school work and extra-curriculars." The drinking age in Quebec is 18 and marijuana is not unheard of, but "the only people who really make a big deal about these things are the American students who come up here and are wowed by it all for their first year. Then they settle down and enjoy things in moderation like everyone else." "Housing is not offered after first year so there is no choice" but to live off campus for most students. Nobody cares, though, because the "relatively cheap," "wildly fun," "quasi-European city" of Montreal is "one of the world's greatest college towns." There are "ethnic quarters with every culture and food imaginable." "Nightlife is incomparable" and "the music scene is really good." "There is never a night when there is nothing to do," says a senior. "This is both a good and bad thing." "Outdoorsy stuff" is also plentiful. "Mount Royal, which is a park just north of campus, has bike and running paths and a beautiful observatory overlooking the city at the top which is great for exercising and exploring when the weather is nice," explains a junior. In the winter months, when the weather is decidedly not so nice, opportunities to hit the slopes are "very close."

Student Body

Students here describe themselves as "very smart." They're also "good looking" and they don't mind telling you so. Beyond those characteristics, the undergraduate population is widely varied. "Diversity is one of McGill's best advantages." It's "a melting pot of eclectic people of different cultures and backgrounds." "This environment doesn't allow for cookie cutters," says a junior. "There are many niches for students to be able to find a place." The international contingent is huge. "McGill recruits students from all over the world" who "speak several languages and have multiple citizenships" "A lot of people seem to take themselves too seriously and always want to win an argument," a junior says. Others are "really down to earth." There are "plenty of preppy students" and "rich, white kids who grew up in Toronto and attended private high school." Other students are emphatically "middle class." There are "jeans-clad, beer-drinking, indie pop-listening" students. There are "academically devoted students, late-night party fiends, hippies," and "elitist, fashion-victim" "scenesters" "adhering to the latest style." Other students are "crunchy," "cry-baby social activists." McGill is also home to "one of the larger openly gay communities in Canada." "We're interesting kids," reflects a sophomore.

FINANCIAL AID: 514-398-6013 • E-MAIL: ADMISSIONS@MCGILL.CA • WEBSITE: WWW.MCGILL.CA

THE PRINCETON REVIEW SAYS

Admissions

Very important factors considered include: Academic GPA, rigor of secondary school record, standardized test scores. *Important factors considered include:* Class rank. *Other factors considered include:* Recommendation(s). ACT with Writing component required; TOEFL required of all international applicants. High school diploma is required and GED is not accepted. *Academic units recommended:* 4 English, 4 mathematics, 3 science, (3 science labs), 3 foreign language, 2 social studies, 2 history.

Financial Aid

Students should submit: Institution's own financial aid form, Provincial Government Loan Applications. Regular filing deadline is 6/30. The Princeton Review suggests that all financial aid forms be submitted as soon as possible after 1/1. *Need-based scholarships/grants offered:* Private scholarships, the school's own gift aid, Canadian (Federal & Provincial) Student Assistance. *Loan aid offered:* FFEL Subsidized Stafford, FFEL Unsubsidized Stafford, FFEL PLUS, college/university loans from institutional funds. Applicants will be notified of awards on a rolling basis beginning 3/1. Institutional employment available. Off-campus job opportunities are fair.

The Inside Word

McGill is as tough as it comes in Canadian higher education. The university is provincially funded. As there are no geographic quotas, competition from applicants around the world is intense. The admissions process is thorough and demanding, and high SAT and SAT Subject Test scores just don't guarantee admission across the board. While English is the language of instruction, French is the language of Montreal, and those who speak it fare much better in everyday life than those who do not.

THE SCHOOL SAYS "..."

From The Admissions Office

"McGill processes more than 30,000 online applications a year. Very few programs are available to non-Quebec students for January admission; consult the Website for details.

"Applicants may submit results from of the SAT (plus at least two appropriate SAT Subject Tests). The ACT is accepted in lieu of the SAT and SAT Subject Test combination. Please note that certain programs can require specific SAT Subject Tests."

SELECTIVITY
Admissions Rating	**86**
# of applicants	21,242
% of applicants accepted	54
% of acceptees attending	44

FRESHMAN PROFILE
Range SAT Critical Reading	640–740
Range SAT Math	650–720
Range SAT Writing	650–730
Range ACT Composite	29–32
Minimum paper TOEFL	577
Minimum computer TOEFL	233
Minimum web-based TOEFL	90
Average HS GPA	3.52

DEADLINES
Regular	
Deadline	1/15
Notification	rolling
Nonfall registration?	yes

APPLICANTS ALSO LOOK AT

AND OFTEN PREFER
Queen's University
New York University
University of Toronto
Concordia University
University of British Columbia
Universite de Montreal

AND SOMETIMES PREFER
Columbia University
University of Western Ontario
University of California—Berkeley
University of Ottawa
University of Waterloo

FINANCIAL FACTS
Financial Aid Rating	**60***
Annual in-state tuition	$1,868
Annual out-of-state tuition	$5,378
Room and board	$10,300
Required fees	$1,450
Books and supplies	$1,000
% UG rec. need-based scholarship or grant aid	18
% UG rec. non-need-based scholarship or grant aid	9
% UG rec. need-based self-help aid	25
% UG rec. any financial aid	28

MERCER UNIVERSITY—MACON

ADMISSIONS OFFICE, 1400 COLEMAN AVENUE, MACON, GA 31207-0001 • ADMISSIONS: 478-301-2650 • FAX: 478-301-2828

CAMPUS LIFE

Quality of Life Rating	**75**
Fire Safety Rating	**78**
Green Rating	**81**
Type of school	private
Affiliation	Baptist
Environment	city

STUDENTS

Total undergrad enrollment	2,228
% male/female	46/54
% from out of state	21
% live on campus	70
% in (# of) fraternities	25 (10)
% in (# of) sororities	29 (7)
% African American	17
% Asian	6
% Caucasian	64
% Hispanic	3
% international	3
# of countries represented	39

SURVEY SAYS . . .

Athletic facilities are great
Low cost of living
Frats and sororities dominate social scene
(Almost) no one smokes
Very little drug use

ACADEMICS

Academic Rating	**87**
Calendar	semester
Student/faculty ratio	13:1
Profs interesting rating	86
Profs accessible rating	85
Most common reg class size	10–19 students
Most common lab size	20–29 students

MOST POPULAR MAJORS

biology/biological sciences
business/commerce
engineering

STUDENTS SAY " . . . "

Academics

Mercer University is a school on the rise, students tell us. Its administration "is moving toward a nationally recognized name" for the school and seems to be taking some critical steps in that direction, by building a reputation for several standout programs, imposing academic rigor throughout the curriculum, and inspiring the sort of student loyalty that translates into alumni donations down the line. Solid offerings in business, pre-pharmacy, engineering, and music lead the way here. All are supported by a solid liberal arts curriculum grounded in the classics; indeed, the school offers an eight-course great books program, "which allows students to read the 'great' books of the accepted literary canon instead of taking general courses." All this takes place in "a small-school atmosphere" that encourages competition with "a strong push for academic success" and nurtures students' development "with a comforting feeling of belonging." "The professors and staff offer exceptional outreach to students, and the relationship between professors and students is unparalleled," students report. Another adds "the administration is very much in touch with the student body and makes itself available to those" who wish to discuss "developing and improving faculties and programs. Student suggestions are taken seriously, and some have even been implemented campus-wide." The combined effect of all of the above is some pretty happy students of the type who insist Mercer creates "the perfect college experience complete with friendly professors, helpful staff, easy accessibility, and student activities to maintain interest."

Life

"There seem to be two main groups who sets the tone for campus life at Mercer: The religious group and the Greek-life group," with some overlap between the two. The difference is fairly simple. "Those who are more interested in religious organizations focus more on social gatherings without alcohol, while sororities and fraternities also focus on social gatherings, but alcohol is present," one student explains. Quadworks, the school's campus activities board, is another major player in the social scene. It "sponsors events from tailgating at basketball games to movies on the lawn, etc." "Quadworks, sponsors so many on-campus activities that there's often little reason to leave," one undergrad writes, "although students are becoming increasingly involved in mixing with the Macon community, especially at the restaurants and shops near to the college." Macon's downtown club scene is popular with some students (easily and safely accessible thanks to the student-government run trolley), but many here complain "there aren't a lot of things to do on the weekends, even around the city of Macon," which explains why "mostly everyone goes home or off campus" when the school week is over.

Student Body

Mercer is a Baptist-affiliated school. "Many students here are religious, mostly Baptist or other Protestants, though you will also find unapologetic atheists and deists mixed in with a small population of Catholics, Orthodox Christians, and various other religious groups. Any student who doesn't happen to have a passionate social or academic interest or a strong commitment to a Christian faith tends to have a hard time belonging, so they leave or fly under the radar for their years here." Some caution that "upon first glance it seems that the entire campus is Greek, when in fact only about 30 percent is. This is because the Greeks hold most high positions in student organizations on campus." Don't come here looking for an alternative community; "There are not many extremely different students i.e. emo, Gothic, etc."

FINANCIAL AID: 478-301-2670 • E-MAIL: ADMISSIONS@MERCER.EDU • WEBSITE: WWW.MERCER.EDU

THE PRINCETON REVIEW SAYS

Admissions

Very important factors considered include: Academic GPA, rigor of secondary school record, standardized test scores, level of applicant's interest. *Important factors considered include:* Character/personal qualities, extracurricular activities, talent/ability, volunteer work. *Other factors considered include:* Class rank, recommendation(s), alumni/ae relation, interview, work experience. SAT or ACT required; ACT with Writing component recommended; TOEFL required of all international applicants. High school diploma is required and GED is accepted. *Academic units required:* 4 English, 4 mathematics, 3 science, (2 science labs), 2 foreign language, 1 social studies, 2 history.

Financial Aid

Students should submit: FAFSA, institution's own financial aid form, state aid form. The Princeton Review suggests that all financial aid forms be submitted as soon as possible after 1/1. *Need-based scholarships/grants offered:* Federal Pell, SEOG, state scholarships/grants, the school's own gift aid, Federal Nursing Scholarships. *Loan aid offered:* Direct Subsidized Stafford, Direct Unsubsidized Stafford, Direct PLUS, Federal Perkins, Federal Nursing, college/university loans from institutional funds. Applicants will be notified of awards on a rolling basis beginning 3/15. Federal Work-Study Program available. Institutional employment available. Off-campus job opportunities are good.

The Inside Word

One student warns that Mercer, "while somewhat lenient in its admission's policy, will give you an excellent education," so "don't come here thinking it will be easy. Plenty of transfer students from major universities have not lasted a semester here." Make sure you're ready to put in the hard work before applying here; getting in is one thing, staying through graduation [is] another. The school works with "a small but growing number of home-schooled applicants."

THE SCHOOL SAYS "..."

From The Admissions Office

"The mission of the Mercer University office of admissions is to attract, admit, and enroll qualified and talented students who will ultimately become happy, successful alumni. We do this by becoming personally involved with each admitted student and family during the admissions process. Mercer admissions staff takes time to know each admitted applicant on a personal level and are concerned about the family's questions regarding financial assistance, campus life, and academic affairs. High school and campus visits, regional receptions, and programs are all conducted by Admissions Staff who are knowledgeable about the high schools and two-year colleges in a particular region. This makes for a truly enjoyable and productive admissions experience for all involved.

"Freshman applicants must take the SAT or the ACT with Writing component."

SELECTIVITY

Admissions Rating	93
# of applicants	4,678
% of applicants accepted	67
% of acceptees attending	19

FRESHMAN PROFILE

Range SAT Critical Reading	530–640
Range SAT Math	550–650
Range SAT Writing	520–630
Range ACT Composite	23–29
Minimum paper TOEFL	550
Minimum computer TOEFL	213
Average HS GPA	3.6
% graduated top 10% of class	42
% graduated top 25% of class	75
% graduated top 50% of class	94

DEADLINES

Early action	
Deadline	11/1
Notification	11/15
Regular	
Priority	4/1
Deadline	7/1
Notification	rolling
Nonfall registration?	no

APPLICANTS ALSO LOOK AT

AND OFTEN PREFER
Samford University
Georgia Institute of Technology
Emory University
University of Georgia

AND SOMETIMES PREFER
Furman University
Auburn University
Florida State University

AND RARELY PREFER
Clemson University
Georgia Southern University

FINANCIAL FACTS

Financial Aid Rating	89
Annual tuition	$28,500
Room and board	$8,450
Required fees	$200
Books and supplies	$1,200
% frosh rec. need-based scholarship or grant aid	69
% UG rec. need-based scholarship or grant aid	64
% frosh rec. non-need-based scholarship or grant aid	25
% UG rec. non-need-based scholarship or grant aid	19
% frosh rec. need-based self-help aid	40
% UG rec. need-based self-help aid	42
% frosh rec. athletic scholarships	9
% UG rec. athletic scholarships	8
% frosh rec. any financial aid	97
% UG rec. any financial aid	95
% UG borrow to pay for school	66
Average cumulative indebtedness	$22,835

MIAMI UNIVERSITY

301 SOUTH CAMPUS AVENUE, OXFORD, OH 45056 • ADMISSIONS: 513-529-2531 • FAX: 513-529-1550

CAMPUS LIFE
Quality of Life Rating	**73**
Fire Safety Rating	**77**
Green Rating	**75**
Type of school	public
Environment	village

STUDENTS
Total undergrad enrollment	14,699
% male/female	46/54
% from out of state	30
% from public high school	71
% live on campus	46
% in (# of) fraternities	20 (28)
% in (# of) sororities	26 (23)
% African American	4
% Asian	3
% Caucasian	85
% Hispanic	2
% Native American	1
% international	2
# of countries represented	49

SURVEY SAYS . . .
Athletic facilities are great
Great food on campus
Low cost of living
Frats and sororities dominate social scene
(Almost) no one smokes

ACADEMICS
Academic Rating	**80**
Calendar	semester
Student/faculty ratio	16:1
Profs interesting rating	75
Profs accessible rating	76
% classes taught by TAs	7
Most common reg class size	20–29 students
Most common lab size	20–29 students

MOST POPULAR MAJORS
finance
marketing/marketing management
zoology/animal biology

STUDENTS SAY ". . ."
Academics
Nestled within a vast expanse of Ohio cornfields, Miami University is a medium-sized public school offering diverse academic programs and a surprisingly close-knit atmosphere. With more than 100 major departments, choice is central to the Miami experience. Whether majoring in humanities or sciences, "students have broad discretion when selecting courses. It is truly up to the individual to decide how far to push oneself academically." In most departments, the workload is sizable; fortunately, "professors at Miami are extremely personable and are always willing to lend an extra hand." A junior tells us, "I've never run into a professor that was not approachable when needing help, and most of them are very passionate about sharing their knowledge with the students." You'll definitely wind up in a number of lecture courses during your first two years (luckily, "most of them are actually pretty good at keeping you awake"). Though only 7% of classes are taught by graduate students, undergrads warn us that these courses are a "hit-or-miss situation." At the same time, many students praise the school's required liberal education courses. A junior shares, "I certainly didn't expect a freshman English class to leave an impact on me. However, the professor awoke so much passion for writing in me that now I work at the writing center on campus." Even so, the academic experience is best during junior and senior year, when upper division courses include "lots of class discussion, projects, no tests, and competent teachers." Not all of the school's administration is known to be as easily accessible or caring as the teaching staff. However, the school's president has made an effort to get personally involved in the student community, and "it is not uncommon to receive a well-developed response from the president if you send him an e-mail."

Life
Offering "countless social, academic, political, and career opportunities," Miami University will offer you a "great college experience" inside and outside the classroom. Academics are definitely taken seriously, and "during the weekdays most people spend their time studying either in their dorms or at the library." When they aren't hitting the books, theatrical or musical performances, movies, parties, speakers, ice hockey games, and campus events create "a good mix of social life and academic life." While academic programs definitely prepare you for the real world, the social life won't. Located in the middle of the cornfields, "many people refer to life at Miami as living in the 'Miami bubble.' It's hard to imagine life outside of Oxford." On that note, Oxford is "a town built for college life," with "wonderful food and activities," that cater specifically to college students. For the socially inclined, "the party scene at Miami is top-notch. There are the ever-present frat parties, but the small size of the town also leaves us with tons of bars and off-campus houses devoted solely to us." With about one third of undergraduates joining fraternities and sororities, "Greek life is enormous, but, with so many students, it doesn't dominate the campus."

Student Body
Stepping onto the Miami University campus, your may not immediately see astounding diversity within the student body. Demographically, the majority of undergraduates hail from a "suburban, generally Mid-Western community," and "there is not much racial diversity on campus." However, students reassure us that the school is working to recruit a more diverse student body, and "each student is very open to diversity and welcomes it with open arms." Due to the overwhelming preference for preppy attire, the "nickname for Miami is J.Crew U," and students admit there are "not many alternative students like you would find in the big city schools." However, the school's predominant dress code doesn't necessarily translate into a totally uniform student body. A sophomore explains, "A lot of the students at Miami are preppy and may seem snobby at first, but once you experience it for yourself, you find all types of people." In fact, "fashion aside, the students here are typically friendly and intelligent, and all seem to apply to the "work-hard, play-hard" mentality." Ambitious and well-rounded, most Miami students are "passionate, driven, very career-oriented, involved around campus, and very social."

FINANCIAL AID: 513-529-8734 • E-MAIL: ADMISSION@MUOHIO.EDU • WEBSITE: WWW.MUOHIO.EDU

THE PRINCETON REVIEW SAYS

Admissions

Very important factors considered include: Class rank, application essay, academic GPA, recommendation(s), rigor of secondary school record, standardized test scores, character/personal qualities, talent/ability. *Other factors considered include:* Alumni/ae relation, extracurricular activities, first generation, geographical residence, state residency, volunteer work, work experience. SAT or ACT required; ACT with Writing component required; TOEFL required of all international applicants. High school diploma is required and GED is accepted. *Academic units recommended:* 4 English, 3 mathematics, 3 science, 2 foreign language, 3 social studies, 1 visual/performing arts.

Financial Aid

Students should submit: FAFSA. The Princeton Review suggests that all financial aid forms be submitted as soon as possible after 1/1. Priority deadline for FAFSA is 2/15. *Need-based scholarships/grants offered:* Federal Pell, SEOG, state scholarships/grants, private scholarships, the school's own gift aid. *Loan aid offered:* Direct Subsidized Stafford, Direct Unsubsidized Stafford, Direct PLUS, Federal Perkins, Federal Nursing, college/university loans from institutional funds, Bank Education Loans. Applicants will be notified of awards on a rolling basis beginning 3/20. Federal Work-Study Program available. Institutional employment available. Off-campus job opportunities are good.

The Inside Word

Admission to Miami University is competitive. In addition to high grades and test scores (50 percent of incoming students at Miami had SAT scores above 1200), Miami University admits students who are active in their schools and communities. Last year, 92 percent of incoming students had volunteered in their communities during high school, and 67 percent participated in varsity sports.

THE SCHOOL SAYS "..."

From The Admissions Office

"At Miami, you'll find a level of involvement—in your classes, in your research, in your extracurricular activities—that you won't find at other schools. What sets Miami apart is the ability to give students a small-college experience within the excitement and opportunities of a large university, all at a public school cost. With more than 100 majors to choose from, and a liberal arts foundation that allows students to explore different areas of interest, finding your true passion—in and out of the classroom—is at the heart of what the MU experience is all about. This deep level of engagement is reflected in the 90 percent freshman to sophomore retention rate and Miami's graduate rate, which is among the top graduation rates for public universities across the country. Miami's reputation for producing outstanding leaders with real-world experience makes us a target school for top national firms, and our graduates' acceptance rate into law and medical school are far above the national average. Students also benefit from small class sizes—90 percent of undergraduate classes have fewer than 50 students—and personal attention from faculty members in the classroom, through research opportunities, and through faculty mentoring programs. Outside of the classroom, students can participate in over 300 student organizations, attend social and cultural events, or get involved with one of the most extensive intramural and club sports program in the country."

SELECTIVITY

Admissions Rating	93
# of applicants	15,009
% of applicants accepted	80
% of acceptees attending	30
# accepting a place on wait list	218
# of early decision applicants	636
% accepted early decision	76

FRESHMAN PROFILE

Range SAT Critical Reading	540–640
Range SAT Math	560–650
Range ACT Composite	24–29
Minimum paper TOEFL	530
Minimum computer TOEFL	200
Minimum web-based TOEFL	72
Average HS GPA	3.66
% graduated top 10% of class	37
% graduated top 25% of class	71
% graduated top 50% of class	98

DEADLINES

Early decision	
Deadline	11/1
Notification	12/15
Early action	
Deadline	12/1
Notification	2/1
Regular	
Deadline	2/1
Notification	3/15
Nonfall registration?	yes

APPLICANTS ALSO LOOK AT
AND OFTEN PREFER
Washington University in St. Louis
University of Notre Dame

AND SOMETIMES PREFER
Purdue University—West Lafayette
University of Wisconsin—Madison

AND RARELY PREFER
Xavier University (OH)

FINANCIAL FACTS

Financial Aid Rating	71
Annual in-state tuition	$11,443
Annual out-of-state tuition	$25,307
Room and board	$9,458
% frosh rec. need-based scholarship or grant aid	35
% UG rec. need-based scholarship or grant aid	22
% frosh rec. non-need-based scholarship or grant aid	25
% UG rec. non-need-based scholarship or grant aid	18
% frosh rec. need-based self-help aid	33
% UG rec. need-based self-help aid	32
% frosh rec. athletic scholarships	2
% UG rec. athletic scholarships	3
% frosh rec. any financial aid	63
% UG rec. any financial aid	59
% UG borrow to pay for school	51
Average cumulative indebtedness	$26,798

MICHIGAN STATE UNIVERSITY

250 ADMINISTRATION BUILDING, EAST LANSING, MI 48824-1046 • ADMISSIONS: 517-355-8332 • FAX: 517-353-1647

CAMPUS LIFE
Quality of Life Rating	**86**
Fire Safety Rating	**60***
Green Rating	**93**
Type of school	public
Environment	town

STUDENTS
Total undergrad enrollment	35,986
% male/female	47/53
% from out of state	8
% live on campus	42
% in (# of) fraternities	8 (31)
% in (# of) sororities	7 (19)
% African American	8
% Asian	5
% Caucasian	76
% Hispanic	3
% Native American	1
% international	5
# of countries represented	134

SURVEY SAYS . . .
Students are friendly
Everyone loves the Spartans
Student publications are popular

ACADEMICS
Academic Rating	**71**
Calendar	semester
Student/faculty ratio	16:1
Profs interesting rating	71
Profs accessible rating	74
Most common reg class size	20–29 students
Most common lab size	20–29 students

STUDENTS SAY ". . ."

Academics

The size of Michigan State University "scares some people," students tell us, but for those comfortable in crowds it's "one of the strongest advantages. Where else do you cut through the Cereal Wing of the Human Nutrition Building to get to a Navigating the Universe class (a class on the parallels between art, philosophy, and physics)?" One student sees it this way: "The size of MSU makes it like training wheels for the real world. Every type of person, value, and belief is here, so you learn just as many street smarts as academic smarts, which is what sets it apart from so many other schools." There are more than "200 majors to choose from" here, including "good engineering and science programs," an "amazing communications program," "the best political science program in Michigan," "the only agriculture school in the state," and "an absolutely amazing school of Hospitality Business." Economies of scale also allow MSU to offer "great study-abroad programs," "a lot of helpful free tutoring in math and other subjects," and "great Web programs that make it very easy to download class materials and view assignments. You can also e-mail the whole class questions or just your professor, through our Angel system." As far as possible downsides to the school's size, MSU students find you have to "fend for yourself." That means potential peril for students who aren't self-motivated. One undergrad explains, "There are two roads you can follow when at MSU. You can study hard and earn a degree in a reputable, challenging setting; or you can soak your brain cells with alcohol instead of academia."

Life

"It requires a lot of studying to keep up with classes" in most disciplines at MSU, but that doesn't mean students bury their heads in the books 24/7. On the contrary, "Michigan State is great because everyone is there to learn but also to have a good time, which is important for any college to flow smoothly." When the weekend arrives, "everyone likes to go out, usually to frats, and have a good time. We do our share of partying, but we know when and how hard to hit the books. We keep our heads very level," except, perhaps, when attending sporting events. Life on campus "generally revolves around the weekend and the basketball or football game. You get through the week looking forward to one of the two." Indeed, "Sports are huge, and nothing beats football Saturdays or basketball nights. Tailgating is a religion." And if neither sports appeal to you, don't sweat it. "If there's something you want to do, someone else does too. You'll be hard pressed to find an activity that doesn't have its own organization and social network." Hometown East Lansing has its own allures; a student explains, "Walking downtown on Grand River is awesome when it gets warmer out," and there are "decent stores and restaurants. Also, in the warm weather you are bound to see people sitting out on their porches. Many of them are having parties or just hanging out, and a lot of times they'll invite you to come on up!" Or you can just enjoy the "breathtaking beauty of the campus," with its "old buildings and beautiful trees and plants that make every walk to class a great one."

Student Body

MSU's size ensures that "this is a fairly diverse campus, especially considering that it is located in the northern Midwest." One student observes, "You can completely immerse yourself among different people in different situations knowing that you have the comfort of your own dorm, and somewhere there is a group just like you." Because "study abroad is emphasized at MSU," there are "a lot of foreign students, and they seem to fit right into the general population." If anything unites students—besides their love of MSU sports—it is that most "are extremely friendly. Random people in classes ask you if you need a ride home, and, even better, random people offer you a seat on the bus. It's comforting to know that these are the people soon entering the workforce and 'the real world.'"

FINANCIAL AID: 517-353-5940 • E-MAIL: ADMIS@MSU.EDU • WEBSITE: WWW.MSU.EDU

THE PRINCETON REVIEW SAYS

Admissions

Very important factors considered include: Academic GPA, rigor of secondary school record, standardized test scores. *Important factors considered include:* Application essay, extracurricular activities, first generation, geographical residence. *Other factors considered include:* Class rank, recommendation(s), alumni/ae relation, character/personal qualities, level of applicant's interest, talent/ability, volunteer work, work experience. SAT or ACT required; ACT with Writing component required; TOEFL required of all international applicants. High school diploma is required and GED is accepted. *Academic units required:* 4 English, 3 mathematics, 2 science, 2 foreign language, 2 social studies, 1 history. *Academic units recommended:* (2 science labs), 2 foreign language, 2 social studies, 2 history.

Financial Aid

Students should submit: FAFSA. The Princeton Review suggests that all financial aid forms be submitted as soon as possible after 1/1. *Need-based scholarships/grants offered:* Federal Pell, SEOG, state scholarships/grants, private scholarships, the school's own gift aid, United Negro College Fund. *Loan aid offered:* Direct Subsidized Stafford, Direct Unsubsidized Stafford, Direct PLUS, Federal Perkins, state loans, college/university loans from institutional funds. Applicants will be notified of awards on a rolling basis beginning 3/15. Federal Work-Study Program available. Institutional employment available. Off-campus job opportunities are excellent.

The Inside Word

Given the extraordinary volume of applications the admissions office receives, it's no wonder that Michigan State relies primarily on numbers. Decisions typically come down to grades, class rank, and test scores. Applicants who have proven to be capable students in college prep courses are relatively likely to find themselves the proud addressees of fat admissions envelopes. Applications are processed on a rolling basis, a process that typically favors early applicants.

THE SCHOOL SAYS "..."

From The Admissions Office

"Although Michigan State University is a graduate and research institution of international stature and acclaim, your undergraduate education is a high priority. More than 2,600 instructional faculty members (90 percent of whom hold a terminal degree) are dedicated to providing academic instruction, guidance, and assistance to our undergraduate students. Our 35,000 undergraduate students are a select group of academically motivated men and women. The diversity of ethnic, racial, religious, and socioeconomic heritage makes the student body a microcosm of the state, national, and international community.

"Students applying for admission to Michigan State University are required to take the new version of the SAT or the ACT exam with the Writing section. The Writing assessment will be considered in the holistic review of the application for admission. SAT Subject Tests are not required."

SELECTIVITY

Admissions Rating	88
# of applicants	25,589
% of applicants accepted	70
% of acceptees attending	42

FRESHMAN PROFILE

Range SAT Critical Reading	480–620
Range SAT Math	540–660
Range SAT Writing	480–610
Range ACT Composite	23–27
Minimum paper TOEFL	550
Minimum computer TOEFL	213
Minimum web-based TOEFL	79
Average HS GPA	3.61
% graduated top 10% of class	30.7
% graduated top 25% of class	72.3
% graduated top 50% of class	96.5

DEADLINES

Early action	
Deadline	10/6
Nonfall registration?	yes

APPLICANTS ALSO LOOK AT AND OFTEN PREFER

Western Michigan University
University of Michigan—Ann Arbor
Central Michigan University

AND SOMETIMES PREFER

Indiana University—Bloomington

FINANCIAL FACTS

Financial Aid Rating	71
Annual in-state tuition	$10,283
Annual out-of-state tuition	$25,613
Room and board	$7,026
Required fees	$884
Books and supplies	$944
% frosh rec. need-based scholarship or grant aid	24
% UG rec. need-based scholarship or grant aid	24
% frosh rec. non-need-based scholarship or grant aid	37
% UG rec. non-need-based scholarship or grant aid	25
% frosh rec. need-based self-help aid	38
% UG rec. need-based self-help aid	37
% frosh rec. athletic scholarships	1
% UG rec. athletic scholarships	1
% frosh rec. any financial aid	45
% UG rec. any financial aid	43
% UG borrow to pay for school	42
Average cumulative indebtedness	$19,488

MICHIGAN TECHNOLOGICAL UNIVERSITY

1400 TOWNSEND DRIVE, HOUGHTON, MI 49931 • ADMISSIONS: 906-487-2335 • FAX: 906-487-2125

CAMPUS LIFE

Quality of Life Rating	**83**
Fire Safety Rating	**94**
Green Rating	**75**
Type of school	public
Environment	village

STUDENTS

Total undergrad enrollment	5,722
% male/female	77/23
% from out of state	25
% from public high school	90
% live on campus	45
% in (# of) fraternities	7 (13)
% in (# of) sororities	12 (8)
% African American	2
% Asian	1
% Caucasian	85
% Hispanic	1
% Native American	1
% international	5
# of countries represented	72

SURVEY SAYS . . .
Athletic facilities are great
Career services are great
Students get along with local
community
Campus feels safe
Lots of beer drinking

ACADEMICS

Academic Rating	**74**
Calendar	semester
Student/faculty ratio	11:1
Profs interesting rating	63
Profs accessible rating	74
% classes taught by TAs	3
Most common reg class size	20–29 students
Most common lab size	10–19 students

MOST POPULAR MAJORS
business administration and
management
civil engineering
mechanical engineering

STUDENTS SAY "..."

Academics

Future engineers looking for an affordable education in a "remote, small location near the woods" flock to Michigan Technological University, a school that "is nationally ranked in almost all its engineering programs, both undergraduate and graduate." MTU offers more than just engineering—the "strong" forest resource and environmental science program "is growing significantly" and the School of Business "is gaining momentum." That being said, most still regard the school primarily as "a winter wonderland for math, science, and computer geeks." The school "offers a real hands-on learning experience, not only in the classroom but in life," all while "dealing with being in the middle of nowhere," which students say "makes you tough." Slackers beware: "Classes are rarely canceled due to inclement weather and with the load of homework that is given, good time-management skills are necessary to succeed." Perhaps this is the reason why "there are so many companies at our career fair that it's hard not to get an interview." As one student reports, "Everyone in the industry I have talked to recruits Tech graduates because of their work ethic and personalities. This goes back to working and suffering all the time. They know what we have been through." Small class sizes facilitate one-on-one contact with professors but also "tend to make for a more competitive environment. It can be hard for those who are below the curve and trying to do better."

Life

MTU is located on the Upper Peninsula in Houghton, a town so remote that "no one goes home on weekends because it's so far away." Students see this as a plus that encourages campus unity. "My college experience would have been so much different if I had gone home on the weekends. It's on the weekends that you get to know people and actually have fun or meet with a group to study," one student explains. "Hockey is a big deal here" and the campus really comes together for games, as "it's our only Division I sport." Intramural broomball is another popular activity, "and a majority of people get involved with it because it is such a fun winter sport." Outdoor activities are also popular; one student points out that "because of its location, Michigan Tech is the only college in the Midwest with its own ski hill right on campus, and many students and faculty utilize this luxury when the winter snows hit." Such snow hit early—"the grass is almost always buried in snow," one student warns. While some here "would probably joke and say that drinking is the only thing to do up here, and for those students it's probably true," those who seek alternative entertainment rarely have trouble finding it. Finding the time for it, given the amount of schoolwork, is another matter.

Student Body

The typical student at Tech "is the smart person from those small towns who really loves the small-town atmosphere." A good number "enjoy doing things outdoors and being active," (hunting, fishing, skiing, and snowmobiling are all popular) but "this is a technical school, so there is a fair share of people who enjoy staying inside and playing a lot of video games." With a male to female ratio of nearly 4:1, MTU has lots of undergrads "wishing there were more females on campus." Although some report optimistically that "more and more women are coming to Tech as well as other ethnic groups, but it needs to grow more."

FINANCIAL AID: 906-487-2622 • E-MAIL: MTU4U@MTU.EDU • WEBSITE: WWW.MTU.EDU

THE PRINCETON REVIEW SAYS

Admissions

Very important factors considered include: Class rank, rigor of secondary school record, standardized test scores. *Important factors considered include:* Academic GPA. *Other factors considered include:* Application essay, recommendation(s), alumni/ae relation, character/personal qualities, extracurricular activities, interview, talent/ability, volunteer work, work experience. SAT or ACT required; TOEFL required of all international applicants. High school diploma is required and GED is accepted. *Academic units required:* 3 English, 3 mathematics, 2 science. *Academic units recommended:* 4 English, 4 mathematics, 3 science, 2 foreign language, 3 social studies, 1 history, 1 visual/performing arts, 1 computer science, 1 academic elective.

Financial Aid

Students should submit: FAFSA. The Princeton Review suggests that all financial aid forms be submitted as soon as possible after 1/1. *Need-based scholarships/grants offered:* Federal Pell, SEOG, state scholarships/grants, private scholarships, the school's own gift aid. *Loan aid offered:* Direct Subsidized Stafford, Direct Unsubsidized Stafford, Direct PLUS, Federal Perkins, state loans, college/university loans from institutional funds, External Private Loans. Applicants will be notified of awards on a rolling basis beginning 3/1. Federal Work-Study Program available. Institutional employment available. Off-campus job opportunities are excellent.

The Inside Word

Michigan Tech makes applying as easy as can be. Admissions decisions are based entirely on your completed application form, your transcripts, and your standardized test scores; there are no essays or personal recommendations to make you sweat here. Best of all, you can apply online free of cost. Admissions decisions are made on a rolling basis with priority given to applications arriving early. Plan to submit your application as early as possible.

THE SCHOOL SAYS "..."

From The Admissions Office

"At Michigan Tech, our students create the future. Our unique Enterprise Program lets students work on real industry problems involving homeland security, wireless technology, communication, environmental sustainability, and nanotechnology. Through student groups like Engineers without Borders and the campus-wide Make A Difference Day, our students impact lives in our community and around the world. Students can choose from 120 degree programs in arts and human sciences, business, computing, engineering, environmental studies, sciences, and technology as they begin their careers here. We offer exciting degree programs in growing fields including biomedical engineering, applied ecology and environmental science, and pre-health studies.

"Outside of the classrooms and labs, students enjoy our golf course, ski hill, trails and recreational forest, and friendly, small-town atmosphere in beautiful Upper Michigan. Located on Portage Waterway, the campus is only minutes from Lake Superior.

"We recommend that students applying for admission take the SAT (or the ACT with the writing section)."

SELECTIVITY

Admissions Rating	88
# of applicants	4,148
% of applicants accepted	84
% of acceptees attending	35

FRESHMAN PROFILE

Range SAT Critical Reading	530–650
Range SAT Math	590–690
Range SAT Writing	500–620
Range ACT Composite	23–28
Minimum paper TOEFL	550
Minimum computer TOEFL	213
Minimum web-based TOEFL	79
Average HS GPA	3.52
% graduated top 10% of class	30
% graduated top 25% of class	61
% graduated top 50% of class	87

DEADLINES

Regular	
Priority	1/15
Nonfall registration?	yes

APPLICANTS ALSO LOOK AT AND SOMETIMES PREFER

Michigan State University
University of Wisconsin—Madison
Kettering University
University of Michigan—Ann Arbor
University of Minnesota—Twin Cities

FINANCIAL FACTS

Financial Aid Rating	78
Annual tuition in-state	$10,762
Annual tuition out-of-state	$22,522
Room and board	$7,738
Books and supplies	$1,000
% frosh rec. need-based scholarship or grant aid	57
% UG rec. need-based scholarship or grant aid	53
% frosh rec. non-need-based scholarship or grant aid	53
% UG rec. non-need-based scholarship or grant aid	37
% frosh rec. need-based self-help aid	56
% UG rec. need-based self-help aid	56
% frosh rec. athletic scholarships	3
% UG rec. athletic scholarships	4
% frosh rec. any financial aid	94
% UG rec. any financial aid	95
% UG borrow to pay for school	65
Average cumulative indebtedness	$14,223

MIDDLEBURY COLLEGE

THE EMMA WILLARD HOUSE, MIDDLEBURY, VT 05753-6002 • ADMISSIONS: 802-443-3000 • FAX: 802-443-2056

CAMPUS LIFE

Quality of Life Rating	99
Fire Safety Rating	90
Green Rating	99
Type of school	private
Environment	village

STUDENTS

Total undergrad enrollment	2,422
% male/female	50/50
% from out of state	94
% from public high school	52
% live on campus	97
% African American	3
% Asian	9
% Caucasian	64
% Hispanic	6
% Native American	1
% international	10
# of countries represented	75

SURVEY SAYS . . .

Lab facilities are great
Athletic facilities are great
School is well run
Great food on campus
Campus feels safe

ACADEMICS

Academic Rating	98
Calendar	4/1/4
Student/faculty ratio	9:1
Profs interesting rating	99
Profs accessible rating	96
Most common	
reg class size	10–19 students

MOST POPULAR MAJORS

economics
English language and literature
psychology

STUDENTS SAY ". . ."

Academics

Home to "smart people who enjoy Aristotelian ethics and quantum physics, but aren't too stuck up to go sledding in front of Mead Chapel at midnight," Middlebury College is a small, exclusive liberal arts school with "excellent foreign language programs" as well as standout offerings in environmental studies, the sciences, theater, and writing. Distribution requirements and other general requirements ensure that a Middlebury education "is all about providing students with a complete college experience including excellent teaching, exposure to many other cultures, endless opportunities for growth and success, and a challenging (yet relaxed) environment." Its "small class size and friendly yet competitive atmosphere make for the perfect college experience," as do "the best facilities of a small liberal arts college in the country. The new library, science center, athletic complex, arts center, and a number of the dining halls and dorms have been built in the past 10 years." Expect to work hard; "it's tough, but this is a mini-Ivy, so what should one expect? There is plenty of time to socialize, and due to the collaborative atmosphere here, studying and socializing can often come hand in hand. The goal of many students here is not to get high grades" but rather "learning in its purest form, and that is perhaps this college's most brightly shining aspect." The collaborative atmosphere is abetted by the fact that "admissions doesn't just bring in geniuses, they bring in people who are leaders and community servants. Think of the guy or girl in your high school whom everybody describes as 'so nice'...that's your typical Middlebury student."

Life

"This high level of involvement in everything translates into an amazing campus atmosphere" at Middlebury, where "most people are very involved. There is a club for just about everything you can imagine, and if you can imagine one that hasn't yet been created, you go ahead and create it yourself." With great skiing and outdoor activity close by, "Almost everyone is athletic in some way. This can translate into anything from varsity sports to intramural hockey (an extremely popular winter pastime!). People are enthusiastic about being active and having fun." Because the school "is set in a very small town, there aren't too many (if any) problems with violence, drugs, [or] crime. It's the ideal college town because of its rural setting, in that there are no real distractions other than those that are provided within the college campus." Of course, the small-town setting also means that "the only real off-campus activity is going out to eat at the town's quaint restaurants or going to the one bar in town," but fortunately "when it comes to on-campus activities, Middlebury provides the student population with tons of great events. Everything from classy music concerts to late-night movies and dance parties can be found as a Midd-supported activity. The student activity board does a fabulous job with entertaining the students virtually every day."

Student Body

"The typical [Middlebury] student is athletic, outdoorsy, and very intelligent." The two most prominent demographics are "very preppy students (popped collars)" and "extreme hippies." One undergrad explains: "The typical students are one of two types: either 'Polo, Nantucket red, pearls, and summers on the Cape,' or 'Birks, wool socks, granola, and suspicious smells about them.' A lot of people break these two molds, but they often fall somewhere on the spectrum between them." There's also "a huge international student population, which is awesome," but some international students, "tend to separate out and end up living in language houses." There's also "a really strong theater/artsy community" here. One student notes, "Other than a few groups, everyone mingles pretty well. We're all too damn friendly and cheerful for our own good."

FINANCIAL AID: 802-443-5158 • E-MAIL: ADMISSIONS@MIDDLEBURY.EDU • WEBSITE: WWW.MIDDLEBURY.EDU

THE PRINCETON REVIEW SAYS

Admissions

Very important factors considered include: Class rank, academic GPA, rigor of secondary school record, character/personal qualities, extracurricular activities, talent/ability. *Important factors considered include:* Application essay, recommendation(s), standardized test scores, racial/ethnic status. *Other factors considered include:* Alumni/ae relation, first generation, geographical residence, interview, level of applicant's interest, volunteer work, work experience. SAT or SAT Subject Tests or ACT required. High school diploma or equivalent is not required. *Academic units recommended:* 4 English, 4 mathematics, 3 science, (3 science labs), 4 foreign language, 3 social studies, 2 history, 1 academic elective, 1 Fine Arts, Music, or Drama courses recommended.

Financial Aid

Students should submit: FAFSA, CSS/Financial Aid PROFILE, noncustodial PROFILE. Regular filing deadline is 2/1. The Princeton Review suggests that all financial aid forms be submitted as soon as possible after 1/1. *Need-based scholarships/grants offered:* Federal Pell, SEOG, state scholarships/grants, private scholarships, the school's own gift aid. *Loan aid offered:* Direct Subsidized Stafford, Direct Unsubsidized Stafford, Direct PLUS, FFEL Subsidized Stafford, FFEL Unsubsidized Stafford, FFEL PLUS, Federal Perkins, college/university loans from institutional funds. Applicants will be notified of awards on or about 4/1. Middlebury is changing its policy and now accepts the College Board's score choice option, which allows applicants to submit only thier highest section scores, across all SAT dates!

The Inside Word

Middlebury gives you options in standardized testing. The school will accept either the SAT or the ACT or three SAT Subject Tests, (the three must be in different subject areas, however). Middlebury is extremely competitive; improve your chances of admission by crafting a standardized test profile that shows you in the best possible light.

THE SCHOOL SAYS "..."

From The Admissions Office

"The successful Middlebury candidate excels in a variety of areas including academics, athletics, the arts, leadership, and service to others. These strengths and interests permit students to grow beyond their traditional 'comfort zones' and conventional limits. Our classrooms are as varied as the Green Mountains, the Metropolitan Museum of Art, or the great cities of Russia and Japan. Outside the classroom, students informally interact with professors in activities such as intramural basketball games and community service. At Middlebury, students develop critical-thinking skills, enduring bonds of friendship, and the ability to challenge themselves.

"Middlebury offers majors and programs in 45 different fields, with particular strengths in languages, international studies, environmental studies, literature and creative writing, and the sciences. Opportunities for engaging in individual research with faculty abound at Middlebury."

SELECTIVITY

Admissions Rating	99
# of applicants	7,823
% of applicants accepted	17
% of acceptees attending	44
# accepting a place on wait list	831
% admitted from wait list	6
# of early decision applicants	927
% accepted early decision	27

FRESHMAN PROFILE

Range SAT Critical Reading	630–740
Range SAT Math	640–740
Range SAT Writing	640–740
Range ACT Composite	29–33
% graduated top 10% of class	86
% graduated top 25% of class	93
% graduated top 50% of class	100

DEADLINES

Early decision	
Deadline	11/1
Notification	12/15
Regular	
Deadline	1/1
Notification	4/1
Nonfall registration?	yes

APPLICANTS ALSO LOOK AT
AND OFTEN PREFER
Harvard College
Dartmouth College
Williams College
Amherst College

AND SOMETIMES PREFER
Pomona College
Duke University
Stanford University
Yale University
Brown University

FINANCIAL FACTS

Financial Aid Rating	95
Comprehensive fee	$50,780
Books and supplies	$1,000
% frosh rec. need-based scholarship or grant aid	48
% UG rec. need-based scholarship or grant aid	45
% frosh rec. need-based self-help aid	45
% UG rec. need-based self-help aid	41
% UG borrow to pay for school	36
Average cumulative indebtedness	$19,981

MILLS COLLEGE

5000 MacArthur Boulevard, Oakland, CA 94613 • Admissions: 510-430-2135 • Fax: 510-430-3314

CAMPUS LIFE
Quality of Life Rating	71
Fire Safety Rating	60*
Green Rating	98
Type of school	private
Environment	metropolis

STUDENTS
Total undergrad enrollment	956
% male/female	0/100
% from out of state	20
% from public high school	80
% live on campus	56
% African American	9
% Asian	8
% Caucasian	44
% Hispanic	14
% Native American	1
% international	3
# of countries represented	15

SURVEY SAYS . . .
Lots of liberal students
Low cost of living
Frats and sororities are unpopular or nonexistent
Political activism is popular
(Almost) no one smokes
Very little drug use

ACADEMICS
Academic Rating	86
Calendar	semester
Student/faculty ratio	11:1
Profs interesting rating	89
Profs accessible rating	82
Most common reg class size	10–19 students
Most common lab size	10–19 students

MOST POPULAR MAJORS
English language and literature
political science and government
psychology

STUDENTS SAY ". . ."

Academics

Mills College is a "socially aware, progressive, academically serious, community-based, and diverse" women's institution, located in Oakland, California. This small school offers 40 major programs to fewer than 1,000 undergraduates, distinguished by uniformly "small class sizes and caring professors." Across the board, students say that "academics are exceptional" at Mills, with passionate instructors, ample class discussion, and plenty of homework. Despite the challenges, "all academic expectations are reasonable and clearly stated, and professors or TA's are available to help with any questions." In complement to their academic programs, Mills "is a school dedicated to social justice and environmental awareness." These concerns are incorporated into the classroom and curriculum; "race, class, sexuality, and gender issues are brought up in almost all classes by students and professors alike, regardless of the discipline." In addition, the school's extensive sustainability initiatives make Mills one of the most "green" campuses in the United States. While a majority of students feel right at home in Mills' unique environment, it is important for prospective students to take note of the school's distinctive flavor, which leans towards the left politically and values quirkiness and experimentation. A senior explains, "Mills may not be for everyone, but if it's the right place for you, you'll know." When it comes to the nuts and bolts, students report occasional administrative glitches, but, for the most part, "the administration is surprisingly organized, and the mechanics all flow well." Given the high tuition costs, however, many feel the school "could provide more student services," such as on-campus health care.

Life

A pretty oasis in the middle of urban Oakland, the Mills campus is a relaxing, quiet, and studious environment that will make a good fit for serious students. Mills' dorms are quiet environments where "people's personal space and peace are respected." The school cafeteria offers "many options for both vegans and vegetarians." Plus, the campus grounds are "good for taking relaxing walks, and the fitness center is inviting." Mills is definitely "not a party school," and students warn us that, "there is nothing within walking distance of the campus." Therefore, weekends tend to be mellow affairs, with many residential students hanging out in the dorms or studying. To combat the Friday night blues, "many students venture beyond campus, utilizing the rich surroundings in the Bay Area to work in the community, attend events to raise awareness for non-profits, and for entertainment and shopping." If they want a night out, "girls go to the UC—Berkeley frat parties" or head to San Francisco for dancing. For those without a car, "the Mills Shuttle Bus will stop by Telegraph Avenue, where many girls go to have fun."

Student Body

At Mills College, students hail from "very diverse cultural and class backgrounds, age ranges from 17 to 63, and life experiences from Cairo to Compton." It might seem like a "culture shock for some at first, but the atmosphere is one of acceptance and personal growth." Mills students describe their classmates as studious, serious, quirky, diverse, and atypical, and many mention that Mills has "a large population of lesbian, queer, bisexual, gender-curious, and transgender students." Acceptance is the rule. As one senior testifies, "I have yet to see any kind of prejudice or intolerance of another person's beliefs. Everyone is polite and courteous when faced with another's points of view." A freshman gushes, "Mills is the most vibrant and diverse community that I have ever been a part of, and from what I can tell, everybody that chooses to be at Mills, fits in at Mills." Reflecting the prevailing perspective in the San Francisco Bay Area, "the student body as a whole is very liberal, socially and politically." In fact, social awareness and political activism is practically a prerequisite among the student population, which principally consists of "environmentally aware, intelligent women who enjoy learning and making a difference."

FINANCIAL AID: 510-430-2000 • E-MAIL: ADMISSION@MILLS.EDU • WEBSITE: WWW.MILLS.EDU

THE PRINCETON REVIEW SAYS

Admissions

Very important factors considered include: Rigor of secondary school record. *Important factors considered include:* Class rank, application essay, academic GPA, recommendation(s), standardized test scores, character/personal qualities, extracurricular activities. *Other factors considered include:* Alumni/ae relation, first generation, interview, level of applicant's interest, talent/ability, volunteer work, work experience. SAT Subject Tests recommended; SAT or ACT required; TOEFL required of all international applicants. High school diploma is required and GED is accepted. *Academic units required:* 4 English, 3 mathematics, 2 science, (2 science labs), 2 foreign language, 2 social studies, 2 history. *Academic units recommended:* 4 English, 4 mathematics, 4 science, (2 science labs), 4 foreign language, 4 social studies, 4 history, 2 visual/performing arts, 2 academic electives.

Financial Aid

Students should submit: FAFSA, institution's own financial aid form, state aid form, noncustodial Parent Statement. The Princeton Review suggests that all financial aid forms be submitted as soon as possible after 1/1. *Need-based scholarships/grants offered:* Federal Pell, SEOG, state scholarships/grants, private scholarships, the school's own gift aid. *Loan aid offered:* FFEL Subsidized Stafford, FFEL Unsubsidized Stafford, FFEL PLUS, Federal Perkins, college/university loans from institutional funds. Applicants will be notified of awards on a rolling basis beginning 3/1. Mills offers a range of merit scholarships including full tuition. Federal Work-Study Program available. Institutional employment available. Off-campus job opportunities are excellent.

Inside Word

Mills strives to create a diverse community of students and welcomes older, nontraditional undergraduates. In fact, a quarter of the Mills undergraduate population is older than 23. In addition to the application, test scores, and transcripts, Mills requests that all first-year applicants submit a graded writing sample. Admissions interviews, though not required, are highly encouraged.

THE SCHOOL SAYS ". . ."

From The Admissions Office

"For more than 150 years, Mills College has shaped women's lives. Offering a progressive liberal arts and sciences curriculum taught by nationally renowned faculty, Mills gives students the personal attention that leads to extraordinary learning. Through intensive, collaborative study in a community of forward-thinking individuals, students gain the ability to make their voices heard, the strength to risk bold visions, an eagerness to experiment, and a desire to change the world.

"Nestled on 135 lush acres in the heart of the San Francisco Bay Area, Mills draws energy from the college's location. Mills students connect with centers of learning, business, and technology; pursue research and internship opportunities; and explore the Bay Area's many sources of cultural, social, and recreational enrichment.

"Ranked fourth among top colleges in the West, Mills offers a renowned education for students who are seeking an intimate, collaborative college experience. You'll learn from distinguished professors who are truly dedicated to teaching. You'll interact with dynamic women of different backgrounds, ethnicities, cultures, ages, and mindsets, making your learning rich and inspiring.

"With more than 40 different majors to choose from—including dual-degree undergraduate and graduate/professional programs in business, public policy, and teacher education–you'll have a wide variety of educational options. The classroom debate will be your intellectual catalyst, but you'll find plenty of opportunities to express yourself, both in and out of the classroom."

SELECTIVITY
Admissions Rating	88
# of applicants	1,127
% of applicants accepted	66
% of acceptees attending	26

FRESHMAN PROFILE
Range SAT Critical Reading	520–650
Range SAT Math	490–590
Range SAT Writing	520–620
Range ACT Composite	20–27
Minimum paper TOEFL	550
Minimum computer TOEFL	213
Average HS GPA	3.65
% graduated top 10% of class	43
% graduated top 25% of class	78
% graduated top 50% of class	98

DEADLINES
Early action	
Deadline	11/15
Notification	12/15
Regular	
Priority	2/1
Deadline	3/1
Notification	rolling
Nonfall registration?	yes

APPLICANTS ALSO LOOK AT
AND OFTEN PREFER
St. Mary's College of California
University of San Francisco
University of California—Berkeley
University of California—San Diego
University of California—Los Angeles
University of California—Riverside

AND SOMETIMES PREFER
Smith College, Scripps College,
University of Redlands, Pitzer College
Occidental College
California State Polytechnic University—
Pomona
University of Puget Sound

AND RARELY PREFER
University of San Diego, Pomona College
University of Wisconsin—Madison
Notre Dame College

FINANCIAL FACTS
Financial Aid Rating	83
Annual tuition	$35,196
Required fees	$1,036
Room and board	$11,480
Books and Supplies	$1,400
% frosh rec. need-based scholarship or grant aid	86
% UG rec. need-based scholarship or grant aid	89
% frosh rec. need-based self-help aid	86
% UG rec. need-based self-help aid	89
% frosh rec. any financial aid	86
% UG rec. any financial aid	89
% UG borrow to pay for school	97
Average cumulative indebtedness	$24,255

MILLSAPS COLLEGE

1701 NORTH STATE STREET, JACKSON, MS 39210-0001 • ADMISSIONS: 601-974-1050 • FAX: 601-974-1059

CAMPUS LIFE
Quality of Life Rating	84
Fire Safety Rating	82
Green Rating	60*
Type of school	private
Affiliation	Methodist
Environment	metropolis

STUDENTS
Total undergrad enrollment	1,013
% male/female	49/51
% from out of state	56
% from public high school	60
% live on campus	83
% in (# of) fraternities	40 (6)
% in (# of) sororities	56 (6)
% African American	11
% Asian	4
% Caucasian	80
% Hispanic	2
% international	1
# of countries represented	19

SURVEY SAYS . . .
No one cheats
Low cost of living
Frats and sororities dominate social scene
Student publications are popular
(Almost) no one smokes

ACADEMICS
Academic Rating	94
Calendar	semester
Student/faculty ratio	10:1
Profs interesting rating	96
Profs accessible rating	93
Most common reg class size	fewer than 10 students
Most common lab size	10–19 students

MOST POPULAR MAJORS
biology/biological sciences
business administration and management
psychology

STUDENTS SAY ". . ."

Academics

You'll get a rigorous undergraduate education at Millsaps College, complimented by a patently student-oriented atmosphere and a satisfying dose of southern charm. Offering 32 major programs, Millsaps' curriculum distinguishes itself through its "emphasis on writing and discussion-based classrooms." Get ready to burn the midnight oil: Preparing for class is indispensable, and life "revolves around doing papers." Fortunately, students say their academic experience is well worth the extra effort. A sophomore tells us that Millsaps is "all about creating an atmosphere in which students are excited to not only learn, but [to also] think." In addition, Millsaps is a highly student-oriented atmosphere. "Professors are extremely impressive with their knowledge and abilities" and their dedication to their students. Small class sizes ensure individual attention, and "the professors really care about the students personally and academically." For those who need an extra hand, Millsaps offers "great academic resources such as the writing center; subject tutors; and numerous opportunities to broaden our horizons through forums, concerts, enrichment programs, and speakers." Academics extend well beyond the classroom, and real-world opportunities abound. A senior shares, "I've worked at a school for the blind in India, studied Mayan ruins in Mexico, written federal grants at a transitional housing facility for people with HIV/AIDS, written a thesis on journalism during the Civil Rights Movement, and worked with a local independent newspaper. I wouldn't have had the chance or the initiative to do any of those things before I came here." Down-to-earth and friendly, administrators, faculty, and staff are "frequently spotted in the cafeteria, the bleachers of a ball game, or the front row of the latest Players (theater) production." Even if there is a problem, students feel involved in the campus community. A student explains, "Some of the decisions made by the administration at Millsaps have been questioned, but several of the Deans are very accessible and constantly seek student input."

Life

Life at Millsaps is busy, fulfilling, fun, and well-rounded. Firing on all pistons, the typical Millsaps undergraduate is "over-committed to various clubs and organizations, hyper-productive in school work, ready to serve the community, and ready to have a good time when the weekend rolls around." On campus, there are more than 80 student clubs and organizations, including "a fencing club, an anime club, a ballroom dancing club, and even a bee-keeping club!" In addition, "the majority of the students at Millsaps participate in intercollegiate or intramural sports." During the weekends, it is easy to find a bit of diversion from your schoolwork; "Whether it is concerts at local pizza joints or bars, fraternity parties, or simply scary movie nights with popcorn in the residence halls, the students find ways to relax and enjoy this unique period of life known as college." Socially, "the Greek system is huge at Millsaps;" however, students insist that the Millsaps Greeks are very different from what you'd find at most schools. With their firm commitment to community service, "everyone can find a place in the Millsaps Greek system, even if you would never have pictured yourself in a fraternity or sorority."

Student Body

Millsaps attracts "intelligent, open-minded, and proactive" students, who might be best described as "over-involved, over-achievers who wouldn't have it any other way." One quality that really distinguishes Millsaps students is their "strong desire to serve the community and be good neighbors to the Jackson area." In fact, "most students work hard at their school work and put academics first, but nearly everyone is involved in service in spite of the heavy workload." While most students hail from the southern states, the student body represents students from 32 states and 19 countries with a majority coming from Mississippi, Louisiana, and Texas. Students "vary in race, socio-economic background, religious traditions and beliefs, and political perspective." Even on such a small campus, "there is enough variety that everyone can find their niche." A freshman agrees, "No matter what you want to do or what you're interested in, you can find someone to appreciate and share your passions with." Friendliness is also a common denominator, as "Millsaps students are very accepting of everyone—real Southern hospitality is evident on campus!"

FINANCIAL AID: 601-974-1220 • E-MAIL: ADMISSIONS@MILLSAPS.EDU • WEBSITE: WWW.GO.MILLSAPS.EDU

THE PRINCETON REVIEW SAYS

Admissions

Very important factors considered include: Academic GPA, rigor of secondary school record, standardized test scores, character/personal qualities. *Important factors considered include:* Class rank, application essay, recommendation(s), extracurricular activities, interview, talent/ability, volunteer work. *Other factors considered include:* Work experience. SAT or ACT required; TOEFL required of all international applicants. High school diploma is required and GED is accepted. *Academic units required:* 4 English, 3 mathematics, 3 science, (1 science lab), 2 social studies, 2 history. *Academic units recommended:* 4 English, 4 mathematics, 4 science, (1 science lab), 2 foreign language, 2 social studies, 2 history, 2 academic electives.

Financial Aid

Students should submit: FAFSA. The Princeton Review suggests that all financial aid forms be submitted as soon as possible after 1/1. *Need-based scholarships/grants offered:* Federal Pell, SEOG, state scholarships/grants, private scholarships, the school's own gift aid. *Loan aid offered:* FFEL Subsidized Stafford, FFEL Unsubsidized Stafford, FFEL PLUS, Federal Perkins, college/university loans from institutional funds. Applicants will be notified of awards on a rolling basis beginning 3/15. Federal Work-Study Program available. Institutional employment available. Off-campus job opportunities are good.

The Inside Word

Millsaps' trademark friendliness begins during the admissions process. The school encourages prospective students to get in touch with an admissions counselor to ask questions, arrange a visit, or connect you with a current student. The admissions staff also maintains a blog to keep prospective students up to date on Millsaps news. For early action admission or scholarships, students need to apply in January. After that, the school admits students on a rolling basis.

THE SCHOOL SAYS "..."

From The Admissions Office

"Millsaps offers outstanding value in nationally ranked liberal arts education. Your academic journey begins with Introduction to Thinking and Writing, a comprehensive freshman experience that develops reasoning, communication, quantitative thinking, historical consciousness, aesthetic judgment, global, and multicultural awareness, and valuing and decision-making. Throughout your Millsaps years you'll be encouraged to think differently; learn critical, analytical skills; embrace independence of thought; and prepare for study in your chosen major. We offer unique opportunities such as study abroad and in the field at our Yucatán Program; an exploration of your personal and professional future in relation to issues of ethics, values, faith, and the common good through our Faith and Work Initiative; highly respected pre-professional programs in law, medicine, and social work; and a 5-year business track leading to an MBA or master's in accountancy with a liberal arts perspective that is accredited by the Association to Advance Collegiate Schools of Business. Our student body included Mississippi's 2003–2004 Rhodes scholar, a 2008–2009 Fulbright Scholar, and the faculty included the Carnegie Foundation's 2006, 2007 and 2008 Mississippi Professor of the Year. Our courses are taught without graduate assistants and our intimate student-faculty-community relationship is a hallmark of a Millsaps education. The emerging cultural climate in Jackson, Mississippi's capital city, provides unique artistic, athletic, and social opportunities in the modern south. We encourage you to look at Millsaps College. You'll appreciate the quality of our educational experience in comparison to the costs you'll discover at other national liberal arts institutions. Millsaps College: 'Are you one?'"

SELECTIVITY

Admissions Rating	87
# of applicants	1,266
% of applicants accepted	77
% of acceptees attending	28

FRESHMAN PROFILE

Range SAT Critical Reading	538–673
Range SAT Math	538–650
Range ACT Composite	23–29
Minimum paper TOEFL	550
Minimum computer TOEFL	220
Minimum web-based TOEFL	80
Average HS GPA	3.46

DEADLINES

Early action	
Deadline	1/8
Notification	rolling
Nonfall registration?	yes

APPLICANTS ALSO LOOK AT

AND OFTEN PREFER
Rhodes College

AND SOMETIMES PREFER
Birmingham-Southern College

FINANCIAL FACTS

Financial Aid Rating	83
Annual tuition	$24,608
Room and board	$9,252
Required fees	$1,632
Books and supplies	$1,050
% frosh rec. need-based scholarship or grant aid	64
% UG rec. need-based scholarship or grant aid	56
% frosh rec. non-need-based scholarship or grant aid	24
% UG rec. non-need-based scholarship or grant aid	14
% frosh rec. need-based self-help aid	39
% UG rec. need-based self-help aid	40
% frosh rec. any financial aid	100
% UG rec. any financial aid	97
% UG borrow to pay for school	62
Average cumulative indebtedness	$26,576

MISSOURI U. OF SCIENCE AND TECHNOLOGY

106 PARKER HALL, ROLLA, MO 65409 • ADMISSIONS: 573-341-4165 • FAX: 573-341-4082

CAMPUS LIFE

Quality of Life Rating	66
Fire Safety Rating	78
Green Rating	74
Type of school	public
Environment	village

STUDENTS

Total undergrad enrollment	4,875
% male/female	78/22
% from out of state	20
% from public high school	85
% live on campus	58
% in (# of) fraternities	21 (21)
% in (# of) sororities	22 (4)
% African American	5
% Asian	3
% Caucasian	83
% Hispanic	2
% Native American	1
% international	3
# of countries represented	49

SURVEY SAYS . . .

Class discussions are rare
Career services are great
Low cost of living
(Almost) no one smokes
Very little drug use

ACADEMICS

Academic Rating	75
Calendar	semester
Student/faculty ratio	15:1
Profs interesting rating	67
Profs accessible rating	71
% classes taught by TAs	12
Most common reg class size	20–29 students
Most common lab size	20–29 students

MOST POPULAR MAJORS

civil engineering
electrical, electronics and communications engineering
mechanical engineering

STUDENTS SAY "..."

Academics

Formerly known as University of Missouri—Rolla, Missouri S&T has undergone a name change, but its "reputation for academic excellence" has remained the same. Its focus on "challenging" academics ensures "the classes are tough," so "don't expect to walk right on through, but be glad that you aren't able to." Luckily, the school offers a "large number of assets" to students, including "lots of opportunities for students to lead" and professors who "really want the students to understand the material." Most students describe the professors as "very knowledgeable" and "willing to help students whenever they are in need of assistance." Some find them "varied," noting that "you have a good chance of getting an excellent professor, but then again some have thick accents, some have thick heads, and some just make you wonder if they really know and believe in what they're talking about." One thing nearly all students agree on is that the "extensive and very strong engineering and science programs" are the school's "biggest strength." "Missouri S&T does a lot of research and funds a lot of experiments and expeditions that give it an edge over other colleges," says one undergrad. They also appreciate Missouri S&T's "cheaper cost" than comparable colleges, as well as the fact their "tuition goes toward academics, not athletics." Opinions on the administration are mixed. Some find they "do a very good job at keeping the students informed about what is going on throughout the school" and "listen heavily to the students." Others aren't so positive, noting "administrators are completely unreachable."

Life

"Classes, studying, and homework dominate the weeks" at Missouri S&T, "so the weekends are when the campus comes alive." But "alive" can be a relative term. Some find life on campus is "great." "Most people get together in large groups and play outside sports for fun, work out together, or play video games in large groups," says one undergrad. "There is a great sense of community." On the other hand, when students are working so hard during the week, sometimes all they want to do with their free time is rest. "What I do for fun is sleep," explains one student, "because I'm always losing it." Either way the wind blows, "there's an organization for everyone" at Missouri S&T, with "fraternities and sororities being a very prominent part of residential life." There are also "a lot of social events that Residential Life puts on." Most agree the town of Rolla "doesn't offer a lot of entertainment." As one student puts it, "It's Rolla. Quarter Bowling night is the most fun thing to do." Many students "leave on the weekends," but most agree "part of that is that there are many different places to go within a three-hour drive." For those who stay, most "have fun with what they learn." While "pranking isn't as prevalent as it was in the past, it still happens." So expect the "normal college pastimes" of "potato cannons" and "siege machines" to take on a "more competitive level when students design equations or create programs to improve their designs."

Student Body

The typical student here is described as "a Midwestern white boy" or, as one student puts it, "a white male, nerdy, who never sees the sun." Either way, one thing is clear, women are "very much in the minority" here. This is reflected on both sides of the gender coin, with guys noting "there aren't many girls here, which stinks," and girls sometimes feeling "harassed" or that they're being "treated differently" by their peers. That said, some say "what once was a huge gap in gender population is now becoming a more respectable margin" and "the ethnic makeup of the student population is quite diverse." Fundamentally, students here are "smart," "welcoming," and "open-minded." They "make their own fun," and a good deal of bonding is done with videogames: *Rock Band*, *Guitar Hero*, and *World of Warcraft* are "hugely popular" here.

MISSOURI UNIVERSITY OF SCIENCE AND TECHNOLOGY

FINANCIAL AID: 800-522-0938 • E-MAIL: ADMISSIONS@UMR.EDU • WEBSITE: WWW.MST.EDU

THE PRINCETON REVIEW SAYS

Admissions

Very important factors considered include: Class rank, academic GPA, rigor of secondary school record, standardized test scores. *Important factors considered include:* Recommendation(s). *Other factors considered include:* Application essay, character/personal qualities, extracurricular activities, interview, talent/ability, volunteer work, work experience. SAT or ACT required; TOEFL required of all international applicants. High school diploma is required and GED is accepted. *Academic units required:* 4 English, 4 mathematics, 3 science, (1 science lab), 2 foreign language, 3 social studies.

Financial Aid

Students should submit: FAFSA. The Princeton Review suggests that all financial aid forms be submitted as soon as possible after 1/1. *Need-based scholarships/grants offered:* Federal Pell, SEOG, state scholarships/grants, private scholarships, the school's own gift aid. *Loan aid offered:* FFEL Subsidized Stafford, FFEL Unsubsidized Stafford, FFEL PLUS, Federal Perkins. Federal Work-Study Program available. Institutional employment available. Off-campus job opportunities are good.

The Inside Word

In line with other leading public universities, gaining entrance to Missouri S&T is largely a numbers game. Applicants who meet class rank and standardized test cut-offs, as well as distribution requirements, will be granted admission. But don't rest on your laurels if you have them—the university draws a competitive, self-selecting pool of applicants, meaning the earlier you apply, the better the advantage you'll have.

THE SCHOOL SAYS ". . ."

From The Admissions Office

"Widely recognized as one of our nation's best universities for engineering, sciences, computer science, and technology, the Missouri University of Science and Technology also offers programs in information science, business, and liberal arts. Personal attention, access to leadership opportunities, research projects, and co-ops and internships mean students are well prepared for the future. A 96 percent career placement rate across all majors and a 90-plus percent placement rate to medical, law, and other professional schools tell the tale; UMR offers a terrific undergraduate experience and value for your money.

"The Missouri University of Science and Technology makes individual admission decisions based primarily on each applicant's standardized test scores and class rank or GPA. In the case of borderline admission situations, additional factors may be considered."

SELECTIVITY

Admissions Rating	96
# of applicants	2,379
% of applicants accepted	92
% of acceptees attending	48

FRESHMAN PROFILE

Range SAT Critical Reading	540–660
Range SAT Math	610–700
Range ACT Composite	24–31
Minimum paper TOEFL	550
Minimum computer TOEFL	213
Average HS GPA	3.7
% graduated top 10% of class	39
% graduated top 25% of class	72
% graduated top 50% of class	94

DEADLINES

Regular	
Priority	12/1
Deadline	7/1
Notification	rolling
Nonfall registration?	yes

FINANCIAL FACTS

Financial Aid Rating	73
Annual tuition in-state	$9,438
Annual tuition ou-of-state	$20,530
Room and board	$7,632
Books and supplies	$960
% frosh rec. need-based scholarship or grant aid	48
% UG rec. need-based scholarship or grant aid	52
% frosh rec. non-need-based scholarship or grant aid	18
% UG rec. non-need-based scholarship or grant aid	11
% frosh rec. need-based self-help aid	32
% UG rec. need-based self-help aid	37
% frosh rec. athletic scholarships	2
% UG rec. athletic scholarships	2

Monmouth University (NJ)

400 CEDAR AVENUE, WEST LONG BRANCH, NJ 07764-1898 • ADMISSIONS: 732-571-3456 • FAX: 732-263-5166

CAMPUS LIFE

Quality of Life Rating	**76**
Fire Safety Rating	**85**
Green Rating	**75**
Type of school	private
Environment	village

STUDENTS

Total undergrad enrollment	4,664
% male/female	43/57
% from out of state	11
% from public high school	84.5
% live on campus	44
% in (# of) fraternities	8 (7)
% in (# of) sororities	10 (6)
% African American	4
% Asian	2
% Caucasian	77
% Hispanic	5
# of countries represented	16

SURVEY SAYS . . .
Great library
Students love West Long Branch, NJ
Great off-campus food
Campus feels safe

ACADEMICS

Academic Rating	**73**
Calendar	semester
Student/faculty ratio	15:1
Profs interesting rating	74
Profs accessible rating	75
Most common	
reg class size	20–29 students

MOST POPULAR MAJORS
business administration and management
communication studies/speech
communication and rhetoric
education

STUDENTS SAY " . . ."

Academics

Monmouth University is "not a large university, but not a tiny one," the sort of place where you "can hang out with friends one day and meet a whole new crowd the next." It's big enough to qualify as "a diverse school with good academics, recognized extracurriculars, and impressive athletics," yet small enough that "students really get to build great academic relationships with their professors and get the attention and education that they need and deserve." Standout departments include communications, business (where most of the professors "have worked for companies prior to teaching so they have a lot of insight"), education, music, criminal justice, and premedical sciences. In all disciplines students must complete "an internship program—what we call the experiential education requirement—that really sets up students for life after college. Many of the students get hired by the people for whom they intern." If there's a drawback here, it's that the student body carries too much dead weight, such as students who "have no interest" in anything but the nearby beach and thus threaten to transform the school into "a post-high school country club." However, "for a student willing to commit himself, Monmouth is a great school. At the same time, it is easy for a student to get by doing marginal work. Basically, you get out of it what you put into it."

Life

Life at Monmouth University "is a totally unique experience for each person. Some people go home every weekend and hate it; others choose to get involved and love it. Personally, I chose the latter choice and couldn't be happier about it." One student reports, "when I'm not endlessly slaving away over my senior thesis, you can find me (or any student my age, really) spending time on the beach, shopping, enjoying my wonderful apartment in Pier Village, or frequenting any one of the local bars." The party scene is not what it once was here; one student reports that "Monmouth somehow still has the reputation as a 'party school,' which was true around ten years ago, but not anymore." Students warn, "The MU police are extremely strict about alcohol consumption. Most parties on campus are busted by RAs or the police." As a result, "off-campus parties are popular. Not a lot of people go home on the weekends, but a good number go to different schools around here." Alternatively, "there is lots of nightlife around the area: Long Branch, Seaside Park, Sayreville, Red Bank, Belmar, etc. Lots of dance clubs allow girls 18 and over in with a small cover charge on select days of the week." Finally, "students often take weekend trips into the city (either New York or Philadelphia) by train or by car" when they want to get off campus.

Students

There's a lot of conspicuous wealth at Monmouth in the form of "various expensive cars in the parking lots" and "designer clothes and bags." Students are typically "very trendy," "extremely image-conscious," and "beautiful and very materialistic." Students "are very in tune with the latest fashion and technology trends." They tend to come from "New Jersey; Pennsylvania; or Staten Island or Long Island, New York. We are all from the suburbs and probably have the same family income." Monmouth's proximity to the beach attracts "many skaters and surfers" as well as "a lot of relaxed people." With three women to every two men, "the male-female ratio totally works out in a guy's favor."

MONMOUTH UNIVERSITY (NJ)

FINANCIAL AID: 732-571-3463 • E-MAIL: ADMISSION@MONMOUTH.EDU • WEBSITE: WWW.MONMOUTH.EDU

THE PRINCETON REVIEW SAYS

Admissions

Very important factors considered include: Academic GPA, rigor of secondary school record, standardized test scores. *Important factors considered include:* Extracurricular activities, volunteer work, work experience. *Other factors considered include:* Application essay, recommendation(s), alumni/ae relation. SAT or ACT required; ACT with Writing component required; TOEFL required of all international applicants. High school diploma is required and GED is accepted. *Academic units required:* 4 English, 3 mathematics, 2 science, (1 science lab), 2 history, 5 academic electives. *Academic units recommended:* 2 foreign language, 2 social studies.

Financial Aid

Students should submit: FAFSA. Regular filing deadline is 6/30. The Princeton Review suggests that all financial aid forms be submitted as soon as possible after 1/1. *Need-based scholarships/grants offered:* Federal Pell, SEOG, state scholarships/grants, private scholarships, the school's own gift aid, Federal Nursing Scholarships. *Loan aid offered:* Direct Subsidized Stafford, Direct Unsubsidized Stafford, Direct PLUS, FFEL PLUS, Federal Perkins, state loans, college/university loans from institutional funds, Alternative Loans. Applicants will be notified of awards on a rolling basis beginning 2/15. Federal Work-Study Program available. Institutional employment available. Off-campus job opportunities are good.

Inside Word

"B" students with slightly above-average SAT or ACT scores should find little impediment to gaining admission to Monmouth. The school's national stature is on the rise, resulting in a more competitive applicant base, but Monmouth must still compete with many heavy hitters for top regional students.

THE SCHOOL SAYS ". . ."

From The Admissions Office

"Monmouth University offers a well-rounded but bold academic environment with plenty of opportunities—personal, professional, and social. Monmouth graduates are poised for success and prepared to assume leadership roles in their chosen professions, because the university invests in students beyond the classroom.

"Monmouth emphasizes hands-on learning, while providing exceptional undergraduate and graduate degree programs. There are programs for medical scholars, honors students, marine scientists, software engineers, teachers, musicians, broadcast producers, and more. Faculty members are lively participants in the education of their students. These teacher/scholars, dedicated to excellence, are often recognized experts in their fields. Students may be in a class with no more than 35 students (half of Monmouth's classes have fewer than 21 students) learning from qualified professors who know each student by name.

"Monmouth recognizes its students are the energy of its campus. The Monmouth community celebrates student life with cultural events, festivals, active student clubs, and organizations that reflect the school's spirit. Athletics play a big part in campus life. A well-established member of the NCAA Division I, Monmouth athletics is a rising tide supported by some of the best fans in the Northeast.

"The president of Monmouth University, Paul G. Gaffney II, believes the reputation of the university starts with the achievements and successes of its students. At Monmouth, students find the support and guidance needed to make their mark in the world."

SELECTIVITY

Admissions Rating	76
# of applicants	7,039
% of applicants accepted	57
% of acceptees attending	24

FRESHMAN PROFILE

Range SAT Critical Reading	490–560
Range SAT Math	510–590
Range SAT Writing	490–570
Range ACT Composite	22–24
Minimum paper TOEFL	550
Minimum computer TOEFL	213
Minimum web-based TOEFL	79
Average HS GPA	3.28
% graduated top 10% of class	18
% graduated top 25% of class	46
% graduated top 50% of class	79

DEADLINES

Early action	
Deadline	12/1
Notification	1/15
Regular	
Priority	12/1
Deadline	3/1
Nonfall registration?	yes

FINANCIAL FACTS

Financial Aid Rating	72
Annual tuition	$23,470
Room and board	$9,221
Required fees	$628
Books and supplies	$1,000
% frosh rec. need-based scholarship or grant aid	60
% UG rec. need-based scholarship or grant aid	56
% frosh rec. non-need-based scholarship or grant aid	3
% UG rec. non-need-based scholarship or grant aid	3
% frosh rec. need-based self-help aid	48
% UG rec. need-based self-help aid	49
% frosh rec. athletic scholarships	3
% UG rec. athletic scholarships	3
% frosh rec. any financial aid	99
% UG rec. any financial aid	93
% UG borrow to pay for school	75
Average cumulative indebtedness	$30,853

MONTANA TECH OF THE UNIVERSITY OF MONTANA

1300 WEST PARK STREET, BUTTE, MT 59701 • ADMISSIONS: 406-496-4256 • FAX: 406-496-4710

CAMPUS LIFE

Quality of Life Rating	**80**
Fire Safety Rating	**88**
Green Rating	**60***
Type of school	public
Environment	town

STUDENTS

Total undergrad enrollment	2,239
% male/female	60/40
% from out of state	12
% from public high school	92
% live on campus	17
% Asian	0
% Caucasian	80
% Hispanic	2
% Native American	2
% international	6
# of countries represented	17

SURVEY SAYS . . .
Career services are great
Students get along with local community
Frats and sororities are unpopular or nonexistent

ACADEMICS

Academic Rating	**79**
Calendar	semester
Student/faculty ratio	11:1
Profs interesting rating	80
Profs accessible rating	82
Most common reg class size	fewer than 10 students
Most common lab size	10–19 students

MOST POPULAR MAJORS
general engineering
petroleum engineering
business and information technology

STUDENTS SAY ". . ."

Academics

A division of the University of Montana public school system, Montana Tech is a "small school with an excellent curriculum in science and engineering, complete with small classes, lots of personal attention, many internship opportunities, nearby recreation, and post-graduate success." The school offers a range of "challenging and rewarding" degree programs in engineering, sciences, and technology, with able professors who "know how to push the students without making them feel inadequate or lost in the material." With an undergraduate enrollment of just 2,200, "it is easy to establish a personal relationship with professors," and "the low student-to-professor ratio allows students to build first-name basis relationships." In fact, "professors are approachable and encourage students to visit them during office hours to discuss anything they would like to." There is no denying the academic rigor of Montana Tech's undergraduate programs; however, the university offers "a lot of support as far as helping you understand anything you're not getting," and "there are always tutors available" at one of the two campus learning centers. While most students admit that they have little contact with the school's administrative offices, most observe that, "the administration seems to be doing a great job of keeping everything running smoothly." In preparing students for life after college, Montana Tech is peerless, giving students "real-world experience while still in an undergraduate learning environment." What's more, with post-graduation job placement at almost 100 percent, "Montana Tech has one of the highest job placement rates in the nation."

Life

To keep up with Montana Tech's demanding coursework, many undergraduates spend a majority of their time with their noses in books. However, many students also get involved in a few extracurricular activities. For example, a sophomore shares, "I'm in the Society of Petroleum Engineers, Ski/Snowboard Club, and an off-campus Homebrewers' Guild." Set in the small mining town of Butte, Montana, halfway between Glacier National Park and Yellowstone, Tech's campus is surrounded by spectacular natural beauty. As a result, "outdoor recreation is popular," and students can easily engage in a range of activities, including "climbing, skiing, snowshoeing, backpacking, hunting, snowmobiling, hiking, mountain biking, and backcountry skiing." On the weekends, Tech students "can usually be found hanging out with large groups of friends at someone's house, just having a good time." Butte also has a number of popular watering holes, and many Tech students "go out to the local bars on the weekend to watch the different bands that come in to play for the locals." A freshman relates, "A lot of time is spent playing pool, having a few drinks, and just getting to know the other students. It can be at the local bar or at a student's house, but it's always a fun time and nothing too crazy."

Student Body

An open and affable vibe permeates the campus atmosphere at Montana Tech and throughout the campus, "students are friendly and always smile and offer a hello when passing by." Generally, Tech undergraduates are neither cliquish nor judgmental, as "most students at Montana Tech are here to study and focus on getting a career instead of how they dress or who they interact with." A junior concurs, "Everyone gets along well because the real measure of a student is not what he or she looks like, but their ability to make connections and see the whole picture." Currently, the school is majority male, and demographically, "Montanans make up most of Tech." In addition to the local men, you'll find "many small town, Canadian, and Middle Eastern Students at Montana Tech," a majority of whom have come to participate in the school's touted petroleum engineering program. While a common interest in math and science unites the student body, the school tends to attract a lot of different personalities. A freshman enthuses, "Everybody's unique and acts that way. We have everybody from cowboy Joe to dreadlock Steve. And they're friends."

FINANCIAL AID: 406-496-4256 • E-MAIL: ENROLLMENT@MTECH.EDU • WEBSITE: WWW.MTECH.EDU

THE PRINCETON REVIEW SAYS

Admissions

Factors considered include: Class rank, academic GPA, standardized test scores. SAT or ACT required; ACT with Writing component required; TOEFL required of all international applicants. High school diploma is recommended and GED is accepted. *Academic units required:* 4 English, 3 mathematics, 2 science, (2 science labs), 3 social studies, 2 combined 2 years of foreign language, visual and performing arts, computer science, or vocational ed. *Academic units recommended:* 4 English, 4 mathematics, 4 science, (2 science labs), 2 foreign language.

Financial Aid

Students should submit: FAFSA, institution's own financial aid form. The Princeton Review suggests that all financial aid forms be submitted as soon as possible after 1/1. *Need-based scholarships/grants offered:* Federal Pell, SEOG, state scholarships/grants, private scholarships, the school's own gift aid. *Loan aid offered:* FFEL Subsidized Stafford, FFEL Unsubsidized Stafford, FFEL PLUS, Federal Perkins, college/university loans from institutional funds. Applicants will be notified of awards on a rolling basis beginning 3/15. Federal Work-Study Program available. Institutional employment available. Off-campus job opportunities are good.

The Inside Word

Under-recognized schools like Montana Tech can be a godsend for students who are strong academically but not likely to be offered admission to nationally renowned technical institutes. In fact, because of its small size and relatively remote location, Montana Tech is a good choice for anyone leaning toward a technical career. You'd be hard-pressed to find many other places that are as low-key and personal in this realm of academia.

THE SCHOOL SAYS "..."

From The Admissions Office

"Characterize Montana Tech by listening to what employers say. They tell us Tech graduates stand out with an incredible work ethic and top-notch technical skills. Last year, 151 employers came to our campus competing for Tech students and graduates. The beneficiaries: the students! Montana Tech has had a ten-year annual average placement rate of 97% or more with exceptional starting salaries. Learning takes place in a personalized environment, in first-class academic facilities, and in the heart of the Rocky Mountains. Students at Tech work hard and play hard. Outdoor recreation provides a great balance to the rigors of the course work at Montana Tech. It's not a large, multifaceted university with lots of frills, but our students get a terrific education, and in the end, great jobs! The SAT (or the ACT with the Writing section) is recommended for all students applying for admission. Students who do not take the tests with the Writing component may be required to take an additional English placement test from the college before they enroll."

SELECTIVITY

Admissions Rating	81
# of applicants	577
% of applicants accepted	90
% of acceptees attending	97

FRESHMAN PROFILE

Range SAT Critical Reading	440–580
Range SAT Math	490–620
Range SAT Writing	430–560
Range ACT Composite	20–25
Minimum paper TOEFL	525
Minimum computer TOEFL	195
Average HS GPA	3.23
% graduated top 10% of class	17
% graduated top 25% of class	37
% graduated top 50% of class	70

DEADLINES

Regular	
Priority	3/1
Notification	rolling
Nonfall registration?	yes

APPLICANTS ALSO LOOK AT
AND SOMETIMES PREFER
The University of Montana
Montana State University—Bozeman

AND RARELY PREFER
Carroll College (MT)

FINANCIAL FACTS

Financial Aid Rating	66
Annual in-state tuition	$5,213
Annual out-of-state tuition	$15,425
Room and board	$6,140
Books and supplies	$1,000
% UG rec. need-based scholarship or grant aid	47
% frosh rec. non-need-based scholarship or grant aid	39
% UG rec. non-need-based scholarship or grant aid	20
% frosh rec. need-based self-help aid	78
% UG rec. need-based self-help aid	64
% frosh rec. athletic scholarships	13
% UG rec. athletic scholarships	5
% frosh rec. any financial aid	80
% UG rec. any financial aid	68
% UG borrow to pay for school	85
Average cumulative indebtedness	$21,000

MORAVIAN COLLEGE

1200 Main Street, Bethlehem, PA 18018 • Admissions: 610-861-1320 • Fax: 610-625-7930

CAMPUS LIFE
Quality of Life Rating	**83**
Fire Safety Rating	**80**
Green Rating	**78**
Type of school	private
Affiliation	Moravian
Environment	city

STUDENTS
Total undergrad enrollment	1,668
% male/female	41/59
% from out of state	39
% from public high school	69
% live on campus	71
% in (# of) fraternities	4 (3)
% in (# of) sororities	9 (4)
% African American	2
% Asian	2
% Caucasian	89
% Hispanic	4
% international	1
# of countries represented	15

SURVEY SAYS . . .
Low cost of living
Students are happy
Musical organizations are popular

ACADEMICS
Academic Rating	**83**
Calendar	semester
Student/faculty ratio	11:1
Profs interesting rating	83
Profs accessible rating	85
Most common reg class size	20–29 students
Most common lab size	10–19 students

MOST POPULAR MAJORS
business/commerce
psychology
sociology

STUDENTS SAY ". . ."

Academics

For those students seeking a place where "everybody knows your name," take a look at Moravian College, a tiny school in eastern Pennsylvania that offers the "liberal arts experience," using a "well-rounded education to mold a well-rounded individual." This "outwardly modest institution" disguises a solid academic environment that is "more geared toward learning rather than just getting good grades on tests," which, combined with the cozy community feel of the surroundings, provides the "perfect peaceful atmosphere for studying and socializing." One student, commenting on the school's relatively low weekend retention rate, describes the school as "Camp Moravian—a lot of people may go home, but those who stay behind have a lot more fun."

For the most part, Moravian's "fairly forgiving" professors "are engaging and provide students with challenging questions concerning the real world." Their availability and willingness to help students understand the material gets praise all around, as does their demeanor; more than one student tells of being invited into a teacher's home for dinner. "Students are able to get the individual attention they need," says one. However, this doesn't mean that there aren't a few points that need to be worked on: "All of my professors are intelligent, but not all of them are meant to be teachers," says one freshman. A few students express some discontent with the administration's level of involvement, but the "college president is a regular fixture on campus," and he "can be seen eating in the student café or sitting on a bench outside the academic building." Though most find the registration process "archaic," the academic advising system helps keep students on track in their course selection.

Life

With such a small undergrad enrollment, students get to know each other's business pretty easily and quickly, and most see this as a positive thing, listing "the chance for strong relationships" as one of the school's greatest strengths. Hanging out with friends, video games, and cards seems to be a pretty big part of relaxing at Moravian, and "there are a lot of different groups and clubs on campus that also plan activities for the rest of the student body to be part of." Almost everything necessary to amuse oneself in this "safe and nurturing environment" is "within walking distance," making it easy to go check out the events offered by the school, such as "movies every week and comedians a few times a semester," and Moravian runs Friday mall trips for those needing supplies. The soccer field and basketball arena are located in the center of the campus, "which makes it easy to attend the home games," and the school has such a wonderful music program that "the recitals are worth checking out, even if you're not a music major." A Greek scene is present on campus but not in an overwhelming way, so that "if you are looking for a party, you can find one. If you are not into the party scene, that's fine."

Student Body

"I'm not going to lie, Moravian's a very white school," confesses a student. Most of the students are from "Pennsylvania, New Jersey, or New York" and come from middle-to-upper-class homes, though "not many people question the economic situations of others." There is, at least, some diversity at Moravian (the "Multicultural Club is one of the best clubs on campus"), and the students that make up this "close-knit community" are a "very open group of people" in how they relate to atypical students. Since there is a separate campus devoted to art and music, there tends to be a fair number of "artsy" students on the south campus to balance out the healthy portion of student athletes that populate mainly the north campus.

MORAVIAN COLLEGE

MORAVIAN COLLEGE

FINANCIAL AID: 610-861-1330 • E-MAIL: ADMISSIONS@MORAVIAN.EDU • WEBSITE: WWW.MORAVIAN.EDU

THE PRINCETON REVIEW SAYS

Admissions

Very important factors considered include: Class rank, academic GPA, rigor of secondary school record, alumni/ae relation, character/personal qualities. *Important factors considered include:* Application essay, recommendation(s), standardized test scores, extracurricular activities, first generation, level of applicant's interest, racial/ethnic status, talent/ability, volunteer work. *Other factors considered include:* Geographical residence, interview, work experience. SAT or ACT required; ACT with Writing component required; TOEFL required of all international applicants. High school diploma is required and GED is accepted. *Academic units required:* 4 English, 3 mathematics, 3 science, (2 science labs), 2 foreign language, 4 social studies. *Academic units recommended:* 4 mathematics, 3 foreign language.

Financial Aid

Students should submit: FAFSA, Monrovian College Financial Aid Application, business/farm supplement. Regular filing deadline is 3/15. The Princeton Review suggests that all financial aid forms be submitted as soon as possible after 1/1. *Need-based scholarships/grants offered:* Federal Pell, SEOG, state scholarships/grants, the school's own gift aid. *Loan aid offered:* FFEL Subsidized Stafford, FFEL Unsubsidized Stafford, FFEL PLUS, Federal Perkins. Applicants will be notified of awards on or about 4/1.

The Inside Word

Moravian is a small liberal arts school with all the bells and whistles. Applicants will find a pretty straightforward admissions process—solid grades and test scores are required. Counselors will look closely to find the extras—community service, extracurricular activities—that make students stand out from the crowd. Moravian has many programs that should not be overlooked, including music, education, and the sciences.

THE SCHOOL SAYS "..."

From The Admissions Office

"Founded in 1742, Moravian is proud of its history as one of the oldest and most respected liberal arts colleges. Students find a supportive environment for self-discovery and academic achievement that nurtures their capacity for leadership, lifelong learning, and positive societal contributions. Moravian enrolls students from a variety of socioeconomic, religious, racial, and ethnic backgrounds. Providing a highly personalized learning experience, the College offers opportunities for students to direct their education toward individual and professional goals. Students are encouraged to collaborate with faculty on original research, pursue honors projects, independent work, internships, and field study. Moravian recently produced 7 Fulbright scholars, a Goldwater scholar, a Rhodes finalist, a Truman Scholarship finalist, and 3 NCAA postgraduate scholars.

"Facilities range from historic to modern, with a $20 million academic complex featuring current educational technology, at the heart of the Main Street Campus. The College is in the process of building a new residence hall on its historic Hurd Campus. The $25 million project will house approximately 230 students, contain classrooms, and other learning spaces that support the academic and co-curricular mission of the College. The Leadership Center fosters student leadership qualities and skills. Moravian encourages the complete college experience for mind, body, and spirit. Its robust varsity sports program, from football to lacrosse, has produced nationally ranked women's softball and track teams, and All-American student athletes—including several Olympic hopefuls—in many sports. Athletes complete on a state-of-the-art synthetic multi-sport field and the eight-lane Olympic track."

SELECTIVITY

Admissions Rating	81
# of applicants	2,098
% of applicants accepted	70
% of acceptees attending	26
# accepting a place on wait list	49
% admitted from wait list	55
# of early decision applicants	176
% accepted early decision	77

FRESHMAN PROFILE

Range SAT Critical Reading	500–600
Range SAT Math	510–610
Range SAT Writing	500–600
Range ACT Composite	19–23
Minimum paper TOEFL	550
Minimum computer TOEFL	213
% graduated top 10% of class	27
% graduated top 25% of class	57
% graduated top 50% of class	85

DEADLINES

Early decision	
Deadline	2/1
Notification	12/15
Regular	
Priority	3/1
Deadline	3/1
Notification	3/15
Nonfall registration?	yes

APPLICANTS ALSO LOOK AT
AND OFTEN PREFER
Lafayette College
Muhlenberg College
AND SOMETIMES PREFER
Gettysburg College
Ursinus College
Susquehanna University

FINANCIAL FACTS

Financial Aid Rating	73
Annual tuition	$30,062
Room and board	$8,312
Required fees	$515
Books and supplies	$900
% frosh rec. need-based scholarship or grant aid	74
% UG rec. need-based scholarship or grant aid	73
% frosh rec. non-need-based scholarship or grant aid	9
% UG rec. non-need-based scholarship or grant aid	7
% frosh rec. need-based self-help aid	66
% UG rec. need-based self-help aid	67
% frosh rec. any financial aid	94
% UG rec. any financial aid	96

MOUNT HOLYOKE COLLEGE

OFFICE OF ADMISSIONS, NEWHALL CENTER, SOUTH HADLEY, MA 01075 • ADMISSIONS: 413-538-2023 • FAX: 413-538-2409

CAMPUS LIFE

Quality of Life Rating	90
Fire Safety Rating	79
Green Rating	82
Type of school	private
Environment	town

STUDENTS

Total undergrad enrollment	3,231
% male/female	0/100
% from out of state	74
% from public high school	61
% live on campus	94
% African American	5
% Asian	12
% Caucasian	48
% Hispanic	5
% Native American	1
% international	18
# of countries represented	67

SURVEY SAYS . . .
Lab facilities are great
Diverse student types on campus
Dorms are like palaces
Campus feels safe
Frats and sororities are unpopular or nonexistent
Musical organizations are popular
Political activism is popular

ACADEMICS

Academic Rating	98
Calendar	semester
Student/faculty ratio	10:1
Profs interesting rating	97
Profs accessible rating	93
Most common reg class size	10–19 students
Most common lab size	10–19 students

MOST POPULAR MAJORS
biology/biological sciences
English language and literature
economics

STUDENTS SAY ". . ."

Academics
Mount Holyoke "is a rigorous all women's college that prepares its students to become the leaders of tomorrow by encouraging them to pursue their passions in a safe, comfortable, and challenging environment," undergrads at this small, prestigious, liberal arts school tell us. Biology, chemistry, the humanities, and international studies are among the strong suits of the school; in nearly all disciplines, professors "are highly respected in their fields, many of them being very prominent figures among their respective academic communities" who are also "very kind; excited to impart their knowledg; very, very accessible outside of class; and willing to spend a lot of time helping individual students." They aren't pushovers, though; "Despite their overall generosity, they hold every student to a very high academic standard (no grade inflation here), and the material covered in each course is always challenging and of high academic caliber." Students may supplement their curricula with classes at other area colleges through the Five College Consortium, but they do say that the consortium is "very underused."

Life
"People are very focused on their academics, sometimes too much so" at Mount Holyoke, and "Much of our time is dedicated to class work." Undergrads typically find time for the "fabulous traditions that help to define" school life, such as "milk and cookies in the evening (a snack put out by dining services at 9:30 on school nights) and class colors and mascots." Otherwise, "Mount Holyoke life is what you make of it. We are an all women's college, but that doesn't mean you are going off to a convent. It is easy to have a social life through the Five College Consortium, and it is easy to go into Boston or New York." Also, "people are active in clubs and sports, and they hang out in the common areas or on the green with friends," and "there are many on-campus events, such as speakers, movie screenings, etc. to keep anyone busy." The campus itself "is so beautiful…between the foliage, the classic brick buildings, and the well kept landscape of the college, I was in love!" Off-campus life offers "movie theaters and restaurants, as well as parties at the other four colleges." Hometown South Hadley "is admittedly not the most happening town ever (to put it mildly)," but Amherst and Northhampton—which are "great for eating, shopping, and anything else imaginable"—"are only a free bus ride away."

Student Body
The Mount Holyoke student body "is extremely diverse, from ethnicity to race to religion to sexual orientation to individual interests. However, the community works as a whole because of the common interest in academics and openness of the students who attend." If there is a "typical" student, it's one who "is female and academically motivated," undergrads tell us. Students are also typically "very aware of world issues, politically active, and open-minded," "very concerned about grades and jobs," and, perhaps, "overly politically correct." Among the subpopulations that stand out, "The most visible opposites are the 'pearls and cardigans,' the 'Carhartts and piercings' types, and the hippies. There are a ton of people, however, who are somewhere in between those."

MOUNT HOLYOKE COLLEGE

FINANCIAL AID: 413-538-2291 • E-MAIL: ADMISSION@MTHOLYOKE.EDU • WEBSITE: WWW.MTHOLYOKE.EDU

THE PRINCETON REVIEW SAYS

Admissions

Very important factors considered include: Class rank, application essay, academic GPA, recommendation(s), rigor of secondary school record. *Important factors considered include:* Character/personal qualities, extracurricular activities, first generation, interview, talent/ability, volunteer work, work experience. *Other factors considered include:* Standardized test scores, alumni/ae relation, geographical residence, level of applicant's interest, racial/ethnic status. TOEFL required of all international applicants. High school diploma is required and GED is accepted. *Academic units recommended:* 4 English, 3 mathematics, 3 science, (3 science labs), 3 foreign language, 3 history, 1 academic elective.

Financial Aid

Students should submit: FAFSA, CSS/Financial Aid PROFILE, noncustodial PROFILE, business/farm supplement, Federal Tax Returns. Regular filing deadline is 3/1. The Princeton Review suggests that all financial aid forms be submitted as soon as possible after 1/1. *Need-based scholarships/grants offered:* Federal Pell, SEOG, state scholarships/grants, private scholarships, the school's own gift aid. *Loan aid offered:* Direct Subsidized Stafford, Direct Unsubsidized Stafford, Direct PLUS, Federal Perkins, college/university loans from institutional funds. Applicants will be notified of awards on or about 4/1. Federal Work-Study Program available. Institutional employment available. Off-campus job opportunities are fair.

The Inside Word

Mount Holyoke has seen a 30 percent increase in the size of its applicant pool in the last decade, allowing what was already a selective institution to become a highly selective one. Matchmaking is a significant factor here; strong academic performance, well written essays, and an understanding of and appreciation for "the Mount Holyoke experience" will usually carry the day.

THE SCHOOL SAYS "..."

From The Admissions Office

"The majority of students who choose Mount Holyoke do so simply because it is an outstanding liberal arts college. After a semester or two, they start to appreciate the fact that Mount Holyoke is a women's college, even though most Mount Holyoke students never thought they'd go to a women's college when they started their college search. Students talk of having 'space' to really figure out who they are. They speak about feeling empowered to excel in traditionally male subjects such as science and technology. They talk about the remarkable array of opportunities—for academic achievement, career exploration, and leadership—and the impressive, creative accomplishments of their peers. If you're looking for a college that will challenge you to be your best, most powerful self and to fulfill your potential, Mount Holyoke should be at the top of your list.

"Submission of standardized test scores is optional for most applicants to Mount Holyoke College. However, the TOEFL is required of students for whom English is not their primary language, and the SAT Subject tests are required for homeschooled students."

SELECTIVITY

Admissions Rating	98
# of applicants	3,127
% of applicants accepted	53
% of acceptees attending	32
# accepting a place on wait list	324
# of early decision applicants	263
% accepted early decision	52

FRESHMAN PROFILE

Range SAT Critical Reading	620–720
Range SAT Math	590–700
Range SAT Writing	625–700
Range ACT Composite	27–31
Minimum paper TOEFL	600
Minimum computer TOEFL	250
Average HS GPA	3.67
% graduated top 10% of class	62
% graduated top 25% of class	91
% graduated top 50% of class	99

DEADLINES

Early decision	
Deadline	11/15
Notification	1/1
Regular	
Deadline	1/15
Notification	4/1
Nonfall registration?	yes

APPLICANTS ALSO LOOK AT
AND OFTEN PREFER
Dartmouth College
Wellesley College
Yale University
Barnard College
AND SOMETIMES PREFER
Bryn Mawr College
Brown University
Smith College
AND RARELY PREFER
Vassar College
University of Massachusetts—Amherst
Middlebury College
Boston University
Skidmore College

FINANCIAL FACTS

Financial Aid Rating	98
Annual tuition	$38,940
% frosh rec. need-based scholarship or grant aid	59
% UG rec. need-based scholarship or grant aid	60
% frosh rec. non-need-based scholarship or grant aid	8
% UG rec. non-need-based scholarship or grant aid	7
% frosh rec. need-based self-help aid	58
% UG rec. need-based self-help aid	60
% frosh rec. any financial aid	69
% UG rec. any financial aid	69
% UG borrow to pay for school	66
Average cumulative indebtedness	$23,841

MUHLENBERG COLLEGE

2400 WEST CHEW STREET, ALLENTOWN, PA 18104-5596 • ADMISSIONS: 484-664-3200 • FAX: 484-664-3234

CAMPUS LIFE

Quality of Life Rating	75
Fire Safety Rating	89
Green Rating	85
Type of school	private
Affiliation	Lutheran
Environment	city

STUDENTS

Total undergrad enrollment	2,372
% male/female	42/58
% from out of state	75
% from public high school	70
% live on campus	92
% in (# of) fraternities	14 (4)
% in (# of) sororities	17 (4)
% African American	2
% Asian	2
% Caucasian	89
% Hispanic	4
# of countries represented	5

SURVEY SAYS . . .

Athletic facilities are great
Students are friendly
Low cost of living
Theater is popular
(Almost) no one smokes

ACADEMICS

Academic Rating	88
Calendar	semester
Student/faculty ratio	11:1
Profs interesting rating	87
Profs accessible rating	88
Most common reg class size	10–19 students
Most common lab size	10–19 students

MOST POPULAR MAJORS
business/commerce
drama and dramatics/theatre arts
psychology

STUDENTS SAY ". . ."

Academics

A small, liberal arts school with a decidedly friendly touch, Muhlenberg College encourages a spirit of community between students, faculty, and staff. Muhlenberg professors are "warm, willing to talk, and really nice," giving students the confidence, resources, and opportunities they seek in an undergraduate education. A senior enthuses, "If you take advantage of it, you can get close with your professors, do independent work, and pave your own way in preparation for whatever you want to eventually do or become." A student in the premedical program adds, "The science classes are very difficult, but there are a lot of resources, such as workshops, tutoring, recitations, and meeting with the professor personally." While academics are challenging, they aren't so rigorous student don't have time for a well-balanced lifestyle. A junior explains, "Muhlenberg allows me to take a full course load each semester while still giving me time to have a job, have a social life, and be connected with the organizations with which I want to be affiliated, in a comfortable and close-knit setting." Things tend to run smoothly, and "the administrators have reached a balanced approach where they are not visible in everyday activities but are clearly in control." At the same time, many students say they've had the opportunity to brush elbows with the school's top administrators. A freshman remembers, "I couldn't believe it when, during the first week of classes, President Helm sat down with my friends and me at brunch and asked us how our first week was going."

Life

Academics are taken seriously, but personal life and extracurricular activities are also an important part of the experience at Muhlenberg College. A sophomore explains, "Academically, Muhlenberg can be rigorous at times, depending on what you place on yourself, but activities outside the classroom are also given a lot of emphasis, so it's not like all you're ever doing is studying." On campus, students participate in intramural sports, attend campus events, or join student clubs. In addition, "all of the sports teams have games nonstop." In dorms, in the suites, in the fraternity houses, or off-campus, "parties are commonplace on the weekends." At the same time, students reassure us "partying happens very often on and off campus, but it is rarely out of control like on bigger campuses." A senior adds, "People definitely work hard here, but then we let loose on the weekends. Saturdays aren't big study days, but Sunday nights in the library are packed." Although first-year students are not allowed to have cars, "there's a shopping center within walking distance," as well as "a shuttle service that will drive students to any place in Allentown, such as the bowling alley, movies, mall, ice skating rink, mini golf, and restaurants." At the same time, students remind us Allentown doesn't offer a multitude of social options for college students. For more cosmopolitan options, the school's location between New York and Philadelphia is unbeatable.

Student Body

Muhlenberg is a patently "friendly campus" where everyone finds a niche and "people smile at you as you walk by them." The overwhelming majority of undergraduates hail from middle-class, suburban families in New Jersey, Long Island, or Pennsylvania, creating a "fairly homogeneous" student body. Preppy is the dominant dress code, though there is also a big group of "artsy, theater-type students" who come to participate in the school's excellent theater program. Fortunately, "the Muhlenberg community is extremely accommodating to all types of students," and varying interests and lifestyles are represented and accepted. A student attests, "Typical students are usually white and middle-class, however, there is a great amount of diversity with people of different religious backgrounds, social backgrounds, and sexual orientations." Adds another, "At first glance we appear to be a very homogeneous campus, but upon closer inspection and by personal experience, it is clear the student body is diverse and is very accepting of that diversity."

FINANCIAL AID: 484-664-3175 • E-MAIL: ADMISSION@MUHLENBERG.EDU • WEBSITE: WWW.MUHLENBERG.EDU

THE PRINCETON REVIEW SAYS

Admissions

Very important factors considered include: Academic GPA, rigor of secondary school record, character/personal qualities. *Important factors considered include:* Extracurricular activities, interview, talent/ability. *Other factors considered include:* Class rank, application essay, recommendation(s), standardized test scores, alumni/ae relation, first generation, level of applicant's interest, racial/ethnic status, volunteer work, work experience. ACT with Writing component required; TOEFL required of all international applicants. High school diploma is required and GED is accepted. *Academic units required:* 4 English, 3 mathematics, 2 science, (2 science labs), 2 foreign language, 1 social studies, 2 history. *Academic units recommended:* 4 mathematics, 4 science, 3 foreign language, 3 history, 2 academic electives.

Financial Aid

Students should submit: FAFSA, institution's own financial aid form, CSS/Financial Aid PROFILE, noncustodial PROFILE. Regular filing deadline is 2/15. The Princeton Review suggests that all financial aid forms be submitted as soon as possible after 1/1. *Need-based scholarships/grants offered:* Federal Pell, SEOG, state scholarships/grants, private scholarships, the school's own gift aid. *Loan aid offered:* FFEL Subsidized Stafford, FFEL Unsubsidized Stafford, FFEL PLUS, Federal Perkins, Private Loans. Applicants will be notified of awards on or about 4/1. Federal Work-Study Program available. Institutional employment available. Off-campus job opportunities are excellent.

The Inside Word

Muhlenberg College accepts only the common application and does not require any supplemental essays, unless you are applying early decision. Muhlenberg is also part of a growing group of colleges that do not require SAT scores or other standardized tests for admission. Students who do not submit test scores are required to appear for an admissions interview and to submit a graded essay from their junior or senior year in high school.

THE SCHOOL SAYS "..."

From The Admissions Office

"Listening to our own students, we've learned that most picked Muhlenberg mainly because it has a long-standing reputation for being academically demanding on one hand but personally supportive on the other. We expect a lot from our students, but we also expect a lot from ourselves in providing the challenge and support they need to stretch, grow, and succeed. It's not unusual for professors to put their home phone numbers on the course syllabus and encourage students to call them at home with questions. Upperclassmen are helpful to underclassmen. 'We really know about collegiality here,' says an alumna who now works at Muhlenberg. 'It's that kind of place.' The supportive atmosphere and strong work ethic produce lots of successes. The premed and pre-law programs are very strong, as are programs in theater arts, English, psychology, the sciences, business, and accounting. 'When I was a student here,' recalls Dr. Walter Loy, now a professor emeritus of physics, 'we were encouraged to live life to its fullest, to do our best, to be honest, to deal openly with others, and to treat everyone as an individual. Those are important things, and they haven't changed at Muhlenberg.'

"Students have the option of submitting SAT or ACT scores (including the Writing sections) or submitting a graded paper with teacher's comments and grade on it from junior or senior year and interviewing with a member of the admissions staff."

SELECTIVITY

Admissions Rating	94
# of applicants	4,846
% of applicants accepted	40
% of acceptees attending	31
# accepting a place on wait list	541
% admitted from wait list	4
# of early decision applicants	428
% accepted early decision	73

FRESHMAN PROFILE

Range SAT Critical Reading	560–660
Range SAT Math	560–660
Range SAT Writing	560–660
Range ACT Composite	24–29
Minimum paper TOEFL	550
Minimum computer TOEFL	213
% graduated top 10% of class	50
% graduated top 25% of class	81
% graduated top 50% of class	98

DEADLINES

Early decision	
Deadline	2/1
Notification	12/1
Regular	
Deadline	2/15
Notification	1/5
Nonfall registration?	yes

APPLICANTS ALSO LOOK AT

AND OFTEN PREFER
Lehigh University
Lafayette College
Bucknell University

AND SOMETIMES PREFER
University of Delaware
Dickinson College
Gettysburg College

AND RARELY PREFER
Rutgers University—Rutgers College
Drew University
Penn State—University Park

FINANCIAL FACTS

Financial Aid Rating	93
Annual tuition	$32,850
Room and board	$7,790
Required fees	$240
Books and supplies	$800
% frosh rec. need-based scholarship or grant aid	44
% UG rec. need-based scholarship or grant aid	42
% frosh rec. non-need-based scholarship or grant aid	12
% UG rec. non-need-based scholarship or grant aid	11
% frosh rec. need-based self-help aid	32
% UG rec. need-based self-help aid	31
% frosh rec. any financial aid	78.5
% UG rec. any financial aid	83.1
% UG borrow to pay for school	82
Average cumulative indebtedness	$18,542

NAZARETH COLLEGE

424 EAST AVENUE, ROCHESTER NY 14618 • ADMISSIONS: 800-462-3944 OR 585-389-2860• FAX: 585-389-2826

CAMPUS LIFE

Quality of Life Rating	93
Fire Safety Rating	60*
Green Rating	60*
Type of school	private
Environment	village

STUDENTS

Total undergrad enrollment	2,188
% male/female	24/76
% from out of state	6
% from public high school	90
% live on campus	53
% African American	5
% Asian	2
% Caucasian	82
% Hispanic	3
% international	1
# of countries represented	13

SURVEY SAYS . . .

Students are friendly
Students get along with local community
Students love Rochester, NY
Great off-campus food
Frats and sororities are unpopular or nonexistent
Musical organizations are popular
Theater is popular

ACADEMICS

Academic Rating	84
Calendar	semester
Student/faculty ratio	12:1
Profs interesting rating	89
Profs accessible rating	88
Most common reg class size	10–19 students
Most common lab size	10–19 students

MOST POPULAR MAJORS

business administration, management and operations
education
physical therapy/therapist

STUDENTS SAY ". . ."

Academics

Nazareth College is "a very personalized school" in the suburbs, "about 10 miles from downtown Rochester, NY." "Education is a huge degree program" and there are quite a few physical therapy and nursing majors. Naz is also great for theater and music. "All of their productions are always spectacular," gushes a sophomore. "I constantly feel like I'm watching a Broadway show whenever I go see one." The academic pace is reasonable. "I would say that our academic program is rigorous but not mental-illness inducing," suggests an English literature major. "I count this as a strength." "Most of the professors are a lot of fun, and try to make classes interesting. Plus, they take the time to get to know you personally, which is great." "Professors care about how you are doing," declares a nursing major. "You are not just a number." Course selection is limited but classes are wonderfully small. "The administration loves student feedback" and receives generally glowing reviews. Nazareth's president frequently walks around campus and greets students. "I think Naz is doing a fine job," proffers a sophomore.

Life

Students here enjoy an "absolutely gorgeous" campus. The residence halls "are very comfortable and quite spacious," and they offer free laundry machines. Socially, there is no Greek system but the student activities council does a fantastic job of having activities planned." Some of these activities are "lame events" but many are widely attended. Intramural and varsity sports are also reasonably big. The surrounding town is a little hamlet right on the Erie Canal "with fun shops and places to eat." "Pittsford, as a town, is very safe and very nice to walk around in," says one student. However, if you attend Nazareth, we recommend that you bring a vehicle with you. "Everyone has a car. It's like a requirement," warns a sophomore. "If you want to find a party, you (usually) can." Older students often frequent the bars and clubs of downtown Rochester for fun. However, "some weekends are slow" and "Nazareth is definitely not a big party school." Road trips are common. "Nazareth isn't really far from anywhere, which makes other colleges, towns, and locations easy to access." Some students also go home on more than a few weekends.

Student Body

"The typical student at Nazareth is a white girl from suburbia"—usually somewhere around Buffalo, Rochester, or Syracuse. Students at Naz are "concerned about their grades." "The same kids you see drunk on Saturday night at the bars are the kids working hard in the library all Sunday." They are a little on the cliquey side but "very friendly," too. "There are a few jerks but nobody likes them, anyway," says one student. "Students here tend to be very liberal." "There are many preppy and sports-oriented people." "There are a lot of artsy and intellectuals," too. "And there are, of course, your weirdoes, but that's normal." There is apparently a notable contingent of gay males as well, "though more straight men are attending as they realize that they have a big sea to fish in."

FINANCIAL AID: 585-389-2310 • E-MAIL: ADMISSIONS@NAZ.EDU • WEBSITE: WWW.NAZ.EDU

THE PRINCETON REVIEW SAYS

Admissions

Very important factors considered include: Class rank, application essay, academic GPA, recommendation(s), rigor of secondary school record. *Important factors considered include:* Character/personal qualities, extracurricular activities, geographical residence, interview, level of applicant's interest, racial/ethnic status, state residency, talent/ability, volunteer work, work experience. *Other factors considered include:* Standardized test scores (if submitted testing is optional), alumni/ae relation, first generation. TOEFL required of all international applicants. High school diploma is required and GED is accepted. *Academic units required:* 4 English, 3 mathematics, 3 science, (2 science labs), 3 foreign language, 3 social studies. *Academic units recommended:* 4 English, 4 mathematics, 4 science, 4 foreign language, 4 social studies.

Financial Aid

Students should submit: FAFSA. Regular filing deadline is 5/1. The Princeton Review suggests that all financial aid forms be submitted as soon as possible after 1/1. *Need-based scholarships/grants offered:* Federal Pell, SEOG, state scholarships/grants, private scholarships, the school's own gift aid. *Loan aid offered:* FFEL Subsidized Stafford, FFEL Unsubsidized Stafford, FFEL PLUS, Federal Perkins. Applicants will be notified of awards on a rolling basis beginning 2/20. Federal Work-Study Program available. Institutional employment available. Off-campus job opportunities are excellent.

The Inside Word

Admissions Officers at Nazareth College are looking for candidates who will enhance the college community as a whole. This means that a special talent in athletics, music, the arts, or leadership areas counts; it can be especially helpful to candidates whose academic records are less than exemplary.

THE SCHOOL SAYS "..."

From The Admissions Office

"Growing interest in Nazareth—applications have grown 32 percent in five years—is a result of many factors. New facilities have increased and improved academic, performing arts, residential, and athletic spaces. Major offerings now include music/business, international business, communication and rhetoric, and music theatre. Nazareth has worked diligently to keep tuition at $5,000 less than the New York State average for private colleges. Our track record is strong—retention and graduation rates exceed national averages; 75 percent of our students participate in a career-related internship with 93 percent of them citing this a very worthwhile experience; and 93 percent of our students are employed or in graduate school within one year of graduation. The College has produced 12 Fulbright scholars and six faculty Fulbrights, in the past decade alone, along with two Thomas R. Pickering Graduate Foreign Affairs Fellowships. The Center for International Education has developed more opportunities for our students to study abroad and for international students to study at Nazareth. With civic engagement and service learning as hallmarks of the Nazareth experience, 91 percent of undergrads participate in community service while at Nazareth. A proactive approach to campus security and state-of-the-art emergency notification system places Nazareth ahead of the curve regarding student safety. Student athletes, veterans of conference and national championships, have one of the highest graduation rates among NCAA Division III institutions. The Nazareth College Arts Center brings an international roster of performing art companies to campus, and provides high-quality facilities for student productions."

SELECTIVITY

Admissions Rating	87
# of applicants	2,181
% of applicants accepted	74
% of acceptees attending	29
# accepting a place on wait list	28
% admitted from wait list	82
# of early decision applicants	45
% accepted early decision	91

FRESHMAN PROFILE

Range SAT Critical Reading	530–630
Range SAT Math	530–630
Range SAT Writing	510–610
Range ACT Composite	23–27
Minimum paper TOEFL	550
Minimum computer TOEFL	213
Minimum web-based TOEFL	79
Average HS GPA	3.3
% graduated top 10% of class	30
% graduated top 25% of class	67
% graduated top 50% of class	91

DEADLINES

Early decision	
Deadline	11/15
Notification	12/15
Early action	
Deadline	12/15
Notification	1/15
Regular	
Priority	12/15
Deadline	2/15
Notification	3/1
Nonfall registration?	yes

FINANCIAL FACTS

Financial Aid Rating	75
Annual tuition	$23,050
Room and board	$9,800
Required fees	$1,000
% frosh rec. need-based scholarship or grant aid	78
% UG rec. need-based scholarship or grant aid	76%
% frosh rec. non-need-based scholarship or grant aid	35
% UG rec. non-need-based scholarship or grant aid	33
% frosh rec. need-based self-help aid	64
% UG rec. need-based self-help aid	65
% UG borrow to pay for school	85
Average cumulative indebtedness	$21,660

NEW COLLEGE OF FLORIDA

5800 BAY SHORE ROAD, SARASOTA, FL 34243-2109 • ADMISSIONS: 941-487-5000 • FAX: 941-487-5010

CAMPUS LIFE
Quality of Life Rating	86
Fire Safety Rating	63
Green Rating	81
Type of school	public
Environment	small city

STUDENTS
Total undergrad enrollment	785
% male/female	38/62
% from out of state	24
% from public high school	80
% live on campus	80
% African American	2
% Asian	3
% Caucasian	78
% Hispanic	10
% Native American	1
# of countries represented	18

SURVEY SAYS . . .
Lots of liberal students
No one cheats
Students are friendly
Students aren't religious
Dorms are like palaces
Campus feels safe
Intercollegiate sports are unpopular or nonexistent
Frats and sororities are unpopular or nonexistent
Student government is popular
Political activism is popular

ACADEMICS
Academic Rating	95
Calendar	4/1/4
Student/faculty ratio	10:1
Profs interesting rating	97
Profs accessible rating	89
Most common reg class size	10–19 students

MOST POPULAR MAJORS
biology/biological sciences
political science and government
psychology

STUDENTS SAY ". . ."

Academics

New College of Florida, a uniquely small and unconventional public institution, "provides challenging courses for highly self-motivated students who want a large amount of control over their academic choices." It's all about "self-directed learning" here ("the student decides what she is going to learn and how she is going to learn it") that leaves undergrads "free to do what they please—with their bodies, their studies, their behavior—but while also being held to high academic standards." Those who choose carefully wind up with "a rounded education that enables them to critically and pragmatically examine and understand the world in which we live…and weird parties." The academics "are undeniably awesome" at NCF, while the small-school setting and the student body "encourage a love of learning, whether it be academic, political, or hobby-related." It's the sort of school where "it is very popular for groups of students to get together to talk about class readings outside of the classroom, usually at the college coffee shop, as a means of socializing." NCF undergrads receive "narrative evaluations instead of grades. These evaluations give advice and help us to become better students." Many here "love having written evaluations in which our process and progress are documented, not only the final outcome. The evaluations force students to fully participate and the professors to pay close attention." All students must write a senior thesis to graduate; reports one undergrad, "recently we had a survey…on which one of the sections dealt with the possibility of making the senior thesis optional. There was an overwhelming response that this was unacceptable. I think that says a lot about how proud we are of our academic standards."

Life

Having fun "in a glorified retirement community requires ingenuity of the New College student population," but "thankfully, most grew up in suburban Florida" and so "know how to navigate a hellhole." It helps that this hellhole includes Lido Beach, "where we enjoy unlimited swimming, sunning, and Frisbee playing," and that "downtown Sarasota isn't that bad either," since it's home to a number of "ethnic eateries. Thai food, in particular, seems to have a strange cult following on campus—constant debate as to which restaurant is the best or most authentic and student events that advertise Thai food are bound to pull in dozens of followers." On campus, students enjoy everything "from club meetings to public speakers to 'hip' bands playing shows. There's usually something to do and usually free food to be found!" There are also "school-wide parties every Friday and Saturday night in a courtyard outside of the dorms. Different students get to decide the theme of each dance party and the music to be played. Most on-campus students never leave campus during the weekend because of these dance parties."

Student Body

New College students share "a few things in common: most…are friendly, passionate about the things they believe in, very hard workers, liberal, and most of all, try to be open to new experiences." They are "largely middle-class, white, and liberal. There are of course exceptions, but the school is rather small,'" there is "a fairly strong queer community here, and many transgendered people who have decided to make New College their coming-out grounds. The student body is generally aware of gender issues and respectful of queer people of all types." There are even "some Republicans on campus. Maybe four. I'm not sure. We're not the type of school that generally attracts heavy right-wingers."

FINANCIAL AID: 941-487-5001 • E-MAIL: ADMISSIONS@NCF.EDU • WEBSITE: WWW.NCF.EDU

THE PRINCETON REVIEW SAYS

Admissions

Very important factors considered include: Application essay, academic GPA, rigor of secondary school record. *Important factors considered include:* Recommendation(s), standardized test scores, character/personal qualities. *Other factors considered include:* Class rank, alumni/ae relation, extracurricular activities, first generation, geographical residence, interview, level of applicant's interest, state residency, talent/ability, volunteer work, work experience. SAT or ACT required; TOEFL required of all international applicants. High school diploma is required and GED is accepted. *Academic units required:* 4 English, 3 mathematics, 3 science, (2 science labs), 2 foreign language, 3 social studies, 3 academic electives. *Academic units recommended:* 4 English, 4 mathematics, 4 science, (2 science labs), 4 foreign language, 4 social studies, 5 academic electives.

Financial Aid

Students should submit: FAFSA. The Princeton Review suggests that all financial aid forms be submitted as soon as possible after 1/1. *Need-based scholarships/grants offered:* Federal Pell, SEOG, state scholarships/grants, private scholarships, the school's own gift aid, Federal Academic Competitiveness Grant. *Loan aid offered:* FFEL Subsidized Stafford, FFEL Unsubsidized Stafford, FFEL PLUS, Alternative Loans. Applicants will be notified of awards on a rolling basis beginning 10/1. Federal Work-Study Program available. Institutional employment available. Off-campus job opportunities are good.

The Inside Word

New College is not your typical public school. The tiny student body allows admissions officers here to review each application carefully; expect a thorough going over of your essays, recommendations, and extracurricular activities. Iconoclastic students tend to thrive here, and the admissions staff knows that. Don't be afraid to let your freak flag fly; it won't get you in here if your academics aren't top flight, but it certainly won't hurt you either.

THE SCHOOL SAYS "..."

From The Admissions Office

"Inspired individualism, with a dash of quirkiness, best describes New College of Florida and its students. At New College, you participate directly in your education by collaborating with faculty to develop an individualized program of classes, seminars, independent research projects, and off-campus experiences designed to meet your personal academic interests and needs. As a result, you receive the high-quality, personalized education of a top-tier private college yet at the affordable cost of a public university. If you are independent, open-minded, and welcome the challenge of a rigorous academic program matched with a relaxed social environment, then New College may be the perfect fit for you.

"Students applying must submit scores from the SAT (or ACT) with the Writing section). We will use the student's best scores from either test."

SELECTIVITY

Admissions Rating	94
# of applicants	1,221
% of applicants accepted	58
% of acceptees attending	31
# accepting a place on wait list	51
% admitted from wait list	12

FRESHMAN PROFILE

Range SAT Critical Reading	630–730
Range SAT Math	590–670
Range SAT Writing	600–690
Range ACT Composite	27–31
Minimum paper TOEFL	560
Minimum computer TOEFL	220
Average HS GPA	3.91
% graduated top 10% of class	38.7
% graduated top 25% of class	78.5
% graduated top 50% of class	92.6

DEADLINES

Regular	
Priority	2/15
Deadline	4/15
Nonfall registration?	yes

APPLICANTS ALSO LOOK AT

AND OFTEN PREFER
University of Central Florida
University of Florida
Florida State University

AND SOMETIMES PREFER
Eckerd College
Hampshire College
University of Miami

AND RARELY PREFER
Truman State University
University of South Florida
St. Mary's College of Maryland

FINANCIAL FACTS

Financial Aid Rating	94
Annual in-state tuition	$4,127
Annual out-of-state tuition	$23,766
Room and board	$7,464
Books and supplies	$800
% frosh rec. need-based scholarship or grant aid	42
% UG rec. need-based scholarship or grant aid	39
% frosh rec. non-need-based scholarship or grant aid	11
% UG rec. non-need-based scholarship or grant aid	8
% frosh rec. need-based self-help aid	30
% UG rec. need-based self-help aid	32
% frosh rec. any financial aid	100
% UG rec. any financial aid	98
% UG borrow to pay for school	24
Average cumulative indebtedness	$13,162

NEW JERSEY INSTITUTE OF TECHNOLOGY

UNIVERSITY HEIGHTS, NEWARK, NJ 07102 • ADMISSIONS: 973-596-3300 • FAX: 973-596-3461

CAMPUS LIFE

Quality of Life Rating	61
Fire Safety Rating	89
Green Rating	83
Type of school	public
Environment	metropolis

STUDENTS

Total undergrad enrollment	5,213
% male/female	80/20
% from out of state	4
% from public high school	80
% live on campus	27
% in (# of) fraternities	8 (15)
% in (# of) sororities	4 (6)
% African American	10
% Asian	21
% Caucasian	35
% Hispanic	19
% Native American	1
% international	5
# of countries represented	102

SURVEY SAYS . . .

Diverse student types on campus
Low cost of living
(Almost) no one smokes
Very little drug use

ACADEMICS

Academic Rating	72
Calendar	semester
Student/faculty ratio	14:1
Profs interesting rating	61
Profs accessible rating	61
Most common reg class size	fewer than 10 students

MOST POPULAR MAJORS

architecture (barch, ba/bs, march, ma/ms, phd)
electrical, electronics and communications engineering
mechanical engineering

STUDENTS SAY "..."

Academics

Mathematics, science, technology, and architecture offerings all shine at New Jersey Institute of Technology. The school is a "leader in the field of technology in the Tri-State Area" whose public school pricing allows students to "graduate without the bank owning our first-borns, which is a definite plus," says a student. As is the case at many prestigious tech-oriented schools, "The professors are generally hired for research rather than teaching ability, [so] there are some who cannot teach, and they aren't that great at grading assignments or handing back papers either." The demanding undergraduate curriculum means "you have to be serious about studies if you are choosing NJIT. There is no time for fun and games." Students groan about the demands made on them but also recognize the benefits. "NJIT is an intense academic university that allows students to be prepared for the working world," explains one architect. Another plus of studying at NJIT is "how well the students interact, especially during exam time. Seniors help juniors, who help sophomores, who help freshman. It's helpful when someone who has taken the courses you're taking at the moment can put things into perspective and give you hints about what may be on the test."

Life

NJIT is "not the best school socially, but few engineering schools are," students concede. Since "a lot of classes give amazing amounts of homework, it is hard to have a normal social life. Most nights are spent doing homework late, then getting a few hours of fun before passing out." Extracurricular life has improved recently with the addition of new recreation facilities; one student notes, "The game room has been improved, with pool tables, bowling, and arcades, and a much-needed pub on campus." NJIT also boasts "a pretty good gym to work out in, and a brand-new soccer field." Undergrads note optimistically that "our team sports are all performing better, and the students are starting to feel a sense of competition building. There are plenty of parties on Thursday nights on campus, organized by frats or clubs," and, of course, "possibilities are endless because New York City is minutes away." Affordable public transportation opens the door to "major league sports, world-class museums, and theater." Hometown Newark, although much maligned by students and locals, offers "great food and restaurants less than half a mile away from campus, in the Ironbound section." Students do appreciate how the "small classes and campus make a 'small-town' atmosphere during the semester," though offset against the school's urban environs.

Student Body

"There are two types of students at NJIT," writes one undergrad, elaborating: "The first are the ones who are involved with athletics, clubs, organizations, and other things. The others are the antisocial ones. These people stay in their dorms and play computer games all day." How many of each category populate this campus? One student offers some pertinent data: "Class attendance dropped 32 percent the day Halo 2 came out." Like the region surrounding it, "NJIT is a total melting pot; the mix of ethnic backgrounds of students is diverse." While many say the various groups interact well, just as many others describe the student body as "clusters of ethnic groups isolated from each other." Because of curricular demands, "Everyone is pretty smart. But you also have the very smart people." When asked in what ways his school could stand to improve, one succinct information technology student wrote "girls!" reflecting a sentiment running through much of the student body. The male:female ratio is about 4:1.

NEW JERSEY INSTITUTE OF TECHNOLOGY

FINANCIAL AID: 973-596-3480 • E-MAIL: ADMISSIONS@NJIT.EDU • WEBSITE: WWW.NJIT.EDU

THE PRINCETON REVIEW SAYS

Admissions

Very important factors considered include: Class rank, rigor of secondary school record, standardized test scores. *Important factors considered include:* Academic GPA. *Other factors considered include:* Application essay, recommendation(s), alumni/ae relation, character/personal qualities, extracurricular activities, geographical residence, interview, level of applicant's interest, racial/ethnic status, religious affiliation/commitment, state residency. SAT or ACT required; TOEFL required of all international applicants. High school diploma is required and GED is accepted. *Academic units required:* 4 English, 4 mathematics, 2 science, (2 science labs). *Academic units recommended:* 2 foreign language, 1 social studies, 1 history, 2 academic electives.

Financial Aid

Students should submit: FAFSA. Regular filing deadline is 5/5. The Princeton Review suggests that all financial aid forms be submitted as soon as possible after 1/1. *Need-based scholarships/grants offered:* Federal Pell, SEOG, state scholarships/grants, private scholarships, the school's own gift aid. *Loan aid offered:* Direct Subsidized Stafford, Direct Unsubsidized Stafford, Direct PLUS, Federal Perkins, state loans, college/university loans from institutional funds. Applicants will be notified of awards on a rolling basis beginning 12/20. Federal Work-Study Program available. Institutional employment available. Off-campus job opportunities are good.

The Inside Word

NJIT is a great choice for students who aspire to technical careers but don't meet the requirements for better-known and more selective universities. To top it off, it's a pretty good buy.

THE SCHOOL SAYS "..."

From The Admissions Office

"Talented high school graduates from across the nation come to NJIT to prepare for leadership roles in architecture, business, engineering, medical, legal, science, and technological fields. Students experience a public research university conducting nearly $90 million in research that maintains a small-college atmosphere at a modest cost. Our attractive 45-acre campus is just minutes from New York City and less than an hour from the Jersey shore. Students find an outstanding faculty and a safe, diverse, and caring learning and residential community. NJIT's academic environment challenges and prepares students for rewarding careers and fulltime advanced study after graduation. The campus is computing-intensive. NJIT is a Top 50 Best Value College, according to The Princeton Review

"Students applying for admission to NJIT may provide scores from either version of the SAT, or the ACT. Writing sample scores will be collected but will not be used for admission purposes. SAT Subject Test scores are not required for any major."

SELECTIVITY

Admissions Rating	**81**
# of applicants	3,429
% of applicants accepted	69
% of acceptees attending	38
# accepting a place on wait list	100
% admitted from wait list	20

FRESHMAN PROFILE

Range SAT Critical Reading	480–590
Range SAT Math	550–650
Range SAT Writing	480–580
Minimum paper TOEFL	550
Minimum computer TOEFL	213
Minimum web-based TOEFL	79
% graduated top 10% of class	25
% graduated top 25% of class	49
% graduated top 50% of class	83

DEADLINES

Regular	
Deadline	4/1
Notification	rolling
Nonfall registration?	yes

APPLICANTS ALSO LOOK AT
AND OFTEN PREFER
Drexel University
Rutgers University—Rutgers College
The College of New Jersey
Rensselaer Polytechnic Institute
AND SOMETIMES PREFER
Virginia Tech
Worcester Polytechnic Institute
Penn State—University Park

FINANCIAL FACTS

Financial Aid Rating	**80**
Annual in-state tuition	$10,500
Annual out-of-state tuition	$19,960
Room and board	$9,206
Required fees	$1,982
Books and supplies	$1,700
% frosh rec. need-based scholarship or grant aid	36
% UG rec. need-based scholarship or grant aid	42
% frosh rec. non-need-based scholarship or grant aid	49
% UG rec. non-need-based scholarship or grant aid	36
% frosh rec. need-based self-help aid	49
% UG rec. need-based self-help aid	50
% frosh rec. athletic scholarships	5
% UG rec. athletic scholarships	4
% frosh rec. any financial aid	70
% UG rec. any financial aid	70
% UG borrow to pay for school	1
Average cumulative indebtedness	$27,930

NEW MEXICO INSTITUTE OF MINING & TECHNOLOGY

CAMPUS STATION, 801 LEROY PLACE, SOCORRO, NM 87801 • ADMISSIONS: 505-835-5424 • FAX: 505-835-5989

CAMPUS LIFE

Quality of Life Rating	71
Fire Safety Rating	60*
Green Rating	60*
Type of school	public
Environment	village

STUDENTS

Total undergrad enrollment	1,138
% male/female	73/27
% from out of state	13
% from public high school	80
% African American	1
% Asian	3
% Caucasian	67
% Hispanic	24
% Native American	3
% international	2
# of countries represented	30

SURVEY SAYS . . .

Students are friendly
Campus feels safe
Low cost of living
Students are happy
Frats and sororities are unpopular or nonexistent

ACADEMICS

Academic Rating	80
Calendar	semester
Student/faculty ratio	11:1
Profs interesting rating	79
Profs accessible rating	79
Most common reg	
class size	fewer than 10 students
Most common	
lab size	10–19 students

MOST POPULAR MAJORS

computer and information sciences
electrical, electronics and communications engineering
mechanical engineering

STUDENTS SAY ". . ."

Academics

New Mexico Institute of Mining and Technology—"Tech" for short—is not your standard-issue, state-run engineering and science degree factory. On the contrary, this small school "is about creating close relationships with actual professors who help students think and grow academically so they can become life-long learners and influential engineers and scientists." Entering students should expect "an intense, rigorous academic experience" designed "for serious students with a love for all things scientific, electronic, or just plain nerdy." The academic program provides "a hands-on education" through "immense internship and experience opportunities, so no person should excuse themselves from achieving an exceptional education in theory and tangible worldly knowledge". Research opportunities also abound, which is another benefit of the school's size. As one student reports, "Within two weeks of attending NMT I was able to obtain a research position working under a professor doing actual research, not grunt work. NMT is a research facility that just so happens to be a university." The workload is tough, but "there are free tutoring centers for nearly every subject, as well as individualized help upon request. Professors are almost always willing to help individual students and love to see students succeed at this school." With all these assets, how does NMT keep the cost of its education so cheap? Public funding is part of the reason, but perhaps "being located in the middle of nowhere"—where property values are traditionally pretty low—also has something to do with it.

Life

Surviving at Tech "involves a lot of work, so students are usually very busy." Undergrads typically immerse themselves in their studies. They "think about school and getting smarter; that's all anyone thinks about. When you walk by people in the cafeteria, they're talking about algorithms. That's not a joke. I didn't know there were places or people like this. I thought people like this were a joke stereotype that you only saw on TV, but they're real." Students do find time for leisure, however. "The more athletic students tend to hike, mountain bike, rock climb, or play rugby," while "the more introverted students tend to play computer games on the campus intranet." Social life here "is not so great. Every weekend, people leave town to go home or they get drunk. there are clubs to join and some things to do, but those activities are limited and often stop around midterms." Hometown Socorro offers "absolutely nothing to do" according to some, although others report that "There are also a few cool hangouts if students really want to get out (Socorro Springs Brewery serves wonderful food)."

Student Body

"At a typical school, you see people listening to music because it's popular, not really because they think it sounds good," one Techie explains. "The clothes they wear, the way they talk, everything is done to try to impress others and try to be as 'cool' as possible. Here however, this is not the concern. No one wears the most expensive 'cool' brand-name clothing, no one listens to the music that's popular. Individuality is absolutely held onto tightly here because no one cares what anyone else thinks of them. I know people who only shower three times a week because they think that's all they need. They're wrong, but they don't care whether you think they're wrong or not. They do because they want." Another student adds that "high school 'popular kids' will probably feel very out of place here. On the other hand, gamers, nerds, geeks, and students who just never fit the mold will find a friendly home." The population "has many Caucasian students, but there are also quite a few students from India and Japan, in particular. Males outweigh females heavily. As a male student, the male-to-female ratio feels like 15:1!"

FINANCIAL AID: 505-835-5333 • E-MAIL: ADMISSION@ADMIN.NMT.EDU • WEBSITE: WWW.NMT.EDU

THE PRINCETON REVIEW SAYS

Admissions

Very important factors considered include: Academic GPA, rigor of secondary school record, standardized test scores. *Other factors considered include:* Class rank, extracurricular activities, talent/ability. SAT or ACT required; ACT recommended; TOEFL required of all international applicants. High school diploma is required and GED is accepted. *Academic units required:* 4 English, 3 mathematics, 2 science, (2 science labs), 2 social studies, 1 history, 3 academic electives. *Academic units recommended:* 4 English, 4 mathematics, 4 science, (3 science labs), 2 foreign language, 3 social studies, 1 history.

Financial Aid

Students should submit: FAFSA, institution's own financial aid form. Regular filing deadline is 3/1. The Princeton Review suggests that all financial aid forms be submitted as soon as possible after 1/1. *Need-based scholarships/grants offered:* Federal Pell, SEOG, state scholarships/grants, private scholarships, the school's own gift aid. *Loan aid offered:* FFEL Subsidized Stafford, FFEL Unsubsidized Stafford, FFEL PLUS, Federal Perkins, state loans. Applicants will be notified of awards on a rolling basis beginning 4/1. Federal Work-Study Program available. Institutional employment available. Off-campus job opportunities are fair.

The Inside Word

Tech sets a minimum requirement of 970 combined SAT score or ACT composite score of 21 for admission, but typically students who thrive here do much better. In fact, the average math score is 610 (average composite ACT is 26, math 26). One student puts it this way: "You have to understand, NMT is a geek school. Even though the admission criteria are not particularly rigorous, you will be expected to focus, work hard, and give it your all." Those unsure whether they can handle the workload are strongly advised to meet with an admissions counselor before deciding whether to apply and/or attend.

THE SCHOOL SAYS ". . ."

From The Admissions Office

"More than a century old, New Mexico Tech has research programs at the cutting edge of today's technology. This is exciting for students because many of them get jobs working for professors or for one of our many research divisions, learning skills they will use in graduate schools or high-tech careers. Pulsars, thunderstorms, volcanoes, lightning, quasars, earthquakes, energetic materials, and caves are just a few of the areas we study. We also teach and work in areas of computer and information security, business management, and several fields of engineering. Many of our research divisions are known worldwide in their fields, including Magdalena Ridge Observatory, the Energetic Materials Research and Testing Center, and Langmuir Laboratory for Atmospheric Research.

"Students are required to submit scores from either the SAT or ACT. New Mexico Institute of Mining and Technology will continue to use the composite score from the ACT and/or the combined score of the Critical Reading and Math components *only* from the SAT for both admission decisions and merit scholarships. The Writing component will not be used for admission decisions and/or merit scholarships. New Mexico Tech does not require the SAT Subject Test for consideration for admission or merit scholarships."

SELECTIVITY

Admissions Rating	**88**
# of applicants	763
% of applicants accepted	55
% of acceptees attending	59

FRESHMAN PROFILE

Range SAT Critical Reading	530–660
Range SAT Math	560–680
Range ACT Composite	23–29
Minimum paper TOEFL	540
Minimum computer TOEFL	207
Average HS GPA	3.6
% graduated top 10% of class	31
% graduated top 25% of class	63
% graduated top 50% of class	91

DEADLINES

Regular	
Priority	3/1
Deadline	8/1
Notification	rolling
Nonfall registration?	yes

APPLICANTS ALSO LOOK AT

AND SOMETIMES PREFER
University of New Mexico
Colorado School of Mines

AND RARELY PREFER
New Mexico State University

FINANCIAL FACTS

Financial Aid Rating	**88**
Annual in-state tuition	$3,543
Annual out-of-state tuition	$11,199
Room and board	$5,300
Required fees	$562
Books and supplies	$1,000
% frosh rec. need-based scholarship or grant aid	17
% UG rec. need-based scholarship or grant aid	26
% frosh rec. non-need-based scholarship or grant aid	26
% UG rec. non-need-based scholarship or grant aid	26
% frosh rec. need-based self-help aid	20
% UG rec. need-based self-help aid	28
% frosh rec. any financial aid	34
% UG rec. any financial aid	39
% UG borrow to pay for school	36
Average cumulative indebtedness	$7,889

NEW YORK UNIVERSITY

22 WASHINGTON SQUARE NORTH, NEW YORK, NY 10011 • ADMISSIONS: 212-998-4500 • FAX: 212-995-4902

CAMPUS LIFE

Quality of Life Rating	72
Fire Safety Rating	79
Green Rating	96
Type of school	private
Environment	metropolis

STUDENTS

Total undergrad enrollment	20,780
% male/female	39/61
% from out of state	64
% from public high school	65
% live on campus	52
% in (# of) fraternities	1 (14)
% in (# of) sororities	2 (10)
% African American	4
% Asian	20
% Caucasian	48
% Hispanic	8
% international	6
# of countries represented	99

SURVEY SAYS . . .

Lots of liberal students
Students love New York, NY
Great off-campus food
Intercollegiate sports are unpopular
or nonexistent
Frats and sororities are unpopular or
nonexistent

ACADEMICS

Academic Rating	83
Calendar	semester
Student/faculty ratio	12:1
Profs interesting rating	62
Profs accessible rating	62
Most common reg class size	10–19 students
Most common lab size	10–19 students

MOST POPULAR MAJORS

drama and dramatics/theatre arts
finance
liberal arts and sciences/liberal
studies

STUDENTS SAY ". . ."

Academics

Located in the heart of Manhattan's Greenwich Village, New York University feeds off its great home city. The school's layout reinforces this relationship; academic buildings and dormitories are scattered around Washington Square Park and are virtually indistinguishable from the private residences, hotels, and restaurants that are its neighbors. Asked to identify the school's greatest asset, so many students respond "location, location, location" that one could be forgiven for thinking that NYU is a training school for real-estate agents. Nonetheless, the school's location "attracts superb professors and well-known researchers and lecturers" and "It's pretty much guaranteed that you'll have a couple good connections in your field when you leave NYU." While at school, you'll find opportunities for "amazing internship possibilities and real-life experiences," and you'll learn the "independence, maturity, and time-management skills" that come with living in an "expensive place where space is limited but you have access to the best of everything." Students note that NYU "offers a great program for nearly anything you want to major in," including a world-renowned arts school, and excellent programs in business, the humanities, and education. The school's weak spot, undergrads agree, is the administration, where "too much red tape" creates an experience reminiscent of "a daily trip to the Department of Motor Vehicles." A relatively small price to pay, most here agree, for the "endless cultural, culinary, musical, artistic, and academic opportunities" that NYU offers.

Life

NYU isn't merely located in "the city that never sleeps." It is, in fact, located in one of the city's hottest social and cultural areas, an agora of restaurants, clubs, concert venues, movie theaters, retail shops, and galleries. Village life ain't cheap, however, and students warn that "money is always an issue. Kids are either worried about getting more money out of their parents or managing what money they have. But money seems to be considerably less of an issue when we're all going out on a Friday night. There is any number of ways to entertain yourself—it's New York City!" Inexpensive diversions include many of the city's famous museums, cheap ethnic eats, and the ever-popular pastime of people-watching. There are also "many free/discounted events put on by the university (like concerts, plays, forums, etc)." Don't expect a typical college party scene here, however, as "There are no frat parties at NYU, as Greek life is virtually non-existent, even frowned upon by many students. Instead, students prefer to go out to bars and clubs on weekends." Dorm and apartment parties also "aren't too abundant, though pre-gaming is very popular." In fact, "NYU doesn't really provide much of an emphasis on campus activities, especially during the weekend. You're basically left to find your own entertainment which, thankfully, is always possible."

Student Body

Students agree that "NYU is just as diverse as the city it is surrounded by," noting that the campus "is a conglomeration of the atypical. If you are looking for a student body wearing J. Crew and discussing the next frat party, this isn't the school for you." Each college has a specific archetype—"The somewhat eccentric theater student in Tisch, the mostly international Stern business students, the Steinhardt musicians reminiscent of the band groups in high school"—but "The vast majority of students are really pretty average, just doing their own thing like everybody else." The community "is known for its acceptance of students of any ethnicity, religion, sexual orientation, gender, or race. We live in New York, so absolutely nothing shocks us, and virtually everything is accepted." The lack of a traditional campus attracts students of an "independent" bent and, on occasion, drives away those who discover they crave a more conventional college experience.

FINANCIAL AID: 212-998-4444 • WEBSITE: WWW.NYU.EDU

THE PRINCETON REVIEW SAYS

Admissions

Very important factors considered include: Application essay, academic GPA, recommendation(s), rigor of secondary school record, standardized test scores, extracurricular activities. *Important factors considered include:* Class rank, character/personal qualities, talent/ability. *Other factors considered include:* Alumni/ae relation, first generation, racial/ethnic status, volunteer work, work experience. SAT or ACT required; ACT with Writing component required; TOEFL required of all international applicants. High school diploma is required and GED is accepted. *Academic units required:* 4 English, 3 mathematics, 3 science, (2 science labs), 2 foreign language, 4 history. *Academic units recommended:* 4 English, 4 mathematics, 4 science, 3 foreign language, 4 history.

Financial Aid

Students should submit: FAFSA, state aid form. Early Decision applicants may submit an institutional form for an estimated award. Regular filing deadline is 2/15. The Princeton Review suggests that all financial aid forms be submitted as soon as possible after 1/1. *Need-based scholarships/grants offered:* Federal Pell, SEOG, state scholarships/grants, private scholarships, the school's own gift aid. *Loan aid offered:* FFEL Subsidized Stafford, FFEL Unsubsidized Stafford, FFEL PLUS, Federal Perkins, Federal Nursing. Applicants will be notified of awards on a rolling basis beginning 4/1. Federal Work-Study Program available. Institutional employment available. Off-campus job opportunities are excellent.

The Inside Word

Undergraduate applicants may apply only to one of NYU's undergraduate schools and colleges. Students applying to the Silver School of Social Work, Steinhardt School of Culture, Education, and Human Development, the Tisch School of the Arts, or the School of Continuing and Professional Studies must indicate an intended major (those applying to the College of Arts and Sciences or the Stern School of Business may indicate that they are undecided on their majors). This is different from the application process at most schools and obviously requires some forethought. Remember that this is a highly competitive school; if your application does not reflect a serious interest in your intended area of study, your chances of getting in will be diminished.

THE SCHOOL SAYS "..."

From The Admissions Office

"Located in Greenwich Village, New York University (NYU) is unlike any other U.S. institution of higher education in the United States. When you enter NYU, you become part of a close-knit community that combines the nurturing atmosphere of a small- to medium-sized college with the myriad offerings and research opportunities of a global, urban university. The energy and resources of New York City serve as an extension of our campus, providing unique opportunities for research, internships, and job placement. With thousands of undergraduate course offerings and over 160 areas of study from which to choose, you can explore and develop your intellectual and professional passions from your very first semester. Along with this extraordinary range of courses and programs, each of our schools offers a strong liberal arts foundation, introducing you to the traditions of scholarship and inquiry that are the keys to success at NYU and throughout life. NYU's intellectual climate is fostered by a faculty of world-famous scholars, researchers, and artists who teach both undergraduate and graduate courses. In addition, an integral element of the NYU academic experience is our study abroad programs. NYU offers ten international academic centers for study abroad—in Berlin, Buenos Aires, Florence, Ghana, London, Madrid, Paris, Prague, Shanghai, and Tel Aviv, along with a complete branch campus in Abu Dhabi scheduled to open in fall 2010.

"At NYU, you will become part of one of the most dynamic universities in the country, in one of the most exciting cities in the world, making NYU's tradition of innovation, learning, and success a part of your future."

SELECTIVITY

Admissions Rating	96
# of applicants	37,245
% of applicants accepted	32
% of acceptees attending	38
# accepting a place on wait list	1,037
% admitted from wait list	52
# of early decision applicants	2,994
% accepted early decision	33

FRESHMAN PROFILE

Range SAT Critical Reading	620–720
Range SAT Math	630–720
Range SAT Writing	620–720
Range ACT Composite	28–31
Average HS GPA	3.6
% graduated top 10% of class	68
% graduated top 25% of class	92
% graduated top 50% of class	100

DEADLINES

Early decision	
Deadline	11/1
Notification	12/15
Regular	
Deadline	1/1
Notification	4/1
Nonfall registration?	no

FINANCIAL FACTS

Financial Aid Rating	77
Annual tuition	$36,586
% frosh rec. need-based scholarship or grant aid	51
% UG rec. need-based scholarship or grant aid	48
% frosh rec. need-based self-help aid	49
% UG rec. need-based self-help aid	47
% frosh rec. any financial aid	58
% UG rec. any financial aid	57
% UG borrow to pay for school	58
Average cumulative indebtedness	$34,850

NORTH CAROLINA STATE UNIVERSITY

BOX 7103, RALEIGH, NC 27695 • ADMISSIONS: 919-515-2434 • FAX: 919-515-5039

CAMPUS LIFE

Quality of Life Rating	76
Fire Safety Rating	85
Green Rating	90
Type of school	public
Environment	metropolis

STUDENTS

Total undergrad enrollment	22,839
% male/female	57/43
% from out of state	7
% from public high school	90
% live on campus	35
% in (# of) fraternities	9 (32)
% in (# of) sororities	12 (17)
% African American	9
% Asian	5
% Caucasian	79
% Hispanic	3
% Native American	1
% international	1
# of countries represented	111

SURVEY SAYS . . .

Lab facilities are great
Everyone loves the Wolfpack
Student publications are popular

ACADEMICS

Academic Rating	74
Calendar	semester
Student/faculty ratio	16:1
Profs interesting rating	74
Profs accessible rating	74
% classes taught by TAs	9
Most common	
reg class size	20–29 students
Most common	
lab size	20–29 students

MOST POPULAR MAJORS

biology/biological sciences
business administration and
management
mechanical engineering

STUDENTS SAY ". . ."

Academics

North Carolina State University provides its student body with a combination of practical experience and theoretical knowledge in a curriculum with a technological bent. It offers strong programs in business, textiles and design, engineering, pre-medical sciences, and a host of agricultural and wildlife sciences. While some here feel the school "offers no liberal arts program," others point out that its college of humanities and social science is "underrated" and "becoming just as important as [the] engineering and agriculture" colleges. There is no doubt, however, the school "emphasiz[es] out-of-classroom experiences." A senior boasts, "All I had to do was ask my professors about opportunities in my field and they heaped internships and research studies so high on me I had to reject six of them." A junior adds, "NCSU really cares about students and provid[es] them with great facilities, community resources, and professors—something you can't really say for many schools of this size." Students report the faculty is "very knowledgeable." "Many people tell you in high school that professors do not care about you [or] your academic success, but from what I have seen here at NCSU, most professors do care as long as you are willing to put forth the effort to ask," a freshman reports. The administration, on the other hand, "is very difficult to get a hold of, unless it's something they themselves care about." Fortunately, many administrative tasks can be handled easily online.

Life

NC State benefits from a great location. "There is always something fun going on" in hometown Raleigh, with "lots of universities within a 30-mile radius, including Duke, UNC, Peace, Meredith, Shaw, and others....There are many people in their early 20s to meet and hang out with." There are also "lots of golf courses, tennis courts, basketball courts, etc., for sports enthusiasts. You will not get bored in Raleigh, [but] if somehow you do...drive to Chapel Hill or Greenville." A slightly longer car trip—approximately two hours—puts you on the beach (east) or the mountains (west). ACC athletics dominate the thoughts of many in the area. NCSU's rivalries with nearby UNC and Duke are long-standing and legendary, especially in basketball, where all three schools typically field competitive teams. "Wolfpack pride is definitely evident throughout campus and even many portions of Raleigh." The school is home to "plenty of on-campus clubs and activities many people participate in during the day. No matter what you are interested in, there is normally a club for it, and NCSU students are very active within their campus organizations and with the community." While "most people stay focused during the week...when the weekend comes they leave that behind for the party scene," which centers on Greek houses and student housing or on bars that "become the hang-out spot." Students point out, however, "this doesn't mean that there aren't other things to do or that you won't have any friends" if "you aren't into drinking."

Student Body

At a school of more than 20,000, you'll find a little of everything, and NCSU is no exception to that rule. "Athletes, computer geeks, frat dogs, sorority girls, skaters, intellects, grad students, goths, exchange students, etc." are peppered among the more populous "agriculture majors who wear overalls and talk with a thick southern accent" or "engineering majors who are kind of geeky." In the same vein, NCSU "is a very conservative campus," but it is not without its "politically liberal students" and homosexual and minority advocacy groups. Atypical students "fit in really well in certain degree programs, especially textiles."

FINANCIAL AID: 919-515-2421 • E-MAIL: UNDERGRAD_ADMISSIONS@NCSU.EDU • WEBSITE: WWW.NCSU.EDU

THE PRINCETON REVIEW SAYS

Admissions

Very important factors considered include: Class rank, academic GPA, rigor of secondary school record, standardized test scores. *Other factors considered include:* Application essay, recommendation(s), alumni/ae relation, character/personal qualities, extracurricular activities, first generation, geographical residence, racial/ethnic status, state residency, talent/ability, volunteer work, work experience. SAT or ACT required; ACT with Writing component required; TOEFL required of all international applicants. High school diploma is required and GED is not accepted. *Academic units required:* 4 English, 4 mathematics, 3 science, (1 science lab), 2 foreign language, 1 social studies, 1 history, 1 academic elective. *Academic units recommended:* 4 English, 4 mathematics, 4 science, (2 science labs), 2 foreign language, 1 social studies, 1 history, 4 academic electives.

Financial Aid

Students should submit: FAFSA, institution's own financial aid form. The Princeton Review suggests that all financial aid forms be submitted as soon as possible after 1/1. *Need-based scholarships/grants offered:* Federal Pell, SEOG, state scholarships/grants, private scholarships, the school's own gift aid, United Negro College Fund. *Loan aid offered:* FFEL Subsidized Stafford, FFEL Unsubsidized Stafford, FFEL PLUS, Federal Perkins, state loans, college/university loans from institutional funds. Applicants will be notified of awards on a rolling basis beginning 4/1. Federal Work-Study Program available. Institutional employment available. Off-campus job opportunities are excellent.

The Inside Word

Soaring tuition rates at private schools and the school's growing reputation in a wide variety of fields have expanded the applicant pool. Freshman applicants must apply to a specific program, and some are more selective than others. Agricultural programs, the College of Textiles, and the College of Natural Resources are not as selective as programs in engineering, mathematics, the sciences, business, and the humanities and social sciences.

THE SCHOOL SAYS "..."

From The Admissions Office

"NC State is arguably the most popular university in the state, with more NC students seeking admission than at any other college or university. More than 17,000 students from across the nation seek one of the 3,600 available freshman spaces. Students choose NC State for its strong and varied academic programs (approximately 90), national reputation for excellence, low cost, location in Raleigh and the Research Triangle Park area, and very friendly atmosphere. Our students like the excitement of a large campus and the many opportunities it offers, such as Cooperative Education, Study Abroad, extensive honors programming, and theme residence halls. Each year, hundreds of NC State graduates are accepted into medical or law schools or other areas of advanced professional study. More corporate and government entities recruit graduates from NC State than from any other university in the United States.

"Freshman applicants must take either the SAT, the ACT with the Writing component."

SELECTIVITY

Admissions Rating	91
# of applicants	17,652
% of applicants accepted	59
% of acceptees attending	45

FRESHMAN PROFILE

Range SAT Critical Reading	520–620
Range SAT Math	560–660
Range SAT Writing	510–610
Range ACT Composite	22–27
Minimum paper TOEFL	550
Minimum computer TOEFL	213
Average HS GPA	4.17
% graduated top 10% of class	40
% graduated top 25% of class	80
% graduated top 50% of class	98

DEADLINES

Early action	
Deadline	11/1
Notification	1/30
Regular	
Priority	11/1
Deadline	2/1
Notification	rolling
Nonfall registration?	yes

APPLICANTS ALSO LOOK AT

AND OFTEN PREFER
University of North Carolina at Chapel Hill

AND SOMETIMES PREFER
University of North Carolina—Charlotte

AND RARELY PREFER
Virginia Tech

FINANCIAL FACTS

Financial Aid Rating	82
Annual in-state tuition	$3,860
Annual out-of-state tuition	$16,158
Room and board	$7,982
Required fees	$1,426
Books and supplies	$930
% frosh rec. need-based scholarship or grant aid	41
% UG rec. need-based scholarship or grant aid	39
% frosh rec. non-need-based scholarship or grant aid	7
% UG rec. non-need-based scholarship or grant aid	4
% frosh rec. need-based self-help aid	21
% UG rec. need-based self-help aid	27
% frosh rec. athletic scholarships	1
% UG rec. athletic scholarships	1
% frosh rec. any financial aid	69
% UG rec. any financial aid	63
% UG borrow to pay for school	49
Average cumulative indebtedness	$14,996

NORTHEASTERN UNIVERSITY

360 HUNTINGTON AVENUE, 150 RICHARDS HALL, BOSTON, MA 02115 • ADMISSIONS: 617-373-2200 • FAX: 617-373-8780

CAMPUS LIFE
Quality of Life Rating	87
Fire Safety Rating	87
Green Rating	99
Type of school	private
Environment	metropolis

STUDENTS
Total undergrad enrollment	15,521
% male/female	49/51
% from out of state	67
% live on campus	47
% in (# of) fraternities	4 (9)
% in (# of) sororities	4 (8)
% African American	5
% Asian	8
% Caucasian	57
% Hispanic	5
% international	7
# of countries represented	94

SURVEY SAYS . . .
Athletic facilities are great
Career services are great
Students love Boston, MA
Great off-campus food
Students are happy
Student publications are popular
Hard liquor is popular

ACADEMICS
Academic Rating	79
Calendar	semester
Student/faculty ratio	15:1
Profs interesting rating	67
Profs accessible rating	75
Most common reg class size	10–19 students

MOST POPULAR MAJORS
business/commerce
engineering
health services/allied health/health sciences

STUDENTS SAY ". . ."

Academics

Northeastern "is all about mixing classroom-based instruction with real-world experience" via a robust, justly renowned co-op program (which places students in real-life major-related internships and jobs for up to 18 months) that provides "meaningful work and life experience" to nearly all undergraduates. While some may quibble co-op "isn't the best thing for all majors, only those oriented toward business, journalism, communications, engineering, some sciences, and architecture," most here insist "the co-op program is Northeastern's bragging right" and "without any doubt the school's greatest strength." As one student explains, "Experiences on co-op lead to better discussion and learning in the classroom as professors tackle real-world applications of their subjects with the knowledge that we have been there before, rather than stay in the theoretical realm." "Northeastern students have some of the strongest post-college resumes in the nation" as a result of their co-op experiences. As you might expect, Northeastern's strengths lie in such solidly pre-professional programs as business, health services, engineering, and computer and information sciences. Students caution it's the type of school "where you get in what you put out…If you sit around and complain about not getting a good job and not having much help from advisors or professors, it's probably because you didn't try very hard. If you put in the effort, you will find many, many people are willing to do a great deal to help you succeed and doors will fly open to ensure your success, and you'll meet a lot of great people (classmates and faculty) and make a lot of friends along the way."

Life

"There is always something to do, either on campus or around the city" at Northeastern, and understandably so; the school is located in Boston, perhaps the nation's preeminent college town. Boston affords "unlimited amounts of things to do like shopping, walking around, movies, etc." Boston is especially accommodating to those over 21, since "there are plenty of bars to enjoy" all across town. For sports fans, "Fenway Park and the TD Banknorth Garden are a short distance away for athletic games," and "Matthews Arena, home of Husky hockey and the men's basketball team," are nearby. On campus, Greek life "is on the rise," and "Greeks…are extremely involved on campus, planning service events, educational speakers or fun events, such as bringing former Red Sox players or popular comedians to campus." Extracurricular clubs "including but not limited to sports, newspaper, religious groups, social awareness, diversity groups, and more" are widely available to students. "The campus has much to offer as far as recreation from an ice rink to multiple gym facilities. It also has a large student center, multiple outdoor quads, and dorm activities. There is never a dull moment on campus, there is always something to do."

Student Body

"Because of our highly attractive location, there is no 'typical' Northeastern student," undergrads here insist, informing us "students come from the local Boston neighborhoods, ivy towns in Connecticut, countries around the world and cities across the country." The university's "wide range of courses to study" further ensures "a wide range of students" on campus. Finally, the school's large population practically ensures a diverse mix, as evidenced by the "250 or so clubs ranging from anime to the Caribbean Student Organization, from fraternities to a gay/lesbian/transsexual organization. You find virtually every race/gender/religious/political type of people here and they all fit in and generally get along." The enticement of co-op, of course, means most everyone here is "looking to obtain a solid education and prepare themselves for the working world." You won't find a lot of ivory-tower intellectuals here.

FINANCIAL AID: 617-373-3190 • E-MAIL: ADMISSIONS@NEU.EDU • WEBSITE: WWW.NORTHEASTERN.EDU

THE PRINCETON REVIEW SAYS

Admissions

Very important factors considered include: Academic GPA, rigor of secondary school record. *Important factors considered include:* Class rank, application essay, recommendation(s), standardized test scores, character/personal qualities, extracurricular activities, first generation, talent/ability. *Other factors considered include:* Alumni/ae relation, geographical residence, racial/ethnic status, state residency, volunteer work, work experience. SAT or ACT required; ACT with Writing component required; TOEFL required of all international applicants. High school diploma is required and GED is accepted. *Academic units required:* 4 English, 3 mathematics, 3 science, (2 science labs), 2 foreign language, 2 social studies, 2 history. *Academic units recommended:* 4 mathematics, 4 science, (4 science labs), 4 foreign language.

Financial Aid

Students should submit: FAFSA, CSS/Financial Aid PROFILE. The Princeton Review suggests that all financial aid forms be submitted as soon as possible after 1/1. *Need-based scholarships/grants offered:* Federal Pell, SEOG, state scholarships/grants, private scholarships, the school's own gift aid, Federal Nursing Scholarships. *Loan aid offered:* FFEL Subsidized Stafford, FFEL Unsubsidized Stafford, FFEL PLUS, Federal Perkins, Federal Nursing, state loans, MEFA, TERI, Signature, Mass, No Interest Loan (NIL), CitiAssist. Applicants will be notified of awards on a rolling basis beginning 2/15. Federal Work-Study Program available. Institutional employment available. Off-campus job opportunities are excellent.

The Inside Word

With more than 35,000 applicants each year, Northeastern admissions officers must wade through an ocean of applications in order to select the incoming class. The volume requires that much of the early winnowing be strictly numbers-based the school has too many applicants with decent test scores and high school grades to bother with substandard candidates. Those who make the first cut should receive a more personalized review that includes a close look at essays, extracurriculars, and recommendations. A campus visit couldn't hurt.

THE SCHOOL SAYS "..."

From The Admissions Office

"Northeastern students take charge of their education in a way you'll find nowhere else, because a Northeastern education is like no other. We integrate challenging liberal arts and professional studies with a variety of experiential learning opportunities anchored by the our signature cooperativeeducation program. Northeastern's dynamic of academic excellence and experience means that our students are better prepared to succeed in the lives they choose. On top of that, they experience all of this on a beautifully landscaped, 73-acre campus in the heart of Boston, where culture, commerce, civic pride, and college students from around the globe are all a part of the mix."

SELECTIVITY

Admissions Rating	**91**
# of applicants	35,848
% of applicants accepted	35
% of acceptees attending	23
# accepting a place on wait list	1,342
% admitted from wait list	27

FRESHMAN PROFILE

Range SAT Critical Reading	570–660
Range SAT Math	610–690
Range ACT Composite	25–29
Minimum paper TOEFL	550
Minimum computer TOEFL	213
% graduated top 10% of class	49
% graduated top 25% of class	83
% graduated top 50% of class	98

DEADLINES

Early action	
Deadline	11/1
Notification	12/31
Regular	
Deadline	1/15
Nonfall registration?	yes

APPLICANTS ALSO LOOK AT

AND OFTEN PREFER
The George Washington University
New York University
Boston College

AND RARELY PREFER
University of Connecticut

FINANCIAL FACTS

Financial Aid Rating	**68**
Annual tuition	$33,320
Room and board	$11,940
Required fees	$401
Books and supplies	$900
% frosh rec. need-based scholarship or grant aid	54
% UG rec. need-based scholarship or grant aid	53
% frosh rec. non-need-based scholarship or grant aid	8
% UG rec. non-need-based scholarship or grant aid	5
% frosh rec. need-based self-help aid	46
% UG rec. need-based self-help aid	47
% frosh rec. athletic scholarships	1
% UG rec. athletic scholarships	1
% frosh rec. any financial aid	90
% UG rec. any financial aid	80

NORTHWESTERN UNIVERSITY

PO BOX 3060, 1801 HINMAN AVENUE, EVANSTON, IL 60208-3060 • ADMISSIONS: 847-491-7271

CAMPUS LIFE

Quality of Life Rating	76
Fire Safety Rating	71
Green Rating	81
Type of school	private
Environment	town

STUDENTS

Total undergrad enrollment	8,176
% male/female	47/53
% from out of state	75
% from public high school	73
% live on campus	65
% in (# of) fraternities	32 (17)
% in (# of) sororities	38 (19)
% African American	6
% Asian	17
% Caucasian	59
% Hispanic	7
% international	5
# of countries represented	42

SURVEY SAYS . . .

Athletic facilities are great
Great off-campus food
Frats and sororities dominate social scene
Musical organizations are popular
Student publications are popular

ACADEMICS

Academic Rating	88
Calendar	quarter
Student/faculty ratio	7:1
Profs interesting rating	74
Profs accessible rating	76
% classes taught by TAs	2
Most common reg class size	fewer than 10 students
Most common lab size	10–19 students

MOST POPULAR MAJORS

economics
engineering
journalism

STUDENTS SAY " . . ."

Academics

"The strength of the school is its range." Northwestern students agree, vowing their school "has everything": "Intelligent but laid-back students, excel[lence] in academic fields," "great extracurriculars and good parties," "strong [Big Ten] sports spirit," and "so many connections and opportunities during and after graduation." Undergrads here brag of "nationally acclaimed programs for almost anything anyone could be interested in, from engineering to theater to journalism to music," and report "everything is given fairly equal weight. Northwestern students and faculty do not show a considerable bias" toward specific fields. The school accomplishes all this while maintaining a manageable scale. While its relatively small size allows for good student-professor interaction, it has "all the perks" of a big school, including "many opportunities" for research and internships. Be aware, however, "Northwestern is not an easy school. It takes hard work to be average here." If you "learn from your failures quickly and love to learn for the sake of learning rather than the grade," students say it is quite possible to stay afloat and even to excel. Helping matters are numerous resources established by administrators and professors, including tutoring programs such as Northwestern's Gateway Science Workshop. Those who take advantage of these opportunities find the going much easier than those who don't.

Life

There are two distinct sections of the Northwestern campus. The North Campus is where "you can find a party every night of the week" and "the Greek scene is strong." The South Campus, about a one-mile trek from the action to the north, is "more artsy and has minimal partying on weeknights," but is closer to town so "it is easy" to "buy dinner, see a show at the movies, and go shopping. People who live on North Campus have a harder time getting motivated to go into Evanston and tap into all that is offered." As one South Campus resident puts it, "South Campus is nice and quiet in its own way. I enjoy reading and watching movies here, and the quietude is appreciated when study time rolls around. But for more exciting fun, a trip north is a must." Regardless of where students live, extracurriculars are "incredible here. There is a group for every interest, and they are amazingly well-managed by students alone. This goes hand-in-hand with how passionate students at Northwestern are about what they love." Many students "are involved in plays, a cappella groups, comedy troupes, and other organizations geared toward the performing arts. Activism is also very popular, with many involved in political groups, human-rights activism, and volunteering." In addition, Northwestern's membership in the Big Ten means students "attend some of the best sporting events in the country." Chicago, of course, "is a wonderful resource. People go into the city for a wide variety of things—daily excursions, jobs, internships, nights out, parties, etc."

Student Body

The typical Northwestern student "was high school class president with a 4.0, swim team captain, and on the chess team." So it makes sense everyone here "is an excellent student who works hard" and "has a leadership position in at least two clubs, plus an on-campus job." Students also tell us "there's [a] great separation between North Campus (think: fraternities, engineering, state school mentality) and South Campus (think: closer to Chicago and its culture, arts and letters, liberal arts school mentality). Students segregate themselves depending on background and interests and it's rare for these two groups to interact beyond a superficial level." The student body here includes sizeable Jewish, Indian, and East-Asian populations.

FINANCIAL AID: 847-491-7400 • E-MAIL: UG-ADMISSION@NORTHWESTERN.EDU • WEBSITE: WWW.NORTHWESTERN.EDU

THE PRINCETON REVIEW SAYS

Admissions

Very important factors considered include: Class rank, application essay, academic GPA, rigor of secondary school record, standardized test scores. *Important factors considered include:* Recommendation(s), character/personal qualities, extracurricular activities, talent/ability. *Other factors considered include:* Alumni/ae relation, first generation, interview, level of applicant's interest, racial/ethnic status, volunteer work, work experience. SAT or ACT required; ACT with Writing component required; TOEFL required of all international applicants. High school diploma or equivalent is not required. *Academic units recommended:* 4 English, 3 mathematics, 2 science, (2 science labs), 2 foreign language, 2 social studies, 1 academic elective.

Financial Aid

Students should submit: FAFSA, CSS/Financial Aid PROFILE, noncustodial PROFILE, business/farm supplement. Parent and student federal tax returns. Regular filing deadline is 2/15. The Princeton Review suggests that all financial aid forms be submitted as soon as possible after 1/1. *Need-based scholarships/grants offered:* Federal Pell, SEOG, state scholarships/grants, private scholarships, the school's own gift aid, United Negro College Fund. *Loan aid offered:* FFEL Subsidized Stafford, FFEL Unsubsidized Stafford, FFEL PLUS, Federal Perkins, college/university loans from institutional funds. Applicants will be notified of awards on or about 4/15. Federal Work-Study Program available. Institutional employment available. Off-campus job opportunities are excellent.

The Inside Word

Northwestern is among the nation's most expensive undergraduate institutions, a fact that dissuades some qualified students from applying. The school is working to attract more low-income applicants by increasing the number of full scholarships available for students whose family income is less than $45,000. Low-income students who score well on the ACT may receive a letter from the school encouraging them to apply. Even if you don't receive this letter, you should consider applying if you've got the goods—you may be pleasantly surprised by the offer you receive from the financial aid office.

THE SCHOOL SAYS "..."

From The Admissions Office

"Consistent with its dedication to excellence, Northwestern provides both an educational and an extracurricular environment that enables its undergraduate students to become accomplished individuals and informed and responsible citizens. To the students in all its undergraduate schools, Northwestern offers liberal learning and professional education to help them gain the depth of knowledge that will empower them to become leaders in their professions and communities. Furthermore, Northwestern fosters in its students a broad understanding of the world in which we live as well as excellence in the competencies that transcend any particular field of study: writing and oral communication, analytical and creative thinking and expression, and quantitative and qualitative methods of thinking.

"Applicants are required to take the SAT or the ACT with the Writing section."

SELECTIVITY

Admissions Rating	98
# of applicants	21,930
% of applicants accepted	27
% of acceptees attending	34
# accepting a place on wait list	1,274
% admitted from wait list	37
# of early decision applicants	1,296
% accepted early decision	44

FRESHMAN PROFILE

Range SAT Critical Reading	670–750
Range SAT Math	680–770
Range SAT Writing	660–750
Range ACT Composite	30–34
Minimum paper TOEFL	600
Minimum computer TOEFL	250
% graduated top 10% of class	85
% graduated top 25% of class	97
% graduated top 50% of class	99

DEADLINES

Early decision	
Deadline	11/1
Notification	12/15
Regular	
Deadline	1/1
Notification	4/15
Nonfall registration?	yes

APPLICANTS ALSO LOOK AT
AND OFTEN PREFER
Harvard College
Yale University

AND SOMETIMES PREFER
University of Chicago
Stanford University

FINANCIAL FACTS

Financial Aid Rating	95
Annual tuition	$36,756
Room and board	$11,295
Required fees	$369
Books and supplies	$1,626
% frosh rec. need-based scholarship or grant aid	41
% UG rec. need-based scholarship or grant aid	41
% frosh rec. need-based self-help aid	36
% UG rec. need-based self-help aid	38
% frosh rec. athletic scholarships	5
% UG rec. athletic scholarships	5
% frosh rec. any financial aid	60
% UG rec. any financial aid	60
% UG borrow to pay for school	46
Average cumulative indebtedness	$18,393

OBERLIN COLLEGE

101 NORTH PROFESSOR STREET, OBERLIN, OH 44074 • ADMISSIONS: 440-775-8411 • FAX: 440-775-6905

CAMPUS LIFE
Quality of Life Rating	**74**
Fire Safety Rating	**60***
Green Rating	**92**
Type of school	private
Environment	rural

STUDENTS
Total undergrad enrollment	2,839
% male/female	45/55
% from out of state	91
% from public high school	60
% live on campus	88
% African American	6
% Asian	7
% Caucasian	75
% Hispanic	5
% Native American	1
% international	6

SURVEY SAYS . . .
Lots of liberal students
No one cheats
Low cost of living
Frats and sororities are unpopular or nonexistent
Musical organizations are popular
Political activism is popular

ACADEMICS
Academic Rating	**93**
Calendar	4/1/4
Student/faculty ratio	9:1
Profs interesting rating	94
Profs accessible rating	97
Most common reg class size	10–19 students
Most common lab size	fewer than 10 students

MOST POPULAR MAJORS
English language and literature
history

STUDENTS SAY "..."

Academics

Oberlin College, a school "for laid-back people who enjoy learning and expanding social norms, allows each and every student to have the undergrad experience for which he or she is looking, all the while challenging the students to change themselves and the world for the better." Oberlin is a place where students "focus on learning for learning's sake rather than making money in a career." As one student explains, "I didn't plan on becoming a scholar when I entered Oberlin....As fate would have it, I ended up loving my college classes and professors. Now I hope to be a professor of religion." At Oberlin, "academics are very highly valued, but balanced with a strong interest in the arts and a commitment to society." Wags might suggest Oberlin puts the "liberal" in "liberal arts," and the school's staunchest supporters agree, stressing the school's emphasis on open-mindedness and the belief that "one person can change the world." Among the school's offerings, "the sciences, English, politics, religion, music, environmental studies, and East-Asian studies are particularly noteworthy." The presence of a prestigious music school imbues the entire campus community. One undergrad writes, "Oberlin's greatest strength is the combination of the college and the conservatory. They are not separated, so students mix with each other all the time." Professors here—the "heart and soul of the school"—are dedicated teachers who "treat you more like collaborators and realize that even with their PhDs, they can learn and grow from you, as well as you from them." They are "excellent instructors and fantastic people" who are "focused on learning instead of deadlines." Undergrads also appreciate "a cooperative learning environment" in which "Students bond over studying together for difficult exams."

Life

Life during the week at Oberlin can be "pretty bland," as "almost everyone has to crack the books and study it up." It's not always bland, though. Some here manage to find time for the many "events [going on] each weekend—operas, plays, organ pumps, etc.," or "rally to stage to help the oppressed." Thursday afternoons at Oberlin means "Classical Thursdays," an event during which "you get free beer from the college if you bring a professor to the on-campus pub." Another feature of campus life is "the musical scene, which has its heart in the conservatory. All of the other arts—performing, studio, whatever—are intertwined with the talent in the conservatory." On weekends, "people let loose, rip out the bong (no pun intended), and drink beer. Not everyone does this every weekend. Some don't do it at all," and "there is absolutely no pressure on those who don't." There are also "tons of student-produced social events like parties, fundraisers, concerts, dances, etc.," keeping students "very connected to each other and to what's going on in the community." Hometown Oberlin "is a small town, and about all there is to do there is go out for pizza or Chinese, see a movie for $2 or $3 at the Apollo, or go to the Feve, the bar in town."

Student Body

"If you're a liberal, artsy, indie loner who likes to throw around the phrase 'heteronormative white privilege,'" then Oberlin might be the place for you. "We're like the Island of Misfit Toys, but together we make a great toy chest." "We're all different and unusual, which creates a common bond between students." "Musicians, jocks, science geeks, creative writing majors, straight, bi, questioning, queer, and trans [students]," all have their place here, alongside "straight-edge, international, local, and joker students." Oberlin has a reputation for a left-leaning and active student body. One undergrad observes, "They are less active politically than they would like to think, but still more active than most people elsewhere." Another adds, "Most students are very liberal, but the moderates and (few) Republicans have a fine time of it. Every student has different interests and isn't afraid to talk about them." Some here worry "Oberlin's student body is becoming more and more mainstream each year."

FINANCIAL AID: 440-775-8142 • E-MAIL: COLLEGE.ADMISSIONS@OBERLIN.EDU • WEBSITE: WWW.OBERLIN.EDU

THE PRINCETON REVIEW SAYS

Admissions

Very important factors considered include: Class rank, academic GPA, rigor of secondary school record, standardized test scores. *Important factors considered include:* Application essay, recommendation(s), character/personal qualities, extracurricular activities, first generation, talent/ability. *Other factors considered include:* Alumni/ae relation, interview, level of applicant's interest, racial/ethnic status, volunteer work, work experience. SAT or ACT required; ACT with Writing component required; TOEFL required of all international applicants. High school diploma is required and GED is accepted. *Academic units required:* 4 English, 4 mathematics, 3 science, 3 foreign language, 3 social studies.

Financial Aid

Students should submit: FAFSA, institution's own financial aid form, CSS/Financial Aid PROFILE, state aid form, noncustodial PROFILE, business/farm supplement. Regular filing deadline is 2/1. The Princeton Review suggests that all financial aid forms be submitted as soon as possible after 1/1. *Need-based scholarships/grants offered:* Federal Pell, SEOG, state scholarships/grants, private scholarships, the school's own gift aid. *Loan aid offered:* FFEL Subsidized Stafford, FFEL Unsubsidized Stafford, FFEL PLUS, Federal Perkins, college/university loans from institutional funds. Applicants will be notified of awards on or about 4/1.

The Inside Word

Oberlin's music conservatory is one of the most elite programs in the nation. Aspiring music students should expect stiff competition for one of the 600 available slots. Other applicants won't have a much easier time of it. Oberlin is a highly selective institution that attracts a highly competitive applicant pool. Your personal statement could be the make-or-break factor here.

THE SCHOOL SAYS "..."

From The Admissions Office

"Oberlin College is an independent, coeducational, liberal arts college. It comprises two divisions, the College of Arts and Sciences, with roughly 2,800 students enrolled, and the Conservatory of Music, with about 600 students. Students in both divisions share one campus; they also share residence and dining halls as part of one academic community. Many students take courses in both divisions. Oberlin awards the Bachelor of Arts and the Bachelor of Music degrees; a five-year program leads to both degrees. Selected master's degrees are offered in the conservatory. Oberlin is located 35 miles southwest of Cleveland. Founded in 1833, Oberlin College is highly selective and dedicated to recruiting students from diverse backgrounds. Oberlin was the first coeducational college in the United States, as well as a historic leader in educating African Americans. Oberlin's 440-acre campus provides outstanding facilities, modern scientific laboratories, a large computing center, a library unexcelled by other college libraries for the depth and range of its resources, and one of the top-5 college- or university-based art museums in the country.

"Freshman applicants must take the SAT the ACT with Writing component."

SELECTIVITY
Admissions Rating	**97**
# of applicants	7,006
% of applicants accepted	33
% of acceptees attending	34
# accepting a place on wait list	354
% admitted from wait list	2
# of early decision applicants	341
% accepted early decision	66

FRESHMAN PROFILE
Range SAT Critical Reading	640–740
Range SAT Math	620–710
Range SAT Writing	640–730
Range ACT Composite	27–32
Minimum paper TOEFL	600
Minimum computer TOEFL	200
Average HS GPA	3.6
% graduated top 10% of class	69
% graduated top 25% of class	91
% graduated top 50% of class	99

DEADLINES
Early decision	
Deadline	11/15
Notification	12/20
Regular	
Deadline	1/15
Notification	4/1
Nonfall registration?	no

APPLICANTS ALSO LOOK AT
AND OFTEN PREFER
Wesleyan University
Brown University
Swarthmore College
AND SOMETIMES PREFER
Vassar College

FINANCIAL FACTS
Financial Aid Rating	**95**
Annual tuition	$38,012
Room and board	$9,870
Required fees	$268
Books and supplies	$1,956
% frosh rec. need-based scholarship or grant aid	52
% UG rec. need-based scholarship or grant aid	52
% frosh rec. non-need-based scholarship or grant aid	29
% UG rec. non-need-based scholarship or grant aid	26
% frosh rec. need-based self-help aid	40
% UG rec. need-based self-help aid	45
% frosh rec. any financial aid	61
% UG rec. any financial aid	60

OCCIDENTAL COLLEGE

1600 CAMPUS ROAD, OFFICE OF ADMISSION, LOS ANGELES, CA 90041 • ADMISSIONS: 800-825-5262 • FAX: 323-341-4875

CAMPUS LIFE

Quality of Life Rating	87
Fire Safety Rating	60*
Green Rating	82
Type of school	private
Environment	metropolis

STUDENTS

Total undergrad enrollment	1,834
% male/female	44/56
% from out of state	54
% from public high school	58
% live on campus	72
% in (# of) fraternities	6 (4)
% in (# of) sororities	13 (4)
% African American	6
% Asian	15
% Caucasian	58
% Hispanic	14
% Native American	1
% international	2
# of countries represented	23

SURVEY SAYS . . .

No one cheats
Students are friendly
Diverse student types on campus
Great food on campus

ACADEMICS

Academic Rating	89
Calendar	semester
Student/faculty ratio	9:1
Profs interesting rating	83
Profs accessible rating	84
Most common reg class size	10–19 students
Most common lab size	10–19 students

MOST POPULAR MAJORS
economics
English language and literature
international relations and affairs

STUDENTS SAY "..."

Academics

"Combine sunny weather with big-city opportunities, amazing professors, a gorgeous campus, and an emphasis on diversity, and you get Oxy!" That's how Occidental College is affectionately known by its "happy, outgoing, and bright" students. Located "just over the hill from bustling Los Angeles," Oxy is "a small school that provides the opportunity to develop one's intellect in a safe, friendly, and mentally challenging environment." This "very prestigious school" is "tough academically. The work is hard, and there's a high level of work expected of all students. But the benefits of getting an education here are worth all the work." Strong instruction is a big part of the equation; Oxy profs "are the absolute best because they are extremely personable toward and available for the students. They have a great desire for all their students to succeed, especially those who are on the pre-medicine track." Profs here don't exist to "publish or perish;" "they actually are at Oxy to teach—and not to teach so they can research." That said, Oxy is no slacker when it comes to research either. Students say it is "really easy" to get "independent study, internships, and grants" that would "not be offered anywhere else to undergraduates." Students love "class sizes [that] are small for the most part" and the school's Center for Academic Excellence, "which provides free tutoring for many academic subjects."

Life

Los Angeles "is an amazing town to learn in," and Oxy exploits this asset. "Every week the school offers trips around southern California." Extracurricular diversions are copious, but most require access to an automobile. "Everyone who doesn't have a car wishes they did and hangs out with people who do," undergrads warn. For those with wheels, "there's so much to do" in Los Angeles "that you can always find something to do on weekends. Old Town Pasadena is only 10 minutes away, and it's a great place to spend a Saturday night." Students also sojourn "to Chinatown, Disneyland, the beach, the movies, plays, museums, the Glendale Galleria, [and] the Santa Monica Promenade. The location definitely has advantages," and so does the Oxy campus, where "there is always something fun going on," such as "a thematic party or just a cool social gathering," more than one "speaker series hosted by departments, movies projected on the dining hall wall, and many other things." Students "stay connected to what's going through our very effective 'daily digest e-mail.'" While most students are "fairly social," Oxy is "not what I would call a party school." Most of the parties "are all just off campus," and "drinks are easy to obtain but also easy to refuse."

Student Body

The typical Oxy undergrad "is politically and globally aware, is passionate about more than one interest, and loves to speak up about any and every issue (both related to the school and outside of it)." Most are "very liberal, studious, hard-working, and playful." Atypical students "are usually conservative or party animals. The conservative students have a bit of a hard time since the college and its students are typically very left-winged, yet they manage. The party animals fit in very well, although [they are] not necessarily liked in all situations, such as group projects, since they are a bit less hard-working." In terms of personality types, "we range from kids who are proud of being hicks to the artsy hipsters to some Goth kids to just your average run-of-the-mill sandwich-eating college kid." Common threads are "intelligence and desire to discuss issues, whatever they may be" and "the laid-back groove of California," which most here embody.

FINANCIAL AID: 323-259-2548 • E-MAIL: ADMISSION@OXY.EDU • WEBSITE: WWW.OXY.EDU

THE PRINCETON REVIEW SAYS

Admissions

Very important factors considered include: Rigor of secondary school record, extracurricular activities, volunteer work, work experience. *Important factors considered include:* Class rank, application essay, recommendation(s), standardized test scores. *Other factors considered include:* Academic GPA, alumni/ae relation, character/personal qualities, first generation, geographical residence, interview, level of applicant's interest, racial/ethnic status, talent/ability. SAT Subject Tests recommended; SAT or ACT required; ACT with Writing component required; TOEFL required of all international applicants. High school diploma is required and GED is accepted. *Academic units recommended:* 4 English, 4 mathematics, 3 science, (2 science labs), 3 foreign language, 2 social studies, 2 history, 2 academic electives.

Financial Aid

Students should submit: FAFSA, CSS/Financial Aid PROFILE, state aid form, noncustodial PROFILE, business/farm supplement. Regular filing deadline is 2/1. The Princeton Review suggests that all financial aid forms be submitted as soon as possible after 1/1. *Need-based scholarships/grants offered:* Federal Pell, SEOG, state scholarships/grants, private scholarships, the school's own gift aid. *Loan aid offered:* FFEL Subsidized Stafford, FFEL Unsubsidized Stafford, FFEL PLUS, Federal Perkins, college/university loans from institutional funds. Applicants will be notified of awards on a rolling basis beginning 4/1. Federal Work-Study Program available. Institutional employment available. Off-campus job opportunities are good.

The Inside Word

The admissions team at Occidental is adamant about not adhering to formulas. They rely heavily on essays and recommendations in their mission to create a talented and diverse incoming class. The college attracts some excellent students, so a demanding course load in high school is essential for the most competitive candidates. Successful applicants tend to be creative and academically motivated.

THE SCHOOL SAYS "..."

From The Admissions Office

"Here's what our students tell us:

'The professors have all been just amazing. They're all very willing to coordinate times to meet and discuss how you feel about a class and what you want to get out of it.'

'I realize the caliber of discussion that occurs at Oxy is not easily matched. I've developed very strong relationships with many professors, and that's something I believe is unique to Oxy.'

'The program has been awesome. Whether you want to go to med school or grad school, it's a great experience. The professors really want you to succeed.'

'I've been working with postdoctoral researchers as an undergraduate. It's very rewarding. Oxy challenges me both inside and outside the classroom.'

'Occidental opened my eyes to different beliefs, values, and ideas. Discussions in class are much more interesting, because you consider things you might not have thought about before.'

'Oxy's close-knit community and its size make me feel this is a place I can call home.'

'Oxy instills curiosity and makes students want to go out and learn a subject on their own. I've gotten a broader sense of self and have been able to fulfill my learning goals."

Occidental requires all applicants (including international students) to take either the SAT or ACT with the Writing component. SAT subject tests are recommended but not required."

SELECTIVITY

Admissions Rating	**94**
# of applicants	5,790
% of applicants accepted	39
% of acceptees attending	20
# accepting a place on wait list	334
% admitted from wait list	5
# of early decision applicants	112
% accepted early decision	45

FRESHMAN PROFILE

Range SAT Critical Reading	590–700
Range SAT Math	600–690
Range SAT Writing	590–690
Range ACT Composite	26–30
Minimum paper TOEFL	600
Minimum computer TOEFL	250
% graduated top 10% of class	65
% graduated top 25% of class	91
% graduated top 50% of class	99

DEADLINES

Early decision	
Deadline	11/15
Notification	12/15
Regular	
Deadline	1/10
Notification	4/1
Nonfall registration?	no

APPLICANTS ALSO LOOK AT
AND OFTEN PREFER
Pomona College
University of Southern California
University of California—Berkeley
University of California—Los Angeles

AND SOMETIMES PREFER
Claremont McKenna College

FINANCIAL FACTS

Financial Aid Rating	**96**
Annual tuition	$37,970
Room and board	$10,780
Required fees	$952
Books and supplies	$1,054
% frosh rec. need-based scholarship or grant aid	51
% UG rec. need-based scholarship or grant aid	50
% frosh rec. non-need-based scholarship or grant aid	7
% UG rec. non-need-based scholarship or grant aid	4
% frosh rec. need-based self-help aid	46
% UG rec. need-based self-help aid	47
% frosh rec. any financial aid	77
% UG rec. any financial aid	78
% UG borrow to pay for school	73
Average cumulative indebtedness	$21,001

OGLETHORPE UNIVERSITY

4484 PEACHTREE ROAD, NORTHEAST, ATLANTA, GA 30319 • ADMISSIONS: 404-364-8307 • FAX: 404-364-8491

CAMPUS LIFE

Quality of Life Rating	87
Fire Safety Rating	60*
Green Rating	72
Type of school	private
Environment	metropolis

STUDENTS

Total undergrad enrollment	943
% male/female	39/61
% from out of state	30
% from public high school	79
% live on campus	61
% in (# of) fraternities	33 (4)
% in (# of) sororities	25 (3)
% African American	23
% Asian	5
% Caucasian	50
% Hispanic	3
% Native American	1
% international	5
# of countries represented	35

SURVEY SAYS . . .

Students are friendly
Diverse student types on campus
Different types of students interact
Students get along with local community
Students love Atlanta, GA
Great off-campus food
Dorms are like palaces
Theater is popular

ACADEMICS

Academic Rating	88
Calendar	semester
Student/faculty ratio	13:1
Profs interesting rating	96
Profs accessible rating	90
Most common reg class size	10–19 students

MOST POPULAR MAJORS

business/commerce
English language and literature
psychology

STUDENTS SAY " . . ."

Academics

Oglethorpe University in Atlanta concerns itself with creating an environment in which students from varying majors can interact so as to broaden each student's experiences. Oglethorpe's liberal arts curriculum naturally lends itself to students learning to be "analytical and engaging in the classroom," and many report it is "so much easier to learn and broaden your mind and opinions while being able to discuss and debate different ideas in a classroom of fewer than 20 students" than in the lecture halls of larger universities. "We also have a rep for being a theater school and we really aren't at all," says a student. Though the "pickings are very slim" as far as class options go, "there are many classes here that you would never find at another school, but they are very interesting and definitely prepare you for the real world."

It can be tough to win students over at such a small school, but the administration here is commended for running the place "professionally," although the financial aid, while "pretty darn fair," is "sloppy," "very slow, and loses stuff all the time." Students also wish for an update of many of the systems, so registration, transcripts, and bill payment can all be done online. The professors, most of whom are experts in their field, are "overall pretty much the bomb, in a very good way," and it shows in the positive experiences every single Oglethorpe student takes away from the classroom. "I come away from class much more enriched than when I went in," says a senior. "You get what you pay for," says a student as a testament to his satisfaction.

Life

"We live in the big city of Atlanta, but still manage to have a real small-town vibe on campus," says a sophomore. Life is made up of strictly school on weekdays, but when the weekend rolls around, students let loose a bit. Theatre is popular, as well as "jamming with musical instruments." Greek life is very popular here, as are their parties on Greek Row, but Oglethorpe has "a much different take on it" than other schools. "It is more based on social fun and networking rather than bordering on a painfully exclusive club." "It's not uncommon to see a group of brothers sitting outside with their beers arguing the nature of humanity or the current applications of Aristotle." There is "a lot of drinking, but you don't have to drink" to have fun. One student says that merely "sitting out in the grass on the quad and talking with friends is the best." There are also many school-sponsored events (usually at least four or five a week), "so no one has any reason to be bored."

Student Body

Diversity is a huge element at Oglethorpe, where a large minority population and many international students mean "ethnicity and gender are almost irrelevant." While many students can still be classified into groups, all "interact with each other easily," and the school as a whole "is such a microcosm that everybody stands out a lot." "Oglethorpe embodies everything from pot-head philosophers, wannabe prep jocks, loud outspoken activists, and just your plain average college nerd," says one student. "It is a small campus so it is impossible to completely avoid someone you do not like, but it is easy enough to just not be around them and hang out with that group," says another. Most people are "refined in either the fine arts or sports or sometimes both," and there's also "a strong minority of LGBT students." The strong theater program does give the school an "artsy" feel, but there's also an athletic and frat/sorority scene.

FINANCIAL AID: 404-364-8356 • E-MAIL: ADMISSION@OGLETHORPE.EDU • WEBSITE: WWW.OGLETHORPE.EDU

THE PRINCETON REVIEW SAYS

Admissions

Very important factors considered include: Academic GPA, rigor of secondary school record, standardized test scores. *Important factors considered include:* Class rank, application essay, recommendation(s), extracurricular activities, interview, level of applicant's interest, volunteer work. *Other factors considered include:* Alumni/ae relation, character/personal qualities, first generation, talent/ability, work experience. SAT or ACT required; ACT with Writing component recommended; TOEFL required of all international applicants. High school diploma is required and GED is accepted. *Academic units required:* 4 English, 3 mathematics, 2 science, 3 social studies. *Academic units recommended:* 2 foreign language.

Financial Aid

Students should submit: FAFSA, institution's own financial aid form, state aid form. The Princeton Review suggests that all financial aid forms be submitted as soon as possible after 1/1. *Need-based scholarships/grants offered:* Federal Pell, SEOG, state scholarships/grants, private scholarships, the school's own gift aid, United Negro College Fund. *Loan aid offered:* Direct Subsidized Stafford, Direct Unsubsidized Stafford, Direct PLUS, FFEL Subsidized Stafford, FFEL Unsubsidized Stafford, FFEL PLUS, Federal Perkins. Applicants will be notified of awards on a rolling basis beginning 4/1. Federal Work-Study Program available. Institutional employment available. Off-campus job opportunities are excellent.

The Inside Word

With rising national interest in the South, it won't be long before the academic strength found at Oglethorpe attracts wider attention and more applicants. At present, it's much easier to gain admission here than at many universities of similar quality. Go to Atlanta for a campus interview—you'll leave impressed.

THE SCHOOL SAYS "..."

From The Admissions Office

"Promising students and outstanding teachers come together at Oglethorpe University in an acclaimed program of liberal arts and sciences. Here you'll find an active intellectual community on a beautiful English Gothic campus just 10 miles from the center of Atlanta, capital of the Southeast, site of the 1996 Summer Olympics, and home to four million people. If you want challenging academics, the opportunity to work closely with your professors, and the stimulation of a great metropolitan area, consider Oglethorpe, a national liberal arts college in a world-class city.

"Applicants are required to take the SAT (or the ACT with the Writing section). It is recommended that students submit scores from two SAT Subject Tests."

SELECTIVITY
Admissions Rating	**82**
# of applicants	1,155
% of applicants accepted	48
% of acceptees attending	32

FRESHMAN PROFILE
Range SAT Critical Reading	510–640
Range SAT Math	500–610
Range SAT Writing	500–610
Range ACT Composite	21–27
Minimum paper TOEFL	550
Minimum computer TOEFL	200
Average HS GPA	3.43
% graduated top 10% of class	23
% graduated top 25% of class	54
% graduated top 50% of class	84

DEADLINES
Early action	
Deadline	12/5
Notification	12/20
Regular	
Notification	rolling
Nonfall registration?	yes

FINANCIAL FACTS
Financial Aid Rating	**79**
Annual tuition	$25,380
Room and board	$9,500
Required fees	$100
Books and supplies	$800
% frosh rec. need-based scholarship or grant aid	62
% UG rec. need-based scholarship or grant aid	61
% frosh rec. non-need-based scholarship or grant aid	8
% UG rec. non-need-based scholarship or grant aid	8
% frosh rec. need-based self-help aid	45
% UG rec. need-based self-help aid	49
% frosh rec. any financial aid	95
% UG rec. any financial aid	95
% UG borrow to pay for school	58
Average cumulative indebtedness	$26,299

OHIO NORTHERN UNIVERSITY

525 SOUTH MAIN STREET, ADA, OH 45810 • ADMISSIONS: 419-772-2260 • FAX: 419-772-2313

CAMPUS LIFE

Quality of Life Rating	**76**
Fire Safety Rating	**60***
Green Rating	**60***
Type of school	private
Affiliation	Methodist
Environment	village

STUDENTS

Total undergrad enrollment	2,591
% male/female	53/47
% from out of state	14
% live on campus	71
% in (# of) fraternities	15 (6)
% in (# of) sororities	20 (4)
% African American	4
% Asian	2
% Caucasian	90
% Hispanic	2
% international	2
# of countries represented	18

SURVEY SAYS . . .

Students are friendly
Campus feels safe
Low cost of living

ACADEMICS

Academic Rating	**78**
Calendar	quarter
Student/faculty ratio	13:1
Profs interesting rating	74
Profs accessible rating	82
Most common reg class size	20–29 students

MOST POPULAR MAJORS

biological and biomedical sciences
business, management, marketing,
and related support services
engineering

STUDENTS SAY ". . ."

Academics

Ohio Northern's premier attraction is its Raabe College of Pharmacy; the school, which enrolls about one-third of all undergraduates here, offers a six-year Pharm.D. option as well as dual majors in pharmacy/biology and pharmacy/law. Students in the program warn that "the academics can be tough" but "the hands-on opportunities available to students are great," and the school's "good reputation for applying for jobs" justifies the work required to succeed. Less prestigious but equally popular (and, according to students, nearly as excellent) are the James F. Dicke College of Business Administration and the T.J. Smull College of Engineering, each claiming between 15 and 20 percent of the student body. Across all five schools at this small university, students report that they "get involved in major-related activities as soon as they arrive on campus. This is much harder to do at a larger school. The opportunities here are almost endless." As are the challenges; decent students find that ONU is entirely easy to get into but more difficult to excel at, as "the school does a good job of weeding out the social-scene-centered students, and by second year most students are overall very academically motivated."

Life

Ohio Northern is located in the town of Ada (app. pop. 5,600), an hour and a half's drive northwest of Columbus. "There isn't a ton of stuff to do off campus unless you want to drive a half an hour" to Lima, so "You really have to make your own fun" at ONU (for those with cars, Lima and Findlay—also a half hour off—"provide lots of eating and shopping places"). Many choose to get involved with campus activities, students tell us that "Life is usually hectic because of classes and organizations students are involved with," and that "There are over 150 student organizations at Ohio Northern, so there always seems to be something going on that you can attend." Others indulge in the party scene, explaining that "Obviously, the social scene is limited in such a small isolated town. The weekend scene is no different than any other college in America, lots of alcohol consumption (but mostly on campus, since there are only three bars in Ada). Random hooking up is also common among the alcohol-impaired. However, "there is a sizeable population of students that keep their fun clean with cards, board games, movies, etc." Some here even insist that "There is a decent amount of drinking that goes on, but not near as much as at some other schools."

Student Body

ONU students are "usually really dedicated to something and have a strong passion for it. It could be politics, music, sports, religion, or anything." They are typically "involved with some organization. Everyone seems to find something that they are good at or interested in, whether it's a club, sports, or Greek life, or all three." Minority students are in short supply; nearly everyone is "white, middle-class, and fairly smart," typically "from a rural or suburban community" where they were "honor or merit roll students." They tend to be "conservative and not very open-minded to different cultures, gender-orientations, etc...There is a small but growing population of students with different ethnicities, cultures, sexual orientations, and political stances that more or less group together to interact within their own subgroup(s)."

FINANCIAL AID: 419-772-2272 • E-MAIL: ADMISSIONS-UG@ONU.EDU • WEBSITE: WWW.ONU.EDU

THE PRINCETON REVIEW SAYS

Admissions

Very important factors considered include: Academic GPA, rigor of secondary school record, standardized test scores. *Important factors considered include:* Class rank, extracurricular activities, interview. *Other factors considered include:* Application essay, recommendation(s), alumni/ae relation, character/personal qualities, first generation, level of applicant's interest, talent/ability, volunteer work. SAT or ACT required; TOEFL required of all international applicants. High school diploma is required and GED is accepted. *Academic units required:* 4 English, 2 mathematics, 2 science, (2 science labs), 2 social studies, 2 history, 4 academic electives. *Academic units recommended:* 4 English, 4 mathematics, 3 science, (2 science labs), 2 foreign language, 3 social studies, 2 history, 1 visual/performing arts, 1 computer science, 4 academic electives.

Financial Aid

Students should submit: FAFSA. Regular filing deadline is 6/1. The Princeton Review suggests that all financial aid forms be submitted as soon as possible after 1/1. *Need-based scholarships/grants offered:* Federal Pell, SEOG, state scholarships/grants, private scholarships, the school's own gift aid, External Scholarships. *Loan aid offered:* FFEL Subsidized Stafford, FFEL Unsubsidized Stafford, FFEL PLUS, Federal Perkins, college/university loans from institutional funds, Alternative Loans, Federal Health Professions Loan. Applicants will be notified of awards on a rolling basis beginning 3/1. Federal Work-Study Program available. Institutional employment available. Off-campus job opportunities are good.

The Inside Word

Solid high school grades and above average standardized test scores will pretty much punch your ticket to Ohio Northern. Admissions standards for the pharmacy school are considerably more stringent. Applicants may qualify for substantial merit-based scholarships based on standardized test scores and high school GPA; see the school's website for details.

THE SCHOOL SAYS "..."

From The Admissions Office

"Ohio Northern's purpose is to help students develop into self-reliant, mature men and women capable of clear and logical thinking and sensitive to the higher values of truth, beauty, and goodness. ONU selects its student body from among those students possessing characteristics congruent with the institution's objectives. Generally, a student must be prepared to use the resources of the institution to achieve personal and educational goals.

"Students applying for admission are urged to submit scores for the SAT or the ACT with the Writing section. The student's best composite scores will be used for scholarship purposes."

SELECTIVITY
Admissions Rating	93
# of applicants	3,032
% of applicants accepted	88
% of acceptees attending	28

FRESHMAN PROFILE
Range SAT Critical Reading	500–620
Range SAT Math	530–650
Range SAT Writing	490–620
Range ACT Composite	23–28
Minimum paper TOEFL	480
Minimum computer TOEFL	157
Minimum web-based TOEFL	54
Average HS GPA	3.62
% graduated top 10% of class	41
% graduated top 25% of class	69
% graduated top 50% of class	89

DEADLINES
Regular	
Priority	12/1
Deadline	8/15
Notification	rolling
Nonfall registration?	yes

APPLICANTS ALSO LOOK AT AND SOMETIMES PREFER
University of Toledo
Wittenberg University
Bowling Green State University
Miami University
The Ohio State University—Columbus

FINANCIAL FACTS
Financial Aid Rating	84
Annual tuition	$31,626
Room and board	$8,280
Required fees	$240
Books and supplies	$1,800
% frosh rec. need-based scholarship or grant aid	79
% UG rec. need-based scholarship or grant aid	55
% frosh rec. non-need-based scholarship or grant aid	43
% UG rec. non-need-based scholarship or grant aid	30
% frosh rec. need-based self-help aid	62
% UG rec. need-based self-help aid	61
% UG borrow to pay for school	83
Average cumulative indebtedness	$45,753

THE OHIO STATE UNIVERSITY—COLUMBUS

110 ENARSON HALL, 54 WEST TWELFTH AVENUE, COLUMBUS, OH 43210 • ADMISSIONS: 614-292-3980 • FAX: 614-292-4818

CAMPUS LIFE
Quality of Life Rating	85
Fire Safety Rating	65
Green Rating	60*
Type of school	public
Environment	metropolis

STUDENTS
Total undergrad enrollment	37,088
% male/female	53/47
% from out of state	10
% from public high school	88
% live on campus	24
% in (# of) fraternities	6 (39)
% in (# of) sororities	6 (21)
% African American	7
% Asian	5
% Caucasian	80
% Hispanic	3
% international	2

SURVEY SAYS . . .
Athletic facilities are great
Great off-campus food
Everyone loves the Buckeyes
Student publications are popular

ACADEMICS
Academic Rating	71
Calendar	quarter
Student/faculty ratio	13:1
Profs interesting rating	66
Profs accessible rating	71

MOST POPULAR MAJORS
biology/biological sciences
political science and government
psychology

STUDENTS SAY ". . ."

Academics
The Ohio State University in Columbus is "a great blend of academics, opportunity, and fun." This is one of the largest universities in the country, and as such, you'll find "every resource you could possibly need" and "unlimited" academic opportunities. "Everything from music to biochemical engineering and anything and everything in between" is available. "You name it and we've got it," guarantees an English major. "The size of campus can be in some ways intimidating," though. It's a "cattle call" here. Classes are often enormous, and it can be hard to get the ones you want. Also, while "the administration seems to run the school fairly smoothly," "red tape" is a problem. "If you want to do anything out of the ordinary, such as apply a scholarship to the summer quarter, or take a leave of absence, it is very difficult." "You have to kind of fend for yourself to figure out how the school works." "OSU is not a school which holds your hand though planning and logistical matters," cautions a business major. The general education curriculum is unpopular with many students, but Ohio State is on a quarter system and coursework moves pretty fast. Any class you don't like will be over relatively quickly. Some professors are "incredibly eager to work with students" and are "as interesting and entertaining as they can be when lecturing." "There are a lot of mediocre professors," too. Still other faculty members are "too wrapped up in their research" and "don't pay attention to whether the students are learning or not." Also, just like at any big state school, there are plenty of teaching assistants here and they are "sometimes sub par."

Life
For many students, life at Ohio State comes down to "drinking and sports." The entire campus is fulled up with "a ton of Buckeye spirit." "Attending the varsity sports events is popular." "Everyone is obsessed with Buckeye football." It's a little bit "like a religion" and the team is "idolized." Students also "party a lot in general." "It's hard to tell exactly how many people really are partying," explains a senior. "It just seems like a lot." For many students, "awesome" house parties "are the preferred medium" for social activity, but there is "always a party, always a bar" "Thursday through Saturday." "There are other scenes than just the party scene," of course. The "great" recreation center here is absolutely gargantuan. "There is always an interesting event, conference, or performance," and OSU brings in plenty of "big entertainment acts." There are about 800 student organizations as well. "Greek life here isn't dominant" but it's noticeable and a few thousand students are involved. "It's impossible to not find something that fits you," promises a senior. "You're never bored." Off campus, Columbus boasts a population of over one million souls and "is its own city." Many students "gallery hop in the art district" or regularly take advantage of the area's "great shopping."

Student Body
"It's hard to categorize students here," says a sophomore. The vibe is "middle class" and "very Midwestern," and just about everyone is either "from small Ohio towns" or from "from a suburban-type setting" around Columbus, Toledo, Cincinnati, or Cleveland. Otherwise, "Ohio State is a melting pot," and "it easy to blend into the crowd." "There is no real homogenous, average student." Several ethnic minorities are solidly represented. Many students dress "like they shopped in a department store, albeit a nice department store," observes a senior. "There is a lot of style and fashion walking around campus," too. There are also hordes of students clad in "OSU clothing." A huge contingent of students is "smart, outgoing, athletic, and involved," but "the stereotypical weird kids at other universities have several hundred like-minded classmates at OSU." There are "drunks, nerds, overachievers, underachievers," "artists," outcasts, and hippies. Many students are "working a job or two." "The large community provides diversity," relates a senior. "However, we have our own smaller communities to help campus feel like home."

THE OHIO STATE UNIVERSITY—COLUMBUS

FINANCIAL AID: 614-292-0300 • E-MAIL: ASKABUCKEYE@OSU.EDU (FRESHMEN AND TRANSFER)• WEBSITE: WWW.OSU.EDU

THE PRINCETON REVIEW SAYS

Admissions

Very important factors considered include: Class rank, academic GPA, rigor of secondary school record, standardized test scores, *Important factors considered include:* Application essay, extracurricular activities, first generation, talent/ability, volunteer work, work experience. *Other factors considered include:* you provide cultural, economic, racial or geograph diversity, SAT or ACT required; ACT with Writing component required. TOEFL required of all international applicants. High school diploma is required and GED is accepted. *Academic units required:* 4 English, 3 mathematics, 3 natural sciences, 2 foreign language, 2 social studies, 1 academic electives, 1 visual/performing arts. *Academic units recommended:* 4 English, 4 mathematics, 3 natural sciences, 3 foreign language, 3 social studies, 1 academic electives, 1 visual/performing arts.

Financial Aid

Students should submit: FAFSA. The Princeton Review suggests that all financial aid forms be submitted as soon as possible after 1/1. Need-based scholarships/grants offered: Federal Pell, SEOG, state scholarships/grants, private scholarships, the school's own gift aid. *Loan aid offered:* Direct Subsidized Stafford, Direct Unsubsidized Stafford, Direct PLUS, Federal Perkins, college/university loans from institutional funds. Applicants will be notified of awards on or about 4/5.

The Inside Word

Though the sheer number of applicants to OSU each year is sizeable, applications are read with more than a cursory glance toward grades and class rank. Standards are high, but OSU is certainly worth a short for the average student. The university's great reputation and affordable cost make it a good choice for anyone looking at large schools.

THE SCHOOL SAYS ". . ."

From The Admissions Office

"The Ohio State University has changed dramatically in the last decade, and, as a result, has seen its academic reputation thrive. A strong focus on helping first-year students make a successful transition to the university, competitive admissions, and a physical transformation (amazing new and renovated facilities across campus) are changes that have increased Ohio State's ability to draw students and faculty of exceptional scholarly talent."

"Once you're on campus, "big school" translates to depth, diversity, and opportunity. Ohio State prides itself on offering about any academic or extracurricular opportunity a student could dream of: 170 majors; 800+ student organizations; 100 study abroad programs; internship, research, and service-learning opportunities in every college; multiple Honors and Scholars programs; and 40+ learning communities. Professional and faculty advisors assigned to each student help identify the opportunities that meet the student's interests and goals.

"Ohio State consistently boasts an impressive first-year retention rate over 90%; the national average is around 75%. Ohio State's focus on the first year is campus-wide, including strong orientation and first-year programs."

SELECTIVITY

Admissions Rating	88
# of applicants	18,286
% of applicants accepted	68
% of acceptees attending	51
# accepting a place on wait list	149
% admitted from wait list	2

FRESHMAN PROFILE

Range SAT Critical Reading	530–640
Range SAT Math	560–670
Range SAT Writing	520–630
Range ACT Composite	24–29
Minimum paper TOEFL	527
Minimum computer TOEFL	197
% graduated top 10% of class	43
% graduated top 25% of class	80
% graduated top 50% of class	98

DEADLINES

Regular	
Deadline	2/1
Notification	rolling
Nonfall registration?	yes

APPLICANTS ALSO LOOK AT AND OFTEN PREFER

University of Cincinnati
Ohio University—Athens
Bowling Green State University
Miami University

FINANCIAL FACTS

Financial Aid Rating	72
Annual tuition in state	$8,679
Annual tuition out-of-state	$21,918
Room and board	$8,073
% frosh rec. need-based scholarship or grant aid	52
% UG rec. need-based scholarship or grant aid	46
% frosh rec. non-need-based scholarship or grant aid	4
% UG rec. non-need-based scholarship or grant aid	2
% frosh rec. need-based self-help aid	46
% UG rec. need-based self-help aid	48
% frosh rec. athletic scholarships	1
% UG rec. athletic scholarships	1
% frosh rec. any financial aid	54
% UG rec. any financial aid	49
% UG borrow to pay for school	58
Average cumulative indebtedness	$17,821

OHIO UNIVERSITY—ATHENS

120 CHUBB HALL, ATHENS, OH 45701 • ADMISSIONS: 740-593-4100 • FAX: 740-593-0560

CAMPUS LIFE

Quality of Life Rating	84
Fire Safety Rating	70
Green Rating	81
Type of school	public
Environment	village

STUDENTS

Total undergrad enrollment	17,231
% male/female	49/51
% from out of state	8
% from public high school	93
% live on campus	45
% in (# of) fraternities	10 (16)
% in (# of) sororities	14 (12)
% African American	5
% Asian	1
% Caucasian	89
% Hispanic	2
% international	2
# of countries represented	126

SURVEY SAYS . . .

Athletic facilities are great
Students are friendly
Students are happy
Student publications are popular
Lots of beer drinking
Hard liquor is popular
(Almost) everyone smokes

ACADEMICS

Academic Rating	72
Calendar	quarter
Student/faculty ratio	19:1
Profs interesting rating	75
Profs accessible rating	77
% classes taught by TAs	15
Most common reg class size	10–19 students
Most common lab size	10–19 students

MOST POPULAR MAJORS

biology/biological sciences
journalism
kinesiology and exercise science

STUDENTS SAY ". . ."

Academics

"Academically, Ohio University has something for everyone, from astrophysics to the history of rock and roll," students at this large state-run university boast. And students have an equally wide range of choices when it comes to committing themselves to academics; "You can take advantage of the vast amount of knowledge and resources directly available, or you can forget studies and party," students tell us, occasionally bemoaning the school's "weak academic reputation" in some of the less rigorous disciplines (the most popular major here is recreation and sports sciences). Those seeking a challenge will have no trouble finding it here, however; OU boasts "a strong engineering faculty," a noteworthy aviation program offered within the university's demanding school of engineering and technology, an "excellent and very selective early childhood education program," and "one of the best journalism schools in the country"— the E.W. Scripps School of Journalism—which offers "frequent opportunities to learn and grow outside the classroom with guest speakers and special events." Scripps houses "a great communications school" offering great hands-on experience; one student informs us that "Southeast Ohio depends on our college television and radio station for their news, weather, and high school sports." As at any large university, unassertive students are in danger of getting lost in the crowd, but those who make the effort to seek out faculty and administrators assure us that "The school is very supportive of the students. I have close relationships with multiple professors, and I think that they generally take a strong interest in the students."

Life

"Ohio University has a beautiful campus with lots of character, both in academia and nightlife," students here report. Greek organizations play a major role in the life of the campus, providing service to the community and serving as a social catalyst. Undergraduates assure us that the school "truly lives up to its reputation as a party school. It is never hard to find a party on any given night, whether in the dorms or off campus." One undergrad writes "a nationwide reputation as a party school is not something I'm proud of," but most accept things as they are, noting that "Ohio University is a school where everyone can find a group of people doing whatever they're particularly interested in," which is to say that partying is hardly the only option here. College athletics are a big draw (especially football, men's basketball, and women's volleyball), as are such annual events as Homecoming and Halloween celebrations, and the school is host to literally hundreds of student clubs and organizations serving interests of every variety. Hometown Athens is a typical small college town with access to a wide variety of outdoor activities. The closest cities of note—Columbus; Ohio and Charleston, West Virginia—are each about a 90-minute drive from the OU campus.

Student Body

The OU student body "is pretty homogenous," with a large contingent of undergrads who are "white, middle- to upper-class, and from Ohio." "We have a small minority population, especially in the undergraduate programs," one student concedes, "but it's easy to interact with other cultures if you seek them out." Students here "try to get involved in community service, especially those involved in Greek life," and they are "generally friendly." Most work hard enough to get by but rarely harder; one student observes that "students totally devoted to their schoolwork are atypical here."

FINANCIAL AID: 740-593-4141 • E-MAIL: ADMISSIONS.FRESHMEN@OHIOU.EDU • WEBSITE: WWW.OHIOU.EDU

THE PRINCETON REVIEW SAYS

Admissions

Very important factors considered include: Academic GPA, rigor of secondary school record. *Important factors considered include:* Class rank, standardized test scores. *Other factors considered include:* Application essay, recommendation(s), alumni/ae relation, character/personal qualities, extracurricular activities, racial/ethnic status, talent/ability, volunteer work, work experience. SAT or ACT required. High school diploma is required and GED is accepted. *Academic units required:* 4 English, 3 mathematics, 3 science, 2 foreign language, 3 social studies, 1 Visual or Performing Arts.

Financial Aid

Students should submit: FAFSA. Regular filing deadline is 3/15. The Princeton Review suggests that all financial aid forms be submitted as soon as possible after 1/1. *Need-based scholarships/grants offered:* Federal Pell, SEOG, state scholarships/grants, private scholarships, the school's own gift aid. *Loan aid offered:* Direct Subsidized Stafford, Direct Unsubsidized Stafford, Direct PLUS, Federal Perkins, Institutional short term loans are repaid in 30–60 days. Applicants will be notified of awards on or about 4/1.

The Inside Word

Admissions requirements vary from school to school at Ohio University. The Honors Tutorial is most selective (you should be in the top 10 percent of your graduating class and earn at least a 30/1300 on your ACT/SAT), followed by the journalism school (top 15 percent, 25/1140), the business school (top 20 percent, 24/1100), media arts and visual studies, engineering, and visual communication. Admissions decisions are numbers-driven; those on the cusp should get in if they've demonstrated academic improvement during their junior and senior years.

THE SCHOOL SAYS "..."

From The Admissions Office

"Pursuing your academic studies at Ohio University means immersing yourself in the quintessential college experience. The tree-lined streets and rolling hills of Athens provide a picture-perfect backdrop for this historic campus beloved for its brick paths and stately Georgian architecture. Live and learn in this classic, residential college town and you join a tight-knit academic community of faculty and student scholars who are welcoming, intellectually challenging, and civic-minded.

"Ohio is highly regarded for the strength of it undergraduate and graduate programs. As the oldest college in Ohio and the entire Northwest Territory, Ohio University offers an irrefutable history of academic excellence and prominence. Our students' success in winning many of the nation's most prestigious and competitive academic awards is at a record high. Our total number of Fulbright winners, for example, currently ranks us first in the state for the fourth straight year and ties us with the likes of Boston College, Princeton, and UCLA. The Honors Tutorial College is the only degree-granting college of its kind in the country and mirrors the same one-on-one tutorial system practiced for centuries at Cambridge and Oxford. Close faculty mentoring and personal involvement is a university value that benefits all Ohio students.

"Visit our campus and you'll discover why students' first and lasting impression of Ohio University is 'It's what I always dreamed college would be.'"

SELECTIVITY

Admissions Rating	81
# of applicants	14,046
% of applicants accepted	78
% of acceptees attending	36

FRESHMAN PROFILE

Range SAT Critical Reading	480–600
Range SAT Math	490–600
Range SAT Writing	470–580
Range ACT Composite	21–26
Average HS GPA	3.37
% graduated top 10% of class	15
% graduated top 25% of class	44
% graduated top 50% of class	85

DEADLINES

Regular	
Deadline	2/1
Notification	rolling
Nonfall registration?	yes

APPLICANTS ALSO LOOK AT
AND OFTEN PREFER

Bowling Green State University
Miami University
Kent State University—Kent Campus
The Ohio State University—Columbus

FINANCIAL FACTS

Financial Aid Rating	68
Annual in-state tuition	$8,907
Annual out-of-state tuition	$17,871
Room and board	$8,946
Books and supplies	$873
% frosh rec. need-based scholarship or grant aid	23
% UG rec. need-based scholarship or grant aid	23
% frosh rec. non-need-based scholarship or grant aid	29
% UG rec. non-need-based scholarship or grant aid	20
% frosh rec. need-based self-help aid	47
% UG rec. need-based self-help aid	44
% frosh rec. athletic scholarships	2
% UG rec. athletic scholarships	2
% frosh rec. any financial aid	55
% UG rec. any financial aid	50
% UG borrow to pay for school	66
Average cumulative indebtedness	$23,041

OHIO WESLEYAN UNIVERSITY

ADMISSIONS OFFICE, 61 SOUTH SANDUSKY STREET, DELAWARE, OH 43015 • ADMISSIONS: 740-368-3020 • FAX: 740-368-3314

CAMPUS LIFE

Quality of Life Rating	73
Fire Safety Rating	60*
Green Rating	60*
Type of school	private
Affiliation	Methodist
Environment	town

STUDENTS

Total undergrad enrollment	1,947
% male/female	47/53
% from out of state	51
% from public high school	79
% live on campus	71
% in (# of) fraternities	28 (11)
% in (# of) sororities	26 (7)
% African American	5
% Asian	2
% Caucasian	81
% Hispanic	1
% international	9
# of countries represented	42

SURVEY SAYS . . .

Lab facilities are great
Students are friendly
Diverse student types on campus
Frats and sororities dominate social scene
Lots of beer drinking

ACADEMICS

Academic Rating	83
Calendar	semester
Student/faculty ratio	12:1
Profs interesting rating	88
Profs accessible rating	86
Most common reg class size	10–19 students
Most common lab size	10–19 students

MOST POPULAR MAJORS
psychology
zoology
economics management

STUDENTS SAY "..."

Academics

With just 550 students in each entering class, it is easy to feel a part of the intimate and friendly Ohio Wesleyan community. Personal attention is key to the OWU experience, and "the 12:1 student-to-faculty ratio allows a great deal of communication, which fosters a better learning environment for each individual." Outside of class, "most professors have an open-door policy and are even willing to come in on the weekends for review sessions." In fact, OWU professors "are very interested in spending time getting to know students personally, which definitely adds a positive experience to academic life." With world-class facilities, small class sizes, and ample one-on-one time with their professors, students have a surprising number of opportunities at this small college. A sophomore tells us, "My coursework often involves hands-on lab experience, and, in the chemistry department, I have even had the opportunity to use equipment that is often only used by graduate students at larger institutions." In this student-oriented environment, OWU undergraduates feel well prepared the meet their educational goals, as well as their dreams for post-college life. A sophomore explains, "OWU fosters the pursuit of each student's interests and goals through various forms of support, including financial support, academic support through our academic skills center, mental support through our counseling program, and help with internships and long-term goals through career services." From the dorms to the dining hall, learning spills out of the classroom; you'll often find students engaged in "some kind of intellectual discussion during lunch." A freshman marvels, "The intellectual atmosphere here exceeds anything I could have dreamed of."

Life

Life at Ohio Wesleyan "is a fantastic combination of academics and extracurriculars, which allows the students to participate in whatever events interest them." When it comes to clubs and activities, OWU has it all: "From the Ultimate Frisbee club to the Medieval Sword Fighting Club, there is just about anything here you can imagine to do." In an unstructured moment, OWU students might "start a pickup game of Frisbee, play piano, go into town to cruise the local mall, [or] take a walk to the park." Students also enjoy the surrounding town Delaware, Ohio, "a cute place to be with fun shops and an old-fashioned movie theater." On the weekends, "the school's campus program board brings in entertainment such as comedians, hypnotists, magicians, and musicians/bands." In addition, fraternities and sororities play a fairly important role in the campus social scene (not to mention, serve as popular watering holes on the weekend); however, students insist that Greek life appeals to people who "cherish the idea of brotherhood and sisterhood and believe in community service," rather than those who simply want to party. Another special part of OWU residential life are the Small Living Units, theme-based houses in which every resident is required to "complete a house project based upon the theme of the house." Themes vary from creative arts to ethnic cultures.

Student Body

Coming from 47 states and 50 countries, Ohio Wesleyan undergrads have "different backgrounds and history," as well as a range of goals and interests. OWU doesn't attract any single type of person, and you'll rub elbows with "shy kids, outgoing kids, creative types, scientific types, people [who] dye their hair, people who have tattoos, [and] people that don't do either." A sophomore adds, "I have friends from China, Japan, Vietnam, Taiwan, and Russia. To be able to hear their perspectives on the world is valuable to me." Despite the diversity, there are some "common threads" throughout the campus, including a general interest in "environmental preservation, community service, [and] political awareness." According to most students, the typical OWU undergraduate participates "in some kind of club or organization" and "cares about their academics and the community." Academics are serious business, but OWU students value their personal time as well. A freshman explains, "I really enjoy the balance between academics and having fun. People respect and understand when someone needs to study, but it is never so stressful that you cannot go out and have fun on the weekends."

OHIO WESLEYAN UNIVERSITY

FINANCIAL AID: 740-368-3050 • E-MAIL: OWUADMIT@OWU.EDU • WEBSITE: WWW.OWU.EDU

THE PRINCETON REVIEW SAYS

Admissions

Very important factors considered include: Application essay, academic GPA, recommendation(s), rigor of secondary school record, character/personal qualities, interview. *Important factors considered include:* Class rank, standardized test scores, extracurricular activities, talent/ability. *Other factors considered include:* Alumni/ae relation, first generation, geographical residence, level of applicant's interest, racial/ethnic status, volunteer work, work experience. SAT or ACT required; TOEFL required of all international applicants. High school diploma is required and GED is accepted. *Academic units required:* 4 English, 3 mathematics, 3 science, 2 foreign language, 3 social studies. *Academic units recommended:* 4 mathematics, 4 science, 3 foreign language, 4 social studies.

Financial Aid

Students should submit: FAFSA, institution's own financial aid form. Regular filing deadline is 5/1. The Princeton Review suggests that all financial aid forms be submitted as soon as possible after 1/1. *Need-based scholarships/grants offered:* Federal Pell, SEOG, state scholarships/grants, private scholarships, the school's own gift aid. *Loan aid offered:* FFEL Subsidized Stafford, FFEL Unsubsidized Stafford, FFEL PLUS, Federal Perkins, college/university loans from institutional funds. Applicants will be notified of awards on a rolling basis beginning 2/15. Federal Work-Study Program available. Institutional employment available. Off-campus job opportunities are excellent.

The Inside Word

In addition to offering loads of information about the school, Ohio Wesleyan's admissions page offers loads of expert advice to high school seniors. Each year, Ohio Wesleyan University receives about 4,200 applications for just 560 spots in the entering class. The average first-year student ranked in the top 30 percent of their high school class, with an average GPA of 3.4.

THE SCHOOL SAYS "..."

From The Admissions Office

"Balance and opportunity describe Ohio Wesleyan. Males make up 48 percent of the student body. There are 35 percent of all students who are members of Greek life. Eight percent of all students are international and 8 percent of them are U.S. minorities. Exceptional teaching and academics are hallmarks of an OWU education, and features such as the Woltemade Center for Economics, Business and Entrepreneurship, and the Arneson Institute for Practical Politics set us apart from other institutions of our kind. OWU houses a newly renovated $34-million science center and newly renovated fine art facilities. Our mission places a premium on community service-learning and interactive learning with more than 85 percent of students participating in community-service activities before graduation. Our annual Sagan National Colloquium is a semester-long program that brings leaders in academics, business, science, and the arts to campus for lectures, panel discussions, readings, exhibits, and performances related to a selected topic of importance to the community and the world. Ohio Wesleyan University is a competitive member of NCAA Division III and the North Coast Athletic Conference, with three National Championships in soccer in the past six years.

"Ohio Wesleyan is located in a small-town setting and is near Columbus, the state capital and the sixteenth-largest city in the United States.

"Applicants may submit the SAT or ACT. Best scores from either test will be considered in the application review."

SELECTIVITY
Admissions Rating	86
# of applicants	4,238
% of applicants accepted	64
% of acceptees attending	21
# accepting a place on wait list	12
% admitted from wait list	50
# of early decision applicants	61
% accepted early decision	30

FRESHMAN PROFILE
Range SAT Critical Reading	520–640
Range SAT Math	520–650
Range ACT Composite	22–28
Minimum paper TOEFL	NA
Minimum computer TOEFL	217
Average HS GPA	3.43
% graduated top 10% of class	30
% graduated top 25% of class	59
% graduated top 50% of class	87

DEADLINES
Early decision	
Deadline	12/1
Notification	12/15
Early action	
Deadline	12/15
Notification	1/15
Regular	
Priority	3/1
Notification	rolling
Nonfall registration?	yes

APPLICANTS ALSO LOOK AT
AND OFTEN PREFER
The College of Wooster
Denison University
Miami University

AND SOMETIMES PREFER
Whittenberg
Ohio State

FINANCIAL FACTS
Financial Aid Rating	82
Annual tuition	$34,570
Room and board	$9,224
Required fees	$460
Books and supplies	$2,402
% frosh rec. need-based scholarship or grant aid	63
% UG rec. need-based scholarship or grant aid	59
% frosh rec. non-need-based scholarship or grant aid	14
% UG rec. non-need-based scholarship or grant aid	8
% frosh rec. need-based self-help aid	50
% UG rec. need-based self-help aid	47
% frosh rec. any financial aid	99
% UG rec. any financial aid	98
% UG borrow to pay for school	77
Average cumulative indebtedness	$26,700

THE BEST 371 COLLEGES ■ 413

PENNSYLVANIA STATE UNIVERSITY—UNIVERSITY PARK

201 SHIELDS BUILDING, BOX 3000, UNIVERSITY PARK, PA 16802-3000 • ADMISSIONS: 814-865-5471 • FAX: 814-863-7590

CAMPUS LIFE

Quality of Life Rating	**87**
Fire Safety Rating	**96**
Green Rating	**97**
Type of school	public
Environment	town

STUDENTS

Total undergrad enrollment	35,876
% male/female	55/45
% from out of state	24
% live on campus	36
% in (# of) fraternities	13 (53)
% in (# of) sororities	11 (34)
% African American	4
% Asian	5
% Caucasian	84
% Hispanic	4
% international	2
# of countries represented	121

SURVEY SAYS . . .

Athletic facilities are great
Everyone loves the Nittany Lions
Student publications are popular
Beer is popular

ACADEMICS

Academic Rating	**74**
Calendar	semester
Student/faculty ratio	17:1
Profs interesting rating	68
Profs accessible rating	68
Most common reg class size	20–29 students
Most common lab size	20–29 students

MOST POPULAR MAJORS

business administration and
management
engineering

STUDENTS SAY ". . ."

Academics

Pennsylvania State University "is everything anyone could ever want in a university," including, but hardly limited to, quality football. As one student explains, "There is so much opportunity here. As a student, your boundaries are limitless. You can do everything you can imagine at Penn State. You can also get one of the best college experiences along with a great education." Best of all, students insist "PSU has the big-city school opportunities for learning and even doing research as an undergrad (and not just as an honors student!) while providing a small-town school atmosphere. The town of State College is very student-friendly as well, since many residents there are PSU grads themselves." And while PSU students enjoy the same level of service as their peers at small schools—"if you don't get involved, it can be easy to get lost in a sea of students," undergrads warn. "Virtually everybody working here for a paycheck—staff and faculty alike—cares about the students' education and experience. It's college, not high school, so you often have to make the first step. But the return on your effort will be worth it," and in that regard, PSU does considerably better than most state schools of similar size. Business and engineering top the list of more than 160 majors available here.

Life

"Fun comes in a variety of forms" at PSU, including "the club scene, student organization activities…attending sporting events, concerts at the Bryce Jordan Center or Eisenhower Auditorium," or "just hanging out with friends." As one student puts it, "At Penn State, there's always something to do. If it's not a sporting event or a concert, there's always a party to fall back on," though parties definitely aren't just backup plans. "There is definitely a huge focus on alcohol here, but if you don't drink, the alcohol scene is easy to escape." Sports are huge; "people are very interested in and astute when regarding sports, both professional and at the collegiate level," and "partially due to the success of the football team, Penn State is great on school unity." A "significant number of students go home on many weekends to reconnect with family and high school friends," but more than enough remain behind to populate a robust extracurricular scene. Greek life is substantial but hardly unavoidable, thanks to the cornucopia of on-campus and in-town alternatives. Nearby road trip destinations are in short supply, but with the campus and University Park offering so many options, few here complain.

Student Body

"At such a huge school" as Penn State "there are so many different descriptions of 'the typical student.' There's the typical Ugg-wearing, legging-donned sorority girl, the Bach-obsessed music students, the math-loving engineers, and the list goes on and on." As one student puts it, "Penn State is so diverse I don't think there is a 'typical student.' Everyone is different in his own way, and there's hardly ever if any discrimination, toward anyone. Everyone fits in here, no matter who you are. One thing I think every student has in common at Penn State is love for our school. We Are Penn State!" A sizeable number of undergrads here are "from a middle- or lower-economic-bracket family, so [they] are here mainly to advance into their chosen careers. But having said that, they each would like to learn a few new and different things about themselves and their world in the process." "Avid football fans" and "partygoers" certainly won't feel at all out of place at PSU.

PENNSYLVANIA STATE UNIVERSITY—UNIVERSITY PARK

FINANCIAL AID: 814-865-6301 • E-MAIL: ADMISSIONS@PSU.EDU • WEBSITE: WWW.PSU.EDU

THE PRINCETON REVIEW SAYS

Admissions

Very important factors considered include: Academic GPA, standardized test scores. *Important factors considered include:* Rigor of secondary school record. *Other factors considered include:* Class rank, application essay, recommendation(s), alumni/ae relation, character/personal qualities, extracurricular activities, talent/ability, volunteer work, work experience. SAT or ACT required; ACT with Writing component required; TOEFL required of all international applicants. High school diploma is required and GED is accepted. *Academic units required:* 4 English, 3 mathematics, 3 science, 2 foreign language, 3 social studies.

Financial Aid

Students should submit: FAFSA. The Princeton Review suggests that all financial aid forms be submitted as soon as possible after 1/1. *Need-based scholarships/grants offered:* Federal Pell, SEOG, state scholarships/grants, private scholarships, the school's own gift aid. *Loan aid offered:* FFEL Subsidized Stafford, FFEL Unsubsidized Stafford, FFEL PLUS, Federal Perkins, college/university loans from institutional funds, Private Loans. Applicants will be notified of awards on a rolling basis beginning 3/1. Federal Work-Study Program available. Institutional employment available. Off-campus job opportunities are good.

The Inside Word

High school GPA is by far the most important factor in the PSU admissions decision. According to the school's Web site, high school grades account for two-thirds of the final decision. Standardized test scores, class rank, extracurricular activities, and other factors make up the final one-third. PSU admits on a rolling basis. It's a popular choice, so applicants are well served to submit their applications as early as possible.

THE SCHOOL SAYS ". . ."

From The Admissions Office

"Unique among large public universities, Penn State combines the over-35,000-student setting of its University Park campus with 20 academically and administratively integrated undergraduate locations—small-college settings ranging in size from 600 to 3,400 students. Each year, more than 60 percent of incoming freshmen begin their studies at these residential and commuter campuses, while nearly 40 percent begin at the University Park campus. The smaller locations focus on the needs of new students by offering the first two years of most Penn State baccalaureate degrees in settings that stress close interaction with faculty. Depending on the major selected, students may choose to complete their degree at University Park or one of the smaller locations. Your application to Penn State qualifies you for review for any of our campuses. Your two choices of location are reviewed in the order given. Entrance difficulty is based, in part, on the demand. Due to its popularity, the University Park campus is the most competitive for admission.

"Freshman applicants may submit the results from the SAT or the ACT with the Writing Component. The Writing portions of these tests will not necessarily be factored into admission decisions."

SELECTIVITY

Admissions Rating	**91**
# of applicants	39,551
% of applicants accepted	51
% of acceptees attending	32
# accepting a place on wait list	1,704
% admitted from wait list	80

FRESHMAN PROFILE

Range SAT Critical Reading	530–630
Range SAT Math	560–670
Minimum paper TOEFL	550
Minimum computer TOEFL	213
Minimum web-based TOEFL	80
Average HS GPA	3.58
% graduated top 10% of class	44.65
% graduated top 25% of class	81.3
% graduated top 50% of class	97.44

DEADLINES

Regular	
Priority	11/30
Notification	rolling
Nonfall registration?	yes

FINANCIAL FACTS

Financial Aid Rating	**63**
Annual in-state tuition	$12,284
Annual out-of-state tuition	$23,152
Room and board	$7,180
Required fees	$560
Books and supplies	$1,168
% frosh rec. need-based scholarship or grant aid	24
% UG rec. need-based scholarship or grant aid	30
% frosh rec. non-need-based scholarship or grant aid	20
% UG rec. non-need-based scholarship or grant aid	17
% frosh rec. need-based self-help aid	37
% UG rec. need-based self-help aid	42
% frosh rec. athletic scholarships	2
% UG rec. athletic scholarships	2
% frosh rec. any financial aid	75
% UG rec. any financial aid	73
% UG borrow to pay for school	67
Average cumulative indebtedness	$26,300

PEPPERDINE UNIVERSITY

24255 PACIFIC COAST HIGHWAY, MALIBU, CA 90263-4392 • ADMISSIONS: 310-456-4861 • FAX: 310-506-4861

CAMPUS LIFE

Quality of Life Rating	92
Fire Safety Rating	69
Green Rating	80
Type of school	private
Affiliation	Churches of Christ
Environment	suburban

STUDENTS

Total undergrad enrollment	3,386
% male/female	46/54
% from out of state	45
% live on campus	58
% in (# of) fraternities	18 (5)
% in (# of) sororities	31 (7)
% African American	7
% Asian	9
% Caucasian	60
% Hispanic	10
% Native American	1
% international	6

SURVEY SAYS . . .

Lab facilities are great
School is well run
Students are friendly
Dorms are like palaces
Campus feels safe
Students are happy

ACADEMICS

Academic Rating	88
Calendar	semester
Student/faculty ratio	14:1
Profs interesting rating	87
Profs accessible rating	88
Most common	
reg class size	10–19 students
Most common	
lab size	fewer than 10 students

MOST POPULAR MAJORS

business administration and
marketing
communication, journalism
interdisciplinary studies

STUDENTS SAY ". . ."

Academics

Pepperdine University, in sunny, "calm" Malibu is a smaller liberal arts school affiliated with the Churches of Christ "where students are given numerous opportunities to mature and develop academically in a spiritually nurturing environment." "Christian values" are unmistakable here. Attendance at chapel is required and the mandatory core curriculum (which includes an optional, highly recommended Great Books sequence) involves religion courses. The faculty is "pretty much all Christian" as well and, while "some of the professors need to be fired," most are "challenging" and "truly passionate." "My professors have all been excellent with the exception of maybe two in all my four years," says a biology major, "and they really look out for their students." The administration is full of "religious zealots" who "tend to shelter students way too much," but staffers all the way up to the top brass are "very easy to communicate with" and the school is "very well managed." "You feel like a student and not a number at Pepperdine," says a journalism major. Study-abroad programs in Germany, Hong Kong, France, Argentina, and a host of other places are reportedly "beyond compare." About half the undergrads here go overseas at least once. "Right now, I'm studying abroad in Switzerland and loving every minute of it," declares an advertising major.

Life

The gym is pretty bad and "the food is far too expensive for its quality." However, "the dorms are very nice," and students at Pepperdine enjoy "amazing weather" and a "uniquely breathtaking" campus "with a killer view" of the ocean. During the week, life is "vibrant." "Speakers and musicians come to campus" frequently, and "students are very active with organizations, clubs, and social life in general." "Sororities and fraternities are really big at Pepperdine," and some students "party like rock stars." Be warned, though: Drug and alcohol policies are "zero tolerance." "Rarely do students drink on campus," says a junior. "It's a big risk." There are "curfew rules" and "restrictions for when opposite genders can be in one another's rooms," too. Mostly, students "go off campus if they want to get wild and crazy," and the parties tend to be "fairly exclusive." Many students avoid the party scene altogether. "Instead we go out to dinner, go stargazing, have political discussions, go shopping, or catch the latest movies," explains a senior. "Church-related functions" are also popular, and there is "a big emphasis on service." The number of volunteer opportunities is "almost overwhelming." Outdoor activities are outrageously abundant, too. "Running into celebs at local restaurants and businesses is pretty cool" in the glitzy surrounding enclave of Malibu, but otherwise it's "pricey" and "everything closes down at 10:00 P.M." "Even the beauty of the Pacific, sadly, can become old." Santa Monica and Hollywood aren't terribly far but Pepperdine often feels "totally isolated." Having your own car is "almost necessary."

Student Body

"There are many students receiving financial aid" here. "It's mostly white and rich and, if not white, just rich." Pepperdine has its "fair share of millionaires' kids and minor celebrities." "Appearances and brand names are important" and the atmosphere is "somewhat superficial." "There are two types at Pepperdine," suggests a sophomore, "the type who has a scholarship or financial aid and is exceedingly intelligent and the type who is pretty stupid but whose parents pay full tuition to the school and give them BMW's and beach houses." Politically, conservatives tend to dominate. Many, many students are "active Christians." Some are "Churches of Christ diehards" "who are totally on fire for God." Pepperdine students are also "sun-kissed," "social," "excited about life," and "high in character" as well. There are surfers, athletes, frat boys, "Barbie girls," quite a few Texans, and some "eclectic" students but, all in all, it's a "slightly preppy" and "typical southern Californian" crowd. "Not very many people who attend this school are unique or radical or experimental in any way."

PEPPERDINE UNIVERSITY

FINANCIAL AID: 310-506-4301 • E-MAIL: ADMISSION-SEAVER@PEPPERDINE.EDU • WEBSITE: WWW.PEPPERDINE.EDU

THE PRINCETON REVIEW SAYS

Admissions

Very important factors considered include: Application essay, academic GPA, recommendation(s), rigor of secondary school record, standardized test scores, character/personal qualities, extracurricular activities, talent/ability. *Important factors considered include:* Religious affiliation/commitment, volunteer work. *Other factors considered include:* Alumni/ae relation, first generation, racial/ethnic status, work experience. SAT or ACT required; ACT with Writing component required; TOEFL required of all international applicants. High school diploma is required and GED is accepted. *Academic units recommended:* 4 English, 4 mathematics, 4 science, (3 science labs), 3 foreign language, 3 social studies, 3 history, 3 academic electives, 1 Speech.

Financial Aid

Students should submit: FAFSA, institution's own financial aid form. Regular filing deadline is 2/15. The Princeton Review suggests that all financial aid forms be submitted as soon as possible after 1/1. *Need-based scholarships/grants offered:* Federal Pell, SEOG, state scholarships/grants, private scholarships, the school's own gift aid, United Negro College Fund. *Loan aid offered:* FFEL Subsidized Stafford, FFEL Unsubsidized Stafford, FFEL PLUS, Federal Perkins, college/university loans from institutional funds. Applicants will be notified of awards on or about 4/15. Federal Work-Study Program available. Institutional employment available. Off-campus job opportunities are good.

The Inside Word

A stunning physical location enables the admissions office to produce beautiful catalogs and viewbooks, which, when combined with the university's reputation for academic quality, help to attract a large applicant pool. In addition to solid grades and test scores, successful applicants typically have well-rounded extracurricular backgrounds. Involvement in school, church, and community is an overused cliché in the world of college admissions, but at Pepperdine it's definitely one of the ingredients in successful applications.

THE SCHOOL SAYS " . . ."

From The Admissions Office

"As a selective university, Pepperdine seeks students who show promise of academic achievement at the collegiate level. However, we also seek students who are committed to serving the university community, as well as others with whom they come into contact. We look for community-service activities, volunteer efforts, and strong leadership qualities, as well as a demonstrated commitment to academic studies and an interest in the liberal arts.

"Seaver College of Pepperdine University requires freshman applicants to submit scores from either the Scholastic Aptitude Test (SAT Reasoning Test including the Writing portion) or the American College Test (ACT) (including the Writing test). The scores are evaluated in conjunction with the grade point average in specific courses completed."

SELECTIVITY

Admissions Rating	94
# of applicants	6,910
% of applicants accepted	34
% of acceptees attending	33
# accepting a place on wait list	410
% admitted from wait list	0

FRESHMAN PROFILE

Range SAT Critical Reading	550–670
Range SAT Math	560–680
Range SAT Writing	550–660
Range ACT Composite	25–30
Minimum paper TOEFL	550
Minimum computer TOEFL	220
Minimum web-based TOEFL	80
Average HS GPA	3.69
% graduated top 10% of class	40
% graduated top 25% of class	75
% graduated top 50% of class	95

DEADLINES

Regular	
Deadline	1/15
Notification	4/1
Nonfall registration?	yes

APPLICANTS ALSO LOOK AT

AND OFTEN PREFER
University of Southern California
University of California—San Diego
University of California—Los Angeles
University of San Diego
Loyola Marymount University

AND SOMETIMES PREFER
Vanderbilt University
New York University

AND RARELY PREFER
Occidental College
Biola University

FINANCIAL FACTS

Financial Aid Rating	88
Annual tuition	$37,730
% frosh rec. need-based scholarship or grant aid	48
% UG rec. need-based scholarship or grant aid	38
% frosh rec. non-need-based scholarship or grant aid	21
% UG rec. non-need-based scholarship or grant aid	14
% frosh rec. need-based self-help aid	49
% UG rec. need-based self-help aid	39
% frosh rec. athletic scholarships	4
% UG rec. athletic scholarships	3
% frosh rec. any financial aid	53
% UG rec. any financial aid	42
% UG borrow to pay for school	61
Average cumulative indebtedness	$31,546

PITZER COLLEGE

1050 North Mills Avenue, Claremont, CA 91711-6101 • Admissions: 909-621-8129 • Fax: 909-621-8770

Quality of Life Rating	**91**
Fire Safety Rating	**76**
Green Rating	**77**
Type of school	private
Environment	town

STUDENTS

Total undergrad enrollment	1,025
% male/female	41/59
% from out of state	45
% live on campus	65
% African American	6
% Asian	9
% Caucasian	41
% Hispanic	15
% international	3
# of countries represented	12

SURVEY SAYS . . .
Lots of liberal students
Students are friendly
Different types of students interact
Students aren't religious
Frats and sororities are unpopular or nonexistent
Student government is popular
Political activism is popular

ACADEMICS

Academic Rating	**92**
Calendar	semester
Student/faculty ratio	12:1
Profs interesting rating	93
Profs accessible rating	95
Most common reg class size	10–19 students

MOST POPULAR MAJORS
political science and government
psychology
sociology

STUDENTS SAY ". . ."

Academics

Though the '60s-style academic buildings on the campus of Pitzer College "are not too visually appealing, progressive learning" and academic flexibility abound. "People have to take courses in a couple of key areas, but within those areas the specific courses are not dictated," explains a history major. As a result, you can chart your own course "within enough of a structure to ensure everyone gets a real liberal arts education." Students can also take courses at the "four other amazing colleges" that make up the Claremont Colleges consortium. "It's a great mix of a classic college experience and a small liberal arts oasis." Classes are "discussion-oriented" and "writing-based." Pitzer's professors are "really great at being accessible outside of class whether you want to talk about things related to the class, or anything else under the sun." "They are fascinating, helpful, warm people, who often have a wicked sense of humor," beams an art history major. While it can be difficult to determine "who is actually in charge of what," the "friendly" administration "makes sure the students play a real part" in everything from planning new construction to faculty tenure. Overall, Pitzer students seem extremely happy with their academic experience. "Pitzer is my own little utopia," confides a sociology major. "It just sucks I'm graduating."

Life

"Life at Pitzer College is very on-campus oriented." "Pitzer and the other Claremont Colleges strongly encourage campus life"—everything from guest lectures to deejays. Students "tend to enjoy the outdoors" as well. Biking is big, along with "surf trips" and hiking at Mount Baldy. "Most people are pretty involved, or at least they show up to a lot of stuff," says one student. "I play soccer and participate in the theater," comments another. "I go to Thursday night Groove at the Grove," says another. Other students "just do their own thing," which is cool too, because Pitzer is "the chillest place on Earth." The lifestyle is "Southern Californian." "The sun is always out and people are always on the mounds," deep in discussion. "There is always music and laughter to be found." "If you talk to the right people you can find the marijuana/free love culture, but on average people are pretty normal. On weekends people mostly hang out in small groups and goof around." While there's no Greek system, the social mood is festive. "Weekends start on Thursdays," though parties "mostly occur on the other campuses." Younger carousers "tend to go on the grand expeditions to find the party around the Five C's." "Upperclassmen tend to go off-campus to house parties." Complaints include the hit-or-miss housing situation. New green dorms were completed recently but "the old dorms are getting a little funky." The "borderline inedible" campus food needs improvement. And "gossip spreads like wildfire" on this small campus. Getting away to the anonymous confines of nearby Los Angeles is always an option, but the trip "can be quite difficult" without a car.

Student Body

Students are "motivated" yet "very laidback." There is a strong sense of "togetherness and community." "Cliques are not as noticeable as in high school. Everyone is simply friends with everyone." "The typical Pitzer student is rarely typical," observes an anthropology major. "Everyone is a bit quirky but it seems like there's a sense of pride that comes with being labeled as a wacky Pitzer student." "We are all oddballs," adds one student. However, "as Pitzer has become increasingly more competitive over the years, the student body has gradually branched out from the 'tree-hugging stoner' prototype to include a wider array of students." "In my freshman class I would say we only have five to 20 true hippies," surveys a first-year student. Politically, while "you can experience a lot of diversity of thought" among the five Claremont Colleges, you'll be experiencing mostly liberalism here. "Pitzer is a haven for those who want to change the world" and students are "passionate about their personal causes." "The few conservatives on campus get a lot of grief, I'm sure," muses one student.

418 ■ THE BEST 371 COLLEGES

FINANCIAL AID: 909-621-8208 • E-MAIL: ADMISSION@PITZER.EDU • WEBSITE: WWW.PITZER.EDU

THE PRINCETON REVIEW SAYS

Admissions

Very important factors considered include: Class rank, application essay, academic GPA, recommendation(s), rigor of secondary school record, character/personal qualities, extracurricular activities, racial/ethnic status. *Important factors considered include:* First generation, geographical residence, interview, level of applicant's interest, talent/ability, volunteer work. *Other factors considered include:* Standardized test scores, alumni/ae relation, work experience. ACT with Writing component recommended; TOEFL required of all international applicants. High school diploma is required and GED is accepted. *Academic units required:* 4 English, 3 mathematics, 3 science, (3 science labs), 3 foreign language, 3 social studies, 1 history, 1 visual/performing arts.

Financial Aid

Students should submit: FAFSA, CSS/Financial Aid PROFILE, state aid form, noncustodial PROFILE, business/farm supplement. Regular filing deadline is 2/1. The Princeton Review suggests that all financial aid forms be submitted as soon as possible after 1/1. *Need-based scholarships/grants offered:* Federal Pell, SEOG, state scholarships/grants, private scholarships, the school's own gift aid, Federal ACG and National SMART. *Loan aid offered:* FFEL Subsidized Stafford, FFEL Unsubsidized Stafford, FFEL PLUS, Federal Perkins, college/university loans from institutional funds. Applicants will be notified of awards on or about 4/1. Federal Work-Study Program available. Institutional employment available. Off-campus job opportunities are fair.

The Inside Word

Pitzer emphasizes admissions essays, and it's no coincidence unique students find themselves admitted here year after year. Let your thoughts flow freely when you write yours. Show the admissions committee what makes you who you are. Be passionate about whatever you are passionate about. What you have to say about yourself will go much further than numbers in determining your fate. Also worth noting: If you graduate in the top 10 percent of your high school class or have a 3.5 GPA (in your serious classes), you don't have to submit standardized test scores. You still can, but it's not required.

THE SCHOOL SAYS "..."

From The Admissions Office

"Pitzer is about opportunities. It's about possibilities. The students who come here are looking for something different from the usual 'take two courses from column A, two courses from column B, and two courses from column C.' That kind of arbitrary selection doesn't make a satisfying education at Pitzer. So we look for students who want to have an impact on their own education, who want the chief responsibility—with help from their faculty advisors—in designing their own futures.

"Pitzer's admission policy uses a test-optional policy. Students in the top 10 percent of their class or those who have an unweighted academic GPA of 3.5 or higher are not required to submit test scores. Others are allowed to choose from a variety of choices, including standardized tests (i.e., the SAT and ACT with the Writing component)."

SELECTIVITY

Admissions Rating	90
# of applicants	4,031
% of applicants accepted	22
% of acceptees attending	29
# accepting a place on wait list	939
# of early decision applicants	133
% accepted early decision	43

FRESHMAN PROFILE

Range SAT Critical Reading	580–690
Range SAT Math	580–680
Range ACT Composite	24.5–30
Minimum paper TOEFL	520
Minimum web-based TOEFL	70
Average HS GPA	3.75
% graduated top 10% of class	51
% graduated top 25% of class	80
% graduated top 50% of class	99

DEADLINES

Early decision	
Deadline	11/15
Notification	1/1
Regular	
Deadline	1/1
Notification	4/1
Nonfall registration?	no

APPLICANTS ALSO LOOK AT AND OFTEN PREFER

Pomona College
Occidental College
University of Southern California
University of California—Berkeley
University of California—Los Angeles
Scripps College
Claremont McKenna College

FINANCIAL FACTS

Financial Aid Rating	97
Annual tuition	$34,500
Room and board	$10,930
Required fees	$3,370
Books and supplies	$1,000
% frosh rec. need-based scholarship or grant aid	42
% UG rec. need-based scholarship or grant aid	37
% frosh rec. need-based self-help aid	39
% UG rec. need-based self-help aid	35
% UG borrow to pay for school	37
Average cumulative indebtedness	$21,044

POMONA COLLEGE

333 NORTH COLLEGE WAY, CLAREMONT, CA 91711-6312 • ADMISSIONS: 909-621-8134 • FAX: 909-621-8952

CAMPUS LIFE
Quality of Life Rating	99
Fire Safety Rating	79
Green Rating	60*
Type of school	private
Environment	village

STUDENTS
Total undergrad enrollment	1,516
% male/female	50/50
% from out of state	67
% from public high school	60
% live on campus	98
% in (# of) fraternities	5 (3)
% African American	8
% Asian	14
% Caucasian	47
% Hispanic	11
% international	4
# of countries represented	24

SURVEY SAYS . . .
No one cheats
School is well run
Students are friendly
Students aren't religious
Dorms are like palaces
Low cost of living
Students are happy
Musical organizations are popular

ACADEMICS
Academic Rating	97
Calendar	semester
Student/faculty ratio	8:1
Profs interesting rating	90
Profs accessible rating	97
Most common reg class size	10–19 students
Most common lab size	10–19 students

MOST POPULAR MAJORS
biology/biological sciences
economics
English language and literature

STUDENTS SAY ". . ."

Academics

"Pomona has much to boast about, including powerhouse academics, state-of-the-art facilities, and a cushy endowment," raves one student. A fellow student describes Pomona as "the best place on earth for a solid, well-rounded, and liberal-tilted education where students pitch each other into fountains on their birthdays." While students are impressed with the "good faculty-to-student ratio," "small class sizes," and access to "a wealth of academic resources and extracurricular opportunities" as part of the Claremont University Consortium, Pomona students reserve their highest compliments for their professors who "are actually glad to be teaching, rather than merely putting up with the teaching so they can research." "It is not uncommon to receive detailed comments on assignments and personal e-mails from professors." One student unequivocally declares, "The professors are the soul of my academic experience." "The school really does run like butter," and "staff and administration really do make an attempt to cater to every student." Students are also impressed by how the school is "making some really amazing efforts at promoting gender, race, sexual, ethnic, and cultural consciousness." Students are generally satisfied with the "very visible" administration, although they admit it "gets bogged down in bureaucracy a bit sometimes."

Life

"Pomona is like the lovechild of a summer camp and a real college." With its "California chill infused with a little East Coast neurosis," Pomona provides a "quality of life that is truly sublime." Everyone agrees, "the sunshine and palm trees make it difficult to stay in a bad mood for too long, even during finals." Another student more abstractly describes the Pomona experience as "climbing academic cliffs with a large group of friends pushing you up from behind holding large jars of marshmallow creme." "The sponsor program, a system where freshmen are housed in sponsor 'groups' with two sophomore advisors, is great because you have a group of friends the moment you set foot on campus." Students also love the "really great quirky Pomona-sponsored traditions" including "Death by Chocolate (recently renamed Chocolate for Change) where Pomona brings in literally tons of chocolate for its students." One student also recalls "during finals the student government brought in 20 puppies to the lawn at the campus center for students to play with and relieve stress." While some students refer to Claremont as a "beautiful bubble where people reciprocally learn and get along," others point out "life inside the bubble is fantastic, but we don't get that many diverse opinions or experiences here." "However, with Scripps, Pitzer, Claremont McKenna, and Harvey Mudd only a quick walk away, you can definitely find a place to fit in."

Student Body

"Basically, Pomona is a school full of really nerdy kids who are relatively good at hiding their nerdy tendencies and are totally accepting of others when they come out anyway," discloses one student. Another student goes one step further and reveals everyone is "nerdily passionate about something whether it be Japanese, Greek gods, chemistry, or music." "The typical student at Pomona has accomplished far more than he or she should have by the age of 18" and is "strongly left-wing, well-read, and appreciative of good tea" as well as "pro-choice, pro-gay marriage, and committed to sustainability." Pomona students seem to share many traits in common including "intelligence, work ethic, let's-forget-work-and-go-party-and-have-fun ethic, political awareness, [and] health awareness." There's also "a certain level of quirkiness and a laid-back attitude." Some students say Pomona is "lacking in racial diversity" and generalize that "everyone comes from a background of privilege and often thoughtless liberalism." However, with its "clique-averse" student population, "there is definitely an unstated philosophy of mutual support, not cut-throat competition."

POMONA COLLEGE

FINANCIAL AID: 909-621-8205 • E-MAIL: ADMISSIONS@POMONA.EDU • WEBSITE: WWW.POMONA.EDU

THE PRINCETON REVIEW SAYS

Admissions

Very important factors considered include: Class rank, application essay, academic GPA, recommendation(s), rigor of secondary school record, standardized test scores, character/personal qualities, extracurricular activities, talent/ability. *Important factors considered include:* Interview. *Other factors considered include:* Alumni/ae relation, first generation, geographical residence, racial/ethnic status, volunteer work, work experience. SAT and SAT Subject Tests or ACT required; ACT with Writing component recommended; TOEFL required of all international applicants. High school diploma or equivalent is not required. *Academic units required:* 4 English, 3 mathematics, 3 science, (2 science labs), 2 foreign language, 2 social studies, 3 history. *Academic units recommended:* 4 mathematics, 4 science, (3 science labs), 3 foreign language, 2 social studies, 3 history.

Financial Aid

Students should submit: FAFSA, CSS/Financial Aid PROFILE, noncustodial PROFILE, business/farm supplement. Tax returns for both the student and parents. Regular filing deadline is 2/1. The Princeton Review suggests that all financial aid forms be submitted as soon as possible after 1/1. *Need-based scholarships/grants offered:* Federal Pell, SEOG, state scholarships/grants, private scholarships, the school's own gift aid. *Loan aid offered:* FFEL Subsidized Stafford, FFEL Unsubsidized Stafford, FFEL PLUS, Federal Perkins, college/university loans from institutional funds. Applicants will be notified of awards on or about 4/1. Federal Work-Study Program available. Institutional employment available. Off-campus job opportunities are good.

The Inside Word

Even though it is tough to get admitted to Pomona, students will find the admissions staff to be accessible and engaging. An applicant pool full of such well-qualified students as those who typically apply, in combination with the college's small size, necessitates that candidates undergo as personal an admissions evaluation as possible. This is how solid matches are made and how Pomona does a commendable job of keeping an edge on the competition.

THE SCHOOL SAYS " . . ."

From The Admissions Office

"Perhaps the most important thing to know about Pomona College is that we are what we say we are. There is enormous integrity between the statements of mission and philosophy governing the college and the reality that students, faculty, and administrators experience. The balance in the curriculum is unusual. Sciences, social sciences, humanities, and the arts receive equal attention, support, and emphasis. Most importantly, the commitment to undergraduate education is absolute. Teaching awards remain the highest honor the trustees can bestow upon faculty. The typical method of instruction is the seminar and the average class size of 14 offers students the opportunity to become full partners in the learning process. Our location in the Los Angeles basin and in Claremont, with five other colleges, provides a remarkable community.

"Pomona College requires the SAT plus two SAT Subject Tests (in different fields) or the ACT with the Writing component."

SELECTIVITY
Admissions Rating	99
# of applicants	6,293
% of applicants accepted	16
% of acceptees attending	39

FRESHMAN PROFILE
Range SAT Critical Reading	700–780
Range SAT Math	690–780
Range SAT Writing	680–770
Range ACT Composite	30–34
Minimum paper TOEFL	600
Minimum computer TOEFL	250

DEADLINES
Early decision	
Deadline	11/1
Notification	12/15
Regular	
Deadline	1/2
Nonfall registration?	no

APPLICANTS ALSO LOOK AT
AND OFTEN PREFER
Harvard College
University of California—Berkeley
Stanford University
Princeton University
AND SOMETIMES PREFER
Dartmouth College
University of California—Los Angeles
Williams College

FINANCIAL FACTS
Financial Aid Rating	96
Annual tuition	$35,318
Room and board	$12,120
Required fees	$307
% frosh rec. need-based scholarship or grant aid	52
% UG rec. need-based scholarship or grant aid	53
% frosh rec. need-based self-help aid	52
% UG rec. need-based self-help aid	53
% frosh rec. any financial aid	53
% UG rec. any financial aid	50
% UG borrow to pay for school	54
Average cumulative indebtedness	$11,300

PRESCOTT COLLEGE

220 GROVE AVENUE, PRESCOTT, AZ 86301 • ADMISSIONS: 877-350-2100 • FAX: 928-776-5242

CAMPUS LIFE

Quality of Life Rating	95
Fire Safety Rating	63
Green Rating	96
Type of school	private
Environment	town

STUDENTS

Total undergrad enrollment	717
% male/female	40/60
% from out of state	62
% from public high school	78
% live on campus	4
% African American	2
% Asian	1
% Caucasian	85
% Hispanic	7
% Native American	1
% international	1

SURVEY SAYS . . .

Lots of liberal students
Class discussions encouraged
No one cheats
Students are friendly
Different types of students interact
Students aren't religious
Great food on campus
Students are happy
Intercollegiate sports are unpopular
or nonexistent
Frats and sororities are unpopular or
nonexistent
Political activism is popular

ACADEMICS

Academic Rating	90
Calendar	semester
Student/faculty ratio	7:1
Profs interesting rating	98
Profs accessible rating	93
Most common	
reg class size	10–19 students

MOST POPULAR MAJORS

education
elementary education and teaching
environmental studies

STUDENTS SAY ". . ."

Academics

Tiny, innovative Prescott College in the Arizona mountains has "a reputation for being about the environment." The wilderness orientation program features a three-week backcountry excursion, just for instance. Undergrads here pursue "experientially-based," highly "self-directed" curricula on an alternating block and quarterly academic schedule. They receive narrative evaluations of their work instead of actual grades (though letter grades are also available). The "truly interdisciplinary" class offerings, "while somewhat limited, can be amazing." "We don't have lecture classes," explains a senior. "Class sizes are limited to the number of people who can fit in a 15-passenger van, which makes for discussions that include everybody." "My first semester, I was down at a field station in Mexico studying marine biology out on boats and islands every day," reminisces another senior. "Personal attention" is ample and Prescott's professors "are passionate about the topics they teach." The personable administration is "very flexible and open when it comes to student ideas." The big gripe here involves the limited amount of resources. There is "very little state-of-the-art" technology, though, the design and sustainability aspects of many of the buildings are top of the line. Those who are seeking out the resources, name recognition, and larger-scale community of a large university may "find it very difficult to survive this educational experience." Freshman orientation is a key element of the school. All willing students attend wilderness orientation, spending some 20 days hiking and living in the field. "This is one of the most formative events in Prescott College culture, and cannot be ignored," says a student.

Life

Political activism and community service are widespread but life at Prescott College is mostly idiosyncratic. "People always seem to be involved with a million projects for classes or just for stuff they are interested in and believe in." Students might attend "a lecture about the ecology of peace, or a workshop on digital storytelling, or someone's presentation of the semester they spent hiking around Thailand for their senior project." "Everyone knows everyone" and virtually all students live off campus. "I live in a yurt," notes a junior. The surrounding town "offers little" except for "a lot of retirees," so students make their own fun. "Adrenaline sports" and outdoor activities are popular. "It is common for students (or classes) to take trips into the wilderness, or to go camping or backpacking." Potluck dinners "are big." Parties are "there if you look for them" and drinking, dancing, bonfires, and "music jams" definitely have their place; however, "not a lot of people get wasted every weekend."

Student Body

"Generally speaking, a 'typical' student is one who prefers a style of life and education that differs with societal norms." "Racial and political diversity are almost non-existent but just about any other minority you could think of is represented here." Many students "attended a different college previously or spent some time in the workforce after high school." Prescott reportedly "puts a lot of effort into being queer friendly" as well and "there are many gay and several transgendered students." Students tell us that most everyone is "diligent in their studies" and "truly interested in bettering the community." They are very intellectual students that happen to wear tye-dye-t-shirts and Chaco sandals that also love the environment and put all their energy into saving it!" says a student. "Most people here are intelligent, caring people who shower at least twice a week," declares a senior. "Almost no one is religious in a traditional sense but there is a spiritual element." Politically, students are "extremely leftwing." Conservatives are exotic. "I had one Republican classmate once," says a senior.

E-MAIL: ADMISSIONS@PRESCOTT.EDU • WEBSITE: WWW.PRESCOTT.EDU

THE PRINCETON REVIEW SAYS

Admissions

Very important factors considered include: Application essay, recommendation(s), rigor of secondary school record. *Important factors considered include:* Academic GPA, standardized test scores, character/personal qualities, extracurricular activities, interview, level of applicant's interest, talent/ability, volunteer work, work experience. *Other factors considered include:* First generation. SAT or ACT required; TOEFL required of all international applicants. High school diploma is required and GED is accepted. *Academic units recommended:* 4 English, 3 mathematics, 2 science, 1 foreign language, 3 social studies, 2 history, 1 visual/performing arts.

Financial Aid

Students should submit: FAFSA. The Princeton Review suggests that all financial aid forms be submitted as soon as possible after 1/1. *Need-based scholarships/grants offered:* Federal Pell, SEOG, state scholarships/grants, private scholarships, the school's own gift aid, ACT & SMART. *Loan aid offered:* FFEL Subsidized Stafford, FFEL Unsubsidized Stafford, FFEL PLUS. Applicants will be notified of awards on a rolling basis beginning 3/15. Federal Work-Study Program available. Institutional employment available. Off-campus job opportunities are good.

The Inside Word

The acceptance rate at Prescott is high. However, the applicant pool is very self-selecting, and Prescott is the kind of place that pays a lot of careful attention to each and every application. Decent grades are important but well-articulated essays are equally vital. Mentioning how dedicated you are to ecological concerns certainly won't hurt your cause. You also want to demonstrate the ability to self-motivate. Students here design their own academic programs and self-direction is nothing less than the bedrock of Prescott's culture. Standardized test score aren't required (though you should definitely send them if you've done well).

THE SCHOOL SAYS ". . ."

From The Admissions Office

"Prescott College highlights the dramatic educational return on investment when experience is at the center of learning. Tucked into a corner of the town in central Arizona of the same name, Prescott College is an evolving experiment in rejecting hierarchical thinking for collaboration and teamwork as the cornerstone of learning. This is an educational institution that puts students at the center in everything it does and is. Optional Grades. Narrative Evaluations. No barriers. Limited bureaucracy. No summa or magna or "best in show" ribbons. Just a peripatetic community of lively intellects and fearless explorers whose connecting threads are a passion for social responsibility and the environment, and a keen sense of adventure.

"At Prescott College, our goal is to fuel your passion and give you a deeper understanding of the world around you through collaborative learning and personal experience. We don't settle for the mundane college experience. Instead, we take learning outside the classroom and into the real world through experiential and field-based learning. From field studies, internships, and independent studies to community service and study abroad opportunities, our students are challenged to think critically, explore the world up close, and form solutions through collaborative efforts.

"If you're looking for a college experience unlike any other—the kind that enables you to take control of your education and truly make a positive impact in your community and in the world—then Prescott College is the ideal college for you."

SELECTIVITY

Admissions Rating	79
# of applicants	365
% of applicants accepted	77
% of acceptees attending	32
# of early decision applicants	16
% accepted early decision	94

FRESHMAN PROFILE

Range SAT Critical Reading	460–660
Range SAT Math	430–600
Range SAT Writing	470–610
Range ACT Composite	18–27
Minimum paper TOEFL	550
Minimum computer TOEFL	213
Minimum web-based TOEFL	61
Average HS GPA	3.09
% graduated top 10% of class	11
% graduated top 25% of class	32
% graduated top 50% of class	57

DEADLINES

Early decision	
Deadline	12/1
Notification	12/15
Regular	
Priority	3/1
Deadline	8/15
Notification	rolling
Nonfall registration?	yes

APPLICANTS ALSO LOOK AT

AND OFTEN PREFER
Mills College
Earlham College
College of the Atlantic

AND SOMETIMES PREFER
Whitman College

AND RARELY PREFER
Hendrix College
Reed College
The Evergreen State College
University of Arizona
Sarah Lawrence College

FINANCIAL FACTS

Financial Aid Rating	77
Annual tuition	$9,864
Books and supplies	$624
% frosh rec. need-based scholarship or grant aid	51
% UG rec. need-based scholarship or grant aid	58
% frosh rec. non-need-based scholarship or grant aid	1
% frosh rec. need-based self-help aid	51
% UG rec. need-based self-help aid	71
% frosh rec. any financial aid	83
% UG rec. any financial aid	83
% UG borrow to pay for school	72
Average cumulative indebtedness	$11,495

PRINCETON UNIVERSITY

PO Box 430, Admission Office, Princeton, NJ 08544-0430 • Admissions: 609-258-3060 • Fax: 609-258-6743

CAMPUS LIFE

Quality of Life Rating	96
Fire Safety Rating	60*
Green Rating	97
Type of school	private
Environment	town

STUDENTS

Total undergrad enrollment	4,878
% male/female	52/48
% from out of state	84
% from public high school	56.2
% live on campus	98
% African American	8
% Asian	15
% Caucasian	51
% Hispanic	8
% Native American	1
% international	10

SURVEY SAYS . . .

No one cheats
Great library
School is well run
Campus feels safe
Low cost of living

ACADEMICS

Academic Rating	98
Calendar	semester
Student/faculty ratio	5:1
Profs interesting rating	84
Profs accessible rating	93
Most common reg class size	10–19 students
Most common lab size	10–19 students

MOST POPULAR MAJORS

economics
history
political science and government

STUDENTS SAY ". . ."

Academics

An Ivy League institution with a singular focus on undergraduate study (and one of the best engineering schools in the Ivy League" to boot), Princeton University upholds every ounce of its reputation, according to students. With top-notch, "endless" resources at each student's disposal, terrific financial aid packages (no student loans!), and a centuries-old reputation, the school provides the "academic and social opportunity of a lifetime," all within the gothic walls of a beautiful, enclosed New Jersey campus. "Princeton is all about learning; every second is an educational experience," one student says. Though the academics can be "grueling," they're also well worth the effort, and work is "never assigned without a reason. [There is] no busywork." The administration's ongoing effort to curb grade inflation means that competition does exist at Princeton, although it's mainly competition with one's self— "discovering the drive and focus to spend time for your academic classes and extracurriculars" is the one of the hardest parts of being a student here. "Princeton is full of opportunities to further your interests, but only if you actively take a role," says a sophomore. Still, students are all supportive of continuing the Princeton tradition of excellence, and the "strong student body" allows for "better class discussions and more meaningful projects." There's no question that the professors (who teach all of the classes) here are all-stars in their fields. "We're using textbooks that they wrote and studying theories that they developed," says a student. "In my biology for non-science majors class, my Nobel-prize winning professor personally taught me how to use a microscope! If that's not passion for teaching, I don't know what is!" says another. The administration has fans in most students; while there are "regular tiffs" with the administration over some aspects of school life (one suggests that "less administrative intervention could improve the school"), those in charge (especially within the school's residential colleges) are "very friendly, accessible, and helpful in resolving student-life issues."

Life

Even though Princetonian lives are lived out mostly on campus, tiny Princeton is "the perfect distance" from NYC, Philadelphia, and some beautiful beaches for those students who do choose to pop out for a bit. Everyone is constantly busy, not just with the large amounts of work but "with a range of extracurricular activities from athletics to dance groups." Princeton's unique "eating clubs"—10 social clubs that are housed in off-campus mansions and that upperclassmen can join and enjoy the right to eat, "hang out, relax, study, party, and everything in between" keep most partying ("once or twice a week") in a safe setting amongst fellow students. There is, however, somewhat of a divide "between students who spend time at eating clubs (80% or so) and students who choose to abstain from partying and prefer to study." Most of the clubs are "very accessible" to all students for events, and "it's nice to have the social scene localized to one [place close to] campus, because everyone always knows where the parties will be." One student refers to a popular saying on campus, "Academics, social life, and sleep: pick two."

Student Body

The typical Princetonian has a work-hard/play-hard mentality—working very, very hard on weeknights, but "willing to put down their books to party on the weekends." Students tend to get "absorbed" in their work at crunch times. Though not even close to a majority, there is definitely a segment of the population that "holes up in their rooms" to study, in direct contrast to the "social" student that one typically meets around campus. This bunch of "competitive, brilliant" students has a mix of typical and atypical and no real problem reconciling the two, though students would like to see diversity increase even further than it has in recent years. "From star athletes to musical prodigies to academic powerhouses, everyone brings something different to the table," says a student. This driven group "thinks about how to be successful in their lives after Princeton, and [they] plan accordingly."

FINANCIAL AID: 609-258-3330 • E-MAIL: UAOFFICE@PRINCETON.EDU •WEBSITE: WWW.PRINCETON.EDU

THE PRINCETON REVIEW SAYS

Admissions

Very important factors considered include: Class rank, application essay, academic GPA, recommendation(s), rigor of secondary school record, standardized test scores, character/personal qualities, talent/ability. *Important factors considered include:* Extracurricular activities. *Other factors considered include:* Alumni/ae relation, first generation, geographical residence, interview, racial/ethnic status, volunteer work, work experience. SAT or ACT required; ACT with Writing component required; TOEFL required of all international applicants. High school diploma or equivalent is not required. *Academic units recommended:* 4 English, 4 mathematics, 4 science, (2 science labs), 4 foreign language, 2 social studies, 2 history.

Financial Aid

Students should submit: FAFSA, institution's own financial aid form, Institutional noncustodial Parent's Form. The Princeton Review suggests that all financial aid forms be submitted as soon as possible after 1/1. *Need-based scholarships/grants offered:* Federal Pell, SEOG, state scholarships/grants, private scholarships, the school's own gift aid. *Loan aid offered:* FFEL Subsidized Stafford, FFEL Unsubsidized Stafford, FFEL PLUS, Federal Perkins, college/university loans from institutional funds. Applicants will be notified of awards on or about 4/1. Federal Work-Study Program available. Institutional employment available. Off-campus job opportunities are good.

The Inside Word

Princeton is much more open about the admissions process than the rest of their Ivy compatriots. The admissions staff evaluates candidates' credentials using a 1–5 rating scale, common among highly selective colleges. Princeton's recommendation to interview should be considered a requirement, given the ultracompetitive nature of the applicant pool. In addition, three SAT Subject Tests are required.

THE SCHOOL SAYS "..."

From The Admissions Office

"Methods of instruction [at Princeton] vary widely, but common to all areas is a strong emphasis on individual responsibility and the free interchange of ideas. This is displayed most notably in the wide use of preceptorials and seminars, in the provision of independent study for all upperclass students and qualified underclass students, and in the availability of a series of special programs to meet a range of individual interests. The undergraduate college encourages the student to be an independent seeker of information and to assume responsibility for gaining both knowledge and judgment that will strengthen later contributions to society.

Princeton offers a distinctive financial aid program that provides grants, which do not have to be repaid, rather than loans. Princeton meets the full demonstrated financial need of all students—domestic and international—offered admission. More than half of Princeton's undergraduates receive financial aid.

"All applicants must submit results for both the SAT as well as SAT Subject Tests in three different subject areas."

SELECTIVITY
Admissions Rating	99
# of applicants	21,370
% of applicants accepted	10
% of acceptees attending	59
# accepting a place on wait list	1,061
% admitted from wait list	14

FRESHMAN PROFILE
Range SAT Critical Reading	690–790
Range SAT Math	700–790
Range SAT Writing	690–780
Range ACT Composite	31–34
Minimum paper TOEFL	600
Minimum computer TOEFL	250
Average HS GPA	3.86
% graduated top 10% of class	97
% graduated top 25% of class	100
% graduated top 50% of class	100

DEADLINES
Regular	
Deadline	1/1
Notification	3/31
Nonfall registration?	no

APPLICANTS ALSO LOOK AT AND SOMETIMES PREFER
Harvard College
Stanford University
Massachusetts Institute of Technology
Yale University

FINANCIAL FACTS
Financial Aid Rating	98
Annual tuition	$35,340
Room and board	$11,680
Books and supplies	$1,200
% frosh rec. need-based scholarship or grant aid	54
% UG rec. need-based scholarship or grant aid	53
% frosh rec. need-based self-help aid	54
% UG rec. need-based self-help aid	53
% frosh rec. any financial aid	57
% UG rec. any financial aid	56
% UG borrow to pay for school	22
Average cumulative indebtedness	$5,955

PROVIDENCE COLLEGE

RIVER AVENUE AND EATON STREET, PROVIDENCE, RI 02918 • ADMISSIONS: 401-865-2535 • FAX: 401-865-2826

CAMPUS LIFE

Quality of Life Rating	**68**
Fire Safety Rating	**96**
Green Rating	**74**
Type of school	private
Affiliation	Roman Catholic
Environment	city

STUDENTS

Total undergrad enrollment	3,938
% male/female	44/56
% from out of state	87
% from public high school	54
% live on campus	76
% African American	2
% Asian	3
% Caucasian	81
% Hispanic	3
% international	1
# of countries represented	21

SURVEY SAYS . . .

Diversity lacking on campus
Everyone loves the Friars
Intramural sports are popular
Frats and sororities are unpopular or nonexistent
Student government is popular
Lots of beer drinking
Hard liquor is popular

ACADEMICS

Academic Rating	**80**
Calendar	semester
Student/faculty ratio	12:1
Profs interesting rating	72
Profs accessible rating	78
Most common reg class size	20–29 students
Most common lab size	10–19 students

MOST POPULAR MAJORS

biology/biological sciences
business administration and management
marketing/marketing management

STUDENTS SAY ". . ."

Academics

Providence College, "a solid, respectable school with a reputation for having fun," appeals both to those who seek an "intense curriculum" ("especially the Development of Western Civilization course" that can be "stressful and time-consuming" though "it offers a great liberal arts background") and to those who simply want "challenging classes" in an atmosphere that balances "academic and personal growth with an incredibly fun social scene." The centerpiece of the PC experience is "the four-semester Civ program, through which the school truly molds the mind with classical training and gives us a basic understanding of how our civilization came to be where it is today." While some students dismiss the sequence as "unnecessary to our success in the future," others appreciate the forced immersion in philosophy, history, art, and theology, noting "I am happy I am forced to take Civ because I would not have enrolled into any other courses that deal with the topics introduced in Civ." PC academics are "demanding," but "the school has great support systems for academics" "even outside the classroom stuff. The library has lots of different resources and there's always someone around to help." Undergrads also appreciate how "being in a smaller school, there are more opportunities to excel in one's chosen field, whether it's getting an internship in a biology lab, writing for the newspaper, or starring in a theatrical production."

Life

Social life at Providence College "revolves around the off-campus bars and the off-campus houses. While there are other activities to participate in, the main focus is drinking." One undergrad reports, "Kids work hard from Sunday night to Thursday afternoon; then the weekend starts, and everyone hits the bars." However, it would be remiss to assume students here do nothing but study and drink—on the contrary, there is "a huge focus on extracurriculars," so much so that students always try to "balance and manage" their time between "schoolwork and a social life." Intercollegiate athletics "are extremely popular (all the hockey games are packed) and bring a great atmosphere to the campus," and intramurals "are lots of fun. There's even a noncompetitive division for students who only want to have fun." Community service "is also really popular. Students are always busy donating their time to different groups." Downtown Providence has a lot to offer; it has "a great music scene, theater, and lots of art venues. The restaurants are good too." Students can access the city easily as "public transportation is free for us. It's only 5 minutes to downtown, and the bus runs right through campus."

Student Body

Though Providence students "are not the most diverse group," "The administration is really emphasizing our need for people who are different" from what some perceive to be the usual "cookie-cutter" student. That said, students report, by and large, that they are "all comfortable with one another and it is easy to fit in," noting a "strong sense of community." The typical student here "is a white, upper-middle class kid who went to a private/Catholic prep school in New England" and "looks as though he stepped off the pages of the Hollister/Abercrombie catalog." Students who do not fit the mold "seem to form their own peer groups for the most part. Interaction between atypical and typical students is not a problem." One student says that "everyone is working together to try to come up with ways to make our student population more diverse, both ethnically and economically." Most here are "friendly and hardworking and are very involved in various organizations, from Student Government to intramural sports to the Board of Multicultural Student Affairs...we are proud of our school."

FINANCIAL AID: 401-865-2286 • E-MAIL: PCADMISS@PROVIDENCE.EDU • WEBSITE: WWW.PROVIDENCE.EDU

THE PRINCETON REVIEW SAYS

Admissions

Very important factors considered include: Academic GPA, recommendation(s), rigor of secondary school record. *Important factors considered include:* Application essay, character/personal qualities, extracurricular activities. *Other factors considered include:* Class rank, standardized test scores, alumni/ae relation, first generation, geographical residence, level of applicant's interest, racial/ethnic status, state residency, talent/ability, volunteer work, work experience. Test optional; TOEFL required of all international applicants. High school diploma is required. *Academic units required:* 4 English, 4 mathematics, 3 science, (2 science labs), 3 foreign language, 2 social studies, 2 history. *Academic units recommended:* 4 English, 4 mathematics, 4 science, (2 science labs), 3 foreign language, 2 social studies, 2 history.

Financial Aid

Students should submit: FAFSA, CSS/Financial Aid PROFILE, business/farm supplement. Regular filing deadline is 2/1. The Princeton Review suggests that all financial aid forms be submitted as soon as possible after 1/1. *Need-based scholarships/grants offered:* Federal Pell, SEOG, state scholarships/grants, private scholarships, the school's own gift aid, Federal Academic Competitive Grant/Smart Grant. *Loan aid offered:* Direct Subsidized Stafford, Direct Unsubsidized Stafford, Direct PLUS, FFEL Subsidized Stafford, FFEL Unsubsidized Stafford, FFEL PLUS, Federal Perkins. Applicants will be notified of awards on or about 4/1. Federal Work-Study Program available. Institutional employment available. Off-campus job opportunities are good.

The Inside Word

Few schools can claim a more transparent admissions process than Providence College. The admissions section of the school's Website includes a voluminous blog authored by the school's senior admissions counselor. Surf on over to http://blogs.targetx.com/providence/ScottSeseske and learn everything you could possibly want to know about the how, what, when, and why of admissions decisions at Providence.

THE SCHOOL SAYS "..."

From The Admissions Office

"Infused with the history, tradition, and learning of a 700-year-old Catholic teaching order, the Dominican Friars, Providence College offers a value-affirming environment where students are enriched through spiritual, social, physical, and cultural growth as well as through intellectual development. Providence College offers more than 51 programs of study plus 49 majors leading to baccalaureate degrees in business, education, the sciences, arts, and humanities. Our faculty is noted for a strong commitment to teaching. A close student/faculty relationship allows for in-depth classwork, independent research projects, and detailed career exploration. While noted for the physical facilities and academic opportunities associated with larger universities, Providence also fosters personal growth through a small, spirited, family-like atmosphere that encourages involvement in student activities and athletics.

"Submission of standardized test scores is optional for students applying for admission. This policy change allows each student to decide whether they wish to have their standardized test results considered as part of their application for admission. Students who choose not to submit SAT or ACT test scores will not be penalized in the review for admission. Additional details about the test-optional policy can be found on our website at Providence.edu/testoptionalpolicy."

SELECTIVITY

Admissions Rating	93
# of applicants	8,844
% of applicants accepted	45
% of acceptees attending	25
# accepting a place on wait list	932
% admitted from wait list	19

FRESHMAN PROFILE

Range SAT Critical Reading	530–630
Range SAT Math	540–640
Range SAT Writing	550–650
Range ACT Composite	23–28
Minimum paper TOEFL	550
Minimum computer TOEFL	215
Minimum web-based TOEFL	80
Average HS GPA	3.47
% graduated top 10% of class	44
% graduated top 25% of class	80
% graduated top 50% of class	98

DEADLINES

Early action	
Deadline	11/1
Notification	1/1
Regular	
Deadline	1/15
Notification	4/1
Nonfall registration?	yes

APPLICANTS ALSO LOOK AT

AND OFTEN PREFER
College of the Holy Cross
Boston College

AND SOMETIMES PREFER
Loyola College in Maryland
Villanova University

AND RARELY PREFER
Fairfield University
University of Connecticut
Fordham University

FINANCIAL FACTS

Financial Aid Rating	74
Annual tuition	$30,800
Room and board	$11,360
Required fees	$800
Books and supplies	$800
% frosh rec. need-based scholarship or grant aid	44
% UG rec. need-based scholarship or grant aid	52
% frosh rec. non-need-based scholarship or grant aid	6
% UG rec. non-need-based scholarship or grant aid	6
% frosh rec. need-based self-help aid	45
% UG rec. need-based self-help aid	46
% frosh rec. athletic scholarships	4
% UG rec. athletic scholarships	3
% frosh rec. any financial aid	75
% UG rec. any financial aid	74
% UG borrow to pay for school	64
Average cumulative indebtedness	$33,297

PURDUE UNIVERSITY—WEST LAFAYETTE

1080 Schleman Hall, West Lafayette, IN 47907 • Admissions: 765-494-1776 • Fax: 765-494-0544

CAMPUS LIFE

Quality of Life Rating	**89**
Fire Safety Rating	**89**
Green Rating	**82**
Type of school	public
Environment	town

STUDENTS

Total undergrad enrollment	31,761
% male/female	58/42
% from out of state	35
% live on campus	33
% in (# of) fraternities	9 (49)
% in (# of) sororities	6 (29)
% African American	3
% Asian	5
% Caucasian	80
% Hispanic	3
% Native American	1
% international	7
# of countries represented	128

SURVEY SAYS . . .

Great food on campus
Students are happy
Everyone loves the Boilermakers
Student publications are popular

ACADEMICS

Academic Rating	**78**
Calendar	semester
Student/faculty ratio	14:1
Profs interesting rating	69
Profs accessible rating	81
% classes taught by TAs	26
Most common reg class size	fewer than 10 students
Most common lab size	10–19 students

MOST POPULAR MAJORS

biology/biological sciences
business administration and management
mechanical engineering

STUDENTS SAY " . . ."

Academics

Purdue University is a large public school in Indiana that has a "hardcore engineering" reputation far and wide. However, there are more than 200 majors here and many students insist that Purdue's liberal arts programs are "underrated" and "much bigger than people think." Programs in pharmacy, nursing, business, hotel management, agriculture, and education are also laudable. The "student-oriented" top brass is reportedly "great." The "archaic" registration process is "a hassle for everyone," but "everything is very organized and the people who work in administration are genuinely there to help the students." While classes do get smaller at the upper levels, Purdue's general education courses are "always packed." The faculty really runs the gamut. "Professors are here to do two things: research and teach, usually in that order," explains a molecular biology major. "As such, they are very intelligent people. Their ability to express their information, however, is a case-by-case situation." There are professors who "only teach classes because they have to" and "there are some teaching assistants who can barely speak English." Other professors "like teaching" and are "willing to help students outside of class." The academic experience at Purdue can also vary wildly from major to major. For engineers "classes are insanely tough, yet satisfying." Getting through the introductory courses is a grueling rite of passage. "While some of the weed-out classes seem difficult and pointless, they really do prepare you for upper level courses," promises a chemical engineering major.

Life

Purdue boasts an "absolutely amazing" freshman orientation program and, with more than 800 clubs and organizations, "there is something for everyone." "Purdue is a party school if you're a partier, a place to succeed for the academically oriented, a Big Ten school for the sports fan, and a place for anyone to completely blend in or stand out," explains a sophomore. Intramural sports are popular. If you enjoy large percussion instruments, Purdue's Big Bass Drum is the planet's largest. The Greek system is also considerable and "fraternity parties are huge." Students who are of age frequently take advantage of a thriving bar scene. Tradition is also a noticeable part of campus life. Purdue students love being Boilermakers. "During football season, we have the great tradition of Breakfast Club, where people dress in ridiculous costumes and wake up at the crack of dawn because the bars open at 7:00 A.M.," explains a sophomore, "but make sure you get there early, because they start lining up around 6:00 A.M." Purdue is located in a "typical college town" "in the middle of cornfields." On campus, "there is a lot of concrete." "You can walk to everything" and "some buildings are wonderful and state of the art." Others could use renovation. Dorm rooms are "a little small." The student recreation facilities are "crowded." "Parking can be a little hectic." Some students also complain that the weather around here is "awful." While the climates in Indianapolis and Chicago aren't any better, both cities are a reasonable drive away.

Student Body

"Many students at Purdue are typical Midwesterners from a suburb of Chicago or Indianapolis." Others are "country kids" from the rural towns that dot Indiana. There are substantially more men here than women, which you will find to be the case at almost any engineering-heavy school. Students note that there are "lots of international students" and they argue that "Purdue is a lot more diverse than it is given credit for." "Students take academics very seriously here." They are "laid back but not lazy." "They're friendly, amiable, and open to many different people and experiences." "The Greeks and non-Greeks mix pretty well." Though there is some tension because "many of the engineering and science students look at anyone else as stupid and destined to work at McDonald's," but everyone else gets along for the most part. Politically, "liberalism is very alive," but Purdue is "a more conservative" campus. Mostly, though, it doesn't matter because "no one is really politically motivated."

PURDUE UNIVERSITY—WEST LAFAYETTE

FINANCIAL AID: 765-494-5050 • E-MAIL: ADMISSIONS@PURDUE.EDU • WEBSITE: WWW.PURDUE.EDU

THE PRINCETON REVIEW SAYS
Admissions
Very important factors considered include: Application essay, rigor of secondary school record, standardized test scores. *Important factors considered include:* Class rank, academic GPA, geographical residence, racial/ethnic status. *Other factors considered include:* Recommendation(s), alumni/ae relation, character/personal qualities, extracurricular activities, first generation, state residency, volunteer work, work experience. SAT or ACT required; ACT with Writing component required; TOEFL required of all international applicants. High school diploma is required and GED is accepted. *Academic units required:* 4 English, 3 mathematics, 2 science, (2 science labs), 2 foreign language, 3 social studies. *Academic units recommended:* 4 mathematics, 3 science, (3 science labs).

Financial Aid
Students should submit: FAFSA. The Princeton Review suggests that all financial aid forms be submitted as soon as possible after 1/1. *Need-based scholarships/grants offered:* Federal Pell, SEOG, state scholarships/grants, private scholarships, the school's own gift aid, Federal Academic Competitiveness Grant (ACG) and National SMART Grant Program. *Loan aid offered:* William D. Ford Federal Direct Loan Program for Stafford, Unsubsidized Stafford and PLUS loans; Federal Perkins; college/university loans from institutional funds. Applicants will be notified of awards on or about 4/15. Federal Work-Study Program available. Institutional employment available. Off-campus job opportunities are good.

The Inside Word
The fact that Purdue holds class rank as one of its most important considerations in the admission of candidates is troublesome. There are far too many inconsistencies in ranking policies and class size among the 25,000-plus high schools in the United States to place so much weight on an essentially incomparable number. The university's high admit rate thankfully renders the issue relatively moot.

THE SCHOOL SAYS "..."
From The Admissions Office
"Although it is one of America's largest universities, Purdue does not 'feel' big to its students. The campus is very compact when compared to universities with similar enrollment. Purdue is a comprehensive university with an international reputation in a wide range of academic fields. A strong work ethic prevails at Purdue. As a member of the Big Ten, Purdue has a strong and diverse athletic program. Purdue offers more than 800 clubs and organizations. The residence halls and Greek community offer many participatory activities for students. Numerous convocations and lectures are presented each year. Purdue is all about people, and allowing students to grow academically as well as socially, preparing them for the real world.

"Applicants seeking admission are required to have their SAT or ACT test score sent from the testing agency. Purdue accepts either test, will use the best score, and requires a Writing score."

SELECTIVITY
Admissions Rating	87
# of applicants	29,952
% of applicants accepted	72
% of acceptees attending	33

FRESHMAN PROFILE
Range SAT Critical Reading	490–610
Range SAT Math	530–660
Range SAT Writing	490–600
Range ACT Composite	23–28
Minimum paper TOEFL	550
Minimum computer TOEFL	213
Minimum web-based TOEFL	79
Average HS GPA	3.5
% graduated top 10% of class	30
% graduated top 25% of class	65
% graduated top 50% of class	93

DEADLINES
Regular	
Priority	3/1
Notification	modified rolling
Nonfall registration?	yes

AND SOMETIMES PREFER
Valparaiso University
University of Illinois at Urbana-Champaign
Indiana University—Bloomington

FINANCIAL FACTS
Financial Aid Rating	82
Annual in-state tuition	$7,750
Annual out-of-state tuition	$23,224
Room and board	$7,930
Required fees	$433
Books and supplies	$1,140
% frosh rec. need-based scholarship or grant aid	27
% UG rec. need-based scholarship or grant aid	27
% frosh rec. non-need-based scholarship or grant aid	23
% UG rec. non-need-based scholarship or grant aid	14
% frosh rec. need-based self-help aid	36
% UG rec. need-based self-help aid	37
% frosh rec. athletic scholarships	1
% UG rec. athletic scholarships	1
% frosh rec. any financial aid	72
% UG rec. any financial aid	75
% UG borrow to pay for school	48
Average cumulative indebtedness	$23,087

QUINNIPIAC UNIVERSITY

275 MOUNT CARMEL AVENUE, HAMDEN, CT 06518 • ADMISSIONS: 203-582-8600 • FAX: 203-582-8906

CAMPUS LIFE
Quality of Life Rating	75
Fire Safety Rating	95
Green Rating	79
Type of school	private
Environment	town

STUDENTS
Total undergrad enrollment	5,747
% male/female	39/61
% from out of state	70
% from public high school	70
% live on campus	75
% in (# of) fraternities	6 (2)
% in (# of) sororities	8 (3)
% African American	3
% Asian	2
% Caucasian	80
% Hispanic	5
% international	1
# of countries represented	23

SURVEY SAYS . . .
Diversity lacking on campus
Low cost of living
Hard liquor is popular
(Almost) no one smokes

ACADEMICS
Academic Rating	82
Calendar	semester
Student/faculty ratio	12:1
Profs interesting rating	76
Profs accessible rating	74
Most common reg class size	10–19 students
Most common lab size	10–19 students

MOST POPULAR MAJORS
business/commerce
physical therapy/therapist
psychology

STUDENTS SAY ". . ."

Academics

Quinnipiac University, "a professional school with the goal of educating its students to succeed in the future," boasts excellent programs in business, communications, and the health sciences, especially in those for nursing, physician's assistant, and physical and occupational therapy. Undergrads insist that QU's physical therapy program "is the best in the region." "The structure of the PT program is so well thought out that each class is working off the other in helping me get a education and actually learn the material," one student reports. Students in all health science fields appreciate QU's regional cache, especially when it comes time to apply to graduate school or to find a job. Communications and journalism majors get plenty of hands-on experience in the school's "full green-screen room as well as editing, media production, and journalist rooms." The departments produce "lively student television programming (news, sports, a game show, a travel show, and soon a cooking show), an excellent student newspaper, and an eclectic student radio station." Future teachers also find a happy home at QU; the school offers "a great five-year teaching program" that confers both a BA and a masters. "It's excellent preparation for teachers," one student tells us. By developing a number of hallmark programs, QU has elevated its national profile considerably, and students approvingly observe that the school "is focused on growing and becoming a school on the rise. There have been a lot of improvements on campus and [administrators] actually are interested in the students' opinions."

Life

According to most students, QU is your prototypical 'work hard, play hard' school. As one undergrad explains, "I spend Monday through Thursday doing loads of homework/studying, and as soon as Friday comes, it's time to party. Almost everyone on campus drinks, and a lot of people take the shuttles to bars and clubs." But while "drinking is definitely the students' most popular activity," it's hardly the only option. "When there is a men's ice hockey game, a lot of people get tickets and attend," students report, and basketball is also popular (both teams play in "a beautiful new arena"). QU offers a number of dry options, and "a lot of students stay sober and still have a great time with their friends or at school-sponsored events." Those looking "for quieter activities" can avail themselves of "the movie theater, bowling allies, and a ton of restaurants in Hamden, North Haven, and New Haven." The campus itself "is consistently described as a country club, and it's not far from the truth. The dorms as well as the campus are gorgeous."

Student Body

"The typical 'Quinnipiac Girl' (yes we say that here)," according to one student, "is very fashion-forward and is from Long Island. She is always in designer clothing, and in the winter she wears Uggs, tight leggings, and a North Face jacket carrying either a really nice, leather Coach bag or a Vera Bradley bag. The typical boy is also from Long Island and is Italian. He also wears fashion clothing." It's easy to dismiss these students as "mostly spoiled [and] rich" at first glace, but students caution against doing that. Says one, "Once you realize that's not everyone, and you actually get involved in the school, you realize the people at QU are amazing! It's a great place to be." True, some bad apples have generated "negative "press due to several racial incidents on campus" in recent years, "but that does not reflect the majority of students at QU," many here assure us. If anything, "students tend to be naive about other ethnicities because the majority of people at Quinnipiac are Caucasian" and "very sheltered."

FINANCIAL AID: 203-582-8750 • E-MAIL: ADMISSIONS@QUINNIPIAC.EDU • WEBSITE: WWW.QUINNIPIAC.EDU

THE PRINCETON REVIEW SAYS

Admissions

Very important factors considered include: Rigor of secondary school record. *Important factors considered include:* Class rank, application essay, academic GPA, standardized test scores. *Other factors considered include:* Recommendation(s), alumni/ae relation, character/personal qualities, extracurricular activities, interview, level of applicant's interest, racial/ethnic status, talent/ability, volunteer work, work experience. SAT or ACT required; ACT with Writing component recommended; TOEFL required of all international applicants. High school diploma is required and GED is accepted. *Academic units required:* 4 English, 3 mathematics, 3 science, (2 science labs), 2 foreign language, 2 social studies, 4 years of Science and Math required in PT,OT, Nursing and PA. *Academic units recommended:* 4 English, 4 mathematics, 4 science, (3 science labs), 2 foreign language, 3 social studies.

Financial Aid

Students should submit: FAFSA. The Princeton Review suggests that all financial aid forms be submitted as soon as possible after 1/1. *Need-based scholarships/grants offered:* Federal Pell, SEOG, state scholarships/grants, private scholarships, the school's own gift aid, Federal Nursing Scholarships. *Loan aid offered:* FFEL Subsidized Stafford, FFEL Unsubsidized Stafford, FFEL PLUS, Federal Perkins, Federal Nursing, state loans. Applicants will be notified of awards on a rolling basis beginning 2/15. Federal Work-Study Program available. Institutional employment available. Off-campus job opportunities are excellent.

The Inside Word

Quinnipiac admits students on a rolling basis, a process that favors those who get their applications in early. Programs in physical therapy, nursing, and physician assistant are quite competitive. The school strongly recommends that those seeking spots in these programs apply no later than early November.

THE SCHOOL SAYS "..."

From The Admissions Office

"The appeal of Quinnipiac University continues to grow each year. Our students come from a variety of states and backgrounds. Seventy-five percent of the freshman class is from out of state. Students come from 25 states and 18 countries. Nearly 30 percent of current undergraduates plan to stay at Quinnipiac to complete their graduate degrees. As admission becomes more competitive and our enrollment remains stable, the university continues to focus on its mission: to provide outstanding academic programs in a student-oriented environment on a campus with a strong sense of community. The development of an honors program, a highly regarded emerging leaders student-life program, and a 'writing across the curriculum' initiative in academic affairs, form the foundation for excellence in business, communications, health sciences, education, liberal arts, and law. The university has a fully digital high-definition production studio in the School of Communications; the Terry Goodwin '67 Financial Technology Center which provides a high-tech simulated trading floor in the School of Business; and a critical care lab for our nursing and physician assistant majors. All incoming students purchase a university-recommended laptop with wireless capabilities supported by a campus-wide network. More than 70 student organizations, 21 Division I teams, recreation and intramurals, community service, student publications, and a strong student government offer a variety of outside-of-class experiences. There are many clubs that get students involved in campus life. Multicultural awareness is supported through the Black Student Union, Asian/Pacific Islander Association, Latino Cultural Society, and GLASS. An active alumni association reflects the strong connection Quinnipiac has with its graduates, and they give the faculty high marks for career preparation. Students are encouraged to apply early in the fall of their senior year and can access our online application or the common application easily from our web site. We use the best individual scores on the SAT Reasoning Test (no Subject Tests required), or the ACT composite. We begin notifying students of our decisions in early January."

SELECTIVITY

Admissions Rating	88
# of applicants	14,994
% of applicants accepted	45
% of acceptees attending	22
# accepting a place on wait list	900
% admitted from wait list	23

FRESHMAN PROFILE

Range SAT Critical Reading	540–610
Range SAT Math	560–630
Range ACT Composite	23–27
Minimum paper TOEFL	550
Minimum computer TOEFL	213
Minimum web-based TOEFL	77
Average HS GPA	3.4
% graduated top 10% of class	25
% graduated top 25% of class	66
% graduated top 50% of class	95

DEADLINES

Regular	
Priority	2/1
Notification	rolling
Nonfall registration?	yes

APPLICANTS ALSO LOOK AT

AND OFTEN PREFER
University of Connecticut
Boston University

AND SOMETIMES PREFER
University of Delaware
Fairfield University
Northeastern University

AND RARELY PREFER
Ithaca College
Sacred Heart University

FINANCIAL FACTS

Financial Aid Rating	66
Annual tuition	$31,100
Room and board	$12,520
Required fees	$1,300
Books and supplies	$800
% frosh rec. need-based scholarship or grant aid	55
% UG rec. need-based scholarship or grant aid	55
% frosh rec. non-need-based scholarship or grant aid	28
% UG rec. non-need-based scholarship or grant aid	22
% frosh rec. need-based self-help aid	46
% UG rec. need-based self-help aid	48
% frosh rec. athletic scholarships	5
% UG rec. athletic scholarships	4
% frosh rec. any financial aid	70
% UG rec. any financial aid	68
% UG borrow to pay for school	70
Average cumulative indebtedness	$37,839

RANDOLPH COLLEGE

2500 RIVERMONT AVENUE, LYNCHBURG, VA 24503-1526 • ADMISSIONS: 434-947-8100 • FAX: 434-947-8996

CAMPUS LIFE
Quality of Life Rating	**88**
Fire Safety Rating	**87**
Green Rating	**73**
Type of school	private
Affiliation	Methodist
Environment	city

STUDENTS
Total undergrad enrollment	549
% male/female	18/82
% from out of state	52
% from public high school	78
% live on campus	88
% African American	9
% Asian	3
% Caucasian	66
% Hispanic	7
% Native American	1
% international	12
# of countries represented	33

SURVEY SAYS . . .
No one cheats
Diverse student types on campus
Different types of students interact
Dorms are like palaces
Campus feels safe
Frats and sororities are unpopular or nonexistent
Student government is popular

ACADEMICS
Academic Rating	**95**
Calendar	semester
Student/faculty ratio	7:1
Profs interesting rating	95
Profs accessible rating	88
Most common reg class size	fewer than 10 students
Most common lab size	fewer than 10 students

MOST POPULAR MAJORS
biology/biological sciences
political science and government
psychology

STUDENTS SAY ". . ."

Academics

Randolph College offers "a combination of great academics, cultural integrity, individuality, and tradition" to its 700-plus students on a "small, yet beautiful" campus. Many chose the school based on "its location," "its reputation," and "the quality of its academics." As one undergrad explains, "I decided to attend Randolph because I wanted a school that melded fun, wacky traditions; strong academics; small classes with teachers who really get to know you well; a family-like community; and a school that makes you feel at home." Expect to "work" here thanks to "rigorous" classes. The school's small size allows students and faculty to "take the time to have conversations." (Some here boast that certain classes have "as few as three students"). In addition to small class sizes, "the professors are excellent, exceptionally so." Though praise for the "fantastic" professors is virtually unanimous, student opinion regarding the administration is decidedly mixed. Some undergrads are quick to assert that the administration is "very caring and helpful with any student they encounter." And one content sophomore highlights that The Dean of College Offices is "accessible...and offers great advice about tackling problems." However, others feel that the school administration sometimes makes decisions "without considering the view point of the rest of the college community."

Life

Thanks to Randolph's "rigorous" coursework, many here note that "there really isn't much time for things other than studying." But you won't find any complaints regarding that here. "My life at school is usually stressful but rewarding," says one undergrad. "I'm in a number of clubs and organizations while still trying to find the time to finish my homework and study for exams." Randolph "is all about being a strong familial community that works hard and has fun traditions that make your life here a little extraordinary." These traditions provide for "a great experience and a lot of fun." For most undergrads, there's "a lot of reading," "hanging out with friends," "attending sporting events," and "trips to other schools on the weekends." Mostly, you get out of your social life what you put into it. "It's entirely up to the individual," explains a student, "unless you proactively go out to do something, it's not going to happen." With that in mind, if you're willing to put the time in, there are plenty of "activities and groups" and a "very diverse social life" to discover.

Student Body

As a rule, students at Randolph "are academically motivated and open to other ideas and cultures." In line with that, "Those that are not serious about academics or that are very close minded will most likely quickly find that this school is not the correct fit for them." This is due to the "great diversity of students" on campus that makes for some "extraordinarily unique" individuals who, despite differences, manage to "fit together perfectly." "There's enough diversity here for everyone to be different," says one undergrad, "but enough conformity for groups of friends to develop and interact with each other." Students are "serious but not very nerdy," "liberal," and "more informed than most." Despite academics being "the number one priority for students," most here are "very involved in a number of clubs and extracurricular activities." There are also "very few cliques," though "a few do exist." Some feel that "after the switch to coeducation...a disproportionate number of athletes" were admitted though the student body's passion for "equality, the environment, and education still prevails." Most students agree that Randolph's "close-knit community" is "a place where everybody really does know your name and everyone smiles at each other."

FINANCIAL AID: 434-947-8128 • E-MAIL: ADMISSIONS@RANDOLPHCOLLEGE.EDU • WEBSITE: WWW.RANDOLPHCOLLEGE.EDU

THE PRINCETON REVIEW SAYS

Admissions

Very important factors considered include: Academic GPA, rigor of secondary school record, character/personal qualities. *Important factors considered include:* Class rank, application essay, recommendation(s), standardized test scores, extracurricular activities. *Other factors considered include:* Alumni/ae relation, first generation, interview, level of applicant's interest, talent/ability, volunteer work, work experience. SAT or ACT required; TOEFL required of all international applicants. High school diploma is required and GED is accepted. *Academic units required:* 4 English, 3 mathematics, 2 science, (2 science labs), 3 foreign language, 2 history, 2 academic electives.

Financial Aid

Students should submit: FAFSA, state aid form. The Princeton Review suggests that all financial aid forms be submitted as soon as possible after 1/1. *Need-based scholarships/grants offered:* Federal Pell, SEOG, state scholarships/grants, private scholarships, the school's own gift aid. *Loan aid offered:* FFEL Subsidized Stafford, FFEL Unsubsidized Stafford, FFEL PLUS, Federal Perkins, college/university loans from institutional funds, Private Loans. Applicants will be notified of awards on a rolling basis beginning 3/1. Federal Work-Study Program available. Institutional employment available. Off-campus job opportunities are good.

The Inside Word

Admitting highly qualified and well-matched students is a top priority at Randolph, and applicants can rest assured that their applications will be given due consideration (something guaranteed not only by the school's small size, but also its recent switch from a women's-only college to a coeducational institution). There's no minimum GPA or standardized test score requirements, but be aware that most successful candidates have impressive classroom credentials. Character also plays an important role in admissions decisions; Randolph is looking for independent, confident students who place a premium on their educations.

THE SCHOOL SAYS "..."

From The Admissions Office

"If you want to live in a world in which your intelligence, energy, and purpose make a difference, Randolph College provides the educational experience you need.

"Nationally ranked and recognized for both its academic programs and affordability, Randolph College offers women and men the best features of an honors education with a global outlook, a wide range of majors, and an emphasis on real world experience. Embedded within the strong, liberal arts foundation are ample opportunities for study abroad, leadership roles, and working closely with faculty on research. All students are encouraged to pursue and achieve goals with personal meaning.

"A graduate of Randolph College understands the intellectual foundations of the arts, sciences, and humanities and has developed critical skills to learn, adapt, and succeed in a rapidly changing global environment. The college's strong emphasis on writing enables students to communicate clearly and persuasively, and our diverse student population and study abroad programs enable students to see and live through the eyes of another culture. The long-standing and unique honor system is a central part of daily life at Randolph and adds to the already close knit community feel.

"A member of the Old Dominion Athletic Conference, Randolph allows student scholar-athletes the opportunity to excel and participate in a variety of sports while focusing on academics. Located in the heart of Virginia, Randolph College's campus is part of the growing college town of Lynchburg and is located within easy driving distance of major cities and beaches, cultural and entertainment opportunities galore, and a variety of recreational activities."

SELECTIVITY

Admissions Rating	88
# of applicants	1,585
% of applicants accepted	84
% of acceptees attending	11

FRESHMAN PROFILE

Range SAT Critical Reading	500–630
Range SAT Math	490–600
Range ACT Composite	23–27
Minimum paper TOEFL	550
Minimum computer TOEFL	213
Minimum web-based TOEFL	79
Average HS GPA	3.3
% graduated top 10% of class	20
% graduated top 25% of class	60
% graduated top 50% of class	90

DEADLINES

Early action	
Deadline	12/1
Notification	12/15
Regular	
Priority	2/1
Deadline	4/1
Notification	4/15
Nonfall registration?	yes

APPLICANTS ALSO LOOK AT

AND OFTEN PREFER
University of Virginia
James Madison University

AND SOMETIMES PREFER
Sweet Briar College
College of William and Mary

AND RARELY PREFER
Randolph-Macon College
Virginia Tech
Hollins University

FINANCIAL FACTS

Financial Aid Rating	85
Annual tuition	$25,350
Room and board	$9,000
Required fees	$510
Books and supplies	$800
% frosh rec. need-based scholarship or grant aid	74
% UG rec. need-based scholarship or grant aid	66
% frosh rec. non-need-based scholarship or grant aid	22
% UG rec. non-need-based scholarship or grant aid	18
% frosh rec. need-based self-help aid	66
% UG rec. need-based self-help aid	58
% frosh rec. any financial aid	99
% UG rec. any financial aid	96
% UG borrow to pay for school	75
Average cumulative indebtedness	$27,218

REED COLLEGE

3203 SOUTHEAST WOODSTOCK BOULEVARD, PORTLAND, OR 97202-8199 • ADMISSIONS: 503-777-7511 • FAX: 503-777-7553

CAMPUS LIFE

Quality of Life Rating	93
Fire Safety Rating	60*
Green Rating	78
Type of school	private
Environment	metropolis

STUDENTS

Total undergrad enrollment	1,408
% male/female	44/56
% from out of state	86
% from public high school	59
% live on campus	64
% African American	3
% Asian	9
% Caucasian	56
% Hispanic	7
% Native American	1
% international	6
# of countries represented	41

SURVEY SAYS . . .

Students aren't religious
Dorms are like palaces
Campus feels safe
Frats and sororities are unpopular or nonexistent

ACADEMICS

Academic Rating	99
Calendar	semester
Student/faculty ratio	10:1
Profs interesting rating	99
Profs accessible rating	95
Most common reg class size	10–19 students
Most common lab size	10–19 students

MOST POPULAR MAJORS

biology/biological sciences
English language and literature
psychology

STUDENTS SAY ". . ."

Academics

Reed College, "offers a serious liberal-arts education in a small, creative, community" where "intellectualism is highly respected" and students pursue "learning for learning's sake" in "a challenging academic atmosphere." "We are a collection of those weird kids in high school who had a passionate interest in learning about something and made that interest academic, even if it wasn't beforehand," one student explains. They're the sort of students who seek out an "academic rigor that definitely prepares us for graduate school and scholarly work." "Small, discussion based classes, frequent interaction with professors, and general intellectual curiosity override all other aspects of the life at Reed," where "studying and going to classes is not somehow the price to pay for staying here (with the ultimate goal being the weekend and, eventually, a diploma); rather, it is the core joy of being at Reed." Unsurprisingly, "students work incredibly hard," but "the school is there for us every step of the way. As freshmen, students meet with their humanities professors after every paper one-on-one for paper conferences." Seniors must complete a thesis project; "When writing one's senior thesis, students meet with professors one-on-one for an hour every week." It's exactly the right sort of place for students who "want to be excited about school again," says one student. "I wanted to be around other people who were both excited about academics and excited about being at a place where academics excited them. I wanted to be in a place where people didn't take themselves too seriously but took their work seriously." Welcome to Reed.

Life

Reed is an academically intense school, so "a great amount of time is spent on academics, even on the weekends" here. "Late at night, it is not uncommon to see Reedies debating the merits of Thucydides and Herodotus or discussing the financial bailout package in the library lobby, dorm common rooms, and at the hotcake house (a nearby 24-hour pancake joint)," one student reports. But although "people are very involved in their studies, especially seniors and their individual theses…everyone keeps his or her own passions alive with student government, various hobbies (baking, knitting, singing, dancing), sports (rugby, ultimate Frisbee, and basketball), and often trips around the multiple neighborhoods of Portland." The city justly is celebrated for its coffee shops, restaurants, and bookstores. Annual campus traditions include Renn Fayre, "a three-day party at the end of the year at which students celebrate the completion of senior theses. Renn Fayre begins with Thesis Parade, in which seniors burn their thesis drafts in a bonfire in front of the library and then march in costume, covered in champagne and confetti through the library across the lawn to the registrar's office to turn in their [completed] theses."

Student Body

Reed students tend to be "smart, intellectually curious, and a little quirky." Politics tilt strongly to the left. One student reports, "There is virtually no political dialogue. The student body is so liberal the only dialogue is really between socialists and communists. For students who regard themselves as liberal and, consequentially, open-minded, there is very little acceptance of people who don't identify themselves as liberal or who simply like political dialogue." The student body is also "overwhelmingly Caucasian" and affluent, although students note there is "a growing population of minority students (minority in various senses) and they are making efforts constantly to establish themselves as a social presence on campus. Student groups like the Latino, Asian, and Black and African Student Unions and places like the Multicultural Resource Center offer places for support."

FINANCIAL AID: 800-547-4750 • E-MAIL: ADMISSION@REED.EDU • WEBSITE: WWW.REED.EDU

THE PRINCETON REVIEW SAYS

Admissions

Very important factors considered include: Application essay, academic GPA, rigor of secondary school record. *Important factors considered include:* Class rank, recommendation(s), standardized test scores, interview, level of applicant's interest. *Other factors considered include:* Alumni/ae relation, character/personal qualities, extracurricular activities, first generation, geographical residence, racial/ethnic status, talent/ability, volunteer work, work experience. SAT Subject Tests recommended; SAT or ACT required; TOEFL required of all international applicants. High school diploma is required and GED is accepted. *Academic units recommended:* 4 English, 4 mathematics, 3 science, 3 foreign language, 1 social studies, 3 history.

Financial Aid

Students should submit: FAFSA, institution's own financial aid form, CSS/Financial Aid PROFILE, noncustodial PROFILE. Regular filing deadline is 1/15. The Princeton Review suggests that all financial aid forms be submitted as soon as possible after 1/1. *Need-based scholarships/grants offered:* Federal Pell, SEOG, state scholarships/grants, private scholarships, the school's own gift aid. *Loan aid offered:* FFEL Subsidized Stafford, FFEL Unsubsidized Stafford, FFEL PLUS, Federal Perkins. Applicants will be notified of awards on or about 4/1. Federal Work-Study Program available. Institutional employment available.

The Inside Word

Reed admissions officers know exactly what type of student will thrive here, and that's who they seek. Being smart isn't enough to get in here. Reedies are fiercely intellectual, and more concerned with academic pursuits for their own sake than for any financial rewards their educations will produce. Successful applicants demonstrate genuine intellectual curiosity as well as the aptitude to handle a demanding curriculum.

THE SCHOOL SAYS "..."

From The Admissions Office

"Reed is animated and energized by its seemingly paradoxical features. Reed has, for example: 1) a traditional, classical, highly structured curriculum—yet, at the same time, a progressive, free-thinking, decidedly unstructured community culture; 2) a powerful emphasis on intellectuality, serious study, and the very highest standards of academic achievement—yet, at the same time, a rich and rewarding program of recreational and extracurricular activity, including a physical education requirement; 3) a refusal to overemphasize grades—yet, third in the nation in the production of future PhDs; 4) a faculty culture absolutely dedicated to superb undergraduate teaching—yet, at the same time, a faculty culture that supports and celebrates high-level research and scholarship at the cutting edge of each academic discipline.

"Reed is not a simple place. It's a complex amalgam of diverse elements. But those elements have been chosen and developed over the years with great care. The result is an intricate—even ornate—but utterly coherent and clearly articulated architecture that has been called by at least one outside observer 'exquisite' and by another 'the most intellectual college in the country.' Reed is not for everyone. But for students who are interested both in exploring great ideas and in developing personal autonomy, it makes very good sense indeed.

"Reed accepts either the ACT or SAT and does not require SAT Subject Tests or the ACT Writing exam. With the SAT, we will continue to look most closely at the Critical Reading and Math sections and think of test scores on a 1,600-point, as opposed to a 2,400-point scale."

SELECTIVITY

Admissions Rating	97
# of applicants	3,485
% of applicants accepted	32
% of acceptees attending	29
# accepting a place on wait list	650
% admitted from wait list	4
# of early decision applicants	214
% accepted early decision	51

FRESHMAN PROFILE

Range SAT Critical Reading	660–760
Range SAT Math	630–710
Range SAT Writing	650–740
Range ACT Composite	29–32
Minimum paper TOEFL	600
Minimum computer TOEFL	250
Minimum web-based TOEFL	100
Average HS GPA	3.9
% graduated top 10% of class	65
% graduated top 25% of class	89
% graduated top 50% of class	99

DEADLINES

Early decision	
Deadline	11/15
Notification	12/15
Regular	
Deadline	1/15
Notification	4/1
Nonfall registration?	no

APPLICANTS ALSO LOOK AT

AND OFTEN PREFER
University of Chicago
University of California—Berkeley

AND SOMETIMES PREFER
Oberlin College
Macalester College

AND RARELY PREFER
Pomona College
Carleton College

FINANCIAL FACTS

Financial Aid Rating	97
Annual tuition	$37,960
Room and board	$9,920
Required fees	$230
Books and supplies	$950
% frosh rec. need-based scholarship or grant aid	48
% UG rec. need-based scholarship or grant aid	46
% frosh rec. need-based self-help aid	46
% UG rec. need-based self-help aid	46
% frosh rec. any financial aid	51
% UG rec. any financial aid	49
% UG borrow to pay for school	53
Average cumulative indebtedness	$17,296

RENSSELAER POLYTECHNIC INSTITUTE

110 EIGHTH STREET, TROY, NY 12180-3590 • ADMISSIONS: 518-276-6216 • FAX: 518-276-4072

CAMPUS LIFE

Quality of Life Rating	**68**
Fire Safety Rating	**72**
Green Rating	**88**
Type of school	private
Environment	city

STUDENTS

Total undergrad enrollment	5,367
% male/female	72/28
% from out of state	59
% from public high school	72
% live on campus	53
% in (# of) fraternities	25 (32)
% in (# of) sororities	18 (5)
% African American	4
% Asian	11
% Caucasian	74
% Hispanic	6
% Native American	1
% international	2
# of countries represented	63

SURVEY SAYS . . .

Lab facilities are great
Students are happy
Frats and sororities dominate social scene
Student publications are popular

ACADEMICS

Academic Rating	**80**
Calendar	semester
Student/faculty ratio	14:1
Profs interesting rating	61
Profs accessible rating	73
Most common	
reg class size	10–19 students
Most common	
lab size	10–19 students

MOST POPULAR MAJORS

business/commerce
computer engineering
electrical, electronics and communications engineering

STUDENTS SAY ". . ."

Academics

Rensselaer Polytechnic Institute, which proud students declare "a small research institute making a large impact on the world," is "essentially a hardcore technical school; oriented toward engineering and the sciences, although the school is trying to expand its offerings" in the humanities and arts. The school has already made some headway; as one student points out, "There are a lot of students who are dedicated to their single major in a science or technology field here, which leads to a somewhat narrow-minded type of person...but RPI's saving grace is that it also offers rigorous degrees in architecture and the arts that make this technical institution more like a liberal arts college, as opposed to a strictly technical college." Students in all disciplines face "rigorous course loads" that provide "a lesson in perseverance and innovation to overcome future challenges." Most programs incorporate "a hands-on studio-based method" supplemented by "top-of-the-line facilities...and numerous resources for all students to use." RPI's identity as a research center helps here; according to one undergrad, "The greatest resource for students at RPI are the researchers. It's easy to go to any top-ranked school and take hard classes. It's much harder to find as many professors who are on the cutting edge of their disciplines and actively taking undergraduate students into their labs. RPI excels in this, and any RPI student who wants a research position can usually find one." RPI's co-op program and Career Development Center "are also outstanding, leading to a high placement rate in excellent jobs," although of the latter some warn that "many engineering firms are familiar with Rensselaer, but employers in other fields still have yet to learn of the students available."

Life

"The academics are challenging" at RPI, making life "stressful, but in a good way. Time management is a key to success here." A few students have trouble walking away from the books, but most "enjoy relaxing through various clubs and intramural sports" available to all. The Greek scene is popular, but it's not your stereotypical Animal House variety; sure, "there are definitely a bunch of parties every weekend if you're into that," but "they're all pretty much very responsible with sober bartenders and sober drivers." RPI's Greek organizations also "do a lot of community service in the area and philanthropy events on campus." Greek or not, many here agree that "one of the greatest things to do for fun is to head up to the field house on a Friday or Saturday night and watch some Division I men's hockey." For those who want something a little more active, "Intramural and inter-fraternity sports are a great way to unwind as well as just hanging out in our student-run union." Hometown Troy "is not the best town to live in, although it has a few cool things to do. But, Albany is only a 20-minute drive away (the bus is free), and there's always something to do there."

Student Body

"There are a lot of very, very nerdy kids here at RPI, as can be imagined at a school with primarily engineering students," but "there are a large number of 'normal' people as well, and each year, the percent of females in each incoming class increases." While the gender gap may be narrowing, it's still pretty wide, meaning that "there [may be] only one typical student at RPI: a white male. They might be into sports, video games, drinking, Greek life, computers, RPG, or whatever, but they're an overwhelming aspect of campus." The minority population includes "many Asian and Indian students." Nearly everyone "comes from the top of their class so they are all very intelligent people" who are "driven and hardworking and think on a global level."

FINANCIAL AID: 518-276-6813 • E-MAIL: ADMISSIONS@RPI.EDU • WEBSITE: WWW.RPI.EDU

THE PRINCETON REVIEW SAYS

Admissions

Very important factors considered include: Class rank, academic GPA, rigor of secondary school record, standardized test scores. *Important factors considered include:* Application essay, recommendation(s), character/personal qualities, extracurricular activities, level of applicant's interest. *Other factors considered include:* Alumni/ae relation, geographical residence, interview, racial/ethnic status, talent/ability, volunteer work, work experience. SAT or ACT required; ACT with Writing component required; TOEFL required of all international applicants. High school diploma is required and GED is accepted. *Academic units required:* 4 English, 4 mathematics, 3 science, 2 social studies. *Academic units recommended:* 4 science, 3 social studies.

Financial Aid

Students should submit: FAFSA, CSS/Financial Aid PROFILE. The Princeton Review suggests that all financial aid forms be submitted as soon as possible after 1/1. *Need-based scholarships/grants offered:* Federal Pell, SEOG, state scholarships/grants, private scholarships, the school's own gift aid, Gates Millennium Scholarship, ACG, Smart Grants. *Loan aid offered:* FFEL Subsidized Stafford, FFEL Unsubsidized Stafford, FFEL PLUS, Federal Perkins, state loans, college/university loans from institutional funds. Applicants will be notified of awards on or about 3/25. Federal Work-Study Program available. Institutional employment available. Off-campus job opportunities are good.

The Inside Word

Outstanding test scores and grades are pretty much a must for any applicant hopeful of impressing the RPI admissions committee. Underrepresented minorities and women—two demographics the school would like to augment—will get a little more leeway than others, but in all cases, the school is unlikely to admit anyone who lacks the skills and background to survive here. RPI offers many students January admission in order to allow them to pursue productive activities (work, travel, volunteering) in the fall semester following high school graduation.

THE SCHOOL SAYS "..."

From The Admissions Office

"The oldest degree-granting technological research university in North America, RPI or Rensselaer was founded in 1824 to instruct students to apply 'science to the common purposes of life.' Rensselaer offers more than 100 programs and 1,000 courses leading to bachelor's, master's, and doctoral degrees. Undergraduates pursue studies in architecture, engineering, humanities, arts, and social sciences, management and technology, science, and information technology (IT). A pioneer in interactive learning, Rensselaer provides real-world, hands-on educational opportunities that cut across academic disciplines. Students have ready access to laboratories and attend classes involving lively discussion, problem solving, and faculty mentoring. The Office of First-Year Experience provides programs for students and their primary support persons that begin even before students arrive on campus. Students are able to take full advantage of Rensselaer's three unique research platforms: the $80 million state-of-the-art Center for Biotechnology and Interdisciplinary Studies (CBIS); one of the world's most powerful academic supercomputers, the Computational Center for Nanotechnology Innovations (CCNI); and the newly-opened Experimental Media and Performing Arts Center (EMPAC), which encourages students to explore the intersection of science, technology, and the arts. Newly renovated residence halls, wireless computing network, and studio-classrooms create a fertile environment for study and learning. Rensselaer offers recreational and fitness facilities plus numerous student-run organizations and activities, including fraternities and sororities, a newspaper, a radio station, drama and musical groups, and more than 160 clubs. In addition to intramural sports, NCAA varsity sports include Division I men's and women's ice hockey teams and 21 Division III men's and women's teams in 13 sports. The new East Campus Athletic Village scheduled to open in October 2009 will further transform athletics on the campus."

SELECTIVITY

Admissions Rating	94
# of applicants	11,249
% of applicants accepted	44
% of acceptees attending	27
# accepting a place on wait list	1,301
% admitted from wait list	29
# of early decision applicants	1,288
% accepted early decision	50

FRESHMAN PROFILE

Range SAT Critical Reading	600–690
Range SAT Math	650–730
Range SAT Writing	580–680
Range ACT Composite	24–29
Minimum paper TOEFL	570
Minimum computer TOEFL	230
Minimum web-based TOEFL	88
% graduated top 10% of class	64
% graduated top 25% of class	92
% graduated top 50% of class	99

DEADLINES

Early decision	
Deadline	11/1
Notification	12/5
Regular	
Deadline	1/15
Notification	3/14
Nonfall registration?	yes

APPLICANTS ALSO LOOK AT

AND OFTEN PREFER
Cornell University
Massachusetts Institute of Technology

AND SOMETIMES PREFER
Carnegie Mellon University
Boston University

AND RARELY PREFER
Clarkson University
Worcester Polytechnic Institute

FINANCIAL FACTS

Financial Aid Rating	85
Annual tuition	$36,950
Room and board	$10,730
Required fees	$1,040
Books and supplies	$1,802
% frosh rec. need-based scholarship or grant aid	66
% UG rec. need-based scholarship or grant aid	64
% frosh rec. non-need-based scholarship or grant aid	17
% UG rec. non-need-based scholarship or grant aid	11
% frosh rec. need-based self-help aid	51
% UG rec. need-based self-help aid	52
% frosh rec. athletic scholarships	1
% UG rec. athletic scholarships	1
% frosh rec. any financial aid	98
% UG rec. any financial aid	94
% UG borrow to pay for school	70
Average cumulative indebtedness	$30,375

RHODES COLLEGE

OFFICE OF ADMISSIONS, 2000 NORTH PARKWAY, MEMPHIS, TN 38112 • ADMISSIONS: 901-843-3700 • FAX: 901-843-3631

CAMPUS LIFE

Quality of Life Rating	**78**
Fire Safety Rating	**80**
Green Rating	**85**
Type of school	private
Affiliation	Presbyterian
Environment	metropolis

STUDENTS

Total undergrad enrollment	1,649
% male/female	42/58
% from out of state	74
% from public high school	50
% live on campus	76
% in (# of) fraternities	45 (7)
% in (# of) sororities	53 (6)
% African American	7
% Asian	5
% Caucasian	79
% Hispanic	2
% international	2
# of countries represented	11

SURVEY SAYS . . .
No one cheats
School is well run
Great off-campus food
Low cost of living
(Almost) no one smokes

ACADEMICS

Academic Rating	**96**
Calendar	semester
Student/faculty ratio	10:1
Profs interesting rating	88
Profs accessible rating	88
Most common	
reg class size	10–19 students
Most common	
lab size	20–29 students

MOST POPULAR MAJORS
biology/biological sciences
business/commerce
English language and literature

STUDENTS SAY "..."

Academics
"There is a true sense of community" at Rhodes College in Memphis. It is a community "fostered by the honor code, good ol' southern hospitality," and "a campus that is beautiful, welcoming, and safe." A "small-college feel in a big-city setting" means Rhodes undergrads benefit from both "small and discussion-based classes that give students the opportunity to understand different opinions" and the "endless social, academic, and professional opportunities for students and alums" afforded by an urban location. "Academics are incredible and challenging" here, so much so they may "drive you mad with all the papers and tests, but at the end of the day you know you're going to graduate with an excellent education that will lead to a great job." Rhodes earns students' plaudits in a broad range of offerings, including the "excellent business department, excellent programs in both political science and international relations," a "good English program," and "strong sciences." Education extends well beyond the classroom at Rhodes. The school "is great at getting students into internships, study-abroad programs, and community service opportunities," undergrads report. The school's "revered" honor code is also highly touted; "Every student signs an honor code promising not [to] lie, cheat, or steal." Students think the honor code is "great because professors trust you to take home a test, and you can leave your backpack virtually anywhere on campus, come back hours, even days later, and it will still be there!"

Life
Students lead a balanced life at Rhodes. "For the most part everybody goes to class and gets their work done during the day or week," then "goes out at night or on the weekends." The city of Memphis "offers plenty of things to do," including "a lot of good music," "a myriad of excellent restaurants" that include some justly world-famous barbecue joints, a great bar scene, and a variety of professional and collegiate sports options. "Greek life is huge" on campus, but "frat parties are always open to non-Greek students, so this makes a social life possible for all students." "The campus is split in half between Greek and non-Greek; regardless of this, Greeks and non-Greeks constantly interact and befriend one another," one student explains. Another major player on campus is "The Big Diehl, [which is] a weekend programming committee [that] plans fun trips, like a free trip to Six Flags in St. Louis or a $20 ski trip to the North Carolina mountains." Most Rhodies "are very outgoing" and "are involved in multiple activities outside of school and even outside sports. Most students are involved in different programs that work with the Memphis community by either helping out at a local hospital, tutoring children at a school, or [participating in a variety of] other ways to help out. Those not helping the Memphis community are helping and improving the Rhodes community."

Student Body
"Rhodes has a reputation for educating rich white kids," and "there are certainly those types present, but there are also kids from working-class families, different cultural and ethnic groups, as well as different religious groups." Some report "those who are not 'the rich kids' may get looked down upon by those who are wealthier, but over a four-year period that distinction becomes less important than [it seems] during the first semester freshman year." While "diversity has really increased over the past couple of years" as the school has implemented new recruiting strategies, many here still bemoan that Rhodes is still perceived as "a heavily white institution." There are lots of "conservative southern belles and gentlemen" who are "generally Christian" but "do not wear their religion on their sleeves."

FINANCIAL AID: 901-843-3810 • E-MAIL: ADMINFO@RHODES.EDU • WEBSITE: WWW.RHODES.EDU

THE PRINCETON REVIEW SAYS

Admissions

Very important factors considered include: Class rank, academic GPA, rigor of secondary school record. *Important factors considered include:* Application essay, recommendation(s), standardized test scores, alumni/ae relation, character/personal qualities, racial/ethnic status. *Other factors considered include:* Extracurricular activities, first generation, geographical residence, interview, level of applicant's interest, state residency, talent/ability, volunteer work, work experience. SAT or ACT required; TOEFL required of all international applicants. High school diploma is required and GED is accepted. *Academic units required:* 4 English, 3 mathematics, 2 science, (2 science labs), 2 foreign language, 2 social studies, 3 academic electives.

Financial Aid

Students should submit: FAFSA, CSS/Financial Aid PROFILE, noncustodial PROFILE. Regular filing deadline is 3/1. The Princeton Review suggests that all financial aid forms be submitted as soon as possible after 1/1. *Need-based scholarships/grants offered:* Federal Pell, SEOG, state scholarships/grants, private scholarships, the school's own gift aid. *Loan aid offered:* Direct Subsidized Stafford, Direct Unsubsidized Stafford, Direct PLUS, FFEL Subsidized Stafford, FFEL Unsubsidized Stafford, FFEL PLUS, Federal Perkins. Federal Work-Study Program available. Institutional employment available. Off-campus job opportunities are good.

The Inside Word

Rhodes' national profile is growing. Even though the majority of students come from Tennessee and nearby states; students from farther-flung points of origination will enjoy a leg up because they add to the geographic diversity. Likewise, the school seems to favor athletes. As with all small, selective schools, applicants are advised to schedule a campus visit and to interview to demonstrate their interest in attending.

THE SCHOOL SAYS ". . ."

From The Admissions Office

"It's not just one characteristic that makes Rhodes different from other colleges; it's a special blend of features that sets us apart. We are a selective liberal arts college yet without a cut-throat atmosphere; we are a small community yet located in a major city; we are in a metropolitan area yet offer one of the most beautiful and serene campuses in the nation. Our students are serious about learning and yet know how to have fun in an atmosphere of trust and respect brought about by adherence to the honor code. And they know that learning at Rhodes doesn't mean sitting in a lecture hall and memorizing the professor's lecture. It means interaction, discussion, and a process of teacher and student discovering knowledge together. Community service is an integral part of the culture at Rhodes. Our students are keenly aware of their social responsibility, and more than 80 percent are involved as volunteers throughout their college years. Rhodes is a place that welcomes new people and new ideas. It's a place of energy and enlightenment, not of apathy and complacency. Everyone who is a part of the Rhodes community is striving to be the best at what she/he does.

"Applicants are required to take the SAT or the ACT. The ACT Writing section is optional. Homeschool students must submit two SAT Subject Tests from areas other than English and Mathematics."

SELECTIVITY

Admissions Rating	95
# of applicants	3,747
% of applicants accepted	50
% of acceptees attending	26
# of early decision applicants	140
% accepted early decision	48

FRESHMAN PROFILE

Range SAT Critical Reading	580–680
Range SAT Math	580–670
Range ACT Composite	26–30
Minimum paper TOEFL	550
Minimum computer TOEFL	213
Average HS GPA	3.73
% graduated top 10% of class	55
% graduated top 25% of class	82
% graduated top 50% of class	98

DEADLINES

Early decision	
Deadline	11/1
Notification	12/1
Regular	
Priority	1/15
Notification	4/1
Nonfall registration?	yes

APPLICANTS ALSO LOOK AT

AND OFTEN PREFER
Davidson College

AND SOMETIMES PREFER
Sewanee—The University of the South
Vanderbilt University
Furman University
Trinity University

AND RARELY PREFER
The University of Memphis
Birmingham-Southern College

FINANCIAL FACTS

Financial Aid Rating	83
Annual tuition	$32,136
Room and board	$7,842
Required fees	$310
Books and supplies	$1,020
% frosh rec. need-based scholarship or grant aid	43
% UG rec. need-based scholarship or grant aid	42
% frosh rec. non-need-based scholarship or grant aid	18
% UG rec. non-need-based scholarship or grant aid	14
% frosh rec. need-based self-help aid	30
% UG rec. need-based self-help aid	29
% frosh rec. any financial aid	80
% UG rec. any financial aid	80
% UG borrow to pay for school	46
Average cumulative indebtedness	$26,064

RICE UNIVERSITY

OFFICE OF ADMISSION MS 17, PO BOX 1892, HOUSTON, TX 77251-1892 • ADMISSIONS: 713-348-7423 • FAX: 713-348-5952

CAMPUS LIFE
Quality of Life Rating	99
Fire Safety Rating	60*
Green Rating	78
Type of school	private
Environment	metropolis

STUDENTS
Total undergrad enrollment	2,995
% male/female	51/49
% from out of state	47
% live on campus	68
% African American	6
% Asian	18
% Caucasian	53
% Hispanic	12
% international	4
# of countries represented	44

SURVEY SAYS . . .
Students are friendly
Great off-campus food
Dorms are like palaces
Students are happy
Frats and sororities are unpopular or nonexistent

ACADEMICS
Academic Rating	96
Calendar	semester
Student/faculty ratio	5:1
Profs interesting rating	83
Profs accessible rating	86
% classes taught by TAs	4
Most common	
reg class size	10–19 students

MOST POPULAR MAJORS
biology/biological sciences
economics
psychology

STUDENTS SAY ". . ."

Academics

Students tell us Rice University provides "an Ivy League education without the Eastern establishment elitism and cut-throat competition." As at the Ivies, there's a lot of high-profile research going on here. Unlike at least some of the Ivies, though, "Many of the top researchers at the school teach intro level classes in their fields." Undergrads here benefit from Rice's relatively small size. As one student explains, the school "is small enough that you're always running into someone you know, but big enough that you can easily do awesome research, be a part of a radio station reaching all of Houston, or get involved in the performing arts." Academically, the school "is heavily focused on the sciences and engineering," and although the school has made efforts to bolster its other disciplines, for at least the time being "the humanities and social sciences are perceived as 'easy' majors. While there are a lot of great resources for these disciplines here, sometimes we who study them feel forgotten in a sea of bioengineers and pre-meds." Perceptions notwithstanding, academics across the board here are "challenging, but there is an extensive support network and it is not a competitive environment." Indeed, undergrads agree "Rice University is dedicated to its students, whether in the classroom through providing topnotch professors who are approachable…or just around campus by catering to students' professed, real needs and desires." Students say the school is run by an administration that is "extremely sensitive to students' needs and concerns."

Life

You can't understand life at Rice without understanding the residential college system, which many, many students say is "hands down the best thing about Rice." Under the system, "you are placed in a dorm and you live there all four years. It's great because it gives you another family and allows you to get to know everyone in your college. Rather than having frats or sororities you have to be approved of to join, your college immediately accepts you without question." Each college "has developed its own personality, traditions, and completely student-led government…When asked 'Where are you from?' students almost always reply not with their hometown but with their college affiliation." Students are equally enthusiastic about Rice's "wet campus" policy, under which "you can have alcohol in your room, you can drink it at Pub, and you can drink it at on-campus public parties. " While this results in "a fairly large drinking culture" on campus, "there are also tons of people who don't ever drink…There's something for everyone at Rice, and there's very little pressure to enter a sphere of activity that makes you uncomfortable." Hometown Houston "is not the prettiest or most pedestrian-friendly city in America, but it is one of the most vibrant, futuristic places you can live right now, and the opportunities for research within the Houston community are unparalleled." Rice wants students to explore the city. Explains one student, "The serveries are closed on Saturday nights, so people have to get off campus…There are shuttles that take you to the Village, a fun place with shops, restaurants, and bars not to far from campus…It's a really great excuse to find out what Houston has to offer."

Student Body

"Everyone at Rice is weird with some talent, oddity, or quirk that would otherwise attract attention in the normal world, but is accepted as totally normal here," students inform us. "Through the madness is how people bond." The residential college system also helps, as it "ensures a lot of mixing among different majors, races, interests, and geographic origins. People are similar enough and smart enough and have enough converging interests to make good friends with each other." Elite schools are best positioned to build a diverse student body, and Rice is no exception to the rule. Here you'll find "people with extremely diverse beliefs and backgrounds. We are not overly Democrat or Republican, we are not overly religious (though we do have a good number of active organizations, particularly Campus Crusade for Christ and Hillel), and we come from anything ranging from public high schools to boarding schools." However, the school "is not very diverse geographically, as 50 percent come from Texas."

FINANCIAL AID: 713-348-4958 • E-MAIL: ADMISSION@RICE.EDU • WEBSITE: WWW.RICE.EDU

THE PRINCETON REVIEW SAYS

Admissions

Very important factors considered include: Class rank, application essay, academic GPA, recommendation(s), rigor of secondary school record, standardized test scores, character/personal qualities, extracurricular activities, talent/ability. *Other factors considered include:* Alumni/ae relation, first generation, geographical residence, interview, level of applicant's interest, racial/ethnic status, state residency, volunteer work, work experience. SAT Subject Tests required; SAT or ACT required; ACT with Writing component required; TOEFL required of all international applicants. High school diploma or equivalent is not required. *Academic units required:* 4 English, 3 mathematics, 2 science, (2 science labs), 2 foreign language, 2 social studies, 3 academic electives. *Academic units recommended:* 4 English, 4 mathematics, 4 science, (3 science labs), 4 foreign language, 2 social studies, 2 academic electives.

Financial Aid

Students should submit: FAFSA, CSS/Financial Aid PROFILE, noncustodial PROFILE, business/farm supplement, tax returns and W-2s. The Princeton Review suggests that all financial aid forms be submitted as soon as possible after 1/1. *Need-based scholarships/grants offered:* Federal Pell, SEOG, state scholarships/grants, private scholarships, the school's own gift aid. *Loan aid offered:* FFEL Subsidized Stafford, FFEL Unsubsidized Stafford, FFEL PLUS, Federal Perkins, state loans. Applicants will be notified of awards on a rolling basis beginning 3/1. Federal Work-Study Program available. Institutional employment available. Off-campus job opportunities are excellent.

The Inside Word

Rice is among the nation's most selective undergraduate institutions. Legacies, athletes, and others thought to bring added value to the campus may receive a few breaks when their applications are assessed. All others need to present a very compelling profile including a challenging high school curriculum, solid grades, and superior test scores.

THE SCHOOL SAYS "..."

From The Admissions Office

"We seek students of keen intellect and diverse backgrounds who show potential to succeed at Rice and will also contribute to the educational environment of those around them.

"Student applications are reviewed within the context of the division to which they apply. Admission committee decisions are based not only on high school grades and test scores but also on such qualities as leadership, participation in extracurricular activities, and personal creativity. Admission is extremely competitive. Rice attempts to seek out and identify those students who have demonstrated exceptional ability and the potential for personal and intellectual growth.

"Our individualized, holistic evaluation process employs many different means to identify these qualities in applicants.

"Required admission testing includes the SAT or ACT with Writing. In addition, Rice requires all freshman applicants to take two SAT Subject Tests. All test scores must be sent to Rice directly from the official testing agency."

SELECTIVITY

Admissions Rating	98
# of applicants	9,813
% of applicants accepted	23
% of acceptees attending	35
# accepting a place on wait list	808
% admitted from wait list	1
# of early decision applicants	674
% accepted early decision	28

FRESHMAN PROFILE

Range SAT Critical Reading	650–750
Range SAT Math	670–780
Range SAT Writing	640–750
Range ACT Composite	30–34
Minimum paper TOEFL	600
Minimum computer TOEFL	250
% graduated top 10% of class	85
% graduated top 25% of class	94
% graduated top 50% of class	99

DEADLINES

Early decision	
Deadline	11/1
Notification	12/15
Early action	
Deadline	12/1
Notification	2/10
Regular	
Deadline	1/10
Notification	4/1
Nonfall registration?	no

APPLICANTS ALSO LOOK AT

AND OFTEN PREFER
Harvard College
Stanford University

AND SOMETIMES PREFER
Duke University

AND RARELY PREFER
Washington University in St. Louis

FINANCIAL FACTS

Financial Aid Rating	96
Annual tuition	$25,960
Room and board	$10,750
Required fees	$526
Books and supplies	$800
% frosh rec. need-based scholarship or grant aid	35
% UG rec. need-based scholarship or grant aid	37
% frosh rec. non-need-based scholarship or grant aid	17
% UG rec. non-need-based scholarship or grant aid	23
% frosh rec. need-based self-help aid	27
% UG rec. need-based self-help aid	24
% frosh rec. athletic scholarships	10
% UG rec. athletic scholarships	7
% frosh rec. any financial aid	65
% UG rec. any financial aid	64
% UG borrow to pay for school	42
Average cumulative indebtedness	$11,108

RIDER UNIVERSITY

2083 LAWRENCEVILLE ROAD, LAWRENCEVILLE, NJ 08648 • ADMISSIONS: 609-896-5042 • FAX: 609-895-6645

CAMPUS LIFE
Quality of Life Rating	70
Fire Safety Rating	60*
Green Rating	88
Type of school	private
Environment	village

STUDENTS
Total undergrad enrollment	4,606
% male/female	39/61
% from out of state	22
% from public high school	80
% live on campus	54
% in (# of) fraternities	7 (5)
% in (# of) sororities	10 (8)
% African American	9
% Asian	3
% Caucasian	71
% Hispanic	5
% international	3
# of countries represented	50

SURVEY SAYS . . .
Athletic facilities are great
Student publications are popular
Lots of beer drinking
(Almost) everyone smokes

ACADEMICS
Academic Rating	74
Calendar	semester
Student/faculty ratio	13:1
Profs interesting rating	76
Profs accessible rating	75
Most common reg class size	10–19 students
Most common lab size	10–19 students

MOST POPULAR MAJORS
accounting
business/commerce
elementary education and teaching

STUDENTS SAY ". . ."

Academics
Rider University is a medium-sized suburban liberal arts school in New Jersey that offers internships galore and a wide variety of majors. Rider's Westminster Choir College (in nearby Princeton) is worth looking into if you can hum a tune exceptionally well, but the biggest draw is probably the "very good business program." Academically, "the classes aren't too big." "Last semester my biggest class had 17 kids in it," notes a public relations major. Coursework is generally "engaging." A few members of the faculty "should not be teaching," but most professors are "intelligent people with a lot to offer." They're "very interested and involved within their respective fields." "Professors are very easy to contact and are always excited to help answer a question even when you don't have them as a professor anymore," relates an accounting major. "It is easy to build close personal relationships with your professors and that really helps students do well in the classroom." Views of the administration differ pretty radically. Some students call management "very efficient" and "simply wonderful," other students say that the staff is "rude and very unhelpful." "It is very hard for me to get a straight answer," gripes an education major.

Life
Rider's main campus is "secluded from town" and full of too many "outdated and jail-like" buildings. Also, some dorms could stand to be "spruced up." The newer residence halls are "great" though, and the gleaming student recreation center is a big hit with many students. There's also a nice on-campus pub. Otherwise, "fun is a touchy topic." Disgruntled students tell us that life at Rider "is not amazingly exciting." It's "a suitcase school," they say, and "a ghost town on the weekends" because so many students drive home on Friday night. "Basically there's not a lot to do around here," laments a sophomore. Happier students report an "overwhelming" number of activities and a good amount of free food at weekend events. "One of the biggest perks about staying on the weekend is that you get a really good parking spot," says an optimistic sophomore. Many students who stick around also participate in the Greek system. "A lot of people party," too, but "the alcohol policies are extreme." As a result, there are "numerous parties off campus." Students also frequent "clubs and bars" in the area. While "there's nothing to do anywhere in Lawrenceville without having a car," Rider is situated "directly between" easily accessible Philadelphia and New York City.

Student Body
"Mostly, everyone is from New Jersey," but ethnic diversity is pretty laudable at Rider and "students come from many different backgrounds." "It's not too hard to fit in." "There are a lot of students who take their work seriously." "There are the weird people who don't really socialize." There are also "slacker types" with "no sense of the real world" who are "trying to float through college" and "are more concerned with the party scene than academics." There are students "from middle-class homes" and wealthy students "with nice cars." You'll see quite a few women with "skinny jeans, Uggs, and poofy hair." There are "many clone students," too. "Your average student looks like your average kid." guesses a junior. "Overall, everyone has a niche" but "you have to join a group to make friends." "There are a lot of cliques," observes a senior. "The athletes stay with the athletes; the Greeks stay with the Greeks; and so on." Many people "stay connected to their high school friends."

FINANCIAL AID: 609-896-5360 • E-MAIL: ADMISSIONS@RIDER.EDU • WEBSITE: WWW.RIDER.EDU

THE PRINCETON REVIEW SAYS

Admissions

Very important factors considered include: Application essay, academic GPA, recommendation(s), rigor of secondary school record, standardized test scores. *Important factors considered include:* Level of applicant's interest. *Other factors considered include:* Class rank, alumni/ae relation, character/personal qualities, extracurricular activities, geographical residence, interview, state residency, talent/ability, volunteer work, work experience. SAT or ACT required; ACT with Writing component required; TOEFL required of all international applicants. High school diploma is required and GED is accepted. *Academic units required:* 4 English, 3 mathematics. *Academic units recommended:* 4 mathematics, 4 science, (2 science labs), 2 foreign language, 2 social studies, 2 history.

Financial Aid

Students should submit: FAFSA. The Princeton Review suggests that all financial aid forms be submitted as soon as possible after 1/1. *Need-based scholarships/grants offered:* Federal Pell, SEOG, state scholarships/grants, private scholarships, the school's own gift aid. *Loan aid offered:* FFEL Subsidized Stafford, FFEL Unsubsidized Stafford, FFEL PLUS, Federal Perkins, state loans, college/university loans from institutional funds, alternative loans. Applicants will be notified of awards on a rolling basis beginning 3/15. Federal Work-Study Program available. Institutional employment available.

The Inside Word

In the admissions world there are two all-important mandates: recruit the college's home state, and recruit Jersey! As a school in the Garden State, Rider deserves some special attention for the diverse group of students it brings in each year. Students who wish to attend need to have a solid academic record and good test scores. A few bumps in your academic past, however, shouldn't pose too much of a threat.

THE SCHOOL SAYS "..."

From The Admissions Office

"Rider students are driven by their dreams of a fulfilling career and a desire to have an impact on the world around them. Rider is a place to apply your imagination, talents and aspirations in ways that will make a difference. A Rider education will prepare you as a leader and as a member of a team. When you graduate from Rider, you'll be a different person, confidently ready for your life's challenges and opportunities.

"We invite you to visit and experience Rider firsthand. Open Houses are offered in the fall and late spring, tours are available daily and Information Sessions are offered most weekends.

"Freshmen applicants are required to submit the results of either the SAT or ACT exam, the writing component is required for both. The highest scores from either test will be considered for admission."

SELECTIVITY

Admissions Rating	78
# of applicants	6,829
% of applicants accepted	74
% of acceptees attending	17
# accepting a place on wait list	27
% admitted from wait list	100
# of early decision applicants	51
% accepted early decision	29

FRESHMAN PROFILE

Range SAT Critical Reading	470–560
Range SAT Math	470–570
Range SAT Writing	460–570
Range ACT Composite	18–24
Minimum paper TOEFL	550
Minimum computer TOEFL	213
Minimum web-based TOEFL	80
Average HS GPA	3.24
% graduated top 10% of class	17
% graduated top 25% of class	37
% graduated top 50% of class	75

DEADLINES

Early decision	
Deadline	11/15
Notification	12/15
Early action	
Deadline	11/15
Notification	12/15
Regular	
Notification	rolling
Nonfall registration?	yes

FINANCIAL FACTS

Financial Aid Rating	73
Annual tuition	$27,140
Room and board	$10,280
Required fees	$590
Books and supplies	$1,400
% frosh rec. need-based scholarship or grant aid	71
% UG rec. need-based scholarship or grant aid	65
% frosh rec. non-need-based scholarship or grant aid	11
% UG rec. non-need-based scholarship or grant aid	10
% frosh rec. need-based self-help aid	55
% UG rec. need-based self-help aid	50
% frosh rec. athletic scholarships	6
% UG rec. athletic scholarships	6
% frosh rec. any financial aid	85
% UG rec. any financial aid	66
% UG borrow to pay for school	74
Average cumulative indebtedness	$33,156

RIPON COLLEGE

300 SEWARD STREET, PO BOX 248, RIPON, WI 54971 • ADMISSIONS: 920-748-8337 • FAX: 920-748-8335

CAMPUS LIFE
Quality of Life Rating	94
Fire Safety Rating	62
Green Rating	73
Type of school	private
Environment	village

STUDENTS
Total undergrad enrollment	1,037
% male/female	48/52
% from out of state	24
% from public high school	75
% live on campus	92
% in (# of) fraternities	33 (5)
% in (# of) sororities	23 (3)
% African American	2
% Asian	1
% Caucasian	85
% Hispanic	3
% Native American	1
% international	2
# of countries represented	14

SURVEY SAYS . . .
Students are friendly
Students get along with local community
Low cost of living
(Almost) no one smokes

ACADEMICS
Academic Rating	86
Calendar	semester
Student/faculty ratio	15:1
Profs interesting rating	96
Profs accessible rating	95
Most common reg class size	10–19 students
Most common lab size	10–19 students

MOST POPULAR MAJORS
business/commerce
history
psychology

STUDENTS SAY ". . ."

Academics

Looking for a school that provides "intensive preparation for grad school" but also a "small and comfortable" and "homey and welcoming" environment? Undergrads at Ripon College think their school is just the place for you. "Everything about this community is warm and open," so even when academics get "competitive and challenging," they are still "surprisingly enjoyable." As one student explains, "What sets the administration apart is the way they treat each student as a person, rather than as a pain. It's the same with the professors. Ripon has some truly amazing teachers and professors that everybody hates, like every other school anywhere. The difference is that each of those professors, love 'em or hate 'em, is willing to sit down one-on-one and treat you like a person with a problem, rather than just a number with a grade." "And most of the professors try to make classes interesting and engaging, whether they succeed or not." Students also appreciate how "opportunities are in surprising abundance here. Faculty connections in the community provide many students with real-world applications of the academic knowledge they are gaining" through internships, community projects, and research projects. Ripon boasts "a wonderful science department" that oversees "a great biology program" and "a decent environmental studies program." Political science and education are among the other top-flight disciplines here.

Life

Ripon is located in a small town that "shuts down at night," and it's "20 minutes from the next closest town," so students "make our own fun," which includes "a lot of sledding, movies, shopping trips, and prairie walks," as well as the requisite campus parties, of course. "Drinking and partying are very common here," students say. "It's easily the most popular pastime," and "whether partying in the frat houses or going to the bars, people are always out and about." The campus also offers "plenty of organizations and extracurriculars to participate in," and "everyone on campus is involved in at least one club or organization." Likewise, "almost the entire student body participates in intramural sports." In short, students find sufficient diversion "whether they are participating in floor activities, all-campus activities, sporting events, school plays, or even just hanging out with friends. There is never a time when you feel as though you have nothing to do." For road trips, "Oshkosh and Fond du Lac are about half an hour away, so if somebody does have a car, these are common weekend activities." Trips to Madison or Milwaukee "are rarer" and are typically reserved for big concerts or major sporting events.

Student Body

There are "a few different groups of students at Ripon College," including "a large portion of athletes who spend a lot of their time dedicated to their respective sports and are thus, for the most part, not involved on campus." There is also a "solid group of intelligent, motivated, involved, and engaged students who make up the vast majority of the clubs," and "a substantial representation of Greek that put a lot of time and effort into being involved on campus. The different Greek organizations host the majority of events around campus." Most students here "come from the areas of Wisconsin that surround Ripon" and "tend to be fairly down-to-earth and friendly. You can make some amazing friends here."

FINANCIAL AID: 920-748-8101 • E-MAIL: ADMINFO@RIPON.EDU • WEBSITE: WWW.RIPON.EDU

THE PRINCETON REVIEW SAYS

Admissions

Very important factors considered include: Rigor of secondary school record, interview. *Important factors considered include:* Class rank, academic GPA, recommendation(s), standardized test scores, character/personal qualities, extracurricular activities. *Other factors considered include:* Application essay, talent/ability, volunteer work. SAT or ACT required; TOEFL required of all international applicants. High school diploma is required and GED is accepted. *Academic units required:* 4 English, 2 mathematics, 2 science, 2 social studies. *Academic units recommended:* 4 mathematics, 4 science, 2 foreign language, 4 social studies.

Financial Aid

Students should submit: FAFSA. The Princeton Review suggests that all financial aid forms be submitted as soon as possible after 1/1. *Need-based scholarships/grants offered:* Federal Pell, SEOG, state scholarships/grants, private scholarships, the school's own gift aid. *Loan aid offered:* FFEL Subsidized Stafford, FFEL Unsubsidized Stafford, FFEL PLUS, Federal Perkins. Applicants will be notified of awards on a rolling basis beginning 3/1. Federal Work-Study Program available. Institutional employment available. Off-campus job opportunities are good.

The Inside Word

Ripon seeks accomplished high school students who have challenged themselves in and out of the classroom. Solid performers—those earning a B+ average in a college prep curriculum and exceeding 1100 SAT/22 ACT—should find a clear path awaiting them, although the school does also consider such peripherals as potential contribution to extracurricular life and the likelihood a candidate will flourish in a small-school environment.

THE SCHOOL SAYS "..."

From The Admissions Office

"Since its founding in 1851, Ripon College has adhered to the philosophy that the liberal arts offer the richest foundation for intellectual, cultural, social, and spiritual growth. Academic strength is a 150-year tradition at Ripon. We attract excellent professors who are dedicated to their disciplines; they in turn attract bright, committed students. Together with the other members of our tightly knit learning community, students at Ripon learn more deeply, live more fully, and achieve more success. Students are surprised to discover that here there are more opportunities—to be involved, to lead, to speak out, to make a difference, to explore new interests—than at a college 10 times our size. Through collaborative learning, group living, teamwork, and networking, students tap into the power of a community where we all work together to ensure success—at Ripon and beyond.

"All of the best residential liberal arts colleges strive to be true learning communities like Ripon. We succeed better than most because our enrollment of about 1,000 students is perfect for fostering connections inside and outside the classroom. Our students flourish in this environment of mutual respect, where shared values are elevated and diverse ideas are valued. If you are seeking academic challenge and want to benefit from an environment of personal attention and support—then you should take a closer look at Ripon.

"Applicants to Ripon College must submit scores from either the ACT (Writing section not required) or the SAT."

SELECTIVITY
Admissions Rating	84
# of applicants	1,081
% of applicants accepted	79
% of acceptees attending	33

FRESHMAN PROFILE
Range SAT Critical Reading	460–610
Range SAT Math	500–630
Range ACT Composite	20–27
Minimum paper TOEFL	550
Minimum computer TOEFL	213
Minimum web-based TOEFL	79
Average HS GPA	3.36
% graduated top 10% of class	26
% graduated top 25% of class	50
% graduated top 50% of class	83

DEADLINES
Regular	
Priority	3/15
Notification	rolling
Nonfall registration?	yes

APPLICANTS ALSO LOOK AT
AND OFTEN PREFER
University of Wisconsin—Oshkosh
University of Wisconsin—Madison
St. Norbert College

AND SOMETIMES PREFER
Carroll College (WI)

AND RARELY PREFER
Lawrence University

FINANCIAL FACTS
Financial Aid Rating	87
Annual tuition	$23,970
Room and board	$6,770
Required fees	$275
Books and supplies	$1,000
% frosh rec. need-based scholarship or grant aid	79
% UG rec. need-based scholarship or grant aid	81
% frosh rec. non-need-based scholarship or grant aid	18
% UG rec. non-need-based scholarship or grant aid	15
% frosh rec. need-based self-help aid	60
% UG rec. need-based self-help aid	65
% frosh rec. any financial aid	91
% UG rec. any financial aid	89
% UG borrow to pay for school	96
Average cumulative indebtedness	$24,795

ROCHESTER INSTITUTE OF TECHNOLOGY

60 LOMB MEMORIAL DRIVE, ROCHESTER, NY 14623-5604 • ADMISSIONS: 585-475-6631 • FAX: 585-475-7424

CAMPUS LIFE
Quality of Life Rating	75
Fire Safety Rating	60*
Green Rating	91
Type of school	private
Environment	city

STUDENTS
Total undergrad enrollment	13,056
% male/female	67/33
% from out of state	45
% from public high school	85
% live on campus	68
% in (# of) fraternities	5 (19)
% in (# of) sororities	5 (10)
# of countries represented	95

SURVEY SAYS . . .
Lab facilities are great
Great library
Athletic facilities are great
Career services are great
Diverse student types on campus

ACADEMICS
Academic Rating	80
Calendar	quarter
Student/faculty ratio	14:1
Profs interesting rating	73
Profs accessible rating	78
Most common reg class size	10–19 students
Most common lab size	10–19 students

MOST POPULAR MAJORS
business/commerce
information technology
photography

STUDENTS SAY ". . ."

Academics

Rochester Institute of Technology is a "serious, no-nonsense school" "with amazing facilities" and a "unique" cooperative education program that is "very good" at "preparing you to work in the real world." The "great technical education" is a main draw for students. Other "high-quality programs" include animation, design, and the "renowned" College of Business. The National Technical Institute for the Deaf "makes for a diverse population." "Hard work" and a "fast pace" define academic life. Courses "go by fast" on RIT's "hard-core" 10-week quarter system. "Classes require a lot of outside work," says a junior. One bonus of attending RIT is that "the best employers in the country hold on-campus interviews frequently." Upon graduation, "job placement is really high" thanks to RIT's co-op program that "is required for many majors and encouraged for all." Co-op students graduate with "hands-on" experience at firms across the country. The "very passionate" professors here "come to teach, not to do research." "Academic support" is ubiquitous. "Even the worst professors I've had in lecture have been helpful after class," says an engineering major. "If you don't do well, it's your own fault." The "visible" administration is "fairly helpful." Some students wish administrators would "listen to their students a little bit more," but "the dean of your college is just an e-mail and appointment away."

Life

"Everything is made of brick" here, and the "freezing" winters can be "very hard to walk through every day." "They should put us in a dome," helpfully suggests a first-year student. The weather notwithstanding, "RIT is a place where you come to work hard and make a lot of money when you graduate," explains a senior. The "competitive academic environment" "makes a lot of the students stress out," and students really "have to study." "On weekends, people tend to relax." "If you're looking for a party school," look elsewhere. "Big parties" are sometimes held "off-campus" but "not like the ones that happen at other schools." "Very intense alcohol-free policies" also stifle the party scene, and Greek organizations "are kept on an annoyingly tight leash." "School spirit" is not the highest, but "there are many different types of activities on campus." "Almost anyone who is looking for something to do can find a place to fit in." Engineering clubs "give students hands-on experience and knowledge that they can apply to both their schoolwork and the career world." The campus "is a great venue for influential speakers" and "The College Activities Board does a great job of getting big acts to come perform." There is also "an amazing gym," and "downtown Rochester is close and has a lot" to offer, including "amazing Indian and sushi restaurants."

Student Body

RIT students are "very hardworking" and "career-motivated." "Grades are taken very seriously." Students say "super-smart" engineering majors and "crazy science students" are typical, as are "ragtag art students, preppy business students, jocks, [and] hippies." Many students "like to fool around with computers." Some students assert that "RIT is a nerd haven." Others complain that RIT has a "reputation of being a dork school when it really isn't." "There is a stereotype that students here are unsocial and like to sit in their room playing video games," complains a senior. Without question, there are "kids who don't come out of their rooms," but those that do leave their confines "are awesome." "The variety of programs offered draws a very diverse group of students that can in no way fit under one general description," explains a junior. "The interaction of these extremely different groups of students is part of what makes life on campus so interesting." That said, RIT is "predominantly male," and many would like to see the male/female ratio improved.

FINANCIAL AID: 585-475-2186 • E-MAIL: ADMISSIONS@RIT.EDU • WEBSITE: WWW.RIT.EDU

THE PRINCETON REVIEW SAYS

Admissions

Very important factors considered include: Academic GPA, rigor of secondary school record. *Important factors considered include:* Class rank, standardized test scores. *Other factors considered include:* Application essay, recommendation(s), alumni/ae relation, character/personal qualities, extracurricular activities, first generation, geographical residence, interview, level of applicant's interest, racial/ethnic status, talent/ability, volunteer work. SAT or ACT required; TOEFL required of all international applicants. High school diploma is required and GED is accepted. *Academic units required:* 4 English, 2 mathematics, 2 science, (1 science lab), 4 social studies, 10 academic electives. *Academic units recommended:* 4 English, 3 mathematics, 3 science, (2 science labs), 3 foreign language, 4 social studies, 5 academic electives.

Financial Aid

Students should submit: FAFSA, institution's own financial aid form, state aid form. The Princeton Review suggests that all financial aid forms be submitted as soon as possible after 1/1. *Need-based scholarships/grants offered:* Federal Pell, SEOG, state scholarships/grants, private scholarships, the school's own gift aid, NACME. *Loan aid offered:* Direct Subsidized Stafford, Direct Unsubsidized Stafford, Direct PLUS, Federal Perkins, RIT Loan program, Alternative loans. Applicants will be notified of awards on a rolling basis beginning 3/15. Federal Work-Study Program available. Institutional employment available. Off-campus job opportunities are excellent.

The Inside Word

Admission here is nowhere near as cutthroat as it is at other top-tier technical schools on the East Coast. But that doesn't mean admission isn't competitive, since RIT's co-op programs and its tremendous record of job placement with prestigious employers all over the country make it an attractive choice for many academically-talented applicants. The relatively high acceptance rate is somewhat deceiving because the applicant pool is largely self-selecting. The applicant pool is also small enough that RIT can go over your application with the finest-toothed of combs, for better or worse.

THE SCHOOL SAYS "..."

From The Admissions Office

"RIT is among the world's leading career-oriented, technological institutions. Ambitious, creative, diverse, and career-oriented students from every state and more than 95 foreign countries find a home in RIT's innovative, vibrant living/learning community. The university's eight colleges offer undergraduate and graduate programs areas such as engineering, computing, information technology, engineering technology, business, hospitality, science, art, design, photography, biomedical sciences, game design and development, and the liberal arts including psychology, advertising and public relations, and public policy Distinctive academic offerings include microelectronic and software engineering, imaging science, film and animation, biotechnology, physician assistant, new media, international business, telecommunications, and the programs in the School for American Crafts. In addition, students may choose from more than 80 different minors to develop personal and professional interests that complement their academic program. As home of the National Technical Institute for the Deaf (NTID), RIT is a leader in providing educational opportunities and access services for deaf and hard-of-hearing students. Experiential learning has been a hallmark of an RIT education since 1912. Every academic program at RIT offers some form of experiential education opportunity which may include cooperative education, internships, study abroad, and undergraduate research. Students work hard, but learning is complemented with plenty of organized and spontaneous events and activities. RIT is a unique blend of rigor and fun, creativity and specialization, intellect and practice that prepares alumni for long-term career success in global society."

SELECTIVITY
Admissions Rating	**84**
# of applicants	12,725
% of applicants accepted	60
% of acceptees attending	34
# accepting a place on wait list	344
% admitted from wait list	100
# of early decision applicants	1,461
% accepted early decision	66

FRESHMAN PROFILE
Range SAT Critical Reading	540–630
Range SAT Math	560–670
Range SAT Writing	520–610
Range ACT Composite	24–29
Minimum paper TOEFL	550
Minimum computer TOEFL	215
Minimum web-based TOEFL	79
% graduated top 10% of class	30.2
% graduated top 25% of class	62
% graduated top 50% of class	91.4

DEADLINES
Early decision	
Deadline	12/1
Notification	1/15
Regular	
Deadline	2/1
Notification	rolling
Nonfall registration?	yes

APPLICANTS ALSO LOOK AT

AND OFTEN PREFER
Cornell University
Carnegie Mellon University

AND SOMETIMES PREFER
Worcester Polytechnic Institute
Rensselaer Polytechnic Institute

AND RARELY PREFER
SUNY at Buffalo

FINANCIAL FACTS
Financial Aid Rating	**91**
Annual tuition	$27,624
Room and board	$9,381
Required fees	$411
Books and supplies	$900
% frosh rec. need-based scholarship or grant aid	71
% UG rec. need-based scholarship or grant aid	65
% frosh rec. non-need-based scholarship or grant aid	20
% UG rec. non-need-based scholarship or grant aid	20
% frosh rec. need-based self-help aid	66
% UG rec. need-based self-help aid	62
% frosh rec. any financial aid	88
% UG rec. any financial aid	77
% UG borrow to pay for school	66
Average cumulative indebtedness	$22,700

ROLLINS COLLEGE

CAMPUS BOX 2720, WINTER PARK, FL 32789-4499 • ADMISSIONS: 407-646-2161 • FAX: 407-646-1502

CAMPUS LIFE
Quality of Life Rating	**82**
Fire Safety Rating	**86**
Green Rating	**72**
Type of school	private
Environment	town

STUDENTS
Total undergrad enrollment	1,785
% male/female	43/57
% from out of state	47
% from public high school	55
% live on campus	69
% in (# of) fraternities	19 (5)
% in (# of) sororities	25 (6)
% African American	4
% Asian	4
% Caucasian	71
% Hispanic	10
% Native American	1
% international	4
# of countries represented	47

SURVEY SAYS . . .
Athletic facilities are great
Students love Winter Park, FL
Great off-campus food
Frats and sororities dominate social scene
Lots of beer drinking
Hard liquor is popular
(Almost) everyone smokes

ACADEMICS
Academic Rating	**89**
Calendar	semester
Student/faculty ratio	10:1
Profs interesting rating	90
Profs accessible rating	88
Most common reg class size	10–19 students

MOST POPULAR MAJORS
economics
international business/trade/commerce
psychology

STUDENTS SAY ". . ."

Academics
Rollins College offers "an amazing campus with great academics surrounded by the richest students around," leading some to describe the school as "a country club for college kids." Rollins' high-end cache means some regard it as academically low impact—even some students believe the school "is above average in regards to academics, but not top echelon since many students do not work hard"—but a strong majority here contends success here requires "a lot of work, much more than some people think. While Rollins is stereotyped for being a 'party school' we also have highly rated academic programs," and professors here "are tough. Some require a lot of reading and work, but if you have problems they are always available outside of class to help." Small classes mean students "are really forced into keeping up-to-date with the reading and with the assigned writings." Classroom work often takes the form of smaller discussion groups. One student explains, "Rollins is also a cool place to learn because many of our classes are taught around tables or in circles to stimulate discussion." The school also offers "many opportunities for studying abroad, and financial aid helps to pay for most of them." Areas of academic strength include "an impressive physics department, a great theater program with professors who are working professionals, a strong pre-law program, [and] a good education department."

Life
Rollins provides "an excellent quality of life for its students. Whether it is relaxing by our lakefront pool, jet skiing on the lake, visiting the beach, shopping, going to the theme parks, or just eating lunch on the patio, we know how to have a good time." While "life at this school can be balanced if you take full advantage of everything that is offered," many here are less interested in balance than in good times, which is why "the party scene is vibrant and dominating on many evenings." Many here concede Rollins "is a pretty big party school." Greek life "is huge," and "fraternity and sorority parties are big." Students point out that "all parties are welcoming to students" and students "may choose to attend any party regardless of their Greek affiliation." Intercollegiate athletics "are not as popular here for some reason. No one knows when games are, or who's playing." When students need to escape campus life, they find themselves fortunate enough to be "in a perfect location in Winter Park. We're close to movies, shopping, parks, museums, and nightlife in downtown Orlando. The beach is only 45 minutes away, Disney World and Universal Studios are only 25 minutes away, and there are golf courses all over the place." "Close" is a relative term, of course. The campus is close to all these destinations for students who have cars, but "If you don't have a car, don't plan on going anywhere. Nothing's in walking distance except a couple of great bars that are loaded with Rollins students 24/7."

Student Body
"The typical student [at Rollins] is rich, white, and preppy," and while "there are obviously different kinds of people who attend Rollins, the above description seems to apply to the majority." As one undergrad observes, "Most students drive a BMW, Mercedes, Land Rover, etc., and only wear or carry Coach, Prada, Ralph Lauren, A&F, etc." Those outside the ranks of the economic elite "don't necessarily have trouble fitting in at school, for most everyone finds their niche." Undergrads warn, however, that while "students generally are friendly...cliques do develop," in part because "Rollins is such a small school." They also concede "there is not much diversity, and diversity is rarely encouraged, particularly by social groups like sororities and fraternities. The few who do stand out find their own crowd and begin their own clubs, such as Pinehurst (for alternative lifestyles) and the Anime Club, and are often stereotyped as 'geeks.'"

FINANCIAL AID: 407-646-2395 • E-MAIL: ADMISSION@ROLLINS.EDU • WEBSITE: WWW.ROLLINS.EDU

THE PRINCETON REVIEW SAYS

Admissions

Very important factors considered include: Academic GPA, rigor of secondary school record. *Important factors considered include:* Application essay, recommendation(s), standardized test scores, extracurricular activities, talent/ability. *Other factors considered include:* Class rank, alumni/ae relation, character/personal qualities, first generation, interview, level of applicant's interest, volunteer work, work experience. ACT with Writing component recommended; TOEFL required of all international applicants. High school diploma is required and GED is accepted. *Academic units required:* 4 English, 3 mathematics, 2 science, 2 foreign language, 2 social studies, 2 history, 2 academic electives. *Academic units recommended:* 4 English, 4 mathematics, 4 science, 3 foreign language, 3 social studies, 3 history, 3 academic electives.

Financial Aid

Students should submit: FAFSA, institution's own financial aid form. Regular filing deadline is 3/1. The Princeton Review suggests that all financial aid forms be submitted as soon as possible after 1/1. *Need-based scholarships/grants offered:* Federal Pell, SEOG, state scholarships/grants, private scholarships, the school's own gift aid. *Loan aid offered:* Direct Subsidized Stafford, Direct Unsubsidized Stafford, Direct PLUS, Federal Perkins, college/university loans from institutional funds. Applicants will be notified of awards on a rolling basis beginning 3/1. Federal Work-Study Program available. Institutional employment available.

The Inside Word

Applicants to Rollins who do not seek academic merit scholarships have the option of including a graded paper in lieu of standardized test scores. It's the school's way of creating another opportunity for students who test poorly but otherwise excel in academics, and it's characteristic of the individualized approach taken here. Each applicant is assigned an admissions officer who acts as his or her liaison, ensuring a personalized admissions experience. Early decision applicants are given priority in admissions as well as in considerations for merit-based scholarships and need-based financial aid.

THE SCHOOL SAYS "..."

From The Admissions Office

"As you begin the college selection process, remember that you are in control of your destiny. Your academic record—course load, grades earned, test scores—are the most important part of your application credentials. But Rollins also pays close attention to your personal dimension—interests, strengths, values, and potential to contribute to college life. Don't sell yourself short in the application process. Be proud of what you've accomplished and who you are, and be honest when you describe yourself. Finally, the admission committee always likes to see candidates who express interest in the college. If we're your first choice, apply early decision. Each year we admit approximately one-third of the entering class through the early decision process. Are you unsure about your choice? If you can, schedule some visits, meet with an admission counselor, tour campus, and spend time in a class so you can see for yourself what Rollins and other colleges are all about. Take control of your destiny, and enjoy the process along the way.

"First-year applicants may submit either SAT or ACT scores for admission consideration. Candidates are strongly encouraged to complete the Writing components, but results without Writing will be considered. Each candidate's best score combination will be used in the selection process; we strongly recommend that candidates consider taking both the SAT and the ACT."

SELECTIVITY
Admissions Rating	89
# of applicants	3,485
% of applicants accepted	53
% of acceptees attending	25
# accepting a place on wait list	330
% admitted from wait list	15
# of early decision applicants	156
% accepted early decision	62

FRESHMAN PROFILE
Range SAT Critical Reading	555–650
Range SAT Math	555–650
Range ACT Composite	24–29
Minimum paper TOEFL	550
Minimum computer TOEFL	213
Minimum web-based TOEFL	80
Average HS GPA	3.4
% graduated top 10% of class	43
% graduated top 25% of class	73
% graduated top 50% of class	91

DEADLINES
Early decision	
Deadline	11/15
Notification	12/15
Regular	
Deadline	2/15
Notification	4/1
Nonfall registration?	yes

APPLICANTS ALSO LOOK AT

AND OFTEN PREFER
University of Richmond

AND SOMETIMES PREFER
Southern Methodist University
University of Miami
University of Florida

AND RARELY PREFER
Stetson University
Florida State University

FINANCIAL FACTS
Financial Aid Rating	88
Annual tuition	$34,520
Room and board	$10,780
% frosh rec. need-based scholarship or grant aid	40
% UG rec. need-based scholarship or grant aid	41
% frosh rec. non-need-based scholarship or grant aid	3
% UG rec. non-need-based scholarship or grant aid	4
% frosh rec. need-based self-help aid	31
% UG rec. need-based self-help aid	33
% frosh rec. athletic scholarships	3
% UG rec. athletic scholarships	4
% frosh rec. any financial aid	70
% UG rec. any financial aid	70
% UG borrow to pay for school	48
Average cumulative indebtedness	$21,904

ROSE-HULMAN INSTITUTE OF TECHNOLOGY

5500 WABASH AVENUE-CM 1, TERRE HAUTE, IN 47803-3999 • ADMISSIONS: 812-877-8213 • FAX: 812-877-8941

CAMPUS LIFE
Quality of Life Rating	**82**
Fire Safety Rating	**92**
Green Rating	**77**
Type of school	private
Environment	town

STUDENTS
Total undergrad enrollment	1,821
% male/female	79/21
% from out of state	58
% from public high school	82.7
% live on campus	60
% in (# of) fraternities	42 (9)
% in (# of) sororities	53 (4)
% African American	2
% Asian	5
% Caucasian	90
% Hispanic	2
% international	2
# of countries represented	20

SURVEY SAYS . . .
Lab facilities are great
Athletic facilities are great
Career services are great
School is well run
Campus feels safe

ACADEMICS
Academic Rating	**85**
Calendar	quarter
Student/faculty ratio	12:1
Profs interesting rating	84
Profs accessible rating	95
Most common reg class size	20–29 students
Most common lab size	20–29 students

MOST POPULAR MAJORS
biomedical/medical engineering
chemical engineering
mechanical engineering

STUDENTS SAY " . . . "

Academics
Rose-Hulman earns its "reputation as an excellent undergraduate engineering school" with a combination of strong academics and "personal attention, small class sizes, and a family atmosphere" a rarity among tech schools. Sure, "The workload is fairly heavy, especially sophomore year with the engineering curriculum." Sometimes students feel "Rose is about beating you up and putting you through hell so when you graduate you'll be the only engineer who knows what it's like to be on a project that completely sucks, but you've been taught that all projects are like that so you're the only engineer who will see it all the way through." However, students enjoy an unusually strong support system, and that mitigates the strain. "The transition is made as smooth as possible from high school to college for freshmen" with "on-campus tutoring in the learning center (an excellent resource for students to get homework help)" and "professors who are always available outside of class." One student elaborates, "Our professors are personal and focus on undergraduate education. They will know your name, ask if you are OK if you miss a class or two, and even pull up a chair next to your table at the bar." Those who make it through four years here enjoy the added benefit of "a great alumni base. With almost 99 percent job placement, if you get a decent GPA you're almost guaranteed a job in the field of your choice."

Life
"Life at Rose is academically demanding," but "the community here is so supportive and safe that you get through it," and while "students do a lot of homework and study a lot," they do occasionally find time to close the books and relax. "It's all work and little play Sunday through Thursday," but come Friday "we play hard.'" Students inform us "there's always something to do on campus, whether it's going to a fraternity party or attending a concert or going to a dance or just watching a movie with friends." Greek life is big, "but it's not your typical Animal House," and both intramural and Division III intercollegiate athletics have their supporters. There are also "tons of different groups to get involved in" on campus. Hometown Terre Haute, on the other hand, isn't so lively. "There isn't much to do" in town other than "go to the shadiest bars and check out the locals." As one student points out, "We are located in the middle of nowhere…not much they can do about it, but it is not so great."

Student Body
"The kids who attend Rose-Hulman are smart, dedicated, and consequently, nerds," but "this is not a negative thing. Within the students here, there are no outcasts, and even our athletes are most likely also math-letes." "Everyone definitely marches to the beat of his own drum," students assure us. Personality types run the gamut from "geniuses, average students, student-athletes, outspoken, quiet, etc." Demographically, undergrads are "mostly white male engineers from the Midwest" (partly a function of Rose-Hulman's location), but "we are slowly expanding the Rose-Hulman name and getting people from all over the U.S. and globe." The population "is mostly boys, although the females are catching up," albeit slowly. About half of the incoming freshman class played varsity sports in high school, which is about as many had been involved in the performing arts.

FINANCIAL AID: 812-877-8259 • E-MAIL: ADMIS.OFC@ROSE-HULMAN.EDU • WEBSITE: WWW.ROSE-HULMAN.EDU

THE PRINCETON REVIEW SAYS

Admissions

Very important factors considered include: Class rank, rigor of secondary school record. *Important factors considered include:* Academic GPA, recommendation(s), standardized test scores, character/personal qualities. *Other factors considered include:* Application essay, alumni/ae relation, extracurricular activities, interview, talent/ability, volunteer work, work experience. SAT or ACT required; TOEFL required of all international applicants. High school diploma is required and GED is not accepted. *Academic units required:* 4 English, 4 mathematics, 2 science, (2 science labs), 2 social studies, 4 academic electives. *Academic units recommended:* 5 mathematics, 3 science.

Financial Aid

Students should submit: FAFSA. The Princeton Review suggests that all financial aid forms be submitted as soon as possible after 1/1. *Need-based scholarships/grants offered:* Federal Pell, SEOG, state scholarships/grants, the school's own gift aid. *Loan aid offered:* Direct Subsidized Stafford, Direct Unsubsidized Stafford, Direct PLUS, Federal Perkins. Applicants will be notified of awards on or about 3/10. Federal Work-Study Program available. Institutional employment available.

The Inside Word

Rose-Hulman attracts an accomplished applicant pool and counselors believe only its less-than-optimally-desirable location prevents it from attracting an even more competitive group. Grades and test scores are paramount in the review process, but the school invites applicants to submit any supporting materials they think will help their case; such as an essay explaining why you want to be an engineer. Qualified women applicants should receive an especially favorable review, as Rose-Hulman—like most engineering schools—would love to reduce its gender imbalance.

THE SCHOOL SAYS "..."

From The Admissions Office

"Rose-Hulman is generally considered one of the premier undergraduate colleges of engineering and science. We are nationally known as an institution that puts teaching above research and graduate programs. At Rose-Hulman, professors (not graduate students) teach the courses and conduct their own labs. Department chairmen teach freshmen. To enhance the teaching at Rose-Hulman, computers have become a prominent addition to not only our labs but also in our classrooms and residence halls. Additionally, all students are now required to purchase laptop computers. Ninety million dollars in new facilities have been added in the last six years.

"Students applying for admission class may submit either the SAT or ACT, and the student's best scores from either test will be considered."

SELECTIVITY

Admissions Rating	97
# of applicants	3,088
% of applicants accepted	70
% of acceptees attending	22

FRESHMAN PROFILE

Range SAT Critical Reading	560–680
Range SAT Math	630–710
Range SAT Writing	550–650
Range ACT Composite	27–31
Minimum paper TOEFL	580
Minimum computer TOEFL	237
Minimum web-based TOEFL	92
% graduated top 10% of class	59.3
% graduated top 25% of class	91.8
% graduated top 50% of class	99.5

DEADLINES

Regular	
Priority	12/1
Deadline	3/1
Notification	rolling
Nonfall registration?	no

APPLICANTS ALSO LOOK AT

AND OFTEN PREFER
Purdue University—West Lafayette
Case Western Reserve University
University of Illinois at Urbana-Champaign

AND SOMETIMES PREFER
Georgia Institute of Technology
Worcester Polytechnic Institute
Rensselaer Polytechnic Institute

AND RARELY PREFER
Kettering University
Rochester Institute of Technology

FINANCIAL FACTS

Financial Aid Rating	75
Annual tuition	$30,243
Room and board	$8,343
Required fees	$480
Books and supplies	$1,500
% frosh rec. need-based scholarship or grant aid	70
% UG rec. need-based scholarship or grant aid	67
% frosh rec. need-based self-help aid	65
% UG rec. need-based self-help aid	62
% frosh rec. any financial aid	100
% UG rec. any financial aid	99
% UG borrow to pay for school	74
Average cumulative indebtedness	$32,612

RUTGERS, THE STATE UNIVERSITY OF NEW JERSEY—NEW BRUNSWICK

65 DAVIDSON ROAD, PISCATAWAY, NJ 08854-8097 • ADMISSIONS: 732-932-4636 • FAX: 732-445-0237

CAMPUS LIFE
Quality of Life Rating	63
Fire Safety Rating	80
Green Rating	60*
Type of school	public
Environment	town

STUDENTS
Total undergrad enrollment	26,479
% male/female	51/49
% from out of state	7
% live on campus	49
% in (# of) fraternities	8 (29)
% in (# of) sororities	6 (15)
% African American	9
% Asian	24
% Caucasian	52
% Hispanic	8
% international	2
# of countries represented	117

SURVEY SAYS . . .
Class discussions are rare
Athletic facilities are great
Diverse student types on campus
Everyone loves the Scarlet Knights
Student publications are popular
Lots of beer drinking
Hard liquor is popular

ACADEMICS
Academic Rating	71
Calendar	semester
Student/faculty ratio	14:1
Profs interesting rating	61
Profs accessible rating	61
% classes taught by TAs	20

MOST POPULAR MAJORS
biology/biological sciences
engineering

STUDENTS SAY ". . ."
Academics
Rutgers, The State University of New Jersey—New Brunswick, "is the kind of university [at which], if you make the effort to create your niche and find opportunities to succeed, you will have one of the best experiences of your life." With "a great study-abroad program, solid academic departments and professors, the vast resources of a large research [school] and lots of scholarship money for honors students," Rutgers "offers boundless opportunity, both educational and professional, but you have to be willing to go out and seek it." Rutgers' immenseness is made more manageable by its subdivision into 13 colleges, "each with its own unique community and environment, all unified under one entity that can afford all the opportunities of a large university." Even so, the university's bureaucracy is legendary. One student writes, "The school seems to take pride in its web of red tape. The famous 'RU Screw' has become so notorious that the university president had to publicly denounce it." It's a good sign that Rutgers "is progressively changing its administrative policies under the administration of its relatively new president. There is a renewed focus on student service, and the changes are evident." As at many state schools, "Good things will not happen at Rutgers by sitting in the corner and waiting for opportunity to knock. It is a big school, so the more you put yourself out and make yourself known, the more likely you'll be able to find help in academics and administration." For self-starters, the rewards can be great. One writes, "I've had the opportunity to [conduct] my own research in the Rutgers facilities." Indeed, "there is a lot of research going on at Rutgers. The topics are numerous, and there are plenty of spots to fill if you look around well enough."

Life
"Weekdays are busy, and you can find places crowded at any time of the day" on the Rutgers campus. "There's always something going on: concerts, free movies, talks. It's all about diversity and going out to find what you want to do." Student government "is huge." Students say there are "always voter registration drives, and we even have Tent State University in the spring, during which a bunch of political student groups set up tents on the main courtyard and camp out for a week handing out literature, having fun stuff (concerts, etc.), and talking to people about what they do and how they can get involved." For some, "drinking is a big thing." One student writes, "If there was no such thing as getting inebriated, there would be nothing to do here." Many refute that position, noting "there are other things you can do as well. There are lots of places to eat and drink coffee…or going to a small discussion group with Jhumpa Lahiri, the Pulitzer Prize–winning writer," to name a few. While weekdays are lively, weekends are another story. One student comments, "Life at Rutgers would feel more college-y if people didn't leave on weekends and it [didn't feel] so deserted."

Student Body
Rutgers "is huge, so there is just about every type of person you could think of here." One undergrad observes, "With so many students, it's hard not to find others with whom you fit in. But the drawback to such a large student body is that you need to go out and make friends; you can't expect them to come to you." Another student adds, "To be fair, sometimes it feels a bit like high school (there are 'skaters' and 'preps' and 'thugs' and all that), but once you're an upperclassmen you kind of learn to ignore it."

RUTGERS, THE STATE UNIVERSITY OF NEW JERSEY—NEW BRUNSWICK

FINANCIAL AID: 732-932-7057 • WEBSITE: WWW.RUTGERS.EDU

THE PRINCETON REVIEW SAYS

Admissions

Very important factors considered include: Class rank, academic GPA, rigor of secondary school record, standardized test scores. *Other factors considered include:* Application essay, recommendation(s), extracurricular activities, first generation, geographical residence, interview, racial/ethnic status, state residency, talent/ability, volunteer work, work experience. SAT or ACT required; TOEFL required of all international applicants. High school diploma is required and GED is accepted. *Academic units required:* 4 English, 3 mathematics, 2 science, 2 foreign language, 5 academic electives. *Academic units recommended:* 4 mathematics, 2 foreign language.

Financial Aid

Students should submit: FAFSA. The Princeton Review suggests that all financial aid forms be submitted as soon as possible after 1/1. *Need-based scholarships/grants offered:* Federal Pell, SEOG, state scholarships/grants, private scholarships, the school's own gift aid, Outside Scholarships. *Loan aid offered:* Direct Subsidized Stafford, Direct Unsubsidized Stafford, Direct PLUS, Federal Perkins, Federal Nursing, state loans, college/university loans from institutional funds, Educational Loans. Applicants will be notified of awards on a rolling basis beginning 2/1.

The Inside Word

With a literal mountain of applications to process each admissions season, Rutgers does not have the luxury of time. The school looks at your grades, the quality of your high school curriculum, your standardized test scores, and your essay to decide whether you can make the grade at Rutgers. Although the school grows more competitive each year, solid students should still find little difficulty getting in.

THE SCHOOL SAYS "..."

From The Admissions Office

"Rutgers, The State University of New Jersey, one of only 62 members of the Association of American Universities, is a research university that attracts students from across the nation and around the world. What does it take to be accepted for admission to Rutgers University? Our primary emphasis is on your past academic performance as indicated by your high school grades (particularly in required academic subjects), your class rank or cumulative average, the strength of your academic program, your standardized test scores on the SAT or ACT, any special talents you may have, and your participation in school and community activities. We seek students with a broad diversity of talents, interests, and backgrounds. Above all else, we're looking for students who will get the most out of a Rutgers education—students with the intellect, initiative, and motivation to make full use of the opportunities we have to offer.

"First-year applicants should take the SAT or the ACT (with Writing component). Test scores are not required for students who graduated high school more than two years ago or have completed more than 12 college credits since graduating."

SELECTIVITY

Admissions Rating	87
# of applicants	28,208
% of applicants accepted	56
% of acceptees attending	35

FRESHMAN PROFILE

Range SAT Critical Reading	530–630
Range SAT Math	560–670
Minimum paper TOEFL	550
Minimum computer TOEFL	213
% graduated top 10% of class	40
% graduated top 25% of class	81
% graduated top 50% of class	99

DEADLINES

Regular	
Priority	12/1
Notification	3/1
Nonfall registration?	yes

APPLICANTS ALSO LOOK AT
AND OFTEN PREFER
University of Virginia
Cornell University
University of Pennsylvania
AND SOMETIMES PREFER
Montclair State University
Boston College
New Jersey Institute of Technology
Penn State—University Park
AND RARELY PREFER
The George Washington University
Seton Hall University

FINANCIAL FACTS

Financial Aid Rating	73
Annual tuition in-state	$9,268
Annual tuition out-of-state	$19,482
Room and board	$9,942
Required fees	$2,294
% frosh rec. need-based scholarship or grant aid	31
% UG rec. need-based scholarship or grant aid	32
% frosh rec. non-need-based scholarship or grant aid	30
% UG rec. non-need-based scholarship or grant aid	25
% frosh rec. need-based self-help aid	44
% UG rec. need-based self-help aid	44
% frosh rec. athletic scholarships	1
% UG rec. athletic scholarships	1
% frosh rec. any financial aid	67
% UG rec. any financial aid	69
% UG borrow to pay for school	65
Average cumulative indebtedness	$16,283

SACRED HEART UNIVERSITY

5151 Park Avenue, Fairfield, CT 06825 • Admissions: 203-371-7880 • Fax: 203-365-7607

STUDENTS SAY "..."

Academics

Looking for an "excellent education" with a Catholic influence in Southern New England? Then Sacred Heart University may be the place for you. As one undergrad says, "I feel as though Sacred Heart offers some of the most brilliant professors available in the academic world." High praise, though as another explains, "at SHU, you can really connect with your professors. It is the kind of school where professors know the names of all of their students and remember them after the semester ends." The net result is an academic atmosphere that is "both stimulating and intellectually fulfilling." Learning is enhanced by SHU's "advanced" technology, which means that "the whole campus is wireless and most professors use this to their advantage by putting notes and assignments online, which saves paper, and students from arthritis." Some students do complain that some upper-level administrators "seem disconnected." Others note that they would like to see the "registration process improve." But, all in all, if you're willing to suffer a few administrative headaches, you just might discover "the academic experience is great!"

Life

"If you don't get involved, then you don't get the most of the life on campus"—and yes, there's plenty to pick from at SHU. According to one freshman, "There's pretty much a club for anyone, making it easy to become involved. There are also community service projects happening all the time." A classmate adds, "Every day they e-mail us with the 'Events of the Day,' and there's always something going on...midnight volleyball, acoustic shows at the Outpost, concerts, sports games, and even Ping-Pong tournaments." Athletics are also a "big part" of student life. "I'm usually at almost every athletic event with my face painted red and a crazy wig on," says an enthusiastic supporter. Though SHU is officially a dry campus, there are many whet appetites here. "It is a big bar school," explains one student. "There are some parties that go on, but the bars are where people go." To get to the bars in nearby Fairfield or Bridgeport, most students take cabs—"and the cabs are very expensive." There's also "a shuttle that takes everyone to the mall and runs on the hour." Other popular weekend destinations include New Haven, only "20 minutes away," and New York is one hour from campus.

Student Body

Your typical SHU student "is either a Yankee or Red Sox fan." In other words, most undergrads hail from the Northeast—"from Massachusetts, New York, and Connecticut," in particular. But if you call some far-off land home, don't worry: "Everyone seems to fit in, even if you're not from these states." A freshman describes her fellow Pioneers as "approachable, kind, courteous, respectful, and outgoing." But another first-year says that the four words that best describe your average SHU undergrad are "white, rich, preppy, and Catholic." Look beyond the "average" undergrad, you'll see "the students at Sacred Heart come in all different shapes and colors, and come from different backgrounds and come from all over the world."

E-MAIL: ENROLL@SACREDHEART.EDU • WEBSITE: WWW.SACREDHEART.EDU

THE PRINCETON REVIEW SAYS

Admissions

Very important factors considered include: Academic GPA, rigor of secondary school record. *Important factors considered include:* Class rank, recommendation(s), standardized test scores, character/personal qualities, extracurricular activities, interview, talent/ability, volunteer work, work experience. *Other factors considered include:* Application essay, alumni/ae relation, first generation, geographical residence, level of applicant's interest, racial/ethnic status, religious affiliation/commitment, state residency. SAT or ACT required; ACT with Writing component required; TOEFL required of all international applicants. High school diploma is required and GED is accepted. *Academic units required:* 4 English, 3 mathematics, 3 science, (1 science lab), 2 foreign language, 3 social studies, 3 history, 3 academic electives. *Academic units recommended:* 4 English, 4 mathematics, 4 science, (2 science labs), 4 foreign language, 4 social studies, 4 history, 4 academic electives.

Financial Aid

Students should submit: FAFSA, CSS/Financial Aid PROFILE, noncustodial PROFILE. The Princeton Review suggests that all financial aid forms be submitted as soon as possible after 1/1. *Need-based scholarships/grants offered:* Federal Pell, SEOG, state scholarships/grants, private scholarships, the school's own gift aid. *Loan aid offered:* Direct Subsidized Stafford, Direct Unsubsidized Stafford, Direct PLUS, FFEL Subsidized Stafford, FFEL Unsubsidized Stafford, FFEL PLUS, Federal Perkins, state loans, Alternative loans. Applicants will be notified of awards on a rolling basis beginning 3/1. Federal Work-Study Program available. Institutional employment available. Off-campus job opportunities are excellent.

The Inside Word

Who's the person behind the application? This is what the admissions officers at student-friendly Sacred Heart University want to know. While they place heavy emphasis on traditional academic indicators like high-school curriculum and GPA, they also spend time reading each applicant's admissions essay. If you really want to make an impact, why not head to Sacred Heart for a campus visit? A strong interview can turn many tides to your favor.

THE SCHOOL SAYS ". . ."

From The Admissions Office

"Sacred Heart University, distinguished by the personal attention it provides its students, is a thriving, dynamic university known for its commitment to academic excellence, cutting-edge technology, and community service. The second-largest Catholic university in New England, Sacred Heart continues to be innovative in its offerings to students; recently launched programs include Connecticut's first doctoral program in physical therapy, an MBA program for liberal arts undergraduates at the newly AACSB-accredited John F. Welch College of Business, and a campus in County Kerry, Ireland. The university's commitment to experiential learning incorporates concrete, real-life study for students in all majors. Drawing on the rich resources in New England and New York City, students are connected with research and internship opportunities ranging from co-ops at international advertising agencies to research with faculty on marine life in the Long Island Sound. These experiential learning opportunities are complemented by a rich student life program offering more than 80 student organizations including strong music programs, media clubs, and academic honor societies. Either the SAT or the ACT (with Writing component) is required for admission. For students taking the SAT more than once, the highest Math score and the highest Critical Reading score will be evaluated by the admissions committee. No current policy exists for the use of the SAT Writing component."

SELECTIVITY

Admissions Rating	83
# of applicants	7,568
% of applicants accepted	65
% of acceptees attending	20
# of early decision applicants	193
% accepted early decision	75

FRESHMAN PROFILE

Range SAT Critical Reading	490–560
Range SAT Math	500–590
Minimum paper TOEFL	500
Minimum computer TOEFL	70
Average HS GPA	3.3
% graduated top 10% of class	16
% graduated top 25% of class	52
% graduated top 50% of class	86

DEADLINES

Early decision	
Deadline	12/1
Notification	12/15
Regular	
Priority	1/15
Notification	rolling
Nonfall registration?	yes

APPLICANTS ALSO LOOK AT

AND OFTEN PREFER
University of Connecticut
Villanova University

AND SOMETIMES PREFER
Fordham University
Providence College

AND RARELY PREFER
Hofstra University
Iona College

FINANCIAL FACTS

Financial Aid Rating	74
Annual tuition	$28,790
Room and board	$11,608
Required fees	$200
Books and supplies	$700
% frosh rec. need-based scholarship or grant aid	67
% UG rec. need-based scholarship or grant aid	64
% frosh rec. non-need-based scholarship or grant aid	6
% UG rec. non-need-based scholarship or grant aid	5
% frosh rec. need-based self-help aid	59
% UG rec. need-based self-help aid	57
% frosh rec. athletic scholarships	6
% UG rec. athletic scholarships	6
% frosh rec. any financial aid	86
% UG rec. any financial aid	92
% UG borrow to pay for school	87
Average cumulative indebtedness	$39,620

SAINT ANSELM COLLEGE

100 SAINT ANSELM DRIVE, MANCHESTER, NH 03102-1310 • ADMISSIONS: 603-641-7500 • FAX: 603-641-7550

CAMPUS LIFE

Quality of Life Rating	86
Fire Safety Rating	60*
Green Rating	60*
Type of school	private
Affiliation	Roman Catholic
Environment	city

STUDENTS

Total undergrad enrollment	1,879
% male/female	42/58
% from out of state	79
% from public high school	45
% live on campus	90
% African American	1
% Asian	1
% Caucasian	86
% Hispanic	2
% Native American	1
% international	1
# of countries represented	18

SURVEY SAYS . . .

Students are friendly
Students get along with local community
Great food on campus
Student government is popular
Political activism is popular

ACADEMICS

Academic Rating	88
Calendar	semester
Student/faculty ratio	12:1
Profs interesting rating	89
Profs accessible rating	86
Most common reg class size	10–19 students
Most common lab size	10–19 students

STUDENTS SAY ". . ."

Academics

If you long for four years of "Catholic faith and hard classes," consider "wonderful, small" Saint Anselm College in Manchester, New Hampshire. The nursing program is reportedly "awesome," but Saint Anselm is best known for providing "a true liberal arts education." In addition to comprehensive exams in every major, all students must complete three courses each in philosophy and theology, two English courses, two science courses, a year of foreign language, and four common humanities courses. "Some people enjoy the humanities program." Others say "the lectures can be absolute torture." Depending on who you talk to, the administration either "functions smoothly" or is "too Catholic" and "takes its time with everything." Students almost universally gush about their "passionate" professors. "I get tons of individual attention," brags a nursing major. "They are always willing to set a time with you outside of class for help." However, "essays are numerous," and "classes are very difficult." "The library is always filled." There is something of a "crusade against grade inflation" on this campus as well. "St. A's is known as St. C's," explains a junior. "Despite how hard you work, you may not see the results you want," warns an English major. Other students tell us "the work is not excruciatingly hard." "It's definitely not impossible," says a biochemistry major. "I'm no rocket scientist, and I'm taking in at least two A's this semester," agrees a classics major. "St. A's requires you to work very hard, but in a warm, friendly, and respectful atmosphere where there are plenty of opportunities to make your college years fantastic," reflects a business major.

Life

This "absolutely gorgeous" campus boasts "spectacular" food. "Internet technology is a joke" though, and the recreational facilities aren't much. A few students complain that Saint Anselm is "a suitcase school" but others say "you can be involved in numerous things." "It is a small, tight-knit school, where if you stick around on campus and get involved you will have the best time ever," declares a senior. "Community service is big." "I've never seen such a giving school," gloats a first-year student. There's mass every day, and you'll always find a few Benedictine monks around campus. "The monks are awesome," says a junior. "For students who are interested, Saint Anselm is a haven for politics." The "really cool" New Hampshire Institute of Politics provides "a lot of speakers and political candidates," particularly when primary season rolls around. "It's a big deal to go to the hockey games." "Intramural sports are very popular," too. "The pub is a great place on campus for juniors and seniors who are 21 to grab a drink and relax." Various campus policies are "strict" though. First-year residence halls are not co-ed and visitation hours for members of the opposite sex are limited. "If you're looking for an intense party scene, Saint Anselm College isn't the place," advises a senior. Nevertheless, "the senior housing always has something going on" and "drinking is very prevalent" on the weekends, "though students must be sneaky." Nearby Boston is "a great option for the weekends" as well.

Student Body

The stereotype at Saint Anselm is definitely a "white, Catholic Red Sox fan." "Most students I've met here have Boston accents, at least half are Irish, and went to a private school," observes a freshman. There's "only a handful of minorities." "The student body is not the most diverse community but most people are very welcoming," adds a senior. "Social groups here tend to be well defined and yet somehow still permeable, or at least, amiable to one another." There are "sheltered, ignorant snobs," but "the majority of students is middle-class and receives some sort of financial aid." Students at Saint A's describe themselves as "smart, hardworking, involved in community service," and "very preppy." "There are a select few who are rebellious, artsy, and try to stand out but they generally get along with the preppy kids." "Most kids are on an athletic team of some type." Many are serious about religion, "but many are not." Politically, opinions "are surprisingly varied for a campus that is pretty conservative."

FINANCIAL AID: 603-641-7110 • E-MAIL: ADMISSION@ANSELM.EDU • WEBSITE: WWW.ANSELM.EDU

THE PRINCETON REVIEW SAYS

Admissions

Very important factors considered include: Application essay, academic GPA, recommendation(s), rigor of secondary school record, standardized test scores, racial/ethnic status. *Other factors considered include:* Class rank, alumni/ae relation, character/personal qualities, extracurricular activities, geographical residence, level of applicant's interest, state residency, talent/ability, volunteer work, work experience. SAT or ACT required; TOEFL required of all international applicants. High school diploma is required and GED is accepted. *Academic units required:* 4 English, 3 mathematics, 3 science, (2 science labs), 2 foreign language, 2 social studies. *Academic units recommended:* 4 mathematics, 4 science, 4 foreign language.

Financial Aid

Students should submit: FAFSA, CSS/Financial Aid PROFILE, noncustodial PROFILE, business/farm supplement. Regular filing deadline is 3/15. The Princeton Review suggests that all financial aid forms be submitted as soon as possible after 1/1. *Need-based scholarships/grants offered:* Federal Pell, SEOG, state scholarships/grants, private scholarships, the school's own gift aid. *Loan aid offered:* FFEL Subsidized Stafford, FFEL Unsubsidized Stafford, FFEL PLUS, Federal Perkins. Applicants will be notified of awards on a rolling basis beginning 3/1. Federal Work-Study Program available. Institutional employment available. Off-campus job opportunities are excellent.

The Inside Word

St. Anselm gets a predominately regional applicant pool, and Massachusetts is one of its biggest suppliers of students. An above-average academic record should be more than adequate to gain admission.

THE SCHOOL SAYS "..."

From The Admissions Office

"Why Saint Anselm? The answer lies with our graduates. Not only do our alumni go on to successful careers in medicine, law, human services, and other areas, but they also make connections on campus that last a lifetime. With small classes, professors are accessible and approachable. The Benedictine monks serve not only as founders of the college but as teachers, mentors, and spiritual leaders.

"Saint Anselm is rich in history, but certainly not stuck in a bygone era. In fact, the college has launched a $50-million fund-raising campaign, which will significantly increase funding for financial aid, academic programs, and technology. New initiatives include the New Hampshire Institute of Politics. Not a political junkie? No problem. The NHIOP is a diverse undertaking that also involves elements of psychology, history, theology, ethics, and statistics.

"Saint Anselm encourages students to challenge themselves academically and to lead lives that are both creative and generous. On that note, more than 40 percent of our students participate in community service locally and globally. Each year, about 150 students take part in Spring Break Alternative to help those less fortunate across the United States and Latin America. High expectations and lofty goals are hallmarks of a Saint Anselm College education, and each student is encouraged to achieve his or her full potential here. Why Saint Anselm? Accept the challenge and soon you will discover your own answers.

"Freshman applicants must take the SAT or the ACT. The best scores from either test will be used in admissions decisions."

SELECTIVITY

Admissions Rating	85
# of applicants	3,835
% of applicants accepted	70
% of acceptees attending	19
# accepting a place on wait list	321
% admitted from wait list	77
# of early decision applicants	79
% accepted early decision	76

FRESHMAN PROFILE

Range SAT Critical Reading	490–580
Range SAT Math	500–590
Range SAT Writing	500–600
Range ACT Composite	21–26
Minimum paper TOEFL	550
Minimum computer TOEFL	213
Minimum web-based TOEFL	80
Average HS GPA	3.13
% graduated top 10% of class	23
% graduated top 25% of class	56
% graduated top 50% of class	91

DEADLINES

Early decision	
Deadline	11/15
Notification	12/1
Regular	
Priority	3/1
Notification	rolling
Nonfall registration?	yes

APPLICANTS ALSO LOOK AT

AND OFTEN PREFER
Fairfield University, College of the Holy Cross, Boston College, Providence College, Stonehill College

AND SOMETIMES PREFER
University of New Hampshire
University of Massachusetts—Amherst

AND RARELY PREFER
Merrimack College

FINANCIAL FACTS

Financial Aid Rating	79
Annual tuition	$29,720
Room and board	$11,240
Required fees	$795
% frosh rec. need-based scholarship or grant aid	72
% UG rec. need-based scholarship or grant aid	69
% frosh rec. non-need-based scholarship or grant aid	6
% UG rec. non-need-based scholarship or grant aid	4
% frosh rec. need-based self-help aid	64
% UG rec. need-based self-help aid	64
% frosh rec. athletic scholarships	1
% UG rec. athletic scholarships	1
% UG borrow to pay for school	77
Average cumulative indebtedness	$35,025

SAINT LOUIS UNIVERSITY

221 NORTH GRAND BOULEVARD, SAINT LOUIS, MO 63103 • ADMISSIONS: 314-977-2500 • FAX: 314-977-7136

CAMPUS LIFE

Quality of Life Rating	**72**
Fire Safety Rating	**86**
Green Rating	**76**
Type of school	private
Affiliation	Roman Catholic
Environment	metropolis

STUDENTS

Total undergrad enrollment	7,635
% male/female	41/59
% from out of state	57
% live on campus	53
% in (# of) fraternities	16 (11)
% in (# of) sororities	24 (7)
% African American	9
% Asian	6
% Caucasian	67
% Hispanic	3
% international	5
# of countries represented	87

SURVEY SAYS . . .

Students are friendly
Student government is popular
Lots of beer drinking
Hard liquor is popular
Very little drug use

ACADEMICS

Academic Rating	**77**
Calendar	semester
Student/faculty ratio	12:1
Profs interesting rating	71
Profs accessible rating	72
% classes taught by TAs	6
Most common reg class size	10–19 students
Most common lab size	10–19 students

MOST POPULAR MAJORS

biology/biological sciences
business administration and management
nursing/registered nurse
(rn, asn, bsn, msn)

STUDENTS SAY ". . ."

Academics

"The Jesuit tradition really resonates in everything that happens at SLU," a place where "Service, social justice, and political awareness are stressed at every level of your education." This "medium-sized Jesuit school with solid academic programs and a campus that feels close-knit" is best known for its "great premedical programs," which include "a great direct-entry physical therapy program" and "a well-respected accelerated nursing program" as well as the school's premed tracks. Students also speak highly of SLU's offerings in business and prelaw, as well as its unique programs in aviation and "the one-of-a-kind nutrition program with a culinary emphasis." Since SLU is a Catholic school, nearly all programs here require a solid core curriculum including classes in religion and ethics. Students praise the way this curriculum "forces you to examine your worldview from the moment you step on campus and helps you discover what your beliefs really are." Academics, especially in the high-profile departments, can be rigorous. In this regard, SLU is "perfect for high achievers and scholars who strive for the best. The professors are nice and professional but are very stern about assignments being turned in on time." One student says, "When it comes to natural sciences, particularly chemistry, biology, etc., I think SLU can be very hard. I guess it works, though. A nursing degree or physical therapy degree from SLU is very highly respected in the health care profession."

Life

"SLU manages to provide everything your parents wish for your college experience and still everything you wouldn't want them to know about," undergrads here confide. Campus life includes "a lot of fun activities the student government puts on...such as outdoor movies, balls, and dances." "Dorm life is very strict and not much fun." The party scene "is decent," because "there are a lot of off-campus living opportunities that are close by and great places to live. The Lofts and Coronado are two great off-campus apartments that are extremely close by." College sports are in the mix. "With the new arena, basketball games are becoming the thing to do." Greek life "is great at SLU." The fraternities and sororities "provide many parties and events for the students and activities such as laser tag and barbecue" to help the students "become involved" and "get to know each other." Being in St. Louis means "great city life around, but most of it is for students that are 21 and above," and "off-campus eateries that are close by and range from Drunken Fish Sushi to Rally's Burgers." Students tell us "safety is a huge importance in SLU since we are so close to the city, [and fortunately] there is usually a DPS officer that is always close by to help students in need." Service is a big part of many students' lives, and "SLU's Jesuit influence encourages the student body to become active in the community. SLU's efforts to encourage community service give many students their first taste of the real world and better prepare them to venture out into it after graduation."

Student Body

SLU "has a pretty homogeneous student population of white, upper-middle class, students coming from a private high school (usually Jesuit, and single-sex) or from the suburbs of bigger Midwestern cities. The girls wear Uggs, North Face fleeces, and dye their hair, while the boys live in their fraternity letters and some American Eagle jeans." Many "have been in the Catholic school system their entire lives," although there are also "quite a few kids who went to public school and kids who are lower-middle-class." Students are generally committed to the concept of service; and they "put forth a lot of community service hours into the surrounding area, from Habitat for Humanity to the Big Brothers/Big Sisters programs. There are plenty of clubs students use to help raise money for their organizations."

FINANCIAL AID: 314-977-2350 • E-MAIL: ADMITME@SLU.EDU • WEBSITE: WWW.SLU.EDU

THE PRINCETON REVIEW SAYS

Admissions

Very important factors considered include: Academic GPA, standardized test scores. *Important factors considered include:* Application essay, rigor of secondary school record, extracurricular activities. *Other factors considered include:* Recommendation(s), alumni/ae relation, character/personal qualities, first generation, interview, level of applicant's interest, talent/ability, volunteer work. SAT or ACT required; TOEFL required of all international applicants. High school diploma is required and GED is accepted. *Academic units required:* 4 English, 4 mathematics, 3 science, 3 foreign language, 3 social studies, 3 academic electives. *Academic units recommended:* 4 English, 4 mathematics, 3 science, 3 foreign language, 3 social studies, 3 academic electives.

Financial Aid

Students should submit: FAFSA. The Princeton Review suggests that all financial aid forms be submitted as soon as possible after 1/1. *Need-based scholarships/grants offered:* Federal Pell, SEOG, state scholarships/grants, private scholarships, the school's own gift aid, Federal Nursing Scholarships. *Loan aid offered:* FFEL Subsidized Stafford, FFEL Unsubsidized Stafford, FFEL PLUS, Federal Perkins, Federal Nursing, college/university loans from institutional funds. Applicants will be notified of awards on a rolling basis beginning 3/1. Federal Work-Study Program available. Institutional employment available. Off-campus job opportunities are good.

The Inside Word

Saint Louis University's student body is primarily regional, but it continually expands its draw so that today nearly 60 percent of all undergrads arrive from out of state. This increase in geographic diversity has brought with it elevated admissions standards. The grades and test scores that got your older brother or sister in here may not be good enough for you (although family ties to the school are a plus). Admissions officers look for students who display a commitment to both scholarship and Jesuit principles. Applicants must demonstrate success in college preparatory classes and a desire to be active participants in the community.

THE SCHOOL SAYS "..."

From The Admissions Office

"A hot Midwestern university with a growing national and international reputation, Saint Louis University gives students the knowledge, skills, and values to build a successful career and make a difference in the lives of those around them. Students live and learn in a safe and attractive campus environment. The beautiful urban, residential campus offers loads of internship, outreach, and recreational opportunities. Ranked as one of the best educational values in the country, the university welcomes students from all 50 states and 80 foreign countries who pursue rigorous majors that invite individualization. Accessible faculty, study-abroad opportunities, and many small, interactive classes make SLU a great place to learn.

"A leading Jesuit, Catholic university, SLU's goal is to graduate men and women of competence and conscience—individuals who are not only capable of making wise decisions but who also understand why they made them. Since 1818, Saint Louis University has been dedicated to academic excellence, service to others, and preparing students to be leaders in society. Saint Louis University truly is the place *where knowledge touches lives.*

"For admission, Saint Louis University will accept either the SAT or the ACT with or without the Writing component."

SELECTIVITY

Admissions Rating	92
# of applicants	10,022
% of applicants accepted	72
% of acceptees attending	21

FRESHMAN PROFILE

Range SAT Critical Reading	530–640
Range SAT Math	540–660
Range ACT Composite	24–29
Minimum paper TOEFL	550
Minimum computer TOEFL	213
Minimum web-based TOEFL	80
Average HS GPA	3.68
% graduated top 10% of class	36
% graduated top 25% of class	65
% graduated top 50% of class	90

DEADLINES

Regular	
Priority	12/1
Deadline	8/1
Notification	rolling
Nonfall registration?	yes

APPLICANTS ALSO LOOK AT

AND OFTEN PREFER
Marquette University
University of Missouri—Columbia
University of Illinois at Urbana-Champaign

AND SOMETIMES PREFER
Truman State University
University of Dayton
Notre Dame College
Creighton University

AND RARELY PREFER
Rockhurst University
Xavier University (OH)
Maryville University of Saint Louis

FINANCIAL FACTS

Financial Aid Rating	72
Annual tuition	$30,330
Room and board	$8,760
Required fees	$398
Books and supplies	$1,040
% frosh rec. need-based scholarship or grant aid	60
% UG rec. need-based scholarship or grant aid	52
% frosh rec. non-need-based scholarship or grant aid	6
% UG rec. non-need-based scholarship or grant aid	5
% frosh rec. need-based self-help aid	49
% UG rec. need-based self-help aid	44
% frosh rec. athletic scholarships	2
% UG rec. athletic scholarships	2
% frosh rec. any financial aid	91
% UG rec. any financial aid	89
% UG borrow to pay for school	67
Average cumulative indebtedness	$29,298

SAINT MARY'S COLLEGE OF CALIFORNIA

PO BOX 4800, MORAGA, CA 94575-4800 • ADMISSIONS: 925-631-4224 • FAX: 925-376-7193

CAMPUS LIFE

Quality of Life Rating	**71**
Fire Safety Rating	**86**
Green Rating	**86**
Type of school	private
Affiliation	Roman Catholic
Environment	village

STUDENTS

Total undergrad enrollment	2,514
% male/female	38/62
% from out of state	13
% from public high school	52
% live on campus	61
% African American	6
% Asian	11
% Caucasian	53
% Hispanic	22
% Native American	1
% international	2
# of countries represented	34

SURVEY SAYS . . .

Lab facilities are great
Campus feels safe
Frats and sororities are unpopular or nonexistent
Lots of beer drinking
Hard liquor is popular

ACADEMICS

Academic Rating	**86**
Calendar	4/1/4
Student/faculty ratio	11:1
Profs interesting rating	82
Profs accessible rating	83
Most common reg class size	10–19 students

MOST POPULAR MAJORS

business administration, management and operations
communication and media studies
psychology

STUDENTS SAY ". . ."

Academics

The "Lasallian tradition" on which Saint Mary's College of California is based "is about quality education, faith, concern for the poor, social justice, respect for all persons, and inclusive community." A junior explains, "It is about learning about all aspects of life and growth through that learning." SMC students tell us time and again that their school truly embodies these ideals, living up to its motto, "enter to learn, leave to serve," through its emphasis on "learning and service." The former is embodied by the school's seminar program, which focuses on classics of Western literature ("You'll like at least 25 percent of the books," promises one student, adding, "as for the rest, you'll have to accept that you're going to be a little confused"); wide-ranging area requirements that ensure "you learn a little bit about everything;" and "seminar-style classes" that "teach critical thinking." Students "enjoy the small class sizes" and appreciate that they "are able to actually go to teachers for help rather than seek the help of some random teacher's aide." Also, "if you're still having trouble in classes, you can seek out the help of a free tutor." Undergrads note that "the facilities could be better, but it is the people, the professors, and the administration that makes academics here so enjoyable."

Life

"Life at Saint Mary's is pretty easygoing." The pace is set by the low (some say "nonexistent") level of activity in hometown Moraga, a "mountain town where everything closes early, even the Jack in the Box." Students report that "due to the small size of the school, there is little to do on campus." "The Program Board is trying but most people don't take the time to check them out." The Lasallian tradition means that students are always "putting on community-service events." Intercollegiate sports are also popular, particularly basketball, which "is really big here." Some students "leave campus for the weekend," while those who "stay usually party." One benefit of the school's location is that students are "very close to Berkeley, San Francisco, and the little up-and-coming Walnut Creek." Many students appreciate that SMC is "close enough to San Francisco to have fun but far enough that you don't have to deal with the issues of city life."

Student Body

SMC offers a "tight-knit community," though as many note, "The typical Saint Mary's student is white and comes from money" and "probably attended a Catholic high school in the Bay Area." However, "There are many other types of people on campus," and one undergrad explains, "The great thing about this school is that everyone is treated the same among teachers and students no matter what their background." Saint Mary's has "a healthy population of international students, many of whom are athletes, and there are a great number of ethnic clubs on campus that host different events throughout the year for anybody to attend." What you won't find here is "many goth types or hippies or anything that's not mainstream. However, that doesn't mean that they wouldn't be accepted into our communities." Some note that "the school is pretty clique-y," though the average students are "athletic and academically oriented," looking to "further themselves."

SAINT MARY'S COLLEGE OF CALIFORNIA

FINANCIAL AID: 925-631-4370 • E-MAIL: SMCADMIT@STMARYS-CA.EDU • WEBSITE: WWW.STMARYS-CA.EDU

THE PRINCETON REVIEW SAYS

Admissions

Very important factors considered include: Academic GPA, rigor of secondary school record, standardized test scores. *Important factors considered include:* Application essay, recommendation(s), first generation. *Other factors considered include:* Class rank, alumni/ae relation, character/personal qualities, extracurricular activities, geographical residence, interview, level of applicant's interest, racial/ethnic status, religious affiliation/commitment, talent/ability, volunteer work, work experience. SAT or ACT required; TOEFL required of all international applicants. High school diploma is required and GED is accepted. *Academic units required:* 4 English, 3 mathematics, 2 science, (1 science lab), 2 foreign language, 1 social studies, 1 history, 2 academic electives. *Academic units recommended:* 4 English, 4 mathematics, 3 science, (1 science lab), 3 foreign language, 1 social studies, 1 history, 2 academic electives.

Financial Aid

Students should submit: FAFSA, state aid form. The Princeton Review suggests that all financial aid forms be submitted as soon as possible after 1/1. *Need-based scholarships/grants offered:* Federal Pell, SEOG, state scholarships/grants, private scholarships, the school's own gift aid. *Loan aid offered:* FFEL Subsidized Stafford, FFEL Unsubsidized Stafford, FFEL PLUS, Federal Perkins. Applicants will be notified of awards on a rolling basis beginning 3/15. Federal Work-Study Program available. Institutional employment available. Off-campus job opportunities are good.

The Inside Word

The Lasallian tradition that Saint Mary's adheres to is an awareness of social and economic injustice. In line with this, Saint Mary's reserves one quarter of its undergraduate population for students from the lowest economic strata. The school will continue to boost its own funding of financial aid in order to help such students attend the school. Saint Mary's commitment to serving the underprivileged provides a great opportunity for low-income students with strong academic potential.

THE SCHOOL SAYS "..."

From The Admissions Office

"Today, Saint Mary's College continues to offer a value-oriented education by providing a classical liberal arts background second to none. The emphasis is on teaching an individual how to think independently and responsibly, how to analyze information in all situations, and how to make choices based on logical thinking and rational examination. Such a program develops students' ability to ask the right questions and to formulate meaningful answers, not only within their professional careers but also for the rest of their lives. Saint Mary's College is committed to preparing young men and women for the challenge of an ever-changing world, while remaining faithful to an enduring academic and spiritual heritage. We believe the purpose of a college experience is to prepare men and women for an unlimited number of opportunities, and that this is best accomplished by educating the whole person, both intellectually and ethically. We strive to recruit, admit, enroll, and graduate students who are generous, faith-filled, and human, and we believe this is reaffirmed in our community of brothers, in our faculty, and in our personal concern for each student.

"For freshman applicants, we will accept the SAT, and the ACT is also accepted. The ACT Writing assessment is optional. The highest critical reading and the highest Math scores attained on the SAT will be used. SAT Subject Tests are not required."

SELECTIVITY

Admissions Rating	87
# of applicants	3,638
% of applicants accepted	81
% of acceptees attending	23
# accepting a place on wait list	70
% admitted from wait list	40

FRESHMAN PROFILE

Range SAT Critical Reading	490–590
Range SAT Math	480–590
Minimum paper TOEFL	527
Minimum computer TOEFL	197
Minimum web-based TOEFL	71
Average HS GPA	3.33

DEADLINES

Early action	
Deadline	11/15
Regular	
Priority	11/15
Deadline	2/1
Notification	3/15
Nonfall registration?	yes

APPLICANTS ALSO LOOK AT

AND OFTEN PREFER
University of California—Berkeley
University of California—Los Angeles

AND SOMETIMES PREFER
University of San Diego
Loyola Marymount University
Santa Clara University
University of California—Davis

AND RARELY PREFER
University of San Francisco
Sonoma State University
University of the Pacific

FINANCIAL FACTS

Financial Aid Rating	74
Annual tuition	$33,100
Room and board	$11,680
Required fees	$150
Books and supplies	$1,206
% frosh rec. need-based scholarship or grant aid	61
% UG rec. need-based scholarship or grant aid	57
% frosh rec. non-need-based scholarship or grant aid	21
% UG rec. non-need-based scholarship or grant aid	25
% frosh rec. need-based self-help aid	58
% UG rec. need-based self-help aid	57
% frosh rec. athletic scholarships	8
% UG rec. athletic scholarships	6
% frosh rec. any financial aid	82
% UG rec. any financial aid	78
% UG borrow to pay for school	71
Average cumulative indebtedness	$23,389

SAINT MICHAEL'S COLLEGE

ONE WINOOSKI PARK, COLCHESTER, VT 05439 • ADMISSIONS: 802-654-3000 • FAX: 802-654-2906

CAMPUS LIFE

Quality of Life Rating	**98**
Fire Safety Rating	**74**
Green Rating	**89**
Type of school	private
Affiliation	Roman Catholic
Environment	city

STUDENTS

Total undergrad enrollment	1,980
% male/female	47/53
% from out of state	80
% from public high school	67.8
% live on campus	96
% African American	1
% Asian	1
% Caucasian	94
% Hispanic	1
% international	1
# of countries represented	30

SURVEY SAYS . . .

Students are friendly
Students get along with local community
Students love Colchester, VT
Great off-campus food
Students are happy
Frats and sororities are unpopular or nonexistent
Student publications are popular

ACADEMICS

Academic Rating	**88**
Calendar	semester
Student/faculty ratio	12:1
Profs interesting rating	89
Profs accessible rating	92
Most common reg class size	10–19 students
Most common lab size	20–29 students

MOST POPULAR MAJORS

business/commerce
English language and literature
psychology

Academics

Saint Michael's College is a Catholic liberal art college that boasts "an absolutely unbeatable location" in the heart of "prime" Vermont ski territory. A reasonably broad set of core course requirements includes two mandatory religion classes. Study abroad is "huge." "Sciences are a very popular." "The education department, in general, is amazing." Coursework at SMC "can be very challenging—by no means is everything a breeze." However, classes tend to be manageably small. "Rarely do you have a class larger than 30 students, which gives you a nice, intimate classroom experience." "The administration and professors at the school are all very open and welcoming to every student," promises a junior. "Like any school, there are the good and the bad teachers." For the most part, though, "professors are really passionate and devoted to the subjects that they teach." They are "available outside of class, open to lots of discussion in the classroom, and always are willing to help." The biggest academic gripe here is probably the "insufficient" course selection, since "the size of the college limits the overall variety of courses."

Life

Saint Mike's is lively. "It's my opinion that you cannot be bored on this campus," asserts one student. "The theater kids, the sports kids, the campus ministry kids, the volunteer program kids, the fire and rescue kids—there are groups for everyone." The community service program is "extremely popular." Rallies and demonstrations are common. "Most people are moderately interested in the outdoors," and the wilderness program runs student-led trips each weekend." Socially, SMC is "really close-knit." "The big family aspect of Saint Mike's makes it easy to meet people and make friends. That boils down to awesome weekends." "Monday through Thursday, people tend to really focus on classes." Thursday marks the beginning of the weekend, which continues until late Saturday night. Mostly, "people get absolutely hammered in their rooms," then amble around campus to "various parties and get-togethers." There's a drug scene, too, if that's your bag. If you choose not to partake in the festivities, it's fine. Virtually all students "are required to live on campus all four years," and the students tell us "overcrowded" dorms are "a mess." Also, the Vermont winters are "brutal." On the plus side, if you ski or snowboard, "several great mountains" are nearby. (Smugglers' Notch offers ridiculously cheap season passes through a special offer to Saint Mike's students.) In warmer weather, "many activities—even parties—happen outside in the beautiful Vermont scenery." For a change of pace, students take the free bus to "artsy," "adorable" Burlington, "a hubbub of fun."

Student Body

"We have little to no ethnic or racial diversity at our school," admits a senior. "For what it's worth, however, the minorities here blend in with the rest of the student body." "A typical student is a solid B student in high school who's really involved" and hails from "20 minutes outside Boston," observes one student. There are plenty of "hockey/rugby player types," and many students are "involved in sports." Quite a few students grew up wealthy. "New, expensive cars" dot the campus. "There is an abundance of preppy kids." You'll know them by their "Ugg boots, North Face fleeces, and Vera Bradley bags." "Hippies" are around but not pervasive. "St Mike's is painted as more of a hippie college than it really is," reports one student. Politically, there are conservatives, but there are a lot more "left-wing liberals who care too much about the environment." Overall, there's an "open, welcoming" vibe. "Everyone is pretty low-key about fitting in." "You can see a hippie hugging a preppie or a Yankees fan and Red Sox fan eating lunch together," swears one student. "Everyone gets along here."

FINANCIAL AID: 802-654-3243 • E-MAIL: ADMISSION@SMCVT.EDU • WEBSITE: WWW.SMCVT.EDU

THE PRINCETON REVIEW SAYS

Admissions

Very important factors considered include: Class rank, academic GPA, rigor of secondary school record. *Important factors considered include:* Application essay, recommendation(s), standardized test scores, character/personal qualities, extracurricular activities, talent/ability. *Other factors considered include:* Alumni/ae relation, first generation, geographical residence, level of applicant's interest, racial/ethnic status, state residency, volunteer work, work experience. SAT or ACT required; ACT with Writing component required; TOEFL required of all international applicants. High school diploma is required and GED is accepted. *Academic units required:* 4 English, 3 mathematics, 3 science, (2 science labs), 3 foreign language, 3 social studies. *Academic units recommended:* 4 English, 4 mathematics, 4 science, (3 science labs), 4 foreign language, 4 social studies.

Financial Aid

Students should submit: FAFSA, Signed copies of Parent's Federal Tax Return, Parent's Federal W-2 forms, Signed copies of Student's Federal Tax Return, Student's Federal W-2 forms, Dependent Verification Worksheet (Please check the Student Financial Services form). The Princeton Review suggests that all financial aid forms be submitted as soon as possible after 1/1. *Need-based scholarships/grants offered:* Federal Pell, SEOG, state scholarships/grants, private scholarships, the school's own gift aid. *Loan aid offered:* FFEL Subsidized Stafford, FFEL Unsubsidized Stafford, FFEL PLUS, Federal Perkins. Applicants will be notified of awards on a rolling basis beginning 1/15. Federal Work-Study Program available. Institutional employment available. Off-campus job opportunities are excellent.

Inside Word

Saint Mike's is a pretty easy admit if you've shown a reasonable level of consistency in solid college prep curriculum. Candidates who goofed around a little too much in high school would be well advised to strongly highlight their extracurricular activities.

THE SCHOOL SAYS "..."

From The Admissions Office

"Saint Michael's is a residential, Catholic, liberal arts college for students who want to make the world a better place.

A Saint Michael's education will prepare you for life, as each of our 30 majors is grounded in our liberal studies core. Our superb faculty is committed first and foremost to teaching and is known for really caring about students while simultaneously challenging them to reach higher than they ever thought possible. Because of our holistic approach, Saint Michael's graduates are prepared for their entire careers, not just their first jobs out of college.

"With nearly 100% of students living on campus, our "24/7" learning environment means exceptional teaching goes beyond the classroom and into the living areas, which include three new suite-style residences, townhouse apartments, and traditional residence halls. The remarkable sense of community encourages students to get involved, take risks, and think differently. A unique passion for social justice issues on campus reflects the heritage of the Edmundite priests who founded Saint Michael's in 1904.

"Saint Michael's is situated just outside of Burlington, Vermont's largest city and a true college town. A unique Cultural Pass program allows students to see an array of music, dance, theater, and Broadway productions at the Flynn Center downtown. Students also take advantage of some of the best skiing in the East through an agreement with Smugglers' Notch ski resort—an all-access season pass is provided to any Saint Michael's student in good academic standing."

SELECTIVITY

Admissions Rating	87
# of applicants	3,618
% of applicants accepted	69
% of acceptees attending	22
# accepting a place on wait list	186
% admitted from wait list	8

FRESHMAN PROFILE

Range SAT Critical Reading	520–620
Range SAT Math	520–610
Range SAT Writing	530–620
Range ACT Composite	22–26
Minimum paper TOEFL	550
Minimum computer TOEFL	213
Average HS GPA	3.4
% graduated top 10% of class	24
% graduated top 25% of class	52
% graduated top 50% of class	82

DEADLINES

Regular	
Priority	11/1
Deadline	2/1
Notification	4/1
Nonfall registration?	yes

APPLICANTS ALSO LOOK AT
AND OFTEN PREFER
College of the Holy Cross
Boston College

AND SOMETIMES PREFER
Fairfield University
University of Vermont
Stonehill College

AND RARELY PREFER
University of New Hampshire
Saint Anselm College

FINANCIAL FACTS

Financial Aid Rating	78
Annual tuition	$32,940
Room and board	$8,280
Required fees	$275
Books and supplies	$1,200
% frosh rec. need-based scholarship or grant aid	57
% UG rec. need-based scholarship or grant aid	61
% frosh rec. non-need-based scholarship or grant aid	14
% UG rec. non-need-based scholarship or grant aid	7
% frosh rec. need-based self-help aid	45
% UG rec. need-based self-help aid	8
% frosh rec. athletic scholarships	1
% UG rec. athletic scholarships	1
% frosh rec. any financial aid	90.7
% UG rec. any financial aid	89.8
% UG borrow to pay for school	74
Average cumulative indebtedness	$26,044

SALISBURY UNIVERSITY

ADMISSIONS OFFICE, 1101 CAMDEN AVENUE, SALISBURY, MD 21801 • ADMISSIONS: 410-543-6161 • FAX: 410-546-6016

CAMPUS LIFE

Quality of Life Rating	**78**
Fire Safety Rating	**71**
Green Rating	**88**
Type of school	public
Environment	town

STUDENTS

Total undergrad enrollment	7,025
% male/female	45/55
% from out of state	14
% from public high school	80
% live on campus	37
% in (# of) fraternities	5 (8)
% in (# of) sororities	5 (5)
% African American	11
% Asian	3
% Caucasian	81
% Hispanic	3
% international	1
# of countries represented	62

SURVEY SAYS . . .

Lab facilities are great
Great food on campus
Intramural sports are popular
Lots of beer drinking
Hard liquor is popular

ACADEMICS

Academic Rating	**73**
Calendar	4/1/4
Student/faculty ratio	16:1
Profs interesting rating	72
Profs accessible rating	76
% classes taught by TAs	2
Most common reg class size	20–29 students
Most common lab size	20–29 students

MOST POPULAR MAJORS
biology/biological sciences
business administration and management
communication studies/speech communication and rhetoric

STUDENTS SAY ". . ."

Academics

Salisbury University has come a long way since it first opened its doors in 1925. Originally a two-year college, Salisbury gradually grew into a four-year BA-conferring school, then added graduate programs in education, business, and nursing. The pace of ascendance has quickened over the past decade, transforming Salisbury from a local school to a regional favorite to, most recently, a university with some national draw. As one student observes, SU is "rapidly gaining respect and a reputation as a challenging, high-level academic institution." Part of the school's allure has to do with cost; SU is extremely affordable for Maryland residents and not much more expensive for out-of-state students. Scale is another factor at this "laid-back, perfectly sized university" small enough to be "your home away from home," but large enough to "offer a top-notch education." Undergraduate business programs are the biggest draw here, attracting nearly 20 percent of all undergrads. Students love that the business curriculum prepares "well-rounded individuals" by "requiring us to have an internship to graduate, which forces one to get some real-world experience." The nursing, education, and communication programs also attract big crowds. In all programs, students enjoy "small class sizes, a compact campus, nice accessible professors, great majors, and fun trips." One student tells us that Salisbury "is about life learning, not just from textbooks and lectures, but from opportunity and diversity." Another adds that the university "is on its way to great things very soon."

Life

Life at SU "depends on what you are looking for. There is a club or organization for everything," and "all kinds of work, volunteer opportunities, and internships available through the school." The Student Office of Activity Programming (SOAP) "brings concerts, comedians, imitations of game shows, and open mic nights to campus and gives us students something fun and constructive to do!" The school's "amazing" Division III sports teams are well supported as well. Even so, many here tell us that life at SU "can get boring a lot of the time though because everything except bars and Taco Bell shuts down early, so many people end up going off campus or to bars and getting drunk." This does not sit well with the conservative rural locals, and as a result, "We have a bad reputation with the Salisbury community. We are known for being a drinking school." And indeed, "Students do drink here at SU. I mean, we are known to be a party school, and it's not a lie. But if you don't do that sort of thing then it's not a big deal. I had a hard time my freshman year first semester because I thought everyone on campus went to parties and that's all there was to do. However, I found people who didn't go to parties, to be friends with, and I started becoming more active in theater and the Honors Student Association, and I found my niche here at SU." As one student sums up, "basically anything you want, SU has."

Student Body

SU undergrads are typically "laid-back and like to hang out with friends, yet they know how and when to get work done when it needs to be done," although there are some here who "drink too much and complain when they don't get the grades they want even though they've skipped most classes due to hangovers. " Most of the latter are presumably gone by sophomore year. There are "a lot of student athletes" here as well as "a D&D crowd who are really nice. They sort of hang out with other Starnet (SciFi club) members." Insofar as diversity, SU apparently has "a department devoted to it."

FINANCIAL AID: 410-543-6165 • E-MAIL: ADMISSIONS@SALISBURY.EDU • WEBSITE: WWW.SALISBURY.EDU

THE PRINCETON REVIEW SAYS

Admissions

Very important factors considered include: Academic GPA, rigor of secondary school record, extracurricular activities, talent/ability. *Important factors considered include:* Class rank, standardized test scores, alumni/ae relation, geographical residence, volunteer work. *Other factors considered include:* Application essay, recommendation(s), character/personal qualities, racial/ethnic status, work experience. TOEFL required of all international applicants. High school diploma is required and GED is accepted. *Academic units required:* 4 English, 3 mathematics, 3 science, (2 science labs), 2 foreign language, 3 social studies. *Academic units recommended:* 4 English, 4 mathematics, 4 science, (3 science labs), 3 foreign language, 3 social studies, 3 academic electives.

Financial Aid

Students should submit: FAFSA. Regular filing deadline is 12/31. The Princeton Review suggests that all financial aid forms be submitted as soon as possible after 1/1. *Need-based scholarships/grants offered:* Federal Pell, SEOG, state scholarships/grants, private scholarships, the school's own gift aid. *Loan aid offered:* Direct Subsidized Stafford, Direct Unsubsidized Stafford, Direct PLUS, Federal Perkins. Applicants will be notified of awards on a rolling basis beginning 3/15. Federal Work-Study Program available. Institutional employment available. Off-campus job opportunities are fair.

The Inside Word

Salisbury has increased its undergraduate population by nearly 20 percent in the past few years which hasn't made admission here any easier. On the contrary, the expansion was a reaction to a growing national profile and corresponding increase in the number of applications. Despite the trend, you can still expect a careful, personalized reading of your application here. It's about a lot more than just the numbers at Salisbury; prepare your application accordingly.

THE SCHOOL SAYS "..."

From The Admissions Office

"Friendly, convenient, safe, and beautiful are just a few of the words used to describe the campus of Salisbury University. The campus is a compact, self-contained community that offers the full range of student services. Beautiful, traditional-style architecture and impeccably landscaped grounds combine to create an atmosphere that inspires learning and fosters student pride. Located just 30 minutes from the beaches of Ocean City, Maryland, SU students enjoy a year-round resort social life as well as an inside track on summer jobs. Situated less than 2 hours from the urban excitement of Baltimore and Washington, D.C., greater Salisbury makes up for its lack of size—its population is about 80,000—by being strategically located. Within easy driving distance of a number of other major cities, including New York City, Philadelphia, and Norfolk, Salisbury is the hub of the Delmarva Peninsula, a mostly rural region flavored by the salty air of the Chesapeake Bay and Atlantic Ocean.

"Submission of SAT and/or ACT scores when applying would be optional to freshman applicants who present a weighted high school grade point average (GPA) of 3.5 or higher on a 4.0 scale. Any student applying with less than a 3.5 would still need to submit a standardized test score to supplement the official high school transcript. Additionally, an applicant may wish to submit a standardized test score subsequent to admission for full scholarship consideration as the majority of the university's scholarships include test scores as a requirement."

SELECTIVITY

Admissions Rating	86
# of applicants	7,275
% of applicants accepted	53
% of acceptees attending	31

FRESHMAN PROFILE

Range SAT Critical Reading	520–600
Range SAT Math	520–610
Range SAT Writing	510–590
Range ACT Composite	21–25
Minimum paper TOEFL	550
Minimum computer TOEFL	213
Average HS GPA	3.53
% graduated top 10% of class	17.5
% graduated top 25% of class	55.3
% graduated top 50% of class	92.3

DEADLINES

Early action	
Deadline	12/1
Notification	1/15
Regular	
Priority	1/15
Notification	3/15
Nonfall registration?	yes

APPLICANTS ALSO LOOK AT AND SOMETIMES PREFER

St. Mary's College of Maryland
Towson University
University of Maryland—Baltimore County

AND RARELY PREFER

University of Maryland—College Park

FINANCIAL FACTS

Financial Aid Rating	67
Annual in-state tuition	$4,814
Annual out-of-state tuition	$13,116
Room and board	$7,798
Required fees	$1,678
Books and supplies	$1,200
% frosh rec. need-based scholarship or grant aid	35
% UG rec. need-based scholarship or grant aid	30
% frosh rec. need-based self-help aid	30
% UG rec. need-based self-help aid	32
% frosh rec. any financial aid	72
% UG rec. any financial aid	68
% UG borrow to pay for school	53.1
Average cumulative indebtedness	$15,939

SAMFORD UNIVERSITY

800 Lakeshore Drive, Birmingham, AL 35229 • Admissions: 205-726-3673 • Fax: 205-726-2171

CAMPUS LIFE

Quality of Life Rating	92
Fire Safety Rating	88
Green Rating	74
Type of school	private
Affiliation	Baptist
Environment	town

STUDENTS

Total undergrad enrollment	2,824
% male/female	36/64
% from out of state	53
% from public high school	53.1
% live on campus	67
% in (# of) fraternities	20 (6)
% in (# of) sororities	31 (6)
% African American	7
% Asian	1
% Caucasian	88
% Hispanic	1
% international	1
# of countries represented	19

SURVEY SAYS . . .

Athletic facilities are great
School is well run
Students are friendly
Students get along with local
community
Students love Birmingham, AL
Great off-campus food
Students are happy
Very little drug use

ACADEMICS

Academic Rating	85
Calendar	4/1/4
Student/faculty ratio	11:1
Profs interesting rating	88
Profs accessible rating	84
Most common reg class size	10–19 students
Most common lab size	10–19 students

MOST POPULAR MAJORS

biology/biological sciences
nursing/registered nurse
(rn, asn, bsn, msn)
teacher education, multiple levels

STUDENTS SAY ". . ."

Academics

Samford University, "a beautiful liberal arts college with Christian values," draws undergrads seeking "a close-knit community in which high value is placed on morality, academic excellence and communication skills." Students tell us that "Samford represents what is great about a Christian university. It provides an environment that is diverse and not typically conservative Christian." A "well-rounded, challenging curriculum" ensures that students transcend indoctrination while experiencing "some aspect of religious discussion…in classes where you would not usually encounter it." High expectations ensure that they don't coast through to an easy degree. As one student explains, "Samford professors expect a lot from their students, and in return we expect a lot from them. It's been said that academics at Samford are quite a bit harder than most universities, so when someone gets a B people see it as an A, when they get a C it's seen as a B, and so forth." Outstanding disciplines here include English, journalism, nursing, pharmacy, business, music, and theater. But perhaps Samford's most outstanding quality is its "incredibly friendly, welcoming, and genuine atmosphere that makes the transition to college life a pleasant one. The campus is positively breathtaking, the facilities are excellent, class sizes are relatively small, and professors are available and helpful…There is an overall feeling of contentment on campus."

Life

"There are people who party and those who don't" at Samford; despite the campus' official "dry" status, "there will always be those few people who break the rules," and furthermore, Birmingham offers "some fun nightlife" that can, and occasionally does, involve intoxicants. As a whole, however, "students generally are not big partiers, but like to have fun. Most weekends are spent hanging out with friends or traveling." "There is a strong Greek presence" on the Samford campus, "and many weekends include Greek parties or fundraisers and activities." Religious groups "are especially popular, and the majority of the student body is involved in at least one college ministry throughout the week." Students enjoy "at least five opportunities a week to worship" and "are very engaged in the community and local churches." These activities include "a strong awareness of global issues: fair trade, Darfur, etc." Samford's gated campus "is located in a very safe part of Birmingham," providing students a secure enclave from which to launch their explorations of the city. Students tell us the city is "awesome," "with plenty of places to eat, shop, and play. There are several movie theaters and shopping centers within a 10-mile radius, as well as a roller skating rink, plenty of gorgeous parks, and a thriving downtown."

Student Body

"The Samford stereotype is a white, wealthy, Southern, Protestant (usually Baptist) female, decked out in country club attire," but "while that accounts for maybe an (admittedly vocal) 20 percent of the school, there is a lot of diversity otherwise, especially outside the Greek system." Students who don't fit the mold "often hang out on the quad and are active in various campus organizations or other activities. There actually are hippies, druggies, minorities, political extremists of all stripes, gay people, and people from all over the world at Samford. Don't be deceived by your first glance." Quite a few respondents told us that while "a wide variety of people attend" Samford, "a large percent were raised in a very sheltered environment" and the majority are "white, upper-class, southern Christians" "with strong Christian values and beliefs." Students tend to be highly ambitious, with "a generally heavy interest in their future and…a plan for achieving their goals."

FINANCIAL AID: 800-888-7245 • E-MAIL: ADMISS@SAMFORD.EDU • WEBSITE: WWW.SAMFORD.EDU

THE PRINCETON REVIEW SAYS

Admissions

Very important factors considered include: Application essay, academic GPA, recommendation(s), rigor of secondary school record, standardized test scores, character/personal qualities, religious affiliation/commitment. *Important factors considered include:* Class rank, alumni/ae relation, extracurricular activities, interview. *Other factors considered include:* Geographical residence, level of applicant's interest, racial/ethnic status, state residency, talent/ability, volunteer work, work experience. SAT or ACT required; TOEFL required of all international applicants. High school diploma is required and GED is accepted. *Academic units required:* 4 English, 3 mathematics, 3 science, 2 foreign language, 2 social studies. *Academic units recommended:* (2 science labs).

Financial Aid

Students should submit: FAFSA. The Princeton Review suggests that all financial aid forms be submitted as soon as possible after 1/1. *Need-based scholarships/grants offered:* Federal Pell, SEOG, state scholarships/grants, private scholarships, the school's own gift aid. *Loan aid offered:* FFEL Subsidized Stafford, FFEL Unsubsidized Stafford, FFEL PLUS, Federal Perkins, college/university loans from institutional funds. Applicants will be notified of awards on or about 4/1. Federal Work-Study Program available. Institutional employment available. Off-campus job opportunities are excellent.

The Inside Word

Samford admits applicants on a rolling basis. The first acceptance letters go out as early as October. As is often the case with rolling admissions, those who apply early in the process are most likely to receive a generous review. The school strongly recommends a campus visit, meaning you ought to make one if at all possible. A campus visit is a great way of signaling your desire to attend the school, which in turn improves your chances of being admitted.

THE SCHOOL SAYS "..."

From The Admissions Office

"Students who are drawn to Samford are well-rounded individuals who not only expect to be challenged but are excited by the prospect. It is the critical and creative way you think, it is the articulate way you write and speak, it is the joy of learning that stays with you throughout your life, and it is the clarity of decision making guided by Christian principles."

SELECTIVITY
Admissions Rating	91
# of applicants	2,153
% of applicants accepted	89
% of acceptees attending	37

FRESHMAN PROFILE
Range SAT Critical Reading	510–630
Range SAT Math	500–610
Range ACT Composite	20–27
Minimum paper TOEFL	550
Minimum computer TOEFL	213
Minimum web-based TOEFL	80
Average HS GPA	3.58
% graduated top 10% of class	36
% graduated top 25% of class	59
% graduated top 50% of class	86

DEADLINES
Regular	
Priority	3/1
Notification	rolling
Nonfall registration?	yes

APPLICANTS ALSO LOOK AT
AND OFTEN PREFER
The University of Alabama at Birmingham
University of Alabama—Tuscaloosa
Auburn University

AND SOMETIMES PREFER
Troy University
Furman University
University of Georgia
Abilene Christian University

FINANCIAL FACTS
Financial Aid Rating	75
Annual tuition	$20,200
Room and board	$6,624
Required fees	$220
% frosh rec. need-based scholarship or grant aid	35
% UG rec. need-based scholarship or grant aid	34
% frosh rec. need-based self-help aid	31
% UG rec. need-based self-help aid	34
% frosh rec. athletic scholarships	8
% UG rec. athletic scholarships	7
% UG borrow to pay for school	46
Average cumulative indebtedness	$18,501

SANTA CLARA UNIVERSITY

500 EL CAMINO REAL, SANTA CLARA, CA 95053 • ADMISSIONS: 408-554-4700 • FAX: 408-554-5255

CAMPUS LIFE

Quality of Life Rating	**89**
Fire Safety Rating	**93**
Green Rating	**96**
Type of school	private
Affiliation	Roman Catholic
Environment	city

STUDENTS

Total undergrad enrollment	5,267
% male/female	47/53
% from out of state	36
% from public high school	43
% live on campus	49
% African American	4
% Asian	16
% Caucasian	47
% Hispanic	13
% international	3
# of countries represented	31

SURVEY SAYS . . .

Athletic facilities are great
Career services are great
School is well run
Students are happy
Lots of beer drinking
Hard liquor is popular

ACADEMICS

Academic Rating	**83**
Calendar	quarter
Student/faculty ratio	12.4:1
Profs interesting rating	86
Profs accessible rating	88
Most common reg class size	20–29 students
Most common lab size	10–19 students

MOST POPULAR MAJORS
business/marketing
social sciences
psychology/engineering

STUDENTS SAY ". . ."

Academics

Santa Clara University is a small Jesuit institution that "teaches Catholic values and strives for global solidarity" while offering "a great academic program that stresses the development of critical thinking" and real-world application of classroom lessons. Here the Jesuit ideals of broad education and competence, conscience and compassion are stressed not only through a thorough core curriculum (which "develops better-rounded students who are more aware of the world around them") but also through "a large emphasis on immersion trips and getting students to volunteer and to go out into the community." Science, business, and engineering are the school's academic fortes, although students identify many other strong points: Art history, English, mathematics, and communications all have their boosters. SCU operates on a quarter system that "is very fast-paced." For some it means "constantly worrying about the next midterm, final, or paper that's due," resulting in "chronic stress." Others, however, "love having classes for ten weeks, plus one week of finals," describing it as "a short enough time that you don't get sick of a course" but long enough to "really develop a relationship with your professor." As one student explains, "The engineering program is notoriously difficult and has a reputation for losing eager freshman to easier majors such as communications or sociology. Other programs are extremely challenging" but manageable. In all areas, the school's small size "fosters an excellent community and strong access to and interaction with faculty." An added bonus: "Professional placement in the Bay Area is extraordinary."

Life

"There are two categories of students" at SCU: "the drinkers and the thinkers." In both camps, "most are very academic and stay in and study during the week," but the former are more likely on weekends to "hit the parties or visit San Francisco. Everyone needs a break sometime!" The latter tend to be "very busy pursuing their careers" through internships, workshops, and interest-related clubs. The party scene typically revs up on Wednesdays, Fridays, and Saturdays. "House parties off campus are a really fun way for everyone to interact" and represent the party venue of choice. Partying is hardly the only leisure alternative, however; as one student explains, "What most students do for fun depends on the person. Many find fun in staying in their dorm playing video games with friends, while others enjoy going to the handful of local bars that cater to SCU students. Also, the Activities Planning Board has concerts and comedy shows…that students can attend for ridiculously cheap prices." Many here are athletically inclined; for spectators, "basketball season is when our student fan group is most active, and a lot of students come out for the men's games. Our volleyball and soccer teams pull a good amount of fans in the fall." Because SCU "is located right next to a Cal Train station; a weekend trip to San Francisco is affordable and fun!" Many take advantage of the opportunity.

Student Body

"The typical student at Santa Clara is probably from an upper-middle-class family," making the student body "somewhat homogenous in terms of economic background, but that is expected since it is a private school in California." Writes one student, "My one problem with Santa Clara is that we have a very limited demographic. The people here are the people who can pay to be here. There are different, atypical people here; you just have to look slightly harder to find them." SCU undergrads typically "work hard and are intelligent but know how to have fun and go out. They have balance in their lives" and are "outgoing and very involved in clubs and organizations." They tend to be "relatively conservative and success-oriented."

FINANCIAL AID: 408-554-4505 • WEBSITE: WWW.SCU.EDU

THE PRINCETON REVIEW SAYS

Admissions

Very important factors considered include: Application essay, academic GPA, recommendation(s), rigor of secondary school record. *Important factors considered include:* Standardized test scores, character/personal qualities, extracurricular activities, racial/ethnic status, talent/ability, volunteer work. *Other factors considered include:* Class rank, alumni/ae relation, first generation, geographical residence, level of applicant's interest, religious affiliation/commitment, state residency, work experience. SAT or ACT required; TOEFL required of all international applicants. High school diploma is required and GED is not accepted. *Academic units required:* 4 English, 3 mathematics, 2 science, 2 foreign language, 3 social studies, 1 academic elective. *Academic units recommended:* 4 English, 4 mathematics, 3 science, 3 foreign language, 3 social studies, 1 visual/performing arts, 1 academic elective.

Financial Aid

Students should submit: FAFSA, CSS/Financial Aid PROFILE. The Princeton Review suggests that all financial aid forms be submitted as soon as possible after 1/1. Early Action Deadline 11/1. *Need-based scholarships/grants offered:* Federal Pell, SEOG, state scholarships/grants, private scholarships, the school's own gift aid. *Loan aid offered:* Direct Subsidized Stafford, Direct Unsubsidized Stafford, Direct PLUS, FFEL PLUS, Federal Perkins, Private alternative loans. Applicants will be notified of awards on or about 4/1. Federal Work-Study Program available. Off-campus job opportunities are good.

The Inside Word

Each year, the Santa Clara admissions office works hard to assemble a diverse incoming class. The result is a student body with large Asian and Hispanic populations; this isn't your typical lily-white private school.

THE SCHOOL SAYS "..."

From The Admissions Office

"Santa Clara University, located one hour south of San Francisco, offers its undergraduates an opportunity to be educated within a challenging, dynamic, and caring community. The university blends a sense of tradition and history (as the oldest college in California) with a vision that values innovation and a deep commitment to social justice. Santa Clara's faculty members are talented scholars who are demanding, supportive, and accessible. The students are serious about academics, are ethnically diverse, and enjoy a full range of athletic, social, community-service, religious, and cultural activities—both on campus and through the many options presented by our northern California location. The undergraduate program includes three divisions: the College of Arts and Sciences, the School of Business, and the School of Engineering.

"Santa Clara University will accept either the SAT or the ACT. The ACT Writing component is optional. The highest verbal and the highest math scores attained on the SAT will be used."

SELECTIVITY
Admissions Rating	90
# of applicants	10,124
% of applicants accepted	58
% of acceptees attending	21
# accepting a place on wait list	870
% admitted from wait list	6

FRESHMAN PROFILE
Range SAT Critical Reading	550–650
Range SAT Math	570–680
Range ACT Composite	25–30
Minimum paper TOEFL	550
Minimum computer TOEFL	213
Average HS GPA	3.53
% graduated top 10% of class	40
% graduated top 25% of class	72
% graduated top 50% of class	94

DEADLINES
Early action	
Deadline	11/1
Notification	12/31
Regular	
Deadline	1/7
Notification	4/1
Nonfall registration?	no

APPLICANTS ALSO LOOK AT
AND OFTEN PREFER
University of Southern California
University of California—Berkeley
University of California—Los Angeles
AND SOMETIMES PREFER
University of California—San Diego
University of San Diego
Loyola Marymount University
AND RARELY PREFER
University of San Francisco
University of California—Santa Cruz

FINANCIAL FACTS
Financial Aid Rating	77
Annual tuition	$36,000
Room and board	$11,400
Books and supplies	$1,638
% frosh rec. need-based scholarship or grant aid	32
% UG rec. need-based scholarship or grant aid	28
% frosh rec. non-need-based scholarship or grant aid	20
% UG rec. non-need-based scholarship or grant aid	13
% frosh rec. need-based self-help aid	24
% UG rec. need-based self-help aid	23
% frosh rec. athletic scholarships	6
% UG rec. athletic scholarships	5
% frosh rec. any financial aid	83
% UG rec. any financial aid	77
% UG borrow to pay for school	43.6
Average cumulative indebtedness	$25,438

SARAH LAWRENCE COLLEGE

ONE MEAD WAY, BRONXVILLE, NY 10708-5999 • ADMISSIONS: 914-395-2510 • FAX: 914-395-2676

CAMPUS LIFE

Quality of Life Rating	**64**
Fire Safety Rating	**90**
Green Rating	**86**
Type of school	private
Environment	metropolis

STUDENTS

Total undergrad enrollment	1,309
% male/female	26/74
% from out of state	75
% from public high school	65
% live on campus	85
% African American	4
% Asian	6
% Caucasian	68
% Hispanic	5
% international	3
# of countries represented	32

SURVEY SAYS . . .

Lots of liberal students
Class discussions encouraged
No one cheats
Students aren't religious
Frats and sororities are unpopular or nonexistent
(Almost) everyone smokes

ACADEMICS

Academic Rating	**98**
Calendar	semester
Student/faculty ratio	9:1
Profs interesting rating	98
Profs accessible rating	89
Most common reg class size	10–19 students

STUDENTS SAY ". . ."

Academics

Offering a unique approach to liberal arts education, Sarah Lawrence College is a "serious academic and artistic environment where individual passion fuels learning." Through SLC's distinctive curriculum, students are the architects of their own educational experience and the school "places a great emphasis on personal research and personal responsibility." In their first year, undergrads meet with their advisors every week to discuss their academic plans, and "besides your don (permanent counselor), you have a slew of people who really want you to be the best that you can be." Of particular note, students benefit from "inordinate amounts of individual time with each professor," who are all "enormously educated, good teachers, and passionate about their subjects." Across disciplines, Sarah Lawrence professors "are generally willing to give over copious amounts of time to undergraduate research papers, projects, ideas, and extracurricular discussion." A student shares this noteworthy story: "I am in a lecture about Epic Poetry but I'm not really interested in poetry, so I talked to the professor and he was totally cool with all my papers being about anthropological elements of the text and not poetic ones." Among other innovations, SLC's unusual (but, some say, inefficient) course registration system allows students to interview teachers before signing up for classes. Fortunately, "all of the classes here are excellent, so if one doesn't get into a desired class, it isn't the end of the world." Unfortunately, many students feel SLC's administration can be bureaucratic and out-of-step with the school's dominant philosophy and culture. When discussing these shortcomings, however, students acknowledge that the administration faces many challenges in that the school is "expensive to run" and funds are more limited than at larger colleges.

Life

Whether you enjoy attending "study parties" or playing Frisbee in your underwear, "life at Sarah Lawrence is about as quirky as the college itself." Club meetings and school-sponsored activities are sometimes lightly attended; however, poetry readings, artistic pursuits, live music shows, and political organizing are widely popular, and "there is a growing athletic community on campus" as well. On campus, there are occasional dance parties, as well as casual get-togethers; however, on the whole, campus life is fairly subdued. A student claims, "The best way to relax is to get together with a few friends, put on some music, and just hang out. Conversations range from deep political or philosophical debates to discussing cartoons." Located near the village of Bronxville, "everybody enjoys the fact that we're a hop, skip and a jump away from wonderful Manhattan," and a majority of students head to the city on the weekend. For those who stay on campus, "weekends include a lot of wandering around, but mostly just sitting and talking in friends dorm rooms about typical stuff, you know, Nietzsche and the importance of green architecture." In addition, students might be found "playing music together, listening to music, throwing dinner parties, drinking beer, playing board games, playing drinking games, talking about music, going to the city, eating a lot of Chinese and Sushi take-out, [or] playing in the snow."

Student Body

With a motto like "we're different, so are you," it's not surprising that "Sarah Lawrence is like Mecca for creative, proactive, outrageous, and independent students who want ultimate freedom in designing their education." Bohemian attire and alternative music are culturally prevalent, and "writers, artists, eccentrics, musicians, academics, activists, and scientists all call Sarah Lawrence home." In fact, many students say that, "the typical Sarah Lawrence student looks like the atypical student at any mainstream university." Students agree that the SLC "environment is very inclusive of all people and walks of life;" however, many complain that the "indie" or bohemian veneer attracts students who are unfriendly, self-absorbed, or who are "so used to being the "different" ones that they can't deal with the fact that they aren't "special" here." While some would like a warmer and friendlier college atmosphere, students reassure us that "there is a wide spectrum of interests and lifestyles so almost everyone can find a crowd of friends that suits them."

FINANCIAL AID: 914-395-2570 • E-MAIL: SLCADMIT@SLC.EDU • WEBSITE: WWW.SARAHLAWRENCE.EDU

THE PRINCETON REVIEW SAYS

Admissions

Very important factors considered include: Application essays, recommendation(s), rigor of secondary school record. *Important factors considered include:* Academic GPA, character/personal qualities, extracurricular activities, talent/ability. *Other factors considered include:* Class rank, alumni/ae relation, first generation, geographical residence, interview, racial/ethnic status, volunteer work, work experience. TOEFL required of all international applicants. High school diploma is required and GED is accepted. *Academic units required:* 4 English, 2 mathematics, 2 science, 2 foreign language, 2 history. *Academic units recommended:* 4 mathematics, 4 science, 4 foreign language, 4 history.

Financial Aid

Students should submit: FAFSA, CSS/Financial Aid PROFILE, state aid form, noncustodial PROFILE. Regular filing deadline is 2/1. The Princeton Review suggests that all financial aid forms be submitted as soon as possible after 1/1. *Need-based scholarships/grants offered:* Federal Pell, SEOG, state scholarships/grants, private scholarships, the school's own gift aid. *Loan aid offered:* FFEL Subsidized Stafford, FFEL Unsubsidized Stafford, FFEL PLUS, Federal Perkins. Applicants will be notified of awards on or about 4/1. Federal Work-Study Program available. Institutional employment available. Off-campus job opportunities are good.

The Inside Word

In addition to three required essay questions, Sarah Lawrence College requests that candidates submit a graded, analytic writing sample. Students say you shouldn't underestimate the importance of this unusual requirement, as SLC's curriculum is writing-based and a good sample can make your application stand out. Sarah Lawrence College doesn't believe that standardized test scores accurately reflect a student's ability to succeed in their academic program, and therefore, they do not review ACT or SAT scores.

THE SCHOOL SAYS " . . ."

From The Admissions Office

"Students who come to Sarah Lawrence are curious about the world, and they have an ardent desire to satisfy that curiosity. Sarah Lawrence offers such students two innovative academic structures: the seminar/conference system and the arts components. Courses in the humanities, social sciences, natural sciences, and mathematics are taught in the seminar/conference style. The seminars enroll an average of 11 students and consist of lecture, discussion, readings, and assigned papers. For each seminar, students also meet one-on-one in biweekly conferences, for which they conceive of individualized projects and shape them under the direction of professors. Arts components let students combine history and theory with practice. Painters, printmakers, photographers, sculptors, filmmakers, composers, musicians, choreographers, dancers, actors, and directors work in readily available studios, editing facilities, and darkrooms, guided by accomplished professionals. The secure, wooded campus is 30 minutes from midtown Manhattan, and the diversity of people and ideas at Sarah Lawrence make it an extraordinary educational environment.

"Sarah Lawrence College no longer uses standardized test scores in the admission process. This decision reflects our conviction that overemphasis on test preparation can distort results and make the application process inordinately stressful, and that academic success is better predicted by the student's course rigor, their grades, recommendations, and writing ability."

SELECTIVITY

Admissions Rating	99
# of applicants	2,785
% of applicants accepted	46
% of acceptees attending	27
# accepting a place on wait list	200
% admitted from wait list	30
# of early decision applicants	137
% accepted early decision	62

FRESHMAN PROFILE

Minimum paper TOEFL	600
Minimum computer TOEFL	250
Average HS GPA	3.7
% graduated top 10% of class	37
% graduated top 25% of class	84
% graduated top 50% of class	98

DEADLINES

Early decision	
Deadline	11/1
Notification	12/15
Regular	
Deadline	1/1
Notification	4/1
Nonfall registration?	no

FINANCIAL FACTS

Financial Aid Rating	82
Annual tuition	$39,450
Room	$8,756
General fee	$700
Student activities	$200
Books and supplies	$600
% frosh rec. need-based scholarship or grant aid	49
% UG rec. need-based scholarship or grant aid	51
% frosh rec. non-need-based scholarship or grant aid	1
% frosh rec. need-based self-help aid	52
% UG rec. need-based self-help aid	52
% frosh rec. any financial aid	50
% UG rec. any financial aid	53
% UG borrow to pay for school	63
Average cumulative indebtedness	$15,581

SCRIPPS COLLEGE

1030 COLUMBIA AVENUE, MAILBOX #1265, CLAREMONT, CA 91711 • ADMISSIONS: 909-621-8149 • FAX: 909-607-7508

CAMPUS LIFE

Quality of Life Rating	**94**
Fire Safety Rating	**70**
Green Rating	**82**
Type of school	private
Environment	town

STUDENTS

Total undergrad enrollment	944
% male/female	0/100
% from out of state	59
% from public high school	59
% live on campus	96
% African American	4
% Asian	13
% Caucasian	50
% Hispanic	8
% Native American	1
% international	1
# of countries represented	12

SURVEY SAYS . . .

No one cheats
Great food on campus
Dorms are like palaces
Frats and sororities are unpopular or nonexistent
Political activism is popular

ACADEMICS

Academic Rating	**98**
Calendar	semester
Student/faculty ratio	10:1
Profs interesting rating	91
Profs accessible rating	90
Most common reg class size	10–19 students
Most common lab size	10–19 students

MOST POPULAR MAJORS

English language and literature
international relations and affairs
psychology

STUDENTS SAY ". . ."

Academics

Scripps College is for serious female students looking "to get away from the preppy, East Coast feeling" of other "top-notch" liberal arts educations. Due to its membership in the Claremont College Consortium, Scripps provides the "intimacy of a small school" environment while boasting "the resources of a large university." With an "emphasis on analytical thinking and creativity" Scripps' unique Core program focuses on "broadening minds and teaching students how to think" while presenting "learning in a way that is socially conscious." Scripps' "humanities-based education" takes an "interdisciplinary approach to learning, which allows the mind to cultivate and [to] make connections amongst all subjects, creating strong, intellectual women" and providing them with "the skills to become leaders in their chosen fields." At Scripps "it's difficult to go 'under the radar'" because "the professors are extremely caring and attentive to their students' needs." Small class sizes are "an instant appeal." According to many students, Scripps "is the best of both worlds…intimacy of a small school with resources of a small-to-medium university, atmosphere of a women's college with the benefits of co-education (through the other Claremont Colleges), [and] small-town feel with L.A. an easy hour away by Metrolink." Dedicated to "turning loose generation after generation of confident, hopeful, courageous, and inspiring women," the school offers "a good variety of courses."

Life

"Scripps is a place where women are challenged to stretch themselves academically, have a strong voice, pursue their passions (whatever they may be), and love every minute of it." What natural luxuries the "warm weather" and "laid-back California atmosphere" provide, the school capitalizes upon: from its "beautiful grounds and dorms," to "the brand-new Sally Tiernan Field House, [which] makes working out fun and easy." "Devoted to creating strong female leaders," as one hard-core Scripps enthusiast proclaims, Scripps "is a playground for the mind, body, and spirit that allows you to learn, grow, and understand yourself and the world." For relaxation, students "will go into town or hang out at the Motley, the school coffeehouse." On a quiet night, students "watch movies, hang out in The Village, go to the theater on campus, and [find] many other extracurricular activates." Though the Five College Consortium offers numerous party options, "for those not interested in the party scene, residence halls often host evening soirees; there are numerous art openings." "Many students enjoy the weather and the opportunity for outdoor activities (surfing, skiing, hiking, etc)." Others who have found their way into the city appreciate "the proximity to movie theaters and L.A."

Student Body

"Inspiring, strong women out to change the world" who are united by curiosity and intellect, all Scripps students "are intelligent and have a passion." Or, as one student humorously put it, Scripps students are "feminist liberals who will go on to change the world with their elite education, but [they] will do so with fun and style." Though the "'typical' student is upper-middle class, overachiever, from SoCal, the pacific northwest, or the East Coast," "there are many exceptions to this." "Each of the 5 C's gets a stereotype, and Scripps' tends to be 'Militant Feminist' or 'Daddy's Girl.' We all sort of laugh at that because neither of those are a majority here." Though the average student is "politically liberal [and] somewhat idealistic [and] enjoys obscure music and literature," "there are all kinds of women—outspoken lesbians, very outdoorsy types, girls who love to party, extreme intellects, etc." The bottom line is: at Scripps "women support women." Even those not specifically looking for an all-female education say, "I didn't intend on going to a women's college, but I am really glad that I did. It's been a great experience; it's helped me to build confidence in a world that is still male-dominated."

FINANCIAL AID: 909-621-8275 • E-MAIL: ADMISSION@SCRIPPSCOLLEGE.EDU • WEBSITE: WWW.SCRIPPSCOLLEGE.EDU

THE PRINCETON REVIEW SAYS

Admissions

Very important factors considered include: Class rank, application essay, academic GPA, recommendation(s), rigor of secondary school record, standardized test scores, alumni/ae relation, character/personal qualities, extracurricular activities, first generation, interview, racial/ethnic status. *Important factors considered include:* Geographical residence. SAT or ACT required; TOEFL required of all international applicants. High school diploma is required and GED is accepted. *Academic units required:* 4 English, 3 mathematics, 3 science, 3 foreign language, 3 social studies. *Academic units recommended:* 4 English.

Financial Aid

Students should submit: FAFSA, CSS/Financial Aid PROFILE, state aid form, noncustodial PROFILE, business/farm supplement. Verification worksheet, signed copies of parent Institution Verification form, parent and student federal tax returns. Regular filing deadline is 5/1. The Princeton Review suggests that all financial aid forms be submitted as soon as possible after 1/1. *Need-based scholarships/grants offered:* Federal Pell, SEOG, state scholarships/grants, private scholarships, the school's own gift aid. *Loan aid offered:* FFEL Subsidized Stafford, FFEL Unsubsidized Stafford, FFEL PLUS, Federal Perkins, college/university loans from institutional funds. Applicants will be notified of awards on or about 4/1. Federal Work-Study Program available. Institutional employment available. Off-campus job opportunities are good.

The Inside Word

Though academic excellence is a prerequisite, when it comes to applying to Scripps, admissions is based on more than just the usual suspects. In lieu of formulas or standardized test minimums, admissions officers aim to establish a diverse and talented freshman class and do so by evaluating a variety of factors. Serious candidates should carve out a unique personal statement while giving equal attention to each facet of their application. Strong writing skills and intellectual curiosity are viewed as essential qualities in successful applicants.

THE SCHOOL SAYS " . . ."

From The Admissions Office

"At Scripps, we believe that learning involves much more than amassing information. The truly educated person is one who can think analytically, communicate effectively, and make confident, responsible choices. Scripps classes are small (the average class size is 15) so that they foster an atmosphere where students feel comfortable participating, testing old assumptions, and exploring new ideas. Our curriculum is based on the traditional components of a liberal arts education: a set of general requirements in a wide variety of disciplines including foreign language, natural science, and writing; a multicultural requirement; a major that asks students to study one particular field in depth; and a variety of electives that allows considerable flexibility. What distinguishes Scripps from other liberal arts colleges is an emphasis on interdisciplinary courses.

"First-year applicants must submit results of the SAT or the ACT. SAT Subject Tests are not required."

SELECTIVITY
Admissions Rating	99
# of applicants	1,931
% of applicants accepted	43
% of acceptees attending	30
# accepting a place on wait list	176
# of early decision applicants	81
% accepted early decision	48

FRESHMAN PROFILE
Range SAT Critical Reading	640–730
Range SAT Math	620–710
Range SAT Writing	650–730
Range ACT Composite	28–32
Minimum paper TOEFL	600
Minimum computer TOEFL	250
Average HS GPA	4.08
% graduated top 10% of class	70
% graduated top 25% of class	92
% graduated top 50% of class	99

DEADLINES
Early decision	
Deadline	11/1
Notification	12/15
Regular	
Deadline	1/1
Notification	4/1
Nonfall registration?	yes

APPLICANTS ALSO LOOK AT
AND OFTEN PREFER
Pomona College
Occidental College
University of Southern California
University of California—Berkeley
Stanford University
Wellesley College

AND SOMETIMES PREFER
University of California—Los Angeles

FINANCIAL FACTS
Financial Aid Rating	98
Annual tuition	$37,736
Room and board	$11,500
Required fees	$214
Books and supplies	$800
% frosh rec. need-based scholarship or grant aid	44
% UG rec. need-based scholarship or grant aid	42
% frosh rec. non-need-based scholarship or grant aid	15
% UG rec. non-need-based scholarship or grant aid	21
% frosh rec. need-based self-help aid	36
% UG rec. need-based self-help aid	35
% frosh rec. any financial aid	44
% UG rec. any financial aid	54
% UG borrow to pay for school	48
Average cumulative indebtedness	$13,207

SEATTLE UNIVERSITY

ADMISSIONS OFFICE, 900 BROADWAY, SEATTLE, WA 98122-4340 • ADMISSIONS: 206-296-2000 • FAX: 206-296-5656

CAMPUS LIFE

Quality of Life Rating	**98**
Fire Safety Rating	**60***
Green Rating	**97**
Type of school	private
Affiliation	Roman Catholic/Jesuit
Environment	metropolis

STUDENTS

Total undergrad enrollment	4,168
% male/female	39/61
% from out of state	40
% from public high school	63
% live on campus	27
% African American	6
% Asian	19
% Caucasian	52
% Hispanic	8
% Native American	1
% international	8
# of countries represented	74

SURVEY SAYS . . .

No one cheats
School is well run
Diverse student types on campus
Students get along with local community
Students love Seattle, WA
Great off-campus food
Frats and sororities are unpopular or nonexistent

ACADEMICS

Academic Rating	**89**
Calendar	quarter
Student/faculty ratio	13:1
Profs interesting rating	90
Profs accessible rating	89
Most common reg class size	10–19 students
Most common lab size	10–19 students

MOST POPULAR MAJORS

finance
marketing/marketing management
nursing/registered nurse
(rn, asn, bsn, msn)

STUDENTS SAY ". . ."

Academics

Seattle University is a midsize Jesuit university that "offers a community experience in which students can learn and grow together." "Between its academic excellence, exceptional facilities, location, and social justice focus, this school offers the holistic Jesuit educational experience in a dynamic setting appropriate for the scholars of the 21st century." Issues of "community and social justice in a complex world" permeate the curriculum here, "pushing students to re-evaluate their presuppositions about the world in a just and humane manner." Academically, SU "is very strong and very challenging," but great support networks—including a writing center, a math lab, and an encouraging faculty help students cope. According to students, professors "all respond to e-mails…leave us their cell phone numbers," and "will meet after hours to talk about an assignment." A "prestigious nursing program" tops a list of outstanding departments that also include public affairs, criminal justice, civil engineering, and business. Throughout the university, "SU believes in emphasizing the human aspect of education, and so access to faculty and administrative staff is seamless. Our president walks around and talks to students, and the entire administration is very visible on campus."

Life

SU students are "lucky enough to live in the middle of one of the most exciting cities in the country," and most take full advantage of the situation. "Being in Capitol Hill, there's more than enough restaurants, theaters, museums, concerts, parks, book stores/libraries to suit anyone's palate," while the greater city "is fun to explore, so weekends are not limited to sitting around drinking." Seattle is a music town, so, "there is a lot of live music—both on campus and off—as well as movies." Students also venture into the city to perform community service, a popular vocation among SU undergrads. Traveling just a bit beyond city limits, students find an area "perfect for outdoorsy things like snowboarding/skiing in the winter or rock climbing/hiking/camping in the fall and spring. The school usually sponsors these types of trips for easy access." On-campus options are "fun for all types of people," with events ranging from concerts, "sporting events, magicians, musical talent, speakers, and lots of different types of food to try," as well as "hundreds of events ranging from community cookie-baking to giant drag shows or cultural festivals. Residence halls have programming daily, and it's always some sort of awareness month or week. This is an active campus." There's also "a party life at Seattle U, but it's smaller than state schools." As one student puts it, "it's definitely not a party school, but those who like to party will be able to find something. There's really a place for everybody."

Student Body

SU attracts a lot of "generally nice, down-to-earth people" who "are using their college experience to launch into their post-college career and not as a four-year vacation before work starts." Students here "are very independent-minded. Everyone has plans set, and they want to succeed at what they're setting out to do. But with that said, we all get along really well, and everyone hangs out with each other. There's little separation between majors, and it helps that the residence halls aren't divided up by academics." They also tend to be the sort of folks who "want to make a difference in the world: business majors, music majors, English majors; we all want to help out." They're "pretty aware of events going on in the world—and care." Environmental awareness "is a huge part of campus community, as is community service." Students pride themselves on SU's "pretty diverse" population, which includes "a lot of international students," a "large gay population," and "quite a few nontraditional [older than 25] students" in the mix.

FINANCIAL AID: 206-296-2000 • E-MAIL: ADMISSIONS@SEATTLEU.EDU • WEBSITE: WWW.SEATTLEU.EDU

THE PRINCETON REVIEW SAYS

Admissions

Very important factors considered include: Rigor of secondary school record, character/personal qualities. *Important factors considered include:* Application essay, academic GPA, recommendation(s), standardized test scores, extracurricular activities. *Other factors considered include:* Class rank, alumni/ae relation, first generation, interview, level of applicant's interest, racial/ethnic status, religious affiliation/commitment, talent/ability, volunteer work, work experience. SAT or ACT required. High school diploma is required and GED is accepted for non traditional students. *Academic units required:* 4 English, 3 mathematics, 2 science, (2 science labs), 2 foreign language, 2 social studies, 1 history, 2 academic electives. *Academic units recommended:* 4 English, 4 mathematics, 3 science, (2 science labs), 2 foreign language, 2 social studies, 1 history, 2 academic electives.

Financial Aid

Students should submit: FAFSA. The Princeton Review suggests that all financial aid forms be submitted as soon as possible after 1/1. *Need-based scholarships/grants offered:* Federal Pell, SEOG, state scholarships/grants, private scholarships, the school's own gift aid, Federal Nursing Scholarships. *Loan aid offered:* Direct Subsidized Stafford, Direct Unsubsidized Stafford, Direct PLUS, Federal Perkins, Federal Nursing. Applicants will be notified of awards on a rolling basis beginning 3/21.

The Inside Word

School has more stringent test score and coursework requirements for certain majors. Because this is a Jesuit school, admissions officers tend to value community service. Those who demonstrate a significant commitment to volunteering will find themselves at an advantage, as will those who convey a clear sense of their academic and career goals.

THE SCHOOL SAYS " . . ."

From The Admissions Office

"Seattle University provides an ideal environment for motivated students interested in self-reliance, awareness of different cultures, social justice, and the fulfillment that comes from making a difference. Our urban setting promotes the development of leadership skills and independence as well as providing a variety of opportunities for students to apply what they learn through internships, clinical experiences, and volunteer work. It is an environment that allows us to 'connect the mind to what matters.

"Our academic offerings are designed to provide leadership opportunities as well as to develop global awareness and enable graduates to serve society through a demanding liberal arts and sciences foundation. In the Jesuit tradition, we teach our students how to think, not what to think. Professional undergraduate offerings include highly respected schools of business, nursing, and science and engineering, as well as career-oriented liberal arts programs such as creative writing, journalism, communications, and criminal justice.

"While located in the center of the city, Seattle University is a true residential campus, including students from 48 states and territories and 76 different nations. Washington State has designated the campus as an 'official backyard sanctuary' for its striking landscaping and environmentally conscious practices—several buildings enjoy official 'green' designations, and the student-run recycling program continually receives national recognition. Additionally, Seattle University is proud of its distinction as the most ethnically diverse institution in the Northwest—all students are valued and respected for their individual strengths, experiences, and worth."

SELECTIVITY

Admissions Rating	87
# of applicants	4,999
% of applicants accepted	65
% of acceptees attending	27

FRESHMAN PROFILE

Range SAT Critical Reading	520–630
Range SAT Math	520–620
Range SAT Writing	510–610
Range ACT Composite	22–28
Minimum paper TOEFL	520
Minimum computer TOEFL	190
Average HS GPA	3.56
% graduated top 10% of class	28
% graduated top 25% of class	64
% graduated top 50% of class	93

DEADLINES

Early action	
Deadline	11/15
Notification	12/23
Regular	
Priority	1/15
Notification	rolling
Nonfall registration?	yes

APPLICANTS ALSO LOOK AT

AND OFTEN PREFER
Santa Clara University
University of Puget Sound

AND SOMETIMES PREFER
Gonzaga University
University of Portland
University of Washington

AND RARELY PREFER
Pacific Lutheran University
Western Washington University

FINANCIAL FACTS

Financial Aid Rating	76
Annual tuition	$28,260
Room and board	$8,340
Books and supplies	$1,350
% frosh rec. need-based scholarship or grant aid	59
% UG rec. need-based scholarship or grant aid	59
% frosh rec. non-need-based scholarship or grant aid	12
% UG rec. non-need-based scholarship or grant aid	61
% frosh rec. need-based self-help aid	46
% UG rec. need-based self-help aid	48
% frosh rec. athletic scholarships	3
% UG rec. athletic scholarships	1
% frosh rec. any financial aid	88
% UG rec. any financial aid	76
% UG borrow to pay for school	81
Average cumulative indebtedness	$16,002

SETON HALL UNIVERSITY

ENROLLMENT SERVICES, 400 SOUTH ORANGE AVENUE, SOUTH ORANGE, NJ 07079 • ADMISSIONS: 973-761-9332 • FAX: 973-275-2040

CAMPUS LIFE
Quality of Life Rating	70
Fire Safety Rating	83
Green Rating	60*
Type of school	private
Affiliation	Roman Catholic
Environment	village

STUDENTS
Total undergrad enrollment	4,951
% male/female	45/55
% from out of state	26
% from public high school	70
% live on campus	44
% African American	11
% Asian	6
% Caucasian	51
% Hispanic	11
% international	1
# of countries represented	71

SURVEY SAYS . . .
Diverse student types on campus
College radio is popular
Student publications are popular

ACADEMICS
Academic Rating	79
Calendar	semester
Student/faculty ratio	14:1
Profs interesting rating	76
Profs accessible rating	74
% classes taught by TAs	4
Most common reg class size	10–19 students
Most common lab size	10–19 students

MOST POPULAR MAJORS
communication studies/speech communication and rhetoric
criminal justice/safety studies
nursing/registered nurse
(rn, asn, bsn, msn)

STUDENTS SAY ". . ."

Academics
"All the colleges within the university are well regarded" at Seton Hall, a prominent Catholic university just down the road from New York City, but the Stillman School of Business and the Whitehead School of Diplomacy and International Relations "are considered the best schools on campus" and thus typically garner the most attention, and understandably so. The former features "a great sports management program" and an attractive, five-year BA/Masters in accounting. Students benefit from proximity to New York, which creates the opportunity for valuable internships, especially in finance. The latter "is directly affiliated with the United Nations," a relationship that "provides students with professors who have had experience with international relations, whether it be ambassadors or foreign correspondents." SHU also excels in nursing, and the university's commitment to keeping pace with technology gives all students a leg up in the modern job market. Indeed, the school works hard "to link the academic world with the real world" through "study abroad, internships, international speakers and events," but without forfeiting the benefits of a more traditional liberal arts education. "The core curriculum gives all students a great foundation beyond their majors so that students are well-rounded individuals with a variety of experiences upon graduation," undergrads report. Students warn that administrative tasks can be onerous; one writes, "there is a lot of red tape at Seton Hall. The bills that are sent out at the end of the semester are never correct, and it takes several phone calls with financial aid to ascertain the correct balance."

Life
Social life at SHU fights an uphill battle. The school is located in South Orange, " a boring town for college-age students." A much more appealing town, New York City, is "a 20-minute train ride [from campus], so a lot of people go to the city for fun." Add to that the fact that "most of the student body lives in North Jersey, so it's easy for them to go home for the weekend," and many do just that. Under these circumstances, SHU does a pretty good job of offering on-campus attractions, students tell us. Greek life "is very popular," and the school's "big-time men's basketball program" is a huge draw, even though the team has not fared especially well in recent seasons. "Students are always attending basketball games" and "praying that the team does not suck." Intramurals "can be very competitive," "the athletic facilities are state-of-the-art," and "the campus lends itself to outdoor activities. Many students play sports outside when it is warm, and when it is cold there are plenty of indoor activities in which to participate."

Student Body
Seton Hall "is sort of a mishmash of different types. There are a lot of jocks who are definitely treated like stars by the administration, although not so much by the average professor," and "there are some very academic students who mostly try to ignore the actual school and focus on internships and study-abroad opportunities." And then there's "the average student, who is from New Jersey, has a major in the School of Arts and Sciences or Business, parties on Thursdays, goes home on weekends, and coasts through college on loans their parents have taken out." "While Seton Hall is a Catholic university, "it is not difficult to find students of other religions," and "the school is accepting of all religious beliefs." Indeed, SHU is big enough that "there are a lot of different kinds of people," and "everyone finds his place by sophomore year." Unfortunately "it also tends to be like high school, in that once you are in a group you're there for the rest of your four years." As one student puts it, "There are definitely cliques here, more so than in my high school. The athletes always sit together, as do people in certain clubs."

FINANCIAL AID: 973-761-9332 • E-MAIL: THEHALL@SHU.EDU • WEBSITE: WWW.SHU.EDU

THE PRINCETON REVIEW SAYS

Admissions

Very important factors considered include: Application essay, academic GPA, recommendation(s), rigor of secondary school record, standardized test scores. *Important factors considered include:* Extracurricular activities, volunteer work, work experience. *Other factors considered include:* Class rank, character/personal qualities, interview, talent/ability. SAT or ACT required; ACT with Writing component required; TOEFL required of all international applicants. High school diploma is required and GED is accepted. *Academic units required:* 4 English, 3 mathematics, 1 science, (1 science lab), 2 foreign language, 2 social studies, 4 academic electives.

Financial Aid

Students should submit: FAFSA. The Princeton Review suggests that all financial aid forms be submitted as soon as possible after 1/1. *Need-based scholarships/grants offered:* Federal Pell, SEOG, state scholarships/grants, private scholarships, the school's own gift aid. *Loan aid offered:* FFEL Subsidized Stafford, FFEL Unsubsidized Stafford, FFEL PLUS, Federal Perkins, state loans. Applicants will be notified of awards on a rolling basis beginning 3/1. Federal Work-Study Program available. Institutional employment available. Off-campus job opportunities are good.

The Inside Word

Students seeking a good school with solid, Catholic roots should consider Seton Hall, whose proximity to New York City helps the school draw prestigious faculty and affords students excellent access to educational, internship, and entertainment opportunities. Applicants who show decent grades in a college preparatory curriculum coupled with strong recommendations should have little trouble gaining admission here. Top students may be pleasantly surprised by the school's financial aid offers.

THE SCHOOL SAYS "..."

From The Admissions Office

"For more than 150 years, Seton Hall University has been a catalyst for leadership, developing the whole student—mind, heart and spirit. As a Catholic university that embraces students of all races and religions, Seton Hall combines the resources of a large university with the personal attention of a small liberal arts college. The University's attractive suburban campus is only 14 miles by train, bus or car to New York City, with the wealth of employment, internship, cultural and entertainment opportunities the city offers. Outstanding faculty, a technologically advanced campus, and a values-centered curriculum challenge Seton Hall students. Students are exposed to a world of ideas from great scholars, opening their minds to the perspectives, history and achievements of many cultures. Our new core curriculum focuses on the need for our students to have common experiences and encourages them to become thinking, caring, communicative and ethically responsible leaders while emphasizing practical proficiencies and intellectual development Our commitment to our students goes beyond textbooks and homework assignments, though. At Seton Hall, developing servant leaders who will make a difference in the world is a priority. That's why all students take classes in ethics and learn in a community informed by Catholic ideals and universal values. While Seton Hall certainly enjoys a big reputation, our campus community is close-knit and inclusive. Students, faculty and staff come from around the world, bringing with them a kaleidoscope of experiences and perspectives to create a diverse yet unified campus environment."

SELECTIVITY

Admissions Rating	86
# of applicants	5,365
% of applicants accepted	77
% of acceptees attending	25

FRESHMAN PROFILE

Range SAT Critical Reading	480–590
Range SAT Math	500–600
Minimum paper TOEFL	550
Minimum computer TOEFL	213
Average HS GPA	3.15
% graduated top 10% of class	28
% graduated top 25% of class	60
% graduated top 50% of class	88

DEADLINES

Regular	
Priority	3/1
Notification	rolling
Nonfall registration?	yes

APPLICANTS ALSO LOOK AT

AND OFTEN PREFER
New York University
William Paterson University
Penn State—University Park

AND SOMETIMES PREFER
Fairfield University
University of Connecticut
Fordham University
Rider University

AND RARELY PREFER
Hofstra University
Monmouth University (NJ)
St. Bonaventure University
Ramapo College of New Jersey

FINANCIAL FACTS

Financial Aid Rating	74
Annual tuition	$22,770
Room and board	$10,466
Required fees	$1,950
% frosh rec. need-based scholarship or grant aid	54
% UG rec. need-based scholarship or grant aid	38
% frosh rec. non-need-based scholarship or grant aid	47
% UG rec. non-need-based scholarship or grant aid	33
% frosh rec. need-based self-help aid	45
% UG rec. need-based self-help aid	45
% frosh rec. athletic scholarships	4
% UG rec. athletic scholarships	4
% frosh rec. any financial aid	91
% UG rec. any financial aid	86
% UG borrow to pay for school	6
Average cumulative indebtedness	$16,160

SEWANEE—THE UNIVERSITY OF THE SOUTH

735 UNIVERSITY AVENUE, SEWANEE, TN 37383-1000 • ADMISSIONS: 931-598-1238 • FAX: 931-538-3248

CAMPUS LIFE

Quality of Life Rating	**87**
Fire Safety Rating	**78**
Green Rating	**88**
Type of school	private
Affiliation	Episcopal
Environment	rural

STUDENTS

Total undergrad enrollment	1,464
% male/female	47/53
% from out of state	76
% from public high school	45
% live on campus	93
% in (# of) fraternities	82 (12)
% in (# of) sororities	88 (9)
% African American	4
% Asian	3
% Caucasian	88
% Hispanic	3
% Native American	1
% international	2
# of countries represented	22

SURVEY SAYS . . .

No one cheats
Students are friendly
Campus feels safe
Students are happy
Frats and sororities dominate social scene
Lots of beer drinking
Hard liquor is popular

ACADEMICS

Academic Rating	**95**
Calendar	semester
Student/faculty ratio	10:1
Profs interesting rating	97
Profs accessible rating	95
Most common reg class size	10–19 students
Most common lab size	10–19 students

MOST POPULAR MAJORS

English language and literature
history
visual and performing arts

STUDENTS SAY ". . ."

Academics

The University of the South is a small, "very demanding" school "in the middle of rural Tennessee." Students describe it as "an oasis of perfection" "dripping with both Southern and academic tradition." "Sewanee embodies what a liberal arts education should," beams a history major. Classes are "small" and there's a "well-rounded curriculum." About a third of all your courses here will be general education requirements, and you have to pass a comprehensive exam in your major. "The volume of work can make you want to pull your hair out," warns an economics major. "Sewanee does not inflate grades," either. "You must work hard to earn an A." "Occasionally a professor or two takes the absent-minded professor stereotype to a ridiculous level," but "it is hard to find a truly bad teacher among the whole lot." Professors here "care about their students." "Their passion for their fields and students is unparalleled." Profs are also very approachable. "We have incredible access to the faculty," gushes a religion major. "Many professors invite students to their homes for social and educational activities somewhat regularly," adds a music major. Students also love the "extremely reachable" administration. The only complaint we hear about academic life concerns the lack of course availability.

Life

Some dorms at Sewanee "really need some work." "Give me air conditioning," demands a sweaty sophomore. The school is generally "behind technologically" as well. The "secluded" town that surrounds the school is "void of any good restaurants, bars, and general distractions a city provides." The campus is "absolutely gorgeous," though. It's a "serene haven" in "an idyllic setting" atop a mountain. Also, the school owns an "incredible amount of land." "Hiking the beautiful perimeter trail" is a favorite pastime, and students can bike, kayak, and "play in the woods" to their hearts' content. Socially, "Sewanee is unique in its quirks." There's a revered honor code. Faculty members wear academic gowns when they teach, and "most Sewanee students follow the tradition of dressing up for class." You'll see men in bow ties and seersucker suits and women in "pointy heels and pearls." There's also an "ever-present" sense of community. "You can't compartmentalize your life here," and for good or ill, "everyone knows what everyone else did last night." Otherwise, this school is "an uncanny combination of academic suicide and rampant partying." During the week, studying is paramount. "We spend a lot of time in the library," notes a sophomore. However, alcohol policies here are "lenient" and "Sewanee is a pretty big party school." Booze is "by no means forced upon you," but "students here drink often and heavily." The frat scene is absolutely massive. "Almost everyone becomes involved in a fraternity or a sorority." "The administration requires all Greek events to be open to the entire campus," but "there is no other social network except the Greek organizations."

Student Body

Even though the administration here is "pushing the diversity card to the nth degree," Sewanee is "strikingly homogenous." "A lot more students here are liberal than you would guess," and Yankees are "not viewed as aliens," but "Sewanee is a Southern and conservative school in every sense of the word." Students are typically "laid-back," "rich, conservative, and fun" "children of the Southern aristocracy" who like to "get drunk on the weekends." Some are "heavily spoiled and coddled." Sewanee is affiliated with the Episcopalian church, and some students are pious, but on the whole, religion is not a big deal here. "We have lots of cookie-cutter, preppy, extreme social drinkers, but then again you can also find people who wear only organic hemp, sleep outside, and have dreadlocks," explains a junior. "There are a lot of outdoorsy styles mixed in as well." While "social arrangements are very cliquish," students tell us they are "relatively peacefully coexisting." "It really is one of the friendliest communities that I have ever seen," declares a sophomore.

FINANCIAL AID: 931-598-1312 • E-MAIL: COLLEGEADMISSION@SEWANEE.EDU • WEBSITE: WWW.SEWANEE.EDU

THE PRINCETON REVIEW SAYS

Admissions

Very important factors considered include: Academic GPA, recommendation(s), rigor of secondary school record. *Important factors considered include:* Application essay, standardized test scores, character/personal qualities, extracurricular activities, volunteer work, work experience. *Other factors considered include:* Class rank, alumni/ae relation, first generation, geographical residence, interview, level of applicant's interest, racial/ethnic status, talent/ability. SAT or ACT required; ACT with Writing component required; TOEFL required of all international applicants. High school diploma is required and GED is not accepted. *Academic units required:* 4 English, 3 mathematics, 2 science, (2 science labs), 2 foreign language, 1 social studies, 1 history. *Academic units recommended:* 4 English, 4 mathematics, 4 science, (3 science labs), 4 foreign language, 2 social studies, 2 history.

Financial Aid

Students should submit: FAFSA, institution's own financial aid form. The Princeton Review suggests that all financial aid forms be submitted as soon as possible after 1/1. *Need-based scholarships/grants offered:* Federal Pell, SEOG, state scholarships/grants, private scholarships, the school's own gift aid. *Loan aid offered:* FFEL Subsidized Stafford, FFEL Unsubsidized Stafford, FFEL PLUS, Federal Perkins, state loans, college/university loans from institutional funds, private alternative loans. Applicants will be notified of awards on or about 4/1. Federal Work-Study Program available. Institutional employment available. Off-campus job opportunities are fair.

The Inside Word

The admissions office at Sewanee is very personable and accessible to students. Its staff includes some of the most well-respected admissions professionals in the South, and it shows in the way they work with students. Despite a fairly high acceptance rate, candidates who take the admissions process here lightly may find themselves disappointed. Applicant evaluation is too personal for a lackadaisical approach to succeed.

THE SCHOOL SAYS " . . ."

From The Admissions Office

"Sewanee is consistently ranked among the top tier of national liberal arts universities. Sewanee is committed to an academic curriculum that focuses on the liberal arts as the most enlightening and valuable form of undergraduate education. Founded by leaders of the Episcopal church in 1857, Sewanee continues to be owned by 28 Episcopal dioceses in 12 states. The university is located on a 10,000-acre campus atop Tennessee's Cumberland Plateau between Chattanooga and Nashville. The university has an impressive record of academic achievement—25 Rhodes scholars and 26 NCAA postgraduate scholarship recipients have graduated from Sewanee.

"Sewanee will require all applicants to take the SAT or the ACT with the Writing test."

SELECTIVITY
Admissions Rating	94
# of applicants	2,488
% of applicants accepted	64
% of acceptees attending	26
# accepting a place on wait list	107
% admitted from wait list	36
# of early decision applicants	185
% accepted early decision	54

FRESHMAN PROFILE
Range SAT Critical Reading	568–680
Range SAT Math	580–680
Range ACT Composite	26–30
Minimum paper TOEFL	550
Minimum computer TOEFL	220
Average HS GPA	3.62
% graduated top 10% of class	49
% graduated top 25% of class	67
% graduated top 50% of class	94

DEADLINES
Early decision	
Deadline	11/15
Notification	12/15
Regular	
Deadline	2/1
Notification	3/17
Nonfall registration?	no

APPLICANTS ALSO LOOK AT AND SOMETIMES PREFER
Vanderbilt University
Davidson College

AND RARELY PREFER
Rhodes College
University of Georgia

FINANCIAL FACTS
Financial Aid Rating	93
Annual tuition	$33,900
Room and board	$9,760
Required fees	$272
Books and supplies	$1,900
% frosh rec. need-based scholarship or grant aid	39
% UG rec. need-based scholarship or grant aid	48
% frosh rec. need-based self-help aid	30
% UG rec. need-based self-help aid	36
% frosh rec. any financial aid	93
% UG rec. any financial aid	95
% UG borrow to pay for school	45
Average cumulative indebtedness	$15,885

SIENA COLLEGE

515 LOUDON ROAD, LOUDONVILLE, NY 12211 • ADMISSIONS: 518-783-2423 • FAX: 518-783-2436

CAMPUS LIFE

Quality of Life Rating	**80**
Fire Safety Rating	**60***
Green Rating	**60***
Type of school	private
Affiliation	Roman Catholic
Environment	town

STUDENTS

Total undergrad enrollment	3,242
% male/female	46/54
% from out of state	14.4
% African American	2
% Asian	3
% Caucasian	82
% Hispanic	4
# of countries represented	7

SURVEY SAYS . . .

Lab facilities are great
Students get along with local community
Students love Loudonville, NY
Frats and sororities are unpopular or nonexistent
Hard liquor is popular

ACADEMICS

Academic Rating	**78**
Calendar	semester
Student/faculty ratio	13:1
Profs interesting rating	80
Profs accessible rating	84
Most common reg class size	20–29 students
Most common lab size	10–19 students

MOST POPULAR MAJORS

accounting
marketing/marketing management
psychology

STUDENTS SAY ". . ."

Academics

The Franciscan tradition "is all about community," and, at Siena College, a small school with "a strong Franciscan atmosphere," students benefit from a friendly community in which "there is always someone to lend a helping hand." That someone may be a professor, a tutor, or, on occasion, a Rollerblading friar in robes. No matter whose hand is extended, however, "Every student really has a lot of opportunities to get any amount of personal academic attention or other scholastic opportunities that they want." Biology and other premedical disciplines are highly regarded, and students especially love the Siena College–Albany Medical College Program, a joint acceptance program that focuses on humanities and community service. In addition, the school's many business undergrads feel their program, which is enhanced by a loyal alumni base that helps newly minted grads quickly find jobs, is the school's "greatest strength." Regardless of discipline, Siena "teachers know who you are and do not just consider you a number, as opposed [to how it is at] larger colleges and universities." An honors program offers "even smaller classes, preferential registration, and seminars" to those seeking an extra challenge.

Life

For many students, recreation time at Siena means it's time for a beer or two, and lately that's become a point of contention with the administration. Students tell us that the administration, in its effort to crack down on underage drinking, has instituted security checkpoints at the townhouses (where upperclassmen live and, in previous years, had hosted parties) and limits on the amount of alcohol allowed in the rooms of students more than 21. Security can be aggressive, we're told, to the point that more than one undergraduate told us that students sometimes feel "like prisoners." Though this has driven the drinking crowd off campus to nearby clubs and the bars of Albany, on-campus drinking still occurs, but it's more often of the pre-gaming or small-quiet-party variety. The campus still bustles during the week, however, because "most people are involved in clubs" and at least "one sport, whether intramural or intercollegiate." Other diversions include a school-sponsored bus that takes students to the Crossgates Mall, which "is pretty large and houses a bunch of amazing stores," and "a whole strip of dining-out places." Still, an English major admits, "If you don't drink, I can see where weekends would be boring, especially in the winter." The school does sponsor activities on campus designed "to draw students away from the drinking scene," but "there is often a stigma about the 'coolness' of these events."

Student Body

There "isn't much diversity" on the Siena campus, where it seems just about everyone "is from an upper-middle-class Catholic family from Long Island" or "upstate New York." There are some who don't fit the mold, but not many; students speculate that they're mostly nontraditional or international students. Minority students tend to "stick together, but all seem well-liked." Many students "are involved either in D1 athletics, intramural teams, or clubs and Student Senate activities"; students in these groups tend to party together on the weekends "and generally create a strong group of friends easily." While there's a solid contingent of folks at Siena who "drink, party, and hardly ever study," there are also students, particularly in the sciences, who work hard but "don't socialize much outside of their departments, due to the nature of their programs."

FINANCIAL AID: 518-783-2427 • E-MAIL: ADMIT@SIENA.EDU • WEBSITE: WWW.SIENA.EDU

THE PRINCETON REVIEW SAYS

Admissions

Very important factors considered include: Academic GPA, rigor of secondary school record. *Important factors considered include:* Recommendation(s), standardized test scores. *Other factors considered include:* Class rank, application essay, alumni/ae relation, character/personal qualities, extracurricular activities, first generation, interview, level of applicant's interest, racial/ethnic status, talent/ability, volunteer work, work experience. SAT or ACT required; ACT with Writing component required; TOEFL required of all international applicants. High school diploma is required and GED is accepted. *Academic units required:* 4 English, 3 mathematics, 3 science, (3 science labs), 1 social studies, 2 history. *Academic units recommended:* 4 English, 4 mathematics, 4 science, (4 science labs), 3 foreign language, 1 social studies, 3 history.

Financial Aid

Students should submit: FAFSA, state aid form. The Princeton Review suggests that all financial aid forms be submitted as soon as possible after 1/1. *Need-based scholarships/grants offered:* Federal Pell, SEOG, state scholarships/grants, private scholarships, the school's own gift aid, Siena Grants, St. Francis Community Grants. *Loan aid offered:* FFEL Subsidized Stafford, FFEL Unsubsidized Stafford, FFEL PLUS, Federal Perkins. Applicants will be notified of awards on or about 4/1.

The Inside Word

Siena's draw is still primarily regional, with the vast majority of students arriving from in state. Standards aren't especially high; the admit rate says as much about the applicant pool as it does about the school's selectivity. Expect to meet higher standards if you indicate an interest in the School of Science, as it is the gateway to the school's desirable premedical programs. The school does applicants a favor here—substandard students stand little chance of surviving the school's science regimen.

THE SCHOOL SAYS "..."

From The Admissions Office

"Siena is a coeducational, independent liberal arts college with a Franciscan tradition. It is a community where the intellectual, personal, and social growth of all students is paramount. Siena's faculty calls forth the best Siena students have to give—and the students do the same for them. Students are competitive, but not at each other's expense. Siena's curriculum includes 23 majors in three schools—liberal arts, science, and business. In addition, there are over a dozen pre-professional and special academic programs. With a student/faculty ratio of 14:1, class size ranges between 15 and 35 students. Siena's 152-acre campus is located in Loudonville, a suburban community within two miles of the New York State seat of government in Albany. With 15 colleges in the area, there is a wide variety of activities on weekends. Regional theater, performances by major concert artists, and professional sports events compete with the activities on the campus. Within 50 miles are the Adirondacks, the Berkshires, and the Catskills, providing outdoor recreation throughout the year. Because the capital region's easy, friendly lifestyle is so appealing, many Siena graduates try to find their first jobs in upstate New York.

"Freshman applicants must submit the SAT or ACT with the Writing component."

SELECTIVITY

Admissions Rating	86
# of applicants	6,490
% of applicants accepted	56
% of acceptees attending	23
# accepting a place on wait list	359
% admitted from wait list	1
# of early decision applicants	167
% accepted early decision	29

FRESHMAN PROFILE

Range SAT Critical Reading	500–590
Range SAT Math	530–630
Range SAT Writing	500–590
Range ACT Composite	23–26
Minimum paper TOEFL	550
Minimum computer TOEFL	213
Minimum web-based TOEFL	79
Average HS GPA	89.7
% graduated top 10% of class	25.1
% graduated top 25% of class	59.1
% graduated top 50% of class	92.9

DEADLINES

Early decision	
Deadline	12/1
Notification	12/15
Early action	
Deadline	12/1
Notification	1/1
Regular	
Priority	3/1
Deadline	3/1
Notification	3/15
Nonfall registration?	yes

APPLICANTS ALSO LOOK AT
AND SOMETIMES PREFER
Fairfield University
AND RARELY PREFER
Le Moyne College

FINANCIAL FACTS

Financial Aid Rating	74
Annual tuition	$22,510
Room and board	$8,875
Required fees	$175
Books and supplies	$930
% frosh rec. need-based scholarship or grant aid	69
% UG rec. need-based scholarship or grant aid	66
% frosh rec. non-need-based scholarship or grant aid	6
% UG rec. non-need-based scholarship or grant aid	4
% frosh rec. need-based self-help aid	57
% UG rec. need-based self-help aid	55
% frosh rec. athletic scholarships	9
% UG rec. athletic scholarships	8
% frosh rec. any financial aid	96.1
% UG rec. any financial aid	95.3
% UG borrow to pay for school	77
Average cumulative indebtedness	$21,800

SIMMONS COLLEGE

300 THE FENWAY, BOSTON, MA 02115 • ADMISSIONS: 617-521-2051 • FAX: 617-521-3190

CAMPUS LIFE
Quality of Life Rating	87
Fire Safety Rating	87
Green Rating	90
Type of school	private
Environment	city

STUDENTS
Total undergrad enrollment	2,023
% male/female	0/100
% from out of state	36
% live on campus	55
% African American	6
% Asian	7
% Caucasian	73
% Hispanic	4
% international	3
# of countries represented	53

SURVEY SAYS . . .
Great library
Students get along with local community
Students love Boston, MA
Great off-campus food
Sororities are unpopular or nonexistent
Student government is popular

ACADEMICS
Academic Rating	86
Calendar	semester
Student/faculty ratio	13:1
Profs interesting rating	83
Profs accessible rating	83
Most common reg class size	10–19 students

MOST POPULAR MAJORS
nursing/registered nurse
(rn, asn, bsn, msn)
psychology

STUDENTS SAY ". . ."

Academics

Simmons College, an "all-women's college located in the Fenway area of Boston," provides students with "lots of opportunities to work closely with faculty and [to] interact with local Boston communities." The school excels in pre-professional programs in nursing and physical therapy, each of which capitalizes on the school's location to "give students opportunities to do internships/clinical placements at world-renowned hospitals that are only a few blocks away (e.g. Children's Hospital Boston, Brigham and Women's, Mass General)." Students also rave about Simmons' offerings in psychology, biology, pre-dental sciences, economics, and management, and they praise the school's "excellent facilities, including an amazing new library" and the "large career resource department." Small classes here "allow great discussions, because those who want to participate have the opportunity to do so," which can be both a blessing and a curse. At Simmons "If you work hard, you get out of it what you put in." One drawback is the study-abroad program. One undergrad gripes, "There just aren't enough choices! And if there are, they are all usually around the same time, making it quite difficult to choose."

Life

Life at Simmons College "is more academic in nature: The classes are teaching-based, and life on campus revolves around schoolwork." One student agrees, "Simmons is pretty much where students go to school. We go elsewhere to have fun/party/live." With downtown Boston outside the school's front door, the options are plentiful. There are museums ("great things to do in the area" include "free gallery talks at the Museum of Fine Arts"), "shopping on Newbury Street," and "eating great food in the North End." Public transportation means "getting around is easy, and exploring the city is amazing." When students seek a party, they typically "go to other local colleges…like MIT, Harvard, Boston University, and Northeastern." On-campus fun is more subdued. There's "a lot of random friendly girl-time things going on, like decorating our doors for the holidays, making paper chains, or watching television. For entertainment here, you really have to turn to your friends, because almost nothing worth attending happens on campus," a female student notes. Most see this as a boon; writes one student, "What's nice about living at Simmons is that it is a peaceful and nice place to live, but when you want to go to a party, Northeastern and BU are just minutes away. After spending a night there, you realize how thankful you are for clean dorms and the lack of boys."

Student Body

The student body at Simmons is "mostly middle- to upper-class women who hail from all over the United States and many other countries. The school is predominately white, but a range of ethnicities are represented." One student reports that her study group consists of "an orthodox Jew, a Saudi Arabian, an African American, a Cambodian, an Indian, and two Caucasians. The UN could take lessons from us." Politically, "most students are liberal and involved with their community." Left-leaning politics dominates to the point that "it can be challenging to express conservative viewpoints." Sexual orientation "tends not to be a question, and it is very common for girls to be open about being straight, gay, or bisexual." While "there are a lot of lesbians here," they are "not at all the majority." Simmons hosts a conspicuous butch subculture. As one women explains, "Even though you know going into it that Simmons is an all-women's college, you may be shocked to see some guys walking around attending your classes…until you realize that they are girls! It's great that everyone is cool with everyone else and the people who are narrow-minded stick to themselves."

FINANCIAL AID: 617-521-2001 • E-MAIL: UGADM@SIMMONS.EDU • WEBSITE: WWW.SIMMONS.EDU

THE PRINCETON REVIEW SAYS

Admissions

Very important factors considered include: Academic GPA, rigor of secondary school record. *Important factors considered include:* Class rank, application essay, recommendation(s), standardized test scores. *Other factors considered include:* Extracurricular activities, interview, talent/ability, volunteer work, work experience. SAT or ACT required; TOEFL required of all international applicants. High school diploma or equivalent is not required. *Academic units required:* 4 English, 3 mathematics, 3 science, 3 foreign language, 3 social studies, 3 history. *Academic units recommended:* 4 English, 4 mathematics, 3 science, 4 foreign language, 4 social studies, 3 history.

Financial Aid

Students should submit: FAFSA. Regular filing deadline is 3/1. The Princeton Review suggests that all financial aid forms be submitted as soon as possible after 1/1. *Need-based scholarships/grants offered:* Federal Pell, SEOG, state scholarships/grants, private scholarships, the school's own gift aid. *Loan aid offered:* FFEL Subsidized Stafford, FFEL Unsubsidized Stafford, FFEL PLUS, Federal Perkins, state loans, college/university loans from institutional funds. Applicants will be notified of awards on a rolling basis beginning 3/15. Federal Work-Study Program available. Institutional employment available. Off-campus job opportunities are excellent.

The Inside Word

Most of the nation's best all-women's colleges are in the Northeast, including those Seven Sister schools (roughly the female equivalent of the formerly all-male Ivies) that remain single-sex institutions. The competition for students is intense, and although Simmons is a solid school, there are at least a half-dozen competitors more appealing to most candidates. Solid high school performers should have little need to worry here. The school's excellent academics and Boston location make Simmons a worthy option for any woman interested in single-sex education.

THE SCHOOL SAYS "..."

From The Admissions Office

"Simmons honors educational values that place students first and helps them build successful careers, lead meaningful lives, and realize a powerful return on their investment. Simmons delivers a quality education and measurable success through a singular approach to professional preparation, intellectual exploration, and community orientation.

"Simmons is a 100-year-old university in Boston, with a tradition of providing women with a collaborative environment that stimulates dialogue, enhances listening, catalyzes action, and spurs personal and professional growth.

"Simmons College accepts both the ACT with the Writing Section and SAT. Additionally, if English is not your native language a TOEFL is required."

SELECTIVITY

Admissions Rating	84
# of applicants	3,222
% of applicants accepted	55
% of acceptees attending	22
# accepting a place on wait list	33
% admitted from wait list	100

FRESHMAN PROFILE

Range SAT Critical Reading	510–600
Range SAT Math	500–590
Range SAT Writing	520–620
Range ACT Composite	22–26
Minimum paper TOEFL	560
Minimum computer TOEFL	220
Minimum web-based TOEFL	83
Average HS GPA	3.17
% graduated top 10% of class	20
% graduated top 25% of class	55
% graduated top 50% of class	91

DEADLINES

Early action	
Deadline	12/1
Notification	1/20
Regular	
Priority	2/1
Deadline	2/1
Notification	4/15
Nonfall registration?	yes

APPLICANTS ALSO LOOK AT

AND OFTEN PREFER
Mount Holyoke College, Boston University
Smith College

AND SOMETIMES PREFER
University of New Hampshire
University of Connecticut
University of Vermont

AND RARELY PREFER
Emmanuel College
University of Massachusetts—Amherst
Quinnipiac University, Suffolk University

FINANCIAL FACTS

Financial Aid Rating	68
Annual tuition	$30,520
Room and board	$12,050
Required fees	$930
% frosh rec. need-based scholarship or grant aid	70
% UG rec. need-based scholarship or grant aid	65
% frosh rec. non-need-based scholarship or grant aid	5
% UG rec. non-need-based scholarship or grant aid	3
% frosh rec. need-based self-help aid	65
% UG rec. need-based self-help aid	64
% frosh rec. any financial aid	72
% UG rec. any financial aid	70
% UG borrow to pay for school	78
Average cumulative indebtedness	$42,174

SIMON'S ROCK COLLEGE OF BARD

84 ALFORD ROAD, GREAT BARRINGTON, MA 01230 • ADMISSIONS: 413-528-7312 • FAX: 413-528-7334

CAMPUS LIFE
Quality of Life Rating	86
Fire Safety Rating	60*
Green Rating	60*
Type of school	private
Environment	village

STUDENTS
Total undergrad enrollment	368
% male/female	43/57
% from out of state	80
% live on campus	85
% African American	7
% Asian	4
% Caucasian	58
% Hispanic	6
% Native American	1
% international	4

SURVEY SAYS . . .
Class discussions encouraged
No one cheats
Athletic facilities are great
Students aren't religious
Campus feels safe
Frats and sororities are unpopular or
nonexistent
Political activism is popular
(Almost) everyone smokes

ACADEMICS
Academic Rating	99
Calendar	semester
Student/faculty ratio	8:1
Profs interesting rating	99
Profs accessible rating	97
Most common reg class size	10–19 students
Most common lab size	10–19 students

MOST POPULAR MAJORS
cell/cellular biology and histology
creative writing
psychology

STUDENTS SAY ". . ."

Academics

Bard College at Simon's Rock is a tiny, "rigorous," and "unique" bastion of the liberal arts and sciences that allows high-school-aged students "the opportunity to start their college careers and broaden their academic horizons a bit earlier than is orthodox." At Simon's Rock, you can enroll after completing tenth or eleventh grade. "I wasn't learning anything in high school," explains an art history major. "Simon's Rock recognizes that and provides you with another option." There's a Lower College and an Upper College. (Students in the Lower College are the ones who would otherwise be in high school.) Both colleges offer an incredible amount of freedom to design your own course of study. There are more than 40 majors. The arts programs are "very strong." Students in the engineering program can spend three years at Simon's Rock and then two years at Columbia University. Several outstanding study-abroad opportunities send students to places such as Istanbul, Ghana, Oxford, and the Sorbonne in Paris. Many people "only stay here two years," long enough to earn an associate's degree. After that, they transfer to a more traditional college. However, you can also stick around at SRC to get your bachelor's degree. Either way, "the academic expectations are formidable." Coursework is "challenging" and "requires a lot of time input out of class." There's quite a bit of reading. Seniors must complete a self-designed thesis. Classes are small—the average size is a mere 10 students—and they are filled with "engaging" discussion. "Simon's Rock professors are generally very supportive and understanding." They provide "up-close and personal attention" and "go out of their way to be available out of the classroom."

Life

The "gorgeous" campus here can be "a bit of a bubble" and, at times, "small to the point of claustrophobia," but students promise that there is much to do. There's "a large number of clubs for the size of the school," and "new clubs and interests are always forming." "The athletic center is top-notch." Winters are hard, but "the spring is pure glory." Hikes "in the beautiful woods" are common, weather permitting. Equally common is "just hanging out." Often, students will "simply sit around talking about random stuff, ranging from the weather to Marx." "Most of campus smokes." "Drugs and alcohol are a major form of recreation and stress relief." However, the party scene is "relatively low-key." Often, it's "sneaking around under night skies" to darkened party spots. Students also emphasize that it is "possible to have fun and attend parties without being pressured" into consuming anything you'd rather avoid. The "very small town" of Great Barrington is a little less than 2 miles away. "Befriending car-endowed people is a good skill." Without or without wheels, though, "there is very little to do off campus." Simon's Rock is "isolated" in the Berkshire Mountains of "rural" western Massachusetts, roughly in "in the middle of nowhere." On the plus side, New York City and Boston are reasonably easy to reach. Older students frequently make treks to those cities on the weekends.

Student Body

For the students here, "Simon's Rock is a blissful release from the institutional hell of high school." Students come here from 40 or so states. They are "brilliant and creative" and "excited to learn." "Lots of people come from their high school used to being the smartest person in the room," explains one student, "and then they realize that, wow, there are lots of really smart people here, and now you have someone to talk to about serious stuff." Students describe themselves as "strong individuals who lean toward nonconformity." They are "a little misunderstood." They "tend to be liberal," and they are "very aware and educated in current politics." "Some people are very, very androgynous." "Many are artists." Many are "hippies." Many are artists and hippies. Ultimately, Simon's Rock is filled with "kids who think outside the box." "Most people walk to their own beat." "Brightly dyed hair, body piercings, tattoos, girls with buzz cuts, guys in skirts, and crazy clothing ensembles are SRC trademarks."

SIMON'S ROCK COLLEGE OF BARD

FINANCIAL AID: 413-528-7297 • E-MAIL: ADMIT@SIMONS-ROCK.EDU • WEBSITE: WWW.SIMONS-ROCK.EDU

THE PRINCETON REVIEW SAYS

Admissions

Very important factors considered include: Application essay, recommendation(s), rigor of secondary school record, character/personal qualities, interview, talent/ability. *Important factors considered include:* Class rank, academic GPA, level of applicant's interest. *Other factors considered include:* Standardized test scores, alumni/ae relation, extracurricular activities, first generation, racial/ethnic status, volunteer work, work experience. TOEFL required of all international applicants. High school diploma or equivalent is not required. *Academic units recommended:* 2 English, 2 mathematics, 2 science, (1 science lab), 2 foreign language, 2 social studies, 2 history.

Financial Aid

Students should submit: FAFSA, CSS/Financial Aid PROFILE, business/farm supplement, Parent and Student Federal Taxes/ Federal Verification Worksheet. The Princeton Review suggests that all financial aid forms be submitted as soon as possible after 1/1. *Need-based scholarships/grants offered:* Federal Pell, SEOG, state scholarships/grants, private scholarships, the school's own gift aid. *Loan aid offered:* FFEL Subsidized Stafford, FFEL Unsubsidized Stafford, FFEL PLUS, Federal Perkins, state loans, Alternative Educational Loans. Applicants will be notified of awards on a rolling basis beginning 4/15. Federal Work-Study Program available. Institutional employment available. Off-campus job opportunities are good.

The Inside Word

Because Simon's Rock boasts healthy application numbers, it is in a position to concentrate on matchmaking. To that end, admissions officers seek students with independent and inquisitive spirits. Applicants who exhibit academic ambition while extending their intellectual curiosity beyond the realm of the classroom are particularly appealing. Successful candidates typically have several honors and advanced placement courses on their transcripts, as well as strong letters of recommendation and well-written personal statements.

THE SCHOOL SAYS "..."

From The Admissions Office

"Simon's Rock is dedicated to one thing: To allow bright, highly motivated students the opportunity to pursue college work leading to the AA and BA degrees at an age earlier than our national norm.

"Simon's Rock College of Bard will accept either the SAT or the ACT with or without the Writing component."

SELECTIVITY

Admissions Rating	99
# of applicants	204
% of applicants accepted	84
% of acceptees attending	74

FRESHMAN PROFILE

Range SAT Critical Reading	560–690
Range SAT Math	530–680
Range ACT Composite	25–30
Minimum paper TOEFL	550
Minimum computer TOEFL	200
Average HS GPA	3.36
% graduated top 10% of class	60
% graduated top 25% of class	82
% graduated top 50% of class	94

DEADLINES

Regular	
Priority	4/15
Deadline	5/31
Notification	rolling
Nonfall registration?	yes

FINANCIAL FACTS

Financial Aid Rating	89
Annual tuition	$34,804
Room and board	$9,260
Required fees	$530
Books and supplies	$1,000
% frosh rec. need-based scholarship or grant aid	51
% UG rec. need-based scholarship or grant aid	39
% frosh rec. non-need-based scholarship or grant aid	50
% UG rec. non-need-based scholarship or grant aid	33
% frosh rec. need-based self-help aid	47
% UG rec. need-based self-help aid	43
% frosh rec. any financial aid	78
% UG rec. any financial aid	71
% UG borrow to pay for school	70
Average cumulative indebtedness	$15,000

SKIDMORE COLLEGE

815 NORTH BROADWAY, SARATOGA SPRINGS, NY 12866-1632 • ADMISSIONS: 518-580-5570 • FAX: 518-580-5584

CAMPUS LIFE
Quality of Life Rating	88
Fire Safety Rating	60*
Green Rating	60*
Type of school	private
Environment	town

STUDENTS
Total undergrad enrollment	2,771
% male/female	40/60
% from out of state	67
% from public high school	61
% live on campus	85
% African American	3
% Asian	8
% Caucasian	66
% Hispanic	5
% Native American	1
% international	3
# of countries represented	46

SURVEY SAYS . . .
Students aren't religious
Students love Saratoga Springs, NY
Great off-campus food
Dorms are like palaces
Frats and sororities are unpopular or nonexistent

ACADEMICS
Academic Rating	89
Calendar	semester
Student/faculty ratio	8.4:1
Profs interesting rating	86
Profs accessible rating	91
Most common reg class size	10–19 students
Most common lab size	10–19 students

MOST POPULAR MAJORS
business/commerce
English language and literature
psychology

STUDENTS SAY ". . ."

Academics

"Creative thought matters" is Skidmore's slogan, and students here echo it frequently enough to convince us that it's more than your standard college hype; nearly one in five undergrads major in the visual or performing arts. Skidmore also boasts "great science programs," a "superb" English Department, and an "excellent" business program. The combined effect produces "a haven for inquisitive, artsy, liberal-minded students looking for a place to get a good education with minimal pretentiousness." Arts students laud the school's "great artistic community, populated by so many musicians, artists, actors, and dancers who are all passionate about what they do. This leads to collaboration in and outside of schoolwork, making it a great place to develop as an artist." Undergrads in more traditional liberal arts and sciences disciplines love the "opportunities for real work"—such as working as a "lab assistant for research projects" or "in local schools"—and "the very enthusiastic professors who are passionate about their work." Those for whom Skidmore is a fit feel it represents the "perfect balance between structure and freedom."

Life

Students tell us that Skidmore's Saratoga Springs location is one of the best things about the school. "The town is great," a senior raves. "The nightlife is fantastic, internships and volunteer opportunities abound, you have access to the Adirondacks and all of the best ski sites, it's a great place for friends and family to visit…everyone loves the place. Most students end up spending a summer or two in Saratoga just so they can enjoy everything about it without being distracted by studies." On campus, life is "very relaxed, and there is generally little pressure on students to do anything. However, the campus is a very involved one and there are countless extracurricular clubs and events going on at any point." Many students "get drunk and go to parties on the weekend," often at upperclassmen's houses, but "It is really easy to find other activities to participate in if partying isn't your scene. There are tons of events every night, and lots of people who don't make partying their number one choice." These activities include "tons of campus concerts, performances, and shows" produced by the campus' glut of artists and performers.

Student Body

"Artistic/liberal kids" and "business major/athletic kids" form the two most conspicuous and readily identifiable populations on the Skidmore campus; one student explains, "You can usually tell who is who by the way they dress." While those two groups do "make a large part of the student body," undergrads point out that "there are all types of students that are not in those categories, or lie somewhere in between the two." For example, "We have kids who double major in business and art, and athletes who are in the orchestra—you can be anyone you want to be and be accepted as an individual and as a part of the Skidmore community." Indeed, "the student body as a whole is extremely open-minded to diversity. There are a number of LGBT students who are strongly supported by the student body." "Although there is not a large amount of ethnic diversity," one student reports, "I have never seen a student of a different ethnicity be discriminated against or even heard another student make any racist statement[s]." Are Skidmore students entirely free of prejudice? No, not entirely; one student explains, "The only discrimination I have seen here is against Republicans. Skidmore is extremely liberal, and I would say it is pretty hard to fit in here with extremely conservative beliefs."

FINANCIAL AID: 518-580-5750 • E-MAIL: ADMISSIONS@SKIDMORE.EDU • WEBSITE: WWW.SKIDMORE.EDU

THE PRINCETON REVIEW SAYS

Admissions

Very important factors considered include: Rigor of secondary school record. *Important factors considered include:* Class rank, application essay, academic GPA, recommendation(s), character/personal qualities, extracurricular activities, talent/ability, volunteer work, work experience. *Other factors considered include:* Standardized test scores, alumni/ae relation, first generation, geographical residence, interview, racial/ethnic status. SAT Subject Tests recommended; SAT or ACT required; ACT with Writing component required; TOEFL required of all international applicants. High school diploma is required and GED is accepted. *Academic units recommended:* 4 English, 4 mathematics, 4 science, (3 science labs), 4 foreign language, 4 social studies.

Financial Aid

Students should submit: FAFSA, CSS/Financial Aid PROFILE. Regular filing deadline is 1/15. The Princeton Review suggests that all financial aid forms be submitted as soon as possible after 1/1. *Need-based scholarships/grants offered:* Federal Pell, SEOG, state scholarships/grants, the school's own gift aid. *Loan aid offered:* FFEL Subsidized Stafford, FFEL Unsubsidized Stafford, FFEL PLUS, Federal Perkins. Applicants will be notified of awards on or about 4/1. Federal Work-Study Program available. Institutional employment available. Off-campus job opportunities are fair.

The Inside Word

Skidmore remains a fallback option for Northeastern kids who don't get into their top choices. Admits are very bright kids and a successful applicant must present the admissions office with a fairly compelling picture. You'll receive friendly, personalized assistance from the admissions office here, especially if you communicate a strong desire to attend Skidmore.

THE SCHOOL SAYS "..."

From The Admissions Office

"Launched in 2005, Skidmore's First-Year Experience (FYE) is a year-long academic, co-curricular, and residential initiative that immediately engages each first-year student with a faculty mentor-advisor, with 14 other students in an innovative Scribner Seminar, and with the entire college community through a series of artistic, cultural, and social events. FYE's centerpiece, 50 distinctive seminars—ranging from the human colonization of space to lessons learned from Hurricane Katrina to British national identity—requires each student to participate actively and creatively in his or her own learning. Seminar instructors function as faculty mentor-advisors for their 15 students and provide curricular and co-curricular perspectives not only on the specific seminar topic but on the liberal arts in general. In most cases, students live in residence halls in close proximity to classmates from their seminar. In terms of skills and habits of mind, seminar participants will learn to distinguish among and formulate the types of questions asked by different disciplines; read critically and gather and interpret evidence; consider and address complexities and ambiguities; recognize choices, examine assumptions, and take a skeptical stance; formulate conclusions based upon evidence; and communicate those conclusions orally and in writing. These are the fundamentals for academic excellence. The First-Year Experience is just the beginning of the expectation that students will creatively craft an experience leading to intensive work in a major field of study, often via a double major or major and minor, supplemented by a semester abroad, collaborative research with a faculty member, and internships. It is also a singular manifestation of Skidmore's commitment to the belief that 'Creative Thought Matters'—that every life, career, and endeavor is made more profound with creative ability at its core.

"Applicants are required to take the SAT or the ACT with the Writing section. We recommend that students provide scores for two SAT Subject Test examinations."

SELECTIVITY

Admissions Rating	**94**
# of applicants	7,316
% of applicants accepted	30
% of acceptees attending	30
# accepting a place on wait list	1,105
% admitted from wait list	7.8
# of early decision applicants	497
% accepted early decision	59

FRESHMAN PROFILE

Range SAT Critical Reading	580–680
Range SAT Math	590–670
Range SAT Writing	590–690
Range ACT Composite	26–29
Minimum paper TOEFL	590
Minimum computer TOEFL	243
Minimum web-based TOEFL	243
Average HS GPA	3.403
% graduated top 10% of class	37.1
% graduated top 25% of class	79.3
% graduated top 50% of class	96.2

DEADLINES

Early decision	
Deadline	11/15
Notification	12/15
Regular	
Deadline	1/15
Notification	4/1
Nonfall registration?	no

APPLICANTS ALSO LOOK AT

AND OFTEN PREFER
Wesleyan University

AND SOMETIMES PREFER
New York University
Connecticut College

AND RARELY PREFER
University of Vermont

FINANCIAL FACTS

Financial Aid Rating	**92**
Annual tuition	$39,600
Room and board	$19,776
Required fees	$820
% frosh rec. need-based scholarship or grant aid	41
% UG rec. need-based scholarship or grant aid	40.5
% frosh rec. non-need-based scholarship or grant aid	16.8
% UG rec. non-need-based scholarship or grant aid	7.7
% frosh rec. need-based self-help aid	41
% UG rec. need-based self-help aid	40.5
% frosh rec. any financial aid	43.6
% UG rec. any financial aid	41.6
Average cumulative indebtedness	$19,163

SMITH COLLEGE

SEVEN COLLEGE LANE, NORTHAMPTON, MA 01063 • ADMISSIONS: 413-585-2500 • FAX: 413-585-2527

CAMPUS LIFE
Quality of Life Rating	**96**
Fire Safety Rating	**72**
Green Rating	**97**
Type of school	private
Environment	town

STUDENTS
Total undergrad enrollment	2,610
% male/female	0/100
% from out of state	77
% from public high school	67
% live on campus	90
% African American	7
% Asian	13
% Caucasian	43
% Hispanic	7
% Native American	1
% international	7
# of countries represented	72

SURVEY SAYS . . .
Great off-campus food
Dorms are like palaces
Frats and sororities are unpopular or nonexistent
Student government is popular
Political activism is popular

ACADEMICS
Academic Rating	**96**
Calendar	semester
Student/faculty ratio	9:1
Profs interesting rating	93
Profs accessible rating	88
Most common reg class size	10–19 students

MOST POPULAR MAJORS
political science and government
psychology

STUDENTS SAY ". . ."

Academics

Smith College isn't for everyone. You have to be a woman to get in, for one, and a highly accomplished one at that—Smith is among the nation's most selective undergraduate institutions. More important still is a capacity for self-direction; Smith has an open curriculum ("no core requirements"), which means students "can make our schedules however we like, leaving lots of freedom to take interesting classes outside our majors." Those who thrive here are those who are "tired of being told that I needed to take things I wasn't interested in. I like being trusted with my own education, and Smith gave me that option," but students needing structure may find the freedom a bit overwhelming. Fortunately, Smith offers undergrads plenty of support; "Both the administration and the faculty at Smith are very invested in the success of students. It is very easy to get support and find someone to help navigate not only your academic career at Smith but also the continuation of a liberal arts education in the real world through internships, jobs, summer experiences, and other programs offered in conjunction with Smith." Students also enjoy "almost limitless resources in terms of libraries, funding, etc., all easily accessible," all in a "small community" setting; "From financial aid officers who've 'found' extra funds to professors who think of an internship you might be interested in, it really seems like everyone here is willing to go the extra mile for students."

Life

Smith's unique housing system—students live in smaller houses rather than dorms—is a much-cherished tradition. Students crow that the system "provides for a strong campus community including friendly rivalries and close friendships. Your house is your lifeline, especially during the first few weeks of school." "Strong self-government within each household" reinforces Smith's academic emphasis on independence. Campus life "provides a variety of activities every night to keep their students entertained, including "great sports teams" and "an organization or group for just about everybody." Hometown Northampton "is a lively town with fun bars, restaurants, and theaters" and is surprisingly active given its size (approximately 30,000). Further opportunities arise from Smith's participation in the Five College Consortium; "Any event on any of the five campuses (Hampshire, UMass Amherst, Amherst, Mount Holyoke, and Smith) is open to all five college's students. Students are able to take classes at all the colleges, join clubs at all the colleges, get into parties at all colleges, and attend any performance or event at any of the colleges. Because of this, you can easily be involved in a wide variety of social engagements (e.g. frat parties at UMass, theater performances at Hampshire, or a night in your living room with housemates at Smith)."

Student Body

Smith fosters "an accepting and intellectual atmosphere" where "students actually enjoy their studies and happily talk about class work outside of class." The women here tend to be "overachievers...who take advantage of the many things Smith has to offer and tend to be constantly busy trying to manage school work and multiple extracurriculars. Smithies are always involved." As an elite school, Smith can attract students "from vastly different backgrounds who thus bring those differences with them to the Smith community," thereby exposing students "to people of different race, religion, socio-economic, cultural, social, gender, [and] sexual backgrounds" whom they might elsewhere not have encountered; undergrads appreciate the opportunity. The student body has a well-earned reputation for being "very open about and accepting of all types of sexual orientation, with active GLBTQ and transgender communities." They also tend to be "very environmentally aware and active," and "the large majority of students are liberal or very liberal politically."

FINANCIAL AID: 413-585-2530 • E-MAIL: ADMISSION@SMITH.EDU • WEBSITE: WWW.SMITH.EDU

THE PRINCETON REVIEW SAYS

Admissions

Very important factors considered include: Academic GPA, recommendation(s), rigor of secondary school record, character/personal qualities. *Important factors considered include:* Class rank, application essay, extracurricular activities, interview, talent/ability. *Other factors considered include:* Standardized test scores, alumni/ae relation, first generation, racial/ethnic status, volunteer work, work experience. TOEFL required of all international applicants. High school diploma or equivalent is not required. *Academic units recommended:* 4 English, 3 mathematics, 3 science, (3 science labs), 3 foreign language, 2 history.

Financial Aid

Students should submit: FAFSA, CSS/Financial Aid PROFILE, noncustodial PROFILE, business/farm supplement. Regular filing deadline is 2/15. The Princeton Review suggests that all financial aid forms be submitted as soon as possible after 1/1. *Need-based scholarships/grants offered:* Federal Pell, SEOG, state scholarships/grants, the school's own gift aid. *Loan aid offered:* Direct Subsidized Stafford, Direct Unsubsidized Stafford, FFEL PLUS, Federal Perkins, state loans, college/university loans from institutional funds. Applicants will be notified of awards on or about 4/1. Federal Work-Study Program available. Institutional employment available. Off-campus job opportunities are excellent.

The Inside Word

Applicants to Smith can expect a careful and thorough review of all application materials. Only students who have successfully pursued rigorous high school curricula and demonstrated unique and compelling talents or personal attributes are likely to get past the gatekeepers here. Standardized test scores are optional here; if yours are sub-par, don't submit them. If they're good, though, include them; they can't hurt.

THE SCHOOL SAYS " . . ."

From The Admissions Office

"Smith students choose from 1,000 courses in more than 50 areas of study. There are no specific course requirements outside the major; students meet individually with faculty advisers to plan a balanced curriculum. Smith programs offer unique opportunities, including the chance to study abroad, or at another college in the United States, and a semester in Washington, D.C. The Ada Comstock Scholars Program encourages women beyond the traditional age to return to college and complete their undergraduate studies. Smith is located in the scenic Connecticut River valley of western Massachusetts near a number of other outstanding educational institutions. Through the Five College Consortium, Smith, Amherst, Hampshire, and Mount Holyoke colleges, and the University of Massachusetts enrich their academic, social, and cultural offerings by means of joint faculty appointments, joint courses, student and faculty exchanges, shared facilities, and other cooperative arrangements. Smith is the only women's college to offer an accredited major in engineering; it's also the only college in the country that offers a guaranteed paid internship program ("Praxis")."

"Smith requires either the SAT or the ACT."

SELECTIVITY

Admissions Rating	98
# of applicants	3,771
% of applicants accepted	48
% of acceptees attending	36
# accepting a place on wait list	353
% admitted from wait list	36
# of early decision applicants	256
% accepted early decision	64

FRESHMAN PROFILE

Range SAT Critical Reading	600–710
Range SAT Math	570–680
Range SAT Writing	590–700
Range ACT Composite	25–31
Minimum paper TOEFL	600
Minimum computer TOEFL	250
Minimum web-based TOEFL	90
Average HS GPA	3.89
% graduated top 10% of class	64
% graduated top 25% of class	91
% graduated top 50% of class	99

DEADLINES

Early decision	
Deadline	11/15
Notification	12/15
Regular	
Deadline	1/15
Notification	4/1
Nonfall registration?	no

APPLICANTS ALSO LOOK AT

AND OFTEN PREFER
Brown University

AND SOMETIMES PREFER
Wellesley College

AND RARELY PREFER
Mount Holyoke College

FINANCIAL FACTS

Financial Aid Rating	94
Annual tuition	$37,510
Room and board	$12,622
% frosh rec. need-based scholarship or grant aid	53
% UG rec. need-based scholarship or grant aid	58
% frosh rec. non-need-based scholarship or grant aid	1
% UG rec. non-need-based scholarship or grant aid	1
% frosh rec. need-based self-help aid	55
% UG rec. need-based self-help aid	60
% frosh rec. any financial aid	67.2
% UG rec. any financial aid	71
% UG borrow to pay for school	71
Average cumulative indebtedness	$20,960

SONOMA STATE UNIVERSITY

1801 EAST COTATI AVENUE, ROHNERT PARK, CA 94928 • ADMISSIONS: 707-664-2778 • FAX: 707-664-2060

CAMPUS LIFE

Quality of Life Rating	69
Fire Safety Rating	60*
Green Rating	98
Type of school	public
Environment	town

STUDENTS

Total undergrad enrollment	7,709
% male/female	39/61
% from out of state	2
% from public high school	81
% live on campus	31
% in (# of) fraternities	5 (5)
% in (# of) sororities	5 (9)
% African American	2
% Asian	5
% Caucasian	67
% Hispanic	12
% Native American	1
% international	1

SURVEY SAYS . . .
Great library
Athletic facilities are great
Low cost of living
(Almost) no one smokes
Very little drug use

ACADEMICS

Academic Rating	77
Calendar	semester
Student/faculty ratio	23:1
Profs interesting rating	74
Profs accessible rating	69
% classes taught by TAs	1
Most common reg class size	20–29 students

MOST POPULAR MAJORS
business/commerce
liberal arts and sciences studies and humanities
psychology

STUDENTS SAY ". . ."

Academics

Sonoma State University is a good place to get a down-to-earth and cost-effective public education, without sacrificing the opportunities and excitement of residential college life. For a state school, SSU's student body is on the smaller side, and the environment is friendly and casual. Major coursework takes a "one-on-one" approach, and, in most departments, "professors make it easy to build a relationship with them outside of the classroom." While SSU professors "enjoy teaching," students admit that class quality is "hit-or-miss," especially in lectures and general education courses. Fortunately, what remains a virtual constant is that the professors "want to see their students succeed and therefore, are willing to go above and beyond in assisting them." A student says, "Not only do my professors know my name, but they actually know my character as well, and whenever I need letters of recommendation, I can always ask actual professors instead of TAs." With the California state finances in turmoil, SSU has taken a noticeable blow. Students warn us that, "classes can be hard to get, especially with budget cuts," making it more difficult to graduate in four years. Budget restriction have also made it more difficult for students who want to take a broad-based curriculum, because many classes are offered exclusively to majors. For example, "all art classes are only available for art majors, and only drama majors are allowed to audition for plays." Many students blame the administration for their registration woes, saying "there is somewhat of a disconnect between the administration and SSU students."

Life

As at many state colleges, a majority of SSU students live off campus and commute to school. However, with more than a quarter of undergraduates living on campus, you can still have the full college experience at Sonoma State. The school's dorms and suites are "beautiful," the gym and recreational center are state-of-the-art, and there are an "abundance of extracurricular activities that make the university setting more than just academics." In the evenings, "the Residential Student Association at SSU puts on many fantastic activities for students to attend, such as weekly movie nights, karaoke, crafts, pizza feeds, comedians, open mic nights, guest speakers, and so on." In addition, the school's attractive atmosphere makes it a great place to kick back, and "a lot of people go to the cafe or just hang around campus" during their spare time. Although fraternities and sororities do not have housing, "the night life around Sonoma State University focuses on Greek events," and for many (though not all) students, "partying is a staple." For those looking for an alternative to the Greek system, "Sonoma State has great leadership opportunities for students on campus." Off campus, the surrounding town of Rohnert Park isn't a favorite with students. However, Sonoma's stellar location makes the school a perfect home base for day trips in Northern California. From SSU, "the beach is less than an hour's drive from campus, as is San Francisco."

Student Body

Nestled amidst Northern California redwoods, Sonoma State attracts students from across the state. In addition to locals, "there are a significant amount of southern California students," who may initially stand out from their Bay Area counterparts. Eventually, however, everyone is "socialized to the laid-back atmosphere" that defines the SSU experience. On this relaxed campus, "most students are politically aware, care about the environment, and are accepting to those who are different." A majority of students come from middle-class families, and students acknowledge that, "there is personality diversity but not ethnic diversity." In any case, "you are bound to have an interesting conversation at least once a day," and everyone is "respectful of others with different opinions." No matter what you like to do, you'll find a niche; "People looking for a social realm can experience that, and those looking for a quiet, academic realm can experience that as well." In most cases, Sonoma State students blend a bit of both, and "the typical students at Sonoma are dedicated to their studies but not afraid to go out and have some fun."

FINANCIAL AID: 707-664-2389 • E-MAIL: ADMITME.@SONOMA.EDU • WEBSITE: WWW.SONOMA.EDU

THE PRINCETON REVIEW SAYS

Admissions

Very important factors considered include: Academic GPA, rigor of secondary school record, standardized test scores. *Other factors considered include:* First generation, geographical residence, state residency. SAT or ACT required; TOEFL required of all international applicants. High school diploma is required and GED is accepted. *Academic units required:* 4 English, 3 mathematics, 2 science, (1 science lab), 2 foreign language, 2 history, 1 visual/performing arts, 1 academic elective, 1 visual/performing arts.

Financial Aid

Students should submit: FAFSA. The Princeton Review suggests that all financial aid forms be submitted as soon as possible after 1/1. *Need-based scholarships/grants offered:* Federal Pell, SEOG, state scholarships/grants, private scholarships, the school's own gift aid, ACG, SMART. *Loan aid offered:* Direct Subsidized Stafford, Direct Unsubsidized Stafford, Direct PLUS, Federal Perkins. Applicants will be notified of awards on a rolling basis beginning 3/15. Federal Work-Study Program available. Institutional employment available. Off-campus job opportunities are good.

The Inside Word

To determine an applicant's eligibility for admission, SSU calculates an admissions index number based on his or her standardized test scores and GPA. Due to the school's budget problems, students applying for admission to impacted majors must submit higher GPAs and test scores than applicants to non-impacted programs. Currently, impacted majors include communication studies, human development, liberal studies, pre-nursing and nursing, and psychology.

THE SCHOOL SAYS "..."

From The Admissions Office

"Sonoma State University occupies 275 acres in the beautiful wine country of Sonoma county, in northern California. Located at the foot of the Sonoma hills, the campus is an hour's drive north of San Francisco and centrally located between the Pacific Ocean to the west and the wine country to the north and east. SSU is deeply committed to the teaching of the liberal arts and sciences. The campus has earned a national reputation as a leader in integrating the use of technology into its curriculum. Within its 32 academic departments, SSU awards bachelor's degrees in 41 areas of specialization and master's degrees in 14 areas. In addition, the university offers a joint master's degree in mathematics with San Francisco State University. The campus ushered in the twenty-first century with the opening of a new library and technology center, the Jean and Charles Schulz Information Center.

"All freshmen applicants are required to provide SAT or ACT scores."

SELECTIVITY

Admissions Rating	77
# of applicants	12,240
% of applicants accepted	76
% of acceptees attending	18

FRESHMAN PROFILE

Range SAT Critical Reading	450–550
Range SAT Math	460–570
Range ACT Composite	20–24
Minimum paper TOEFL	500
Minimum computer TOEFL	173
Average HS GPA	3.23

DEADLINES

Regular	
Priority	11/30
Deadline	11/30
Notification	rolling
Nonfall registration?	yes

FINANCIAL FACTS

Financial Aid Rating	72
Annual out-of-state tuition	$9,357
Room and board	$10,115
Required fees	$4,272
Books and supplies	$1,656
% frosh rec. need-based scholarship or grant aid	13
% UG rec. need-based scholarship or grant aid	23
% frosh rec. non-need-based scholarship or grant aid	5
% UG rec. non-need-based scholarship or grant aid	7
% frosh rec. need-based self-help aid	17
% UG rec. need-based self-help aid	27
% frosh rec. any financial aid	63
% UG rec. any financial aid	53
% UG borrow to pay for school	37
Average cumulative indebtedness	$14,410

SOUTHERN METHODIST UNIVERSITY

PO Box 750181, Dallas, TX 75275-0181 • Admissions: 214-768-0103 • Fax: 214-768-2507

CAMPUS LIFE
Quality of Life Rating	**76**
Fire Safety Rating	**60***
Green Rating	**69**
Type of school	private
Affiliation	Methodist
Environment	metropolis

STUDENTS
Total undergrad enrollment	6,172
% male/female	47/53
% from out of state	45
% from public high school	61
% live on campus	31
% in (# of) fraternities	23 (15)
% in (# of) sororities	31 (13)
% African American	5
% Asian	6
% Caucasian	74
% Hispanic	8
% Native American	1
% international	6
# of countries represented	92

SURVEY SAYS . . .
Athletic facilities are great
School is well run
Students love Dallas, TX
Great off-campus food
Frats and sororities dominate social scene
Lots of beer drinking
Hard liquor is popular

ACADEMICS
Academic Rating	**78**
Calendar	semester
Student/faculty ratio	12:1
Profs interesting rating	71
Profs accessible rating	65
Most common reg class size	10–19 students
Most common lab size	20–29 students

MOST POPULAR MAJORS
business administration and management
public relations/image management
social sciences
corporate communications and public affairs

STUDENTS SAY ". . ."

Academics

Southern Methodist University seeks "to challenge and develop students intellectually and socially in order to provide a fulfilling higher education." Others agree that students here are "making valuable connections that can serve [them] well in the working world." They "work hard and play hard," so it's all about finding balance between "making the grades and having fun." Good news for grads: Future opportunities abound as "You won't struggle to find a job because of SMU's outstanding reputation in the Dallas market. Its strong name has also branched out into the greater south. Most of the alums are very successful, and they seek out SMU students." The school works its magic most effectively in such popular disciplines as business, advertising, pre-law, and premedical study; its Meadows School of Arts is home to "an incredible music program" and equally strong programs in dance, theater, arts administration, and advertising. Students are keen to brag that SMU professors "go above and beyond their duties" and are always "looking after your best interests." Combine this with a "great administration" that "really strives to stay in touch with their students and uses their feedback to make beneficial changes." SMU's Dallas address means "there are a lot of ways to get involved in the community or resources for your career path." As one student explains, "My school does a great job at helping students decide what they want out of their future and assisting them on making it possible."

Life

"School is hard," notes one student, "but you make it through somehow" thanks to "parties, movies, clubs, bars, [and a] very Greek" campus. In fact, the typical student is described as "sporting a Greek affiliation" (and they don't mean the nationality). The Greeks serve as the nexus of social life and account for a large "sense of community" among students. In short, writes one Greek student, "We run this place. Everyone who is anyone is in it. Tailgating wouldn't happen without us. Homecoming wouldn't happen without us." Togas aside, SMU's "beautiful" campus garners even more accolades. "It is definitely the prettiest campus in Texas and one of the greatest in the south," says a student. Beyond campus awaits Dallas, where "there is always a party going on, whether it is downtown or at a local bar. Because of the location (in upscale Highland Park), bars are always new and safe with the best DJs. There are more places to eat near SMU than anywhere I have ever been."

Student Body

First, let's address the stereotypes. The typical SMU student is described largely as "upper-class, white, and wealthy—though looks can be deceiving." That said, many note that SMU could use "more diversity," and "typical students can feel left out." Another student claims that the school has "a huge mix of students," though "you have to look hard." As with most Texas schools, there is a huge sense of pride in the state. "You'll see Texas flags in all the dorm rooms. But it's more of a statement of the genteel southern style of living people appreciate. Everyone is Republican...and very conservative." Though many agree that a majority of students "come from high-income households," SMU is a "dynamic community" that manages "to offer something for everyone. You just have to find your niche."

FINANCIAL AID: 214-768-2058 • E-MAIL: UGADMISSION@SMU.EDU • WEBSITE: WWW.SMU.EDU/ADMISSION

THE PRINCETON REVIEW SAYS

Admissions

Very important factors considered include: Class rank, application essay, academic GPA, recommendation(s), rigor of secondary school record, standardized test scores. *Important factors considered include:* Character/personal qualities, extracurricular activities, talent/ability, volunteer work, work experience. *Other factors considered include:* Alumni/ae relation, first generation, interview, level of applicant's interest. SAT or ACT required; TOEFL required of all international applicants. High school diploma is required and GED is not accepted. *Academic units required:* 4 English, 3 mathematics, 3 science, (2 science labs), 2 foreign language, 1 social studies, 2 history. *Academic units recommended:* 4 English, 4 mathematics, 4 science, (3 science labs), 3 foreign language, 2 social studies, 3 history.

Financial Aid

Students should submit: FAFSA, CSS/Financial Aid PROFILE, noncustodial PROFILE, business/farm supplement. The Princeton Review suggests that all financial aid forms be submitted as soon as possible after 1/1. *Need-based scholarships/grants offered:* Federal Pell, SEOG, state scholarships/grants, private scholarships, the school's own gift aid. *Loan aid offered:* FFEL Subsidized Stafford, FFEL Unsubsidized Stafford, FFEL PLUS, Federal Perkins, state loans, college/university loans from institutional funds. Applicants will be notified of awards on a rolling basis beginning 3/15. Off-campus job opportunities are good.

The Inside Word

With a potent combination of high-caliber academics, Texan weather, and classic architecture, admissions standards at SMU have been steadily rising over the last decade, meaning that securing a seat here is getting more and more competitive. Solid high school grades and a roster of activities will usually do the trick, but keep in mind that performing arts majors must audition. Interestingly, all other applicants, regardless of declared major, are listed as "pre-majors" to the Dedman College of Humanities and Sciences.

THE SCHOOL SAYS "..."

From The Admissions Office

"SMU students balance challenging academic programs with a total campus experience that enables them to choose their own path of achievement. Small classes ensure that students receive personal attention. Classes are taught by professors who are dedicated to teaching undergraduates while producing new knowledge, enriching the classroom. Students also have access to visiting dignitaries ranging from former presidents to Nobel laureates. Reflecting its student-centered focus, SMU is one of the few universities to have a voting student member on its Board of Trustees. Internships, community service, student research opportunities, and study abroad programs abound. SMU also offers a thriving honors program and one of the top merit scholarship programs in the nation. More than 400 arts events each year add a special vitality to campus life, and nearly 200 student organizations provide opportunities for leadership. SMU welcomes a diverse student body from every state and over 90 countries; 72 percent of students receive some form of financial aid. Graduates attend some of the best graduate and professional schools in the nation. They find promising career opportunities through SMU's close ties with Dallas, a center of commerce and culture and gateway to the global community.

"SMU requires either the ACT or SAT. Assessment of written communication skills remains an important component of the SMU application review process. To that end, it is recommended that applicants use every opportunity, including the ACT or SAT, to display their writing skills in the application process."

SELECTIVITY

Admissions Rating	89
# of applicants	8,270
% of applicants accepted	50
% of acceptees attending	34
# accepting a place on wait list	415
% admitted from wait list	19

FRESHMAN PROFILE

Range SAT Critical Reading	560–660
Range SAT Math	590–680
Range SAT Writing	560–660
Range ACT Composite	25–30
Minimum paper TOEFL	550
Minimum computer TOEFL	213
Average HS GPA	3.57
% graduated top 10% of class	42
% graduated top 25% of class	73
% graduated top 50% of class	94

DEADLINES

Early action	
Deadline	11/1
Notification	12/31
Regular	
Priority	1/15
Deadline	3/15
Notification	rolling
Nonfall registration?	yes

APPLICANTS ALSO LOOK AT
AND SOMETIMES PREFER
The University of Texas at Austin
AND RARELY PREFER
Texas Christian University

FINANCIAL FACTS

Financial Aid Rating	78
Annual tuition	$31,200
Room and board	$12,445
Required fees	$3,960
Books and supplies	$800
% frosh rec. need-based scholarship or grant aid	24
% UG rec. need-based scholarship or grant aid	27
% frosh rec. non-need-based scholarship or grant aid	25
% UG rec. non-need-based scholarship or grant aid	20
% frosh rec. need-based self-help aid	28
% UG rec. need-based self-help aid	30
% frosh rec. athletic scholarships	5
% UG rec. athletic scholarships	5
% frosh rec. any financial aid	82
% UG rec. any financial aid	65
% UG borrow to pay for school	38
Average cumulative indebtedness	$20,883

SOUTHWESTERN UNIVERSITY

ADMISSIONS OFFICE, PO BOX 770, GEORGETOWN, TX 78627-0770 • ADMISSIONS: 512-863-1200 • FAX: 512-863-9601

CAMPUS LIFE

Quality of Life Rating	83
Fire Safety Rating	78
Green Rating	73
Type of school	private
Affiliation	Methodist
Environment	town

STUDENTS

Total undergrad enrollment	1,259
% male/female	39/61
% from out of state	6
% from public high school	81
% live on campus	81
% in (# of) fraternities	29 (4)
% in (# of) sororities	30 (4)
% African American	3
% Asian	5
% Caucasian	75
% Hispanic	15
% Native American	1
# of countries represented	9

SURVEY SAYS . . .
No one cheats
Career services are great
School is well run
Students are friendly
Dorms are like palaces
Campus feels safe
Students are happy

ACADEMICS

Academic Rating	92
Calendar	semester
Student/faculty ratio	10:1
Profs interesting rating	93
Profs accessible rating	92
Most common reg class size	10–19 students
Most common lab size	2–9 students

MOST POPULAR MAJORS
business
communication studies
political science and government
psychology

STUDENTS SAY " . . ."

Academics
"Camouflaged behind a directional name," Southwestern University offers "a lot of personal attention" and seriously generous financial aid. However, "Southwestern's greatest asset" is its "enthusiastic" and "delightfully eccentric" faculty. They are "extraordinary teachers" who "really care" and "form close and long-lasting friendships" with students. "Professors will meet with you outside of class every day," promises a history major. While course selection is "limited," students also rave about their "really small" classes. The "responsive" administration is "extremely involved," and the career services staff is reportedly "outstanding." Newly-minted SU grads have a great track record at finding real jobs and getting into graduate and professional schools. If you come here, though, be prepared for a "crazy hard" academic experience. Class attendance is required. Homework is ample. While "getting A's is definitely not impossible, it does require work." "There is almost no such thing as a blow-off class," and the broad core curriculum typically culminates in "a sizable research thesis" or a special project. "You learn a whole lot and are insanely prepared for whatever you want to do when you leave," reports a psychology major.

Life
Southwestern's campus is "absolutely beautiful." "The dorms don't completely suck." On the other hand, the "mediocre" food "gets old pretty fast." Campus life is largely "self contained," and despite "constant drama," it's "predictable." In a nutshell, "life at Southwestern is a struggle to maintain the fine balance between a very heavy workload and a very fun social life." SU students "spend a near-absurd amount of time studying" every weeknight. On Wednesday nights and on the weekends, though, they find time to party. "Greek life really is a large part of Southwestern's campus" and fraternities definitely "drive the social scene." However, "students not involved in Greek life are still welcome at Greek events and go often." There are also various house parties and "big themed parties" in the student apartments. For sober students, "there are tons of plays and concerts all the time," and "the school does a good job of providing some form of entertainment every weekend." Extracurricular activities are also abundant. "It's all a pretty open, nonexclusive atmosphere where pretty much anybody is welcome to participate in the sports, organizations, or whatever," relates a senior. Off campus, the city of Georgetown lacks excitement and "the townies don't like the students very much." Luckily, the "much cooler" environs of Austin are just a short drive away.

Student Body
Students come to Southwestern "from any number of small towns" and from "suburbia" but "it seems like everybody is from Texas." It seems like everyone is white, too. "There are definitely not enough minorities here, that's for sure," asserts a senior. "The school is not as racially diverse as the administration likes to pretend." Many females also lament the male "shortage." "It's a guy's paradise," says a freshman. "You will see the most gorgeous girls with the geekiest guys." "There's also a pretty open gay population." Students at SU describe themselves as "highly motivated," "very eclectic," and "quirky." "Unconventional appearances" are common. There aren't too many jocks here. It's mostly a "nerdy, skinny, non-athletic" crowd. "Most of us are the brainy, slightly eccentric kid you sat behind in any AP or IB class you took in high school," admits a sophomore. Most students are Christian, but at the same time, "not very religious." Some students are "ultra conservative." Others are "liberal as hell." Many are "loaded, money-wise." "The typical student is either an extremely conservative trust fund baby, or a lip-service hippie trust fund baby," suggests a junior. However, a very large contingent of students is also here "on scholarship" or thanks to Southwestern's generous financial aid packages.

SOUTHWESTERN UNIVERSITY

FINANCIAL AID: 512-863-1259 • E-MAIL: ADMISSION@SOUTHWESTERN.EDU • WEBSITE: WWW.SOUTHWESTERN.EDU

THE PRINCETON REVIEW SAYS

Admissions

Very important factors considered include: Class rank, application essay, academic GPA, recommendation(s), rigor of secondary school record, standardized test scores. *Important factors considered include:* Alumni/ae relation, character/personal qualities, extracurricular activities, first generation, geographical residence, interview, level of applicant's interest, racial/ethnic status, talent/ability, volunteer work, work experience. SAT or ACT required; ACT with Writing component required; TOEFL required of all international applicants. High school diploma is required and GED is accepted. *Academic units required:* 4 English, 4 mathematics, 3 science, (2 science labs), 2 foreign language, 2 social studies, 1 history, 1 academic elective. *Academic units recommended:* 4 English, 4 mathematics, 4 science, (3 science labs), 3 foreign language, 3 social studies, 2 history.

Financial Aid

Students should submit: FAFSA. Regular filing deadline is 3/1. The Princeton Review suggests that all financial aid forms be submitted as soon as possible after 1/1. *Need-based scholarships/grants offered:* Federal Pell, SEOG, state scholarships/grants, private scholarships, the school's own gift aid. *Loan aid offered:* FFEL Subsidized Stafford, FFEL Unsubsidized Stafford, FFEL PLUS, Federal Perkins, state loans, college/university loans from institutional funds. Applicants will be notified of awards on a rolling basis beginning 3/1. Federal Work-Study Program available. Institutional employment available. Off-campus job opportunities are good.

The Inside Word

Southwestern is one of the best "sleepers" in the nation. Admissions standards are high, but they would be even higher if more people knew about this place. Academic excellence abounds, the administration is earnest and helpful, and financial aid packages are frequently tremendous. If you could thrive in a small-town, close-knit environment, Southwestern definitely deserves a look.

THE SCHOOL SAYS "..."

From The Admissions Office

"Southwestern University, the state's first institution of higher learning. On the outskirts of Texas's vibrant capital city of Austin. Southwestern is committed to helping students achieve personal and professional success as well as a passion for lifelong learning. The Paideia Program, funded in 2002 by an $8.5 million grant, is a distinctive new option for select students beginning their sophomore year that provides opportunities to compare, contrast, and integrate knowledge and skills gained in various areas of study. In addition to their regular studies, students work with the same Paideia professor over a three-year period in seminar groups of 10. They work to discover the powerful connections between Southwestern's rigorous academic experience and the dynamic programs available outside the classroom—through leadership, service, intercultural learning, and collaborative research or creative works. All Southwestern students discover that a premier liberal arts education leads to high acceptance rates into prestigious graduate and professional programs and careers right out of college. Southwestern is today what it has always been: a highly personal liberal arts experience that equips students with the strengths they need to develop fulfilling lives.

"Southwestern University will accept SAT scores. The Writing component will be considered in a comprehensive manner, along with overall academic record, application essay, extracurricular activities, recommendations, and a personal interview."

SELECTIVITY

Admissions Rating	89
# of applicants	1,923
% of applicants accepted	65
% of acceptees attending	28
# accepting a place on wait list	4
% admitted from wait list	0
# of early decision applicants	64
% accepted early decision	88

FRESHMAN PROFILE

Range SAT Critical Reading	550–670
Range SAT Math	560–660
Range ACT Composite	24–29
Minimum paper TOEFL	570
Minimum computer TOEFL	230
% graduated top 10% of class	51
% graduated top 25% of class	77
% graduated top 50% of class	96

DEADLINES

Early decision	
Deadline	11/1
Notification	12/15
Regular	
Priority	2/15
Deadline	2/15
Notification	4/1
Nonfall registration?	yes

APPLICANTS ALSO LOOK AT

AND OFTEN PREFER
Trinity University
Rice University

AND SOMETIMES PREFER
Texas A&M University—College Station
The University of Texas at Austin

AND RARELY PREFER
Baylor University
Austin College
Texas Christian University

FINANCIAL FACTS

Financial Aid Rating	88
Annual tuition	$27,940
Room and board	$8,870
Books and supplies	$1,000
% frosh rec. need-based scholarship or grant aid	58
% UG rec. need-based scholarship or grant aid	53
% frosh rec. non-need-based scholarship or grant aid	38
% UG rec. non-need-based scholarship or grant aid	34
% frosh rec. need-based self-help aid	48
% UG rec. need-based self-help aid	46
% frosh rec. any financial aid	87
% UG rec. any financial aid	83
% UG borrow to pay for school	43
Average cumulative indebtedness	$23,601

THE BEST 371 COLLEGES ■ 495

SPELMAN COLLEGE

350 SPELMAN LANE, SOUTHWEST, ATLANTA, GA 30314 • ADMISSIONS: 404-270-5193 • FAX: 404-270-5201

CAMPUS LIFE
Quality of Life Rating	69
Fire Safety Rating	95
Green Rating	79
Type of school	private
Environment	metropolis

STUDENTS
Total undergrad enrollment	2,337
% male/female	0/100
% from out of state	69
% from public high school	84
% live on campus	48
% in (# of) sororities	NR (4)
% African American	96
% international	2
# of countries represented	18

SURVEY SAYS . . .
Lab facilities are great
Career services are great
Campus feels safe
Students are happy
Frats and sororities dominate social
scene
Musical organizations are popular
Student government is popular
Very little drug use

ACADEMICS
Academic Rating	75
Calendar	semester
Student/faculty ratio	12:1
Profs interesting rating	66
Profs accessible rating	62
Most common reg class size	10–19 students
Most common lab size	20–29 students

MOST POPULAR MAJORS
political science and government
psychology

STUDENTS SAY ". . ."

Academics

In a nutshell, sums up a senior, small Spelman College in Atlanta is "political awareness, intellectual nirvana, and warm sisterhood in a pair of Prada shoes." It's also "the premier college for black women in the United States." The hard sciences are especially notable, but "academics are very strong" across the board. Spelman makes you analyze every situation," emphasizes a sociology major. "It makes you think." "Small classes" allow for plenty of "individual attention." Outside of class, professors are "easy to talk to" as well. The women of Spelman are split in their views of the administration. Proponents say that management is "friendly and as available as regular professors, sometimes more so." Critics charge that the staff can be "rude." "At times, school administration takes patience," says a junior, "but I guess you could look at it as another thing Spelman instills in you." Most students tend to agree that "Spelman could stand to improve financial aid." The curriculum here is strongly oriented toward the liberal arts and sciences, and there is something of a "lack of relevant career-based majors." For programs not offered on campus, though, Spelman belongs to the Atlanta University Center, "the largest consortium" of historically black colleges in the nation," and students can take classes and utilize resources at a handful of schools nearby.

Life

"The food is horrible," and parking needs to improve, but overall, students here are very pleased with their "sisterly community." "Spelman College allows for its students to participate in a lot of different things," says a junior. There are "comedy shows, concerts (for all tastes), coronation ball, pageants—everything you can think of." On Market Friday, "there is music, and vendors come to sell their merchandise. Students from Morehouse College and Clark Atlanta University come over, and occasionally a celebrity walks through." Greek life is noticeable, but "Spelman's campus really isn't the place to be for great parties or socializing." In fact, it's "practically a ghost town on the weekends." Older students often go to house parties or frequent Atlanta's nightclubs. "You have the city of Atlanta at your disposal, which never allows for a dull moment." "It is mandatory for first-year students to live on campus," and they can't have cars, "so the shuttle buses wait outside to pick them up and take them to the party," wherever it is. If you have an interest in men, don't worry. "I don't want anyone to be afraid to come to Spelman because it's a women's college and they're afraid they'll never see men," admonishes a senior. "A lot of times I forget that I go to a women's college. The social scene is never lacking. Morehouse—an HBCU and a men's college—is literally right across the street from us, and they take classes with us, join in activities and clubs with us, and throw parties with us." There's also a joint homecoming, which is "ridiculously fun."

Student Body

"Because most of us are women of African descent, people believe that we will all be the same, but at times I believe Spelman is more diverse than many other schools," suggests a sophomore. "We have students of many different ethnic backgrounds (Jamaican, Trinidadian, Nigerian, etc.). Students come from various socioeconomic backgrounds. This is contrary to what many people think about the typical Spelmanite." "The only things that I'd say are common to nearly all Spelman students are that we are (1) black and (2) female," agrees a senior. "Other than that, everyone's different, and I don't mean to make that a cliché. You'd be surprised how much diversity can be found at a historically black college for women." The students here describe themselves as "hardworking, friendly, competitive, and fashionable." They often come "from a middle-class to upper-middle-class background." "People think Spelman women have a lot of money and are generally stuck up," observes one senior. Students here are also "politically active." "Our school has historically been involved in a lot of political movements," relates another senior, "and it's a joke around Morehouse and Spelman that every year we have a new issue."

FINANCIAL AID: 404-270-5212 • E-MAIL: ADMISS@SPELMAN.EDU • WEBSITE: WWW.SPELMAN.EDU

THE PRINCETON REVIEW SAYS

Admissions

Very important factors considered include: Application essay, academic GPA, rigor of secondary school record, standardized test scores, character/personal qualities. *Important factors considered include:* Recommendation(s), extracurricular activities. *Other factors considered include:* Class rank, alumni/ae relation, first generation, geographical residence, level of applicant's interest, volunteer work, work experience. SAT or ACT required; TOEFL required of all international applicants. High school diploma is required and GED is accepted. *Academic units required:* 4 English, 3 mathematics, 3 science, (2 science labs), 2 foreign language, 3 social studies, 2 history, 2 academic electives. *Academic units recommended:* 4 English, 4 mathematics, 4 science, (3 science labs), 4 foreign language, 4 social studies, 3 history, 2 academic electives.

Financial Aid

Students should submit: Institution's own financial aid form, CSS/Financial Aid PROFILE. The Princeton Review suggests that all financial aid forms be submitted as soon as possible after 1/1. *Need-based scholarships/grants offered:* Federal Pell, SEOG, state scholarships/grants, private scholarships, the school's own gift aid, United Negro College Fund. *Loan aid offered:* FFEL Subsidized Stafford, FFEL Unsubsidized Stafford, FFEL PLUS. Federal Work-Study Program available. Institutional employment available. Off-campus job opportunities are good.

The Inside Word

No Historically Black College in the country has more competitive admissions process than Spelman. Successful candidates show strong academic records with challenging course loads and solid grades. Applicant evaluation is very personal; it is quite important to show depth of character and social consciousness.

THE SCHOOL SAYS "..."

From The Admissions Office

"As an outstanding Historically Black College for women, Spelman strives for academic excellence in liberal arts education. This predominantly residential private college provides students with an academic climate conducive to the full development of their intellectual and leadership potential. The college is a member of the Atlanta University Center consortium, and Spelman students enjoy the benefits of a small college while having access to the resources of the other three participating institutions. The purpose extends beyond intellectual development and professional career preparation of students. It seeks to develop the total person. The college provides an academic and social environment that strengthens those qualities that enable women to be self-confident as well as culturally and spiritually enriched. This environment attempts to instill in students both an appreciation for the multicultural communities of the world and a sense of responsibility for bringing about positive change in those communities.

"Applicants for are required to submit standardized test scores from an appropriate venue (i.e. ACT, TOEFL, SAT). The highest composite score will be used in admissions decisions. Writing scores from either the SAT or ACT will not be taken into consideration in the admission process."

SELECTIVITY

Admissions Rating	92
# of applicants	5,656
% of applicants accepted	33
% of acceptees attending	30

FRESHMAN PROFILE

Range SAT Critical Reading	500–580
Range SAT Math	490–570
Range ACT Composite	21–25
Minimum paper TOEFL	500
Minimum computer TOEFL	250
Average HS GPA	3.59
% graduated top 10% of class	40
% graduated top 25% of class	73
% graduated top 50% of class	95

DEADLINES

Early decision	
Deadline	11/1
Notification	12/15
Early action	
Deadline	11/15
Notification	12/31
Regular	
Deadline	2/1
Notification	4/1
Nonfall registration?	no

APPLICANTS ALSO LOOK AT

AND OFTEN PREFER
Georgia Institute of Technology

AND SOMETIMES PREFER
Tuskegee University
Clark Atlanta University
Howard University
Hampton University
Florida A&M University

FINANCIAL FACTS

Financial Aid Rating	67
Annual tuition	$14,470
Room and board	$8,750
Required fees	$2,535
Books and supplies	$1,150
% frosh rec. need-based scholarship or grant aid	80
% UG rec. need-based scholarship or grant aid	54
% frosh rec. non-need-based scholarship or grant aid	49
% UG rec. non-need-based scholarship or grant aid	21
% frosh rec. need-based self-help aid	11
% UG rec. need-based self-help aid	72
% frosh rec. any financial aid	82
% UG rec. any financial aid	75
% UG borrow to pay for school	75

ST. BONAVENTURE UNIVERSITY

PO BOX D, ST. BONAVENTURE, NY 14778 • ADMISSIONS: 716-375-2400 • FAX: 716-375-4005

CAMPUS LIFE

Quality of Life Rating	**73**
Fire Safety Rating	**60***
Green Rating	**60***
Type of school	private
Affiliation	Roman Catholic
Environment	village

STUDENTS

Total undergrad enrollment	1,905
% male/female	50/50
% from out of state	24
% from public high school	70
% live on campus	77
% African American	4
% Asian	2
% Caucasian	18
% Hispanic	2
% international	2
# of countries represented	24

SURVEY SAYS . . .

Athletic facilities are great
Students are friendly
Frats and sororities are unpopular or nonexistent
College radio is popular
Student publications are popular
Lots of beer drinking
Hard liquor is popular

ACADEMICS

Academic Rating	**77**
Calendar	semester
Student/faculty ratio	14:1
Profs interesting rating	81
Profs accessible rating	82
Most common reg class size	10–19 students
Most common lab size	10–19 students

MOST POPULAR MAJORS

business/commerce
elementary education and teaching
journalism

STUDENTS SAY "..."

Academics

St. Bonaventure is "a small-town university with a lot to offer," including a "simply stellar" journalism and mass communications program that features "an amazing faculty" that "wants you to get the best job possible." SBU's business program is also "very strong," and its education department "has a good reputation." A new science building should bolster the university's small but growing biology, chemistry, and computer science departments. Regardless of major, all students must complete a core curriculum offered through SBU's Clare College. While a few here insist that "Clare College is not that bad, and a lot of the classes are interesting," the majority complain that the "required Catholic core curriculum" is "a complete drag and a waste of students' time and effort, in addition to being a GPA reducer." Somewhere in between are those pragmatists who tell us that "Clare College courses are annoying but not over demanding. If you didn't want to learn about Catholic heritage, you shouldn't come to a Catholic school." Amen! While SBU undergrads may not agree on the value of the core curriculum, nearly all concur that professors here "are easy to talk to and are always available after class and outside of class. They make students feel comfortable and want to get to know the students. We are not just numbers." They also agree that their degree provides them access to "great connections with alumni" and that, all things considered, SBU leaves them "as well equipped to take the jobs of their choosing out of college as students at any other college, period."

Life

"When the weekend arrives, the general consensus of the students is one thing: partying. Off-campus houses host triple keggers every weekends; and the four local bars begin to draw crowds on Wednesday nights." Almost everyone agrees that "Drinking is huge...and so are basketball games"—as one student explains it, "we all love love love basketball games; the entire student population will be at a basketball game on a Saturday night, without fail"—but undergrads add that "there are lots of other things to keep busy" for those outliers to whom neither beer nor hoops appeals. Winter sports such as snowboarding and skiing are quite popular, and students have access to numerous parks and trails for hiking during the warm months. Furthermore, "the radio station and Campus Activities Board work very hard to bring in an up-and-coming band probably once a week." Students add that "the radio station is also a great thing to do, it's very easy to get involved in." Finally, the school's many community-spirited undergrads can participate in "the oldest student-run soup kitchen in the country" or "a program called Bona Buddies that matches up students with underprivileged local kids to mentor them."

Student Body

The typical Bona undergrad "is white and Catholic, with a desire to do well and succeed but a stronger desire to have fun while doing so." Most "wear jeans and a North Face jacket or something very similar." Students are "trendy" but casual. A great number "hail from within three hours of the school, mostly in the Rochester and Buffalo area." Western New York is conservative terrain, so SBU "has a good number of conservative students." They are typically "involved, whether it be in our soup kitchen or radio station." While the demographic is largely white, "there are more and more minority students every year," and the school offers "a plethora of activities, groups and policies that seem to provide a soaring number of opportunities for minority students."

FINANCIAL AID: 716-375-2528 • E-MAIL: ADMISSIONS@SBU.EDU • WEBSITE: WWW.SBU.EDU

THE PRINCETON REVIEW SAYS

Admissions

Very important factors considered include: Academic GPA, recommendation(s), rigor of secondary school record, character/personal qualities, interview. *Important factors considered include:* Application essay, standardized test scores, extracurricular activities, level of applicant's interest, talent/ability, volunteer work. *Other factors considered include:* Class rank, alumni/ae relation, first generation, work experience. SAT recommended; SAT or ACT required; ACT recommended; essay required; TOEFL required of all international applicants. High school diploma is required and GED is accepted for transfer students. *Academic units required:* 4 English, 3 mathematics, 3 science, 2 foreign language, 4 social studies. *Academic units recommended:* 4 English, 3 mathematics, 3 science, (3 science labs), 2 foreign language, 4 social studies.

Financial Aid

Students should submit: FAFSA, state aid form. The Princeton Review suggests that all financial aid forms be submitted as soon as possible after 1/1. *Need-based scholarships/grants offered:* Federal Pell, SEOG, state scholarships/grants, private scholarships, the school's own gift aid. *Loan aid offered:* FFEL Subsidized Stafford, FFEL Unsubsidized Stafford, FFEL PLUS, Federal Perkins, college/university loans from institutional funds. Applicants will be notified of awards on a rolling basis beginning 3/15.

The Inside Word

Above-average students should meet little resistance from the St. Bonaventure admissions office; nearly nine in ten applicants here are accepted, and the academic profile of the median admitted student is respectable but hardly overwhelming. A personal essay is required, and an interview is optional; barring a misstep of catastrophic proportions, both can only improve your chances of getting in.

THE SCHOOL SAYS ". . ."

From The Admissions Office

"The St. Bonaventure University family has been imparting an extraordinary Franciscan tradition to men and women of a rich diversity of backgrounds for more than 130 years. This tradition encourages all who become a part of it to face the world confidently, respect the earthly environment, and work for productive change in the world. The charm of our campus and the inspirational beauty of the surrounding hills provide a special place where growth in learning and living is abundantly realized. The Richter Student Fitness Center, which opened in 2004, provides all students with state-of-the-art facilities for athletics and wellness. Academics at St. Bonaventure are challenging. Small classes and personalized attention encourage individual growth and development. St. Bonaventure's nationally known Schools of Arts and Sciences, Business Administration, Journalism/Mass Communication, and Education offer majors in 31 disciplines. The School of Graduate Studies also offers several programs leading to the master's degree.

"Applicants can submit scores from either the SAT or the ACT. The biology Subject Test is required only for students applying to one of our dual-admission medical programs."

SELECTIVITY
Admissions Rating	76
# of applicants	1,914
% of applicants accepted	83
% of acceptees attending	35

FRESHMAN PROFILE
Range SAT Critical Reading	480–570
Range SAT Math	480–500
Range ACT Composite	19–23
Minimum paper TOEFL	550
Minimum computer TOEFL	213
Average HS GPA	3.13
% graduated top 10% of class	12
% graduated top 25% of class	32
% graduated top 50% of class	66

DEADLINES
Regular	
Priority	2/1
Deadline	4/15
Notification	rolling
Nonfall registration?	yes

APPLICANTS ALSO LOOK AT
AND OFTEN PREFER
State University of New York at Geneseo
AND SOMETIMES PREFER
Niagara University

FINANCIAL FACTS
Financial Aid Rating	81
Annual tuition	$24,928
Room and board	$9,100
Required fees	$865
Books and supplies	$709
% frosh rec. need-based scholarship or grant aid	73
% UG rec. need-based scholarship or grant aid	71
% frosh rec. non-need-based scholarship or grant aid	13
% UG rec. non-need-based scholarship or grant aid	12
% frosh rec. need-based self-help aid	60
% UG rec. need-based self-help aid	59
% frosh rec. athletic scholarships	3
% UG rec. athletic scholarships	4
% UG borrow to pay for school	72
Average cumulative indebtedness	$16,900

ST. JOHN'S COLLEGE (MD)

PO BOX 2800, ANNAPOLIS, MD 21404 • ADMISSIONS: 1-800-727-9238 • FAX: 410-269-7916

CAMPUS LIFE

Quality of Life Rating	**91**
Fire Safety Rating	**85**
Green Rating	**78**
Type of school	private
Environment	town

STUDENTS

Total undergrad enrollment	489
% male/female	53/47
% from out of state	85
% from public high school	74
% live on campus	77
% African American	1
% Asian	2
% Caucasian	87
%. Hispanic	5
% international	2
# of countries represented	17

SURVEY SAYS . . .

Class discussions encouraged
No one cheats
Registration is a breeze
Frats and sororities are unpopular or
nonexistent
(Almost) everyone smokes

ACADEMICS

Academic Rating	**99**
Calendar	semester
Student/faculty ratio	8:1
Profs interesting rating	98
Profs accessible rating	97
Most common reg class size	10–19 students

MOST POPULAR MAJORS

liberal arts and sciences studies and
humanities

STUDENTS SAY ". . ."

Academics

Tiny St. John's College specializes in a four-year curriculum that is an "exhilarating and exhausting" survey of intellectual history, starting with ancient Greece and ending in modern times. Virtually all classes are required. There are no majors. There are no textbooks. And there are no tests, except for "occasional grammar and vocab quizzes" in ancient Greek and French. Grades are based on papers and class participation. Students encounter the works of "the greatest minds of Western Civilization" in their original, unadulterated form. While students at other schools may occasionally think outside the box, students at St. John's critically examine "the eternal questions of this world," namely "what it is to be a human." It's "certainly not the best education for everyone (especially students who want to learn certain technical skills)." For these students, though, it is a little slice of heaven. Classes are small—"never larger than 20 students"—and "discussion-based." Professors (called "tutors") are "deeply intelligent" and "can bounce from Newton to Leibniz to Baudelaire to Bach" with ease. They "do little or no lecturing," favoring instead to "facilitate discussion." Students engage in conversation, "instead of sitting through lectures on other people's interpretations." "There's a wonderful sense of camaraderie that develops in the classroom, as we wrestle with the great questions of the ages," enthuses one student.

Life

Despite the "overbearing" workload, "there is an almost snuggly feeling of community at St. John's." "The academic atmosphere is immersing and supportive, especially since everyone is in, or has had, or will have all the same classes." Social life is "alarmingly insular." "We at St. John's are removed from the world to a truly shocking degree," elaborates one student. "The campus feels not like a campus, but a miniature world, which actually is not very much like the real world." Extracurricular activities include "heaps of clubs." "Most everyone attends the Shakespeare plays and classical music concerts." Intramural sports are "incredibly fun" and a big part of Johnnie life. "Skill is optional but enthusiasm is required." "It is a great stress reliever," explains one student. "The books tear your soul apart," but sports here are a way of "pasting it back together." Campus-wide parties on the weekends include "raucous" reality dance parties as well as waltz and swing dancing parties. Drinking is popular. Coffee and cigarettes are big. Johnnies also "sail, watch movies," and play board games. Or they just hang out, "finding adventures where they pop up." Students also talk late into the night "about set theory, socks, art history, *Moby Dick*, why macaroni is so orange," and pretty much everything except politics. "Johnnies are extraordinarily uninterested in politics." While the food on campus "sucks," students find epicurean delights in "Annapolis, Baltimore, Washington, D.C., or New York."

Student Body

"St. John's is a unique program, and it takes a unique group of people to keep it going." "The one thing Johnnies have in common is their love of learning and their love for thought," says a junior. "A Johnnie is a bookworm, socially awkward in some fashion, and an intense thinker." Eyeglasses are common. "This campus may have the worst collective eyesight in America." "Many students are quite intelligent, and most are highly eccentric." "'Intellectual elitism' can be a problem." "Upperclassmen especially have an esprit de corps and traditionalist spirit that borders on crotchetiness." "Most people here are strange." Many are "brash and freakish." "There is definitely a certain type of person who picks St. John's, but how that quality reveals itself is different for every person," notes one student. "St. John's is entirely made up of atypical students, so none of them fit in, and they don't feel like they need to." Johnnies are "an amazing conglomeration of artists, mathematicians, jocks, role-playing enthusiasts, poets, iconoclasts, activists, and some who are all of these." That said, there's a serious lack of "ethnic diversity." However, intellectual diversity abounds. Students are "willing to assert opinions, and, more importantly, to reconsider them."

FINANCIAL AID: 410-626-2502 • E-MAIL: ADMISSIONS@SJCA.EDU • WEBSITE: WWW.STJOHNSCOLLEGE.EDU

THE PRINCETON REVIEW SAYS

Admissions

Very important factors considered include: Application essay. *Important factors considered include:* Recommendation(s), rigor of secondary school record, character/personal qualities. *Other factors considered include:* Class rank, academic GPA, standardized test scores, alumni/ae relation, extracurricular activities, first generation, interview, racial/ethnic status, talent/ability. TOEFL required of all international applicants. High school diploma is required and GED is accepted. *Academic units required:* 3 mathematics, 2 foreign language. *Academic units recommended:* 4 English, 4 mathematics, 3 science, (3 science labs), 4 foreign language, 2 social studies, 2 history.

Financial Aid

Students should submit: FAFSA, CSS/Financial Aid PROFILE, state aid form, noncustodial PROFILE, business/farm supplement. The Princeton Review suggests that all financial aid forms be submitted as soon as possible after 1/1. *Need-based scholarships/grants offered:* Federal Pell, SEOG, state scholarships/grants, private scholarships, the school's own gift aid. *Loan aid offered:* FFEL Subsidized Stafford, FFEL Unsubsidized Stafford, FFEL PLUS, Federal Perkins, college/university loans from institutional funds. Applicants will be notified of awards on a rolling basis beginning 12/1. Federal Work-Study Program available. Institutional employment available. Off-campus job opportunities are good.

The Inside Word

St. John's has one of the most personal admissions processes in the country. The applicant pool is highly self-selected and extremely bright, so don't be fooled by the high acceptance rate—every student who is offered admission deserves to be here. Candidates who don't give serious thought to the kind of match they make with the college and devote serious energy to their essays are not likely to be accepted.

THE SCHOOL SAYS ". . ."

From The Admissions Office

"The purpose of the admission process is to determine whether an applicant has the necessary preparation and ability to complete the St. John's program satisfactorily. The essays are designed to enable applicants to give a full account of themselves. They can tell the committee much more than statistical records reveal. Previous academic records show whether an applicant has the habits of study necessary at St. John's. Letters of reference, particularly those of teachers, are carefully read for indications that the applicant has the maturity, self-discipline, ability, energy, and initiative to succeed in the St. John's program. St. John's attaches little importance to 'objective' test scores, and no applicant is accepted or rejected because of such scores.

"St. John's College does not require the results of standardized tests, except in the case of international students, homeschooled students, and those who will not receive a high school diploma. Results of the ACT or SAT are sufficient for these students."

SELECTIVITY
Admissions Rating	94
# of applicants	460
% of applicants accepted	81
% of acceptees attending	42

FRESHMAN PROFILE
Range SAT Critical Reading	640–740
Range SAT Math	590–680
Minimum paper TOEFL	600
Minimum computer TOEFL	270
Minimum web-based TOEFL	100
% graduated top 10% of class	34
% graduated top 25% of class	63
% graduated top 50% of class	89

DEADLINES
Regular	
Priority	3/1
Nonfall registration?	yes

APPLICANTS ALSO LOOK AT
AND OFTEN PREFER
University of Virginia
University of Chicago
Swarthmore College

AND SOMETIMES PREFER
Oberlin College
Reed College
Kenyon College
Smith College

AND RARELY PREFER
Bard College

FINANCIAL FACTS
Financial Aid Rating	89
Annual tuition	$39,992
Room and board	$9,600
Required fees	$400
Books and supplies	$280
% frosh rec. need-based scholarship or grant aid	56
% UG rec. need-based scholarship or grant aid	55
% frosh rec. non-need-based scholarship or grant aid	1
% UG rec. non-need-based scholarship or grant aid	2
% frosh rec. need-based self-help aid	62
% UG rec. need-based self-help aid	55
% frosh rec. any financial aid	79
% UG rec. any financial aid	73

ST. JOHN'S COLLEGE (NM)

1160 CAMINO CRUZ BLANCA, SANTA FE, NM 87505 • ADMISSIONS: 505-984-6060 • FAX: 505-984-6162

CAMPUS LIFE
Quality of Life Rating	**92**
Fire Safety Rating	**60***
Green Rating	**80**
Type of school	private
Environment	city

STUDENTS
Total undergrad enrollment	431
% male/female	60/40
% from out of state	93
% from public high school	70
% African American	1
% Asian	3
% Caucasian	83
% Hispanic	5
% Native American	1
% international	4
# of countries represented	12

SURVEY SAYS . . .
Class discussions encouraged
No one cheats
Registration is a breeze
Students are happy
Intercollegiate sports are unpopular or nonexistent
Frats and sororities are unpopular or nonexistent

ACADEMICS
Academic Rating	**99**
Calendar	semester
Student/faculty ratio	8:1
Profs interesting rating	95
Profs accessible rating	98
Most common reg class size	10–19 students

STUDENTS SAY "..."

Academics

The "mind-blowing," all-mandatory curriculum at "incredibly small" St. John's College in Santa Fe, New Mexico, includes "copious amounts" of philosophy, literature, language, math, and science. Students "read only primary texts as opposed to textbooks." "There are no majors." There are no lectures. "Every class is a discussion." There are few tests. Grades are based almost exclusively on papers. While students love the academic experience, they caution that it is full of "relentless intellectual duress." "The program is very difficult and you get kicked out if you can't keep up," warns a senior. "You have to be prepared to work hard without being rewarded with simple answers." Professors at St. John's are called tutors "because they are not professing anything." Instead, they guide students through a few thousand years of Western thought, starting with ancient Greece and ending in modern times, and allow you "to form your own opinions." Some faculty members "are terrible" but most are "insightful, brilliant, and dedicated." Virtually all of them are "absurdly accessible" as well. "Students meet with the dean all the time." However, when difficulties arise, the administration sometimes causes "an ordeal far out of proportion to the problem." "Financial aid is scarce," too. Other complaints include the "often less [than] modern" condition of the campus. There are some "shabby" classrooms, and the Internet connection "needs to be upgraded by an order of magnitude."

Life

Campus life at St. John's in Santa Fe is "a strange boot camp" where "the dating scene is a nightmare" and "the food needs improvement." The "life-consuming" curriculum here forces students to put in many hours of difficult reading. "We read the great, earthshaking books all the time, which necessarily takes a toll on our psychology," explains a junior. "You can only have your conception of the world shattered so many times before you feel emotionally drained." "Social life in general tends to be a less formal (frequently rather irreverent) extension of our classroom life," explains a junior. "A typical dining hall conversation might cycle between Star Wars, the Roman Empire, various videogames, Socrates, world religions, and the nature and existence of divine truth." Beyond stimulating banter, "there is no universally popular activity." "There are lectures every Friday night." "Pickup sports are popular." Martial arts are reasonably big, "as is fencing." "Organized trips for skiing, hiking, rafting," and other outdoor activities are common. Many students "tend to drink now and then, some smoke pot with more frequency, or occasionally use other drugs." There's no pressure to participate, though. "There are definitely people, like myself, who don't drink or smoke or do other drugs," asserts a senior. Surrounding Santa Fe boasts "excellent restaurants" and a nice view of the mountains. Otherwise, it's "a town for rich, retired hippies."

Student Body

"This is a school for super geeks." Everyone is a "voracious reader" and "kind of neurotic." "For many students, St. John's is a funny interlude—a bizarre and startlingly wonderful place to reflect on the world around them and think about themselves and how they want to live their own lives." "People here tend to have considered the big questions," suggests a senior. "How can I be a good person? Why does the world work the way it does?" Some students suffer from "academic haughtiness." "Johnnies tend to have an underlying pretension regarding their role in the world as philosophers and avant-garde thinkers and writers." A lot of people smoke cigarettes, too. "If you're not a smoker before you come here, you will be when you leave." "The population is not diverse ethnically, but it is tolerant politically, religiously, and socially." There are "churchgoing Christians and radical atheists." "Every St. John's student is atypical in one way or another." "Although they might not fit in elsewhere, they feel quite comfortable at St. John's." "People here go after what they want," agrees a sophomore, "whether it's getting too stoned to think or finding a job as a ranch hand in the middle of nowhere."

ST. JOHN'S COLLEGE (NM)

FINANCIAL AID: 505-984-6058 • E-MAIL: ADMISSIONS@MAIL.SJCSF.EDU • WEBSITE: WWW.SJCSF.EDU

THE PRINCETON REVIEW SAYS

Admissions

Very important factors considered include: Application essay. *Important factors considered include:* Recommendation(s), rigor of secondary school record, character/personal qualities, level of applicant's interest. *Other factors considered include:* Class rank, academic GPA, standardized test scores, alumni/ae relation, extracurricular activities, first generation, interview, racial/ethnic status, talent/ability, volunteer work, work experience. TOEFL required of all international applicants. High school diploma is required and GED is accepted. High school diploma or equivalent is not required. *Academic units required:* 3 mathematics, 2 foreign language. *Academic units recommended:* 4 English, 1 mathematics, 3 science, (3 science labs), 4 foreign language, 2 history.

Financial Aid

Students should submit: FAFSA, CSS/Financial Aid PROFILE, noncustodial PROFILE, business/farm supplement. The Princeton Review suggests that all financial aid forms be submitted as soon as possible after 1/1. *Need-based scholarships/grants offered:* Federal Pell, SEOG, state scholarships/grants, private scholarships, the school's own gift aid, academic competitiveness grant. *Loan aid offered:* FFEL Subsidized Stafford, FFEL Unsubsidized Stafford, FFEL PLUS, Federal Perkins, college/university loans from institutional funds. Applicants will be notified of awards on a rolling basis beginning 12/10. Federal Work-Study Program available. Institutional employment available. Off-campus job opportunities are excellent.

The Inside Word

Self-selection drives this admissions process—more than one-half of the entire applicant pool each year indicates that St. John's is their first choice, and half of those admitted send in tuition deposits. Even so, no one in admissions takes things for granted, and neither should any student considering an application. The admissions process is highly personal on both sides of the coin. Only the intellectually curious and highly motivated need apply.

THE SCHOOL SAYS "..."

From The Admissions Office

"St. John's appeals to students who value good books, love to read, and are passionate about discourse and debate. There are no lectures and virtually no tests or electives. Instead, classes of 16–20 students occur around conference tables where professors are as likely to be asked to defend their points of view as are students. Great books provide the direction, context, and stimulus for conversation. The entire student body adheres to the same, all-required arts and science curriculum. Someone once said, 'A classic is a house we still live in,' and at St. John's, students and professors alike approach each reading on the list as if the ideas it holds were being expressed for the first time—questioning the logic behind a geometrical proof, challenging the premise of a scientific development, or dissecting the progression of modern political theory as it unfolds."

SELECTIVITY

Admissions Rating	**91**
# of applicants	323
% of applicants accepted	81
% of acceptees attending	45
# accepting a place on wait list	13
% admitted from wait list	50

FRESHMAN PROFILE

Range SAT Critical Reading	620–730
Range SAT Math	570–680
Range ACT Composite	25–31
Minimum paper TOEFL	600
Minimum computer TOEFL	270
% graduated top 10% of class	27
% graduated top 25% of class	64
% graduated top 50% of class	86

DEADLINES

Regular	
Priority	3/1
Nonfall registration?	yes

APPLICANTS ALSO LOOK AT

AND OFTEN PREFER
Stanford University
Deep Springs College

AND SOMETIMES PREFER
University of Chicago
Rice University
Bard College

AND RARELY PREFER
Oberlin College

FINANCIAL FACTS

Financial Aid Rating	**93**
Annual tuition	$39,992
Room and board	$9,600
Required fees	$400
Books and supplies	$300
% frosh rec. need-based scholarship or grant aid	43
% UG rec. need-based scholarship or grant aid	57
% frosh rec. need-based self-help aid	47
% UG rec. need-based self-help aid	53
% frosh rec. any financial aid	47
% UG rec. any financial aid	63
% UG borrow to pay for school	45
Average cumulative indebtedness	$20,428

ST. JOHN'S UNIVERSITY

8000 UTOPIA PARKWAY, QUEENS, NY 11439 • ADMISSIONS: 718-990-2000 • FAX: 718-990-5728

CAMPUS LIFE

Quality of Life Rating	75
Fire Safety Rating	92
Green Rating	89
Type of school	private
Affiliation	Roman Catholic
Environment	metropolis

STUDENTS

Total undergrad enrollment	12,326
% male/female	46/54
% from out of state	20
% from public high school	65
% live on campus	23
% in (# of) fraternities	6 (16)
% in (# of) sororities	7 (17)
% African American	16
% Asian	17
% Caucasian	37
% Hispanic	15
% international	4
# of countries represented	122

SURVEY SAYS . . .

Athletic facilities are great
Diverse student types on campus
Students get along with local
community
Students love Queens, NY
Everyone loves the Red Storm

ACADEMICS

Academic Rating	71
Calendar	semester
Student/faculty ratio	17:1
Profs interesting rating	63
Profs accessible rating	61
Most common reg class size	20–29 students
Most common lab size	20–29 students

MOST POPULAR MAJORS

liberal studies
finance
pharmacy (pharmd [USA], pharmd
or bs/bpharm [Canada])
psychology

STUDENTS SAY ". . ."

Academics

Like its hometown of Queens, NY, St. John's moves inexorably forward without forgetting its history and traditions. The school's administration is committed to constantly "updating the university's facilities." Recent improvements include "a state-of-the-art athletic training facility and revamped cafeterias," as well as an upgrade to science facilities, added town-house residences for students, and a new University Center. In addition, the school distributes "brand-new laptops to all incoming students" and has "done a tremendous job of implementing technology throughout the campus," which "is completely wireless except for a few athletic fields and parking lots." On the traditions side of the balance, the school maintains "a lot of policies and politics opposed by typical college students [such as] the visitor policies in the dorms." Many praise St. John's' study abroad programs and Institute for Writing Studies, which provides writing support to all students. When it comes to classroom experience, "professors are professors. Like [at] any school, some are better than others." Students report that "the experience you have at St. John's really depends on what you do with it. Don't take a professor just because he/she is easy—chances are that means they suck! If you are self-motivated…you will find challenging professors." Big-picture people will see that St. John's offers "a quality private education" and, in many instances, a "generous" financial aid package that translates to an overall "low cost."

Life

Historically, St. John's has been known as "basically a school for commuters." Although the number of resident students is growing, some students still think "on the weekends this place is a ghost town." Others counter that "Recently there has been an amazing effort" by the school's Residence Life Department "to bring back campus life," an effort that includes posting "weekly calendars informing us about campus events and activities." For those who prefer off-campus activities in their spare time, the school helps to make that possible, too. There are "shuttles that can take us into the city [aka Manhattan, to those outside New York City] and on weekends…to the mall." In addition, the "school runs programs to see Broadway shows for free." Even without the school's help, however, New York is at students' fingertips; almost everything the city has to offer "is just a subway ride away." "Clubs, sports events, parties, restaurants"—you name it, NYC's got it, and St. John's students sample it. The faithful will be happy to know that "St. John's makes it easy to incorporate a spiritual life with an academic one." For the altruistic, there are "community-service initiatives galore."

Student Body

Because it is "located in Queens, the most diverse place on Earth," it's no surprise that St. John's itself is "very, very diverse." Though "everyone gets along exceptionally well," getting along well doesn't equal total integration. Each "ethnic group tends [to] hang around with itself. Yet students' external differences belie less visible similarities. Many are may be the first in their family to attend college, so a strong work ethic is pervasive. Everyone "wants to achieve something greater than their parents." The second major similarity stems from the first: "students here generally have many responsibilities outside of their schoolwork."

ST. JOHN'S UNIVERSITY

FINANCIAL AID: 1-888-9-STJOHNS • E-MAIL: ADMISSIONS@STJOHNS.EDU • WEBSITE: WWW.STJOHNS.EDU

THE PRINCETON REVIEW SAYS

Admissions

Very important factors considered include: Academic GPA, standardized test scores. *Important factors considered include:* Rigor of secondary school record. *Other factors considered include:* Class rank, application essay, recommendation(s), alumni/ae relation, character/personal qualities, extracurricular activities, geographical residence, interview, level of applicant's interest, volunteer work, work experience. SAT or ACT required; TOEFL required of all international applicants. High school diploma is required and GED is accepted. *Academic units required:* 4 English. *Academic units recommended:* 3 mathematics, 2 science, (2 science labs), 2 foreign language, 2 history, 1 Social Studies.

Financial Aid

Students should submit: FAFSA. The Princeton Review suggests that all financial aid forms be submitted as soon as possible after 1/1. *Need-based scholarships/grants offered:* Federal Pell, SEOG, state scholarships/grants, private scholarships, the school's own gift aid. *Loan aid offered:* FFEL Subsidized Stafford, FFEL Unsubsidized Stafford, FFEL PLUS. Applicants will be notified of awards on a rolling basis beginning 3/15. Federal Work-Study Program available. Institutional employment available. Off-campus job opportunities are good.

The Inside Word

The admissions process at St. John's doesn't include many surprises. High school grades and standardized test scores are undoubtedly the most important factors though volunteer work and extracurricular activities are also highly regarded. What is surprising is that this Catholic university doesn't consider religious affiliation at all when making admissions decisions; there are students of every religious stripe here (see the "Student Body" section).

THE SCHOOL SAYS "..."

From The Admissions Office

"Founded by the Vincentian Fathers in 1870, St. John's is a world-class Catholic university that prepares students for ethical leadership in today's global society. St. John's offers quality academics, high-tech resources and confidence-building service activities enlivened by the vast opportunities available only in exciting New York City. Representing 44 states and 122 foreign countries, students pursue more than 100 programs in the arts, sciences, business, education, pharmacy, and allied health. Professors are internationally respected scholars, 87% holding a Ph.D. or comparable degree. The 17:1 student-faculty ratio ensures personal attention in class.

"St. John's also offers these advantages:

- Dynamic freshman year features "Learning Communities"—themed groupings of like-minded students sharing classes, activities and residence suites.
- Unique core courses like Discover New York use the city as a "living class room."
- All entering students receive wireless laptop computers with access to our award-winning network.
- Reflecting our Vincentian heritage, course-related service activities provide real-world experience while serving those in need.
- Amazing global studies programs like Discover the World allow students to earn 15 credits while studying in three foreign cities in a single semester.

"St. John's has three residential New York City campuses—our flagship campus in Queens; the wooded Staten Island campus; and a "vertical" campus in lower Manhattan. St. John's also has a location in Oakdale, NY; a learning center in Paris, France; and a campus in Rome, Italy."

SELECTIVITY

Admissions Rating	81
# of applicants	40,970
% of applicants accepted	46
% of acceptees attending	18
# accepting a place on wait list	1,933
% admitted from wait list	26

FRESHMAN PROFILE

Range SAT Critical Reading	480–580
Range SAT Math	490–610
Minimum paper TOEFL	500
Minimum computer TOEFL	173
Minimum web-based TOEFL	61
Average HS GPA	3.2
% graduated top 10% of class	18
% graduated top 25% of class	42
% graduated top 50% of class	71

DEADLINES

Regular	
Notification	rolling
Nonfall registration?	yes

APPLICANTS ALSO LOOK AT
AND OFTEN PREFER

State University of New York—Stony Brook University
City University of New York—Baruch College

AND SOMETIMES PREFER

Fordham University
New York University

FINANCIAL FACTS

Financial Aid Rating	70
Annual tuition	$28,100
Room and board	$12,570
Required fees	$690
Books and supplies	$1,000
% frosh rec. need-based scholarship or grant aid	72
% UG rec. need-based scholarship or grant aid	67
% frosh rec. non-need-based scholarship or grant aid	69
% UG rec. non-need-based scholarship or grant aid	67
% frosh rec. need-based self-help aid	63
% UG rec. need-based self-help aid	62
% frosh rec. athletic scholarships	1
% UG rec. athletic scholarships	2
% frosh rec. any financial aid	97
% UG rec. any financial aid	97
% UG borrow to pay for school	70
Average cumulative indebtedness	$29,657

St. Lawrence University

PAYSON HALL, CANTON, NY 13617 • ADMISSIONS: 315-229-5261 • FAX: 315-229-5818

CAMPUS LIFE
Quality of Life Rating	80
Fire Safety Rating	68
Green Rating	87
Type of school	private
Environment	village

STUDENTS
Total undergrad enrollment	2,187
% male/female	45/55
% from out of state	56
% from public high school	70
% live on campus	98
% in (# of) fraternities	2 (1)
% in (# of) sororities	20 (4)
% African American	3
% Asian	2
% Caucasian	68
% Hispanic	3
% Native American	1
% international	5
# of countries represented	49

SURVEY SAYS . . .
Lab facilities are great
Athletic facilities are great
Low cost of living
(Almost) no one smokes

ACADEMICS
Academic Rating	87
Calendar	semester
Student/faculty ratio	11:1
Profs interesting rating	89
Profs accessible rating	85
Most common reg class size	10–19 students
Most common lab size	10–19 students

MOST POPULAR MAJORS
economics
political science and government
psychology

STUDENTS SAY ". . ."

Academics
Students at St. Lawrence love their professors. "All of my professors have been extremely accessible and willing to help out if I've ever had questions. The quality of the professors is very high;" "The professors for the most part are very receptive to feedback and love teaching their students," and "if you're showing effort, they will do everything they can to help you." "Showing effort" might be the operative phrase; "one could coast through...by choosing easy classes. However, there are plenty of opportunities to really challenge yourself and succeed with the support of grants, professors, and advisors." Students rave about the small class sizes, "even lectures, and not only does this contribute to a more comfortable, discussion-based learning experience, it ensures that every professor is available and interested, at almost any time." A few students admit that "as a first-year student it can be frustrating trying to get the classes of your choice;" but others say, "if you talk to the teachers beforehand, you can usually get the classes you want if they are offered that semester." Regarding the administration, some students claim it "leaves a bit to be desired" and "is not always on the same page as the students." Most are very happy with the administration, though. "If you reach out to them, they will give you as much information as they can," and they "care a lot about our safety and make sure that all of our needs are well-met." "Some deans also teach classes—I had my first-year seminar with an academic dean, and it was great. They seem like they're always available if a student has an issue."

Life
Because Canton is small and the winter is long, "all of the fun and events happen on the campus [because] there is not much to do in town." "The student center is always full of people, and it's hard to not to stay there all day." "Theme houses," in which small groups of students focused on particular issues or activities live, receive high marks both from their residents and the students who come to the dorms for events. "The Java Barn is a small music venue located on campus that is completely run by 11 students that live together in a theme house on campus" and features popular live music events almost every weekend. Hockey games are huge, as are outdoor activities. "At St. Lawrence the natural world is our playground," "and there are lots of people and groups who carpool up to Whiteface in Lake Placid and go downhill skiing. During the warm months there is always something going on on the quad, and many people go on trips to the near by Adirondack Mountains for hiking and other outdoor activities." The rope swing on the Grasse River is also a popular destination, as are Ottawa and Montreal for day trips. If it's too cold to venture outside, students hit the gym: "Our athletic facilities are amazing with an indoor track, squash courts, gym, and climbing wall." As is typical for small schools in similar locales, drinking is popular on weekends. "There are many parties at St. Lawrence, but it is not the only thing to do on campus!" "People go to sporting, singing, and comedy events on campus," and "SLU students are creative with their fun."

Student Body
"A lot of students at St. Lawrence University are athletic and from the East Coast." "There are a lot of the classic Abercrombie & Fitch types...until you take a better look around." Though "preppy" seems to describe many students at St. Lawrence, "There are multitudes of clubs that provide a social scene for all students no matter their interests." "Everyone seems happy and has found some group [to] fit in with." "Most students join an extracurricular activity like art, music, sports, community service, etc." "A typical St. Lawrence student is easy-going, approachable, and likes to have a good time." "There are always a few atypical types, but they make the school more interesting. There's a place here for everyone."

FINANCIAL AID: 315-229-5265 • E-MAIL: ADMISSIONS@STLAWU.EDU • WEBSITE: WWW.STLAWU.EDU

THE PRINCETON REVIEW SAYS

Admissions

Very important factors considered include: Application essay, academic GPA, class rank, recommendation(s), character/personal qualities. *Important factors considered include:* Rigor of secondary school record, extracurricular activities, interview, racial/ethnic status. *Other factors considered include:* Standardized test scores, alumni/ae relation, first generation, geographical residence, level of applicant's interest, talent/ability, volunteer work, work experience. TOEFL required of all international applicants. High school diploma is required and GED is accepted. *Academic units recommended:* 4 English, 4 mathematics, 4 science, 4 foreign language, 2 social studies, 2 history.

Financial Aid

Students should submit: FAFSA, noncustodial PROFILE, business/farm supplement. Income Tax Returns/W-2s. Regular filing deadline is 2/1. The Princeton Review suggests that all financial aid forms be submitted as soon as possible after 1/1. *Need-based scholarships/grants offered:* Federal Pell, SEOG, state scholarships/grants, private scholarships, the school's own gift aid. *Loan aid offered:* Direct Subsidized Stafford, Direct Unsubsidized Stafford, Direct PLUS, Federal Perkins, college/university loans from institutional funds. Applicants will be notified of awards on or about 3/30. Federal Work-Study Program available. Institutional employment available. Off-campus job opportunities are poor.

The Inside Word

St. Lawrence is "test-optional," which means you're not required to submit scores from the SAT or the ACT, but that means your high school transcript and teacher recommendations better be stellar. If you're an international student seeking financial aid, or a home-schooled student, it's probably a good idea to submit some standardized test scores. Scholarship selection is based on overall academic profile, so good scores can help.

THE SCHOOL SAYS ". . ."

From The Admissions Office

"In an ideal location, St. Lawrence is a diverse liberal arts learning community of inspiring faculty and talented students guided by tradition and focused on the future. The students who live and learn at St. Lawrence are interesting and interested; they enroll with myriad accomplishments and talents, as well as desire to explore new challenges. Our faculty has chosen St. Lawrence intentionally because they know that there is institutional commitment to support great teaching. They are dedicated to making each student's experience challenging and rewarding. Our graduates make up one of the strongest networks of support among any alumni body and are ready, willing, and able to connect with students and help them succeed.

"Which students are happiest at St. Lawrence? Students who like to be actively involved. Students who are open-minded and interested in meeting people with backgrounds different from their own. Students who value having a voice in decisions that affect them. Students who appreciate all that is available to them and cannot wait to take advantage of both the curriculum and the co-curricular options. Students who want to enjoy their college experience and are able to find joy in working hard.

"You can learn the facts about us from this guidebook: We have about 2,200 students; we offer more than 30 majors; the average class size is 16 students; a great new science center; close to 50 percent of our students study abroad; and we have an environmental consciousness that fits our natural setting between the Adirondack Mountains and St. Lawrence River. You must visit, meet students and faculty, and sense the energy on campus to begin to understand just how special St. Lawrence University is.

"The submission of standardized test scores (SAT or ACT) is optional. Students must indicate on the St. Lawrence Common Application supplement which scores, if any, they wish to have considered in the application process."

SELECTIVITY

Admissions Rating	**87**
# of applicants	5,419
% of applicants accepted	34
% of acceptees attending	34
# accepting a place on wait list	186
% admitted from wait list	9
# of early decision applicants	245
% accepted early decision	82

FRESHMAN PROFILE

Range SAT Critical Reading	570–640
Range SAT Math	570–640
Range SAT Writing	560–650
Range ACT Composite	25–29
Minimum paper TOEFL	600
Minimum computer TOEFL	250
Average HS GPA	3.55
% graduated top 10% of class	44
% graduated top 25% of class	74
% graduated top 50% of class	96

DEADLINES

Early decision	
Deadline	11/15
Notification	12/15
Regular	
Deadline	2/1
Notification	3/30
Nonfall registration?	yes

APPLICANTS ALSO LOOK AT
AND SOMETIMES PREFER
Colby College
Colgate University

AND RARELY PREFER
Ithaca College

FINANCIAL FACTS

Financial Aid Rating	**87**
Annual tuition	$37,675
Room and board	$5,185
Required fees	$240
Books and supplies	$650
Insurance	$1,650
% frosh rec. need-based scholarship or grant aid	61
% UG rec. need-based scholarship or grant aid	62
% frosh rec. non-need-based scholarship or grant aid	17
% UG rec. non-need-based scholarship or grant aid	12
% frosh rec. need-based self-help aid	55
% UG rec. need-based self-help aid	58
% frosh rec. athletic scholarships	1
% UG rec. athletic scholarships	2
% frosh rec. any financial aid	85
% UG rec. any financial aid	82
% UG borrow to pay for school	68
Average cumulative indebtedness	$29,941

ST. MARY'S COLLEGE OF MARYLAND

ADMISSIONS OFFICE, 18952 EAST FISHER ROAD, ST. MARY'S CITY, MD 20686-3001 • ADMISSIONS: 240-895-5000 • FAX: 240-895-5001

CAMPUS LIFE
Quality of Life Rating	**93**
Fire Safety Rating	**77**
Green Rating	**91**
Type of school	public
Environment	rural

STUDENTS
Total undergrad enrollment	1,988
% male/female	42/58
% from out of state	17
% from public high school	70
% live on campus	82
% African American	6
% Asian	3
% Caucasian	59
% Hispanic	3
% international	2
# of countries represented	37

SURVEY SAYS . . .
Athletic facilities are great
Students are friendly
Different types of students interact
Great food on campus
Campus feels safe
Students are happy
Frats and sororities are unpopular or nonexistent

ACADEMICS
Academic Rating	**89**
Calendar	semester
Student/faculty ratio	12:1
Profs interesting rating	96
Profs accessible rating	96
Most common reg class size	10–19 students
Most common lab size	fewer than 10 students

MOST POPULAR MAJORS
economics
English language and literature
psychology

STUDENTS SAY ". . ."

Academics

Set on the "beautiful St. Mary's River," St. Mary's College of Maryland is a "humble oasis" that "has all of the intellectual stimulation of a private liberal arts school with none of the academic rivalry." The blissfully content students at SMCM throw around the word "community" like rice at a wedding, and they always precede it with some sort of positive lead-in: "small," "open-minded," "social justice minded, environmentally-friendly, hippie-loving, and very diverse and accepting" are just some of the descriptors used. Classes here are "rigorous" and "very engaging, requiring participation and input from all of the students," and the "amazing" professors are lauded for their brilliance, love of the material, and sheer accessibility. Students talk of having seen professors "at school events not related to their classes and students have been invited to class dinners at their houses." Not only does the small size of the school mean that the faculty knows each student's name—"you are NEVER a number"—but "you get to know your professors on a personal level, which is great when it comes time for them to write recommendations for scholarships, graduate school, or future jobs." The administration gets positive reviews with just a few naysayers. The deans are commended for being "everywhere, participating in athletics, music programs, etc." and making it clear " that the students are the first priority," but a few students still say that the administration "can be a little bit withdrawn from the student body." Although there are complaints of too much construction around the campus, most students know that improvements and growth are necessary for the growth of the college, though they do wish to see more immediate changes to the health services, which "need some serious work."

Life

The phrase "summer camp setting" doesn't just refer to how the campus looks; Frisbee golf, sailing, bonfires, sun tanning, and kayaking in the school-provided kayaks are some of the main activities for students taking a break from their studies (which often occur outside). The river seems to be the hub of student life, not only acting as a "tremendous stress reliever,"" but a sort of ad hoc campus center." Since the "very outdoorsy" campus is located in a remote location, "most of the fun that happens occurs on campus," and "the cold winter months are often difficult to bear and result in cabin fever." The lack of metropolitan areas (the nearest being Annapolis) means SMCM is "very residential," and "you really develop your own home and nest here with your friends as family." "There is a decent party scene on campus" with "parties on the weekends studying during the week," but "students are rarely pressured to drink [and] and many don't do it all." The plethora of clubs and other activities means no one goes home bored. "I couldn't ask for a better college experience," says a junior.

Student Body

The diversity rate here isn't all that high (though it's not expected to be at such a small school), but no one has any real complaints. Most here are very environmentally oriented, "both in terms of their leisure activities and in terms of their political leanings." Some affectionately refer to their "hippie" classmates, but the "very accepting" student body has plenty of "pearl-wearing preps" and jocks in its "big social mosh pit," so "even the non-tree huggers amongst us can find a comfortable niche with little trouble." "It's entirely acceptable to be a bit quirky," says a junior. SMCM "is truly its own place," and this extreme love of the campus and its surroundings creates a sort of communal understanding that those who don't contribute to the betterment of the campus community will find themselves answering to the angry masses. "Word gets around on a small campus, and if you are mean or vandalize or something, people will know and shun you for that bad action."

FINANCIAL AID: 240-895-3000 • E-MAIL: ADMISSIONS@SMCM.EDU • WEBSITE: WWW.SMCM.EDU

THE PRINCETON REVIEW SAYS

Admissions

Very important factors considered include: Academic GPA, rigor of secondary school record. *Important factors considered include:* Application essay, recommendation(s), standardized test scores, extracurricular activities, first generation, talent/ability, volunteer work. *Other factors considered include:* Alumni/ae relation, geographical residence, interview, racial/ethnic status, state residency, work experience. SAT or ACT required; TOEFL required of all international applicants. High school diploma is required and GED is accepted. *Academic units required:* 4 English, 3 mathematics, 3 science, (2 science labs), 2 foreign language, 2 social studies, 1 history, 3 academic electives. *Academic units recommended:* 4 mathematics, 4 foreign language.

Financial Aid

Students should submit: FAFSA. Regular filing deadline is 3/1. The Princeton Review suggests that all financial aid forms be submitted as soon as possible after 1/1. *Need-based scholarships/grants offered:* Federal Pell, SEOG, state scholarships/grants, private scholarships, the school's own gift aid. *Loan aid offered:* FFEL Subsidized Stafford, FFEL Unsubsidized Stafford, FFEL PLUS, Federal Perkins. Applicants will be notified of awards on or about 4/1. Federal Work-Study Program available. Institutional employment available. Off-campus job opportunities are good.

The Inside Word

There are few better choices than St. Mary's for better-than-average students who are not likely to get admitted to extremely selective colleges in the country. It is likely that if funding for public colleges is able to stabilize, or even grow, that this place will soon be joining the ranks of the best. Now is the time to take advantage, before the academic expectations of the admissions committee start to soar.

THE SCHOOL SAYS "..."

From The Admissions Office

"St. Mary's College of Maryland occupies a distinctive niche and represents a real value in American higher education. It is a public college, dedicated to the ideal of affordable, accessible education but committed to quality teaching and excellent programs for undergraduate students. The result is that St. Mary's offers the small college experience of the same high caliber usually found at prestigious private colleges, but at public college prices. Designated by the state of Maryland as 'a public honors college,' one of only two public colleges in the nation to hold that distinction, St. Mary's has become increasingly attractive to high school students. Admission is very selective.

"Applicants must take the SAT; the ACT with the Writing section is also accepted."

SELECTIVITY

Admissions Rating	90
# of applicants	2,723
% of applicants accepted	52
% of acceptees attending	32
# accepting a place on wait list	214
% admitted from wait list	14
# of early decision applicants	369
% accepted early decision	44

FRESHMAN PROFILE

Range SAT Critical Reading	580–680
Range SAT Math	570–660
Range SAT Writing	570–680
Range ACT Composite	24–29
Minimum paper TOEFL	550
Minimum computer TOEFL	250
Minimum web-based TOEFL	90
Average HS GPA	3.56
% graduated top 10% of class	47
% graduated top 25% of class	78
% graduated top 50% of class	95

DEADLINES

Early decision	
Deadline	11/1
Notification	12/1
Regular	
Deadline	1/1
Notification	4/1
Nonfall registration?	yes

FINANCIAL FACTS

Financial Aid Rating	86
Annual tuition in-state	$13,234
Annual tuition-out-of-state	$24,627
Room and board	$9,955
Books and supplies	$1,000
% frosh rec. need-based scholarship or grant aid	17
% UG rec. need-based scholarship or grant aid	19
% frosh rec. non-need-based scholarship or grant aid	17
% UG rec. non-need-based scholarship or grant aid	19
% frosh rec. need-based self-help aid	17
% UG rec. need-based self-help aid	19
% frosh rec. any financial aid	59
% UG rec. any financial aid	61
% UG borrow to pay for school	70
Average cumulative indebtedness	$17,125

ST. OLAF COLLEGE

1520 St. Olaf Avenue, Northfield, MN 55057 • Admissions: 507-786-3025 • Fax: 507-786-3832

CAMPUS LIFE
Quality of Life Rating	98
Fire Safety Rating	65
Green Rating	87
Type of school	private
Affiliation	Lutheran
Environment	village

STUDENTS
Total undergrad enrollment	3,014
% male/female	45/55
% from out of state	45
% from public high school	82
% live on campus	96
% African American	1
% Asian	5
% Caucasian	86
% Hispanic	2
% International	1
# of countries represented	30

SURVEY SAYS . . .
Athletic facilities are great
Students get along with local community
Great food on campus
Frats and sororities are unpopular or nonexistent
Musical organizations are popular

ACADEMICS
Academic Rating	94
Calendar	4/1/4
Student/faculty ratio	12.8:1
Profs interesting rating	87
Profs accessible rating	91
Most common reg class size	10–19 students
Most common lab size	20–29 students

MOST POPULAR MAJORS
biology/biological sciences
English language and literature
mathematics

STUDENTS SAY ". . ."

Academics

St. Olaf, a small Lutheran liberal arts school located 40 miles south of downtown Minneapolis, provides a "great liberal arts education rich with musical, academic, and social opportunities in a tight-knit, caring community." The school is renowned for its "amazing and extensive" music department (with which "most students are involved somehow"), but that's hardly the school's only asset. On the contrary, St. Olaf offers "excellent vocational training programs in nursing, social work, and education" (supplemented by "great…hands-on learning in addition to classroom learning through internships") as well as "an amazing science and math program. The new 200,000 square foot of Natural and Mathematical Sciences opened last year. One of the best things about this school is the broad range of academics and academic experiences you can have." For most here, those experiences include study abroad; the school's numerous study abroad programs mean that "almost everyone goes abroad for at least a month." Writes one student, "St. Olaf has an amazing study abroad program. I've ridden camels in Egypt, climbed the Great Wall in China, seen the ruins of the Acropolis, and gone drinking in Switzerland all in the same semester!" Many students here complete a five-course sequence called "the Great Conversation Program, which provides a rigorous introduction to college, exploring the many 'Great Books' of western culture. The liberal arts requirements make everyone somewhat knowledgeable on every field."

Life

"There isn't much to do in Northfield," so life at St. Olaf "is very centered on campus." The school and student organizations make sure that "there is always something to do on campus, despite the small size of the student body. Bands are brought in to the student nightclub; there are more than 100 concerts a year. The theater and dance programs put on frequent shows, and sports events are happening constantly. Students have the ability to participate in most of these activities, usually without too much prior experience, either." Also, undergraduates are "very focused on clubs and special interest groups. For about 3,000 students there are more than 100 clubs on campus, serving everything from religious beliefs to environmental concerns to just having fun." Undergraduates "are very progressive…Their passion for creating progressive social and political change often springs from their religious convictions." Intramural sports "are huge, so if varsity sports aren't your thing there are outside options," and because students "walk absolutely everywhere…the freshman 15 is more like the freshman five, if that. We're very healthy." When students need some big-city diversion, the Twin Cities are only about 45 minutes away. "Many students go up there to eat, see a play, sporting event, concert, or just to shop on weekends."

Student Body

"The stereotype that St. Olaf is completely made up of blond-haired, blue-eyed, Scandinavian Lutherans is not true," students insist, although they quickly admit that "We do have a large number of them!" As one student explains, "We joke about how it seems like every girl is 5-foot-4, blond, and fair-skinned, but that isn't totally true. There is a place for more diverse students. It seems like the typical St. Olaf student's mindset is open enough to embrace different religions, races, ideas, and beliefs." The true common ground here is that most St. Olaf undergraduates are "highly motivated toward success, whether academic or vocational," and are "also likely…type-A personalities" who are "involved in many extracurricular events yet maintain good grades under a full academic load." While St. Olaf is a college of the Evangelical Lutheran Church in America, its student body is quite diverse when it comes to religious orientation. One student notes, the population is not particularly conservative or evangelical. They are more liberal politically and ideologically."

FINANCIAL AID: 507-786-3019 • E-MAIL: ADMISSIONS@STOLAF.EDU • WEBSITE: WWW.STOLAF.EDU

THE PRINCETON REVIEW SAYS

Admissions

Very important factors considered include: Application essay, academic GPA, rigor of secondary school record. *Important factors considered include:* recommendation(s), standardized test scores, character/personal qualities, extracurricular activities, talent/ability. *Other factors considered include:* Class rank, alumni/ae relation, first generation, geographical residence, interview, level of applicant's interest, racial/ethnic status, religious affiliation/commitment, state residency, volunteer work, work experience. SAT or ACT required; TOEFL required of all international applicants. High school diploma is required and GED is accepted. *Academic units required:* 4 English, 2 mathematics, 2 science, (1 science labs), 2 foreign language, 1 social studies, 1 history, 2 academic electives. *Academic units recommended:* 4 English, 4 mathematics, 4 science, (2 science labs), 4 foreign language, 2 social studies, 2 history, 4 academic electives.

Financial Aid

Students should submit: FAFSA, CSS/Financial Aid PROFILE, noncustodial PROFILE, business/farm supplement. Regular filing deadline is 4/15. The Princeton Review suggests that all financial aid forms be submitted as soon as possible after 1/1. *Need-based scholarships/grants offered:* Federal Pell, SEOG, state scholarships/grants, private scholarships, the school's own gift aid. *Loan aid offered:* FFEL Subsidized Stafford, FFEL Unsubsidized Stafford, FFEL PLUS, Federal Perkins, Federal Nursing, state loans, college/university loans from institutional funds. Applicants will be notified of awards on a rolling basis beginning 3/1. Federal Work-Study Program available. Off-campus job opportunities are fair.

The Inside Word

St. Olaf's national reputation is sharply on the rise. This elevated prominence means St. Olaf must compete for candidates with more prestigious schools; hence, the acceptance rate hasn't dropped as dramatically as one might expect, as these days the school loses more of its admits to the Harvards and Northwesterns of the world than it did in the past. The artificially high acceptance rate masks a highly selective, highly competitive admissions process. Bring your A game.

THE SCHOOL SAYS ". . ."

From The Admissions Office

"Recognized as one of the nation's leading liberal arts colleges, St. Olaf offers an academically rigorous education with a vibrant faith tradition as a college of the Lutheran church. Widely known for its programs in mathematics, natural sciences, and music, St. Olaf also provides dynamic opportunities for interdisciplinary study. Committed to global education, more than two-thirds of St. Olaf students study off campus during part of their four years of study. Since 1996, St. Olaf has produced five Rhodes scholars, more than any other liberal arts college in the nation, and 49 Fulbright recipients. St. Olaf ranks eighth overall among baccalaureate colleges in the number of graduates who go on to earn doctoral degrees, placing first in mathematics and statistics, second in religion/theology, and third in art/music and foreign language. Chemistry, physics, and biological sciences also fall within the top ten."

SELECTIVITY

Admissions Rating	96
# of applicants	3,964
% of applicants accepted	59
% of acceptees attending	35
# accepting a place on wait list	114
% admitted from wait list	3
# of early decision applicants	151
% accepted early decision	93

FRESHMAN PROFILE

Range SAT Critical Reading	590–700
Range SAT Math	590–710
Range SAT Writing	580–680
Range ACT Composite	27–31
Minimum paper TOEFL	550
Minimum computer TOEFL	213
Average HS GPA	3.65
% graduated top 10% of class	59
% graduated top 25% of class	85
% graduated top 50% of class	99

DEADLINES

Early Decision	
Deadline	11/15
Notification	12/15
Regular	
Priority	1/15
Nonfall registration?	no

APPLICANTS ALSO LOOK AT
AND SOMETIMES PREFER

Gustavus Adolphus College
Lawrence University
Macalester College
University of Wisconsin—Madison
Carleton College
University of Minnesota—Twin Cities
Grinnell College
Northwestern University

FINANCIAL FACTS

Financial Aid Rating	97
Annual tuition	$35,500
Room and board	$8,200
% frosh rec. need-based scholarship or grant aid	64
% UG rec. need-based scholarship or grant aid	65
% frosh rec. non-need-based scholarship or grant aid	31
% UG rec. non-need-based scholarship or grant aid	30
% frosh rec. need-based self-help aid	64
% UG rec. need-based self-help aid	65
% frosh rec. any financial aid	86
% UG rec. any financial aid	86
% UG borrow to pay for school	65
Average cumulative indebtedness	$25,273

STANFORD UNIVERSITY

UNDERGRAD. ADMISSION, 355 GALVEZ ST, MONTAG HALL, STANFORD, CA 94305 • ADMISSIONS: 650-723-2091 • FAX: 650-725-2846

CAMPUS LIFE

Quality of Life Rating	**98**
Fire Safety Rating	**81**
Green Rating	**92**
Type of school	private
Environment	city

STUDENTS

Total undergrad enrollment	6,502
% male/female	51/49
% from out of state	58
% from public high school	60
% live on campus	89
% in (# of) fraternities	NR (17)
% in (# of) sororities	NR (11)
% African American	10
% Asian	23
% Caucasian	38
% Hispanic	12
% Native American	3
% international	7
# of countries represented	68

SURVEY SAYS . . .

School is well run
Students are friendly
Dorms are like palaces
Campus feels safe

ACADEMICS

Academic Rating	**99**
Calendar	quarter
Student/faculty ratio	6:1
Profs interesting rating	95
Profs accessible rating	86
% classes taught by TAs	5
Most common reg class size	10–19 students
Most common lab size	10–19 students

MOST POPULAR MAJORS
biology/biological sciences
economics
international relations

STUDENTS SAY ". . ."

Academics

Students insist that Stanford is "the most amazing school in the country, with a great mix of academics, athletics, and weather," and it's hard to argue with them. The school really does offer it all to the laid-back-but-ambitious crowd lucky enough to receive an invite to attend; as one student puts it, "Stanford essentially disproves the theorem that if it sounds too good to be true, it probably is." Undergrads here "can and are able to do so much." Take, for example, the anthropology major who reported "great opportunities such as researching over the summer in the Peruvian Amazon and working with the Center for Ecotourism and Sustainable Development to create a network of indigenous leaders interested in ecotourism." Or the myriad of super-curious here who extol "the many interdisciplinary majors: human biology; history, literature, and the arts; materials science and engineering; symbolic systems; science technology and society; public policy; modern thought and literature; urban studies.... It's amazing how many different fields you can combine." And perhaps best of all, "there is not any counter productive cut-throat competition. Staff and students are all very supportive of each other, and it's really an environment where you can explore and succeed."

Life

"Everyone studies all the time, and a lot of people work and are involved with extracurriculars" at Stanford. They also "work out and volunteer. Basically, people try to be perfect." The school "offers so many extracurriculars that it's impossible for students to not be involved and feel welcome," helping to "offset academic stresses" that can be considerable, especially for engineers and premeds. Indeed, "It would be easy to be at Stanford, not take classes, and still be busy. There is always something going on: theater performances, a cappella concerts, small-scale concerts every Thursday, major concerts at least once a year, row house parties every weekend.... It's possible to go out Wednesday through Saturday night." Day to day life here "revolves around the amazing sense of dorm community and the great athletic teams." Stanford prides itself on its robust intercollegiate athletic programs, and "everyone at Stanford lives and breathes Cardinal red." Residential choices "vary. You can live in a great row house with a huge room and a private chef, or a one-room double in a dorm with awful food. There are a lot of options: dorms, houses, co-ops, apartments, and suites." Students generally avoid Palo Alto ("It's soooo expensive!"), but do find the cash to visit equally pricey San Francisco when their schedules permit.

Student Body

Stanford undergrads describe each other in terms so rapturous it makes one wonder whether there isn't something a little funny about the campus water supply. These "ambitions, driven, and incredibly intelligent" people include every form of high achiever; writes one, "I have been fortunate enough to meet a professional cartoonist, several Olympic athletes, an international math Olympiad participant, a professional rapper, a concert violinist, an equestrian champion, a national rugby champion, and so many other talented people just in my 89-person dorm. There are people who have run with the bulls in Pamplona, ski race every weekend, have written published books, and that ever-elusive person who actually won the national science fair in eighth grade." The vibe is "definitely chill....There isn't any of the East Coast snobbery/aristocracy here that I picture at the Ivies." Is there anything negative one can say about these people? "There are barely any fat people," one student offers. Ah ha, but there are some. That will likely have to do.

FINANCIAL AID: 650-723-3058 • E-MAIL: ADMISSION@STANFORD.EDU • WEBSITE: WWW.STANFORD.EDU

THE PRINCETON REVIEW SAYS

Admissions

Very important factors considered include: Class rank, application essay, academic GPA, recommendation(s), rigor of secondary school record, standardized test scores, character/personal qualities, extracurricular activities, talent/ability. *Other factors considered include:* alumni/ae relation, first generation, geographical residence, racial/ethnic status, volunteer work, work experience. SAT or ACT required; ACT with Writing component required. High school diploma is required and GED is accepted. *Academic units recommended:* 4 English, 4 mathematics, 3 science, (3 science labs), 3 foreign language, 2 social studies, 1 history.

Financial Aid

Students should submit: FAFSA, CSS/Financial Aid PROFILE. The Princeton Review suggests that all financial aid forms be submitted by 2/15. *Need-based scholarships/grants offered:* Federal Pell, SEOG, state scholarships/grants, private scholarships, Academic Competitive Grants, SMART Grants, and the school's own gift aid. *Loan aid offered:* FFEL Subsidized Stafford, FFEL Unsubsidized Stafford, FFEL PLUS, and Federal Perkins. Applicants will be notified of awards on a rolling basis beginning 4/3. Federal Work-Study Program available. Institutional employment available. Off-campus job opportunities are good.

The Inside Word

Stanford admissions is justly praised for its compassionate approach toward applicants, not only those it accepts but those many, many highly qualified candidates whom it must reject. The admissions staff here may be the nation's best at saying "no" without breaking hearts. Applicants should remember that the vast majority of their competition is qualified to attend this school, yet fewer than 10% of them will receive the thick envelope. Good luck!

THE SCHOOL SAYS "..."

From The Admissions Office

"Stanford looks for distinctive students who exhibit energy, personality, a sense of intellectual vitality and extraordinary impact outside the classroom. While there is no minimum grade point average, class rank, or test score one needs to be admitted to Stanford, the vast majority of successful applicants will be among the strongest students (academically) in their secondary schools. The most compelling applicants for admission will be those who have thus far achieved state, regional, national, and international recognition in their academic and extracurricular areas of interest.

"Stanford currently accepts the Common Application as its exclusive application for admission. In addition to the on-line version of the Common Application, all applicants must submit an on-line Stanford-specific supplement to be considered for admission. The online supplement allows candidates to: detail information about an experience they find intellectually engaging; write a note to their freshman year roommate sharing a personal experience they have had; and explain why they feel Stanford is a good fit for them.

"While the SAT or ACT is required for admission, SAT subject tests are not required (and only recommended). AP scores are also not required but may be influential in admission decisions and can be used for placement/credit purposes if an applicant decides to enroll."

SELECTIVITY

Admissions Rating	99
# of applicants	25,299
% of applicants accepted	9
% of acceptees attending	71
# accepting a place on wait list	1,002

FRESHMAN PROFILE

Range SAT Critical Reading	650–760
Range SAT Math	680–780
Range SAT Writing	670–760
Range ACT Composite	30–34
% graduated top 10% of class	92
% graduated top 25% of class	99
% graduated top 50% of class	100

DEADLINES

Early action	
Deadline	11/1
Notification	12/15
Regular	
Deadline	1/1
Notification	4/1
Nonfall registration?	no

APPLICANTS ALSO LOOK AT
AND OFTEN PREFER
Harvard College
Yale University
Princeton University
AND SOMETIMES PREFER
University of California—Berkeley

FINANCIAL FACTS

Financial Aid Rating	96
Annual tuition	$37,380
Room and board	$11,463
Books and supplies	$1,455
% frosh rec. need-based scholarship or grant aid	43
% UG rec. need-based scholarship or grant aid	43
% frosh rec. non-need-based scholarship or grant aid	2
% UG rec. non-need-based scholarship or grant aid	2
% frosh rec. need-based self-help aid	27
% UG rec. need-based self-help aid	32
% frosh rec. athletic scholarships	7
% UG rec. athletic scholarships	7
% UG rec. any financial aid	77
% UG borrow to pay for school	40
Average cumulative indebtedness	$15,724

STATE UNIVERSITY OF NEW YORK AT BINGHAMTON

PO Box 6000, Binghamton, NY 13902-6001 • Admissions: 607-777-2171 • Fax: 607-777-4445

CAMPUS LIFE

Quality of Life Rating	74
Fire Safety Rating	75
Green Rating	99
Type of school	public
Environment	city

STUDENTS

Total undergrad enrollment	11,760
% male/female	52/48
% from out of state	9
% from public high school	89
% live on campus	65
% in (# of) fraternities	9 (24)
% in (# of) sororities	11 (19)
% African American	5
% Asian	13
% Caucasian	44
% Hispanic	7
% international	9
# of countries represented	102

SURVEY SAYS . . .

Diverse student types on campus
Campus feels safe
Student publications are popular
Lots of beer drinking

ACADEMICS

Academic Rating	76
Calendar	semester
Student/faculty ratio	20:1
Profs interesting rating	64
Profs accessible rating	69
% classes taught by TAs	9
Most common reg class size	20–29 students
Most common lab size	10–19 students

MOST POPULAR MAJORS

business administration and
management
English language and literature
engineering

STUDENTS SAY ". . ."

Academics

With fewer than 12,000 undergraduates, Binghamton University is "a decent sized school that doesn't feel that big." It's thanks to this that "you get to know people easily" here. Yet the school is also large enough to accommodate "a great education in a variety of fields, ranging from the liberal arts to engineering to business to education to nursing." Students report that "the school does the best it can to prepare its students at an Ivy level. It knows that it does not have the name recognition of others but teaches its students the values of hard work so that they can compete with Ivy students for jobs. Students aim for these jobs and are often successful getting them." Professional programs, which are among the most popular here, are "amazing" and "the connection with alumni is great," not to mention "the career development center is awesome," all huge pluses when it comes time for the job search. And the school accomplishes all this at a very reasonable cost. "Everyone here says value is a huge strength for this school," one student explains. Similar to many state schools, students sometimes complain about problems on the administrative level. Administrators "can sometimes be frustrating to deal with. It seems like if you have a problem, you end up getting sent to another office." Fortunately, Binghamton has begun to address these issues by hiring more staff, offering new advising services, and installing an integrated student service system.

Life

Students tell us that "campus life is really great" at Binghamton, offering "tons of activities to participate in, including club or intramural sports, student government, fraternities/sororities (both social and professional), student groups, and more." Dorms are "convenient" and "clean" (although "living off-campus is less expensive"), and undergrads are kept busy "trying to balance classes, school work, jobs, volunteer work, and sports…. There's never enough time for everything you want to do." Some complain that "the weekends can get pretty dull on campus," which is why they opt for beer-soaked fraternity parties or "the bars downtown." According to the drinking crowd, "The weeks can be stressful with a lot of classes, papers and tests, so students tend to unwind on the weekends. Once the frats run out of alcohol, people generally walk about 10 minutes to the bars." However, the drinking scene is by no means the only weekend alternative. As one student explains, "For people not interested in that, there is late night Binghamton," which "shows movies; has hypnotists, magicians, or comedians come; [and] has crafts to do, and it's all free." Binghamton is also experiencing a resurgence, and students frequently patronize many of the cafes, restaurants, and galleries found downtown.

Student Body

The typical BU undergrad "is someone who was smart in high school"—they had to be to get in here—but was "well-rounded enough so as to not be only invested in academics. In general, although people are relatively smart, they have other things on their mind than pure academics." The campus is "very ethnically diverse," with "a lot of Jewish students and a lot of Asians" factoring into the mix. Geographically, Long Island and New York City are extremely well represented, "but there are many others from around the country and the world." Class background and local weather conspire to make "The North Face" a conspicuous brand on campus.

STATE UNIVERSITY OF NEW YORK AT BINGHAMTON

FINANCIAL AID: 607-777-2428 • E-MAIL: ADMIT@BINGHAMTON.EDU • WEBSITE: WWW.BINGHAMTON.EDU

THE PRINCETON REVIEW SAYS

Admissions

Very important factors considered include: academic GPA, rigor of secondary school record, standardized test scores. *Important factors considered include:* Class rank, application essay, recommendation(s), extracurricular activities, first generation. *Other factors considered include:* alumni/ae relation, character/personal qualities, geographical residence, level of applicant's interest, racial/ethnic status, state residency, talent/ability, volunteer work, work experience. SAT or ACT required; ACT with Writing component required. TOEFL required of all international applicants. High school diploma is required and GED is accepted. *Academic units required:* 4 English, 3 mathematics, 2 science, 3 foreign language, 2 social studies. *Academic units recommended:* 4 mathematics, 4 science, 4 history.

Financial Aid

Students should submit: FAFSA, state aid form. The Princeton Review suggests that all financial aid forms be submitted as soon as possible after 1/1. *Need-based scholarships/grants offered:* Federal Pell, SEOG, state scholarships/grants, private scholarships, academic competitveness grant, the school's own gift aid. *Loan aid offered:* Direct Subsidized Stafford, Direct Unsubsidized Stafford, Direct PLUS, Federal Perkins, Federal Nursing, college/university loans from institutional funds. Applicants will be notified of awards on a rolling basis beginning 4/1. Federal Work-Study Program available. Institutional employment available. Off-campus job opportunities are excellent.

The Inside Word

Binghamton receives nearly 11 applications for every slot in its freshman class. That's bad news for marginal candidates, who should probably start looking elsewhere in the SUNY system if they have their hearts set on attending one. With competition this stiff, you'll need solid test scores and high school grades just to get past the first winnowing stage.

THE SCHOOL SAYS "..."

From The Admissions Office

"Binghamton has established itself as the premier public university in the Northeast, because of our outstanding undergraduate programs, vibrant campus culture, and committed faculty. Students are academically motivated, but there is a great deal of mutual help as they compete against the standard of a class rather than each other. Faculty and students work side by side in research labs or on artistic pursuits. Achievement, exploration, and leadership are hallmarks of a Binghamton education. Add to that a campus wide commitment to internationalization that includes a robust study abroad program, cultural offerings, languages and international studies, and you have a place where graduates leave prepared for success. Binghamton University graduates lead the nation in top starting salaries among public universities, demonstrating that our students are recognized by employers and recruiters for having strong abilities to be leaders, critical thinkers, decision-makers, analysts and researchers in many fields and industries."

SELECTIVITY

Admissions Rating	**94**
# of applicants	26,666
% of applicants accepted	40
% of acceptees attending	24
# accepting a place on wait list	730
% admitted from wait list	12

FRESHMAN PROFILE

Range SAT Critical Reading	580–660
Range SAT Math	610–690
Range ACT Composite	26–29
Minimum paper TOEFL	550
Minimum computer TOEFL	213
Minimum web-based TOEFL	80
Average HS GPA	3.7
% graduated top 10% of class	48
% graduated top 25% of class	83
% graduated top 50% of class	97

DEADLINES

Fall Admission	
Freshman	
Priority	1/15
Notification	4/1
Transfers	
Priority	3/15
Notification	rolling

APPLICANTS ALSO LOOK AT

AND OFTEN PREFER
Cornell University

AND SOMETIMES PREFER
New York University
Boston University

AND RARELY PREFER
State University of New York—Stony Brook University
University of Rochester

FINANCIAL FACTS

Financial Aid Rating	**84**
Annual in-state tuition	$4,970
Annual out-of-state tuition	$12,870
Room and board	$10,612
Required fees	$1,798
Books and supplies	$800
% frosh rec. need-based scholarship or grant aid	34
% UG rec. need-based scholarship or grant aid	38
% frosh rec. non-need-based scholarship or grant aid	13
% UG rec. non-need-based scholarship or grant aid	12
% frosh rec. need-based self-help aid	39
% UG rec. need-based self-help aid	42
% frosh rec. athletic scholarships	3
% UG rec. athletic scholarships	2
% frosh rec. any financial aid	79
% UG rec. any financial aid	68
% UG borrow to pay for school	54
Average cumulative indebtedness	$14,541

STATE UNIVERSITY OF NEW YORK AT GENESEO

ONE COLLEGE CIRCLE, GENESEO, NY 14454-1401 • ADMISSIONS: 585-245-5571 • FAX: 585-245-5550

CAMPUS LIFE
Quality of Life Rating	**81**
Fire Safety Rating	**85**
Green Rating	**87**
Type of school	public
Environment	village

STUDENTS
Total undergrad enrollment	5,441
% male/female	42/58
% from out of state	2
% from public high school	58
% live on campus	57
% in (# of) fraternities	8 (8)
% in (# of) sororities	11 (11)
% African American	2
% Asian	6
% Caucasian	72
% Hispanic	4
% international	3
# of countries represented	26

SURVEY SAYS . . .
Lab facilities are great
Students are friendly
Campus feels safe
Low cost of living
Students are happy
Student publications are popular
Lots of beer drinking
Hard liquor is popular

ACADEMICS
Academic Rating	**80**
Calendar	semester
Student/faculty ratio	19:1
Profs interesting rating	73
Profs accessible rating	79
Most common reg class size	20–29 students
Most common lab size	10–19 students

MOST POPULAR MAJORS
business administration and management
elementary education and teaching
psychology

STUDENTS SAY ". . ."

Academics

State University of New York—Geneseo, the school that considers itself the Honors College of the SUNY system, offers "challenging academics in a very home-like atmosphere" where "you don't get lost in the crowd like bigger schools." As one student puts it, "Geneseo is all about the classic college experience: a small town, rigorous academics, and having fun at the same time." One in five students pursues a teaching degree here, leading some to conclude that "Geneseo focuses mainly on training future teachers, but for the rest of us, they are preparing us for our next step into employment or further education." Nearly as many study business and marketing; the "best academic departments are by far the natural sciences," however, where "the students are the brightest, the courses are the toughest, and the professors really know their stuff." Geneseo also provides "great pre-professional (medical, dental, pharmacological) preparation in sciences." Students here enjoy a small-school experience that includes "superior academics, small, intimate classes, and professors who truly care about students and will offer them every opportunity to succeed" as well as "many study-abroad options (students are encouraged to explore the world)." They also point out that "leadership and research are also a great focus at SUNY Geneseo. If a student wants to do individual research, professors are more than willing to help students organize projects and carry them out." For these and other reasons, students describe Geneseo as a school "for the academically inclined non-rich citizen. It's the Harvard of the SUNY system."

Life

"The great thing about Geneseo is that there's always a party to go to if you want, but there's no pressure to go," and "it's perfectly acceptable to stay home and watch movies with friends on the weekends or even study on Saturday nights." Indeed, students tell us that "there is so much more to do than just party. The college always has amazing activities going on in the union. Every weekend there are crafts and games, and sometimes they bring in comedians or performers…. At the Halloween Monster Mash Bash, there is a costume ball and activities as well as a raffle for really great prizes. There are far too many activities to list here!" Intercollegiate hockey games "are a big hit, and lots of students go to them on weekends." There are "also many different organizations you can get involved in, including several volunteer organizations, intramural sports, and different hobbies." On the weekends, students "know how to party." The town of Geneseo provides little distraction; "There is nothing to do in town, and the closest city is a 45-minute drive away (Rochester, NY)."

Student Body

"The typical student here at SUNY Geneseo is much like that of the ordinary New York State public high school," except that "Most of the school is white (the college is making efforts to diversify). Despite the majority being white, there is still a wide diversity of student types, be it that they are from different backgrounds, economic classes, or simply around the nation." Undergrads "spend most of their time studying in Milne Library, and those who choose not to study usually don't make it to graduation." There are "a few minority and gay/lesbian/bisexual students" here, "but they really are the minority and often have difficulty adjusting. Many students feel like outsiders and transfer before graduating." Students tell us that "the two largest minorities are Asian and African American…the different ethnic groups tend to clump together."

THE PRINCETON REVIEW SAYS

Admissions

Very important factors considered include: rigor of secondary school record, standardized test scores. *Important factors considered include:* Class rank, application essay, academic GPA, recommendation(s), extracurricular activities, racial/ethnic status, talent/ability. *Other factors considered include:* alumni/ae relation, character/personal qualities, first generation, level of applicant's interest, volunteer work, work experience. SAT or ACT required; TOEFL required of all international applicants. High school diploma is required and GED is accepted. *Academic units recommended:* 4 English, 4 mathematics, 4 science, 4 foreign language, 4 social studies.

Financial Aid

Students should submit: FAFSA, state aid form. Regular filing deadline is 2/15. The Princeton Review suggests that all financial aid forms be submitted as soon as possible after 1/1. *Need-based scholarships/grants offered:* Federal Pell, SEOG, state scholarships/grants, private scholarships, the school's own gift aid. *Loan aid offered:* FFEL Subsidized Stafford, FFEL Unsubsidized Stafford, FFEL PLUS, Federal Perkins, alternative loans. Applicants will be notified of awards on a rolling basis beginning 3/15. Federal Work-Study Program available. Institutional employment available. Off-campus job opportunities are poor.

The Inside Word

Geneseo is the most selective of SUNY's 13 undergraduate colleges and more selective than three of SUNY's university centers. No formulaic approach is used here. Expect a thorough review of your academic accomplishments (over half the student body graduated in the top 10 percent of their class) and your extracurricular/personal side. Admissions standards are tempered only by a somewhat low yield of admits who enroll. The school competes for students with some big-time schools, meaning it must admit many more students than it expects will attend.

THE SCHOOL SAYS "..."

From The Admissions Office

"Geneseo has carved a distinctive niche among the nation's premier public liberal arts colleges. Geneseo is the only undergraduate college in the state of New York system to be granted a chapter of Phi Beta Kappa. The college now competes for students with some of the nation's most selective private colleges, including Colgate, Vassar, Hamilton, and Boston College. Founded in 1871, the college occupies a 220-acre hillside campus in the historic Village of Geneseo, overlooking the scenic Genesee Valley. As a residential campus—with nearly two-thirds of the students living in college residence halls—it provides a rich and varied program of social, cultural, recreational, and scholarly activities. Geneseo is noted for its distinctive core curriculum and the extraordinary opportunities it offers undergraduates to pursue independent study and research with faculty who value close working relationships with talented students. Equally impressive is the remarkable success of its graduates, nearly one-third of whom study at leading graduate and professional schools immediately following graduation.

"SUNY Geneseo will use either SAT or ACT test results in the admission selection process. The SAT Writing test result will not be used. SAT Subject Test results are not required but will be considered if the applicant submits the test results."

SELECTIVITY

Admissions Rating	94
# of applicants	10,588
% of applicants accepted	37
% of acceptees attending	28
# accepting a place on wait list	312
# of early decision applicants	339
% accepted early decision	39

FRESHMAN PROFILE

Range SAT Critical Reading	610–690
Range SAT Math	620–690
Range ACT Composite	29–30
Minimum paper TOEFL	525
Minimum computer TOEFL	197
Minimum web-based TOEFL	71
Average HS GPA	3.7
% graduated top 10% of class	50
% graduated top 25% of class	83
% graduated top 50% of class	99

DEADLINES

Early Decision	
Deadline	11/15
Notification	12/15
Regular	
Deadline	1/1
Notification	3/1
Nonfall registration?	yes

APPLICANTS ALSO LOOK AT

AND OFTEN PREFER
Hamilton College
Cornell University
Colgate University

AND SOMETIMES PREFER
Vassar College
Boston College
Skidmore College
State University of New York at Binghamton
University of Rochester

FINANCIAL FACTS

Financial Aid Rating	87
Annual in-state tuition	$4,970
Annual out-of-state tuition	$12,870
Room and board	$9,070
Required fees	$1,308
Books and supplies	$800
% frosh rec. need-based scholarship or grant aid	18
% UG rec. need-based scholarship or grant aid	41
% frosh rec. non-need-based scholarship or grant aid	23
% UG rec. non-need-based scholarship or grant aid	13
% frosh rec. need-based self-help aid	18
% UG rec. need-based self-help aid	34
% frosh rec. any financial aid	60
% UG rec. any financial aid	70
% UG borrow to pay for school	67
Average cumulative indebtedness	$18,700

STATE UNIVERSITY OF NEW YORK—PURCHASE COLLEGE

ADMISSIONS OFFICE, 735 ANDERSON HILL ROAD, PURCHASE, NY 10577 • ADMISSIONS: 914-251-6300 • FAX: 914-251-6314

CAMPUS LIFE

Quality of Life Rating	63
Fire Safety Rating	60*
Green Rating	86
Type of school	public
Environment	town

STUDENTS

Total undergrad enrollment	3,790
% male/female	45/55
% from out of state	20
% live on campus	68
% African American	8
% Asian	3
% Caucasian	56
% Hispanic	10
% international	2
# of countries represented	21

SURVEY SAYS . . .

Diverse student types on campus
Students aren't religious
Frats and sororities are unpopular or
nonexistent
Musical organizations are popular
Student publications are popular
Student government is popular
Political activism is popular
Hard liquor is popular
(Almost) everyone smokes

ACADEMICS

Academic Rating	77
Calendar	semester
Student/faculty ratio	17:1
Profs interesting rating	77
Profs accessible rating	65
% classes taught by TAs	1
Most common	
reg class size	10–19 students
Most common	
lab size	fewer than 10 students

MOST POPULAR MAJORS

liberal arts and sciences/
liberal studies
visual/performing arts

STUDENTS SAY ". . ."

Academics

Purchase College is the SUNY system's answer to the region's many high-priced conservatories and arts schools set within a public liberal arts and sciences college. While it may not have the cache of Julliard or Rhode Island School of Design, students here don't feel they're getting shorted. On the contrary, they laud the teachers with professional experience (the school's proximity to New York City helps here) who "are caring, inspirational, and focused." They also appreciate the fact that access to Purchase's School of Liberal Arts and Sciences provides "a diverse curriculum" with a greater liberal arts focus than you'll find at most arts schools. Of course, they also love how they're "paying state tuition for a school full of ex-Ivy League teachers who were all too eccentric for Ivy schools, so now they teach at Purchase!" The school's more conventional liberal arts and science offerings notwithstanding, Purchase is primarily "an artistic community." Peer "work in the dance, music, photography, film, art, and acting conservatories is amazing, and it is wonderful to be able to experience the work of these students." Classes tend to be small "with a heavy emphasis on writing skills." Students "are usually well-read and prepared for discussion," and, because "Class sizes are not too large," they "are able to contribute to both the structure of the class and the content." Outside the creative arts, Purchase excels in psychology, journalism, pre-med, biology, and creative writing.

Life

"Campus activities are amazing" at Purchase, a result of the art school/proximity-to-New York combo, which helps bring "nationally recognized figures in the arts to speak on a regular basis, including Art Speigelman and Tony Kushner. There are also free shows several days a week performed by excellent indie bands like My Brightest Diamond and Gregory and the Hawk" as well as numerous events featuring student performances, such as "Fall Ball, a major campus event [that] features a drag show performed by students. Given that many people who dance or sing are in one of the conservatories, it's very entertaining." And then there's New York City, "just a 40-minute train ride away" and "the most popular destination for entertainment." When students "plan on doing something special, [they] plan on going there for the weekend." Purchase has the requisite college parties, but "excessive drinking is probably far less common at Purchase than at a more frat-oriented school." Students tend to keep very busy with schoolwork, especially those in the conservatories, who "spend a great deal of time practicing and studying."

Student Body

At Purchase, "many students who would be stereotyped as 'freaks' are not that freaky." This group includes "the 'artsy' type" who has "green hair" and "piercings" and is "blatantly alternative to pop culture." Such students "comprise a good half of the student population," and, as a result, "they make everyone else considered 'normal' look weird." That being said, the student body here is "extremely diverse." There's "an outspoken gay community and a ton of different ethnicities." Because of the school's "urban feel, racism is virtually obsolete, and there is no hostility towards those of different sexual orientations." "Most everyone finds a niche at Purchase." In all areas, students "like to dive deep into their interests...Purchase is where the dancers, musicians, actors, visual artists, liberal arts and science majors, etc. are all interacting with one another to create a really interesting group of students."

STATE UNIVERSITY OF NEW YORK—PURCHASE COLLEGE

FINANCIAL AID: 914-251-6350 • E-MAIL: ADMISSIONS@PURCHASE.EDU • WEBSITE: WWW.PURCHASE.EDU

THE PRINCETON REVIEW SAYS

Admissions

Very important factors considered include: Application essay, academic GPA, talent/ability, *Important factors considered include:* Standardized test scores. *Other factors considered include:* Class rank, recommendation(s), rigor of secondary school record, character/personal qualities, extracurricular activities, interview, SAT recommended; SAT or ACT required; TOEFL required of all international applicants. High school diploma is required and GED is accepted.

Financial Aid

Students should submit: FAFSA, state aid form. The Princeton Review suggests that all financial aid forms be submitted as soon as possible after 1/1. *Need-based scholarships/grants offered:* Federal Pell, SEOG, state scholarships/grants, private scholarships, the school's own gift aid. *Loan aid offered:* FFEL Subsidized Stafford, FFEL Unsubsidized Stafford, FFEL PLUS. Federal Perkins. Applicants will be notified of awards on a rolling basis beginning 3/1. Federal Work-Study Program available. Institutional employment available. Off-campus job opportunities are excellent.

The Inside Word

About one-third of Purchase College undergraduates enroll in the School of the Arts. All must undergo some type of audition or portfolio review to gain admission; this is the most important piece of the application. Traditional application components—such as high school transcript, test scores, and personal essay—are also considered, but do not figure as prominently. Applicants to the School of Liberal Arts and Sciences undergo a more conventional application review.

THE SCHOOL SAYS ". . ."

From The Admissions Office

"At Purchase College, you're encouraged to 'Think Wide Open.' The campus combines the energy and excitement of professional training in the performing and the visual arts with the intellectual traditions and spirit of discovery of the humanities and sciences. A Purchase College education emphasizes creativity, individual accomplishment, openness, and exploration. It culminates in a senior research or creative project that may focus on civic engagement or interdisciplinary work to become an excellent springboard to a career or to graduate or professional school. The Conservatories of Art and Design, Dance, Music, and Theatre Arts and Film that make up the School of the Arts deliver a cohort-based education with apprenticeships and other professional opportunities in nearby New York City.

"You'll find a unique and engaging atmosphere at Purchase, whether you are a student in the arts, humanities, natural sciences, or social sciences. You choose among a wide variety of programs, including arts management, journalism, creative writing, environmental science, new media, dramatic writing, premed, pre-law, and education. You'll attend performances by your friends, see world-renowned artists on stage at the Performing Arts Center, and experience the artworks on display in the Neuberger Museum of Art (one of the largest campus art museums in the country)—all without leaving campus. The new student services building, along with an enhanced student services website, is making Purchase a lot more user-friendly for its students.

"Admissions requirements vary with each program in the college and can include auditions, portfolio reviews, essays, writing samples, and interviews.

"In addition to individual program requirements, Purchase College requires SAT or ACT scores to complete your application."

SELECTIVITY

Admissions Rating	84
# of applicants	8,905
% of applicants accepted	24
% of acceptees attending	33
# of early decision applicants	34
% accepted early decision	29

FRESHMAN PROFILE

Range SAT Critical Reading	520–620
Range SAT Math	490–590
Range SAT Writing	510–610
Range ACT Composite	22–26
Minimum paper TOEFL	550
Minimum computer TOEFL	213
Average HS GPA	3.2
% graduated top 10% of class	10
% graduated top 25% of class	39
% graduated top 50% of class	81

DEADLINES

Early Decision	
Deadline	11/1
Notification	12/5
Regular	
Priority	3/1
Deadline	7/15
Notification	5/1
Nonfall registration?	yes

APPLICANTS ALSO LOOK AT

AND SOMETIMES PREFER
State University of New York—Stony Brook University

AND RARELY PREFER
Emerson College

FINANCIAL FACTS

Financial Aid Rating	65
Annual in-state tuition	$4,970
Annual out-of-state tuition	$12,870
Room and board	$9,908
Required fees	$1,461
Books and supplies	$1,100
% frosh rec. need-based scholarship or grant aid	42
% UG rec. need-based scholarship or grant aid	42
% frosh rec. non-need-based scholarship or grant aid	3
% UG rec. non-need-based scholarship or grant aid	3
% frosh rec. need-based self-help aid	51
% UG rec. need-based self-help aid	48
% UG borrow to pay for school	59
Average cumulative indebtedness	$20,209

STATE UNIVERSITY OF NEW YORK—STONY BOOK UNIVERSITY

OFFICE OF ADMISSIONS, STONY BROOK, NY 11794-1901 • ADMISSIONS: 631-632-6868 • FAX: 631-632-9898

CAMPUS LIFE

Quality of Life Rating	62
Fire Safety Rating	60*
Green Rating	90
Type of school	public
Environment	town

STUDENTS

Total undergrad enrollment	15,596
% male/female	51/49
% from out of state	6
% from public high school	90
% live on campus	53
% in (# of) fraternities	1 (17)
% in (# of) sororities	1 (15)
% African American	7
% Asian	22
% Caucasian	35
% Hispanic	8
% international	6
# of countries represented	106

SURVEY SAYS . . .

Class discussions are rare
Great library
Diverse student types on campus
Low cost of living
Lots of beer drinking

ACADEMICS

Academic Rating	70
Calendar	semester
Student/faculty ratio	18:1
Profs interesting rating	62
Profs accessible rating	61
Most common reg class size	10–19 students
Most common lab size	20–29 students

MOST POPULAR MAJORS

biology/biological sciences
health professions and related clinical sciences,
psychology

STUDENTS SAY ". . ."

Academics

Stony Brook University "is a great place for ambitious, focused students who actually want to learn something" at a "great research university in which classes are challenging and interesting." Nearly half the undergraduates here pursue traditionally punishing majors such as biology, computer science ("one of the best undergraduate computer science programs," according to at least one student), and engineering. The school also boasts "a strong marine biology program," a popular undergraduate business program, and a solid selection of liberal arts majors. Students in the science and tech majors describe the school as "challenging but worth it," noting that "the sciences here are amazing. Now that I'm interviewing for medical schools, I'm seeing just how highly they think of Stony Brook's undergraduate science programs!" Professors are accomplished and, while "They can be boring, they know what they're teaching like the back of their hand. They will be very helpful in office hours, as long as you ask questions that show them you're trying." As at similar schools, "The only thing you have to watch out for, occasionally, is getting a professor who does not speak English well; that can cause some problems!" Students have "plenty of research opportunities" here, which is another plus. Stony Brook's administration "may consist of nice people, but it's pretty poorly organized. When there is some sort of paperwork involved, nothing ever goes right the first time around. Also, nothing is convenient, and you'll usually have to go in circles to get something done." Most students find the difficulties worth enduring and focus instead on how the school delivers "a great education for a reasonable price."

Life

"Life at Stony Brook depends on whom you surround yourself with," students tell us. While "a lot of students complain that there's nothing to do on campus," others counter that "the problem is that students aren't willing to put in the effort to find those activities." One undergrad explains, "There are many activities in campus life. However, you won't be aware of them at all if you don't...look them up. There are a lot of places where you can go play sports, and most dorms have places to play pool, ping-pong, or just watch TV." The school is home to "lots of student clubs with something for everyone" and Division I intercollegiate athletic teams. In the past, students have noted that athletic games weren't well attended. Hometown Stony Brook "is basically suburban. It is not the best college town. There are a few clubs and bars in the area that some students go to on Thursday nights. However, you have to have a car to get there....If I want to have fun, I generally have to go into the city [NYC]. The city is about 2 hours away by train."

Student Body

The typical student at Stony Brook University "is a middle-class Long Island or Queens kid of Jewish, East Asian, or Indian background." Minority populations are large across a broad demographic range; the school is home to many who are "either Asian, African American, or Hispanic and very, very liberal." Subpopulations "tends to stick to themselves....The atypical students are probably quite miserable at Stony Brook. There is definitely a very Long Island high school-like atmosphere," in part because of the large commuter population and in part because the student body is so large. This may be changing as more and more students are from out of state. In addition 87% of freshman and 60% of transfer students live on campus. One student writes, "All students fit in, but the student body is often impersonal, and it is very difficult to develop lasting friendships and relationships as a result."

STATE UNIVERSITY OF NEW YORK—STONY BROOK UNIVERSITY

FINANCIAL AID: 631-632-6840 • E-MAIL: ENROLL@STONYBROOK.EDU • WEBSITE: WWW.STONYBROOK.EDU

THE PRINCETON REVIEW SAYS

Admissions

Very important factors considered include: Academic GPA, rigor of secondary school record, standardized test scores. *Important factors considered include:* Class rank. *Other factors considered include:* Application essay, recommendation(s), alumni/ae relation, character/personal qualities, extracurricular activities, interview, level of applicant's interest, state residency, talent/ability, volunteer work, work experience. SAT Subject Tests recommended; SAT or ACT required; ACT with Writing component required. TOEFL required of all international applicants. High school diploma is required and GED is accepted. *Academic units required:* 4 English, 3 mathematics, 3 science, 2 foreign language, 4 social studies. *Academic units recommended:* 4 mathematics, 4 science, 3 foreign language.

Financial Aid

Students should submit: FAFSA Program Specific Forms. The Princeton Review suggests that all financial aid forms be submitted as soon as possible after 1/1. *Need-based scholarships/grants offered:* Federal Pell, SEOG, state scholarships/grants, the school's own gift aid. *Loan aid offered:* Direct Subsidized Stafford, Direct Unsubsidized Stafford, Direct PLUS, Federal Perkins. Applicants will be notified of awards on a rolling basis beginning 3/1. Federal Work-Study Program available. Institutional employment available. Off-campus job opportunities are excellent.

The Inside Word

Liberal arts and social science candidates with above-average grades and test scores should encounter little difficulty gaining entry to SUNY—Stony Brook. Students in technical fields (engineering, applied mathematics, computer science), in business, and in music must clear some higher hurdles. You can indicate "undecided" for your major on your application, but know that this does not guarantee you entry into these more competitive majors; you'll still have to meet the admissions requirements when you finally declare a major.

THE SCHOOL SAYS "..."

From The Admissions Office

"Our graduates include Carolyn Porco, the leader of the Imaging Team for the Cassini mission to Saturn; John Hennessy, the president of Stanford University; and Scott Higham, a Pulitzer Prize-winning investigative journalist for the Washington Post who has come to speak to students at our new School of Journalism. Situated on 1,100 wooded acres on the North Shore of Long Island, Stony Brook offers more than 150 majors, minors, and combined-degree programs for undergraduates, including our Fast Track MBA program, a thriving research environment, and a dynamic first-year experience in one of six small undergraduate communities. Stony Brook Southampton is our new residential campus focused on sustainability. Faculty include four members of our School of Marine and Atmospheric Sciences who are recent co-winners of the Nobel Peace Prize. Students enjoy comfortable campus housing, outstanding recreational facilities that include a new stadium, modern student activities center, and indoor sports complex. In addition, the Staller Center for the Arts offers spectacular theatrical and musical performances throughout the year. We invite students who possess both intellectual curiosity and academic ability to explore the countless exciting opportunities available at Stony Brook. Freshmen applying for admission to the university are required to take the SAT (or the ACT with the Writing section). SAT Subject Test scores are recommended, but not required."

SELECTIVITY

Admissions Rating	**77**
# of applicants	25,590
% of applicants accepted	43
% of acceptees attending	26
# accepting a place on wait list	529
% admitted from wait list	2

FRESHMAN PROFILE

Range SAT Critical Reading	520–610
Range SAT Math	570–660
Range SAT Writing	510–610
Minimum paper TOEFL	550
Minimum computer TOEFL	213
Minimum web-based TOEFL	80
% graduated top 10% of class	36
% graduated top 25% of class	72
% graduated top 50% of class	97

DEADLINES

Regular	
Deadline	12/1
Notification	2/1
Nonfall registration?	yes

APPLICANTS ALSO LOOK AT

AND OFTEN PREFER
New York University
Rensselaer Polytechnic Institute

AND SOMETIMES PREFER
Rutgers, The State University of New Jersey—New Brunswick

AND RARELY PREFER
Hofstra University
Pace University

FINANCIAL FACTS

Financial Aid Rating	**68**
Annual in-state tuition	$4,970
Annual out-of-state tuition	$12,870
Room and board	$9,132
Required fees	$1,460
Books and supplies	$900
% frosh rec. need-based scholarship or grant aid	50
% UG rec. need-based scholarship or grant aid	49
% frosh rec. non-need-based scholarship or grant aid	2
% UG rec. non-need-based scholarship or grant aid	1
% frosh rec. need-based self-help aid	36
% UG rec. need-based self-help aid	40
% frosh rec. athletic scholarships	2
% UG rec. athletic scholarships	1
% frosh rec. any financial aid	74
% UG rec. any financial aid	65
% UG borrow to pay for school	63
Average cumulative indebtedness	$17,336

STATE UNIVERSITY OF NEW YORK—UNIVERSITY AT ALBANY

OFFICE OF UNDERGRAD ADMISSIONS, 1400 WASHINGTON AVE., ALBANY, NY 12222 • ADMISSIONS: 518-442-5435 • FAX: 518-442-5383

CAMPUS LIFE

Quality of Life Rating	61
Fire Safety Rating	82
Green Rating	79
Type of school	public
Environment	city

STUDENTS

Total undergrad enrollment	12,937
% male/female	52/48
% from out of state	5
% live on campus	57
% in (# of) fraternities	3 (11)
% in (# of) sororities	6 (18)
% African American	9
% Asian	6
% Caucasian	57
% Hispanic	8
% international	2
# of countries represented	84

SURVEY SAYS . . .

Class discussions are rare
Diverse student types on campus
Lousy food on campus
Lots of beer drinking
Hard liquor is popular
(Almost) everyone smokes

ACADEMICS

Academic Rating	61
Calendar	semester
Student/faculty ratio	19:1
Profs interesting rating	61
Profs accessible rating	61
% classes taught by TAs	11
Most common reg class size	20–29 students
Most common lab size	10–19 students

MOST POPULAR MAJORS

business administration and management
English language and literature
psychology

STUDENTS SAY ". . ."

Academics

Is SUNY Albany (UAlbany to those in the know) the perfect-sized school? Many here think so. Students describe it as "a big school numbers-wise that feels small." Notes one student, "It has a very broad range of quality academic programs, which is very important for an undecided senior in high school." Another adds, "If you know what you want and are motivated, the sky is the limit." The school exploits its location in the state capital to bolster programs in political science, criminal justice, and business, and it "offers internship opportunities to college students that very few schools can." Other standout departments include psychology, Japanese studies, mathematics, and many of the hard sciences. Professors here vary widely in quality, but a surprising number "are receptive, active, and engaging"—in other words, "a lot more accessible than I would have thought for a school this big." Teachers are especially willing to "go out of their way to help students who are interested in learning, come to class regularly, and care about their academic work." The administration, as at most state-run schools, "is basically an over-bloated bureaucracy. Students are sent from department to department in each of their endeavors. It is advisable to avoid [the] administration if at all possible."

Life

There are three distinct social orbits on the Albany campus. Some students take the initiative "by joining one of the many clubs or groups or getting involved with the student government." Others "party for a good time," telling us that "any night of the week you can find people to go out to the bars and clubs with you" and that "the average night ends between 2:30–4:00 A.M." Both of these groups are likely to tell you that "there is a lot to do in Albany and the surrounding area," including "a great arts district, tons of awesome restaurants, museums, [and] a state park." A third, sizable group primarily complains about the cold weather and asserts that "there's nothing to do in Albany." The school works to excite these students with "fun programs and entertainers who come to the campus. We have had a series of comedians, rappers/singers, guests from MTV and VH1, authors, political figures, musical performances, sporting events, spirit events, and many other things around campus." School spirit is on the rise among all groups, we're told. The reason? "A few years ago, basketball team began winning, and everyone came out of the woodwork to support them—it was really a great thing to see."

Student Body

Undergrads here believe that the student body is very diverse in terms of ethnicity and also in terms of personality type; one student observes, "You have your motivated students [who] get good grades, are involved, and get amazing jobs in NYC after college. Then you have your unmotivated kids [who] complain, don't go to class, and blame a bad grade on the professor (when really it is because they crammed the night before and didn't go to class)." Geographically, the school is less diverse. Nearly everyone is a New York State resident, with many coming from "downstate New York"—Long Island, New York City, and Westchester County. There's a fair amount of upstate kids as well, and "a lot of people have certain stereotypes in their heads when they first come to Albany. The Long Islander has his idea about the upstater and vice versa. After a few weeks, though, people see that these aren't always true. I think people from anywhere get along pretty well." The international students, who form a small but noticeable contingent, "tend to keep to themselves," perhaps "due to a culture or language barrier." About one-quarter of the campus population is Jewish.

STATE UNIVERSITY OF NEW YORK—UNIVERSITY AT ALBANY

FINANCIAL AID: 518-442-5757 • E-MAIL: UGADMISSIONS@ALBANY.EDU • WEBSITE: WWW.ALBANY.EDU

THE PRINCETON REVIEW SAYS

Admissions

Very important factors considered include: Class rank, academic GPA, recommendation(s), rigor of secondary school record, standardized test scores, character/personal qualities. *Important factors considered include:* Application essay. *Other factors considered include:* alumni/ae relation, extracurricular activities, first generation, geographical residence, talent/ability, volunteer work, work experience. SAT or ACT required; ACT with Writing component required. TOEFL or IELTS required of all international applicants. High school diploma is required and GED is accepted. *Academic units required:* 4 English, 2 mathematics, 2 science, (2 science labs), 1 foreign language, 3 social studies, 2 history, 4 academic electives. *Academic units recommended:* 4 mathematics, 3 science, (3 science labs), 3 foreign language.

Financial Aid

Students should submit: FAFSANY State residents should apply for TAP on-line. The Princeton Review suggests that all financial aid forms be submitted as soon as possible after 1/1. *Need-based scholarships/grants offered:* Federal Pell, SEOG, state scholarships/grants, private scholarships, the school's own gift aid. *Loan aid offered:* FFEL Subsidized Stafford, FFEL Unsubsidized Stafford, FFEL PLUS. Federal Perkins. Applicants will be notified of awards on a rolling basis beginning 3/15. Federal Work-Study Program available. Institutional employment available. Off-campus job opportunities are good.

The Inside Word

The Wall Street Journal has noted a growing trend among students who, in the past, had limited their postsecondary options to high-end private schools: More such students, the paper reported, have broadened their vision to include prestigious state schools such as SUNY Albany. The driving force, unsurprisingly, is economic. In the event of an unlikely decline in the cost of private education, expect admissions at schools like UAlbany to grow more competitive in coming years.

THE SCHOOL SAYS ". . ."

From The Admissions Office

"Increasing numbers of well-prepared students are discovering the benefits of study in UAlbany's nationally ranked programs and are taking advantage of outstanding internship and employment opportunities in upstate New York's 'Tech Valley.' The already strong undergraduate program is being further enhanced by the recently established Honors College, a university-wide program for ambitious students. The Honors College offers enhanced honors courses and co-curricular options including honors housing.

"Ten schools and colleges, including the nation's first College of Nanoscale Science and Engineering, offer bachelor's, master's, and doctoral programs to more than nearly 13,000 undergraduates and 5,000 graduate students. An award-winning advisement program helps students take advantage of all these options by customizing the undergraduate experiences. More than two-thirds of Albany graduates go on for advanced degrees, and acceptance to law and medical school is above the national average.

"Student life on campus includes 200 clubs, honor societies, and other groups, and 19 Division I varsity teams. With 19 other colleges in the region, Albany is a great college town, adjacent to the spectacular natural and recreational centers of New York and New England.

"Freshmen are awarded more than $800,000 in merit scholarships each year and nearly three-quarters of our students receive financial aid."

SELECTIVITY

Admissions Rating	83
# of applicants	21,892
% of applicants accepted	50
% of acceptees attending	22

FRESHMAN PROFILE

Range SAT Critical Reading	490–580
Range SAT Math	520–610
Range ACT Composite	22–26
Minimum paper TOEFL	550
Minimum computer TOEFL	213
Minimum web-based TOEFL	79
Average HS GPA	3.6
% graduated top 10% of class	15
% graduated top 50% of class	90

DEADLINES

Early action	
Deadline	11/15
Notification	1/1
Regular	
Priority	3/1
Deadline	3/1
Notification	rolling
Nonfall registration?	yes

FINANCIAL FACTS

Financial Aid Rating	74
Annual in-state tuition	$4,660
Annual out-of-state tuition	$11,740
Room and board	$9,778
Required fees	$1,728
Books and supplies	$1,000
% frosh rec. need-based scholarship or grant aid	49
% UG rec. need-based scholarship or grant aid	50
% frosh rec. non-need-based scholarship or grant aid	2
% UG rec. non-need-based scholarship or grant aid	2
% frosh rec. need-based self-help aid	45
% UG rec. need-based self-help aid	47
% frosh rec. athletic scholarships	2
% UG rec. athletic scholarships	1
% frosh rec. any financial aid	64
% UG rec. any financial aid	62
Average cumulative indebtedness	$18,189

STATE UNIVERSITY OF NEW YORK—UNIVERSITY AT BUFFALO

15 CAPEN HALL, BUFFALO, NY 14260-1660 • ADMISSIONS: 716-645-6900 • FAX: 716-645-6411

CAMPUS LIFE

Quality of Life Rating	**74**
Fire Safety Rating	**60***
Green Rating	**60***
Type of school	public
Environment	metropolis

STUDENTS

Total undergrad enrollment	17,509
% male/female	54/46
% from out of state	4
% live on campus	40
% in (# of) fraternities	2 (19)
% in (# of) sororities	4 (14)
% African American	7
% Asian	9
% Caucasian	60
% Hispanic	4
% international	10
# of countries represented	113

SURVEY SAYS . . .

Diverse student types on campus
Student publications are popular
Lots of beer drinking
Hard liquor is popular

ACADEMICS

Academic Rating	**71**
Calendar	semester
Student/faculty ratio	16:1
Profs interesting rating	62
Profs accessible rating	67
% classes taught by TAs	12
Most common reg class size	20–29 students
Most common lab size	20–29 students

MOST POPULAR MAJORS
business/commerce
engineering
psychology

STUDENTS SAY " . . ."

Academics

Offering "more academic programs per dollar than any other university in the state," SUNY Buffalo (UB for short) "is about choices. You can choose many different…combinations of academics and social activities with the support in place." Students brag that UB's "programs are all of the highest quality, translating [into] a best-value education for students." The School of Engineering and Applied Science in particular "is well respected" and "works with corporate partners in a variety of ways that range from joint-research ventures to continuing education to co-op work arrangements for our students." Other stand-out offerings include: pharmacy, physical therapy, a popular business and management school "that is ranked highly," "a solid undergrad and grad architecture program," and "one of the top nursing programs in the state." Of course, a school with this much to offer is bound to be large, making it "easy not to attend class and fall through the cracks, so one must be self-motivated to do well." Administrative tasks are occasionally Kafkaesque, with "a lot of red tape to go through to get anything done. I feel like a pebble being kicked around when trying to get support or services," notes one student. Many students point out that support services and contact with professors improves during junior and senior years when students are pursuing their majors and forging stronger relationships within their departments.

Life

UB is divided into two campuses. Traditionally, South Campus in Northeast Buffalo has been where "the parties are," though students say, "it's much less safe than North Campus," which is located in the suburban enclave of Amherst. The recent closing of several bars near South Campus has made it less of a party destination than it was in years past; these days many students report going to downtown Buffalo "to go clubbing." Students living on North Campus describe it as "its own little city. We have food services, our own bus system, a highway, even our own zip codes. If you know how to play, North Campus is just as much fun as Main Street [which runs by South Campus]; you just need to know where to go." The North Campus, which features "a lake and a nice bike path for when you want to escape from the hectic [atmosphere]" of academic life, is the more populous of the two; the inter-campus bus system is "convenient," although a car is preferred. Students tell us that "between all of the clubs and organizations, the Office of Student Life, athletics, and the Student Association, there is always something to do" on campus. The school's Division I sports teams "are a big hit around here. Even if we are the worst in the division, we still cheer hard and go crazy for our guys and girls." Those who explore Buffalo extol its "amazing art and music scene."

Student Body

Because of UB's size, "You can find just about every kind of person there is here. Everyone has a place in this large and diverse student population." As one student notes, "Although the typical student is of traditional college age, there really isn't a 'typical' student—the student body is very diverse in terms of religion, ethnicity, nationality, age, gender, and orientation. 'Atypical' students fit in well because of the diversity of the student population." Another student adds, "There are a lot of foreign and minority students, to the point that the actual 'majority' is the minority here at UB." Geographically, UB draws "from urban areas, rural areas, NYC, Long Island, and most every country in the world." As a state school, "a lot of the students are from New York State, but with differing areas of the state, there are many different types of students."

STATE UNIVERSITY OF NEW YORK—UNIVERSITY AT BUFFALO

FINANCIAL AID: 866-838-7257 • E-MAIL: UB-ADMISSIONS@BUFFALO.EDU • WEBSITE: WWW.BUFFALO.EDU

THE PRINCETON REVIEW SAYS

Admissions

Very important factors considered include: Class rank, rigor of secondary school record, standardized test scores. *Other factors considered include:* Application essay, recommendation(s), character/personal qualities, extracurricular activities, geographical residence, racial/ethnic status, talent/ability, volunteer work, work experience. SAT or ACT required; ACT with Writing component required. TOEFL required of all international applicants. High school diploma is required and GED is accepted. *Academic units recommended:* 4 English, 3 mathematics, 3 science, 3 foreign language, 4 social studies.

Financial Aid

Students should submit: FAFSA. The Princeton Review suggests that all financial aid forms be submitted as soon as possible after 1/1. *Need-based scholarships/grants offered:* Federal Pell, SEOG, state scholarships/grants, private scholarships, the school's own gift aid, Federal Nursing Scholarships. *Loan aid offered:* Direct Subsidized Stafford, Direct Unsubsidized Stafford, Direct PLUS, Federal Perkins, Federal Nursing, college/university loans from institutional funds. Applicants will be notified of awards on a rolling basis beginning 2/1.

The Inside Word

As students point out, UB "is famous for its architecture, nursing, and pharmacy schools"; as such, it makes sense that "those majors are a harder to get into." In fact, admissions standards at UB have grown more demanding across all programs in recent years. Despite the school's large applicant pool, it takes a close look at applications, searching for evidence of special talents and experiences that will enrich campus life.

THE SCHOOL SAYS ". . ."

From The Admissions Office

"The University at Buffalo (UB) is among the nation's finest public research universities—a learning community where you'll work side by side with world-renowned faculty, including Nobel, Pulitzer, National Medal of Science, and other award winners. As the largest, most comprehensive university center in the State University of New York (SUNY) system, UB offers more undergraduate majors than any public university in New York or New England. Through innovative resources like our Undergraduate Research and Creative Activities, Discovery Seminars, and Undergraduate Academics, you'll be free to chart an academic course that meets your individual goals. At UB you can even design your own major. Our unique University Honors College and University Scholars Program scholarship programs offer an enhanced academic experience, including opportunities for independent study, advanced research, and specialized advisement. The university is committed to providing the latest information technology—and is widely considered to be one of the most wired (and wireless) universities in the country. UB also places a high priority on offering an exciting campus environment. With nonstop festivals, Division I sporting events, concerts, and visiting lecturers, you'll have plenty to do outside of the classroom. We encourage you and your family to visit campus to see UB up close and in person. Our Visit UB campus tours and presentations are offered year-round.

"Freshman applicants must take the SAT (or the ACT with Writing component)."

SELECTIVITY

Admissions Rating	85
# of applicants	19,831
% of applicants accepted	48
% of acceptees attending	35
# accepting a place on wait list	344
% admitted from wait list	80
# of early decision applicants	512
% accepted early decision	69

FRESHMAN PROFILE

Range SAT Critical Reading	500–610
Range SAT Math	540–650
Range ACT Composite	23–27
Minimum paper TOEFL	550
Minimum computer TOEFL	213
Average HS GPA	3.2
% graduated top 10% of class	24
% graduated top 25% of class	62
% graduated top 50% of class	93

DEADLINES

Early Decision	
Deadline	11/1
Notification	12/15
Regular	
Priority	11/1
Notification	rolling
Nonfall registration?	yes

FINANCIAL FACTS

Financial Aid Rating	81
Annual in-state tuition	$4,350
Annual out-of-state tuition	$10,610
Room and board	$9,132
Required fees	$1,867
Books and supplies	$947
% frosh rec. need-based scholarship or grant aid	35
% UG rec. need-based scholarship or grant aid	33
% frosh rec. non-need-based scholarship or grant aid	21
% UG rec. non-need-based scholarship or grant aid	11
% frosh rec. need-based self-help aid	52
% UG rec. need-based self-help aid	50
% frosh rec. athletic scholarships	1
% UG rec. athletic scholarships	1
% frosh rec. any financial aid	67
% UG rec. any financial aid	75
% UG borrow to pay for school	69
Average cumulative indebtedness	$17,657

STEVENS INSTITUTE OF TECHNOLOGY

CASTLE POINT ON HUDSON, HOBOKEN, NJ 07030 • ADMISSIONS: 201-216-5194 • FAX: 201-216-8348

CAMPUS LIFE
Quality of Life Rating	77
Fire Safety Rating	60*
Green Rating	70
Type of school	private
Environment	town

STUDENTS
Total undergrad enrollment	2,040
% male/female	74/26
% from out of state	35
% from public high school	80
% live on campus	85
% in (# of) fraternities	19 (10)
% in (# of) sororities	20 (3)
% African American	4
% Asian	11
% Caucasian	53
% Hispanic	9
% international	6
# of countries represented	47

SURVEY SAYS . . .
Class discussions are rare
Career services are great
Students love Hoboken, NJ
Great off-campus food
Campus feels safe
Frats and sororities dominate
social scene
Lots of beer drinking

ACADEMICS
Academic Rating	70
Calendar	semester
Student/faculty ratio	8:1
Profs interesting rating	61
Profs accessible rating	62
Most common reg class size	20–29 students
Most common lab size	10–19 students

MOST POPULAR MAJORS
business administration and
management
computer/information technology
services administration and
management,
mechanical engineering

STUDENTS SAY ". . ."

Academics

Students at the Stevens Institute of Technology tell us time and again that "Stevens' reputation among some of the world's best employers is outstanding." This leads to a "high job placement [rate] and great starting salaries," which, for many, are the primary charms of this small Hoboken, N. J. school. Engineering disciplines claim about two-thirds of all Stevens undergraduates, and "a huge number participate in the co-op program," which "allows students a break from the theoretical nonsense while putting it to use." In this program, "students spend 5 years getting their undergraduate degree [while] work[ing] three semesters at a company getting experience and pay." That's three semesters of work on top of a 156-credit program that awards a "bachelor's of engineering, not [a] bachelor's of science in engineering. (Offered by [fewer] than half a dozen schools in the country.)" It's a calendar that is not for the faint of heart, since it means a freshman "can have eight classes in [his or her] first semester." Stevens also delivers in mathematics and the sciences; students in the latter area brag that Stevens "always gets a high percent[age] of students accepted...to medical school." As at most tech and science schools, students here complain that, while "the professors are very intelligent," "Sometimes we get professors who are unable to communicate the material." This is often attributed to professors whose first language is not English; some say it's "50/50" whether you'll be able to understand your professor. Even so, most agree that "the juice is worth the squeeze...you'll get a good job" if you graduate.

Life

Stevens is situated in the town of Hoboken, which is "located right on the doorstep of New York City." Hoboken boosters believe that "there is simply no better spot in the world to have a college." In truth, this small town close to the capital of the world pleases multiple tastes: "Those who don't enjoy the city are quite content in Hoboken, [and] the more city-slicker-type students feel very at home with the Manhattan skyline as a backdrop." Because the train to New York City is only "a 7-minute walk from campus," it's easy for students to touch as well as look. Despite its great location, Stevens' "highly demanding" academics play the largest role in student life, which is driven by the ebb and flow—usually the latter—of course work. Nevertheless, "students are very involved [on] campus. Whether it [is] a sports team or Greek life, the vast majority of students do at least one extracurricular activity." Stevens boasts "a very good Division III athletic program," and its teams "have been getting larger fan turnouts" in recent years. Students tell us that there's also "no lack of parties and alcohol [at] this school. You can count on a party every Thursday." A 3:1 male/female ratio drives some male students off campus in search of companionship.

Student Body

Like most tech schools, Stevens "is a nerd school, no doubt about it." It's home to many students who are "very smart but lacking social skills," preferring to "play World of Warcraft in their rooms or watch anime on a Friday night." Students point out that you'll also find "musicians, theater junkies, sports fanatics, and bookworms" on campus. And "just about everybody here has a secret hobby or talent you would have never thought of." In addition, Stevens also has a substantial number of international students—and "lots of minorities" who boost the diversity factor. On the downside, students tend to be very cliquish and "don't associate with each other outside of class" unless they are part of "the group."

FINANCIAL AID: 201-216-5194 • E-MAIL: ADMISSIONS@STEVENS.EDU • WEBSITE: WWW.STEVENS.EDU

THE PRINCETON REVIEW SAYS

Admissions

Very important factors considered include: Application essay, academic GPA, recommendation(s), rigor of secondary school record, standardized test scores, character/personal qualities, extracurricular activities, interview, volunteer work, work experience. *Important factors considered include:* Class rank, talent/ability. *Other factors considered include:* alumni/ae relation, SAT or ACT required; TOEFL required of all international applicants. High school diploma is required and GED is not accepted. *Academic units required:* 4 English, 4 mathematics, 3 science, (3 science labs). *Academic units recommended:* 4 science, (4 science labs), 2 foreign language, 2 social studies, 2 history, 1 computer science, 4 academic electives.

Financial Aid

Students should submit: FAFSA. The Princeton Review suggests that all financial aid forms be submitted as soon as possible after 1/1. *Need-based scholarships/grants offered:* Federal Pell, SEOG, state scholarships/grants, private scholarships, the school's own gift aid. *Loan aid offered:* Direct Subsidized Stafford, Direct Unsubsidized Stafford, Direct PLUS, FFEL Subsidized Stafford, Federal Perkins, state loans, Signature Loans, TERI Loans, NJ CLASS, CitiAssist. Applicants will be notified of awards on a rolling basis beginning 3/30. Federal Work-Study Program available. Institutional employment available. Off-campus job opportunities are excellent.

The Inside Word

Stevens is among the most desirable "second tier" engineering/science/math schools; its location and cachet with employers guarantee the school's status. It's a good choice for those who can't get through the door at MIT or Caltech but who are nonetheless extremely smart and unafraid of hard work. Such students will find the Stevens admissions office quite sympathetic to their applications.

THE SCHOOL SAYS "..."

From The Admissions Office

"Founded in 1870 as the first American college to devote itself exclusively to engineering education based on scientific principles, Stevens Institute of Technology is a prestigious independent university for study and research. In past year, Stevens has been ranked by the Princeton Review as one of the nation's 'Most Entrepreneurial Campuses' for having tailored their undergraduate business and technology curricula to encourage young entrepreneurs, providing them with the training and guidance they need to start their own businesses. Stevens has also been ranked among the nation's top-20 'Most Wired Campuses' by *PC Magazine* and *The Princeton Review*. In 2007 Stevens' office of Career Development has also been ranked among the nation's top 20 by The Princeton Review.

"At the undergraduate level, Stevens' broad-based education leads to prestigious degrees in business, science, computer science, engineering, or humanities. Research activities are vital to the university's educational mission, thus Stevens attracts world-renowned faculty to complement its exceptional on-campus facilities. In addition, Stevens maintains an honor system that has been in existence since 1908. Stevens' more than 2,000 undergraduates come from more than 42 states and 65 countries, creating a diverse, dynamic environment. Stevens also boasts an outstanding campus life—students will find more than 150 student organizations and 25 NCAA Division III athletics teams.

"Stevens requires the SAT or ACT for all applicants. We recommend that all students take SAT Subject Tests to show their strength in English, math, and a science of their choice. Accelerated premed and pre-dentistry applicants must take the SAT as well as two SAT Subject Tests in math (Level I or II), and biology or chemistry. Accelerated law applicants must take two SAT Subject Tests of their choice."

SELECTIVITY

Admissions Rating	93
# of applicants	3,058
% of applicants accepted	49
% of acceptees attending	38
# accepting a place on wait list	328
% admitted from wait list	17
# of early decision applicants	287
% accepted early decision	78

FRESHMAN PROFILE

Range SAT Critical Reading	550–650
Range SAT Math	620–710
Range ACT Composite	24–30
Minimum paper TOEFL	550
Minimum computer TOEFL	213
Minimum web-based TOEFL	82
Average HS GPA	3.7
% graduated top 10% of class	49
% graduated top 25% of class	86
% graduated top 50% of class	97

DEADLINES

Early Decision	
Deadline	11/15
Notification	12/15
Regular	
Priority	11/15
Deadline	2/1
Notification	3/15
Nonfall registration?	no

APPLICANTS ALSO LOOK AT

AND OFTEN PREFER
Cornell University
Massachusetts Institute of Technology
Carnegie Mellon University
Princeton University

AND SOMETIMES PREFER
Johns Hopkins University
New York University

AND RARELY PREFER
Rensselaer Polytechnic Institute

FINANCIAL FACTS

Financial Aid Rating	71
Annual tuition	$34,900
Room and board	$11,000
Required fees	$1,800
Books and supplies	$900
% frosh rec. need-based scholarship or grant aid	66
% UG rec. need-based scholarship or grant aid	54
% frosh rec. non-need-based scholarship or grant aid	62
% UG rec. non-need-based scholarship or grant aid	55
% frosh rec. need-based self-help aid	65
% UG rec. need-based self-help aid	57
% frosh rec. any financial aid	82.4
% UG rec. any financial aid	75.3
% UG borrow to pay for school	65.7
Average cumulative indebtedness	$35,319

STONEHILL COLLEGE

320 WASHINGTON STREET, EASTON, MA 02357-5610 • ADMISSIONS: 508-565-1373 • FAX: 508-565-1545

CAMPUS LIFE
Quality of Life Rating	**97**
Fire Safety Rating	**92**
Green Rating	**76**
Type of school	private
Affiliation	Roman Catholic
Environment	suburban

STUDENTS
Total undergrad enrollment	2,408
% male/female	40/60
% from out of state	46
% live on campus	84
% African American	2
% Asian	1
% Caucasian	92
% Hispanic	4
# of countries represented	11

SURVEY SAYS . . .
Students are friendly
Students get along with local community
Dorms are like palaces
Students are happy
Frats and sororities are unpopular or nonexistent
Student government is popular

ACADEMICS
Academic Rating	**90**
Calendar	semester
Student/faculty ratio	13:1
Profs interesting rating	93
Profs accessible rating	91
Most common reg class size	20–29 students
Most common lab size	10–19 students

MOST POPULAR MAJORS
biology/biological sciences
English language and literature
psychology

STUDENTS SAY ". . ."

Academics

"Stonehill is a small liberal arts college" "focused on educating the mind and soul" in the Roman Catholic tradition. "With a great small, interactive classroom experience" and "amazing" professors who "will help you no matter what," the academic experience here is distinctly "personal." "You won't be lost in the crowd at Stonehill. Professors know who you are and want to help you succeed." (Dare we say they will also notice when you are absent and may call you to find out why?) But that does not mean professors don't expect students to work hard. To the contrary, they "challenge you to question; question your readings, your professors, yourself." The whole point is to teach "how to be a critical thinker, and to look more in depth on ideas and topics." Faculty and administrators are extremely accessible."Many [faculty members] give students not only their school e-mail addresses, but their cell phone or home phone numbers as well as their AIM screen names if they have them!" Students also appreciate the learning opportunities off campus. "Stonehill has an amazing focus on internships and studying abroad, and is known for having connections in the working world. The internships and opportunities given to students are pretty unique."

Life

"Being in the middle of Boston and Providence as well as having more than 70 clubs and organizations on campus that most two events a semester, there is always something to do" at Stonehill. "During the week, most people are considerate and allow you to get work done." "We have quiet hours at 10 p.m. on the weekdays and 1 A.M. on the weekends." But on the weekends, students cut loose. "For fun, people head into Boston a lot; the school has a shuttle to take us to the metro T station so it's very accessible if you don't have a car." On campus, "each night of the week there are different events sponsored by different groups on campus or by the Student Activities building. Some of the more widely attended events include our mixers (dances) which are held at various points throughout the year." "If you're looking for the frat/sorority party school, this isn't the place for you. It's much more laid-back, with drinking in the dorm rooms or in the 21-plus common rooms." And it should be noted that alcohol is taken seriously here; many call the school's alcohol policy "way too strict," though it's possible to "learn the ways around it." The dorms here "are beautiful and you get to choose your housing based on a point system. You get points for being active in the school (sports, clubs, attending lectures, etc.) so the more you participate the better housing you get. You can lose points for misbehavior, so the best housing goes to the best students, which is a huge plus!"

Student Body

"Stonehill is a pretty homogeneous place." Most students are "Caucasian and from middle-class families in New England." They tend to be "preppy" and "love to party on the weekends." However, they "also know how to crack down during the week and excel in class." "The typical student at Stonehill is kind, considerate, friendly and smart. At Stonehill we hold doors, sometimes for an akwardly long time," but the friendly population makes everyone feel welcome." "There are some minorities, but the one thing that does not deviate from this mold is the expected college 'look."

FINANCIAL AID: 508-565-1088 • E-MAIL: ADMISSIONS@STONEHILL.EDU • WEBSITE: WWW.STONEHILL.EDU

THE PRINCETON REVIEW SAYS

Admissions

Very important factors considered include: Class rank, academic GPA, rigor of secondary school record, character/personal qualities, talent/ability. *Important factors considered include:* Application essay, recommendation(s), extracurricular activities, level of applicant's interest, volunteer work, work experience. *Other factors considered include:* Standardized test scores, alumni/ae relation, first generation, geographical residence, racial/ethnic status, religious affiliation/commitment, ACT with Writing component recommended. TOEFL required of all international applicants. High school diploma is required and GED is accepted. *Academic units required:* 4 English, 3 mathematics, 1 science, (1 science lab), 2 foreign language, 3 history, 3 academic electives. *Academic units recommended:* 4 English, 4 mathematics, 3 science, (2 science labs), 3 foreign language, 3 history, 3 academic electives.

Financial Aid

Students should submit: FAFSA, CSS/Financial Aid PROFILE, noncustodial PROFILE, business/farm supplement. The Princeton Review suggests that all financial aid forms be submitted as soon as possible after January 1. *Need-based scholarships/grants offered:* Federal Pell, SEOG, state scholarships/grants, private scholarships, the school's own gift aid *Loan aid offered:* Direct Subsidized Stafford, Direct Unsubsidized Stafford, Direct PLUS, Federal Perkins, state loans. Applicants will be notified of awards on or about 3/15. Federal Work-Study Program available. Institutional employment available. Off-campus job opportunities are good.

The Inside Word

Though not nearly as selective as some of its fellow Boston-area colleges, Stonehill students are no dummies. Half of them graduated in the 10 ten percent of their high school classes. Members of ethnic minorities may feel a bit isolated here.

THE SCHOOL SAYS "..."

From The Admissions Office

"Located 22 miles south of Boston, Stonehill is a selective Catholic college with an academically challenging, welcoming community on a beautiful, active campus. With an average class size of 20, Stonehill's dedicated and supportive faculty make personal connections with each of our 2,400 students and mentor them throughout all four years and beyond. Stonehill offers more than 70 diverse majors and minors in the liberal arts, sciences, and business. Nearly 90% of our students participate in enriching opportunities such as competitive international and U.S. internships; nationally ranked study abroad programs; and top-notch undergraduate research, practicum, and field work experiences. Our proximity to America's premier college town allows you to join a network of 250,000 students and offers easy access to theatres, museums, professional sports games, restaurants, and more. But most importantly, Stonehill is a vibrant community where many minds come together for one purpose: to educate students for lives that make a difference."

SELECTIVITY

Admissions Rating	93
# of applicants	6,838
% of applicants accepted	45
% of acceptees attending	21
# accepting a place on wait list	587
% admitted from wait list	41
# of early decision applicants	67
% accepted early decision	66

FRESHMAN PROFILE

Range SAT Critical Reading	550–640
Range SAT Math	550–650
Range ACT Composite	24–28
Minimum paper TOEFL	550
Minimum computer TOEFL	213
Minimum web-based TOEFL	78
Average HS GPA	3.44
% graduated top 10% of class	57
% graduated top 25% of class	93
% graduated top 50% of class	99

DEADLINES

Early decision	
Deadline	11/1
Notification	12/15
Early action	
Deadline	11/1
Notification	1/15
Regular	
Deadline	1/15
Notification	3/15
Nonfall registration?	yes

APPLICANTS ALSO LOOK AT

AND OFTEN PREFER
Boston University, Villanova University
Northeastern University

AND SOMETIMES PREFER
Boston College, Union College

AND RARELY PREFER
Assumption College, Marist College

FINANCIAL FACTS

Financial Aid Rating	74
Annual tuition	$31,210
Room and Board	$12,240
% frosh rec. need-based scholarship or grant aid	65
% UG rec. need-based scholarship or grant aid	62
% frosh rec. non-need-based scholarship or grant aid	12
% UG rec. non-need-based scholarship or grant aid	9
% frosh rec. need-based self-help aid	54
% UG rec. need-based self-help aid	56
% frosh rec. athletic scholarships	3
% UG rec. athletic scholarships	3
% frosh rec. any financial aid	89
% UG rec. any financial aid	88
% UG borrow to pay for school	75
Average cumulative indebtedness	$25,603

SUFFOLK UNIVERSITY

EIGHT ASHBURTON PLACE, BOSTON, MA 02108 • ADMISSIONS: 617-573-8460 • FAX: 617-742-4291

CAMPUS LIFE

Quality of Life Rating	79
Fire Safety Rating	99
Green Rating	91
Type of school	private
Environment	metropolis

STUDENTS

Total undergrad enrollment	5,639
% male/female	44/56
% from out of state	32
% from public high school	66
% live on campus	24
% in (# of) fraternities	NR (1)
% in (# of) sororities	NR (1)
% African American	3
% Asian	6
% Caucasian	58
% Hispanic	6
% international	10
# of countries represented	105

SURVEY SAYS . . .

Great library
Diverse student types on campus
Students love Boston, MA
Great off-campus food
Dorms are like palaces
Student government is popular
(Almost) everyone smokes

ACADEMICS

Academic Rating	72
Calendar	semester
Student/faculty ratio	13:1
Profs interesting rating	73
Profs accessible rating	72
% classes taught by TAs	1
Most common reg class size	20–29 students
Most common lab size	10–19 students

MOST POPULAR MAJORS

business/corporate communications
interior design
sociology

STUDENTS SAY ". . ."

Academics

"A small classroom university in the heart of a big city," Boston's Suffolk University "is small enough that you actually recognize students from their pictures in the admissions booklets [and] big enough to attract national speakers." It's also a school with a huge international component, thanks to its campuses in Madrid, Spain, and Dakar, Senegal and "a unique partnership with Charles University in Prague," all of which "provide students an easy opportunity to study abroad without the usual hassle of all the paperwork." Academic life on the home campus "includes "down-to-earth professors" who "are always available outside of class and are very helpful" and the Balloti Learning Center, which "offers extra help to students who want or need it." Make no mistake: The family is "incredibly student-oriented" here—"the student and [his or her] concerns come first." Top programs include communications, psychology, government, history, and sociology, which "offers concentrations in crime and justice or health and human services as opposed to just a general major."

Life

Suffolk lacks a traditional sprawling suburban campus. Simply put, Suffolk students know they ain't in Kansas any more! The university consists of a collection of buildings located in swanky Beacon Hill, literally steps from Boston Common and the Public Gardens. So, if you're a city lover you my have just found heaven! You'll find "constant entertainment available," though some students are quick to point out that their urban existence can make some feel "disconnected" compounded by the fact that many students choose to live off campus. One commuter writes, "It's sometimes difficult for me to join in some of the activities that they have going on at the school." Even so, many here are satisfied with the status quo; they'll skip the conventional campus activities and the rah-rah campus unity, preferring to spend their free time enjoying the city of Boston. "Most people have lots of friends [at] other schools" and take advantage of the multitude of fun activities in Boston such as "movies at the Museum of Fine Arts" and "local concerts." Undergrads agree that "lots of people party for fun," and being in Boston. "What you lose in the lack of campus, you gain with the city."

Student Body

Suffolk's overseas ties draw a large international population to the Boston campus, to the point that "in some classes, almost half of the students are foreign-born. Interacting with students from different backgrounds or cultures isn't an option—it's a daily occurrence. In my international business classes it leads to fascinating discussions because, rather than read about business in different cultures, we have firsthand experiences." Most of the American student body comes from Boston and the surrounding area, and "the minority is pretty eclectic," and "very independent." This minority includes "art-school hipsters" and a "relatively large gay community." Each group also features a lot of "preppy" students who use "Boston as their playground." Students report that there "isn't a real strong sense of community, unless you live in the dorms" (about one in five does).

FINANCIAL AID: 617-573-8470 • E-MAIL: ADMISSION@SUFFOLK.EDU • WEBSITE: WWW.SUFFOLK.EDU

THE PRINCETON REVIEW SAYS

Admissions

Very important factors considered include: Rigor of secondary school record. *Important factors considered include:* Class rank, application essay, academic GPA, standardized test scores, character/personal qualities. *Other factors considered include:* recommendation(s), alumni/ae relation, extracurricular activities, first generation, geographical residence, interview, level of applicant's interest, talent/ability, volunteer work, work experience. SAT or ACT required; TOEFL required of all international applicants. High school diploma is required and GED is accepted. *Academic units required:* 4 English, 3 mathematics, 2 science, (1 science labs), 2 foreign language, 1 history, 4 academic electives. *Academic units recommended:* 4 English, 4 mathematics, 4 science, (1 science labs), 3 foreign language, 4 history, 4 academic electives.

Financial Aid

Students should submit: FAFSA, institution's own financial aid form. Regular filing deadline is 3/1. The Princeton Review suggests that all financial aid forms be submitted as soon as possible after 1/1. *Need-based scholarships/grants offered:* Federal Pell, SEOG, state scholarships/grants, private scholarships, the school's own gift aid. *Loan aid offered:* Direct Subsidized Stafford, Direct Unsubsidized Stafford, Direct PLUS, Federal Perkins. Applicants will be notified of awards on a rolling basis beginning 2/5. Federal Work-Study Program available. Institutional employment available. Off-campus job opportunities are excellent.

The Inside Word

Suffolk is unapologetic about its mission to provide access and opportunity to college bound students. That said, test scores and high school GPA requirements are average. Applicants who are borderline based on straight numbers should make their case to the admissions office directly.

THE SCHOOL SAYS "..."

From The Admissions Office

"Ask any student, and they'll tell you: The best thing about Suffolk is the professors. They go the extra mile to help students to succeed. Suffolk faculty members are noted scholars and experienced professionals, but first and foremost, they are teachers and mentors. Suffolk's faculty is of the highest caliber. Ninety-four percent of the faculty hold PhDs. Suffolk maintains a 13:1 student/faculty ratio with an average class size of 19.

"Career preparation is a high priority at Suffolk. Many students work during the school year in paid internships, co-op jobs, or work-study positions. Suffolk has an excellent job placement record. More than 94 percent of recent graduates are either employed or enrolled in graduate school at the time of graduation.

"The university's academic programs emphasize quality teaching, small class size, real-world career applications, and an international experience. There are more than 50 study abroad sites available to students. The undergraduate academic program offers more than 70 majors and 1,000 courses.

"We require applicants to submit the SAT with the essay score or the ACT taken with the Writing component. Standardized tests are used for both placement and assessment. International students may submit any of the following tests for admission: the TOEFL or ELPT, IELTS, CPE, CAE, and FCE. The role of standardized testing is still a secondary role when considering admission to the university. The candidate's grades and the overall strength of curriculum are primary factors in the admission decision."

SELECTIVITY

Admissions Rating	77
# of applicants	9,171
% of applicants accepted	79
% of acceptees attending	21
# accepting a place on wait list	22
% admitted from wait list	10

FRESHMAN PROFILE

Range SAT Critical Reading	450–550
Range SAT Math	450–560
Range SAT Writing	450–560
Range ACT Composite	20–24
Minimum paper TOEFL	525
Minimum computer TOEFL	197
Minimum web-based TOEFL	71
Average HS GPA	3.1
% graduated top 10% of class	11
% graduated top 25% of class	32
% graduated top 50% of class	70

DEADLINES

Early action	
Deadline	11/15
Notification	12/20
Regular	
Deadline	3/1
Nonfall registration?	yes

FINANCIAL FACTS

Financial Aid Rating	66
Annual tuition	$27,100
Room and board	$7,408
% frosh rec. need-based scholarship or grant aid	66
% UG rec. need-based scholarship or grant aid	68
% frosh rec. non-need-based scholarship or grant aid	26
% UG rec. non-need-based scholarship or grant aid	23
% frosh rec. need-based self-help aid	75
% UG rec. need-based self-help aid	77
% frosh rec. any financial aid	81
% UG rec. any financial aid	82

SUSQUEHANNA UNIVERSITY

514 University Avenue, Selinsgrove, PA 17870 • Admissions: 570-372-4260 • Fax: 570-372-2722

CAMPUS LIFE

Quality of Life Rating	**81**
Fire Safety Rating	**89**
Green Rating	**79**
Type of school	private
Affiliation	Lutheran
Environment	town

STUDENTS

Total undergrad enrollment	2,066
% male/female	47/53
% from out of state	44.9
% from public high school	81
% live on campus	74
% in (# of) fraternities	13 (4)
% in (# of) sororities	19 (5)
% African American	3
% Asian	2
% Caucasian	91
% Hispanic	2
% international	1
# of countries represented	8

SURVEY SAYS . . .

Athletic facilities are great
Dorms are like palaces
Campus feels safe
Musical organizations are popular

ACADEMICS

Academic Rating	**85**
Calendar	semester
Student/faculty ratio	13:1
Profs interesting rating	81
Profs accessible rating	87
Most common reg class size	10–19 students
Most common lab size	10–19 students

MOST POPULAR MAJORS

business administration and management
communication studies/speech
communication and rhetoric
creative writing

STUDENTS SAY ". . ."

Academics

Students tell us that Susquehanna University's small size makes it "the perfect university to give students the opportunity to excel in all aspects of school—academics, research, athletics, clubs, and many other activities." Located in rural central Pennsylvania, SU is regarded by students as "an oasis of quirky in the middle of nowhere." This quirkiness emanates from the school's strong programs in the fine arts (including a "big music program," solid departments in creative writing and graphic design, and an active theatre program). Less quirky and more populous is the school's popular School of Business—one in four students here pursues a business major. Students note that "This is a liberal arts university requiring you to take classes from many areas," meaning that all here receive a well-rounded education. They also point out that "It is understandable that you aren't going to be the best at all of those areas. The professors know this as well and are there to help." Indeed, what students love most about SU is the sense that "It is all about the student here. There are no graduate students teaching the undergraduates, the advisers want to make sure how you are doing, and the relationships formed with professors are priceless."

Life

SU's hometown of Selinsgrove "doesn't have the most exciting night life," but that "doesn't really matter" because students "don't have much money to spend on nightlife anyway" and "there's a ton of free stuff to do on campus." Popular campus options include TRAX, "a place were students can go and dance and have a few drinks if they are 21," and Charlie's Coffeehouse, a venue "that provides entertainment like live bands, movies, or games on Friday and Saturday nights." Students are also kept busy with the "abundance of student organizations and campus activities. Not only does it seem like students at Susquehanna are eager to get involved in probably more things than they realistically have time for, but the staff in our student life and campus activities office are amazing." As one student explains, "SU tries to provide as many options as it can because there is literally nothing to do around Selinsgrove." Well, maybe not exactly nothing. Some here concede that the town provides "close proximity to restaurants and stores" and a "decent-sized mall just a couple miles away, as well as everything else from Wall-Mart to every type of fast food restaurant you could think of, all within five miles of school." When small town life gets to be too much, students take advantage of "one-day bus trips to big cities like New York."

Student Body

While there is "a broad mix of students in the sense that there are those that relish in the fine arts, others that are greatly involved in the sciences, and others that enjoy the analytical business aspect of Susquehanna," SU undergrads concede that the typical student is "white and moderately well-off financially" and that "atypical students fit in because they hang out with other atypical students." Overall, students here are "somewhat preppy, but with their own style" and "are hard-working" individuals "who are involved in a ton of activities and sports, but still go out on the weekends."

FINANCIAL AID: 570-372-4450 • E-MAIL: SUADMISS@SUSQU.EDU • WEBSITE: WWW.SUSQU.EDU

THE PRINCETON REVIEW SAYS

Admissions

Very important factors considered include: Academic GPA, rigor of secondary school record. *Important factors considered include:* Class rank, application essay, recommendation(s), standardized test scores, alumni/ae relation, character/personal qualities, extracurricular activities, interview, level of applicant's interest, racial/ethnic status, talent/ability, volunteer work, work. *Other factors considered include:* First generation, geographical residence, religious affiliation/commitment, state residency. TOEFL required of all international applicants. High school diploma is required and GED is accepted. *Academic units required:* 4 English, 3 mathematics, 3 science, (2 science labs), 2 foreign language, 2 social studies, 2 history, 2 academic electives. *Academic units recommended:* 4 English, 4 mathematics, 4 science, (3 science labs), 4 foreign language, 4 social studies, 2 history, 3 academic electives.

Financial Aid

Students should submit: FAFSA, CSS/Financial Aid PROFILE, business/farm supplement. Prior year Federal tax return. Regular filing deadline is 5/1. The Princeton Review suggests that all financial aid forms be submitted as soon as possible after 1/1. *Need-based scholarships/grants offered:* Federal Pell, SEOG, state scholarships/grants, private scholarships, the school's own gift aid. *Loan aid offered:* FFEL Subsidized Stafford, FFEL Unsubsidized Stafford, FFEL PLUS, Federal Perkins, college/university loans from institutional funds. Applicants will be notified of awards on or about 3/1. Federal Work-Study Program available. Institutional employment available. Off-campus job opportunities are good.

The Inside Word

Susquehanna competes with a number of similar area schools for its student body, and as a result cannot afford to be as selective as it might like, thus creating an opportunity for high school underachievers to attend a challenging and prestigious school. Further improving the odds, Susquehanna does not require standardized test scores of applicants. Those who choose not to submit SAT/ACT scores must instead submit two graded writing samples.

THE SCHOOL SAYS "..."

From The Admissions Office

"Susquehanna University prepares its graduates to achieve, lead and serve in a diverse and interconnected world. Graduates consistently say their Susquehanna experiences give them a competitive edge over other recent graduates entering the workplace. Susquehanna's new central curriculum includes GO (Global Opportunities). This distinctive program allows every student to have a cross-cultural experience away from campus, either in the United States or abroad. A cross-cultural experience is designed to take students out of their everyday environment. It might include a traditional semester study-abroad program (GO Long), a short-term faculty/staff-led program (GO Short), a self-designed experience proposed and accepted in advance, or service in a cross-cultural setting."

"With more than 50 majors and minors, students find a fine balance of liberal arts and professional studies, and state-of-the-art facilities to support intellectual and personal growth. The Sigmund Weis School of Business is accredited by the Association to Advance Collegiate Schools of Business (AACSB). A new "green" science facility will open in the fall of 2010. As the largest academic building on campus, it will include 19 teaching and research labs, 30 prep and support spaces and a rooftop greenhouse."

"Susquehanna's success is demonstrated by its graduation rate—80 percent of its students graduate within four years, a rate cited among the top in the nation, and far above the national average. And 96 percent of Susquehanna's graduates have a job or are attending graduate school within six months of graduation."

SELECTIVITY

Admissions Rating	86
# of applicants	2,777
% of applicants accepted	73
% of acceptees attending	31
# accepting a place on wait list	195
% admitted from wait list	11
# of early decision applicants	173
% accepted early decision	83

FRESHMAN PROFILE

Range SAT Critical Reading	500–610
Range SAT Math	520–600
Range SAT Writing	500–610
Range ACT Composite	21–26
Minimum paper TOEFL	550
Minimum computer TOEFL	213
Minimum web-based TOEFL	81
Average HS GPA	3.22
% graduated top 10% of class	25
% graduated top 25% of class	60
% graduated top 50% of class	87

DEADLINES

Early Decision	
Deadline	11/15
Notification	12/1
Regular	
Priority	3/1
Deadline	3/1
Notification	rolling
Nonfall registration?	yes

APPLICANTS ALSO LOOK AT

AND OFTEN PREFER
Dickinson College
Gettysburg College
Lafayette College
Muhlenberg College
Franklin & Marshall College

AND SOMETIMES PREFER
University of Delaware
Ithaca College
Lehigh University

AND RARELY PREFER
Lebanon Valley College
Lycoming College

FINANCIAL FACTS

Financial Aid Rating	82
Annual tuition	$32,050
Room and board	$8,800
Required fees	$400
% frosh rec. need-based scholarship or grant aid	61
% UG rec. need-based scholarship or grant aid	58
% frosh rec. non-need-based scholarship or grant aid	9
% UG rec. non-need-based scholarship or grant aid	7
% frosh rec. need-based self-help aid	56
% UG rec. need-based self-help aid	54
% frosh rec. any financial aid	96.4
% UG rec. any financial aid	90.6

SWARTHMORE COLLEGE

500 COLLEGE AVENUE, SWARTHMORE, PA 19081 • ADMISSIONS: 610-328-8300 • FAX: 610-328-8580

CAMPUS LIFE
Quality of Life Rating	**89**
Fire Safety Rating	**89**
Green Rating	**83**
Type of school	private
Environment	town

STUDENTS
Total undergrad enrollment	1,477
% male/female	48/52
% from out of state	87
% from public high school	55
% live on campus	95
% in (# of) fraternities	5 (2)
% African American	9
% Asian	17
% Caucasian	44
% Hispanic	11
% Native American	1
% international	7
# of countries represented	35

SURVEY SAYS . . .
No one cheats
Lab facilities are great
School is well run
Low cost of living
Musical organizations are popular
Political activism is popular

ACADEMICS
Academic Rating	**99**
Calendar	semester
Student/faculty ratio	8:1
Profs interesting rating	97
Profs accessible rating	95
Most common reg class size	10–19 students
Most common lab size	fewer than 10 students

MOST POPULAR MAJORS
biology/biological sciences
economics
political science and government

STUDENTS SAY ". . ."

Academics

Swarthmore College "has a lovely campus, the people are almost unbelievably friendly, it's a safe environment, and it's really, really challenging academically," and "although it's not one of the most well-known schools, those who do know of it also know of its wonderful reputation. It's where to go for a real education—for learning for the sake of truly learning, rather than just for grades." Students warn that "academics here are definitely stressful, especially when you sign up for extracurricular activities that take up some more time—and almost everyone here's involved in something outside of just classes, because you don't want to just go to class, study, and sleep every day here." As a result, "Swarthmore is truly challenging. It teaches its students tough lessons not only about classes but about life, and though it may be extremely, almost unbearably difficult sometimes, it's totally worth it." Undergrads also note that "there are tons of resources to help you—professors, academic mentors, writing associates (who are really helpful to talk to when you have major papers), residential assistants, psychological counseling, multicultural support groups, queer/trans support groups—basically, whenever you need help with something, there's someone you can talk to." Swatties also love how "Swarthmore is amazingly flexible. The requirements are very limited, allowing you to explore whatever you are interested in and change your mind millions of times about your major and career path. If they don't offer a major you want, you can design your own with ease."

Life

The Swarthmore community is "a family of students who are engaged in academics, learning, politics, activism, and civic responsibility, with a work-hard, play-hard, intense mentality, who don't get enough sleep because they're too busy doing all they want to do in their time here, and who (this is kind of cheesy, but true) when you really think about it are really just smart students who care about the world and want to make it better." There "is a misconception that Swarthmore students do nothing but study, [but] while we certainly do a lot of it, we still find many ways to have fun." Not so much in hometown Swarthmore—"there isn't a lot to do right in the area"—but "with a train station on campus, Philly is very accessible." Additionally, "there are so many organizations and clubs on campus that you'd be pressed to find none of the activities interesting. Even then, you can start your own club, so that takes care of it." The small size of the school means that "opportunities to participate in many different programs" are usually available. On-campus activities "are varied, and there is almost always something to do on the weekend. There are student musical performances, drama performances, movies, speakers, and comedy shows," as well as "several parties every weekend, with and without alcohol, and a lot of pre-partying with friends." One student sums up, "While it is tough to generalize on the life of a Swarthmore student, one word definitely applies to us all: busy. All of us are either working on extracurriculars, studying, or fighting sleep to do more work."

Student Body

Students are "not sure if there is a typical Swattie" but suspect that "the defining feature among us is that each person is brilliant at something: maybe dance, maybe quantum physics, maybe philosophy. Each person here has at least one thing that [he or she does] extraordinarily well." A Swattie "is [typically] liberal, involved in some kind of activism group or multicultural group, talks about classes all the time, was labeled a nerd by people in high school, and is really smart—one of those people where you just have to wonder, how do they get all their homework done and manage their extracurriculars and still have time for parties?" The campus "is very diverse racially but not in terms of thought—in other words, pretty much everyone's liberal, you don't get many different points of view. Multicultural and queer issues are big here, but you don't have to be involved in that to enjoy Swarthmore. You just have to accept it."

FINANCIAL AID: 610-328-8358 • E-MAIL: ADMISSIONS@SWARTHMORE.EDU • WEBSITE: WWW.SWARTHMORE.EDU

THE PRINCETON REVIEW SAYS

Admissions

Very important factors considered include: Class rank, application essay, academic GPA, recommendation(s), rigor of secondary school record, character/personal qualities. *Important factors considered include:* Standardized test scores, extracurricular activities. *Other factors considered include:* Alumni/ae relation, first generation, geographical residence, interview, level of applicant's interest, racial/ethnic status, talent/ability, volunteer work, work experience. Either SAT and SAT Subject Tests or ACT or ACT with Writing component required. High school diploma or equivalent is not required.

Financial Aid

Students should submit: FAFSA, institution's own financial aid form, CSS/Financial Aid PROFILE, state aid form, noncustodial PROFILE, business/farm supplement. Federal Tax Return, W-2 Statements, Year-end paycheck stub. Regular filing deadline is 2/15. The Princeton Review suggests that all financial aid forms be submitted as soon as possible after 1/1. *Need-based scholarships/grants offered:* Federal Pell, SEOG, state scholarships/grants, private scholarships, the school's own gift aid. *Loan aid offered:* Swarthmore College financial aid awards are designed to meet a student's demonstrated financial need loan free; however, students and their families have access to Federal Stafford and PLUS loan programs should they wish to borrow to fund the student's education. Applicants will be notified of awards on or about 4/1. Federal Work-Study Program available. Institutional employment available. Off-campus job opportunities are good.

The Inside Word

Competition for admission to Swarthmore remains fierce, as the school consistently receives applications from top students across the country. Applicants should understand that Swarthmore receives more than enough applications from well-qualified students to fill its classrooms. At some point, perfectly good candidates get rejected simply because there's no more room. Admissions officers comb applications carefully for evidence of intellectually curious, highly motivated, and creative-minded candidates.

THE SCHOOL SAYS "..."

From The Admissions Office

"Swarthmore College, a highly selective college of liberal arts and engineering, celebrates the life of the mind. Since its founding in 1864, Swarthmore has given students of uncommon intellectual ability the knowledge, insight, skills, and experience to become leaders for the common good. The College is private, yet open to all regardless of financial need; American, yet decidedly global in outlook and diversity, drawing students from around the world and all 50 states. So much of what Swarthmore stands for, from its commitment to curricular breadth and rigor to its demonstrated interest in facilitating discovery and fostering ethical intelligence among exceptional young people, lies in the quality and passion of its faculty. A student/faculty ratio of 8:1 ensures that students have close, meaningful engagement with their professors, preparing them to translate the skills and understanding gained at Swarthmore into the mark they want to make on the world. The College's Honors program features small groups of dedicated and accomplished students working closely with faculty; an emphasis on independent learning; students entering into a dialogue with peers, teachers, and examiners; a demanding program of study in major and minor fields; and an examination at the end of two years' study by outside scholars. Located 11 miles southwest of Philadelphia, Swarthmore's idyllic, 357-acre campus is a designated arboretum, complete with rolling lawns, creek, wooded hills, and hiking trails."

SELECTIVITY

Admissions Rating	99
# of applicants	6,121
% of applicants accepted	16
% of acceptees attending	39
# of early decision applicants	480
% accepted early decision	34

FRESHMAN PROFILE

Range SAT Critical Reading	680–760
Range SAT Math	670–760
Range SAT Writing	660–760
Range ACT Composite	28–33
% graduated top 10% of class	86.5
% graduated top 25% of class	97.5
% graduated top 50% of class	100

DEADLINES

Early Decision	
Deadline	11/15
Notification	12/15
Regular	
Deadline	1/2
Notification	4/1
Nonfall registration?	no

FINANCIAL FACTS

Financial Aid Rating	99
Annual tuition	$36,154
Room and board	$11,314
Required fees	$336
Books and supplies	$1,110
% frosh rec. need-based scholarship or grant aid	49
% UG rec. need-based scholarship or grant aid	47
% frosh rec. need-based self-help aid	47
% UG rec. need-based self-help aid	46
% frosh rec. any financial aid	49
% UG rec. any financial aid	48
% UG borrow to pay for school	All Swarthmore aid awards are loan-free

SWEET BRIAR COLLEGE

PO Box B, Sweet Briar, VA 24595 • Admissions: 434-381-6142 • Fax: 434-381-6152

CAMPUS LIFE

Quality of Life Rating	**88**
Fire Safety Rating	**97**
Green Rating	**81**
Type of school	private
Environment	rural

STUDENTS

Total undergrad enrollment	647
% male/female	0/100
% from out of state	49
% from public high school	72
% live on campus	90
% African American	3
% Asian	1
% Caucasian	87
% Hispanic	3
% Native American	1
% international	1
# of countries represented	16

SURVEY SAYS . . .

No one cheats
Career services are great
School is well run
Students are friendly
Students get along with local
community
Dorms are like palaces
Campus feels safe
Students are happy
Student government is popular

ACADEMICS

Academic Rating	**99**
Calendar	semester
Student/faculty ratio	9:1
Profs interesting rating	99
Profs accessible rating	99
Most common	
reg class size	10–19 students
Most common	
lab size	fewer than 10 students

MOST POPULAR MAJORS

biology/biological sciences
business/commerce
psychology

STUDENTS SAY ". . ."

Academics

"A traditional all-girl's school providing exceptional educational opportunities on one of the most beautiful campuses in the nation," Sweet Briar is a tiny liberal arts college that "allows women to do it all; it provides a rigorous academic program as well as a flourishing co-curricular life" that includes "activities and leadership opportunities." A "prestigious riding program" attracts many who want to make equestrian pursuits a part of their academic experience. The small campus is another enticing feature, making it possible "to become involved in any and all aspects of campus life, whether it be academic, social, physical, or extracurricular" while also facilitating "the support of the professors." The faculty here "may not live up to the publishing powerhouses," explains one student, "but they are some of the best teachers with whom I have ever interacted. The small size of the school lends to a very close-knit community, even with the professors, deans, and president." Sweet Briar is strong in education, with a program that is enhanced by "an on-campus kindergarten and preschool, so students interested in being teachers can get teaching experience their first year." The small-school setting is not without its drawbacks; there are problems with course availability "The courses I would like to enroll in are not offered," says, one student, and limited funding means that the school still needs to "bring many of the buildings up to date and [to] work on getting the campus completely wireless." Students say those problems are worth enduring for the personal attention they receive. "From the administration to the professors, these professionals devote countless hours to being accessible to students, and [they allow] the school to run as an institution for its pupils."

Life

Life at Sweet Briar "is firmly established in traditions. This is one of the most attractive features of the college: The many traditions that build a strong sense of community, whether it be convocation, lantern bearing, step singing, or the many tap clubs active on campus." Socially, the campus "is fairly quiet most of the time. There are a couple of parties a week, but most of the partying (especially on the weekend) is done off campus" at schools like UVA and Hampden-Sydney. Students say "this is not a bad thing," as it allows them to "have our fun and not deal with the mess." The surrounding area is also quiet, because the school "is in a very rural area." Students stay busy during the week; "A lot of girls over-commit themselves to clubs and sports." The school's legendarily beautiful campus continues to live up to its reputation; one student writes, "This is my fourth year at Sweet Briar, and the campus still takes my breath away every morning when I wake up. It's exquisite."

Student Body

Writes one eloquent Sweet Briar student, "Many people stereotype the students at Sweet Briar College. Being a women's college in Southern Virginia allows some to believe us all to be Southern belles interested solely in getting an MRS. We're portrayed as those girls in pink with pearls and ribbons. This, however, could not be further from the truth." While there are some on campus who might fit that stereotype, they are "strongly overpowered" by those who don't. Besides being different from the assumed stereotype, students are also varied among themselves. One students says, "My friends and I, a group of our class leaders, are a random and eclectic group. Our one common trait is that each of us has a little bit of strangeness that we love about ourselves." Another student agrees, "In reality, we are diverse. Many of us do not wear pearls, and not all of us ride horses, but we all share an enthusiasm for our academics." The college works to bring many different types of people together, "and each person is respected for her own unique characteristics."

FINANCIAL AID: 434-381-6156 • E-MAIL: ADMISSIONS@SBC.EDU • WEBSITE: WWW.SBC.EDU

THE PRINCETON REVIEW SAYS

Admissions

Very important factors considered include: academic GPA, rigor of secondary school record. *Important factors considered include:* Application essay, recommendation(s), standardized test scores, interview. *Other factors considered include:* Class rank, alumni/ae relation, character/personal qualities, extracurricular activities, first generation, racial/ethnic status, talent/ability, volunteer work, work experience. SAT or ACT required; TOEFL required of all international applicants. High school diploma is required and GED is accepted. *Academic units required:* 4 English, 3 mathematics, 3 science, (2 science labs), 2 foreign language, 3 social studies, *Academic units recommended:* 4 English, 4 mathematics, 4 science, (3 science labs), 4 foreign language, 4 social studies.

Financial Aid

Students should submit: FAFSA, noncustodial PROFILE. The Princeton Review suggests that all financial aid forms be submitted as soon as possible after 1/1. *Need-based scholarships/grants offered:* Federal Pell, SEOG, state scholarships/grants, private scholarships, the school's own gift aid. *Loan aid offered:* Direct Subsidized Stafford, Direct Unsubsidized Stafford, Direct PLUS, Federal Perkins, college/university loans from institutional funds. Applicants will be notified of awards on or about 3/1. Federal Work-Study Program available. Institutional employment available. Off-campus job opportunities are fair.

The Inside Word

A tiny applicant pool allows Sweet Briar to consider each application closely. The school looks not only for evidence of academic achievement and ability but also for "fit" with the school. How well will you fit into/fill out the Sweet Briar community? How well can the school deliver quality academics in your areas of interest? (A school this small can't provide in-depth instruction in every discipline, after all.) These are the questions that will determine your admissions status as Sweet Briar, especially if your test scores and/or high school grades are borderline.

THE SCHOOL SAYS "..."

From The Admissions Office

"The woman who applies to Sweet Briar is mature and far-sighted enough to know what she wants from her college experience. She is intellectually adventuresome, more willing to explore new fields, and more open to challenging her boundaries. Sweet Briar attracts the ambitious, confident woman who enjoys being immersed not only in a first-rate academic program, but in a variety of meaningful activities outside the classroom. Our students take charge and revel in their accomplishments. This attitude follows graduates, enabling them to compete confidently in the corporate world and in graduate school.

"The faculty and staff do not simply give students individual attention; rather they pay attention to individuals. As an institution, we commit to every student, and our mission is to provide a learning community that prepares her to be successful in whatever she chooses to do after college."

SELECTIVITY	
Admissions Rating	87
# of applicants	629
% of applicants accepted	83
% of acceptees attending	38
# of early decision applicants	63
% accepted early decision	98

FRESHMAN PROFILE	
Range SAT Critical Reading	510–630
Range SAT Math	470–600
Range ACT Composite	20–26
Minimum paper TOEFL	550
Minimum computer TOEFL	213
Minimum web-based TOEFL	79
Average HS GPA	3.53
% graduated top 10% of class	28
% graduated top 25% of class	53
% graduated top 50% of class	88

DEADLINES	
Early Decision	
Deadline	12/1
Notification	12/15
Regular	
Priority	2/1
Deadline	2/1
Notification	3/15
Nonfall registration?	yes

**APPLICANTS ALSO LOOK AT
AND SOMETIMES PREFER**
University of Virginia
Agnes Scott College

FINANCIAL FACTS	
Financial Aid Rating	91
Annual tuition	$28,860
Room and board	$10,460
Required fees	$275
Books and supplies	$900
% frosh rec. need-based scholarship or grant aid	62
% UG rec. need-based scholarship or grant aid	53
% frosh rec. non-need-based scholarship or grant aid	33
% UG rec. non-need-based scholarship or grant aid	40
% frosh rec. need-based self-help aid	62
% UG rec. need-based self-help aid	53
% frosh rec. any financial aid	90
% UG rec. any financial aid	93
% UG borrow to pay for school	50
Average cumulative indebtedness	$20,118

SYRACUSE UNIVERSITY

100 CROSS-HINDS HALL, 900 SOUTH CROUSE AVE., SYRACUSE, NY 13244 • ADMISSIONS: 315-443-3611 • FAX: 315-443-4226

CAMPUS LIFE
Quality of Life Rating	**63**
Fire Safety Rating	**83**
Green Rating	**94**
Type of school	private
Environment	metropolis

STUDENTS
Total undergrad enrollment	13,105
% male/female	44/56
% from out of state	54
% from public high school	75
% live on campus	75
% in (# of) fraternities	NR (27)
% in (# of) sororities	NR (20)
% African American	7
% Asian	9
% Caucasian	59
% Hispanic	6
% Native American	1
% international	5
# of countries represented	119

SURVEY SAYS . . .
Everyone loves the Orange
Frats and sororities dominate social scene
Student publications are popular
Lots of beer drinking
Hard liquor is popular

ACADEMICS
Academic Rating	**82**
Calendar	semester
Student/faculty ratio	15:1
Profs interesting rating	70
Profs accessible rating	73
% classes taught by TAs	6
Most common reg class size	10–19 students
Most common lab size	20–29 students

MOST POPULAR MAJORS
business administration and management
commercial and advertising art
radio and television

STUDENTS SAY " . . ."

Academics

Syracuse University "is very strong academically" and boasts "some of the nation's top programs" in a broad range of disciplines. Students are especially bullish on the "prestigious" S. I. Newhouse School of Public Communications, which "has some amazing professors who have worked out in the field and are eager to share all of their experiences with their students," as well as the School of Architecture, "an energetic, sleepless journey of collaboration and individuality in an amazingly cool atmosphere." SU's programs in advertising, art, business, music, political science, engineering, and the life sciences also earn plaudits from undergraduates. Best of all, students say, SU delivers the benefits of "both large schools and small schools," which means it can offer the ability "to concentrate in an area while also taking a variety of other classes that do not have to be within your major or college," as well as plenty of research faculty who put "SU at the front of [the] material" and "professors who are always available to meet during office hours [or] by appointment." One undergrad sums it up: "SU is big enough to have a wealth of resources but small enough so that you always fit in." Another adds, "SU is about academics and preparing us as best as possible for our future careers, along with a little bit of men's basketball."

Life

Students tell us that "the social life at Syracuse is the epitome of the great American college experience. Local bars, frats, and house parties are all popular. Partying takes place from Thursday through Sunday, and close friendships are easily cultivated during the recovery period in between." However, it's important to note that "the school is great about providing other activities" as well. "You don't need to drink to find something fun to do at night or on weekends." "People climb trees on the quad, go rock climbing on the weekends, [and] take ballet classes. We're notorious for our frat parties, but, at the same time, the library is packed every Saturday night." "The student union also provides free movies on weekends, and there are loads of speakers, concerts, and cultural events throughout the week." Of course, SU sports "are huge"—"Syracuse Basketball is going to win the national championship!" Students are mixed on the city of Syracuse. Some tell us "It's pretty much dead" and "The weather sucks," while others aver that "upstate New York is a great location with lots of outdoor activities, unless you hate sub-Arctic climates."

Student Body

While SU undergrads report that a typical peer would be "fashionable," "wealthy," and "trend-driven," they also point out that "there are also tons of students who don't fit that description." Indeed there are upstate, out-of-state, and international students in addition to an abundance from Long Island and New Jersey. While the student body includes "a large frat/sorority presence," there's also a fair share of "neo-hippies." Although SU's student population appears homogenous to some, other students say "[This] seems to be proven wrong on many occasions. For example, the guy living next to me is from St. Thomas. I have friends from all over the world...All religions, sexual orientations, and ethnic groups are strongly represented."

FINANCIAL AID: 315-443-1513 • E-MAIL: ORANGE@SYR.EDU • WEBSITE: WWW.SYRACUSE.EDU

THE PRINCETON REVIEW SAYS

Admissions

Very important factors considered include: Class rank, application essay, academic GPA, recommendation(s), rigor of secondary school record, standardized test scores, character/personal qualities, level of applicant's interest. *Important factors considered include:* extracurricular activities, interview, talent/ability, volunteer work, work experience. *Other factors considered include:* alumni/ae relation, first generation, geographical residence, racial/ethnic status, state residency, SAT or ACT required; ACT with Writing component required. TOEFL required of all international applicants. High school diploma is required and GED is accepted. *Academic units required:* 4 English, 4 mathematics, 4 science, (4 science labs), 3 foreign language, 4 social studies.

Financial Aid

Students should submit: FAFSA, CSS/Financial Aid PROFILE, business/farm supplement. Regular filing deadline is 2/1. The Princeton Review suggests that all financial aid forms be submitted as soon as possible after 1/1. *Need-based scholarships/grants offered:* Federal Pell, SEOG, state scholarships/grants, private scholarships, the school's own gift aid. *Loan aid offered:* FFEL Subsidized Stafford, FFEL Unsubsidized Stafford, FFEL PLUS, Federal Perkins. Applicants will be notified of awards on or about 3/21. Federal Work-Study Program available. Institutional employment available. Off-campus job opportunities are good.

The Inside Word

Syracuse University is divided into 9 colleges, and applicants apply to the college in which they are interested. Some colleges make specific requirements of applicants (for example: a portfolio, an audition, or specific high school course work) in addition to SU's general admissions requirements. Applicants are allowed to indicate a second and third choice—you may still gain admission even if you don't get into your first-choice program.

THE SCHOOL SAYS " . . . "

From The Admissions Office

"Syracuse University provides a dynamic learning environment with a focus on scholarship in action, in which excellence is connected to ideas, problems, and professions in the world. Students at SU focus on interactive, collaborative, and interdisciplinary learning while choosing their course of study from more than 200 options. About half of undergraduates study abroad. SU operates centers in Beijing, Florence, Hong Kong, London, Madrid, Santiago, and Strasbourg. New facilities continue to expand scholarship in action opportunities for students. The Newhouse 3 building houses various facilities for public communications students, including research centers, a high-tech convergence lab, and meeting rooms for student activities. A $107 million Life Sciences Complex will promote interdisciplinary research and education, signaling a new era in scientific research.

"A distinction of the SU education is the breadth of opportunity combined with individualized attention. Average class size is less than 20 students. Only 3 percent of all classes have more than 100 students. Faculty members are experts in their field, who are dedicated to teaching while conducting research, writing, and experiments they can share with students to aid in the learning process.

"Outside of the classroom, students are encouraged to immerse themselves in organizations and take advantage of the opportunities available in the city of Syracuse. The University community collaborates with city residents, organizations, and businesses in such areas as the arts, entrepreneurship and economic development, and scientific research. The Connective Corridor, a 3 mile pedestrian pathway and shuttle bus circuit, links SU and downtown Syracuse's arts institutions, entertainment venues, and public spaces."

SELECTIVITY

Admissions Rating	92
# of applicants	22,079
% of applicants accepted	53
% of acceptees attending	27
# accepting a place on wait list	1,550
% admitted from wait list	33
# of early decision applicants	826
% accepted early decision	77

FRESHMAN PROFILE

Range SAT Critical Reading	520–620
Range SAT Math	550–650
Range SAT Writing	530–630
Range ACT Composite	23–28
Minimum paper TOEFL	550
Minimum computer TOEFL	213
Minimum web-based TOEFL	80
Average HS GPA	3.6
% graduated top 10% of class	38.6
% graduated top 25% of class	74.1
% graduated top 50% of class	96.5

DEADLINES

Early Decision	
Deadline	11/15
Notification	12/15
Regular	
Deadline	1/1
Notification	rolling
Nonfall registration?	yes

APPLICANTS ALSO LOOK AT AND SOMETIMES PREFER

University of Maryland—College Park
New York University
Cornell University
Boston University
Penn State—University Park

FINANCIAL FACTS

Financial Aid Rating	87
Annual tuition	$32,180
Room and board	$11,656
Required fees	$1,260
Books and supplies	$1,268
% frosh rec. need-based scholarship or grant aid	54
% UG rec. need-based scholarship or grant aid	52
% frosh rec. non-need-based scholarship or grant aid	3
% UG rec. non-need-based scholarship or grant aid	3
% frosh rec. need-based self-help aid	51
% UG rec. need-based self-help aid	51
% frosh rec. athletic scholarships	2
% UG rec. athletic scholarships	3
% frosh rec. any financial aid	79
% UG rec. any financial aid	80
% UG borrow to pay for school	64
Average cumulative indebtedness	$27,455

TEMPLE UNIVERSITY

1801 North Broad Street, Philadelphia, PA 19122-6096 • Admissions: 215-204-7200 • Fax: 215-204-5694

CAMPUS LIFE
Quality of Life Rating	**71**
Fire Safety Rating	**93**
Green Rating	**85**
Type of school	public
Environment	metropolis

STUDENTS
Total undergrad enrollment	25,598
% male/female	46/54
% from out of state	19
% from public high school	71.7
% live on campus	19
% in (# of) fraternities	1 (11)
% in (# of) sororities	1 (9)
% African American	17
% Asian	10
% Caucasian	58
% Hispanic	4
% international	3
# of countries represented	117

SURVEY SAYS . . .
Diverse student types on campus
Low cost of living
(Almost) no one smokes
Very little drug use

ACADEMICS
Academic Rating	**76**
Calendar	semester
Student/faculty ratio	18:1
Profs interesting rating	67
Profs accessible rating	68
Most common reg class size	20–29 students
Most common lab size	20–29 students

MOST POPULAR MAJORS
elementary education and teaching
marketing/marketing management
psychology

STUDENTS SAY ". . ."

Academics

Temple University is "a large school" that "makes you feel at home in the city of Philadelphia" and offers "rigorous academic classes and many outside activities." This "wonderful" school is "located right in the city," and students praise the campus as being "one of the most diverse in the country." "Temple University is a place where everyone fits in and walks away with a little more knowledge than they had the day before," says one undergrad. This diversity also extends to classes. There's a "wide variety of classes" and "lots of awesome majors," all of which are supported by a "helpful and passionate set of professors who learn right along with students." There's also the "top-notch" honors program, which is a "favorite part of Temple by far," explains one student. "It's an outstanding program, and I feel very fortunate to be a part of it." Most here agree their academic experience has been "amazing." In the words of one undergrad, "Temple's standard of access and excellence is evident in its students' success." The "knowledgeable" professors "really want to see students succeed." While some feel that the administration "doesn't always run so smoothly," noting that "Temple is pretty much a small city, and it often runs like a bureaucracy," overall, students agree that administrators are "accessible at any time" and are "helpful when you need them."

Life

As you'd expect from a big school in a big city, "Temple has something for everyone." Whether you're looking for "city life," "friendly people," or "a million and one clubs or groups to join," you'll find it here at Temple. "There are tons of things to do," says one student. "If students get bored on campus, they were probably boring to begin with." Life on campus is "very interconnected," and "there's usually always something going on" thanks to "student organizations that appeal to every interest and social group." Most students keep busy during by "studying," "going to the gym," and "playing intramural sports," but even if nothing is happening on campus, "there's much to do in the city." Not surprisingly, Philadelphia plays a substantial part in students' social lives. "There are amazing bars in the city," says one undergrad. "The only nights that students do not go out for drinks are Sunday and Monday." That said, if imbibing isn't your cup of tea, not to worry—there's plenty more on offer than watering holes. "You can have tons of fun on campus without drinking," explains a student. "There are lots of fun things to do because of our close proximity to Center City Philadelphia." Some examples are "great clubs, shopping, hookah bars, and restaurants." Also, if you get tired of Temple's campus you can always check out another—"Drexel, LaSalle, and UPenn's campuses are close by."

Student Body

Diversity isn't just a word at Temple; it's a fact. "At Temple, the atypical students are the typical students," explains an undergrad. "The majority population is made up of ethnic minorities." The student body here is made up of "many different kinds of ethnicities, sexual orientations, and economic and political stances," all of whom "contribute to the overall sense of school spirit and pride." Students agree that everyone here is "unique," and that makes for a place where "everyone becomes comfortable with each other's differences." "Every student brings their own light to Temple, which is what makes the school shine so bright," says one student. Despite this "huge mixture of types," students here do share similarities, particularly in their "motivation" to do well. Students here fill their time with "studying" and "extracurricular activities," all while also "experiencing life in the city of Philadelphia." One thing that all students agree on is that "The typical student at Temple University is approachable and greatly accepts diversity." As one undergrad says, "Everyone just kind of fits in, which is why the students like Temple so much."

FINANCIAL AID: 215-204-2244 • E-MAIL: TUADM@TEMPLE.EDU • WEBSITE: WWW.TEMPLE.EDU

THE PRINCETON REVIEW SAYS

Admissions

Very important factors considered include: academic GPA, rigor of secondary school record. *Important factors considered include:* Class rank, standardized test scores. *Other factors considered include:* Application essay, recommendation(s), alumni/ae relation, character/personal qualities, extracurricular activities, talent/ability, volunteer work, work experience. SAT or ACT required; ACT with Writing component required. TOEFL required of all international applicants. High school diploma is required and GED is accepted. *Academic units required:* 4 English, 3 mathematics, 2 science, (1 science labs), 2 foreign language, 2 social studies, 1 history, 1 academic electives, *Academic units recommended:* 4 English, 4 mathematics, 3 science, (2 science labs), 2 foreign language, 2 social studies, 2 history, 3 academic electives.

Financial Aid

Students should submit: FAFSA. The Princeton Review suggests that all financial aid forms be submitted as soon as possible after 1/1. *Need-based scholarships/grants offered:* Federal Pell, SEOG, state scholarships/grants, private scholarships, the school's own gift aid, Federal Nursing Scholarships. *Loan aid offered:* FFEL Subsidized Stafford, FFEL Unsubsidized Stafford, FFEL PLUS, Federal Perkins, Federal Nursing, state loans, college/university loans from institutional funds. Applicants will be notified of awards on a rolling basis beginning 2/15. Federal Work-Study Program available. Institutional employment available. Off-campus job opportunities are excellent.

The Inside Word

Temple is a well-recognized name in higher education, and its location is one of the nation's most popular cities only adds to this, meaning that competition can be steep when it comes to admissions, particularly if you aren't a resident of Pennsylvania. Admissions officers are fairly objective about their approach to application assessment in that they focus primarily on the solid numbers: class rank, GPA, and standardized test scores. That said, keep in mind that there are no minimum requirements, so if you have skills and talents that can't be mathematically calculated, it would behoove you to point them out in your application.

THE SCHOOL SAYS "..."

From The Admissions Office

"Temple combines the academic resources and intellectual stimulation of a large research university with the intimacy of a small college. The university experienced record growth in attracting new students from all 50 states and more than 125 countries: up 60 percent in 3 years. Students choose from 125 undergraduate majors. Special academic programs include honors, learning communities for first-year undergraduates, co-op education, and study abroad. Temple has 7 regional campuses, including Main Campus and the Health Sciences Center in historic Philadelphia, suburban Temple University, Ambler, and overseas campuses in Tokyo and Rome. Main Campus is home to the Tuttleman Learning Center, with 1,000 computer stations linked to Paley Library. Our TECH Center has more than 600 computer workstations, 100 laptops, and a Starbucks. The Liacouras Center is a state-of-the-art entertainment, recreation, and sports complex that hosts concerts, plays, trade shows, and college and professional athletics. It also includes the Independence Blue Cross Student Recreation Center, a major fitness facility for students now and in the future. Students can also take advantage of our Student Fieldhouse. The university has constructed two new dorms, built to meet an unprecedented demand for main campus housing.

"Applicants are required to take the new version of the SAT (or the ACT with Writing) and will be considered using the 2400 scale. The best Critical Reading, Math and Writing scores from either test will be considered."

SELECTIVITY

Admissions Rating	83
# of applicants	18,670
% of applicants accepted	61
% of acceptees attending	36
# accepting a place on wait list	500
% admitted from wait list	100

FRESHMAN PROFILE

Range SAT Critical Reading	500–600
Range SAT Math	510–610
Range SAT Writing	490–590
Range ACT Composite	21–26
Minimum paper TOEFL	550
Minimum computer TOEFL	213
Minimum web-based TOEFL	79
Average HS GPA	3.37
% graduated top 10% of class	20
% graduated top 25% of class	53
% graduated top 50% of class	91

DEADLINES

Regular	
Deadline	3/1
Notification	rolling
Nonfall registration?	yes

APPLICANTS ALSO LOOK AT

AND OFTEN PREFER
Rutgers, The State University of New Jersey—Newark Campus
West Chester University of Pennsylvania
Penn State—University Park

AND SOMETIMES PREFER
University of Maryland—College Park
Howard University
Syracuse University

AND RARELY PREFER
Holy Family University
Northeastern University

FINANCIAL FACTS

Financial Aid Rating	76
Annual in-state tuition	$10,858
Annual out-of-state tuition	$19,878
Room and board	$8,884
Required fees	$590
Books and supplies	$1,000
% frosh rec. need-based scholarship or grant aid	72
% UG rec. need-based scholarship or grant aid	63
% frosh rec. non-need-based scholarship or grant aid	45
% UG rec. non-need-based scholarship or grant aid	32
% frosh rec. need-based self-help aid	60
% UG rec. need-based self-help aid	55
% frosh rec. athletic scholarships	1
% UG rec. athletic scholarships	1
% frosh rec. any financial aid	72
% UG rec. any financial aid	63
% UG borrow to pay for school	72
Average cumulative indebtedness	$26,064

TEXAS A&M UNIVERSITY—COLLEGE STATION

ADMISSIONS COUNSELING, COLLEGE STATION, TX 77843-1265 • ADMISSIONS: 979-845-3741 • FAX: 979-847-8737

CAMPUS LIFE
Quality of Life Rating	**92**
Fire Safety Rating	**60***
Green Rating	**86**
Type of school	public
Environment	city

STUDENTS
Total undergrad enrollment	38,341
% male/female	52/48
% from out of state	3
% live on campus	24
% in (# of) fraternities	5 (33)
% in (# of) sororities	12 (23)
% African American	3
% Asian	5
% Caucasian	77
% Hispanic	14
% Native American	1
% international	1
# of countries represented	125

SURVEY SAYS . . .
Athletic facilities are great
Students are friendly
Everyone loves the Aggies
Student publications are popular

ACADEMICS
Academic Rating	**73**
Calendar	semester
Student/faculty ratio	19:1
Profs interesting rating	71
Profs accessible rating	78
% classes taught by TAs	25
Most common reg class size	20–29 students
Most common lab size	20–29 students

MOST POPULAR MAJORS
biological and physical sciences
multi-/interdisciplinary studies
operations management and
supervision

STUDENTS SAY ". . ."

Academics
"The excellence of a great research university filled with many traditions and the warm hospitality of a safe, small town" are the hallmarks of a Texas A&M education. United by the school's hallowed traditions, undergrads at this agriculture and engineering powerhouse "are the most fiercely loyal people to the school and other Aggies," and they can't stop bragging about how great their academic and extracurricular lives are. One student writes, "During the college search, I always heard about colleges looking for 'the well-rounded student.' Texas A&M's strength is being a 'well-rounded university,'" particularly for those interested in veterinary science, agricultural science, construction and engineering, business, and life sciences. Most departments hold students to "very high standards." As one student puts it, "At Texas A&M University, students generally get what they give. An A is well earned, [and] an F is deserved." Another adds, "Classes are extremely hard, but the Aggie ring is worth more this way." That ring provides access to "the Aggie network," alumni of A&M who "help make a lot of things possible," especially "finding a job. I've heard stories of some people getting hired at the sight of their Aggie ring." With A&M "taking many steps, especially in the past few years, to really make A&M an even stronger university and research institution"—including "hiring a lot of new faculty" and "construction of new facilities on campus"—there are now more reasons than ever to love being an Aggie. How great is it? Ultimately you have to find out for yourself, because "From the outside looking in, you can't understand it, and from the inside looking out, you can't explain it!"

Life
A&M "is rich in tradition such as the Twelfth Man, Muster, Silvertaps, Reveille, 'Howdy,' the Corps of Cadets, Elephant Walk, and Maroon Out, just to name a few." If you're already familiar with these terms, you probably know how deeply they permeate campus life. Others should check out the school's website to learn more about them; how you feel about the traditions will strongly impact how much you enjoy life at A&M. Aggies tend to be enthusiastic about sports, both attending games and participating in club, intramural, and pick-up games. Although social activities are bound to be extremely diverse at a campus this large, many students here tell us that Northgate, a "row of bars and restaurants off the north side of campus," is the place to go; live music ("Texas country music is real big at A&M"), drinks, and dancing are all on the menu. Hometown College Station "is a small city, so there aren't many activities available off campus, but the city is at the crossroads to the three major areas in Texas: Houston, Dallas–Fort Worth, and the Austin–San Antonio area. Weekend trips to these areas are fairly common."

Student Body
While "It is true that there is a very large Caucasian population at TAMU," there are also "large numbers of Middle Eastern, Asian, and Hispanic students" as well, providing a good deal of diversity on campus. It's Texas, and it's not Austin, so it should come as no surprise that A&M students tend to be politically conservative. Some point out that "conservative students are probably the most vocal, making it appear our school is more conservative [than it is]. From my experience, most students place themselves in the middle of left and right, making informed decisions when it comes to politics." Many here "are involved in student organizations and have a good social life as well." About 5 percent of the student body participates in the Corps of Cadets, "a senior military academy within the university." One cadet tells us that he and his peers "are the most visible people on campus and live with a structured military lifestyle."

FINANCIAL AID: 979-845-3236 • E-MAIL: ADMISSIONS@TAMU.EDU • WEBSITE: WWW.TAMU.EDU

THE PRINCETON REVIEW SAYS

Admissions

Very important factors considered include: Class rank, academic GPA, rigor of secondary school record, standardized test scores, extracurricular activities, talent/ability. *Important factors considered include:* Application essay, first generation, geographical residence, state residency, volunteer work, work experience. *Other factors considered include:* recommendation(s), character/personal qualities, SAT or ACT required; ACT with Writing component required. TOEFL required of all international applicants. High school diploma is required and GED is accepted. *Academic units required:* 4 English, 3 mathematics, 3 science, (2 science labs), 2 foreign language, 2 social studies, 1 history. *Academic units recommended:* 4 English, 3 mathematics, 3 science, (2 science labs), 2 foreign language, 2 social studies, 1 history, 1 computer course.

Financial Aid

Students should submit: FAFSA, institution's own financial aid formFinancial Aid Transcripts (for transfer students). The Princeton Review suggests that all financial aid forms be submitted as soon as possible after 1/1. *Need-based scholarships/grants offered:* Federal Pell, SEOG, state scholarships/grants, private scholarships, the school's own gift aid. *Loan aid offered:* FFEL Subsidized Stafford, FFEL Unsubsidized Stafford, FFEL PLUS, Federal Perkins, state loans, college/university loans from institutional funds. Applicants will be notified of awards on a rolling basis beginning 4/1. Federal Work-Study Program available. Institutional employment available. Off-campus job opportunities are excellent.

The Inside Word

Texas A&M uses some cut-and-dried admissions criteria: Students graduating in the top 10 percent of a recognized public or private high school in the state of Texas are automatically in; all they have to do is get their applications in on time. Applicants in the top quarter of their graduating class who have a combined SAT Math/Critical Reading score of 1300 (minimum score of 600 in each component) are also automatically in, as are such students who earn a composite ACT score of 30 (minimum 27 on the Math and English sections). All other applications are deemed "Review Admits" to be sorted through by the admissions committee.

THE SCHOOL SAYS "..."

From The Admissions Office

"Established in 1876 as the first public college in the state, Texas A&M University has become a world leader in teaching, research, and public service. Located in College Station in the heart of Texas, it is centrally situated among three of the country's 10 largest cities: Dallas, Houston, and San Antonio. Texas A&M is ranked nationally in these four areas: enrollment, enrollment of top students, value of research, and endowment.

"Freshman applicants are required to take the SAT or the ACT. We will use the applicant's best single testing date score in decision-making."

SELECTIVITY

Admissions Rating	90
# of applicants	20,887
% of applicants accepted	70
% of acceptees attending	55
# accepting a place on wait list	357
% admitted from wait list	73

FRESHMAN PROFILE

Range SAT Critical Reading	520–630
Range SAT Math	560–670
Range SAT Writing	500–610
Range ACT Composite	23–29
Minimum paper TOEFL	550
% graduated top 10% of class	54
% graduated top 25% of class	86
% graduated top 50% of class	99

DEADLINES

Regular	
Deadline	2/1
Notification	rolling
Nonfall registration?	yes

APPLICANTS ALSO LOOK AT AND SOMETIMES PREFER

The University of Texas at Austin

FINANCIAL FACTS

Financial Aid Rating	85
Annual in-state tuition	$4,898
Annual out-of-state tuition	$19,238
Room and board	$8,000
Required fees	$2,946
Books and supplies	$1,200
% frosh rec. need-based scholarship or grant aid	34
% UG rec. need-based scholarship or grant aid	30
% frosh rec. non-need-based scholarship or grant aid	5
% UG rec. non-need-based scholarship or grant aid	3
% frosh rec. need-based self-help aid	20
% UG rec. need-based self-help aid	25
% frosh rec. athletic scholarships	1
% UG rec. athletic scholarships	1
% frosh rec. any financial aid	68.1
% UG rec. any financial aid	61.3
% UG borrow to pay for school	53.7
Average cumulative indebtedness	$19,940

TEXAS CHRISTIAN UNIVERSITY

OFFICE OF ADMISSIONS, TCU BOX 297013, FORT WORTH, TX 76129 • ADMISSIONS: 817-257-7490 • FAX: 817-257-7268

CAMPUS LIFE

Quality of Life Rating	**86**
Fire Safety Rating	**91**
Green Rating	**83**
Type of school	private
Affiliation	Disciples of Christ
Environment	metropolis

STUDENTS

Total undergrad enrollment	7,369
% male/female	41/59
% from out of state	20
% from public high school	72
% live on campus	45
% in (# of) fraternities	37 (13)
% in (# of) sororities	39 (16)
% African American	5
% Asian	3
% Caucasian	75
% Hispanic	8
% international	5
# of countries represented	86

SURVEY SAYS . . .

Athletic facilities are great
Students love Fort Worth, TX
Frats and sororities dominate social scene

ACADEMICS

Academic Rating	**79**
Calendar	semester
Student/faculty ratio	15:1
Profs interesting rating	84
Profs accessible rating	84
% classes taught by TAs	2
Most common	
reg class size	10–19 students
Most common	
lab size	20–29 students

MOST POPULAR MAJORS
biology/biological sciences
business administration and management

STUDENTS SAY ". . ."

Academics

The popular conception of Texas is that everything there is big, big, big, but Texas Christian University is one Lone Star institution that bucks this trend, insisting on "smaller classroom sizes" that allows professors to be "very interested in [students] personally." One undergrad explains: "If I have a problem and need to talk with the profs, they go out of their way to meet with me, especially when it comes to career options and what my best options are in terms of what I want to do. They are very helpful." While "there are some programs with more students than others, overall the academic experience at TCU is very personal and rewarding. Many students are easily able to latch onto a professor's lab research…Getting involved in the academic programs at TCU will really pay off." Students enjoy a strong support network; the school "offers many resources such as the library, writing center, career center, student support services, and other educational and personal resources," and alumni "are really involved and give a lot back to the school." Business, education, and physical therapy are among the standout offerings here. Access to the Dallas-Fort Worth business community means plenty of good internship and networking opportunities.

Life

"Greek life is one of the most popular activities" at TCU; some say "the Greeks rule the social scene at the school," while others see slightly more diverse options. The school "puts a lot of its money to good use, such as new residence halls, a nice recreational facility, funding for numerous clubs and organizations, and great activities to bring the campus community together," creating "a focus on the student community" that extends beyond the Greek houses. TCU football is another pillar of campus life, and students "have a lot of pride" in both the program and the school itself. Beyond these choices, life at TCU "is what you make it. If you want to make grades your top priority, it's very easy to do so. If you want to go out and party a lot, it's very easy to do [that] as well. Lots of people drink on campus, but not everyone makes that their life. It's all about what your priorities are because it is easy to go either way." Off-campus opportunities are plentiful thanks to access to Dallas-Fort Worth, a major metropolis.

Student Body

"The student body is very Greek" at TCU. Students differ on how this impacts social dynamics; some insist that "if you aren't in a fraternity or sorority, it is very hard to fit in," while others point out that "there are other types of people on campus", and "if you are open-minded and have a good personality overall you won't find it hard to make friends inside and outside of Greek life and find yourself belonging at TCU." While "the student population is mostly made up of Caucasian students," there is "a growing minority student population," the largest segment of which is Latina. Undergrads tend to be "middle- to upper-class…in good physical shape, and like to have a good time." Many, "but not all, dress extremely well…First impressions mean a lot here, so do not mess up." Some complain about the pervasive materialism, but others think the issue is overblown; one tells us, "Some may find the money an issue, but that's only because they make it an issue. I've never been ashamed that I can't buy the latest Prada handbag, and no one has ever looked down on me because of that. If you don't bring it up, nobody cares. A lack of character may make these people feel left out."

TEXAS CHRISTIAN UNIVERSITY

FINANCIAL AID: 817-257-7858 • E-MAIL: FROGMAIL@TCU.EDU • WEBSITE: WWW.TCU.EDU

THE PRINCETON REVIEW SAYS

Admissions

Very important factors considered include: Class rank, application essay, academic GPA, recommendation(s), rigor of secondary school record, standardized test scores, character/personal qualities. *Important factors considered include:* extracurricular activities, first generation, geographical residence, level of applicant's interest, racial/ethnic status, religious affiliation/commitment, talent/ability, volunteer work, work experience. *Other factors considered include:* alumni/ae relation, interview, SAT or ACT required; ACT with Writing component recommended. TOEFL required of all international applicants. High school diploma is required and GED is not accepted. *Academic units required:* 4 English, 3 mathematics, 3 science, 2 foreign language, 3 social studies, 2 academic electives. *Academic units recommended:* 4 English, 4 mathematics, 4 science, 4 foreign language, 4 social studies, 4 academic electives.

Financial Aid

Students should submit: FAFSA Regular filing deadline is 5/1. The Princeton Review suggests that all financial aid forms be submitted as soon as possible after 1/1. *Need-based scholarships/grants offered:* Federal Pell, SEOG, state scholarships/grants, private scholarships, the school's own gift aid. *Loan aid offered:* FFEL Subsidized Stafford, FFEL Unsubsidized Stafford, FFEL PLUS, Federal Perkins, Federal Nursing, state loans. Applicants will be notified of awards on a rolling basis beginning 3/15. Federal Work-Study Program available. Institutional employment available. Off-campus job opportunities are good.

The Inside Word

The sheer volume of applications sent to TCU—the school receives about 12,000 each year—requires the school to apply some baseline criteria for winnowing out unlikely candidates. That said, the school works hard to consider applications holistically and to find mitigating evidence to offset subpar performance in any one category (e.g. standardized test scores).

THE SCHOOL SAYS "..."

From The Admissions Office

"TCU is a major teaching and research university with the feel of a small college. The TCU academic experience includes small classes with top faculty; cutting-edge technology; a liberal arts and sciences core curriculum; and real-life application though faculty-directed research, group projects, and internships. While TCU faculty members are recognized for research, their main focus is on teaching and mentoring students. The friendly campus community welcomes new students at Frog Camp before classes begin, where students find three days of fun meeting new friends, learning campus traditions, and serving the community. Campus life includes 200 clubs and organizations, a spirited NCAA Division I athletics program, and numerous productions from professional schools of the arts. More than half of the students participate in a wide array of intramural sports, and about 35 percent are involved in Greek organizations, including ones emphasizing ethnic diversity as well as the Christian faith. The historic relationship to the Christian Church (Disciples of Christ) means that instead of teaching a particular viewpoint, TCU encourages students to consider and follow their own beliefs. The university's mission—to educate individuals to think and act as ethical leaders and responsible citizens in a global community—influences everything from course work to study abroad to the way Horned Frogs act and interact. From National Merit Scholars to those just now realizing their academic potential, TCU attracts and serves students who are learning to change the world.

"TCU will accept either the SAT or the ACT (with or without the Writing component) in admission and scholarship processes. The Writing sections will be considered alongside the TCU application essay."

SELECTIVITY
Admissions Rating	86
# of applicants	12,212
% of applicants accepted	50
% of acceptees attending	26
# accepting a place on wait list	304
% admitted from wait list	90

FRESHMAN PROFILE
Range SAT Critical Reading	520–630
Range SAT Math	540–640
Range SAT Writing	530–640
Range ACT Composite	23–28
Minimum paper TOEFL	550
Minimum computer TOEFL	213
Minimum web-based TOEFL	80
% graduated top 10% of class	32
% graduated top 25% of class	63
% graduated top 50% of class	92

DEADLINES
Early action	
Deadline	11/1
Notification	1/1
Regular	
Priority	11/1
Deadline	2/15
Notification	4/1
Nonfall registration?	yes

FINANCIAL FACTS
Financial Aid Rating	76
Annual tuition	$28,250
Room and board	$9,800
Required fees	$48
Books and supplies	$880
% frosh rec. need-based scholarship or grant aid	33
% UG rec. need-based scholarship or grant aid	36
% frosh rec. non-need-based scholarship or grant aid	6
% UG rec. non-need-based scholarship or grant aid	5
% frosh rec. need-based self-help aid	25
% UG rec. need-based self-help aid	29
% frosh rec. athletic scholarships	4
% UG rec. athletic scholarships	4
% frosh rec. any financial aid	75
% UG rec. any financial aid	72
% UG borrow to pay for school	59
Average cumulative indebtedness	$26,503

THOMAS AQUINAS COLLEGE

10000 NORTH OJAI ROAD, SANTA PAULA, CA 93060 • ADMISSION: 800-634-9797 • FAX: 805-525-9342

CAMPUS LIFE
Quality of Life Rating	94
Fire Safety Rating	88
Green Rating	61
Type of school	private
Affiliation	Roman Catholic
Environment	rural

STUDENTS
Total undergrad enrollment	340
% male/female	48/52
% from out of state	65
% from public high school	16
% live on campus	99
% Asian	3
% Caucasian	76
% Hispanic	6
% Native American	1
% international	7
# of countries represented	7

SURVEY SAYS . . .
Lots of conservative students
Class discussions encouraged
No one cheats
Students are very religious
Dorms are like palaces
Low cost of living
Intercollegiate sports are unpopular
or nonexistent
Frats and sororities are unpopular or
nonexistent
Very little drug use

ACADEMICS
Academic Rating	99
Calendar	semester
Student/faculty ratio	11:1
Profs interesting rating	98
Profs accessible rating	92
Most common	
reg class size	10–19 students

MOST POPULAR MAJORS
business administration and
management
communication studies/speech
communication and rhetoric
English/language arts teacher
education

STUDENTS SAY ". . ."

Academics

Thomas Aquinas College is a "Great Books" school, which means it is a place where students all follow an identical curriculum that requires "reading the original works of some of the greatest thinkers in history" including, of course, Thomas Aquinas. The goal here is "to discover the truth by studying the greatest minds of Western thought," and students agree that this approach "far outstrips most others because eternal truth is the end goal, not just some credentials for a job later. Not accidentally, this does actually produce more capable, honest, and self-giving individuals." Undergrads here appreciate "the integration of the curriculum" and are "amazed at the way it all fits together....That it is one integrated program followed by all greatly contributes to the unity" of the TAC community. Of course, any program, no matter how well designed, is only as good as those who execute it; fortunately, at TAC "the academic experience is amazing....This journey, when it is not self-inspiring, receives infallible impetus from all the professors at the school, who are inspiring models of inquiry, wonder, and disciplined understanding." Teachers, called tutors here, "are incredibly well-rounded people." As one student sums up the TAC approach, the program is all about "teaching students that reason can help them enlighten and hone their faith and that they don't have to be afraid to encounter the big philosophical questions as a Catholic, because their worldview is well thought-out enough to take on even the biggest challengers."

Life

Life at TAC "centers around the curriculum....Consequently, we are always talking about the ideas in those books, and even more everyday conversations are influenced by what we read. Some of the more weighty discussions are, for example: Is Newtonian physics legitimate in the light of Aristotelian physics and metaphysics? Does Kant really prove that you can't prove that God exists? Is a line made up of points? Does God predestine people to Hell? What is the order of charity? What is law? And there are many others." Though "this may not sound like fun" to some, students agree that "when conversations like these are placed in the context of a wonderful social and spiritual life and a myriad of activities, whether sports or the performing arts or volunteer work in the local community, the potential for true growth and true betterment of self and others is huge, and this is what we actually experience." It's thanks to this perspective that many here thrive "in an atmosphere of selflessness and progress in grace and understanding." Some here bristle at the administration's "strongly enforced" rules, and others find it "annoying that we're so far from town," but most accept these strictures as an acceptable cost of a TAC education.

Student Body

The typical student at Thomas Aquinas College, according to one among their ranks, "is a devout Catholic, solidly Aristotelian in philosophy and Thomistic in theology, perhaps even to the point of automatically assuming everything they say (except when Aristotle contradicts Thomas Aquinas!)....A large number could be said, perhaps, to have their views shaped primarily by the Republican platform." He or she "studies a lot, because if you want to stay you've got to study hard since we take at least 18 credits per semester, and you can't drop any classes." In addition, "The typical student also believes in what he/she is doing, because if you don't, why do all that work?" Home schoolers are well represented here. Students tell us that those uncomfortable with the restrictive rules and "with the extreme geographical isolation...end up withdrawing from the program."

FINANCIAL AID: 800-634-9797 • E-MAIL: ADMISSIONS@THOMASAQUINAS.EDU • WEBSITE: WWW.THOMASAQUINAS.EDU

THE PRINCETON REVIEW SAYS

Admissions

Very important factors considered include: Application essay, recommendation(s), rigor of secondary school record, standardized test scores, character/personal qualities, level of applicant's interest. *Important factors considered include:* Academic GPA. *Other factors considered include:* Class rank, extracurricular activities, interview, religious affiliation/commitment, talent/ability, volunteer work, work experience. SAT or ACT required; TOEFL required of all international applicants. High school diploma is required and GED is accepted. *Academic units required:* 4 English, 3 mathematics, 2 science, 2 foreign language, 2 history. *Academic units recommended:* 4 English, 4 mathematics, 3 science, (2 science labs), 2 history, 3 academic electives.

Financial Aid

Students should submit: FAFSA, institution's own financial aid form, state aid formTax return, Noncustodial Parent Statement. Regular filing deadline is 3/2. The Princeton Review suggests that all financial aid forms be submitted as soon as possible after 1/1. *Need-based scholarships/grants offered:* Federal Pell, state scholarships/grants, private scholarships, the school's own gift aid. *Loan aid offered:* FFEL Subsidized Stafford, FFEL Unsubsidized Stafford, FFEL PLUS, college/university loans from institutional funds, Canadian student Loans. Applicants will be notified of awards on a rolling basis beginning 1/1. Off-campus job opportunities are fair.

The Inside Word

Thomas Aquinas admits applicants on a rolling basis. Apply early to improve your chances. Because of the school's unique curriculum, candidates must demonstrate a penchant for scholarship and a love of learning for its own sake. Students will get a chance to demonstrate both in four admission essays (successful candidates' essays typically run 7 to 10 pages in length, according to the school). The Great Books summer program for high school juniors offers a great way to get to know the college from the inside.

THE SCHOOL SAYS "..."

From The Admissions Office

"Thomas Aquinas College holds with confidence that the human mind is capable of knowing the truth about reality, that living according to the truth is necessary for human happiness, and that truth is best comprehended through the harmonious work of faith and reason. The intellectual virtues are understood to be essential, and the college considers the cultivation of those virtues the primary work of Catholic liberal education.

"The academic program designed to achieve this goal is comprehensive and unified—and it includes no textbooks or lecture classes. In every subject—from philosophy, theology, mathematics, and science to language, music, literature, and history—students read the greatest written works in those disciplines, both ancient and modern: Homer, Plato, Aristotle, Augustine, Aquinas, Newton, Maxwell, Einstein, the Founding Fathers of the American Republic, Shakespeare, and T. S. Eliot, to name just a few. Instead of attending lecture classes, students gather in small tutorials, seminars, and laboratories for Socratic-style discussions.

"One mark of the program's success is the variety of professions and careers that graduates enter. Many attend graduate and professional schools in a wide array of disciplines; among them, philosophy, theology, law, literature, and the sciences are most often chosen.

"SAT or ACT scores are required, and the Writing component on each test is encouraged. However, scores in Critical Reading and Math (SAT), or English and Mathematics (ACT) are more central in the consideration of that aspect of a student's application."

SELECTIVITY

Admissions Rating	98
# of applicants	232
% of applicants accepted	64
% of acceptees attending	68
# accepting a place on wait list	63
% admitted from wait list	40

FRESHMAN PROFILE

Range SAT Critical Reading	600–720
Range SAT Math	550–640
Range SAT Writing	600–680
Range ACT Composite	26–28
Minimum paper TOEFL	570
Minimum computer TOEFL	230
Average HS GPA	3.67
% graduated top 10% of class	75
% graduated top 25% of class	75
% graduated top 50% of class	100

DEADLINES

Regular	
Notification	rolling
Nonfall registration?	no

APPLICANTS ALSO LOOK AT AND SOMETIMES PREFER

Thomas More College of Liberal Arts
University of Dallas
Franciscan University of Steubenville
University of Notre Dame
The Catholic University of America
Benedictine College
Christendom College

FINANCIAL FACTS

Financial Aid Rating	99
Annual tuition	$22,400
Room and board	$7,400
Books and supplies	$450
% frosh rec. need-based scholarship or grant aid	56
% UG rec. need-based scholarship or grant aid	59
% frosh rec. non-need-based scholarship or grant aid	2
% UG rec. non-need-based scholarship or grant aid	1
% frosh rec. need-based self-help aid	67
% UG rec. need-based self-help aid	68
% frosh rec. any financial aid	70
% UG rec. any financial aid	75
% UG borrow to pay for school	71
Average cumulative indebtedness	$14,000

TRANSYLVANIA UNIVERSITY

300 NORTH BROADWAY, LEXINGTON, KY 40508-1797 • ADMISSIONS: 859-233-8242 • FAX: 859-233-8797

CAMPUS LIFE

Quality of Life Rating	**86**
Fire Safety Rating	**84**
Green Rating	**73**
Type of school	private
Affiliation	Christian
(Nondenominational)	
Environment	city

STUDENTS

Total undergrad enrollment	1,158
% male/female	40/60
% from out of state	18
% from public high school	79
% live on campus	75
% in (# of) fraternities	50 (4)
% in (# of) sororities	50 (4)
% African American	3
% Asian	2
% Caucasian	83
% Hispanic	1
# of countries represented	3

SURVEY SAYS . . .
No one cheats
Athletic facilities are great
Students love Lexington, KY
Great off-campus food
Frats and sororities dominate social scene

ACADEMICS

Academic Rating	**92**
Calendar	4/1/4
Student/faculty ratio	12.6:1
Profs interesting rating	93
Profs accessible rating	91
Most common reg class size	10–19 students
Most common lab size	10–19 students

MOST POPULAR MAJORS
biology/biological sciences
business/commerce
psychology

STUDENTS SAY " . . ."

Academics

Transylvania University "in the middle of" Lexington, is a small and "very challenging" bastion of the liberal arts and sciences with a "strong pre-med program," "a remarkable pre-law program," and a broad core curriculum. "You take a variety of courses even though you might not be interested in them," and "writing is an integral part of the academic experience." "Even business, science, and math students must take writing-intensive classes." "The academic standards here are high." Dedication is "required if you want to excel," and studying is definitely a must. "Basically, I spend a lot of time in the library," reports a biochemistry major. "This school is very time-consuming." Classes are very small, though, "which makes it very easy to work with the professors and develop a relationship with them." The "quirky" faculty is "by far the best aspect of the school." They "are really concerned about helping you learn" and are "great to just sit down and talk with during their office hours." The conservative administration "tends to micromanage," but it's accessible as well. "If you have a complaint, going straight to the top will probably get you somewhere." Still, "they can make you jump through way too many hoops," and getting the classes you want can be a major hassle. "We are still in the middle ages when it comes to registration," gripes a French major.

Life

The campus here is "wonderfully historic" and "beautiful," but "some of the buildings are getting a little run down." "Food services are usually hit or miss." "The Internet is really, really bad. A lot of people complain about the speed and the restrictions on file sharing." "The dorms are popular," and most everyone lives on campus. "Once you're inside the Transy bubble, it's very hard to get out." "Students are often completely absorbed by this community." "The small college atmosphere allows students to participate in many arenas," relates a sophomore. "At many schools, a math major would never be able to sing in the choir, work on the school newspaper, and be a resident assistant." However, the most prominent aspect of Transylvania's social life is the "overwhelming" Greek system. "Everything that happens on campus has some sort of affiliation with sororities or fraternities." "New students almost feel pressured into joining," and if you don't pledge, "it's generally up to you to make your own fun." "Not every student can handle going to school in this environment," cautions a junior, but "others absolutely flourish in it." "Loud" parties are popular, and a strong contingent of students gets "rowdy" on the weekends. "Alcohol laws are lenient." "We are a wet campus," explains a senior, "so, if you are 21, it is legal to have a small amount of alcohol in your room." "People respect you if you say you don't drink but, at the same time, you feel left out if you don't." The "medium-sized city" of Lexington also offers a decent number of options. The downtown area is within "walking distance." The proximity of the University of Kentucky is another plus. "We have access to their library and social scene," notes a sophomore.

Student Body

"Upper-middle-class white suburbanites" constitute the vast majority of the student body. "There are a few odd students who just don't fit in" but "most students have similar backgrounds and get along with each other rather well." "You have your occasional jock and the occasional guy who looks like he just walked out of the country club." However, the typical student here is reportedly "a nerd deep down and was probably called that in high school." Virtually everyone takes academics pretty seriously. Politically, "there is quite a divide between those who are conservative and those who are liberal." Transylvania students also divide themselves by their frats and sororities. Students "have a very strong tendency to associate mostly with members of their Greek chapters." There's still quite a bit of intermingling, though. "It's just too small to be exclusive."

FINANCIAL AID: 859-233-8239 • E-MAIL: ADMISSIONS@TRANSY.EDU • WEBSITE: WWW.TRANSY.EDU

THE PRINCETON REVIEW SAYS

Admissions

Very important factors considered include: academic GPA, rigor of secondary school record, standardized test scores, *Important factors considered include:* Application essay, recommendation(s), extracurricular activities. *Other factors considered include:* Class rank, alumni/ae relation, character/personal qualities, first generation, geographical residence, interview, talent/ability, volunteer work, work experience. SAT or ACT required; TOEFL required of all international applicants. High school diploma is required and GED is accepted. *Academic units required:* 4 English, 3 mathematics, 3 science, 2 social studies. *Academic units recommended:* 4 English, 4 mathematics, 4 science, (2 science labs), 2 foreign language, 2 social studies, 1 history, 1 academic electives.

Financial Aid

Students should submit: FAFSA. The Princeton Review suggests that all financial aid forms be submitted as soon as possible after 1/1. *Need-based scholarships/grants offered:* Federal Pell, SEOG, state scholarships/grants, private scholarships, the school's own gift aid. *Loan aid offered:* FFEL Subsidized Stafford, FFEL Unsubsidized Stafford, FFEL PLUS, Federal Perkins, college/university loans from institutional funds. Applicants will be notified of awards on a rolling basis beginning 3/15. Federal Work-Study Program available. Institutional employment available. Off-campus job opportunities are excellent.

Inside Word

Applicants who become successful students at TU have the wherewithal to rise to challenging academic demands and the discipline to do so in an ethical fashion. If you're looking for a place to disappear into an ocean of faces, try the University of Kentucky down the road.

THE SCHOOL SAYS "..."

From The Admissions Office

"Bright, highly motivated students choose Transylvania for our personal approach to learning and our record of success in preparing them for rewarding careers and fulfilling lives. They attend small classes (many have fewer than 10 students) with highly qualified professors (no teaching assistants) and tackle faculty-directed student research projects in intriguing subjects like neurotransmitters and receptors, computer animation, and local Hispanic culture. Transylvania graduates have won prestigious scholarships and distinguished themselves at highly selective graduate and professional schools.

"Transylvania students consider the world their classroom. They enjoy May term travel courses studying the ancient polis in Greece, language and culture in France, and tropical ecology in Hawaii. Study abroad takes them to Germany, England, Japan, Mexico, and other destinations for a summer, a semester, or a year.

"You'll find Transylvania, a small college, nestled in a big city. Transylvania students soak up the advantages of Lexington, Kentucky, with its population of 270,000, numerous internships and job opportunities, and lots of entertainment. On campus, we have more than 50 co-curricular activities, and 18 varsity teams competing in NCAA Division III.

"While Transylvania is the nation's sixteenth-oldest college and proud of its rich history, its commitments to the exploration of a variety of disciplines, to intellectual inquiry, and to critical thinking have never been more relevant than in today's rapidly changing twenty-first-century world.

"Applicants are not required to submit Writing scores from the ACT or the SAT."

SELECTIVITY
Admissions Rating	92
# of applicants	1,334
% of applicants accepted	80
% of acceptees attending	30

FRESHMAN PROFILE
Range SAT Critical Reading	530–640
Range SAT Math	530–640
Range ACT Composite	24–29
Minimum paper TOEFL	550
Minimum computer TOEFL	213
Average HS GPA	3.66
% graduated top 10% of class	40
% graduated top 25% of class	66
% graduated top 50% of class	91

DEADLINES
Early action	
Deadline	12/1
Notification	1/15
Regular	
Priority	12/1
Deadline	2/1
Notification	3/1
Nonfall registration?	yes

APPLICANTS ALSO LOOK AT
AND OFTEN PREFER
Miami University
AND SOMETIMES PREFER
University of Kentucky
Centre College

FINANCIAL FACTS
Financial Aid Rating	82
Annual tuition	$24,250
Room and board	$7,770
Required fees	$1,030
Books and supplies	$1,000
% frosh rec. need-based scholarship or grant aid	68
% UG rec. need-based scholarship or grant aid	64
% frosh rec. non-need-based scholarship or grant aid	30
% UG rec. non-need-based scholarship or grant aid	34
% frosh rec. need-based self-help aid	51
% UG rec. need-based self-help aid	50
% frosh rec. any financial aid	98
% UG rec. any financial aid	98
% UG borrow to pay for school	63.6
Average cumulative indebtedness	$17,885

TRINITY COLLEGE (CT)

300 SUMMIT STREET, HARTFORD, CT 06016 • ADMISSIONS: 860-297-2180 • FAX: 860-297-2287

CAMPUS LIFE

Quality of Life Rating	61
Fire Safety Rating	86
Green Rating	60*
Type of school	private
Environment	metropolis

STUDENTS

Total undergrad enrollment	2,243
% male/female	50/50
% from out of state	83
% from public high school	44
% live on campus	95
% in (# of) fraternities	20 (7)
% in (# of) sororities	16 (3)
% African American	6
% Asian	5
% Caucasian	61
% Hispanic	6
% international	4
# of countries represented	30

SURVEY SAYS . . .

Great library
Students aren't religious
Everyone loves the Bantams
Frats and sororities dominate social scene
Student publications are popular
Lots of beer drinking
Hard liquor is popular

ACADEMICS

Academic Rating	90
Calendar	semester
Student/faculty ratio	10:1
Profs interesting rating	82
Profs accessible rating	81
Most common reg class size	10–19 students
Most common lab size	10–19 students

MOST POPULAR MAJORS

economics
history
political science and government

STUDENTS SAY ". . ."

Academics

Connecticut's Trinity College "offers a rare combination of high academic standards, a balanced political climate, intense athletic competitiveness/participation, awesome financial aid," and, last but not least, "a huge party scene," prompting some students to opine that "Trinity offers the most even balance of academics (amazing professors, room to find your niche) and social life" among U.S. colleges. Here, "Monday through Thursday everyone goes to class, studies, and gets their work done," but, "come the weekend, people let loose and party just as hard as they study." Weekdays offer "a great learning experience that provides ample opportunities," thanks in part to the school's small size (which means undergraduates have opportunities for research), a faculty staffed by "brilliant and caring" professors who "prioritize teaching above publishing," and a library that is "nothing less than phenomenal." Students also appreciate Trinity's urban setting, noting that "the city of Hartford [is used] as a valuable learning tool" and pointing out that, unlike "the majority of top liberal arts schools...[where] internship opportunities are limited, Trinity offered me the opportunity [for] many hands-on experiences." This may be particularly true if your field of interest is politics (Trinity's "location in a capital city means lots of opportunities for political internships," explains one student). Other standout departments include English (both literature and creative writing), engineering, theater, French, and the interdisciplinary program in human rights.

Life

For many Trinity undergrads, "The fraternities dominate the weekend social scene," and because these groups can be "fairly elitist" when it comes to allowing people into their late-night soirees, "sometimes it's hard to find something to do." Other students take a broader view of campus life. Such students tell us that new groups are "gaining social power," among them "The Fred (named after late professor Fred Pfiel)," which hosts "open mic evenings, nonalcoholic competitions, [and] theme nights," among other events. They also call out Trinity's Cinestudio, "one of the best on-campus, student-run movie theaters in the country." While campus theater, orchestra, a cappella, and chamber groups have limited participation, their performances are often well attended by the student body. Students note that "everything is available on campus so there is minimal effort to find things off campus." Those who have cars "often travel to nicer parts of Hartford or other Connecticut towns." One student observes, "Hartford, Connecticut is not as bad as people make it out to be. It has a lot to offer as long as you are willing to leave campus. There are some great restaurants and lots of shows to go to. Don't let yourself get stuck on campus every weekend."

Student Body

"Despite admissions' efforts, Trinity is still characterized by the New England boarding-school grad in polos and pink pants," undergrads here tell us, although some assert that "what many see as the typical student is actually a minority." Still, "the picture that immediately comes to mind is a blond, blue-eyed girl buying Coach...with daddy's money." Adding some diversity is "a growing population of 'Wesleyan-types,' who probably got rejected from our fellow Connecticut school. There's [been] an influx of intelligent, down-to-earth people at Trinity who are passionate about a lot more than getting wasted Thursday through Sunday." Students tend to be "over-wired" when not in class, attached to a "cell phone, IM, computer, [or] iPod, and therefore socially awkward or impolite....In class, they are overachievers, very articulate and competitive. Most spend an impressive amount of time studying."

FINANCIAL AID: 860-297-2046 • E-MAIL: ADMISSIONS.OFFICE@TRINCOLL.EDU • WEBSITE: WWW.TRINCOLL.EDU

THE PRINCETON REVIEW SAYS

Admissions

Very important factors considered include: rigor of secondary school record, *Important factors considered include:* Class rank, application essay, academic GPA, recommendation(s), standardized test scores, character/personal qualities, extracurricular activities, interview, racial/ethnic status, talent/ability. *Other factors considered include:* alumni/ae relation, first generation, geographical residence, level of applicant's interest, volunteer work, work experience. SAT or ACT required; ACT with Writing component recommended. High school diploma is required and GED is accepted. *Academic units required:* 4 English, 3 mathematics, 2 science, (2 science labs), 3 foreign language, 2 history.

Financial Aid

Students should submit: FAFSA, CSS/Financial Aid PROFILE, noncustodial PROFILE, business/farm supplement. Federal Income tax returns. Regular filing deadline is 3/1. The Princeton Review suggests that all financial aid forms be submitted as soon as possible after 1/1. *Need-based scholarships/grants offered:* Federal Pell, SEOG, state scholarships/grants, private scholarships, the school's own gift aid. *Loan aid offered:* Direct Subsidized Stafford, Direct Unsubsidized Stafford, Direct PLUS, FFEL Subsidized Stafford, FFEL Unsubsidized Stafford, FFEL PLUS, Federal Perkins, college/university loans from institutional funds. Applicants will be notified of awards on or about 4/1. Federal Work-Study Program available. Institutional employment available. Off-campus job opportunities are good.

The Inside Word

Students describe Trinity as "the home of Yale rejects," an appraisal that accurately characterizes the school's rep as an Ivy safety (if not the actual makeup of the student body). The school's high price tag ensures that a large percentage of the student body is made up of wealthy prepsters, but the school does offer generous financial aid packages to top candidates who can't afford the hefty price of attending. The school would love to broaden its student demographic, so competitive minority students should receive a very receptive welcome here.

THE SCHOOL SAYS "..."

From The Admissions Office

"An array of distinctive curricular options—including an interdisciplinary neuroscience major and a professionally accredited engineering degree program, a unique Human Rights Program, a Health Fellows Program, and interdisciplinary programs such as the Cities Program, Interdisciplinary Science Program, and InterArts—is one reason record numbers of students are applying to Trinity. In fact, applications are up 80 percent over the past 5 years. In addition, the college has been recognized for its commitment to diversity; students of color have represented approximately 20 percent of the freshman class for the past 4 years, setting Trinity apart from many of its peers. Trinity's capital city location offers students unparalleled 'real-world' learning experiences to complement classroom learning. Students take advantage of extensive opportunities for internships for academic credit and community service, and these opportunities extend to Trinity's global learning sites in cities around the world. Trinity's faculty is a devoted and accomplished group of exceptional teacher-scholars; our 100-acre campus is beautiful; Hartford is an educational asset that differentiates Trinity from other liberal arts colleges; our global connections and foreign study opportunities prepare students to be good citizens of the world; and our graduates go on to excel in virtually every field. We invite you to learn more about why Trinity might be the best choice for you.

"Students applying for admission may submit the following testing options: SAT, ACT with Writing."

SELECTIVITY

Admissions Rating	95
# of applicants	5,950
% of applicants accepted	34
% of acceptees attending	28
# accepting a place on wait list	460
% admitted from wait list	37
# of early decision applicants	412
% accepted early decision	69

FRESHMAN PROFILE

Range SAT Critical Reading	600–690
Range SAT Math	610–690
Range SAT Writing	608–700
Range ACT Composite	26–29
% graduated top 10% of class	61
% graduated top 25% of class	88
% graduated top 50% of class	96

DEADLINES

Early Decision	
Deadline	11/15
Notification	12/15
Regular	
Deadline	1/1
Notification	4/1
Nonfall registration?	no

APPLICANTS ALSO LOOK AT

AND OFTEN PREFER
Boston College
Boston University

AND SOMETIMES PREFER
Wesleyan University
Middlebury College

FINANCIAL FACTS

Financial Aid Rating	98
Annual tuition	$35,110
Room and board	$9,420
Required fees	$1,760
Books and supplies	$900
% frosh rec. need-based scholarship or grant aid	35
% UG rec. need-based scholarship or grant aid	36
% frosh rec. non-need-based scholarship or grant aid	11
% UG rec. non-need-based scholarship or grant aid	9
% frosh rec. need-based self-help aid	28
% UG rec. need-based self-help aid	31
% frosh rec. any financial aid	39
% UG rec. any financial aid	40
% UG borrow to pay for school	43
Average cumulative indebtedness	$19,835

TRINITY UNIVERSITY (TX)

ONE TRINITY PLACE, SAN ANTONIO, TX 78212 • ADMISSIONS: 210-999-7207 • FAX: 210-999-8164

CAMPUS LIFE

Quality of Life Rating	93
Fire Safety Rating	91
Green Rating	77
Type of school	private
Environment	metropolis

STUDENTS

Total undergrad enrollment	2,475
% male/female	47/53
% from out of state	27
% from public high school	72
% live on campus	71
% in (# of) fraternities	14 (7)
% in (# of) sororities	26 (6)
% African American	4
% Asian	7
% Caucasian	60
% Hispanic	11
% Native American	1
% international	6
# of countries represented	66

SURVEY SAYS . . .

Great library
School is well run
Great off-campus food
Dorms are like palaces
Campus feels safe

ACADEMICS

Academic Rating	89
Calendar	semester
Student/faculty ratio	9.5:1
Profs interesting rating	90
Profs accessible rating	90
Most common reg class size	10–19 students
Most common lab size	10–19 students

MOST POPULAR MAJORS

business administration,
English, modern languages
and literature

STUDENTS SAY ". . ."

Academics

Trinity University is a small private school that, despite its size, offers "a diversity of good programs." The school is "known for its good science and premed programs, but has decent arts programs, too." And students point out that "Not many other schools this size have their own radio station and television stations with a full communications department." Throw in "a really good program in education" ("you can graduate with a masters in five years, and teachers graduated from Trinity are well-known" in the area), a "really great business program," and "a great study-abroad program" and you understand why students say "it's rare to have such a well-rounded school of this size." On top of its academic variety Trinity adds "a diverse population, small classes, and a very active social scene; in other words—there's something for everyone!" Students don't forfeit the benefits of a small school here, though. On the contrary, they enjoy "the ability to really get to know our professors and the administration and to work up to leadership positions and opportunities.... No one holds your hand here, yet everyone really has the drive to do well. There are very few people who just show up to class and then "peace out" when it's over. Everyone interacts and really makes an effort to engage in class time." The school's location in the nation's seventh-largest city also means that there are "great opportunities" for graduates.

Life

Trinity students form "a pretty small, close-knit community, so students spend a lot of time with each other. People study here a lot, but people also go out a lot and know how to have a good time." Campus fun includes "parties, club sports, various organizations to join, good school sport teams (especially soccer), intramural sports, and all sorts of events going on like dances, concerts, and other things." Big-city life dampens the enthusiasm of some for campus events. As one student explains, "Trinity has many on-campus activities such as Trinity Idol, the Tigers Den, and the Roast, but San Antonio is a city full of cultural and unique restaurants and activities. We go to the zoo, the many restaurants, downtown, the many parks, and venues to hear music." One student sizes up the situation this way: "San Antonio has everything you could want in terms of food, clubs, and shopping. First Fridays is the best part of San Antonio. Once a month they have a sort of festival with plenty of art and crafts for sale." Trinity's dormitories earn good marks as they "are pretty big, and we have walk-in closets, and the bathrooms are big as well," although some complain that "all of them are the same" and that "there are no single rooms.... It gets tiring sharing a small room with another person for three years (there's a three-year residency requirement)."

Student Body

Trinity undergrads are "smart," "friendly," and "very dedicated to doing well in school" while also maintaining a healthy social life. As one undergrad puts it, "For the most part, students at Trinity have managed to find that delicate balance between an academic and social life (often through trial and error)." Most here "come from well-to-do families," are "talented in unique ways," and "worked hard in high school." While "the majority is Caucasian," "there are tons of international students who enhance the university" by broadening the perspectives represented in Trinity classrooms.

FINANCIAL AID: 210-999-8315 • E-MAIL: ADMISSIONS@TRINITY.EDU • WEBSITE: WWW.TRINITY.EDU

THE PRINCETON REVIEW SAYS

Admissions

Very important factors considered include: academic GPA, Class rank, rigor of secondary school record, *Important factors considered include:* Application essay, recommendation(s), standardized test scores, character/personal qualities, extracurricular activities, interview, talent/ability. *Other factors considered include:* alumni/ae relation, first generation, geographical residence, level of applicant's interest, racial/ethnic status, volunteer work, work experience. SAT or ACT required; TOEFL required of all international applicantswhose first language is not English. High school diploma is required and GED is accepted. *Academic units required:* 4 English, 3 mathematics, 3 science, (2 science labs), 2 foreign language, 3 social studies. *Academic units recommended:* 4 English, 3 mathematics, 3 science, (2 science labs), 3 foreign language, 3 social studies, 3 academic electives.

Financial Aid

Students should submit: FAFSA Preferred filing deadline is 2/15. The Princeton Review suggests that all financial aid forms be submitted as soon as possible after 1/1. *Need-based scholarships/grants offered:* Federal Pell, SEOG, state scholarships/grants, private scholarships, the school's own gift aid. *Loan aid offered:* FFEL Subsidized Stafford, FFEL Unsubsidized Stafford, FFEL PLUS, Federal Perkins, state loans, college/university loans from institutional funds. Applicants will be notified of awards by 4/1. Federal Work-Study Program available. Institutional employment available. Off-campus job opportunities are good.

The Inside Word

As Trinity embraces a small close-knit community of student scholars, admissions counselors are looking for the complete picture: bright, capable, motivated students who are ready to take advantage of all the school has to offer. While an applicant's academic performance is the factor considered most heavily in the admissions process, standardized test scores, essay, recommendations, and extracurricular activities also play a big role. Trinity accepts the Common Application.

THE SCHOOL SAYS "..."

From The Admissions Office

"Three qualities separate Trinity University from other selective, academically challenging institutions around the country. First, Trinity is unusual in the quality and quantity of resources devoted almost exclusively to its undergraduate students. Those resources give rise to a second distinctive aspect of Trinity—its emphasis on undergraduate research. Our students prefer being involved over observing. With superior laboratory facilities and strong, dedicated faculty, our undergraduates fill many of the roles formerly reserved for graduate students, and our professors often go to their undergraduates for help with their research. Other hands-on learning experiences including internships, study-abroad, and service projects are also available to students. Finally, Trinity stands apart for the attitude of its students. In an atmosphere of academic camaraderie and fellowship, our students work together to stretch their minds and broaden their horizons across academic disciplines. For quality of resources, for dedication to undergraduate research, and for the disposition of its student body, Trinity University holds a unique position in American higher education.

"Students applying for admission must submit either the SAT or the ACT. The highest composite test scores from one or multiple dates are evaluated. The SAT Writing section and ACT Writing component are not required."

SELECTIVITY

Admissions Rating	93
# of applicants	3,754
% of applicants accepted	58
% of acceptees attending	30
# accepting a place on wait list	104
% admitted from wait list	34
# of early decision applicants	50
% accepted early decision	72

FRESHMAN PROFILE

Range SAT Critical Reading	600–690
Range SAT Math	610–690
Range ACT Composite	27–31
Minimum paper TOEFL	600
Minimum computer TOEFL	250
Average HS GPA	3.55
% graduated top 10% of class	50
% graduated top 25% of class	80
% graduated top 50% of class	97

DEADLINES

Early Decision	
Deadline	11/1
Notification	12/1
Early action	
Deadline	12/1
Notification	2/1
Regular	
Deadline	2/1
Notification	4/1
Nonfall registration?	no

APPLICANTS ALSO LOOK AT
AND OFTEN PREFER
The University of Texas at Austin
Rice University

AND SOMETIMES PREFER
Tulane University
Texas A&M University—College Station

FINANCIAL FACTS

Financial Aid Rating	89
Annual tuition	$28,272
Room and board	$8,895
Required fees	$1,045
% frosh rec. need-based scholarship or grant aid	40
% UG rec. need-based scholarship or grant aid	36
% frosh rec. non-need-based scholarship or grant aid	10
% UG rec. non-need-based scholarship or grant aid	7
% frosh rec. need-based self-help aid	31
% UG rec. need-based self-help aid	30
% frosh rec. any financial aid	87
% UG rec. any financial aid	83

TRUMAN STATE UNIVERSITY

McCLAIN HALL 205, 100 EAST NORMAL, KIRKSVILLE, MO 63501 • ADMISSIONS: 660-785-4114 • FAX: 660-785-7456

CAMPUS LIFE

Quality of Life Rating	**80**
Fire Safety Rating	**76**
Green Rating	**79**
Type of school	public
Environment	village

STUDENTS

Total undergrad enrollment	5,497
% male/female	42/58
% from out of state	21
% from public high school	76
% live on campus	50
% in (# of) fraternities	23 (16)
% in (# of) sororities	19 (11)
% African American	5
% Asian	2
% Caucasian	82
% Hispanic	2
% Native American	1
% international	5
# of countries represented	46

SURVEY SAYS . . .

Students are friendly
Campus feels safe
Low cost of living
Students are happy
(Almost) no one smokes
Very little drug use

ACADEMICS

Academic Rating	**87**
Calendar	semester
Student/faculty ratio	16:1
Profs interesting rating	80
Profs accessible rating	86
% classes taught by TAs	1
Most common reg class size	20–29 students
Most common lab size	fewer than 10 students

MOST POPULAR MAJORS

biology/biological sciences
business administration and management
English language and literature

STUDENTS SAY ". . ."

Academics

Truman students aren't shy about discussing their school's "extremely well deserved academic reputation," referring to it as "superior," "excellent," "the best public university in the state of Missouri," and even "the Harvard of the Midwest." Truman students are here to work, and many cite the school's financial aid and scholarships as allowing them to do so. "Truman State offers many scholarships that make getting a great education very affordable," says a freshman biology major, and a senior linguistics major says "they gave me scholarships that ended up essentially paying me to come here." Students enjoy Truman's focus on its study-abroad options, and they use the school's financial accessibility to participate. "I wanted to get a world-class education, but I didn't want the price of tuition to prevent me from exploring the world itself. I'm doing an internship in Tanzania this summer, which quite frankly would not have been financially possible" otherwise. Many Truman students choose to study English, business, and accounting, but as one junior told us "I wanted a school that was well-rounded so that, regardless of what I ended up majoring [in], I knew it would be a solid program." Students also appreciate the ability to take classes outside their majors, as one junior tells us, "Even though I am an exercise science major, I have taken many classes in other majors such as art and literature."

Life

Students almost unanimously love life at Truman State. "The campus is beautiful, and the atmosphere is very welcoming." However, at a school of Truman's caliber one can expect students to spend most of their time studying. "Many people here really care about their education, so they do schoolwork and study," and "the thing that stands out the most is how everyone here is pretty grade conscious." Students have noticed that other students "would rather go to class hung-over than miss lectures." Students do have reservations about hometown Kirksville; "there is not a lot to do. It really is a rural town, but people make fun things to do on campus." Some students participate in Greek life and "go to planned social events with fraternities and sororities. There are also a few bars in town that of-age students go to on a regular basis." But Truman's social scene is far from one-sided; "some people say there's nothing to do but drink, but from the amount of school organizations and activities, that's obviously not true. People make their own fun." "The trick to making life at Truman interesting is to find your niche, whether it's on a sports team…or in a musical ensemble…I got involved with the campus newspaper." Students also undertake social responsibility. "You can be a huge political advocate, involved in protests on the quad. You can become involved in community service locally and nation-wide."

Student Body

All of the students at Truman are bonded by one thing; their respect for other students' academic abilities, and all students are here to study. Therefore, "it is easy to get to know other classmates and have study groups or friends to lean on in times of need." "Most people strive to excel here, so there is a healthy focus on academics within friends," and the "typical student is an over-achiever with big dreams and goals." Also, many are "from Missouri, specifically St. Louis, and a high proportion are from Catholic, private schools." As one student tells us, "The typical student can be described as the typical American…there is no distinct description to identify the typical person."

FINANCIAL AID: 660-785-4130 • E-MAIL: ADMISSIONS@TRUMAN.EDU • WEBSITE: WWW.TRUMAN.EDU

THE PRINCETON REVIEW SAYS

Admissions

Very important factors considered include: Class rank, academic GPA, rigor of secondary school record, standardized test scores, *Important factors considered include:* Application essay. *Other factors considered include:* recommendation(s), alumni/ae relation, character/personal qualities, extracurricular activities, first generation, geographical residence, racial/ethnic status, state residency, talent/ability, volunteer work, work experience. SAT or ACT required; TOEFL required of all international applicants. High school diploma is required and GED is accepted. *Academic units required:* 4 English, 3 mathematics, 3 science, (1 science labs), 2 foreign language, 2 social studies, 1 history, 1 visual/performing arts. *Academic units recommended:* 4 mathematics, (2 science labs).

Financial Aid

Students should submit: FAFSA, institution's own financial aid form. The Princeton Review suggests that all financial aid forms be submitted as soon as possible after 1/1. *Need-based scholarships/grants offered:* Federal Pell, SEOG, state scholarships/grants, private scholarships, the school's own gift aid, Federal ACG and SMART. *Loan aid offered:* FFEL Subsidized Stafford, FFEL Unsubsidized Stafford, FFEL PLUS, Federal Perkins, Federal Nursing, college/university loans from institutional funds, alternative loans. Applicants will be notified of awards on a rolling basis beginning 3/1. Federal Work-Study Program available. Institutional employment available. Off-campus job opportunities are good.

The Inside Word

Those interested in studying at Truman State had better get to work; the school places a large emphasis on GPA, class rank, and academic rigor. The selectivity and quality of education numbers are high, but annual tuition is low for all students. The early admissions decision is nonbinding, so you have the best chance of getting in if you apply early.

THE SCHOOL SAYS "..."

From The Admissions Office

"Truman's talented student body enjoys small classes where undergraduate research and personal interaction with professors are the norm. Truman's commitment to providing an exemplary liberal arts and sciences education with over 250 student organizations and outstanding internship and study abroad opportunities allows students to compete in top graduate schools and the job market.

"Truman offers a variety of competitive scholarships and there is no seperate scholarship application. Students wishing to be considered for all scholarship programs are strongly encouraged to apply for admission by December 15th.

"Students applying for admission to Truman State University can submit scores from both the ACT and the SAT. The best scores from either test will be considered. The Writing section is not currently required for admission to Truman."

SELECTIVITY	
Admissions Rating	**97**
# of applicants	4,280
% of applicants accepted	79
% of acceptees attending	40

FRESHMAN PROFILE	
Range SAT Critical Reading	540–700
Range SAT Math	570–690
Range ACT Composite	25–31
Minimum paper TOEFL	550
Minimum computer TOEFL	213
Minimum web-based TOEFL	79
Average HS GPA	3.76
% graduated top 10% of class	50
% graduated top 25% of class	80
% graduated top 50% of class	98

DEADLINES	
Regular	
Priority	12/15
Nonfall registration?	yes

APPLICANTS ALSO LOOK AT
AND OFTEN PREFER
Saint Louis University
Missouri State University
University of Missouri—Columbia
AND SOMETIMES PREFER
Washington University in St. Louis

FINANCIAL FACTS	
Financial Aid Rating	**89**
Annual tuition in-state	$6,458
Annual tuition out-of-state	$11,308
Room and board	$6,854
Required fees	$539
Books and supplies	$1,000
% frosh rec. need-based	
scholarship or grant aid	29
% UG rec. need-based	
scholarship or grant aid	28
% frosh rec. non-need-based	
scholarship or grant aid	37
% UG rec. non-need-based	
scholarship or grant aid	31
% frosh rec. need-based	
self-help aid	30
% UG rec. need-based	
self-help aid	30
% frosh rec. athletic scholarships	7
% UG rec. athletic scholarships	6
% frosh rec. any financial aid	98
% UG rec. any financial aid	95
% UG borrow to pay for school	51
Average cumulative	
indebtedness	$16,858

TUFTS UNIVERSITY

BENDETSON HALL, MEDFORD, MA 02155 • ADMISSIONS: 617-627-3170 • FAX: 617-627-3860

CAMPUS LIFE
Quality of Life Rating	85
Fire Safety Rating	96
Green Rating	88
Type of school	private
Environment	town

STUDENTS
Total undergrad enrollment	5,029
% male/female	49/51
% from out of state	75.2
% from public high school	59
% in (# of) fraternities	10 (11)
% in (# of) sororities	3 (3)
% African American	6
% Asian	13
% Caucasian	55
% Hispanic	6
% international	6
# of countries represented	93

SURVEY SAYS . . .
Great food on campus
Campus feels safe
Student publications are popular
Political activism is popular

ACADEMICS
Academic Rating	89
Calendar	semester
Student/faculty ratio	7:1
Profs interesting rating	83
Profs accessible rating	80
% classes taught by TAs	1
Most common reg class size	10–19 students
Most common lab size	10–19 students

MOST POPULAR MAJORS
economics
English language and literature
international relations and affairs

STUDENTS SAY ". . ."

Academics

Tufts University boasts a "small-campus feel;" a "globally recognized" reputation; and "engaging," "personable" faculty. Professors here "know what they are talking about" and "seem to go out of their way to make themselves accessible." These very same professors, however, "flood" students "with tons of work." Lower-level classes can be huge on occasion, but upper-level classes are "small and well-focused." The "transparent" administration tends "to grapple with technology and change," but it is "incredibly helpful" and very well liked, despite "militant political correctness." "President Bacow will generally respond to any e-mail sent to him by a student within about 20 minutes." Academically, while you can choose from a massive number of stellar majors in the liberal arts and engineering, Tufts is probably best known for its "very strong" science programs (especially premed) and its prestigious international relations programs. "Tufts is internationalism," declares one student. "From the music department's ethnomusicology [major] to political science and international relations, every facet of Tufts, both in and out of the classroom, revolves around thinking globally." Studying abroad "is highly encouraged;" about 40 percent of students take advantage of awesome study-abroad programs in a host of exotic locales including an "amazing" summer program in the Alps.

Life

At Tufts, the campus is "gorgeous," "the food is incredible," and course work is time-consuming, so it's no surprise that social life is basically centered on campus. Students here "know each other." "It's a nice feeling," an undergrad says, but "if you want to be anonymous, Tufts is not for you." The "fabulous extracurricular opportunities" include "a daily paper, a dozen student magazines," and "countless service and activism organizations." In addition, a vast array of large-scale, free campus events helps to keep students entertained. While "drinking is very popular on the weekends," undergrads report that "there is not always a party guaranteed on a Friday or Saturday night, which is unthinkable at bigger schools." When there is one, it can seem as if "The campus police break everything up." This may be why "as you get older and you meet more people, you begin to go to more parties and social events off campus," a more seasoned student tells us. Many feel that the surrounding town of Medford leaves a lot to be desired, but fortunately, "you have the greatest college city in the nation a subway ride away" if "you get tired [of] the Tufts scene." It should be noted, however, that public transportation into Boston takes "like an hour (counting waiting)." "We're not in Boston," cautions one student. "Don't let the admissions folks fool you."

Students

Some students tell us that Tuft's reputation as a haven for the "Ivy League reject" is accurate. Others vehemently disagree. "The Tufts Ivy complex is over," argues one student. "Anyone here could get into Cornell!" Students describe themselves as "genuinely nice," "painfully liberal," and "very goal-oriented." They are "laid-back" and only "competitive with themselves." One undergrad asserts, "The typical student here is very intelligent and ambitious, but they don't want you to think that." Another adds, "They get their work done so they can have fun too." Ethnic diversity is notable; traditionally underrepresented minorities on campus have a strong presence. However, "people tend to separate into their little cliques after first semester and rarely interact with other people." "Almost all Tufts students are rich" as well. "The frustrating thing is not the lack of ethnic diversity, but the lack of socioeconomic diversity," an English major writes. This student body features "a lot of smart kids in Lacoste polos who are looking to save the world" (or, at least, "convince others they are looking to save to world") and a lot of "preppy," "rich kids" "Louis V. bag," "North Face fleece," and "big sunglasses," There are also "the stoners, the die-hard partiers, the activists, the coffeehouse philosophers," and a slew of "obscenely wealthy international kids."

FINANCIAL AID: 617-627-2000 • E-MAIL: ADMISSIONS.INQUIRY@ASE.TUFTS.EDU • WEBSITE: WWW.TUFTS.EDU

THE PRINCETON REVIEW SAYS

Admissions

Very important factors considered include: Application essay, academic GPA, rigor of secondary school record, character/personal qualities. *Important factors considered include:* Class rank, recommendation(s), standardized test scores, extracurricular activities, talent/ability, volunteer work, work experience. *Other factors considered include:* alumni/ae relation, first generation, geographical residence, interview, racial/ethnic status, SAT and SAT Subject Tests or ACT required; ACT with Writing component required. TOEFL required of all international applicants. High school diploma is required and GED is accepted. *Academic units recommended:* 4 English, 4 mathematics, 4 science, 4 foreign language, 4 social studies.

Financial Aid

Students should submit: FAFSA, CSS/Financial Aid PROFILE, noncustodial PROFILE, business/farm supplement. Parent and Student Federal Income Tax Returns. Regular filing deadline is 2/15. The Princeton Review suggests that all financial aid forms be submitted as soon as possible after 1/1. *Need-based scholarships/grants offered:* Federal Pell, SEOG, state scholarships/grants, private scholarships, the school's own gift aid. *Loan aid offered:* FFEL Subsidized Stafford, FFEL Unsubsidized Stafford, FFEL PLUS, Federal Perkins, state loans, college/university loans from institutional funds. Applicants will be notified of awards on or about 4/1. Federal Work-Study Program available. Institutional employment available. Off-campus job opportunities are good.

The Inside Word

The admissions process is rigorous. With an acceptance rate hovering not much over 25 percent and average SAT section scores in the low 700s, you'll need to demonstrate fairly extraordinary academic accomplishments and submit a thorough and well-prepared application in order to get admitted to Tufts. On the bright side, Tufts is still a little bit of a safety school for aspiring Ivy Leaguers. Since many applicants who also get into an Ivy League school will pass on Tufts, it has spots for "mere mortals" at the end of the day.

THE SCHOOL SAYS "..."

From The Admissions Office

"Tufts University, on the boundary between Medford and Somerville, sits on a hill overlooking Boston, five miles northwest of the city. The campus is a tranquil New England setting within easy access by subway and bus to the cultural, social, and entertainment resources of Boston and Somerville. Since its founding in 1852 by members of the Universalist church, Tufts has grown from a small liberal arts college into a nonsectarian university of more than 8,000 students with undergraduate programs in arts & sciences and engineering. By 1900 the college had added a medical school, a dental school, and graduate studies. The university now also includes the Fletcher School of Law and Diplomacy, the Graduate School of Arts & Sciences, the Cummings School of Veterinary Medicine, the Friedman School of Nutrition Science and Policy, the Sackler School of Graduate Biomedical Sciences, and the Gordon Institute of Engineering Management.

"Applicants are required to submit scores (including the Writing assessment) from either the SAT or ACT. If an applicant submits the SAT, SAT Subject Tests are also required (candidates for the School of Engineering are encouraged to submit math and either chemistry or physics)."

SELECTIVITY

Admissions Rating	**97**
# of applicants	15,619
% of applicants accepted	26
% of acceptees attending	33
# of early decision applicants	1,321
% accepted early decision	32

FRESHMAN PROFILE

Range SAT Critical Reading	670–750
Range SAT Math	670–750
Range SAT Writing	670–760
Range ACT Composite	30–33
Minimum paper TOEFL	600
Minimum computer TOEFL	100
% graduated top 10% of class	85
% graduated top 25% of class	98.5
% graduated top 50% of class	100

DEADLINES

Early Decision	
Deadline	11/1
Notification	12/15
Regular	
Deadline	1/1
Notification	4/1
Nonfall registration?	no

FINANCIAL FACTS

Financial Aid Rating	**94**
Annual tuition	$38,840
Room and board	$10,518
Books and supplies	$2,042
% frosh rec. need-based scholarship or grant aid	36
% UG rec. need-based scholarship or grant aid	35
% frosh rec. non-need-based scholarship or grant aid	1
% UG rec. non-need-based scholarship or grant aid	1
% frosh rec. need-based self-help aid	34
% UG rec. need-based self-help aid	35
% frosh rec. any financial aid	40
% UG rec. any financial aid	41
% UG borrow to pay for school	40
Average cumulative indebtedness	$23,687

TULANE UNIVERSITY

6823 St. Charles Avenue, New Orleans, LA 70118 • Admissions: 504-865-5731 • Fax: 504-862-8715

CAMPUS LIFE

Quality of Life Rating	**91**
Fire Safety Rating	**87**
Green Rating	**83**
Type of school	private
Environment	city

STUDENTS

Total undergrad enrollment	6,749
% male/female	46/54
% live on campus	51
% in (# of) fraternities	13 (15)
% in (# of) sororities	15 (10)
% African American	8.7
% Asian	4.8
% Caucasian	58
% Hispanic	4
% Native American	1
% international	3
# of countries represented	45

SURVEY SAYS . . .

Athletic facilities are great
Students love New Orleans, LA
Great off-campus food
Students are happy
Lots of beer drinking
Hard liquor is popular

ACADEMICS

Academic Rating	**84**
Calendar	semester
Profs interesting rating	82
Profs accessible rating	86
Most common reg class size	10–19 students
Most common lab size	10–19 students

MOST POPULAR MAJORS

business/commerce
health services/allied health/health sciences
psychology

STUDENTS SAY ". . ."

Academics

In 2005, Hurricane Katrina sent Tulane students on a forced semester in exile. For most schools, this move would have been a death sentence. Tulane, however, is not most schools; it is uniquely Tulane, "the ultimate work-hard, play-hard school" whose strong academics and laid-back approach make it the place where all the "cool smart kids" go, a place that inspires the type of student devotion rarely found at schools that lack powerhouse sports programs. Student after student praises the school's recovery efforts, observing that "Tulane's administration brought us through Katrina and is helping New Orleans through this time as well," and that "in post-Katrina New Orleans, the professors who have returned are the ones who really want to be here and really have a desire to help students learn." Katrina has actually strengthened students' allegiance to the school; as one put it, "This is the most amazing, out-of-this-world place to be—a college experience that no other school could top. And we know it because we experienced other schools during [the] Hurricane Katrina [hiatus]." The Tulane academic experience is distinguished by small classes, mostly "10 to 20 students," "one of the best study abroad programs in the country," and, of course, New Orleans, the "best city in the country," which allows Tulane to offer "a one-of-a-kind out-of-classroom experience." Standout programs include premed, business, economics, architecture, and exercise and sports science.

Life

Tulane students love New Orleans—and love to explore it—a city full of "art galleries and museums," "amazing" shopping on Magazine Street, "family-owned restaurants in the uptown area," "touristy" places in the French Quarter, and "a lot [of] different bars near campus." The city also boasts Audubon Park, "a really fun place to get exercise or spend some time," and, of course, an "unparalleled music scene." None of this, however, stops "about 30 percent of the campus" from getting involved in Greek life, or "most students" from getting involved "in at least two student organizations." In addition, "community service [and] volunteer work," always "very popular at Tulane," have become "especially popular post-Katrina." Those concerned about safety—New Orleans has traditionally had one of the higher crime rates in the nation—should note that "Tulane is located in a major city, but not in downtown New Orleans." By all accounts, campus security does "an excellent job of making sure campus is secure, and students have the opportunity to be escorted anywhere." As an added bonus, "The weather is nice—you can wear flip flops year round."

Student Body

The typical Tulane student "is serious about academics, but isn't holed up in the library all the time." Similar to students at other big-city schools, Tulane undergrads tend to be "self-reliant, motivated, [and] forward-looking." They point out that the school is "one of the most geographically diverse schools in the country," observing that "75 percent of the students come from more than 500 miles away....In my 8-person suite, there are two girls from Boston, one from New York, one from Texas, one from Baton Rouge, one from Florida, and I'm from Chicago. It's great!" Diversity is further represented in the "tons of very large, very active, very vocal groups on campus for every minority, including ethnicities, political beliefs, religious beliefs, and sexual orientations. Everyone here manages to find [a] niche." A strong Jewish Studies program helps Tulane draw one of the largest Jewish student populations in the South; about 25 percent of the student body is Jewish.

FINANCIAL AID: 504-865-5723 • E-MAIL: UNDERGRAD.ADMISSION@TULANE.EDU • WEBSITE: WWW.TULANE.EDU

THE PRINCETON REVIEW SAYS

Admissions

Very important factors considered include: Class rank, academic GPA, rigor of secondary school record, standardized test scores. *Important factors considered include:* Application essay, recommendation(s). *Other factors considered include:* alumni/ae relation, character/personal qualities, extracurricular activities, interview, talent/ability, volunteer work, work experience. SAT or ACT required; ACT with Writing component required. TOEFL required of all international applicants. High school diploma is required and GED is accepted. *Academic units recommended:* 4 English, 4 mathematics, 4 science, (4 science labs), 3 foreign language, 3 social studies, 3 academic electives.

Financial Aid

Students should submit: FAFSA, CSS/Financial Aid PROFILE, noncustodial PROFILE, business/farm supplement. Regular filing deadline is 2/1. The Princeton Review suggests that all financial aid forms be submitted as soon as possible after 1/1. *Need-based scholarships/grants offered:* Federal Pell, SEOG, state scholarships/grants, private scholarships, the school's own gift aid, Academic Competitiveness Grant, SMART Grant. *Loan aid offered:* FFEL Subsidized Stafford, FFEL Unsubsidized Stafford, FFEL PLUS, Federal Perkins. Applicants will be notified of awards on a rolling basis beginning 2/1. Federal Work-Study Program available. Institutional employment available. Off-campus job opportunities are good.

The Inside Word

Admission to Tulane is extremely competitive, and the admissions committee looks for high levels of achievement from potential students. The school receives tons of applications, so do all you can to stand out in the crowd.

THE SCHOOL SAYS "..."

From The Admissions Office

"More than 6,700 full-time undergraduate students in five schools, Tulane University offers the personal attention and teaching excellence traditionally associated with small colleges together with the facilities and interdisciplinary resources found only at major research universities. Following Hurricane Katrina, the university underwent a spectacular renewal: renovating facilities and restructuring academic programs. The opportunities for students to be involved in the rebirth of New Orleans offer an experience unavailable at any other place, at any other time.

"Tulane is committed to undergraduate education. Senior faculty members teach most introductory and lower-level courses, and most classes have 25 or fewer students. The close student-teacher relationship pays off. Tulane graduates are among the most likely to be selected for several prestigious fellowships that support graduate study abroad. Founded in 1834 and reorganized as Tulane University in 1884, Tulane is one of the major private research universities in the South.

"The Tulane campus offers a traditional collegiate setting in an attractive residential neighborhood, which is now thriving after Hurricane Katrina."

SELECTIVITY

Admissions Rating	94
# of applicants	34,125
% of applicants accepted	27
% of acceptees attending	17
# accepting a place on wait list	207
% admitted from wait list	33

FRESHMAN PROFILE

Range SAT Critical Reading	630–720
Range SAT Math	620–700
Range SAT Writing	640–720
Range ACT Composite	29–32
Minimum paper TOEFL	550
Minimum computer TOEFL	213
Average HS GPA	3.49
% graduated top 10% of class	59
% graduated top 25% of class	88
% graduated top 50% of class	98

DEADLINES

Early action	
Deadline	11/1
Notification	12/15
Regular	
Priority	11/1
Deadline	1/15
Notification	4/1
Nonfall registration?	yes

APPLICANTS ALSO LOOK AT

AND OFTEN PREFER
Vanderbilt University
Duke University
Emory University

AND SOMETIMES PREFER
Washington University in St. Louis

FINANCIAL FACTS

Financial Aid Rating	92
Annual tuition	$35,500
Room and board	$9,296
Required fees	$3,164
Books and supplies	$1,200
% frosh rec. need-based scholarship or grant aid	35
% UG rec. need-based scholarship or grant aid	37
% frosh rec. non-need-based scholarship or grant aid	15
% UG rec. non-need-based scholarship or grant aid	12
% frosh rec. need-based self-help aid	20
% UG rec. need-based self-help aid	25
% frosh rec. athletic scholarships	1
% UG rec. athletic scholarships	2
% UG borrow to pay for school	48
Average cumulative indebtedness	$23,819

TUSKEGEE UNIVERSITY

OLD ADMINISTRATION BUILDING, SUITE 101, TUSKEGEE, AL 36088 • ADMISSIONS: 334-727-8500 OR 800-622-65311 • FAX: 334-727-4402

CAMPUS LIFE

Quality of Life Rating	**61**
Fire Safety Rating	**60***
Green Rating	**60***
Type of school	private
Environment	rural

STUDENTS

Total undergrad enrollment	2,541
% male/female	44/56
% from out of state	65
% live on campus	55
% in (# of) fraternities	6 (5)
% in (# of) sororities	5 (6)
% African American	89
% international	1
# of countries represented	90

SURVEY SAYS . . .

Registration is a pain
Students are friendly
Students don't like Tuskegee, AL
Low cost of living
Everyone loves the Golden Tigers
Frats and sororities dominate social scene
Musical organizations are popular
Student government is popular
Hard liquor is popular

ACADEMICS

Academic Rating	**72**
Calendar	semester
Student/faculty ratio	11:1
Profs interesting rating	65
Profs accessible rating	61
Most common	
reg class size	10–19 students

MOST POPULAR MAJORS

electrical, electronics and communications engineering
veterinary medicine (dvm)

STUDENTS SAY ". . ."

Academics

Tuskegee University is a smaller, historically black college steeped in "pride, history," "heritage, and tradition." Students here declare that theirs is "the most prestigious HBCU in the nation." A required core curriculum in the liberal arts and sciences ensures a well-rounded education, but this place is primarily known for its excellence in the hard sciences and its "top-notch" engineering programs. Tuskegee produces more African American aerospace science engineers than any other school in the country. The chemical, electrical, and mechanical engineering programs are also notable. (Incidentally, some three-quarters of the African American veterinarians on the planet went here as well.) Students tell us that the academic atmosphere is "wonderful." "Class sizes are small," explains a senior, "only slightly larger than the average high school class at times." Opportunities for undergraduate research are definitely available. Professors are "always accessible" and "mostly good." Many are nothing less than "enlightening." Faculty members "are also very good mentors." They "break their necks to help students outside the class." In the past, the administration has not received the same reviews. Though some students have noted that Tuskegee is run "as smoothly as possible," other felt that the administrators were "hard to find." However, in 2008 a Vice President for Student Affairs was hired to recognize these issues. Additionally, a new online registration process has been implemented.

Life

Tuskegee is located in eastern Alabama, in an affordable but "boring" town "in the middle of nowhere." There are "very few distractions." "The students have a great sense of school spirit and unity," though, and they "make their own fun" on this "laidback" campus. You can participate in more than 100 clubs and organizations. There are "all sorts of student activities, such as fashion shows, basketball tournaments, concerts," and game nights. "A lot of school clubs have movie nights and show really great movies," too. Tuskegee is home to "a great football team" that is "overwhelmingly supported." Don't leave your seat at halftime either, or you'll miss the Marching Crimson Pipers—"the Best Band in the Land." Percentage-wise, Greek life isn't huge, but fraternities and sororities are extremely visible. Frat parties are common. House parties are also abundant. Drugs and alcohol are "available, but if it's not your style then you don't have to take part." When students grow tired of the campus scene, the relatively bright lights of Montgomery aren't far, and Auburn "is right up the road, so you can always go mingle with the Auburn University students."

Student Body

"As an HBCU, Tuskegee's student population is composed almost completely of African Americans." The only obvious exception is the smattering of white students who are enrolled in the veterinary school. "The typical student at Tuskegee is outgoing" "and easy to get along with." Most are very diligent when it comes to academics. "There may be a few slackers," one student says. Some Tuskegee students tell us that "everyone has their own style" here. According to them, "you have the fraternity/sorority types, athletes," and all manner of other subgroups. Others beg to differ. They say that there isn't a lot of individuality. "Students at this university tend to dress the same." Either way, though, pretty much everyone agrees that "it's not hard to fit in unless you're just totally lame."

FINANCIAL AID: 334-727-8210 OR 800-416-2831 • E-MAIL: ADMI@TUSKEGEE.EDU • WEBSITE: WWW.TUSKEGEE.EDU

THE PRINCETON REVIEW SAYS

Admissions

Very important factors considered include: Class rank, academic GPA, recommendation(s), rigor of secondary school record, standardized test scores, talent/ability. *Important factors considered include:* alumni/ae relation, character/personal qualities. *Other factors considered include:* Application essay, extracurricular activities, first generation, geographical residence, interview, state residency, volunteer work, work experience. SAT or ACT required; TOEFL required of all international applicants. High school diploma is required and GED is accepted. *Academic units required:* 4 English, 3 mathematics, 2 science, 3 social studies, 4 academic electives.

Financial Aid

Students should submit: FAFSA, institution's own financial aid form. The Princeton Review suggests that all financial aid forms be submitted as soon as possible after 1/1. *Need-based scholarships/grants offered:* Federal Pell, SEOG, state scholarships, the school's own gift aid, United Negro College Fund. *Loan aid offered:* FFEL Subsidized Stafford, FFEL Unsubsidized Stafford, FFEL PLUS, Federal Perkins. The Federal Work-Study Program is available and Institutional employment is available. Off-campus job opportunities are good.

The Inside Word

Tuskegee presents its students with a myriad of opportunities for discovery and research. Therefore, Tuskegee seeks applicants who have proven themselves successful in the classroom. Admissions counselors consider each application holistically individually. What they really like to see, though, is a GPA of at least 3.0 and a composite ACT score of 21 or better. Note also that requirements for the nursing and engineering programs are more stringent. For example, you'll probably need four years of high school math if you want to major in engineering here. Prospective students interested in either field should investigate the specific criteria.

THE SCHOOL SAYS "..."

From The Admissions Office

"Tuskegee University, located in central Alabama, was founded in 1881 under the dynamic and creative leadership of Booker T. Washington. As a state-related, independent institution, Tuskegee offers undergraduate and graduate programs in five major areas: The College of Agriculture, Environmental, and Natural Sciences; the College of Engineering, Architecture, and Physical Sciences; the College of Business and Information Sciences; the College of Liberal Arts and Education; and the College of Veterinary Medicine, Nursing, and Allied Health. Substantial research and service programs make Tuskegee University an effective comprehensive institution, geared toward preparing tomorrow's leaders today.

"First-year applicants must take the SAT or ACT; the SAT is preferred. International applicants must complete the TOEFL. Nursing applicants must complete the National League of Nursing exam."

SELECTIVITY

Admissions Rating	80
# of applicants	2,827
% of applicants accepted	58
% of acceptees attending	44

FRESHMAN PROFILE

Range SAT Critical Reading	390–500
Range SAT Math	380–490
Range ACT Composite	17–21
Minimum paper TOEFL	500
Minimum computer TOEFL	62
Average HS GPA	3.0
% graduated top 10% of class	20
% graduated top 25% of class	59
% graduated top 50% of class	100

DEADLINES

Regular	
Priority	3/31
Deadline	7/15
Notification	rolling
Nonfall registration?	yes

FINANCIAL FACTS

Financial Aid Rating	84
Annual tuition	$15,630
Room and board	$7,350
Required fees	$650
Books and supplies	$949
% frosh rec. need-based scholarship or grant aid	66
% UG rec. need-based scholarship or grant aid	77
% frosh rec. non-need-based scholarship or grant aid	44
% UG rec. non-need-based scholarship or grant aid	26
% frosh rec. need-based self-help aid	51
% UG rec. need-based self-help aid	58
% frosh rec. athletic scholarships	8
% UG rec. athletic scholarships	5
% frosh rec. any financial aid	80
% UG rec. any financial aid	92
% UG borrow to pay for school	91
Average cumulative indebtedness	$28,000

UNION COLLEGE (NY)

GRANT HALL, SCHENECTADY, NY 12308 • ADMISSIONS: 518-388-6112 • FAX: 518-388-6986

CAMPUS LIFE

Quality of Life Rating	63
Fire Safety Rating	84
Green Rating	85
Type of school	private
Environment	town

STUDENTS

Total undergrad enrollment	2,199
% male/female	51/49
% from out of state	59
% from public high school	70
% live on campus	88
% in (# of) fraternities	29 (12)
% in (# of) sororities	22 (5)
% African American	4
% Asian	6
% Caucasian	82
% Hispanic	4
% international	3
# of countries represented	30

SURVEY SAYS . . .

Athletic facilities are great
Frats and sororities dominate social
scene
Lots of beer drinking
Hard liquor is popular

ACADEMICS

Academic Rating	88
Calendar	trimester
Student/faculty ratio	10:1
Profs interesting rating	85
Profs accessible rating	86
Most common reg class size	10–19 students
Most common lab size	10–19 students

MOST POPULAR MAJORS

history
political science and government
psychology

STUDENTS SAY ". . ."

Academics

Immersing a bunch of engineers and premeds in an accelerated trimester calendar should be a formula for a high-stress campus, but somehow Union College manages to keep the situation under control. A highly capable student body helps, as does, perhaps, the availability of quality liberal arts classes to intersperse among the science- and math-heavy classes; as one student puts it, "There aren't too many schools that do a good job combining engineering with liberal arts, [but it's] important if you actually want to communicate with people." In fact, many students here believe Union is actually an "excellent liberal arts school with a solid footing in the hard sciences—I wasn't sure exactly what I wanted to do with my life after graduation, [and] Union gave me a myriad of options." Those options include not only "great Science and Engineering Departments" but also strong programs in economics, political science, and psychology, all taught by top-notch professors. An economics major writes, "I was really amazed and pleasantly surprised when I saw the caliber of the professors here. They are all interested in their particular field of research, and their enthusiasm in the classroom rubs off on the students and makes for interesting and fun-filled learning exercises." Students even love the trimester system, which "allows a normal course load of only three classes a term." Some feel this allows for "lots of free time." Others caution, "The amount of work is increased, and in addition we must complete courses in only 10 weeks as opposed to the normal 12 to 14. By nature, Union is an accelerated school."

Life

For as long as anyone can remember, the Greeks have dominated the social scene at Union College, and while the frats are still "a big scene on the weekends (30–40 percent of campus is involved in Greek life)," the school has increased attempts to provide more alternatives. The creation of seven Minerva Houses—each incoming student is assigned to one—represents the most significant effort; the houses are intended "to provide a nonexclusive (i.e., [non-] Greek) space for students to live and work." Some report that the Minervas are "a great idea," while others see them as "creat[ing] tension over the distribution of funds" or, worse yet, "rapidly becoming small [frat-like] cliques themselves. For example, almost the entire ultimate Frisbee team lives in Orange House." There's no disagreement over the city of Schenectady; everyone agrees it is less than ideal, and worse, there is "nothing to do." General consensus is that fun means "staying on campus and drinking" or "maybe an excursion to Albany (20 minutes away) for a concert." Campus perks up whenever the hockey team plays, as "hockey games are huge events here" and football also draws a crowd. While students concede that drinking is big at Union, they also report that "there are other options for students. Every weekend at least one Minerva has to hold an event, [and] there are speakers, lecturers, movies, [and] performances. We always have a lot going on!"

Student Body

While "you can find a variety of people at Union," students say there is definitely "a typical Union student," who can be described as "preppy, Northeastern, [and] middle- to upper-class." By all accounts, you'll find "a lot of athletes, a lot of frat boys," and a lot of students who "wear Polo and Abercrombie" here. Atypical students are those who "find their place on campus in the Minerva House activities and clubs such as Women's Union, Black Student Union, performing arts groups, the college's radio station—WRUC, ultimate Frisbee, and others." The "terribly cliquish nature of the social scene makes it difficult to provide a decent analysis of individual students."

FINANCIAL AID: 518-388-6123 • E-MAIL: ADMISSIONS@UNION.EDU • WEBSITE: WWW.UNION.EDU

THE PRINCETON REVIEW SAYS

Admissions

Very important factors considered include: academic GPA, rigor of secondary school record. *Important factors considered include:* Class rank, recommendation(s), character/personal qualities, extracurricular activities, talent/ability. *Other factors considered include:* Application essay, standardized test scores, alumni/ae relation, first generation, geographical residence, interview, level of applicant's interest, racial/ethnic status, state residency, volunteer work, work experience. TOEFL required of all international applicants. High school diploma is required and GED is not accepted. *Academic units required:* 4 English, 3 mathematics, 2 science, (2 science labs), 2 foreign language, 1 social studies, 1 history. *Academic units recommended:* 4 English, 4 mathematics, 4 science, (4 science labs), 4 foreign language, 2 social studies, 2 history.

Financial Aid

Students should submit: FAFSA, CSS/Financial Aid PROFILE, state aid form, noncustodial PROFILE, business/farm supplement. Regular filing deadline is 2/1. The Princeton Review suggests that all financial aid forms be submitted as soon as possible after 1/1. *Need-based scholarships/grants offered:* Federal Pell, SEOG, state scholarships/grants, private scholarships, the school's own gift aid. *Loan aid offered:* FFEL Subsidized Stafford, FFEL Unsubsidized Stafford, FFEL PLUS, Federal Perkins, college/university loans from institutional funds. Applicants will be notified of awards on or about 4/1. Federal Work-Study Program available. Institutional employment available. Off-campus job opportunities are good.

The Inside Word

Hoping to produce world-historical progeny some day? Attending Union College may improve your odds; the school is alma mater to Franklin D. Roosevelt's father and Winston Churchill's grandfather. Craft your application package carefully here. Since Union does not require standardized test scores, there is no need to submit these scores unless they strengthen your application.

THE SCHOOL SAYS "..."

From The Admissions Office

"The Union academic program is characterized by breadth and flexibility across a range of disciplines and interdisciplinary programs in the liberal arts and engineering. With nearly 1,000 courses to choose from, Union students may major in a single field, combine work in two or more departments or create their own organizing-theme major. Opportunities for undergraduate research are robust and give students a chance to work closely with professors year-round, take part in professional-level conferences and use sophisticated scientific equipment. More than half of Union's students take advantage of the college's extensive international study program, with new opportunities created regularly. A rich array of service learning programs and strong athletic, cultural and social activities also enhance the overall Union experience. Union's seven student-run Minerva Houses are lively hubs for intellectual and social activities. They bring together students, faculty and staff for hundreds of events, from dinners with invited speakers, lectures, and live bands to trips to local attractions.

"The Union community welcomes talented and diverse students, and we work closely with each one to help identify and cultivate their passions. Admission to the College is based on excellent academic credentials as reflected in the high school transcript, quality of courses selected, teacher and counselor recommendations, personal essays and writing samples. Personal interviews are strongly recommended. All candidates who apply to Union receive a thorough and thoughtful review of their application. Submission of SAT and ACT scores is optional except for the law and medicine programs."

SELECTIVITY

Admissions Rating	95
# of applicants	5,271
% of applicants accepted	39
% of acceptees attending	28
# accepting a place on wait list	298
% admitted from wait list	5
# of early decision applicants	327
% accepted early decision	77

FRESHMAN PROFILE

Range SAT Critical Reading	570–660
Range SAT Math	600–680
Range SAT Writing	560–670
Range ACT Composite	26–30
Minimum paper TOEFL	600
Minimum computer TOEFL	250
Minimum web-based TOEFL	90
Average HS GPA	3.5
% graduated top 10% of class	57
% graduated top 25% of class	82
% graduated top 50% of class	96

DEADLINES

Early Decision	
Deadline	11/15
Notification	12/15
Regular	
Deadline	1/15
Notification	4/1
Nonfall registration?	no

APPLICANTS ALSO LOOK AT

AND OFTEN PREFER
Cornell University
Colgate University
Tufts University

AND SOMETIMES PREFER
Hamilton College
Lehigh University
Skidmore College

AND RARELY PREFER
Hobart and William Smith Colleges
University of Rochester
Syracuse University

FINANCIAL FACTS

Financial Aid Rating	97
Comprehensive fee	$48,552
Books and supplies	$450
% frosh rec. need-based scholarship or grant aid	44
% UG rec. need-based scholarship or grant aid	47
% frosh rec. non-need-based scholarship or grant aid	5
% UG rec. non-need-based scholarship or grant aid	2
% frosh rec. need-based self-help aid	42
% UG rec. need-based self-help aid	47
% frosh rec. any financial aid	58
% UG rec. any financial aid	60
% UG borrow to pay for school	52
Average cumulative indebtedness	$23,000

UNITED STATES AIR FORCE ACADEMY

2304 CADET DRIVE, SUITE 2500, USAF ACADEMY, CO 80840-5025 • ADMISSIONS: 719-333-2520 • FAX: 719-333-3012

CAMPUS LIFE

Quality of Life Rating	**77**
Fire Safety Rating	**80**
Green Rating	**76**
Type of school	public
Environment	metropolis

STUDENTS

Total undergrad enrollment	4,537
% male/female	81/19
% from out of state	85
% from public high school	99
% live on campus	100
% African American	5
% Asian	8
% Caucasian	77
% Hispanic	7
% Native American	2
% international	1
# of countries represented	35

SURVEY SAYS . . .
No one cheats
Lab facilities are great
Athletic facilities are great
Career services are great
Campus feels safe
Frats and sororities are unpopular or nonexistent
Very little drug use

ACADEMICS

Academic Rating	**99**
Calendar	semester
Student/faculty ratio	9:1
Profs interesting rating	88
Profs accessible rating	99
Most common reg class size	10–19 students
Most common lab size	10–19 students

MOST POPULAR MAJORS
aerospace, aeronautical, and astronautical engineering
business/commerce
social sciences

STUDENTS SAY "..."

Academics

The United States Air Force Academy is "a leadership laboratory" and "an incredibly prestigious institution" that provides "rigorous academic and military training" for future Air Force officers. Students here have "the opportunity to travel the world, making a difference in lives and in history." There's military free-fall parachute training, combat survival, skydiving, internships at national labs, and, of course, the best flying programs in the solar system. Everyone leaves here with a really cool skill set. There's "free tuition," too (and a nominal monthly stipend). "Very tough" professors bring "a lot of real-world experience" and "rival those of any of the top schools in the country." "Class sizes are very small," and extra help is copious. "The teachers are always there," promises a physics major. "The professors and officers who teach classes go the extra mile to make themselves available." "If you can get in, the tools are here to help you stay." You'll "owe at least five years of service" as an active-duty officer upon graduation, though, and nothing about this place is easy. The "very broad" core curriculum is "hard and tedious" and heavy on science and engineering. "Courses and course loads are very demanding." "You have to be on top of your game 24/7," cautions a first-year cadet. "Slacking is not tolerated, and constant professionalism is the minimum standard."

Life

"The Air Force Academy will break you down mentally and physically and then build you into something greater than you ever could have imagined." Like the other military academies, though, Air Force is "better to be from than to go to." "The campus has a pretty cold, sterile feel to it." "The dining facility and food quality are not the greatest." The "stressful, time-crunched environment" "challenges each cadet academically, militarily, and athletically." In addition to tons of homework, "there is military training almost every day." Rules are "strict." There are "room inspections." There are "random urine tests." "It's really easy to get in trouble." The "grueling" first year is especially difficult. You can leave the confines of the campus only rarely. "Your life is miserable, and the upperclassmen treat you with contempt." "Every action and word is under scrutiny." Life becomes a little easier, and free time becomes somewhat more abundant as you rise through the ranks. "Weekends offer a good time to relax or get away, provided the weekend does not include military training." "Snowboarding and skiing are very popular in the winter." Drinking simply doesn't happen on campus, but "the cadets that are of age go out drinking a lot" when they can. Some students just catch up on sleep during their free time. "USAFA has made me appreciate and enjoy doing nothing," one cadet says.

Student Body

"We are all a bunch of college kids in a very different environment," explains one cadet. "This school forces you to grow up and obtain a more mature outlook on life, yet, at the same time, the kids are normal kids who know when and how to have fun." The population at Air Force is overwhelmingly male. It's a "tight-knit community," and people tend to be "similar in beliefs and backgrounds." The military aspect limits how "atypical" anyone can really be. "You probably will not do well here" if you don't fit the mold. Cadets describe themselves as "hardworking and motivated," "fairly conservative," and "very patriotic." "The sense of pride and duty that comes from serving your country is something that you cannot explain to a civilian," one student says. They're "inventive," "studious," "physically fit," and "smart as a whip." "The typical cadet is tired of being here and wants to go home on break" as well.

E-MAIL: RR_WEBMAIL@USAFA.AF.MIL • WEBSITE: WWW.USAFA.AF.MIL

THE PRINCETON REVIEW SAYS

Admissions

Very important factors considered include: Class rank, application essay, academic GPA, rigor of secondary school record, standardized test scores, character/personal qualities, interview, level of applicant's interest. *Important factors considered include:* recommendation(s), extracurricular activities, talent/ability, volunteer work, work experience. *Other factors considered include:* alumni/ae relation, first generation, racial/ethnic status, SAT or ACT required; ACT with Writing component recommended. High school diploma is required and GED is accepted. *Academic units recommended:* 4 English, 4 mathematics, 4 science, (4 science labs), 2 foreign language, 3 social studies, 3 history, 1 computer science.

Financial Aid

The Princeton Review suggests that all financial aid forms be submitted as soon as possible after 1/1.

The Inside Word

The Air Force Academy promises a demanding four years, and the fainthearted need not apply. Due to the arduous nature of the school, it's no wonder that applicants face stringent requirements right at the outset. Aside from an excellent academic record, successful candidates need to be physically fit. They also must win a nomination from their congressperson. Honor is a valued quality at the academy, and admissions officers will accept only those with the strength of character and determination necessary to succeed at one of the country's most elite institutions.

THE SCHOOL SAYS ". . ."

From The Admissions Office

"The Air Force Academy offers one of the most prestigious and respected undergraduate programs available. Each cadet completes a balanced sequence of core curriculum, which includes courses in basic sciences, engineering, humanities and social sciences. Air Force Academy graduates earn a Bachelor of Science degree from one of 32 majors and two minors. The Academy education is tailored to develop future Air Force officers with innovative, analytical and resourceful minds. Upon graduation from the Academy, one receives a commission as a second lieutenant in the United States Air Force.

"The Academy's extensive athletic program includes intercollegiate or intramural sports, physical education courses and physical fitness tests. These programs are tailored to help prepare you for Air Force leadership by building confidence, emotional control, physical courage and the ability to perform under pressure. The 27 men and 10 women intercollegiate teams compete in the NCAA Division I and are members of the Mountain West Conference.

"The Academy experience requires cadets to become active participants in leadership roles and opportunities that give a sense of honor and duty. The Academy is a leadership laboratory, and our mission is to educate, train and inspire men and women to become officers of character motivated to lead the United States Air Force in service to our nation. If you choose to accept the challenges, you will be rewarded with unique experiences and opportunities incomparable to any other college experience."

SELECTIVITY

Admissions Rating	96
# of applicants	9,001
% of applicants accepted	18
% of acceptees attending	81

FRESHMAN PROFILE

Range SAT Critical Reading	595–680
Range SAT Math	620–700
Range SAT Writing	560–660
Range ACT Composite	25–29
Average HS GPA	3.86
% graduated top 10% of class	52
% graduated top 25% of class	80
% graduated top 50% of class	99

DEADLINES

Regular	
Deadline	1/31
Notification	rolling
Nonfall registration?	no

APPLICANTS ALSO LOOK AT AND SOMETIMES PREFER

United States Naval Academy
United States Military Academy

FINANCIAL FACTS

Financial Aid Rating	60*

*Tuition covered by full scholarship.

UNITED STATES COAST GUARD ACADEMY

31 MOHEGAN AVENUE, NEW LONDON, CT 06320-8103 • ADMISSIONS: 800-883-8724 • FAX: 860-701-6700

CAMPUS LIFE
Quality of Life Rating	62
Fire Safety Rating	76
Green Rating	77
Type of school	public
Environment	city

STUDENTS
Total undergrad enrollment	996
% male/female	72/28
% from out of state	94
% from public high school	81
% live on campus	100
% African American	3
% Asian	5
% Caucasian	86
% Hispanic	5
% Native American	1
% international	1
# of countries represented	9

SURVEY SAYS . . .
No one cheats
Career services are great
Campus feels safe
Everyone loves the Bears
Intramural sports are popular
Frats and sororities are unpopular or nonexistent
Political activism is unpopular or nonexistent
Very little drug use

ACADEMICS
Academic Rating	87
Calendar	semester
Student/faculty ratio	9:1
Profs interesting rating	68
Profs accessible rating	96
Most common reg class size	10–19 students
Most common lab size	10–19 students

MOST POPULAR MAJORS
oceanography, chemical and physical engineering
political science and government

STUDENTS SAY ". . ."

Academics

If you're ready to "deal with military rules and discipline along with a rigorous engineering education" so that "in four years you get the job you've always wanted" (provided that job involves military, maritime, or multi-mission humanitarian service), the United States Coast Guard Academy may be the place for you. "Rigorous academics and military training" prepare cadets "for success as junior officers in the [Coast Guard] as ship drivers, pilots, and marine safety officers." The workload is considerable. Students must take a minimum of 19 credits per semester while also handling military training and athletics. Cadets note that this regimen "builds character through intense physical and mental training," although some opine that "It's like a cup of boiling hot chocolate: It smells good, you know it tastes good, but you have wait a long time to let it cool down in order to enjoy it fully." Others simply say that the demands make USCGA "a great place to be from but not always the greatest place to be." The school offers eight majors, most heavily in science, technology, engineering, and math, including operations research, management, and government. In all disciplines, "The academic program is extremely difficult, but most instructors are willing to work with you one-on-one if necessary."

Life

Life at USCGA, unsurprisingly, is highly regimented. One student sums it up: "We have to wake up at 0600 every day whether we have class or not. We have to have our doors open whether we're in our rooms or not from 0600 to 1600. They tell us exactly what we can and can't do and what we can wear and what we can't. We have military training period from 0700 to 0800 and class from 0800 to1600. We all eat lunch together at the same time in a family-style fashion. Sports period is from 1600 to 1800. Military training periods from 1900 to 2000. Study hour-from 2000 to 2200. We all have to stand duty and play sports and get a certain number of community-service hours. We can't drink on base, and we can't leave during the week. We have to make our own fun, which involves some creativity sometimes (and demerits), but our fun wouldn't appeal to most college students because it's silly and doesn't involve alcohol." Cadets warn that "The school can be very rigid with the rules. It hurts to see one of your friends get kicked out after having made a stupid decision, as almost all college students do," but students recognize that "that goes with the territory of being a military institution." Students "can only leave campus on the weekends." When they do "there is a bus system that takes cadets to familiar places in the New London area" as well as "a nearby Amtrak station that takes cadets to New York City or Boston when cadets are allowed to leave the Academy for an extended period of time (rare), usually holiday weekends."

Student Body

Service academies tend to attract students from particular demographics, and the USCGA is no exception. Most here are "fairly conservative," "extremely athletic," "very smart," and "were leaders of their schools while in high school." They tend to be "type-A personalities" who are "very disciplined or looking for discipline" in their lives. Students tell us that "although there are exceptions, almost everyone here is very selfless, and willing to take one for the team or to sacrifice to help out a buddy. As the saying goes, 'Ship, shipmates, self.' Along those same lines, everyone is held to a high standard by both comrades and superiors. Both have a low tolerance for slacking."

UNITED STATES COAST GUARD ACADEMY

E-MAIL: ADMISSIONS@USCGA.EDU • WEBSITE: WWW.USCGA.EDU

THE PRINCETON REVIEW SAYS

Admissions

Very important factors considered include: Class rank, academic GPA, rigor of secondary school record, standardized test scores, character/personal qualities, extracurricular activities. *Important factors considered include:* Application essay, recommendation(s), talent/ability. *Other factors considered include:* alumni/ae relation, interview, level of applicant's interest, volunteer work, work experience. SAT or ACT required; ACT with Writing component required. TOEFL required of all international applicants. High school diploma is required and GED is accepted. *Academic units required:* 4 English, 4 mathematics, 3 science, (3 science labs).

Financial Aid

The Princeton Review suggests that all financial aid forms be submitted as soon as possible after 1/1.

The Inside Word

Though USCGA has a low level of public recognition, gaining admission is still a steep uphill climb. Candidates must go through the rigorous multi-step admissions process as do their other service-academy peers (although no congressional nomination is required) and will encounter a serious roadblock if they fall short on any step. Those who pass muster join a proud, if somewhat under-recognized, student body, virtually equal in accomplishment to those at other service academies.

THE SCHOOL SAYS " . . ."

From The Admissions Office

"Founded in 1876, the United States Coast Guard Academy enjoys a proud tradition of graduating leaders of character. The academy experience melds academic rigor, leadership development, and athletic participation to prepare you to graduate as a commissioned officer. Character development of cadets is founded on the core values of honor, respect, and devotion to duty. You build friendships that last a lifetime, study with inspiring professors in small classes, and train during the summer aboard America's tall ship *Eagle*, as well as the service's ships and aircraft. Top performers spend their senior summer traveling on exciting internships around the nation and overseas. Graduates serve for 5 years and have unmatched opportunities to attend flight school and graduate school, all funded by the Coast Guard.

"Appointments to the Academy are based on a selective admissions process; Congressional nominations are not required. Your leadership potential and desire to serve your country are what counts. Our student body reflects the best America has to offer—with all its potential and diversity!

"Applicants are required to take the SAT (or the ACT with the Writing section)."

SELECTIVITY
Admissions Rating	**96**
# of applicants	1,633
% of applicants accepted	24
% of acceptees attending	70

FRESHMAN PROFILE
Range SAT Critical Reading	570–670
Range SAT Math	610–680
Range ACT Composite	25–29
Minimum paper TOEFL	560
Minimum computer TOEFL	220
Average HS GPA	3.76
% graduated top 10% of class	50
% graduated top 25% of class	90
% graduated top 50% of class	99

DEADLINES
Early action	
Deadline	11/1
Notification	12/15
Regular	
Priority	12/15
Deadline	3/1
Notification	rolling
Nonfall registration?	no

FINANCIAL FACTS
Financial Aid Rating	**60***

*Tuition covered by full scholarship.

UNITED STATES MERCHANT MARINE ACADEMY

OFFICE OF ADMISSIONS, KINGS POINT, NY 11024-1699 • ADMISSIONS: 516-773-5391 • FAX: 516-773-5390

CAMPUS LIFE

Quality of Life Rating	63
Fire Safety Rating	60*
Green Rating	60*
Type of school	public
Environment	village

STUDENTS

Total undergrad enrollment	985
% male/female	88/12
% from out of state	86
% from public high school	71
% live on campus	100
% African American	3
% Asian	5
% Caucasian	84
% Hispanic	5
% Native American	1
% international	3
# of countries represented	5

SURVEY SAYS . . .

Class discussions are rare
Career services are great
Lousy food on campus
Low cost of living
Frats and sororities are unpopular or
nonexistent
Political activism is unpopular or
nonexistent
(Almost) no one smokes
Very little drug use

ACADEMICS

Academic Rating	74
Calendar	trimester
Student/faculty ratio	11:1
Profs interesting rating	61
Profs accessible rating	66
Most common reg class size	10–19 students
Most common lab size	10–19 students

MOST POPULAR MAJORS

engineering
naval architecture and
marine engineering
transportation and materials moving

STUDENTS SAY ". . ."

Academics

"The Merchant Marine Academy produces officers, leaders, and good citizens of honor and integrity to serve the economic and defense interests of the United States through the maritime industry and armed forces." A "prestigious academy, paid for by the federal government," has free tuition. With "strong alumni support," and "100% job placement," the USMMA offers "opportunities upon graduation [that] are endless." After gradation, students are automatically qualified to enter any branch of the armed forces as an officer, including: Army, Navy, Air Force, Marines, Coast Guard, or NOAA. Students who choose to pursue civilian jobs post graduation are quick to note that the school provides the "best marine engineering education available," chock full of skills that are "highly sought after in the engineering industry." Known for having "the hardest academics out of all the military academies," "the school is regimented and very disciplined. The class load is very rigorous." Beyond the regular course load, "spending a year studying at sea on merchant vessels gives the students a hands-on perspective that not many other engineering schools offer." Professors are "undoubtedly more than qualified in their fields of study (ranging from former NASA scientists to highly decorated and accomplished officers in the military). However, sometimes they experience difficulty in attempting to convey the subject matter." As one student notes, The United States Merchant Marine Academy "is academically challenging, which will push you far beyond what you thought you could do; it will also train you to assume a leadership role in any company."

Life

Life at the Merchant Marine Academy fosters "an environment that pushes you to the limit," and students say that it is "tough as hell, but worth every minute." Many midshipmen view "sea year" as the apex of their college experience because it is often considered "a gigantic study-abroad term" during which students spend their time "traveling the world on merchant ships." Because of the school's focus on "teaching time-management, integrity, leadership, and discipline," students are "getting the best education in the field, while making the best friends of your life, all under stressful [and] sometimes pain-staking conditions." For fun, students "will work out or play basketball or football." There are also "several clubs and activities to be involved in" and "several intramural tournaments held throughout the year." Because "New York City is 16 miles east of school...students take frequent trips on the weekends and enjoy the city life." With their sights set on the future, many say, The Merchant Marine Academy is "a tough place to be at but the best place to be from."

Student Body

Students are quick to form a "mutual bond with one another" and "get along very well." "Outgoing and focused," "everyone is strong-willed and generally respectful." The vast majority of students describe themselves as "white, male, intelligent, athletic, conservative, and competitive." Students are bonded by a fraternal patriotism and a strong work ethic. Regiments inspire an "esprit d'corps. "We are tight. We know everybody, and we are dedicated to everyone's success." Freshman year "is tough, both regimentally and academically." "As a plebe, a freshmen, you are an outcast from the rest of the regiment in order to build unity among their class. [Plebes] must complete a long series of steps before they become recognized." "Most time is spent doing: academics, sports, and regiment. The few remaining hours a week are spent socializing with friends outside of school at bars."

UNITED STATES MERCHANT MARINE ACADEMY

FINANCIAL AID: 516-773-5295 • E-MAIL: ADMISSIONS@USMMA.EDU • WEBSITE: WWW.USMMA.EDU

THE PRINCETON REVIEW SAYS

Admissions

Very important factors considered include: rigor of secondary school record, standardized test scores, character/personal qualities. *Important factors considered include:* Class rank, application essay, academic GPA, recommendation(s), extracurricular activities, level of applicant's interest, talent/ability. *Other factors considered include:* geographical residence, interview, racial/ethnic status, state residency, volunteer work, work experience. SAT or ACT required; TOEFL required of all international applicants. High school diploma is required and GED is accepted. *Academic units required:* 4 English, 3 mathematics, 3 science, (1 science labs), 8 academic electives. *Academic units recommended:* 4 English, 4 mathematics, 4 science, (2 science labs), 2 foreign language, 4 social studies.

Financial Aid

Students should submit: FAFSA, institution's own financial aid form Regular filing deadline is 5/1. The Princeton Review suggests that all financial aid forms be submitted as soon as possible after 1/1. *Need-based scholarships/grants offered:* Federal Pell, private scholarships, Federal SMART Grants and Federal Academic Competitiveness Grants. *Loan aid offered:* Direct PLUS, FFEL Subsidized Stafford, FFEL Unsubsidized Stafford, FFEL PLUS Applicants will be notified of awards on a rolling basis beginning 1/31. Off-campus job opportunities are poor.

The Inside Word

Prospective midshipmen face demanding admission requirements. The USMMA assesses scholastic achievement, strength of character, and stamina (applicants must meet specific physical standards). Candidates must also be nominated by a proper nominating authority, typically a state representative or senator.

THE SCHOOL SAYS " . . ."

From The Admissions Office

"What makes the U.S. Merchant Marine Academy different from the other federal service academies? The difference can be summarized in two phrases that appear in our publications. The first: 'The World Is Your Campus.' You will spend a year at sea—a third of your sophomore year and two-thirds of your junior year—teamed with a classmate aboard a U.S. merchant ship. You will visit an average of 18 foreign nations while you work and learn in a mariner's true environment. You will graduate with seafaring experience and as a citizen of the world. The second phrase is 'Options and Opportunities.' Unlike students at the other federal academies, who are required to enter the service connected to their academy, you have the option of working in the seagoing merchant marine and transportation industry or applying for active duty in the Navy, Coast Guard, Marine Corps, Air Force, or Army. Nearly 25 percent of our most recent graduating class entered various branches of the armed forces with an officer rank. As a graduate of the U.S. Merchant Marine Academy, you will receive a Bachelor of Science degree, a government-issued merchant marine officer's license, and a Naval Reserve commission (unless you have been accepted for active military duty). No other service academy offers so attractive a package.

"Applicants must take the SAT or the ACT with the Writing component. For homeschooled students, we recommend they also submit scores from SAT Subject Tests in Chemistry and/or Physics."

SELECTIVITY
Admissions Rating	93
# of applicants	1,734
% of applicants accepted	18
% of acceptees attending	100

FRESHMAN PROFILE
Range SAT Critical Reading	540–640
Range SAT Math	600–660
Range ACT Composite	25–29
Minimum paper TOEFL	533
Minimum computer TOEFL	200
Minimum web-based TOEFL	73
Average HS GPA	3.6
% graduated top 10% of class	18
% graduated top 25% of class	23
% graduated top 50% of class	85

DEADLINES
Regular	
Deadline	3/1
Notification	rolling
Nonfall registration?	no

APPLICANTS ALSO LOOK AT
AND OFTEN PREFER
United States Naval Academy
AND SOMETIMES PREFER
United States Air Force Academy
United States Coast Guard Academy
United States Military Academy
AND RARELY PREFER
State University of New York—Maritime College

FINANCIAL FACTS
Financial Aid Rating	94
Required fees	$2,843

*Tuition covered by full scholarship.

UNITED STATES MILITARY ACADEMY

600 THAYER ROAD, WEST POINT, NY 10996-1797 • ADMISSIONS: 845-938-4041 • FAX: 845-938-3021

CAMPUS LIFE

Quality of Life Rating	**71**
Fire Safety Rating	**85**
Green Rating	**60***
Type of school	public
Environment	village

STUDENTS

Total undergrad enrollment	4,553
% male/female	85/15
% from out of state	93
% from public high school	86
% live on campus	100
% African American	6
% Asian	7
% Caucasian	75
% Hispanic	8
% Native American	1
% international	1
# of countries represented	37

SURVEY SAYS . . .

No one cheats
Athletic facilities are great
Career services are great
School is well run
Campus feels safe
Frats and sororities are unpopular or nonexistent
Very little drug use

ACADEMICS

Academic Rating	**96**
Calendar	semester
Student/faculty ratio	7:1
Profs interesting rating	89
Profs accessible rating	99
Most common reg class size	10–19 students
Most common lab size	10–19 students

MOST POPULAR MAJORS

business administration and management
economics
engineering/industrial management

STUDENTS SAY ". . ."

Academics

A United States Military Academy education "is not easy and not always fun, but it is a great experience to be proud of," and one that is designed "to educate tomorrow's world leaders." Don't come to West Point expecting the typical college experience. As one student explains, "The military atmosphere makes everything different. Teachers are usually commissioned Army officers and strict discipline is maintained within the classroom at all times. Disciplinary actions ensure that students turn in assignments on time, arrive to class on time, and do not miss class." Also, USMA uses "the Thayer method" of education, under which "Cadets are required to teach themselves the material before coming to class and then spend class time clarifying what was self-taught the night before." Though some find the system "unrealistic," most agree that "it is not really enjoyable to endure, but it does help foster individual academic responsibility." It also contributes to the sense that USMA "give you 28 hours of things to do in a 24-hour day." Expect to be "busy," but know that "every teacher makes an explicit point of stating that any help that a cadet needs will be given. If you want to do well here and are willing to work for it, the path is available for you to do so." Take heart; though the program "is as grueling as can be for the first 2 years," you'll find that in the final 2 years "You have a lot more time to do what you want to do."

Life

"Life at West Point is very regimented" and "just about every hour of every day is busy." As one student puts it, "West Point tries to make sure that we have little free time and are always doing something (physical, academic, or military)." Another adds that there is "not much room for fun." "Physical fitness is a big part of every student's life," as "West Point has corps-wide physical testing events. From the APFT (Army Physical Fitness Test) to the infamous and dreaded IOCT (Indoor Obstacle Course Test), this place will make you stay in shape or get rid of you." In order to leave campus overnight, students need a pass. "During the first year, you are only guaranteed one pass to leave a semester, but everyone is allowed to go on trip sections, plebes included. Plebes are also allowed to go to the mall, visit sponsors' houses, play sports, and go to their own club to hang out—all without having to take pass." Also, "passes are awarded for grades, physical fitness, attitude, special activities, etc." So as long as you are a "good person" and "take care of your business," the school is "more than happy to reward you and let you get off post for the weekend." Cadets love to "go to New York City on the weekend." Fitness doesn't end with the school day as many "enjoy the thrill of the outdoors and taking things to the extreme."

Student Body

Being a military school, it should come as no surprise that things as USMA are "uniform." "Most students are the same," notes a senior. They're "intelligent, athletic, honest, and committed to serving in the Army." And while it is a coed institution, expect a greater number of "male students." Gender aside, students are "very alike as far as life goals and ambitions...all are very intellectual and bring their own views to the school." There are "a lot of type-A personalities" here, all "prepared to do anything and everything to be the best." However, some find that the school "still has a long way to go" in terms of "ethnic diversity." But being part of "The Long Gray Line" comes with a "unifying, competitive spirit" that "levels the playing field" for these "soldiers and students."

UNITED STATES MILITARY ACADEMY

FINANCIAL AID: 845-938-4041 • E-MAIL: ADMISSIONS@USMA.EDU • WEBSITE: WWW.WESTPOINT.EDU

THE PRINCETON REVIEW SAYS

Admissions

Very important factors considered include: Class rank, application essay, academic GPA, recommendation(s), rigor of secondary school record, standardized test scores, character/personal qualities, extracurricular activities, talent/ability. *Important factors considered include:* geographical residence, interview, level of applicant's interest, racial/ethnic status, volunteer work. *Other factors considered include:* alumni/ae relation, state residency, work experience. SAT or ACT required; High school diploma is required and GED is accepted. *Academic units recommended:* 4 English, 4 mathematics, 4 science, (2 science labs), 2 foreign language, 3 social studies, 1 history, 3 academic electives.

Financial Aid

All students attend West Point on the equivalent of a full-scholarship. Additionally, all students receive an annual salary of approximately $10,000. Room and board, medical and dental care are provided by the institution. A one-time deposit of $2,000 is required upon admission to supplement the initial issue of uniforms, books, supplies, equipment and fees. Loan aid offered: Loans for the deposit are available from $100 to $2,000.

The Inside Word

America's military academies experienced an increase in applicants after 9/11 and although applications have dropped slightly, they are still above pre-9/11 levels. Entrance to West Point is highly competitive, but if you have the desire to serve and be a leader of character then West Point is the place for you. The admissions process must start in your junior year in order to get the requisite nomination. You'll need to excel in school, be physically fit, and participate in extracurricular activities to be considered. Students immediately start a rewarding leadership experience and receive a competitive salary upon graduating.

THE SCHOOL SAYS "..."

From The Admissions Office

"Are you a physically fit, morally sound, adventurous high achiever? Are you looking for superior academics, top-notch faculty, and small classes? Do you dream of leading in the 21st century? Then West Point is for you. For more than 200 years our faculty and staff have had one goal: producing leaders of character. West Point isn't easy, but don't worry; if we accept you, you can succeed here. Our graduation rate, 80%, is among the nation's highest. Consistently rated in the top ten in the nation, our academic program has 31 core courses that provide a balanced education in the arts and sciences. You will graduate with a Bachelor of Science degree in one of more-than 40 majors ranging from electrical engineering to physics to history to philosophy. Every cadet participates in an intercollegiate, club, or intramural-level sport every semester, and every summer you will receive military training ranging from marksmanship to parachuting. The fully-funded four-year college education includes tuition, room, board, and full medical and dental care. In return, you will be commissioned as an Army officer with an 8-year commitment, five on active duty. As a new graduate you will have responsibilities your peers can only dream of—leading tens of Soldiers with millions of dollars worth of equipment and making decisions with worldwide implications. When you leave West Point you will be a member of the famed Long Gray Line, with friends and experiences to last a lifetime and prepared to fulfill your dreams."

SELECTIVITY

Admissions Rating	96
# of applicants	10,140
% of applicants accepted	14
% of acceptees attending	77

FRESHMAN PROFILE

Range SAT Critical Reading	570–670
Range SAT Math	600–690
Range ACT Composite	21–36
Average HS GPA	3.75
% graduated top 10% of class	43
% graduated top 25% of class	75
% graduated top 50% of class	96

DEADLINES

Regular	
Deadline	2/28
Notification	rolling
Nonfall registration?	no

APPLICANTS ALSO LOOK AT AND OFTEN PREFER

United States Naval Academy
United States Air Force Academy

FINANCIAL FACTS

Financial Aid Rating	60*

*Tuition covered by full scholarship.

UNITED STATES NAVAL ACADEMY

117 DECATUR ROAD, ANNAPOLIS, MD 21402 • ADMISSIONS: 410-293-4361 • FAX: 410-295-1815

CAMPUS LIFE

Quality of Life Rating	84
Fire Safety Rating	60*
Green Rating	60*
Type of school	public
Environment	town

STUDENTS

Total undergrad enrollment	4,489
% male/female	80/20
% from out of state	95
% from public high school	60
% live on campus	100
% African American	4
% Asian	3
% Caucasian	75
% Hispanic	10
% Native American	1
% international	1
# of countries represented	27

SURVEY SAYS . . .

Lab facilities are great
Athletic facilities are great
Career services are great
Campus feels safe
Everyone loves the Navy
Frats and sororities are unpopular or
nonexistent
Very little drug use

ACADEMICS

Academic Rating	89
Calendar	semester
Student/faculty ratio	8.5:1
Profs interesting rating	81
Profs accessible rating	99
Most common reg class size	10–19 students

MOST POPULAR MAJORS

economics
political science and government
systems engineering

STUDENTS SAY ". . ."

Academics

The United States Naval Academy is "a rugged, in-your-face" "leadership laboratory" that "teaches you to think critically and develops your skills as a future combat leader." You'll find "the highest ideals of duty, honor, and loyalty" here. You'll find "unreal" facilities, too. Few colleges can boast a sub-critical nuclear reactor, just for example. All midshipmen get "a full-ride scholarship" that includes tuition, room and board, medical care, and a stipend. And you'll "have a guaranteed job when you graduate" as a Navy or Marine Corps officer. "Classes are extremely small." Academics "pile on fast." Regardless of major, you'll take a ton of core courses in the humanities, the hard sciences, engineering, and naval science and weapons systems. Though the experience is "grueling," the professors at the Academy are "some of the most caring and well educated people in the world." They "are always accessible outside of class," and "they do whatever it takes for the students to understand the material." To put it mildly, the top brass "practices tough love." "Think of Stalin and Hitler having a child, and then that child running your school." On one hand, "the administration has obligations to the military and the United States government" to train future officers. On the other hand, "there are too many stupid policies." While the atmosphere "tends to brew cynicism," major reform is unlikely. "The administration is what it is," muses a chemistry major. "Deal with it."

Life

Ultimately, the Naval Academy "gives you a great education, a job, and financial security, but at the cost of your freedom for four years." "To quote a popular slogan: 'We're here to defend liberty, not enjoy it,'" quips one midshipman. During the summer before classes start, first-year students get indoctrinated with "yelling, physical training," and basic seamanship. The entire first year is a "stressful" "crucible-type experience," and it's "no fun." Older students have it only slightly better. Life is "extremely micromanaged." "Midshipmen are never allowed outside the walls during the week." "Each day begins for every student at 6:30 A.M. and ends well past 11:00 at night." "You have to wear a uniform almost all the time." There are "mandatory meals, formations," and sports and study periods. "Most people work out, watch movies, and play various videogames." "On weekends, you may or may not be allowed to leave for a night or two, depending on which class year you are." Older midshipmen often spend that time soaking up "the great bar scene" in Annapolis. "Catching up on sleep" is also popular. Graduates usually leave with "at least some degree of spite." "The food will always suck." Nevertheless, a "strong camaraderie" is pervasive. "Even though people complain, there is no place we'd rather be," declares a junior. "Nobody here was drafted."

Student Body

The overwhelmingly male population here represents "every state and a lot of foreign countries." "Everyone is 100 percent equal regardless of gender, race, or religion." "The only intolerance is that open homosexuals are not allowed in the military under federal law." Politically, there's "a fair share of liberals," but the majority is "conservative-minded." "You can usually point out a midshipman in a crowd." Students "are pretty much the same person" because they are "made to conform." "We try to kick out the 'individuals' early on," dryly notes a junior. Many midshipmen were "the best from where they came from." "The school is full of enormous egos." "Fiercely competitive," "type-A" personalities proliferate. "Almost everyone was a sports star in high school," and "everyone is in great physical condition." At the same time, "there are many students who play a lot of videogames and are socially awkward." Deep down, "everyone here is a dork or a geek, even the most macho of athletic commandos." they're "resilient," "hardworking," "intellectual," and "pretty straightedge." They have "a good sense of humor and a level head." The average midshipman is also "a little jaded," and, on some days, "a zombie that just tries to make it to the meals."

E-MAIL: WEBMAIL@GWMAIL.USNA.EDU • WEBSITE: WWW.USNA.EDU

THE PRINCETON REVIEW SAYS

Admissions

Very important factors considered include: Class rank, application essay, academic GPA, recommendation(s), rigor of secondary school record, standardized test scores, character/personal qualities, extracurricular activities, interview, level of applicant's interest. *Important factors considered include:* talent/ability. *Other factors considered include:* alumni/ae relation, first generation, geographical residence, racial/ethnic status, volunteer work, work experience. SAT or ACT required; TOEFL required of all international applicants. High school diploma or equivalent is not required. *Academic units recommended:* 4 English, 4 mathematics, 2 science, (1 science labs), 2 foreign language, 2 history, 1 Introductory computer courses.

Financial Aid

The Princeton Review suggests that all financial aid forms be submitted as soon as possible after 1/1.

The Inside Word

It doesn't take a genius to recognize that getting admitted to the USNA requires true strength of character; simply completing the arduous admissions process is an accomplishment worthy of remembrance. Those who have successful candidacies are strong, motivated students, and leaders in both school and community. Perseverance is an important character trait for anyone considering the life of a midshipman—the application process is only the beginning of a truly challenging and demanding experience.

THE SCHOOL SAYS "..."

From The Admissions Office

"The Naval Academy offers you a unique opportunity to associate with a broad cross-section of the country's finest young men and women. You will have the opportunity to pursue a 4-year program that develops you mentally, morally, and physically as no civilian college can. As you might expect, this program is demanding, but the opportunities are limitless and more than worth the effort. To receive an appointment to the academy, you need 4 years of high school preparation to develop the strong academic, athletic, and extracurricular background required to compete successfully for admission. You should begin preparing in your freshman year and apply for admission at the end of your junior year. Selection for appointment to the academy comes as a result of a complete evaluation of your admissions package and completion of the nomination process. Complete admissions guidance may be found online."

SELECTIVITY

Admissions Rating	96
# of applicants	10,960
% of applicants accepted	14
% of acceptees attending	83
# accepting a place on wait list	70
% admitted from wait list	21

FRESHMAN PROFILE

Range SAT Critical Reading	560–670
Range SAT Math	600–700
% graduated top 10% of class	56
% graduated top 25% of class	81
% graduated top 50% of class	96

DEADLINES

Regular	
Deadline	1/31
Notification	rolling
Nonfall registration?	no

**APPLICANTS ALSO LOOK AT
AND OFTEN PREFER**
United States Air Force Academy

AND SOMETIMES PREFER
United States Military Academy

FINANCIAL FACTS

Financial Aid Rating	60*
Books and supplies	$1,000

*Tuition covered by full scholarship.

THE UNIVERSITY OF ALABAMA AT BIRMINGHAM

1530 3RD AVENUE SOUTH, BIRMINGHAM AL, 35294 • ADMISSIONS: 205-934-8221 • FAX: 205-975-7114

CAMPUS LIFE

Quality of Life Rating	89
Fire Safety Rating	93
Green Rating	60*
Type of school	public
Environment	metropolis

STUDENTS

Total undergrad enrollment	9,989
% male/female	40/60
% from out of state	7
% live on campus	19
% in (# of) fraternities	6 (9)
% in (# of) sororities	6 (8)
% African American	27
% Asian	4
% Caucasian	60
% Hispanic	2
% international	2
# of countries represented	89

SURVEY SAYS . . .

Registration is a breeze
Lab facilities are great
Athletic facilities are great
School is well run
Diverse student types on campus
Different types of students interact
Students get along with local community
Dorms are like palaces
Students are happy

ACADEMICS

Academic Rating	80
Calendar	semester
Student/faculty ratio	17:1
Profs interesting rating	81
Profs accessible rating	87
Most common reg class size	20–29 students
Most common lab size	20–29 students

MOST POPULAR MAJORS
biology/biological sciences
nursing/registered nurse
(rn, asn, bsn, msn)
psychology

STUDENTS SAY ". . ."

Academics

University of Alabama at Birmingham is a refreshingly friendly public college, boasting a strong reputation in pre-health and science, plenty of personalized attention for undergraduate students, and a "faculty that really cares and want you to do your best." "Integrating culture, education, and 'real world' experience into a college degree," the school encourages students to pursue research, internships, or other opportunities by "working in the field they aspire to have a career in, whether it be art history, biomedical engineering, or medicine." A senior enthuses, "No matter what you want to do, the faculty and administration will see to it that you get the experience you want and need. Nothing is too big or off-limits; you can do it all here." Like faculty, UAB's "administration is very helpful and seems very focused on student satisfaction, personally and academically." A sophomore boasts, "I've eaten dinner with the family of several of my professors and the dean as well. Need I say more?"

Life

"Traditionally a commuter school," UAB has recently stepped up efforts to create a more dynamic campus atmosphere, with good results. A junior enthuses, "From the free movie showings, campus dining, volunteer activities, and cultural events, I find myself enjoying my college life." Other popular extracurricular pursuits include intramural sports, campus ministry, research, honors activities, campus jobs, and fraternities and sororities. In addition, UAB is an NCAA Division I school, so many students "love going to sporting events, such as the basketball and football games." Striking a balance between study and relaxation, UAB students "have far too much coursework to have major parties midweek; but on the weekends, no one is in the library, unless its finals week." But when you're ready to go out, "UAB is located close to downtown Birmingham and is right next to Five Points South and the Lakeview District, so nightlife is pretty easy to come across."

Student Body

With diverse academic and extracurricular opportunities, UAB is a school that "fits most every type of person." As a result, the student body is "truly a great American melting pot of different cultures, religions, and races." "Students work together for the common goals of getting an education and understanding and appreciating the diversity of others," one student says. As the school's reputation grows in fields other than medicine and science, the campus demographics have also been changing. A senior elaborates, "UAB was once a commuter college with a med school but has since become a very undergraduate and non-medicine-student-friendly campus. Most students will be entering into some sort of health related profession, but a great number of students are theater, art, history, and psychology majors." No matter what your interests, "everyone tends to get along with each other, since there is always something to talk about—be it UAB sports or some of the current events on campus."

THE UNIVERSITY OF ALABAMA AT BIRMINGHAM

FINANCIAL AID: 205-934-8223 • E-MAIL: UNDERGRADADMIT@UAB.EDU • WEBSITE: MAIN.UAB.EDU

THE PRINCETON REVIEW SAYS

Admissions

Very important factors considered include: academic GPA, rigor of secondary school record, standardized test scores, SAT or ACT required; TOEFL required of all international applicants. High school diploma is required and GED is accepted. *Academic units required:* 4 English, 3 mathematics, 3 science, (2 science labs), 1 foreign language, 3 social studies, 3 academic electives.

Financial Aid

Students should submit: FAFSA. The Princeton Review suggests that all financial aid forms be submitted as soon as possible after 1/1. Need-based scholarships/grants offered: Federal Pell, SEOG, state scholarships/grants, private scholarships, the school's own gift aid, United Negro College Fund. *Loan aid offered:* Direct Subsidized Stafford, Direct Unsubsidized Stafford, Direct PLUS, Federal Perkins, state loans, college/university loans from institutional funds. Applicants will be notified of awards on a rolling basis beginning 4/1. Federal Work-Study Program available. Institutional employment available. Off-campus job opportunities are excellent.

The Inside Word

It's not very hard to get admitted to UAB and the process is refreshingly uncomplicated. Basically, you need to get either a 20 on the ACT or a combined score of 950 on the critical reading and math sections of the SAT. To complement this, a high school GPA of at least 2.25 is also required.

THE SCHOOL SAYS "..."

From The Admissions Office

"BREAKTHROUGH...it's a great word to describe UAB. From undergraduate research and interest-specific honors programs to a cutting-edge medical center known internationally for discovery, UAB is a place where great minds come together to make a difference. We are an energetic, exciting place; one of the state's largest universities with eight undergraduate schools, a large graduate school, four medical professional schools, and a renowned medical center.

"UAB is the place for students who seek a world-class research university in the heart of a fun and diverse city and for students who want to take what they learn in the classroom directly to the best companies, career options, and graduate schools available. UAB is also for students who seek diversity in culture and thought, and who are creative, inquisitive, and motivated to get involved and to make a difference.

"On campus you'll discover more than 150 active student organizations and countless activities. And off campus, Alabama's largest city—recently named one of the most livable in America by a national organization—offers must-see attractions and can't-miss events just down the street or mere minutes away. So it's easy to explore your interests, try new experiences, create memories, enjoy old friends and make new ones.

"UAB...for students who expect more from college—students who take achievement seriously—students who want to make a BREAKTHROUGH."

SELECTIVITY

Admissions Rating	86
# of applicants	3,257
% of applicants accepted	85
% of acceptees attending	46

FRESHMAN PROFILE

Range ACT Composite	21–27
Minimum paper TOEFL	500
Minimum computer TOEFL	173
Minimum web-based TOEFL	61
Average HS GPA	3.51
% graduated top 10% of class	27
% graduated top 25% of class	52
% graduated top 50% of class	79

DEADLINES

Regular	
Deadline	3/1
Nonfall registration?	yes

FINANCIAL FACTS

Financial Aid Rating	70
Annual in-state tuition	$3,792
Annual out-of-state tuition	$9,480
Room and board	$7,820
Required fees	$872
Books and supplies	$900
% frosh rec. need-based scholarship or grant aid	28
% UG rec. need-based scholarship or grant aid	30
% frosh rec. non-need-based scholarship or grant aid	22
% UG rec. non-need-based scholarship or grant aid	13
% frosh rec. need-based self-help aid	32
% UG rec. need-based self-help aid	37
% frosh rec. athletic scholarships	6
% UG rec. athletic scholarships	4

THE UNIVERSITY OF ALABAMA—TUSCALOOSA

Box 870132, Tuscaloosa, AL 35487-0132 • Admissions: 205-348-5666 • Fax: 205-348-9046

CAMPUS LIFE

Quality of Life Rating	**86**
Fire Safety Rating	**75**
Green Rating	**81**
Type of school	public
Environment	city

STUDENTS

Total undergrad enrollment	22,046
% male/female	47/53
% from out of state	27
% in (# of) fraternities	22 (30)
% in (# of) sororities	29 (24)
% African American	11
% Asian	1
% Caucasian	84
% Hispanic	2
% Native American	1
% international	1
# of countries represented	72

SURVEY SAYS . . .

Athletic facilities are great
Everyone loves the Crimson Tide
Frats and sororities dominate social scene
Student publications are popular

ACADEMICS

Academic Rating	**74**
Calendar	semester
Student/faculty ratio	20:1
Profs interesting rating	80
Profs accessible rating	80
% classes taught by TAs	12
Most common reg class size	10–19 students
Most common lab size	20–29 students

MOST POPULAR MAJORS
elementary education and teaching
finance
nursing/registered nurse
(rn, asn, bsn, msn)

STUDENTS SAY " . . . "

Academics

The University of Alabama is a ridiculously affordable, "technologically advanced," "student-centered" institution that enjoys an outrageous degree of alumni support. "Course offerings are pretty diverse," and there are "tons of majors." Highlights include a "great" engineering college and three honors programs. Other standout programs include business, communication studies, and nursing. Some students say that the "bold and visionary" top brass runs the school "fairly well." Others gripe that the administration is "very bogged down in red tape." "Working with the administration is really terrible sometimes," undergrads say. Professors here are "top researchers or writers in their fields," and some are "very enthusiastic about having undergraduate students helping them with research." The faculty as a whole is also "approachable" and "generally very easy to get in touch with for outside assistance." Teaching ability is "hit-or-miss," though. While there are many professors who are "very animated and interesting to listen to," "others do not have the same talent." "Being a great researcher does not necessarily make a person a good teacher," notes one student.

Life

"An atmosphere of almost antebellum charm" permeates this "pretty" campus. "On sunny days in the fall and spring, students enjoy studying and playing on the quad." Recreational facilities are "excellent." "Life during football season revolves around football." So does morale. Win or lose, though, UA boasts "one of the best college football atmospheres in the country. On Saturdays when the Crimson Tide plays at home, the campus is "a sea of tents for tailgating," "and Alabama fans are singing the fight song." Otherwise, "the Greek organizations rule this campus." They wield "an inordinate amount of power" in student government as well. Whether you pledge or not, though, students promise "an outstanding social atmosphere." "While not everyone participates in the party scene on campus, it is very popular." In addition to the house parties and the festivities at the frat houses, "people enjoying going to the bars on the strip." "Comfort" abounds in surrounding Tuscaloosa, and it is "definitely a college town." People are "very open and courteous" to the students, and virtually everything you need is within "walking distance." When students at UA hanker for more urban environs, "Birmingham is only an hour away, and there is plenty to do there."

Student Body

Students here are "extremely friendly" and "usually well dressed and well mannered." "People tend to be a bit conservative," and "a lot are religious." "The typical student is active in a few organizations, makes decent grades, and finds time to relax, too." African American students are the largest minority group. They represent more than ten percent of the student body. Some students maintain that UA is "not diverse socially, ideologically, and culturally." "The different ethnic groups stick together," they say. They look around campus and see "frat boys or sorority girls for the most part"—"same hair, same sunglasses with a string on the back, and stupid visors." Other students vigorously disagree. "We truly aren't a university filled with cookie-cutter people," asserts one student. "There are many diverse groups of students who all have their own roles on campus." "It is easy for someone to come from up north and say this campus is full of close-minded southern Baptist Republicans, just like it is easy for someone to come from a small town...and think this campus is full of liberal heathens," points out another student. "Few people are really atypical, because no matter where you fall in any category, there are people around you who you can connect with."

THE UNIVERSITY OF ALABAMA—TUSCALOOSA

FINANCIAL AID: 205-348-6756 • E-MAIL: ADMISSIONS@UA.EDU • WEBSITE: WWW.UA.EDU

THE PRINCETON REVIEW SAYS

Admissions

Very important factors considered include: academic GPA, rigor of secondary school record, standardized test score. *Important factors considered include:* Class rank. *Other factors considered include:* Application essay, recommendation(s), alumni/ae relation, character/personal qualities, extracurricular activities, first generation, interview, talent/ability, volunteer work, work experience. SAT or ACT required; ACT with Writing component required. TOEFL required of all international applicants. High school diploma is required and GED is accepted. *Academic units required:* 4 English, 3 mathematics, 3 science, (2 science labs), 1 foreign language, 3 social studies, 1 history, 5 academic electives.

Financial Aid

Students should submit: FAFSA. The Princeton Review suggests that all financial aid forms be submitted as soon as possible after 1/1. *Need-based scholarships/grants offered:* Federal Pell, SEOG, state scholarships/grants, private scholarships, the school's own gift aid, Federal Nursing Scholarships. *Loan aid offered:* Direct Subsidized Stafford, Direct Unsubsidized Stafford, Direct PLUS, Federal Perkins, college/university loans from institutional funds. Applicants will be notified of awards on a rolling basis beginning 4/1. Federal Work-Study Program available. Institutional employment available. Off-campus job opportunities are good.

The Inside Word

The University of Alabama relies heavily on objective data in the application process. Admission is not highly competitive, and applicants with satisfactory grades and modest test scores are likely to be accepted.

THE SCHOOL SAYS "..."

From The Admissions Office

"Since its founding in 1831 as the first public university in the state, the University of Alabama has been committed to providing the best, most complete education possible for its students. Our commitment to that goal means that as times change, we sharpen our focus and methods to keep our graduates competitive in their fields. By offering outstanding teaching in a solid core curriculum enhanced by multimedia classrooms and campus-wide computer labs, the University of Alabama keeps its focus on the future while maintaining a traditional college atmosphere. Extensive international study opportunities, internship programs, and cooperative education placements help our students prepare for successful futures. Consisting of 11 colleges and schools offering 220 degrees in more than 100 fields of study, the university gives its students a wide range of choices and offers courses of study at the bachelor's, master's, specialist, and doctoral levels. The university emphasizes quality and breadth of academic opportunities and challenging programs for well-prepared students through its Honors College, including the University Honors Program, International Honors Program, and Computer-Based Honors Programs and Blount Undergraduate Initiative (liberal arts program). Twenty-four percent of undergraduates are from out of state, providing an enriching social and cultural environment.

"Applicants may submit either the SAT or the ACT. The Writing component is not required for admission beginning in 2010."

SELECTIVITY

Admissions Rating	84
# of applicants	18,500
% of applicants accepted	60
% of acceptees attending	46

FRESHMAN PROFILE

Range SAT Critical Reading	490–600
Range SAT Math	500–610
Range ACT Composite	21–27
Minimum paper TOEFL	500
Minimum computer TOEFL	173
Minimum web-based TOEFL	61
Average HS GPA	3.4
% graduated top 10% of class	42.2
% graduated top 25% of class	54.8
% graduated top 50% of class	79.9

DEADLINES

Regular	
Priority	2/1
Notification	rolling
Nonfall registration?	yes

APPLICANTS ALSO LOOK AT
AND OFTEN PREFER
University of Tennessee—Knoxville
Florida State University
University of Georgia

AND SOMETIMES PREFER
Auburn University

FINANCIAL FACTS

Financial Aid Rating	73
Annual in-state tuition	$6,400
Annual out-of-state tuition	$18,000
Room and board	$6,430
Books and supplies	$1,000
% frosh rec. need-based scholarship or grant aid	13
% UG rec. need-based scholarship or grant aid	17
% frosh rec. non-need-based scholarship or grant aid	13
% UG rec. non-need-based scholarship or grant aid	10
% frosh rec. need-based self-help aid	25
% UG rec. need-based self-help aid	30
% frosh rec. athletic scholarships	2
% UG rec. athletic scholarships	2
% frosh rec. any financial aid	60
% UG rec. any financial aid	61
% UG borrow to pay for school	48.7
Average cumulative indebtedness	$18,896

UNIVERSITY OF ARIZONA

PO Box 210040, Tucson, AZ 85721-0040 • Admissions: 520-621-3237 • Fax: 520-621-9799

CAMPUS LIFE

Quality of Life Rating	**70**
Fire Safety Rating	**60***
Green Rating	**60***
Type of school	public
Environment	metropolis

STUDENTS

Total undergrad enrollment	28,670
% male/female	47/53
% from out of state	31
% from public high school	90
% live on campus	20
% in (# of) fraternities	10 (25)
% in (# of) sororities	11 (20)
% African American	3
% Asian	6
% Caucasian	68
% Hispanic	17
% Native American	4
% international	3
# of countries represented	123

SURVEY SAYS . . .

School is well run
Everyone loves the Wildcats
Student publications are popular

ACADEMICS

Academic Rating	**70**
Calendar	semester
Student/faculty ratio	18:1
Profs interesting rating	63
Profs accessible rating	64
% classes taught by TAs	22
Most common reg class size	10–19 students
Most common lab size	10–19 students

MOST POPULAR MAJORS

cell/cellular and molecular biology
political science and government
psychology

STUDENTS SAY ". . ."

Academics

The weather's warm and the learning is there for the taking at the University of Arizona—come on in. Giving its students the "absolute full package," the U of A provides a quality, affordable education, with "great school spirit and an all-around positive college environment." Though students don't shy away from the fact that the school's fun-loving environment might move their studies to the backseat on the weekends, most still hit the books plenty during the week, and "there are plenty of opportunities to work hard and succeed, academically and otherwise, if you seek them out." "You have to be willing to put time and effort into it," says a sophomore business major. The large university also "has some outstanding programs" for undergraduate research experience, including BRAVO, a program that provides funding for students who want to do scientific research abroad.

Though lectures (especially in the intro levels) can be large, the "amazing" professors make sure they are accessible to students and conduct their classes in a way that "provides real-life scenarios instead of the textbook jargon." Also, all large general education classes have weekly breakout sessions limited to 30 students each. There "is always a bad apple," but on the whole, students are thrilled with their instructors. "You might not know it just from meeting them, but some of our professors are absolute legends in their field," says a junior. Academic advising is also a strong suit at U of A, as are the science programs, and there are many sections of general education classes offered, making scheduling "very flexible, and allowing classes at the times you want." The administration, "although it is a bureaucracy," still manages to function well, and one can even send an e-mail to the president and receive a real answer in return.

Life

People here enjoy an active social life on top of their studies, and "everyone drinks socially and goes wild on the weekends, but buckles down again come Monday." The "Greek community rules the school," if not in membership numbers than in influence over weekend plans. Popular options include "house parties, frat parties, and definitely 4th Avenue for the bar scene." Everyone on campus gets into Pac-10 sporting events. One student claims to "have lined up four hours before a men's basketball game to get good seats in the student section (this is a common occurrence)." People here are very politically active, and clubs like the Young Democrats and the Young Republicans attract large numbers. "There is always something to do both on campus and off." Tucson is great for the lover of outdoors, as there are "numerous hiking and biking trails that go through the Sonoran Desert," as well as rock climbing and golf. "Life at the University of Arizona is mostly busy, but busy in a good way," says a student.

Student Body

A giant unifying factor on campus is that "everyone shares a love for this school." Combine that with the large student body, and you'll find each of the groups on campus "interact very well and in a dignified manner." It's "a good-looking campus," and people "generally care about what they look like and are wearing." The number of activities available to each student means that "no one is an outcast," and "finding a group of friends that is right for you is easy." "If you want to fit in, you find a group of people like yourself. We have the atypical groups, but not the atypical person" says a freshman. Most hail from Tucson, Phoenix, or California, and are pretty laid-back, and "go along with the relaxed Tucson atmosphere at the U of A."

FINANCIAL AID: 520-621-1858 • E-MAIL: APPINFO@ARIZONA.EDU • WEBSITE: WWW.ARIZONA.EDU

THE PRINCETON REVIEW SAYS

Admissions

Very important factors considered include: academic GPA, rigor of secondary school record. *Other factors considered include:* Class rank, application essay, recommendation(s), standardized test scores, character/personal qualities, extracurricular activities, first generation, geographical residence, interview, racial/ethnic status, state residency, talent/ability, volunteer wor SAT or ACT recommended; High school diploma is required and GED is accepted. *Academic units required:* 4 English, 3 mathematics, 3 science, (3 science labs), 2 foreign language, 1 social studies, 1 history, 1 Fine Art. *Academic units recommended:* 4 English, 3 mathematics, 3 science, (3 science labs), 2 foreign language, 2 social studies, 1 history, 1 Fine Art.

Financial Aid

The Princeton Review suggests that all financial aid forms be submitted as soon as possible after 1/1. *Need-based scholarships/grants offered:* Federal Pell, SEOG, state scholarships/grants, private scholarships, the school's own gift aid, Federal Nursing Scholarships. *Loan aid offered:* FFEL Subsidized Stafford, FFEL Unsubsidized Stafford, FFEL PLUS, Federal Perkins, Federal Nursing, college/university loans from institutional funds. Federal Work-Study Program available. Institutional employment available. Off-campus job opportunities are good.

The Inside Word

The sun never sets for an Arizona resident—particularly if they're applying to the University of Arizona and have a solid academic record. The university offers "assured admission" for in-state freshmen applicants. This essentially guarantees all applicants immediate admission provided they have fulfilled the following requirements, as detailed on the school's Website: They must be "an Arizona resident, attend a regionally accredited high school, rank in the top 25 percent of their class, and have no course work deficiencies as prescribed by the Arizona Board of Regents."

THE SCHOOL SAYS "..."

From The Admissions Office

"Surrounded by mountains and the dramatic beauty of the Sonoran Desert, the University of Arizona offers a top-drawer education in a resort-like setting. Some of the nation's highest-ranked departments make their homes at this oasis of learning in the desert. In addition to producing cloudless sunshine 350 days per year, the clear Arizona skies provide an ideal setting for one of the country's best astronomy programs. Other nationally rated programs include nursing, sociology, management information systems, anthropology, creative writing, and computer and aerospace engineering. The university balances a strong research component with an emphasis on teaching—faculty rolls include Nobel and Pulitzer Prize winners. Famous Chinese astrophysicist and political dissident Fang Lizhi continues his landmark studies here; he now teaches physics to undergraduates. A wealth of academic choices—the university offers 114 majors, with myriad academic concentration options within those majors—is supplemented by an active, progressive campus atmosphere; conference-winning and national title-winning basketball, baseball, swimming, softball, and football teams; and countless recreational opportunities."

SELECTIVITY
Admissions Rating	88
# of applicants	25,449
% of applicants accepted	77
% of acceptees attending	45

FRESHMAN PROFILE
Range SAT Critical Reading	480–600
Range SAT Math	490–620
Range ACT Composite	21–26
Average HS GPA	3.39
% graduated top 10% of class	35
% graduated top 25% of class	65
% graduated top 50% of class	90

DEADLINES
Regular	
Deadline	5/1
Notification	rolling
Nonfall registration?	yes

APPLICANTS ALSO LOOK AT
AND RARELY PREFER
Northern Arizona University
Arizona State University at the Tempe campus

FINANCIAL FACTS
Financial Aid Rating	64
Annual in-state tuition	$6,090
Annual out-of-state tuition	$21,300
Room and board	$7,934
Required fees	$400
Books and supplies	$1,000
% frosh rec. need-based scholarship or grant aid	33
% UG rec. need-based scholarship or grant aid	34
% frosh rec. non-need-based scholarship or grant aid	39
% UG rec. non-need-based scholarship or grant aid	26
% frosh rec. need-based self-help aid	17
% UG rec. need-based self-help aid	25
% UG borrow to pay for school	45
Average cumulative indebtedness	$18,241

UNIVERSITY OF ARKANSAS—FAYETTEVILLE

232 SILAS HUNT HALL, FAYETTEVILLE, AR 72701 • ADMISSIONS: 479-575-5346 • FAX: 479-575-7515

CAMPUS LIFE

Quality of Life Rating	**84**
Fire Safety Rating	**60***
Green Rating	**94**
Type of school	public
Environment	town

STUDENTS

Total undergrad enrollment	15,426
% male/female	51/49
% from out of state	26.5
% from public high school	84
% in (# of) fraternities	17.5 (16)
% in (# of) sororities	23.6 (11)
% African American	5
% Asian	3
% Caucasian	83
% Hispanic	3
% Native American	2
% international	3
# of countries represented	106

SURVEY SAYS . . .
Athletic facilities are great
Students love Fayetteville, AR
Everyone loves the Razorbacks
Frats and sororities dominate social
scene

ACADEMICS

Academic Rating	**72**
Calendar	semester
Student/faculty ratio	17:1
Profs interesting rating	71
Profs accessible rating	72
% classes taught by TAs	27
Most common	
reg class size	20–29 students
Most common	
lab size	20–29 students

MOST POPULAR MAJORS
finance
journalism
marketing/marketing management

STUDENTS SAY "..."

Academics

The University of Arkansas is affordable, "student-centered," and large but not gargantuan. Though you'll see some sizeable lectures during your first year, most classes are "relatively small." "The facilities are exceptional" and otherwise "state-of-the-art." More than 100 undergraduate majors and programs are available. The Sam Walton College of Business is awash in cash and "one of the strongest assets." Engineering majors can participate in cutting-edge research. Agricultural programs are strong and diverse. The honors college is "wonderful." Also, some 25 percent of all Arkansas students study abroad. There are summer programs available in China and Egypt, just to a name two examples. Programs during the academic year take place in every nook and cranny of the globe. Student opinion is split with regard to the administration. Some students call the management "very friendly." "Things run pretty smoothly," they say. Others contend that UA is "overly bureaucratic." "The odds of being sent to three different buildings, none of which are right, are pretty much even," wagers one malcontent. Despite "a few really atrocious instructors," students generally praise Arkansas's "dynamic faculty." "The professors are almost always good teachers," and they "know their material." Outside of class, professors tend to be "accessible" and "willing to do anything it takes for the success of their students."

Life

"Parking is horrible," but UA boasts a "beautiful," "well-defined campus with lots of green space." The rolling hills provide plenty of "great exercise," too. Students here are reportedly enjoy a "vibrant extracurricular and social scene." "There are lots of things to do that don't involve booze." With more than 300 clubs and groups to choose from, "the vast majority of students participate in at least a few campus organizations." "Greek life is prevalent" according to some students. "Intramural sports are popular." Razorback football "is the big highlight of the fall," and the campus has "a lot of spirit" for the beloved Hogs. There are ample activities that do involve booze as well. "Parties are everywhere." "A lot of people will go to the fraternity houses" for revelry. There's also "great nightlife" and "a very enthusiastic bar scene" off campus. "Funky," "charming," and "not-too-expensive" Fayetteville is, by all accounts, a "pretty neat town." Eclectic restaurants and live music venues are ample. "The always-enticing Dickson Street," "located a couple blocks away," is the hub of it all. "On the weekends, it borders on insanity." For outdoorsy types, wilderness activities abound throughout northwestern Arkansas. "The nearby mountains" provide numerous opportunities for climbing, biking, and hiking.

Students

They typical student here is "overly friendly," "fun-loving," "at least somewhat religious, and has a southern accent." Most students come "from either Arkansas or Texas." There are "a lot of international students," but "there is little ethnic diversity." Like at virtually every other flagship state university, you'll find "all kinds of students" on this campus. Fayetteville is called "the melting pot of Arkansas." Politics range from "conservative" to "incredibly liberal." "Students come from all walks of life and have many different experiences to share with others." "Party-frat kids abound," as do "southern sorority girls who walk to class in pearls and heels." However, you'll also find "hicks;" "artists; musicians; nerds;" and "NPR listening, sandal-wearing, health-food-shopping people," as well as the occasional "middle-aged boomer returning to school to start a whole new career." "There is always someone just as weird as you to run with," and students generally "mesh well" even if "groups don't often commingle."

FINANCIAL AID: 479-575-3806 • E-MAIL: UOFA@UARK.EDU • WEBSITE: WWW.UARK.EDU/ADMISSIONS

THE PRINCETON REVIEW SAYS

Admissions

Very important factors considered include: Class rank, academic GPA, rigor of secondary school record, standardized test scores. *Other factors considered include:* recommendation(s), alumni/ae relation, character/personal qualities, extracurricular activities, first generation, geographical residence, racial/ethnic status, state residency, talent/ability, volunteer work, work experience. SAT or ACT required; TOEFL required of all international applicants. High school diploma is required and GED is accepted. *Academic units required:* 4 English, 4 mathematics, 3 science, (2 science labs), 3 social studies, 2 academic electives. *Academic units recommended:* 2 foreign language.

Financial Aid

Students should submit: FAFSA. The Princeton Review suggests that all financial aid forms be submitted as soon as possible after 1/1. *Need-based scholarships/grants offered:* Federal Pell, SEOG, state scholarships/grants, private scholarships, the school's own gift aid. *Loan aid offered:* FFEL Subsidized Stafford, FFEL Unsubsidized Stafford, FFEL PLUS, Federal Perkins, state loans, college/university loans from institutional funds, alternative loans. Applicants will be notified of awards on a rolling basis beginning 4/1. Federal Work-Study Program available. Institutional employment available.

The Inside Word

The admissions policy at the University of Arkansas is very straightforward. You need a 3.0 grade-point average (on a 4.0 scale) in your serious academic coursework and at least a 20 on the ACT. The SAT is fine, too, as long as get a comparable minimum score. If you fail to meet these requirements, you still may gain admission based on a case-by-case review process. Also, UA has a rolling admissions policy. As such, candidates will find it in their best interest to apply early.

THE SCHOOL SAYS "..."

From The Admissions Office

"The University of Arkansas, the flagship campus of the University of Arkansas System, is located in Fayetteville and overlooks the beautiful Ozark Mountains. The university is both the major land-grant university for Arkansas and the state university, encompassing more than 130 buildings on 345 acres and providing more than 200 graduate and undergraduate academic programs—more than some universities twice its size.

"At the same time, the University of Arkansas maintains a low student-to-faculty ratio—currently 17:1—that makes personal attention possible. The university aggressively promotes undergraduate research in virtually every discipline and makes higher education affordable with competitively priced tuition and generous financial aid. Over the past two decades, university undergraduates have earned many honors: 30 received Goldwater Scholarships; 12 have been recognized by the *USA Today* All-USA College Academic Team. There have been 16 National Science Foundation graduate fellows; 10 Fulbright scholars; 11 British Marshall scholars and six Truman scholars. Five undergraduates have received Udall scholarships; three earned Madison scholarships; three have received Tylenol scholarships; and one was named a Rhodes scholar. Quality programs, affordable tuition and the level of student achievement all contribute to the University of Arkansas consistently being ranked in the top tier of national universities.

"The city of Fayetteville is home to more than 62,000 people and is growing every day. Northwest Arkansas is the headquarters to several major international corporations that have close ties to the university: Tyson Foods, the world's largest protein producer; J.B. Hunt Transport Services Inc., a major transportation and logistics company; and Wal-Mart Stores Inc., the world's largest corporation. Fayetteville has been named "One of America's Most Livable Cities," "One of America's 'Hottest' Cities," one of the nation's "least stressful" metro areas, and among the "Best Places to Live in America" by publications such as *Forbes, Frommer's Guide,* and *Money* magazine."

SELECTIVITY

Admissions Rating	85
# of applicants	12,045
% of applicants accepted	58
% of acceptees attending	43

FRESHMAN PROFILE

Range SAT Critical Reading	500–630
Range SAT Math	520–640
Range ACT Composite	23–28
Minimum paper TOEFL	550
Minimum computer TOEFL	213
Minimum web-based TOEFL	80
Average HS GPA	3.59
% graduated top 10% of class	30
% graduated top 25% of class	30
% graduated top 50% of class	89

DEADLINES

Early action	
Deadline	11/15
Notification	12/15
Regular	
Priority	11/15
Deadline	8/1
Notification	rolling
Nonfall registration?	yes

FINANCIAL FACTS

Financial Aid Rating	76
Annual in-state tuition	$4,772
Annual out-of-state tuition	$13,226
Room and board	$7,017
Required fees	$1,266
Books and supplies	$966
% frosh rec. need-based scholarship or grant aid	30
% UG rec. need-based scholarship or grant aid	27
% frosh rec. non-need-based scholarship or grant aid	6
% UG rec. non-need-based scholarship or grant aid	3
% frosh rec. need-based self-help aid	24
% UG rec. need-based self-help aid	28
% frosh rec. athletic scholarships	3
% UG rec. athletic scholarships	3
% frosh rec. any financial aid	71
% UG rec. any financial aid	65
% UG borrow to pay for school	43.8
Average cumulative indebtedness	$19,248

UNIVERSITY OF CALIFORNIA—BERKELEY

110 SPROUL HALL #5800, BERKELEY, CA 94720-5800 • ADMISSIONS: 510-642-3175 • FAX: 510-642-7333

CAMPUS LIFE
Quality of Life Rating	**76**
Fire Safety Rating	**75**
Green Rating	**99**
Type of school	public

STUDENTS
Total undergrad enrollment	25,151
% male/female	47/53
% from out of state	7
% from public high school	85
% live on campus	35
% in (# of) fraternities	10 (38)
% in (# of) sororities	10 (19)
% African American	4
% Asian	42
% Caucasian	31
% Hispanic	12
% international	4

SURVEY SAYS . . .
Great library
Great off-campus food
Everyone loves the Golden Bears
Student publications are popular
Political activism is popular

ACADEMICS
Academic Rating	**91**
Calendar	semester
Student/faculty ratio	15:1
Profs interesting rating	73
Profs accessible rating	62
Most common reg class size	fewer than 10 students

MOST POPULAR MAJORS
computer engineering
English language and literature
political science and government

STUDENTS SAY ". . ."

Academics

"Tough and competitive" University of California—Berkeley "is the epitome of cultural, political, and intellectual diversity," both in its diverse student body (both in background and interests) and its substantial academic offerings. With "many departments ranked in the top five in their field," UCB has the "stunning ability to accommodate nearly every interest and demand of students." One student explains, "The freedom is incredible; there are a great array of majors and minors that all boast excellence in their departments. I feel like no matter what I choose to do at Cal, I will get the best of everything." It won't be handed to you, however; "UCB is a buffet. The opportunities are plentiful, and the education is great, but you have to serve yourself." The many standout departments (featuring "many professors who are Nobel laureates and award winners") include the "top-tier science departments," the "very strong business and engineering departments," "the main humanities (history, English, political science)," mathematics, computer science, and music. No matter what you study here, there's a good chance your professors will "have done great things in their fields." "My organic chemistry professor helped name molecules at an international convention," says one student. "My other organic chemistry professor just won an award for finding a drug to help with cancer research. These are real people with amazing lives, and I get to learn the tricks of the trade from them." Ambitious students can get in on the ground-breaking work, as the school "provides optimal research experience for students and constantly seeks students [who] can bring fresh ideas and new perspectives to the table."

Life

For many, "Life is mostly centered around academic-related activities, if not classes and studying, then internships or jobs, or something of that sort." More than a few, in fact, live in a near-perpetual state of academic immersion; they "get too sucked in to their work" and "don't take full advantage of their surroundings," but "if you can get your head out of the books for long enough, there's always a movie to catch, a good game of Frisbee going on, or a party in one of the co-ops or fraternities." The city of Berkeley is "amazing." "There are so many great restaurants and booktores and interesting people and just so much stuff to experience and to explore." Better still, San Francisco is "a 30-minute BART ride away" and is "always exciting" with tons of "shopping, eating, concerts, theater, and all the culture of the big city." Around campus, "Many students participate in sports or clubs for fun. Football games are probably the main reason students have school spirit, and the games bring the students together for memorable experiences." The university community provides "a lot of opportunities for everyone: clubs, sports, jobs, internships, sororities, fraternities, dance, art, journalism, etc. There are so many opportunities to meet people and have fun inside the Berkeley campus and out of it," as well as an "endless number of events going on any given day. Art shows, benefits, plays, operas, live bands (local and touring), [and] there are volunteer events and free classes. There is not enough time to do everything."

Student Body

"The only real common factor among most Berkeley students is that they are studious hard workers." Undergrads here "come from all different socioeconomic and cultural backgrounds…It is such a big school that you are always likely to be able to find someone else like you." The mix includes "a lot of emo grad students, Asian premeds, a handful of jocks, and frat scenesters," "nerds who never leave the library, environmental activists, ground-breaking scientists, party animals," and "new age hippies," among many others. In short, "Everyone here is unique, from the run-of-the-mill preppy kids to the neo-hippie and goth crowd, to the guy wearing a kilt in your 8 A.M. Japanese class." Asian students "make up a plurality of the student body, and there are loads of Asian cultural groups on campus. Other ethnic groups—such as African-Americans and Hispanics—can be seen on campus" but are not as well represented. The Berkeley area "is quite liberal," and many students here fit in well with the surrounding community.

FINANCIAL AID: 510-642-6442 • E-MAIL: OUARS@UCLINK.BERKELEY.EDU • WEBSITE: WWW.BERKELEY.EDU

THE PRINCETON REVIEW SAYS

Admissions

Very important factors considered include: Application essay, academic GPA, rigor of secondary school record, state residency. *Important factors considered include:* standardized test scores, character/personal qualities, extracurricular activities, talent/ability, volunteer work, work experience. *Other factors considered include:* first generation, geographical residence, SAT and SAT Subject Tests or ACT required; ACT with Writing component required. TOEFL required of all international applicants. High school diploma is required and GED is accepted. *Academic units required:* 4 English, 3 mathematics, 2 science, (2 science labs), 2 foreign language, 2 history, 1 visual/performing arts, 1 academic electives. *Academic units recommended:* 4 English, 4 mathematics, 3 science, (3 science labs), 3 foreign language, 2 history, 1 visual/performing arts, 1 academic electives.

Financial Aid

Students should submit: FAFSA, state aid form Regular filing deadline is 3/2. The Princeton Review suggests that all financial aid forms be submitted as soon as possible after 1/1. *Need-based scholarships/grants offered:* Federal Pell, SEOG, state scholarships/grants, private scholarships, the school's own gift aid. *Loan aid offered:* Direct Subsidized Stafford, Direct Unsubsidized Stafford, Direct PLUS, Federal Perkins, college/university loans from institutional funds. Applicants will be notified of awards on or about 4/15. Federal Work-Study Program available. Institutional employment available. Off-campus job opportunities are excellent.

The Inside Word

The entire UC system is competitive, and Berkeley is the most competitive of the UC campuses. In-state applicants need to be exceptional; out-of-state applicants must be exceptionally exceptional. The 22% acceptance rate tells you that a lot of highly qualified applicants receive a very disappointing letter in late March.

THE SCHOOL SAYS "..."

From The Admissions Office

"One of the top public universities in the nation and the world, the University of California—Berkeley offers a vast range of courses and a full menu of extracurricular activities. Berkeley's academic programs are internationally recognized for their excellence. Undergraduates can choose one of 100 majors. Thirty-five departments are top ranked, more than any other college or university in the country. Access to one of the foremost university libraries enriches studies. There are 23 specialized libraries on campus and distinguished museums of anthropology, paleontology, and science.

"All applicants must take the ACT plus Writing or the SAT Reasoning Test. In addition, all applicants must take two SAT Subject Tests in two different subject areas. (If a math SAT Subject Test is chosen by the applicant, he/she must take the math Level II exam.)"

SELECTIVITY

Admissions Rating	97
# of applicants	48,263
% of applicants accepted	22
% of acceptees attending	41

FRESHMAN PROFILE

Range SAT Critical Reading	580–710
Range SAT Math	620–750
Range SAT Writing	590–710
Minimum paper TOEFL	550
Minimum computer TOEFL	213
Average HS GPA	3.9
% graduated top 10% of class	98
% graduated top 25% of class	100
% graduated top 50% of class	100

DEADLINES

Regular Deadline	11/30
Nonfall registration?	yes

APPLICANTS ALSO LOOK AT

AND OFTEN PREFER
Stanford University

AND SOMETIMES PREFER
University of California—Los Angeles

AND RARELY PREFER
University of California—San Diego
University of California—Santa Cruz
University of California—Santa Barbara
University of California—Davis

FINANCIAL FACTS

Financial Aid Rating	86
Annual tuition in-state	$8,932
Annual tuition out-of-state	$20,607
Room and board	$14,494
Books and supplies	$1,268
% frosh rec. need-based scholarship or grant aid	44
% UG rec. need-based scholarship or grant aid	45
% frosh rec. non-need-based scholarship or grant aid	1
% UG rec. non-need-based scholarship or grant aid	1
% frosh rec. need-based self-help aid	40
% UG rec. need-based self-help aid	39
% frosh rec. athletic scholarships	2
% UG rec. athletic scholarships	2
% UG borrow to pay for school	47
Average cumulative indebtedness	$13,171

UNIVERSITY OF CALIFORNIA—DAVIS

178 MRAK HALL, DAVIS, CA 95616 • ADMISSIONS: 530-752-2971 • FAX: 530-752-1280

CAMPUS LIFE

Quality of Life Rating	**89**
Fire Safety Rating	**83**
Green Rating	**95**
Type of school	public
Environment	town

STUDENTS

Total undergrad enrollment	24,017
% male/female	44/56
% from out of state	2
% from public high school	84
% live on campus	20
% in (# of) fraternities	9 (28)
% in (# of) sororities	8 (21)
% African American	3
% Asian	40
% Caucasian	35
% Hispanic	13
% Native American	1
% international	2
# of countries represented	121

SURVEY SAYS . . .
Athletic facilities are great
Student publications are popular

ACADEMICS

Academic Rating	**75**
Calendar	quarter
Student/faculty ratio	19:1
Profs interesting rating	72
Profs accessible rating	73
Most common reg class size	20–29 students
Most common lab size	20–29 students

MOST POPULAR MAJORS
biology/biological sciences
economics
psychology

STUDENTS SAY ". . ."

Academics

"UC—Davis is a huge research university with the atmosphere of an intimate community." The campus known for its cows, and the agricultural and food sciences programs are indeed excellent. There are more than 100 majors. Research opportunities for undergraduates are abundant. Study-abroad and internship programs are "fantastic." "Registration is very nerve-racking," but on the whole, management is "invisible." "Things seem to work magically around here." "The administration is like Atlantis," offers a linguistics major; "it's rumored to exist, but you've never actually seen it." "As for your academic experience, 90 percent of it is dependent upon who your professor is, and 100 percent is dependent upon your personal interest," explains an international relations major. "I know that adds up to 190 percent. You can blame my statistics professor." UCD's quarter system affords "no time to fool around." "It is not really a school for a slacker." "Although the pace is fast, it's very doable," asserts a communications major. Classes can be quite large here, and the classrooms themselves "could do with some better desks." Some members of the "world-class faculty" are "very enthusiastic" and "really profound." "I have consistently found my professors to be wonderful teachers who care deeply about their students," boasts a biology major. "Professors vary a lot depending on subject." As a rule, "upper-division professors are generally far better than lower-division ones."

Life

UC—Davis is located in a "cozy," "rural," and "relaxed" college town in northern California not too far from Sacramento. Most students report a pretty high level of satisfaction with the atmosphere, though a few tell us that Davis "is boring, and ugly." "Downtown Davis is a great place that is located within walking distance of the dorms and most off-campus housing," says a sophomore. It's "filled with interesting non-chain stores" and "great places to eat all types of food." "There are bicycles everywhere." And "if Davis isn't your thing, you can always go to Sacramento or San Francisco." "Tahoe is about two hours away, so it's pretty easy to go snowboarding or skiing," too. On the "sprawling" campus "the food is repetitive," but Davis has "excellent" recreational facilities and "a wide variety of activities, clubs, and groups to get involved in." "The sense of community is pretty good." "Greek life is big;" and "keggers at frats" are definitely available. "There is a demographic that enjoys going to parties at the fraternities, but other people who do not enjoy that can easily stay out of it." "Davis is not mainly about parties," though. Mostly, "Davis is a place where you can really sit down and study," and "the best part is just finding a good group of people." "There is a niche for everyone."

Student Body

"Students here are the hardworking, studious, responsible kids," says a sophomore. "The student body is mostly made up of white and Asian students," but "Davis is a melting pot." "Many different cultures, ethnicities, and religions are present," and "everybody is really accepting." Students here describe themselves as "goal-orientated," "down-to-earth, well-rounded, balanced, amiable, and intelligent." "Some seem shy and timid." "There are some atypical students who care more about their looks and having fun than just studying, but I feel like they are a minority," says a sophomore. There are "the uber-serious premed students who spend all of their waking time in class or in the library having an aneurism." There's "the sorority girl; the band geek, the jock; the crazy, outspoken chick;" and "a lot of hippies," too. A pretty high percentage of these students is "really concerned about environmental issues," and many UCD students "take an active stand" on politics.

FINANCIAL AID: 530-752-2390 • E-MAIL: FRESHMANADMISSIONS@UCDAVIS.EDU • WEBSITE: WWW.UCDAVIS.EDU

THE PRINCETON REVIEW SAYS

Admissions

Very important factors considered include: academic GPA, rigor of secondary school record, standardized test scores. *Important factors considered include:* Application essay, character/personal qualities, extracurricular activities, first generation, talent/ability. *Other factors considered include:* state residency, volunteer work, work experience. SAT Subject Tests required; SAT or ACT required; ACT with Writing component required. TOEFL required of all international applicants. High school diploma is required and GED is accepted. *Academic units required:* 4 English, 3 mathematics, 2 science, (2 science labs), 2 foreign language, 2 social studies, 1 visual/performing arts, 1 academic electives. *Academic units recommended:* 4 English, 4 mathematics, 3 science, (3 science labs), 3 foreign language, 2 social studies, 1 visual/performing arts, 1 academic electives.

Financial Aid

Students should submit: FAFSA. The Princeton Review suggests that all financial aid forms be submitted as soon as possible after 1/1. *Need-based scholarships/grants offered:* Federal Pell, SEOG, state scholarships/grants, private scholarships, the school's own gift aid, specify):Academic Competitiveness Grant (ACG) and National Science and Mathematics Access to Retain Talent Grant. *Loan aid offered:* Direct Subsidized Stafford, Direct Unsubsidized Stafford, Direct PLUS, Federal Perkins, college/university loans from institutional funds. Applicants will be notified of awards on a rolling basis beginning 3/15.

The Inside Word

Admission to UC—Davis is considerably easier than, say, admission to Berkeley. Nevertheless, every school in the UC system is world-class, and the UC system in general is geared toward the best and brightest of California's high school students.

THE SCHOOL SAYS "..."

From The Admissions Office

"UC—Davis is characterized by a distinguished faculty of scholars, scientists, and artists; a treasured sense of community; and a dedication to innovative teaching, research, and public service. Students follow a philosophy of learning, discovery, and engagement. Their involvement in academic, leadership, and honors programs, as well as internships, education abroad, and research, typify the undergraduate experience. Students can earn degrees in more than 100 majors, interact with the university's professional schools through select minor programs, and receive pregraduate advising in nearly any field imaginable.

"The friendly, supportive nature of the campus and Davis community also defines the undergraduate experience. UC—Davis offers its active student body more than 450 student organizations; NCAA Division I athletics; and stunning cultural, academic, and recreational facilities such as the Mondavi Center for the Performing Arts, the Genome Center, and the Activities and Recreation Center.

"UC—Davis also provides many resources to help undergraduates build social and career networks before they graduate, so that students are well connected by the time they don their cap and gown.

"All applicants must take the ACT plus Writing or the SAT Reasoning Test. In addition, all applicants must take two SAT Subject Tests in two different subject areas. (If a math SAT Subject Test is chosen by the applicant, he/she must take the math Level II exam.)"

SELECTIVITY

Admissions Rating	98
# of applicants	40,605
% of applicants accepted	53
% of acceptees attending	23

FRESHMAN PROFILE

Range SAT Critical Reading	500–630
Range SAT Math	550–670
Range SAT Writing	510–640
Range ACT Composite	22–28
Minimum paper TOEFL	550
Minimum computer TOEFL	213
Minimum web-based TOEFL	60
Average HS GPA	3.79
% graduated top 10% of class	96
% graduated top 25% of class	100
% graduated top 50% of class	100

DEADLINES

Regular	
Deadline	11/30
Notification	3/15
Nonfall registration?	no

APPLICANTS ALSO LOOK AT AND OFTEN PREFER

University of California—Berkeley
University of California—San Diego
University of California—Los Angeles

FINANCIAL FACTS

Financial Aid Rating	74
Annual out-of-state tuition	$21,021
Room and board	$11,978
Required fees	$8,635
Books and supplies	$1,544
% frosh rec. need-based scholarship or grant aid	56
% UG rec. need-based scholarship or grant aid	50
% frosh rec. non-need-based scholarship or grant aid	1
% UG rec. non-need-based scholarship or grant aid	1
% frosh rec. need-based self-help aid	41
% UG rec. need-based self-help aid	37
% frosh rec. athletic scholarships	2
% UG rec. athletic scholarships	1
% frosh rec. any financial aid	46
% UG rec. any financial aid	59
% UG borrow to pay for school	46
Average cumulative indebtedness	$14,372

UNIVERSITY OF CALIFORNIA—LOS ANGELES

405 HILGARD AVENUE, BOX 951436, LOS ANGELES, CA 90095-1436 • ADMISSIONS: 310-825-3101 • FAX: 310-206-1206

CAMPUS LIFE
Quality of Life Rating	95
Fire Safety Rating	85
Green Rating	88
Type of school	public
Environment	metropolis

STUDENTS
Total undergrad enrollment	26,536
% male/female	45/55
% from out of state	6
% from public high school	78
% live on campus	40
% in (# of) fraternities	13 (36)
% in (# of) sororities	13 (28)
% African American	4
% Asian	38
% Caucasian	34
% Hispanic	15
% international	4
# of countries represented	132

SURVEY SAYS . . .
Athletic facilities are great
Students love Los Angeles, CA
Great food on campus
Great off-campus food
Everyone loves the Bruins
Student publications are popular

ACADEMICS
Academic Rating	80
Calendar	quarter
Student/faculty ratio	16:1
Profs interesting rating	65
Profs accessible rating	63
Most common reg class size	10–19 students
Most common lab size	20–29 students

MOST POPULAR MAJORS
biology/biological sciences
political science and government
psychology

STUDENTS SAY "..."

Academics

It's all about diversity in activities, academics, athletics, race, religion, and sexuality at UCLA; or, as one student puts it, "academically competitive, athletically dominated, and overcrowded." One of the most vaunted schools in the UC system, Bruins take advantage of the school's location and opportunities in order to "learn as much as you want in whatever field you desire, while being engaged in non-academic endeavors that are equally as stimulating and interesting." Students here "have a lot of things going on that are not always academic or on-campus," and "their outside experiences and passions are reflected in their contributions in class and on campus."

Being a large university can be a double-edged sword, and while those enrolled here are thrilled to be able to "take classes in practically any subject you can imagine," many do wish class sizes were smaller, and "it's very difficult to get classes, especially in competitive majors." "In Chinese, most classes get filled very quickly because econ, business, and everyone else wants to learn Chinese right now," says a junior. Though there are a few complaints of disinterested professors at lower levels, once students reach upper-division courses, "the professors are extremely knowledgeable and often have written the book, literally, on the topics they are teaching." With such a wide selection of courses and departments, reviews range from "not always the greatest teachers" to "very smart [who] make themselves very available." The curve can be tough, and students begin to think of their learning as "studying longer and getting better scores than the person next to you in order to place higher on the curve." As far as step-by-step guidance goes, you "do have to be self-driven at UCLA," but "if you're determined enough you will be able to accomplish whatever you need (within reason, of course)." "It's all on you to get your stuff done," says a sophomore biology major.

Life

While at times, the school can seem large, "there are always programs going on in the buildings to help you meet new people," and most people use some form of club, organization, or sorority/fraternity to narrow down their circles. Since most of the apartments are within walking distance of the dorms, which are all grouped together, "there's a sense of community. You don't lose track of your friends in the crowd." Students here are "really concerned about academics and getting into graduate/professional schools," but on weekends, many still go to parties at the frats or off-campus apartments. "There seem to be times when no one does work, at other times everyone is busy and stays up studying for days at a time," says a student. Westwood offers everything a college student could want, from shopping, movie premieres, going to the beach, or attending the "great concerts in the area, most of which are very well priced." Naturally, sporting events are "a huge part" of the school, and all "take great pride in being part of such great tradition."

Student Body

UCLA's a tough school to get into, and everyone here "was accepted for a reason," so most students are "well-rounded" and "extremely driven," whether it be academically, athletically, or dramatically. That being said, they also chose to go to school in one of the liveliest cities in the US, so the typical student "regards academic success highly but does not make studying the central focus of their lives," and there's a "balance of work and play." There's a "very strong Asian presence," and most people are involved in extracurricular activities, but beyond that, it's difficult to find any other common characteristics of a UCLA student, other than that they "study hard and hate USC." "Everyone, and I mean everyone, belongs here," says a sophomore, referring to the extraordinarily broad student spectrum. "It doesn't matter; there will be a group of people who are EXACTLY like you, and they will probably have formed a club for it already."

UNIVERSITY OF CALIFORNIA—LOS ANGELES

FINANCIAL AID: 310-206-0400 • E-MAIL: UGADM@SAONET.UCLA.EDU • WEBSITE: WWW.UCLA.EDU

THE PRINCETON REVIEW SAYS

Admissions

Very important factors considered include: Application essay, academic GPA, rigor of secondary school record, standardized test scores. *Important factors considered include:* character/personal qualities, extracurricular activities, talent/ability, volunteer work, work experience. *Other factors considered include:* first generation, geographical residence, SAT Subject Tests required; SAT or ACT required; ACT with Writing component required. TOEFL required of all international applicants. High school diploma is required and GED is accepted. *Academic units required:* 4 English, 3 mathematics, 2 science, (2 science labs), 2 foreign language, 2 history, 1 academic electives, 1 visual/performing arts. *Academic units recommended:* 4 English, 4 mathematics, 3 science, (3 science labs), 3 foreign language, 2 history, 1 academic electives, 1 visual/performing arts.

Financial Aid

Students should submit: FAFSA. The Princeton Review suggests that all financial aid forms be submitted as soon as possible after 1/1. *Need-based scholarships/grants offered:* Federal Pell, SEOG, state scholarships/grants, private scholarships, the school's own gift aid, United Negro College Fund, Federal Nursing Scholarships, National Merit. *Loan aid offered:* FFEL Subsidized Stafford, FFEL Unsubsidized Stafford, FFEL PLUS, Federal Perkins, Federal Nursing, state loans, college/university loans from institutional funds. Applicants will be notified of awards on a rolling basis beginning 3/15. Federal Work-Study Program available. Institutional employment available. Off-campus job opportunities are good.

The Inside Word

A powerhouse within the California system, UCLA has its applicants face a stringent and comprehensive assessment. Each application is evaluated within the context of three categories: academics, personal achievement, and life challenges, and each is reviewed by multiple admissions officers. Academic success is a must for any serious contender and enrollment in honors and Advanced Placement courses is highly recommended. Additionally, officers pay close attention to level of commitment in regards to extracurricular activities.

THE SCHOOL SAYS "..."

From The Admissions Office

"Undergraduates arrive at UCLA from throughout California and around the world with exceptional levels of academic preparation. They are attracted by our acclaimed degree programs, distinguished faculty, and the beauty of a park-like campus set amid the dynamism of the nation's second-largest city. UCLA's highly ranked undergraduate programs incorporate cutting-edge technology and teaching techniques that hone the critical-thinking skills and the global perspectives necessary for success in our rapidly changing world. The diversity of these programs draws strength from a student body that mirrors the cultural and ethnic vibrancy of Los Angeles. Generally ranked among the nation's top half-dozen universities, UCLA is at once distinguished and dynamic, academically rigorous and responsive.

"All applicants must take the ACT plus Writing or the SAT Reasoning Test. In addition, all applicants must take two SAT Subject Tests in two different subject areas. (If a math SAT Subject Test is chosen by the applicant, he/she must take the math Level II exam.)"

SELECTIVITY
Admissions Rating	98
# of applicants	55,437
% of applicants accepted	23
% of acceptees attending	37

FRESHMAN PROFILE
Range SAT Critical Reading	570–680
Range SAT Math	600–730
Range SAT Writing	580–700
Range ACT Composite	25–31
Minimum paper TOEFL	550
Minimum computer TOEFL	220
Average HS GPA	4.22
% graduated top 10% of class	97
% graduated top 25% of class	100
% graduated top 50% of class	100

DEADLINES
Regular Deadline	11/30
Notification	rolling
Nonfall registration?	no

FINANCIAL FACTS
Financial Aid Rating	81
Annual out-of-state tuition	$20,021
Room and board	$12,891
Required fees	$8,310
Books and supplies	$1,515
% frosh rec. need-based scholarship or grant aid	47
% UG rec. need-based scholarship or grant aid	46
% frosh rec. non-need-based scholarship or grant aid	1
% UG rec. non-need-based scholarship or grant aid	1
% frosh rec. need-based self-help aid	36
% UG rec. need-based self-help aid	37
% frosh rec. athletic scholarships	2
% UG rec. athletic scholarships	2
% frosh rec. any financial aid	47
% UG rec. any financial aid	46
% UG borrow to pay for school	46
Average cumulative indebtedness	$15,996

UNIVERSITY OF CALIFORNIA—RIVERSIDE

1138 HINDERAKER HALL, RIVERSIDE, CA 92521 • ADMISSIONS: 951-827-3411 • FAX: 951-827-6344

CAMPUS LIFE

Quality of Life Rating	62
Fire Safety Rating	85
Green Rating	96
Type of school	public
Environment	city

STUDENTS

Total undergrad enrollment	15,708
% male/female	48/52
% from out of state	2
% from public high school	88
% live on campus	30
% in (# of) fraternities	6 (20)
% in (# of) sororities	6 (20)
% African American	8
% Asian	40
% Caucasian	17
% Hispanic	28
% international	2
# of countries represented	66

SURVEY SAYS . . .

Great library
Athletic facilities are great
Diverse student types on campus
Different types of students interact
Frats and sororities dominate social
scene
Student publications are popular
(Almost) everyone smokes

ACADEMICS

Academic Rating	73
Calendar	quarter
Student/faculty ratio	18.5:1
Profs interesting rating	62
Profs accessible rating	65
Most common reg class size	20–29 students
Most common lab size	20–29 students

MOST POPULAR MAJORS
biology/biological sciences
business administration
and management
psychology

STUDENTS SAY ". . ."

Academics

The University of California—Riverside is an "underrated" and "research-oriented" school with an "extensive library" and heaps of "very up-to-date" technology. There are nearly 80 majors available. Premed and the biological sciences are noteworthy strengths. Computer science, engineering, and business administration are also solid. "The honors program is fantastic." Cutting-edge research opportunities for undergraduates are ample "in virtually any area." If you have a passion for creepy crawly things, UCR boasts one of the best entomology departments in the nation. (The bug collection is astounding.) UCR is also a leader in agricultural research. "Lectures are huge" at the introductory level, and "overworked" teaching assistants are a fact of life. "Classes are smaller" as you get further along in your major, though, particularly in comparison to other UC schools. The academic atmosphere varies widely by department. "Fast-paced, challenging" coursework is common in the hard sciences. "Most science students are always in the libraries." Other students report a radically different experience. "Some of my classes are a joke," gripes a history major. Similarly, "professors are either great or awful." There are "some very excellent teachers" here who "go out of their way to help students learn both inside and outside the classroom." Other professors "treat teaching as just a requirement. Student opinion regarding the administration also differs. Some undergrads declare them to be "helpful" and diligent about "keeping students on track." Others, however, assert that some administrators act as if helping the students is a burden."

Life

UCR students enjoy a "beautiful" campus with a lot of newer buildings and "a forest feel to it." This campus is also as wired (and wireless) as any in the country. With nearly 300 clubs and organizations, there are "plenty of extracurricular activities." The Greek system has a noticeable presence on campus. If you are athletic, the huge student recreation center is dreamy. Many intercollegiate athletic teams are formidable, too, though student support is generally low. The party scene isn't very happening. Many students are commuters, and on the weekends, "the campus is empty." The city of Riverside has a few advantages. For example, "the cost of living is cheap off campus." Just down the street from campus, there's also University Village, which has "a movie theater and food places." Riverside is also a mere "40 minutes from the snow at Big Bear." However, the general sentiment among students here is that the surrounding area is "lackluster" and "freaking boring." "UCR needs to be transplanted to another town," suggests one visionary student.

Student Body

UCR is "one of the most diverse of all the UC campuses" and, for that matter, one of the most diverse campuses anywhere. "It's hard to describe the typical student, because there are so many different types of people." Asian and Asian American students constitute the largest ethnic bloc. There are "the fraternity freaks, the overachievers, the geeks, the recluses, the trendy people," and many other subgroups. At the same time, UCR is mostly full of "average college students." "Everybody is pretty relaxed and friendly." Sure, there "weirdoes here and there, "maybe a few people with green hair," but "no one is out of the ordinary." Just about everyone here is from California, and it's largely a middle-class crowd. Some 70 percent of all students receive financial aid. "Most of the students seem serious about being in college and are here for the right reasons," though not all of them. "There are the extremely bright students who spend all day studying," relates a sophomore. "There are also students who barely got in and do nothing at all."

FINANCIAL AID: 951-827-3878 • E-MAIL: UGADMISS@UCR.EDU • WEBSITE: WWW.UCR.EDU

THE PRINCETON REVIEW SAYS

Admissions

Very important factors considered include: academic GPA, rigor of secondary school record, standardized test scores, state residency. *Important factors considered include:* Application essay, first generation. *Other factors considered include:* talent/ability, SAT Subject Tests required; SAT or ACT required; ACT with Writing component required. TOEFL required of all international applicants. High school diploma is required and GED is accepted. *Academic units required:* 4 English, 3 mathematics, 2 science, (2 science labs), 2 foreign language, 2 history, 1 visual/performing arts, 1 academic electives. *Academic units recommended:* 4 mathematics, 3 science, (3 science labs), 3 foreign language.

Financial Aid

Students should submit: FAFSA, state aid form Regular filing deadline is 3/2. The Princeton Review suggests that all financial aid forms be submitted as soon as possible after 1/1. *Need-based scholarships/grants offered:* Federal Pell, SEOG, state scholarships/grants, private scholarships, the school's own gift aid. *Loan aid offered:* Direct Subsidized Stafford, Direct Unsubsidized Stafford, Direct PLUS, Federal Perkins, college/university loans from institutional funds. Applicants will be notified of awards on a rolling basis beginning 3/1. Federal Work-Study Program available. Institutional employment available. Off-campus job opportunities are excellent.

The Inside Word

The UC—Riverside admissions process is based heavily on quantitative factors. Applicants who have strong GPAs and standardized test scores should have no problem gaining acceptance. There is a priority filing period, so students should apply as early as possible.

THE SCHOOL SAYS "..."

From The Admissions Office

"The University of California—Riverside offers the quality, rigor, and facilities of a major research institution, while assuring its undergraduates personal attention and a sense of community. Academic programs, teaching, advising, and student services all reflect the supportive attitude that characterizes the campus. Among the exceptional opportunities are the UC—Riverside/UCLA Thomas Haider Program in Biomedical Sciences, which provides an exclusive path to UCLA's Geffen School of Medicine; the University Honors Program; an extensive undergraduate research program; UC's only oldest and most comprehensive undergraduate degree program in business administration in Southern California; and UC's only bachelor's degree in creative writing. More than 300 student clubs and organizations and a variety of athletic and arts events give students a myriad of ways to get involved and have fun.

"All applicants must take the ACT plus Writing or the SAT Reasoning Test. In addition, all applicants must take two SAT Subject Tests in two different subject areas. (If a math SAT Subject Test is chosen by the applicant, he/she must take the math Level II exam.)"

SELECTIVITY

Admissions Rating	99
# of applicants	21,453
% of applicants accepted	78
% of acceptees attending	26

FRESHMAN PROFILE

Range SAT Critical Reading	450–560
Range SAT Math	470–610
Range SAT Writing	450–570
Range ACT Composite	19–24
Minimum paper TOEFL	550
Minimum computer TOEFL	213
Average HS GPA	3.44
% graduated top 10% of class	94
% graduated top 25% of class	100
% graduated top 50% of class	100

DEADLINES

Regular	
Deadline	11/30
Notification	rolling
Nonfall registration?	no

APPLICANTS ALSO LOOK AT
AND OFTEN PREFER
University of California—Berkeley
University of California—San Diego
University of California—Los Angeles

AND SOMETIMES PREFER
University of California—Irvine
University of California—Santa Barbara
University of California—Davis

AND RARELY PREFER
University of California — Merced
University of California—Santa Cruz

FINANCIAL FACTS

Financial Aid Rating	80
Annual in-state tuition	$7,126
Annual out-of-state tuition	$27,734
Room and board	$10,850
Required fees	$720
Books and supplies	$1,700
% frosh rec. need-based scholarship or grant aid	60
% UG rec. need-based scholarship or grant aid	59
% frosh rec. non-need-based scholarship or grant aid	1
% UG rec. non-need-based scholarship or grant aid	1
% frosh rec. need-based self-help aid	54
% UG rec. need-based self-help aid	49
% frosh rec. athletic scholarships	1
% UG rec. athletic scholarships	1
% frosh rec. any financial aid	80
% UG rec. any financial aid	75
% UG borrow to pay for school	62
Average cumulative indebtedness	$15,414

UNIVERSITY OF CALIFORNIA—SAN DIEGO

9500 GILMAN DRIVE, 0021, LA JOLLA, CA 92093-0021 • ADMISSIONS: 858-534-4831 • FAX: 858-534-5723

CAMPUS LIFE
Quality of Life Rating	**71**
Fire Safety Rating	**83**
Green Rating	**97**
Type of school	public
Environment	metropolis

STUDENTS
Total undergrad enrollment	22,518
% male/female	48/52
% from out of state	3
% live on campus	33
% in (# of) fraternities	10 (19)
% in (# of) sororities	10 (14)
% African American	2
% Asian	45
% Caucasian	27
% Hispanic	12
% international	4
# of countries represented	70

SURVEY SAYS . . .
Class discussions are rare
Great library
Athletic facilities are great
Low cost of living
(Almost) no one smokes
Very little drug use

ACADEMICS
Academic Rating	**79**
Calendar	quarter
Student/faculty ratio	19:1
Profs interesting rating	62
Profs accessible rating	63
Most common reg class size	10–19 students
Most common lab size	20–29 students

MOST POPULAR MAJORS
biology
economics
psychology

STUDENTS SAY ". . ."

Academics

UCSD is one of the world's premier research institutions, and the economic downturn hasn't diminished its importance or vitality. What began as an oceanography school that expanded into a university in the early 1960s has grown into a haven for neurosciences, chemistry, medicine, engineering, ocean studies, and even theater and dance. The faculty, filled with Nobel laureates, earns across-the-board praise from students for their knowledge and dedication. "My professors are amazing and truly want to teach every student," one says. "My professors have been phenomenal; always accessible, enthusiastic, and encouraging." Others say their classes got smaller and the instruction better as they progressed in their degree programs. "It's especially cool when you take a class on poli-sci immigration from the leader in the field, or take a physics class taught by (astronaut) Sally Ride." However, a common complaint is that some professors don't appear to be fully invested in the classroom experience: "A number of professors seemed to be focused more on their research rather than sharing knowledge with students." Libraries and research facilities get high marks. Best of all, students say, the school has a sterling reputation, so "I know my degree won't be meaningless." There's "always a good job market with so many biotech companies close by."

Life

Students are divided on whether this school in scenic but sleepy La Jolla has a boring social scene ("Some joke that UCSD stands for the University of California—Socially Dead/Sleep Deprived"), or that one simply has to look hard to find recreation ("There is always something to do on campus, and it is always changing! I never get bored!"). But one thing is certain: Some students work way too hard to afford the luxury of a social life, and this causes some friction between the science and non-science students. One student summed up the dichotomy perfectly: "My school is all about science and the beach." Trying to study the hard sciences despite the distraction of the Pacific only a few blocks away is a mammoth task. And a fine public transit system makes downtown San Diego very accessible. "If you enjoy constant fair weather and beautiful beaches, then this is the place for you," one student gushes. The school has tried to make campus a fun place to be. Price Center, the campus hub, is under expansion, and there are three free concerts per quarter, including the eagerly anticipated Sun God Festival in May. Then there's that cool outdoor art: 17 commissioned installations (and counting), including a giant teddy bear made of boulders. Several students wish the NCAA Division II school would spring for a football team to create more campus unity. But to others, the six-college setup "makes everyone feel like they belong to a close-knit community within such a populous school."

Student Body

Of the more than 22,000 undergrads at UCSD, more than 45 percent are Asian, and about 12 percent are Hispanic. With whites in the minority, some stereotypes and misunderstandings have flourished. "The typical student at our school is Asian American and studious," one student reports. Another says: "It's really a shame when I smile at someone on a sunny day, and they shrink away in fear." Many students, however, are thankful for the diversity and the fact that students aren't cut from the same mold as those at other large schools. "Great professors and nice, dorky kids," is how one student sums up the demographic. "UCSD has very smart people doing really incredible things." They can "surf and dance and loads of other things, so it just goes to show that intelligence comes in all kinds of packages." As has been established, some view the nightlife as a dead zone, but many find kindred spirits through sports teams, whether it's university-sponsored or intramural. There are many campus groups, but some students wish there were a higher level of political involvement. "Many students are into their studies and hardly venture out of their comfort zone to take advantage of what college has to offer," one says.

FINANCIAL AID: 858-534-4480 • E-MAIL: ADMISSIONSINFO@UCSD.EDU • WEBSITE: WWW.UCSD.EDU

THE PRINCETON REVIEW SAYS

Admissions

Very important factors considered include: Application essay, academic GPA, rigor of secondary school record, standardized test scores, character/personal qualities, state residency, talent/ability. *Important factors considered include:* extracurricular activities, volunteer work. *Other factors considered include:* first generation, work experience. SAT Subject Tests required; SAT or ACT required; ACT with Writing component required. TOEFL required of all international applicants. High school diploma is required and GED is accepted. *Academic units required:* 4 English, 3 mathematics, 2 science, (2 science labs), 2 foreign language, 2 history, 1 visual/performing arts, 1 academic electives. *Academic units recommended:* 4 English, 4 mathematics, 3 science, (3 science labs), 3 foreign language, 2 history, 1 academic electives.

Financial Aid

Students should submit: FAFSA, state aid form Regular filing deadline is 6/1. The Princeton Review suggests that all financial aid forms be submitted as soon as possible after 1/1. *Need-based scholarships/grants offered:* Federal Pell, SEOG, state scholarships/grants, private scholarships, the school's own gift aid. *Loan aid offered:* FFEL Subsidized Stafford, FFEL Unsubsidized Stafford, FFEL PLUS, Federal Perkins, college/university loans from institutional funds, alternative loans. Applicants will be notified of awards on a rolling basis beginning 3/15. Federal Work-Study Program available. Institutional employment available. Off-campus job opportunities are good.

The Inside Word

While not as lauded as Berkeley or UCLA, UCSD is quickly earning its place as one of the gems of the UC system. It continues to distinguish itself in a number of ways, including its individualized approach to admissions. Although admissions officers do implement a formula, they factor in extracurricular pursuits and personal experiences. Applicants will need to be strong in all areas if they hope to attend UCSD.

THE SCHOOL SAYS "..."

From The Admissions Office

"UCSD is recognized for the exceptional quality of its academic programs. UCSD ranks fifth in the nation and first in the University of California system for the amount of federal research dollars spent on research and development; and the university ranks tenth in the nation in the excellence of its graduate programs and the quality of its faculty, according to the most recent National Research Council college rankings."

"About 40 percent of UCSD's undergraduates participate in research, developing critical thinking and effective communication skills as well as greater cultural understanding. Their faculty mentors are in the divisions and schools of arts and humanities, biology, engineering, medicine, pharmacy, physical sciences, social sciences, and UCSD's Scripps Institution of Oceanography, California Institute for Telecommunications and Information Technology and the San Diego Supercomputer Center. Undergraduates also participate in research at the Salk Institute for Biological Studies and other nearby research institutes and biotechnology companies."

"All applicants must take the ACT plus Writing or the SAT Reasoning Test. In addition, all applicants must take two SAT Subject Tests in two different subject areas. (If a math SAT Subject Test is chosen by the applicant, he/she must take the math Level II exam.)"

SELECTIVITY

Admissions Rating	99
# of applicants	47,365
% of applicants accepted	42
% of acceptees attending	22

FRESHMAN PROFILE

Range SAT Critical Reading	540–660
Range SAT Math	600–710
Range SAT Writing	560–670
Range ACT Composite	24–30
Minimum paper TOEFL	550
Average HS GPA	3.94
% graduated top 10% of class	100
% graduated top 25% of class	100
% graduated top 50% of class	100

DEADLINES

Regular	
Deadline	11/30
Notification	rolling
Nonfall registration?	yes

APPLICANTS ALSO LOOK AT
AND OFTEN PREFER

University of Southern California
University of California—Berkeley
University of California—Los Angeles
Stanford University
University of California—Santa Barbara
University of California—Davis

AND SOMETIMES PREFER

Stanford University

FINANCIAL FACTS

Financial Aid Rating	72
Annual in-state tuition	$8,798
Annual out-of-state tuition	$21,669
Room and board	$11,057
Required fees	$8,062
Books and supplies	$1,523
% frosh rec. need-based scholarship or grant aid	54
% UG rec. need-based scholarship or grant aid	49
% frosh rec. non-need-based scholarship or grant aid	1
% frosh rec. need-based self-help aid	48
% UG rec. need-based self-help aid	43
% frosh rec. athletic scholarships	2
% UG rec. athletic scholarships	1
% frosh rec. any financial aid	77
% UG rec. any financial aid	63
% UG borrow to pay for school	50
Average cumulative indebtedness	$15,904

UNIVERSITY OF CALIFORNIA—SANTA BARBARA

OFFICE OF ADMISSIONS, 1210 CHEADLE HALL, SANTA BARBARA, CA 93106-2014 • ADMISSIONS: 805-893-2881 • FAX: 805-893-2676

CAMPUS LIFE

Quality of Life Rating	**90**
Fire Safety Rating	**87**
Green Rating	**94**
Type of school	public
Environment	city

STUDENTS

Total undergrad enrollment	18,888
% male/female	46/54
% from out of state	4
% from public high school	86
% live on campus	33
% in (# of) fraternities	6 (17)
% in (# of) sororities	12 (18)
% African American	3
% Asian	17
% Caucasian	51
% Hispanic	21
% Native American	1
% international	1
# of countries represented	72

SURVEY SAYS . . .

Athletic facilities are great
Students are friendly
Student publications are popular
Lots of beer drinking
Hard liquor is popular

ACADEMICS

Academic Rating	**81**
Calendar	quarter
Profs interesting rating	75
Profs accessible rating	78
Most common reg class size	fewer than 10 students
Most common lab size	20–29 students

MOST POPULAR MAJORS

biology/biological sciences
economics
psychology

STUDENTS SAY ". . ."

Academics

One student response effectively sums up how most students feel about The University of California—Santa Barbara: "I like the relaxed and non-competitive environment. Don't get me wrong, though; UCSB's academics are top-rate, and some of the professors are jaw-droppingly amazing. Plus, you can't beat getting to relax on the beach 2 minutes after a lecture given by a Nobel Laureate." Laid-back and top-rate are some of the comments that most students tell us when describing their educations at UCSB; from "the perfect balance between academics and social atmosphere," to "beautiful location, active social life and night life...and some of the top engineering and science programs in the country." Some detractors tend to focus on the school's predilection for partying but, at the end of the day, most students are here to study. Many students cite the faculty as their favorite part of UCSB. One declares, "all of my professors so far are Ivy League alumni, and I have learned an incredible amount from them," while another states, "I was impressed by the Nobel prizes the faculty had." Other students focus on UCSB's farther-reaching upside such as its "exceptional research opportunities and great networking to help students obtain internships and jobs," or its "enthusiastic alumni." "The typical students here are intelligent and academically inclined but also enjoy balancing their time with many nonacademic activities." And, "The best thing about UCSB is that the students know how to keep a balance between having fun and getting their work done."

Life

Life at UCSB is centered on outdoor activities, and rightly so; "The campus is situated in an area that allows for many fun outdoor activities such as hiking, surfing, and much more." "The campus is by the beach and the mountains in a beautiful setting." Some students object to the view of UCSB as a party school, "people need to get past the party reputation and realize that this is an excellent school academically." Santa Barbara attracts smart students searching for a "collaborative, non-competitive learning environment. Everyone at UCSB is so laidback and friendly, but we still take our academics very seriously." Or, as one student puts it, "UCSB does not disappoint its reputation as a party school, our claim to being the Harvard of party schools is well founded." Had enough partying? Many "people think about the environment and ways to be sustainable and green." Students can also find "lots of surfing and going to the beach," "great hiking in the mountains, ocean kayaking, [and] rock climbing." Overall, most students are thrilled to be at Santa Barbara.

Student Body

As you'd expect, "the typical student is an outgoing person by nature who loves to party. There are plenty of others as well, but we all tend to fit in somewhere because the weather here brings out the best in everyone." "There are a lot of surfers and people who like to party a lot, but there seems to be a place for everyone whether you're studious, or love computers, or are even religious." One student explains, "our community is so diverse and so replete with different academic and social opportunities," and another adds, "UCSB is a WONDERFUL environment for queer students. There are lots of organizations for many different types of students, and I haven't been discriminated [against] in the least." As with any large group of people, at least some aren't thrilled. One tells us, "The typical student at UCSB is spoiled [and] snobby." However, this disgruntled student's feelings are definitely in the minority. "For the level of intelligence students at UCSB display, most students are not overly 'nerdy or socially inept.'"

UNIVERSITY OF CALIFORNIA—SANTA BARBARA

FINANCIAL AID: 805-893-2432 • E-MAIL: ADMISSIONS@SA.UCSB.EDU • WEBSITE: WWW.UCSB.EDU

THE PRINCETON REVIEW SAYS

Admissions

Very important factors considered include: Application essay, academic GPA, rigor of secondary school record, standardized test scores. *Other factors considered include:* Class rank, character/personal qualities, extracurricular activities, level of applicant's interest, state residency, talent/ability, volunteer work, work experience. SAT Subject Tests required; SAT or ACT required; ACT with Writing component required. TOEFL required of all international applicants. High school diploma is required and GED is accepted. *Academic units required:* 4 English, 3 mathematics, (2 science labs), 2 foreign language, 2 history, 1 visual/performing arts, 1 academic electives. *Academic units recommended:* 4 mathematics, (3 science labs), 3 foreign language.

Financial Aid

Students should submit: FAFSA Regular filing deadline is 5/31. The Princeton Review suggests that all financial aid forms be submitted as soon as possible after 1/1. *Need-based scholarships/grants offered:* Federal Pell, SEOG, state scholarships/grants, private scholarships, the school's own gift aid, Work Study is also available as need-based aid. *Loan aid offered:* Direct Subsidized Stafford, Direct Unsubsidized Stafford, Direct PLUS, Federal Perkins. Applicants will be notified of awards on a rolling basis beginning 3/15. Federal Work-Study Program available. Institutional employment available. Off-campus job opportunities are good.

The Inside Word

As you might expect, a large state school with a reputation like UCSB's attracts a lot of applicants, and this number is growing every year. Those wishing to be future Gauchos need solid test scores, GPAs, and extracurriculars; all of UCSB's current freshman class finished in the top 50 percent of their high school classes.

THE SCHOOL SAYS "..."

From The Admissions Office

"The University of California—Santa Barbara is a major research institution offering undergraduate and graduate education in the arts, humanities, sciences and technology, and social sciences. Large enough to have excellent facilities for study, research, and other creative activities, the campus is also small enough to foster close relationships among faculty and students. The faculty numbers more than 900. A member of the most distinguished system of public higher education in the nation, UC—Santa Barbara is committed equally to excellence in scholarship and instruction. Through the general education program, students acquire good grounding in the skills, perceptions, and methods of a variety of disciplines. In addition, because they study with a research faculty, they not only acquire basic skills and broad knowledge but also are exposed to the imagination, inventiveness, and intense concentration that scholars bring to their work. UCSB is one of 62 members of the prestigous Association of American Universities.

"All applicants must take the ACT plus Writing or the SAT Reasoning Test. In addition, all applicants must take two SAT Subject Tests in two different subject areas. (If a math SAT Subject Test is chosen by the applicant, he/she must take the math Level II exam.)"

SELECTIVITY

Admissions Rating	95
# of applicants	47,083
% of applicants accepted	49
% of acceptees attending	19

FRESHMAN PROFILE

Range SAT Critical Reading	530–650
Range SAT Math	550–670
Range SAT Writing	530–650
Range ACT Composite	23–29
Minimum paper TOEFL	550
Minimum computer TOEFL	213
Minimum web-based TOEFL	80
Average HS GPA	3.84

DEADLINES

Regular	
Deadline	11/30
Notification	3/1
Nonfall registration?	no

APPLICANTS ALSO LOOK AT

AND OFTEN PREFER
University of California—Berkeley
University of California—Davis

AND SOMETIMES PREFER
University of California—Los Angeles

AND RARELY PREFER
University of California—Santa Cruz
California Polytechnic State University—
San Luis Obispo

FINANCIAL FACTS

Financial Aid Rating	78
Annual tuition out-of-state	$21,021
Room and board	$12,405
Required fees	$7,788
Books and supplies	$1,596
% frosh rec. need-based scholarship or grant aid	38
% UG rec. need-based scholarship or grant aid	36
% frosh rec. non-need-based scholarship or grant aid	1
% frosh rec. need-based self-help aid	31
% UG rec. need-based self-help aid	31
% frosh rec. athletic scholarships	2
% UG rec. athletic scholarships	1
% frosh rec. any financial aid	46
% UG rec. any financial aid	44
% UG borrow to pay for school	48
Average cumulative indebtedness	$15,201

UNIVERSITY OF CALIFORNIA—SANTA CRUZ

ADMISSIONS, COOK HOUSE, 1156 HIGH STREET, SANTA CRUZ, CA 95064 • ADMISSIONS: 831-459-4008 • FAX: 831-459-4452

CAMPUS LIFE
Quality of Life Rating	**89**
Fire Safety Rating	**78**
Green Rating	**95**
Type of school	public
Environment	city

STUDENTS
Total undergrad enrollment	15,125
% male/female	46/54
% from out of state	2.68
% from public high school	85
% live on campus	47
% in (# of) fraternities	1 (7)
% in (# of) sororities	1 (13)
% African American	3
% Asian	21
% Caucasian	50
% Hispanic	17
% Native American	1
% international	1
# of countries represented	72

SURVEY SAYS . . .
Students are friendly
Students are happy
Political activism is popular

ACADEMICS
Academic Rating	**80**
Calendar	quarter
Student/faculty ratio	19:1
Profs interesting rating	74
Profs accessible rating	77
% profs teaching UG courses	100
% classes taught by TAs	0
Most common	
reg class size	20–29 students
Most common	
lab size	10–19 students

MOST POPULAR MAJORS
psychology
economics/business
literature/letters

STUDENTS SAY "..."
Academics
The University of California—Santa Cruz offers one of the nation's best combinations of "focus on scholastic endeavors in a beautiful forest setting" and is, by all accounts "a great place to live and study!" Students attribute their enthusiasm to "intelligent, eloquent, and easily accessible professors," academics that are "impressive and challenging," and fellow students who are "happy, open-minded, and a little bit crazy." This school is best suited to those who can motivate themselves in a "chill" environment and the sort of student whose motto might be: "There's no point in learning if you're too stressed to enjoy it." The sciences are "world-class" at UCSC, and the school also boasts "one of the finest engineering programs in the UC's" as well as "a great marine biology program." While the "professors all do research," what sets them apart from those at the typical research-driven university is that "they are very passionate about their subject even when teaching undergrads" and "also tend to be quite approachable despite having large class sizes and allow students to attend their office hours for extra help." The school also offers undergrads "a lot of opportunities in terms of internships, research opportunities, job opportunities, and networking." "There's a focus on undergraduate study" here, one student contentedly reports.

Life
Undergrads rave about the "take-your-breath-away beauty" of the heavily wooded UCSC campus; one says it's like "taking paths through the forest that resemble Endor only to find a lecture hall at the end." Another adds, "Almost every time my friends and I walk around outside, someone comments on how lucky we are to be surrounded by such beauty. Whether the silvery ocean, the fog in the trees, the wind in the fields of green, the wildlife such as deer, raccoons, squirrels, newts, etc., it all comes together like a painting." The school's setting means "there is much to do recreationally, such as hiking, biking, swimming, trail running, tree climbing, or rock climbing. You can walk in any direction and find some hiking trail that leads to some other part of the forest." Students note that, "It is also nice to get off campus from time to time and enjoy the city of Santa Cruz. Downtown is lively and usually has something fun going on such as local farmer's markets and cultural festivals." Ambitious students "may head to San Jose or San Francisco on the weekend for a more rowdy bar or club scene." Both cities are "readily accessible via public transportation." The party scene on and off campus consists of "mostly decentralized, smaller parties, due to the near-absence of fraternities and sororities." It also includes "a lot of drug use" that is limited to "specific locations" and "easy to avoid" for abstaining students.

Student Body
"The 'stereotypical' Santa Cruz student is a hippie," and the school certainly has its fair share of those "The typical student is very hard-working until about 9 p.m., when hikes to the forest are common practice and returning to your room smelling like reefer is acceptable," one undergrad explains—but "there are many different types who attend UCSC." "It seems that almost every student here has a personal passion, whether it be an activism or cause of some sort, etc.," one student writes. "Everyone is so...alive." "Most are liberal" and there's a definite propensity for earnestness; it's the sort of place where students declare without irony that they "not only possess a great respect for one another but the world and life in general. The world to an average UCSC student is a sacred and beautiful place to be shared and enjoyed by all its inhabitants."

UNIVERSITY OF CALIFORNIA—SANTA CRUZ

FINANCIAL AID: 831-459-2963 • E-MAIL: ADMISSIONS@UCSC.EDU • WEBSITE: WWW.ADMISSIONS.UCSC.EDU

THE PRINCETON REVIEW SAYS

Admissions

Very important factors considered include: Application essay, academic GPA, rigor of secondary school record, standardized test scores, state residency. *Important factors considered include:* Class rank, character/personal qualities, extracurricular activities, first generation, geographical residence, talent/ability. *Other factors considered include:* volunteer work, work experience. SAT Subject Tests required; SAT or ACT required; ACT with Writing component required. TOEFL required of all international applicants. High school diploma is required and GED is accepted. *Academic units required:* 4 English, 3 mathematics, 2 science, (2 science labs), 2 foreign language, 1 social studies, 1 history, 1 visual/performing arts, 1 academic electives. *Academic units recommended:* 4 English, 4 mathematics, 3 science, (3 science labs), 3 foreign language, 1 social studies, 1 history, 1 visual/performing arts, 1 academic electives.

Financial Aid

Students should submit: FAFSA Regular filing deadline is 6/1. The Princeton Review suggests that all financial aid forms be submitted as soon as possible after 1/1. *Need-based scholarships/grants offered:* Federal Pell, SEOG, state scholarships/grants, private scholarships, the school's own gift aid. *Loan aid offered:* Direct Subsidized Stafford, Direct Unsubsidized Stafford, Direct PLUS, Federal Perkins. Applicants will be notified of awards on a rolling basis beginning 4/1. Federal Work-Study Program available. Institutional employment available. Off-campus job opportunities are excellent.

The Inside Word

UC—Santa Cruz scores all applicants on a 10,000-point scale encompassing 14 criteria. High school GPA accounts for 4,400 of those points; standardized test scores, 2,400 points; up to 700 points for academic accomplishment within life experiences; and lower point amounts in such areas as special talents, achievement, awards, geographic location, and outstanding performance in a particular academic discipline. UCSC's acceptance rate belies the high caliber of applicants it regularly receives.

THE SCHOOL SAYS ". . ."

From The Admissions Office

"UC—Santa Cruz students, faculty, and researchers are working together to make a world of difference. Within our extraordinary educational community, students participate in the creation of new knowledge, new technologies, and new forms of expressing and understanding cultures. From helping teachers improve their skills to building more efficient solar cells and working to save endangered sea turtles, our focus is on improving our planet and the lives of all its inhabitants. The academic programs at UCSC are challenging and rigorous, and many of them are in newer fields that focus on interdisciplinary thinking. At UCSC, undergraduates conduct and publish research, working closely with faculty on leading-edge projects. Taking advantage of the campus' proximity to centers of industry and innovation such as the Monterey Bay National Marine Sanctuary and Silicon Valley, many students at UC—Santa Cruz take part in fieldwork and internships that complement their studies and provide practical experience in their fields."

"All fresh applicants must take the ACT Assessment plus the ACT Writing Test or the new SAT Reasoning Test. In addition, all frosh applicants must take two SAT Subject Tests in two different subject areas. (If a Math SAT Subject Test is chosen by the applicant, they must take the Math Level II exam). Starting with fall 2012 admissions, the University of California will no longer require the SAT Subject Tests."

SELECTIVITY

Admissions Rating	99
# of applicants	27,837
% of applicants accepted	73
% of acceptees attending	23

FRESHMAN PROFILE

Range SAT Critical Reading	510–630
Range SAT Math	530–640
Range SAT Writing	500–620
Range ACT Composite	22–27
Minimum paper TOEFL	550
Minimum computer TOEFL	220
Minimum web-based TOEFL	83
Average HS GPA	3.5
% graduated top 10% of class	96
% graduated top 25% of class	100
% graduated top 50% of class	100

DEADLINES

Regular	
Deadline	11/30
Notification	rolling
Nonfall registration?	yes

APPLICANTS ALSO LOOK AT

AND OFTEN PREFER
University of California—Sant Barbara
University of California—Davis

AND SOMETIMES PREFER
University of California—San Diego
University of California—Los Angeles
University of California—Irvine

FINANCIAL FACTS

Financial Aid Rating	84
Annual out-of-state tuition	$21,423
Room and board	$13,641
Required fees	$10,131
Books and supplies	$1,392
% frosh rec. need-based scholarship or grant aid	46.5
% UG rec. need-based scholarship or grant aid	46.5
% UG rec. non-need-based scholarship or grant aid	1
% frosh rec. need-based self-help aid	41.5
% UG rec. need-based self-help aid	41
% frosh rec. any financial aid	48
% UG rec. any financial aid	48

UNIVERSITY OF CENTRAL FLORIDA

PO Box 160111, Orlando, FL 32816-0111 • Admissions: 407-823-3000 • Fax: 407-823-5625

CAMPUS LIFE

Quality of Life Rating	**90**
Fire Safety Rating	**82**
Green Rating	**85**
Type of school	public
Environment	city

STUDENTS

Total undergrad enrollment	42,642
% male/female	45/55
% from out of state	5
% live on campus	21
% in (# of) fraternities	11 (21)
% in (# of) sororities	9 (18)
% African American	9
% Asian	5
% Caucasian	67
% Hispanic	14
% international	1
# of countries represented	141

SURVEY SAYS . . .

Athletic facilities are great
Great off-campus food
Student publications are popular
Student government is popular

ACADEMICS

Academic Rating	**73**
Calendar	semester
Student/faculty ratio	30:1
Profs interesting rating	69
Profs accessible rating	71
% classes taught by TAs	6
Most common	
reg class size	20–29 students
Most common	
lab size	20–29 students

MOST POPULAR MAJORS

health services/allied health/health
sciences
marketing/marketing management
psychology

Academics

The University of Central Florida is "a growing school with a solid academic image." "Its reputation needs to catch up with how it actually is," urges a junior. The engineering and science programs are renowned, and students laud the hospitality, management, and business programs. UCF undergrads also benefit from "awesome technology" all over campus. The Internet is everywhere. Much like the surrounding city of Orlando, UCF has experienced explosive growth in recent decades. Today, UCF is really quite gargantuan. "It's one of the largest schools in the nation." "The massive size of UCF can be intimidating for students who need a personal approach to higher education." "It is easy to feel a bit lost," admits a freshman. Classes are large, and most note that professors can be "hit-or-miss." "Some professors are amazing" and "willing to go out of their way to make sure you understand the lectures." Others "just stand in front of the class and read off PowerPoint slides." The foreign professors, while "highly-specialized," can "be hard to understand." On the bright side, upper-level courses are "fun and taught by professors who are good and know what they're doing." "The administration seems to genuinely care but, because there are so many students, it is hard for them to really do anything about your concerns." Registration is pretty awful. "When you get to the end of your degree, you better plan out your schedule carefully because there are a lot of important classes that are only offered every three semesters," advises one student. In terms of initials, students used to say that "UCF" stood for "U Can't Finish." Now, it stands for "Under Construction Forever," but most don't mind "because the newer facilities are beautiful!"

Life

UCF boasts a "very scenic," "comfortable" campus. "Everything is relatively close together," which is great when it comes to getting to your next class, but not so much when parking your car. "No matter how many garages UCF builds, somehow parking still sucks." Socially, if you're bored here, you just aren't trying very hard. "The campus organizes a wide variety of social events." "We have a ridiculous number of clubs and organizations," boasts a sophomore. "There are about a million events going on at any given time." There is almost every imaginable intramural sport. There is "a huge three-story gym" that features "every kind of workout machine." "Football game days are amazing" as students root for the perennially "up-and-coming" team. Fraternities and sororities are here too, but they "constitute a minority of the culture." UCF's location is a big hit with students. Hot, sunny Orlando is "a large, thriving city," but the area around UCF has "the feel of a college town." "If you live in the dorms your first year, you will definitely get the typical college experience." The "many bars with dance floors around campus" are "a breeding ground for drunken debauchery." They "get packed every night." "Downtown Orlando is a different story, which "provides a nice refuge for upperclassmen trying to break away."

Student Body

"The only real thing that many students share in common is sandals," observes a business major. "At a given time, 75 percent of the campus is probably wearing sandals." "The typical student also applied to the University of Florida but didn't get in," claims a UCF Spanish major, "and also to South Florida, but had a grain of sense and avoided Tampa like the plague." UCF students hail overwhelmingly from in-state, too. And "the girls are insanely pretty." Otherwise, "it is difficult to generalize" about some 42,000 undergrads. "There is no possible way to describe a typical student." Students tend to have "their own set of friends, activities, and experiences at UCF." There are vast differences among students in the different schools (business, health and public affairs, communication, hospitality, engineering, etc.) and also within the schools themselves. "This is a melting pot of culture," says one student. "Walking around campus you see a little bit of every culture, every race, and every ethnicity." "There are strong subcultures for the minorities" and ages, ranging from students "right out of high school" and those "older in years [who] are looking to further their careers."

FINANCIAL AID: 407-823-2827 • E-MAIL: ADMISSION@MAIL.UCF.EDU • WEBSITE: WWW.UCF.EDU

THE PRINCETON REVIEW SAYS

Admissions

Very important factors considered include: academic GPA, rigor of secondary school record, standardized test scores. *Important factors considered include:* Application essay, recommendation(s). *Other factors considered include:* Class rank, alumni/ae relation, character/personal qualities, extracurricular activities, first generation, geographical residence, interview, level of applicant's interest, state residency, talent/ability, volunteer work, work experience. SAT or ACT required; ACT with Writing component required. TOEFL required of all international applicants. High school diploma is required and GED is accepted. *Academic units required:* 4 English, 3 mathematics, 3 science, (2 science labs), 2 foreign language, 3 social studies, 3 academic electives.

Financial Aid

Students should submit: FAFSA Regular filing deadline is 6/30. The Princeton Review suggests that all financial aid forms be submitted as soon as possible after 1/1. *Need-based scholarships/grants offered:* Federal Pell, SEOG, state scholarships/grants, private scholarships, the school's own gift aid, University scholarships and grants. *Loan aid offered:* FFEL Subsidized Stafford, FFEL Unsubsidized Stafford, FFEL PLUS, Federal Perkins. Applicants will be notified of awards on a rolling basis beginning 3/15. Federal Work-Study Program available. Institutional employment available.

Inside Word

As is the case at many state schools, it's all a numbers game here; students aren't required to interview or submit essays. It's also worth noting that when calculating your GPA, which is a very important criterion for admission, the Admissions Committee weights honors, AP, dual enrollment, and International Baccalaureate academic classes more heavily than regular classes.

THE SCHOOL SAYS "..."

From The Admissions Office

"The University of Central Florida offers competitive advantages to its student body. We're committed to teaching, providing advisement, and academic support services for all students. Our undergraduates have access to state-of-the-art wireless buildings, high-tech classrooms, research labs, web-based classes, and an undergraduate research and mentoring program.

"Our Career Services professionals help students gain practical experiences at NASA, schools, hospitals, high-tech companies, local municipalities, and the entertainment industry. With an international focus to our curricula and research programs, we enroll international students from 126 nations. Our study abroad programs and other study and research opportunities include agreements with 98 institutions and 36 countries.

"UCF's 1,415-acre campus provides a safe and serene setting for learning, with natural lakes and woodlands. The bustle of Orlando lies a short distance away: the pro sport teams, the Kennedy Space Center, film studios, Walt Disney World, Universal Orlando, Sea World, and sandy beaches are all nearby.

"Applicants are required to take the SAT (or the ACT with the Writing section). We will student's best scores from either test."

SELECTIVITY

Admissions Rating	89
# of applicants	28,659
% of applicants accepted	48
% of acceptees attending	46
# accepting a place on wait list	436
% admitted from wait list	6

FRESHMAN PROFILE

Range SAT Critical Reading	530–630
Range SAT Math	550–640
Range SAT Writing	510–600
Range ACT Composite	23–27
Minimum paper TOEFL	550
Minimum computer TOEFL	213
Average HS GPA	3.67
% graduated top 10% of class	35
% graduated top 25% of class	77
% graduated top 50% of class	95

DEADLINES

Regular	
Priority	1/1
Deadline	5/1
Notification	rolling
Nonfall registration?	yes

FINANCIAL FACTS

Financial Aid Rating	73
Annual in-state tuition	$3,947
Annual out-of-state tuition	$19,427
Room and board	$8,492
Books and supplies	$924
% frosh rec. need-based scholarship or grant aid	23
% UG rec. need-based scholarship or grant aid	28
% frosh rec. non-need-based scholarship or grant aid	38
% UG rec. non-need-based scholarship or grant aid	25
% frosh rec. need-based self-help aid	16
% UG rec. need-based self-help aid	22
% frosh rec. athletic scholarships	1
% UG rec. athletic scholarships	1
% frosh rec. any financial aid	95
% UG rec. any financial aid	80
% UG borrow to pay for school	43.7
Average cumulative indebtedness	$14,601

UNIVERSITY OF CHARLESTON

2300 MacCorkle Ave SE, Charleston, WV 25304 • Admissions: 304-357-4750 • Fax: 304-357-4781

CAMPUS LIFE

Quality of Life Rating	**75**
Fire Safety Rating	**60***
Green Rating	**70**
Type of school	private
Environment	city

STUDENTS

Total undergrad enrollment	1,102
% male/female	42/58
% from out of state	34
% live on campus	59
% in (# of) fraternities	NR (2)
% in (# of) sororities	NR (3)
% African American	7
% Asian	1
% Caucasian	58
% Hispanic	1
% international	10
# of countries represented	16

SURVEY SAYS . . .

Diverse student types on campus
Students get along with local community
Low cost of living
(Almost) no one smokes
Very little drug use

ACADEMICS

Academic Rating	**78**
Calendar	semester
Student/faculty ratio	13:1
Profs interesting rating	79
Profs accessible rating	78
Most common reg class size	10–19 students
Most common lab size	fewer than 10 students

MOST POPULAR MAJORS

biology/biological sciences
business administration and management
health services/allied health/health sciences

STUDENTS SAY ". . ."

Academics

University of Charleston is a perfect place to prepare for life in the real world while benefiting from the friendliness and comfort of a small college environment. A private school in West Virginia's capital city, UC offers 22 undergraduate majors, including interior design, education, pre-pharmacy, science, and nursing. A sophomore enthuses, "I had high expectations, and those have been met. My dream [is] to attend medical school, and UC and the staff is there to make it happen." For those who don't have graduate programs in mind, the "school is located in an area where internships are plentiful and jobs are easy to find. Our job placement percentages are nearly at 100 percent every year." With about 1,100 undergraduates, class sizes are uniformly small, and "the professors are very open to interaction with students outside the classroom." You'll never feel like a face in the crowd at this small school, where "professors and administrators are always on hand and get to know you on a personal basis." Despite their accessibility, some feel that administrators "don't listen to students' concerns," particularly in the financial aid department.

Life

Even though it is a small campus community, everybody at UC "finds ways to have their own fun, whether it comes in the form of playing video games, watching television sitcom reruns, or dabbling into an alcoholic beverage. It's all about individual tastes and preferences." Students lament the fact that "Charleston is a small town that usually stops functioning at about 8." Even so, "there is plenty to do on weekends," both on and off campus. In their free time, UC undergraduates "go shopping at the mall, watch movies, and go bowling, and sometimes we go dancing." For penny-pinching college students, "several local bars and dance clubs offer discount prices to UC students, and UC sponsored sports games and social events are always free to students." The Student Life department also offers activities "like dance lessons and Zumba classes." In addition, "many have on-campus and off-campus jobs" to help offset the high price of their educations.

Student Body

The typical UC student is "smart, social, and friendly;" invested in the campus community; and "truly cares about their academic success." Sports are a big part of campus life, and most students are "very involved throughout the university through various clubs, activities, or athletics." Students hail from more than 30 states, though predominantly from West Virginia and Ohio. There is also a smattering of international students from China, India, Jamaica, and Haiti, among other countries. UC offers financial aid and scholarship packages (including athletic scholarships); however, tuition is pricey, and "students are typically from the middle- or upper-class." At the same time, there are also a "growing number of single parents and older students." No matter what your background, "98 percent of students fit in here at the University of Charleston and feel welcomed by the university residents and staff."

FINANCIAL AID: 304-357-4759 • E-MAIL: ADMISSIONS@UCWV.EDU • WEBSITE: HTTP://WWW.UCWV.EDU/

THE PRINCETON REVIEW SAYS

Admissions

Very important factors considered include: standardized test scores. *Important factors considered include:* rigor of secondary school record, character/personal qualities, extracurricular activities. *Other factors considered include:* Class rank, application essay, recommendation(s), interview, talent/ability, volunteer work, work experience. SAT or ACT required; TOEFL required of all international applicants. High school diploma is required and GED is accepted. *Academic units required:* 1 Algebra for BS Nursing. *Academic units recommended:* 4 English, 3 mathematics, 3 science, 1 foreign language, 3 social studies, 2 history.

Financial Aid

Students should submit: FAFSA, state aid form. The Princeton Review suggests that all financial aid forms be submitted as soon as possible after 1/1. *Need-based scholarships/grants offered:* Federal Pell, SEOG, state scholarships/grants, private scholarships, the school's own gift aid. *Loan aid offered:* FFEL Subsidized Stafford, FFEL Unsubsidized Stafford, FFEL PLUS, Federal Perkins, Federal Nursing Applicants will be notified of awards on a rolling basis beginning 3/1. Federal Work-Study Program available. Off-campus job opportunities are good.

The Inside Word

"Since our founding in 1888, the University of Charleston has been providing a dynamic educational experience in a welcoming environment that nurtures the strengths of each student to help them reach their highest potential. Our mission is to educate each student for a life of productive work, enlightened living, and community involvement. Our educational program focuses on "learning your way" where each student is allowed to demonstrate what they have learned in order to earn the credits necessary for graduation. This curriculum is a unique blend of learning outcomes, student needs, course delivery, experiential education, and continuous quality improvement.

"Our 40-acre campus is located directly across from the State Capital Complex along the banks of the Kanawha River in the beautiful city of Charleston, West Virginia. Our location offers students the best of both worlds with all the amenities of a major metropolitan community and renowned outdoor recreational attractions found in the Mountain State. Housing facilities for residential students are very modern and student-friendly. We offer students many living options from traditional double, single, suite, and apartment style rooms. Because the University believes that students learn from their involvement in the community and campus activities, students are strongly encouraged to participate in one or more of the forty co-curricular organizations found at the University. The Community Service program provides opportunities for students to help both on campus and in the Charleston area. The varsity sports program has become one of the University's most valuable assets with teams competing in Division II of the NCAA."

SELECTIVITY

Admissions Rating	78
# of applicants	1,647
% of applicants accepted	66
% of acceptees attending	28

FRESHMAN PROFILE

Range SAT Critical Reading	430–530
Range SAT Math	440–580
Range ACT Composite	19–25
Minimum paper TOEFL	550
Minimum computer TOEFL	213
Minimum web-based TOEFL	79
Average HS GPA	3.36
% graduated top 10% of class	25
% graduated top 25% of class	43
% graduated top 50% of class	70

DEADLINES

Regular	
Notification	rolling
Nonfall registration?	yes

FINANCIAL FACTS

Financial Aid Rating	78
Annual tuition	$24,000
Room and board	$8,700
Books and supplies	$1,500
% frosh rec. need-based scholarship or grant aid	75
% UG rec. need-based scholarship or grant aid	56
% frosh rec. non-need-based scholarship or grant aid	58
% UG rec. non-need-based scholarship or grant aid	30
% frosh rec. need-based self-help aid	77
% UG rec. need-based self-help aid	84
% frosh rec. athletic scholarships	3
% UG rec. athletic scholarships	2
% frosh rec. any financial aid	98
% UG rec. any financial aid	97
% UG borrow to pay for school	89
Average cumulative indebtedness	$21,530

THE UNIVERSITY OF CHICAGO

1101 EAST FIFTY-EIGHTH STREET, ROSENWALD HALL, SUITE 105, CHICAGO, IL 60637 • ADMISSIONS: 773-702-8650 • FAX: 773-702-4199

CAMPUS LIFE
Quality of Life Rating	83
Fire Safety Rating	60*
Green Rating	86
Type of school	private
Environment	metropolis

STUDENTS
Total undergrad enrollment	5,027
% male/female	50/50
% from out of state	79
% from public high school	63
% in (# of) fraternities	NR (10)
% in (# of) sororities	NR (3)
% African American	6
% Asian	14
% Caucasian	45
% Hispanic	9
% international	8
# of countries represented	59

SURVEY SAYS . . .
No one cheats
Lab facilities are great
Great library
Athletic facilities are great
School is well run
Students love Chicago, IL
Dorms are like palaces

ACADEMICS
Academic Rating	97
Calendar	quarter
Student/faculty ratio	6:1
Profs interesting rating	82
Profs accessible rating	81
Most common reg class size	fewer than 10 students
Most common lab size	10–19 students

MOST POPULAR MAJORS
biology/biological sciences
economics
political science and government

STUDENTS SAY "..."

Academics
"Dedication to enriching the 'life of the mind' is palpable" at the "incomparable" University of Chicago. It is home to "the best economics department in the country," and one of the best (and most monstrously ugly) main libraries on Earth. Chicago students believe that "no university offers a better academic experience," and there is "an unexpectedly vibrant school spirit that comes not from athletics, but [a] shared academic involvement." Undergraduates must complete an intense, "interdisciplinary" core curriculum that "teaches them how to think about literature and philosophy and science." The core is "rigorous" and "you will spend about a third of your time here on it. But it's [also] fantastic, and you come out an incredibly well-rounded thinker with opinions on a wide variety of subjects." Naturally, "courses are tough." "Once you're out of the fire," though, "you realize how much more enriched you've become intellectually, with respect [as] to how to learn and...knowledge itself." Professors at Chicago "are the best in the world" and are "real celebrities in their fields of study," but they "make every effort to help every student who asks." Still, "there are duds." "Not everyone with the intelligence to do amazing research is capable of teaching." The "incredibly supportive" administration "takes pains to engage the entire campus in a sort of collective, community-wide conversation....They bring in all sorts of speakers, allow student groups almost absolute freedom, and are very supportive of student initiatives."

Life
The quarter system "makes for a particularly fast-paced" schedule. "We wear t-shirts that say 'U of C: Where fun comes to die,' and we're proud of it," explains a first-year student. "Don't come here if you don't plan to work very hard," an economics major warns. "We spend a large chunk of our time studying and should be studying much of the time that we are not." However, according to one student, "As much as a lot of people complain about the extremely rigorous academics at this school, we all secretly love it or we wouldn't be here." And "contrary to popular belief," students "certainly do know how to have fun." There are "concerts, plays, movies," and "tons of truly brilliant events on campus." Students also spend a lot of time "just talking" with "fascinating" classmates "who can hold their own on any topic under the sun." "The frat party scene is not much at all compared to other schools, but it's still there. Room parties with extended friends and random people from the building are usually more popular." While "scorn for the lovely neighborhood" surrounding the campus is "exceedingly common," downtown Chicago is "very accessible." The city "is a huge asset and resource," "whether it's for an internship," "a night out," or "just a day away from campus."

Student Body
Students at Chicago are "intense," "opinionated," "engaged with the world around them," and "somewhat zany." "Most everyone has a quirk," a senior reports, "like the center on the football team who's really into Dungeons & Dragons." Without question, "the popular stereotype" of the Chicago student is "a nerdy, socially awkward person." Living up to the hype are an abundance of students "religiously dedicated to academic performance" and "a bunch of strange people," "usually clutching some fantastic book." However, "there aren't as many extremely strange and nerdy students as there have been in the past." "A portion of the student body at the U of C [are] actually talented, cool, and (gasp!) attractive." "There are loads of people who are fascinating," a sophomore writes. There are "artists, communists, fashionistas, activists," and even "some who aren't posing at all." "Everyone who is at the University of Chicago considers themselves at the best possible university," concludes one student. "It's a self-selecting group," and most people are "happy to be here." Chicago students "look down on other schools, particularly the Ivies."

THE UNIVERSITY OF CHICAGO

FINANCIAL AID: 773-702-8666 • WEBSITE: WWW.UCHICAGO.EDU

THE PRINCETON REVIEW SAYS

Admissions

Very important factors considered include: Application essays, recommendations(s), rigor of secondary school record, character/personal qualities, talent/ability. *Important factors considered include:* Class rank, academic GPA, extracurricular activities, volunteer work. *Other factors considered include:* standardized test scores, alumni/ae relation, first generation, interview, level of applicant's interest, racial/ethnic status, work experience. SAT or ACT required; TOEFL required of all international applicants. High school diploma or equivalent is not required. *Academic units recommended:* 4 English, 4 mathematics, 4 science, 3 foreign language, 2 social studies, 2 history.

Financial Aid

Students should submit: FAFSA, institution's own financial aid form, CSS/Financial Aid PROFILE, noncustodial PROFILE, business/farm supplement. Regular filing deadline is 2/1. The Princeton Review suggests that all financial aid forms be submitted as soon as possible after 1/1. *Need-based scholarships/grants offered:* Federal Pell, SEOG, state scholarships/grants, private scholarships, the school's own gift aid. *Loan aid offered:* FFEL Subsidized Stafford, FFEL Unsubsidized Stafford, FFEL PLUS, Federal Perkins. Applicants will be notified of awards on or about 4/15.

The Inside Word

The University of Chicago now uses the common application. Essay topics will continue to be of the thought provoking "uncommon" type, keeping the spirit of fun and inquiry in the application's supplement. People here dwell on deep thoughts and big ideas. In your application you'll need to demonstrate outstanding grades in the tough courses and, most of all, that you will fit in with a bunch of thinkers. Think really hard before you write your three essays, and try to say really intelligent things during your interview. Interviews are recommended but are not required.

THE SCHOOL SAYS "..."

From The Admissions Office

"The University of Chicago is a place where talented young people—writers, politicians, activists, artists, mathematicians, and scientists—come to learn in a setting that rewards interesting thought and prizes initiative and creativity. Chicago is also a place where collegiate life is urban, yet friendly and open, and free of empty traditionalism and snobbishness. Chicago is the right choice for students who know that they would thrive in an intimate classroom setting. Classes at Chicago are small, emphasizing discussion with faculty members whose research is always testing the limits of their chosen fields. Students at Chicago take chances—delighting professors when they pursue a topic on their own for the fun of it—and display an articulate voice in papers and in discussion. Their good times include the normal collegiate good times – a highly successful Division III sports program, small but active Greek life, 40 student theatrical productions a year, a rich musical life—and the extraordinary opportunities a major city offers our students, who enjoy the politics, music, theater, commerce, architecture, and neighborhood life of Chicago."

SELECTIVITY

Admissions Rating	98
# of applicants	12,376
% of applicants accepted	28
% of acceptees attending	38
# accepting a place on wait list	1,453
% admitted from wait list	2

FRESHMAN PROFILE

Range SAT Critical Reading	660–770
Range SAT Math	650–760
Range ACT Composite	28–33
Minimum paper TOEFL	600
Minimum computer TOEFL	250
% graduated top 10% of class	86
% graduated top 25% of class	96
% graduated top 50% of class	100

DEADLINES

Early action	
Deadline	11/1
Notification	12/15
Regular	
Deadline	1/2
Notification	4/1
Nonfall registration?	no

APPLICANTS ALSO LOOK AT

AND OFTEN PREFER
Harvard College
Yale University
Northwestern University
University of Pennsylvania

AND SOMETIMES PREFER
Washington University in St. Louis
University of California—Berkeley

AND RARELY PREFER
New York University
Georgetown University

FINANCIAL FACTS

Financial Aid Rating	95
Annual tuition	$36,891
Room and board	$11,697
Required fees	$741
Books and supplies	$1,100
% frosh rec. need-based scholarship or grant aid	48
% UG rec. need-based scholarship or grant aid	45
% frosh rec. need-based self-help aid	38
% UG rec. need-based self-help aid	37
% frosh rec. any financial aid	48.7
% UG rec. any financial aid	45.8
% UG borrow to pay for school	41
Average cumulative indebtedness	$27,562

UNIVERSITY OF CINCINNATI

OFFICE OF ADMISSIONS, PO BOX 210091, CINCINNATI, OH 45221-0091 • ADMISSIONS: 513-556-1100 • FAX: 513-556-1105

CAMPUS LIFE

Quality of Life Rating	**71**
Fire Safety Rating	**78**
Green Rating	**87**
Type of school	public
Environment	metropolis

STUDENTS

Total undergrad enrollment	20,183
% male/female	49/51
% from out of state	10
% live on campus	20
% in (# of) fraternities	NR (23)
% in (# of) sororities	NR (10)
% African American	11
% Asian	3
% Caucasian	78
% Hispanic	2
% international	1
# of countries represented	115

SURVEY SAYS . . .

Athletic facilities are great
Diverse student types on campus

ACADEMICS

Academic Rating	**72**
Calendar	quarter
Student/faculty ratio	15:1
Profs interesting rating	65
Profs accessible rating	65
Most common	
reg class size	20–29 students

MOST POPULAR MAJORS

communication studies/speech communication and rhetoric
marketing/marketing management
psychology

STUDENTS SAY ". . ."

Academics

The University of Cincinnati is "an urban university" "in the midst of a renaissance." The expansive campus includes 12 separate colleges, each of which is like a "different world." Even "each major within the individual colleges provides and entirely different experience than the next." The "great" engineering programs afford opportunities for "lots of cutting edge research." The "renowned" Conservatory of Music offers "intense practical experience in the arts." There's "a real sense of ambition and drive" within the "stellar" College of Design, Architecture, Art, and Planning. Also, internships and co-op programs are "huge." As a result, many students "have extensive experience in their fields before obtaining a degree." UC's professors run the gamut from "very helpful" to "total crap." Profs are often overly concerned with research and "not as accessible to students as they should be." "Seventy percent of my professors could be classified as very good, with 20 percent being classified as excellent, and the other 10 percent being less than very good," assesses a senior. "Overall, my academic experience at UC has been more defined by my own initiative to seek good faculty and good outside programs (internships, study abroad, etc.)." "The administration is famous for lack of intra-office coordination; they have great intentions, but students are always talking about getting 'the UC run-around.'" Nevertheless, "there are vast opportunities available to students if they are just willing to put in some effort."

Life

Many students praise the "modern and nice" campus as "an urban oasis of amazing architecture" with amenities galore. The campus itself is "usually pretty safe." However, the "shady" surrounding neighborhood "can be extraordinarily hostile." There's "way too much crime." While there's been "a rebirth of on-campus interest and activity" in recent years, UC largely remains "a big commuter school with little cohesive force." A lot of students are from Cincinnati and often spend weekends "at home rather than around campus." Football and basketball games are the biggest extracurricular draws but, otherwise, "people don't have a lot of enthusiasm for campus events." The frat scene is noticeable but not huge. On the weekends, "drinking is inevitable." "For fun we party at houses and in bars," explains one student. Downtown bars are popular destinations." "The urban setting adds excitement to the atmosphere." The Cincinnati area also "has a huge variety of excellent employers and offers an excellent environment for raising a family." It's "a great city for art museums and restaurants," too.

Student Body

Most students here "probably did a little bit above average in high school." Beyond that, few characteristics unite these undergrads. Without question, the University of Cincinnati "does not lack diversity." There are "lots of minority students, particularly Asian and African American students." "UC attracts many older students" as well. "Different money backgrounds" proliferate. The campus is "a vibrant quilt of culture" that feels "very realistic." "It really could be considered the melting pot college of the Midwest." Students tend to be really cliquish, though, and disparate little groups "keep to themselves." "Some people are really into partying." Others are very serious about academics. "Everyone has their own group of friends," observes a psychology major. "Ethnic groups stick together and rarely interact outside of their own group." "Engineers hang out with other engineers." The "suburbanite commuter students" stick together. So, too, do the "artsy, hardworking types," "frat-boy jock" types, and the "fashionable, mature" architecture students.

FINANCIAL AID: 513-556-1000 • E-MAIL: TRANSFER@UC.EDU • WEBSITE: WWW.ADMISSIONS.UC.EDU

THE PRINCETON REVIEW SAYS

Admissions

Very important factors considered include: Class rank, academic GPA, rigor of secondary school record, standardized test scores. *Other factors considered include:* Application essay, extracurricular activities, SAT or ACT required; ACT with Writing component required. TOEFL required of all international applicants. High school diploma is required and GED is accepted. *Academic units required:* 4 English, 3 mathematics, 2 science, 2 foreign language, 2 social studies, 2 academic electives. *Academic units recommended:* 4 mathematics, 3 science, 1 history.

Financial Aid

Students should submit: FAFSA. The Princeton Review suggests that all financial aid forms be submitted as soon as possible after 1/1. *Need-based scholarships/grants offered:* Federal Pell, SEOG, state scholarships/grants, private scholarships, the school's own gift aid, United Negro College Fund, Federal Nursing Scholarships, ACG, SMART, TEACH. *Loan aid offered:* FFEL Subsidized Stafford, FFEL Unsubsidized Stafford, FFEL PLUS, Federal Perkins, Federal Nursing, state loans, college/university loans from institutional funds. Applicants will be notified of awards on a rolling basis beginning 3/10. Federal Work-Study Program available. Institutional employment available. Off-campus job opportunities are excellent.

The Inside Word

One the University of Cincinnati's greatest strengths is that it boasts several smaller and completely unique colleges within a single large university setting. Each school maintains some autonomy, and this extends to admissions policies. Requirements vary among programs and candidates will need to do their research before completing their applications. Competitive programs tend to fill up rather quickly, so interested students should submit their materials as early as possible.

THE SCHOOL SAYS "..."

From The Admissions Office

"Remarkable architecture, park-like open spaces, engaging student tour guides, and a welcoming admissions staff make the University of Cincinnati a must-visit destination. UC campus has been transformed over the past 10 years and is drawing national and international attention for blending student life, learning, research, and recreation in a unique urban environment.

"Freshman application materials include high school transcripts, test scores, a personal statement, and a list of co-curricular activities. Some academic programs require additional materials.

"Sign up for a visit, become a Bearcat VIP, and apply online. Information about all UC majors is linked from the website. We also have Tuesday-night online chat sessions for students and parents. Nothing beats a visit, however, for assessing how well you'll fit in here.

"Either the SAT or ACT is required for students applying to bachelor's degree programs; the ACT Writing component is required. SAT Subject Tests are not required."

SELECTIVITY

Admissions Rating	**80**
# of applicants	14,333
% of applicants accepted	61
% of acceptees attending	36

FRESHMAN PROFILE

Range SAT Critical Reading	500–610
Range SAT Math	520–640
Range SAT Writing	490–600
Range ACT Composite	22–27
Minimum paper TOEFL	515
Average HS GPA	3.4
% graduated top 10% of class	22
% graduated top 25% of class	49
% graduated top 50% of class	81

DEADLINES

Regular	
Priority	1/15
Deadline	9/1
Nonfall registration?	yes

FINANCIAL FACTS

Financial Aid Rating	**66**
Annual in-state tuition	$7,896
Annual out-of-state tuition	$22,419
Room and board	$9,240
Required fees	$1,503
Books and supplies	$1,275
% frosh rec. need-based scholarship or grant aid	25
% UG rec. need-based scholarship or grant aid	23
% frosh rec. non-need-based scholarship or grant aid	27
% UG rec. non-need-based scholarship or grant aid	22
% frosh rec. need-based self-help aid	21
% UG rec. need-based self-help aid	18
% frosh rec. athletic scholarships	1
% UG rec. athletic scholarships	1
% frosh rec. any financial aid	80
% UG rec. any financial aid	73
% UG borrow to pay for school	65
Average cumulative indebtedness	$24,431

UNIVERSITY OF COLORADO—BOULDER

552 UCB, BOULDER, CO 80309-0552 • ADMISSIONS: 303-492-6301 • FAX: 303-492-7115

CAMPUS LIFE

Quality of Life Rating	**83**
Fire Safety Rating	**85**
Green Rating	**88**
Type of school	public
Environment	city

STUDENTS

Total undergrad enrollment	26,111
% male/female	53/47
% from out of state	33
% live on campus	25
% in (# of) fraternities	8 (21)
% in (# of) sororities	13 (16)
% African American	2
% Asian	6
% Caucasian	78
% Hispanic	6
% Native American	1
% international	2
# of countries represented	111

SURVEY SAYS . . .

Athletic facilities are great
Students love Boulder, CO
Great off-campus food
Everyone loves the The Colorado
Buffaloes
Lots of beer drinking
Hard liquor is popular

ACADEMICS

Academic Rating	**73**
Calendar	semester
Student/faculty ratio	17.5:1
Profs interesting rating	70
Profs accessible rating	71
% classes taught by TAs	10
Most common	
reg class size	10–19 students
Most common	
lab size	20–29 students

MOST POPULAR MAJORS
English language and literature
physiology
psychology

STUDENTS SAY ". . ."

Academics

"It is all about the total college experience" at the University of Colorado; students enjoy both "excellent academics and a great social atmosphere." "The University of Colorado is all about getting an education for five days and spending the other two in the mountains," students repeatedly tell us, noting that "CU is an amazing place because you can find an array of challenges and opportunities whether your drive is research, the arts, sports, a job, or tough class work. However, at the same time, you can find a great social life outside of school being in an amazing place like Boulder." The sciences "are a huge strength" here, with students singling out chemistry, biology, and engineering for praise. "As an undergraduate student at CU—Boulder, I am able to research in one of my professor's labs while receiving a great education," one student explains; another points out that "being in a class taught by a Nobel laureate is not something everyone gets to experience." Business studies also excel. As at most large schools, CU has "a wide range when it comes to the quality of professors" but "for the most part [they are] very engaging in their lectures and encouraging of discussion. They are also very good about returning e-mails and [hanging] office hours." The administration can be cumbersome, but students generally appreciate how "In a tough economic climate and a gross lack of state funding, CU's administration does its best to make cuts without hurting the student body's quality of education."

Life

"The University of Colorado and the city of Boulder have so much to offer," students say. "The campus is gorgeous, as are most of the students, and there is always something to do," much of it outdoors. "People are very active in Boulder. Hiking, kayaking, mountain biking, and skiing or snowboarding is popular weekend (or weekday) activities." As one student puts it, "The mountains are a huge attraction, and during ski season the campus is considerably quieter on the weekends." CU football is also "huge, and so is the partying that is associated with it." Students concede that "the partying is pretty widespread" on and around campus but also note that "there are plenty of fun things to do that don't involve alcohol or drugs." The school "really encourages students to get involved with the ceaseless amounts of activities, groups, and clubs. Also, CU does a fantastic job of keeping students up-to-date on the goings-on and important news around school, town, and the world." Hometown Boulder is full of coffee shops and quaint shopping areas; students agree that they are blessed with "a beautiful campus and town."

Student Body

Most CU students "are very outdoors-prone" —it's what attracted them to the school in many cases—and tend to be "attractive, health-conscious," "liberal, [and] environmentally motivated" and they "live a bohemian-like lifestyle." The school is huge, so plenty students do not fit that description, of course; as one student observes, "Boulder is known for being a crazy, hippie town, but when I came here, I was surprised at the number of 'preppie kids' who are politically apathetic and more concerned with how they look than how the world around them looks." Most here "care about school but aren't super-academic." "Being social is extremely important to many people, and because of this, schoolwork sometimes takes a backseat." One student sums it up this way: "If you came to get a good education, then you will get one, but a lot of the students came here for the skiing and don't take school seriously." CU has "a large GLBTQ population, and the school is very supportive."

UNIVERSITY OF COLORADO—BOULDER

FINANCIAL AID: 303-492-5091 • E-MAIL: APPLY@COLORADO.EDU • WEBSITE: WWW.COLORADO.EDU

THE PRINCETON REVIEW SAYS

Admissions

Very important factors considered include: Class rank, application essay, academic GPA, recommendation(s), rigor of secondary school record. *Important factors considered include:* standardized test scores, character/personal qualities, first generation, state residency. *Other factors considered include:* alumni/ae relation, extracurricular activities, geographical residence, level of applicant's interest, talent/ability, volunteer work, work experience. SAT or ACT required; TOEFL required of all international applicants. High school diploma is required and GED is accepted. *Academic units required:* 4 English, 4 mathematics, 3 science, (2 science labs), 3 foreign language, 3 social studies, 1 history, 1 geography.

Financial Aid

Students should submit: FAFSATax return required. The Princeton Review suggests that all financial aid forms be submitted as soon as possible after 1/1. *Need-based scholarships/grants offered:* Federal Pell, SEOG, state scholarships/grants, private scholarships, the school's own gift aid. *Loan aid offered:* Direct Subsidized Stafford, Direct Unsubsidized Stafford, Direct PLUS, Federal Perkins, college/university loans from institutional funds, private lenders. Applicants will be notified of awards on a rolling basis beginning 2/1. Federal Work-Study Program available. Institutional employment available. Off-campus job opportunities are excellent.

The Inside Word

Applicants must indicate the school within CU to which they wish to be admitted. Engineering and Applied Science is most competitive, followed by the College of Music, the Leeds School of Business, and the College of Architecture and Planning. The College of Arts and Sciences is the least competitive; those applying to and rejected by the more competitive schools are automatically entered into consideration for admission to the College of Arts and Sciences. With nearly one-third of the student body from out of state, CU boasts far more geographic diversity than most state schools.

THE SCHOOL SAYS "..."

From The Admissions Office

""The University of Colorado—Boulder is a place of beauty and academic prominence at the foot of the Rocky Mountains. A sense of vitality and curiosity fills the campus, and yet it's comfortable and relaxed. It's a place you can be yourself and let your imagination soar. We have programs for you if you seek leadership training, research experience, academic honors, international experience (one in four graduates has studied abroad), community involvement, and more. There are a number of enrichment programs that give exceptionally talented and intellectually committed students the opportunity to expand their education outside the classroom, build a sense of community, and help prepare for post-graduate opportunities. Residential Academic Programs (RAPs) and Living and Learning Communities (LLCs) in several residence halls provide undergraduates with shared learning and living experiences.

"Getting involved is easy at CU—Boulder. If you are interested in student government, clubs, athletics, recreation, Greek life, volunteer work, theater, dance, film, exhibits, planetarium shows, or concerts, you will find them here.

"To find out if CU—Boulder is the place for you, we encourage you to visit. Contact the office of admissions, or take a virtual tour online.

"The University of Colorado at Boulder requires either SAT or ACT scores for admissions; the Writing tests are currently not used in making decisions. SAT Subject Test scores are not required."

SELECTIVITY	
Admissions Rating	**89**
# of applicants	23,004
% of applicants accepted	78
% of acceptees attending	33
# accepting a place on wait list	292
% admitted from wait list	2

FRESHMAN PROFILE	
Range SAT Critical Reading	520–630
Range SAT Math	550–650
Range ACT Composite	24–28
Minimum paper TOEFL	500
Minimum computer TOEFL	173
Minimum web-based TOEFL	61
Average HS GPA	3.57
% graduated top 10% of class	27
% graduated top 25% of class	61
% graduated top 50% of class	93

DEADLINES	
Early action	
Deadline	12/15
Notification	2/15
Regular	
Priority	12/15
Deadline	2/15
Notification	4/1
Nonfall registration?	yes

FINANCIAL FACTS	
Financial Aid Rating	**87**
Annual in-state tuition	$5,922
Annual out-of-state tuition	$23,580
Room and board	$9,860
Required fees	$1,356
Books and supplies	$1,749
% frosh rec. need-based scholarship or grant aid	29
% UG rec. need-based scholarship or grant aid	28
% frosh rec. non-need-based scholarship or grant aid	1
% UG rec. non-need-based scholarship or grant aid	1
% frosh rec. need-based self-help aid	30
% UG rec. need-based self-help aid	29
% frosh rec. athletic scholarships	1
% UG rec. athletic scholarships	1
% frosh rec. any financial aid	66
% UG rec. any financial aid	56
% UG borrow to pay for school	42
Average cumulative indebtedness	$18,361

UNIVERSITY OF CONNECTICUT

2131 HILLSIDE ROAD, UNIT 3088, STORRS, CT 06268-3088 • ADMISSIONS: 860-486-3137 • FAX: 860-486-1476

CAMPUS LIFE
Quality of Life Rating	74
Fire Safety Rating	84
Green Rating	96
Type of school	public
Environment	town

STUDENTS
Total undergrad enrollment	16,459
% male/female	50/50
% from out of state	23
% from public high school	95
% live on campus	71
% in (# of) fraternities	8 (16)
% in (# of) sororities	9 (13)
% African American	5
% Asian	8
% Caucasian	64
% Hispanic	5
% international	1
# of countries represented	106

SURVEY SAYS . . .
Low cost of living
Everyone loves the Huskies
Student publications are popular
(Almost) no one smokes

ACADEMICS
Academic Rating	74
Calendar	semester
Student/faculty ratio	17:1
Profs interesting rating	65
Profs accessible rating	68
% classes taught by TAs	25
Most common reg class size	10–19 students
Most common lab size	10–19 students

MOST POPULAR MAJORS
business/commerce
political science and government
psychology

STUDENTS SAY ". . ."

Academics
Brimming with sincere Husky pride, students at the University of Connecticut eagerly dole out praise for their school's fabulous athletic programs, world-class academics, friendly atmosphere, and remarkable affordability. At this large research university, professors are "extremely in-tune with recent developments in their fields" and "research opportunities are outstanding," even on the under-graduate level. A political science major shares, "My professors are the ones invited to the White House to discuss the Middle East crisis, flying across the world to solve issues of border disputes, and more. The professors bring their life experiences to the classroom, and it brings the material to life." While most professors maintain their professional pursuits outside the classroom, teaching is taken seriously at UConn, and instructors and administrators "genuinely care and want you to succeed." By all accounts, faculty is easily accessible during office hours and, "if you can't make those, they'll work out a different time for you." Like professors, UConn's leadership is surprising friendly, down-to-earth, and accessible. Well loved by all, "president Hogan rides the student bus to the football games, is always seen around campus, and even keeps a blog letting students know what he is up to." Even so, students remind us that UConn is a big school, and students must take responsibility for their own educations. A senior explains, "UConn doesn't spoon-feed you education. Students do have to take the initiative to communicate with professors and the other resources on campus." "You have to put into it what you want to get out."

Life
UConn's "vibrant school spirit" is one of the university's most distinctive qualities, and Huskies are enthusiastically involved in the campus community. Most UConn undergraduates are "in a million clubs, do community service, play sports, or simply have Husky pride and attend UConn events." Socially and academically, you'll find a mix: "Some students are all about academics, and they live in Babbidge Library, others are all about partying and can be found at the off-campus apartments or the bar throughout the week." In general, most students strike a balance between work and play. A sophomore elaborates, "From Sunday to Thursday, almost all students work diligently. Thursday nights bring some partying, followed by mass amounts of parties on Friday and Saturday nights." If you aren't interested in parties, there are plenty other options, "from athletics, to musical and theatrical performances, to events in the Student Union, UConn has so many different things to do!" In addition, there are more than "350 clubs and organizations," as well as an active intramural sports league, which is a great way to blow off steam. No summary of life at UConn would be complete without mentioning the competitive Division I athletics, which are the "heart of campus spirit." In their free time, UConn students (along with faculty and alumni) "love to go cheer on our nationally ranked UConn Huskies." In fact, student tickets for sporting events sell out months in advance.

Student Body
Considering the school's attractive in-state tuition, it's no surprise that 80 percent of UConn undergraduates come from Connecticut. While that fact may diminish the demographic diversity on campus, students reassure us that "there's a great mix at UConn. With more than 16,000 students enrolled, you're bound to run into just about every type of person." Students say you'll see a lot of students wearing North Face jackets and Ugg boots, but you'll also find an "animal science club, in which the students walk around with squirrel tails on." While UConn students exhibit varying degrees of academic seriousness, "the majority care about their grades, and the library is always packed during exams, midterms, and finals." More than anything else, "the real tie [among] students is the pride that we all have in our university." A senior insists, "I have not met one person who is unhappy and dislikes the university."

FINANCIAL AID: 860-486-2819 • E-MAIL: BEAHUSKY@UCONN.EDU • WEBSITE: WWW.UCONN.EDU

THE PRINCETON REVIEW SAYS

Admissions

Very important factors considered include: Class rank, academic GPA, rigor of secondary school record, standardized test scores, talent/ability. *Important factors considered include:* Application essay, recommendation(s), character/personal qualities, extracurricular activities, first generation, racial/ethnic status, volunteer work. *Other factors considered include:* alumni/ae relation, geographical residence, level of applicant's interest, state residency, work experience. SAT or ACT required; ACT with Writing component required. TOEFL required of all international applicants. High school diploma is required and GED is accepted. *Academic units required:* 4 English, 3 mathematics, 2 science, (2 science labs), 2 foreign language, 2 social studies, 3 academic electives. *Academic units recommended:* 3 foreign language.

Financial Aid

Students should submit: FAFSA. The Princeton Review suggests that all financial aid forms be submitted as soon as possible after 1/1. *Need-based scholarships/grants offered:* Federal Pell, SEOG, state scholarships/grants, private scholarships, the school's own gift aid. *Loan aid offered:* FFEL Subsidized Stafford, FFEL Unsubsidized Stafford, FFEL PLUS, Federal Perkins. Applicants will be notified of awards on a rolling basis beginning 3/1. Federal Work-Study Program available. Institutional employment available. Off-campus job opportunities are good.

The Inside Word

When reviewing applications, the UConn admissions committee evaluates students based on a wide range of factors, including standardized test scores, rigor of high school curriculum, classroom performance, extracurricular activities, and community involvement. Honors and advanced placement classes are not required, but they are viewed favorably by the admissions committee. Competitive applicants have a cumulative grade point average of 3.3 on a 4.0 scale and usually rank in the top quarter of their high school class.

THE SCHOOL SAYS "..."

From The Admissions Office

"Thanks to a $2.8-billion construction program that is impacting every area of university life, the University of Connecticut provides students a high-quality and personalized education on one of the most attractive and technologically advanced college campuses in the United States. Applications are soaring nationally as an increasing number of high-achieving students from diverse backgrounds are making UConn their school of choice. From award-winning actors to governmental leaders, students enjoy an assortment of fascinating speakers each year, while performances by premier dance, jazz, and rock musicians enliven student life. Our beautiful New England campus is convenient and safe, and most students walk to class or ride university shuttle buses. State-of-the-art residential facilities include interest-based learning communities and honors housing as well as on-campus suite-style and apartment living. Championship Division I athletics have created fervor known as Huskymania among UConn students.

"Freshman applicants seeking admittance are required to submit official score reports from the SAT or ACT with Writing component."

SELECTIVITY
Admissions Rating	89
# of applicants	21,058
% of applicants accepted	54
% of acceptees attending	31
# accepting a place on wait list	1,839
% admitted from wait list	1

FRESHMAN PROFILE
Range SAT Critical Reading	540–630
Range SAT Math	570–660
Range SAT Writing	550–640
Range ACT Composite	24–28
Minimum paper TOEFL	550
Minimum computer TOEFL	213
Minimum web-based TOEFL	79
% graduated top 10% of class	39
% graduated top 25% of class	78
% graduated top 50% of class	98

DEADLINES
Early action	
Deadline	12/1
Notification	2/1
Regular	
Deadline	2/1
Notification	rolling
Nonfall registration?	yes

APPLICANTS ALSO LOOK AT
AND OFTEN PREFER
University of Delaware
University of Maryland—College Park
AND SOMETIMES PREFER
Northeastern University
Boston University
AND RARELY PREFER
Rutgers, The State University of New Jersey—New Brunswick

FINANCIAL FACTS
Financial Aid Rating	70
Annual in-state tuition	$7,632
Annual out-of-state tuition	$23,232
Room and board	$10,120
Required fees	$2,254
Books and supplies	$800
% frosh rec. need-based scholarship or grant aid	37
% UG rec. need-based scholarship or grant aid	34
% frosh rec. non-need-based scholarship or grant aid	37
% UG rec. non-need-based scholarship or grant aid	24
% frosh rec. need-based self-help aid	36
% UG rec. need-based self-help aid	38
% frosh rec. athletic scholarships	2
% UG rec. athletic scholarships	2
% frosh rec. any financial aid	49
% UG rec. any financial aid	48
% UG borrow to pay for school	61
Average cumulative indebtedness	$21,521

UNIVERSITY OF DALLAS

1845 EAST NORTHGATE DRIVE, IRVING, TX 75062 • ADMISSIONS: 972-721-5266 • FAX: 972-721-5017

CAMPUS LIFE
Quality of Life Rating	**78**
Fire Safety Rating	**93**
Green Rating	**69**
Type of school	private
Affiliation	Roman Catholic
Environment	city

STUDENTS
Total undergrad enrollment	1,289
% male/female	48/52
% from out of state	50
% from public high school	45
% live on campus	50
% African American	1
% Asian	5
% Caucasian	68
% Hispanic	16
% international	2
# of countries represented	20

SURVEY SAYS . . .
Students are friendly
Students are very religious
Low cost of living
Frats and sororities are unpopular or nonexistent
(Almost) no one smokes
Very little drug use

ACADEMICS
Academic Rating	**84**
Calendar	semester
Student/faculty ratio	13:1
Profs interesting rating	89
Profs accessible rating	88
Most common reg class size	20–29 students
Most common lab size	10–19 students

MOST POPULAR MAJORS
business administration and management
English language and literature
psychology

STUDENTS SAY ". . ."

Academics

This "Catholic University for independent thinkers" prides itself on its core curriculum, in which students undertake "a deep and penetrating study of the Western tradition, from Ancient Greece to today" by reading "the greatest works of literature in all subjects." Students love the focus on primary sources throughout their four years. "The idea of learning politics from the writings of the democratic world's greatest minds is much more appealing to me than learning from a textbook," says one freshman. UD students are encouraged to approach everything—including their own faith—from a critical perspective. "The spirit of truth-seeking that pervades everything and everyone, both in and out of the classroom," can make for an "intense" environment. "I had one professor freshman year who said he was up until 3 A.M. doing the reading, so we better have done it, too," says a sophomore politics major. But it's easy to get motivated "when your professors care so much about what the students gain from the class discussions and the texts themselves." The small size of the school also adds to the academic intensity and makes students "feel like part of a big family." The administration gets poor marks: "They seem to be more concerned with keeping us from drinking and having sex than providing basic services all other college students take for granted." But any grumbling is overshadowed by enthusiasm for the school's unique character, including a study-abroad program that sends most sophomores to Rome. The semester in Italy "brings our studies to life and helps us to connect what we learn in the classrooms with real, on-site visits to places like ancient Greece and Pompeii."

Life

At UD, "you're either studying, praying, or going to parties." The administration can be "very strict," and underage students are often written up for drinking. But that doesn't mean life here is boring. There are boisterous and popular celebrations for Groundhog Day and other holidays, weeknights bring "many, many on-campus activities organized by clubs, academic departments, or residence hall associations," and many students attend parties at off-campus apartments on weekends. Although Dallas is accessible by car, "undergraduate students (especially freshmen and sophomores) spend most of their time hanging out on campus." Students complain that the campus is in need of an overhaul: "A lot of the buildings are pretty ugly," and the school "needs to provide better facilities, [such as] library, computer lab, and study areas." But students find ways to have fun despite the barren surroundings. "We love to play intramurals, especially flag football and ultimate Frisbee. We like dancing, as evidenced by our very popular swing dancing club." And then there's that semester in Rome: "If you haven't gone yet, you're thinking about it, and if you have gone, you're talking about it and posting your photos."

Student Body

The typical UD student "studies one of the humanities (preferably English, history, or philosophy), is very, very studious and strongly committed to the Catholic faith but also knows how to have a good time." Of course, a good time at UD may be slightly different than at other schools: "It is not uncommon to encounter deep theological or philosophical discussions in diverse extracurricular settings—such as cross-country meets or weekend parties!" Students here take their studies seriously, and "few who are not enthusiastic about this intellectual pursuit come to the school." UD students are also serious about their faith: "Those who aren't very Catholic become more so; some of those who aren't [Catholic] convert." Campus nightlife is fun but not wild; most students "drink moderately or not at all," and there is no Greek scene. The student body is conservative politically, but everyone is "welcoming toward the liberal minority and dignifies alternative stances with respect and with very philosophical and very friendly discussions." Despite any differences, the core program unites the student body: "No matter what year you are, you have the same academic background as every student when it comes to discussing literary traditions, such as Dante or Homer, philosophy, politics, and more."

FINANCIAL AID: 972-721-5266 • E-MAIL: UGADMIS@UDALLAS.EDU • WEBSITE: WWW.UDALLAS.EDU

THE PRINCETON REVIEW SAYS

Admissions

Very important factors considered include: Application essay, academic GPA, recommendation(s), rigor of secondary school record, standardized test scores, character/personal qualities. *Important factors considered include:* Class rank, talent/ability. *Other factors considered include:* alumni/ae relation, extracurricular activities, first generation, interview, level of applicant's interest, volunteer work, work experience. SAT or ACT required; ACT with Writing component required. TOEFL required of all international applicants. High school diploma is required and GED is accepted. *Academic units required:* 4 English, 3 mathematics, 3 science, 2 foreign language, 3 social studies, 3 history, 2 visual/performing arts, 4 academic electives. *Academic units recommended:* 4 English, 4 mathematics, 3 science, (3 science labs), 3 foreign language, 4 social studies, 4 history, 2 visual/performing arts, 4 academic electives.

Financial Aid

Students should submit: FAFSA. The Princeton Review suggests that all financial aid forms be submitted as soon as possible after 1/1. *Need-based scholarships/grants offered:* Federal Pell, SEOG, state scholarships/grants, the school's own gift aid. *Loan aid offered:* FFEL Subsidized Stafford, FFEL Unsubsidized Stafford, FFEL PLUS, state loans Applicants will be notified of awards on a rolling basis beginning 3/30. Federal Work-Study Program available. Institutional employment available. Off-campus job opportunities are fair.

The Inside Word

The university's conservative nature means that UD admissions officers place significant emphasis on the "fit" part of the admissions process. Having a solid academic background counts for a lot, but a dedication to Catholicism, the classics, or just serious academic inquiry can be even more important.

THE SCHOOL SAYS "..."

From The Admissions Office

"Quite unabashedly, the curriculum at the University of Dallas is based on the supposition that truth and virtue exist and are the proper objects of search in an education. The curriculum further supposes that this search is best pursued through an acquisition of philosophical and theological principles on the part of a student and has for its analogical field a vast body of great literature—perhaps more extensive than is likely to be encountered elsewhere—supplemented by a survey of the sweep of history and an introduction to the political and economic principles of society. An understanding of these subjects, along with an introduction to the quantitative and scientific worldview and a mastery of a language, is expected to form a comprehensive and coherent experience, which, in effect, governs the intellect of a student in a manner that develops independence of thought in its most effective mode.

"Students applying for admission are required to take the SAT Reasoning Test or the ACT with Writing Assessment."

SELECTIVITY

Admissions Rating	95
# of applicants	1,593
% of applicants accepted	53
% of acceptees attending	35

FRESHMAN PROFILE

Range SAT Critical Reading	560–680
Range SAT Math	550–650
Range SAT Writing	530–670
Range ACT Composite	24–29
Minimum paper TOEFL	550
Minimum computer TOEFL	213
Minimum web-based TOEFL	79
Average HS GPA	3.69
% graduated top 10% of class	29
% graduated top 25% of class	63
% graduated top 50% of class	87

DEADLINES

Early action	
Deadline	12/1
Notification	1/15
Regular	
Priority	1/15
Deadline	8/1
Notification	rolling
Nonfall registration?	yes

APPLICANTS ALSO LOOK AT

AND OFTEN PREFER
University of Notre Dame
Southern Methodist University

AND SOMETIMES PREFER
Trinity University
Austin College
Texas Christian University

AND RARELY PREFER
Saint Louis University
Loyola University New Orleans
Texas A&M University—College Station
The University of Texas at Austin

FINANCIAL FACTS

Financial Aid Rating	82
Annual tuition	$24,646
Room and board	$8,220
Required fees	$1,648
Books and supplies	$1,700
% frosh rec. need-based scholarship or grant aid	65
% UG rec. need-based scholarship or grant aid	62
% frosh rec. non-need-based scholarship or grant aid	80
% UG rec. non-need-based scholarship or grant aid	80
% frosh rec. need-based self-help aid	53
% UG rec. need-based self-help aid	52
% frosh rec. any financial aid	95
% UG rec. any financial aid	95
% UG borrow to pay for school	70
Average cumulative indebtedness	$24,000

UNIVERSITY OF DAYTON

300 COLLEGE PARK, DAYTON, OH 45469-1300 • ADMISSIONS: 937-229-4411 • FAX: 937-229-4729

CAMPUS LIFE

Quality of Life Rating	95
Fire Safety Rating	60*
Green Rating	74
Type of school	private
Affiliation	Roman Catholic
Environment	city

STUDENTS

Total undergrad enrollment	7,731
% male/female	50/50
% from out of state	38
% from public high school	51
% live on campus	75
% in (# of) fraternities	12.5 (13)
% in (# of) sororities	12.5 (9)
% African American	3
% Asian	1
% Caucasian	86
% Hispanic	2
% international	2
# of countries represented	50

SURVEY SAYS . . .

School is well run
Students are friendly
Students get along with local community
Students are happy
Intramural sports are popular
Lots of beer drinking

ACADEMICS

Academic Rating	80
Calendar	semester
Student/faculty ratio	14:1
Profs interesting rating	81
Profs accessible rating	90
% classes taught by TAs	7
Most common	
reg class size	20–29 students
Most common	
lab size	10–19 students

MOST POPULAR MAJORS

business/commerce
engineering

STUDENTS SAY ". . ."

Academics

The University of Dayton, a school "known for friendly students, strong academics, and Flyer basketball," is "academically challenging yet unpretentious [and] casual yet fun as hell." Students at this midsize Catholic school enjoy a "relaxed atmosphere. Academics are important at Dayton, but people aren't engaged in cut-throat rivalries with people to get ahead in the classroom. If you're struggling, it's easy to find someone to offer a helping hand." One student observes, "Dayton is about academics, but the school also stresses getting to know the people you study with. I thought the community aspect they repeated endlessly during my visit was just a way to get me to enroll at Dayton, but everyone is genuinely interested" in making sure that overall everyone around them has "a good college experience." Both academics and service "are taken very seriously" at UD. One undergrad notes, "You earn what you deserve. As long as you work hard, and your teachers can see that, you won't have a problem." Top programs include "a great pre-med program," "a wonderful engineering department," "an amazing teacher education program," and an "awesome business school" that includes the Davis Center for Portfolio Management, a "student-run fund that invests more than three million of the university's endowment." The number of options is unusual for an institution with such a small-school feel; students describe UD as "small enough that you get to know people very well, and you are always seeing someone you know, yet big enough that there are always new people to meet."

Life

"On top of great academic programs, the University of Dayton offers the full college experience—exciting athletic events, good dorm life, and the Ghetto," one student writes, alluding to UD's well-known student neighborhood, where "Porch sitting is a must on sunny days." One student explains, "Porches are symbolic of UD. Everyone sits out on the porch. It's one huge neighborhood where everyone is welcome to party or to chill. And when we party, everyone leaves their door wide open for anyone to come." As one student puts it, "Community is probably the first word that comes to the majority of the student body's minds." UD is situated near "a poverty-stricken area," but students point out that "It's never necessary to leave campus, even on the weekends," so the neighborhood isn't as large a factor as it might be. One student writes, "Going out to eat and seeing movies is the basic activity for when we get bored of hanging out at each other's houses on campus, but normally, we are content with going to the bars, going to house parties, or just staying in to watch a movie on the weekends…it just depends on the mood." And let's not forget Dayton basketball, "the gem of the community." True to its Marianist tradition, UD also has "the largest campus ministry in the country. We help both the local and global community with things ranging from one-time service days to immersion trips and even an entire year of service."

Student Body

"Many will say that the typical UD student comes from an upper-middle class suburb, went to a Catholic high school, and owns a North Face jacket," one student writes. "However, I know quite a few people who don't fit that description, and I think compared to similar schools, UD is much more diverse. Even though many people come from affluent backgrounds, many are also in need of a lot of financial aid, and it doesn't really matter. The idea of community and inclusiveness really helps everyone feel united." The typical undergrad here tends to be "semi-religious, overly friendly, welcoming, and accepting of the few diverse students who are here." He or she also "loves UD basketball, community service, beer, and most of all, holding the door for the person behind them." Because of the school's Catholic focus, "The majority of students are Catholic, and some students who are not Catholic feel that the university incorporates too much religion in service-type activities."

FINANCIAL AID: 937-229-4311 • E-MAIL: ADMISSION@UDAYTON.EDU • WEBSITE: WWW.UDAYTON.EDU

THE PRINCETON REVIEW SAYS

Admissions

Very important factors considered include: Academic GPA. *Important factors considered include:* Class rank, rigor of secondary school record, standardized test scores, talent/ability. *Other factors considered include:* Application essay, recommendation(s), alumni/ae relation, character/personal qualities, extracurricular activities, first generation, interview, racial/ethnic status, volunteer work, work experience. SAT or ACT required; TOEFL required of all international applicants. High school diploma is required and GED is accepted. *Academic units required:* 2 2 units of foreign language are required for admission to the College of Arts and Sciences. *Academic units recommended:* 4 English, 3 mathematics, 2 science, (1 science labs), 3 social studies, 4 academic electives.

Financial Aid

Students should submit: FAFSA. The Princeton Review suggests that all financial aid forms be submitted as soon as possible after 1/1. *Need-based scholarships/grants offered:* Federal Pell, SEOG, state scholarships/grants, private scholarships, the school's own gift aid, ACG, SMART. *Loan aid offered:* FFEL Subsidized Stafford, FFEL Unsubsidized Stafford, FFEL PLUS, Federal Perkins, GATE. Applicants will be notified of awards on a rolling basis beginning 2/20. Federal Work-Study Program available. Institutional employment available. Off-campus job opportunities are good.

The Inside Word

University of Dayton is an excellent option for students who want to attend a Catholic university but don't meet the stringent criteria of Georgetown or Notre Dame. UD gives "balanced consideration" to all academic factors—e.g., class rank, GPA—on the application. Candidates who demonstrate a modicum of success in the classroom and intellectual promise will most likely be accepted. Applicants must apply to one of the university's four divisions (they do not, however, have to apply for a specific major); admissions criteria vary slightly among the different divisions.

THE SCHOOL SAYS ". . ."

From The Admissions Office

"The University of Dayton is a Catholic leader in higher education. We offer the resources and diversity of a comprehensive university and the attention and accessibility of a small college. More than 70 challenging academic programs are offered in the College of Arts and Sciences and the Schools of Business Administration, Education and Allied Professions, Engineering, and Law. Classes are small—26 students on average. Our more than 800 full-time and part-time faculty are committed to teaching undergraduate students and involving them in their research projects. The University of Dayton Research Institute ranks second in the nation in the amount of materials research performed annually. Technology-enhanced learning and the student computer initiative ensure students gain expertise in the tools that will prepare them for the future. All university-owned housing is fully wired for direct high-speed Internet access, and a wireless network covers several academic buildings, the student union, library, outdoor plazas, and residential buildings. Recent campus construction provides a modern home for the university's cutting-edge academic programs. New facilities include ArtStreet, Marianist Hall, and the Science Center. A new fitness and recreation complex, the RecPlex, provides 130,000 square feet of space for classrooms, courts, a natatorium, offices, and other recreational facilities. A strong sense of community is a hallmark feature of the university; a dual emphasis on leadership and service contributes to students' participation in more than 170 clubs and organizations. Division I intercollegiate athletics and club and intramural sports are also popular.

"Students applying for admission may provide scores from either the SAT or the ACT. The highest composite scores from either test will be used in admission decisions."

SELECTIVITY
Admissions Rating	85
# of applicants	11,610
% of applicants accepted	74
% of acceptees attending	23
# accepting a place on wait list	71
% admitted from wait list	30

FRESHMAN PROFILE
Range SAT Critical Reading	520–620
Range SAT Math	530–640
Range ACT Composite	23–28
Minimum paper TOEFL	523
Minimum computer TOEFL	193
Minimum web-based TOEFL	70
Average HS GPA	3.52
% graduated top 10% of class	21
% graduated top 25% of class	51
% graduated top 50% of class	84

DEADLINES
Regular	
Early action	12/15
Regular	3/1
Nonfall registration decision	.yes

APPLICANTS ALSO LOOK AT
AND OFTEN PREFER
University of Notre Dame
AND SOMETIMES PREFER
Saint Louis University
Marquette University
Miami University
Case Western
The Ohio State University—Columbus
AND RARELY PREFER
Purdue University—West Lafayette
Xavier University (OH)
University of Cincinnati
Ohio University—Athens
John Carroll University

FINANCIAL FACTS
Financial Aid Rating	88
Annual tuition	$27,330
Room and board	$9,680
% frosh rec. need-based scholarship or grant aid	56
% UG rec. need-based scholarship or grant aid	52
% frosh rec. non-need-based scholarship or grant aid	50
% UG rec. non-need-based scholarship or grant aid	43
% frosh rec. need-based self-help aid	47
% UG rec. need-based self-help aid	50
% frosh rec. athletic scholarships	1
% UG rec. athletic scholarships	1
% UG borrow to pay for school	59
Average cumulative indebtedness	$19,162

UNIVERSITY OF DELAWARE

ADMISSIONS OFFICE, 116 HULLIHEN HALL, NEWARK, DE 19716-6210 • ADMISSIONS: 302-831-8123 • FAX: 302-831-6905

CAMPUS LIFE

Quality of Life Rating	**75**
Fire Safety Rating	**97**
Green Rating	**85**
Type of school	public
Environment	town

STUDENTS

Total undergrad enrollment	15,407
% male/female	42/58
% from out of state	64
% from public high school	80
% live on campus	46
% in (# of) fraternities	10 (22)
% in (# of) sororities	14 (19)
% African American	5
% Asian	4
% Caucasian	80
% Hispanic	5
% international	1
# of countries represented	100

SURVEY SAYS . . .
Great library
Great off-campus food
Students are happy
Student publications are popular
Lots of beer drinking
Hard liquor is popular

ACADEMICS

Academic Rating	**79**
Calendar	4/1/4
Student/faculty ratio	12:1
Profs interesting rating	73
Profs accessible rating	77
% classes taught by TAs	5
Most common reg class size	20–29 students
Most common lab size	10–19 students

MOST POPULAR MAJORS
biology/biological sciences
finance
nursing/registered nurse
(rn, asn, bsn, msn)

STUDENTS SAY ". . ."

Academics

In a departure from their typically balanced assessments of UD, undergrads maintain an exceptionally positive view of their school's "absolutely beautiful" campus and its "phenomenal" study-abroad program. "Registration however, is a nightmare," making it "near impossible to get the exact schedule you want." Students describe a middle-of-the-road academic experience overall. Regarding professors: some "are experts in their fields and are excellent at teaching," while others "are purely there for research," or "have no clue how to teach a class." While most may be "genuinely interested in meeting with students and talking about the class material," "They won't hunt you down" to make sure you're getting it. In other words, there is a willingness to help "as long as the student takes the initiative." The same can be said of the administration. Students generally consider it to be of "average quality." It "can be a pain with some administrative tasks (financial aid, anything that involves going to student services), but it's probably par for the course."

Life

Student life at UD is characterized by the timeless effort "to balance partying and studying." During the week, which runs from Sunday through Wednesday, "life usually remains centered around studies." "You will find the libraries [and] computer labs filled," and "quiet hours are enforced." For many, working out is part of their weekday work regimen: "A lot of people enjoy going to the gym." Come Thursday, however, "those with good schedules start going out." "Parties are what everyone looks for," especially house parties, and they are reportedly in abundant supply. Those who aren't into drinking but want to stay on campus can take advantage of "a movie theater right on campus that shows fairly current movies for only $3." The SCPAB (Student-Centered Programming Advisory Board) also "books some pretty good musicians and comedians." Many students "hang out on Main Street," which "intersects campus" and includes "endless restaurants, the book stores, a bowling alley, and a movie theater." Because "the campus is close to Baltimore, D.C., and Philly, road trips to museums and other universities [are] always possible."

Student Body

Budding psychologists take note: Undergrads here report a collective "tunnel vision," and it's focused on "success." According to a junior, "Most of us come from upper-middle-class homes and won't be satisfied with anything less than what we already have." As a means to an end, "academics are important." But only so much—course work "won't stop anyone from going out," an international relations major reports. Geographically, students mainly hail "from the New Jersey, Delaware, Maryland, and Pennsylvania region." Sartorially, "People care what they look like," and those "who have money flaunt it by what they wear." Temperamentally, people are "relaxed, friendly, and generally very approachable." There are very few categories UD students can be sorted into, but an in-state/out-of-state divide exists. Students "from Delaware are not considered as smart as those not from Delaware because it is easier for them to get in," and there is also a widespread perception that those from in-state "are not as well-off financially."

FINANCIAL AID: 302-831-8761 • E-MAIL: ADMISSIONS@UDEL.EDU • WEBSITE: WWW.UDEL.EDU

THE PRINCETON REVIEW SAYS

Admissions

Very important factors considered include: Academic GPA, rigor of secondary school record, state residency. *Important factors considered include:* Application essay, recommendation(s), standardized test scores, character/personal qualities, extracurricular activities, talent/ability, volunteer work, work experience. *Other factors considered include:* Class rank, alumni/ae relation, first generation, geographical residence, interview, level of applicant's interest, racial/ethnic status, SAT Subject Tests recommended; SAT or ACT required; ACT with Writing component required. TOEFL required of all international applicants. High school diploma is required and GED is accepted. *Academic units required:* 4 English, 3 mathematics, 3 science, (2 science labs), 2 foreign language, 2 social studies, 2 history, 2 academic electives. *Academic units recommended:* 4 English, 4 mathematics, 4 science, (3 science labs), 4 foreign language, 2 social studies, 2 history.

Financial Aid

Students should submit: FAFSA Regular filing deadline is 3/15. The Princeton Review suggests that all financial aid forms be submitted as soon as possible after 1/1. *Need-based scholarships/grants offered:* Federal Pell, SEOG, state scholarships/grants, private scholarships, the school's own gift aid. *Loan aid offered:* Direct Subsidized Stafford, Direct Unsubsidized Stafford, Direct PLUS, Federal Perkins, Federal Nursing Applicants will be notified of awards on a rolling basis beginning 3/15. Federal Work-Study Program available. Institutional employment available. Off-campus job opportunities are excellent.

Inside Word

It's rare that a flagship state university enrolls more students from out of state than in state, but the University of Delaware does. It is situated near many more-populous states on the East Coast, which makes it a viable and desirable alternative for those states' residents. The school is sensitive to this fact, and in-state students will find admission to UD significantly easier than out-of-state students will.

THE SCHOOL SAYS "..."

From The Admissions Office

"The University of Delaware is a major national research university with a long-standing commitment to teaching and serving undergraduates. It is one of only a few universities in the country designated as a land-grant, sea-grant, urban-grant, and space-grant institution. The academic strength of this university is found in its highly selective honors program, nationally recognized Undergraduate Research Program, study abroad opportunities on all seven continents, and its successful alumni, including three Rhodes Scholars since 1998. The University of Delaware offers the wide range of majors and course offerings expected of a university but in spirit remains a small place where you can interact with your professors and feel at home. The beautiful green campus is ideally located at the very center of the East Coast 'megacity' that stretches from New York City to Washington, D.C. All of these elements, combined with an endowment approaching $1 billion and a spirited Division I athletics program, make the University of Delaware a tremendous value.

"Freshman applicants are required to take the SAT (or the ACT with the Writing section). Two SAT Subject Tests are recommended for applicants to the University Honors Program."

SELECTIVITY

Admissions Rating	93
# of applicants	22,491
% of applicants accepted	56
% of acceptees attending	28
# accepting a place on wait list	527
% admitted from wait list	55

FRESHMAN PROFILE

Range SAT Critical Reading	550–640
Range SAT Math	570–660
Range SAT Writing	560–650
Range ACT Composite	25–28
Minimum paper TOEFL	550
Minimum computer TOEFL	213
Minimum web-based TOEFL	80
Average HS GPA	3.6
% graduated top 10% of class	42
% graduated top 25% of class	78
% graduated top 50% of class	97

DEADLINES

Regular	
Priority	12/1
Deadline	1/15
Notification	3/15
Nonfall registration?	yes

FINANCIAL FACTS

Financial Aid Rating	79
Annual in-state tuition	$7,780
Annual out-of-state tuition	$20,260
Room and board	$8,478
Required fees	$866
Books and supplies	$800
% frosh rec. need-based scholarship or grant aid	27
% UG rec. need-based scholarship or grant aid	25
% frosh rec. non-need-based scholarship or grant aid	22
% UG rec. non-need-based scholarship or grant aid	12
% frosh rec. need-based self-help aid	31
% UG rec. need-based self-help aid	30
% frosh rec. athletic scholarships	2
% UG rec. athletic scholarships	2
% frosh rec. any financial aid	57
% UG rec. any financial aid	55
% UG borrow to pay for school	44
Average cumulative indebtedness	$17,200

UNIVERSITY OF DENVER

UNIVERSITY HALL, ROOM 110, 2197 SOUTH UNIVERSITY BOULEVARD, DENVER, CO 80208 • ADMISSIONS: 303-871-2036 • FAX: 303-871-3301

CAMPUS LIFE

Quality of Life Rating	82
Fire Safety Rating	83
Green Rating	86
Type of school	private
Environment	metropolis

STUDENTS

Total undergrad enrollment	5,305
% male/female	44/56
% from out of state	42
% live on campus	42
% in (# of) fraternities	19 (9)
% in (# of) sororities	11 (5)
% African American	3
% Asian	6
% Caucasian	72
% Hispanic	7
% Native American	1
% international	5
# of countries represented	80

SURVEY SAYS . . .
Athletic facilities are great
Students love Denver, CO
Low cost of living
(Almost) no one smokes

ACADEMICS

Academic Rating	84
Calendar	quarter
Student/faculty ratio	9:1
Profs interesting rating	83
Profs accessible rating	82
Most common reg class size	10–19 students
Most common lab size	10–19 students

MOST POPULAR MAJORS
business, management, marketing,
and related support services
business/commerce
psychology

STUDENTS SAY ". . ."

Academics
The University of Denver runs on a 10-week quarter system rather than the traditional semester schedule, which is "ideal to learn about many different subjects, since we take 12 to 13 classes a year." "All of [the professors] seem to enjoy teaching," though they receive some mixed remarks from students, who aren't thrilled with their required classes but are very happy with the upper-level classes in their majors. The International Studies Department and Daniels School of Business receive special mention, and "opportunities to work with professors on their research have been abundant." "If you want to learn, professors will bend over backwards to accommodate you and your interests," and "almost all professors want to see their students succeed." Many students comment that "The academic experience at the University of Denver is whatever you want it to be. It can be as rigorous or as easy as the student wants." "If you just want to show up and count the minutes until you hit the mountains, you can. Or, if you really want to learn, you can do that, too." As is the case at many schools, student experiences with the administration vary wildly, which may be due to recent transitions in leadership. "I think that DU is becoming more organized. They have long-term goals, and they are in the middle of that transition." "The administration seems committed to academics while at the same time placing much effort in expansion."

Life
At DU, "The people are very interested in playing outside, which is understandable with all the sunshine Denver gets." "Most people take advantage of the fact that we are only one hour away from some of the best skiing and snowboarding in the world." "There are free classes at the gym (which are GREAT), a fantastic work-out facility, a beautiful park nearby to go running, great skiing within an hour of school, hiking trails, and camping sites." Students' lives generally consist of a shifting ratio of four activities: "skiing, hiking, drinking, and studying." "Substances may be used but, for the most part, with discretion." "Many kids go clubbing and go to parties. Others just enjoy hanging out and hitting the town. There is a good mix of the two here." "DU is a great size: big enough to never give off that small-town, high school feeling, but small enough to ensure that you will see friendly, recognizable faces everywhere." Life on campus is very active, with strong participation in intramural and club sports and a significant Greek presence. "Greek life can either be your whole social life, or you can not be involved in it at all and have a very active social life." Denver receives high marks as a college town: "Downtown Denver is...only 18 minutes away by light rail, which has everything you would ever want to do or see that isn't right next to campus."

Student Body
Students at DU are pretty comfortable with themselves and each other. "Most people are just normal, friendly people who all have certain areas that they choose to be involved in, whether it is student government, alpine club, or Greek life." Also, most are probably "skiers or...snowboarders or involved in some sort of physical activity relating to Colorado, such as hiking, fishing, camping, etc." "There are not too many exclusive 'groups' on campus, and most people are very accepting of others." "Everyone is very laid-back." Though some students comment on the upper-middle-class majority—"the students are motivated but seem to be used to lives of accommodation..."—many acknowledge that "DU puts a lot of emphasis on diversity," and "Denver has a combination of traditional students and non-traditional students, domestic and international students, liberals and conservatives." "There [is] a significant number of international students, which really adds to the university experience." "In general, everyone is friendly and gets along. Most people are a little quirky in their own way."

FINANCIAL AID: 303-871-4020 • E-MAIL: ADMISSION@DU.EDU • WEBSITE: WWW.DU.EDU/ADMISSION

THE PRINCETON REVIEW SAYS

Admissions

Very important factors considered include: Academic GPA, rigor of secondary school record, standardized test scores, character/personal qualities, *Important factors considered include:* Application essay, recommendation(s), extracurricular activities, interview, level of applicant's interest, talent/ability, volunteer work, work experience. SAT or ACT required; TOEFL required of all international applicants. High school diploma is required and GED is accepted. *Academic units recommended:* 4 English, 3-4 mathematics, 3-4 science, (2 science labs), 2-4 foreign language, 2 social studies, 2-4 history.

Financial Aid

Students should submit: FAFSA plus CSS profile. Regular filing deadline is 3/1. The Princeton Review suggests that all financial aid forms be submitted as soon as possible after 1/1. *Need-based scholarships/grants offered:* Federal Pell, SEOG, state scholarships/grants, private scholarships, the school's own gift aid. *Loan aid offered:* FFEL Subsidized Stafford, FFEL Unsubsidized Stafford, FFEL PLUS, Federal Perkins, college/university loans from institutional funds. Applicants will be notified of awards on or about 3/25. Federal Work-Study Program available. Institutional employment available. Off-campus job opportunities are excellent.

The Inside Word

DU admissions gives academic achievement top billing when reviewing applications. Last year's incoming freshman class had an average GPA of 3.7, but that's not all that counts: The admissions committee wants to see a roster of challenging classes as well. In particular, applicants to math or science programs and to the Daniels College of Business are expected to have strong quantitative skills. ACT and SAT scores are also important, though the writing components are not considered. Applicants are strongly encouraged to schedule an interview, which DU alumni, faculty, and staff conduct in 30 cities nation-wide.

THE SCHOOL SAYS " . . ."

From The Admissions Office

"Founded in 1864, the University of Denver offers an educational experience characterized by adventurous learning and innovative mentoring from a caring faculty. Our undergraduate students come from all across the United States and from more than 80 countries to study in an environment that nurtures potential and passion. The Hyde Interview, which is strongly encouraged, provides all applicants the opportunity to give a voice to their application while assisting DU with admission decisions. DU is continually developing educational initiatives that help students prepare for an ever-changing world. Among our offerings: residence-based learning communities that provide extracurricular and co-curricular programming in particular areas; a grant program for students that funds everything from research to creative endeavors; and hundreds of internship opportunities that put students in laboratories, corporate offices, government agencies, and cultural settings. In addition, one of the signature offerings is the Cherrington Global Scholars program which allows students to study abroad at the same cost of a term at DU. More than 70 percent of DU students study abroad at some point in their years in school—which ranks DU second nationally among doctoral and research institutions for percentage of students participating. DU students enjoy an active lifestyle with plenty of opportunities to enjoy recreation in the Rockies, cheer on one of the city's many professional sports teams, or explore the city's lively arts and entertainment scene. Many DU students partake in these activities by using the new light rail system, an above-ground train that is free to all DU students. There is a station conveniently located on our campus and provides students a great mode of transportation for a variety of purposes such as entertainment, internships, and jobs in the Denver area. Applicants may submit either the ACT or SAT."

SELECTIVITY
Admissions Rating	92
# of applicants	7,144
% of applicants accepted	64
% of acceptees attending	25
# accepting a place on wait list	478
% admitted from wait list	59

FRESHMAN PROFILE
Range SAT Critical Reading	540–640
Range SAT Math	540–660
Range ACT Composite	24–29
Minimum paper TOEFL	525
Minimum computer TOEFL	193
Average HS GPA	3.66
% graduated top 10% of class	43
% graduated top 25% of class	76
% graduated top 50% of class	96

DEADLINES
Early action	
Deadline	11/1
Notification	1/15
Regular	
Deadline	1/15
Notification	3/15
Nonfall registration?	yes

APPLICANTS ALSO LOOK AT
AND OFTEN PREFER
University of Colorado—Boulder
Colorado College
Colorado State University
AND SOMETIMES PREFER
University of Puget Sound
University of Vermont
Boston University

FINANCIAL FACTS
Financial Aid Rating	72
Annual tuition	$32,976
Room and board	$9670
Fees	$834
% frosh rec. need-based scholarship or grant aid	43
% UG rec. need-based scholarship or grant aid	42
% frosh rec. non-need-based scholarship or grant aid	5
% UG rec. non-need-based scholarship or grant aid	4
% frosh rec. need-based self-help aid	30
% UG rec. need-based self-help aid	31
% frosh rec. athletic scholarships	4
% UG rec. athletic scholarships	5
% frosh rec. any financial aid	81
% UG rec. any financial aid	85
% UG borrow to pay for school	45
Average cumulative indebtedness	$25,375

UNIVERSITY OF FLORIDA

201 CRISER HALL, BOX 114000, GAINESVILLE, FL 32611-4000 • ADMISSIONS: 352-392-1365 • FAX: 352-392-3987

CAMPUS LIFE

Quality of Life Rating	79
Fire Safety Rating	72
Green Rating	97
Type of school	public
Environment	city

STUDENTS

Total undergrad enrollment	34,656
% male/female	46/54
% from out of state	4
% from public high school	81
% live on campus	26
% in (# of) fraternities	15 (NR)
% in (# of) sororities	15 (NR)
% African American	10
% Asian	8
% Caucasian	63
% Hispanic	14
% international	1

SURVEY SAYS . . .

Athletic facilities are great
Everyone loves the Gators
Intramural sports are popular
Frats and sororities dominate social scene
Student publications are popular
Student government is popular
Lots of beer drinking
Hard liquor is popular

ACADEMICS

Academic Rating	72
Calendar	semester
Student/faculty ratio	20:3
Profs interesting rating	64
Profs accessible rating	73
% classes taught by TAs	29
Most common reg class size	10–19 students
Most common lab size	10–19 students

MOST POPULAR MAJORS

psychology
finance
political science
health science
English

STUDENTS SAY ". . ."

Academics

"A top-tier research institute" that "is full of bright students who still know how to have fun," the University of Florida offers "an environment unparalleled by any other university in the world with its first-class amenities, athletics, academics, campus, and students," enthusiastic students insist. The school "has excellent academic programs all across the board: You're not limited to just a great engineering program or journalism program" here; the sciences (including premedical studies, which piggyback on "a strong teaching hospital on campus"), business, education, communications, and engineering are among the many standout offerings. In short, "UF is a great school" that's "not expensive, even for out-of-state students. Plus, there is a great sense of family here: You really are a part of the Gator Nation!" It is, of course, a very large university that at times "runs more [like] a machine than a place that fosters learning and growth." As one student reports, "The school never even knew I had a name. The first thing anyone ever asks you is 'What's your UF-ID?'" Also, students must be prepared for "the annoyance of the size of the more generalized prerequisite courses, e.g., lower-level courses required by two or three majors." Still, "the professors are almost always wonderful: They are helpful and definitely know their stuff."

Life

"The greatest strength [of this school] is UF's spirit," students agree, telling us that "there's just something about being a Gator. It doesn't matter where you are in the world, UF students and alumni are everywhere and ready to greet you with open arms and a hearty 'Go Gators!' You belong there." While here, you can party to your heart's content; the university "certainly lives up to its role of number 1 party school. Every day is a weekend in Gainesville, and you will always find something going on Sunday through Saturday. There's midtown, a strip right across from the stadium that has the infamous Swamp restaurant, clubs, bars, and plenty of food to satiate hunger in between classes. There's also 'downtown' Gainesville, which houses more bars, clubs, and restaurants and shopping to keep you busy throughout the entire semester." And "if you're not into the party scene, there's the Hippodrome Theatre, Lake Wauberg, and the local mall and movie theaters to keep you occupied. Gainesville is definitely a college town, and it is perfect for anyone looking for the true college experience." College sports are huge, "and there are hardly any people that aren't proud of Gator athletes and always ready to sport the orange and blue." UF's Greek community "is very prominent, and a large number of students belong [to] a fraternity/sorority or associate with students who do."

Student Body

The typical UF student "has a popular major like engineering or business," "is witty, loves Gator football, and likes to party. An atypical student may be someone who doesn't party or may deviate from mainstream beliefs, practices, or political parties, but for the most part, any student is accepted as a member of the Gator nation," and most "seem to maintain a well-balanced life of studying and socializing." While "the sorority/fraternity people are the most dominant group on campus," there's also "a really strong indie scene (the two never interact)." In fact, "there are people all over the spectrum," although the place is so big that "half of them you may never meet." "We are one of the most diverse campuses in the nation," one student explains, "and we are all Gators at heart, first and foremost."

THE PRINCETON REVIEW SAYS

Admissions

Very important factors considered include: Academic GPA, rigor of secondary school record, *Important factors considered include:* Application essay, character/personal qualities, extracurricular activities, first generation, talent/ability. *Other factors considered include:* Class rank, standardized test scores, alumni/ae relation, geographical residence, level of applicant's interest, state residency, volunteer work, work experience. SAT or ACT required; ACT with Writing component required. High school diploma is required and GED is accepted. *Academic units required:* 4 English, 3 mathematics, 3 science, (2 science labs), 2 foreign language, 3 social studies, 3 academic electives.

Financial Aid

Students should submit: FAFSA. The Princeton Review suggests that all financial aid forms be submitted as soon as possible after 1/1. *Need-based scholarships/grants offered:* Federal Pell, SEOG, state scholarships/grants, private scholarships, the school's own gift aid State, Academic, Creative arts/performance, Special achievements/activities, Special characteristics, Athletic and ROTC. *Loan aid offered:* Direct Subsidized Stafford, Direct Unsubsidized Stafford, Direct PLUS, Federal Perkins, college/university loans from institutional funds. Applicants will be notified of awards on a rolling basis beginning 4/1. Federal Work-Study Program available. Institutional employment available. Off-campus job opportunities are fair.

The Inside Word

First-generation college students from disadvantaged backgrounds qualify for the Florida Opportunity Scholars program, which fully covers four years of educational costs. The program is not limited to minority students; in 2008, about 39 percent of recipients were African American, 27 percent Hispanic, 21 percent white, and 11 percent Asian American. The average family income of recipients is just less than $25,000 per year.

THE SCHOOL SAYS "..."

From The Admissions Office

"University of Florida students come from more than 100 countries, all 50 states, and every one of the 67 counties in Florida. Twenty-two percent of the student body is comprised of graduate students. Approximately 4,300 African American students, 6,300 Hispanic students, and 4,000 Asian American students attend UF. Ninety percent of the entering freshmen rank above the national mean of scores on standard entrance exams. UF consistently ranks near the top among public universities in the number of new National Merit and Achievement scholars in attendance.

"Students must submit the SAT or ACT with the writing section. UF considers your highest section scores across all SAT test dates."

SELECTIVITY

Admissions Rating	95
# of applicants	47,622
% of applicants accepted	35.2
% of acceptees attending	56.2

FRESHMAN PROFILE

Range SAT Critical Reading	570–680
Range SAT Math	590–700
Range ACT Composite	25–30

DEADLINES

Regular	
Deadline	11/1
Nonfall registration?	yes

FINANCIAL FACTS

Financial Aid Rating	83
Annual in-state tuition	$3,777
Annual out-of-state tuition	$20,622
Room and board	$7,150
Books and supplies	$960
% frosh rec. need-based scholarship or grant aid	26
% UG rec. need-based scholarship or grant aid	23
% frosh rec. non-need-based scholarship or grant aid	39
% UG rec. non-need-based scholarship or grant aid	28
% frosh rec. need-based self-help aid	15
% UG rec. need-based self-help aid	19
% frosh rec. athletic scholarships	1
% UG rec. athletic scholarships	1
% frosh rec. any financial aid	86.1
% UG rec. any financial aid	84.3
% UG borrow to pay for school	41
Average cumulative indebtedness	$15,318

UNIVERSITY OF GEORGIA

TERRELL HALL, ATHENS, GA 30602 • ADMISSIONS: 706-542-8776 • FAX: 706-542-1466

CAMPUS LIFE

Quality of Life Rating	85
Fire Safety Rating	82
Green Rating	89
Type of school	public
Environment	city

STUDENTS

Total undergrad enrollment	25,150
% male/female	42/58
% from out of state	12
% from public high school	76
% live on campus	27
% in (# of) fraternities	20 (34)
% in (# of) sororities	25 (24)
% African American	7
% Asian	7
% Caucasian	82
% Hispanic	2
% international	1
# of countries represented	127

SURVEY SAYS . . .

Athletic facilities are great
Great food on campus
Great off-campus food
Low cost of living
Everyone loves the Bulldogs

ACADEMICS

Academic Rating	73
Calendar	semester
Student/faculty ratio	18:1
Profs interesting rating	74
Profs accessible rating	65
% classes taught by TAs	19
Most common reg class size	20–29 students

MOST POPULAR MAJORS

art/art studies
biology/biological sciences
psychology

STUDENTS SAY ". . ."

Academics

As at many large universities, UGA has a "mixed bag of professors," but there are "more good teachers" than bad. Though students don't love the core curriculum classes due to their large size and the prevalence of TAs, "once [you're] in your particular program, the teachers are outstanding and easy to reach." "The professors really do want to see you at office hours if you have questions," and they "want to share their love of learning with you." "My major-related classes are very small, and each student receives individual attention." The honors program also receives raves: "Many of my best classes and favorite teachers have come from the honors program, but non-honors classes are generally good as well." "The study spaces are well-equipped and quiet," but "the school of social work is still housed in an old dorm." "Administration is a pain (not the people, only the requirements), but I think that describes academia in general." In general students "feel that the administration can be very accommodating at times, but at other times it can seem like it is full of red tape." Registration technology "needs to be brought out of the 1980s and into the 21st century." "The administration [can] seem like a bunch of penny-pinchers, but they must be to run a major research facility."

Life

Life at UGA seems to be a good mix of the two different worlds of sports and arts: football, frats, and tailgating on campus come together nicely with the coffee shops and music scene in downtown Athens. "On Saturday afternoons in the fall, nearly everyone on campus is at the football game. It's a way of life here." "Everybody really gets behind the team, and Saturdays in Athens feel like mini vacations." Fraternities and sororities dominate the party scene, but "there is definitely plenty to do, even if you don't go Greek." Students love to brag about the high number of bars per capita in Athens, but there's plenty more to boast about. "The Athens music and art scene is very inspiring, and there are tons of opportunities for creativity here." "Downtown Athens is fabulous! Whether you drink or don't drink, all are welcome and all congregate there." Campus life offers plenty of activity, too. "Fun is a part of daily life…with a dozen intramural sports each semester…and many community activities (multiple movie theaters, bowling allies, golf course)." "Ultimate Frisbee, walks around the multiple parks, days lounging on North Campus, and spending LOTS of time downtown are a couple ways I like to have fun at school." "There are so many organizations that everyone can find a place that will feel like home or find a place to meet new people." "It's no secret that UGA knows how to party. However, most of the students know how to manage social and academic time."

Student Body

"Students are generally white, upper-middle class, smart, [and] involved, and [they] have a good time," "seem to be predominantly conservative," and "are usually involved in at least one organization whether it be Greek, a club, or sports." "The typical student at UGA is one who knows how and when to study but allows himself or herself to have a very active social life." The majority are Southerners, with many students from within Georgia. "The stereotype is southern, Republican, football-loving, and beer-drinking. While many, many of UGA's students do not fit this description, there is no lack of the above," and "there is a social scene for everyone in Athens." "There are a great number of atypical students in the liberal arts," which "creates a unique and exciting student body with greatly contrasting opinions."

FINANCIAL AID: 706-542-6147 • E-MAIL: UNDERGRAD@ADMISSIONS.UGA.EDU • WEBSITE: WWW.UGA.EDU

THE PRINCETON REVIEW SAYS

Admissions

Very important factors considered include: Academic GPA, rigor of secondary school record, *Important factors considered include:* standardized test scores. *Other factors considered include:* Application essay, recommendation(s), character/personal qualities, extracurricular activities, talent/ability, volunteer work, work experience. SAT or ACT required; ACT with Writing component required. TOEFL required of all international applicants. High school diploma is required and GED is accepted. *Academic units required:* 4 English, 4 mathematics, 3 science, (2 science labs), 2 foreign language, 3 social studies. *Academic units recommended:* 4 English, 4 mathematics, 3 science, (2 science labs), 3 foreign language, 1 social studies, 2 history, 1 academic electives.

Financial Aid

Students should submit: FAFSA. The Princeton Review suggests that all financial aid forms be submitted as soon as possible after 1/1. *Need-based scholarships/grants offered:* Federal Pell, SEOG, state scholarships/grants, private scholarships, the school's own gift aid. *Loan aid offered:* Direct Subsidized Stafford, Direct Unsubsidized Stafford, Direct PLUS, Federal Perkins, state loans, college/university loans from institutional funds. Applicants will be notified of awards on a rolling basis beginning 5/15.

The Inside Word

A school as large as UGA must start winnowing applicants by the numbers. If you fail to meet certain baseline curricular, GPA, and standardized-test-score floors, only exceptional talent elsewhere (a gift for the arts or, better still, throwing a football) will get you past the first cut. Many students here are Georgia residents reaping the benefits of the state's HOPE scholarship program, which pays tuition and most school-related fees for state residents who earn at least a 3.0 GPA in high school, so long as they maintain at least a 3.0 in college.

THE SCHOOL SAYS "..."

From The Admissions Office

"The University of Georgia offers students the advantages and resources of a top public research university, including a wide range of majors and exceptional academic facilities such as the 200,000-square-foot Miller Learning Center. At the same time, UGA provides opportunities more common to smaller, private schools, such as first-year seminars led by distinguished faculty and learning communities that connect students with similar academic interests. The university is committed to challenging its academically superior students in the classroom and beyond, with increased emphasis on undergraduate research, service-learning, and study abroad. UGA students taking advantage of such offerings find themselves well positioned to compete with the best undergraduates in the country, as evidenced by their recent string of successes in winning Rhodes, Marshall, Truman, and other major scholarships.

"The UGA campus, considered one of the most beautiful in the nation, adjoins vibrant downtown Athens. "While Athens is renowned for its local music scene, UGA also houses the Performing Arts Center, the Hugh Hodgson School of Music, the Lamar Dodd School of Art, and the Georgia Museum of Art." Sports—from football to gymnastics—are also a major attraction, with UGA teams perennially ranked among the best in the country.

"To experience the excitement of UGA, most prospective students visit campus, a 90-minute drive northeast of the Atlanta airport. See the Admissions website to sign up for a tour with the Visitors Center, view the weekday schedule of admissions information sessions, and find application details.

"Applicants for first-year admission will be required to submit either the SAT or ACT. Students submitting only the ACT must also submit the optional ACT Writing Test."

SELECTIVITY

Admissions Rating	93
# of applicants	17,207
% of applicants accepted	56
% of acceptees attending	51
# accepting a place on wait list	813
% admitted from wait list	69

FRESHMAN PROFILE

Range SAT Critical Reading	560–660
Range SAT Math	570–660
Range SAT Writing	560–660
Range ACT Composite	24–29
Minimum paper TOEFL	550
Minimum computer TOEFL	213
Average HS GPA	3.8
% graduated top 10% of class	52
% graduated top 25% of class	85
% graduated top 50% of class	98

DEADLINES

Early action	
Deadline	10/15
Notification	12/15
Regular	
Priority	10/15
Deadline	1/15
Nonfall registration?	yes

APPLICANTS ALSO LOOK AT
AND OFTEN PREFER
Georgia Institute of Technology
AND SOMETIMES PREFER
Emory University
University of North Carolina at Chapel Hill
AND RARELY PREFER
University of South Carolina—Columbia
Clemson University

FINANCIAL FACTS

Financial Aid Rating	79
Annual tuition in-state	$6,130
Annual tuition out-of-state	$22,442
Room and board	$7,528
Books and supplies	$900
% frosh rec. need-based scholarship or grant aid	29
% UG rec. need-based scholarship or grant aid	24
% frosh rec. non-need-based scholarship or grant aid	9
% UG rec. non-need-based scholarship or grant aid	5
% frosh rec. need-based self-help aid	15
% UG rec. need-based self-help aid	18
% frosh rec. athletic scholarships	2
% UG rec. athletic scholarships	2
% frosh rec. any financial aid	37
% UG rec. any financial aid	32
% UG borrow to pay for school	39
Average cumulative indebtedness	$14,343

UNIVERSITY OF IDAHO

IDAHO ADMISSIONS OFFICE, PO BOX 444264, MOSCOW, ID 83844-4264 • ADMISSIONS: 208-885-6326 • FAX: 208-885-9119

CAMPUS LIFE

Quality of Life Rating	**71**
Fire Safety Rating	**60***
Green Rating	**89**
Type of school	public
Environment	town

STUDENTS

Total undergrad enrollment	8,471
% male/female	54/46
% from out of state	38
% from public high school	90
% in (# of) fraternities	NR (18)
% in (# of) sororities	NR (9)
% African American	1
% Asian	2
% Caucasian	84
% Hispanic	5
% Native American	1
% international	2

SURVEY SAYS . . .

Athletic facilities are great
Frats and sororities dominate social scene
Lots of beer drinking
Hard liquor is popular

ACADEMICS

Academic Rating	**73**
Calendar	semester
Student/faculty ratio	16:1
Profs interesting rating	69
Profs accessible rating	66
% classes taught by TAs	15
Most common reg class size	10–19 students
Most common lab size	10–19 students

MOST POPULAR MAJORS

elementary education and teaching
mechanical engineering
psychology

STUDENTS SAY ". . ."

Academics

While huge lectures and inaccessible administrators beleaguer many other state schools, the University of Idaho comes with a friendly and intimate academic environment. Even better, this school comes with a tremendously affordable price tag. Idaho residents attend UI for a pittance, and students from more than a dozen other states pay only a little more. "We don't cost a lot," dryly notes a senior. All students must complete a straightforward core curriculum. Beyond that, you can choose from more than 150 majors. The engineering programs here are nationally recognized. The College of Natural Resources boasts excellent forestry and ecology programs as well as one of the biggest genetics laboratories in the country. Students describe the academic atmosphere here as "relaxed," and they report a high level of satisfaction with their academic experiences. "The administration is an active and visible." Many facilities are world-class. Classes are usually small, particularly once you get past the introductory courses. "With a few exceptions," the faculty is "very knowledgeable" and generally "incredible." Professors are "pretty easy to get a hold of after class and are always willing to help you." Also, many are "constantly involved in doing research," in a good way. As a result, undergraduate research opportunities are ample.

Life

The University of Idaho's "beautiful" campus is chock full of trees, expansive lawns, and traditionally collegiate buildings. Students laud the fact that UI "isn't too big or too small." Students portray a lively campus atmosphere and a thriving party scene. Cultural events include the Lionel Hampton Jazz Festival, which attracts big name musicians each year. Intramural sports are popular. The student recreation center boasts saunas, professional massage therapy, and a massive 55-foot climbing wall. There are "many student organizations"—more than 200, in fact. When it comes to social life, though, "Greek life rules the school." Some students are thrilled about this situation. Others call it "pretty positive." Still others find the focus on frats and sororities to be a bit much. Whether you pledge or not, though, "the main entertainment on the weekends is drinking." Students here "party a lot." Off campus, "podunk" Moscow "is not and will never be a big city," but students assure us that it is "the perfect college town." Restaurants and bars are plentiful. Coffee shops are "numerous." "Good music" abounds. You can't really beat Moscow for organic food. Also, the social amenities at Washington State University are "right next door" (about 10 miles west). Another big draw here is the great outdoors. The plethora of nearby rivers, lakes, and mountains provides opportunities galore for adrenaline sports and wilderness recreation.

Student Body

The student population at UI has a "laid-back" vibe. "It is really easy to meet people." If you are having any trouble, just head over to the famed Hello Walk, a sidewalk on campus where it's customary for students and everyone else to greet "one another with a friendly hello." "A lot of UI students are Greek," and they more or less fit the basic fraternity and sorority mold. There are also plenty of rugged, "earthy-hippie, outdoorsy types." You'll find every personality type, though, "from cowboys to cosmopolitan city residents." That said, pretty much everyone is "white, middle-class," and "from the Northwest." There are few minorities. Some students lament the lack of ethnic diversity. Others call our attention to the school's geographic limitations in this regard. "It's Idaho," says a senior. "Idaho just isn't diverse."

FINANCIAL AID: 208-885-6312 • E-MAIL: ADMAPPL@UIDAHO.EDU • WEBSITE: WWW.UIDAHO.EDU

THE PRINCETON REVIEW SAYS

Admissions

Very important factors considered include: Academic GPA, standardized test scores. *Other factors considered include:* recommendation(s), SAT or ACT required; TOEFL required of all international applicants. High school diploma is required and GED is accepted. *Academic units required:* 4 English, 3 mathematics, 3 science, (1 science labs), 1 foreign language, 2 social studies, 1 academic electives.

Financial Aid

Students should submit: FAFSA. The Princeton Review suggests that all financial aid forms be submitted as soon as possible after 1/1. *Need-based scholarships/grants offered:* Federal Pell, SEOG, state scholarships/grants, private scholarships, the school's own gift aid. *Loan aid offered:* Direct Subsidized Stafford, Direct Unsubsidized Stafford, Direct PLUS, Federal Perkins, college/university loans from institutional funds. Applicants will be notified of awards on a rolling basis beginning 3/30. Federal Work-Study Program available. Institutional employment available. Off-campus job opportunities are good.

The Inside Word

The University of Idaho's straightforward approach to admissions is a welcome change for students completing more involved applications. In a way that's typical of large, public universities; admissions officers arrive at decisions based upon high school GPA and test scores. Most applicants are admitted and welcome the opportunity to attend a strong school at an affordable price.

THE SCHOOL SAYS "..."

From The Admissions Office

"The University of Idaho, in the rolling Palouse Hills of northern Idaho, is one of the leading public universities in the Northwest. Idaho attracts nearly 12,000 students and has become known for its academic excellence, exceptional student living and learning environment, outstanding creative and research opportunities, and proven track record of high-achieving graduates. It continues to educate students in fields important to the mountain West and beyond, such as agriculture, water resources, environmental science and Native American studies. Idaho also offers highly-regarded programs in engineering, business, natural resources, architecture, biotechnology, teaching, and foreign languages, among others. Through insight and innovation, and a legacy of leadership, the University of Idaho enriches the lives of people throughout the region and the world.

"Students applying for admission are required to take either the SAT or the ACT. The Writing component is not required from the ACT. SAT Subject Test scores are not used for admission purposes."

SELECTIVITY
Admissions Rating	**82**
# of applicants	4,577
% of applicants accepted	77
% of acceptees attending	47

FRESHMAN PROFILE
Range SAT Critical Reading	480–600
Range SAT Math	480–600
Range SAT Writing	450–570
Range ACT Composite	20–25
Minimum paper TOEFL	525
Minimum computer TOEFL	193
Minimum web-based TOEFL	70
Average HS GPA	3.39
% graduated top 10% of class	18
% graduated top 25% of class	42
% graduated top 50% of class	74

DEADLINES
Regular	
Priority	2/15
Deadline	8/1
Nonfall registration?	yes

APPLICANTS ALSO LOOK AT
AND OFTEN PREFER
Utah State University
AND RARELY PREFER
Idaho State University

FINANCIAL FACTS
Financial Aid Rating	**75**
Annual in-state tuition	$4,932
Annual out-of-state tuition	$15,012
Room and board	$7,242
Required fees	$4,410
Books and supplies	$1,474
% frosh rec. need-based scholarship or grant aid	34
% UG rec. need-based scholarship or grant aid	37
% frosh rec. non-need-based scholarship or grant aid	44
% UG rec. non-need-based scholarship or grant aid	39
% frosh rec. need-based self-help aid	44
% UG rec. need-based self-help aid	50
% frosh rec. athletic scholarships	3
% UG rec. athletic scholarships	3
% frosh rec. any financial aid	56.3
% UG rec. any financial aid	57.6
% UG borrow to pay for school	66
Average cumulative indebtedness	$21,609

UNIVERSITY OF ILLINOIS AT URBANA-CHAMPAIGN

901 WEST ILLINOIS STREET, URBANA, IL 61801 • ADMISSIONS: 217-333-0302 • FAX: 217-333-9758

CAMPUS LIFE

Quality of Life Rating	79
Fire Safety Rating	63
Green Rating	92
Type of school	public
Environment	city

STUDENTS

Total undergrad enrollment	30,395
% male/female	53/47
% from out of state	7
% from public high school	75
% live on campus	50
% in (# of) fraternities	22 (60)
% in (# of) sororities	23 (36)
% African American	7
% Asian	13
% Caucasian	66
% Hispanic	7
% international	5
# of countries represented	123

SURVEY SAYS . . .

Athletic facilities are great
Everyone loves the Fighting Illini
Frats and sororities dominate social scene
Student publications are popular
Lots of beer drinking
Hard liquor is popular

ACADEMICS

Academic Rating	72
Calendar	semester
Student/faculty ratio	17:1
Profs interesting rating	66
Profs accessible rating	68
% classes taught by TAs	26
Most common reg class size	20–29 students
Most common lab size	20–29 students

MOST POPULAR MAJORS

cell/cellular and molecular biology
political science and government
psychology

STUDENTS SAY ". . ."

Academics

The epically large flagship campus of the University of Illinois "is very challenging and gives you freedom to do anything." Students here enjoy "all the benefits of a great public university." There are more than 150 undergraduate programs. The colleges of engineering and business are of the "most prestigious and hardest to get into," but there are dozens of other "very strong and reputable" departments as well. "The research resources are amazing," raves a Russian literature major. "The library has almost any resource an undergraduate or even an advanced researcher would ever need." However, the drawbacks that come with such an expansive campus are present as well. Lower-level class sizes "are horrendously large." "My largest class had 800 students," says a biochemistry major. "The massive bureaucracy" is a constant source of irritation. "Simple things like adding or dropping a class a few weeks into a semester can require five or six trips to different buildings to talk to different people, each time requiring you to explain your situation." "Professors are more impersonal to freshmen but seem to warm up to upperclassmen," explains one student. "There are some professors that should not be teaching anywhere," though. "A lot of times, it's a toss-up with bad/good professors," counsels a geology major. "You can learn a lot and have a great teacher, but you need to ask around and find out who that good teacher is." "There are professors and classes that you come across that certainly leave something to be desired," agrees a women's studies major. "But overall, I am very pleased with my academic experience at UIUC, and I have met some astoundingly intelligent, influential professors."

Life

At the University of Illinois, there is "never a dull moment, despite the surrounding cornfields." More than a thousand clubs and organizations provide students with a wide array of options. "Anything that you are interested in, you can do," gloats an engineering major. "It's a huge campus, but it's not too spread out," says a Spanish major. "You can get around anywhere by bike or bus, and you don't need a car." "The campus is very Greek-oriented," and the students who pledge the myriad of frats and sororities "love the Greek life." Some students notice serious animosity between the independent students and students involved in the frat scene. "It seems at times to take over our campus," says one independent. Other students just don't see the problem. "I think plenty of non-Greeks associate with Greeks," asserts a finance major. "Drinking is a big thing at U of I." Apartment parties and frat parties rage on the weekends. There is an "outstanding bar culture," too. "If you don't want to party all the time, there are plenty of other options." "Intramural sports and playing sports on the quad and in frat park are popular." The campus is "alive with the Big Ten spirit" and students are very supportive of their beloved Illini. "Awesome concerts" proliferate, and "there is a really good artsy theater which runs foreign and indie films."

Student Body

The U of I has a decidedly Midwestern feel, and "Midwestern hospitality" is abundant. "Kids from out-of-state and small-town farm students" definitely have a presence, but, sometimes, it seems like "practically everyone is from the northwest suburbs of Chicago." There's a lot of ethnic diversity "visible on campus." There are many Asian and Asian-American students. On the whole, the majority of students are "very smart kids who like to party." "The typical student is involved and really good at balancing schoolwork, clubs and organizations, and a social life." "They really study fairly hard, and when you ask, it turns out that they're majoring in something like rocket science." Ultimately, there's something for everyone here with students who think about "nothing but drinking" to those who "never miss a class" and are "in the library every night." "There is a niche for everyone."

UNIVERSITY OF ILLINOIS AT URBANA-CHAMPAIGN

FINANCIAL AID: 217-333-0100 • E-MAIL: ADMISSIONS@OAR.UIUC.EDU • WEBSITE: WWW.UIUC.EDU

THE PRINCETON REVIEW SAYS

Admissions

Very important factors considered include: Class rank, application essay, academic GPA, rigor of secondary school record, standardized test scores, *Important factors considered include:* character/personal qualities, extracurricular activities, first generation, talent/ability, volunteer work, work experience. *Other factors considered include:* geographical residence, racial/ethnic status, state residency, SAT or ACT required; ACT with Writing component required. TOEFL required of all international applicants. High school diploma is required and GED is accepted. *Academic units required:* 4 English, 3 mathematics, 2 science, (2 science labs), 2 foreign language, 2 social studies, 2 academic electives.

Financial Aid

Students should submit: FAFSA. The Princeton Review suggests that all financial aid forms be submitted as soon as possible after 1/1. *Need-based scholarships/grants offered:* Federal Pell, SEOG, state scholarships/grants, private scholarships, the school's own gift aid, United Negro College Fund. *Loan aid offered:* Direct Subsidized Stafford, Direct Unsubsidized Stafford, Direct PLUS, Federal Perkins, college/university loans from institutional funds. Other Federal Work-Study Program available. Institutional employment available. Off-campus job opportunities are excellent.

The Inside Word

Few candidates are deceived by Illinois's relatively high acceptance rate; the university has a well-deserved reputation for expecting applicants to be strong students, and those who aren't usually don't bother to apply. Despite a jumbo applicant pool, the admissions office reports that every candidate is individually reviewed, which deserves mention as rare in universities of this size.

THE SCHOOL SAYS " . . ."

From The Admissions Office

"The campus has been aptly described as a collection of neighborhoods constituting a diverse and vibrant city. The neighborhoods are of many types: students and faculty within a department; people sharing a room or house; the members of a professional organization, a service club, or an intramural team; or simply people who, starting out as strangers sharing a class or a study lounge or a fondness for a weekly film series, have become friends. And the city of this description is the university itself—a rich cosmopolitan environment constructed by students and faculty to meet their educational and personal goals. The quality of intellectual life parallels that of other great universities, and many faculty and students who have their choice of top institutions select Illinois over its peers. While such choices are based often on the quality of individual programs of study, another crucial factor is the 'tone' of the campus life that is linked with the virtues of Midwestern culture. There is an informality and a near-absence of pretension, which, coupled with a tradition of commitment to excellence, creates an atmosphere that is unique among the finest institutions.

"Applicants are required to take the SAT or the ACT with the Writing section."

SELECTIVITY

Admissions Rating	94
# of applicants	21,645
% of applicants accepted	71
% of acceptees attending	45
# accepting a place on wait list	633
% admitted from wait list	96

FRESHMAN PROFILE

Range SAT Critical Reading	540–670
Range SAT Math	630–740
Range ACT Composite	26–31
Minimum paper TOEFL	550
Minimum computer TOEFL	213
Minimum web-based TOEFL	79
% graduated top 10% of class	55
% graduated top 25% of class	89
% graduated top 50% of class	99

DEADLINES

Early action	
Deadline	11/10
Notification	12/14
Regular	
Priority	11/10
Deadline	1/2
Notification	12/14
Nonfall registration?	no

APPLICANTS ALSO LOOK AT

AND OFTEN PREFER
University of Michigan—Ann Arbor
Northwestern University

AND SOMETIMES PREFER
Washington University in St. Louis
University of Iowa
University of Wisconsin—Madison
Indiana University at Bloomington

AND RARELY PREFER
Purdue University—West Lafayette

FINANCIAL FACTS

Financial Aid Rating	78
Annual in-state tuition	$8,502
Annual out-of-state tuition	$21,895
Room and board	$8,196
Required fees	$2,001
Books and supplies	$1,200
% frosh rec. need-based scholarship or grant aid	36
% UG rec. need-based scholarship or grant aid	39
% frosh rec. non-need-based scholarship or grant aid	13
% UG rec. non-need-based scholarship or grant aid	12
% frosh rec. need-based self-help aid	34
% UG rec. need-based self-help aid	36
% frosh rec. athletic scholarships	1
% UG rec. athletic scholarships	1
% frosh rec. any financial aid	69
% UG rec. any financial aid	72
% UG borrow to pay for school	51
Average cumulative indebtedness	$17,057

UNIVERSITY OF IOWA

107 CALVIN HALL, IOWA CITY, IA 52242 • ADMISSIONS: 319-335-3847 • FAX: 319-333-1535

CAMPUS LIFE

Quality of Life Rating	85
Fire Safety Rating	81
Green Rating	89
Type of school	public
Environment	city

STUDENTS

Total undergrad enrollment	20,079
% male/female	49/51
% from out of state	37
% from public high school	90
% live on campus	29
% in (# of) fraternities	8 (18)
% in (# of) sororities	13 (18)
% African American	2
% Asian	4
% Caucasian	85
% Hispanic	3
% international	2
# of countries represented	116

SURVEY SAYS . . .

Low cost of living
Everyone loves the Hawkeyes
Lots of beer drinking
Hard liquor is popular
(Almost) no one smokes

ACADEMICS

Academic Rating	72
Calendar	semester
Student/faculty ratio	15:1
Profs interesting rating	63
Profs accessible rating	70
Most common reg class size	10–19 students
Most common lab size	20–29 students

MOST POPULAR MAJORS

business/commerce
engineering
psychology

STUDENTS SAY ". . ."

Academics

Students get the "best of both worlds" at University of Iowa thanks to "very strong academics" and a student body that likes "to have a lot of fun." As one undergrad explains, "On one hand it's a huge party school, but on the other hand it's very academically challenging." Fundamentally, the school offers "a great community that knows how to have fun while succeeding." But don't expect to breeze on through classes. Academics are "challenging," and most students agree "you get out what you put in." "If a student is motivated and wants to do well, there is an army of people here to help them improve in all areas of their academic needs," says one student. A substantial part of that support team is comprised of "great professors who encourage you to live life and always learn with passion." While some professors "are more interested in research than teaching, all are very knowledgeable and attempt to help their students." The "research facilities" and "solid programs in a variety of fields" are cited as two of Iowa's "greatest strengths." On the administration side of things, students find little common ground. Some say that that administration is "pretty good" and that it has done "a wonderful job handling the flood damages and changes, which occurred this past summer." Others feel the administration is "a little strict" and "has made some bad decisions in the past year." One student notes, "The president of the university seems both in and out of sync with the problems and challenges which lay ahead—she had a rocky start but seems to be getting better."

Life

How best to explain what University of Iowa has to offer its students once classes are out? As one student concisely puts it, "great times, amazing friends, awesome partying, chances of a lifetime, no regrets, intense moments, and rewarding futures." It's no secret that Iowa has a "rather large party scene" with students "heading downtown for happy hour on the weekends." However, some students complain that "social life is starting to head downhill with harsh alcohol policies aimed at students' wallets and cracking down on parties." Despite this, most here report that they lose interest in partying as they "mature" and find plenty to do thanks to "student groups, lots of interesting public lectures," and "free night activities to attend." Iowa City "has a great local music scene" and offers a "plethora of restaurants, shops, nightlife, and cultural events." The proximity of downtown is "an advantage" to students, who not only "breathe a breath of life" into all the local businesses but also "work in businesses" themselves. The university's hospitals and clinics provide "amazing" opportunities to "volunteer or get a part-time job." That said, when the chips are down, "football games take precedence over everything else" at this "Big Ten school with a smaller campus feel."

Student Body

Most students here come from either "small-town Iowa or the Chicago area" and are "committed to learning but at the same time still want to enjoy college life." Indeed, "work hard, play hard" is echoed by the majority of students. Most note that while "Iowa is ethnically homogenous," there's "more diversity socially" thanks to a "combination of different types" who all "find their place here." Students do report that there are "many" international students and "a lot of political activism and artistic expression" among "minority students," along with "communities for people with many different hobbies and lifestyles." Overall, what binds these Hawkeyes is a "very strong sense of community" (as evidenced recently "during the flooding over the summer") and "a lot of school spirit," meaning that ultimately "the majority of Iowa students find their niche."

FINANCIAL AID: 319-335-1450 • E-MAIL: ADMISSIONS@UIOWA.EDU • WEBSITE: WWW.UIOWA.EDU

THE PRINCETON REVIEW SAYS

Admissions

Very important factors considered include: Class rank, academic GPA, rigor of secondary school record, standardized test scores. *Other factors considered include:* recommendation(s), character/personal qualities, state residency, talent/ability, SAT or ACT required; ACT with Writing component recommended. TOEFL required of all international applicants. High school diploma is required and GED is accepted. *Academic units required:* 4 English, 3 mathematics, 3 science, 2 foreign language, 3 social studies. *Academic units recommended:* 4 mathematics, 4 foreign language.

Financial Aid

Students should submit: FAFSA, institution's own financial aid form. The Princeton Review suggests that all financial aid forms be submitted as soon as possible after 1/1. *Need-based scholarships/grants offered:* Federal Pell, SEOG, state scholarships/grants, private scholarships, the school's own gift aid. *Loan aid offered:* Direct Subsidized Stafford, Direct Unsubsidized Stafford, Direct PLUS, Federal Perkins, Federal Nursing, state loans, college/university loans from institutional funds. Applicants will be notified of awards on a rolling basis beginning 3/15. Federal Work-Study Program available. Institutional employment available. Off-campus job opportunities are good.

The Inside Word

As a large public university, there should be little surprise that the application process at University of Iowa is fairly formulaic and impersonal. That said, there's nothing wrong with knowing what to expect. Admission is automatically granted to applicants who meet secondary school course requirements and class-rank and entrance-exam minimums. The cutoffs are fairly high, and Iowa's growing popularity has only enhanced the quality of its applicant pool. With this in mind, it's best to put your best foot forward—and early on—especially if you're an out-of-state applicant or applying to the engineering school.

THE SCHOOL SAYS " . . ."

From The Admissions Office

"The University of Iowa has outstanding programs in the creative arts, notably the Iowa Writers' Workshop and the world-renowned International Writing Program. It also has strong programs in business, communication studies, journalism, English, engineering, political science, and psychology, and was the birthplace of the discipline of speech pathology and audiology. It offers excellent programs in the basic health sciences and health care programs, led by the top ranked College of Medicine and the closely associated University Hospitals and Clinics.

"The University of Iowa will accept either the SAT or the ACT. The ACT Writing test is not required but we recommend you take it."

SELECTIVITY

Admissions Rating	89
# of applicants	15,582
% of applicants accepted	82
% of acceptees attending	33

FRESHMAN PROFILE

Range SAT Critical Reading	510–660
Range SAT Math	560–680
Range ACT Composite	23–28
Minimum paper TOEFL	530
Minimum computer TOEFL	197
Minimum web-based TOEFL	71
Average HS GPA	3.56
% graduated top 10% of class	22
% graduated top 25% of class	55
% graduated top 50% of class	93

DEADLINES

Regular	
Deadline	4/1
Notification	rolling
Nonfall registration?	yes

APPLICANTS ALSO LOOK AT
AND OFTEN PREFER
University of Illinois at Urbana-Champaign

AND SOMETIMES PREFER
Iowa State University
University of Northern Iowa
Indiana University at Bloomington

FINANCIAL FACTS

Financial Aid Rating	89
Annual in-state tuition	$5,782
Annual out-of-state tuition	$21,156
Room and board	$8,004
Required fees	$1,042
Books and supplies	$1,090
% frosh rec. need-based scholarship or grant aid	32
% UG rec. need-based scholarship or grant aid	30
% frosh rec. non-need-based scholarship or grant aid	26
% UG rec. non-need-based scholarship or grant aid	17
% frosh rec. need-based self-help aid	39
% UG rec. need-based self-help aid	42
% frosh rec. athletic scholarships	2
% UG rec. athletic scholarships	2
% frosh rec. any financial aid	80
% UG rec. any financial aid	82
% UG borrow to pay for school	61
Average cumulative indebtedness	$22,856

UNIVERSITY OF KANSAS

OFFICE OF ADMISSIONS & SCHOLARSHIPS, 1502 IOWA STREET, LAWRENCE, KS 66045 • ADMISSIONS: 785-864-3911 • FAX: 785-864-5017

CAMPUS LIFE

Quality of Life Rating	**88**
Fire Safety Rating	**80**
Green Rating	**81**
Type of school	public
Environment	city

STUDENTS

Total undergrad enrollment	21,073
% male/female	50/50
% from out of state	23
% live on campus	23
% in (# of) fraternities	12 (26)
% in (# of) sororities	17 (16)
% African American	4
% Asian	4
% Caucasian	81
% Hispanic	4
% Native American	1
% international	3
# of countries represented	110

SURVEY SAYS . . .
Athletic facilities are great
Great off-campus food
Everyone loves the Jayhawks
Student publications are popular

ACADEMICS

Academic Rating	**75**
Calendar	semester
Student/faculty ratio	19:1
Profs interesting rating	76
Profs accessible rating	77
% classes taught by TAs	17
Most common reg class size	20–29 students
Most common lab size	10–19 students

MOST POPULAR MAJORS
biology/biological sciences
business/commerce
psychology

STUDENTS SAY "..."

Academics

"Strong in traditions both sports and academics," the University of Kansas (KU to those in the know) is "paradise for sports fans, academics, liberals, and partiers alike." Students stress that KU provides "the full college experience" through "many amazing research opportunities, supportive faculty, and strong academics, as well as a great social scene." KU boasts a wealth of solid nationally ranked programs, including an "amazing hands-on architecture program," a "fantastic journalism program," a highly reputed program in speech language and hearing, a "good nursing school," and solid science departments. As one student sees it, "My school can offer an Ivy-League education to those who are willing to be the best they can be." No matter what discipline you pursue, "The price is amazing for everything that you receive. The buildings, the classrooms, the technology, the campus…and the location were all what I was looking for." While KU's class sizes "can be a bit overwhelming," professors "are interested in seeing their students succeed and make themselves readily available to students." "Discussions or labs help make [the large lectures] bearable." Those seeking a more intimate academic experience should consider the honors program; "The people who run it are all super-nice and helpful, and the honors classes themselves are much smaller and more discussion-based, which lets the students think more and become better friends."

Life

"Tradition is a big strength" of KU life. "Singing the alma mater and reciting the Rock Chalk chant before games and other events is awesome," students tell us. For many, "Life revolves around basketball from November to April," especially in 2008 when KU won its fifth national championship and tens of thousands of fans celebrated in the streets. Reports one undergrad, "Going to games is great. I've never experienced anything like [it]. I love sitting in the student section. The energy radiating off of everyone is amazing. Camping out in line on the day of basketball games will be one of my greatest memories. You gotta love KU basketball." If you don't, though, you needn't despair, because "Lawrence offers a great downtown with bars, clubs, shops, coffeehouses, and music. There's always something to do, even if you're not 21." The town has "a big music scene, and bands like Pat Green, James Blunt, and Mat Kearney have played numerous shows. Smaller indie-rock bands come through as well. Liberty Hall in downtown hosts concerts and projection movies, and the student union always brings in acts like Ben Folds or other celebrities." There's an active party scene on and off campus; according to one undergrad, "The majority of us bust our [butts] during the week, and party the weekend away. There are a lot of places for students to go on weekends to forget about how [crappy] their week was."

Student Body

KU students tell us there are "a lot of fraternity and sorority types at our school, and they're very active on (and off) campus," but there's also "a large number of alternative, indie, and minority students present, and they all fit into a niche as well. Overall, I would say it's a very pleasant coexistence between the two types of people," as "most people are really easygoing and enjoy getting to know people who are different from them." Demographically, KU is made up of "pretty much plain-vanilla Midwestern college students." They're among the most liberal in the state, but, one student quips, "that isn't saying much, seeing as it is Kansas." However, "Most everyone here is very open-minded and willing to accept people for who they are." As one student puts it, "Nothing surprises me anymore. When I first came to KU it was interesting to see same-sex couples, rocker guys, and girls with their collars popped walking around the same campus. Now, it's just life."

FINANCIAL AID: 785-864-4700 • E-MAIL: ADM@KU.EDU • WEBSITE: WWW.KU.EDU

THE PRINCETON REVIEW SAYS

Admissions

Very important factors considered include: Class rank, academic GPA, standardized test scores, SAT or ACT required; High school diploma is required and GED is accepted. *Academic units required:* 4 English, 3 mathematics, 3 science, 3 social studies, 1 Computer Technology (one unit). *Academic units recommended:* 4 English, 4 mathematics, 3 science, 2 foreign language, 3 social studies, 1 Computer Technology (one unit).

Financial Aid

Students should submit: FAFSA. The Princeton Review suggests that all financial aid forms be submitted as soon as possible after 1/1. *Need-based scholarships/grants offered:* Federal Pell, SEOG, state scholarships/grants, private scholarships, the school's own gift aid. *Loan aid offered:* Direct Subsidized Stafford, Direct Unsubsidized Stafford, Direct PLUS, FFEL Subsidized Stafford, FFEL Unsubsidized Stafford, FFEL PLUS, Federal Perkins, college/university loans from institutional funds. Applicants will be notified of awards on a rolling basis beginning 4/1. Federal Work-Study Program available. Institutional employment available. Off-campus job opportunities are excellent.

The Inside Word

KU can process your application to its College of Liberal Arts and Sciences or its School of Engineering (architecture program excluded) in 48 hours. In-state students can be admitted to the College of Liberal Arts and Sciences if they achieve a 21/980 on the ACT/SAT (writing section excluded) or earn at least a 2.0 on the Kansas Board of Regents curriculum. Out-of-state students need a 24/1090 or at least a 2.5 on the board curriculum. No matter where you're from, a top-third high school class rank will do the trick. The School of Engineering requires a minimum 28/640 ACT/SAT Math section score for out-of-state students. In-state students need a minimum Math score of 22/540.

THE SCHOOL SAYS "..."

From The Admissions Office

"The University of Kansas has a long and distinguished tradition for academic excellence. Outstanding students from Kansas and across the nation are attracted to KU because of its strong academic reputation, beautiful campus, affordable cost of education, and contagious school spirit. KU provides students extraordinary opportunities in honors programs, service learning, research, internships, and study abroad. The university is located in Lawrence (40 minutes from Kansas City), a community of 88,000 regarded as one of the nation's best small cities for its arts scene, live music, and historic downtown.

"Students applying for admissions may submit an ACT or SAT score, and KU will only look at Math and Critical Reading (verbal) section of SAT for admissions purposes."

SELECTIVITY
Admissions Rating	89
# of applicants	10,902
% of applicants accepted	92
% of acceptees attending	45

FRESHMAN PROFILE
Range ACT Composite	22–27
Average HS GPA	3.4
% graduated top 10% of class	27
% graduated top 25% of class	60
% graduated top 50% of class	90

DEADLINES
Regular	
Deadline	4/1
Notification	rolling
Nonfall registration?	yes

FINANCIAL FACTS
Financial Aid Rating	73
Annual in-state tuition	$6,195
Annual out-of-state tuition	$16,272
Room and board	$6,474
Required fees	$847
Books and supplies	$800
% frosh rec. need-based scholarship or grant aid	24
% UG rec. need-based scholarship or grant aid	26
% frosh rec. non-need-based scholarship or grant aid	15
% UG rec. non-need-based scholarship or grant aid	11
% frosh rec. need-based self-help aid	33
% UG rec. need-based self-help aid	33
% frosh rec. athletic scholarships	2
% UG rec. athletic scholarships	2
% frosh rec. any financial aid	61
% UG rec. any financial aid	51
% UG borrow to pay for school	46
Average cumulative indebtedness	$20,902

UNIVERSITY OF KENTUCKY

100 FUNKHOUSER BUILDING, LEXINGTON, KY 40506 • ADMISSIONS: 859-257-2000 • FAX: 859-257-3823

CAMPUS LIFE

Quality of Life Rating	**70**
Fire Safety Rating	**83**
Green Rating	**60***
Type of school	public
Environment	city

STUDENTS

Total undergrad enrollment	18,960
% male/female	49/51
% from out of state	17
% live on campus	22
% in (# of) fraternities	15 (19)
% in (# of) sororities	19 (16)
% African American	5
% Asian	2
% Caucasian	88
% Hispanic	1
% international	1
# of countries represented	117

SURVEY SAYS . . .

Great library
Athletic facilities are great
Everyone loves the Wildcats
Student publications are popular

ACADEMICS

Academic Rating	**71**
Calendar	semester
Student/faculty ratio	17:1
Profs interesting rating	68
Profs accessible rating	63
% classes taught by TAs	20
Most common reg class size	20–29 students
Most common lab size	20–29 students

STUDENTS SAY ". . ."

Academics

The University of Kentucky in Lexington is "all about making a name for yourself by preparing for and getting involved in future career goals while having fun and enjoying what college is all about." "Making a name for yourself" here requires distinguishing yourself in a crowd of almost 19,000 undergraduates; daunting as that sounds, students tell us it can be done. "Getting involved in future career goals" is easy enough, given the "great selection of courses and majors" available. Kentucky offers undergraduate degrees in 12 of its 19 divisions. Choices include the College of Agriculture (with popular majors in animal science, agricultural economics, and hospitality management), the College of Business and Management, the College of Education, the College of Engineering, the College of Communications and Information Studies (advertising, journalism, and library science), and the College of Arts and Sciences (biology, history, and political science). Students here laud the "impressive teaching staff, dedicated to enhancing student knowledge and teaching students about the future." UK's brand-new library "is also quite amazing. It is the perfect place to go study because usually the dorms can be a bit too distracting." All told, go-getters willing to take initiative will find UK offers "a safe and fun atmosphere where you have unlimited opportunities to get involved at a reasonable price."

Life

"Everyone is a Wildcat" at UK, because "UK has tremendous sports programs and big fans all around the United States." Men's basketball fans "are among the craziest in the nation," and students "would be football fanatics if our team would win a game every now and then." "Because UK is dry, most parties are held off campus." Social life for many revolves around the off-campus Greek houses where "There is always a party going on, but you have to be a part of a fraternity or sorority to really know about it and attend." Some students report "there are a lot of nonalcoholic parties in the dorms that might be crazier than the alcoholic parties," although others advise, "it's better to live off campus because the residence halls are pretty bad (except for the new ones), the meal plan is awful, and everything off campus is a lot cheaper." Hometown Lexington "is a great city with much to do and lots of opportunities. It offers many different clubs, bars, and restaurants that college students can go to as well as horse racing. All of these venues have a 'College Day' where students get discounts." One sophomore warns, however, that "small-town students can become distracted by the lights of the city."

Student Body

"The typical UK student has a Southern accent, likes to party, and often shops at J. Crew," but, "as the undergraduate population is about 19,000, there are a lot of people who do not fit that description." True, one of the most common "types"—or at least the most conspicuous one—are the "beautiful people, the hot girls and guys who roam the campus and dress up to go to class." But for every "collar-popping, stuck-up frat boy" there is also "your typical country Kentucky boy, boots and all." What you won't find many of at UK are "liberals—they are few and far between—and the type of atypical student with wild hair colors or other style extremes." Most "lean right politically, but generally the student body is apathetic." School spirit is rampant, so much so that "on an average day, one in three students will have some sort of UK clothing on."

FINANCIAL AID: 859-257-3172 • E-MAIL: ADMISSION@UKY.EDU • WEBSITE: WWW.UKY.EDU

THE PRINCETON REVIEW SAYS

Admissions

Very important factors considered include: Academic GPA, rigor of secondary school record, standardized test scores. *Other factors considered include:* Class rank, application essay, recommendation(s), alumni/ae relation, character/personal qualities, extracurricular activities, first generation, geographical residence, interview, racial/ethnic status, talent/ability, volunteer work, SAT or ACT required; TOEFL required of all international applicants. High school diploma is required and GED is accepted. *Academic units required:* 4 English, 3 mathematics, 3 science, 2 foreign language, 3 social studies, 5 academic electives, 2 Fine or Performing Arts (1), Health (.5), and Physical Ed. (.5). *Academic units recommended:* 4 English, 4 mathematics, 4 science, 2 foreign language, 3 social studies, 3 academic electives, 2 Fine or Performing Arts (1), Health (.5), and Physical Ed. (.5).

Financial Aid

Students should submit: FAFSA Regular filing deadline is 2/15. The Princeton Review suggests that all financial aid forms be submitted as soon as possible after 1/1. *Need-based scholarships/grants offered:* Federal Pell, SEOG, state scholarships/grants, private scholarships, the school's own gift aid. *Loan aid offered:* Direct Subsidized Stafford, Direct Unsubsidized Stafford, Direct PLUS, FFEL Subsidized Stafford, FFEL Unsubsidized Stafford, FFEL PLUS, Federal Perkins, state loans, college/university loans from institutional funds. Applicants will be notified of awards on a rolling basis beginning 4/1. Federal Work-Study Program available.

The Inside Word

The University of Kentucky's admissions team is about as objective as they come. If you have the GPA, class rank, and test scores, you will in all likelihood be welcomed into the Wildcat community. The university is continually looking to improve its selectivity, so hitting the books is a must if you want to be a serious contender.

THE SCHOOL SAYS ". . ."

From The Admissions Office

"The University of Kentucky offers you an outstanding learning environment and quality instruction through its excellent faculty. Of the 1,892 full-time faculty, 98 percent hold the doctorate degree or the highest degree in their field of study. Many are nationally and internationally known for their research, distinguished teaching, and scholarly service to Kentucky, the nation, and the world. UK's scholars (students, faculty, and alumni) have been honored by Nobel, Pulitzer, Rhodes, Fulbright, Guggenheim, and Grammy awards, and most recently the Metropolitan Opera and the Marshall Foundation. Yet, with a student to teacher ratio of only 17:1, UK faculty are accessible and willing to answer your questions and discuss your interests.

"UK will accept the SAT. The Writing sections of the ACT and SAT will not be used in the admission process."

SELECTIVITY

Admissions Rating	84
# of applicants	10,024
% of applicants accepted	81
% of acceptees attending	52

FRESHMAN PROFILE

Range SAT Critical Reading	490–610
Range SAT Math	500–630
Range ACT Composite	21–26
Minimum paper TOEFL	527
Minimum computer TOEFL	197
Average HS GPA	3.48
% graduated top 10% of class	23
% graduated top 25% of class	50
% graduated top 50% of class	79

DEADLINES

Regular	
Priority	2/15
Deadline	2/15
Notification	rolling
Nonfall registration?	yes

APPLICANTS ALSO LOOK AT

AND OFTEN PREFER
Transylvania University
Centre College
Miami University
Indiana University at Bloomington

AND SOMETIMES PREFER
University of Tennessee—Knoxville
Western Kentucky University
Bellarmine University
Eastern Kentucky University
University of Louisville

AND RARELY PREFER
Purdue University—West Lafayette
University of Florida
University of Illinois at Urbana-
Champaign
Florida State University
The Ohio State University—Columbus

FINANCIAL FACTS

Financial Aid Rating	85
Annual tuition in-state	$8,358
Annual tuition out-of-state	$16,901
% frosh rec. need-based scholarship or grant aid	20
% UG rec. need-based scholarship or grant aid	24
% frosh rec. non-need-based scholarship or grant aid	35
% UG rec. non-need-based scholarship or grant aid	25
% frosh rec. need-based self-help aid	26
% UG rec. need-based self-help aid	29
% frosh rec. athletic scholarships	2
% UG rec. athletic scholarships	2
% frosh rec. any financial aid	40
% UG rec. any financial aid	38
% UG borrow to pay for school	67.6
Average cumulative indebtedness	$17,692

UNIVERSITY OF LOUISIANA AT LAFAYETTE

PO DRAWER 41210, LAFAYETTE, LA 70504 • ADMISSIONS: 337-482-6457 • FAX: 337-482-6195

CAMPUS LIFE

Quality of Life Rating	84
Fire Safety Rating	86
Green Rating	60*
Type of school	public
Environment	city

STUDENTS

Total undergrad enrollment	14,240
% male/female	42/58
% from out of state	4
% live on campus	12
% in (# of) fraternities	4 (11)
% in (# of) sororities	5 (9)
% African American	19
% Asian	2
% Caucasian	74
% Hispanic	2
% international	2
# of countries represented	97

SURVEY SAYS . . .
Students are friendly
Diverse student types on campus
Students get along with local
community
Students love Lafayette, LA
Great off-campus food
Student publications are popular
Student government is popular
(Almost) everyone smokes

ACADEMICS

Academic Rating	70
Calendar	semester
Student/faculty ratio	23:1
Profs interesting rating	70
Profs accessible rating	70
Most common	
reg class size	20–29 students

MOST POPULAR MAJORS
biology/biological sciences
business administration and
management
nursing/registered nurse
(rn, asn, bsn, msn)

STUDENTS SAY ". . ."

Academics
At the "medium-sized" University of Louisiana at Lafayette—in "the heart of Cajun country"—many students feel "under the shadow" of their mammoth cousin, LSU. We really don't know why. UL Lafayette offers "serious bang for your buck"; tremendously generous grant and scholarship programs and out-of-state fee waivers make UL Lafayette one of the best bargains in the country. Programs in "education, computer science, and engineering" are "ranked as some of the best in the nation." The nursing program is the "third largest" in the country and "one of the best" anywhere. "Seasoned" and "overwhelmingly helpful" professors are "friendly, fun" and "honestly interested in having you learn." "The experience has been absolutely wonderful academically," gushes a senior. "In more than 120 hours of course study, I cannot remember hav[ing] one bad professor." Other students disagree; they remember a "couple of bad apples." A perennial complaint among students at UL Lafayette is that many professors from other countries "cannot be understood by the students." The administration is generally unpopular. "The bureaucracy is ridiculous," reports a general studies major. "The university is run like an out-of-date chicken farm," adds a finance major. "No one knows the answer to anything" and "Getting financial aid in a timely manner is a real problem." Students are generally very satisfied, though. "My overall college experience at University of Louisiana at Lafayette has been terrific," asserts a junior. "I would recommend this college to anyone."

Life
UL Lafayette's "beautiful campus" is "full of big trees and handsome Southern architecture." Unfortunately, "It always floods when it rains," some "lousy buildings" "need updating," and the parking situation is just "painful." Nevertheless, "school spirit is really high." "Football games are huge events," and Lafayette is, by all accounts, a "great" college town. "Believe me," swears a wide-eyed first-year student, "it is an experience." The Strip "is right by campus" and "lined with numerous bars and clubs." "Most people," however, "congregate downtown," where it's "almost like Bourbon Street in New Orleans." The local music scene is hopping, and festivals are frequent, including a very large International Music Festival and a gigantic Mardi Gras celebration. If partying isn't your bag, or if you get sick of it, Lafayette also offers an "abundance of coffee shops" and "numerous art venues." "There is so much history and culture in Louisiana" that, frankly, it's hard to "ever be bored or without something fun to do on any day of the week." and you can find "great food anywhere." "If you're looking for a good, inexpensive college education that is packed with good food, cold beer, and excitement, look no further than UL Lafayette."

Student Body
Students at UL Lafayette are "friendly and fun" and "always seem to be in a good mood." They have "southern flair with a little bit of our Cajun cayenne," a marketing major quips. They're also "very strongly rooted in their religions"; in that regard, "Catholic conservatives" seem to dominate. Many "are from the surrounding area of Acadiana," are "lower- to upper-middle class," and "receive some financial support from [their] parents." Many also "have part-time job[s]." Beyond that, "there are many different types of people" and "everyone seems to get along together." One undergrad reports, "Our campus includes a very diverse group of students from various religious and racial backgrounds." There are also "a few oddballs" who "try to get themselves noticed by the way they dress and their eccentric hair." For the most part, however, "everyone blends in." "No one really points out or harasses other students here at UL Lafayette, unless that student happens to be wearing LSU paraphernalia."

UNIVERSITY OF LOUISIANA AT LAFAYETTE

FINANCIAL AID: 337-482-6506 • E-MAIL: ADMISSIONS@LOUISIANA.EDU • WEBSITE: WWW.LOUISIANA.EDU

THE PRINCETON REVIEW SAYS

Admissions

Very important factors considered include: Class rank, academic GPA, rigor of secondary school record, standardized test scores. *Other factors considered include:* state residency, SAT or ACT required; TOEFL required of all international applicants. High school diploma is required and GED is accepted. *Academic units required:* 4 English, 4 mathematics, 3 science, (0 science labs), 2 foreign language, 1 social studies, 2 history, 1 visual/performing arts, 1 Computer Science/Literacy.

Financial Aid

Students should submit: FAFSA. The Princeton Review suggests that all financial aid forms be submitted as soon as possible after 1/1. *Need-based scholarships/grants offered:* Federal Pell, SEOG, state scholarships/grants, private scholarships, the school's own gift aid, Federal Nursing Scholarships. *Loan aid offered:* FFEL Subsidized Stafford, FFEL Unsubsidized Stafford, FFEL PLUS, Federal Perkins, Federal Nursing Applicants will be notified of awards on a rolling basis beginning 4/1. Federal Work-Study Program available. Institutional employment available. Off-campus job opportunities are good.

The Inside Word

UL Lafayette is still a fallback school for many applicants. You are pretty much guaranteed admission if you carry an ACT score of at least 18 and complete a basic college-prep high school curriculum with a GPA of 2.5 or better. If your numbers are a little lower, you can submit an essay and some other credentials for possible admission through UL Lafayette's admission by committee. It should be noted, however, that admission by committee is limited to 7 percent of each incoming class.

THE SCHOOL SAYS "..."

From The Admissions Office

"The University of Louisiana at Lafayette offers students from throughout the United States and more than 90 countries strong academic training and personal enrichment opportunities in a friendly, comfortable, student-centered environment. UL Lafayette students are taught, mentored, and advised by some of the brightest and most accomplished faculty members in the United States. Although UL Lafayette offers more than 100 programs of study and the research opportunities, internship possibilities, and facilities of a major research-intensive university, average class size is approximately the same as that at many high schools and smaller higher education institutions.

"UL students receive a good deal of individual attention and support—both personal and academic—from faculty and staff.

"A wide range of cultural, recreational, and social activities are available on and off campus, including more than 150 campus organizations and clubs, NCAA Division I and intramural athletics, a state-of-the-art aquatic center, a thriving arts scene, a wide range of live music venues, shopping, a great variety of excellent restaurants, theaters, the second largest Mardi Gras in the nation, and an international music festival. In fact, *Utne Reader* magazine selected the city of Lafayette as Louisiana's 'Most Enlightened Town.'

"Our relatively low tuition and generous financial aid and scholarship programs, including an out-of-state tuition waiver for qualified students, make UL Lafayette one of the most affordable universities in the nation.

"Students who have completed the required college preparatory core curriculum in high school may qualify for admission on the basis of a combination of their high school cumulative grade point average and ACT or SAT scores. Writing scores are not required."

SELECTIVITY
Admissions Rating	74
# of applicants	7,634
% of applicants accepted	68
% of acceptees attending	50

FRESHMAN PROFILE
Range ACT Composite	20–24
Minimum paper TOEFL	525
Minimum computer TOEFL	195
Average HS GPA	3.23
% graduated top 10% of class	15
% graduated top 25% of class	39
% graduated top 50% of class	73

DEADLINES
Regular	
Priority	7/20
Nonfall registration?	yes

FINANCIAL FACTS
Financial Aid Rating	70
Annual in-state tuition	$3,402
Annual out-of-state tuition	$9,582
Room and board	$3,820
Books and supplies	$1,200
% frosh rec. need-based scholarship or grant aid	46
% UG rec. need-based scholarship or grant aid	41
% frosh rec. non-need-based scholarship or grant aid	9
% UG rec. non-need-based scholarship or grant aid	4
% frosh rec. need-based self-help aid	22
% UG rec. need-based self-help aid	30
% frosh rec. athletic scholarships	2
% UG rec. athletic scholarships	3
% frosh rec. any financial aid	87
% UG rec. any financial aid	72

UNIVERSITY OF MAINE

5713 CHADBOURNE HALL, ORONO, ME 04469-5713 • ADMISSIONS: 207-581-1561 • FAX: 207-581-1213

CAMPUS LIFE

Quality of Life Rating	74
Fire Safety Rating	86
Green Rating	98
Type of school	public
Environment	village

STUDENTS

Total undergrad enrollment	8,868
% male/female	53/47
% from out of state	16
% live on campus	42
% in (# of) fraternities	NR (13)
% in (# of) sororities	NR (6)
% African American	1
% Asian	1
% Caucasian	79
% Hispanic	1
% Native American	1
% international	1
# of countries represented	67

SURVEY SAYS . . .

Athletic facilities are great
Everyone loves the Black Bears
Student publications are popular
Lots of beer drinking
Hard liquor is popular

ACADEMICS

Academic Rating	74
Calendar	semester
Student/faculty ratio	15:1
Profs interesting rating	68
Profs accessible rating	70
% classes taught by TAs	17
Most common	
reg class size	10–19 students
Most common	
lab size	fewer than 10 students

MOST POPULAR MAJORS

business/commerce
education
engineering

STUDENTS SAY ". . ."

Academics

The University of Maine boasts "a phenomenal engineering school" and notable programs in ecology, marine science, and forestry. "The campus is beautiful," says a sophomore, "melding scenery, history, and modernity." "The resources available through the library are quite staggering." There are also some "very fancy new labs." "It can be disheartening to see the beauty and grand scale of the engineering and science buildings, and then walk back to the buildings where most of your classes are held and see the lack of basic upkeep," gripes a history major. The academic atmosphere here is "challenging but not overwhelming." "Classes range in size from 20-200." "Professors can vary noticeably." There are "some rather dull professors." There are also plenty of "intelligent, kind, realistic human beings" on the faculty who are "quite flexible about meeting with and accommodating students." Some students say the top brass is "reasonable," "decently efficient," and "personable." Others see "layers of administration" and "terrible" management.

Life

Prepare for "bitter, arctic-like cold" and "a lot of snow" if you attend UMaine. Prepare for "unhealthy" food, too. "Ninety percent of it is deep fried or covered in a dairy-based something," protests a junior. On the bright side, campus life is active. There are "tons of things to do." "Musicians, comedians, and other artists" perform frequently. Sports keep many students busy. "Intramurals are great." The recreation center is "state of the art" and "hugely popular." Naturally, "hockey is crazy." "The campus is usually buzzing on game day," and the arena is "generally packed." Students are probably "too obsessed with the Red Sox" as well. "The party scene isn't too shabby." All in all, "consuming large quantities of cheap beer" is pretty common. There's a decent Greek presence, and, for some students, the frat houses are "the place to go on the weekends." There are also "house parties" and "a few local bars." More intimate get-togethers happen, too. "There's a tremendous amount of small-scale social drinking," notes a junior. The "rural community" of Orono "maintains that remote appeal" but it's "boring." "There is a ton of natural beauty around." though. "The extensive wilderness between campus and Canada" provides hiking, kayaking, and hunting opportunities galore. "Ventures to Sugarloaf are abundant."

Student Body

"Most of the students are Maine natives" or New Englanders. To put it diplomatically, the "minority percentage reflects that of the state." To put it bluntly, "this school is almost all white." "The typical student at UMaine is one who loves the outdoors, embraces the cold, is not too concerned with fashion, and lives in North Face or Patagonia clothes," reflects a sophomore. However, students report that you can find "every type of white person imaginable" on this campus. "There are tons of unique styles and groups that mix together." You've got "Carhartt-wearing, wood-chopping, straight-from-the-sticks, true-blue Mainers." There are "hockey rowdies" and "obnoxious frat boys." "There are a lot of hippies" and people who "care about the environment." There are "rare, wild-looking characters" and nontraditional students as well. The atmosphere is "relaxed" and "laidback." "People are friendly up here." Some students tell us that "out-of-staters have a really hard time." Others disagree. "The in-state kids will totally accept you," promises a junior. "An out-of-stater can be distinguished from a Mainer fairly easily," explains a junior. "They can't drive, dress inappropriately for the weather, or wonder why school isn't cancelled during a blizzard. But we get used to them, and eventually, just maybe, by the time they graduate, part of them is Mainer, too."

FINANCIAL AID: 207-581-1324 • E-MAIL: UM-ADMIT@MAINE.EDU • WEBSITE: WWW.UMAINE.EDU

THE PRINCETON REVIEW SAYS

Admissions

Very important factors considered include: Class rank, academic GPA, rigor of secondary school record, standardized test scores, *Important factors considered include:* Application essay, recommendation(s). *Other factors considered include:* character/personal qualities, extracurricular activities, geographical residence, interview, talent/ability, volunteer work, work experience. SAT or ACT required; TOEFL required of all international applicants. High school diploma is required and GED is accepted. *Academic units required:* 4 English, 3 mathematics, 2 science, (2 science labs), 2 foreign language, 2 social studies, 4 academic electives, 1 Physical education for Education Majors. *Academic units recommended:* 4 English, 4 mathematics, 4 science, (3 science labs), 2 foreign language, 3 social studies, 1 history, 4 academic electives, 1 Physical education for Education Majors.

Financial Aid

Students should submit: FAFSA. The Princeton Review suggests that all financial aid forms be submitted as soon as possible after 1/1. *Need-based scholarships/grants offered:* Federal Pell, SEOG, state scholarships/grants, private scholarships, the school's own gift aid. *Loan aid offered:* FFEL Subsidized Stafford, FFEL Unsubsidized Stafford, FFEL PLUS, Federal Perkins, state loans Applicants will be notified of awards on a rolling basis beginning 3/15. Federal Work-Study Program available. Institutional employment available. Off-campus job opportunities are good.

The Inside Word

The University of Maine is much smaller than most public flagship universities, and its admissions process reflects this; it is a much more personal approach than many others use. Candidates are reviewed carefully for fit with their choice of college and major, and the committee will contact students regarding a second choice if the first doesn't seem to be a good match. Prepare your application as if you are applying to a private university.

THE SCHOOL SAYS " . . . "

From The Admissions Office

"The University of Maine offers you the best of both worlds—the excitement, breadth and depth that are available at a land grant, sea grant, research university with the personal attention and community feel of a smaller college. Five academic colleges and an Honors College offer you the chance to belong to a supportive academic community, while providing the specialization, resources and opportunities for research, internships and scholarly activity you would expect at a major university. Academics are a priority at UMaine; most programs hold the highest level of accreditation possible, setting UMaine apart nationally.

"And at UMaine there is always something to do—there are more than 200 clubs and student organizations, lots of volunteer opportunities, an active student government, a new multi-million dollar student recreation center with an busy intramural schedule and Division I varsity athletics to keep you busy. A special First Year Residence Experience (FYRE) will help support your transitions to college—this unique program includes special activities and theme living communities. It is located between the new Student Recreation Center and the newly renovated Hilltop dining complex. Check out our website to learn more—or better yet, come visit us in person and see the campus for yourself!"

SELECTIVITY

Admissions Rating	82
# of applicants	7,407
% of applicants accepted	77
% of acceptees attending	36

FRESHMAN PROFILE

Range SAT Critical Reading	480–580
Range SAT Math	480–600
Range SAT Writing	470–570
Range ACT Composite	19–25
Minimum paper TOEFL	530
Minimum computer TOEFL	197
Minimum web-based TOEFL	71
Average HS GPA	3.22
% graduated top 10% of class	21
% graduated top 25% of class	52
% graduated top 50% of class	86

DEADLINES

Early action	
Deadline	12/15
Notification	1/31
Regular	
Priority	2/1
Notification	rolling
Nonfall registration?	yes

APPLICANTS ALSO LOOK AT
AND OFTEN PREFER

University of New Hampshire
University of Vermont
University of Southern Maine

AND SOMETIMES PREFER

University of Connecticut
University of Massachusetts—Amherst
University of Rhode Island

FINANCIAL FACTS

Financial Aid Rating	79
Annual in-state tuition	$7,170
Annual out-of-state tuition	$20,580
Room and board	$8,008
Required fees	$1,930
Books and supplies	$700
% frosh rec. need-based scholarship or grant aid	53
% UG rec. need-based scholarship or grant aid	46
% frosh rec. non-need-based scholarship or grant aid	4
% UG rec. non-need-based scholarship or grant aid	3
% frosh rec. need-based self-help aid	52
% UG rec. need-based self-help aid	52
% frosh rec. any financial aid	76
% UG rec. any financial aid	93
% UG borrow to pay for school	76
Average cumulative indebtedness	$22,630

UNIVERSITY OF MARY WASHINGTON

1301 COLLEGE AVENUE, FREDERICKSBURG, VA 22401 • ADMISSIONS: 540-654-2000 • FAX: 540-654-1857

CAMPUS LIFE

Quality of Life Rating	**80**
Fire Safety Rating	**81**
Green Rating	**74**
Type of school	public
Environment	city

STUDENTS

Total undergrad enrollment	4,070
% male/female	34/66
% from out of state	22
% from public high school	81
% live on campus	59
% African American	4
% Asian	4
% Caucasian	64
% Hispanic	4
# of countries represented	28

SURVEY SAYS . . .
No one cheats
Athletic facilities are great
Students are friendly
Great off-campus food
Students are happy
Frats and sororities are unpopular or nonexistent
Student publications are popular
Student government is popular
Political activism is popular

ACADEMICS

Academic Rating	**79**
Calendar	semester or continuous
Student/faculty ratio	15:1
Profs interesting rating	92
Profs accessible rating	92
Most common reg class size	20–29 students
Most common lab size	20–29 students

MOST POPULAR MAJORS
business administration and management
English language and literature
psychology

STUDENTS SAY " . . ."

Academics
The University of Mary Washington is a public bastion of the liberal arts in Virginia. It's "not too big and not too small," and it offers "a private school education at half the cost." Students here complain loudly about their "slow," "unfriendly," and "very unresponsive" administration. Financial aid is a perennial gripe, although the school has embarked on a capital campaign with scholarships as a major focus. "Sometimes, I feel students could do better than they do," wagers an English major. As long as students here don't have to deal with the staff, though, they're pretty happy. There are "great research opportunities." The academic experience is challenging and intimate. "This is an undergrad institution, so the professors are here for the sole purpose of teaching," explains a psychology major. "I like the fact that not a single class is taught by a teaching assistant," adds an international affairs major. "Most middle- to upper-level courses have fewer than 20 students," and "smaller class sizes help create closer relationships with faculty." There are some "run of the mill" teachers, but, for the most part, "the professors at this school are absolutely amazing." "Each one has their own quirks that everyone loves." They are "usually quite approachable," too. "Professors greet their students by names semesters after having them in class," observes a Spanish major.

Life
The Internet connection and the food are "both terrible," though the school is working to improve them, students say that Mary Washington's "beautiful" campus "feels homey." It's fun to "sit on the benches all around campus and just socialize." "The atmosphere of our school is its greatest strength," relates a junior. "You don't get lost here." "Everyone can find a niche with great friends." Intramural and intercollegiate sports are popular, but "school spirit (in the artificial, beer-chugging, football-watching, pennant-waving sense) is not required." There are school-sponsored events, though they tend to "vary in success." "You need to join a club or sport or else you will go insane or go home every weekend," advises a junior. Luckily, "it is extremely easy to get as involved as your heart desires." There's no official Greek scene, and alcohol and drug policies are "hard ass and zero tolerance." "The drinking scene is predominantly run by sports teams." "Fake fraternities" routinely throw parties as well. However, get-togethers are small (typically "between 20 and 40 people") and, on the whole, "this is not a party school." For a strong contingent of students, movies and relaxed dinners are very common. Off campus, Fredericksburg's Central Park shopping complex is a frequent destination. The "quaint" downtown area is "gorgeous to wander around," too. There are "some cool local bookstores and such," but, mostly, the surrounding area is "designed for the older tourist." Some students spend their weekends "traveling to other universities in Virginia." "It's an easy drive to the mountains, the beach, or D C" as well.

Students
"A lot of people will complain that we are not ethically diverse," says one sophomore. "But I think that the fact that we have such a wide range of political, religious, and sexual backgrounds here makes up for [it]." "There is a strong influence of the preppy" here. However, "students freely mingle with each other without regard to social standing," and they are quick to point out that "there's no real cookie-cutter Mary Wash student." It's "an eclectic mix," they say. "There is your typical preppy polo- and Sperry-wearing guy and Vera Bradley-carrying girl, but there are also a lot of other types of people." "There isn't a push to just wear designer clothing." "If you walk on campus you are more apt to notice the preppy southern girls walking around, but once you're in class and living in the residence halls you notice that everyone is pretty different," says a senior. "I absolutely loathe the idea that ethnic diversity is the be-all, end-all of diversity," agrees a sophomore. "There are so many people from so many different social structures and outlooks—ranging from hardcore neo-cons to pansy liberals to militant anarchists to theater majors."That being said, UMW seems to be working to increase the diversity on campus.

Financial Aid: 800-468-5614 • E-mail: admit@umw.edu • Website: www.umw.edu

THE PRINCETON REVIEW SAYS

Admissions

Very important factors considered include: Academic GPA, rigor of secondary school record, standardized test scores. *Important factors considered include:* Class rank, application essay, recommendation(s), extracurricular activities. *Other factors considered include:* alumni/ae relation, character/personal qualities, first generation, geographical residence, racial/ethnic status, state residency, talent/ability, volunteer work, work experience. SAT or ACT required; High school diploma is required and GED is accepted. *Academic units required:* 4 English, 3 mathematics, 3 science, (3 science labs), 2 foreign language, 2 social studies, 1 history. *Academic units recommended:* 4 English, 4 mathematics, 4 science, (4 science labs), 4 foreign language, 2 social studies, 2 history.

Financial Aid

Students should submit: FAFSA, institution's own financial aid form. Regular filing deadline is 5/31. The Princeton Review suggests that all financial aid forms be submitted as soon as possible after 1/1. *Need-based scholarships/grants offered:* Federal Pell, SEOG, state scholarships/grants, private scholarships, the school's own gift aid, unendowed gifts. *Loan aid offered:* FFEL Subsidized Stafford, FFEL Unsubsidized Stafford, FFEL PLUS, Federal Perkins. Applicants will be notified of awards on or about 4/15. Federal Work-Study Program available. Institutional employment available. Off-campus job opportunities are good.

The Inside Word

It's hard to beat small, selective public colleges like Mary Washington for quality and cost. The admissions process is very selective and, with the exception of preferential treatment for Virginia residents, functions in virtually the same manner as small private college Admissions Committees do. Students who are interested need to focus on putting their best into all aspects of the application.

THE SCHOOL SAYS "..."

From The Admissions Office

"The University of Mary Washington has long been known for its commitment to providing a stellar undergraduate, liberal arts education. Our faculty are devoted to teaching—without teaching assistants—and are able to provide individualized attention to their students. An education at UMW, with multiple opportunities for student research and service learning, prepares graduates for outstanding careers or for entry into graduate school. Internship opportunities abound not only in Fredericksburg, but also an hour's drive away in either Washington, D.C. or Richmond, VA. A wide range of programs includes strong majors in political science/international affairs, English, biology, psychology, earth/environmental science, history, visual and performing arts, economics, and business. Also distinctive are historic preservation and a new concentration in creative writing. UMW's campus is one of the nation's most beautiful, with classic Jeffersonian architecture, spacious grounds, and a park-like character. Historic Fredericksburg's 40-square-block historic district is walking distance from campus. Several large, modern shopping and entertainment complexes are nearby. UMW provides a variety of residential options, from traditional residence halls to modern apartments. Currently under development is a new retail and garden apartment complex next to campus. More than 100 clubs and organizations are offered along with a top NCAA Division III athletic program. The University recently opened Lee Hall, with an expanded facility providing enhanced student services, a new bookstore, and 'Underground' snack bar/coffee house. UMW students are bright, multitalented, and involved. The University environment is friendly and welcoming, and UMW places great value on diversity within its student body."

SELECTIVITY

Admissions Rating	85
# of applicants	4,600
% of applicants accepted	71
% of acceptees attending	28
# accepting a place on wait list	219
% admitted from wait list	90

FRESHMAN PROFILE

Range SAT Critical Reading	550–650
Range SAT Math	540–620
Range SAT Writing	540–640
Range ACT Composite	24–28
Minimum paper TOEFL	580
Minimum computer TOEFL	230
Minimum web-based TOEFL	88
Average HS GPA	3.59

DEADLINES

Early action	
Deadline	1/15
Notification	2/15
Regular	
Priority	1/15
Deadline	2/1
Notification	4/1
Nonfall registration?	yes

APPLICANTS ALSO LOOK AT

AND OFTEN PREFER
University of Virginia
College of William and Mary

AND SOMETIMES PREFER
University of Richmond
James Madison University

FINANCIAL FACTS

Financial Aid Rating	64
Annual in-state tuition	$3,750
Annual out-of-state tuition	$16,200
Room and board	$7,700
Required fees	$3,750
Books and supplies	$1,000
% frosh rec. need-based scholarship or grant aid	14
% UG rec. need-based scholarship or grant aid	12
% frosh rec. non-need-based scholarship or grant aid	12
% UG rec. non-need-based scholarship or grant aid	6
% frosh rec. need-based self-help aid	20
% UG rec. need-based self-help aid	21
% frosh rec. any financial aid	56
% UG rec. any financial aid	58
% UG borrow to pay for school	57
Average cumulative indebtedness	$16,000

UNIVERSITY OF MARYLAND—BALTIMORE COUNTY

1000 HILLTOP CIRCLE, BALTIMORE, MD 21250 • ADMISSIONS: 410-455-2291 • FAX: 410-455-1094

CAMPUS LIFE

Quality of Life Rating	**69**
Fire Safety Rating	**85**
Green Rating	**88**
Type of school	public
Environment	metropolis

STUDENTS

Total undergrad enrollment	9,468
% male/female	55/45
% from out of state	6.9
% in (# of) fraternities	3.4 (9)
% in (# of) sororities	3.6 (11)
% African American	17
% Asian	22
% Caucasian	52
% Hispanic	4
% international	4
# of countries represented	131

SURVEY SAYS . . .
Great library
Diverse student types on campus
Campus feels safe

ACADEMICS

Academic Rating	**75**
Calendar	4/1/4
Student/faculty ratio	18:1
Profs interesting rating	68
Profs accessible rating	67
% classes taught by TAs	1.3
Most common reg class size	20–29 students
Most common lab size	10–19 students

MOST POPULAR MAJORS
biology/biological sciences
computer and information sciences
psychology

STUDENTS SAY ". . ."

Academics
Students agree that University of Maryland—Baltimore County "is a great school for scientific and information technology people" that boasts "very good programs in biology and mechanical engineering." Undergrads here find themselves immersed in "a science-y environment with some good departments and some not-so-good, but if you find the right niche you'll do fantastically." Provided, you can survive the "discouragingly difficult exams" and "very strict and/or too harsh grading of papers and exams" typically encountered in the school's trademark disciplines. Students of political science and government benefit from the fact that "The school is located near Baltimore and is a train ride from DC, which opens up internship and learning opportunities. (One political science professor takes kids to embassies related to the class he's teaching every semester; I've met the Iraqi and Indonesian ambassadors to the USA.)" Students in the liberal arts, on the other hand, complain that "the school has no concern for us. All the money in the school only goes to the Science and Tech departments," which explains the "amazing technology" undergrads brag about. "There's a lot of focus on research" at UMBC, so "the professors and the library are a great strength" here. Professors "are required to do research in their fields, so they are always up-to-date on material they teach. Even if they are mean or difficult, they all know what they are talking about." The library "has a great deal of research assistance and access to a consortium of millions of books."

Life
"For the most part, campus is quiet" because "people take studying seriously," and "during the weekend many students go home." Add the large commuter population and the school's proximity to some attractive social destinations (downtown Baltimore, DC, Columbia) and you begin to understand why "it may seem as if there's nothing going on" on the UMBC campus. Students assure us that, perceptions to the contrary, "someone is usually having a party or get together" on or around campus, most frequently in the apartment-style residences. Undergrads also enjoy about "200 clubs to join such as dancing, bike riding, football and even juggling" as well as "the game room or the Sports Zone if a person just wants to relax." Mostly, though, students find their fun away from school grounds. The school sponsors "shuttle buses to go to the clubs in Baltimore, so it's great that they promote safety in regards to drinking and driving." Fells Point, a bar district near Baltimore's Inner Harbor, is a popular destination, as is the University of Maryland's College Park campus. All in all, this is not a highly social campus; "Everybody really dances to his own beat" we're told.

Student Body
"There is no typical student" on the "very diverse" UMBC campus. "Everyone varies, from preppy cheerleaders and jocks to antisocial art nerds to normal human beings to religious fanatics to animal rights activists to overachievers to underachievers to foreigners to truly gifted kids to how-did-they-pass-their-SATs kids to druggies to good people and everything in between." The campus is also "full of nontraditional students who are married/engaged, have kids, and work." The Asian population is so large at UMBC that "some folks describe UMBC as 'U Must Be Chinese,' but the majority are Caucasians, with minority black/African-Americans, and a noticeable number of Indian/Pakistani ethnic groups." The student body tends to form cliques along lines of background and academic field; this is hardly unusual for a predominantly commuter campus (only about one-third of students live on campus, more than half of whom are freshmen).

UNIVERSITY OF MARYLAND—BALTIMORE COUNTY

FINANCIAL AID: 410-455-2387 • E-MAIL: ADMISSIONS@UMBC.EDU • WEBSITE: WWW.UMBC.EDU

THE PRINCETON REVIEW SAYS

Admissions

Very important factors considered include: Academic GPA, rigor of secondary school record, standardized test scores. *Important factors considered include:* Application essay. *Other factors considered include:* Class rank, recommendation(s), character/personal qualities, extracurricular activities, talent/ability, volunteer work, SAT required; SAT or ACT required; ACT required; TOEFL required of all international applicants. High school diploma is required and GED is accepted. *Academic units required:* 4 English, 3 mathematics, 3 science, 2 foreign language, 3 social studies, 3 Social Studies and History. *Academic units recommended:* 1 mathematics.

Financial Aid

Students should submit: FAFSA. The Princeton Review suggests that all financial aid forms be submitted as soon as possible after 1/1. *Need-based scholarships/grants offered:* Federal Pell, SEOG, state scholarships/grants, private scholarships, the school's own gift aid. *Loan aid offered:* FFEL Subsidized Stafford, FFEL Unsubsidized Stafford, FFEL PLUS, Federal Perkins. Applicants will be notified of awards on a rolling basis beginning 4/1. Federal Work-Study Program available. Institutional employment available. Off-campus job opportunities are excellent.

The Inside Word

UMBC is an Honors College within the University of Maryland system. After the College Park campus, it is perhaps the most prestigious state-run undergraduate institution in Maryland. Selectivity is somewhat hampered by the school's inability to accommodate residents; about 70 percent of students commute. Even so, the densely populated Baltimore metropolitan area gives the school plenty of top-flight candidates to choose from. Your high school transcript must show a challenging curriculum (and success in your most demanding courses) if you hope to attend this school.

THE SCHOOL SAYS "..."

From The Admissions Office

"When it comes to universities, a mid-sized school can be just right. Some students want the resources of a large community. Others are looking for the attention found at a smaller one. With an undergraduate population of over 9,000, UMBC can offer the best of both. There are always new people to meet and things to do—from Division I sports to more than 170 student clubs. As a research university, we offer an abundance of programs, technology, and opportunities for hands-on experiences. Yet we are small enough that students don't get lost in the shuffle. More than 80 percent of our classes have fewer than 40 students. Among public research universities, UMBC is recognized for its success in placing students in the most competitive graduate programs and careers. Of course, much of the success of UMBC has to do with the students themselves—highly motivated students who get involved in their education."

"Freshman applicants are required to take the SAT or ACT."

SELECTIVITY
Admissions Rating	86
# of applicants	5,820
% of applicants accepted	72
% of acceptees attending	38
# accepting a place on wait list	171
% admitted from wait list	43

FRESHMAN PROFILE
Range SAT Critical Reading	520–630
Range SAT Math	560–670
Range SAT Writing	520–630
Range ACT Composite	22–27
Minimum paper TOEFL	550
Minimum computer TOEFL	213
Minimum web-based TOEFL	80
Average HS GPA	3.57
% graduated top 10% of class	25.9
% graduated top 25% of class	54.5
% graduated top 50% of class	82.8

DEADLINES
Early action	
Deadline	11/1
Notification	12/15
Regular	
Priority	11/1
Deadline	2/1
Notification	rolling
Nonfall registration?	yes

APPLICANTS ALSO LOOK AT
AND OFTEN PREFER
Virginia Tech, Johns Hopkins University
AND SOMETIMES PREFER
Virginia Tech, Johns Hopkins University
University of Maryland—College Park
Penn State—University Park
AND RARELY PREFER
Towson University

FINANCIAL FACTS
Financial Aid Rating	80
Annual tuition in-state	$8,780
Annual tuition iout-of-state	$17,512
% frosh rec. need-based scholarship or grant aid	40
% UG rec. need-based scholarship or grant aid	39
% frosh rec. non-need-based scholarship or grant aid	10
% UG rec. non-need-based scholarship or grant aid	5
% frosh rec. need-based self-help aid	40
% UG rec. need-based self-help aid	43
% frosh rec. athletic scholarships	5
% UG rec. athletic scholarships	4
% frosh rec. any financial aid	80
% UG rec. any financial aid	58
% UG borrow to pay for school	50
Average cumulative indebtedness	$20,228

UNIVERSITY OF MARYLAND—COLLEGE PARK

MITCHELL BUILDING, COLLEGE PARK, MD 20742-5235 • ADMISSIONS: 800-422-5867 • FAX: 301-314-9693

CAMPUS LIFE
Quality of Life Rating	69
Fire Safety Rating	82
Green Rating	95
Type of school	public
Environment	metropolis

STUDENTS
Total undergrad enrollment	25,852
% male/female	52/48
% from out of state	24
% live on campus	41
% in (# of) fraternities	13 (31)
% in (# of) sororities	10 (25)
% African American	13
% Asian	15
% Caucasian	57
% Hispanic	6
% international	2
# of countries represented	149

SURVEY SAYS . . .
Athletic facilities are great
Diverse student types on campus
Everyone loves the Terrapins
Student publications are popular
Lots of beer drinking

ACADEMICS
Academic Rating	75
Calendar	semester
Student/faculty ratio	18:1
Profs interesting rating	71
Profs accessible rating	68
% classes taught by TAs	15
Most common reg class size	20–29 students
Most common lab size	20–29 students

MOST POPULAR MAJORS
criminology
economics
political science and government

STUDENTS SAY ". . ."

Academics
The University of Maryland—College Park is a grand mix of "20-minute walks to class across one of the country's most beautiful campuses, [an introduction] to high-level courses taught by the nation's top researchers, [and] a motivated 'green' campus" as well as "crowded, smelly frat parties, [and] living-learning communities that can make the gigantic campus much smaller." Students are quick to boast about sports, too, especially the school's titles as "the 2008 national champions in men's soccer and women's field hockey." In short: It's a quintessential large university, offering "a great experience with a variety of opportunities that are what you make of them." Students crow about Maryland's "nationally recognized business program," a "top-ranked criminology program," a solid engineering school, a great political science department that capitalizes on the school's proximity to Washington, D.C., and the "top-notch honors program." Most of all, they love the "great price. This school gives you a great education for a really cheap price." Low cost doesn't translate to budget accommodations. On the contrary, "the administration shows a desire to always upgrade facilities, as can be witnessed by the tremendous business school and the brand new engineering building." In conclusion, students applaud "the widely diverse opportunities available at UMD. You can never get bored because there is always something to do."

Life
"Life at UMD is awesome," with "a good mix of fun activities" including "school-sponsored parties, games," a "campus recreation center that has virtually everything you could wish for, including pools, an extensive gym, a rock wall, squash courts, an indoor track," and a student union "loaded with fun places like the arcade area, bowling alley," and "tons of places to eat as well." In addition, "there are always open games of soccer, football, or ultimate Frisbee being played on the mall and elsewhere." There are bars close to campus, and "students are always having parties," especially along College Park's raucous Frat Row. Terrapin sports are a passion for many. And if all that isn't enough, "the proximity to D.C., makes clubbing, nights out on the town, and general visits to D.C. frequent." With all this going on, no wonder students say that "the social life at UMD is unsurpassed." Some warn the surrounding area is dicey; "It's pretty annoying and scary to get crime alerts from the police informing us of incidents close to campus," one student explains. Undergrads also warn that parking regulations are brutal. "Bus transportation around campus provided by the university is great, but for students and visitors with cars, it's a huge hassle. Permits are expensive, and free parking for visitors is impossible to find. School officials are strict with violations, and tickets are $75. They are hard to refute and very costly."

Student Body
"The University of Maryland is a very large school," so "there is no 'typical' student here. Everyone will find that they can fit in somewhere." Better still, "different groups are very accepting of other groups. Students in Greek life are just as accepting of students in non-Greek life. Athletes blend in with non-athletes. UMD provides a great environment for students to meet people they would normally not know and helps to provide great connections with these people." UMD is "an especially diverse school," and this makes people "more tolerant and accepting of people from different backgrounds and cultures." A student from New Jersey explains it this way: "Coming from a very diverse area, I thought it was going to be hard to find a school that had that same representation of minority and atypical students until I found Maryland. I don't think I have ever learned so much about different religions, cultures, orientations, or lifestyles. All of them are accepted and even celebrated" at UMD.

FINANCIAL AID: 301-314-9000 • E-MAIL: UM-ADMIT@UMD.EDU • WEBSITE: WWW.MARYLAND.EDU

THE PRINCETON REVIEW SAYS

Admissions

Very important factors considered include: Academic GPA, rigor of secondary school record, standardized test scores, *Important factors considered include:* Class rank, application essay, recommendation(s), first generation, state residency, talent/ability. *Other factors considered include:* alumni/ae relation, character/personal qualities, extracurricular activities, geographical residence, racial/ethnic status, volunteer work, work experience. SAT or ACT required; ACT with Writing component required. TOEFL required of all international applicants. High school diploma is required and GED is accepted. *Academic units required:* 4 English, 3 mathematics, 3 science, (2 science labs), 2 foreign language, 3 social studies, *Academic units recommended:* 4 mathematics.

Financial Aid

Students should submit: FAFSA. The Princeton Review suggests that all financial aid forms be submitted as soon as possible after 1/1. *Need-based scholarships/grants offered:* Federal Pell, SEOG, state scholarships/grants, private scholarships, the school's own gift aid. *Loan aid offered:* FFEL Subsidized Stafford, FFEL Unsubsidized Stafford, FFEL PLUS, Federal Perkins. Applicants will be notified of awards on a rolling basis beginning 4/1. Federal Work-Study Program available. Institutional employment available. Off-campus job opportunities are good.

The Inside Word

Maryland admissions officers don't simply crunch numbers and apply a formula. The school considers no fewer than 25 factors when determining who's in and who's out. Essays, recommendations, extracurricular activities, talents and skills, and demographic factors all figure into the mix along with high school transcript and standardized test scores. Give all aspects of your application your utmost attention; admissions are very competitive.

THE SCHOOL SAYS "..."

From The Admissions Office

"Commitment to excellence, to diversity, to learning—these are the hallmarks of a Maryland education. As the state's flagship campus and one of the nation's leading public universities, Maryland offers students and faculty the opportunity to come together to explore and create knowledge, to debate and discover our similarities and our differences, and to serve as a model of intellectual and cultural excellence for the state and the nation's capital. With leading programs in engineering, business, journalism, architecture, and the sciences, the university offers an outstanding educational value."

SELECTIVITY

Admissions Rating	96
# of applicants	28,054
% of applicants accepted	39
% of acceptees attending	36

FRESHMAN PROFILE

Range SAT Critical Reading	570–680
Range SAT Math	600–700
Minimum paper TOEFL	575
Average HS GPA	3.92
% graduated top 10% of class	73
% graduated top 25% of class	91
% graduated top 50% of class	99

DEADLINES

Early action	
Deadline	12/1
Notification	2/15
Regular	
Priority	12/1
Deadline	1/20
Notification	4/1
Nonfall registration?	yes

APPLICANTS ALSO LOOK AT
AND RARELY PREFER
University of Maryland—Baltimore County

FINANCIAL FACTS

Financial Aid Rating	68
Annual tuition in-state	$8,005
Annual tution out-of-state	$23,076
Room and board	$5,402
Books and supplies	$1,025
% frosh rec. need-based scholarship or grant aid	25
% UG rec. need-based scholarship or grant aid	26
% frosh rec. non-need-based scholarship or grant aid	21
% UG rec. non-need-based scholarship or grant aid	14
% frosh rec. need-based self-help aid	23
% UG rec. need-based self-help aid	26
% frosh rec. athletic scholarships	1
% UG rec. athletic scholarships	1
% frosh rec. any financial aid	67.8
% UG rec. any financial aid	59.5
% UG borrow to pay for school	44
Average cumulative indebtedness	$20,091

UNIVERSITY OF MASSACHUSETTS—AMHERST

UNIVERSITY ADMISSIONS CENTER, AMHERST, MA 01003-9291 • ADMISSIONS: 413-545-0222 • FAX: 413-545-4312

CAMPUS LIFE

Quality of Life Rating	**62**
Fire Safety Rating	**72**
Green Rating	**84**
Type of school	public
Environment	town

STUDENTS

Total undergrad enrollment	19,964
% male/female	50/50
% from out of state	19
% live on campus	63
% in (# of) fraternities	5 (21)
% in (# of) sororities	6 (15)
% African American	5
% Asian	8
% Caucasian	72
% Hispanic	4
% international	1
# of countries represented	44

SURVEY SAYS . . .

Lots of liberal students
Class discussions are rare
Great library
Students aren't religious
Great off-campus food
Low cost of living
Student publications are popular

ACADEMICS

Academic Rating	**70**
Calendar	semester
Student/faculty ratio	18:1
Profs interesting rating	63
Profs accessible rating	62
Most common reg class size	20–29 students
Most common lab size	20–29 students

MOST POPULAR MAJORS

communication studies/speech
communication and rhetoric
hospitality administration/
management
psychology

STUDENTS SAY ". . ."

Academics

It's all about "finding out where you fit in" at the University of Massachusetts Amherst, where students say the experience is "all what you make of it. If you want to party, there is one available to you almost every night," but a pre-law student warns that "academics are challenging," and other students agree, especially in the engineering program, the hard sciences, the sports management program ("one of the oldest and best in the country"), and at the Isenberg School of Management. As at many big schools, "It is easy to not go to class because they are so large, although many teachers now use the PRS [a handheld wireless interactive remote unit], which quizzes you and is a method of [taking] attendance during each class." You will also have the opportunity to get a degree with an "individual concentration" that allows you to design your own interdisciplinary majors. Students can also enroll—at no extra charge—in courses at Amherst, Hampshire, Mount Holyoke, and Smith colleges through the Five College Consortium. The consortium includes open library borrowing, a meal exchange, and a free bus system connecting the campuses. Unlike many major research institutions, UMass Amherst has a surprising number of professors who "show a passion for teaching. I have yet to see a professor who just teaches for money," a sports management major reports. By all accounts, "More than half of the professors are awesome." Students agree that "UMass Amherst has countless opportunities for one to get involved and improve his or her leadership and responsibilities."

Life

"There is so much to do on campus here that you rarely have to leave the school to find something," students report, pointing out that, in addition to attending one of the school's ubiquitous sporting events, "You can go ice skating on campus, go to a play, see bands play, see a movie, etc." Are you sitting down? "Most of these things are also free of charge, or available for a reduced fee." When the weather permits, "Numerous people are outside doing some sort of activity, whether it's playing catch, playing a sport with a bunch of people, or just laying out in the sun. In the Southwest Residential area, there is a horseshoe that people call Southwest Beach because on nice days it is packed with hundreds of people." If you're into socializing, "There is something going on every night of the week somewhere." One student says, "Drinking is big here but not totally out of control like some say." And another student assures us that, "It is more than possible to stay in on a Friday night, do your laundry, and watch a movie with friends. Parties are available, but not required." More students seem to want to live on campus now, lured perhaps by the new apartment style residence halls and dining services. Hometown Amherst provides "great restaurants and shows." Northampton and Holyoke, both close by, are "good places to go shopping."

Student Body

"There is no such thing as a typical student at UMass Amherst." An undergraduate population of over 20,000 makes that impossible; however, students do seem to fall into a few readily identified groups. There are "plenty of students who are here strictly for academics," people who are here for the party scene," and a "lot of people who came here for academics but fell into the party scene." Most learn to balance fun and work; those who don't exit long before graduation. Students also "tend to fit the mold of their residence," undergrads tell us. one student writes, "Southwest houses students of mainstream culture. Students there can be seen wearing everything from UMass—Amherst sweats to couture. Students in Central (especially Upper Central) tend to be the 'hippie' or scene type kid[s]. Northeast houses...the more reserved types.reserved types. Orchard Hill typically houses the more quiet types as well."

FINANCIAL AID: 413-545-0801 • E-MAIL: MAIL@ADMISSIONS.UMASS.EDU • WEBSITE: WWW.UMASS.EDU

THE PRINCETON REVIEW SAYS

Admissions

Very important factors considered include: Academic GPA, rigor of secondary school record, *Important factors considered include:* Class rank, standardized test scores. *Other factors considered include:* Application essay, recommendation(s), character/personal qualities, extracurricular activities, first generation, geographical residence, level of applicant's interest, racial/ethnic status, state residency, talent/ability, volunteer work, work experience SAT or ACT required; ACT with Writing component recommended. TOEFL required of all international applicants. High school diploma is required and GED is accepted. *Academic units required:* 4 English, 3 mathematics, 3 science, (2 science labs), 2 foreign language, 2 social studies, 2 academic electives.

Financial Aid

Students should submit: FAFSA. The Princeton Review suggests that all financial aid forms be submitted as soon as possible after 1/1. *Need-based scholarships/grants offered:* Federal Pell, SEOG, state scholarships/grants, private scholarships, the school's own gift aid. *Loan aid offered:* Direct Subsidized Stafford, Direct Unsubsidized Stafford, Direct PLUS, Federal Perkins, state loans Applicants will be notified of awards on a rolling basis beginning 3/1. Federal Work-Study Program available. Institutional employment available.

The Inside Word

University of Massachusetts Amherst requires applicants to identify a first-choice and a second-choice major; admissions standards are tougher in the school's most prestigious programs (such as engineering, business, communications and journalism, economics, computer science, and sports management). It is possible to be admitted for your second-choice major but not your first; it is also possible to be admitted as an "undeclared" student if you fail to gain admission via your chosen majors. You can transfer into either major later, although doing so will require you to excel in your freshman and sophomore classes.

THE SCHOOL SAYS "..."

From The Admissions Office

"The University of Massachusetts—Amherst is the largest public university in New England, offering its students an almost limitless variety of academic programs and activities. Over 85 majors are offered, including a unique program called Bachelor's Degree with Individual Concentration (BDIC) in which students create their own program of study. (If you are a legal resident of Connecticut, Maine, New Hampshire, Rhode Island or Vermont, and the major you want at UMass—Amherst is not available at your public college, you may qualify for reduced tuition through the New England Regional Student Program.)The outstanding full-time faculty of over 1,100 is the best in their fields and they take teaching seriously. Students can take courses through the honors program and sample classes at nearby Amherst, Hampshire, Mount Holyoke, and Smith Colleges at no extra charge. First-year students participate in the Residential First-Year Year Experience with opportunities to explore every possible interest through residential life. The extensive library system is the largest at any public institution in the Northeast. The Center for Student Development brings together more than 200 clubs and organizations, fraternities and sororities, multicultural and religious centers. The campus completes in NCAA Division I sports for men and women, with teams winning national recognition. Award-winning student-operated businesses, the largest college daily newspaper in the region, and an active student government provide hands-on experience. About 5,000 students a year participate in the intramural sports program. The picturesque New England Town of Amherst offers shopping and dining, and the ski slopes of western Massachusetts and southern Vermont are close by. SAT or ACT scores are required for admission to the university. The school takes a holistic view of the student's application package and considers these scores as only part of the evaluation criteria. Additionally, any Advanced Placement, Honors, and SAT Subject Test scores are considered when reviewing each applicant. Increased applications in recent years have made admission more selective. "

SELECTIVITY

Admissions Rating	86
# of applicants	28,931
% of applicants accepted	64
% of acceptees attending	22
# accepting a place on wait list	113
% admitted from wait list	81

FRESHMAN PROFILE

Range SAT Critical Reading	510–620
Range SAT Math	540–640
Minimum paper TOEFL	550
Minimum computer TOEFL	213
Average HS GPA	3.56
% graduated top 10% of class	25
% graduated top 25% of class	65
% graduated top 50% of class	96

DEADLINES

Early action	
Deadline	11/1
Notification	12/15
Regular	
Deadline	1/15
Notification	March–mid-April
Nonfall registration?	yes

APPLICANTS ALSO LOOK AT
AND OFTEN PREFER
Boston College, Boston University
Tufts University

AND SOMETIMES PREFER
Northeastern University
University of Connecticut
Syracuse University

AND RARELY PREFER
University of Hartford, University of New Hampshire, University of Rhode Island

FINANCIAL FACTS

Financial Aid Rating	72
Annual tuition in-state	$11,732
Annual tuition out-of-state	$23,229
Room and board	$8,276
Books and supplies	$1,000
% frosh rec. need-based scholarship or grant aid	44
% UG rec. need-based scholarship or grant aid	38
% frosh rec. non-need-based scholarship or grant aid	4
% UG rec. non-need-based scholarship or grant aid	2
% frosh rec. need-based self-help aid	44
% UG rec. need-based self-help aid	42
% frosh rec. athletic scholarships	2
% UG rec. athletic scholarships	1
% frosh rec. any financial aid	84
% UG rec. any financial aid	82
% UG borrow to pay for school	66
Average cumulative indebtedness	$21,614

UNIVERSITY OF MIAMI

OFFICE OF ADMISSION, PO BOX 248025, CORAL GABLES, FL 33124-4616 • ADMISSIONS: 305-284-4323 • FAX: 305-284-2507

CAMPUS LIFE
Quality of Life Rating	93
Fire Safety Rating	83
Green Rating	90
Type of school	private
Environment	town

STUDENTS
Total undergrad enrollment	10,008
% male/female	47/53
% from out of state	50
% live on campus	44
% in (# of) fraternities	14 (15)
% in (# of) sororities	14 (13)
% African American	8
% Asian	5
% Caucasian	46
% Hispanic	23
% international	7

SURVEY SAYS . . .
thletic facilities are great
Diverse student types on campus
Low cost of living
(Almost) no one smokes

ACADEMICS
Academic Rating	83
Calendar	semester
Student/faculty ratio	11:1
Profs interesting rating	75
Profs accessible rating	81
Most common reg class size	10–19 students
Most common lab size	10–19 students

STUDENTS SAY ". . ."

Academics

"A force, much like a real hurricane, to be reckoned with academically and in athletics," the "heavily sports-oriented" University of Miami offers "academic excellence along with cultural diversity." the reputation is a result of the efforts of the university's president, Donna Shalala, whose "forward thinking" has "transformed this university into an academic leader." In addition to its "top-notch" nursing program, the school's other notable programs include business and communications. "Coursework is often challenging, even for those students who got straight A's in high school." Class size ranges from "200+ person class-es" to "small interactive classes," and students are generally pleased with their professors who "are always available and very willing to talk to students." One student says, "The majority of the teachers were good, and those that weren't made up for it with sheer enthusiasm." The school's administration is both "very visible and approachable" and "is working hard to improve the quality of the university through facility improvements and additions, as well as program restructuring and evaluation." "It is not uncommon to see multiple administra-tors showing their support at school events and club meetings." During final exams, "faculty, trustees, and student government executives served free break-fast to students from 9 p.m. [to] past midnight" and also "strung up 30-some hammocks between the palm trees behind the library for [students] to study or sleep." One satisfied student sums up, "Students here are respected, and seem-ingly no one rests until every pupil is academically satiated."

Life

Depending on which student you talk to, the University of Miami "can be the hottest party spot" or "the ideal place to gain experience in almost any field of work or research while living in a beautiful place with a culture mix that is truly unique." One international student raves that "the school's rich culture and proud spirit acted like a sponge and soaked me into the Canes culture." Students compare their "very mellow" campus to "a country club" that is "secluded from the poverty and sham politics of Miami, where students live in a party-life bubble, protected from the real world." The "vibrant student life" includes "going out clubbing" as well as "following the football team" and "tailgating." Students also agree that "sorority/fraternity life is also a major part of life." "Every day, there are dozens of programs (cultural, social, physi-cal, or academic) to participate in," and students can get involved in "theater productions, musical performances, cultural events, student shows and show-cases, on-campus movie showings, service events, leadership opportunities, and seminars." For off-campus fun, "the beach is a popular weekend destina-tion," and "people either go to Coconut Grove or South Beach."

Student Body

At first glance, "it can appear that the University of Miami admits only super-thin or super-buff students looking for the perfect spot for a tan while cruising in their Mercedes down the ritzy streets of Coral Gables." University of Miami students "all love warm weather and not wearing an excess amount of cloth-ing" and "develop an urge to wear shades at one point or another." However, "the students at Miami are not all about tanning and partying; [they] are a com-petitive bunch." "The typical Miami student is probably from either Miami-Dade/Broward Counties or the Northeast" and is "into athletics." Students seem to fall into three categories: "those who go to South Beach, those who just have fun and party, and those who choose to remain for the most part academ-ic." "While "students are not politically active," "most students perform com-munity service." The student body "is very diverse," with students from more than "90 countries," and "international students have formed various cultural organizations that reach out to their respective cultures." Although "it can seem that people are a little 'clique-y' when it comes to their culture," University of Miami students seem "widely accepting of many cultural groups" and manage to "all live together symbiotically."

FINANCIAL AID: 305-284-5212 • WEBSITE: WWW.MIAMI.EDU/ADMISSIONS

THE PRINCETON REVIEW SAYS

Admissions

Very important factors considered include: Class rank, application essay, academic GPA, recommendation(s), rigor of secondary school record, standardized test scores, extracurricular activities, *Important factors considered include:* volunteer work. *Other factors considered include:* alumni/ae relation, character/personal qualities, first generation, geographical residence, racial/ethnic status, talent/ability, work experience. SAT or ACT required; TOEFL required of all international applicants. High school diploma is required and GED is accepted. *Academic units recommended:* 4 English, 4 mathematics, 3 science, (2 science labs), 2 foreign language, 3 social studies, 2 history, 1 visual/performing arts, 1 computer science.

Financial Aid

Students should submit: FAFSA. The Princeton Review suggests that all financial aid forms be submitted as soon as possible after 1/1. *Need-based scholarships/grants offered:* Federal Pell, SEOG, state scholarships/grants, private scholarships, the school's own gift aid, Federal Nursing Scholarships, Federal Academic Competitiveness Grant Federal SMART Grant. *Loan aid offered:* FFEL Subsidized Stafford, FFEL Unsubsidized Stafford, FFEL PLUS, Federal Perkins, Federal Nursing, college/university loans from institutional funds, Private Alternative Education Loans. Applicants will be notified of awards on a rolling basis beginning 3/1. Federal Work-Study Program available. Institutional employment available. Off-campus job opportunities are excellent.

The Inside Word

The University of Miami's campaign to overcome its reputation as a "football school" is an unqualified success. Each recent academic year has seen an increase in applications, and UM's selectivity is on the rise. The school partially attributes this accomplishment to its alumni and gladly repays them by giving legacies a boost during the admissions process. Of course, having a Cane for a parent isn't enough; students must demonstrate achievement in arduous classes, intellectual promise, and strong moral character.

THE SCHOOL SAYS "..."

From The Admissions Office

"The University of Miami in Coral Gables, is an innovative private research university in a location unlike any other in the country. Located 10 miles from the vibrant international city of Miami, UM's more than 9,000 undergraduates come from every state and 114 nations, allowing people of many cultures to challenge and champion each other. Faculty work closely with students, and internships and research experiences are integral to academic life. Students work hard as community volunteers and exert leadership in a range of lively clubs and organizations, including the student-managed TV station, radio station, and newspaper.

"The University of Miami will accept the critical reading and math scores from the SAT, as well as the ACT with or without the Writing component."

SELECTIVITY
Admissions Rating	96
# of applicants	21,773
% of applicants accepted	39
% of acceptees attending	24
# of early decision applicants	1,210
% accepted early decision	22

FRESHMAN PROFILE
Range SAT Critical Reading	580–680
Range SAT Math	610–710
Range SAT Writing	580–670
Range ACT Composite	27–31
Minimum paper TOEFL	550
Minimum computer TOEFL	213
Minimum web-based TOEFL	80
Average HS GPA	4.2
% graduated top 10% of class	66
% graduated top 25% of class	90
% graduated top 50% of class	97

DEADLINES
Early Decision	
Deadline	11/1
Notification	12/15
Early action	
Deadline	11/1
Notification	2/1
Regular	
Deadline	5/1
Notification	4/15
Nonfall registration?	yes

APPLICANTS ALSO LOOK AT AND SOMETIMES PREFER
Vanderbilt University, New York University
University of Southern California
Boston University

AND RARELY PREFER
Florida State University

FINANCIAL FACTS
Financial Aid Rating	81
Annual tution	$35,540
Room and board	$10,800
Required fees	$648
% frosh rec. need-based scholarship or grant aid	45
% UG rec. need-based scholarship or grant aid	45
% frosh rec. non-need-based scholarship or grant aid	15
% UG rec. non-need-based scholarship or grant aid	13
% frosh rec. need-based self-help aid	36
% UG rec. need-based self-help aid	39
% frosh rec. athletic scholarships	2
% UG rec. athletic scholarships	3
% UG borrow to pay for school	56
Average cumulative indebtedness	$24,500

UNIVERSITY OF MICHIGAN—ANN ARBOR

1220 STUDENT ACTIVITIES BUILDING, ANN ARBOR, MI 48109-1316 • ADMISSIONS: 734-764-7433 • FAX: 734-936-0740

CAMPUS LIFE
Quality of Life Rating	85
Fire Safety Rating	87
Green Rating	89
Type of school	public
Environment	city

STUDENTS
Total undergrad enrollment	25,865
% male/female	50/50
% from out of state	36
% live on campus	37
% in (# of) fraternities	17 (37)
% in (# of) sororities	17 (22)
% African American	6
% Asian	13
% Caucasian	69
% Hispanic	5
% Native American	1
% international	4
# of countries represented	120

SURVEY SAYS . . .
Students love Ann Arbor, MI
Great off-campus food
Everyone loves the Wolverines
Student publications are popular
Political activism is popular

ACADEMICS
Academic Rating	83
Calendar	semester
Student/faculty ratio	15:1
Profs interesting rating	65
Profs accessible rating	71
% classes taught by TAs	39
Most common reg class size	10–19 students
Most common lab size	20–29 students

MOST POPULAR MAJORS
business administration and
management
mechanical engineering
psychology

STUDENTS SAY "..."

Academics

Among the many allures of the University of Michigan—Ann Arbor is that the school offers "a great environment both academically and socially." One student explains, "It has the social, fun atmosphere of any Big Ten university, but most people are still incredibly focused on their studies. It's great to be at a place where there is always something to do, but your friends completely understand when you have to stay in and get work done." With "an amazing honors program," a "wide range of travel-abroad opportunities," and "research strength" all available "at a low cost," it's no wonder students tell us that UM "provides every kind of opportunity at all times to all people." Academically, Michigan "is very competitive, and the professors have high academic standards for all the students." In fact, some here insist that "Michigan is as good as Ivy League schools in many disciplines." Standout offerings include business ("We have access to some of the brightest leaders" in the business world, students report), a "great engineering program," and "a good undergraduate program for medical school preparation." Those seeking add-on academic experiences here will find "a vast amount of resources. Internships, career opportunities, tutoring, community service projects, a plethora of student organizations, and a wealth of other resources" are all available, but "you need to make the first move" because no one "will seek you out."

Life

Michigan is a huge university, meaning that students have endless extracurricular options here. One explains: "If you seek it out, you can find organizations for ANY interest. There are always people out there who share your interests. That's part of the benefit of 40,000+ students!" There is a robust party scene. Students tell us that "most students go to house parties [or] hit the bars." There's also a vigorous social scene for the non-drinking crowd, with "great programs like UMix…phenomenal cultural opportunities in Ann Arbor especially music and movies," and "the hugely popular football Saturdays. The sense of school spirit here is impressive." Michigan students tend to be both academically serious and socially outgoing, which "is great because you can have a stimulating conversation with someone one day, and, the next day, be watching a silly movie or playing video games with this person."

Student Body

The Michigan student body "is hugely diverse," which "is one of the things Michigan prides itself on." "If you participate in extracurricular activities and make an effort to get to know other students in class and elsewhere, you'll definitely end up with a pretty diverse group of friends," undergrads assure us. Although varied, students tend to be similar in that they "are social but very academically driven." A number of students "are on the cutting edge of both research and progressive thinking," and there is a decided liberal tilt to campus politics. Even so, there's a place for everyone here, because "there are hundreds of mini-communities within the campus, made of everything from service fraternities to political organizations to dance groups. If you have an interest, you can find a group of people who enjoy the same thing."

FINANCIAL AID: 734-763-6600 • WEBSITE: WWW.ADMISSIONS.UMICH.EDU, WWW.FINAID.UMICH.EDU

THE PRINCETON REVIEW SAYS

Admissions

Very important factors considered include: rigor of secondary school record, *Important factors considered include:* Application essay, academic GPA, recommendation(s), standardized test scores, character/personal qualities, first generation. *Other factors considered include:* Class rank, alumni/ae relation, extracurricular activities, geographical residence, level of applicant's interest, state residency, talent/ability, volunteer work, work experience. SAT or ACT required; ACT with Writing component required. TOEFL required of all international applicants. High school diploma is required and GED is accepted. *Academic units required:* 4 English, 3 mathematics, 3 science, (1 science labs), 2 foreign language, 3 social studies, 1 academic electives. *Academic units recommended:* 4 English, 4 mathematics, 4 science, (1 science labs), 4 foreign language, 3 social studies, 2 history, 2 visual/performing arts, 1 computer science, 1 academic electives.

Financial Aid

Students should submit: FAFSA, CSS/Financial Aid PROFILE Regular filing deadline is 5/29. The Princeton Review suggests that all financial aid forms be submitted as soon as possible after 1/1. *Need-based scholarships/grants offered:* Federal Pell, SEOG, state scholarships/grants, private scholarships, the school's own gift aid, Academic Competitive Grant (ACG); National SMART. *Loan aid offered:* Direct Subsidized Stafford, Direct Unsubsidized Stafford, Direct PLUS, Federal Perkins, Federal Nursing, college/university loans from institutional funds, Health Professional student loans. Applicants will be notified of awards on a rolling basis beginning 3/14. Federal Work-Study Program available. Institutional employment available. Off-campus job opportunities are excellent.

The Inside Word

Michigan admissions are extremely competitive. Just to give you an idea of how competitive: 28 percent of the 2008 incoming freshman class graduated in the top one percent of their high school class. The volume of applications—Michigan received nearly 30,000 applications for the aforementioned class—means the admissions office must rely heavily on numbers to make its decision, so do what you can to get those test scores and GPAs as high as you can. Michigan admits on a rolling basis, a process that favors those who apply early.

THE SCHOOL SAYS "..."

From The Admissions Office

"Michigan is a place of incredible possibility. Students shape that possibility according to their diverse interests, goals, energy, and initiative. Undergraduate education is in the academic spotlight at Michigan, offering more than 220 fields of study in 12 schools and colleges; more than 150 first-year seminars with 20 or fewer students taught by senior faculty; composition classes of 20 or fewer students; more than 1,200 first- and second-year students in undergraduate research partnerships with faculty; and numerous service learning programs linking academics with volunteerism. Some introductory courses have large lectures, but these are combined with labs or small group discussions where students get plenty of individualized attention. A Michigan degree is one of distinction and promise; graduates are successful in medical, law, and graduate schools all over the nation and world. A year after graduation, more than 95 percent of UM alumni report that they are in the "next step" of their career—whether that is graduate or professional school, working, or volunteering."

SELECTIVITY
Admissions Rating	99
# of applicants	29,105
% of applicants accepted	41
% of acceptees attending	47

FRESHMAN PROFILE
Range SAT Critical Reading	610–720
Range SAT Math	660–760
Range SAT Writing	610–720
Range ACT Composite	28–32
Minimum paper TOEFL	570
Minimum computer TOEFL	230
Minimum web-based TOEFL	88
Minimum IELTS	6.5
Average HS GPA	3.75
% graduated top 10% of class	94
% graduated top 25% of class	99
% graduated top 50% of class	100

DEADLINES
Early action	
Deadline	11/1
Notification	12/24
Regular	
Deadline	2/1
Notification	rolling
Nonfall registration?	yes

APPLICANTS ALSO LOOK AT
AND OFTEN PREFER
Michigan State University
University of Illinois at Urbana-Champaign
Northwestern University

AND SOMETIMES PREFER
Washington University in St. Louis
New York University
Cornell University

AND RARELY PREFER
University of Wisconsin—Madison
University of California—Berkeley

FINANCIAL FACTS
Financial Aid Rating	91
Annual in-state tuition	$11,549
Annual out-of-state tuition	$34,041
Room and board	$8,590
Required fees	$189
Books and supplies	$1,048
% frosh rec. need-based scholarship or grant aid	24
% UG rec. need-based scholarship or grant aid	24
% frosh rec. non-need-based scholarship or grant aid	70
% UG rec. non-need-based scholarship or grant aid	53
% frosh rec. need-based self-help aid	40
% UG rec. need-based self-help aid	46
% frosh rec. athletic scholarships	2
% UG rec. athletic scholarships	2
% UG borrow to pay for school	46
Average cumulative indebtedness	$25,586

UNIVERSITY OF MINNESOTA—TWIN CITIES

240 WILLIAMSON HALL, 231 PILLSBURY DRIVE SOUTHEAST, MINNEAPOLIS, MN 55455-0213 • ADMISSIONS: 612-625-2008

CAMPUS LIFE

Quality of Life Rating	**81**
Fire Safety Rating	**60***
Green Rating	**91**
Type of school	public
Environment	metropolis

STUDENTS

Total undergrad enrollment	28,505
% male/female	47/53
% from out of state	26
% live on campus	22
% in (# of) fraternities	NR (22)
% in (# of) sororities	NR (12)
% African American	5
% Asian	10
% Caucasian	76
% Hispanic	2
% Native American	1
% international	3

SURVEY SAYS . . .

Students love Minneapolis, MN
Great off-campus food
Student publications are popular

ACADEMICS

Academic Rating	**73**
Calendar	semester
Student/faculty ratio	19:1
Profs interesting rating	70
Profs accessible rating	69
Most common reg class size	10–19 students
Most common lab size	10–19 students

MOST POPULAR MAJORS
biology/biological sciences
journalism
psychology

STUDENTS SAY ". . ."

Academics

The University of Minnesota is an "insanely huge" "research institution" "in the heart of" the Twin Cities. You'll find a wealth of majors here. Business is "superb." Engineering is strong across the board. The U is also "a great place to study an obscure language" or virtually anything else you can imagine. There are more than 300 opportunities to work and study abroad. Local internships "and hands-on opportunities" are also ample. "The professors run the whole gamut." "There are some amazing ones and some really terrible ones," says a civil engineering major. Some faculty members are "brilliant" and "inspired people" who "enjoy teaching the material and getting to know the students personally." Other professors "are knowledgeable but not always great at conveying the concepts." "There are a few who can really be GPA wreckers," too. Lower-level classes can be full of "massive crowds of students." though freshman seminars have 15 to 20 students. The teaching assistants who "do the dirty work" are frequently "from foreign countries" and "have really thick accents," especially in the hard sciences. "As your progress into upper-division course, the lectures rarely eclipse 100," though, and you have more interaction with real professors. "The administration really seems to care about the students" and "the U is run very well for a university of its size." Also, advising can be "beyond terrible."

Life

The "beautiful," "very environmentally friendly" campus here is "spread over two cities and a river." "Frigid," "crazy winters" are perennial. "By January, all you can see of students is their eyes," observes a sophomore. "The rest of them are wrapped in coats, hats, and scarves." "The snow is great for outdoor fun like sledding and ice skating" but "don't come here if you can't handle the cold." Socially, "the U has everything, plain and simple." You can have a "totally different experience than someone else." "There's a group for just about every interest," and "there is always something to do, even on a random Tuesday night." The campus provides a variety of events and "always has something going on during the weekends." "Hockey games are always great" and sports are a "big thing." "Partying is very popular but there are also a lot of people who don't" participate. If you want to imbibe, though, "keggers," house parties, and frat blowouts are frequent. There's also quite a bit happening off campus. According to students here, "Minneapolis is one of the greatest places in the country." "The music scene is unreal." "Great art" and "gorgeous parks" abound. "Shopping at the Mall of America" is another favorite pastime. In some areas, "it is scary walking around at night," but the neighborhoods near campus are generally "very young and energetic" and public transportation is "readily available and cheap."

Student Body

"Students are generally from the Midwest somewhere." More often than not, they are "right out of suburbia" or from "small to medium-sized towns" in "Minnesota or Wisconsin." There are a lot of "tall," "blond," "pasty, white people" who "are 'Minnesota Nice.'" "The U of M is a human zoo," though. "It's a school that embraces diversity." "There are a lot of different ethnicities." Some people are "snooty." Others "grew up poor." Some are "bubbly." Some are "antisocial." Also, "there is a microcosm for just about every subculture imaginable." There are "the math nerds," the "frat boys," and "lots of hippies and artsy people." There's "a huge gay population." "Preppy, athletic, emo," and nontraditional students are also visible. Politically, "the conservatives add a good balance to the grand scheme of things," but the campus leans left. Some students are "very politically aware." "There always seems to be some group protesting or trying to convince me of something," notes one student. Not surprisingly, "there is a limited sense of community" at the U. "It is too easy to get lost in the mass of people here, wandering among so many faces without knowing one," laments a forlorn junior. Sooner or later, most everyone "is able to find their niche." After that, "most people stick to their cliques."

Fax: 612-626-1693 • Financial Aid: 612-624-1665 • Website: ADMISSIONS.TC.UMN.EDU

THE PRINCETON REVIEW SAYS

Admissions

Very important factors considered include: Class rank, academic GPA, rigor of secondary school record, standardized test scores. *Other factors considered include:* alumni/ae relation, character/personal qualities, extracurricular activities, first generation, geographical residence, racial/ethnic status, talent/ability, volunteer work, work experience. SAT or ACT required; ACT with Writing component required. TOEFL required of all international applicants. High school diploma is required and GED is accepted. *Academic units required:* 4 English, 3 mathematics, 3 science, 2 foreign language, 3 social studies, 1 visual or performing arts.

Financial Aid

Students should submit: FAFSA, institution's own financial aid form. The university of Minnesota has a priority deadline of March 1 by which they encourage students to submit their FAFSA. *Need-based scholarships/grants offered:* Federal Pell, SEOG, state scholarships/grants, private scholarships, the school's own gift aid, Federal Nursing Scholarships. *Loan aid offered:* Direct Subsidized Stafford, Direct Unsubsidized Stafford, Direct PLUS, Federal Perkins, Federal Nursing, state loans, college/university loans from institutional funds. Federal Work-Study Program available. Institutional employment available.

The Inside Word

Despite what looks to be a fairly choosy admissions rate, it's the sheer volume of applicants that creates a selective situation at Minnesota.

THE SCHOOL SAYS "..."

From The Admissions Office

"The University of Minnesota is one of the nation's top public research universities. That means your college experience will be enhanced by world-renowned faculty, state-of-the-art learning facilities, and an unprecedented variety of options (such as 140 majors). 83 percent of our classes have fewer than 50 students, and our caring advisers will help you find the courses and opportunities that are right for you and your goals.

"Hands-on courses, volunteer opportunities, internships, and undergraduate research are part of the U of M experience. You will find one of the nation's largest study abroad programs, with 300 opportunities in more than 60 countries. You will find historic architecture, and breathtaking views of the Minneapolis skyline right on campus. Just minutes from campus you can intern at Fortune 500 company, volunteer major hospital, head to a professional sporting event, jog around the beautiful chain of lakes, get inspired at one of our many museums, and much more! With a wealth of cultural, career, and recreational opportunities in the Twin Cities, there's no better place to earn your college degree!

"The University of Minnesota offers a fantastic education and prestigious degree at a competitive price. Residents of Minnesota benefit from in-state tuition. Minnesota residents may also qualify for the University of Minnesota Founders Free Tuition Program, which covers 100 percent of tuition and fees for eligible students.

"Residents of North Dakota, South Dakota, Wisconsin, or Manitoba qualify for special reciprocity tuition rates. Out-of-state students benefit from the lowest nonresident tuition in the Big 10. Last year, we awarded over $9 million in 4-year scholarship packages."

SELECTIVITY	
Admissions Rating	**89**
# of applicants	29,159
% of applicants accepted	53
% of acceptees attending	33

FRESHMAN PROFILE	
Range SAT Critical Reading	530–670
Range SAT Math	580–710
Range ACT Composite	24–29
Minimum paper TOEFL	550
Minimum computer TOEFL	213
% graduated top 10% of class	45
% graduated top 25% of class	83
% graduated top 50% of class	98

DEADLINES	
Regular	
Priority	12/15
Nonfall registration?	yes

FINANCIAL FACTS	
Financial Aid Rating	**81**
Annual tuition in-state	$10,090
Annual tuition out-of-state	$14,590
% frosh rec. need-based scholarship or grant aid	50
% UG rec. need-based scholarship or grant aid	46
% frosh rec. non-need-based scholarship or grant aid	17
% UG rec. non-need-based scholarship or grant aid	13
% frosh rec. need-based self-help aid	43
% UG rec. need-based self-help aid	44
% UG borrow to pay for school	64
Average cumulative indebtedness	$23,811

UNIVERSITY OF MISSISSIPPI

145 MARTINDALE, UNIVERSITY, MS 38677 • ADMISSIONS: 662-915-7226 • FAX: 662-915-5869

CAMPUS LIFE

Quality of Life Rating	82
Fire Safety Rating	60*
Green Rating	79
Type of school	public
Environment	village

STUDENTS

Total undergrad enrollment	12,609
% male/female	47/53
% from out of state	34
% from public high school	70
% live on campus	33
% in (# of) fraternities	32 (19)
% in (# of) sororities	34 (12)
% African American	13
% Asian	1
% Caucasian	80
% Hispanic	1
% international	1
# of countries represented	65

SURVEY SAYS . . .

Great off-campus food
Everyone loves the Ole Miss Rebels
Frats and sororities dominate social
scene
Student publications are popular
Lots of beer drinking
Hard liquor is popular

ACADEMICS

Academic Rating	74
Calendar	semester
Student/faculty ratio	18:1
Profs interesting rating	70
Profs accessible rating	72
Most common reg class size	10–19 students
Most common lab size	20–29 students

MOST POPULAR MAJORS
accounting
elementary education and teaching
marketing/marketing management

STUDENTS SAY ". . ."

Academics

The University of Mississippi (or "Ole Miss," as it is familiarly known) is an institution "steeped in rich traditions" that its students praise for having "great people, a beautiful campus, and a hospitable community." Familial connections and affection for the school's past (which includes graduating "numerous senators and representatives, among them Trent Lott, Thad Cochran, and Roger Wicker") draw many to Ole Miss, but that doesn't mean the school is content to rest on its laurels. On the contrary, in recent years the school has taken major strides toward "making itself one of America's great public universities." The 1997 establishment of the Croft Institute for International Studies, "recently ranked second best in the nation by the State Department in the areas of job placement," represents one such step. Another was the 1999 creation of the Lott Leadership Institute; together the two resources "provide unique and challenging fields of study that help distinguish Ole Miss academically." Solid programs in journalism, music, accounting, forensic chemistry, engineering, pharmacy, premedicine, and Southern studies help round out the academic picture. Those who can gain access to the Sally McDonnell Barkesdale Honors College should take advantage of the opportunity. The program "is so strongly supported by the administration and alumni that you can literally eat dinner with 14 other honor students and a visiting senator, and then the next day go talk with a visiting ambassador about opportunities for working with the State Department. Honors college students receive many perks, including the chance to go on a 'ventures' trip to a major city, paid for by the Honors College."

Life

Undergrads at Mississippi are generally a content lot. As one student happily exclaimed, "The school spirit and pride people have at Ole Miss is contagious!." Indeed, many undergrads view the university as, "a great Southern school with amazing traditions and great standards that knows how to have a good time." Popular traditions include pregaming in The Grove, "a social setting jam-packed with friends and families all bound by the same values of hospitality and friendship." An "extremely popular" Greek system is another tradition that hasn't lost any steam. For many undergrads, "most activities outside of class or studying are centered on Greek life," which includes not only "an enormous amount of drinking and partying," but also "being among the most involved and active people on campus." Hometown Oxford "may be small, but there is always something to do. Oxford has some of the best restaurants in the South. Also, Oxford gets great live music, poetry readings, and famous authors frequently. Lake Sardis is also nearby. Many people go boating on free days."

Student Body

Ole Miss is home to more than 12,000 undergraduates, a size that makes generalizations about the entire population difficult and necessarily imprecise. That said, students detect an undeniable presence of "students who are pretty wealthy and take pride in that." This group is personified by the "preppy girl or boy wearing expensive labels and going to school to follow in his or her mom or dad's footsteps. "Sums up one undergrad, "Ole Miss students are charming and very social; it is as if everyone has been raised attending cocktail parties and debutante balls forever. We are primarily conservative, white southerners who are unashamed of our Southern culture and heritage. Those who fit this mold love Ole Miss; [others] seem to view the Southern elitism as 'snobbery.'" This perceived snobbery may be at least a partial result of the fact that the school is "not very diverse."

FINANCIAL AID: 662-915-7175 • E-MAIL: ADMISSIONS@OLEMISS.EDU • WEBSITE: WWW.OLEMISS.EDU

THE PRINCETON REVIEW SAYS

Admissions

Very important factors considered include: Academic GPA, rigor of secondary school record, *Important factors considered include:* Class rank, standardized test scores. *Other factors considered include:* alumni/ae relation, state residency, talent/ability, TOEFL required of all international applicants. High school diploma is required and GED is accepted. *Academic units required:* 4 English, 3 mathematics, 3 science, (2 science labs), 1 foreign language, 1 social studies, 2 history, 1 academic electives. *Academic units recommended:* 4 mathematics, 4 science, 2 foreign language, 2 social studies.

Financial Aid

Students should submit: FAFSA. The Princeton Review suggests that all financial aid forms be submitted as soon as possible after 1/1. *Need-based scholarships/grants offered:* Federal Pell, SEOG, state scholarships/grants, private scholarships, the school's own gift aid. *Loan aid offered:* FFEL Subsidized Stafford, FFEL Unsubsidized Stafford, FFEL PLUS, Federal Perkins, college/university loans from institutional funds. Applicants will be notified of awards on a rolling basis beginning 4/1. Federal Work-Study Program available. Institutional employment available. Off-campus job opportunities are good.

The Inside Word

While Ole Miss offers students tremendous educational opportunities, the university's admissions policies are less than strenuous. Applicants who demonstrate moderate success in college prep curricula will most likely secure admittance.

THE SCHOOL SAYS "..."

From The Admissions Office

"The flagship university of the state, The University of Mississippi, widely known as Ole Miss, offers extraordinary opportunities through more than 100 areas of study, including programs such as the Sally McDonnell Barksdale Honors College and the Croft Institute for International Studies. UM students are the only public university students in the state who have the opportunity to be tapped by the nation's oldest and most prestigious honor society, Phi Beta Kappa. Strong academic programs and a rich and varied campus life have helped Ole Miss graduate 24 Rhodes Scholars, and 11 Truman Scholars. Since 1998 alone, UM has produced five Goldwater Scholars, a Marshall Scholar, and four Fulbright Scholars.

"The campus is diverse; 32 percent come from other states and countries and 13 percent are black American. Recent significant campus improvements include the $25 million Gertrude Ford Performing Arts Center and the privately funded Paris-Yates Chapel and Peddle Bell Tower. UM ranks 33rd in the nation among public universities for endowment per student. Ole Miss is home to 20 research centers, including the National Center for Justice and the Rule of Law, which provides training on investigating and prosecuting cybercrime; the William Winter Institute for Racial Reconciliation; and the National Center for Natural Products Research.

"The university is located in Oxford, consistently recognized as a great college town and as a center for writers and other artists. Like Ole Miss, Oxford is modest in size and large in the opportunities it provides residents, offering many of the advantages of a larger place in a friendly and open environment.

"Students applying will be allowed to take the SAT or the ACT but are not required to take the ACT Writing section. The university will not consider the writing section of either exam when evaluating students for admission, but certain specialty programs may request these scores."

SELECTIVITY

Admissions Rating	60*
# of applicants	7,946
% of applicants accepted	83
% of acceptees attending	37

FRESHMAN PROFILE

Range SAT Critical Reading	450–580
Range SAT Math	460–580
Range ACT Composite	20–26
Minimum paper TOEFL	550
Minimum computer TOEFL	213

DEADLINES

Regular	
Priority	6/15
Deadline	7/20
Notification	rolling
Nonfall registration?	yes

FINANCIAL FACTS

Financial Aid Rating	73
Annual tuition in-state	$5,180
Annual tuition ou-of state	$7,024
Room and board	$7,778
Books	$1,200
% frosh rec. need-based scholarship or grant aid	24
% UG rec. need-based scholarship or grant aid	26
% frosh rec. non-need-based scholarship or grant aid	26
% UG rec. non-need-based scholarship or grant aid	24
% frosh rec. need-based self-help aid	20
% UG rec. need-based self-help aid	28
% frosh rec. athletic scholarships	3
% UG rec. athletic scholarships	3
% frosh rec. any financial aid	69
% UG rec. any financial aid	72
% UG borrow to pay for school	41
Average cumulative indebtedness	$19,183

THE UNIVERSITY OF MONTANA—MISSOULA

101 LOMMASSON CENTER, MISSOULA, MT 59812 • ADMISSIONS: 406-243-6266 • FAX: 406-243-5711

CAMPUS LIFE

Quality of Life Rating	**83**
Fire Safety Rating	**79**
Green Rating	**96**
Type of school	public
Environment	city

STUDENTS

Total undergrad enrollment	12,196
% male/female	47/53
% from out of state	25
% from public high school	44
% live on campus	29
% in (# of) fraternities	6 (5)
% in (# of) sororities	6 (4)
% African American	1
% Asian	2
% Caucasian	83
% Hispanic	2
% Native American	4
% international	2
# of countries represented	65

SURVEY SAYS . . .

Athletic facilities are great
Students love Missoula, MT
Low cost of living
Student publications are popular
(Almost) no one smokes

ACADEMICS

Academic Rating	**71**
Calendar	semester
Student/faculty ratio	19:1
Profs interesting rating	71
Profs accessible rating	67
% classes taught by TAs	9
Most common reg class size	10–19 students
Most common lab size	10–29 students

MOST POPULAR MAJORS

business administration and
management
education
psychology

STUDENTS SAY " . . ."

Academics

Perhaps it stands to reason a school boasting "the best wildlife program in the country" would be found in Missoula, a "beautiful city" that is "five minutes from a designated wilderness area." While the wildlife biology program has garnered the most acclaim from students, the university is no one-trick pony. The school also boasts "great anthropology, biology, forestry, and nursing programs" taught by professors who are "nationally known." Raves one student, "I feel like I have [an] Ivy-League professor for Montana prices." Indeed, there is nearly unanimous agreement that "academics at UM are facilitated by great instructors" who would do "anything and everything for their students." Despite the university's size, "professors provide individual attention and provide numerous methods for contact (some including home phone numbers)." While TA's are spoken of in lesser terms, ranging from "[not] quite as good" to "horrible," the enthusiasm for the university's professors seems to carry the day. In addition to "great professors that care about your education," the university also has "tutors for many subjects that students may need help with" and "really encourages internships, studying abroad, and community service."

Life

"Life at UM combines a love for the Grizzlies with the outdoors." "And while "football is very popular, [it] does not overshadow academic progress." Indeed, Missoula seems to offer the best of many worlds, as "you can be in a good-sized city with 65,000 people and be completely isolated on a hiking trail looking across a beautiful landscape." For every activity, there is a season. "In the summer, hundreds of college kids grab tubes and float the river. In the winter, snowboarding is popular. Longboarding, cycling, and golf are also popular." And while the university clearly appeals to the outdoorsy types, one needn't fear a lack of choice. "There are a great number of social and academic clubs available for students to partake in" as well as "great art shows downtown on Friday nights, and the bar life is fun on weekends, too." While some feel that the administration could be "more strict with underage drinking," students who are "21 or older have a wide choice of small bars downtown to attend." And though "The University of Montana prides itself for having a beautiful campus," the most common complaint relates to the recent and disruptive "construction at every corner of campus."

Student Body

A certain level of diversity can be expected from students living in "a barnacle of liberalism and intellectual pursuits in the red state of Montana." While the school is sometimes described as being split into the two factions of "Montanans who love football and big trucks and out-of-state hippies who love the mountains," the truth is that "Missoula is a very accepting town. People don't have to fit in here; they simply are who they choose to be. The diversity makes for a more interesting experience." The student body is demographically dominated by students who are "Caucasian, middle-class, outdoor-orientated, environmentally conscious," some of whom "are very active in the volunteer community, school organizations, political campaigns and much more. They are very open to different views and pursue healthy interactions about opinions." On campus, "there seems to be very little pressure to act or dress a certain way," and students tend to appreciate "the libertarian 'Live and Let Live' mentality of many of the people in this area."

FINANCIAL AID: 406-243-5373 • E-MAIL: ADMISS@UMONTANA.EDU • WEBSITE: WWW.UMT.EDU

THE PRINCETON REVIEW SAYS

Admissions

Very important factors considered include: Class rank, academic GPA, rigor of secondary school record, standardized test scores, *Important factors considered include:* extracurricular activities, talent/ability. *Other factors considered include:* Application essay, recommendation(s), SAT or ACT required; ACT with Writing component recommended. TOEFL required of all international applicants. High school diploma is required and GED is accepted. *Academic units required:* 4 English, 3 mathematics, 2 science, (2 science labs), 3 social studies, 2 history. *Academic units recommended:* 2 foreign language, 2 visual/performing arts, 2 computer science, 2 Foreign language or vocational education.

Financial Aid

Students should submit: FAFSA UM Supplemental Information Sheet. The Princeton Review suggests that all financial aid forms be submitted as soon as possible after 1/1. Need-based scholarships/grants offered: Federal Pell, SEOG, state scholarships/grants, private scholarships, the school's own gift aid. *Loan aid offered:* FFEL Subsidized Stafford, FFEL Unsubsidized Stafford, FFEL PLUS, Federal Perkins. Applicants will be notified of awards on a rolling basis beginning 4/1. Federal Work-Study Program available. Institutional employment available. Off-campus job opportunities are good.

The Inside Word

The University of Montana operates on a rolling admissions basis, and the admissions game here is relatively straightforward. Decisions are based largely upon numbers. Applicants who enrolled in a college prep curriculum and earned average or better grades should be able to secure entry—especially if they apply earlier in the admissions cycle.

THE SCHOOL SAYS "..."

From The Admissions Office

"There's something special about this place. It's something different for each person. For some, it's the blend of academic quality and outdoor recreation. The University of Montana ranks fifth in the nation among public institutions for producing Rhodes scholars, and *Outside Magazine* lists Missoula in its 'Top Ten Amazing Places for Outdoor Recreation." For others, it's size—not too big, not too small. The University of Montana is a midsized university in the heart of the Rocky Mountains—accessible in both admission and tuition bills—that produces graduates considered among the best and brightest in the world. It is located in a community that could pass for a cozy college town or a bustling big city, depending on your point of view. There's a lot happening, but you won't get lost. People are friendly and diverse. They come from all over the world to study and learn and to live a good life. They come to a place to be inspired, a place where they feel comfortable yet challenged. Some never leave. Most never want to."

SELECTIVITY

Admissions Rating	83
# of applicants	4,631
% of applicants accepted	95
% of acceptees attending	47

FRESHMAN PROFILE

Range SAT Critical Reading	480–580
Range SAT Math	480–590
Range SAT Writing	450–580
Range ACT Composite	20–26
Minimum paper TOEFL	500
Minimum computer TOEFL	173
Average HS GPA	3.22
% graduated top 10% of class	17
% graduated top 25% of class	39
% graduated top 50% of class	71

DEADLINES

Regular	
Priority	3/1
Notification	rolling
Nonfall registration?	yes

FINANCIAL FACTS

Financial Aid Rating	68
Annual in-state tuition	$3,936
Annual out-of-state tuition	$15,576
Room and board	$6,258
Required fees	$1,441
Books and supplies	$850
% frosh rec. need-based scholarship or grant aid	35
% UG rec. need-based scholarship or grant aid	36
% frosh rec. non-need-based scholarship or grant aid	2
% UG rec. non-need-based scholarship or grant aid	1
% frosh rec. need-based self-help aid	46
% UG rec. need-based self-help aid	46
% frosh rec. athletic scholarships	2
% UG rec. athletic scholarships	2
% frosh rec. any financial aid	28
% UG rec. any financial aid	73
% UG borrow to pay for school	67
Average cumulative indebtedness	$17,527

UNIVERSITY OF NEBRASKA—LINCOLN

313 NORTH THIRTEENTH STREET, VAN BRUNT VISITORS CENTER, LINCOLN, NE 68588-0256 • ADMISSIONS: 402-472-2023

CAMPUS LIFE
Quality of Life Rating	**90**
Fire Safety Rating	**70**
Green Rating	**70**
Type of school	public
Environment	city

STUDENTS
Total undergrad enrollment	18,053
% male/female	54/46
% from out of state	17
% live on campus	41
% in (# of) fraternities	15 (27)
% in (# of) sororities	18 (18)
% African American	2
% Asian	3
% Caucasian	83
% Hispanic	3
% Native American	1
% international	3
# of countries represented	117

SURVEY SAYS . . .
Athletic facilities are great
Everyone loves the Cornhuskers
Intramural sports are popular
Student publications are popular

ACADEMICS
Academic Rating	**72**
Calendar	semester
Student/faculty ratio	19:1
Profs interesting rating	70
Profs accessible rating	75
% classes taught by TAs	18
Most common	
reg class size	20–29 students
Most common	
lab size	20–29 students

MOST POPULAR MAJORS
business administration and
management
finance
psychology

STUDENTS SAY ". . ."

Academics
"A big research university with a small school feel," the University of Nebraska—Lincoln provides "the best of both worlds...the benefits and amenities of a large school, but the community atmosphere of a smaller school." At UNL, "If you have questions about anything, it is so easy to find the answer." With "lots of amenities" and "ample opportunities for research and growth, both academically and socially in a college-town environment, second to none," UNL students enjoy "the strong sense of community" of this large state school, and say "it's amazingly personal for such a large amount of students." The community-like feel extends to how students regard those who run the school. Students say the administration is "very accessible and always friendly," and the members of the faculty "care enough to know more than your name." Students are also very positive when it comes to their professors. "Most of my professors are genuinely interested in the well-being of their students and want to aid in learning." In addition, when classes prove quite challenging, there are "plenty of available resources" at students' disposal. Students come to UNL for "the range of academic strengths" and to pursue a variety of majors including strong business and engineering programs. "Academically, the honors program is a real challenge—and it has the added benefit of small class sizes." It also "provides above-average classroom experience and education." At UNL, according to the students, "if you want to make an excellent educational experience for yourself, the opportunities here make it possible."

Life
Life in Lincoln is "all about the Husker spirit," because "nearly the entire student body...rallies around Husker football," and "being a Husker really is a big deal for most people at UNL." In addition to strong student of support of athletics, UNL boasts several fun intramural sports opportunities year-round, and students are eagerly awaiting the updates to the health and fitness centers, "luckily, plans are being made." "The amount and variety of organizations and activities that UNL has is outrageous," and such offerings go so far as to include ballroom dancing. And "the fact that each student is given the opportunity to create their own [organization] if they wish leaves no room for complaint." When asked for an area of improvement, students mentioned that UNL "can work on being conscious about the environment a bit more," because being located "in such an agriculturally-based state, there is very little awareness of environmental issues," but, students have already noted that they are "seeing more and more recycling bins around campus." UNL is a dry campus, and "off-campus house parties are popular" and "for those of age, there's a large bar-scene a few blocks from campus." The school's location in Nebraska's capital city is "convenient for almost anything you want to do." "Just a short walk away from city campus," students also venture into Lincoln since "the downtown scene has a lot to offer: theaters, bars, boutiques, coffee shops, restaurants, etc."

Student Body
At UNL, "students here like to socialize and better their communities," and most "students are friendly, willing to meet new friends and...help out even a perfect stranger." Though according to students, UNL's student body is comprised of "typical Midwestern people" and "a lot of white students that are relatively religious," "there are a lot of international students," and "differences are pretty well tolerated, even though, we aren't the most ethnically diverse student body." Students also mention a division between those "that are Greek and those that aren't." Also, "groups of students seem to be localized in dorms—the honors students in Neihardt, the international and music students at Selleck, the athletes at Harper-Schramm-Smith, the partiers at Abel, etc." The majority of students "try their best while still being able to have fun on the weekends."

FAX: 402-472-0670 • FINANCIAL AID: 402-472-2030 • E-MAIL: NUHUSKER@UNL.EDU • WEBSITE: WWW.UNL.EDU

THE PRINCETON REVIEW SAYS

Admissions

Very important factors considered include: Class rank, standardized test scores, *Important factors considered include:* rigor of secondary school record. *Other factors considered include:* Academic GPA, recommendation(s), first generation, talent/ability, SAT or ACT required; ACT recommended; TOEFL required of all international applicants. High school diploma is required and GED is accepted. *Academic units required:* 4 English, 4 mathematics, 3 science, (1 science labs), 2 foreign language, 3 social studies. *Academic units recommended:* 1 history.

Financial Aid

Students should submit: FAFSA. The Princeton Review suggests that all financial aid forms be submitted as soon as possible after 1/1. *Need-based scholarships/grants offered:* Federal Pell, SEOG, state scholarships/grants, private scholarships, the school's own gift aid. *Loan aid offered:* Direct Subsidized Stafford, Direct Unsubsidized Stafford, Direct PLUS, FFEL Subsidized Stafford, FFEL Unsubsidized Stafford, FFEL PLUS, Federal Perkins, college/university loans from institutional funds. Applicants will be notified of awards on a rolling basis beginning 4/1. Federal Work-Study Program available. Institutional employment available. Off-campus job opportunities are excellent.

The Inside Word

UNL offers 150 majors and 285 programs of study. All applications will be weighed on the combined strength of coursework, GPA's, and test scores. In order to gain direct acceptance to a specific school of study at UNL, interested applicants should take into account those school's specialized requirements as they may include additional high school coursework than what is required by UNL's general studies program.

THE SCHOOL SAYS " . . ."

From The Admissions Office

"The University of Nebraska—Lincoln offers one of today's most dynamic college experiences. The university has developed a national reputation for its substantial out-of-state scholarship program. As a result, more students nationwide are finding that the university, with its strength in undergraduate education, its tradition of student engagement, its lively campus atmosphere and its connection to downtown Lincoln, is uniquely suited to provide an enriching student experience. The university delivers on the promise of the friendliness of a private college with major university resources. It is no wonder alumni stay connected years after graduating and thousands of miles from campus.

"Established in 1869, the University of Nebraska—Lincoln has a rich tradition of excellence. Students join more than 200,000 alumni who have made their mark as industry leaders in business, engineering, the arts, journalism, education, and the sciences. A degree from Nebraska opens doors. UNL recently accepted positions with national companies like the Walt Disney Company, ESPN, Caterpillar, Ritz-Carlton, the Ellen Degeneres Show, Garmin, and Mitsubishi. Attending UN—Lincoln also means you will have built-in connections with 116 graduate degree programs, including those in University of Nebraska Law, Dental, and Medical Centers located either on campus or 50 miles east in Omaha.

"Freshmen students seeking admission should either be ranked in the upper one-half of their high school class, or have received an ACT composite score of 20 or higher or an SAT total score of 950 or higher (Critical Reading and Math only; Writing portion not considered)."

SELECTIVITY	
Admissions Rating	76
# of applicants	9,598
% of applicants accepted	62
% of acceptees attending	71

FRESHMAN PROFILE	
Range SAT Critical Reading	500–650
Range SAT Math	530–670
Range ACT Composite	22–28
Minimum paper TOEFL	525
Minimum computer TOEFL	193
% graduated top 10% of class	27
% graduated top 25% of class	53
% graduated top 50% of class	83

DEADLINES	
Regular	
Priority	1/15
Deadline	5/1
Notification	rolling
Nonfall registration?	yes

FINANCIAL FACTS	
Financial Aid Rating	78
Annual in-state tuition	$6,315
Annual out-of-state tuition	$17,028
Books and supplies	$950
% frosh rec. need-based scholarship or grant aid	36
% UG rec. need-based scholarship or grant aid	33
% frosh rec. non-need-based scholarship or grant aid	5
% UG rec. non-need-based scholarship or grant aid	3
% frosh rec. need-based self-help aid	30
% UG rec. need-based self-help aid	34
% frosh rec. athletic scholarships	2
% UG rec. athletic scholarships	3
% frosh rec. any financial aid	41
% UG rec. any financial aid	36
% UG borrow to pay for school	61
Average cumulative indebtedness	$19,075

UNIVERSITY OF NEW HAMPSHIRE

FOUR GARRISON AVENUE, DURHAM, NH 03824 • ADMISSIONS: 603-862-1360 • FAX: 603-862-0077

CAMPUS LIFE

Quality of Life Rating	**67**
Fire Safety Rating	**97**
Green Rating	**99**
Type of school	public
Environment	village

STUDENTS

Total undergrad enrollment	11,845
% male/female	44/56
% from out of state	43
% from public high school	78
% live on campus	57
% in (# of) fraternities	8 (10)
% in (# of) sororities	8 (7)
% African American	1
% Asian	2
% Caucasian	82
% Hispanic	2
% international	1
# of countries represented	51

SURVEY SAYS . . .

Great library
Athletic facilities are great
Diversity lacking on campus
Frats and sororities dominate social scene
Lots of beer drinking
Hard liquor is popular

ACADEMICS

Academic Rating	**72**
Calendar	semester
Student/faculty ratio	18:1
Profs interesting rating	62
Profs accessible rating	62
% classes taught by TAs	1
Most common reg class size	10–19 students
Most common lab size	20–29 students

MOST POPULAR MAJORS

business administration and management
communication, journalism, and related programs
psychology

STUDENTS SAY ". . ."

Academics

The benefits of going to a large, well-established state school, such as the University of New Hampshire, are exactly what one expects—its low in-state tuition, firmly established reputation, and place in the system allow it to offer "many resources to help students out in life." Located in tiny, beautiful Durham, the school "emphasizes research in every field, including non-science fields," and a lot of importance is placed "on the outdoors and the environment." The small town really fosters "lots of school spirit," and the laid-back denizens of UNH make it known that "having a good time" is a priority in their lives: "Weekends are for the Warriors."

Most professors "truly care" about the students' learning so that "you never feel like a number at the school but rather a respected student," and professors "will get down and dirty when it comes to experiencing what they're teaching first-hand." Though there are definitely complaints that some can be "subpar," a student "just needs to posses the initiative to go to their office hours" and they will get all the help they need. Some of the general education classes "are HUGE," and TA's can be difficult to understand, but for the most part, students report that they've had a "good experience" and that their academic careers has been "very successful." The Honors program is particularly challenging (in a very positive way) and offers "great seminar/inquiry classes that have about 15 students." Students universally pan the administration, claiming it "is a massive bureaucracy that gets little done," partially due to poor communication, or one student puts it that "the left hand has no idea what the right hand is doing." "The school is way more challenging than I thought it would be because the administration makes things harder than they need to be," says a sophomore.

Life

The school is just "15 minutes to the beach, one hour to the mountains, and one hour to Boston," making the world a Wildcat's oyster. Partying is big here, and the weekends are crazy; "Everyone goes out pretty much every Thursday, Friday, and Saturday night." The small number of bars in town "makes the age limit pretty well enforced." After a hard night out, "there are many late night convenience stores and food places to go to." In fact, it can be "difficult to find activities to do on the weekend that don't involve drinking," though UNH does a good job of bringing in "popular comedians, musicians, bands, political figures, etc.," and the school has tons of "amazing" a capella groups, so there is "almost always something to go see." Sports are also big here: "We love our hockey and football," says a student. Though there's a pretty big housing crunch, the oft-used athletic and recreational facilities here are both convenient and excellent, and since everything on this "beautiful" campus is only about 10 minutes away, "you walk pretty much everywhere," though public transportation and school-provided buses run often. Students do a lot of socializing over meals at the "eight cafes or in any of the three dining halls."

Student Body

This being New Hampshire, people are "very politically and socially aware." Students here are mostly middle-class and hail from New England (especially from New Hampshire, naturally), and a main point of contention among students is that there "is not a lot of ethnic/racial diversity," though the school is working on it. The size of UNH means that "even the most unique individual will find a group of friends," and even the most atypical students "fit in perfectly well." Most of these "laid-back" and "easy-to-get-along-with" Wildcats party, and it can be "hard to find one that doesn't." "EVERYONE skis or snowboards," and in the cold weather "Uggs and North Face fleece jackets abound."

FINANCIAL AID: 603-862-3600 • E-MAIL: ADMISSIONS@UNH.EDU • WEBSITE: WWW.UNH.EDU

THE PRINCETON REVIEW SAYS

Admissions

Very important factors considered include: Class rank, academic GPA, rigor of secondary school record. *Important factors considered include:* recommendation(s). *Other factors considered include:* Application essay, standardized test scores, alumni/ae relation, character/personal qualities, extracurricular activities, first generation, geographical residence, racial/ethnic status, state residency, talent/ability, volunteer work, work experience. SAT or ACT required; ACT with Writing component required. TOEFL required of all international applicants. High school diploma is required and GED is accepted. *Academic units required:* 4 English, 3 mathematics, 3 science, (2 science labs), 2 foreign language, 3 social studies. *Academic units recommended:* 4 English, 4 mathematics, 4 science, (3 science labs), 3 foreign language, 3 social studies, 1 academic electives.

Financial Aid

Students should submit: FAFSA Regular filing deadline is 3/1. The Princeton Review suggests that all financial aid forms be submitted as soon as possible after 1/1. *Need-based scholarships/grants offered:* Federal Pell, SEOG, state scholarships/grants, private scholarships, the school's own gift aid, Veterans Educational Benefits. *Loan aid offered:* FFEL Subsidized Stafford, FFEL Unsubsidized Stafford, FFEL PLUS, Federal Perkins, college/university loans from institutional funds. Applicants will be notified of awards on a rolling basis beginning 3/1. Federal Work-Study Program available. Institutional employment available. Off-campus job opportunities are excellent.

The Inside Word

New Hampshire's emphasis on academic accomplishment in the admissions process makes it clear that the admissions committee is looking for students who have taken high school seriously. Standardized tests take as much of a backseat here as is possible at a large, public university.

THE SCHOOL SAYS "..."

From The Admissions Office

"The University of New Hampshire is an institution best defined by the students who take advantage of its opportunities. Enrolled students who are willing to engage in a high-quality academic community in some meaningful way, who have a genuine interest in discovering or developing new ideas, and who believe in each person's obligation to improve the community they live in typify the most successful students at UNH. Undergraduate students practice these three basic values in a variety of ways: by undertaking their own, independent research projects; by collaborating in faculty research; and by participating in study abroad, residential communities, community service, and other cultural programs.

"University of New Hampshire will require all high school graduates to submit results from the new SAT or the ACT (with the Writing component). The Writing portions will not be used for admissions decisions during the first 2–3 admissions cycles. Students graduating from high school prior to 2006 can submit results from the old SAT or ACT. The UNH admissions process does not require SAT Subject tests."

SELECTIVITY

Admissions Rating	83
# of applicants	16,246
% of applicants accepted	65
% of acceptees attending	25

FRESHMAN PROFILE

Range SAT Critical Reading	510–610
Range SAT Math	520–620
Minimum paper TOEFL	550
Minimum computer TOEFL	213
Minimum web-based TOEFL	80
% graduated top 10% of class	24
% graduated top 25% of class	73
% graduated top 50% of class	97

DEADLINES

Early action	
Deadline	11/15
Notification	1/15
Regular	
Deadline	2/1
Notification	rolling
Nonfall registration?	yes

APPLICANTS ALSO LOOK AT

AND OFTEN PREFER
University of Connecticut
University of Vermont
University of Massachusetts—Amherst

AND SOMETIMES PREFER
Northeastern University
Boston University
Providence College
University of Rhode Island

AND RARELY PREFER
Boston College
University of Maine
Syracuse University

FINANCIAL FACTS

Financial Aid Rating	74
Annual in-state tuition	$9,420
Annual out-of-state tuition	$22,900
Room and board	$8,596
Required fees	$2,336
Books and supplies	$1,400
% frosh rec. need-based scholarship or grant aid	36
% UG rec. need-based scholarship or grant aid	39
% UG rec. non-need-based scholarship or grant aid	3
% frosh rec. need-based self-help aid	58
% UG rec. need-based self-help aid	56
% frosh rec. athletic scholarships	2
% UG rec. athletic scholarships	2
% frosh rec. any financial aid	84
% UG rec. any financial aid	79
% UG borrow to pay for school	75
Average cumulative indebtedness	$27,516

UNIVERSITY OF NEW MEXICO

OFFICE OF ADMISSIONS, PO BOX 4895, ALBUQUERQUE, NM 87196-4895 • ADMISSIONS: 505-277-2446 • FAX: 505-277-6686

CAMPUS LIFE

Quality of Life Rating	71
Fire Safety Rating	70
Green Rating	60*
Type of school	public
Environment	metropolis

STUDENTS

Total undergrad enrollment	18,395
% male/female	44/56
% from out of state	8.931
% live on campus	10
% in (# of) fraternities	1 (9)
% in (# of) sororities	2 (10)
% African American	3
% Asian	4
% Caucasian	45
% Hispanic	36
% Native American	7
% international	1
# of countries represented	66

SURVEY SAYS . . .

Diverse student types on campus
Different types of students interact
Students get along with local
community
Great off-campus food
Low cost of living
Students are happy
Student publications are popular
(Almost) no one smokes

ACADEMICS

Academic Rating	70
Calendar	semester
Student/faculty ratio	19:1
Profs interesting rating	65
Profs accessible rating	61
Most common	
reg class size	20–29 students
Most common	
lab size	10–19 students

MOST POPULAR MAJORS

biology/biological sciences
business administration and
management
psychology

STUDENTS SAY " . . ."

Academics

Offering a "solid education" in a beautiful setting, the University of New Mexico offers "academic excellence...through some of the best teachers and tough classes." Students also cited affordability and excellent scholarships awarded to both in-state and out-of-state applicants as a decisive factor in attending UNM. The affordability also extends to "amazing opportunities to travel abroad." At UNM, "there is something here for everyone." The education program and variety of science programs—including Earth and planetary sciences, biology, and the pre-med and nursing programs—also attract students. Some students express frustration with it at times being "difficult to work your way around the student services system," but the "very knowledgeable" teaching faculty are roundly praised as "teachers who care." UNM students also agree that "professors are helpful [and] genuinely interested in your personal success." Professors are approachable both in class and out and "talk to and with you and not just at you." "It's very easy to come to instructors outside of class with questions," and "most professors are willing to meet with you at your convenience." As for UNM's greatest strengths, students cite both the "research-oriented staff" and "the research opportunities available. Oftentimes the research can be done with top-of-the-line equipment" nearby at Sandia National Labs, Los Alamos National Labs, and other well-known research institutes. In UNM's collaborative environment, students also often work together and "are eager to form study groups." Also, students who need additional help can rely on academic support with "tutoring, study groups and, supplemental instruction for most courses."

Life

With "ways for everyone to get involved," UNM offers "hundreds of great student organizations" providing "opportunities for fun events." There is a student group "that will fit everyone," and at UNM, "everyone seems to find their niche." Offering another opportunity to become more involved on campus, the Greek community "makes up a lot of the senate and other extracurricular activities" and "with them, any activity has fun attached." UNM students are divided in their support of the school's athletics program. With some thinking "this school should concentrate less on sports and more on academics," other students feel "attending games is a must." Students enjoy spending time at the Student Union Building (SUB), because "there is always something going on." Even with a dry campus, "a lot of people drink, just like at any college." Students often leave campus for Albuquerque and its "excellent night life." UNM students also mentioned attending concerts and art shows for fun. Students also go to the weekly free movies at The Cellar, and to stay active, students frequent the Johnson Gym. Outdoors, students say and"hanging out at the duck pond is a great way to pass time between classes in warmer months" and, "during the winter season, there are numerous ski resorts and places to go snowboarding that are not far away."

Student Body

Time and time again, students select UNM's "diversity" as its greatest strength, and one student even stated "no one will ever feel ethnically alone since there are so many different kinds of people." This also means at UNM, "people never get boring," and "you meet someone different every day." In addition to the diversity, the prevailing atmosphere is a friendly one where "people get along regardless of origin," but "like any school there are cliques...but that does not mean they do not interact with each other." One student reserved special praise for the university, "UNM is sensitive and very engaged with its diverse population of students...concerned with facilitating in-depth inquiry and learning," and more than one student observed that at UNM, "everyone brings something to the table."

FINANCIAL AID: 505-277-2041 • E-MAIL: APPLY@UNM.EDU • WEBSITE: WWW.UNM.EDU

THE PRINCETON REVIEW SAYS

Admissions

Very important factors considered include: Academic GPA, rigor of secondary school record, *Important factors considered include:* Class rank, standardized test scores. *Other factors considered include:* Application essay, recommendation(s), character/personal qualities, extracurricular activities, first generation, volunteer work, work experience. SAT or ACT required; ACT with Writing component recommended. TOEFL required of all international applicants. High school diploma is required and GED is accepted. *Academic units required:* 4 English, 3 mathematics, 2 science, (1 science labs), 2 foreign language, 1 social studies, 1 history.

Financial Aid

Students should submit: FAFSA. The Princeton Review suggests that all financial aid forms be submitted as soon as possible after 1/1. *Need-based scholarships/grants offered:* Federal Pell, SEOG, state scholarships/grants, private scholarships, the school's own gift aid, United Negro College Fund, Federal Nursing Scholarships. *Loan aid offered:* Direct Subsidized Stafford, Direct Unsubsidized Stafford, Direct PLUS, Federal Perkins, Federal Nursing, state loans, college/university loans from institutional funds. Applicants will be notified of awards on a rolling basis beginning 4/15. Federal Work-Study Program available.

The Inside Word

UNM offers online applications through its website, and you will also find specific scholastic standards for traditional and non-traditional students interested in applying to UNM. Traditional applicants should have completed core coursework, taken the ACT or SAT exam and have an average or above-average GPA if they would like to be considered for admission at UNM.

THE SCHOOL SAYS "..."

From The Admissions Office

"The University of New Mexico is a major research institution nestled in the heart of multicultural Albuquerque on one of the nation's most beautiful and unique campuses. Students learn in an environment graced by distinctive Southwestern architecture, beautiful plazas and fountains, spectacular art and a national arboretum...all within view of the 10,000-foot Sandia Mountains. At UNM, diversity is a way of learning with education enriched by a lively mix of students being taught by a world-class research faculty that includes a Nobel laureate, a MacArthur Fellow, and members of several national academies. UNM offers more than 225 degree programs and majors and has earned national recognition in dozens of disciplines, ranging from primary care medicine and clinical law to engineering, photography, Latin American history, and intercultural communications. Research and the quest for new knowledge fuels the university's commitment to an undergraduate education where students work side-by-side with many of the finest scholars in their fields.

"The university will continue to accept SAT or ACT scores, but the University of New Mexico does not require the Writing component at this time. The SAT Critical Reading portion will be used with the SAT Math to be considered in any admission decision based on formula. The use of ACT composite remains unchanged. These requirements are subject to change."

SELECTIVITY

Admissions Rating	79
# of applicants	8,788
% of applicants accepted	68
% of acceptees attending	54

FRESHMAN PROFILE

Range SAT Critical Reading	470–610
Range SAT Math	460–600
Range ACT Composite	19–25
Minimum paper TOEFL	520
Minimum computer TOEFL	190
Minimum web-based TOEFL	68
Average HS GPA	3.33
% graduated top 10% of class	20
% graduated top 25% of class	45
% graduated top 50% of class	77

DEADLINES

Regular	
Deadline	6/15
Nonfall registration?	yes

FINANCIAL FACTS

Financial Aid Rating	60*
Annual in-state tuition	$4,834
Annual out-of-state tuition	$15,708

UNIVERSITY OF NEW ORLEANS

AD 103, LAKEFRONT, NEW ORLEANS, LA 70148 • ADMISSIONS: 504-280-6595 • FAX: 504-280-5522

CAMPUS LIFE
Quality of Life Rating	**64**
Fire Safety Rating	**60***
Green Rating	**60***
Type of school	public
Environment	metropolis

STUDENTS
Total undergrad enrollment	8,628
% male/female	48/52
% from out of state	5
% from public high school	63
% live on campus	5
% in (# of) fraternities	1 (9)
% in (# of) sororities	1 (8)
% African American	18
% Asian	6
% Caucasian	59
% Hispanic	7
% Native American	1
% international	4
# of countries represented	89

SURVEY SAYS . . .
Athletic facilities are great
Diverse student types on campus
Students get along with local
community
(Almost) everyone smokes

ACADEMICS
Academic Rating	**70**
Calendar	semester
Student/faculty ratio	18:1
Profs interesting rating	66
Profs accessible rating	66
% classes taught by TAs	34
Most common	
reg class size	10–19 students

MOST POPULAR MAJORS
business administration and
management
communication studies/speech
communication and rhetoric
general studies

STUDENTS SAY "..."

Academics

The University of New Orleans is "recovering at a snail's pace since Hurricane Katrina," but continues to provide "an equal opportunity for all people to get a superior education at an affordable price." You'll find a "diverse community of students" and "some of the best academics in the country." Classes are "challenging," "rewarding," and "offered at a variety of times, so it is easier for working students to attend class," but there are few bells and whistles. UNO "is geared to get students an education and doesn't fool around with extras." While "it is easy to get in" to UNO, it can be "hard to get out." "Classes are not easy." "UNO is for hard workers," a computer science major asserts. "It isn't an escalator for rich people to send their spoiled kids like the other schools in New Orleans." Faculty members are "accessible," "dedicated," and "extremely knowledgeable." They "have had extensive careers" and retain "good connections to the real world." Students note, however, that the bad professors are "really bad." Also, "since the hurricane," UNO has shut down "many programs," and many academic services "are only a fraction of what they were." UNO still excels in many areas including engineering, and naval architecture. business, and hotel, restaurant, and tourism administration. There is also a "great jazz program."

Life

"Hurricane Katrina has left our campus a mess," warns a junior. "UNO is getting back to normal, but it will be awhile before it will get better." "Areas of campus are still not rebuilt" and the campus was "a hideous sprawl" even before the storm. While "more people are living on campus" now, UNO remains "primarily a commuter campus." Students here are "almost completely focused on academics." Generally, when classes end, students "leave ASAP." "Job opportunities for college students are pretty good," and "most students work either full- or part-time." "The overall experience at UNO is a very independent one," an English major reports. "There are clubs and organizations in which to be involved," but "it is hard to get people involved in extracurricular activities." "If you want a college life, you must join a fraternity or sorority or some type of group on campus," a business major ventures. On the plus side, UNO boasts a "world-class" gym, and, of course, the "amazing" city of New Orleans is still brimming "with a lot of opportunity." "It's New Orleans. My god!" exclaims a junior. The campus is "less than 10 minutes to the French Quarter." "There's so much to do" and the food "is unmatched anywhere." "We live in a city that is immersed in culture and entertainment so fun is not too hard to find," says a senior. "You can find an open bar at any time of any day, but it isn't impossible to find a quiet spot and work out some math."

Student Body

UNO boasts "an eclectic assortment of students" who are "very serious" about academics, yet "very friendly." "Many different ethnic and social backgrounds" are represented here and it's definitely not "a regular 'all-American' college." "Because the school is a commuter school, the student population is made up mostly of local folks," observes an anthropology major. "But that doesn't stop the school from being extremely diverse." "Classmates range from high school grads to grandparents." "It's just a big gumbo of people," a sophomore writes. "The typical student" at UNO is probably "mid-20s, working full- or part-time while attending classes, [and] living off-campus in New Orleans." "I think the typical student at UNO is one who is excited to be in college, often entering or returning to college after spending some time in the workforce," a political science major reports. Many students are "married, have kids, and live in the suburbs," and many are "making a second or third try at college." In recent years, though, "the contingency of on-campus, fresh-out-of-high-schoolers" has grown by "leaps and bounds."

FINANCIAL AID: 504-280-6603 • E-MAIL: ADMISSIONS@UNO.EDU • WEBSITE: WWW.UNO.EDU

THE PRINCETON REVIEW SAYS

Admissions

Very important factors considered include: Class rank, academic GPA, rigor of secondary school record, standardized test scores. *Other factors considered include:* recommendation(s), geographical residence, state residency, SAT or ACT required; TOEFL required of all international applicants. High school diploma is required and GED is accepted. *Academic units required:* 4 English, 3 mathematics, 3 science, 2 foreign language, 1 social studies, 2 history, 1 visual/performing arts, 1 additional math or science, .5 computer science.

Financial Aid

Students should submit: FAFSA. The Princeton Review suggests that all financial aid forms be submitted as soon as possible after 1/1. *Need-based scholarships/grants offered:* Federal Pell, SEOG, state scholarships/grants, private scholarships, the school's own gift aid. *Loan aid offered:* Direct Subsidized Stafford, Direct Unsubsidized Stafford, Direct PLUS, FFEL Subsidized Stafford, FFEL Unsubsidized Stafford, FFEL PLUS, Federal Perkins, college/university loans from institutional funds. Applicants will be notified of awards on a rolling basis beginning 4/20. Federal Work-Study Program available. Institutional employment available.

The Inside Word

Admission is straightforward here. Complete a basic college-bound high school curriculum with a GPA of at least 2.5, get at least an 23 on your ACT, or graduate in the top 25 percent of your high school class. Nontraditional students who don't want to pay the exorbitant prices of the more well-known private universities in New Orleans can find their niche at UNO; if you are 25 or older, the only requirement for admission is a legitimate high school diploma or a GED.

THE SCHOOL SAYS " . . ."

From The Admissions Office

"The University of New Orleans returned to its Lakefront campus after Katrina with a full array of academic programs and an enhanced student life program, which includes a campus bar, first-run movies, and a host of exciting student activities.

"The university has served as a central player in the rebuilding of one of America's most unique and diverse cities. Many academic offerings will focus on the aftermath of Hurricane Katrina and provide students with a living laboratory to address these issues across many disciplines. UNO embraces its mission by providing the best educational opportunities for undergraduate and graduate students, conducting world-class research, and serving a diverse and cultured community in critical areas. UNO's most outstanding offerings include a doctoral program in conservation biology, providing training in the most advanced molecular biological techniques; the largest U.S. undergraduate program in Naval Architecture and Marine Engineering; a leading jazz studies program; one of the top five film programs in the country; and the only graduate arts administration program in the Gulf South.

"UNO will use the total score from the Critical Reading/Verbal and Math sub sections of the SAT or the composite score for the ACT. The Writing components of the ACT and SAT will be used for placement purposes, but not for admission purposes, at the time."

SELECTIVITY	
Admissions Rating	72
# of applicants	3,615
% of applicants accepted	55
% of acceptees attending	63

FRESHMAN PROFILE	
Range SAT Critical Reading	470–600
Range SAT Math	490–650
Range SAT Writing	460–580
Range ACT Composite	20–24
Minimum paper TOEFL	525
Minimum computer TOEFL	195
Minimum web-based TOEFL	71
Average HS GPA	3.12
% graduated top 10% of class	16
% graduated top 25% of class	35
% graduated top 50% of class	67

DEADLINES	
Regular	
Priority	7/1
Deadline	8/20
Notification	rolling
Nonfall registration?	yes

FINANCIAL FACTS	
Financial Aid Rating	66
Annual in-state tuition	$3,488
Annual out-of-state tuition	$10,884
Room and board	$6,130
Required fees	$818
Books and supplies	$1,200
% frosh rec. need-based scholarship or grant aid	47
% UG rec. need-based scholarship or grant aid	41
% frosh rec. non-need-based scholarship or grant aid	28
% UG rec. non-need-based scholarship or grant aid	17
% frosh rec. need-based self-help aid	23
% UG rec. need-based self-help aid	31
% frosh rec. athletic scholarships	2
% UG rec. athletic scholarships	2
% frosh rec. any financial aid	75
% UG rec. any financial aid	66
% UG borrow to pay for school	9
Average cumulative indebtedness	$14,911

THE UNIVERSITY OF NORTH CAROLINA AT ASHEVILLE

CPO #1320, 117 UNIVERSITY HALL, ASHEVILLE, NC 28804-8510 • ADMISSIONS: 828-251-6481 • FAX: 828-251-6482

CAMPUS LIFE

Quality of Life Rating	92
Fire Safety Rating	82
Green Rating	85
Type of school	public
Environment	town

STUDENTS

Total undergrad enrollment	3,150
% male/female	42/58
% from out of state	13
% from public high school	87
% live on campus	35
% in (# of) fraternities	2 (1)
% in (# of) sororities	3 (2)
% African American	3
% Asian	1
% Caucasian	88
% Hispanic	3
% international	1
# of countries represented	19

SURVEY SAYS . . .
No one cheats
Students are friendly
Students get along with local community
Students love Asheville, NC
Great off-campus food
Dorms are like palaces
Students are happy
Political activism is popular

ACADEMICS

Academic Rating	85
Calendar	semester
Student/faculty ratio	13:1
Profs interesting rating	89
Profs accessible rating	84
Most common reg class size	10–19 students
Most common lab size	20–29 students

MOST POPULAR MAJORS
English language and literature
environmental studies
psychology

STUDENTS SAY "..."

Academics

Undergrads at UNC—Asheville rave about their top-notch academic experience. Professors are "devoted and passionate [about] their fields of study, and it shows in the classroom." Importantly, "even though you may not be totally fascinated by the subject initially, the professors' enthusiasm for each course is contagious." Students also appreciate Asheville's "liberal arts ideology." As one senior English lit major says, "It's wonderful when every semester, at least two seemingly unrelated classes end up teaching the same lessons through different means and subjects." Though "course material is challenging," students take solace in knowing that "an A is totally achievable." This is due in part to the fact that "professors are available and more than willing to assist students outside of class." And one environmental studies major adds, "The classes are small enough that the professors know you by name and seem to care if you do well." Furthermore, "tutoring sessions…are free and plentiful" for those undergrads who feel that they require more assistance. The school's administration garners decidedly mixed reviews. While there are some undergrads who feel that they are "relatively detached from school life" and "out of touch with the students," others taut the deans as being "unusually accessible."

Life

With roughly "two-thirds of [the] student [body] living off-campus," some undergrads warn that life "can be slow on the weekends." Fortunately, one senior confidently declares that campus life "has started to pick up in the last few years." Freshman are now required to live on campus their first year and another third of students live within 1 mile of campus in non-university housing. Indeed, "students enjoy a wide range of activities" from playing "Frisbee golf on the quad" to attending one of many "lectures" or "basketball games" held on campus. While there is a Greek system, "partying does not define the school." Many students are "environmentally conscious" and spend a lot of energy helping shape "campus policies, including [instituting] new, reusable take-out boxes from the school cafeteria." Naturally, many of these activists are also outdoor enthusiasts, and undergrads love the fact that they are nestled "in the Blue Ridge Mountains." The university offers a fantastic "outdoors program that [hosts] popular rock climbing, caving, hiking, and kayaking [trips]." Students also give hometown Asheville high marks. As one impressed sophomore recounts, "You can't take three steps downtown without tripping over some kind of festival or street performance." A favorite Asheville activity for many students is "the drum circle" where "people gather every Friday evening (in warm weather), circulating, dancing, thrumming & drumming. Drummers, amateur to experienced, bring their own instruments to bang upon. People without personal beat abilities twist through the crowds to dance or simply watch from the sidelines."

Student Body

UNC—Asheville seems to hold appeal for self-described "hippies." As one sophomore expounds, "This school attracts the sort of people who get excited about local, organic, dairy-free muffins and sandals made from recycled flax." Indeed many undergrads "care about the environment, [are] liberal-leaning, enjoy the outdoors, [and are] pretty sociable." Happily, the university "fosters the idea that individuality is essential," and students assure us that everyone "is easily accepted here" regardless of political affiliation. Perhaps this acceptance stems from the fact that the campus welcomes students from a variety of "economic backgrounds, religious backgrounds and sexual orientations." The only area lacking, lament some undergrads, is racial diversity. While the school is mostly white, one senior reveals that the university is making a valiant effort "to try and increase diversity on campus." However, Asheville does manage to attract both a large number of "commuter students" as well as "a lot of non-traditional students."

THE UNIVERSITY OF NORTH CAROLINA AT ASHEVILLE

FINANCIAL AID: 828-251-6535 • E-MAIL: ADMISSIONS@UNCA.EDU • WEBSITE: WWW.UNCA.EDU

THE PRINCETON REVIEW SAYS

Admissions

Very important factors considered include: Class rank, academic GPA, rigor of secondary school record, *Important factors considered include:* Application essay, recommendation(s), standardized test scores. *Other factors considered include:* alumni/ae relation, extracurricular activities, first generation, geographical residence, interview, level of applicant's interest, racial/ethnic status, state residency, talent/ability, volunteer work, work experience. SAT or ACT required; ACT with Writing component required. TOEFL or SAT or ACT required of all international applicants. High school diploma is required and GED is not accepted. *Academic units required:* 4 English, 4 mathematics including 1 with algebra II as prerequisite, 3 sciences (1 physical, 1 biological and 1 lab), 2 foreign language (2 units of the same language), 2 social studies (1 must be U.S. history). *Academic units recommended:* 4 academic electives.

Financial Aid

Students should submit: FAFSA. The Princeton Review suggests that all financial aid forms be submitted as soon as possible after 1/1. Need-based scholarships/grants offered: Federal Pell, SEOG, state scholarships/grants, private scholarships, the school's own gift aid. *Loan aid offered:* Direct Subsidized Stafford, Direct Unsubsidized Stafford, Direct PLUS, Federal Perkins, state loans, college/university loans from institutional funds. Applicants will be notified of awards on a rolling basis beginning 3/15. Federal Work-Study Program available. Institutional employment available. Off-campus job opportunities are good.

The Inside Word

UNC—Asheville provides a sound public education in a small campus atmosphere, and an increasing number of students are setting their sights on it each year. In kind, the school works diligently to create a diverse student body and thoroughly analyzes each application it receives. Although selectivity is rising, candidates who demonstrate reasonable academic success and involvement in a variety of extracurricular activities should be able to secure admittance.

THE SCHOOL SAYS "..."

From The Admissions Office

"If you want to learn how to think, how to analyze and solve problems on your own, and how to become your own best teacher then, a broad-based liberal arts education is the key. UNC Asheville focuses on undergraduates, with a core curriculum covering natural science, math, social sciences, humanities, language and culture, arts and ideas, and health and fitness. Students thrive in small classes, with a faculty dedicated first of all to teaching. The liberal arts emphasis develops discriminating thinkers, expert and creative communicators with a passion for learning. These are qualities you need for today's challenges and the changes of tomorrow.

"The University of North Carolina at Asheville requires the SAT or for students submitting an ACT score, the ACT with the Writing component."

SELECTIVITY

Admissions Rating	87
# of applicants	2,464
% of applicants accepted	73
% of acceptees attending	32

FRESHMAN PROFILE

Range SAT Critical Reading	530–640
Range SAT Math	520–630
Range SAT Writing	510–620
Range ACT Composite	21–27
Minimum paper TOEFL	550
Minimum computer TOEFL	213
Minimum web-based TOEFL	79
Average HS GPA	3.9
% graduated top 10% of class	22
% graduated top 25% of class	59
% graduated top 50% of class	97

DEADLINES

Early action	
Deadline	11/15
Notification	12/15
Regular	
Priority	
Deadline	2/15
Notification	3/15
Nonfall registration?	yes

FINANCIAL FACTS

Financial Aid Rating	84
Annual in-state tuition	$2,339
Annual out-of-state tuition	$13,669
Room and board	$6,620
Required fees	$1,916
Books and supplies	$850
% frosh rec. need-based scholarship or grant aid	36
% UG rec. need-based scholarship or grant aid	39
% frosh rec. non-need-based scholarship or grant aid	6
% UG rec. non-need-based scholarship or grant aid	5
% frosh rec. need-based self-help aid	24
% UG rec. need-based self-help aid	31
% frosh rec. athletic scholarships	4
% UG rec. athletic scholarships	3
% frosh rec. any financial aid	66
% UG rec. any financial aid	58
% UG borrow to pay for school	50
Average cumulative indebtedness	$14,685

THE UNIVERSITY OF NORTH CAROLINA AT CHAPEL HILL

JACKSON HALL 153A, CAMPUS BOX #2200, CHAPEL HILL, NC 27599 • ADMISSIONS: 919-966-3621 • FAX: 919-962-3045

CAMPUS LIFE
Quality of Life Rating	95
Fire Safety Rating	87
Green Rating	96
Type of school	public
Environment	town

STUDENTS
Total undergrad enrollment	17,422
% male/female	41/59
% from out of state	17
% from public high school	82
% in (# of) fraternities	15 (32)
% in (# of) sororities	17 (22)
% African American	11
% Asian	7
% Caucasian	71
% Hispanic	5
% Native American	1
% international	1
# of countries represented	133

SURVEY SAYS . . .
Low cost of living
Everyone loves the Tar Heels
Student publications are popular

ACADEMICS
Academic Rating	84
Calendar	semester
Student/faculty ratio	14:1
Profs interesting rating	79
Profs accessible rating	73
% classes taught by TAs	25
Most common reg class size	10–19 students
Most common lab size	10–19 students

MOST POPULAR MAJORS
biology/biological sciences
business administration and management
psychology

STUDENTS SAY " . . ."
Academics
It's quite an understatement to say students at UNC—Chapel Hill are proud of their school. One calls it his "dream school," while another calls it the "perfect mixture of academics, sports, and social life." Although its relative low cost makes UNC a great bargain in higher education, academic rigor doesn't take a back seat, and the vast majority of students say it's one of the main reasons they chose the school. The journalism, business, and nursing programs are ranked among the best in the country, but the students hail the overall liberal arts curriculum because it creates well-rounded adults who "can handle any intellectual obstacle." In describing the instructors, students use words like "world-class," "brilliant," and "incredible," while also noting that they're "warm," "welcoming," and "passionate" about their work and their students. "Most of my professors have been great, and some have been phenomenal." Faculty members are generous with their time outside of class, patiently explaining "even the most difficult material" and using e-mail to announce changes. Some complain about large classes and warn incoming students that they will have to take the initiative and "speak up," because they won't be "coddled." The school's academic-advising system still comes in for sharp criticism. "Students are on their own there," one student says.

Life
With more than 17,000 undergrads, UNC is large enough that students rarely are lacking for something to do. Tar Heel men's basketball probably is at the top of the list; indeed, for many rabid fans, the Dean Smith Center is the center of the universe, especially when Duke is the opponent. One student sums up the school's essence this way: "It's the feeling of running through the beautiful old quad by Davie Poplar on the way to Franklin Street after a big win." The consensus is maintaining grades requires such an effort, letting off steam on weekends is a reward. "Life at UNC is full throttle. People work hard and play hard." Many flock to the bars, restaurants and coffee shops of Franklin Street, but others prefer the music scene in nearby Carrboro or staying on campus to participate in a function sponsored by one of the hundreds of student groups. The campus itself is gorgeous and filled with history. Although only 17 percent of students belong to a fraternity or sorority, the Greek organizations are a big part of the social scene. "When you're writing 30-page papers on 20th-century German philosophy and working two jobs, a night where you get to dress up as a biker chick and listen to AC/DC all night at the bar is a welcome reprieve," one sorority member says.

Student Body
One student after another comments about the feeling of generosity that pervades UNC—"the epitome of Southern hospitality"—and how it extends beyond mere school spirit and the wearing of Carolina blue and white on game days. "Carolina is family," one student says. "Most of us here are crazy about sports, but most will do anything at all to help a fellow UNC student." "Although the student body is very diverse, a commonality among students is the desire to serve others and work for humanitarian efforts." One reason for the closeness is that the vast majority of students hail from the Tar Heel state. So there are "lots of down-home, North Carolina types who excelled in their rural high schools." Students and faculty are viewed as leaning liberal politically, which makes for some interesting exchanges. "Political activism is huge here," a student says. But even though it's a vast school, "it has a place for everyone." "There are really only two common denominators: commitment to some kind of excellence (academic, extracurricular, etc.) and rooting against Duke."

THE UNIVERSITY OF NORTH CAROLINA AT CHAPEL HILL

FINANCIAL AID: 919-962-8396 • E-MAIL: UNCHELP@ADMISSIONS.UNC.EDU • WEBSITE: WWW.UNC.EDU

THE PRINCETON REVIEW SAYS

Admissions

Very important factors considered include: Class rank, application essay, academic GPA, recommendation(s), rigor of secondary school record, standardized test scores, character/personal qualities, extracurricular activities, state residency, talent/ability, *Important factors considered include:* alumni/ae relation, first generation, racial/ethnic status, volunteer work, work experience. SAT or ACT required; ACT with Writing component required. TOEFL required of all international applicants. High school diploma is required and GED is not accepted. *Academic units required:* 4 English, 4 mathematics, 3 science, (1 science labs), 2 foreign language, 2 social studies, 2 academic electives, 1 Social Science course must be U.S. History. *Academic units recommended:* 4 English, 4 mathematics, 4 science, (1 science labs), 4 foreign language, 3 social studies.

Financial Aid

Students should submit: FAFSA, CSS/Financial Aid PROFILE The Princeton Review suggests that all financial aid forms be submitted as soon as possible after 1/1. Need-based scholarships/grants offered: Federal Pell, SEOG, state scholarships/grants, private scholarships, the school's own gift aid, State Grants. *Loan aid offered:* FFEL Subsidized Stafford, FFEL Unsubsidized Stafford, FFEL PLUS, Federal Perkins, state loans, college/university loans from institutional funds, alternative loans. Applicants will be notified of awards on a rolling basis beginning 3/15. Federal Work-Study Program available. Institutional employment available. Off-campus job opportunities are good.

The Inside Word

UNC's admissions process is highly selective. North Carolina students compete against other students from across the state for 82 percent of all spaces available in the freshman class; out-of-state students compete for the remaining 18 percent of the spaces. State residents will find the admissions standards high, and out-of-state applicants will find that it's one of the hardest offers of admission to come by in the country.

THE SCHOOL SAYS "..."

From The Admissions Office

"One of the leading research and teaching institutions in the world, UNC Chapel Hill offers first-rate faculty, innovative academic programs, and students who are smart, friendly, and committed to public service. Students take full advantage of extensive undergraduate research opportunities, a study abroad program with programs on every continent except Antarctica, and 600-plus clubs and organizations. We offer all this in Chapel Hill, one of the greatest and most welcoming college towns anywhere.

"Carolina's commitment to excellence, access, and affordability is reflected in premier scholarships, such as the prestigious Morehead and Robertson Scholarships, as well the Carolina Covenant, a national model that enables students from low-income families to graduate from Carolina debt-free. We invite you to visit—talk with our professors, attend a class, spend time with some students, and walk across the campus on which public education was born.

"All freshman applicants are required to submit an SAT or an ACT Writing component score. While test scores are important, our holistic review process includes other important factors such course work, grades, and extracurricular activities."

SELECTIVITY

Admissions Rating	98
# of applicants	21,543
% of applicants accepted	34
% of acceptees attending	53
# accepting a place on wait list	1,420
% admitted from wait list	32

FRESHMAN PROFILE

Range SAT Critical Reading	590–690
Range SAT Math	620–700
Range SAT Writing	590–690
Range ACT Composite	26–31
Average HS GPA	4.4
% graduated top 10% of class	79
% graduated top 25% of class	96
% graduated top 50% of class	99

DEADLINES

Early action	
Deadline	11/1
Notification	1/15
Regular	
Deadline	1/15
Nonfall registration?	no

APPLICANTS ALSO LOOK AT
AND SOMETIMES PREFER
University of Virginia
Duke University

AND RARELY PREFER
Wake Forest University
North Carolina State University

FINANCIAL FACTS

Financial Aid Rating	92
Annual in-state tuition	$3,705
Annual out-of-state tuition	$20,603
Room and board	$7,334
Required fees	$1,692
Books and supplies	$1,000
% frosh rec. need-based scholarship or grant aid	32
% UG rec. need-based scholarship or grant aid	32
% frosh rec. non-need-based scholarship or grant aid	16
% UG rec. non-need-based scholarship or grant aid	10
% frosh rec. need-based self-help aid	13
% UG rec. need-based self-help aid	17
% frosh rec. athletic scholarships	2
% UG rec. athletic scholarships	2

THE UNIVERSITY OF NORTH CAROLINA AT GREENSBORO

1400 SPRING GARDEN STREET, GREENSBORO, NC 27402-6170 • ADMISSIONS: 336-334-5243 • FAX: 336-334-4180

CAMPUS LIFE

Quality of Life Rating	84
Fire Safety Rating	69
Green Rating	60*
Type of school	public
Environment	city

STUDENTS

Total undergrad enrollment	13,678
% male/female	33/67
% from out of state	8
% from public high school	95
% live on campus	31
% in (# of) fraternities	NR (8)
% in (# of) sororities	NR (10)
% African American	22
% Asian	4
% Caucasian	65
% Hispanic	3
% international	1
# of countries represented	90

SURVEY SAYS . . .

Diverse student types on campus
Different types of students interact
Students get along with local community
Students are happy

ACADEMICS

Academic Rating	74
Calendar	semester
Student/faculty ratio	15.6:1
Profs interesting rating	76
Profs accessible rating	74
Most common reg class size	20–29 students
Most common lab size	20–29 students

MOST POPULAR MAJORS

biology/biological sciences
elementary education and teaching
psychology

STUDENTS SAY ". . ."

Academics

Students describe the University of North Carolina at Greensboro as "about a half-and-half commuter school with great specialized programs and schools such as nursing, education, dance, and music." Undergrads here praise the "high quality of education at a significantly reduced rate, while having the smaller classes allowing closer bonds between faculty and students" than one could reasonably expect for the tuition charged. The key here is the faculty, because according to one student, "UNCG places a big emphasis on having great teachers. There are some duds, but overall, more of them are fantastic than anything else." The school excels in some off-the-beaten-path areas like programs in Kinesiology, deaf education, human development and family studies, which all receive enthusiastic praise from students. Undergrads also love the "opportunities that are given to network with businesses and people outside of campus" and the "great internships" the school helps them find. Nontraditional students appreciate the "great support system for adult students." As the school's reputation continues to improve, some worry this "historically moderate-sized university where student well-being was the first priority…will change into a large research university where the focus is raising more and more money." One undeniable upside of the school's increased stature is that "you feel like you are respected in the community when you tell someone that you are a student at UNCG."

Life

UNCG is conveniently located "a mile from downtown and close to surrounding schools: Guilford College, NC A&T, Greensboro College, Elon, UNC, NC State." One student observes, "With six colleges around UNCG, a metropolis of 250,000-plus (1.1 million in the metro area), and access within a three-hour drive to both beaches and mountains, there is always something to do." On campus "UNCG makes it easy for anyone and everyone to fit in and feel included. Through clubs, students have the ability to offer ideas and have them implemented. There's also intramural sports and free events." The high-profile arts programs on campus yield some wonderful cultural opportunities. "The Weatherspoon Museum of Art is amazing at showcasing the most modern American art and keeps this provincial little town on its toes," writes one artist. A performing arts student adds, "There are wonderful concerts and plays and lectures here. It's a great cultural center and you can always have something to do as long as you look for it." Intercollegiate athletics, students tell us, "are not as popular as they could be, even though they are often ranked nationally, or at least ranked in the conference." Many here feel the addition of a football team (the school has none) would change that. "It would really bring the school spirit up," opines one undergrad. The school's many commuters warn that "parking is horrendous. Prepare to get here an hour before class if you want to find a space on time."

Student Body

UNCG is a big school with "many people from all walks of life, social/cultural backgrounds, etc. The university promotes cultural diversity and acceptance and tolerance of people of different backgrounds." One student reports, "One minute you see a bunch of music majors talking about how much Bach has affected their life, and the next minute, you see a bunch of sorority girls discussing the Gap. Mainly, I have observed that sorority girls stick together, jocks stick together, etc." Two-in-three students are female, and there is a widespread perception that "many of the males are either married or gay. The straight, young, chill male is a minority here." As at many state schools, "about half of the students at UNCG came here to party. The other half consists of hardworking students who are generally frustrated with the slacker mentality in a lot of our classes. This is less of a problem once you get past the intro-level lectures."

THE UNIVERSITY OF NORTH CAROLINA AT GREENSBORO

FINANCIAL AID: 336-334-5702 • E-MAIL: ADMISSIONS@UNCG.EDU • WEBSITE: WWW.UNCG.EDU

THE PRINCETON REVIEW SAYS

Admissions

Very important factors considered include: academic GPA, rigor of secondary school record, *Important factors considered include:* standardized test scores. *Other factors considered include:* recommendation(s), SAT or ACT required; ACT with Writing component required. TOEFL required of all international applicants. High school diploma is required and GED is not accepted. *Academic units required:* 4 English, 4 mathematics, 3 science, (1 science labs), 2 foreign language, 2 social studies.

Financial Aid

Students should submit: FAFSA. The Princeton Review suggests that all financial aid forms be submitted as soon as possible after 1/1. Need-based scholarships/grants offered: Federal Pell, SEOG, state scholarships/grants, private scholarships, the school's own gift aid. *Loan aid offered:* FFEL Subsidized Stafford, FFEL Unsubsidized Stafford, FFEL PLUS, Federal Perkins, college/university loans from institutional funds. Applicants will be notified of awards on a rolling basis beginning 3/15. Federal Work-Study Program available. Institutional employment available. Off-campus job opportunities are good.

The Inside Word

UNCG has yet to gain much attention outside of regional circles so, at least for the moment, gaining admission is not particularly difficult. The usual public university considerations apply; expect the admissions office to focus on grades and test scores, and not much else. Out-of-staters will find a much smoother path to admission here than at Chapel Hill and will still be within reasonable reach of internship and career possibilities in the Research Triangle.

THE SCHOOL SAYS " . . ."

From The Admissions Office

"UNCG is committed to helping students discover how they can make their mark in the world. Exceptional teaching and first-rate academic programs provide a solid learning foundation. Hands-on experiences in internships, leadership opportunities, and service-learning programs prepare students to take on the challenges of the 21st century. Students can broaden their experience by taking advantage of one of the most extensive and affordable study abroad programs in the country. The Lloyd International Honors College offers a genuinely unique opportunity for talented students in any major to benefit from an enriched and supportive intellectual life with a global perspective. UNCG's ideal size and close-knit campus atmosphere enable students to excel as individuals while discovering how they can have an impact on the larger community. Students get connected through more than 180 student organizations, intramural, club and intercollegiate sports, Greeks, outdoor adventures, residential colleges, and a friendly Southern city that quickly starts to feel like home.

"Freshmen applicants must submit at least one SAT or ACT score (including the Writing component)."

SELECTIVITY

Admissions Rating	**82**
# of applicants	10,488
% of applicants accepted	63
% of acceptees attending	38

FRESHMAN PROFILE

Range SAT Critical Reading	460–560
Range SAT Math	470–570
Range SAT Writing	450–550
Minimum paper TOEFL	550
Minimum computer TOEFL	213
Minimum web-based TOEFL	79
Average HS GPA	3.58
% graduated top 10% of class	13.39
% graduated top 25% of class	44.94
% graduated top 50% of class	85.21

DEADLINES

Regular	
Priority	11/1
Deadline	3/1
Notification	rolling
Nonfall registration?	yes

FINANCIAL FACTS

Financial Aid Rating	**75**
Annual in-state tuition	$2,632
Annual out-of-state tuition	$14,351
Room and board	$6,506
Required fees	$1,644
Books and supplies	$1,282
% frosh rec. need-based scholarship or grant aid	33
% UG rec. need-based scholarship or grant aid	33
% frosh rec. non-need-based scholarship or grant aid	53
% UG rec. non-need-based scholarship or grant aid	49
% frosh rec. need-based self-help aid	24
% UG rec. need-based self-help aid	39
% frosh rec. athletic scholarships	1
% UG rec. athletic scholarships	1
% frosh rec. any financial aid	74
% UG rec. any financial aid	67
% UG borrow to pay for school	65
Average cumulative indebtedness	$16,326

UNIVERSITY OF NORTH DAKOTA

PO Box 8135, Grand Forks, ND 58202 • Admissions: 800-225-5863 • Fax: 701-777-4857

CAMPUS LIFE

Quality of Life Rating	77
Fire Safety Rating	76
Green Rating	82
Type of school	public
Environment	town

STUDENTS

Total undergrad enrollment	10,129
% male/female	55/45
% from out of state	48
% from public high school	92
% live on campus	31
% in (# of) fraternities	8 (13)
% in (# of) sororities	8 (7)
% African American	1
% Asian	1
% Caucasian	87
% Hispanic	1
% Native American	3
% international	4
# of countries represented	68

SURVEY SAYS . . .

Athletic facilities are great
Students are friendly
Everyone loves the Fighting Sioux
Student publications are popular
Lots of beer drinking
Hard liquor is popular

ACADEMICS

Academic Rating	70
Calendar	semester
Student/faculty ratio	18:1
Profs interesting rating	66
Profs accessible rating	66
Most common reg class size	20–29 students
Most common lab size	fewer than 10 students

MOST POPULAR MAJORS

airline/commercial/professional pilot
and flight crew
nursing/registered nurse
(rn, asn, bsn, msn)
psychology

STUDENTS SAY ". . ."

Academics

"Size and affordability are very nice draws" at the University of North Dakota. The number of undergrads here is ideal, and UND offers "the best bang for the buck anywhere." North Dakota residents can attend for a song and reciprocity agreements provide enticing tuition breaks for students from a number of Western states. There are nearly 90 undergraduate majors. Nursing and engineering are reportedly solid. The aviation and aerospace programs are some of the very best anywhere in the world. UND owns the biggest non-military fleet of training aircraft on the planet, and students boast that a UND degree has quite a bit of prestige among airlines and in the aviation industry generally. "If you're considering air-traffic control, this is the school to be at," advises one student. Another unique program is the Center for Innovation, which provides internships for undergrads who want to launch a business. Additionally, there are more than 30 specialized academic programs for American Indians. Students describe the overall academic experience at UND as "pretty good" "and not too stressful." Despite some frustrating bureaucracy, most students appreciate the "helpful" administration. The faculty is "highly qualified" but sometimes hit-or-miss in the classroom. Some professors are "excellent teachers who genuinely care for their students." Others "seem to be distant at times." As a result, courses can range "from absolutely awesome to really annoying."

Life

UND's "very safe" campus is "pretty no matter what time of year," and the "rural" locale of Grand Forks serves up plenty of "small-town atmosphere." It's important to understand this school is "located in the tundra of the world," though. Winters are long and brutal. "It's way too cold up here" (like "grimacing-in-pain" cold). Student activities at UND run the gamut. There are more than 200 clubs and organizations. The student recreation center is enormous and state of the art. Intramural sports are quite popular, and many students are "huge supporters of the Fighting Sioux," the intercollegiate athletic teams. Specifically, "hockey is king here." The team is formidable year in and year out, and it has won several national championships. Home games in the "breathtaking" arena are well attended and "extremely fun." About 10 percent of the student population is involved in the Greek scene. Students report the fraternities and sororities loom large in the social scheme of things, though, so that percentage often seems higher. Beginning on Friday (or maybe Thursday), "everybody is on a quest to entertain themselves, usually through alcohol consumption." Many students "drink every weekend," either at the frats or at "bars or house parties."

Student Body

Students here describe themselves as "really friendly." They "have their head on straight," and they know how to handle seriously frigid weather. According to UND, there's somebody on this campus from every state. However, the overwhelming majority of students come "from rural areas in the Midwest." A little more than half of the undergrads are North Dakota residents. Nearly one-third hails from neighboring Minnesota. (The school is essentially located on the state line.) South Dakota residents have a presence, too. Students from anywhere else usually end up at UND because of the aviation program, and those students tend to form their own little worlds. "This is Scandinavian country," so you'll see "a lot of Nordic-descended people." Tall, blue-eyed blonds are pretty common. Native Americans make up the largest non-white ethnic group. "There are not too many minority students," but that information shouldn't be surprising given UND's rural location and the regional demographics.

FINANCIAL AID: 701-777-3121 • E-MAIL: ENROLLMENTSERVICES@MAIL.UND.EDU • WEBSITE: WWW.UND.EDU

THE PRINCETON REVIEW SAYS

Admissions

Very important factors considered include: Academic GPA, standardized test scores. *Other factors considered include:* Class rank, rigor of secondary school record, SAT or ACT required; TOEFL required of all international applicants. High school diploma is required and GED is accepted. *Academic units required:* 4 English, 3 mathematics, 3 science, (3 science labs), 3 social studies, *Academic units recommended:* 1 foreign language.

Financial Aid

Students should submit: FAFSA. The Princeton Review suggests that all financial aid forms be submitted as soon as possible after 1/1. *Need-based scholarships/grants offered:* Federal Pell, SEOG, state scholarships/grants, private scholarships, the school's own gift aid, Federal Nursing Scholarships. *Loan aid offered:* FFEL Subsidized Stafford, FFEL Unsubsidized Stafford, FFEL PLUS, Federal Perkins, Federal Nursing, alternative commercial loans. Applicants will be notified of awards on a rolling basis beginning 5/15. Federal Work-Study Program available. Institutional employment available. Off-campus job opportunities are excellent.

The Inside Word

UND's loose admissions standards belie the national reputation it has earned. Akin to most state schools, it's all about meeting GPA and standardized test minimums. The lack of subjective criteria makes for a relatively painless application process, and a majority of students are admitted.

THE SCHOOL SAYS ". . ."

From The Admissions Office

"More than 10,000 students come to the University of North Dakota each year, from every state in the nation and more than 60 countries. They're impressed by our academic excellence, more than 190 programs, our dedication to the liberal arts mission, and alumni success record. Nearly all of the university's new students rank in the top half of their high school classes, with about half in the top quarter. As the oldest and most diversified institution of higher education in the Dakotas, Montana, Wyoming, and western Minnesota, UND is a comprehensive teaching and research university. Yet the university provides individual attention that may be missing at very large universities. UND graduates are highly regarded among prospective employers. Representatives from more than 200 regional and national companies recruit UND students every year. Our campus is approximately 98 percent accessible.

"Students applying for admission to UND are required to take either the ACT or SAT unless they are older than 25. The ACT Writing component is not a requirement for admission, and SAT results considered include only the Math and Verbal sections."

SELECTIVITY

Admissions Rating	80
# of applicants	4,069
% of applicants accepted	75
% of acceptees attending	63

FRESHMAN PROFILE

Range ACT Composite	20.5–25.5
Minimum paper TOEFL	525
Minimum computer TOEFL	195
Average HS GPA	3.38
% graduated top 10% of class	16
% graduated top 25% of class	40
% graduated top 50% of class	73

DEADLINES

Regular	
Notification	rolling
Nonfall registration?	yes

APPLICANTS ALSO LOOK AT
AND OFTEN PREFER
University of Minnesota—Duluth
Saint Cloud State University
AND SOMETIMES PREFER
University of Minnesota—Crookston
Concordia College
Minot State University

FINANCIAL FACTS

Financial Aid Rating	72
Annual tuition in-state	$6,514
Annual tuition out-of-state	$15,324
Room and board	$5,404
Books and supplies	$800
% frosh rec. need-based scholarship or grant aid	50
% UG rec. need-based scholarship or grant aid	39
% frosh rec. non-need-based scholarship or grant aid	10
% UG rec. non-need-based scholarship or grant aid	8
% frosh rec. need-based self-help aid	70
% UG rec. need-based self-help aid	66
% frosh rec. athletic scholarships	4
% UG rec. athletic scholarships	4
% frosh rec. any financial aid	67
% UG rec. any financial aid	78
% UG borrow to pay for school	76
Average cumulative indebtedness	$21,743

UNIVERSITY OF NOTRE DAME

220 MAIN BUILDING, NOTRE DAME, IN 46556 • ADMISSIONS: 574-631-7505 • FAX: 574-631-8865

CAMPUS LIFE

Quality of Life Rating	88
Fire Safety Rating	90
Green Rating	89
Type of school	private
Affiliation	Roman Catholic
Environment	city

STUDENTS

Total undergrad enrollment	8,354
% male/female	53/47
% from out of state	92
% from public high school	50
% live on campus	76
% African American	4
% Asian	7
% Caucasian	77
% Hispanic	9
% Native American	1
% international	3
# of countries represented	89

SURVEY SAYS . . .

School is well run
Great food on campus
Everyone loves the Fighting Irish
Frats and sororities are unpopular or
nonexistent
Student publications are popular

ACADEMICS

Academic Rating	93
Calendar	semester
Student/faculty ratio	12:1
Profs interesting rating	85
Profs accessible rating	93
% classes taught by TAs	7
Most common	
reg class size	10–19 students
Most common	
lab size	10–19 students

MOST POPULAR MAJORS
finance
political science and government
psychology

STUDENTS SAY ". . ."

Academics

Notre Dame has many traditions, including a "devotion to undergraduate education" you might not expect from a school with such an athletic reputation. Professors here are, by all accounts, "wonderful": "Not only are they invested in their students," they're "genuinely passionate about their fields of study," "enthusiastic and animated in lectures," and "always willing to meet outside of class to give extra help." Wary that distance might breed academic disengagement, professors ensure "large lectures are broken down into smaller discussion groups once a week to help with class material and…give the class a personal touch." For its part, "the administration tries its best to stay on top of the students' wants and needs." They make it "extremely easy to get in touch with anyone." Like the professors, administrators try to make personal connections with students. For example, "our president (a priest), as well as both of our presidents emeritus, make it a point to interact with the students in a variety of ways—teaching a class, saying mass in the dorms, etc." Overall, "while classes are difficult," "students are competitive against one another," and "it's necessary to study hard and often, [but] there's also time to do other things."

Life

Life at Notre Dame is centered around two things—"residential life" and "sports." The "dorms on campus provide the social structure" and supply undergrads with tons of opportunities to get involved and have fun." "During the school week" students "study a lot, but on the weekends everyone seems to make up for the lack of partying during the week." The school "does not have any fraternities or sororities, but campus is not dry, and drinking/partying is permitted within the residence halls." The administration reportedly tries "to keep the parties on campus due to the fact that campus is such a safe place and they truly do care about our safety." In addition to parties the dorms are really competitive in the Interhall Sport System, and "virtually every student plays some kind of sport [in] his/her residence hall." Intercollegiate sports, to put it mildly, "are huge." "If someone is not interested in sports upon arrival, he or she will be by the time he or she leaves." "Everybody goes to the football games, and it's common to see 1,000 students at a home soccer game." Beyond residential life and sports, "religious activities," volunteering, "campus publications, student government, and academic clubs round out the rest of ND life."

Student Body

Undergrads at Notre Dame report "the vast majority" of their peers are "very smart" "white kids from upper- to middle-class backgrounds from all over the country, especially the Midwest and Northeast." The typical student "is a type-A personality that studies a lot, yet is athletic and involved in the community. They are usually the outstanding seniors in their high schools," the "sort of people who can talk about the BCS rankings and Derrida in the same breath." Additionally, something like "85 percent of Notre Dame students earned a varsity letter in high school." "Not all are Catholic" here, though most are, and it seems that most undergrads "have some sort of spirituality present in their daily lives." "ND is slowly improving in diversity concerning economic backgrounds, with the university's policy to meet all demonstrated financial need." As things stand now, those who "don't tend to fit in with everyone else hang out in their own groups made up by others like them (based on ethnicity, sexual orientation, etc.)."

FINANCIAL AID: 574-631-6436 • E-MAIL: ADMISSIONS@ND.EDU • WEBSITE: WWW.ND.EDU

THE PRINCETON REVIEW SAYS

Admissions

Very important factors considered include: rigor of secondary school record. *Important factors considered include:* Class rank, application essay, academic GPA, recommendation(s), standardized test scores, alumni/ae relation, character/personal qualities, extracurricular activities, talent/ability, volunteer work. *Other factors considered include:* first generation, level of applicant's interest, racial/ethnic status, religious affiliation/commitment, work experience. SAT or ACT required; TOEFL required of all international applicants. High school diploma is required and GED is not accepted. *Academic units required:* 4 English, 3 mathematics, 2 science, (2 science labs), 2 foreign language, 2 history, 3 academic electives, *Academic units recommended:* 4 English, 4 mathematics, 4 science, (2 science labs), 4 foreign language, 4 history.

Financial Aid

Students should submit: FAFSA, CSS/Financial Aid PROFILE, business/farm supplement. As may be requested on individual basis, signed Federal income tax return and W-2 forms, Student Federal income tax return. Regular filing deadline is 2/15. The Princeton Review suggests that all financial aid forms be submitted as soon as possible after 1/1. *Need-based scholarships/grants offered:* Federal Pell, SEOG, private scholarships, the school's own gift aid, Federal ACG and SMART Grants. *Loan aid offered:* FFEL Subsidized Stafford, FFEL Unsubsidized Stafford, FFEL PLUS, Federal Perkins, Federal Nursing, Notre Dame Undergraduate Loan (NDUL). Applicants will be notified of awards on or about 4/1. Off-campus job opportunities are fair.

The Inside Word

Notre Dame is one of the most selective colleges in the country. Almost everyone who enrolls is in the top 10 percent of their graduating class and possesses test scores in the highest percentiles. But, as the student respondents suggest, strong academic ability isn't enough to get you in here. The school looks for students with other talents, and seems to have a predilection for athletic achievement. Legacy students get a leg up but are by no means assured of admission.

THE SCHOOL SAYS " . . . "

From The Admissions Office

"Notre Dame is a Catholic university, which means it offers unique opportunities for academic, ethical, spiritual, and social service development. The First Year of Studies program provides special assistance to our students as they make the adjustment from high school to college. The first-year curriculum includes many core requirements, while allowing students to explore several areas of possible future study. Each residence hall is home to students from all classes; most will live in the same hall for all their years on campus. An average of 93 percent of entering students will graduate within five years.

"The highest Critical Reading score and the highest Math score from either test will be accepted; the Writing component score is not required. The ACT is also accepted (with or without Writing component) in lieu of the SAT."

SELECTIVITY

Admissions Rating	98
# of applicants	13,945
% of applicants accepted	27
% of acceptees attending	54

FRESHMAN PROFILE

Range SAT Critical Reading	650–740
Range SAT Math	670–760
Range SAT Writing	640–730
Range ACT Composite	31–34
Minimum paper TOEFL	560
Minimum computer TOEFL	250
Minimum web-based TOEFL	100
% graduated top 10% of class	86
% graduated top 25% of class	95
% graduated top 50% of class	100

DEADLINES

Early action	
Deadline	11/1
Notification	12/20
Regular	
Deadline	12/31
Notification	4/10
Nonfall registration?	yes

APPLICANTS ALSO LOOK AT
AND SOMETIMES PREFER
Duke University
Georgetown University
Northwestern University

AND RARELY PREFER
Boston College

FINANCIAL FACTS

Financial Aid Rating	95
Annual tuition	$36,340
Room and board	$9,828
Required fees	$507
Books and supplies	$950
% frosh rec. need-based scholarship or grant aid	45
% UG rec. need-based scholarship or grant aid	44
% frosh rec. non-need-based scholarship or grant aid	32
% UG rec. non-need-based scholarship or grant aid	29
% frosh rec. need-based self-help aid	36
% UG rec. need-based self-help aid	41
% frosh rec. athletic scholarships	6
% UG rec. athletic scholarships	5
% UG borrow to pay for school	57
Average cumulative indebtedness	$27,569

UNIVERSITY OF OKLAHOMA

1000 ASP AVENUE, NORMAN, OK 73019-4076 • ADMISSIONS: 405-325-2252 • FAX: 405-325-7124

CAMPUS LIFE

Quality of Life Rating	**83**
Fire Safety Rating	**98**
Green Rating	**91**
Type of school	public
Environment	city

STUDENTS

Total undergrad enrollment	20,350
% male/female	48/52
% from out of state	25
% live on campus	32
% in (# of) fraternities	19 (20)
% in (# of) sororities	23 (28)
% African American	6
% Asian	6
% Caucasian	75
% Hispanic	4
% Native American	7
% international	2
# of countries represented	100

SURVEY SAYS . . .

Athletic facilities are great
Low cost of living
Everyone loves the Sooners
(Almost) no one smokes

ACADEMICS

Academic Rating	**72**
Calendar	semester
Student/faculty ratio	18:1
Profs interesting rating	69
Profs accessible rating	72
% classes taught by TAs	20
Most common reg class size	10–19 students
Most common lab size	20–29 students

MOST POPULAR MAJORS

journalism
management science
zoology/animal biology

STUDENTS SAY ". . ."

Academics

The University of Oklahoma—students prefer the abbreviation OU—"is about academics and football," and in that order, too, although when students start gushing about their Sooners it's hard to be sure. Get them to stop talking football long enough, though, and OU undergrads will fill your ears with praise of their school's "nationally recognized theater department," its "best meteorology program in the nation," and the outstanding programs in engineering, journalism, business, visual communication, aviation, interior design, and a host of other disciplines. Or they'll remind you of the "nearly limitless" opportunities "in course and extracurricular selection" at OU, a school that "has resources for almost anything you want," including "probably the best library in the region" and "exceptional undergraduate research opportunities." Or they'll tell you that OU "is also constantly looking to improve its status, which helps students because it will receive better professors, research programs, new buildings, etc." Or they'll brag about how OU encourages study overseas; "receiving financial aid to study abroad is not difficult," demonstrating the school's commitment to providing "real-world experience. They encourage us to get out of the Bible Belt and experience the real world as much as possible." In the end, though, they usually come back to football; "the athletic department brings fame to the school, and with that, more money for the university as a whole," one student explains.

Life

How big is Sooner football? "My parents sent me here so I could buy them Sooner tickets," one student reports, perhaps joking. Undergrads agree that "Sooner football team is very important here at OU. Most everyone gets involved on game days," a full-day commitment that includes pre-game tailgates, the game itself, and post-game celebration (or, rarely, commiseration). Otherwise, students frequent Campus Corner, "the area of town very close to campus with bars, restaurants, and shops. It has a very old-town feel, and it's where most people go on the weekends." The Greek community is also big; "the majority of the campus is involved with Greek life, whether that comes in the form of national sororities and fraternities or in the form of ethic or volunteer-based fraternities," one student tells us. And, as at most large universities, "there is always something to do on campus: theater productions, choir concerts, OU improv, free movies and snacks in the Union, art exhibits….There is truly something for everyone." When students need a big-city escape, "Oklahoma City is only 20 minutes away."

Student Body

"It is easy to become overwhelmed by the large group of sorority and fraternity members that seem to control the university when you are a freshman," students tell us, but despite the initial perception that this is a "go Greek or go home type of school," undergrads eventually "learn that there is a whole world of students that don't participate" and that OU has "quite a diverse student body nowadays. Just in my hall there are foreign exchange students from Uganda, Peru, China, UK, Nepal, and Palestine….By no means are we just a bunch of white Republicans." Another student agrees: "What makes OU special is our large foreign exchange program and special scholarship opportunities that bring student here from all over the country. It is not unusual to get on a bus and hear at least three different languages." That said, don't expect to encounter East Coast attitudes here; "being in Oklahoma, there are definitely a lot of very conservative Christians. But, out of everywhere in Oklahoma, Norman is the most liberal."

FINANCIAL AID: 405-325-4521 • E-MAIL: ADMREC@OU.EDU • WEBSITE: WWW.OU.EDU

THE PRINCETON REVIEW SAYS

Admissions

Very important factors considered include: Class rank, academic GPA, rigor of secondary school record, standardized test scores. *Other factors considered include:* Application essay, recommendation(s), state residency, SAT or ACT required; TOEFL required of all international applicants. High school diploma is required and GED is accepted. *Academic units required:* 4 English, 3 mathematics, 2 science, (2 science labs), 2 social studies, 1 history, 3 academic electives, *Academic units recommended:* 2 foreign language, 1 computer science.

Financial Aid

Students should submit: FAFSA. The Princeton Review suggests that all financial aid forms be submitted as soon as possible after 1/1. *Need-based scholarships/grants offered:* Federal Pell, SEOG, state scholarships/grants, private scholarships, the school's own gift aid, United Negro College Fund. *Loan aid offered:* FFEL Subsidized Stafford, FFEL Unsubsidized Stafford, FFEL PLUS, Federal Perkins, Federal Nursing, college/university loans from institutional funds. Applicants will be notified of awards on a rolling basis beginning 3/15. Federal Work-Study Program available. Institutional employment available. Off-campus job opportunities are excellent.

The Inside Word

The OU admissions office applies formulas, published at the admissions section of the school's website, to determine who gets in. Standards are more stringent for out-of-state applicants than for Oklahoma natives; in all cases, students must exceed minimums in two of three categories (class rank, unweighted high school GPA, standardized test scores) to gain admission. You should be able to tell whether you'll get in before you even submit your application.

THE SCHOOL SAYS "..."

From The Admissions Office

"Ask yourself some significant questions. What are your ambitions, goals, and dreams? Do you desire opportunity, and are you ready to accept challenge? What do you hope to gain from your educational experience? Are you looking for a university that will provide you with the tools, resources, and motivation to convert ambitions, opportunities, and challenges into meaningful achievement? To effectively answer these questions you must carefully seek out your options, look for direction, and make the right choice. The University of Oklahoma combines a unique mixture of academic excellence, varied social cultures, and a variety of campus activities to make your educational experience complete. At OU, comprehensive learning is our goal for your life. Not only do you receive a valuable classroom learning experience, but OU is also one of the finest research institutions in the United States. This allows OU students the opportunity to be a part of technology in progress. It's not just learning, it's discovery, invention, and dynamic creativity, a hands-on experience that allows you to be on the cutting edge of knowledge. Make the right choice and consider the University of Oklahoma!

"The SAT (or ACT) will be used when considering freshman applicants for admission. The Writing component of either test is not required of students and is not used in determining admission to the university. The student's best composite score from any one test will be used."

SELECTIVITY
Admissions Rating	92
# of applicants	9,764
% of applicants accepted	82
% of acceptees attending	48
# accepting a place on wait list	1,704
% admitted from wait list	52

FRESHMAN PROFILE
Range SAT Critical Reading	520–640
Range SAT Math	540–650
Range ACT Composite	23–28
Minimum paper TOEFL	550
Minimum computer TOEFL	213
Minimum web-based TOEFL	79
Average HS GPA	3.62
% graduated top 10% of class	36
% graduated top 25% of class	72
% graduated top 50% of class	94

DEADLINES
Regular	
Deadline	4/1
Nonfall registration?	yes

FINANCIAL FACTS
Financial Aid Rating	82
Annual in-state tuition	$2,830
Annual out-of-state tuition	$10,814
Room and board	$7,376
Required fees	$2,415
Books and supplies	$958
% frosh rec. need-based scholarship or grant aid	5
% UG rec. need-based scholarship or grant aid	13
% frosh rec. non-need-based scholarship or grant aid	48
% UG rec. non-need-based scholarship or grant aid	36
% frosh rec. need-based self-help aid	39
% UG rec. need-based self-help aid	37
% frosh rec. athletic scholarships	1
% UG rec. athletic scholarships	1
% frosh rec. any financial aid	80
% UG rec. any financial aid	73
% UG borrow to pay for school	46
Average cumulative indebtedness	$20,341

UNIVERSITY OF OREGON

1217 UNIVERSITY OF OREGON, EUGENE, OR 97403-1217 • ADMISSIONS: 541-346-3201 • FAX: 541-346-5815

CAMPUS LIFE
Quality of Life Rating	**79**
Fire Safety Rating	**70**
Green Rating	**96**
Type of school	public
Environment	city

STUDENTS
Total undergrad enrollment	17,356
% male/female	49/51
% from out of state	30
% live on campus	21
% in (# of) fraternities	8 (12)
% in (# of) sororities	11 (9)
% African American	2
% Asian	7
% Caucasian	75
% Hispanic	4
% Native American	1
% international	5
# of countries represented	83

SURVEY SAYS . . .
Athletic facilities are great
Everyone loves the Ducks
Student publications are popular

ACADEMICS
Academic Rating	**72**
Calendar	quarter
Student/faculty ratio	19:1
Profs interesting rating	69
Profs accessible rating	74
% classes taught by TAs	16
Most common reg class size	20–29 students
Most common lab size	20–29 students

MOST POPULAR MAJORS
business/commerce
journalism
psychology

STUDENTS SAY ". . ."

Academics

Ask University of Oregon students what they like best about their school and a surprising number will mention intercollegiate athletics. Press them a bit harder, however, and they'll start to identify the school's many outstanding academic programs: a business school with "a great faculty" and "amazing facilities;" solid and popular foreign language programs, including robust offerings in Japanese and Chinese; an "esteemed" and "extremely challenging" journalism school; a "very strong program in psychology and neuroscience"; an architecture program that "is increasing in popularity"; and a music program that students tout as "one of the best in the country." The school also offers "a strong study-abroad program" that provides a "good outlet for all of the creative types at the university to pursue wild adventures or projects around the world," "tons of opportunities for internships," and "a whole world of unrecognized undergraduate lab research opportunities. Any, let alone all of these opportunities would give any student a foot in the door for a future in research." In other words, an ocean of opportunities awaits anyone here willing to seek it out. UO "is a place where you can get involved as deeply as you care to in social causes/politics, where you can become closely connected to your professors and their research, and where a sense of community (on campus and off) permeates your entire educational career." University of Oregon: come for the football and basketball, stay for the "incredible academics."

Life

"Life at UO is amazing all year round," undergrads report. In the fall "there is football, warm but crisp weather, and our campus is gorgeous." During the winter "there are basketball games and a lot of indoor parties." Spring and summer "are gorgeous" and the best time to enjoy the area's many outdoor opportunities, because "the rain keeps people inside during the fall and winter." Hometown Eugene "is great for the outdoors…. There are mountains to hike, rivers to float, and lakes to swim in all within 15 minutes. The coast is an hour away; the mountains are only an hour away (if you ski during the winter)." The school's outdoor program "has several trips each week. Depending on the season, they have rock climbing, snow excursions, white water rafting, and camping trips." Eugene is also great for cultural life. "The Hult Center and other venues host extensive arts and entertainment opportunities including the annual Bach Festival, numerous other music festivals, art walks, the Saturday Market crafts fair—the list is extensive." Enthusiasm for sports permeates the campus, and "there's always a party going on" if that's what you're looking for. In short, "Whatever interests students hold, Eugene and the university usually have something going on that captures their attention."

Student Body

"There is a significant blend of students with different ethnicities, religious views, sexual orientations, and genders" at the University of Oregon, where students tend to be "laid-back, environmentally conscious, and politically inclined…usually to the left." The population includes "more than its fair share of nerds, preps, theater kids, hippies, and maybe more pot smokers, but everyone seems to be super friendly, and most people just want to get along." The student body is "pretty white-bread," though, partly in reflection of the state of Oregon's demographics (the state is 93 percent white). "If they lowered out-of-state costs, more people would attend who are from ethnically diverse cities," one student suggests. A "large Asian and Middle Eastern population" accounts for much of the racial diversity here.

UNIVERSITY OF OREGON

FINANCIAL AID: 541-346-3211 • E-MAIL: UOADMIT@OREGON.UOREGON.EDU • WEBSITE: WWW.UOREGON.EDU

THE PRINCETON REVIEW SAYS

Admissions

Very important factors considered include: Academic GPA, rigor of secondary school record. *Other factors considered include:* Application essay, recommendation(s), standardized test scores, extracurricular activities, first generation, geographical residence, racial/ethnic status, state residency, talent/ability, volunteer work, work experience. SAT or ACT required; ACT with Writing component required. TOEFL required of all international applicants. High school diploma is required and GED is accepted. *Academic units required:* 4 English, 3 mathematics, 2 science, 2 foreign language, 3 social studies, *Academic units recommended:* (1 science labs), 2 additional units in required college preparatory areas recommended.

Financial Aid

Students should submit: FAFSA. The Princeton Review suggests that all financial aid forms be submitted as soon as possible after 1/1. *Need-based scholarships/grants offered:* Federal Pell, SEOG, state scholarships/grants, private scholarships, the school's own gift aid. *Loan aid offered:* Direct Subsidized Stafford, Direct Unsubsidized Stafford, Direct PLUS, Federal Perkins, college/university loans from institutional funds. Applicants will be notified of awards on a rolling basis beginning 4/15. Federal Work-Study Program available. Institutional employment available. Off-campus job opportunities are good.

The Inside Word

Give your grades, rank, and serial number—sorry, make that test scores—and wait for the admissions office to crunch the numbers. A GPA of 3.00 in a college prep curriculum pretty much guarantees entry here; the school is willing to overlook substandard test scores for anyone meeting this threshold. Applicants whose personal circumstances may have hindered their academic achievement should inform the school, as the admissions office may show leniency in their cases.

THE SCHOOL SAYS "..."

From The Admissions Office

"At the UO, you'll be part of a community dedicated to making a difference in the world. Whether you want to change a community, a law, or one person's mind, the UO will provide you with the inspiration and resources you'll need to succeed. You'll attend classes alongside students from all 50 states, 4 U.S. territories, and 84 other countries, learn from people with diverse cultural, ethnic, and spiritual heritages, and have opportunities to participate in cutting-edge research and engage in intellectual dialog with renowned faculty. You'll graduate from the UO with the knowledge, experience, and research, writing, and critical thinking skills necessary to succeed in an increasingly global and diverse community. Set in a 295-acre arboretum, the UO is literally green. Both academic and outdoor programs will bring you into contact with forests, mountains, rivers, and lakes. The first facilities of their kind in the nation, the Green Chemistry Laboratory uses only nontoxic materials and the Tyler Instrumentation Center provides the full range of instruments needed in green chemistry. The Lillis Business Complex is the country's most environmentally friendly business school facility, and nationally recognized programs in sustainable business, architecture, and technology demonstrate the UO's ongoing commitment to the environment. With a student-teacher ratio of 18:1, average class size of 22 students, 273 academic programs, and more than 250 student organizations, you'll find that the UO is uniquely able to provide the advantages of a smaller liberal arts university in addition to all the resources of a major research institution. To be eligible for freshman admission, you must have a high school GPA of at least 3.00, be a graduate of a standard or accredited high school, and submit SAT or ACT scores. A cumulative GPA of 3.25 or better on a 4.00 scale and completion of at least 16 units of academic course work qualifies you for guaranteed admission."

SELECTIVITY
Admissions Rating	88
# of applicants	15,013
% of applicants accepted	85
% of acceptees attending	33

FRESHMAN PROFILE
Range SAT Critical Reading	489–607
Range SAT Math	499–612
Minimum paper TOEFL	500
Minimum computer TOEFL	173
Minimum web-based TOEFL	61
Average HS GPA	3.48
% graduated top 10% of class	26
% graduated top 25% of class	58
% graduated top 50% of class	90

DEADLINES
Early action	
Deadline	11/1
Notification	12/15
Regular	
Priority	11/1
Deadline	1/15
Notification	rolling
Nonfall registration?	yes

APPLICANTS ALSO LOOK AT
AND OFTEN PREFER
University of California—Berkeley
University of California—Santa Cruz
University of California—Santa Barbara
University of California—Davis
AND SOMETIMES PREFER
University of Puget Sound
University of Washington
Willamette University
AND RARELY PREFER
University of Colorado—Boulder
Oregon State University
University of Arizona

FINANCIAL FACTS
Financial Aid Rating	71
Annual in-state tuition	$5,202
Annual out-of-state tuition	$18,759
Room and board	$8,211
Required fees	$1,233
Books and supplies	$1,050
% frosh rec. need-based scholarship or grant aid	16
% UG rec. need-based scholarship or grant aid	21
% frosh rec. non-need-based scholarship or grant aid	18
% UG rec. non-need-based scholarship or grant aid	11
% frosh rec. need-based self-help aid	28
% UG rec. need-based self-help aid	32
% UG rec. athletic scholarships	2
% frosh rec. any financial aid	64.3
% UG rec. any financial aid	61.9
% UG borrow to pay for school	55
Average cumulative indebtedness	$18,805

UNIVERSITY OF THE PACIFIC

3601 PACIFIC AVENUE, STOCKTON, CA 95211 • ADMISSIONS: 209-946-2211 • FAX: 209-946-2413

CAMPUS LIFE
Quality of Life Rating	76
Fire Safety Rating	88
Green Rating	84
Type of school	private
Environment	city

STUDENTS
Total undergrad enrollment	3,457
% male/female	44/56
% from out of state	12.8
% from public high school	82
% in (# of) fraternities	16 (8)
% in (# of) sororities	18 (7)
# of countries represented	66

SURVEY SAYS . . .
Low cost of living
(Almost) no one smokes
Very little drug use

ACADEMICS
Academic Rating	85
Calendar	semester, trimester quarter by program
Profs interesting rating	85
Profs accessible rating	84

MOST POPULAR MAJORS
biology/biological sciences
business/commerce
engineering

STUDENTS SAY ". . ."

Academics

University of the Pacific is "a student-centered school with opportunities for growth" in "many areas" of students' "academic, social, and professional" lives. The school places a premium on "very strong" academics and "personalized learning" that is bolstered by "the relationships between students and faculty" being "really good." "If you ever have any questions, there's always someone there to answer them and help you out academically and socially," says one undergrad. "You won't get lost at Pacific." Indeed, the "small school" atmosphere "creates a sense of community on campus" which allows plenty of "opportunities for students to be somebody…instead of just another person at a large university." Overall, students here praise the "great academics," "small classes," "beautiful campus," "amazing faculty," "strong alumni support," and "great student involvement." However, on every college education a little rain must fall. In line with that, reviews of the administration are decidedly mixed. Some students feel that it's "pretty awesome" and that it is "always working to make sure the school is running properly." The administration makes "informed and useful choices based on student need," explains one student. Others aren't as convinced, noting that the administration can be a "mess of petitions." One thing that all students do agree on is that Pacific is "a school that you can be proud of going to." As one undergrad explains, "I grew up in Stockton, and this school made me realize all the great opportunities that Pacific offers in the way of career development and networking."

Life

Most students at Pacific agree that "life at this school revolves around studying and attending classes." Due to the "rigorous curriculum" offered in any major, "most of the time people are talking about when the next exam is and when they are going to study." That said, this "work hard" atmosphere fades on the weekend, when students "tend to relieve stress and party." "There are always parties on the weekends," explains one student, "usually at Greek houses, but if not there then in the dorms." Outside of parties, many "balance" their academic workloads "by joining social clubs and participating in many volunteer services." Some find the "small campus" "awesome" because "you always run into someone you know when walking from class to class." Off campus, the social options decidedly lessen because many students view Stockton as being "unsafe." Many at Pacific wish the school would "reach out to more students when it comes to activities" and that they would "work with the [city] community to develop activities off campus." On the weekends, a fair amount of the student body heads "home, or to San Francisco if home isn't close enough."

Student Body

At first glance, the typical Pacific student can be described most broadly as "very friendly, active, and sociable." However, beyond that, the descriptions run the gamut from those who "like to party all the time" to those who are "solely focused on academics." "It's a very diverse student body," says one undergrad. "Various ethnic, academic, religious, and personal backgrounds are represented." Others agree, noting that "the greatest strength of the school would have to be the diversity," which is supported by "many out-of-state and international students." Despite all the "different types" of students, everyone "fits into their respective niche on campus." One thing that they share is a tendency to "be quite studious" and "very active in the community and extracurricular activities." The small campus means that students "can recognize a lot of faces around campus even if they aren't friends with them."

FINANCIAL AID: 209-946-2421 • E-MAIL: ADMISSIONS@PACIFIC.EDU • WEBSITE: WWW.PACIFIC.EDU

THE PRINCETON REVIEW SAYS

Admissions

Very important factors considered include: rigor of secondary school record. *Important factors considered include:* Application essay, academic GPA, recommendation(s), standardized test scores, extracurricular activities, first generation. *Other factors considered include:* Class rank, alumni/ae relation, character/personal qualities, geographical residence, level of applicant's interest, talent/ability, volunteer work, work experience. SAT Subject Tests recommended; SAT or ACT required; SAT and SAT Subject Tests or ACT recommended; ACT with Writing component recommended. TOEFL required of all international applicants. High school diploma is required and GED is accepted. *Academic units recommended:* 4 English, 2 foreign language, 2 social studies, 1 history, 1 visual/performing arts, 1 academic electives.

Financial Aid

Students should submit: FAFSA. The Princeton Review suggests that all financial aid forms be submitted as soon as possible after 1/1. *Need-based scholarships/grants offered:* Federal Pell, SEOG, state scholarships/grants, private scholarships, the school's own gift aid, ACG, SMART. *Loan aid offered:* Direct Subsidized Stafford, Direct Unsubsidized Stafford, Direct PLUS, FFEL Subsidized Stafford, FFEL Unsubsidized Stafford, FFEL PLUS, Federal Perkins, Direct Graduate/Professional PLUS Loans. Applicants will be notified of awards on a rolling basis beginning 3/15.

The Inside Word

As you'd expect in a state as educationally-rich as California, the competition between colleges for students is fierce, meaning that high acceptance rates don't necessarily correlate with low entrance requirements. In fact, it's often the reverse, as is the case with University of the Pacific. While the admissions officers consider a variety of factors when considering applicants, a challenging course load is of utmost importance. In other words, enroll in all the honors and advanced placement courses you can if you're keen on making Pacific the place where you'll hang your graduation cap.

THE SCHOOL SAYS ". . ."

From The Admissions Office

"One of the most concise ways of describing the University of the Pacific is that it is 'a major university in a small college package.' Our 3,400 undergraduates get the personal attention that you would expect at a small, residential college. But they also have the kinds of opportunities offered at much larger institutions, including more than 90 majors and programs; hundreds of student organizations; drama, dance, and musical productions; 16 NCAA Division I athletic teams; and two dozen club and intramural sports. We offer undergraduate major programs in the arts, sciences and humanities, business, education, engineering, international studies, music, pharmacy, and health sciences. Some of the unique aspects of our academic programs include the following: We have the only independent, coed, nonsectarian liberal arts and sciences college located between Los Angeles and central Oregon; we have the only undergraduate professional school of international studies in California—and it's the only one in the nation that actually requires you to study abroad; we have the only engineering program in the West that requires students to complete a year's worth of paid work experience as part of their degree; our Conservatory of Music focuses on performance but also offers majors in music management, music therapy, and music education; and we offer several accelerated programs in business, dentistry, dental hygiene, education, law, engineering, and pharmacy. Our beautiful New England-style main campus is located in Stockton (population: 287,245) and is within 2 hours or less of San Francisco, Santa Cruz, Yosemite National Park, and Lake Tahoe. SAT Subject Tests recommended: Mathematics, Chemistry (natural science majors only)."

SELECTIVITY

Admissions Rating	89
# of applicants	5,450
% of applicants accepted	69
% of acceptees attending	23
# accepting a place on wait list	30
% admitted from wait list	100

FRESHMAN PROFILE

Range SAT Critical Reading	500–620
Range SAT Math	530–670
Range SAT Writing	500–620
Range ACT Composite	22–28
Minimum paper TOEFL	475
Minimum computer TOEFL	150
Minimum web-based TOEFL	52
Average HS GPA	3.46
% graduated top 10% of class	39
% graduated top 25% of class	75
% graduated top 50% of class	93

DEADLINES

Early action	
Deadline	11/15
Notification	1/15
Regular	
Priority	11/15
Deadline	1/15
Notification	rolling
Nonfall registration?	yes

FINANCIAL FACTS

Financial Aid Rating	74
Annual tuition	$30,380
Room and board	$10,118
Required fees	$500
Books and supplies	$1,566
% frosh rec. need-based scholarship or grant aid	68
% UG rec. need-based scholarship or grant aid	65
% frosh rec. need-based self-help aid	64
% UG rec. need-based self-help aid	63
% frosh rec. athletic scholarships	2
% UG rec. athletic scholarships	4
% frosh rec. any financial aid	86
% UG rec. any financial aid	81

UNIVERSITY OF PENNSYLVANIA

ONE COLLEGE HALL, PHILADELPHIA, PA 19104 • ADMISSIONS: 215-898-7507 • FAX: 215-898-9670

CAMPUS LIFE

Quality of Life Rating	88
Fire Safety Rating	70
Green Rating	93
Type of school	private
Environment	metropolis

STUDENTS

Total undergrad enrollment	9,756
% male/female	50/50
% from out of state	83
% from public high school	55
% live on campus	62
% in (# of) fraternities	30 (35)
% in (# of) sororities	27 (13)
% African American	8
% Asian	18
% Caucasian	43
% Hispanic	6
% international	10
# of countries represented	103

SURVEY SAYS . . .

Athletic facilities are great
Diverse student types on campus
Great off-campus food
Students are happy
Student publications are popular
Student government is popular
Hard liquor is popular

ACADEMICS

Academic Rating	87
Calendar	semester
Student/faculty ratio	6:1
Profs interesting rating	74
Profs accessible rating	80
% classes taught by TAs	5
Most common	
reg class size	10–19 students

MOST POPULAR MAJORS

business administration and
management
finance
nursing/registered nurse
(rn, asn, bsn, msn)

STUDENTS SAY ". . ."

Academics

At the University of Pennsylvania, everyone shares an intellectual curiosity and top-notch resources, but doesn't "buy into the stigma of being an Ivy League school." Still, no one turns down the opportunity to rave about the school's strong academic reputation or the large alumni network. Students here are also "very passionate about what they do outside the classroom" and the opportunities presented to them through attending UPenn. The university is composed of four undergraduate schools (and "a library for pretty much any topic"), and students tend to focus on what they'll do with their degree pretty early on. Wharton, UPenn's "highly competitive undergraduate business school," creates a "tremendous pre-professional atmosphere" that keeps students competitive and somewhat stressed with their studies during the week. This "career-oriented" attitude spills over into other factions of the university, leaving some desiring more grounds for creativity and less climbing over each other. "It's when individuals' grades are on the line when the claws come out," says a student.

Professors can "sometimes seem to be caught up more in their research than their classes," but "there are very few other institutions where you can take every one of your classes with a professor who is setting the bar for research in his or her field." If you are willing to put in the time and effort, your professors "will be happy to reciprocate." In general, the instructors here are "very challenging academically," and one student says "some of them have been excellent, but all of them have at least been good." The administration is "very professional and efficient" and "truly interested in students' well being." "Academically, I have access to opportunities unparalleled elsewhere," says a student.

Life

Penn kids don't mind getting into intellectual conversations during dinner, but "partying is a much higher priority here than it is at other Ivy League schools." Many students schedule their classes so as to not have class on Fridays, making the weekend "officially" start on Thursday night, and frat parties and Center City bars and clubs are popular destinations. However, when it comes down to midterms and finals, "people get really serious and...buckle down and study." Between weekend jaunts to New York and Philadelphia ("a city large enough to answer the needs of any type of person"), students have plenty of access to restaurants, shopping, concerts, and sports games, as well as plain old "hanging out with hallmates playing Mario Kart." The school provides plenty of guest speakers, cultural events, clubs, and organizations for students to channel their energies, and seniors can even attend "Feb Club" in the month of February, which is essentially an event every night. It's a busy life at UPenn, and "people are constantly trying to think about how they can balance getting good grades academically and their weekend plans."

Student Body

This "determined" bunch is very career-oriented, "takes classes pretty seriously," leans to the left, and "personality-wise tends to be type A." "There is always someone smarter than you are," says a Chemical Biomolecular engineering major. Everyone has "a strong sense of personal style and his or her own credo," but no group deviates too far from the more mainstream stereotypes. There's a definite lack of "emos" and hippies. There's "the career-driven Wharton kid who will stab you in the back to get your interview slot" and "the nursing kid who's practically non-existent," but on the whole, there is "tremendous school diversity," and whatever kind of person you are, "you will find a group of people like you."

FINANCIAL AID: 215-898-1988 • E-MAIL: INFO@ADMISSIONS.UGAO.UPENN.EDU • WEBSITE: WWW.UPENN.EDU

THE PRINCETON REVIEW SAYS

Admissions

Very important factors considered include: recommendation(s), rigor of secondary school record, character/personal qualities. *Important factors considered include:* Class rank, application essay, academic GPA, standardized test scores, extracurricular activities, work experience. *Other factors considered include:* alumni/ae relation, first generation, geographical residence, interview, racial/ethnic status, talent/ability, volunteer work, SAT and SAT Subject Tests or ACT required; ACT with Writing component required. TOEFL required of all international applicants. High school diploma or equivalent is not required. *Academic units required:* 4 English, 4 mathematics, 3 science, (3 science labs), 4 foreign language, 3 history.

Financial Aid

Students should submit: FAFSA, institution's own financial aid form, CSS/Financial Aid PROFILE, noncustodial PROFILE, business/farm supplement. Parents' and student's most recently completed income tax. The Princeton Review suggests that all financial aid forms be submitted as soon as possible after 1/1. *Need-based scholarships/grants offered:* Federal Pell, SEOG, state scholarships/grants, private scholarships, the school's own gift aid *Loan aid offered:* FFEL Subsidized Stafford, FFEL Unsubsidized Stafford, FFEL PLUS, Federal Perkins, Federal Nursing, college/university loans from institutional funds, Supplemental 3rd Party Loans guaranteed by institution. Applicants will be notified of awards on or about 4/1. Federal Work-Study Program available. Institutional employment available. Off-campus job opportunities are excellent.

The Inside Word

After a small decline four cycles ago, applications are once again climbing at Penn—the fifth increase in six years. The competition in the applicant pool is formidable. Applicants can safely assume that they need to be one of the strongest students in their graduating class in order to be successful.

THE SCHOOL SAYS ". . ."

From The Admissions Office

"The nation's first university, the University of Pennsylvania, had its beginnings in 1740, some 36 years before Thomas Jefferson, Benjamin Franklin (Penn's founder), and their fellow revolutionaries went public in Philadelphia with incendiary notions about life, liberty and the pursuit of happiness. Today, Penn continues in the spirit of the Founding Fathers, developing the intellectual, discussion-oriented seminars that comprise the majority of our course offerings, shaping innovative new courses of study, and allowing a remarkable degree of academic flexibility to its undergraduate students. Penn is situated on a green, tree-lined, 260-acre urban campus, four blocks west of the Schuylkill River in Philadelphia. The broad lawns that connect Penn's stately halls embody a philosophy of academic freedom within our undergraduate schools. Newly developed interdisciplinary programs fusing classical disciplines with practical, professional options enable Penn to define cutting-edge academia in and out of the classroom. Students are encouraged to partake in study and research that may extend into many of the graduate and professional schools. Penn students are part of a dynamic community that includes a traditional campus, a lively neighborhood, and a city rich in culture and diversity. Whether your interests include artistic performance, community involvement, student government, athletics, fraternities and sororities, or cultural and religious organizations, you'll find many different options. Most importantly, students at Penn find that their lives in and out of the classroom compliment each other and are full, interesting and busy. We invite you to visit Penn in Philadelphia. You'll enjoy the revolutionary spirit of the campus and city. Penn requires either the SAT plus two SAT Subject Tests (in different fields) or the ACT."

SELECTIVITY
Admissions Rating	99
# of applicants	22,935
% of applicants accepted	17
% of acceptees attending	63
# accepting a place on wait list	2,381
% admitted from wait list	7
# of early decision applicants	3,912
% accepted early decision	29

FRESHMAN PROFILE
Range SAT Critical Reading	650–740
Range SAT Math	680–780
Range SAT Writing	670–760
Range ACT Composite	30–33
Minimum paper TOEFL	600
Minimum computer TOEFL	220
Minimum web-based TOEFL	100
Average HS GPA	3.83
% graduated top 10% of class	99
% graduated top 25% of class	100
% graduated top 50% of class	100

DEADLINES
Early Decision	
Deadline	11/1
Notification	12/15
Regular	
Deadline	1/1
Notification	4/1
Nonfall registration?	no

APPLICANTS ALSO LOOK AT
AND OFTEN PREFER
Harvard College, Stanford University
Massachusetts Institute of Technology
Yale University, Princeton University

AND SOMETIMES PREFER
Duke University
Columbia University
Brown University

AND RARELY PREFER
Cornell University, Georgetown University

FINANCIAL FACTS
Financial Aid Rating	96
Annual tuition	$34,868
Room and board	$11,016
Required fees	$4,102
% frosh rec. need-based scholarship or grant aid	37
% UG rec. need-based scholarship or grant aid	39
% frosh rec. need-based self-help aid	38
% UG rec. need-based self-help aid	41
% frosh rec. any financial aid	60
% UG rec. any financial aid	55
% UG borrow to pay for school	41
Average cumulative indebtedness	$19,085

UNIVERSITY OF PITTSBURGH—PITTSBURGH CAMPUS

4227 Fifth Avenue, First Floor, Alumni Hall, Pittsburgh, PA 15260 • Admissions: 412-624-7488 • Fax: 412-648-8815

CAMPUS LIFE

Quality of Life Rating	**91**
Fire Safety Rating	**83**
Green Rating	**78**
Type of school	public
Environment	metropolis

STUDENTS

Total undergrad enrollment	17,054
% male/female	49/51
% from out of state	17
% live on campus	45
% in (# of) fraternities	8 (22)
% in (# of) sororities	8 (16)
% African American	8
% Asian	5
% Caucasian	80
% Hispanic	1
% international	1
# of countries represented	44

SURVEY SAYS . . .
Athletic facilities are great
Low cost of living
Student publications are popular
(Almost) no one smokes

ACADEMICS

Academic Rating	**80**
Calendar	semester
Profs interesting rating	71
Profs accessible rating	81
Most common reg class size	10–19 students
Most common lab size	20–29 students

MOST POPULAR MAJORS
marketing/marketing management
psychology
speech and rhetorical studies

STUDENTS SAY ". . ."

Academics

Students at the University of Pittsburgh call their school an "underrated academic powerhouse." It's "a premier research university," they say, with "resources and opportunities" galore. "A lot of Pitt's departments are nationally recognized," and there are more than 100 degree programs and areas of study available—with majors ranging the gamut from "Swahili to premed." The engineering school is "very good," the nursing program is "excellent." physical therapy, philosophy, and business are also especially noteworthy. Pitt is "a big school, so sometimes you run into red tape and bureaucratic hassles." "Registration is very hectic, and even upperclassmen have a hard time getting the classes they want/need." This may change however, with the online registration system. Though some students feel the advising system "could be improved," overall, students say the administration is "good" and anything that "needs to be worked on is addressed." Faculty members at Pitt are "extremely well versed in their subject areas." Many are "internationally renowned in their fields." However, the in-class experience gets mixed reviews. "Some professors will change your world," says an economics major. "some will make you hate the class. It can be hit-or-miss." "There are some pretty boring lecturers who are just there to do research." On the other hand, many professors are "really inspiring, passionate," and "extremely accessible." As one student says, "Granted it is a bigger school, so you [may] have to seek help yourself, but that is what I like because it has made me a more assertive person, which is a skill that will benefit me post graduation." "If you are talented and work hard, you'll get what you are after."

Life

Pitt students enjoy a "fun, beautiful, urban" campus that is "secluded enough to feel like college" and, at the same time, fully integrated into the "vibrant," "affordable," and "extremely friendly" city of Pittsburgh. Students take great pride in "the Burgh," and they have "infectious school spirit." "The party scene is excellent." The "smorgasbord of nightlife" available includes "a great college bar scene in Oakland." Students also frequent "parties at the frat houses or at people's off-campus houses." "Pittsburgh offers students more than just a party scene," though. Clubs and student organizations are "copious." The Greek system has a presence, but it's "not overpowering." "There's lots of artsy things to do" like plays, musicals, and symphonies. "It's easy to do anything from free tango lessons to four-square competitions to watching major speakers," relates a sophomore. Off campus, good grub and "unique dining experiences" are available (and often necessary because the campus food "could be better than it is important.)" Students get free admission to a number of "amazing" museums and "a lot of attractions throughout Pittsburgh." They can take the bus all over town gratis, too. Discounted tickets to Penguins hockey games and Pirates baseball games are still another perk. Basically, students assure us, it's "impossible to be bored."

Student Body

Roughly three-quarters of the students here hail from Pennsylvania, and, overall, "the school is pretty middle-class" and "unpretentious." Students here are "moderately to very devoted to academics." They are "friendly and ambitious." They are "scrappy and smarter than you think." Most of them seem to be "enjoying the culture of the city of Pittsburgh." Beyond, that, "it is hard to categorize a Pitt student because it is such a large school." The sheer number of students "allows for a wide range of tastes." "There is a good bit of ethnic diversity." "People from all walks of life" attend Pitt. "This isn't a school where you have to conform to any one norm," explains a senior. "The student body is made of individuals who can successfully keep their own identity while not feeling lost in the mix." "No matter what category a student fits into, they will completely be comfortable on Pitt's campus," promises a junior. "Everyone finds a group of people to hang out with."

UNIVERSITY OF PITTSBURGH—PITTSBURGH CAMPUS

FINANCIAL AID: 412-624-7488 • E-MAIL: OAFA@PITT.EDU • WEBSITE: WWW.PITT.EDU

THE PRINCETON REVIEW SAYS

Admissions

Very important factors considered include: Academic GPA, rigor of secondary school record, standardized test scores. *Other factors considered include:* Class rank, application essay, recommendation(s), character/personal qualities, extracurricular activities, first generation, geographical residence, interview, level of applicant's interest, racial/ethnic status, state residency, talent/ability, volunteer SAT or ACT required; TOEFL required of all international applicants. High school diploma is required and GED is not accepted. *Academic units required:* 4 English, 3 mathematics, 3 science, 2 foreign language, 2 social studies, 3 academic electives. *Academic units recommended:* 4 English, 4 mathematics, 4 science, 3 foreign language, 3 social studies, 5 academic electives.

Financial Aid

Students should submit: FAFSA. The Princeton Review suggests that all financial aid forms be submitted as soon as possible after 1/1. *Need-based scholarships/grants offered:* Federal Pell, SEOG, state scholarships/grants, private scholarships, the school's own gift aid, Federal Nursing Scholarships. *Loan aid offered:* FFEL Subsidized Stafford, FFEL Unsubsidized Stafford, FFEL PLUS, Federal Perkins, Federal Nursing, college/university loans from institutional funds. Applicants will be notified of awards on a rolling basis beginning 3/15. Federal Work-Study Program available. Off-campus job opportunities are excellent.

The Inside Word

Despite the large number of applications that Pitt receives, admissions counselors review each application individually with a holistic perspective. Essays and recommendation are taken into consideration. That said, strong secondary school records and test scores rank high on the admit list. Applicants with honors classes, advanced placement classes, and solid grades have the best chance of admission.

THE SCHOOL SAYS "..."

From The Admissions Office

"The University of Pittsburgh is one of 62 members of the Association of American Universities, a prestigious group whose members include the major research universities of North America. There are nearly 400 degree programs available at the 16 Pittsburgh campus schools (two offering only undergraduate degree programs, four offering graduate degree programs, and ten offering both) and four regional campuses, allowing students a wide latitude of choices, both academically and in setting and style, size and pace of campus. Programs ranked nationally include philosophy, history and philosophy of science, chemistry, economics, English, history, physics, political science, and psychology. "Some of the company the University of Pittsburgh keeps: Pitt ranks in the very top cluster of U.S. public research universities according to the 2007 edition of The Top American Research Universities annual report, issued by The Center for Measuring University Performance, along with Berkeley, Illinois, Michigan, UCLA, UNC, Wisconsin; it has a notable record of high achieving graduates—since 1995 Pitt undergraduates have won two Rhodes, six Marshal, five Truman, four Udall, one Churchill, one Gates Cambridge, 33 Goldwater scholarships, and three Mellon Humanities Fellowships. In research, Pitt ranks sixth among all U.S. universities in terms of competitive grants awarded to faculty by the National Institutes of Health. In international education, only 17 American universities can claim four or more area studies programs that have been competitively designated National Resource Centers by the U.S. Department of Education. In intercollegiate athletics, Pitt's football and men's basketball teams are consistently considered among the finest."

SELECTIVITY

Admissions Rating	92
# of applicants	20,685
% of applicants accepted	55
% of acceptees attending	30
# accepting a place on wait list	300
% admitted from wait list	14

FRESHMAN PROFILE

Range SAT Critical Reading	570–680
Range SAT Math	590–680
Range ACT Composite	25–30
Minimum paper TOEFL	550
Minimum computer TOEFL	213
Minimum web-based TOEFL	80
Average HS GPA	3.95
% graduated top 10% of class	48
% graduated top 25% of class	85
% graduated top 50% of class	98

DEADLINES

Regular	
Notification	rolling
Nonfall registration?	yes

APPLICANTS ALSO LOOK AT

AND OFTEN PREFER
Carnegie Mellon University
Boston University

AND SOMETIMES PREFER
University of Delaware
University of Maryland—College Park
Penn State—University Park

AND RARELY PREFER
Duquesne University
Temple University

FINANCIAL FACTS

Financial Aid Rating	78
Annual tuition in-state	$12,832
Annual tuition out-of-state	$22,480
Required fees	$810
% frosh rec. need-based scholarship or grant aid	41
% UG rec. need-based scholarship or grant aid	37
% frosh rec. non-need-based scholarship or grant aid	25
% UG rec. non-need-based scholarship or grant aid	17
% frosh rec. need-based self-help aid	40
% UG rec. need-based self-help aid	43
% frosh rec. athletic scholarships	1
% UG rec. athletic scholarships	1

UNIVERSITY OF PUGET SOUND

1500 NORTH WARNER STREET, TACOMA, WA 98416-1062 • ADMISSIONS: 253-879-3211 • FAX: 253-879-3993

CAMPUS LIFE
Quality of Life Rating	**91**
Fire Safety Rating	**73**
Green Rating	**60***
Type of school	private
Environment	city

STUDENTS
Total undergrad enrollment	2,531
% male/female	42/58
% from out of state	71
% from public high school	76
% live on campus	62
% in (# of) fraternities	23 (4)
% in (# of) sororities	22 (4)
% African American	3
% Asian	9
% Caucasian	75
% Hispanic	3
% Native American	1
# of countries represented	14

SURVEY SAYS . . .
Lab facilities are great
School is well run
Musical organizations are popular

ACADEMICS
Academic Rating	**94**
Calendar	semester
Student/faculty ratio	11:1
Profs interesting rating	95
Profs accessible rating	98
Most common reg class size	10–19 students
Most common lab size	10–19 students

MOST POPULAR MAJORS
business/commerce
English language and literature
psychology

STUDENTS SAY "..."

Academics

Set "in the shadows of the Cascades" and just down the road from Washington State's Commencement Bay, the University of Puget Sound "offers a strong (and getting stronger) liberal arts education." A junior explains, "We are a very student-centered school," which means that teaching is top priority for this highly qualified faculty. Not only are professors "intelligent, well versed, [and] articulate," they're also concerned about the well-being of their students. "Many professors want to have conversations about what is going on in your life," writes a senior. "They make this school." So does the strong allotment of academic offerings. Students point to the Asian studies, biology, international political economy, and music offerings as the crème de la crème. You won't find the standard "huge lecture classes" at Puget Sound; "Even intro-level lectures have maybe 30 people in them." Despite the friendly atmosphere in class, professors tend to set high expectations for their students. "Coasting by on natural ability doesn't work anymore," warns a senior. Opinions of the administration vary, but most find it to be "caring and supportive of the students. If you have an idea, they say go for it." Students are hoping the new president of the university will help put UPS on the map. As a psychology major puts it, "The university is academically strong, but needs to be recognized for that across the country, not just in the Pacific Northwest."

Life

Whether you're a city slicker or a rugged outdoorsman, Puget Sound's location ensures you'll find something to satisfy your interests. Seattle is a short drive away and has everything from pro sports teams to world-class art exhibits. With beaches, the Puget Sound, the Cascades, and the Olympic Rain Forest all nearby, outdoor enthusiasts are never at a loss for adventure. "Outdoor interests are really popular, [including] ultimate Frisbee, soccer, biking, and hiking." "Athletics are huge," too, and with 21 varsity teams, 14 intramural sports, and three club sports, athletes have plenty of opportunities to flex their muscles. Sports aside, "there are tons of activities (presentations, volunteer opportunities, meetings, movies, talks, concerts, and clubs) every night of the week." In total, Puget Sound offers about 75 student clubs, and "most people are involved in a ton of groups." When they're not involved in parties, that is. "There are always plenty [parties] going on, either at Greek houses or in other nearby campus houses." But beware, warns an undergrad: "The administration can have a Gestapo-esque feel when it comes to parties and drinking on campus." Nonetheless, some students line up at the keg, while others fill the seats for the popular "one-dollar movies" on campus. Regardless of what you're doing, "If you're not doing anything in the evening, you're either lazy or antisocial…or dead."

Student Body

"There are three groups of students" at Puget Sound, according to a senior: " the preppies, the hippies, and the Hawaiians." Among the first two groups, you're likely to find "a lot of 'trustafarians' and rich kids." There's no doubt liberalism rules the roost here, which causes one junior to note that "the least accepted student organization is, ironically, the Republican majority." But political differences—or any differences, for that matter—don't cause irreparable rifts in this student body. According to a sophomore, "Everyone gets along extremely well, no matter what gender, religion, race, ethnicity, [or] social class. Puget Sound has a great atmosphere that I sincerely appreciate." Another classmate adds, "Overall, students are accepting and curious about other beliefs. And students here are open-minded." They're open-hearted, as well as many students reported participating in community service.

FINANCIAL AID: 800-396-7192 • E-MAIL: ADMISSION@PUGETSOUND.EDU • WEBSITE: WWW.PUGETSOUND.EDU

THE PRINCETON REVIEW SAYS

Admissions

Very important factors considered include: Academic GPA, rigor of secondary school record, standardized test scores. *Important factors considered include:* Application essay, recommendation(s), alumni/ae relation, character/personal qualities, extracurricular activities, racial/ethnic status, talent/ability. *Other factors considered include:* Class rank, first generation, interview, level of applicant's interest, volunteer work, work experience. SAT or ACT required; ACT with Writing component recommended. TOEFL required of all international applicants. High school diploma is required and GED is accepted. *Academic units recommended:* 4 English, 4 mathematics, 4 science, (4 science labs), 3 foreign language, 3 social studies, 3 history, 1 fine/visual/performing Arts.

Financial Aid

Students should submit: FAFSA. The Princeton Review suggests that all financial aid forms be submitted as soon as possible after 1/1. *Need-based scholarships/grants offered:* Federal Pell, SEOG, state scholarships/grants, private scholarships, the school's own gift aid. *Loan aid offered:* FFEL Subsidized Stafford, FFEL Unsubsidized Stafford, FFEL PLUS, Federal Perkins. Applicants will be notified of awards on a rolling basis beginning 3/15. Federal Work-Study Program available. Institutional employment available. Off-campus job opportunities are excellent.

The Inside Word

The University of Puget Sound is on the right track with its willingness to supply students with detailed information about how the selection process works. If universities in general were more forthcoming about candidate evaluation, college admission wouldn't be the angst-ridden exercise that it is for so many students. Students should be aware that their academic background is the primary consideration of every admissions committee. How students are considered as individuals remains mysterious. At Puget Sound, it is clear people mean more to the university than its freshman profile, and candidates can count on a considerate and caring attitude before, during, and after the review process.

THE SCHOOL SAYS "..."

From The Admissions Office

"For over more than 100 years, students from many locations and backgrounds have chosen to join our community. It is a community committed to excellence—excellence in the classroom and excellence in student organizations and activities. Puget students are serious about rowing and writing, management and music, skiing and sciences, leadership and languages. At Puget Sound you'll be challenged—and helped—to perform at the peak of your ability.

"Applicants are required to submit the SAT or the ACT. For the foreseeable future, Puget Sound will record the SAT or ACT Writing component score, but will not require it as a part of a completed freshman admission application."

SELECTIVITY

Admissions Rating	93
# of applicants	5,231
% of applicants accepted	65
% of acceptees attending	20
# accepting a place on wait list	132
% admitted from wait list	25
# of early decision applicants	158
% accepted early decision	91

FRESHMAN PROFILE

Range SAT Critical Reading	570–690
Range SAT Math	550–660
Range SAT Writing	560–660
Range ACT Composite	25–30
Minimum paper TOEFL	550
Minimum computer TOEFL	213
Average HS GPA	3.54
% graduated top 10% of class	40
% graduated top 25% of class	69
% graduated top 50% of class	95

DEADLINES

Early Decision	
Deadline	11/15
Notification	12/15
Regular	
Priority	2/15
Deadline	2/15
Notification	4/1
Nonfall registration?	yes

APPLICANTS ALSO LOOK AT

AND OFTEN PREFER
Stanford University

AND SOMETIMES PREFER
Lewis & Clark College
University of Washington
Colorado College, Willamette University
Whitman College

FINANCIAL FACTS

Financial Aid Rating	81
Annual tuition	$35,440
Room	$5,130
Board	$4,060
Student government fee	$195
Books and supplies	$1,000
% frosh rec. need-based scholarship or grant aid	56
% UG rec. need-based scholarship or grant aid	58
% frosh rec. non-need-based scholarship or grant aid	29
% UG rec. non-need-based scholarship or grant aid	29
% frosh rec. need-based self-help aid	44
% UG rec. need-based self-help aid	48
% frosh rec. any financial aid	88
% UG rec. any financial aid	90
% UG borrow to pay for school	88
Average cumulative indebtedness	$27,648

UNIVERSITY OF REDLANDS

1200 EAST COLTON AVENUE, REDLANDS, CA 92373 • ADMISSIONS: 909-335-4074 • FAX: 909-335-4089

CAMPUS LIFE

Quality of Life Rating	85
Fire Safety Rating	75
Green Rating	85
Type of school	private
Environment	town

STUDENTS

Total undergrad enrollment	2,819
% male/female	44/56
% from out of state	33
% live on campus	72
% in (# of) fraternities	5 (5)
% in (# of) sororities	8 (5)
% African American	4
% Asian	5
% Caucasian	57
% Hispanic	13
% Native American	1
% international	2
# of countries represented	17

SURVEY SAYS . . .
Lab facilities are great
Athletic facilities are great
Students are happy
Musical organizations are popular

ACADEMICS

Academic Rating	86
Calendar	semester
Student/faculty ratio	13:1
Profs interesting rating	86
Profs accessible rating	86
Most common reg class size	10–19 students

MOST POPULAR MAJORS
business/commerce
liberal arts and sciences/liberal
studies
psychology

STUDENTS SAY " . . . "

Academics

The University of Redlands is essentially two undergraduate programs in one. Through the College of Arts and Sciences (CAS), the majority of students follow a relatively conventional undergraduate curriculum, declaring majors and meeting the related requirements in order to graduate. About 200 students take a more independent approach through the Johnston Center for Integrative Studies "where students who are accepted can create their own major with the help of their professors." These Johnston students write contracts for their courses and receive narrative evaluations of their work (rather than letter grades). This structure "allows students to learn in a way that is the most efficient for each individual." Because Johnston is a residential community, "Everyone works together to strengthen their education," much to the delight of participants. But regardless of the track they choose, Redlands undergrads enjoy a "personable, student-oriented" school that's "just small enough to have incredible personal attention, yet large enough to still see different people almost every day." Students also appreciate a study-abroad program that "is strongly emphasized and encouraged. If there's anywhere in the world you've had an interest in going—for a month or semester to a year—the University of Redlands is the perfect place to do it. Many students go to Austria because it's a wonderful program, and all your credits transfer when you come back." Redlands excels in a number of areas including business, music, creative writing, and biology, but they don't do it without a bit of sweat. Undergrads warn, "The academics at Redlands are demanding; I find myself reading, writing, and studying with extremely high degrees of intensity."

Life

Redlands is close to a lot of great places, but the town of Redlands itself "isn't much," students say. A number of them use the nickname "Dead Lands" to sum up their attitude, and a freshman gripes that "we can't just go into town to read at a coffee shop because there is no town!" So while "there's not much to do if you don't have a car," for the automobile-enabled, "everything is within an hour: the beach, LA, Palm Springs, and the mountains. Trips to the desert in Joshua Tree National Park are also common. Many people like to snowboard or ski in Big Bear in the winter." This nature-rich setting attracts outdoorsy types, and unsurprisingly Redlands "has a very involved outdoor activities group on campus that takes students kayaking, rock climbing and backpacking to destinations throughout the country." The Redlands campus "is beautiful for its Roman-style buildings and pillars, especially in the winter with the snow-capped mountains in the background," and it stays reasonably busy for a school of Redland's size. "Usually, there's something happening on campus, whether it's a philosophical discussion, a screening of a movie, karaoke night, or a basketball game." Still, "on weekends, most people end up drinking and going to parties," which the school frowns upon. Students wish the administration would be "a little more relaxed when it comes to party scenes. It seems like everyone is always getting in trouble. And even the frats have to be really careful and always have huge fines."

Student Body

Because of the CAS/Johnston academic fault line at Redlands, "the school is somewhat divided," with "ultra-liberal Johnston students who meander about the campus on long boards, leaving behind a perpetual smell of hemp and patchouli" on one side, and "more conservative Abercrombie-wearing NCAA athletes, Greeks, and California-skater types" on the other. The CAS student body also includes "math/science geeks, philosophy brains, the artists and musicians, business people, and whimsical lit majors." Many "regard the Johnston kids with complete suspicion and mistrust," in part because some of the Johnston kids seem to look down on the CAS majority. Johnston undergrads are known for being drawn to "a high-energy community of creativity, inhibition, and at times, spurts of college randomness. They are notorious for doing strange things!"

FINANCIAL AID: 909-335-4047 • E-MAIL: ADMISSIONS@REDLANDS.EDU • WEBSITE: WWW.REDLANDS.EDU

THE PRINCETON REVIEW SAYS

Admissions

Very important factors considered include: Academic GPA, recommendation(s), rigor of secondary school record, character/personal qualities, talent/ability. *Important factors considered include:* Application essay, standardized test scores. *Other factors considered include:* alumni/ae relation, extracurricular activities, first generation, geographical residence, interview, racial/ethnic status, volunteer work, work experience. SAT or ACT required; ACT with Writing component recommended. TOEFL required of all international applicants. High school diploma is required and GED is accepted. *Academic units required:* 4 English, 3 mathematics, 2 science, (1 science labs), 2 foreign language, 2 social studies. *Academic units recommended:* 4 English, 4 mathematics, 3 science, (1 science labs), 3 foreign language, 2 social studies, 1 history.

Financial Aid

Students should submit: FAFSA, state aid form. GPA Verification form for California Residents. The Princeton Review suggests that all financial aid forms be submitted as soon as possible after 1/1. *Need-based scholarships/grants offered:* Federal Pell, SEOG, state scholarships/grants, private scholarships, the school's own gift aid. *Loan aid offered:* FFEL Subsidized Stafford, FFEL Unsubsidized Stafford, FFEL PLUS, Federal Perkins, college/university loans from institutional funds. Applicants will be notified of awards on a rolling basis beginning 2/28. Federal Work-Study Program available. Off-campus job opportunities are fair.

The Inside Word

The University of Redlands is a solid admit for any student with an above-average high school record. Candidates who are interested in pursuing self-designed programs through the University's Johnston Center will find the admissions process to be distinctly more personal than it generally is. The center is interested in intellectually curious, self-motivated students and puts a lot of energy into identifying and recruiting them.

THE SCHOOL SAYS " . . ."

From The Admissions Office

"We've created an unusually blended curriculum of the liberal arts and pre-professional study because we think education is about learning how to think and learning how to do. For example, our environmental studies students have synthesized their study of computer science, sociology, biology, and economics to develop an actual resource management plan for the local mountain communities. Our creative writing program encourages internships with publishing or television production companies so that when our graduates send off their first novel, they can pay the rent as magazine writers. We educate managers, poets, environmental scientists, teachers, musicians, and speech therapists to be reflective about culture and society so that they can better understand and improve the world they'll enter upon graduation.

"First-year students applying for admission are required to submit the results of either the SAT or the ACT. We do not require the Writing section of either test."

SELECTIVITY

Admissions Rating	88
# of applicants	3,443
% of applicants accepted	68
% of acceptees attending	25

FRESHMAN PROFILE

Range SAT Critical Reading	520–620
Range SAT Math	540–620
Range ACT Composite	21–27
Minimum paper TOEFL	550
Minimum computer TOEFL	213
Average HS GPA	3.58
% graduated top 10% of class	31
% graduated top 25% of class	69
% graduated top 50% of class	92

DEADLINES

Regular	
Priority	12/15
Deadline	6/1
Notification	rolling
Nonfall registration?	yes

APPLICANTS ALSO LOOK AT

AND OFTEN PREFER
Occidental College

AND SOMETIMES PREFER
University of Southern California
San Diego State University

AND RARELY PREFER
University of California—Riverside

FINANCIAL FACTS

Financial Aid Rating	86
Annual tuition	$31,994
Room and board	$10,122
Required fees	$300
Books and supplies	$1,566
% frosh rec. need-based scholarship or grant aid	60
% UG rec. need-based scholarship or grant aid	63
% frosh rec. non-need-based scholarship or grant aid	8
% UG rec. non-need-based scholarship or grant aid	7
% frosh rec. need-based self-help aid	45
% UG rec. need-based self-help aid	52
% frosh rec. any financial aid	82
% UG rec. any financial aid	81
% UG borrow to pay for school	69.9
Average cumulative indebtedness	$17,290

UNIVERSITY OF RHODE ISLAND

14 UPPER COLLEGE ROAD, KINGSTON, RI 02881-1391 • ADMISSIONS: 401-874-7100 • FAX: 401-874-5523

CAMPUS LIFE

Quality of Life Rating	66
Fire Safety Rating	81
Green Rating	94
Type of school	public
Environment	village

STUDENTS

Total undergrad enrollment	12,520
% male/female	44/56
% from out of state	39
% live on campus	45
% in (# of) fraternities	11 (11)
% in (# of) sororities	11 (9)
% African American	5
% Asian	3
% Caucasian	73
% Hispanic	5
# of countries represented	64

SURVEY SAYS . . .
Great library
Frats and sororities dominate social scene
Student publications are popular
Lots of beer drinking
Hard liquor is popular
(Almost) everyone smokes

ACADEMICS

Academic Rating	70
Calendar	semester
Student/faculty ratio	16.5:1
Profs interesting rating	62
Profs accessible rating	62
% classes taught by TAs	2.8
Most common reg class size	20–29 students
Most common lab size	10–19 students

MOST POPULAR MAJORS
nursing
communication studies
psychology
physical education

STUDENTS SAY " . . ."

Academics

The University of Rhode Island "is a pretty decent middle-sized school in a great location." Notable majors include "nursing, engineering, or anything science." Film media, languages and textiles program are also popular within the liberal arts fields. The "excellent" pharmacy program at URI is competitive and nationally recognized. Students also laud the great film media program. Many classes are "very rigorous." Others are "wicked easy." For both, "there are many resources available to get help." The faculty really runs the gamut. "There are some really good ones, but some are just awful." The good profs "genuinely care about teaching" and "willingly offer their time" outside of class. "All of my teachers have had considerable experience in their field and bring a lot to the classroom," says an impressed freshman. As for the bad professors, "there are some serious horror stories." Some students think the subpar professors "cancel class almost too much," some bemoan the lack of outside help and the brief periods of time that qualify as office hours, and some have a hard time understanding the accents of foreign professors. URI's administration receives similarly mixed reviews. "I have had very few problems with administration," says one student. "They are happy to sit down and talk with you about any concerns that you have, and they will help solve your problems." Other students see "an ardent bureaucracy" "too obsessed with drinking policies to pay attention to what really matters."

Life

"URI is a gorgeous school—especially in the fall—on a big hill." It's located in a "safe" and "rural" area. "Parking is horrible," though the university has recently opened 1,400 new student parking space and set a shuttle bus system into place so as to make pedestrian traffic safer. The school has recently renovated 12 undergrad residence halls and added new suite and apartment style living quarters. For some students, URI is a "suitcase school." "A lot of students do go home on the weekends just because they live so close by." "If you get involved on campus you will love it," says a psychology major. "If not, you will want to transfer." Intramurals and varsity sports are popular. "Basketball is huge; so is hockey" "There are beautiful beaches right down the road from campus where you can surf, swim, or just sit and read," weather permitting. "Greek life is very popular, and if you live on campus it feels like everyone is part of it (but they're not)." The campus is ostensibly dry, but the alcohol policy certainly "hasn't stopped URI students from getting wasted." "One thing I didn't know coming to URI was how much of the social life happens off campus," discloses an English major. Parties occur 15 minutes away—"down the line," as students here say. On weekends, there are "house parties" in Narragansett by the beach. Bars are also popular. Students looking for more urban pursuits often travel 30 miles north to Providence.

Student Body

"The University of Rhode Island is an affordable option for in-state students." "Most out-of-state residents are from wealthy families or have scholarships." There are "a lot of generic college kids who go to college for the social aspect." "URI is mostly made up of guys that want to party and drive BMWs and girls that wear North Face jackets, Ugg boots, and big Dior sunglasses," stereotypes one student. Politically, it's a "pretty liberal" but mostly "apathetic" crowd. "However, if you search you can find some cool people who don't fit the mold." "There are many different students here," attests a nutrition major, "from jocks and jockettes to artists to frat boys and sorority girls." Ethnic diversity is not unreasonable but URI is cliquish. "People here do tend to hang out with people who are more similar to them." "Ethnicities mostly do not mix." Rhode Islanders often "stick to" high school friends.

FINANCIAL AID: 401-874-9500 • E-MAIL: URIADMIT@ETAL.URI.EDU • WEBSITE: WWW.URI.EDU/ADMISSIONS

THE PRINCETON REVIEW SAYS

Admissions

Very important factors considered include: rigor of secondary school record. *Important factors considered include:* Class rank, application essay, academic GPA, standardized test scores. *Other factors considered include:* recommendation(s), alumni/ae relation, character/personal qualities, extracurricular activities, first generation, geographical residence, level of applicant's interest, racial/ethnic status, state residency, talent/ability, volunteer work, work experienc SAT or ACT required; ACT with Writing component recommended. TOEFL required of all international applicants. High school diploma is required and GED is accepted. *Academic units required:* 4 English, 3 mathematics, 2 science, (1 science labs), 2 foreign language, 2 social studies, 5 academic electives.

Financial Aid

Students should submit: FAFSA. The Princeton Review suggests that all financial aid forms be submitted as soon as possible after 1/1. *Need-based scholarships/grants offered:* Federal Pell, SEOG, state scholarships/grants, private scholarships, the school's own gift aid. *Loan aid offered:* Direct Subsidized Stafford, Direct Unsubsidized Stafford, Direct PLUS, Federal Perkins, Federal Nursing, state loans, college/university loans from institutional funds. Applicants will be notified of awards on a rolling basis beginning 3/31. Federal Work-Study Program available. Institutional employment available. Off-campus job opportunities are good.

The Inside Word

Any candidate with solid grades is likely to find the university's Admissions Committee to be welcoming. The yield of admits who enroll is low and the state's population small. Out-of-state students are attractive to URI because they are sorely needed to fill out the student body. Students who graduate in the top 10 percent of their class are good scholarship bets. If you are a resident of a New England state other then Rhode Island, you get a tuition discount, but only if you enroll in certain degree programs.

THE SCHOOL SAYS "..."

From The Admissions Office

"Outstanding freshman candidates admission with a minimum SAT score of 1200 (combined Critical Reading and Math) or ACT composite score of 25 who rank in the top quarter of their high school class are eligible to be considered for a Centennial Scholarship. These merit-based scholarships range up to full tuition and are renewable each semester if the student maintains full-time continuous enrollment and a 3.0 average or better. In order to be eligible for consideration, all application materials must be received in the Admission Office by the December 1, early-action deadline. Applications are not considered complete until the application fee, completed application, official high school transcript, list of senior courses, personal essay, and SAT or ACT scores (sent directly from the testing agency) are received.

"If a student is awarded a Centennial Scholarship, and his or her residency status changes from out-of-state to regional or in-state, the amount of the award will be reduced to reflect the reduced tuition rate.

"The SAT Math and Critical Reading scores are used for admission evaluation and Centennial Scholarship consideration. The Writing score is not currently used for admission evaluation or Centennial Scholarship consideration."

SELECTIVITY

Admissions Rating	83
# of applicants	15,887
% of applicants accepted	77
% of acceptees attending	26

FRESHMAN PROFILE

Range SAT Critical Reading	480–570
Range SAT Math	500–590
Minimum paper TOEFL	550
Minimum computer TOEFL	213
Minimum web-based TOEFL	79
Average HS GPA	3.09
% graduated top 10% of class	16

DEADLINES

Early action	
Deadline	12/1
Notification	1/31
Regular	
Deadline	2/1
Notification	rolling
Nonfall registration?	yes

APPLICANTS ALSO LOOK AT

AND OFTEN PREFER
Northeastern University
University of Connecticut
University of Massachusetts—Amherst

AND SOMETIMES PREFER
Providence College

FINANCIAL FACTS

Financial Aid Rating	71
Annual in-state tuition	$7,454
Annual out-of-state tuition	$23,552
Room and board	$8,826
Required fees	$1,224
Books and supplies	$1,200
% frosh rec. need-based scholarship or grant aid	53
% UG rec. need-based scholarship or grant aid	55
% frosh rec. non-need-based scholarship or grant aid	5
% UG rec. non-need-based scholarship or grant aid	5
% frosh rec. need-based self-help aid	50
% UG rec. need-based self-help aid	52
% frosh rec. any financial aid	57
% UG rec. any financial aid	57
% UG borrow to pay for school	71
Average cumulative indebtedness	$22,500

UNIVERSITY OF RICHMOND

28 WESTHAMPTON WAY, RICHMOND, VA 23173 • ADMISSIONS: 804-289-8640 • FAX: 804-287-6003

CAMPUS LIFE

Quality of Life Rating	85
Fire Safety Rating	71
Green Rating	89
Type of school	private
Environment	metropolis

STUDENTS

Total undergrad enrollment	2,689
% male/female	49/51
% from out of state	83
% from public high school	61
% live on campus	91
% in (# of) fraternities	28 (5)
% in (# of) sororities	49 (8)
% African American	6
% Asian	4
% Caucasian	71
% Hispanic	3
% international	5
# of countries represented	74

SURVEY SAYS . . .

Athletic facilities are great
Great food on campus
Campus feels safe
Low cost of living

ACADEMICS

Academic Rating	91
Calendar	semester
Student/faculty ratio	8:1
Profs interesting rating	91
Profs accessible rating	93
Most common reg class size	10–19 students
Most common lab size	fewer than 10 students

MOST POPULAR MAJORS

English language and literature
political science and government

STUDENTS SAY ". . ."

Academics

Undergrads at the University of Richmond are quick to gush about their academic experience. Students find life inside (and out) of the classroom extremely "challenging and rewarding." Though professors "actively research," one junior assures us that "this is without a doubt a teaching campus." A fellow classmate echoes this sentiment sharing that the "[professors'] top priority is the students." "Classes are small," which ensures that "professors get to know you on a personal level." Undergrads also applaud their teachers for their sheer accessibility. As one senior notes, "professors will give you their school e-mail, home e-mail, office phone number, cell phone number, home number and tell you to contact them if you ever have questions." They've also been known to "invite classes over for dinner."

While a few students gripe about the administration's "misplaced priorities," most undergrads feel that those who make up the faculty are "a pretty good bunch that seem genuinely concerned with making the school a better place for everyone." And one elated freshman adds that the administration is always "looking to improve things, whether it be the facilities, course options or the living/scholarship opportunities." This praise extends even to the university's new president who students tell us is "actively involved in all aspects of Richmond."

Life

The academically driven students at Richmond tell us that they "work hard throughout the week…essentially living in the library." Luckily, they still manage to strike a balance between work and play. Sports are highly popular at this school—the football team won the Division 1 Championship in 2008—and "almost everyone is involved in an IM, club, or varsity sport." Fraternities and sororities dominate the weekend social scene, as one senior reveals that "the majority of the parties are affiliated with Greek life." Don't worry, these Kappas and Delts are an inclusive lot. The same senior assures that "you by no means need to be Greek to participate." Undergrads seem to love the fact that the "frats have lodges instead of houses." The lodges "are essentially a large dance floor with an area to serve beer, a deck, and a backyard," and "everyone hangs out there." However, those looking for a respite from the frat scene can easily attend one of the myriad of "school-run programs, [from] concerts [and] plays [to] just silly things that they put together." Students can also easily take advantage of hometown Richmond. It's a "great city, filled with fun restaurants, festivals, and [even] fitness events. The Monument 10-K is one of the most popular events of the year, and many UR students train and run together."

Student Body

Richmond undergrads admit that, on the surface, the school is dominated by "white, preppy, upper-middle-class northeasterners" who are often "walking [ads] for Abercrombie and J.Crew." However, if you're willing to look past the exteriors, you'll likely find "some very down-to-earth people." While backgrounds might be similar, one content junior tells us that, "there's a lot of diversity [of] ideas, [ensuring that] discussions in class and out are always interesting." Additionally, "there are a growing number of international students," which helps to foster a vibrant campus atmosphere. And even "atypical" students can rest assured that "everyone…can find some place where they fit in and be comfortable with their peers." Moreover, Richmond students define their fellow undergrads as "typical overachievers" who are "self-motivated to do [their] best." Fortunately, though, "no one is overly competitive." The school does seem to attract an athletic crowd, and one freshman alerts us to the fact that "the gym is always packed." Perhaps this junior best sums up his peers by stating that they "try to be Mr. or Ms. Well-Rounded all while looking good and making it look easy."

FINANCIAL AID: 804-289-8438 • E-MAIL: ADMISSIONS@RICHMOND.EDU • WEBSITE: WWW.RICHMOND.EDU

THE PRINCETON REVIEW SAYS

Admissions

Very important factors considered include: Academic GPA, rigor of secondary school record. *Important factors considered include:* Class rank, application essay, standardized test scores, character/personal qualities, first generation, talent/ability. *Other factors considered include:* recommendation(s), alumni/ae relation, extracurricular activities, geographical residence, interview, racial/ethnic status, first generation college status, state residency, volunteer work, work experience. SAT or ACT required; TOEFL required of all international applicants. High school diploma is required and GED is accepted. *Academic units required:* 4 English, 3 mathematics, 2 science, (2 science labs), 2 foreign language, 2 social studies, *Academic units recommended:* 4 English, 4 mathematics, 4 science, (4 science labs), 4 foreign language, 4 history.

Financial Aid

Students should submit: FAFSA, institution's own financial aid form. Regular filing deadline is 2/15. The Princeton Review suggests that all financial aid forms be submitted as soon as possible after 1/1. *Need-based scholarships/grants offered:* Federal Pell, SEOG, state scholarships/grants, private scholarships, the school's own gift aid. *Loan aid offered:* Direct Subsidized Stafford, Direct Unsubsidized Stafford, Direct PLUS, Federal Perkins. Applicants will be notified of awards on or about 4/1.

The Inside Word

The admissions officers at the University of Richmond seek applicants that will contribute to a dynamic incoming class. Therefore, the personal qualities of each candidate do factor heavily into decisions. Of course, academic rigor is of utmost importance and high school transcripts are heavily scrutinized. The school makes sure that all applications are read at least two times before a final decision is made.

THE SCHOOL SAYS "..."

From The Admissions Office

"The University of Richmond combines the characteristics of a small college with the dynamics of a large university. The unique size, beautiful suburban campus, and world-class facilities offer students an extraordinary mix of opportunities for personal growth and intellectual achievement. At Richmond, students are encouraged to engage themselves in their environment. Discussion and dialogue are the forefront of the academic experience, while research, internships, and international experiences are important components of students' co-curricular lives. The university is committed to providing undergraduate students with a rigorous academic experience, while integrating these studies with opportunities for experiential learning and promoting total individual development. The university also places a high value on diversity and believes in taking full advantage of the rich benefits of learning in a community of individuals from varied backgrounds.

"The University of Richmond requires either the SAT or the ACT. We do not prefers either test. We evaluate all three sections of the SAT (Critical Reading, Math, and Writing); the Writing section of the ACT is optional. If multiple tests are submitted, the admission committee considers those results that are most favorable to the applicant. We do not require or recommend SAT Subject Tests."

SELECTIVITY

Admissions Rating	95
# of applicants	7,970
% of applicants accepted	32
% of acceptees attending	29
# accepting a place on wait list	810
% admitted from wait list	17
# of early decision applicants	364
% accepted early decision	60

FRESHMAN PROFILE

Range SAT Critical Reading	580–680
Range SAT Math	590–680
Range SAT Writing	590–690
Range ACT Composite	26–30
Minimum paper TOEFL	550
Minimum computer TOEFL	213
Minimum web-based TOEFL	80
% graduated top 10% of class	58
% graduated top 25% of class	31
% graduated top 50% of class	99

DEADLINES

Early Decision	
Deadline	11/15
Notification	12/15
Regular	
Deadline	1/15
Notification	4/1
Nonfall registration?	no

APPLICANTS ALSO LOOK AT

AND OFTEN PREFER
University of Virginia
College of William & Mary
Georgetown University

AND SOMETIMES PREFER
Wake Forest University
Boston College

FINANCIAL FACTS

Financial Aid Rating	94
Annual tuition	$40,010
Room and board	$8,480
Books and supplies	$1,050
% frosh rec. need-based scholarship or grant aid	42
% UG rec. need-based scholarship or grant aid	40
% frosh rec. non-need-based scholarship or grant aid	5
% UG rec. non-need-based scholarship or grant aid	4
% frosh rec. need-based self-help aid	35
% UG rec. need-based self-help aid	34
% frosh rec. athletic scholarships	6
% UG rec. athletic scholarships	7
% frosh rec. any financial aid	60
% UG rec. any financial aid	66
% UG borrow to pay for school	43
Average cumulative indebtedness	$20,915

UNIVERSITY OF ROCHESTER

300 WILSON BOULEVARD, PO BOX 270251, ROCHESTER, NY 14627 • ADMISSIONS: 585-275-3221 • FAX: 585-461-4595

CAMPUS LIFE

Quality of Life Rating	**71**
Fire Safety Rating	**70**
Green Rating	**87**
Type of school	private
Environment	metropolis

STUDENTS

Total undergrad enrollment	5,178
% male/female	49/51
% from out of state	48
% from public high school	75
% live on campus	83
% in (# of) fraternities	6 (18)
% in (# of) sororities	6 (13)
% African American	4
% Asian	10
% Caucasian	56
% Hispanic	4
% international	7
# of countries represented	52

SURVEY SAYS . . .
Great library
Low cost of living
Musical organizations are popular
(Almost) no one smokes
Very little drug use

ACADEMICS

Academic Rating	**84**
Calendar	semester
Student/faculty ratio	9:1
Profs interesting rating	73
Profs accessible rating	77
Most common reg class size	10–19 students

MOST POPULAR MAJORS
biology/biological sciences
economics
psychology

STUDENTS SAY ". . ."

Academics

Students at the University of Rochester praise its "great atmosphere, superior academics," and "beautiful campus" by simply saying: "What more could you want?" Indeed, this college "couples strong academics without the cut-throat competitive atmosphere" meaning that students feel "relaxed" while being "pushed to do their best and forge their own paths." As one undergrad explains, "Rochester balances the academic prestige of an Ivy League school with a small, close-knit community and the drive to ensure that every student reaches their full potential." The "intimate" classes allow students to get to know their "knowledgeable and enthusiastic" professors, who "on the whole" are "stellar in terms of their qualifications, their accessibility, and their ability to teach." The faculty is widely known for "making time for students," however some students note "most science professors are here to do research as a first priority, not to teach." Also worth mentioning are the "great" career center and study-abroad offices. The administration is "usually helpful," and most note that they have "open doors and ears to students." Others feel that while the administration "does a good job of running the university," they're a bit lacking when it comes to "communicating with the students." Despite this, students agree the "academic experience" at Rochester leaves "very little to be desired." After all, notes one student, "You cannot escape this place without learning a hell of a lot."

Life

At this "academic school" expect life to be "very busy" thanks to "a lot of studying," but don't worry: "There's always time for fun." Whether your interests involve "movies, music, parties," or "bars," you'll find something to occupy your time away from the books. "There's always something to do at school," says one undergrad, "which is in large part due to the student-run clubs. There are clubs in almost all areas of interest, and each club makes a true effort to organize interesting programs for the student population." When the weekend arrives "most people hang out at the frat quad," which is "generally bustling with parties." "There's drinking just like [at] any college," says one student, "but generally people are much more in control than at a big state school." For those less inclined to imbibe there are "bajillions of clubs and organizations" on campus, and then there's always the city of Rochester itself. The school has a "bus system" that provides free access for students to "various places around town." The city boasts a "pretty awesome" music scene, and "there's always a show or concert on the weekends." And while Rochester's notoriously brutal winters might make some stay indoors, outdoor enthusiasts will find plenty on offer in any season, including lots of "hiking" and "skiing."

Student Body

Most students at Rochester are hard-pressed to describe the "typical" student here. Expect a "very high level" of "ethnic, religious, and social" diversity here thanks to the "wide variety of opportunities" the school offers. However, despite differences the student body has many shared traits. "Rochester is all about smart, fun, and interesting people who take their classes and their work seriously but still know how to have a good time," says one undergrad. These "driven" and "hard-working" students often have "a unique set of interests and are dedicated to pursing them" within "the university and the outside community." Because of this wide range of interests "everyone finds their niche" here. Though this can yield a "sometimes cliquish" atmosphere, students note "there's plenty of opportunity for interaction between different groups."

UNIVERSITY OF ROCHESTER

FINANCIAL AID: 585-275-3226 • E-MAIL: ADMIT@ADMISSIONS.ROCHESTER.EDU • WEBSITE: WWW.ROCHESTER.EDU

THE PRINCETON REVIEW SAYS

Admissions

Very important factors considered include: recommendation(s), rigor of secondary school record, character/personal qualities. *Important factors considered include:* Application essay, academic GPA, standardized test scores, extracurricular activities, interview, talent/ability. *Other factors considered include:* Class rank, alumni/ae relation, first generation, geographical residence, racial/ethnic status, level of applicant's interest, volunteer work, work experience. SAT or ACT required; TOEFL required of all international applicants. High school diploma is required and GED is accepted.

Financial Aid

Students should submit: FAFSA, CSS/Financial Aid PROFILE, state aid form, noncustodial PROFILE, business/farm supplement. Regular filing deadline is 2/1. The Princeton Review suggests that all financial aid forms be submitted as soon as possible after 1/1. *Need-based scholarships/grants offered:* Federal Pell, SEOG, state scholarships/grants, the school's own gift aid. *Loan aid offered:* Direct Subsidized Stafford, Direct Unsubsidized Stafford, Direct PLUS, Federal Perkins, Federal Nursing, college/university loans from institutional funds. Applicants will be notified of awards on or about 4/1. Federal Work-Study Program available. Institutional employment available. Off-campus job opportunities are excellent.

The Inside Word

With nearly 5,200 undergrads, applicants to Rochester can expect a highly individualized academic experience—something that not only makes this school a great place to learn, but also an increasingly competitive institution when it comes to admissions. The most important consideration for admission is grades and standardized test scores, followed closely by the rigor of class work and recommendations. Keep in mind that Rochester is looking for students who will fit well within the school's academic environment and demonstrate a true interest in attending—i.e., scheduling an interview could go a long way in increasing your odds.

THE SCHOOL SAYS "..."

From The Admissions Office

"Rochester believes that excellence requires freedom. In the Rochester curriculum, students are free to select courses that appeal to them most. There are no required subjects; students' interests drive their educations. Students major in either sciences and engineering, humanities, or social sciences and complete a cluster of at least three related courses in arts and science or any one of the other two areas. Because Rochester's nationally schools of engineering, medicine, nursing, music, education and business."

SELECTIVITY

Admissions Rating	95
# of applicants	11,633
% of applicants accepted	43
% of acceptees attending	24
# accepting a place on wait list	390
# of early decision applicants	583
% accepted early decision	49

FRESHMAN PROFILE

Range SAT Critical Reading	600–700
Range SAT Math	620–730
Range SAT Writing	590–700
Range ACT Composite	27–31
Minimum paper TOEFL	600
Minimum computer TOEFL	250
Minimum web-based TOEFL	100
Average HS GPA	3.7
% graduated top 10% of class	75
% graduated top 25% of class	94
% graduated top 50% of class	100

DEADLINES

Early Decision	
Deadline	11/1
Notification	12/15
Regular	
Deadline	1/1
Notification	4/1
Nonfall registration?	yes

APPLICANTS ALSO LOOK AT
AND RARELY PREFER
Franklin & Marshall College

FINANCIAL FACTS

Financial Aid Rating	89
Annual tuition	$37,870
Room and board	$11,200
% frosh rec. need-based scholarship or grant aid	56
% UG rec. need-based scholarship or grant aid	55
% frosh rec. non-need-based scholarship or grant aid	5
% UG rec. non-need-based scholarship or grant aid	4
% frosh rec. need-based self-help aid	49
% UG rec. need-based self-help aid	51
% frosh rec. any financial aid	92
% UG rec. any financial aid	88
% UG borrow to pay for school	55
Average cumulative indebtedness	$27,121

UNIVERSITY OF SAN DIEGO

5998 ALCALA PARK, SAN DIEGO, CA 92110-2492 • ADMISSIONS: 619-260-4506 • FAX: 619-260-6836

CAMPUS LIFE

Quality of Life Rating	**92**
Fire Safety Rating	**74**
Green Rating	**83**
Type of school	private
Affiliation	Roman Catholic
Environment	metropolis

STUDENTS

Total undergrad enrollment	4,946
% male/female	40/60
% from out of state	40
% from public high school	53
% live on campus	49
% in (# of) fraternities	17 (5)
% in (# of) sororities	26 (6)
% African American	2
% Asian	8
% Caucasian	68
% Hispanic	13
% Native American	1
% international	2
# of countries represented	56

SURVEY SAYS . . .

Lab facilities are great
Students get along with local community
Students love San Diego, CA
Great off-campus food
Dorms are like palaces
Campus feels safe
Students are happy

ACADEMICS

Academic Rating	**83**
Calendar	4/1/4
Student/faculty ratio	15:1
Profs interesting rating	85
Profs accessible rating	88
Most common reg class size	30–39 students
Most common lab size	10–19 students

MOST POPULAR MAJORS

business administration and management
communication studies/speech communication and rhetoric
psychology

STUDENTS SAY " . . ."

Academics

If you want "sun, surf, and professors who actually care about your work and your life," check out the University of San Diego. Everyone at this "relatively small" Catholic school must complete a demanding and "well-rounded" set of general education requirements. You won't get out of here without a heaping helping of English, math, science, foreign language, and, of course, religion. Beyond the core curriculum, the selection of majors is very good. The exceedingly popular business administration program is among the best in the country. Other popular and solid programs include communications, psychology, and accounting. "Academically, USD is challenging, but not ridiculously so." Classes are "comfortable" and small. "It's virtually impossible to get lost in the shuffle," and "it isn't like a state school where your teacher wouldn't notice that you're not there." Students avoid a few professors "like the plague" but the faculty as a whole is "magnificent" and "very passionate about teaching." "Their enthusiasm shows in the classroom," and they "practically beg for you to come visit them during office hours." "They make me feel like I matter to them," says an industrial engineering major. Views of management are more mixed. Some students tell us "very helpful" administration "takes care of things right away." Others contend the staff is "overly politically correct," cluttered, unorganized, helpless, and mad at you."

Life

"USD is studying in paradise." The "pristine, manicured" campus looks like "a resort" and "when it's 60 to 65 degrees and sunny in December, you tend to be happier." "School spirit is lackluster at best," but "clubs are big on campus and intramural sports are popular." The Greek scene looms large as well. If you seek spiritual growth, opportunities are ample. "You can be as involved or as uninvolved in the Catholic religion as you choose." Complaints include parking. "On bad days, it can take up to an hour" to find a spot. Still, as one senior warns, "having a car or a friend with one is a necessity." Also, USD's alcohol and drug policies are strict. The resident assistants in the dorms are often "too into their jobs," and campus security is a severe bunch. As a result, "partying on campus is nearly impossible." Students aren't too upset about any of this, though, because the real fun is at the beach. There's a genuine "beach culture atmosphere" here. Many upperclassmen live near the shore, and "most people go down to Mission Beach and Pacific Beach" for "day kegs," the bar scene, and parties galore. Students also tell us that the city of San Diego is "to die for." "You won't find a better spot for a school." "There are two state colleges within driving distance, so a lot of kids from each school intermingle at parties." "Padres and Chargers games are a fun way to hang out depending on cash flow or the season." And for really crazy nights, "there is always Tijuana."

Student Body

Ethnic diversity at USD is reasonably admirable. By far, Hispanics constitute the largest minority group. There are considerably more women than men. "The guys are very handsome." The women are "very hot." "There is a strong majority of Catholics," explains a first-year student, "but I don't get the impression that they tend to be deeply religious." There are "lots of Orange County kids" and "surfer dudes." "Most people are laidback," "down to earth," "outgoing, and friendly." They're "typical Southern Californians, really." "I wouldn't say there are many wildly atypical students," observes a freshman. More than two-thirds of the students here receive financial aid, and "there are many students who are not wealthy." Others, however, "have a lot of money;" USD sarcastically called the "University of Spoiled Daughters." "The 'rich white girl' idea is a stereotype USD is working hard to break," but there is definitely a noticeable "flock of bleached-blond" "size zeros with BMWs" "dressed like they're on a runway." "Juicy sweats, Chanel shades, and name-brand handbags" are too common for some students' tastes. "The Ugg boot situation" is grave as well.

FINANCIAL AID: 619-260-4514 • E-MAIL: ADMISSIONS@SANDIEGO.EDU • WEBSITE: WWW.SANDIEGO.EDU/ADMISSIONS/UNDERGRADUATE

THE PRINCETON REVIEW SAYS

Admissions

Very important factors considered include: Academic GPA, rigor of secondary school record, standardized test scores. *Important factors considered include:* Class rank, application essay, recommendation(s), character/personal qualities, extracurricular activities, talent/ability, volunteer work. *Other factors considered include:* alumni/ae relation, first generation, geographical residence, level of applicant's interest, racial/ethnic status, religious affiliation/commitment, work experience. SAT or ACT required; ACT with Writing component required. TOEFL required of all international applicants. High school diploma is required and GED is accepted. *Academic units required:* 4 English, 3 mathematics, 3 science, (2 science labs), 2 foreign language, 3 social studies. *Academic units recommended:* 4 English, 4 mathematics, 4 science, (3 science labs), 3 foreign language, 4 social studies.

Financial Aid

Students should submit: FAFSA Regular filing deadline is 3/2. The Princeton Review suggests that all financial aid forms be submitted as soon as possible after 1/1. *Need-based scholarships/grants offered:* Federal Pell, SEOG, state scholarships/grants, private scholarships, the school's own gift aid, Federal Nursing Scholarships. *Loan aid offered:* FFEL Subsidized Stafford, FFEL Unsubsidized Stafford, FFEL PLUS, Federal Perkins, college/university loans from institutional funds. Applicants will be notified of awards on a rolling basis beginning 3/1. Federal Work-Study Program available. Institutional employment available. Off-campus job opportunities are good.

The Inside Word

The University of San Diego offers a broad liberal arts core, small classes, and close interaction between students and professors. The dazzling campus and an unbeatable location are just gravy. As such, admission here is competitive. Solid test scores and outstanding grades should be a given for applicants.

THE SCHOOL SAYS "..."

From The Admissions Office

"Looking at the University of San Diego is easy on the eyes. But really seeing our true character demands a little work. It is easy to focus on the obvious: the incredible beauty of the campus, the region's unparalleled climate and livability, long lists of recreational and co-curricular opportunities, the vitality of students walking through the central plaza, or even the obvious expressions of USD's Catholic character. But to focus on the superficial would be misleading. "While the beach is nearby, USD is a serious academic institution. While the campus is stunning, the people make the difference. More than 10,000 candidates vie for 1,100 freshman openings. But to see the 'average' freshman as a 3.8 GPA or a 1220 SAT score would miss the person. Each is unique—selected on expressions of diversity, leadership, service, talent, and essential human character. Faculty, too, are rigorously screened. USD draws more than 100 candidates for every faculty opening, and this screening goes well beyond their lists of publications or the names on their diplomas. To challenge and inspire, they bring innovative approaches to undergraduate research, experiential learning, and faculty mentoring. While often compared to much larger institutions, USD seeks to be recognized for undergraduate teaching and residential learning. In comparison to schools of similar character, USD's academic offerings are truly impressive; a small sample includes marine biology, environmental studies, Latino studies, communication studies, e-commerce, and professional programs in engineering, business, and education, each of which complements a rigorous liberal arts base. New facilities demonstrate this diversity, including a state-of-the-art science center, the Kroc Institute for Peace and Justice, and the Jenny Craig Sports Pavilion. Freshman applicants must submit scores from the SAT or the ACT exam with Writing. As always, these scores will be used in conjunction with many other factors; in particular, the student's grade point average, curriculum, extra curricular activities, and letters of recommendation."

SELECTIVITY

Admissions Rating	92
# of applicants	10,584
% of applicants accepted	33
% of acceptees attending	36
# accepting a place on wait list	351

FRESHMAN PROFILE

Range SAT Critical Reading	540–630
Range SAT Math	560–650
Range SAT Writing	550–650
Range ACT Composite	24–29
Minimum paper TOEFL	550
Minimum computer TOEFL	213
Minimum web-based TOEFL	80
Average HS GPA	3.79
% graduated top 10% of class	39
% graduated top 25% of class	78
% graduated top 50% of class	98

DEADLINES

Early action	
Deadline	11/15
Notification	1/31
Regular	
Priority	1/15
Deadline	3/1
Notification	4/15
Nonfall registration?	yes

APPLICANTS ALSO LOOK AT

AND OFTEN PREFER
University of Southern California

AND SOMETIMES PREFER
University of California—San Diego

AND RARELY PREFER
Santa Clara University

FINANCIAL FACTS

Financial Aid Rating	76
Annual tuition	$35,870
Room and board	$12,602
Required fees	$422
Books and supplies	$1,638
% frosh rec. need-based scholarship or grant aid	47
% UG rec. need-based scholarship or grant aid	41
% frosh rec. non-need-based scholarship or grant aid	29
% UG rec. non-need-based scholarship or grant aid	21
% frosh rec. need-based self-help aid	32
% UG rec. need-based self-help aid	33
% frosh rec. athletic scholarships	3
% UG rec. athletic scholarships	3
% frosh rec. any financial aid	70
% UG rec. any financial aid	64
% UG borrow to pay for school	49
Average cumulative indebtedness	$23,343

UNIVERSITY OF SAN FRANCISCO

2130 FULTON STREET, SAN FRANCISCO, CA 94117 • ADMISSIONS: 415-422-6563 • FAX: 415-422-2217

CAMPUS LIFE
Quality of Life Rating	**86**
Fire Safety Rating	**60***
Green Rating	**82**
Type of school	private
Affiliation	Roman Catholic
Environment	metropolis

STUDENTS
Total undergrad enrollment	4,934
% male/female	36/64
% from out of state	41
% from public high school	51
% live on campus	47
% in (# of) fraternities	1 (4)
% in (# of) sororities	1 (4)
% African American	5
% Asian	21
% Caucasian	37
% Hispanic	14
% Native American	1
% international	8
# of countries represented	78

SURVEY SAYS . . .
Great library
Athletic facilities are great
Diverse student types on campus
Students get along with local
community
Students love San Francisco, CA
Great off-campus food
(Almost) everyone smokes

ACADEMICS
Academic Rating	**85**
Calendar	semester
Student/faculty ratio	15:1
Profs interesting rating	83
Profs accessible rating	79
Most common	
reg class size	10–19 students
Most common	
lab size	10–19 students

MOST POPULAR MAJORS
business/commerce
nursing/registered nurse
(rn, asn, bsn, msn)
psychology

STUDENTS SAY "..."

Academics

The University of San Francisco is a smallish Jesuit school "in an urban setting" with a "very liberal" "social justice slant." Global awareness programs and seminars are routine, and a strong community-service ethic permeates the atmosphere. Class sizes are small, and students report that their academic experience is "intimate and intellectual." Some members of the faculty at USF "seem to just skate through the workday" and are "not necessarily the best teachers." On the whole, though, "the shining star of USF is its professors." They are "ridiculously generous with their time" and are "really the best reason" to enroll. Like at most Catholic schools, "you're required to take everything from English to philosophy to religion" here. "The core curriculum is a bitch," but it does expose you to considerable wisdom. Beyond all the mandatory coursework, USF offers a breadth of options typical of a much larger university. Highlights include the business school and "a very popular nursing program." Education is "also very strong," and there's a four-year Great Books program. Administratively, "the school is run quite well," but there are "disgruntled types who like to make things difficult." Also, "registration is frustrating at times," and advising can be hit-or-miss. "I've had great advisers who have guided me through registration over the years," says a math major, "but others aren't as lucky."

Life

"Housing is a catastrophe" at USF. Students feel "really crammed" and complain that the people in charge "just put people together with no thought to whether they are compatible." There's a nice gym, though, with a pool that "basically covers an entire city block." Socially, "there is no sense of community." "Student groups consist of only the hardcores," and "the lack of school spirit can be quite a downer." "Going to USF is definitely the nontraditional college experience because everyone is pretty much doing their own thing." "Drinking is prevalent," and students "smoke a lot of weed," but "there isn't a big party scene other than little get-togethers in the dorms." House parties are rare "and usually never work out." On-campus activities are sparse, "but who would go anyway?" USF is located "in the heart of San Francisco," and "there is always something going on" in this "vibrant," "distracting" city. Most students "go off-campus on the weekends to explore" and "have adventures." On sunny days, "the best place to be is either Golden Gate Park or the beach." "Stellar museums, numerous theaters, national landmarks, shopping, world-class dining, funky art houses," and pretty much anything else is readily available. "Getting around on the buses is super easy," and public transportation passes are built into the tuition price. "The university is totally integrated into the city, and those who come to USF new to San Francisco will leave feeling like they belong here," promises a senior.

Student Body

USF is home to "one of the most ethnically diverse schools in the country." The Asian and Latino populations are especially high, and there's a noticeable international contingent. According to many females, though, the ratio of women to men is "pitiful." It's "pretty hard to date or even hook up" if you are straight because "most guys are taken or gay." "Students tend to stick with a small, close-knit group of friends," but virtually everyone is "able to fit in easily in the USF community no matter how eccentric." Except possibly conservatives. Liberal politics pervade, and USF "may not be the place for more right-leaning students." Some students "dress in alternative or funky clothing" and are "experimental (with everything from sexuality and music to drugs)." "Many students are Catholic but aren't necessarily strictly practicing." A lot of people smoke cigarettes. There are "science nerds," "hippies," and the occasional "shopping addict." Some students are "outspoken and outgoing." Others "have their iPods on *all the time*." "There are a lot of super-wealthy kids" from Southern California. Others are on scholarships and loans "and barely making it." "People are passionate. Some are lazy. A few are beautifully artistic. A bunch are athletic. A couple are phony. Some are damn smart. Others are pretty ignorant. But at least we got it all," muses a sophomore.

UNIVERSITY OF SAN FRANCISCO

FINANCIAL AID: 415-422-6303 • E-MAIL: ADMISSION@USFCA.EDU • WEBSITE: WWW.USFCA.EDU

THE PRINCETON REVIEW SAYS

Admissions

Very important factors considered include: Academic GPA, recommendation(s), rigor of secondary school record, standardized test scores. *Important factors considered include:* Class rank, application essay. *Other factors considered include:* alumni/ae relation, character/personal qualities, extracurricular activities, interview, racial/ethnic status, talent/ability, volunteer work, SAT or ACT required; ACT with Writing component required. TOEFL required of all international applicants. High school diploma is required and GED is accepted. *Academic units recommended:* 4 English, 3 mathematics, 2 science, (2 science labs), 2 foreign language, 3 social studies, 6 academic electives, 1 chemistry and 1 biology or physics is required of nursing and science applicants.

Financial Aid

Students should submit: FAFSA. The Princeton Review suggests that all financial aid forms be submitted as soon as possible after 1/1. School wnats to point out Feb. 1 deadline for FAFSA. *Need-based scholarships/grants offered:* Federal Pell, SEOG, state scholarships/grants, private scholarships, the school's own gift aid, Federal Nursing Scholarships. *Loan aid offered:* Direct Subsidized Stafford, Direct Unsubsidized Stafford, Direct PLUS, FFEL PLUS, Federal Perkins, Federal Nursing, college/university loans from institutional funds. Note: FFEL Loans are for Graduate students only. Applicants will be notified of awards on a rolling basis beginning 4/1. Federal Work-Study Program available. Institutional employment available. Off-campus job opportunities are excellent.

The Inside Word

The admissions committee at USF is not purely numbers-focused. They'll evaluate your full picture here, using your academic strengths and weaknesses along with your personal character strengths, essays, and recommendations to assess your suitability for admission. It's matchmaking. If you fit well in the USF community, you'll be welcome.

THE SCHOOL SAYS "..."

From The Admissions Office

"The University of San Francisco has experienced a significant increase in applications for admission over the past 5 years. This has made the application evaluation process more challenging. Ultimately, it gives those who read the applications the opportunity to find applicants who can make the most of the university's academic opportunities, location in San Francisco, and its mission to educate minds and hearts to change the world. Community outreach and service to others, along with academic excellence are characteristics that help distinguish those offered admission.

"The university has cancelled complete administrative system upgrade. New housing software will provide the students with the capability to 'compatibility match.

"Applicants are required to take the SAT Reasoning test (or the ACT with the Writing section). The Writing sections will be used for advising and placement purposes. SAT Subject Test scores will also be accepted."

SELECTIVITY

Admissions Rating	85
# of applicants	8,485
% of applicants accepted	64
% of acceptees attending	19

FRESHMAN PROFILE

Range SAT Critical Reading	510–620
Range SAT Math	520–620
Range SAT Writing	510–620
Range ACT Composite	22–27
Minimum paper TOEFL	550
Minimum computer TOEFL	213
Minimum web-based TOEFL	79
Average HS GPA	3.53
% graduated top 10% of class	25
% graduated top 25% of class	61
% graduated top 50% of class	91

DEADLINES

Early action	
Deadline	11/15
Notification	1/16
Regular	
Priority	1/15
Notification	4/1
Nonfall registration?	yes

APPLICANTS ALSO LOOK AT

AND OFTEN PREFER
University of Southern California
University of California—Berkeley
Santa Clara University
Stanford University
University of California—Davis

AND SOMETIMES PREFER
University of San Diego
University of California—Santa Cruz
Loyola Marymount University
Seattle University

AND RARELY PREFER
Fordham University
Boston College

FINANCIAL FACTS

Financial Aid Rating	70
Annual tuition	$34,430
Room and board	$11,540
Required fees	$340
Books and supplies	$1,000
% frosh rec. need-based scholarship or grant aid	48
% UG rec. need-based scholarship or grant aid	47
% frosh rec. non-need-based scholarship or grant aid	12
% UG rec. non-need-based scholarship or grant aid	9
% frosh rec. need-based self-help aid	50
% UG rec. need-based self-help aid	50
% frosh rec. athletic scholarships	3
% UG rec. athletic scholarships	3
% UG borrow to pay for school	64.8
Average cumulative indebtedness	$27,260

UNIVERSITY OF SCRANTON

800 LINDEN STREET, SCRANTON, PA 18510-4699 • ADMISSIONS: 570-941-7540 FAX: 570-941-5928

CAMPUS LIFE

Quality of Life Rating	**78**
Fire Safety Rating	**81**
Green Rating	**71**
Type of school	private
Affiliation	Roman Catholic/Jesuit
Environment	city

STUDENTS

Total undergrad enrollment	4,010
% male/female	43/57
% from out of state	51
% live on campus	53
% African American	1
% Asian	2
% Caucasian	80
% Hispanic	4
% international	1
# of countries represented	23

SURVEY SAYS . . .

School is well run
Students are friendly
Frats and sororities are unpopular or nonexistent
Lots of beer drinking
Hard liquor is popular

ACADEMICS

Academic Rating	**79**
Calendar	semester
Student/faculty ratio	11.3:1
Profs interesting rating	77
Profs accessible rating	81
Most common reg class size	10–19 students
Most common lab size	10–19 students

MOST POPULAR MAJORS
biology/biological sciences
elementary education and teaching
marketing/marketing management

STUDENTS SAY "..."

Academics

With "an outstanding record for admission to graduate programs, not only in law and medicine but also in several other fields," the University of Scranton is a good fit for ambitious students seeking "a Jesuit school in every sense of the word. If you come here, expect to be challenged to become a better person, to develop a strong concern for the poor and marginalized, and to grow spiritually and intellectually." The school manages to accomplish this without "forcing religion upon you, which is nice." Undergraduates also approve of the mandatory liberal-arts-based curriculum that "forces you to learn about broader things than your own major." Strong majors here include "an amazing occupational therapy program, [an] excellent special education program," business, and biology. "This is a great place for premeds and other sciences," students agree. While the workload can be difficult, "a tutoring center provides free tutoring for any students who may need it, and also provides work-study positions for students who qualify to tutor." Need more help? Professors "are extremely accessible. They will go to any lengths to help you understand material and do well," while administrators "are here for the students, and show that every day inside and outside of the classroom." Community ties here are strong; as one student points out, "the Jesuits live in our dorms, creating an even greater sense of community, because we don't view them as just priests, we view them as real people who can relate on our level."

Life

"There is a whole range of activities to do on the weekends" at University of Scranton, including "frequent trips, dances, and movies that are screened for free." Students tell us "the school and student organizations provide plenty of options, such as retreats, talent shows, and other various activities." There are also "many intramurals to become involved in, and the varsity sports (specifically the women's) are very successful." Furthermore, "being a Jesuit school, social justice issues are huge. They are taught in the classroom, and students spend a lot of time volunteering." Hometown Scranton is big enough to provide "movie theaters, two malls, parks, a zoo, a bowling alley, and a skiing/snowboarding mountain." In short, there are plenty of choices for the non-partier at Scranton. Many we heard from in our survey reported busy extracurricular schedules. But those seeking a party won't be disappointed here, either. Scranton undergrads "party a lot, but they balance it with studying. Parties are chances to go out, see people, dance, and drink if you want." You "can find a party any time of day, seven days a week" here, usually with a keg tapped and pouring. Few here feel the party scene is out of hand, however a typical student writes, "It's very different than at schools with Greek systems. It is a lot more laid-back, and all about everyone having a good time."

Students

While "the typical Scranton student is white, Catholic, and from the suburbs," students hasten to point out "within this sameness, there is much diversity. There are people who couldn't care at all about religion, and there are people who are deeply religious. Even in the Catholic atmosphere of the school, the school only requires that you learn about Catholicism as it stands. Theology classes...are prefaced with the idea that 'You do not have to believe this!'" Undergrads here are generally "friendly and welcoming. Cliques are pretty much nonexistent, and anyone who would be classified as 'popular' is only considered so because they are extremely friendly, outgoing, and seek out friendships with as many people as possible." Students tend to be on the Abercrombie-preppy side, with lots of undergrads of Italian, Irish, and Polish descent.

FINANCIAL AID: 570-941-7700 • E-MAIL: ADMISSIONS@SCRANTON.EDU • WEBSITE: WWW.SCRANTON.EDU

THE PRINCETON REVIEW SAYS

Admissions

Very important factors considered include: Class rank, academic GPA, rigor of secondary school record, standardized test scores. *Important factors considered include:* extracurricular activities. *Other factors considered include:* Application essay, recommendation(s), alumni/ae relation, character/personal qualities, interview, level of applicant's interest, talent/ability, volunteer work, work experience. SAT or ACT required; TOEFL required of all international applicants. High school diploma is required and GED is accepted. *Academic units required:* 4 English, 3 mathematics, 3 science, (1 science labs), 2 foreign language, 2 social studies, 2 history, 4 academic electives. *Academic units recommended:* 4 English, 4 mathematics, 3 science, (1 science labs), 2 foreign language, 3 social studies, 3 history, 4 academic electives.

Financial Aid

Students should submit: FAFSA. The Princeton Review suggests that all financial aid forms be submitted as soon as possible after 1/1. *Need-based scholarships/grants offered:* Federal Pell, SEOG, state scholarships/grants, private scholarships, the school's own gift aid. *Loan aid offered:* FFEL Subsidized Stafford, FFEL Unsubsidized Stafford, FFEL PLUS, Federal Perkins, Federal Nursing Applicants will be notified of awards on a rolling basis beginning 3/15. Federal Work-Study Program available. Institutional employment available. Off-campus job opportunities are good.

The Inside Word

Admission to Scranton gets harder each year. A steady stream of smart kids from the tristate area keeps classes full and the admit rate low. Successful applicants will need solid grades and test scores. As with many religiously affiliated schools, students should be a good match philosophically as well.

THE SCHOOL SAYS "..."

From The Admissions Office

"A Jesuit institution in Pennsylvania's Pocono Northeast, the University of Scranton is known for its outstanding academics, state-of-the art campus, and exceptional sense of community. Founded in 1888, the university offers more than 80 undergraduate and graduate academic programs of study through four colleges and schools.

"The Princeton Review included Scranton among *The Best Colleges* in the nation in past years. For years, Scranton was the only college in Pennsylvania and the only Jesuit university to have a student named to the first academic team.

"Freshman applicants are required to take the SAT or ACT exam. The writing scores will not be considered in the admissions decision process. Students are encouraged to apply early for admission and can do so online with no application fee."

SELECTIVITY
Admissions Rating	87
# of applicants	7,890
% of applicants accepted	66
% of acceptees attending	19
# accepting a place on wait list	582
% admitted from wait list	9

FRESHMAN PROFILE
Range SAT Critical Reading	510–600
Range SAT Math	520–610
Minimum paper TOEFL	500
Minimum computer TOEFL	173
Average HS GPA	3.36
% graduated top 10% of class	30
% graduated top 25% of class	64
% graduated top 50% of class	91.4

DEADLINES
Early action	
Deadline	11/15
Notification	12/15
Regular	
Priority	3/1
Deadline	3/1
Notification	rolling
Nonfall registration?	yes

APPLICANTS ALSO LOOK AT
AND OFTEN PREFER
University of Delaware
Fairfield University
Villanova University
Saint Joseph's University (PA)

AND SOMETIMES PREFER
Loyola College in Maryland
Penn State—University Park

FINANCIAL FACTS
Financial Aid Rating	70
Annual Tuition	$32,824
Room and board	$9,572
Required fees	$300
% frosh rec. need-based scholarship or grant aid	67
% UG rec. need-based scholarship or grant aid	63
% frosh rec. non-need-based scholarship or grant aid	6
% UG rec. non-need-based scholarship or grant aid	4
% frosh rec. need-based self-help aid	59
% UG rec. need-based self-help aid	56
% frosh rec. any financial aid	85
% UG rec. any financial aid	82
% UG borrow to pay for school	76
Average cumulative indebtedness	$26,169

UNIVERSITY OF SOUTH CAROLINA—COLUMBIA

UNIVERSITY OF SOUTH CAROLINA, COLUMBIA, SC 29208 • ADMISSIONS: 803-777-7700 • FAX: 803-777-0101

CAMPUS LIFE

Quality of Life Rating	74
Fire Safety Rating	87
Green Rating	95
Type of school	public
Environment	city

STUDENTS

Total undergrad enrollment	19,458
% male/female	45/55
% from out of state	26
% live on campus	36
% in (# of) fraternities	14 (18)
% in (# of) sororities	15 (14)
% African American	12
% Asian	3
% Caucasian	73
% Hispanic	2
% international	1
# of countries represented	107

SURVEY SAYS . . .

Athletic facilities are great
Everyone loves the Fighting
Gamecocks
Frats and sororities dominate social
scene
Student publications are popular
Lots of beer drinking
Hard liquor is popular

ACADEMICS

Academic Rating	71
Calendar	semester
Student/faculty ratio	18:1
Profs interesting rating	67
Profs accessible rating	69
% classes taught by TAs	16
Most common	
reg class size	10–19 students
Most common	
lab size	20–29 students

MOST POPULAR MAJORS

biology/biological sciences
experimental psychology
nursing/registered nurse
(rn, asn, bsn, msn)

STUDENTS SAY ". . ."

Academics

With a large in-state population and a proud football tradition, "The University of South Carolina is all about pride—in academics, athletics, and in life." Undergrads at this large research university embrace the entire USC experience, bragging of "an awesome mix of challenging academics and social activities." As at most large state universities, your academic experience at USC "is what you make of it." You can "blow off your classes," or you can "dive in and try and learn as much as you want to." A few students warn that "most departments are more research-oriented than education-oriented. The philosophy is that research pays the bills, not the students, and therefore more emphasis should be placed on research." Even so, the academic experience is not an impersonal one; on the contrary, professors "will do everything they can to help you out with any problem, personal or academic. The people here are amazing. A stranger is as likely to be friendly and helpful as your best friend." Students tell us that USC excels in business; mathematics; nursing; education; technology; library service; journalism; psychology; and hotel, restaurant, and tourism management. One USC booster sums up: "The University of South Carolina offers the complete student experience: A variety of student organizations and student activities, a great nightlife in the state capital, challenging classes taught by great professors, and opportunities for research—all within a great environment on a beautiful campus."

Life

USC "is a fun place," especially for sports fans, as life here "mostly revolves around football and basketball. Everyone's always talking about the upcoming game or what next season is going to hold. There's a great sense of school pride." Undergrads proudly assert that "USC is probably the best college for tailgating. Football game days are so fun!" But students don't need a sporting event to have a good time; on the contrary, "Many people party every weekend (beginning Thursday nights)." When they do, "A lot of people hang out in Five Points"—which "offers many nightlife and dining options for college students"—"or the Vista"—which is similar to Five Points, but a bit more upscale. Aesthetes have plenty of options as well; on campus "The Koger Center for the Arts brings [in] great performers every year," while the city's Colonial Center "offers big concerts…from Elton John to Jimmy Buffett." Other Columbia highlights include "a very nice zoo" as well as plenty of options for hunting and fishing within 25 miles of the city. Beyond the immediate vicinity, "the mountains are an hour away and so is the beach. A weekend in Charleston, shopping in Charlotte, [and] going to the mountains in [North Carolina]" are excursions "you hear about every weekend (when there's not a football game going on)."

Student Body

With an undergraduate student body of more than 19,000, USC is home to "so many different types of people…involved in so many different activities." When pressed to describe a typical student, undergrads identify "a fun-loving football fan who is a business student or a bio major" and explain that "most students are Southerners who come from a similar Christian, suburban background (although not all remain in that mindset)." However, students also report that USC is home to a "diverse minority and international communities" who "are becoming more and more recognized by the rest of the students." One undergrad sums up: "There isn't a typical student at USC, [but] there are different…group[s] that students could be classified into. There are the frat guys and the sorority girls; the good ol' boys who love to hunt and fish; the debutantes [who] are only here to get a MRS degree; the northerners who came down to USC and had no idea what they were getting themselves into; and then there are the athletes, who pretty much interact only with other athletes."

UNIVERSITY OF SOUTH CAROLINA—COLUMBIA

FINANCIAL AID: 803-777-8134 • E-MAIL: ADMISSIONS-UGRAD@SC.EDU • WEBSITE: WWW.SC.EDU

THE PRINCETON REVIEW SAYS

Admissions

Very important factors considered include: Academic GPA, rigor of secondary school record, standardized test scores. *Important factors considered include:* Class rank. *Other factors considered include:* Class rank, application essay, recommendation(s), alumni/ae relation, character/personal qualities, extracurricular activities, first generation, racial/ethnic status, state residency, talent/ability, volunteer work, work experience. SAT or ACT required; ACT with Writing component required. TOEFL required of all international applicants. High school diploma is required and GED is accepted. *Academic units required:* 4 English, 3 mathematics, 3 science, (3 science labs), 2 foreign language, 2 social studies, 1 history, 4 academic electives, 1 PE or ROTC.

Financial Aid

Students should submit: FAFSA. The Princeton Review suggests that all financial aid forms be submitted as soon as possible after 1/1. *Need-based scholarships/grants offered:* Federal Pell, SEOG, state scholarships/grants, private scholarships, the school's own gift aid, United Negro College Fund, Federal Nursing Scholarships, Univeersity Gamecock Guarantee. *Loan aid offered:* FFEL Subsidized Stafford, FFEL Unsubsidized Stafford, FFEL PLUS, Federal Perkins, Federal Nursing Applicants will be notified of awards on a rolling basis beginning 1/4. Federal Work-Study Program available. Institutional employment available. Off-campus job opportunities are good.

The Inside Word

Students tell us that "the admissions process at USC is very fair. The school takes everything into consideration." This is good news for applicants with spotty high school transcripts or poor standardized test scores. Others need not worry—the school bulletin reports that applicants with a B average in college preparatory courses and SAT section scores between 550 and 600 "are normally competitive for admission."

THE SCHOOL SAYS "..."

From The Admissions Office

"In just 6 years, the number of annual undergraduate applicants to USC has doubled, making it more critical than ever for students to meet the university's priority application deadline. The University of South Carolina's national prominence in academics and research activities also has increased. USC is one of only 62 public research institutions to earn a designated status of 'very high research activity' by the Carnegie Foundation. As early as their freshman year, undergraduates are encouraged to compete for research grants. As South Carolina's flagship institution, USC offers more than 350 degree programs. More than 27,000 students seek baccalaureate, masters, or doctoral degrees. USC is known for its top-ranked academic programs, including its international business and exercise science programs—both rated number one nationally. Other notable programs include chemical and nuclear engineering; health education; hotel, restaurant, and tourism; marine science; law; medicine; nursing; and psychology, among others. USC is recognized for its pioneering efforts in freshman outreach. Its honors college is one of the nation's best, offering an Ivy League–caliber education at state college costs. USC offers student support in such areas as career development, disability services, pre-professional planning, and study abroad. On campus, students enjoy a state-of-the-art fitness center, an 18,000-seat arena, an 80,000-seat stadium, and nearly 300 student organizations. Off campus, South Carolina's world-famous beaches and the Blue Ridge Mountains are each less than a 3-hour drive away. The University of South Carolina is located in the state's capital city, making it a great place for internships and job opportunities."

SELECTIVITY

Admissions Rating	88
# of applicants	17,018
% of applicants accepted	58
% of acceptees attending	39

FRESHMAN PROFILE

Range SAT Critical Reading	540–630
Range SAT Math	550–650
Range ACT Composite	24–28
Minimum paper TOEFL	550
Minimum computer TOEFL	210
Minimum web-based TOEFL	77
Average HS GPA	3.9
% graduated top 10% of class	30
% graduated top 25% of class	69
% graduated top 50% of class	91

DEADLINES

Early action	
Deadline	10/15
Regular	
Priority	12/1
Deadline	12/1
Nonfall registration?	yes

APPLICANTS ALSO LOOK AT
AND OFTEN PREFER
University of North Carolina at Chapel Hill

AND SOMETIMES PREFER
Clemson University

FINANCIAL FACTS

Financial Aid Rating	76
Annual in-state tuition	$8,438
Annual out-of-state tuition	$22,508
Room and board	$7,318
Required fees	$400
Books and supplies	$936
% frosh rec. need-based scholarship or grant aid	17
% UG rec. need-based scholarship or grant aid	23
% frosh rec. non-need-based scholarship or grant aid	37
% UG rec. non-need-based scholarship or grant aid	28
% frosh rec. need-based self-help aid	33
% UG rec. need-based self-help aid	38
% frosh rec. athletic scholarships	3
% UG rec. athletic scholarships	3
% frosh rec. any financial aid	93
% UG rec. any financial aid	90
% UG borrow to pay for school	45
Average cumulative indebtedness	$21,315

THE UNIVERSITY OF SOUTH DAKOTA

414 EAST CLARK, VERMILLION, SD 57069 • ADMISSIONS: 605-677-5434 • FAX: 605-677-6323

CAMPUS LIFE
Quality of Life Rating	65
Fire Safety Rating	91
Green Rating	73
Type of school	public
Environment	village

STUDENTS
Total undergrad enrollment	6,036
% male/female	37/63
% from out of state	25
% from public high school	89
% live on campus	30
% in (# of) fraternities	15 (9)
% in (# of) sororities	8 (4)
% African American	2
% Asian	1
% Caucasian	85
% Hispanic	1
% Native American	2
# of countries represented	29

SURVEY SAYS . . .
Low cost of living
Student publications are popular
Lots of beer drinking
(Almost) no one smokes
Very little drug use

ACADEMICS
Academic Rating	72
Calendar	semester
Student/faculty ratio	15:1
Profs interesting rating	72
Profs accessible rating	71
% classes taught by TAs	5
Most common reg class size	20–29 students
Most common lab size	20–29 students

MOST POPULAR MAJORS
business/commerce
education
psychology

STUDENTS SAY ". . ."

Academics

With an honors program that is "the best-kept secret in the country" and professors who are "nearly always willing to go the extra mile for students," the University of South Dakota offers a "great student to faculty communicative experience at a reasonable price." Numerous departments garner praise from students, and the University boasts winners "almost every year for big scholarships like the Goldwater and Truman, competing with big, Ivy League, private colleges that charge quadruple the amount for the same education." While the nursing school is the most frequently praised, the "business, biology, pre-med, law, and psychology classes are very solid," and the "dental hygiene, music, and journalism schools" also stand out, with the most copious laurels heaped on the music department's professors who are "some of the best." All told, the wide selection of quality academics "gives students many options as far as majors go," and for students willing to throw themselves into their studies "the odds of getting into a professional or graduate program are good."

Life

"We work hard, so we can play hard," sums up the undergraduate philosophy at USD. "Although there is a lot of partying that happens, the students keep themselves occupied with school work, intramural sports, and hanging out with their friends." Vermillion's small size seems to be a double-edged sword; some insist that "the size of the town means no one is more than a 10-minute walk/bike ride away!" and that "since it is a smaller campus students have more opportunities to be involved in internships and various other activities." But the fact remains that "Many of the upperclassmen live in the larger cities to the north and south." In general, "students have to make their own fun, which often involves partying or taking small road trips to other cities in the area." For those planning to roam further afield, "Vermillion is located very close to Yankton, Sioux City (IA), and Sioux Falls (all within an hour). They are bigger cities and offer everything a person would want to do (shopping, movies, entertainment)."

Student Body

A typical USD student "would be a conservative Midwesterner. He or she would be Caucasian" and would most likely have originated in "small towns in South Dakota, Iowa, and Nebraska." "Many people join a Greek system or are athletes or musicians. Those who do not fit into these three main groups seem to focus on their academics" and "[fit] in fine with the majority because of the open mindedness of most students." For example, "Gay students are able to get along with the rest of student population," although in some circles, "Homosexuality is still spoken of as if it is shameful." There's no denying that "partying is a definite part of the culture, though many of the 'smart' kids both party and work hard." Student organizations call out to many, and "it seems like every person on campus is part of at least one of them. It is a great way to meet new people and [to participate in] activities."

FINANCIAL AID: 605-677-5446 • E-MAIL: ADMISS@USD.EDU • WEBSITE: WWW.USD.EDU

THE PRINCETON REVIEW SAYS

Admissions

Very important factors considered include: Class rank, academic GPA, rigor of secondary school record, standardized test scores, *Important factors considered include:* alumni/ae relation. *Other factors considered include:* Application essay, recommendation(s), character/personal qualities, extracurricular activities, geographical residence, racial/ethnic status, state residency, talent/ability, volunteer work, work experience. SAT or ACT required; SAT and SAT Subject Tests or ACT required; TOEFL required of all international applicants. High school diploma is required and GED is accepted. *Academic units required:* 4 English, 3 mathematics, 3 science, (3 science labs), 3 social studies, 1 fine arts. *Academic units recommended:* 4 English, 4 mathematics, 4 science, (3 science labs), 2 foreign language, 3 social studies, 1 fine arts.

Financial Aid

Students should submit: FAFSA. The Princeton Review suggests that all financial aid forms be submitted as soon as possible after 1/1. Need-based scholarships/grants offered: Federal Pell, SEOG, private scholarships, the school's own gift aid, Federal Nursing Scholarships. ACG and SMART grants. *Loan aid offered:* FFEL Subsidized Stafford, FFEL Unsubsidized Stafford, FFEL PLUS, Federal Perkins, Federal Nursing, college/university loans from institutional funds. Applicants will be notified of awards on a rolling basis beginning 3/1. Federal Work-Study Program available. Institutional employment available. Off-campus job opportunities are fair.

The Inside Word

To be a candidate for general admission to USD, you must meet one of three general requirements: rank in the top 50% of your graduating class or obtain an ACT/SAT composite score of 21/990 or higher or have a minimum grade point average of at least 2.6 on a 4.0 scale in all high school courses. An applicant's high school curricula must also meet certain minimum requirements.

THE SCHOOL SAYS "..."

From The Admissions Office

"The University of South Dakota is the perfect fit for students looking for a smart educational investment. The U is South Dakota's only designated liberal arts university and is consistently rated among the top doctoral institutions in the country. Annually, The U awards scholarships to more than 800 first-year students, and more than 80 percent of U students receive some form of financial aid through grants, loans, and work-study jobs.

"U students earn the nation's most prestigious scholarships. Our quality of teaching and research prepares students to pursue their passions all over the world, at institutions such as Columbia, Johns Hopkins, The University of Chicago, and beyond. Fifty-nine U students have been awarded prestigious Fulbright, Rhodes, National Science Foundation, Boren, Truman, Udall, Gilman, and Goldwater scholarships and grants for graduate study. Personal attention from our award-winning faculty and our welcoming environment makes students feel right at home.

"As the flagship liberal arts institution in South Dakota, The University of South Dakota—founded in 1862—has long been regarded as a leader in the state and the region. Notable undergraduate and postgraduate alumni include journalist Ken Bode, author and former news anchor Tom Brokaw, writer and Emmy Award–winner Dorothy Cooper Foote, U.S. Senator Tim Johnson, *USA Today* Founder Al Neuharth, and U.S. Senator John Thune.

"Applicants are not required to take the writing test for either SAT or ACT. USD recommends taking the ACT over the SAT. Students who wish to send their SAT scores will have their scores converted to ACT scores for placement and scholarship consideration."

SELECTIVITY

Admissions Rating	78
# of applicants	3,349
% of applicants accepted	83
% of acceptees attending	42

FRESHMAN PROFILE

Range SAT Critical Reading	470–660
Range SAT Math	480–610
Range ACT Composite	20–25
Minimum paper TOEFL	550
Minimum computer TOEFL	213
Average HS GPA	3.28
% graduated top 10% of class	11
% graduated top 25% of class	35
% graduated top 50% of class	69

DEADLINES

Regular	
Notification	rolling
Nonfall registration?	yes

APPLICANTS ALSO LOOK AT

AND OFTEN PREFER
University of Nebraska—Lincoln

AND SOMETIMES PREFER
South Dakota State University
Augustana College (SD)

AND RARELY PREFER
Dakota State University

FINANCIAL FACTS

Financial Aid Rating	84
Annual in-state tuition	$2,646
Annual out-of-state tuition	$3,966
Room and board	$5,442
Required fees	$3,182
Books and supplies	$900
% frosh rec. need-based scholarship or grant aid	26
% UG rec. need-based scholarship or grant aid	28
% frosh rec. non-need-based scholarship or grant aid	26
% UG rec. non-need-based scholarship or grant aid	19
% frosh rec. need-based self-help aid	48
% UG rec. need-based self-help aid	55
% frosh rec. athletic scholarships	6
% UG rec. athletic scholarships	5
% frosh rec. any financial aid	92
% UG rec. any financial aid	87

UNIVERSITY OF SOUTH FLORIDA

4202 EAST FOWLER AVENUE, SVC-1036, TAMPA, FL 33620-9951 • ADMISSIONS: 813-974-3350 • FAX: 813-974-9689

CAMPUS LIFE
Quality of Life Rating	76
Fire Safety Rating	60*
Green Rating	88
Type of school	public
Environment	metropolis

STUDENTS
Total undergrad enrollment	35,104
% male/female	42/58
% from out of state	3.06
% from public high school	95
% live on campus	12
% in (# of) fraternities	8 (16)
% in (# of) sororities	6 (22)
% African American	12
% Asian	6
% Caucasian	65
% Hispanic	14
% international	1
# of countries represented	132

SURVEY SAYS . . .
Diverse student types on campus
Different types of students interact
Students get along with local
community
Great off-campus food
Everyone loves the Bulls
Student publications are popular
Student government is popular

ACADEMICS
Academic Rating	73
Calendar	semester
Student/faculty ratio	27.5:1
Profs interesting rating	68
Profs accessible rating	70
% classes taught by TAs	17
Most common reg class size	20–29 students
Most common lab size	20–29 students

MOST POPULAR MAJORS
biomedical sciences
business/commerce
psychology

STUDENTS SAY ". . ."

Academics
The University of South Florida is "an enormous and comprehensive research university." A huge range of majors" is available. The "amazing" honors college "is definitely something students should try to get into if possible." There's "a great nursing program,." but pre-med, business, education, engineering, and environmental science are notable as well. "Everything seems to run fairly smoothly and is well organized" at USF, but the "distant" administration is "blissfully unaware of student opinions" and "hard to track down." Don't try calling anyone, "You end up in a permanent prompt loop." Lectures can be "very large," especially in introductory courses. Students report a "mix of good and bad professors." "It all comes down to the luck of the draw." Many professors are "very friendly, down to earth, and easily accessible." Other faculty members "are there mainly for research" and "just have no business teaching" or "struggle with the English language." "There are some professors who blow me away with how great they teach and explain material," observes an environmental science major, "but then there are others who blow me away because I hate them so much."

Life
USF has a handful of regional campuses, but the main one is in Tampa. It's very spread out and full of "open green spaces." The Tampa campus "could stand to be a little more aesthetically pleasing," though, and it "isn't located in the best neighborhood." "Campus security is a big issue." Also, USF is "a heavy commuter school," and "trying to park every day is hell." Socially, "it's not easy to just walk out and meet people" due to the mammoth size of this institution. However, "there are hundreds of campus activities to get involved in." "The school paper is awesome." Movies on the lawn are "tons of fun." "There is always something going on" at the student union. Busch Gardens—a theme park—is located just down the street from campus. Students here are "diehard Bulls football fans" in the fall and they "have a lot of school pride and spirit." There's also a decent smattering of Greek life. "USF students enjoy a party" and "large, loud, long" gatherings are abundant on Thursday nights and throughout the weekend. Many students also opt for the "world famous" club scene in Ybor City, a historic-district-turned-night-clubbing-district in Tampa's Latin Quarter. However, the overall caliber of the festivities here doesn't approach the scene at some other Florida schools. "I don't think we're a major party school," opines a senior.

Student Body
This campus is "full of Floridians," and "flip flops are a mandatory staple in any USF student's wardrobe." That's about all that unites the undergraduate population. "The thing about the University of South Florida is that there is no typical student." This is "a very diverse population of students by any standard." "We come from very different backgrounds and are headed in very different directions," says a senior. "Interests, talents, study habits, and hobbies vary greatly." "You've got the preps, the boozers, the druggies, the philosophers, the theater kids, etc." There are the "overachievers who like sit in circles and pat each other on the back." Other students "always wait until the last minute to complete assignments." "There is a large population of nontraditional and commuter students." A strong contingent works "at least part time." Many students "appear to be on a mission" and "just want to finish their school work and get out of here." There are "a lot of African Americans and significant Muslim, Hispanic, and international student minorities." "It is a beautiful thing to walk across campus and see so many different types of people," beams a sophomore. There is a lot of ethnic self-segregation, though. "It's awkward to see the group of black people hanging out in one corner while the Hispanics stand over there and the white kids sit at that table over there," observes a sophomore.

FINANCIAL AID: 813-974-4700 • WEBSITE: WWW.USF.EDU

THE PRINCETON REVIEW SAYS

Admissions

Very important factors considered include: Academic GPA, rigor of secondary school record, standardized test scores. *Important factors considered include:* Class rank, talent/ability. *Other factors considered include:* character/personal qualities, extracurricular activities, first generation, geographical residence, state residency, volunteer work, work experience. SAT or ACT required; ACT with Writing component required. TOEFL required of all international applicants. High school diploma is required and GED is accepted. *Academic units required:* 4 English, 3 mathematics, 3 science, (2 science labs), 2 foreign language, 3 social studies, 3 academic electives.

Financial Aid

Students should submit: FAFSA. The Princeton Review suggests that all financial aid forms be submitted as soon as possible after 1/1. *Need-based scholarships/grants offered:* Federal Pell, SEOG, state scholarships/grants, private scholarships, the school's own gift aid. *Loan aid offered:* FFEL Subsidized Stafford, FFEL Unsubsidized Stafford, FFEL PLUS, Federal Perkins, college/university loans from institutional funds. Applicants will be notified of awards on a rolling basis beginning 3/15. Federal Work-Study Program available. Institutional employment available. Off-campus job opportunities are good.

The Inside Word

A traditional college-prep high school course load is required for admission to USF. Beyond making sure that you complete all prerequisite classes, however, keep two other things in mind when applying to USF. First, admissions decisions are made on a rolling basis, so the earlier one applies, the better his or her chance of acceptance since there are more unfilled seats early in the admissions cycle. Second, advanced placement (AP) and International Baccalaureate (IB) classes are looked upon favorably in the admissions office, so if your school offers them, load up on them and do well.

THE SCHOOL SAYS ". . ."

From The Admissions Office

"Located in the Tampa Bay metropolitan area, USF is recognized as one of the nation's top research universities. USF takes great pride in its faculty. Professors in all academic areas are responsible for discovering new solutions to existing and emerging problems. As an undergraduate at USF, you can participate actively in the creation of the knowledge that will be taught on other college campuses for decades to come. And, the faculty at USF is diverse as well. Among top tier research universities, USF ranks third in the number of Black faculty, seventh in the number of Hispanic faculty, and first in the number of female faculty.

"As students begin the application process, they should become familiar with USF's admission requirements. USF used extensive institutional research to validate that the high school GPA coupled with grade trends and the rigor of student's curriculum in high school are the most critical factors in student academic success at USF. Preference in admission, therefore, is given to students who complete at least three AP or IB courses, at least two college-level courses through dual enrollment, and additional coursework in math, science or foreign language beyond minimum requirements.

"SAT and ACT scores, while important, are less critical in USF's admission decisions when the high school GPA and rigor of curriculum are both strong. USF does use the SAT Writing and the ACT English/Writing components to make decisions, as scores of 550 and 24 respectively are additional indicators of potential for academic success. USF also takes into account special talents in and outside of the classroom as well as whether a student would be in the first generation of the family to attend college.

"With some of the best weather in the country, it's always a great time to visit USF. Campus tours, information sessions and tours of the residence halls are offered on weekdays throughout the year and on most Saturday mornings from September through April. Reservations are strongly encouraged."

SELECTIVITY

Admissions Rating	**87**
# of applicants	27,017
% of applicants accepted	46
% of acceptees attending	30

FRESHMAN PROFILE

Range SAT Critical Reading	510–610
Range SAT Math	530–630
Range SAT Writing	490–580
Range ACT Composite	23–28
Minimum paper TOEFL	550
Minimum computer TOEFL	213
Average HS GPA	3.67
% graduated top 10% of class	25
% graduated top 25% of class	60
% graduated top 50% of class	81

DEADLINES

Regular	
Priority	3/1
Deadline	4/15
Notification	rolling
Nonfall registration?	yes

APPLICANTS ALSO LOOK AT

AND OFTEN PREFER
University of Florida

AND SOMETIMES PREFER
University of Central Florida
Florida State University

FINANCIAL FACTS

Financial Aid Rating	**63**
Annual in-state tuition	$3,917
Annual out-of-state tuition	$16,634
Room and board	$8,080
Required fees	$74
Books and supplies	$1,500
% frosh rec. any financial aid	98
% UG rec. any financial aid	76
% UG borrow to pay for school	49.64
Average cumulative indebtedness	$18,568

UNIVERSITY OF SOUTHERN CALIFORNIA

700 CHILDS WAY, LOS ANGELES, CA 90089-0911 • ADMISSIONS: 213-740-1111 • FAX: 213-740-6364

CAMPUS LIFE

Quality of Life Rating	**78**
Fire Safety Rating	**96**
Green Rating	**90**
Type of school	private
Environment	metropolis

STUDENTS

Total undergrad enrollment	16,283
% male/female	50/50
% from out of state	37
% from public high school	58
% in (# of) fraternities	17 (30)
% in (# of) sororities	20 (25)
% African American	5
% Asian	23
% Caucasian	47
% Hispanic	12
% Native American	1
% international	9
# of countries represented	138

SURVEY SAYS . . .

Everyone loves the Trojans
Frats and sororities dominate social scene
Musical organizations are popular
Student publications are popular

ACADEMICS

Academic Rating	**87**
Calendar	semester
Student/faculty ratio	9:1
Profs interesting rating	78
Profs accessible rating	77
Most common reg class size	10–19 students
Most common lab size	20–29 students

MOST POPULAR MAJORS

business administration and management
communication studies/speech
communication and rhetoric
psychology

STUDENTS SAY ". . ."

Academics

The University of Southern California boasts "a dynamic and culturally diverse campus located in a world-class city which is equally dynamic and culturally diverse." Everything related to cinema is "top notch." Among the other 150 or so majors here, programs in journalism, business, engineering, and architecture are particularly notable. The honors programs are "very good," too. One of the best perks about USC is its "large and enthusiastic alumni network." Becoming "part of the Trojan Family" is a great way to jumpstart your career because USC graduates love to hire other USC graduates. "Almost everyone talks about getting job offers based solely on going to USC." "The school seems to run very smoothly, with few administrative issues ever being problematic enough to reach the awareness of the USC student community," says an international relations major. The top brass "is a bit mysterious and heavy handed," though. Also, "they milk every dime they can get from you." Academically, some students call the general education courses "a complete waste of time." There are a few "real narcissists" on the faculty as well as some professors "who seem to just be there because they want to do research." Overall, though, students report professors "make the subject matter come alive" and make themselves "very available" outside the classroom. "My academic experience at USC is fabulous," gushes an aerospace engineering major. "I would not choose any other school."

Life

Students at USC complain quite a bit about their "smelly, ugly" housing. Recreation facilities aren't much, either. "For such an athletic school, the student gym is embarrassing." Also, students stress the fact that the area around USC is "impoverished" and "notoriously unsafe." "People get mugged all the time." On campus, though, life is "vibrant." There are more than 600 student organizations. Theatrical and musical productions are "excellent." School spirit is "extreme" and "infectious." "Football games are huge." "There is absolutely nothing that can top watching our unbelievable football team throttle the competition," says a merciless sophomore. "Drinking is a big part of the social scene" as well. "We definitely have some of the sickest parties ever," claims an impressed freshman. "Greek life is very big" and, on the weekends, a strong contingent of students "religiously" visits "The Row, the street lined with all the fraternity and sorority houses." Students also have "the sprawling city of Los Angeles as their playground." It's an "eclectic place with both high and low culture and some of the best shopping in the world." "Hollywood clubs and downtown bars" are popular destinations. Art exhibits, concerts, and "hip restaurants" are everywhere. However, "you need a car." L.A. traffic may be "a buzz kill" but students report that it's considerably preferable to the "absolutely terrible" public transportation system.

Student Body

The one thing that unites everyone here is "tons of Trojan pride." USC students are also "intensely ambitious" and, while there are some "complete slackers," many students hit the books "harder than they let on." Otherwise, students insist that, "contrary to popular belief, USC has immense diversity." "The stereotypical USC student is a surfer fraternity bro or a tan, trendy sorority girl from the O.C." You'll find plenty of those. Many students are also "extremely good looking." Ethnic minorities and a high number of international students make up sizeable contingents of the undergraduate population as well. If you're gay, you shouldn't have any problems. "No one cares what your gender orientation is," says a first-year student. There are "prissy L.A. types" and "spoiled" kids. In some circles, "family income and the brands of clothes you wear definitely matter." However, "though there are quite a few who come from mega wealth, there are also many who are here on a great deal of financial aid." There are "lots of nerds," too, and a smattering of "band geeks and film freaks." Most students don't stray too far from the mainstream, though. "You have to go out of your way to find funky people," advises a sophomore.

UNIVERSITY OF SOUTHERN CALIFORNIA

FINANCIAL AID: 213-740-1111 • E-MAIL: ADMITUSC@USC.EDU • WEBSITE: WWW.USC.EDU

THE PRINCETON REVIEW SAYS

Admissions

Very important factors considered include: Application essay, academic GPA, recommendation(s), rigor of secondary school record, standardized test scores. *Important factors considered include:* extracurricular activities, talent/ability. *Other factors considered include:* Class rank, alumni/ae relation, character/personal qualities, first generation, interview, racial/ethnic status, volunteer work, work experience. SAT or ACT required; ACT with Writing component required. High school diploma is required and GED is not accepted. *Academic units required:* 4 English, 3 mathematics, 2 science, (2 science labs), 2 foreign language, 2 social studies, 3 academic electives. *Academic units recommended:* 4 English, 4 mathematics, 3 science, (3 science labs), 3 foreign language, 3 social studies, 3 academic electives.

Financial Aid

Students should submit: FAFSA, CSS/Financial Aid. PROFILE Parent and student Federal Income Tax form with all schedules and W-2s. USC Non-filing Forms for those not required to file. The Princeton Review suggests that all financial aid forms be submitted as soon as possible after 1/1. *Need-based scholarships/grants offered:* Federal Pell, SEOG, state scholarships/grants, private scholarships, the school's own gift aid. *Loan aid offered:* FFEL Subsidized Stafford, FFEL Unsubsidized Stafford, FFEL PLUS, Federal Perkins, "Credit Ready" and Credit Based loans. Applicants will be notified of awards on a rolling basis beginning 3/15. Federal Work-Study Program available. Institutional employment available. Off-campus job opportunities are excellent.

The Inside Word

USC doesn't have the toughest admissions standards in California but it's up there. Your grades and test scores need to be outstanding to compete. Even if you are a borderline candidate, though, USC is certainly worth a shot. Few schools on the planet have a better alumni network and the "Trojan Family" really does create all kinds of opportunities for its members upon graduation.

THE SCHOOL SAYS "..."

From The Admissions Office

"One of the best ways to discover if USC is right for you is to walk around campus, talk to students, and get a feel for the area both as a place to study and a place to live. If you can't visit, we hold admission information programs around the country. Watch your mailbox for an invitation, or send us an e-mail if you're interested.

"Freshman applicants are required to submit a standardized Writing exam. We will accept either the SAT or the ACT with its optional Writing section."

SELECTIVITY

Admissions Rating	98
# of applicants	35,900
% of applicants accepted	22
% of acceptees attending	35

FRESHMAN PROFILE

Range SAT Critical Reading	620–720
Range SAT Math	650–750
Range SAT Writing	640–730
Range ACT Composite	28–33
Average HS GPA	3.71
% graduated top 10% of class	87
% graduated top 25% of class	97
% graduated top 50% of class	100

DEADLINES

Regular	
Priority	12/10
Deadline	1/10
Notification	4/1
Nonfall registration?	yes

APPLICANTS ALSO LOOK AT
AND OFTEN PREFER
Harvard College, Duke University
Columbia University, Stanford University
California Institute of Technology

AND SOMETIMES PREFER
Washington University in St. Louis
University of Virginia
Johns Hopkins University
University of California—Berkeley
Cornell University
Rice University
Georgetown University

NAND RARELY PREFER
Emory University
Vanderbilt University
New York University

FINANCIAL FACTS

Financial Aid Rating	96
Annual tuition	$38,570
Room and board	$11,458
Required fees	$614
Books and supplies	$1,500
% frosh rec. need-based scholarship or grant aid	35
% UG rec. need-based scholarship or grant aid	36
% frosh rec. non-need-based scholarship or grant aid	25
% UG rec. non-need-based scholarship or grant aid	18
% frosh rec. need-based self-help aid	40
% UG rec. need-based self-help aid	40
% frosh rec. athletic scholarships	3
% UG rec. athletic scholarships	2
% frosh rec. any financial aid	76
% UG rec. any financial aid	69
% UG borrow to pay for school	51
Average cumulative indebtedness	$27,692

THE UNIVERSITY OF TENNESSEE AT KNOXVILLE

320 STUDENT SERVICE BUILDING, CIRCLE PARK DRIVE, KNOXVILLE, TN 37996-0230 • ADMISSIONS: 865-974-2184

CAMPUS LIFE

Quality of Life Rating	**74**
Fire Safety Rating	**83**
Green Rating	**85**
Type of school	public
Environment	city

STUDENTS

Total undergrad enrollment	21,378
% male/female	50/50
% from out of state	13
% live on campus	32
% in (# of) fraternities	14 (23)
% in (# of) sororities	14 (18)
% African American	8
% Asian	3
% Caucasian	85
% Hispanic	2
% international	1
# of countries represented	113

SURVEY SAYS . . .
Great library
Athletic facilities are great
Students are happy
Everyone loves the Volunteers
Student publications are popular

ACADEMICS

Academic Rating	**71**
Calendar	semester
Student/faculty ratio	16:1
Profs interesting rating	64
Profs accessible rating	69
% classes taught by TAs	9
Most common reg class size	20–29 students
Most common lab size	20–29 students

MOST POPULAR MAJORS
finance
political science and government
psychology

STUDENTS SAY "..."

Academics

The "large, dynamic," and "very affordable" University of Tennessee is a "southern football school" with "rich" traditions and "a vibrant academic and social atmosphere." "It is also a school that has something to offer everyone." The profusion of majors and minors includes several "very innovative programs." There are "excellent research facilities" and ample undergraduate research opportunities. There's also a "huge and awesome library." As with virtually every mammoth flagship state university, the faculty at UT is "a mixed bag." Professors here are "active in their fields" and usually "very passionate" about their subjects. "Overall, most faculty members are accessible and eager to help or talk with you," says an art history major. "You get the odd ones," though, and the occasional "horrible" one. "I have absolutely loved some of my professors and also wished I had the ability to fire some," reflects a marketing major. Some students feel that the top brass "genuinely tries to connect" with them. For the majority, though, "the administration is frustrating." "We call it the 'Big Orange Screw,'" maintains a sophomore. "You might get the runaround a little bit," warns a senior. "It's always best to get everything in writing."

Life

"Down by the river is gorgeous" but, on the whole, this concrete-ridden campus is "not very aesthetically pleasing." In fact, "aside from some of the buildings on the outside" and the "top-notch athletic facilities," it's "ugly." "There is never enough parking," either. Those are the complaints. In just about every other way, "the University of Tennessee is a fun place to be." It's definitely a "big campus atmosphere." "Greek life is very prevalent." "Clubs, interest groups, leadership organizations," and the like absolutely run the gamut. "Vol spirit" is also alive and well. "Practically every campus group lives up to the 'Volunteer' name by donating time and resources to our campus and community," boasts a junior. Social life is rollicking. "UT is a party school," declares a senior. "No one in their right mind would look around on the weekend and say otherwise." "Most students drink at least occasionally" at frat houses, at house parties, and at the bars on "The Strip." Intercollegiate athletics also dominate. The student body "bleeds orange." "Whether you're a hippie or a sorority girl," explains a junior, "everyone loves UT sports." The Lady Vols are a perennial basketball powerhouse. Men's basketball is also popular. Football is king, though. "During the fall, most students attend football games on Saturdays." "Huge parties on frat row" precede each one. Tailgating is a lifestyle. It's also worth noting "Knoxville is a great college town" overflowing with entertainment options. The food is great, and there is "a lot of variety within walking distance." The Great Smoky Mountains are "close" as well.

Student Body

The predominantly "middle-class, conservative" students at UT describe themselves as "physically active" and "very school spirited." They "generally harbor the good manners of Southern tradition and are very friendly." If you want to blend into the crowd, bring "at least one North Face jacket, a pair of Sperry shoes, and plenty of Ralph Lauren clothes." "Walking to class, it is a wave of the exact same person in the exact same clothes just in a different color combination," observes a sophomore. Naturally, though, with more than 20,000 undergrads, "UT is made up of many groups" and "a broad range of students." "This campus is full of interesting people who will really add to your life," promises a first-year student. "Artistic types, liberal crunchy types," and all manners of other types have their constituencies. "Everyone can find their niche," even if it might take some "effort and persistence." "If you are interested in any hobby, passion, or interest, whether it be acting, dance, intramurals, being a lawyer, college football, advancing the LGBT cause, or being Greek, the path is there."

THE UNIVERSITY OF TENNESSEE AT KNOXVILLE

FAX: 865-974-1182 • FINANCIAL AID: 865-974-3131 • E-MAIL: ADMISSIONS@UTK.EDU • WEBSITE: WWW.UTK.EDU

THE PRINCETON REVIEW SAYS

Admissions

Very important factors considered include: Academic GPA, rigor of secondary school record, standardized test scores. *Other factors considered include:* Class rank, application essay, recommendation(s), alumni/ae relation, character/personal qualities, extracurricular activities, first generation, geographical residence, level of applicant's interest, racial/ethnic status, state residency, talent/ability, SAT or ACT required; TOEFL required of all international applicants. High school diploma is required and GED is accepted. *Academic units required:* 4 English, 3 mathematics, 2 science, (1 science labs), 2 foreign language, 1 social studies, 1 history, 1 visual/performing arts.

Financial Aid

Students should submit: FAFSA. The Princeton Review suggests that all financial aid forms be submitted as soon as possible after 1/1. *Need-based scholarships/grants offered:* Federal Pell, SEOG, state scholarships/grants, private scholarships, the school's own gift aid, Federal Nursing Scholarships. *Loan aid offered:* FFEL Subsidized Stafford, FFEL Unsubsidized Stafford, FFEL PLUS, Federal Perkins, college/university loans from institutional funds. Applicants will be notified of awards on a rolling basis beginning 3/15. Federal Work-Study Program available. Off-campus job opportunities are good.

The Inside Word

UT must winnow through almost 14,000 freshman applications each year. That sort of volume doesn't allow for nuance. Students with above-average high school GPAs (achieved in a reasonable college prep curriculum) and above-average standardized test scores pretty much all make the cut. The school considers peripherals—extracurriculars, essays, special talents—when deciding which marginal candidates to admit.

THE SCHOOL SAYS "..."

From The Admissions Office

"The University of Tennessee at Knoxville is the place where you belong if you're interested in outstanding resources and unlimited opportunities to foster your personal and academic growth. Nine colleges offer more than 110 majors to students from all 50 states and 106 foreign countries. More than 400 clubs and organizations on campus offer opportunities for fun, challenge, and service. UTK is a place where students take pride in belonging to a 200-year-old tradition and celebrate the excitement of 'the Volunteer spirit.' We invite you to explore the many advantages UTK has to offer.

"Freshman applicants to the University of Tennessee are required to submit ACT or SAT scores. The essay is not required."

SELECTIVITY

Admissions Rating	89
# of applicants	13,894
% of applicants accepted	65
% of acceptees attending	47

FRESHMAN PROFILE

Range SAT Critical Reading	530–630
Range SAT Math	540–640
Range ACT Composite	24–29
Minimum paper TOEFL	523
Minimum computer TOEFL	193
Minimum web-based TOEFL	70
Average HS GPA	3.65
% graduated top 10% of class	41
% graduated top 25% of class	71
% graduated top 50% of class	93

DEADLINES

Regular	
Deadline	12/1
Notification	3/15
Nonfall registration?	yes

FINANCIAL FACTS

Financial Aid Rating	78
Annual in-state tuition	$5,428
Annual out-of-state tuition	$18,086
Room and board	$6,888
Required fees	$827
Books and supplies	$1,326
% frosh rec. need-based scholarship or grant aid	45
% UG rec. need-based scholarship or grant aid	38
% frosh rec. need-based self-help aid	22
% UG rec. need-based self-help aid	28
% frosh rec. athletic scholarships	2
% UG rec. athletic scholarships	2
% frosh rec. any financial aid	47
% UG rec. any financial aid	45
% UG borrow to pay for school	51
Average cumulative indebtedness	$24,690

THE UNIVERSITY OF TEXAS AT AUSTIN

PO Box 8058, Austin, TX 78713-8058 • Admissions: 512-475-7440 • Fax: 512-475-7475

CAMPUS LIFE
Quality of Life Rating	**88**
Fire Safety Rating	**60***
Green Rating	**60***
Type of school	public
Environment	metropolis

STUDENTS
Total undergrad enrollment	36,711
% male/female	48/52
% from out of state	4.2
% in (# of) fraternities	9.4 (26)
% in (# of) sororities	12.1 (22)
% African American	5
% Asian	18
% Caucasian	54
% Hispanic	18
% international	4
# of countries represented	125

SURVEY SAYS . . .
Athletic facilities are great
Students love Austin, TX
Everyone loves the Longhorns
Student publications are popular
Political activism is popular

ACADEMICS
Academic Rating	**75**
Calendar	semester
Student/faculty ratio	17:1
Profs interesting rating	69
Profs accessible rating	63
Most common reg class size	10–19 students
Most common lab size	10–19 students

MOST POPULAR MAJORS
biology/biological sciences
business/commerce
liberal arts and sciences/liberal studies

STUDENTS SAY ". . ."

Academics

Students insist that the University of Texas at Austin has "everything you want in a college: academics, athletics, social life, location," and it's hard to argue with them. UT is "a huge school and has a lot to offer," meaning students have "an infinite number of possibilities open to them and can use them in their own way to figure out what they want for their lives." As one student tells us about arriving on campus, "I did not realize how much was available to me just as an enrolled student. There is free tutoring, gym membership, professional counseling, doctors visits, legal help, career advising, and many distinguished outside speakers. The campus is crawling with experts in every field you can imagine." Standout academic departments are numerous: from the sciences to the humanities to creative arts, UT makes a strong bid for the much-sought-after mantle of "Harvard of the south." Also, the school does a surprisingly good job of avoiding the factory-like feel of many large schools. One student observes: "Coming to a large university, there was a prejudgment that the huge classes will make it impossible to know your professor and vice versa. The university has dispelled that myth with professors who want to know you and [who] provide opportunities to get to know them." And while professors "can vary greatly across a spectrum from 'I'm smarter than him' to 'I want to follow in his footsteps,'" "the class offerings at UT are generally vast and diverse, and students can often avoid taking the less-qualified professors with a little research."

Life

Life at UT—Austin is "very relaxed…. Students usually wear shorts and a T-shirt to class. When the weather gets cold, you might find students wearing the same shorts and T-shirt with a sweatshirt. Students and faculty frequently picnic all over campus. There are plenty of outdoor tables and grassy areas to sit." Undergrads "are often found throwing a Frisbee outside the tower or taking a nap under a tree. It's truly what you see in one of those cheesy brochures with everyone studying and smiling. Of course, the smiles aren't so bright during finals. We switch to an over-caffeinated, glazed-eye look instead." Hometown Austin "provides a social education that a college student newly out on his own would not find anywhere else," with "festivals or fairs of some kind going on downtown all the time" and "the infamous 6th Street with nightlife that dies down only after the bars close." Campus and the surrounding area offer "many hike-and-bike trails and fitness organizations. It's possible for students to train for marathons, half marathons, and triathlons while in school. Barton Springs pool is a natural spring that is very popular year-round. On any giving Saturday you will find students throwing a football, going for a run, biking through the hills, kayaking in the river, having a late lunch at one of Austin's great restaurants, or just sleeping in."

Student Body

"Because of the huge Greek life at UT, a 'typical student' would be a sorority girl or fraternity boy," but—and it's a big but—such students "are hardly the majority, since UT is actually made of more 'atypical' people than most other schools. Everyone here has his own niche, and I could not think of any type of individual who would not be able to find one of his own." Indeed, "Everyone at Texas is different! When you walk across campus, you see every type of ethnicity. There are a lot of minorities at Texas. Also, I see many disabled people, whom the school accommodates well. Everyone seems to get along. The different types of students just blend in together." Especially by Texas standards, "Austin is known for being 'weird.' If you see someone dressed in a way you've never seen before, you just shrug it off and say 'That's Austin!'"

THE PRINCETON REVIEW SAYS

Admissions

Very important factors considered include: Class rank, rigor of secondary school record, *Important factors considered include:* Application essay, standardized test scores, extracurricular activities, talent/ability, volunteer work, work experience. *Other factors considered include:* recommendation(s), character/personal qualities, first generation, level of applicant's interest, racial/ethnic status, state residency, SAT or ACT required; ACT with Writing component required. TOEFL required of all international applicants. High school diploma is required and GED is accepted. *Academic units required:* 4 English, 3 mathematics, 2 science, (2 science labs), 2 foreign language, 3 social studies. *Academic units recommended:* 4 English, 4 mathematics, 4 science, (3 science labs), 3 foreign language, 3 social studies.

Financial Aid

Students should submit: FAFSA. The Princeton Review suggests that all financial aid forms be submitted as soon as possible after 1/1. Need-based scholarships/grants offered: Federal Pell, SEOG, state scholarships/grants, private scholarships, the school's own gift aid. *Loan aid offered:* FFEL Subsidized Stafford, FFEL Unsubsidized Stafford, FFEL PLUS, Federal Perkins, state loans. Applicants will be notified of awards on a rolling basis beginning 3/15. Federal Work-Study Program available. Off-campus job opportunities are fair.

The Inside Word

Texans who graduate in the top 10 percent of their high school class are guaranteed admission to any public university in Texas. However, they are not guaranteed admission to the department of their choice, so even these students should put in the effort necessary to submit the strongest possible application; those who fail to do so risk being admitted as an undeclared major, making the road to their intended major more difficult. Everyone else should do likewise; admissions are quite competitive here. Space for out-of-state students is limited, meaning they'll have even higher hurdles to clear.

THE SCHOOL SAYS "..."

From The Admissions Office

"For more than 120 years, students from all over the world have come to The University of Texas at Austin to obtain a first-class education. Recognized for research, teaching, and public service, the university boasts more than 130 undergraduate academic programs, more than 350 study-abroad programs, outstanding student services, cultural centers, and volunteer and leadership opportunities designed to prepare students to make a difference in the world. Along with its nationally ranked athletic programs, the university's spirit is enhanced by cultural, artistic, and scientific opportunities that help to make Austin one of the most inviting destinations in the country. The Performing Arts Center hosts plays, Austin's opera and symphony, and visiting musical and dance groups. Students access more than 8 million volumes in the university's 17 libraries and study prehistoric fossils at the Texas Memorial Museum, Renaissance and Baroque paintings in the Blanton Museum, original manuscripts at the Ransom Center, and life in the 1960s at the Lyndon B. Johnson Library and Museum. Each year the university enrolls about 50,000 students from richly varied ethnic and geographic backgrounds. Every day graduates contribute to the world community as volunteers, teachers, journalists, artists, engineers, business leaders, scientists, and lawyers. With world-renowned faculty, top-rated academic programs, successful alumni, and such an enticing location, it's no surprise that The University of Texas at Austin ranks among the best universities in the world. Freshman applicants must submit official scores from the new version of the SAT or the ACT with the optional Writing exam. SAT Subject test scores are required only for applicants to the College of Engineering who need to submit scores to meet the math readiness requirement."

SELECTIVITY

Admissions Rating	**92**
# of applicants	29,501
% of applicants accepted	44
% of acceptees attending	52

FRESHMAN PROFILE

Range SAT Critical Reading	540–660
Range SAT Math	570–690
Range SAT Writing	540–670
Range ACT Composite	24–30
Minimum paper TOEFL	550
Minimum computer TOEFL	213
Minimum web-based TOEFL	79
% graduated top 10% of class	75.2
% graduated top 25% of class	94.7
% graduated top 50% of class	99.2

DEADLINES

Regular	
Deadline	12/15
Nonfall registration?	yes

FINANCIAL FACTS

Financial Aid Rating	**90**
Annual in-state tuition	$8,532
Annual out-of-state tuition	$27,760
Room and board	$9,246
Books and supplies	$818
% frosh rec. need-based scholarship or grant aid	57
% UG rec. need-based scholarship or grant aid	44
% frosh rec. need-based self-help aid	60
% UG rec. need-based self-help aid	51
% frosh rec. any financial aid	60
% UG rec. any financial aid	54
% UG borrow to pay for school	42
Average cumulative indebtedness	$17,000

UNIVERSITY OF TORONTO

315 BLOOR STREET WEST, TORONTO, ON M5S1A3 • ADMISSIONS: 416-978-2190 • FAX: 416-978-7022

CAMPUS LIFE
Quality of Life Rating	**73**
Fire Safety Rating	**60***
Green Rating	**60***
Type of school	public
Environment	metropolis

STUDENTS
Total undergrad enrollment	52,703
% male/female	45/55
% from out of state	6
% live on campus	15
% international	10
# of countries represented	162

SURVEY SAYS . . .
Class discussions are rare
Great library
Diverse student types on campus
Students love Toronto, ON
Great off-campus food
Student publications are popular

ACADEMICS
Academic Rating	**73**
Student/faculty ratio	27:1
Profs interesting rating	62
Profs accessible rating	61

STUDENTS SAY "..."

Academics

With "an excellent reputation and a huge selection of courses" as well as "a world-class city" to call home, the University of Toronto "provides expert knowledge in every field" to its 50,000+ undergraduates and nearly 11,000 graduate students. True, it can be "hard to relate to the instructors given that the class sizes are so huge," and those looking for an intimate and supportive academic environment might not find a good fit at U of T. "The general attitude is one of professionalism and very little mercy [here]." Still, self-starters will find the limitless opportunities outweigh the drawbacks. As one puts it, "Most of the professors are premier representatives of their respective industries." Another adds, "The fact that you are learning from Nobel Prize winners in a city full of adventures is unbeatable." "Excellent research facilities" are among the other assets here. The school also capitalizes on its location in the center of Toronto: "The city and the university draw on each other in a variety of ways—clinical opportunities and research flow in both directions." On top of that, industrious undergrads tell us, "The libraries and other research facilities here are excellent and contribute much to the overall academic experience."

Life

When they aren't hitting the books, University of Toronto students enjoy life in "one of the coolest cities in North America" where "there's always something new happening: the Toronto International Film Festival, skating in Nathan Phillips Square, etc." Students benefit from the fact that "the Royal Ontario Museum is on campus, a ton of pubs and art galleries are within walking distance, and a nightlife to suit just about any type of person" can be found in Toronto. When it comes to campus life, many students feel the school's spirit and unity is negatively affected by the large number of commuter students. "Off-campus students, of whom there are many, rarely participate in extracurricular activities," one student complains adds that "Interest in varsity sports is just pathetic" among all undergraduates. Others focus on the positives, pointing out the social and recreational opportunities available to those willing to look. A junior says, "Getting involved here takes some research in terms of navigating the 300 clubs and endless academic/research opportunities, but once I did some searching, I found several places where I fit in well and have fun." For those who live on campus, sororities and fraternities help nurture social bonds, and "most of the residential colleges have tons of events, from campus-wide capture the flag [games] to movie nights" or "intramural sports."

Student Body

At this large public school, the demographics on campus reflect those of surrounding Toronto, "one of the most diverse cities around." As one junior puts it, "It can be said that all students here have in common an excellent academic record prior to university. Beyond that, anything goes: There are huge variances in race, religion, sexual orientation, academic focus, postgraduate aspirations, socioeconomic background, disability, nationality, athleticism, and community involvement." A freshman chimes in, "On my floor alone there are kids from at least 10 different countries and, even with the different cultures, we have blended together to make a big family." Most students say it's relatively easy to find a social group among like-minded individuals, despite the school's impressive size and diversity. According to one senior, "Most students will find a niche where they feel comfortable; there's a place for everyone."

FINANCIAL AID: 416-978-2190 • E-MAIL: ADMISSIONS.HELP@UTORONTO.CA • WEBSITE: WWW.UTORONTO.CA

THE PRINCETON REVIEW SAYS

Admissions

Very important factors considered include: Academic GPA, standardized test scores. SAT or ACT required; SAT and SAT Subject Tests or ACT required; ACT with Writing component required. TOEFL required of all international applicants. High school diploma is required and GED is accepted.

Financial Aid

The Princeton Review suggests that all financial aid forms be submitted as soon as possible after 1/1.

The Inside Word

University of Toronto takes a numbers-based approach to admissions. American students must submit not only high-school transcripts and SAT/ACT scores but also results for three SAT subject tests/APs/IBs. Only those who perform well by all these metrics are likely to gain admission. Candidates should be aware that qualifications vary from program to program, and as an international student you'll have more paperwork to file. U.S. students can apply for financial assistance from the U.S. Federal Family Education Program (FFELP). The University of Toronto is a recognized post-secondary institution for Federal Stafford Loans. All applicants are automatically considered for admission scholarships.

THE SCHOOL SAYS "..."

From The Admissions Office

"The University of Toronto is committed to being an internationally significant research university with undergraduate, graduate, and professional programs of study.

"Students educated at U.S. schools should present good scores on the SAT or ACT examinations. Students must present the Writing component for both tests. Applicants must also present at least three SAT Subject Tests scores or AP scores in subjects appropriate to their proposed area of study. Those seeking admission to science or business/commerce programs are strongly advised to complete AP Calculus AB or BC or IB Mathematics.

"Scores lower than 500 on any part of the SAT Reasoning or Subject Tests are not acceptable. While many of our programs require higher scores, students normally present scores of at least 1700 out of a possible 2400 on the SAT and 26 on the ACT."

SELECTIVITY

Admissions Rating	60*
# of applicants	60,776
% of applicants accepted	77
% of acceptees attending	26

FRESHMAN PROFILE

Minimum paper TOEFL	600
Minimum computer TOEFL	250

DEADLINES

Regular	
Deadline	3/1
Notification	rolling
Nonfall registration?	no

FINANCIAL FACTS

Financial Aid Rating	60*
Tuition (in Canadian Dollars)	
Canadian citizens	$4,776
International	$19,404

THE UNIVERSITY OF TULSA

800 SOUTH TUCKER DRIVE, TULSA, OK 74104 • ADMISSIONS: 918-631-2307 • FAX: 918-631-5003

CAMPUS LIFE

Quality of Life Rating	94
Fire Safety Rating	89
Green Rating	85
Type of school	private
Affiliation	Presbyterian
Environment	metropolis

STUDENTS

Total undergrad enrollment	2,981
% male/female	52/48
% from out of state	41
% from public high school	78
% live on campus	70
% in (# of) fraternities	21 (7)
% in (# of) sororities	23 (9)
% African American	6
% Asian	3
% Caucasian	63
% Hispanic	4
% Native American	4
% international	12
# of countries represented	57

SURVEY SAYS . . .

Athletic facilities are great
Students are friendly
Students get along with local
community
Students are happy

ACADEMICS

Academic Rating	84
Calendar	semester
Student/faculty ratio	10:1
Profs interesting rating	89
Profs accessible rating	90
% classes taught by TAs	4
Most common reg class size	10–19 students
Most common lab size	10–19 students

MOST POPULAR MAJORS

marketing/marketing management
petroleum engineering
psychology

STUDENTS SAY ". . ."

Academics

The University of Tulsa is a mid-size, private school that provides a superior learning environment and a myriad of academic opportunities to its 3,000 undergraduate students. Across disciplines, the academic experience is high quality and stimulating, incorporating "rigorous and invigorating lectures and well instructed lab periods." In addition to coursework, undergraduates benefit from unmatched "academic and professional opportunities reserved only for graduate students at other schools." A current student attests, "I had no trouble getting undergraduate research experience in biochemistry as early as sophomore year." Students rave about TU's outgoing professors, saying that "the faculty and staff at TU seem to take a personal interest in the students here. They are accessible and love to help students in any way possible, not only academically, but professionally and personally as well." How's this for involved? "I have even received a text message from a professor when I forgot to turn in a homework assignment," reports a sophomore. While course selection is occasionally limited by the school's size, "professors will frequently tailor independent study projects with students." When it comes to the administration, some students worry that they are too preoccupied with improving the college's rankings. Others insist that the administrative offices are just as student-friendly as the teaching staff. A sophomore shares, "I became involved in student government my third semester here, and I am so impressed by how accessible the administration is. The deans and president of the university really care about students."

Life

Student life at TU reflects the school's unequivocal emphasis on academics. Studious undergraduates agree that the University of Tulsa "is definitely not a big party school. Most of the students here are focused on studies." Nonetheless, there are plenty of opportunities for extracurricular involvement, and campus clubs range "from honor societies to multi-cultural groups to religious gatherings." The campus isn't too big, so students looking for leadership experience will be pleased to learn that "anyone can be involved and 'be someone' on campus." In addition to student clubs, "collegiate, intramural, and pick-up sports are really popular." About 20 percent of the campus is involved in a Greek organization, and "a lot of student life revolves strongly around sororities and fraternities." However, students reassure us that "even non-Greek students can visit the houses and hang out on a Friday night." If you don't feel like partying at fraternities, there's plenty more to do, on and off campus. A sophomore shares, "For fun my friends and I go bowling, explore the parks of Tulsa, watch movies, do arts and crafts, and go to the occasional party." While students readily admit that Tulsa isn't New York City, they appreciate the myriad of pleasures of their manageable mid-size city, which boasts "some really great restaurants and coffee shops around TU and in historic Tulsa."

Student Body

Defined in broad strokes, most TU undergraduates hail from affluent, Christian families in the Midwest. However, TU students insist that, while there are some similarities within the campus community, they cannot be summed up so easily. In addition to the array of "jocks, computer geeks, fashionistas, 'good' students, loners, and partygoers," University of Tulsa has a "strong international community. Programs such as the petroleum engineering department attract a diverse international populace. One can hear five different languages simply walking to class!" Thanks, in part, to the international students, there is "a diverse religious life on campus (we even have a mosque!), several activist groups that meet on campus, and countless student organizations." No matter what your background, "the majority of students I know at TU are very open and accepting of everyone else, regardless of religion, race, sexual orientation, athletic ability, major, and Greek affiliation." In fact, it's easy to feel at home on the TU campus. A junior explains, "Because the campus is small, even if you don't know somebody's name, you normally recognize their face from somewhere; this leads to a great sense of community."

FINANCIAL AID: 918-631-2526 • E-MAIL: ADMISSION@UTULSA.EDU • WEBSITE: WWW.UTULSA.EDU

THE PRINCETON REVIEW SAYS

Admissions

Very important factors considered include: Class rank, academic GPA, rigor of secondary school record, standardized test scores, interview, level of applicant's interest, *Important factors considered include:* Application essay, recommendation(s), character/personal qualities, extracurricular activities, talent/ability. *Other factors considered include:* alumni/ae relation, first generation, racial/ethnic status, volunteer work, work experience. SAT or ACT required; TOEFL required of all international applicants. High school diploma is required and GED is accepted. *Academic units recommended:* 4 English, 3 mathematics, 3 science, (2 science labs), 2 foreign language, 1 social studies, 2 history, 1 academic electives.

Financial Aid

Students should submit: FAFSA, institution's own financial aid form. The Princeton Review suggests that all financial aid forms be submitted as soon as possible after 1/1. Need-based scholarships/grants offered: Federal Pell, SEOG, state scholarships/grants, private scholarships, the school's own gift aid. *Loan aid offered:* FFEL Subsidized Stafford, FFEL Unsubsidized Stafford, FFEL PLUS, Federal Perkins. Applicants will be notified of awards on a rolling basis beginning 3/1. Federal Work-Study Program available. Institutional employment available. Off-campus job opportunities are good.

The Inside Word

TU is a university with solid academic offerings, a strong sense of community, lots of student-faculty interaction, and attainable admission standards. The school's commitment to undergrads is clear. One of TU's most impressive programs, The Tulsa Undergraduate Research Challenge (TURC), allows undergrads to complete research along with faculty.

THE SCHOOL SAYS "..."

From The Admissions Office

"The University of Tulsa is a private university with a comprehensive scope. Students choose from more than 80 majors offered through three undergraduate colleges—Arts and Sciences, Business Administration, and Engineering and Natural Sciences. Curricula can be customized with collaborative research, joint undergraduate and graduate programs, and an honors program, among others. Professors are equally committed to teaching undergraduates and to scholarly research. This results in extraordinary individual achievement, resulting in the nationally competitive scholarships students have won since 1995: 42 Goldwaters, 27 National Science Foundation scholars, 8 Trumans, 7 Department of Defense scholars, 6 Fulbrights, 6 Phi Kappa Phi, 5 Udalls, and 4 British Marshalls. Over the past decade over 700,000 square feet of facilities have been added costing over $100 million. These include athletic venues, 400 additional apartments, fitness center, Legal Information Center and new computer facility. Over 160 registered clubs, and interest groups, including intramural and recreational sports teams exist along with 6 fraternities and 9 sororities. The 8,300 seat Reynolds Center is home to the standout Golden Hurricane NCAA Division I men's basketball team, campus events, and concerts. A 40-acre sports complex includes the fitness center and indoor tennis center that hosted the 2008 NCAA Division I Men's and Women's tennis finals. An outdoor freshman orientation program launches an entire first-year experience dedicated to developing students' full potential.

"Applicants are required to submit the SAT or ACT. The Writing component is not required. For admission and scholarship review, the best composite score of submitted tests will be used."

SELECTIVITY

Admissions Rating	94
# of applicants	4,714
% of applicants accepted	46
% of acceptees attending	32
# accepting a place on wait list	293
% admitted from wait list	54

FRESHMAN PROFILE

Range SAT Critical Reading	540–700
Range SAT Math	550–690
Range ACT Composite	25–31
Minimum paper TOEFL	500
Minimum computer TOEFL	173
Minimum web-based TOEFL	61
Average HS GPA	3.75
% graduated top 10% of class	64
% graduated top 25% of class	82
% graduated top 50% of class	95

DEADLINES

Regular	
Priority	2/1
Notification	rolling
Nonfall registration?	yes

APPLICANTS ALSO LOOK AT

AND OFTEN PREFER
Oklahoma State University
Southern Methodist University
Texas Christian University
University of Oklahoma

AND SOMETIMES PREFER
Washington University in St. Louis
Tulane University
Baylor University

AND RARELY PREFER
University of Missouri—Columbia
University of Kansas
Texas A&M University—College Station

FINANCIAL FACTS

Financial Aid Rating	87
Annual tuition	$23,860
Room and board	$7,776
Required fees	$80
Books and supplies	$1,200
% frosh rec. need-based scholarship or grant aid	17
% UG rec. need-based scholarship or grant aid	20
% frosh rec. non-need-based scholarship or grant aid	43
% UG rec. non-need-based scholarship or grant aid	38
% frosh rec. need-based self-help aid	34
% UG rec. need-based self-help aid	34
% frosh rec. athletic scholarships	10
% UG rec. athletic scholarships	12
% frosh rec. any financial aid	91
% UG rec. any financial aid	88
% UG borrow to pay for school	36
Average cumulative indebtedness	$28,364

UNIVERSITY OF UTAH

201 SOUTH 1460 EAST, ROOM 250 S, SALT LAKE CITY, UT 84112 • ADMISSIONS: 801-581-7281 • FAX: 801-585-7864

CAMPUS LIFE
Quality of Life Rating	82
Fire Safety Rating	84
Green Rating	89
Type of school	public
Environment	metropolis

STUDENTS
Total undergrad enrollment	20,475
% male/female	55/45
% from out of state	17
% from public high school	93
% live on campus	8
% in (# of) fraternities	2 (7)
% in (# of) sororities	2 (6)
% African American	1
% Asian	6
% Caucasian	79
% Hispanic	5
% Native American	1
% international	3
# of countries represented	113

SURVEY SAYS . . .
Registration is a breeze
Great library
Students get along with local community
Students love Salt Lake City, UT
Great off-campus food
Campus feels safe
Students are happy
Everyone loves the Utes
Student publications are popular

ACADEMICS
Academic Rating	75
Calendar	semester
Student/faculty ratio	13:1
Profs interesting rating	73
Profs accessible rating	64
% classes taught by TAs	14
Most common reg class size	10–19 students
Most common lab size	10–19 students

MOST POPULAR MAJORS
communication, journalism, economics
political science and government

STUDENTS SAY "..."

Academics

Nestled amid Salt Lake City's snowcapped mountains, the University of Utah is a large public school that offers extensive academic programs, ample research opportunities, and a surprisingly student-friendly atmosphere. No matter what your interests, you'll find like minds at U of U. "I have studied everything from Tai Chi/Yoga movement and stage combat to differential equations and linear algebra," says a junior. "The one thing that has remained consistent throughout is the appreciation and dedication the people have for the topic they are involved in." U of U is a research university that actually takes teaching seriously, and "every teacher that I've had shows incredible knowledge in their area, as well as personality and wit." "Classes are informative, challenging, and genuinely enjoyable." As is the case in many larger universities, "most general education courses are taught by grad students," whose teaching abilities can range from great to below average. "Ninety percent of my professors are fantastic; the ones that aren't are usually grad students," explains a junior. On this large campus, students have little contact with the school's administration and "there's definitely no hand-holding at the U of U. If you're unsure of your major or career plans, it's easy to slip through the cracks." However, students assure us. "The administration puts student interests first whenever possible with a focus on keeping tuition low, creating a diverse environment, and providing opportunities and experience in order to prepare students to be productive citizens."

Life

While a large percentage of the undergraduate community at the University of Utah commutes to campus, there are still plenty of activities for the school's 2,000 resident students. There are many people "active in politics, environmental issues, and international issues," and, after hours, "the school holds different events throughout the year, such as Crimson Nights that feature activities such as bowling, crafts, games, food, and music." Socially, "Greek life is not as large as at other schools but is definitely a lot of fun and the best way to get to know more people your age." In addition, "during football season there are great tailgate parties with friends, drinks, and food." Right off campus, there are a range of great restaurants, and "the nightlife is hard to keep up with." There's always something good going on—whether it's at the bars and clubs downtown, or at small music venues." For outdoorsy types, U of U is a paradise. "We have all four seasons and some of the best outdoors in the nation," explains one student. "Killer snow, amazing hills, mountains, lakes, and streams." In this natural wonderland, "hiking, biking, boating, snow-skiing, and snowboarding are just a few of the hundreds of activities available to students."

Student Body

Located in Salt Lake City, hometown to the Church of Latter Day Saints, "a majority of students at the U of U are Mormon, but not a vast majority. There are plenty of social niches to fall into, and none of them are rigidly exclusive." A current student adds, "About half the student body is the typical Utah Mormon, and the other half is a mix of everything. The two halves usually stay separate but they get along." If you like a little cultural mix-up, U of U students agree that "there is more diversity here than in any other part of the state." However, out-of-state students are uncommon, and "those of us not from Utah are definitely in the minority." While there are a number of residential students, a very large percentage of students also chose to commute to school while living with their parents or family. In addition, "there are a lot of older students and a lot of married students." Academically, however, U of U undergraduates share a true dedication to studies, and are "independent, smart, and come to class ready to discuss ideas."

FINANCIAL AID: 801-581-6211 • E-MAIL: FAWIN1@SA.UTAH.EDU • WEBSITE: WWW.UTAH.EDU

THE PRINCETON REVIEW SAYS

Admissions

Very important factors considered include: Academic GPA, rigor of secondary school record, standardized test scores. *Important factors considered include:* talent/ability. *Other factors considered include:* Class rank, recommendation(s), extracurricular activities, interview, racial/ethnic status, SAT required; SAT or ACT required; ACT required; TOEFL required of all international applicants. High school diploma is required and GED is accepted. *Academic units required:* 4 English, 2 mathematics, 3 science, (1 science labs), 2 foreign language, 1 history, 4 academic electives.

Financial Aid

Students should submit: FAFSA, institution's own financial aid form. The Princeton Review suggests that all financial aid forms be submitted as soon as possible after 1/1. *Need-based scholarships/grants offered:* Federal Pell, SEOG, state scholarships/grants, private scholarships, the school's own gift aid, SMART and ACG Grants. *Loan aid offered:* FFEL Subsidized Stafford, FFEL Unsubsidized Stafford, FFEL PLUS, Federal Perkins, Federal Nursing, college/university loans from institutional funds, private alternative loans. Applicants will be notified of awards on a rolling basis beginning 4/15. Federal Work-Study Program available. Institutional employment available. Off-campus job opportunities are excellent.

The Inside Word

Utah is another state in which low numbers of high school grads keep selectivity down at its public flagship university. Admission is based primarily on the big three: Course selection, grades, and test scores. If you have a 3.0 GPA or better and average test scores, you're close to a sure bet for admission.

THE SCHOOL SAYS "..."

From The Admissions Office

"The University of Utah is a distinctive community of learning in the American West. Today's 20,000 students are from every state and 113 foreign countries. The University has research ties worldwide, with national standing among the top comprehensive research institutions. The University offers majors in 73 undergraduate and 94 graduate subjects. Nationally recognized honors and undergraduate research programs stimulate intellectual inquiry. Undergraduates collaborate with faculty on important investigations. The University's intercollegiate athletes compete in the NCAA Division I Mountain West Conference. The men's basketball team has been nationally ranked for several years, as have our women's gymnastics and skiing teams. The University's location in Salt Lake City provides easy access to the arts, theater, Utah Jazz basketball, and hockey. Utah's Great Outdoors—skiing, hiking, and five national parks—are nearby. The university was the site for the opening and closing ceremonies and the Athletes Village for the 2002 Winter Olympic Games.

"Residential Living has greatly expanded the opportunity for students to live on campus with a new and wide variety of housing. Heritage Commons, located in historic Fort Douglas on campus, consists of 21 newly constructed buildings, including three residence hall-style facilities, which accommodate more than 2,500 students.

"Applicants are required to submit ACT scores. SAT scores are also accepted, although ACT scores are preferred. Students are urged to take the ACT near the end of their junior year or early in the senior year of high school."

SELECTIVITY

Admissions Rating	86
# of applicants	7,234
% of applicants accepted	81
% of acceptees attending	51

FRESHMAN PROFILE

Range SAT Critical Reading	490–610
Range SAT Math	500–635
Range SAT Writing	470–610
Range ACT Composite	21–27
Minimum paper TOEFL	500
Minimum computer TOEFL	173
Average HS GPA	3.52
% graduated top 10% of class	28.6
% graduated top 25% of class	48.5
% graduated top 50% of class	76.2

DEADLINES

Regular	
Priority	2/15
Deadline	4/1
Nonfall registration?	yes

FINANCIAL FACTS

Financial Aid Rating	68
Annual in-state tuition	$4,526
Annual out-of-state tuition	$15,841
Room and board	$5,972
Required fees	$759
Books and supplies	$1,080
% frosh rec. need-based scholarship or grant aid	24
% UG rec. need-based scholarship or grant aid	26
% frosh rec. non-need-based scholarship or grant aid	2
% UG rec. non-need-based scholarship or grant aid	1
% frosh rec. need-based self-help aid	19
% UG rec. need-based self-help aid	28
% frosh rec. any financial aid	22
% UG rec. any financial aid	28
% UG borrow to pay for school	40
Average cumulative indebtedness	$11,749

UNIVERSITY OF VERMONT

194 SOUTH PROSPECT STREET, BURLINGTON, VT 05401-3596 • ADMISSIONS: 802-656-3370 • FAX: 802-656-8611

CAMPUS LIFE
Quality of Life Rating	83
Fire Safety Rating	90
Green Rating	96
Type of school	public
Environment	town

STUDENTS
Total undergrad enrollment	9,867
% male/female	44/56
% from out of state	65
% from public high school	70
% live on campus	53
% in (# of) fraternities	6 (9)
% in (# of) sororities	5 (5)
% African American	1
% Asian	2
% Caucasian	92
% Hispanic	2
% international	1
# of countries represented	46

SURVEY SAYS . . .
Students are friendly
Students love Burlington, VT
Great off-campus food
Political activism is popular
Lots of beer drinking
Hard liquor is popular

ACADEMICS
Academic Rating	76
Calendar	semester
Student/faculty ratio	16:1
Profs interesting rating	75
Profs accessible rating	77
% classes taught by TAs	2
Most common reg class size	10–19 students
Most common lab size	10–19 students

MOST POPULAR MAJORS
business administration and management
English language and literature
psychology

STUDENTS SAY ". . ."

Academics

Quality of life issues are important to most University of Vermont undergrads; when discussing their reasons for choosing UVM, they're as likely to cite the "laid-back environment," the "proximity to skiing facilities," the "great parties," and their "amazing" hometown of Burlington as they are to mention the academics. But, students remind us, "That doesn't mean that there are not strong academics [at UVM]." On the contrary, UVM is made up of several well-established colleges and offers "a wide variety of majors." "You can jump around between majors, and then leave with a recognized diploma in hand for something you love to do." Students single out the business school, the "top-notch" education program, the psychology department, premedical sciences, and "the amazing animal science program" for praise, and are especially proud of The Rubenstein School of Natural Resources. It is home to UVM's environmental science majors; students tell us it "is a great college that feels like it's much smaller, [more] separate, and just cozier than the rest of the school." No matter which discipline, "you get out what you put in." "Teachers are readily available and are willing to help you do well in your classes. They encourage you to get help if you need it and are enthusiastic about what they teach. It's all there; you just have to take advantage of it." The size of the university, we're told, is just right. UVM is "a moderately-large school," and it allows undergrads "to feel at home while still offering just about any activity possible."

Life

"UVM is known to be a party school," "even though the university has cracked down on drinking." Indeed, students tell us that one can find "a good balance of having fun and academics" at UVM, "but it's tough, because there's always a party going on somewhere." Students who want to dodge the party scene will find "there is always something" happening in Burlington. The town has "lots of wonderful restaurants, a few movie theaters, a rockin' music scene, several bars, some dancing, and various environmental and social activities downtown." "On campus, there is typically at least one university-sponsored event each night, including interesting lectures, movies, games, or social events." Students love outdoor activities. "When it snows, it's very popular to go to the ski resorts around here and ski or snowboard for the day. When it's still warm out, going to the waterfront and swimming in Lake Champlain is popular too." UVM is an intercollegiate hockey powerhouse, and "in the fall and winter, hockey games are huge social events." They're so popular "that you have to get tickets to them the Monday before the game, or they will be sold out!"

Student Body

There's a "great variety of students" at UVM "because it's a big university," undergrads report, but they also note that "students at UVM are mostly white" and there's "a lot of money at this school." While the most prevalent UVM archetype is "the guitar-loving, earth-saving, relaxed hippie" who "care[s] strongly about the environment" and "social justice," the student body also includes "your athletic types, your artsy people, and a number of other groups" including "vocal LGBTQ and ALANA populations" who, "usually hang out in their own groups," but "are also active in all sorts of clubs across campus." Not surprisingly, there are many "New England types," "potheads," and "snow bums." Students report they "pretty much get along well with everyone." They either come here loving the outdoors or learn to love the outdoors by the time they leave.

FINANCIAL AID: 802-656-3156 • E-MAIL: ADMISSIONS@UVM.EDU • WEBSITE: WWW.UVM.EDU

THE PRINCETON REVIEW SAYS

Admissions

Very important factors considered include: rigor of secondary school record. *Important factors considered include:* Class rank, application essay, academic GPA, standardized test scores, character/personal qualities, state residency. *Other factors considered include:* recommendation(s), alumni/ae relation, extracurricular activities, first generation, geographical residence, interview, level of applicant's interest, racial/ethnic status, talent/ability, volunteer work, work experience. SAT or ACT required; ACT with Writing component required. TOEFL required of all international applicants. High school diploma is required and GED is accepted. *Academic units required:* 4 English, 3 mathematics, 2 science, (1 science labs), 2 foreign language, 3 social studies.

Financial Aid

Students should submit: FAFSA. The Princeton Review suggests that all financial aid forms be submitted as soon as possible after 1/1. *Need-based scholarships/grants offered:* Federal Pell, SEOG, state scholarships/grants, private scholarships, the school's own gift aid, Federal Nursing Scholarships. *Loan aid offered:* FFEL Subsidized Stafford, FFEL Unsubsidized Stafford, FFEL PLUS, Federal Perkins, Federal Nursing, college/university loans from institutional funds. Applicants will be notified of awards on a rolling basis beginning 3/15. Federal Work-Study Program available. Institutional employment available. Off-campus job opportunities are good.

The Inside Word

UVM is a very popular choice among out-of-state students, whom the school welcomes; more than half the student body originates from outside of Vermont. While admissions standards are significantly more rigorous for out-of-staters, solid candidates (B-plus/A-minus average, about a 600 on each section of the SAT) should do fine here. The school assesses applications holistically, meaning students who are weak in one area may be able to make up for it with strengths or distinguishing skills and characteristics in other areas.

THE SCHOOL SAYS "..."

From The Admissions Office

"The University of Vermont blends the close faculty-student relationships most commonly found in a small liberal arts college with the dynamic exchange of knowledge associated with a research university. This is not surprising, because UVM is both. A comprehensive research university offering nearly 100 undergraduate majors and extensive offerings through its Graduate College and College of Medicine, UVM is one of the nation's premier public research universities. UVM prides itself on the richness of its undergraduate experience. Distinguished senior faculty teach introductory courses in their fields. They also advise not only juniors and seniors, but also first- and second-year students, and work collaboratively with undergraduates on research initiatives. Students find extensive opportunities to test classroom knowledge in field through practicums, academic internships, and community service. More than 100 student organizations (involving 80 percent of the student body), 20 Division I varsity teams, 15 intercollegiate club and 14 intramural sports programs, and a packed schedule of cultural events fill in where the classroom leaves off.

"Applicants for the entering class and beyond are required to take the SAT, or the ACT with the Writing section, and they must submit official test scores. SAT Subject Tests are neither required nor recommended for the admission application."

SELECTIVITY

Admissions Rating	87
# of applicants	21,062
% of applicants accepted	65
% of acceptees attending	18
# accepting a place on wait list	1,214

FRESHMAN PROFILE

Range SAT Critical Reading	540–640
Range SAT Math	550–650
Range SAT Writing	540–640
Range ACT Composite	23–28
Minimum paper TOEFL	550
Minimum computer TOEFL	213
% graduated top 10% of class	29
% graduated top 25% of class	72
% graduated top 50% of class	98

DEADLINES

Early action	
Deadline	11/1
Notification	12/15
Regular	
Deadline	1/15
Notification	3/31
Nonfall registration?	yes

FINANCIAL FACTS

Financial Aid Rating	75
Annual in-state tuition	$11,048
Annual out-of-state tuition	$27,886
Room and board	$8,534
Required fees	$1,796
Books and supplies	$990
% UG rec. need-based scholarship or grant aid	48
% UG rec. non-need-based scholarship or grant aid	2
% UG rec. need-based self-help aid	44
% UG rec. athletic scholarships	2
% frosh rec. any financial aid	93
% UG rec. any financial aid	80
% UG borrow to pay for school	60
Average cumulative indebtedness	$25,599

UNIVERSITY OF VIRGINIA

OFFICE OF ADMISSION, PO BOX 400160, CHARLOTTESVILLE, VA 22906 • ADMISSIONS: 434-982-3200 • FAX: 434-924-3587

CAMPUS LIFE

Quality of Life Rating	82
Fire Safety Rating	64
Green Rating	92
Type of school	public
Environment	city

STUDENTS

Total undergrad enrollment	13,869
% male/female	44/56
% from out of state	28
% from public high school	75
% live on campus	43
% in (# of) fraternities	30 (31)
% in (# of) sororities	30 (15)
% African American	9
% Asian	11
% Caucasian	63
% Hispanic	4
% international	5
# of countries represented	169

SURVEY SAYS . . .

Athletic facilities are great
Low cost of living
(Almost) no one smokes

ACADEMICS

Academic Rating	98
Calendar	semester
Student/faculty ratio	15.2:1
Profs interesting rating	79
Profs accessible rating	77
% classes taught by TAs	19
Most common reg class size	10–19 students
Most common lab size	10–19 students

MOST POPULAR MAJORS

business/commerce
economics
psychology

STUDENTS SAY "..."

Academics

Founded by Thomas Jefferson, the University of Virginia takes its history and traditions seriously, but that doesn't mean it's trapped in the past. The school "ranks among the world's best and offers every imaginable subject," combining "the academic advantages of the Ivy League" with the social life—and price—of a large state school. Academics here are "definitely tough" but "straightforward:" "Go to class, do the reading, [and] you'll get the grade you deserve." Although class sizes can be large and it can take "some maneuvering to get into the more popular courses," students rave about their professors. "My professors have been my heroes; they are personable, wise, funny, prepared, engaging, and inspiring." However, that doesn't mean they'll hand your education to you on a platter: Professors "are really willing to help out students after class" if you have "the guts to go up to them." The expectation of student involvement extends across university life; student bodies administer the honor code, "which says that you will not lie, cheat, or steal while at the university." While sanctions for violations like plagiarism can be harsh, one student points out that "it is nice to be able to leave my stuff in the library or dining hall while I get up for a little while and not worry about it getting stolen."

Life

UVA students embody the "work hard, play hard" ethos. Life here "is all about balance between studying and partying. The same students who talk nonstop about how much they drank last weekend are the ones who ace their chem exams and dream of med school." The Greek scene is popular, and alcohol "is definitely a big and visible part of campus life." But there is also "lots going on in Charlottesville" and plenty to do off campus, like "hiking at Old Rag or Humpback Rock, apple picking at Carter Mountain, and other fun, outdoorsy things. There is always the downtown mall for shopping and cool places to eat." And then, of course, there is UVA athletics. Students here "go crazy for football games," which take up "most of a Saturday" during football season. But it's not all party, all the time: "Volunteering is big. Most students are involved in a variety of activities, [like] adopt-a-grandparent, student council, or honor committee." Students complain about the lack of parking and the "bland and repetitive" dining hall food, but they rave about the "beautiful grounds" and "historical architecture." The central location of dorms is "really convenient and good for social interaction."

Student Body

Students here "often get typecast as homogeneous and preppy." While this type certainly exists on campus, "there is a place for everyone at UVA. There are a lot of preppy kids, but there are also tomboys, Goths, skaters, and I even know of one kid who wears a kilt on a regular basis." Some students say that UVA has "room for improvement" when it comes to diversity: "There is some truth behind the rumor that the majority of students here are white, but by no means does this mean that the other ethnic groups here are segregated," since people here are "incredibly friendly" and the school is "a bastion of southern gentility." The student body is a happy group: "Everyone here loves it—you can't find a school with more enthusiastic and dedicated students." UVA students "are really serious about succeeding, but they want to get all they can out of every part of college, too." They're apt to "party Thursday through Saturday" and spend the rest of the week hitting the books and participating in the many clubs and organizations on campus.

FINANCIAL AID: 434-982-6000 • E-MAIL: UNDERGRADADMISSION@VIRGINIA.EDU • WEBSITE: WWW.VIRGINIA.EDU

THE PRINCETON REVIEW SAYS

Admissions

Very important factors considered include: Class rank, academic GPA, recommendation(s), rigor of secondary school record, alumni/ae relation, first generation, racial/ethnic status, state residency. *Important factors considered include:* Application essay, standardized test scores, character/personal qualities, extracurricular activities, talent/ability. *Other factors considered include:* geographical residence, volunteer work, work experience. SAT Subject Tests recommended; SAT or ACT required; ACT with Writing component required. TOEFL required of all international applicants. High school diploma is required and GED is accepted. *Academic units required:* 4 English, 4 mathematics, 2 science, 2 foreign language, 1 social studies. *Academic units recommended:* 5 mathematics, 4 science, 5 foreign language, 4 social studies.

Financial Aid

Students should submit: FAFSA, institution's own financial aid form. The Princeton Review suggests that all financial aid forms be submitted as soon as possible after 1/1. *Need-based scholarships/grants offered:* Federal Pell, SEOG, state scholarships/grants, private scholarships, the school's own gift aid, Federal Nursing Scholarships. *Loan aid offered:* FFEL Subsidized Stafford, FFEL Unsubsidized Stafford, FFEL PLUS, Federal Perkins, Federal Nursing, college/university loans from institutional funds, Alternative / Private Loans. Applicants will be notified of awards on or about 4/5. Federal Work-Study Program available. Institutional employment available.

The Inside Word

As one of the premier public universities in the country, UVA holds its applicants to high standards. While admissions officers don't set minimum requirements, all viable candidates have stellar academic records. Intellectual ability is imperative, and prospective students are expected to have taken a rigorous course load in high school. Applicants should be aware that geographical location and legacies hold significant weight, as Virginia residents and children of alums are given preference.

THE SCHOOL SAYS ". . ."

From The Admissions Office

"Admission to competitive schools requires strong academic credentials. Students who stretch themselves and take rigorous courses (honors-level and Advanced Placement courses, when offered) are significantly more competitive than those who do not. Experienced admissions officers know that most students are capable of presenting superb academic credentials, and the reality is that a very high percentage of those applying do so. Other considerations, then, come into play in important ways for academically strong candidates, as they must be seen as 'selective' as well as academically competitive.

"SAT scores are preferred. The ACT test will also be accepted if the optional ACT Writing Test is also taken. It is strongly recommended that applicants take two SAT Subject Tests of the applicant's choice."

No

SELECTIVITY

Admissions Rating	99
# of applicants	18,363
% of applicants accepted	37
% of acceptees attending	48
# accepting a place on wait list	2,159
% admitted from wait list	3
# of early decision applicants	2,404
% accepted early decision	0

FRESHMAN PROFILE

Range SAT Critical Reading	600–710
Range SAT Math	620–730
Range SAT Writing	610–720
Range ACT Composite	27–32
Average HS GPA	4.09
% graduated top 10% of class	88
% graduated top 25% of class	98
% graduated top 50% of class	99

DEADLINES

Regular	
Deadline	1/2
Notification	4/1
Nonfall registration?	no

APPLICANTS ALSO LOOK AT

AND OFTEN PREFER
Virginia Tech
College of William and Mary

AND SOMETIMES PREFER
Duke University
University of North Carolina at Chapel Hill

AND RARELY PREFER
James Madison University

FINANCIAL FACTS

Financial Aid Rating	91
Annual in-state tuition	$9,490
Annual out-of-state tuition	$29,790
% frosh rec. need-based scholarship or grant aid	23
% UG rec. need-based scholarship or grant aid	22
% frosh rec. non-need-based scholarship or grant aid	13
% UG rec. non-need-based scholarship or grant aid	13
% frosh rec. need-based self-help aid	17
% UG rec. need-based self-help aid	18
% frosh rec. athletic scholarships	4
% UG rec. athletic scholarships	3
% frosh rec. any financial aid	55
% UG rec. any financial aid	35
% UG borrow to pay for school	33
Average cumulative indebtedness	$19,016

UNIVERSITY OF WASHINGTON

1410 NORTHEAST CAMPUS PARKWAY, 320 SCHMITZ BOX 355840, SEATTLE, WA 98195-5840 • ADMISSIONS: 206-543-9686

CAMPUS LIFE
Quality of Life Rating	82
Fire Safety Rating	92
Green Rating	99
Type of school	public
Environment	metropolis

STUDENTS
Total undergrad enrollment	26,509
% male/female	48/52
% from out of state	13
% live on campus	20
% in (# of) fraternities	6 (30)
% in (# of) sororities	5 (16)
% African American	3
% Asian	28
% Caucasian	53
% Hispanic	5
% Native American	1
% international	4
# of countries represented	107

SURVEY SAYS . . .
Great library
Athletic facilities are great
Students love Seattle, WA
Great off-campus food
Everyone loves the Huskies
Student publications are popular

ACADEMICS
Academic Rating	78
Calendar	quarter
Student/faculty ratio	12:1
Profs interesting rating	68
Profs accessible rating	70
% classes taught by TAs	7
Most common reg class size	20–29 students
Most common lab size	20–29 students

MOST POPULAR MAJORS
economics
political science and government
psychology

STUDENTS SAY ". . ."

Academics
Students find "a great combination of high-powered academics, an excellent social life, and a wide variety of courses, all in the midst of the exciting Seattle life" at the University of Washington, the state's flagship institution of higher learning. UW offers "a lot of really stellar programs and the best bang for the buck, especially for in-state students or those in the sciences." Indeed, science programs "are incredible. The research going on here is cutting-edge and the leaders of biomedical sciences, stem cell research, etc. are accessible to students." Undergrads warn, however, that science programs are extremely competitive, "high pressure," and "challenging," with "core classes taught in lectures that seat more than 500 people," creating the sense that "professors don't seem to care too much whether you succeed." Pre-professional programs in business, law, nursing, medicine and engineering all earn high marks, although again with the caveat that the workload is tough and the hand-holding nominal. As one student puts it, "The University of Washington provides every resource and opportunity for its students to succeed. You just have to take advantage of them. No one will do it for you." For those fortunate enough to get in, the Honors Program "creates a smaller community of highly motivated students….It puts this school on top."

Life
UW students typically "have a good balance in their lives of education and fun." They "generally study hard and work in the libraries, but once the nighttime hits, they look forward to enjoying the night with their friends." Between the large university community and the surrounding city of Seattle, undergrads have a near-limitless selection of extracurricular choices. As one student explains, "There are tons of options for fun in Seattle. Going down to Pike's Market on a Saturday and eating your way through is always popular. There are tons of places to eat on 'The Ave,'" the shopping district that abuts campus, "and the UVillage shopping mall is a five minute walk from campus with chain-store comfort available. Intramural sports are big for activities, and going to undergraduate theater productions is never a disappointing experience. And during autumn or spring renting a canoe and paddling around lake Washington down by the stadium is fun." Husky football games "are amazing," and the Greek community "is very big" without dominating campus social life. In short, "the UW has anything you could want to do in your free time."

Student Body
"At such a large university, there is no 'typical' student," undergrads tell us, observing "one can find just about any demographic here and there is a huge variety in personalities." There "are quite a lot of yuppies, but then again, it's Seattle," and by and large "the campus is ultraliberal. Most students care about the environment, are not religious, and are generally accepting of other diverse individuals." Otherwise, "You've got your stereotypes: the Greeks, the street fashion pioneers, the various ethnic communities, the Oxford-looking grad students, etc." In terms of demographics, "the typical student at UW is white, middle-class, and is from the Seattle area," but "there are a lot of African American students and a very large number of Asian students." All groups "seem to socialize with each other."

FAX: 206-685-3655 • FINANCIAL AID: 206-543-6101 • E-MAIL: ASKUWADM@U.WASHINGTON.EDU • WEBSITE: WWW.WASHINGTON.EDU

THE PRINCETON REVIEW SAYS

Admissions

Very important factors considered include: Application essay, academic GPA, rigor of secondary school record. *Important factors considered include:* standardized test scores, character/personal qualities, extracurricular activities, first generation, talent/ability, volunteer work, work experience. *Other factors considered include:* state residency, SAT or ACT required; ACT with Writing component required. TOEFL required of all international applicants. High school diploma or equivalent is not required. *Academic units required:* 4 English, 3 mathematics, 2 science, (1 science labs), 2 foreign language, 3 social studies. *Academic units recommended:* 4 English, 4 mathematics, 3 science, (3 science labs), 3 foreign language, 4 social studies, 1 history, 1 visual/performing arts, 1 computer science.

Financial Aid

Students should submit: FAFSA. The Princeton Review suggests that all financial aid forms be submitted as soon as possible after 1/1. *Need-based scholarships/grants offered:* Federal Pell, SEOG, state scholarships/grants, private scholarships, the school's own gift aid. *Loan aid offered:* Direct Subsidized Stafford, Direct Unsubsidized Stafford, Direct PLUS, Federal Perkins, Federal Nursing, college/university loans from institutional funds. Applicants will be notified of awards on or about 3/31. Federal Work-Study Program available. Institutional employment available. Off-campus job opportunities are excellent.

The Inside Word

In recent years, UW committed to a thorough review of all freshman applications, abandoning the previous process by which a formula was used to rank applicants according to high school GPA and standardized test scores. The new, holistic approach allows admissions officers to take into account a student's background, the degree to which he or she has overcome personal adversity, and such intangibles as leadership quality and special skills. The move has so far resulted in increased racial and socioeconomic diversity, a result praised by some and criticized by others, who regard the new system as a poorly disguised affirmative action program.

THE SCHOOL SAYS ". . ."

From The Admissions Office

"Are you curious about everything, from comet dust to computer game design, salmon to Salman Rushdie, ancient Rome to the atmospherics of Mars? Do you seek the freedom to chart your own course—and work on breakthrough research? Are you ready to cheer on the Division I Huskies and spend your weekends sea kayaking? Would you like to walk to class on a 700-acre stunning, ivy-covered campus, yet be only 15 minutes from downtown Seattle? If the answers are yes, then the University of Washington may be the place for you. Offering more than 140 majors and 450 student organizations, the UW is looking for students who are both excited about the vast academic and social possibilities available to them and eager to contribute to the campus' cultural and intellectual life.

"We encourage you to take advantage of every opportunity in the application, especially the personal statement and activities summary, to tell us why Washington would be good fit for you and how you will contribute to the freshman class.

"Freshman applicants to the University of Washington are required to submit scores from either the SAT or ACT (with the Writing component)."

SELECTIVITY

Admissions Rating	94
# of applicants	17,777
% of applicants accepted	65
% of acceptees attending	46
# accepting a place on wait list	773
% admitted from wait list	43

FRESHMAN PROFILE

Range SAT Critical Reading	530–650
Range SAT Math	560–670
Range SAT Writing	520–630
Range ACT Composite	23–29
Minimum paper TOEFL	537
Minimum computer TOEFL	207
Average HS GPA	3.69
% graduated top 10% of class	86
% graduated top 25% of class	11
% graduated top 50% of class	100

DEADLINES

Regular	
Deadline	1/15
Notification	rolling
Nonfall registration?	yes

APPLICANTS ALSO LOOK AT

AND OFTEN PREFER
University of Southern California

AND SOMETIMES PREFER
Western Washington University
Gonzaga University

AND RARELY PREFER
Washington State University

FINANCIAL FACTS

Financial Aid Rating	79
Annual in-state tuition	$6,385
Annual out-of-state tuition	$22,131
% frosh rec. need-based scholarship or grant aid	22
% UG rec. need-based scholarship or grant aid	26
% frosh rec. non-need-based scholarship or grant aid	3
% UG rec. non-need-based scholarship or grant aid	3
% frosh rec. need-based self-help aid	25
% UG rec. need-based self-help aid	29
% frosh rec. athletic scholarships	2
% UG rec. athletic scholarships	2
% frosh rec. any financial aid	45
% UG rec. any financial aid	45
% UG borrow to pay for school	49
Average cumulative indebtedness	$16,100

UNIVERSITY OF WISCONSIN—MADISON

716 LANGDON STREET, MADISON, WI 53706-1481 • ADMISSIONS: 608-262-3961 • FAX: 608-262-7706

CAMPUS LIFE

Quality of Life Rating	89
Fire Safety Rating	60*
Green Rating	60*
Type of school	public
Environment	city

STUDENTS

Total undergrad enrollment	29,153
% male/female	48/52
% from out of state	32
% live on campus	24
% in (# of) fraternities	9 (26)
% in (# of) sororities	8 (11)
% African American	3
% Asian	6
% Caucasian	79
% Hispanic	4
% Native American	1
% international	5
# of countries represented	105

SURVEY SAYS . . .

Students love Madison, WI
Great off-campus food
Everyone loves the Badgers
Student publications are popular
Political activism is popular
Lots of beer drinking
Hard liquor is popular

ACADEMICS

Academic Rating	79
Calendar	semester
Student/faculty ratio	14:1
Profs interesting rating	71
Profs accessible rating	70
% classes taught by TAs	22
Most common reg class size	10–19 students
Most common lab size	20–29 students

MOST POPULAR MAJORS

biology/biological sciences
history
political science and government

STUDENTS SAY ". . ."

Academics

"The resources are phenomenal" at University of Wisconsin—Madison. "If you are proactive, you basically have the means and resources to pursue any academic or creative feat," promises a journalism major. "The liberal arts majors are fantastic." However, Madison is mostly known as "an amazing research institution," and the hard sciences and engineering programs get most of the pub. They iodized salt here, after all, and cultivated the first lab-based embryonic stem cells. The school of business is "excellent" as well and boasts "some of the best facilities on campus." Overall the school runs surprisingly smoothly" despite some "red tape." Many lecture courses are large and "impersonal." But class sizes often "plummet" after the intro courses, and the academic atmosphere is "challenging." Madison "definitely makes you earn your grades." "Some professors are amazing, and some suck." Also, "a lot of the classes for the undergrads are taught by teaching assistants who are not so good." "It becomes clear within the first few weeks which of your professors actually have lectures that are worthwhile for you to attend, which is probably about half," suggests a first-year student.

Life

UW—Madison's "reputation as a party school" is legendary. Halloween and the Mifflin Street Block Party are epic. "The weekend pretty much starts on Thursday night" as the streets of Madison "fill to the brim with drunk co-eds." There are house parties and frat parties galore. "Getting up at 9:00 A.M." to "bong a few beers for breakfast" before football games in the fall is common, and "nothing—absolutely nothing—can beat being in the student section at a Badger home football game." "The stadium is usually full" for hockey games, too. However, "no one looks at you differently if you choose not to drink" or attend sporting events. And, for everyone, "if you don't have a strong dedication to your education, you will slip up." Beyond the party and sports scene, UW is "energetic" and mammoth. "No one's going to hold your hand and point you to what it is you want." At the same time, whoever you are, "there is a group for you and a ton of activities for you." Two daily student newspapers "serve as the penultimate example of free speech in action." UW's lakefront campus provides "gorgeous" scenery. Many of the buildings "aren't that appealing," though, and some dorms are "absolutely horrible." Off-campus, "having the streets crawling with the homeless isn't so great," but Madison is teeming with culture, "live music," "late-night coffee shops," and "exceptional" chow from around the globe.

Student Body

Ethnic diversity at Madison is in the eye of the beholder. "If you're from a big city, it's pretty white," proposes a sophomore. "But, then again, I've met people here who had one black person in their high school and had never met a Jewish person." Without question, socioeconomic diversity flourishes. "There is a prevalent rivalry between [Wisconsin] students (sconnies) and the coasties who are generally wealthier and from the East or West Coast." "People from the Midwest think people from the coasts are stuck up. People from the coasts think people from the Midwest are hicks." Beyond that, it's impossible to generalize. "All types of people make up the student body here, ranging from the peace-preaching grass-root activist, to the protein-shake-a-day jock, to the overly privileged coastie, to the studious bookworm, to the computer geek," explains a first-year student. "There is a niche for everyone." "There are a lot of atypical students, but that is what makes UW—Madison so special," adds a senior. "Normal doesn't exist on this campus." Politically, "Madison is a hotbed for political and social debate." "Many people are passionate about many things, and it provides a great opportunity to see things from others' points of view." You'll find conservatives, but "left-wing, environmentally conscious nut jobs" who "stage protests" are more common.

FINANCIAL AID: 608-262-3060 • E-MAIL: ONWISCONSIN@ADMISSIONS.WISC.EDU • WEBSITE: WWW.WISC.EDU

THE PRINCETON REVIEW SAYS

Admissions

Very important factors considered include: Class rank, academic GPA, rigor of secondary school record. *Important factors considered include:* Application essay, standardized test scores, state residency. *Other factors considered include:* recommendation(s), alumni/ae relation, character/personal qualities, extracurricular activities, first generation, level of applicant's interest, racial/ethnic status, talent/ability, volunteer work, work experience. SAT or ACT required; ACT with Writing component required. TOEFL required of all international applicants. High school diploma is required and GED is accepted. *Academic units required:* 4 English, 3 mathematics, 3 science, 2 foreign language, 3 social studies, 2 academic electives. *Academic units recommended:* 4 English, 4 mathematics, 4 science, 4 foreign language, 4 social studies, 2 academic electives.

Financial Aid

Students should submit: FAFSA, institution's own financial aid form The Princeton Review suggests that all financial aid forms be submitted as soon as possible after 1/1. *Need-based scholarships/grants offered:* Federal Pell, SEOG, state scholarships/grants, private scholarships, the school's own gift aid. *Loan aid offered:* FFEL Subsidized Stafford, FFEL Unsubsidized Stafford, FFEL PLUS, Federal Perkins, Federal Nursing, state loans Applicants will be notified of awards on a rolling basis beginning 4/1. Federal Work-Study Program available. Institutional employment available. Off-campus job opportunities are excellent.

The Inside Word

Though it's not at the top tier of selectivity, Wisconsin has high expectations of its candidates. Admissions officers are most concerned with the high school transcript (course selection and grades), although test scores are also important. And they won't ignore compelling essays, recommendations, or extracurricular achievements.

THE SCHOOL SAYS "..."

From The Admissions Office

"UW—Madison is the university of choice for some of the best and brightest students. Our freshman class has an average ACT score of 28 and an average SAT of 1276. Almost 60% are from the top 10 percent of their high school class, and nearly all are from the top quarter.

"These factors combine to make admission to UW—Madison both competitive and selective. We consider academic record, course selection, strength of curriculum (honors, AP, IB, etc.), grade trend, class rank, results of the ACT/SAT, and non-academic factors. There is no prescribed minimum test score, GPA, or class rank criteria. Rather, we admit the best and most well-prepared students-students who have challenged themselves and who will contribute to Wisconsin's strength and diversity—for the limited space available.

"Each application is personally reviewed by our admission counselors. All domestic freshman applications completed by February 1 receive full and equal consideration. We offer two notification periods for domestic freshman applicants. To receive a decision during the First Notification Period, you must complete the application and submit all required materials (application fee, official high school transcript, official test scores, personal statements, and recommendations) postmarked by November 1. Admission decisions for these students will be made on or by January 15. All students who complete their applications during the Second Notification Period (after November 1 but before the February 1 deadline) will have decision made on or by March 15. All students receive equal consideration for admission whether they apply during the First or Second Notification Periods."

SELECTIVITY

Admissions Rating	96
# of applicants	25,478
% of applicants accepted	53
% of acceptees attending	43

FRESHMAN PROFILE

Range SAT Critical Reading	540–670
Range SAT Math	620–730
Range SAT Writing	570–670
Range ACT Composite	26–30
Minimum paper TOEFL	550
Minimum computer TOEFL	213
Average HS GPA	3.69
% graduated top 10% of class	58
% graduated top 25% of class	93
% graduated top 50% of class	99

DEADLINES

Regular	
Priority	2/1
Deadline	2/1
Notification	rolling
Nonfall registration?	yes

FINANCIAL FACTS

Financial Aid Rating	75
Annual tuition in-state	$8,020
Annual tuition out-of-state	$22,270
Room and board	$8,040
Books and supplies	$1,040
% frosh rec. need-based scholarship or grant aid	25
% UG rec. need-based scholarship or grant aid	26
% frosh rec. non-need-based scholarship or grant aid	18
% UG rec. non-need-based scholarship or grant aid	13
% frosh rec. need-based self-help aid	26
% UG rec. need-based self-help aid	28
% frosh rec. athletic scholarships	2
% UG rec. athletic scholarships	2
% UG borrow to pay for school	52
Average cumulative indebtedness	$21,123

UNIVERSITY OF WYOMING

DEPARTMENT 3435, 1000 EAST UNIVERSITY AVENUE, LARAMIE, WY 82071 • ADMISSIONS: 307-766-5160 • FAX: 307-766-4042

CAMPUS LIFE

Quality of Life Rating	75
Fire Safety Rating	60*
Green Rating	87
Type of school	public
Environment	town

STUDENTS

Total undergrad enrollment	9,140
% male/female	48/52
% from out of state	28
% live on campus	21
% in (# of) fraternities	5 (8)
% in (# of) sororities	6 (6)
% African American	1
% Asian	1
% Caucasian	83
% Hispanic	3
% Native American	1
% international	2
# of countries represented	74

SURVEY SAYS . . .

Athletic facilities are great
Students are friendly
Students get along with local
community
Everyone loves the Cowboys
Lots of beer drinking
Hard liquor is popular

ACADEMICS

Academic Rating	73
Calendar	semester
Student/faculty ratio	15:1
Profs interesting rating	73
Profs accessible rating	77
% classes taught by TAs	11
Most common reg class size	20–29 students
Most common lab size	20–29 students

MOST POPULAR MAJORS

elementary education and teaching
nursing/registered nurse
(rn, asn, bsn, msn)
psychology

STUDENTS SAY " . . ."

Academics

The University of Wyoming is "about getting a great education with an inexpensive price tag." A wide range of strong programs includes traditional fare (e.g., education, nursing, and majors across the arts and sciences) as well as majors aimed at more idiosyncratic populations (e.g., rangeland ecology and watershed management and agricultural economics). The engineering college is "a big draw," though future engineers here caution that you should expect to put in considerable "blood, sweat, and tears." UW's faculty truly runs the gamut. "Some of my teachers have the enthusiasm of people who have been truly inspired," says a first-year student. Others are "a bit dry." Still others are "just horrible teachers." "There are some of the best teachers in the country at the University of Wyoming," reports a sophomore. "There are also some of the worst." Overall, classes tend to be lectures, and there is "little to no discussion." And while professors "are very much available for you" outside of class, you should expect "to make little effort" to get individual attention. Student opinion differs concerning the administration. Embittered students tell us that management is "one big, unorganized mess." Satisfied students call that the administration "very approachable." "They haven't done anything outrageous or heinous," reflects a senior. Most everyone seems to agree that "registering for classes is hell." "I am having a hard time getting into anything," vents a sophomore.

Life

"Parking is a joke," and "the surrounding area is very poorly lit," but "everything you would ever want to do is right on" UW's "stunningly beautiful" campus. School spirit is high. "Athletic events are electric and the hottest ticket in town." Football games in particular bring out a "rowdy crowd." The Friday Night Fever program "offers something different every Friday night for students for free." Intramurals are "very popular" as well and extracurricular activities are plentiful even if "not everyone chooses to participate." The bar scene can get "very crazy and hectic" Thursday through Saturday. "All the cowboys, athletes, and other students hang out in the same places, which is really fun." Beyond Laramie, UW's "proximity to mountains" makes for "spectacular" opportunities. "Most people enjoy winter sports like skiing and snowboarding." Rock climbing is big. "Fishing locally is great, and the fall is filled with hunting." Be warned, though, that it's "freakin' cold and windy" much of the time. "Students who don't tolerate cold well will be disappointed attending this school." Urban cities such as Fort Collins, Denver, and Cheyenne aren't impossibly far but "during the snowy season, Laramie can become sort of an island" because so many roads are closed.

Student Body

"Most of the students here are from Wyoming and the neighboring states." "These states are, in fact, quite ethnically monochromatic," but the few minority students at UW reportedly "assimilate well." The population "definitely has a small Wyoming feel." "There are many agriculture students." "There are the rancher students who like Coors Light, rodeo, tight Wranglers, and Copenhagen," but "it is a definite overstatement if anyone says that the majority of students are chewing, buckle-wearing cowboys." "There aren't as many hicks at UW as a person might think." The vast majority is "just normal college students who are interested in learning." These "outdoorsy" students describe themselves as "genuine," "independent," and "friendly and practical." They are "mostly laid-back (except around finals) and unpretentious." They "have tons of pride in the state and the school," too. "There are very few loners and, if they are loners, it is by choice," asserts a first-year student. Politically, students are "more conservative." "Laramie is one of the most liberal cities in the state of Wyoming, but Wyoming is one of the most conservative states." Mostly, though, people are "generally libertarian in behavior," and political activity is minimal.

FINANCIAL AID: 307-766-2116 • E-MAIL: WHY-WYO@UWYO.EDU • WEBSITE: WWW.UWYO.EDU

THE PRINCETON REVIEW SAYS

Admissions

Very important factors considered include: Academic GPA, rigor of secondary school record, standardized test scores. *Important factors considered include:* level of applicant's interest. *Other factors considered include:* Application essay, recommendation(s), character/personal qualities, extracurricular activities, interview, state residency, talent/ability, SAT or ACT required; TOEFL required of all international applicants. High school diploma is required and GED is accepted. *Academic units required:* 4 English, 3 mathematics, 3 science, (3 science labs), 3 Cultural Context Electives recommended, 3 behavioral or social sciences, 3 visual or performing arts, 3 humanities or earth/space sciences. *Academic units recommended:* 4 English, 4 mathematics, 4 science, (3 science labs), 2 foreign language, 3 Cultural Context Electives—Recomended—3 behavioral or social sciences, 3 visual or performing arts, 3 humanities or earth/space sciences.

Financial Aid

Students should submit: FAFSA. The Princeton Review suggests that all financial aid forms be submitted as soon as possible after 1/1. *Need-based scholarships/grants offered:* Federal Pell, SEOG, state scholarships/grants, private scholarships, the school's own gift aid. *Loan aid offered:* FFEL Subsidized Stafford, FFEL Unsubsidized Stafford, FFEL PLUS, Federal Perkins. Applicants will be notified of awards on a rolling basis beginning 3/1. Federal Work-Study Program available. Institutional employment available. Off-campus job opportunities are good.

The Inside Word

The admissions process at Wyoming is fairly formula-driven. State residents need a minimum 2.75 high school GPA to gain admission. Nonresidents have to have a 3.0 GPA. That and some solid test scores will open the door to the university.

THE SCHOOL SAYS "..."

From The Admissions Office

"The University of Wyoming and the town of Laramie are relatively small, affording students the opportunity to get the personal attention and develop a close rapport with their professors. They can easily make friends and find peers with similar interests and values. More than 200 student organizations offer students a great way to get involved and encourage growth and learning. Couple the small size with a great location, and you have a winning combination. Laramie sits between the Laramie and Snowy Range Mountains. There are numerous outdoor activities in which one can participate. Furthermore, the university works hard to attract other great cultural events. Major-label recording artists come to UW as well as some of today's great minds. In all, the University of Wyoming is a great place to be because of its wonderful blend of small-town atmosphere with 'big city' activities.

"The University of Wyoming requires first-time, incoming freshmen to submit scores from either the ACT or SAT. The Writing component of the ACT and SAT is not required, but is reviewed if submitted."

SELECTIVITY

Admissions Rating	88
# of applicants	3,371
% of applicants accepted	95
% of acceptees attending	51

FRESHMAN PROFILE

Range SAT Critical Reading	480–610
Range SAT Math	500–630
Range ACT Composite	21–26
Minimum paper TOEFL	525
Minimum computer TOEFL	197
Average HS GPA	3.459
% graduated top 10% of class	20
% graduated top 25% of class	50
% graduated top 50% of class	80

DEADLINES

Regular	
Deadline	8/10
Nonfall registration?	yes

FINANCIAL FACTS

Financial Aid Rating	73
Annual in-state tuition	$2,820
Annual out-of-state tuition	$10,230
% frosh rec. need-based scholarship or grant aid	23
% UG rec. need-based scholarship or grant aid	26
% frosh rec. non-need-based scholarship or grant aid	44
% UG rec. non-need-based scholarship or grant aid	37
% frosh rec. need-based self-help aid	40
% UG rec. need-based self-help aid	52
% frosh rec. athletic scholarships	5
% UG rec. athletic scholarships	5
% frosh rec. any financial aid	95
% UG rec. any financial aid	87
% UG borrow to pay for school	49
Average cumulative indebtedness	$16,005

URSINUS COLLEGE

URSINUS COLLEGE, ADMISSIONS OFFICE, COLLEGEVILLE, PA 19426 • ADMISSIONS: 610-409-3200 • FAX: 610-409-3662

CAMPUS LIFE

Quality of Life Rating	**85**
Fire Safety Rating	**88**
Green Rating	**91**
Type of school	private
Environment	city

STUDENTS

Total undergrad enrollment	1,655
% male/female	45/55
% from out of state	42
% from public high school	61
% live on campus	95
% in (# of) fraternities	10 (7)
% in (# of) sororities	13 (7)
% African American	6
% Asian	4
% Caucasian	73
% Hispanic	3
% international	1
# of countries represented	13

SURVEY SAYS . . .

Athletic facilities are great
Lots of beer drinking
Students are happy

ACADEMICS

Academic Rating	**95**
Calendar	semester
Student/faculty ratio	12:1
Profs interesting rating	85
Profs accessible rating	86
Most common reg class size	fewer than 10 students
Most common lab size	10–19 students

MOST POPULAR MAJORS
biology/biological sciences
economics
psychology

STUDENTS SAY ". . ."

Academics

Ursinus College, a small liberal arts school in aptly named Collegeville, PA. offers a wide array of courses and "has the facilities of a much larger school." "I truly believe that Ursinus is a transformative experience," declares an international relations major. "If you embrace the liberal arts education, this is the institution to be at." "Academic rigor is demanding." A required pair of first-year courses called "the Common Intellectual Experience" "create a bonding experience for the students, and it gets them to think about some extremely important issues." Beyond that, students must complete a host of core requirements in addition to their majors. You'll "do your fair share of 10- to 15-page term papers; usually a couple per semester." "But it pays off in the end." The small size allows for "discussion-based classes" and professors "really try to get students involved." "Some professors are full of themselves," admits a neuroscience major. However, they are "great teachers and certainly know what they're talking about." "I have loved all of my professors," gushes a math major. "They've been friendly, helpful, and knowledgeable. They're eager to get students involved in research." Management is "accessible" as well. The "down-to-earth" administrators "are often seen about the campus attending lectures, concerts, and sporting events." Strong majors here include biology and chemistry. Ursinus boasts an impressive 90-plus percent acceptance rate with medical schools. Students also laud the economics and arts programs.

Life

Ursinus boasts "a very beautiful campus." Some of the older dorms cry out for refurbishing, though, and newer ones are "faintly reminiscent of a hospital." The food isn't great, either. "They stop carting out the good food after the second week," warns a biology major. Also, wireless Internet is spotty. Despite these complaints, students tell us they are extremely happy. "People overall love the school," says a freshman. Ursinus students are proud of their ability to have fun. "There are parties almost every night," especially Thursday through Saturday." The administration tries to crack down, but students persevere, and the drinking scene remains rollicking. House parties or suite parties are options but the Greek system "rules campus life." "The keggers held by Greek organizations" are the most widely attended bashes. Not everyone drinks, of course, "not by a long shot." "The cool thing about Ursinus is that regardless of whether you drink or not, you can still go to the parties and have a great time." Some students warn that "Ursinus can be a little dull" if you insist on avoiding the party scene altogether. Others disagree saying, "there is an incredible availability of activities and clubs on campus." Intramural and varsity athletics are also very popular. Students "love to go to all the food places in Collegeville" as well. It is "difficult" to get too far off campus without a car, though. (And first-year students can't have them.) While "there is no shame inherent in taking the bus" to Philadelphia, few students do.

Students

By and large, while ethnic diversity isn't terrible for a small liberal arts school, Ursinus is "homogenous." "Most people come from wealthier families" and grew up in the comfortable suburbs of "New Jersey, Pennsylvania, and New York." Ursinus students are "very hardworking" and "have similar values." Politically, there's a mildly liberal slant. "Most students on this campus are active and highly involved, although those who do not engage in clubs and activities do seem to find each other." The prototypical Ursinus student is a "somewhat clean-cut, friendly, occasionally drunk," "Hollister-clad, Ugg-wearing" prepster. "Different cliques are evident," though. There are "smart jocks and wonderfully weird nerds." There are "stereotypical frat boys." "There are many weirdoes and there are many average Joes." "Ursinus somehow seems to provide a safe and comfortable environment for people of all different interests," remarks one student.

FINANCIAL AID: 610-409-3600 • E-MAIL: ADMISSIONS@URSINUS.EDU • WEBSITE: WWW.URSINUS.EDU

THE PRINCETON REVIEW SAYS

Admissions

Very important factors considered include: Class rank, rigor of secondary school record, extracurricular activities. *Important factors considered include:* Application essay, academic GPA, recommendation(s), standardized test scores, alumni/ae relation, racial/ethnic status, talent/ability, volunteer work, work experience. *Other factors considered include:* character/personal qualities, first generation, geographical residence, interview, level of applicant's interest, ACT with Writing component recommended. TOEFL required of all international applicants. High school diploma is required and GED is accepted. *Academic units required:* 4 English, 3 mathematics, 1 science, (1 science labs), 2 foreign language, 1 social studies. *Academic units recommended:* 4 English, 4 mathematics, 4 science, (2 science labs), 4 foreign language, 4 social studies.

Financial Aid

Students should submit: FAFSA, institution's own financial aid form, CSS/Financial Aid. PROFILE Regular filing deadline is 2/15. The Princeton Review suggests that all financial aid forms be submitted as soon as possible after 1/1. *Need-based scholarships/grants offered:* Federal Pell, SEOG, state scholarships/grants, private scholarships, the school's own gift aid. *Loan aid offered:* FFEL Subsidized Stafford, FFEL Unsubsidized Stafford, FFEL PLUS, Federal Perkins. Applicants will be notified of awards on or about 4/1. Federal Work-Study Program available. Institutional employment available. Off-campus job opportunities are excellent.

The Inside Word

Grades, test scores, and class rank count for more than anything else, and unless you are academically inconsistent, you'll likely get good news. If you are hoping to snag a scholarship, it's really essential that you visit campus and get yourself interviewed. Students in the top 10 percent of their graduating classes aren't required to submit SAT score.

THE SCHOOL SAYS "..."

From The Admissions Office

"Located a half-hour from center-city Philadelphia, the college boasts a beautiful 168-acre campus that includes the Residential Village (renovated Victorian-style homes that decorate the Main Street and house our students) and the nationally recognized Berman Museum of Art. Ursinus is a member of the Centennial Conference, competing both in academics and in intercollegiate athletics with institutions such as Dickinson, Franklin & Marshall, Gettysburg, and Muhlenberg. The academic environment is enhanced with such fine programs as a chapter of Phi Beta Kappa, an early assurance program to medical school with the Medical College of Pennsylvania, and myriad student exchanges both at home and abroad. A heavy emphasis is placed on student research—an emphasis that can only be carried out with the one-on-one attention Ursinus students receive from their professors.

"Ursinus will continue to ask applicants for writing samples—both a series of application essays and a graded high school paper. The Writing portion of the SAT will not affect admissions decisions. The ACT with the writing component is recommended."

SELECTIVITY
Admissions Rating	**92**
# of applicants	6,192
% of applicants accepted	55
% of acceptees attending	32
# accepting a place on wait list	260
% admitted from wait list	3
# of early decision applicants	197
% accepted early decision	62

FRESHMAN PROFILE
Range SAT Critical Reading	570–680
Range SAT Math	570–670
Range SAT Writing	560–660
Range ACT Composite	25–29
Minimum paper TOEFL	500
Minimum computer TOEFL	173
Average HS GPA	3.67
% graduated top 10% of class	48
% graduated top 25% of class	78
% graduated top 50% of class	96

DEADLINES
Early Decision	
Deadline	1/15
Notification	2/15
Early action	
Deadline	12/1
Regular	
Priority	2/15
Deadline	2/15
Notification	4/1
Nonfall registration?	yes

FINANCIAL FACTS
Financial Aid Rating	**89**
Annual tution	$38,500
Room and board	$9,250
Books and supplies	$1,000
% frosh rec. need-based scholarship or grant aid	64
% UG rec. need-based scholarship or grant aid	66
% frosh rec. non-need-based scholarship or grant aid	17
% UG rec. non-need-based scholarship or grant aid	16
% frosh rec. need-based self-help aid	50
% UG rec. need-based self-help aid	55
% frosh rec. any financial aid	92
% UG rec. any financial aid	91
% UG borrow to pay for school	75
Average cumulative indebtedness	$21,171

VALPARAISO UNIVERSITY

KRETZMANN HALL, 1700 CHAPEL DRIVE, VALPARAISO, IN 46383 • ADMISSIONS: 219-464-5011 • FAX: 219-464-6898

CAMPUS LIFE
Quality of Life Rating	**76**
Fire Safety Rating	**63**
Green Rating	**81**
Type of school	private
Affiliation	Lutheran
Environment	town

STUDENTS
Total undergrad enrollment	2,824
% male/female	47/53
% from out of state	60
% live on campus	68
% in (# of) fraternities	23 (9)
% in (# of) sororities	19 (7)
% African American	5
% Asian	2
% Caucasian	82
% Hispanic	4
% international	3
# of countries represented	48

SURVEY SAYS . . .
Great library
Students are friendly
Campus feels safe
Students are happy
Musical organizations are popular
Very little drug use

ACADEMICS
Academic Rating	**88**
Calendar	semester
Student/faculty ratio	12:1
Profs interesting rating	80
Profs accessible rating	83
Most common reg class size	10–19 students
Most common lab size	10–19 students

MOST POPULAR MAJORS
elementary education and teaching
mechanical engineering
nursing/registered nurse
(rn, asn, bsn, msn)

STUDENTS SAY ". . ."

Academics

Valparaiso University, a small Lutheran university, "is a serious academic community with strong, but not forceful, religious background" that "prepares, motivates, and challenges tomorrow's leaders, engineers, nurses, and teachers while giving the opportunity for religious growth." Business, education, and engineering are the most popular majors, and are among Valpo's most celebrated departments. Other standout disciplines include nursing, music, theater ("the department involves touring professional directors a couple times a year, which speaks for itself" and "puts on great plays"), and one of the nation's largest meteorology programs (which "just erected a state-of-the-art Doppler radar, putting Valpo at the forefront for undergrad meteorology"). Undergrads here appreciate the breadth of excellent offerings as well as "the school's ability to integrate the liberal arts with a variety of majors... As a student, I have been able to study engineering as well as hermeneutics, child development, and read classic texts ranging from Aristotle and Plato to Chuang Tzu and Derrida." Valpo operates under an honor code students say, "creates an environment of trust and high moral responsibility." "People follow the honor code, especially because the punishments are strict, such as failing the class for a first offense," one student tells us. A few dissenters feel "the honor code may reduce some cheating, but I don't think it comes near to eliminating it." Outstanding students may enroll in Christ College, an honors college, which they describe as "very intense but very rewarding."

Life

"There are several activities to choose from on Valparaiso's campus on a typical weekend, ranging from philanthropic dance parties at fraternity houses to music recitals to special guests speakers (to name just a few)," students tell us. Religious groups are active, and not just the Lutherans. The Catholic Church "is very active" here, offering "a student mass Sunday nights with a meal afterward, which is very nice" and "at least three events each week." Athletics are also popular. "We have Division I athletics, so it's fun to watch if you don't play, but Valpo also offers club sports (like Ultimate Frisbee) and intramurals for all student to participate in." The VU campus is officially dry, but that doesn't mean students don't drink. An aggressive campus police force means "there is lots of fear of getting arrested when drinking, but people do it anyway." Fraternities "have parties every Friday night," which helps to offset the perception that "the city of Valpo is horrible" because "there's not much to do" there. "If you can't entertain yourself, this is not the place for you," students warn. When they need big-city diversion, students will "hop on the train to go over to Chicago, an hour ride, for about $6, and get a CTA day pass for $4 (to ride Chicago's transit all day)." Another popular daytrip destination is the Indiana Dunes, which border Lake Michigan.

Student Body

The majority of Valpo students "are Caucasians who come from a well-off family, of extremely religious Lutherans, and are very conservative." One student estimates that "conservative, churchgoing studiers" make up about two-thirds of the student body. Most "come from somewhere in the Midwest," with many "from the Chicagoland area." The typical student is "here to learn. There are some who are just here for the party, but there are not many." Because "meteorology and engineering are large areas of study, there are some students who are 'nerdy,' but no one is left out of university activities." Valpo has "few minority students," and "it would be nice to have a little bit more diversity."

FINANCIAL AID: 219-464-5015 • E-MAIL: UNDERGRAD.ADMISSIONS@VALPO.EDU • WEBSITE: WWW.VALPO.EDU

THE PRINCETON REVIEW SAYS

Admissions

Very important factors considered include: Academic GPA, rigor of secondary school record, *Important factors considered include:* Class rank, standardized test scores, alumni/ae relation, character/personal qualities, extracurricular activities, talent/ability. *Other factors considered include:* Application essay, recommendation(s), first generation, interview, level of applicant's interest, racial/ethnic status, religious affiliation/commitment, volunteer work, SAT or ACT required; ACT with Writing component recommended. TOEFL required of all international applicants. High school diploma is required and GED is accepted. *Academic units required:* 4 English, 3 mathematics, 2 science, (2 science labs), 2 foreign language, 2 history, 3 academic electives, *Academic units recommended:* 4 English, 4 mathematics, 3 science, (3 science labs), 2 foreign language, 1 social studies, 2 history, 3 academic electives.

Financial Aid

Students should submit: FAFSA. The Princeton Review suggests that all financial aid forms be submitted as soon as possible after 1/1. *Need-based scholarships/grants offered:* Federal Pell, SEOG, state scholarships/grants, private scholarships, the school's own gift aid. *Loan aid offered:* Direct Subsidized Stafford, Direct Unsubsidized Stafford, Direct PLUS, Federal Perkins, college/university loans from institutional funds. Applicants will be notified of awards on a rolling basis beginning 3/1. Federal Work-Study Program available. Institutional employment available. Off-campus job opportunities are good.

The Inside Word

Valparaiso's nearly 90 percent admit rate suggests a pretty generous admissions office. The figure is somewhat misleading; Valpo's applicant pool consists largely of students familiar enough with the school to know whether it's worth their while to apply here. In other words, the school doesn't receive a lot of 'reach' applications. Applicants indicating an interest in meteorology should expect a more rigorous review, as space in the program is limited.

THE SCHOOL SAYS "..."

From The Admissions Office

"Valpo provides students a blend of academic excellence, social experience, and spiritual exploration. The concern demonstrated by faculty and administration for the total well-being of students reflects a long history as a Lutheran-affiliated university."

SELECTIVITY

Admissions Rating	92
# of applicants	3,022
% of applicants accepted	92
% of acceptees attending	24

FRESHMAN PROFILE

Range SAT Critical Reading	490–600
Range SAT Math	500–630
Range SAT Writing	480–590
Range ACT Composite	22–28
Minimum paper TOEFL	550
Minimum computer TOEFL	213
Minimum web-based TOEFL	80
Average HS GPA	3.33
% graduated top 10% of class	31
% graduated top 25% of class	61
% graduated top 50% of class	87

DEADLINES

Early action	
Deadline	11/1
Notification	12/1
Regular	
Priority	1/15
Deadline	8/15
Notification	rolling
Nonfall registration?	yes

APPLICANTS ALSO LOOK AT

AND OFTEN PREFER
Purdue University—West Lafayette
Butler University
Indiana University at Bloomington

AND SOMETIMES PREFER
Marquette University
Bradley University
Ball State University

AND RARELY PREFER
DePauw University
Illinois State University

FINANCIAL FACTS

Financial Aid Rating	81
Annual tuition	$26,070
Room and board	$7,620
Required fees	$880
Books and supplies	$1,200
% frosh rec. need-based scholarship or grant aid	76
% UG rec. need-based scholarship or grant aid	69
% frosh rec. non-need-based scholarship or grant aid	12
% UG rec. non-need-based scholarship or grant aid	9
% frosh rec. need-based self-help aid	58
% UG rec. need-based self-help aid	56
% frosh rec. athletic scholarships	2
% UG rec. athletic scholarships	3
% frosh rec. any financial aid	98
% UG rec. any financial aid	94
% UG borrow to pay for school	73
Average cumulative indebtedness	$28,784

VANDERBILT UNIVERSITY

2305 West End Avenue, Nashville, TN 37203 • Admissions: 615-322-2561 • Fax: 615-343-7765

CAMPUS LIFE
Quality of Life Rating	90
Fire Safety Rating	98
Green Rating	82
Type of school	private
Environment	metropolis

STUDENTS
Total undergrad enrollment	6,598
% male/female	48/52
% from out of state	83
% from public high school	57
% live on campus	90
% in (# of) fraternities	35 (19)
% in (# of) sororities	50 (12)
% African American	9
% Asian	7
% Caucasian	59
% Hispanic	6
% international	3
# of countries represented	55

SURVEY SAYS . . .
Lab facilities are great
School is well run
Students love Nashville, TN
Great off-campus food
Frats and sororities dominate social scene
Student publications are popular
Student government is popular

ACADEMICS
Academic Rating	92
Calendar	semester
Student/faculty ratio	9:1
Profs interesting rating	86
Profs accessible rating	83
Most common reg class size	10–19 students
Most common lab size	10–19 students

MOST POPULAR MAJORS
engineering science
psychology
sociology

STUDENTS SAY ". . ."

Academics

The word "balance" pops up a lot in students' descriptions of Vanderbilt University. Most often it's used to describe the amalgamation of "high academic standards" and "myriad" "social, service, and leadership opportunities" that characterizes so many students' experiences here. It is also used to describe the school's well-balanced mix of academic strengths; no surprise there, as Vandy excels in such diverse areas as premedicine, engineering, mathematics, sociology, psychology, and education. Sometimes the word refers to the balance between the "big city" benefits of Nashville—which include not only a world-class music scene but also "great opportunities for jobs, internships, [and] service"—and Vandy's "campus feel." In whatever context, students' numerous references to balance are a testimony to their comfort and satisfaction with the Vanderbilt experience. Undergrads here report a convivial atmosphere that takes away "a lot of the pressure" created by the "academically rigorous" curriculum. Professors "are generally good teachers who make themselves available through prompt responses to e-mail and through office hours," while administrators "are very accessible—you can see them in their office or spot them walking through campus." Fellow students "aren't competitive and are constantly helping each other."

Life

Vanderbilt's campus life is "stimulating, challenging, [and] fun." "There is always something going on," a sophomore reports. Greek life is "a very large part of Vanderbilt's social scene," as most "Fraternity parties are open to everyone." These parties "rival no other," and they "always have bands or themes or activities, so it's not just a crowd of people getting drunk." But there's more than the just the Greek scene for students to participate in. Students tout "clubs for every interest, sports for every level of ability," and "student theater every night of the week." Students also tell us "Christian and other religious organizations are a big part of Vanderbilt campus life" and "service organizations are really important at Vanderbilt, and the majority of students are involved in volunteer work in the Nashville community." As for intercollegiate sports, "attending sporting events is popular, though I wouldn't go so far as to say everyone is a devoted fan." Just about everyone has nice things to say about hometown Nashville. One student writes, "Nashville is a great place to live—there is always something going on. Centennial Park is right across the street; it's a great place to study, walk, or hang out. Downtown has an awesome party scene" that, of course, includes lots of live music. One student adds, "The weather is a pretty nice perk too."

Student Body

"Vanderbilt has come a long way from the stereotypical Southern, wealthy, white student," undergrads here assure us, noting "there are students from all over the country." While there is "definitely still a strong presence of Polo-clad fraternity guys and sorority girls, the image of Vanderbilt has become so much more than that and now encompasses students from different ethnicities, religions, and geographical regions." Today, the glue that binds the student body is that "everyone is involved." It seems like every student has at least one passion [he or she] pursue[s] actively on campus or off campus. Everyone is in at least one student organization. No one here is only about academics." Students also tend to be "religious," "very approachable, and friendly, [and] passionate about their studies."

FINANCIAL AID: 615-322-3591 • E-MAIL: ADMISSIONS@VANDERBILT.EDU • WEBSITE: WWW.VANDERBILT.EDU

THE PRINCETON REVIEW SAYS

Admissions

Very important factors considered include: Class rank, application essay, academic GPA, rigor of secondary school record, standardized test scores, character/personal qualities, extracurricular activities, *Important factors considered include:* recommendation(s), talent/ability. *Other factors considered include:* alumni/ae relation, first generation, geographical residence, interview, racial/ethnic status, state residency, volunteer work, work experience. SAT or ACT required; ACT with Writing component required. TOEFL required of all international applicants. High school diploma is required and GED is accepted. *Academic units required:* 4 English, 3 mathematics, 3 science, (2 science labs), 2 foreign language, 2 social studies, 1 history, 3 academic electives. *Academic units recommended:* 4 English, 4 mathematics, 4 science, (3 science labs), 2 foreign language, 3 social studies, 1 history.

Financial Aid

Students should submit: FAFSA, CSS/Financial Aid. The Princeton Review suggests that all financial aid forms be submitted as soon as possible after 1/1. *Need-based scholarships/grants offered:* Federal Pell, SEOG, state scholarships/grants, private scholarships, the school's own gift aid. *Loan aid offered:* FFEL Subsidized Stafford, FFEL Unsubsidized Stafford, FFEL PLUS, Federal Perkins, Federal Nursing, college/university loans from institutional funds, Undergrad Education Loan. Applicants will be notified of awards on or about 4/1. Federal Work-Study Program available. Institutional employment available. Off-campus job opportunities are excellent.

The Inside Word

Vanderbilt receives 25 percent more and more early decision applications each academic year than it did for the previous academic year, and as a result, competition has increased for those spaces. Still, if you consider early decision here (or anywhere, for that matter), remember that you will not learn about financial aid until long after you've received your binding decision.

THE SCHOOL SAYS "..."

From The Admissions Office

"Vanderbilt is one of a very small number of colleges that makes a dual promise: Applications are considered without regard for financial need (need-blind), and every admitted U.S. applicant's demonstrated financial need will be fully met. Early decision applicants who submit the CSS PROFILE at the time of application will be provided with a provisional award of need-based financial aid.

"Exceptional accomplishment and high promise in some field of intellectual endeavor are essential. The student's total academic and non-academic record is reviewed in conjunction with recommendations and personal essays. For students at the Blair School of Music, the audition is a prime consideration.

"Living on campus is a crucial element of the Vanderbilt experience. With the opening of the Commons fall 2008, all students will be expected to live on campus for four year. The Commons is Vanderbilt's new living-learning area for first-year students. The Commons includes five recently renovated and five newly constructed residence halls, which will allow the university to house all first year students in the same area of campus. Each residence hall (or "house") will also have a faculty member in residence, who will serve as a mentor to students and oversee programming for the house.

"The Vanderbilt undergraduate experience is often described as uniquely balanced. Students are encouraged to participate in a broad spectrum of campus organizations (more than 350) among an increasingly diverse population. This diversity is also evident from recent survey data which reveals that Vanderbilt first-year students self-identify almost equally as liberal, conservative, or moderate. Recent additions to campus include the Schulman Center for Jewish Life, a newly renovated Black Cultural Center, and the Studio Arts Building."

SELECTIVITY

Admissions Rating	99
# of applicants	16,944
% of applicants accepted	25
% of acceptees attending	37
# accepting a place on wait list	1,390
% admitted from wait list	15
# of early decision applicants	1,468
% accepted early decision	36

FRESHMAN PROFILE

Range SAT Critical Reading	652–740
Range SAT Math	680–760
Range SAT Writing	650–730
Range ACT Composite	30–33
Minimum paper TOEFL	570
Average HS GPA	4
% graduated top 10% of class	84
% graduated top 25% of class	97
% graduated top 50% of class	99

DEADLINES

Early Decision	
Deadline	11/1
Notification	12/15
Regular	
Priority	1/3
Deadline	3/1
Notification	4/1
Nonfall registration?	no

APPLICANTS ALSO LOOK AT

AND OFTEN PREFER
Harvard College
Notre Dame de Namur University
Stanford University

AND SOMETIMES PREFER
Columbia University
Washington University in St. Louis

AND RARELY PREFER
Tulane University, Wake Forest University
Georgia Institute of Technology

FINANCIAL FACTS

Financial Aid Rating	97
Annual tuition	$36,100
Room and board	$1,208
% frosh rec. need-based scholarship or grant aid	38
% UG rec. need-based scholarship or grant aid	37
% frosh rec. non-need-based scholarship or grant aid	25
% UG rec. non-need-based scholarship or grant aid	19
% frosh rec. need-based self-help aid	18
% UG rec. need-based self-help aid	24
% frosh rec. athletic scholarships	2
% UG rec. athletic scholarships	4
% frosh rec. any financial aid	62
% UG rec. any financial aid	62
% UG borrow to pay for school	38
Average cumulative indebtedness	$19,839

VASSAR COLLEGE

124 RAYMOND AVENUE, POUGHKEEPSIE, NY 12604 • ADMISSIONS: 845-437-7300 • FAX: 845-437-7063

CAMPUS LIFE

Quality of Life Rating	**80**
Fire Safety Rating	**81**
Green Rating	**96**
Type of school	private
Environment	town

STUDENTS

Total undergrad enrollment	2,343
% male/female	42/58
% from out of state	73
% from public high school	61
% live on campus	95
% African American	5
% Asian	10
% Caucasian	72
% Hispanic	7
% international	6
# of countries represented	43

SURVEY SAYS . . .
No one cheats
Students aren't religious
Frats and sororities are unpopular or nonexistent
Theater is popular
Political activism is popular

ACADEMICS

Academic Rating	**96**
Calendar	semester
Student/faculty ratio	8:1
Profs interesting rating	90
Profs accessible rating	89
Most common reg class size	10–19 students
Most common lab size	10–19 students

MOST POPULAR MAJORS
English language and literature
political science and government
psychology

STUDENTS SAY "..."

Academics

Vassar College gives students "the chance to experiment with [their] life in an encouraging and stimulating environment," providing an unusual amount of academic freedom because "there's no real core curriculum. All you need in the way of requirements are one quantitative class and one foreign language credit. Plus, one-quarter of your credits must be outside of your major." This approach, students agree, "really encourages students to think creatively and pursue whatever they're passionate about, whether medieval tapestries, neuroscience, or unicycles. Not having a core curriculum is great because it gives students the opportunity to delve into many different interests." Of course, a system like this only works if students are motivated and teachers are dedicated. Fortunately, that's exactly how it shakes out at Vassar. The school boasts "world-class professors, small classes, and a faculty that really is interested in us as students. Every teacher and member of the faculty goes the extra mile to [be] available outside of class and [to] meet students for lunch or dinner." Vassar places "a real focus on the undergraduate students. There is big-time research just like at major universities, but there are no graduate students to fill all the spots. All assisting positions go to undergraduates." The school excels in the visual and performing arts—the "drama department is huge"—as well as in English, psychology, history, life sciences, and natural sciences.

Life

"Life is very campus-centered" at Vassar; the farthest off campus people regularly go is the 24-hour diner two blocks north of campus. This is partly because hometown Poughkeepsie "does not offer much in the way of entertainment." For whatever reason, insularity is a defining characteristic of life at Vassar, so much so that students speak of "The Vassar Bubble. This is a term any student will immediately become familiar with. Essentially, Vassar is an island closed off from the rest of the town and community. It would be entirely possible (and not even rare) for a student to not leave campus once in an entire semester. While this is good for some, others will likely go a little crazy stuck on campus." Some escape to New York City whenever possible, but unfortunately the trip to the city is a relatively "expensive endeavor for weekly entertainment; it's about $35 round-trip, and that doesn't include doing stuff once you get there." Fortunately, "there is a huge array of things to do every night on campus. Comedy shows, improv, an incredibly wide array of theater productions"—including "several shows a year and three student groups devoted to drama"—"four comedy groups, five a cappella groups," and "interesting lectures create numerous opportunities to get out of the dorms at night." Weekends are for parties; there's "no Greek life, so lots of parties are awesome, school-sponsored, theme events." There's also "lots of socializing at senior housing," and "Halloween is huge. People really go all out."

Student Body

There are "lots of hipsters" at Vassar including kids who are "very left-wing politically" and "very into the music scene." The school is "not entirely dominated by hipsters," however; there are "lots of different groups" on campus. "Walking around you'll see students who walked out of a thrift store next to students who walked out of a J.Crew catalog," one student tells us. Another adds that Vassar is a comfortable respite for "indie-chic students who revel in obscurity, some socially awkward archetypes, and some prep school pin-ups with their collars popped. But the majority of kids on campus are a mix of these people, which is why we mesh pretty well despite the cliques that inevitably form." What students share is having "an amazing talent or something they passionately believe in" that makes them distinctive. "Vassar admissions works tremendously hard to ensure every student at Vassar is unique and mold-breaking," students brag.

FINANCIAL AID: 845-437-5230 • E-MAIL: ADMISSIONS@VASSAR.EDU • WEBSITE: WWW.VASSAR.EDU

THE PRINCETON REVIEW SAYS

Admissions

Very important factors considered include: rigor of secondary school record, *Important factors considered include:* Class rank, application essay, academic GPA, recommendation(s), standardized test scores, character/personal qualities. *Other factors considered include:* alumni/ae relation, extracurricular activities, first generation, geographical residence, interview, level of applicant's interest, racial/ethnic status, talent/ability, volunteer work, work experience. SAT and SAT Subject Tests or ACT required; ACT with Writing component recommended. TOEFL required of all international applicants. High school diploma is required and GED is accepted. *Academic units required:* 4 English, 4 mathematics, 4 science, (3 science labs), 3 foreign language, 2 social studies, 2 history, 4 academic electives, *Academic units recommended:* 4 English, 4 mathematics, 4 science, (3 science labs), 4 foreign language, 4 social studies, 2 history.

Financial Aid

Students should submit: FAFSA, CSS/Financial Aid, state aid form, noncustodial PROFILE, business/farm supplement. Regular filing deadline is 2/1. The Princeton Review suggests that all financial aid forms be submitted as soon as possible after 1/1. *Need-based scholarships/grants offered:* Federal Pell, SEOG, state scholarships/grants, private scholarships, the school's own gift aid. *Loan aid offered:* FFEL Subsidized Stafford, FFEL Unsubsidized Stafford, FFEL PLUS, Federal Perkins, Loans for Non-citizens with need. Applicants will be notified of awards on or about 3/30. Federal Work-Study Program available. Institutional employment available. Off-campus job opportunities are fair.

The Inside Word

With acceptance rates hitting record lows, stellar academic credentials are a must for any serious Vassar candidate. Importantly, the college prides itself on selecting students who will add to the vitality of the campus. Once admissions officers see you meet their rigorous scholastic standards, they'll closely assess your personal essay, recommendations, and extracurricular activities. Demonstrating an intellectual curiosity that extends outside the classroom is as important as success within it.

THE SCHOOL SAYS "..."

From The Admissions Office

"Vassar presents a rich variety of social and cultural activities, clubs, sports, living arrangements, and regional attractions. Vassar is a vital, residential college community recognized for its respect for the rights and individuality of others.

"Candidates must submit either the SAT Reasoning Test and two SAT Subject Tests taken in different subject fields, or the ACT exam (the optional ACT writing component is recommended)."

SELECTIVITY

Admissions Rating	97
# of applicants	7,361
% of applicants accepted	25
% of acceptees attending	35
# accepting a place on wait list	550
% admitted from wait list	15
# of early decision applicants	582
% accepted early decision	38

FRESHMAN PROFILE

Range SAT Critical Reading	670–750
Range SAT Math	650–720
Range SAT Writing	660–750
Range ACT Composite	29–33
Minimum paper TOEFL	600
Minimum computer TOEFL	250
Minimum web-based TOEFL	100
Average HS GPA	3.75
% graduated top 10% of class	70
% graduated top 25% of class	96
% graduated top 50% of class	99

DEADLINES

Early Decision	
Deadline	11/15
Notification	12/15
Regular	
Deadline	1/1
Notification	4/1
Nonfall registration?	no

APPLICANTS ALSO LOOK AT

AND OFTEN PREFER
Harvard College
Williams College
Yale University
Brown University
Amherst College

AND SOMETIMES PREFER
Columbia University
Wesleyan University
Tufts University

AND RARELY PREFER
New York University
Skidmore College

FINANCIAL FACTS

Financial Aid Rating	98
Annual tuition	$37,570
Room and board	$8,570
Required fees	$545
Books and supplies	$860
% frosh rec. need-based scholarship or grant aid	57
% UG rec. need-based scholarship or grant aid	55
% frosh rec. any financial aid	56
% UG rec. any financial aid	54
% UG borrow to pay for school	50
Average cumulative indebtedness	$19,910

VILLANOVA UNIVERSITY

800 LANCASTER AVENUE, VILLANOVA, PA 19085-1672 • ADMISSIONS: 610-519-4000 • FAX: 610-519-6450

CAMPUS LIFE

Quality of Life Rating	96
Fire Safety Rating	89
Green Rating	92
Type of school	private
Affiliation	Roman Catholic
Environment	village

STUDENTS

Total undergrad enrollment	6,884
% male/female	49/51
% from out of state	75
% from public high school	55
% live on campus	70
% in (# of) fraternities	18 (10)
% in (# of) sororities	25 (9)
% African American	5
% Asian	7
% Caucasian	76
% Hispanic	6
% international	3
# of countries represented	48

SURVEY SAYS . . .

School is well run
Low cost of living
Everyone loves the Wildcats
(Almost) no one smokes

ACADEMICS

Academic Rating	88
Calendar	semester
Student/faculty ratio	11:1
Profs interesting rating	86
Profs accessible rating	89
Most common reg class size	10–19 students
Most common lab size	10–19 students

MOST POPULAR MAJORS

communication studies/speech
communication and rhetoric
finance
nursing/registered nurse
(rn, asn, bsn, msn)

STUDENTS SAY ". . ."

Academics

"Villanova emphasizes not only the importance of academics but also service and connection with the community," is how one student sums up life at this Catholic university just outside Philadelphia. Most students agree the school's emphasis on community and "dedication to service" was an important factor as was its excellent academic reputation. That said, Villanova's "well-rounded academic focus," "excellent nursing and business school programs," and "outstanding" faculty are definitely strong draws for students who choose to attend. Villanova "requires students to take classes based on a core curriculum, which [leads] to a well-rounded education." "You will work hard," warns one student, "but if you put in the work, you will do well." "The professors at Villanova are fantastic!" says another. "I've had professors give out e-mail addresses, cell, home and office numbers, even an AIM screenname in order to make contacting them as easy as possible." The professors for the most are "PhDs and love to teach. You are never taught by a grad student." Even the harshest critique has an element of praise in it: "You either get someone you completely click with and is very interactive with students, or you get a PhD who just has to teach a class and isn't very good at teaching, but is really, really smart." The administration gets high marks as well. "If I wanted to meet with Father Peter, the president of Villanova, I could go see him tomorrow. Everyone is accessible." Keep in mind, though, that a little initiative is not a bad thing. "You need to be your own advocate—you can get anything you want if you ask nicely (or not so nicely, if need be), but nothing will happen if you don't ask."

Life

The "idea of community is extremely important" at Villanova, and student life, both on campus and off, tends to reflect that. "The average student works hard four days a week, parties harder two days a week, and spends the seventh day working for some cause," explains one student. "Life at Villanova seems to be a work hard during the day, play hard during the night atmosphere," says another. "People are serious about their schoolwork and do many activities. However, once it becomes nighttime, especially Thursday through Saturday, many people drink and throw parties. People generally like to have a good time." "Basketball and frat parties" seem to make up a majority of the social life. But, "there is always stuff to do for fun that does not involve partying." "Sporting events are huge here at the school as our basketball program is fantastic." It's worth pointing out "if you don't like basketball, you will learn to like it even if you never actually understand it." Villanova is only 12 miles and a short train ride away from Center City Philadelphia, where "many people go out to dinner or shopping," or to watch (of course) basketball at the Wachovia Center. The school also provides free shuttle buses to the huge King of Prussia mall nearby. There is a Greek presence at Villanova, but because "there are no frat, sorority, or sports houses on campus," much of the Greek life takes place at off-campus houses and apartments, and "parties are usually hard to get to." Ultimately, "the community of students is very tight-knit," and "there are always activities on campus that involve volunteer work or group projects in the surrounding areas."

Student Body

"Good-looking, white, over-achievers who like to have a good time" seems to be the prevailing consensus. "However, that seems to be changing more and more every year," one student says. "We are starting to see many more minorities, which obviously is a great and refreshing thing to see." "Villanova is not as preppy, conservative, or homogeneous as it was….The newer students seem a bit more liberal and academic than the students of years before." Regardless of race or politics, the typical Villanova student "is very service oriented and excels academically," not to mention a "basketball fanatic." "In general, everyone gets along nicely, and the multitude of student organizations and trips foster school unity." Many people note, although Villanova is not a huge university, "students outside the Villanova norm can easily find their own niche in the community."

VILLANOVA UNIVERSITY

FINANCIAL AID: 610-519-4010 • E-MAIL: GOTOVU@VILLANOVA.EDU • WEBSITE: WWW.VILLANOVA.EDU

THE PRINCETON REVIEW SAYS

Admissions

Very important factors considered include: Class rank, academic GPA, rigor of secondary school record, standardized test scores, *Important factors considered include:* Application essay, recommendation(s), character/personal qualities, extracurricular activities, talent/ability, volunteer work, work experience. *Other factors considered include:* alumni/ae relation, first generation, geographical residence, level of applicant's interest, racial/ethnic status, state residency, SAT or ACT required; ACT with Writing component required. TOEFL required of all international applicants. High school diploma is required and GED is accepted. *Academic units required:* 4 English, 4 mathematics, 4 science, (2 science labs), 2 foreign language, 2 academic electives, *Academic units recommended:* 4 English, 4 mathematics, 4 science, (3 science labs), 4 foreign language, 2 academic electives.

Financial Aid

Students should submit: FAFSA, institution's own financial aid form. Regular filing deadline is 2/7. The Princeton Review suggests that all financial aid forms be submitted as soon as possible after 1/1. *Need-based scholarships/grants offered:* Federal Pell, SEOG, state scholarships/grants, private scholarships, the school's own gift aid. *Loan aid offered:* FFEL Subsidized Stafford, FFEL Unsubsidized Stafford, FFEL PLUS, Federal Perkins, Federal Nursing. Applicants will be notified of awards on or about 4/1. Federal Work-Study Program available. Institutional employment available. Off-campus job opportunities are excellent.

The Inside Word

Villanova's growing academic reputation means its application process is growing more competitive as well: 86 percent of the most recent freshman class ranked in the top 25 percent of their high school graduating class. But while academic achievement is important, the university looks at the whole package when considering applicants and expects candidates to do the same. As a private university, Villanova is not exactly cheap, but the school offers a wide variety of scholarships and aid to qualifying students.

THE SCHOOL SAYS "..."

From The Admissions Office

"Villanova is the oldest and largest Catholic university in Pennsylvania, founded in 1842 by the Order of Saint Augustine. Students of all faiths are welcome. The university tends to attract students who are interested in volunteerism. Villanovans provide more than 64,000 hours of service annually and host the largest student-run Special Olympics in the nation. Villanova's scenic campus is located 12 miles west of Philadelphia. The university offers programs through four undergraduate colleges: Liberal Arts and Sciences, Engineering, Nursing, and the Villanova School of Business. There are 250 student organizations and 32 National Honor Societies at Villanova. Incoming freshmen can opt to be part of a Learning Community, through which student groups live together in specially-designated residence halls and learn together in courses and co-curricular programs. The university offers Naval and Marine Reserve Officers Training Corps (ROTC) programs and hundreds of options for studying abroad. 'Nova's alumni body is comprised of 90,000 people. Some prominent grads include: Maria Bello, Golden Globe-Nominated Actress; Rear Admiral Christine Bruzek-Kohler, Director of the U.S. Navy Nurse Corps and Chief of Staff for the Navy Bureau of Medicine and Surgery; Nnenna Lynch, Olympian and Rhodes Scholar; Robert Moran, President and COO of PetSmart; James O'Donnell, CEO of American Eagle Outfitters; and Dianna Sugg, Pulitzer Prize Recipient for Journalism.

"If you're looking to join 'Nova Nation, be prepared: the competition for admission is getting much tougher every year."

SELECTIVITY

Admissions Rating	96
# of applicants	15,102
% of applicants accepted	39
% of acceptees attending	27
# accepting a place on wait list	2,771
% admitted from wait list	6

FRESHMAN PROFILE

Range SAT Critical Reading	580–680
Range SAT Math	620–710
Range SAT Writing	590–680
Range ACT Composite	28–31
Minimum paper TOEFL	550
Minimum computer TOEFL	213
Average HS GPA	3.86
% graduated top 10% of class	60
% graduated top 25% of class	86
% graduated top 50% of class	96

DEADLINES

Early action	
Deadline	11/1
Notification	12/20
Regular	
Priority	12/15
Deadline	1/7
Notification	4/1
Nonfall registration?	no

APPLICANTS ALSO LOOK AT

AND OFTEN PREFER
University of Notre Dame
Georgetown University

AND SOMETIMES PREFER
Lehigh University
Bucknell University
Boston College
Boston University

AND RARELY PREFER
University of Delaware
Drexel University
Loyola College in Maryland

FINANCIAL FACTS

Financial Aid Rating	70
Annual tuition	$35,950
Room and board	$10,070
Required fees	$580
Books and supplies	$950
% frosh rec. need-based scholarship or grant aid	42
% UG rec. need-based scholarship or grant aid	39
% frosh rec. non-need-based scholarship or grant aid	11
% UG rec. non-need-based scholarship or grant aid	11
% frosh rec. need-based self-help aid	43
% UG rec. need-based self-help aid	40
% frosh rec. athletic scholarships	2
% UG rec. athletic scholarships	3
% UG borrow to pay for school	56
Average cumulative indebtedness	$29,812

VIRGINIA POLYTECHNIC INSTITUTE AND STATE UNIVERSITY (VIRGINIA TECH)

UNDERGRADUATE ADMISSIONS, 201 BURRUSS HALL, BLACKSBURG, VA 24061 • ADMISSIONS: 540-231-6267 • FAX: 540-231-3242

CAMPUS LIFE

Quality of Life Rating	95
Fire Safety Rating	80
Green Rating	93
Type of school	public
Environment	town

STUDENTS

Total undergrad enrollment	23,447
% male/female	57/43
% from out of state	25
% from public high school	95
% live on campus	38
% in (# of) fraternities	13 (31)
% in (# of) sororities	20 (12)
% African American	4
% Asian	8
% Caucasian	74
% Hispanic	3
% international	2
# of countries represented	112

SURVEY SAYS . . .

Athletic facilities are great
Great food on campus
Everyone loves the Hokies
Student publications are popular

ACADEMICS

Academic Rating	76
Calendar	semester
Student/faculty ratio	16:1
Profs interesting rating	75
Profs accessible rating	79
Most common reg class size	20–29 students
Most common lab size	20–29 students

MOST POPULAR MAJORS
biology/biological sciences
engineering

STUDENTS SAY ". . ."

Academics

Students at tech schools don't typically brag about their quality of life, but then again, Virginia Polytechnic Institute and State University, otherwise known as Virginia Tech, is not your typical tech school. Here, students happily discover that they can enjoy "a diverse community," "an accepting atmosphere," "a football program that takes priority for all but the most dedicated students," and the opportunity "to have a blast in college while still staying focused on their education." Without losing access to "a great science program" (in which "undergraduate research is huge"), strong engineering programs, and outstanding offerings in architecture, agricultural science, forestry, and business. Throughout this large school, undergrads are pleasantly surprised to find this school offers a well-rounded experience. Profesors "who are always willing to help answer questions," although they warn that "there are a few classes where you can't understand anything the professor says, and he can't figure out how to explain it." Sometimes the result of a language barrier, other times the result of the difficulty of the concept being taught. Fortunately, "even if your teacher can't help you understand something, is not very hard to find someone who can." About 1 in 5 students here pursues engineering, a degree that "provides a mixture of practical and theoretical teaching in the classes, experimental labs, a design capstone" and "a cooperative education program that places great value on applying knowledge in the real world."

Life

Virginia Tech may be located "in the middle of nowhere," but students don't seem to mind, because "the people you meet and the cozy town of Blacksburg can be so much fun. Being part of the Hokie nation is really special." That's especially true during football season, because the football team "is king in Blacksburg. It's hard not to be excited about football when you are tailgating with friends and seeing 60,000 people pack the stadium." While "most people are very serious about school work," they "still have time to go party" or "to have fun in a place called the Break Zone, where you can go bowling, play pool, or just hang out." Greek life is also "pretty big and a really great thing." Whenever weather permits, "you can always find people outside playing volleyball or basketball, or using the drillfield for games of pickup soccer and football" at Tech; lots of students exploit the "perfect location for outdoor activities." According to one undergrad, "Within 30 minutes from campus, you can be hiking on the Appalachian Trail, floating down the New River, picnicking in the Jefferson National Forest, or listening to live old-time music at the Floyd Country Store on Friday nights." Shopping has been a problem in the past, but students report that "they are beginning to bring more sites into Blacksburg" and that there's "some shopping in Christianburg," which is about 10 miles away.

Student Body

School spirit is strong at Virginia Tech, where students "are typically clad head to toe in maroon and orange with a Virginia Tech/HokieBird logo at least somewhere on their outfit." Students regard themselves as "well-rounded and friendly," the sort of people who "enjoy going out and partying but also know when to study and get their work done." There are lots of folks who fit the description: "Caucasian; middle class; and from the Northern Virginia, Richmond, or Virginia Beach areas," but the school is "very open to student diversity. That's actually an aspect that is being pushed in the student population," where you'll also find "a lot of students from other countries like India and China." With more than 23,000 undergraduates, Virginia Tech's "large student body makes it easy to find many people that have the same interests and are able to become good friends."

VIRGINIA POLYTECHNIC INSTITUTE AND STATE UNIVERSITY (VIRGINIA TECH)

FINANCIAL AID: 540-231-5179 • E-MAIL: VTADMISS@VT.EDU • WEBSITE: WWW.VT.EDU

THE PRINCETON REVIEW SAYS

Admissions

Very important factors considered include: Academic GPA, rigor of secondary school record, standardized test scores. *Other factors considered include:* recommendation(s), alumni/ae relation, character/personal qualities, extracurricular activities, first generation, geographical residence, racial/ethnic status, state residency, talent/ability, volunteer work, work experience. SAT or ACT required; ACT with Writing component required. TOEFL required of all international applicants. High school diploma is required and GED is accepted. *Academic units required:* 4 English, 3 mathematics, 2 science, (2 science labs), 1 social studies, 1 history, 4 academic electives, *Academic units recommended:* 4 mathematics, 3 science, 3 foreign language.

Financial Aid

Students should submit: FAFSAGeneral Scholarship Application. The Princeton Review suggests that all financial aid forms be submitted as soon as possible after 1/1. *Need-based scholarships/grants offered:* Federal Pell, SEOG, state scholarships/grants, private scholarships, the school's own gift aid, cadet scholarships/grants. *Loan aid offered:* Direct Subsidized Stafford, Direct Unsubsidized Stafford, Direct PLUS, Federal Perkins, college/university loans from institutional funds. Applicants will be notified of awards on a rolling basis beginning 3/30. Federal Work-Study Program available. Off-campus job opportunities are excellent.

The Inside Word

It's a numbers game at Virginia Tech, a byproduct of the more than 20,000 applications that flood into the admissions office each year. High school grades and curriculum figure most prominently into the admissions decision, followed by standardized test scores. There are no published cutoffs, but solid performers should expect little resistance here, except perhaps in more competitive disciplines (e.g. engineering, architecture).

THE SCHOOL SAYS "..."

From The Admissions Office

"Virginia Tech offers the opportunities of a large research university in a small-town setting. Undergraduates choose from more than 70 majors in seven colleges, including nationally ranked architecture, business, forestry, and engineering schools, as well as excellent computer science, biology, and communication studies, and architecture programs. Technology is a key focus, both in classes and in general. All first-year students are required to own a personal computer, each residence hall room has Ethernet connections, and every student is provided e-mail and Internet access. Faculty incorporate a wide variety of technology into class, utilizing chat rooms, online lecture notes, and multimedia presentations. The university offers cutting-edge facilities for classes and research, abundant opportunities for advanced study in the honors program, undergraduate research opportunities, study abroad, internships, and cooperative education. Students enjoy more than 600 organizations which offer something for everyone. Tech offers the best of both worlds—everything a large university can provide and a small-town atmosphere.

"Freshman applicants must take the SAT or ACT with Writing section. We will use the highest scores from any SAT or ACT test scores submitted."

SELECTIVITY

Admissions Rating	93
# of applicants	20,615
% of applicants accepted	65
% of acceptees attending	40
# accepting a place on wait list	1,286
# of early decision applicants	2,292
% accepted early decision	55

FRESHMAN PROFILE

Range SAT Critical Reading	540–630
Range SAT Math	570–670
Range SAT Writing	530–630
Minimum paper TOEFL	550
Minimum computer TOEFL	207
Average HS GPA	3.86
% graduated top 10% of class	42
% graduated top 25% of class	81
% graduated top 50% of class	97

DEADLINES

Early Decision	
Deadline	11/1
Notification	12/15
Regular	
Deadline	1/15
Notification	4/1
Nonfall registration?	yes

APPLICANTS ALSO LOOK AT

AND OFTEN PREFER
University of Virginia
College of William and Mary

AND RARELY PREFER
College of William and Mary
University of North Carolina at Chapel Hill

FINANCIAL FACTS

Financial Aid Rating	72
Annual in-state tuition	$6,332
Annual out-of-state tuition	$18,789
Room and board	$5,476
Required fees	$1,866
Books and supplies	$1,080
% frosh rec. need-based scholarship or grant aid	29
% UG rec. need-based scholarship or grant aid	29
% frosh rec. non-need-based scholarship or grant aid	8
% UG rec. non-need-based scholarship or grant aid	6
% frosh rec. need-based self-help aid	27
% UG rec. need-based self-help aid	28
% frosh rec. athletic scholarships	2
% UG rec. athletic scholarships	2
% frosh rec. any financial aid	36
% UG rec. any financial aid	35
% UG borrow to pay for school	52
Average cumulative indebtedness	$21,678

WABASH COLLEGE

PO Box 352, 301 West Wabash Avenue, Crawfordsville, IN 47933 • Admissions: 765-361-6225 • Fax: 765-361-6437

CAMPUS LIFE

Quality of Life Rating	**90**
Fire Safety Rating	**82**
Green Rating	**70**
Type of school	private
Environment	village

STUDENTS

Total undergrad enrollment	903
% male/female	100/0
% from out of state	24
% from public high school	91
% live on campus	86
% in (# of) fraternities	53 (9)
% African American	6
% Asian	1
% Caucasian	79
% Hispanic	5
% Native American	1
% international	5
# of countries represented	16

SURVEY SAYS . . .

Lab facilities are great
Athletic facilities are great
Career services are great
School is well run
Everyone loves the Little Giants
Intramural sports are popular
Frats dominate social scene

ACADEMICS

Academic Rating	**98**
Calendar	semester
Student/faculty ratio	10:1
Profs interesting rating	98
Profs accessible rating	99
Most common reg class size	10–19 students
Most common lab size	10–19 students

MOST POPULAR MAJORS

history
psychology
religion/religious studies

STUDENTS SAY "..."

Academics

There's only one rule at Wabash College, a small Indiana all men's school: "A Wabash man is to conduct himself as a gentleman both on and off campus." The administration typically takes a hands-off approach to enforcing this "Gentleman's Rule," meaning that "students are forced to take ownership over their experiences here and be involved on campus." The young men here "have the freedom to make their own life choices and the freedom to face the real-life implications of those choices." While some feel this system fosters "an atmosphere that is hyper-masculine, overly conservative, sports-centric, sexist, and generally intolerant of diversity," the vast majority wouldn't have it any other way, telling us that it "molds average boys into successful men," in the same way that "when pressure is applied to common coal it can become a diamond." All agree that a Wabash education is top-notch, with a strong liberal arts focus that "educates men to think critically, act responsibly, lead effectively, and live humanely." Classes "are challenging, and through the course of four years [students learn] to love pushing [themselves] both in and out of the classroom to rise to the occasion." For those who can't handle the pressure, however, "the 'do-your-own-thing' approach means that you can crash and burn, because you're working without a net. If you really nosedive, professors will notice and step in, but a long slow spiral will continue unabated." Those who survive enjoy the benefit of "good alumni connections."

Life

"Wabash is stressful at times" because "the school is very tough academically, and you get those weeks when it just keeps piling up." It's the sort of place where "students usually devote much of the week studying or attending campus-wide lectures or productions" and where "weekends are usually devoted to partying or visiting friends at other schools." Life is "very fraternity-oriented" with "some big fraternity parties after the football games" on weekends, and "if nothing is going on, you just relax and hang out with your brothers." The administration's laissez-faire governance "is usually great; people can actually do their own thing. If you want to build a trebuchet in your front lawn and launch paint cans over your fraternity, have fun. If you want to organize a communal bike program or a brewing club or a Tuvan throat-singing appreciation society, fine, here's a pile of cash." The drawback is that "the campus can also get pretty anarchic at times." "Get used to running belligerent drunks off your property, to taking your own measures against petty theft, and to hewing civilization out of chaos with bellowing and intimidation and a strong right arm. Thucydides would love it here."

Student Body

The typical Wabash student "is a loud, ruddy-cheeked Midwestern kid who in high school was a bit too brainy to fit in with the jocks and a bit too rowdy to fit in with the nerds" and "is smarter than other people think he is, but probably not quite as smart as he thinks he is." He tends to hit all three C's—Caucasian, Christian, and conservative—but students insist those outside the mainstream "have few problems fitting in." The archetypal student joins a fraternity; independents, we're told, "are much more diverse. There is no typical independent student because you have physics nerds, homosexuals, African Americans, international students from Asia, Europe, and South America, evangelical Christians, atheists, and the list goes on, all contained in the minority of an 900-person campus." Students warn that "open homosexuals, unfortunately, will not feel terribly welcome, although this area has shown recent improvement" in recent years, with "some fraternities [being] outspoken about welcoming homosexuals as members. Others are, to say the least, not."

FINANCIAL AID: 765-361-6370 • E-MAIL: ADMISSIONS@WABASH.EDU • WEBSITE: WWW.WABASH.EDU

THE PRINCETON REVIEW SAYS

Admissions

Very important factors considered include: Class rank, academic GPA, rigor of secondary school record, *Important factors considered include:* recommendation(s), standardized test scores, extracurricular activities, interview, level of applicant's interest, talent/ability. *Other factors considered include:* Application essay, alumni/ae relation, character/personal qualities, first generation, geographical residence, racial/ethnic status, volunteer work, work experience. SAT or ACT required; TOEFL required of all international applicants. High school diploma is required and GED is accepted. *Academic units recommended:* 4 English, 4 mathematics, 2 science, (2 science labs), 2 foreign language, 2 social studies, 2 history, 3 academic electives.

Financial Aid

Students should submit: FAFSA, CSS/Financial Aid, noncustodial Federal tax returns and W-2 statements. Regular filing deadline is 3/1. The Princeton Review suggests that all financial aid forms be submitted as soon as possible after 1/1. *Need-based scholarships/grants offered:* Federal Pell, state scholarships/grants, private scholarships, the school's own gift aid. *Loan aid offered:* FFEL Subsidized Stafford, FFEL Unsubsidized Stafford, FFEL PLUS, college/university loans from institutional funds. Applicants will be notified of awards on or about 4/1. Institutional employment available. Off-campus job opportunities are good.

The Inside Word

Wabash is one of the few remaining all-male colleges in the country, and like the rest it has a small applicant pool. The pool is highly self-selected, and the academic standards for admission, while selective, aren't especially demanding. Graduating is a whole other matter. Don't consider applying if you aren't ready to do the grueling work required for success here.

THE SCHOOL SAYS "..."

From The Admissions Office

"Wabash College is different—and distinctive—from other liberal arts colleges. Different in that Wabash is an outstanding college for men only. Distinctive in the quality and character of the faculty, in the demanding nature of the academic program, in the farsightedness and maturity of the men who enroll, and in the richness of the traditions that have evolved throughout its 174-year history. Wabash is preeminently a teaching institution, and fundamental to the learning experience is the way faculty and students talk to each other—with mutual respect for the expression of informed opinion. For example, students who collaborate with faculty on research projects are considered their peers in the research—an esteem not usually extended to undergraduates. The college takes pride in the sense of community that such a learning environment fosters. But perhaps the single most striking aspect of student life at Wabash is personal freedom. The college has only one rule: 'The student is expected to conduct himself at all times, both on and off the campus, as a gentleman and a responsible citizen.' Wabash College treats students as adults, and such treatment attracts responsible freshmen and fosters their independence and maturity.

"For students seeking admission, Wabash will accept the SAT or the ACT. Wabash will use the student's best scores from either examination and will accept the SAT or ACT Writing portions in place of an essay. Wabash does not require SAT Subject Tests."

SELECTIVITY

Admissions Rating	89
# of applicants	1,365
% of applicants accepted	49
% of acceptees attending	38
# accepting a place on wait list	53
% admitted from wait list	9
# of early decision applicants	63
% accepted early decision	75

FRESHMAN PROFILE

Range SAT Critical Reading	500–620
Range SAT Math	540–650
Range SAT Writing	480–610
Range ACT Composite	22–28
Minimum paper TOEFL	550
Minimum computer TOEFL	213
Average HS GPA	3.6
% graduated top 10% of class	35
% graduated top 25% of class	65
% graduated top 50% of class	95

DEADLINES

Early Decision	
Deadline	11/15
Notification	12/15
Early action	
Deadline	12/15
Notification	1/31
Regular	
Priority	12/15
Notification	rolling
Nonfall registration?	yes

APPLICANTS ALSO LOOK AT AND OFTEN PREFER

Purdue University—West Lafayette
Indiana University at Bloomington

AND SOMETIMES PREFER

DePauw University
Hanover College

FINANCIAL FACTS

Financial Aid Rating	99
Annual tuition	$27,500
Room and board	$7,900
Required fees	$450
Books and supplies	$800
% frosh rec. need-based scholarship or grant aid	87
% UG rec. need-based scholarship or grant aid	72
% frosh rec. non-need-based scholarship or grant aid	33
% UG rec. non-need-based scholarship or grant aid	14
% frosh rec. need-based self-help aid	85
% UG rec. need-based self-help aid	71
% frosh rec. any financial aid	93
% UG rec. any financial aid	88
% UG borrow to pay for school	90
Average cumulative indebtedness	$21,423

WAGNER COLLEGE

One Campus Road, Staten Island, NY 10301-4495 • Admissions: 718-390-3411 • Fax: 718-390-3105

CAMPUS LIFE

Quality of Life Rating	75
Fire Safety Rating	86
Green Rating	75
Type of school	private
Environment	metropolis

STUDENTS

Total undergrad enrollment	1,924
% male/female	38/62
% from out of state	52
% live on campus	71
% in (# of) fraternities	13 (5)
% in (# of) sororities	15 (4)
% African American	5
% Asian	2
% Caucasian	85
% Hispanic	6
% international	1
# of countries represented	22

SURVEY SAYS . . .

Athletic facilities are great
Students are friendly
Campus feels safe
Musical organizations are popular
Theater is popular
Student publications are popular
Student government is popular
Lots of beer drinking
Hard liquor is popular
(Almost) everyone smokes

ACADEMICS

Academic Rating	80
Calendar	semester
Student/faculty ratio	14:1
Profs interesting rating	75
Profs accessible rating	79
Most common reg class size	10–19 students
Most common lab size	fewer than 10 students

MOST POPULAR MAJORS

biology/biological sciences
business/commerce
psychology

STUDENTS SAY ". . ."

Academics

Wagner College on Staten Island boasts one of the most pastoral campuses New York City has to offer. The college is also a pioneer in "practical liberal arts education." All students here must complete a pretty broad curriculum. Interdisciplinary courses for first-year students focus on a unifying theme and include about 30 hours of course-related fieldwork. Seniors must complete a thesis or a big project within their major. Also, "Wagner requires senior-year internships" and "most" students end up working somewhere pretty cool in Manhattan. Classes "never really exceed 30 people." Some students tell us "this school is very strong academically." Others say Wagner's coursework is "absolutely cake." The difficulty level really varies from class to class. There are "very personable" professors who "really know what they're talking about," and there are "terrible ones." "It all depends on who you get." Virtually the entire faculty is "constantly available," though. "The administration, up to the president, is very accessible and conscious of students' needs," relates a biology major. "You can generally walk in without an appointment and get whatever help you need." However, the "mean old women" in the bursar's office are a problem. Also, advising can be hit or miss. "Make sure you get a good adviser," counsels an arts administration major, "because mine blows."

Life

Some students at Wagner contend "the dining hall is excellent." Others disagree. "The food here is terrible," gripes a sophomore. "I hate it." Critics also point out "there are really no fast food places" near campus. "Some of the facilities are a little out of date," too. "Campus maintenance and upkeep would be my biggest complaint," says a first-year student. "If they fixed things like clogged drains and broken lights faster, it would be nice." Also, while it's unquestionably "safe" around campus, that's only because "the overprotective security feels like a Gestapo." On the plus side, students relish their "gorgeous" dorm-room views of the Lower Manhattan skyline. They also love their location. "Wagner represents a unique mix of big city and small town." "Rumors are atrocious and spread quickly," but on the whole it's "a friendly and small campus where you pretty much know everyone." "There's always a sporting event of some kind going on." The coffeehouse on campus "is a great place to meet new people and play a game of pool or hear great local bands." Otherwise, "Greek life and the theater program seem to dominate." "Parties are really not too extensive on campus but we get it done," says a sophomore. Local bars and clubs on Staten Island are popular for students who are 21. When students tire of the local scene, there's always Manhattan. A free shuttle "runs to the ferry quite often" and "almost all of the students" take advantage frequently. "The city can sometimes be expensive," but "you're never bored."

Student Body

While there is clear and growing diversity in Wagner's numbers, one student notes there are "a lot of Staten Islanders and Jersey people." There are substantially more women than men here, and there's a decent gay population. As a result, "there just aren't that many guys who are actively pursuing girls." Overall, it's a "very cliquey" scene. There are "tanning princess types" and "spoiled rich kids" "who'd rather party than study." Other students "are your average go-to-class, hang-out-with-friends, and study kind of people." The biggest social divide is between thespians and jocks. "There are two main groups of students at Wagner," explains a senior. So expect some show tune humming mixed in with Sports Center recaps—and everything in between. Suprised? Didn't your mom tell ya New York City was a big melting pot?

WAGNER COLLEGE

FINANCIAL AID: 718-390-3183 • E-MAIL: ADMISSIONS@WAGNER.EDU • WEBSITE: WWW.WAGNER.EDU

THE PRINCETON REVIEW SAYS

Admissions

Very important factors considered include: Class rank, academic GPA, rigor of secondary school record, *Important factors considered include:* Application essay, recommendation(s), standardized test scores, extracurricular activities, interview. *Other factors considered include:* character/personal qualities, geographical residence, level of applicant's interest, talent/ability, volunteer work, work experience. SAT or ACT required; TOEFL required of all international applicants. High school diploma is required and GED is accepted. *Academic units required:* 4 English, 3 mathematics, 2 science, (1 science labs), 2 foreign language, 1 social studies, 3 history, 6 academic electives.

Financial Aid

Students should submit: FAFSA, institution's own financial aid form, state aid form The Princeton Review suggests that all financial aid forms be submitted as soon as possible after 1/1. *Need-based scholarships/grants offered:* Federal Pell, SEOG, state scholarships/grants, private scholarships. *Loan aid offered:* FFEL Subsidized Stafford, FFEL Unsubsidized Stafford, FFEL PLUS, Federal Perkins, Federal Nursing Applicants will be notified of awards on a rolling basis beginning 3/1. Federal Work-Study Program available. Institutional employment available. Off-campus job opportunities are good.

The Inside Word

As far as grades and test scores, the profile of the average freshman class at Wagner is solid but not spectacular. Don't take the application process too lightly, though. The admissions staff here is dedicated to finding the right students for their school. An interview is definitely a good idea.

THE SCHOOL SAYS "..."

From The Admissions Office

"At Wagner College, we attract and develop active learners and future leaders. Wagner College has received national acclaim (*Time* magazine, American Association of Colleges and Universities) for its innovative curriculum, The Wagner Plan for the Practical Liberal Arts. At Wagner, we capitalize on our unique geography; we are a traditional, scenic, residential campus, which happens to sit atop a hill on an island overlooking lower Manhattan. Our location allows us to offer a program that couples required off-campus experiences (experiential learning), with 'learning community' clusters of courses. This program begins in the first semester and continues through the senior capstone experience in the major. Fieldwork and internships, writing-intensive reflective tutorials, connected learning, 'reading, writing, and doing': At Wagner College our students truly discover 'the practical liberal arts in New York City.'"

SELECTIVITY

Admissions Rating	88
# of applicants	3,012
% of applicants accepted	60
% of acceptees attending	26
# accepting a place on wait list	120
% admitted from wait list	42
# of early decision applicants	90
% accepted early decision	63

FRESHMAN PROFILE

Range SAT Critical Reading	530–640
Range SAT Math	540–650
Range SAT Writing	530–650
Range ACT Composite	24–28
Minimum paper TOEFL	550
Minimum computer TOEFL	217
Minimum web-based TOEFL	17
Average HS GPA	3.52
% graduated top 10% of class	18
% graduated top 25% of class	70
% graduated top 50% of class	92

DEADLINES

Early Decision	
Deadline	1/1
Notification	1/15
Regular	
Priority	2/15
Deadline	3/1
Notification	3/1
Nonfall registration?	yes

APPLICANTS ALSO LOOK AT

AND OFTEN PREFER
New York University
Fairfield University

AND SOMETIMES PREFER
Hobart and William Smith Colleges
Muhlenberg College

AND RARELY PREFER
Manhattan College

FINANCIAL FACTS

Financial Aid Rating	81
Annual tuition	$30,900
Room and board	$9,250
Books and supplies	$725
% frosh rec. need-based scholarship or grant aid	62
% UG rec. need-based scholarship or grant aid	56
% frosh rec. non-need-based scholarship or grant aid	32
% UG rec. non-need-based scholarship or grant aid	29
% frosh rec. need-based self-help aid	48
% UG rec. need-based self-help aid	43
% frosh rec. athletic scholarships	6
% UG rec. athletic scholarships	6
% frosh rec. any financial aid	96
% UG rec. any financial aid	85
% UG borrow to pay for school	56
Average cumulative indebtedness	$34,326

WAKE FOREST UNIVERSITY

Box 7305, Reynolda Station, Winston-Salem, NC 27109 • Admissions: 336-758-5201 • Fax: 336-758-4324

CAMPUS LIFE
Quality of Life Rating	**76**
Fire Safety Rating	**89**
Green Rating	**83**
Type of school	private
Environment	city

STUDENTS
Total undergrad enrollment	4,405
% male/female	49/51
% from out of state	75
% from public high school	65
% live on campus	69
% in (# of) fraternities	35 (14)
% in (# of) sororities	48 (9)
% African American	7
% Asian	5
% Caucasian	83
% Hispanic	2
% Native American	1
% international	1

SURVEY SAYS . . .
Great library
Students are happy
Everyone loves the Demon Deacons
Intramural sports are popular
Frats and sororities dominate social
scene
Lots of beer drinking
Hard liquor is popular

ACADEMICS
Academic Rating	**88**
Calendar	semester
Student/faculty ratio	10:1
Profs interesting rating	85
Profs accessible rating	84
Most common reg class size	10–19 students
Most common lab size	10–19 students

MOST POPULAR MAJORS
business/commerce
political science and government
psychology

STUDENTS SAY ". . ."

Academics

Wake Forest University is a smaller, private school with a Baptist heritage that offers "the best of both worlds—a big university's resources with small liberal arts college's sense of community." Business and accounting are probably the most notable programs, but you really can't go wrong with any of the various majors available. The alumni network is "incredible," and technology is fabulous. Upon enrollment, "every student receives a laptop." "Studying abroad is a huge deal at Wake Forest," too. More than half of the students participate at some point, taking courses in exotic locales all over the world. The especially cool EuroTour offers the chance to see a dozen cities in 10 countries during about a month in the summer. Students at Wake proudly assert theirs are "perhaps the hardest working" students attending a school with the "most beautiful campus in the country." There's definitely quite a bit of "academic rigor" here. "The workload is excessive at times," and professors are "committed to both grade and ego deflation." "Small classes with a lot of discussion are common," though, and students rave about the "wonderful" faculty. "They make class interesting and people rarely skip." "Contacting them out of class is a piece of cake" as well. The administration is also "very easily accessible," and "the school seems to be run well." "There are no needs that are not met by the administration," says a finance major, "and there are no wants by the majority of the students."

Life

Academic pressures are "intense," and students tend to really let loose when they are finally done hitting the books. "Drinking is pretty big at Wake, especially hard liquor." "Frat parties are wildly popular" "on the weekends (and Wake Wednesdays)." The Greek scene is massive. "A large portion of the student body is a member of a fraternity or sorority." "All of the frats and sororities have really different personalities," explains a senior, "so you can find a group that fits you no matter what." Intercollegiate sports are another big pastime, "basketball, field hockey, and football in particular." Wake students love their Demon Deacons, and the teams fight well above their weight, pulling down ACC championships against far larger and less academically renowned schools. Intramurals are also very popular. Students are split regarding the appeal of hometown Winston-Salem. On one hand, it's "a very spread-out city" located in a residential area with no easy access to commerce. On the other hand, it's also "a perfectly gorgeous southern location" filled with "plenty of art galleries, theaters, coffeehouses, bookstores, shops, etc."

Student Body

"There is a lot of Southern prep at Wake Forest" and "a slight air of materialism." "Most people fit into the preppy white kid stereotype," observes a first-year student, "even the non-white students." The typical undergrad is basically "your all-American" kid. Nearly two-thirds of the students here receive some form of financial aid. At the same time, many students come from "well-to-do" families. "Pearl-wearing, North Face jacket-owning, Kate Spade-toting, Greek letter-wearing" types are quite common. Students tell us they range from "really friendly" to "exceedingly perky." They also tend to be athletic. "Everyone works out a bunch, and the few overweight students do stick out." "Politically, most kids are moderates—perhaps a bit right of center, but not drastically so," and "rightwing and leftwing groups tend to be vocal about their views." Some students suggest that Wake "could do with more diversity." At the same time, there is general agreement that atypical students assimilate just fine. "They seem to enjoy themselves, and they did choose to attend our school," relates a senior. "However, there are certainly not many of them."

FINANCIAL AID: 336-758-5154 • E-MAIL: ADMISSIONS@WFU.EDU • WEBSITE: WWW.WFU.EDU

THE PRINCETON REVIEW SAYS

Admissions

Very important factors considered include: Class rank, application essay, academic GPA, rigor of secondary school record, standardized test scores, character/personal qualities, *Important factors considered include:* recommendation(s), extracurricular activities, talent/ability. *Other factors considered include:* alumni/ae relation, first generation, geographical residence, interview, level of applicant's interest, racial/ethnic status, religious affiliation/commitment, state residency, volunteer work, SAT or ACT required; ACT with Writing component required. TOEFL required of all international applicants. High school diploma is required and GED is accepted. *Academic units required:* 4 English, 3 mathematics, 1 science, 2 foreign language, 2 social studies, *Academic units recommended:* 4 English, 4 mathematics, 4 science, 4 foreign language, 4 social studies.

Financial Aid

Students should submit: FAFSA, CSS/Financial Aid, state aid form, noncustodial PROFILE. Regular filing deadline is 3/1. The Princeton Review suggests that all financial aid forms be submitted as soon as possible after 1/1. *Need-based scholarships/grants offered:* Federal Pell, SEOG, state scholarships/grants, private scholarships, the school's own gift aid. *Loan aid offered:* FFEL Subsidized Stafford, FFEL Unsubsidized Stafford, FFEL PLUS, Federal Perkins, state loans, college/university loans from institutional funds. Other Applicants will be notified of awards on a rolling basis beginning 4/1. Federal Work-Study Program available. Institutional employment available. Off-campus job opportunities are excellent.

The Inside Word

Wake Forest's considerable application numbers afford admissions officers the opportunity to be rather selective. In particular, admissions officers remain diligent in their matchmaking efforts—finding students who are good fits for the school—and their hard work is rewarded by a high graduation rate. Candidates will need to be impressive in all areas to gain admission, since all areas of their applications are considered carefully. A relatively large number of qualified students find themselves on Wake Forest's wait list.

THE SCHOOL SAYS "..."

From The Admissions Office

"Wake Forest University has been dedicated to the liberal arts for over a century and a half; this means education in the fundamental fields of human knowledge and achievement. It seeks to encourage habits of mind that ask why, that evaluate evidence, that are open to new ideas, that attempt to understand and appreciate the perspective of others, that accept complexity and grapple with it, that admit error, and that pursue truth.

"Wake Forest is among a small, elite group of American colleges and universities recognized for their outstanding academic quality. It offers small classes taught by full-time faculty—not graduate assistants—and a commitment to student interaction with those professors. Students are provided ThinkPad computers and color printer/scanner/copiers. Classrooms and residence halls are fully networked. Wake Forest maintains a need-blind admissions policy by which qualified students are admitted regardless of their financial circumstances.

"Applicants are required to submit scores from the SAT Reasoning Test and/or the ACT plus Writing. SAT Subject Tests are strongly recommended for students planning to apply for merit-based scholarships."

SELECTIVITY	
Admissions Rating	95
# of applicants	7,177
% of applicants accepted	42
% of acceptees attending	37
# of early decision applicants	630
% accepted early decision	59

FRESHMAN PROFILE	
Range SAT Critical Reading	610–700
Range SAT Math	630–710
Range ACT Composite	27–31
Minimum paper TOEFL	600
Minimum computer TOEFL	250
% graduated top 10% of class	64
% graduated top 25% of class	91
% graduated top 50% of class	99

DEADLINES	
Early Decision	
Deadline	11/15
Notification	12/15
Regular	
Deadline	1/15
Notification	4/1
Nonfall registration?	yes

APPLICANTS ALSO LOOK AT AND SOMETIMES PREFER
University of Virginia
Duke University
University of North Carolina at Chapel Hill

FINANCIAL FACTS	
Financial Aid Rating	84
Annual tuition	$36,560
Room and board	$9,867
Required fees	$415
Books and supplies	$850
% frosh rec. need-based scholarship or grant aid	26
% UG rec. need-based scholarship or grant aid	31
% frosh rec. non-need-based scholarship or grant aid	19
% UG rec. non-need-based scholarship or grant aid	22
% frosh rec. need-based self-help aid	23
% UG rec. need-based self-help aid	28
% frosh rec. athletic scholarships	5
% UG rec. athletic scholarships	4
% frosh rec. any financial aid	39
% UG rec. any financial aid	34
% UG borrow to pay for school	37
Average cumulative indebtedness	$23,397

WARREN WILSON COLLEGE

PO Box 9000, ASHEVILLE, NC 28815-9000 • ADMISSIONS: 828-771-2073 • FAX: 828-298-1440

CAMPUS LIFE
Quality of Life Rating	**92**
Fire Safety Rating	**60***
Green Rating	**96**
Type of school	private
Affiliation	Presbyterian
Environment	village

STUDENTS
Total undergrad enrollment	900
% male/female	38/62
% from out of state	89
% from public high school	71
% live on campus	85
% African American	1
% Asian	1
% Caucasian	90
% Hispanic	3
% international	3
# of countries represented	12

SURVEY SAYS . . .
Lots of liberal students
Students are friendly
Low cost of living
Frats and sororities are unpopular or nonexistent
Political activism is popular
(Almost) no one smokes

ACADEMICS
Academic Rating	**81**
Calendar	semester
Student/faculty ratio	13:1
Profs interesting rating	85
Profs accessible rating	84
Most common reg class size	10–19 students

MOST POPULAR MAJORS
environmental science
creative writing
outdoor leadership
English
global studies

STUDENTS SAY ". . ."

Academics

Warren Wilson's unique approach to education is encapsulated in its "Triad program." This distinctive curriculum combines academics with "work and service." And though this program might demand more of your time, undergrads here speak quite highly of it. As one psych major shares, Triad "allows students to deepen their understanding of the world's needs and prepares them for a lifestyle of service beyond college." Additionally, it's an "active style of learning" that "really pushes students...to become well-rounded individuals." Undergrads are especially enthusiastic about the college's "environmental focus and strong science programs." There is "a working farm on campus that students run, and it [lends] excellent opportunity for hands-on experience." Undergrads also laud the "good creative writing department." Importantly, "the majority of the faculty are genuinely interested in the well-being of each and every student." Professors are "easy to talk to and highly available." This accessibility extends to the administration as well. As one impressed junior tells us that, "we know our administration by first name, and if we want to talk to them, it's no problem to schedule an appointment or have the admin attend a student government meeting."

Life

Undergrads at Warren Wilson tend to lead hectic lives. Many concur that "students are really busy during the week" and therefore view the weekend as "a time for release." However, the intellectual debates don't just stop because it's leisure time. As one freshman shares, life often "revolves around political arguments and philosophical discussions held over cans of Pabst Blue Ribbon." Of course, activities extend beyond delightful and thought-provoking conversation. Students "greatly enjoy" the outdoors, and many can often be found "exploring trails, visiting the animals on the farm, swimming, kayaking, and canoeing on the Swannanoa River." Additionally, "fall soccer games, Friday night themed dance parties...and Thursday night contra dances" are all well attended. And one senior adds that "poetry slams, talent shows, theatrical productions, and parties that are held in the common areas of the dorms" are all great fun. Students are also "very politically and environmentally active, and community service" is extremely popular. Venturing into downtown Asheville is common as well. The town center is only "a 15-minute ride from campus, and there is a bus that goes back and forth during specific hours." The "funky" area has "a great arts and music scene," and "there are lots of concerts, performances, restaurants and local stores to visit."

Student Body

Warren Wilson is a college that "is very open to the idea of individuality" and thus manages to attract "a wide range of students." Many undergrads proclaim their peers to be "dynamic people" who are all "atypical." As a sophomore proudly boasts, "The great thing about this school is that a person, in all their weirdness, is loved and embraced by the community." Of course, for all this diversity, some commonalities do seep through. The "vast majority of people who go here are liberal" and are concerned "with social justice issues." Indeed, the mantle "hippie" is frequently bandied about. While some might object to this stereotype, many undergrads are "committed to environmental awareness." And a freshman notes that his fellow students "care about the outdoors, recycle, unplug appliances not in use, and would rather eat an organic salad than a steak." Additionally, most undergrads are hard-working and very industrious, constantly thinking of new projects to do and coming up with interesting ideas." But perhaps this math major sums up his peers best, "If you like people with weird haircuts, people with a different gender identity, vegans, feminists, and future organic farmers—or are one of these people—you will probably fit right in."

FINANCIAL AID: 828-298-3325 • E-MAIL: ADMIT@WARREN-WILSON.EDU • WEBSITE: WWW.WARREN-WILSON.EDU

THE PRINCETON REVIEW SAYS

Admissions

Very important factors considered include: Application essay, rigor of secondary school record, standardized test scores, character/personal qualities, interview, volunteer work, work experience. *Important factors considered include:* Class rank, recommendation(s). *Other factors considered include:* alumni/ae relation, extracurricular activities, state residency, talent/ability, SAT or ACT required; TOEFL required of all international applicants. High school diploma is required and GED is accepted. *Academic units required:* 4 English, 3 mathematics, 2 science, (2 science labs), 3 history, *Academic units recommended:* 2 foreign language.

Financial Aid

Students should submit: FAFSA, institution's own financial aid form, state aid form The Princeton Review suggests that all financial aid forms be submitted as soon as possible after 1/1. *Need-based scholarships/grants offered:* Federal Pell, SEOG, state scholarships/grants, the school's own gift aid. *Loan aid offered:* FFEL Subsidized Stafford, FFEL Unsubsidized Stafford, FFEL PLUS, Federal Perkins, college/university loans from institutional funds. Applicants will be notified of awards on a rolling basis beginning 3/2.

The Inside Word

At Warren Wilson College, one's sense of social commitment is as vital to the admissions process as one's high school transcript—the college desires students who are actively engaged in their communities. Admissions officers are interested in applicants who seek to make connections and who understand how to apply what they learn in the classroom to outside projects and activities.

THE SCHOOL SAYS "..."

From The Admissions Office

"This book is *The Best 371 Colleges*, but Warren Wilson College may not be the best college for many students. There are 3,500 colleges in the U.S., and there is a best place for everyone. The 'best college' is one that has the right size, location, programs, and above all, the right feel for you, even if it is not listed here. Warren Wilson College may be the best choice if you think and act independently, actively participate in your education, and want a college that provides a sense of community. Your hands will get dirty here, your mind will be stretched, and you'll not be anonymous. If you are looking for the traditional college experience with football and frats and a campus on a quad, this probably is not the right place. However, if you want to be a part of an academic community that works and serves together, this might be exactly what you are looking for.

"Students applying for fall admission should provide results of the SAT or ACT."

SELECTIVITY

Admissions Rating	87
# of applicants	1,300
% of applicants accepted	75
% of acceptees attending	37
# of early decision applicants	77
% accepted early decision	90

FRESHMAN PROFILE

Range SAT Critical Reading	540–670
Range SAT Math	500–610
Range SAT Writing	530–640
Minimum paper TOEFL	550
Average HS GPA	3.43
% graduated top 10% of class	22
% graduated top 25% of class	42
% graduated top 50% of class	83

DEADLINES

Early Decision	
Deadline	11/15
Notification	12/1
Regular	
Deadline	2/15
Nonfall registration?	yes

APPLICANTS ALSO LOOK AT AND OFTEN PREFER
Earlham College

FINANCIAL FACTS

Financial Aid Rating	70
Annual tuition	$24,195
Room and board	$7,730
Required fees	$300
Books and supplies	$870
% frosh rec. need-based scholarship or grant aid	47
% UG rec. need-based scholarship or grant aid	48
% frosh rec. non-need-based scholarship or grant aid	33
% UG rec. non-need-based scholarship or grant aid	27
% frosh rec. need-based self-help aid	51
% UG rec. need-based self-help aid	54
% UG borrow to pay for school	29
Average cumulative indebtedness	$20,554

WASHINGTON COLLEGE

300 WASHINGTON AVENUE, CHESTERTOWN, MD 21620 • ADMISSIONS: 410-778-7700 • FAX: 410-778-7287

CAMPUS LIFE

Quality of Life Rating	70
Fire Safety Rating	96
Green Rating	60*
Type of school	private
Environment	rural

STUDENTS

Total undergrad enrollment	1,275
male/female	41/59
% from out of state	49
% from public high school	63
% live on campus	82
% in (# of) fraternities	8 (3)
% in (# of) sororities	14 (3)
% African American	5
% Asian	1
% Caucasian	85
% Hispanic	1
% international	2
# of countries represented	28

SURVEY SAYS . . .

Lab facilities are great
Students are friendly
Student government is popular
Lots of beer drinking
Hard liquor is popular

ACADEMICS

Academic Rating	84
Calendar	semester
Student/faculty ratio	11:1
Profs interesting rating	88
Profs accessible rating	87
Most common reg class size	10–19 students
Most common lab size	10–19 students

MOST POPULAR MAJORS

business management
psychology
english

STUDENTS SAY ". . ."

Academics

Washington College is a small, private liberal arts college in eastern Maryland that is "steeped in history." It's the tenth oldest college in the United States. Undergraduate research is commonplace here, and internships are tremendous. Study abroad is "really big" and available in about two dozen destinations around the world. The creative writing program is "well respected." Other notable majors include business and theater. Course selection "isn't that great," but academics are "challenging." Some classes "have upwards of 50 people in them" but most are pretty intimate. Usually, "there is a great deal of individualized attention," and "there is no hiding in the back of the classroom." Washington College's "caring" professors are "ridiculously eager about their subjects." Most are "willing to meet outside of class or chat through e-mail" and "willing to go the extra mile." "My professors treat me as an individual and more than just the kid they have to grind the information into," relates an English major. Complaints include the library, which isn't much. Some students also grumble about tuition and call WAC "a money pit." The "ambitious" administration "does everything possible to keep students happy in most aspects of life," but the top brass can be "out of touch" and, sometimes, things "just don't run very smoothly."

Life

"The food on campus is usually not very good and sometimes difficult to eat." Some students say they like the way Washington College "combines colonial charm with modern facilities." Others disagree. "Concrete plus brick equals ugly," asserts a senior. Socially, WAC is "close-knit." "The general atmosphere is comfortable and laid-back." "Pretty much everything happens on campus." "Numerous speakers and musical events" are frequent. There are "strong" athletic programs. Men's lacrosse is especially huge. Fraternities and sororities aren't overwhelming here but they are certainly noticeable. On the weekends, "parties are plentiful." "If you don't drink alcohol, this school isn't for you," advises a junior. The festivities around May Day get especially crazy. Off campus, "there really is nothing to do at all" in "sleepy," "remote," and "very rural" Chestertown. "Many old people live there." "The waterfront area of town is nice." If you want to, you can wakeboard, water ski, and sail to your heart's content. Otherwise, there are a few "little trinket and book shops," but that's about it. "The closet mall is 45 minutes" away. There's "a shuttle that runs to D.C. and Annapolis on the weekends," but "transportation is highly recommended." Many students with cars head to Baltimore and Philadelphia for day trips.

Student Body

"I find this school to be extremely diverse," indicates a first-year student. "Granted, we might have had four black kids in my high school." There's "a fun bunch" of international students and smattering of minorities but "Washington College, embodied in a human would be white." Some students "come from a rural way of life," and there are many middle-class students who "depend on fairly generous scholarships." However, a large contingent of students comes "from private high schools" in "wealthy suburbs" in "New Jersey, Maryland, or Pennsylvania." "Most of us are pretty smart, go to class, and participate in extracurriculars," says a junior. There are "meathead athletes and musicians with tweed jackets." There also "tree huggers, rock climbers, wannabe rockers, dramatists, philosophers, future business leaders," and "your average goths and freaks." On the whole, though, the culture is very preppy. "It would be possible to believe Polo sponsors our students, because it is everywhere," explains a sophomore. "The kids are generic." "Cliques" are reportedly noticeable on this campus, and "boundaries are definitely defined." However, "there is a real sense of community" as well. "Everyone knows everyone," says a junior, "so it's very hard to be excluded."

FINANCIAL AID: 410-778-7214 • WEBSITE: HTTP://ADMISSIONS.WASHCOLL.EDU

THE PRINCETON REVIEW SAYS

Admissions

Very important factors considered include: Academic GPA, rigor of secondary school record, interview, *Important factors considered include:* Class rank, standardized test scores, level of applicant's interest. *Other factors considered include:* Application essay, recommendation(s), alumni/ae relation, character/personal qualities, extracurricular activities, first generation, geographical residence, racial/ethnic status, state residency, talent/ability, volunteer work, work experience. SAT or ACT required; High school diploma is required and GED is accepted. *Academic units required:* 4 English, 3 mathematics, 3 science, (2 science labs), 2 foreign language, 2 social studies, 2 history, *Academic units recommended:* 4 English, 4 mathematics, 4 science, (3 science labs), 4 foreign language, 4 social studies.

Financial Aid

Students should submit: FAFSA, institution's own financial aid form The Princeton Review suggests that all financial aid forms be submitted as soon as possible after 1/1. *Need-based scholarships/grants offered:* Federal Pell, SEOG, state scholarships/grants, private scholarships, the school's own gift aid. *Loan aid offered:* FFEL Subsidized Stafford, FFEL Unsubsidized Stafford, FFEL PLUS, Federal Perkins, college/university loans from institutional funds. Applicants will be notified of awards on a rolling basis beginning 3/15. Federal Work-Study Program available. Institutional employment available. Off-campus job opportunities are good.

The Inside Word

Though Washington's acceptance rate hovers just less than 70 percent, the statistic belies the competitive nature of the applicants. Prospective students who view WC as one of their top choices should do themselves a favor and complete their application ahead of the prescribed deadline. Interviews are also highly recommended and those who decline the opportunity will be putting themselves at a disadvantage.

THE SCHOOL SAYS "..."

From The Admissions Office

"We tell our students, 'Your revolution starts here,' because the person who graduates from Washington College is not the same one who matriculated 4 years earlier, and because through your experiences here, you will be empowered and emboldened to change the world. Your education reflects the maxims of our founder, George Washington: The strength of America's democracy depends on the success of students like you to evolve as a critical and independent thinker, to persevere in the face of challenge, to assume the responsibilities and privileges of informed citizenship. That's where we come in, providing a truly personalized education that tests—and stretches—the limits of each student's talents and potentials. We reach beyond the classroom to create challenges and opportunities that expand your brainpower and creativity through collaborative research with faculty, through independent and self-directed study, and through the rigor of creating a senior project that demonstrates the power of a maturing intellect. All this happens in a wonderfully distinct setting—in historic Chestertown, on the Chester River, amid the ecological bounty of Maryland's Chesapeake Bay—that helps define who we are, and that will shape your own college experience.

"Freshman applicants with a cumulative high school grade point average of 3.50 or better (on a 4.00 scale) or with a top ten percent class rank can request and be granted a 'score optional' admission review."

SELECTIVITY

Admissions Rating	88
# of applicants	3,413
% of applicants accepted	69
% of acceptees attending	18
# accepting a place on wait list	245
% admitted from wait list	60
# of early decision applicants	68
% accepted early decision	93

FRESHMAN PROFILE

Range SAT Critical Reading	530–630
Range SAT Math	510–610
Range SAT Writing	520–620
Range ACT Composite	22–26
Average HS GPA	3.39
% graduated top 10% of class	29
% graduated top 25% of class	65
% graduated top 50% of class	88

DEADLINES

Early Decision	
Deadline	11/1
Notification	12/1
Early action	
Deadline	11/15
Notification	12/15
Regular	
Priority	2/1
Deadline	3/1
Notification	rolling
Nonfall registration?	yes

FINANCIAL FACTS

Financial Aid Rating	90
Annual tuition	$34,690
Room and board	$7,460
Required fees	$660
Books and supplies	$1,250
% frosh rec. need-based scholarship or grant aid	50
% UG rec. need-based scholarship or grant aid	50
% frosh rec. non-need-based scholarship or grant aid	28
% UG rec. non-need-based scholarship or grant aid	32
% frosh rec. need-based self-help aid	29
% UG rec. need-based self-help aid	42
% frosh rec. any financial aid	40
% UG rec. any financial aid	78
% UG borrow to pay for school	79
Average cumulative indebtedness	$20,611

WASHINGTON & JEFFERSON COLLEGE

OFFICE OF ADMISSIONS, 60 SOUTH LINCOLN STREET, WASHINGTON, PA 15301 • ADMISSIONS: 888-W-AND-JAY OR 724-223-6025

CAMPUS LIFE

Quality of Life Rating	72
Fire Safety Rating	85
Green Rating	85
Type of school	private
Environment	village

STUDENTS

Total undergrad enrollment	1,488
% male/female	54/46
% from out of state	25
% from public high school	83
% live on campus	95
% in (# of) fraternities	40 (6)
% in (# of) sororities	44 (4)
% African American	3
% Asian	1
% Caucasian	86
% Hispanic	1
# of countries represented	11

SURVEY SAYS . . .

Low cost of living
Frats and sororities dominate social
scene
(Almost) no one smokes
Very little drug use

ACADEMICS

Academic Rating	85
Calendar	4/1/4
Student/faculty ratio	12:1
Profs interesting rating	86
Profs accessible rating	88
Most common reg class size	10–19 students
Most common lab size	10–19 students

MOST POPULAR MAJORS

business/commerce
English language and literature
psychology

STUDENTS SAY ". . ."

Academics

Washington & Jefferson College is an "intimate" and "prestigious" bastion of the liberal arts in western Pennsylvania. The 4-1-4 academic calendar here is fairly unique. In addition to two conventional semesters, a January term allows students to focus on a single course or to pursue an internship or study abroad in places like Japan, Germany, and Tanzania. A broad set of graduation requirements and "the liberal arts aspect creates well-rounded individuals." More than 40 majors and programs are available. W&J boasts "a great track record with law school admissions." Premed is also "excellent." The academic atmosphere is "wonderfully rigorous." "Small classes make for some good discussions." Coursework ranges from "intense" to "outrageously challenging." Students rarely miss class. "Absences are regarded as strange." The faculty receives high marks. "There are a few who really ought to retire," but most professors are "very knowledgeable and seem to fully enjoy the classes they are teaching." They are "dedicated" and "really personable." They "go out of their way to make themselves accessible" and "do whatever they can to help you." "They all care about me," says a satisfied econ major. "They want me to do well. They want me to learn a lot." The administration is "down-to-earth" and "always looking for student input." Career Services is "extremely helpful" as well. Employment placement is "impressive." "Great alumni connections" definitely help in this regard. "Alumni are always offering to take students under their wings," notes a biology major.

Life

"Someone once described W&J to me as a "mullet," remembers a sophomore. "Business in the front with a party in the back." During the week, students are "very busy." Academics are "pivotal." Scores of students play varsity, club, or intramural sports as well. "Almost everyone is involved in a couple different activities." "Sunday through Friday afternoon is all work, for sure," counsels a junior. "When the weekend rolls around," justifies a junior, "we deserve to have some fun." As such, "most of the students drink themselves into a stupor." "Going to the frats is the most common weekend fun." "It gets repetitive, but it's all we have," relates a sophomore. The Greek system here is the primary organizing force of social life, and it's "very popular." However, "If the party scene is not for a student, there are usually other forms of entertainment offered by the school." "If you don't drink, it's not hard to find things to do," says a first-year student. "But it's hard to find fun things to do." The hilly campus here is "beautiful" and traditional-looking. Several buildings need renovation, though. The dorms in particular "could be updated and made a lot nicer." "Other than the new dorms built a few years ago for seniors, living conditions are absolutely terrible." Also, the four-year residency requirement really rankles. "They force you to live on campus," explains a junior. "Getting off campus is like fighting your own personal war." Other complaints include "limited" wireless internet access and the meal plans, which are "a rip off." Off-campus, the surrounding town is "dull" at best and "scary" at worst. Pittsburgh is "only 30 minutes away," though, and expeditions there are "a frequent thing."

Student Body

W&J is "extremely homogenous." "We're pretty much all the same," admits a junior. "Although the school promotes diversity, there isn't a lot of it." "Mostly, the school consists of white students from relatively average or high socioeconomic backgrounds." You'll fit in especially well if you come from "suburban" "western Pennsylvania or Ohio." "If you are 'different' or eclectic in personal expression in some way and really want to develop that, then I would pick a different school," advises a senior. "If you like to wear sweats to class all the time but don't mind looking cute every now and then, then this is a good school for you." Students here are "fit" and "preppy." Many are "athletes who really break the dumb-jock mold." They are "laid-back but ambitious." They are "goal-oriented." They "take their academics fairly seriously" and have a "great work ethic." Some students tell us the campus is "close-knit." Others say "there are a lot of cliques." Whatever the case, "everyone seems to get along."

FAX : 724-223-6534 • FINANCIAL AID: 724-223-6019 • E-MAIL: ADMISSION@WASHJEFF.EDU • WEBSITE: WWW.WASHJEFF.EDU

THE PRINCETON REVIEW SAYS

Admissions

Very important factors considered include: Class rank, application essay, academic GPA, recommendation(s), rigor of secondary school record, character/personal qualities, interview, *Important factors considered include:* standardized test scores, extracurricular activities. *Other factors considered include:* alumni/ae relation, geographical residence, level of applicant's interest, racial/ethnic status, state residency, talent/ability, volunteer work, SAT or ACT required; TOEFL required of all international applicants. High school diploma is required and GED is accepted. *Academic units required:* 3 English, 3 mathematics, 2 foreign language, 1 history, 6 or more academic courses from English, Mathematics, Foreign Language, History (Social or Natural).

Financial Aid

Students should submit: FAFSA. The Princeton Review suggests that all financial aid forms be submitted as soon as possible after 1/1. *Need-based scholarships/grants offered:* Federal Pell, SEOG, state scholarships/grants, private scholarships, the school's own gift aid, ACG and SMART Grants. *Loan aid offered:* FFEL Subsidized Stafford, FFEL Unsubsidized Stafford, FFEL PLUS, Federal Perkins, college/university loans from institutional funds. Applicants will be notified of awards on a rolling basis beginning 3/1. Federal Work-Study Program available. Institutional employment available. Off-campus job opportunities are good.

The Inside Word

In a reflection of the students the school aims aim to admit, Washington & Jefferson College takes a well-rounded approach to admissions. Academic record, class rank, personal statement, and extracurricular activities are all thoroughly evaluated. Most prospective students work diligently to secure admittance. The lucky applicants who receive a fat letter in the mail are welcomed into a distinctive community that promises to broaden their horizons and to prepare them for a successful future.

THE SCHOOL SAYS "..."

From The Admissions Office

"There is a palpable sense of momentum and energy at Washington & Jefferson. Enrollment has grown significantly over the past 5 years. Additional faculty members have been hired, and academic programs have been added and expanded to accommodate the increased enrollment. The student-centered teaching and learning community that has always distinguished W&J remains our top priority. It is no surprise that 100 percent of our graduates who took the bar exam in the last three years passed, or that 90 percent of our graduates recommended for medical and law school are admitted. The college has added almost $100 million dollars in new facilities since 2002, including new residence halls, new athletic facilities, a state-of-the-art technology center, and the Howard J. Burnett Center, which houses our programs in accounting, business, economics, education, entrepreneurial studies, and modern languages. The new $33 million John A. Swanson Science Center, dedicated to the physical sciences, including physics, chemistry, biochemistry, and bioinformatics, is on track to open in 2010. Also, unique to W&J is the Magellan Project, which provides stipends for innovative internships, prestigious research fellowships, and independent study-travel programs either domestically or abroad. Despite an almost fourfold increase in applications in this time, the Admission Staff remains committed to reviewing each application individually. Our students are balanced, goal oriented, active, engaged and involved and we look for evidence of these traits in prospective students. We encourage students to use every aspect of the application process to demonstrate that they possess these qualities. If you are the kind of student who thrives on challenge, who wants a close personal relationship with top-notch faculty, and who values being a member of a true college community, then we encourage you to consider W&J. W&J recommends but does not require students to submit scores from the SAT (or ACT). We will use the student's best scores from either test."

SELECTIVITY

Admissions Rating	92
# of applicants	6,826
% of applicants accepted	38
% of acceptees attending	15
# accepting a place on wait list	30
% admitted from wait list	60
# of early decision applicants	8
% accepted early decision	50

FRESHMAN PROFILE

Range SAT Critical Reading	510–610
Range SAT Math	530–630
Range ACT Composite	22–26
Minimum paper TOEFL	567
Minimum computer TOEFL	227
Minimum web-based TOEFL	86
Average HS GPA	3.39
% graduated top 10% of class	39
% graduated top 25% of class	74
% graduated top 50% of class	97

DEADLINES

Early Decision	
Deadline	12/1
Notification	12/15
Early action	
Deadline	1/15
Notification	2/15
Regular	
Priority	1/15
Deadline	3/1
Notification	rolling
Nonfall registration?	yes

FINANCIAL FACTS

Financial Aid Rating	74
Annual tuition	$32,495
Room and board	$9,110
Required fees	$450
Books and supplies	$800
% frosh rec. need-based scholarship or grant aid	70
% UG rec. need-based scholarship or grant aid	57
% frosh rec. non-need-based scholarship or grant aid	70
% UG rec. non-need-based scholarship or grant aid	62
% frosh rec. need-based self-help aid	68
% UG rec. need-based self-help aid	65
% frosh rec. any financial aid	99
% UG rec. any financial aid	96
% UG borrow to pay for school	75
Average cumulative indebtedness	$20,000

WASHINGTON STATE UNIVERSITY

370 LIGHTY STUDENT SERVICES, PULLMAN, WA 99164-1067 • ADMISSIONS: 888-468-6978 • FAX: 509-335-4902

CAMPUS LIFE

Quality of Life Rating	**71**
Fire Safety Rating	**81**
Green Rating	**89**
Type of school	public
Environment	town

STUDENTS

Total undergrad enrollment	20,690
% male/female	48/52
% from out of state	8
% from public high school	99
% live on campus	36
% in (# of) fraternities	15 (25)
% in (# of) sororities	20 (15)
% African American	2
% Asian	6
% Caucasian	75
% Hispanic	5
% Native American	1
% international	3
# of countries represented	91

SURVEY SAYS . . .

Athletic facilities are great
Everyone loves the Cougars
Frats and sororities dominate social scene
Student publications are popular
Lots of beer drinking
Hard liquor is popular

ACADEMICS

Academic Rating	**70**
Calendar	semester
Student/faculty ratio	14:1
Profs interesting rating	64
Profs accessible rating	67
% classes taught by TAs	8
Most common reg class size	10–19 students

MOST POPULAR MAJORS

marketing/marketing management
social sciences

STUDENTS SAY "..."

Academics

"A moderately large research university with some very good programs," Washington State University delivers quality and value in a pleasant small-town environment to Washington residents and out-of-state students alike. The Edward R. Murrow College of Communications is among WSU's major drawing cards. The university also boasts a veterinary program "that is one of the leading programs in the nation," a business school whose offerings include a "great MIS program," a "very good agriculture program," solid offerings in plant sciences, zoology, and molecular biosciences, and programs in material science and engineering in which "students have good contact with professors." In fact, throughout the university professors are typically "extremely accessible and work very well with the students. My math professor even plays basketball with all the students at our state-of-the-art rec center every week." As at any school, "when you get a bad professor, look out, but fortunately the majority of professors at WSU are good and want you to do well." Even the administration, often the whipping boy of students at large state schools, earns mostly good marks. One undergrad writes, "The administration— the criticisms of some students notwithstanding—is actually working hard to improve the school's quality, which is noticeable and appreciated." Some even report sensing that "staff actually cares about you as a person, and not just as another random number who pays $20,000 a year. They care about my success, and I appreciate that."

Life

"The weekends are thriving" at WSU, where some head to small house parties while others beat a path to Greek Row, a popular destination. One student writes, "Every night of the weekend (and sometimes during the week) there is a party you can go to...People who are 21 go to one of the three bars near campus around 11 P.M. and can dance and drink the rest of the night. I love the party scene at WSU, it's a great way to meet friends and potential interests." Some contend "if you don't like to party, options are a bit limited," but others point to a broad range of athletic events ("Student camaraderie is outstanding at basketball and football games!") and extracurriculars as alternate options. Hometown Pullman "is tiny, with only 27,000 people, of whom 20,000 are students." Many here relish the environment, pointing out "it is such a small community, you know it is safe to walk around by yourself at night" and noting "while some people complain about boredom here, they usually are not very social. With 20,000-plus undergraduates you have to lock yourself in your room to not find something to do."

Students

"It's hard to define a typical student" at WSU, as "there are a lot of students from rural areas of Washington and quite a few from suburban areas" along with what students say seems like a fair share of "rich white kids from Seattle." Students tell us "it's definitely not a yuppie school. Most people are down -to-earth and lean a little conservative politically," but there's a substantial liberal population as well. Most importantly, "most of these people are very tolerant, so there is no real worry about expressing your beliefs and being attacked for them." Minorities "are definitely outnumbered on campus, but the school has numerous cultural events to encourage diversity and to get everyone to interact. The largest ethnic groups on campus (after Caucasian) include Hawaiian, Asian, Hispanic, and African American." One minority student reports, "All in all, it's not hard to fit in here. Students are extraordinarily friendly, and the guys constantly open doors for the ladies, or vice versa. Little things like that indicate how fun, friendly, and welcoming people are here."

FINANCIAL AID: 509-335-9711 • E-MAIL: ADMISS2@WSU.EDU • WEBSITE: WWW.WSU.EDU

THE PRINCETON REVIEW SAYS

Admissions

Very important factors considered include: Academic GPA, standardized test scores, *Important factors considered include:* Class rank, application essay, rigor of secondary school record. *Other factors considered include:* recommendation(s), character/personal qualities, extracurricular activities, talent/ability, volunteer work, work experience. SAT or ACT required; TOEFL required of all international applicants. High school diploma is required and GED is accepted. *Academic units required:* 4 English, 3 mathematics, 2 science, (1 science labs), 2 foreign language, 3 social studies, 1 visual/performing arts, 1 academic electives, *Academic units recommended:* 4 English, 4 mathematics, 2 science, (1 science labs), 2 foreign language, 3 social studies, 1 visual/performing arts, 1 academic electives.

Financial Aid

Students should submit: FAFSA. The Princeton Review suggests that all financial aid forms be submitted as soon as possible after 1/1. *Need-based scholarships/grants offered:* Federal Pell, SEOG, state scholarships/grants, private scholarships, the school's own gift aid, United Negro College Fund, Federal Nursing Scholarships. *Loan aid offered:* FFEL Subsidized Stafford, FFEL Unsubsidized Stafford, FFEL PLUS, Federal Perkins, Federal Nursing Applicants will be notified of awards on a rolling basis beginning 4/15. Federal Work-Study Program available. Institutional employment available. Off-campus job opportunities are good.

The Inside Word

The huge number of applications WSU must process each year should leave Admissions Officers little time to consider anything other than grades, quality of curriculum, and standardized test scores. Yet WSU also encourages applicants to submit a personal statement and, presumably, takes the time to read them. Herein lies your chance to make up for an inconsistent high school record or less-than-optimal test scores. Make the most of your opportunity.

THE SCHOOL SAYS " . . ."

From The Admissions Office

"At Washington State University, you work side by side with nationally renowned faculty who help you succeed. Many academic programs rank among the nation's best. Programs are designed to give you real-world experience through internships, community service, in-depth labs, and study-abroad experiences. Plus, many disciplines encourage you to participate in faculty research or conduct your own. If you have top grades and a passion for learning, the highly acclaimed Honors College challenges you with interdisciplinary studies, rich classroom discussions, and research opportunities.

"The campus forms the heart of a friendly college town where faculty and peers help you achieve your greatest potential. More than 200 campus organizations connect you with others who share your interests and empower you to build leadership skills. Year after year, employers return to campus seeking Washington State University graduates and regard them as the best prepared in the state.

"In addition to the Pullman campus, WSU has three nonresidential urban campuses in Spokane, the TriCities (Richland), and Vancouver.

"The priority date to apply for admission and the deadline to apply for scholarships is January 31. For your candidacy to be considered, you must complete the high school core curriculum and provide official scores from the SAT or the ACT. We also urge you to deliver a strong personal statement (essay)."

SELECTIVITY

Admissions Rating	87
# of applicants	11,983
% of applicants accepted	72
% of acceptees attending	43
# accepting a place on wait list	515
% admitted from wait list	8

FRESHMAN PROFILE

Range SAT Critical Reading	490–600
Range SAT Math	510–610
Range ACT Composite	21–26
Minimum paper TOEFL	520
Minimum computer TOEFL	190
Minimum web-based TOEFL	68
Average HS GPA	3.48
% graduated top 10% of class	44
% graduated top 25% of class	61
% graduated top 50% of class	84

DEADLINES

Regular	
Priority	1/31
Notification	rolling
Nonfall registration?	yes

APPLICANTS ALSO LOOK AT

AND OFTEN PREFER

Eastern Washington University
Central Washington University
Western Washington University
University of Washington

AND SOMETIMES PREFER

Oregon State University
University of Oregon
University of Portland
Seattle University
University of Idaho
Gonzaga University

AND RARELY PREFER

Pacific Lutheran University
Seattle Pacific University
Arizona State University at the Tempe Campus

FINANCIAL FACTS

Financial Aid Rating	74
Annual tuition in-state	$6,720
Annual tuitions out-of-state	$17,756
% frosh rec. need-based scholarship or grant aid	24
% UG rec. need-based scholarship or grant aid	33
% frosh rec. non-need-based scholarship or grant aid	29
% UG rec. non-need-based scholarship or grant aid	17
% frosh rec. need-based self-help aid	33
% UG rec. need-based self-help aid	42
% frosh rec. athletic scholarships	2
% UG rec. athletic scholarships	2
% frosh rec. any financial aid	81
% UG rec. any financial aid	67

WASHINGTON UNIVERSITY IN ST. LOUIS

CAMPUS BOX 1089, ONE BROOKINGS DRIVE, ST. LOUIS, MO 63130-4899 • ADMISSIONS: 314-935-6000 • FAX: 314-935-4290

CAMPUS LIFE

Quality of Life Rating	**99**
Fire Safety Rating	**86**
Green Rating	**60***
Type of school	private
Environment	city

STUDENTS

Total undergrad enrollment	6,339
% male/female	49/51
% from out of state	90
% from public high school	63
% live on campus	74
% in (# of) fraternities	25 (12)
% in (# of) sororities	25 (6)
% African American	10
% Asian	13
% Caucasian	61
% Hispanic	3
% international	4
# of countries represented	90

SURVEY SAYS . . .

Lab facilities are great
School is well run
Students are friendly
Great food on campus
Great off-campus food
Dorms are like palaces

ACADEMICS

Academic Rating	**96**
Calendar	semester
Student/faculty ratio	7:1
Profs interesting rating	83
Profs accessible rating	85
Most common reg class size	fewer than 10 students
Most common lab size	10–19 students

MOST POPULAR MAJORS

biology/biological sciences
finance
psychology

STUDENTS SAY ". . ."

Academics

"Rigorous but very rewarding," Washington University boasts a "strong" premed program, a "very intense" curriculum, and a "very, very stressful" academic atmosphere. "Teachers are tough," warns a biology major. "They have high expectations." "Architecture majors for instance, have so much work that they go for days without sleeping," observes a junior. Overall, though, students at Wash U wouldn't have it any other way. "I've had an amazing time since my first day of class," declares an English major. However, students aren't without complaints. "Distribution requirements are complicated and difficult for students to understand." "The engineering professors are very poor teachers." However, "All of my professors have been brilliant," says a chemistry major. "My only problem with them is some of them are so smart that they can't even conceive how I don't understand an idea." Professors "really care though." They "love to talk to their students," and they are remarkably accessible. Management is a huge hit. "Administrators realize that their first priority should be the students." "This school is also very wealthy and therefore offers greater opportunities than some schools would be able to." "From building amazing new facilities to creating world-class programs from scratch, it really feels like the sky is the limit."

Life

The food is "really amazing" on this "gorgeous campus." Dorms are reportedly fabulous, too. "Things are way too expensive," though. Outside of class, Wash U students hit the books hard. "The library is always incredibly crowded." "Campus involvement is big" as well, and "no one social scene dominates the campus." "Wash U is a bit of a bubble," describes a senior, "When you're here, the school experience shapes your entire lifestyle. It's a pleasant world, but [it's] hard to divorce yourself from the happy beauty of the campus and take note of the greater world and its problems." "Not every weekend is buck wild," but, of course, debauchery does happen. Some students "seem to live this strange double life of intense studying and partying." "A lot of students go to parties at the fraternities." There is little pressure to drink, though. "If you just want to stay in and watch a movie or play board games with friends," it's not a problem. The eclectic area next to campus—fondly called "The Loop"—is "a great neighborhood to walk to for restaurants, boutiques, and bars," though sketchy neighborhoods are mere blocks away. "St. Louis is a great sports town, so there are always great baseball, football, and hockey games," and there is some culture here but much of the city "shuts down after about 1 A.M."

Student Body

"Some people may say the typical student is a Jew from Long Island, but really this is just a hyped-up stereotype," says a junior. East Coasters definitely have a presence at Wash U, but Midwesterners predominate. The campus is "very ethnically diverse." However, "self-segregation is a big issue." "People who are very wealthy tend to hang out together," too. There is "a frantic premed culture," and, overall, the campus is "a little nerdy." "I hadn't seen so many hot geeks in one place until I came to Wash U," claims a first-year student. Jocks, punks, and goths are rare. "A lot of people look exactly the same. This isn't really the best place to explore your education or figure out what you want to do with your life," reflects a senior. "The typical students here have a plan and a goal they are working toward." These "overcommitted, fun-loving high-school all stars" are "pretty politically apathetic," but they have an array of other interests. "I think the thing that connects everyone is passion," suggests a sophomore. "Every student brings something different." "There are the students involved in way too many activities just for the sake of activities, the premeds, the counterculture and counter-counterculture art students, B-school partiers, intense architecture students, frat boys, sorority girls who promised themselves they would never join one, the ethnicity-obsessed, and then a huge melting pot of all of those mixed together."

FINANCIAL AID: 888-547-6670 • E-MAIL: ADMISSIONS@WUSTL.EDU • WEBSITE: WUSTL.EDU

THE PRINCETON REVIEW SAYS

Admissions

Very important factors considered include: Class rank, application essay, academic GPA, recommendation(s), rigor of secondary school record, standardized test scores, character/personal qualities, extracurricular activities, talent/ability, volunteer work, work experience. *Other factors considered include:* alumni/ae relation, first generation, interview, level of applicant's interest, racial/ethnic status, SAT or ACT required; TOEFL required of all international applicants. High school diploma is required and GED is accepted. *Academic units recommended:* 4 English, 4 mathematics, 4 science, (4 science labs), 2 foreign language, 4 social studies, 4 history.

Financial Aid

Students should submit: FAFSA, CSS/Financial Aid PROFILE, noncustodial PROFILE. Student and parent 1040 tax return or signed waiver if there is no tax return. Regular filing deadline is 2/15. The Princeton Review suggests that all financial aid forms be submitted as soon as possible after 1/1. *Need-based scholarships/grants offered:* Federal Pell, SEOG, state scholarships/grants, private scholarships, the school's own gift aid, United Negro College Fund, Federal Academic Competitive Grant, Federal SMART Grant. *Loan aid offered:* FFEL Subsidized Stafford, FFEL Unsubsidized Stafford, FFEL PLUS, Federal Perkins, state loans, college/university loans from institutional funds. Applicants will be notified of awards on or about 4/1. Federal Work-Study Program available. Institutional employment available. Off-campus job opportunities are excellent.

The Inside Word

The fact that Washington U doesn't have much play as a nationally respected car-window decal is about all that prevents it from being among the most selective universities. In every other respect—that is, in any way that really matters—this place is hard to beat and easily ranks as one of the best. No other university with as impressive a record of excellence across the board has a more accommodating admissions process. Not that it's easy to get in here, but lack of instant name recognition does affect Wash U's admission rate. Students with above-average academic records who are not quite Ivy material are the big winners. Marginal candidates with high financial need may find difficulty; the admissions process at Washington U is not need-blind and may take into account candidates' ability to pay if they are not strong applicants.

THE SCHOOL SAYS "..."

From The Admissions Office

"Washington University in St. Louis is a research university that offers a unique environment for undergraduate students to learn and grow. Unparalleled curriculum flexibility and learning opportunities in a friendly and supportive community inspire undergraduates to explore their interests and to develop new ones. Working with their advisors, undergraduates may choose a traditional single major, as many do. Others combine majors with minors, second majors, and pre-professional programs—all within their four-year undergraduate experience. We encourage our students to participate in internships, study-abroad programs, research and scholarship, and more than 200 clubs and organizations, rounding out Washington University's commitment to help each student identify and pursue his or her passion. Our students pursue their passions every day. Visit campus and ask them about their experiences. As part of this commitment to help our students, Washington University is working to eliminate need-based loans as part of its undergraduate financial aid awards to students from low-income families. This new initiative and its goal of helping families with the most need will not lessen our desire, responsibility, or ability to work with all families to ensure they have the financial resources they need. We remain committed to a flexible and independent approach to delivering financial aid to those who need it most. Applicants are required to submit scores from either the SAT or ACT test. Applicants who submit scores from the ACT test may submit with or without the Writing component."

SELECTIVITY

Admissions Rating	99
# of applicants	22,005
% of applicants accepted	22
% of acceptees attending	30

FRESHMAN PROFILE

Range SAT Critical Reading	680–760
Range SAT Math	700–780
Range ACT Composite	31–34
Minimum paper TOEFL	550
Minimum computer TOEFL	213
Minimum web-based TOEFL	79
% graduated top 10% of class	96
% graduated top 25% of class	100
% graduated top 50% of class	100

DEADLINES

Early Decision	
Deadline	11/15
Notification	12/15
Regular	
Deadline	1/15
Notification	4/1
Nonfall registration?	no

APPLICANTS ALSO LOOK AT

AND OFTEN PREFER
Harvard College
Stanford University
Yale University
University of Pennsylvania

AND SOMETIMES PREFER
Duke University
Northwestern University

FINANCIAL FACTS

Financial Aid Rating	99
Annual tuition	$37,800
Room and board	$12,465
Required fees	$1,064
Books and supplies	$1,280
% frosh rec. need-based scholarship or grant aid	36
% UG rec. need-based scholarship or grant aid	39
% frosh rec. non-need-based scholarship or grant aid	4
% UG rec. non-need-based scholarship or grant aid	3
% frosh rec. need-based self-help aid	28
% UG rec. need-based self-help aid	28
% frosh rec. any financial aid	38
% UG rec. any financial aid	40
% UG borrow to pay for school	40

WEBB INSTITUTE

298 CRESCENT BEACH ROAD, GLEN COVE, NY 11542 • ADMISSIONS: 516-671-2213 • FAX: 516-674-9838

CAMPUS LIFE

Quality of Life Rating	97
Fire Safety Rating	64
Green Rating	60*
Type of school	private
Environment	village

STUDENTS

Total undergrad enrollment	90
% male/female	82/18
% from out of state	78
% from public high school	76
% live on campus	100
% Asian	4
% Caucasian	91
% Hispanic	2

SURVEY SAYS . . .

Registration is a breeze
Career services are great
Different types of students interact
Dorms are like palaces
Frats and sororities are unpopular or nonexistent
Student government is popular
Political activism is unpopular or nonexistent
Very little drug use

ACADEMICS

Academic Rating	96
Calendar	semester
Profs interesting rating	89
Profs accessible rating	99
Most common reg class size	20–29 students

STUDENTS SAY ". . ."

Academics

Webb Institute on Long Island is a very small school that focuses on the complex field of ship design engineering. If you feel destined to become one of "America's future ship designers and engineers," enroll here. Every student receives a four-year, full-tuition scholarship. The only costs are books and supplies, room and board, and personal expenses. Everyone majors in naval architecture and marine engineering, although non-engineering electives are available to juniors and seniors. Webbies are exposed to a smattering of the liberal arts and a ton of advanced math and physics. Virtually every other course involves ship design. There's also a senior thesis and a "required internship program." In January and February, all students get real, paying jobs in the marine industry. Job prospects are phenomenal. Newly minted Webb graduates enjoy "a 100 percent placement rate in grad schools and careers." Coursework is "rigorous," but the academic atmosphere is very intimate. "A huge plus of Webb's small size is that everyone knows everyone," relates a junior. "You're not just another number." "The administration, professors, and students all work in the same building every day, every week." "The [President] can get carried away when he perceives a problem," but the faculty is "approachable," "always accessible," and "very dedicated to the school and students." "Professors have a great deal of respect for the students and work closely with us to accomplish our goals," says a sophomore. "If you're passionate about architecture and engineering, you cannot hope for a better learning environment."

Life

Webb has a "family-like atmosphere." It's "a tiny student body living, eating, sleeping, and learning ship design in a mansion" "in a residential area overlooking the beautiful Long Island Sound." There's an honor code "that is strictly adhered to by all students." Cheating and stealing just don't happen here. "You can leave your wallet lying in the reception room, and if someone doesn't return it to you just because they know what your wallet looks like compared to the other 90 wallets in the school, it will still be there the next day and even the next week." Life at Webb "revolves around course load and the attempts to find distractions from it." "We average about five to seven hours of homework per night," advises a freshman. At the end of the semesters, life [can get crazy] due to a ton of projects." "People generally think about homework and spend most of their time discussing class assignments." When students find some down time, movies and unorganized sports are common. Not surprisingly, "many people turn to the water" for amusement as well. "Sailing is popular." "The school has a skiff and sailboats, which are frequently used during the warm months," says a sophomore. Annual whitewater rafting and ski trips are well attended. New York City is a little less than an hour away, and "a bunch of people venture into" Manhattan on the weekends. "A lot of spontaneous and off-the-wall things occur" too, and "a fair amount of partying goes on at least once a week."

Student Body

The average Webbie is a "middle-class, white male who enjoys engineering and sciences." "Everyone is motivated and works hard." Basically, you have your bookworms who "don't socialize as much" and your more social students who get their work done but also play sports and "have a good time." "The differences in these two groups are by far the most visible division within the student body." Camaraderie is reportedly easy due to the academic stress and Webb's small size. Everyone interacts with everyone else, regardless of background. With fewer than 100 students, it's "impossible to completely isolate yourself." "There are no social cliques, and everyone is included in anything they'd like to be included in." As at most engineering schools, the ratio between males and females is pretty severely lopsided here. "We want more women!" plead many students.

FINANCIAL AID: 516-671-2213 • E-MAIL: ADMISSIONS@WEBB-INSTITUTE.EDU • WEBSITE: WWW.WEBB-INSTITUTE.EDU

THE PRINCETON REVIEW SAYS

Admissions

Very important factors considered include: Class rank, academic GPA, rigor of secondary school record, standardized test scores, character/personal qualities, interview, level of applicant's interest, *Important factors considered include:* recommendation(s), extracurricular activities. *Other factors considered include:* talent/ability, volunteer work, work experience. SAT required; SAT Subject Tests required; High school diploma is required and GED is not accepted. *Academic units required:* 4 English, 4 mathematics, 2 science, (2 science labs), 2 social studies, 4 academic electives.

Financial Aid

Students should submit: FAFSA Regular filing deadline is 7/1. The Princeton Review suggests that all financial aid forms be submitted as soon as possible after 1/1. *Need-based scholarships/grants offered:* Federal Pell, state scholarships/grants, private scholarships, the school's own gift aid. *Loan aid offered:* FFEL Subsidized Stafford, FFEL Unsubsidized Stafford, FFEL PLUS Applicants will be notified of awards on or about 8/1. Off-campus job opportunities are fair.

The Inside Word

Let's not mince words; admission to Webb is mega-tough. Webb's Admissions Counselors are out to find the right kid for their curriculum—one that can survive the school's rigorous academics. The applicant pool is highly self-selected because of the focused program of study: naval architecture and marine engineering.

THE SCHOOL SAYS "..."

From The Admissions Office

"Webb, the only college in the country that specializes in the engineering field of naval architecture and marine engineering, seeks young men and women of all races from all over the country who are interested in receiving an excellent engineering education with a full-tuition scholarship. Students don't have to know anything about ships, they just have to be motivated to study how mechanical, civil, structural, and electrical engineering come together with the design elements that make up a ship and all its systems. Being small and private has its major advantages. Every applicant is special and the President will interview all entering students personally. The student/faculty ratio is 8:1, and since there are no teaching assistants, interaction with the faculty occurs daily in class and labs at a level not found at most other colleges. The college provides each student with a high-end laptop computer. The entire campus operates under the Student Organization's honor system that allows unsupervised exams and 24-hour access to the library, every classroom and laboratory, and the shop and gymnasium. Despite a total enrollment of between 70 and 80 students and a demanding workload, Webb manages to field six intercollegiate teams. Currently more than 60 percent of the members of the student body play on one or more intercollegiate teams. Work hard, play hard and the payoff is a job for every student upon graduation. The placement record of the college is 100 percent every year.

"Freshman applicants must take the SAT. We also require scores from two SAT Subject Tests: Math Level I or II and either physics or chemistry."

SELECTIVITY

Admissions Rating	98
# of applicants	73
% of applicants accepted	41
% of acceptees attending	73
# of early decision applicants	8
% accepted early decision	38

FRESHMAN PROFILE

Range SAT Critical Reading	610–670
Range SAT Math	670–740
Range SAT Writing	610–680
Average HS GPA	3.9
% graduated top 10% of class	71
% graduated top 25% of class	93
% graduated top 50% of class	100

DEADLINES

Early Decision	
Deadline	10/15
Notification	12/15
Regular	
Priority	10/15
Deadline	2/15
Notification	rolling
Nonfall registration?	no

APPLICANTS ALSO LOOK AT

AND OFTEN PREFER
United States Naval Academy
United States Coast Guard Academy

AND SOMETIMES PREFER
Virginia Tech
The Cooper Union for the Advancement of Science and Art

AND RARELY PREFER
University of Michigan—Ann Arbor
State University of New York—Maritime College

FINANCIAL FACTS

Financial Aid Rating	86
Tuition	$0
Room and board	$10,200
Books and supplies	$750
% frosh rec. need-based scholarship or grant aid	8
% UG rec. need-based scholarship or grant aid	14
% frosh rec. non-need-based scholarship or grant aid	4
% UG rec. non-need-based scholarship or grant aid	10
% frosh rec. need-based self-help aid	21
% UG rec. need-based self-help aid	11
% frosh rec. any financial aid	25
% UG rec. any financial aid	20
% UG borrow to pay for school	20
Average cumulative indebtedness	$7,303

WELLESLEY COLLEGE

BOARD OF ADMISSION, 106 CENTRAL STREET, WELLESLEY, MA 02481-8203 • ADMISSIONS: 781-283-2270 • FAX: 781-283-3678

CAMPUS LIFE

Quality of Life Rating	**96**
Fire Safety Rating	**84**
Green Rating	**87**
Type of school	private
Environment	town

STUDENTS

Total undergrad enrollment	2,191
% male/female	0/100
% from out of state	84
% from public high school	63
% live on campus	98
% African American	7
% Asian	27
% Caucasian	46
% Hispanic	7
% Native American	1
% international	8
# of countries represented	70

SURVEY SAYS . . .

No one cheats
Lab facilities are great
School is well run
Diverse student types on campus
Dorms are like palaces
Campus feels safe
Sororities are unpopular or nonexistent
Student government is popular
Political activism is popular

ACADEMICS

Academic Rating	**98**
Calendar	semester
Student/faculty ratio	8:1
Profs interesting rating	99
Profs accessible rating	98
Most common reg class size	10–19 students
Most common lab size	10–19 students

MOST POPULAR MAJORS

economics
political science and government
psychology

STUDENTS SAY ". . ."

Academics

Wellesley College, "a small liberal arts institution with the intimacy of a family and the academic excellence of a top-rank university," provides its all-female student body with "an excellent education to make women independent individuals" while "preparing ambitious women to succeed in the professional world." This elite school located just outside Boston offers "undergraduate research opportunities, close relationships with professors, a suburban environment," and much more. One student explains, "Wellesley has everything I was looking for. It was a small, liberal arts school in New England with small class sizes, excellent professors, and an amazing reputation. I also appreciated the culture within the student body, the dedicated alumnae network, and the academic challenge." "Class work is rigorous" at Wellesley as teachers here "have incredibly high expectations, but there are lots of resources available to help you if you need it." Professors "hold a large amount of office hours and even provide you with their home phone numbers and cell phone numbers in case you have any questions, whether about the class, the assignment, or life. The dedication of the Wellesley community is what I find to be stand out about the school." Spending part of junior year abroad is a staple of a Wellesley education. One student reports, "more than 50 percent of Wellesley students travel abroad." Indeed, at home or abroad Wellesley offers "unlimited opportunities" and "takes the steps necessary" to help young women "realize [their] potential."

Life

At Wellesley, "the focus is all on academics," especially during the week. "You won't see students partying here on weekdays! Instead, you'll find students attending lectures, or discussing the news or issues on campus and what homework they have." The school's "close-knit atmosphere and location" make for an "unbelievably rich" college experience. While it's true "there are no males around, at least not to the degree that there would be on a co-ed campus," students see this as a benefit. A freshman says, "This simply makes me focus more on what I'm really at college for: To get the most out of the educational opportunities available to me. In class, I am able to focus wholeheartedly on the subject matter, which is sometimes more difficult to do if there's a cute guy sitting in the class with me who is looking at me or whom I like." When it's time to chill, "students attend cultural shows and plays on campus but mostly head into Boston." Social connections in this city dictate that eventually "everyone ends up knowing someone else who goes to school in Boston and from that person, develops an additional social network in the city. This gives students a much-needed break on weekends from the often stressful Wellesley environment."

Students

Students describe the typical Wellesley undergrad (aka "Wendy Wellesley) as "an overachiever balancing two majors, 10 extracurricular activities, and several volunteer jobs." She is "passionate, hardworking, and wants to have an impact on the world around her." One student notes that "strong personalities," "diverse" individuals, and a "large range of interests" do not "allow the existence of absolutely typical students." Though "trends do occur," the "common denominator" among students is their "commitment to academic excellence." Beyond these traits, "students are extremely diverse—ethnically, geographically, and socioeconomically. Because students come from so many backgrounds, no students are truly in the minority, and it is therefore easy for anyone to fit in."

FINANCIAL AID: 781-283-2360 • E-MAIL: ADMISSION@WELLESLEY.EDU • WEBSITE: WWW.WELLESLEY.EDU

THE PRINCETON REVIEW SAYS

Admissions

Very important factors considered include: Application essay, academic GPA, recommendation(s), rigor of secondary school record, standardized test scores, character/personal qualities, *Important factors considered include:* Class rank, extracurricular activities. *Other factors considered include:* alumni/ae relation, first generation, geographical residence, interview, level of applicant's interest, racial/ethnic status, state residency, talent/ability, volunteer work, work experience. SAT and SAT Subject Tests or ACT required; ACT with Writing component required. High school diploma or equivalent is not required. *Academic units recommended:* 4 English, 4 mathematics, 3 science, (2 science labs), 4 foreign language, 4 social studies, 4 history.

Financial Aid

Students should submit: FAFSA, institution's own financial aid form, CSS/Financial Aid PROFILE noncustodial PROFILE, business/farm supplement. Business taxes, if applicable. The Princeton Review suggests that all financial aid forms be submitted as soon as possible after 1/1. *Need-based scholarships/grants offered:* Federal Pell, SEOG, state scholarships/grants, private scholarships, the school's own gift aid, Federal ACG Grant, SMART Grant. *Loan aid offered:* FFEL Subsidized Stafford, FFEL Unsubsidized Stafford, FFEL PLUS, Federal Perkins, state loans, college/university loans from institutional funds. Applicants will be notified of awards on or about 4/1. Federal Work-Study Program available. Institutional employment available. Off-campus job opportunities are excellent.

The Inside Word

As the number of women's colleges diminishes—*The New York Times* recently reported that the U.S. now has only about 60 all-women's schools, down from more than 300 in the 1960s—competition for admission to the remaining single-sex institutions stiffens. Wellesley has always been an elite institution, but it grows ever more so as its number of competitors for top women students shrinks. If you submit your application materials to Wellesley by November 1, the school will provide you with an early evaluation, giving you some idea of your chances for admission.

THE SCHOOL SAYS "..."

From The Admissions Office

"Widely acknowledged as the nation's best women's college, Wellesley College provides students with numerous opportunities on campus and beyond. With a long-standing commitment to and established reputation for academic excellence, Wellesley offers more than 1,000 courses in 53 established majors and supports 180 clubs, organizations, and activities for its students. The college is easily accessible to Boston, a great city in which to meet other college students and to experience theater, art, sports, and entertainment. Considered one of the most diverse colleges in the nation, Wellesley students hail from 70 countries and all 50 states.

"As a community, we are looking for students who possess intellectual curiosity: the ability to think independently, ask challenging questions, and grapple with answers. Strong candidates demonstrate both academic achievement and an excitement for learning. They also display leadership, an appreciation for diverse perspectives, and an understanding of the college's mission to educate women who will make a difference in the world.

"The SAT and SAT Subject Tests or ACT with Writing component are required. Two SAT Subject Tests are required, one of which should be quantitative (Math or Science). We strongly recommend that students planning to apply early decision complete the tests before the end of their junior year and no later than October of their senior year."

SELECTIVITY

Admissions Rating	97
# of applicants	4,001
% of applicants accepted	36
% of acceptees attending	41
# accepting a place on wait list	421
% admitted from wait list	3
# of early decision applicants	208
% accepted early decision	51

FRESHMAN PROFILE

Range SAT Critical Reading	640–740
Range SAT Math	630–725
Range SAT Writing	650–740
Range ACT Composite	29–32
% graduated top 10% of class	76
% graduated top 25% of class	97
% graduated top 50% of class	100

DEADLINES

Early Decision	
Deadline	11/1
Notification	12/15
Regular	
Deadline	1/15
Notification	4/1
Nonfall registration?	no

FINANCIAL FACTS

Financial Aid Rating	98
Annual tuition	$37,826
Room and board	$11,786
Required fees	$236
% frosh rec. need-based scholarship or grant aid	56
% UG rec. need-based scholarship or grant aid	58
% frosh rec. need-based self-help aid	49
% UG rec. need-based self-help aid	54
% frosh rec. any financial aid	58
% UG rec. any financial aid	61
% UG borrow to pay for school	53
Average cumulative indebtedness	$12,639

WELLS COLLEGE

ROUTE 90, AURORA, NY 13026 • ADMISSIONS: 315-364-3264 • FAX: 315-364-3227

CAMPUS LIFE

Quality of Life Rating	**74**
Fire Safety Rating	**82**
Green Rating	**81**
Type of school	private
Environment	rural

STUDENTS

Total undergrad enrollment	544
% male/female	23/77
% from out of state	31
% from public high school	88
% live on campus	86
% African American	5
% Asian	2
% Caucasian	68
% Hispanic	4
% Native American	1
% international	2
# of countries represented	13

SURVEY SAYS . . .

No one cheats
Lousy food on campus
Low cost of living
Frats and sororities are unpopular or nonexistent
Musical organizations are popular
(Almost) no one smokes
Very little drug use

ACADEMICS

Academic Rating	**87**
Calendar	semester
Student/faculty ratio	9:1
Profs interesting rating	91
Profs accessible rating	90
Most common	
reg class size	10–19 students

MOST POPULAR MAJORS

English language and literature
history
psychology

STUDENTS SAY ". . ."

Academics

Undergrads at Wells are full of praise for their academic experience. The "intimate" size of the college ensures a "personal" education that stresses "individual attention." The professors "genuinely care about their students" and often "form lasting friendships" with them. However, this doesn't mean the classroom is a cakewalk. One junior stressed the professors "set very high academic standards for their students." And a freshman revealed the workload, at times, can be "overwhelming." Indeed, it's "not a school where you will be able to get an easy A." Luckily, it's a supportive environment, and professors are "almost always willing to go the extra step to make sure you understand the material." Moreover, "they encourage you to explore beyond their own subject and connect your subjects with each other." It's clearly evident to these undergrads their profs "teach for the love it." While acclaim for the academics is virtually unanimous, opinions regarding the administrators definitely run the gamut. Some undergrads feel "the administration tend to do as they please with little regard for the students." And one senior adds that they "make it very obvious they are running a business." However, another undergrad counters by saying "students are allowed to have a voice, and can meet with the administration to discuss changes to controversial policies."

Life

Wells students agree "there isn't a lot to do" in "rural" hometown Aurora. Fortunately, that just means entertainment is centered around the college. One junior reveals, "The traditions on campus are superior and amazing!" In turn, they foster "a great sense of community." The school sponsors a number of activities such as "concerts, parties, dances, and guest speakers." Additionally the college theater is pretty popular because the "performing arts are very high quality" at Wells. Of course many students love to simply "chill out with close friends, have an intellectual conversation, or host their own dance party." And a number of students "get creative" and "make their own fun." Indeed, an intrepid freshman regales with tales of "riding mattresses down stairs," and another shares that when it snows "students ride sleds or make snowmen or other types of sculptures." Though Aurora is "small," one sophomore gushes "the surrounding area is beautiful and there are lots of places to go hiking." When undergrads are itching to get a little farther away, they typically head to either "Ithaca or Auburn." Both towns offer ample opportunity for fun such as "movies, bowling, ice skating, a mall, [and] dining out."

Student Body

When Wells made the decision to go co-ed back in 2005, the college was forced to "restructure its student identity." Naturally, the transition was fraught with some growing pains. And while there's still some lingering tension, especially with "recruited male athletes," many undergrads assure us "one of the beautiful things about Wells is that, in general, everyone is welcome." A content English major expands upon this sentiment stating, "Everyone is important and has a place here." This can partly be attributed to the fact the college "has a strong emphasis on community." Additionally, Wells seems to attract "friendly, eccentric people" who are "socially and politically conscious, academic minded, and tolerant." And these "fun" students "aren't afraid to be different." Undergrads find common ground in that most everyone is "concerned about their education." Indeed, the "typical student at Wells is very studious [and] spends many hours studying or in the library." Perhaps this happy freshman sums up by sharing, "It is a diverse environment, but everyone can find someone that is like them. There is no such thing as not fitting in!"

FINANCIAL AID: 315-364-3289 • E-MAIL: ADMISSIONS@WELLS.EDU • WEBSITE: WWW.WELLS.EDU

THE PRINCETON REVIEW SAYS

Admissions

Very important factors considered include: Academic GPA, recommendation(s), rigor of secondary school record, standardized test scores, extracurricular activities, *Important factors considered include:* Application essay, interview. *Other factors considered include:* Class rank, alumni/ae relation, character/personal qualities, level of applicant's interest, talent/ability, volunteer work, work experience. SAT or ACT required; TOEFL required of all international applicants. High school diploma is required and GED is accepted. *Academic units required:* 4 English, 3 mathematics, 2 science, (2 science labs), 1 social studies, 3 history, 2 academic electives, *Academic units recommended:* 4 mathematics, 3 science, (3 science labs), 2 foreign language, 2 social studies, 2 history, 3 academic electives, 2 music, art, computer science.

Financial Aid

Students should submit: FAFSACSS/Financial Aid Profile for Early Decision Applicants only. The Princeton Review suggests that all financial aid forms be submitted as soon as possible after 1/1. *Need-based scholarships/grants offered:* Federal Pell, SEOG, state scholarships/grants, private scholarships, the school's own gift aid. *Loan aid offered:* FFEL Subsidized Stafford, FFEL Unsubsidized Stafford, FFEL PLUS, Federal Perkins. Applicants will be notified of awards on a rolling basis beginning 3/1. Federal Work-Study Program available. Institutional employment available. Off-campus job opportunities are poor.

The Inside Word

Wells is engaged in that age-old admissions game called matchmaking. There are no minimums or cutoffs in the admissions process here. But don't be fooled by the high admit rate. The admissions committee will look closely at your academic accomplishments. However, they will also give attention to your essay, recommendations, and extracurricular pursuits. The committee also recommends an interview; we suggest taking them up on it.

THE SCHOOL SAYS "..."

From The Admissions Office

"Wells College believes the 21st century needs well-educated individuals with the ability, self-confidence, and vision to contribute to an ever-changing world. Wells offers an outstanding classroom experience and innovative liberal arts curriculum that prepares students for leadership in a variety of fields, including business, government, the arts, sciences, medicine, and education. By directly connecting the liberal arts curriculum to experience and career development through internships, off-campus study, study abroad, research with professors, and community service, each student has an ideal preparation for graduate and professional school as well as for the 21st century.

"Wells College requires freshman applicants to submit scores from SAT scores. Students may also choose to submit scores from the ACT (with or without the Writing component) in lieu of the SAT."

SELECTIVITY

Admissions Rating	85
# of applicants	1,148
% of applicants accepted	64
% of acceptees attending	24
# of early decision applicants	16
% accepted early decision	63

FRESHMAN PROFILE

Range SAT Critical Reading	510–640
Range SAT Math	490–590
Range ACT Composite	23–27
Minimum paper TOEFL	550
Minimum computer TOEFL	213
Average HS GPA	3.5
% graduated top 10% of class	25
% graduated top 25% of class	60
% graduated top 50% of class	92

DEADLINES

Early Decision	
Deadline	12/15
Notification	1/15
Early action	
Deadline	12/15
Notification	2/1
Regular	
Priority	12/15
Deadline	3/1
Notification	4/1
Nonfall registration?	no

APPLICANTS ALSO LOOK AT
AND OFTEN PREFER
Hobart and William Smith Colleges
Mount Holyoke College
AND SOMETIMES PREFER
State University of New York at Binghamton
AND RARELY PREFER
Le Moyne College
Elmira College

FINANCIAL FACTS

Financial Aid Rating	78
Annual tuition	$17,580
Room and board	$8,420
Required fees	$1,900
Books and supplies	$800
% frosh rec. need-based scholarship or grant aid	71
% UG rec. need-based scholarship or grant aid	76
% frosh rec. non-need-based scholarship or grant aid	37
% UG rec. non-need-based scholarship or grant aid	34
% frosh rec. need-based self-help aid	71
% UG rec. need-based self-help aid	75
% frosh rec. any financial aid	71
% UG rec. any financial aid	76
% UG borrow to pay for school	77
Average cumulative indebtedness	$20,355

WESLEYAN COLLEGE

4760 FORSYTH ROAD, MACON, GA 31210-4462 • ADMISSIONS: 478-757-5206 • FAX: 912-757-4030 • 800-447-6610

CAMPUS LIFE

Quality of Life Rating	86
Fire Safety Rating	60*
Green Rating	83
Type of school	private
Affiliation	Methodist
Environment	suburban

STUDENTS

Total undergrad enrollment	629
% male/female	0/100
% from out of state	10
% from public high school	81
% live on campus	82
% African American	33
% Asian	3
% Caucasian	46
% Hispanic	2
% international	14
# of countries represented	22

SURVEY SAYS . . .

*Lab facilities are great
Diverse student types on campus
Low cost of living
(Almost) no one smokes
Very little drug use*

ACADEMICS

Academic Rating	97
Calendar	semester
Student/faculty ratio	8:1
Profs interesting rating	93
Profs accessible rating	87
Most common reg class size	fewer than 10 students

MOST POPULAR MAJORS

psychology
business/economics
biology
marketing communication, education

STUDENTS SAY " . . ."

Academics

The Wesleyan College motto, "First for Women," encompasses the school's commitment to women's education since it was founded in 1836. The first accredited college to offer degrees to women, this small school is not your typical college environment, maintaining a strong focus on sisterhood between students, rigorous academic programs, and an intimate and interactive academic atmosphere. With an excellent faculty-to-student ratio, "you get one-on-one time with your professors," and "most classes are done discussion-style, with many diverse viewpoints presented." At the same time, the close-knit atmosphere does not translate into slack academic expectations. A junior explains, "The overall academic experience is tough due to the small classes and extra attention; teachers expect you to turn [in] quality work on time." Fortunately, students appreciate the benefits of their unique education, saying, "Everyone brings something different to the table, which enriches the academic experience." Tuition is a bit more reasonable at Wesleyan College than at other private schools, and more than half of current students receive some form of financial assistance. Despite affordability, "the campus facilities are impressive, especially for such a small school" and the 200-acre campus includes athletic and equestrian facilities, as well as a new, world-class science center. When it comes to the nuts and bolts, many students feel the school's administration, though friendly, could improve its organizations skills. A student points out, "Getting to the administration is the easy, but the paperwork can be difficult."

Life

Academics take center stage at Wesleyan and, because "the academic load can be quite stressful, a lot of time is spent studying." Even in their downtime, students like to "talk about the interesting things we discussed in classes or about plays or art shows we've recently been to." Those who do have wheels often "leave campus to party and drink because alcohol is not allowed on campus." In the surrounding city, the "Cherry Blossom festival is also a great program to enjoy during the spring semester," and students "frequent many of the clubs on Cherry Street in downtown Macon." Wesleyan is affiliated with the United Methodist Church, and many students take part in community service activities, religious groups, and campus clubs. In addition, "the sense of sisterhood and camaraderie on campus" is one of the school's distinguishing characteristics. Wesleyan promotes class spirit and frequently organizes "pep rallies and different events that get students involved." In fact, "during lunch in the cafeteria you can usually hear class cheers." A sophomore enthuses, "Sisterhood enables you to make friends and interact with people you would have never met otherwise." On the other hand, if you want to fraternize with the opposite sex, "boys (and students from neighboring colleges) rarely come to our campus events!"

Student Body

There are just 700 undergraduates at Wesleyan College, yet "Wesleyan students come from all kinds of backgrounds, countries, ethnic groups, and religions." Within the Wesleyan community, you'll meet "artsy kids, hippies, science geeks, religious girls, political activists." No matter where you fit in, "Wesleyan truly embraces how you are, no matter who you are." A junior attests, "Everybody is different here, but since diversity is so celebrated, there are very few people who just don't fit in." Academics are the first priority for most Wesleyan undergraduates, and "the top students are strong-willed [and] outspoken and passionately love the work they do." At the same time, the average student "maintains a balance between their academics, extracurricular activities, and community service." On that note, most students are involved in their school and community, as the student body's small size "allows for you to be involved in student activities as much as you want."

FINANCIAL AID: 800-447-6610 • E-MAIL: ADMISSION@WESLEYANCOLLEGE.EDU • WEBSITE: WWW.WESLEYANCOLLEGE.EDU

THE PRINCETON REVIEW SAYS

Admissions

Very important factors considered include: rigor of secondary school record. *Important factors considered include:* Class rank, academic GPA, recommendation(s), standardized test scores, extracurricular activities, interview, talent/ability. *Other factors considered include:* Application essay, alumni/ae relation, level of applicant's interest, volunteer work, work experience. SAT or ACT required; TOEFL required of all international applicants. High school diploma is required and GED is accepted. *Academic units required:* 4 English, 3 mathematics, 3 science, (2 science labs), 2 foreign language, 3 social studies, *Academic units recommended:* 4 English, 4 mathematics, 4 science, (3 science labs), 4 foreign language, 4 social studies, 2 academic electives.

Financial Aid

Students should submit: FAFSA, institution's own financial aid form, state aid form. Regular filing deadline is 6/3. The Princeton Review suggests that all financial aid forms be submitted as soon as possible after 1/1. *Need-based scholarships/grants offered:* Federal Pell, SEOG, state scholarships/grants, private scholarships, the school's own gift aid. *Loan aid offered:* FFEL Subsidized Stafford, FFEL Unsubsidized Stafford, FFEL PLUS, Federal Perkins, state loans, college/university loans from institutional funds, CitiAssist, Wells FARGO,Collegiate Loans, key alternative loans. Applicants will be notified of awards on a rolling basis beginning 3/1. Federal Work-Study Program available. Off-campus job opportunities are good.

The Inside Word

Wesleyan College values diversity. At this small college, you'll find students from 25 countries and 21 states, with a wide range of interests. To evaluate a student's qualitative characteristics, Wesleyan recommends that applicants submit a teacher recommendation and have a personal interview with the admissions staff (though neither is required.) Students are also encouraged to submit samples of their creative work, such as poetry, music, or research projects.

THE SCHOOL SAYS "..."

From The Admissions Office

"Mention the term 'women's college' and most people envision ivy-covered towers in the Northeastern U.S. However, Wesleyan College in Macon, Georgia was founded in 1836 as the first college in the world chartered to grant degrees to women. Today it is recognized as one of the nation's most diverse and affordable selective 4-year liberal arts colleges. Students value the college's tradition of service and rigorous academic program renowned for its quality. An exceptional faculty teaches classes in seminar style. A student/faculty ratio of 10:1 ensures that students are known by more than just a grade or a number. The acceptance rate of Wesleyan students into medical, law, business, and other graduate programs is exemplary. Undergraduate degrees are offered in 32 majors and 29 minors including self-designed majors and interdisciplinary programs, plus eight pre-professional programs that include seminary, engineering, medicine, pharmacy, veterinary medicine, health sciences, dental, and law. A $12.5 million science center added to the college's offerings for 2007. Master of Arts degrees in education and an accelerated Executive Master of Business Administration program enroll both men and women.

"Beyond the academic, Wesleyan offers a thriving residence life program, NCAA Division III athletics, championship IHSA equestrian program, and meaningful opportunities for community involvement and leadership. The college's beautiful 200-acre wooded campus, along with 30 historically significant buildings, is listed in the National Register of Historic Places as the Wesleyan College Historic District. Wesleyan is nestled in a northern suburb of Macon, the third largest city in the state.

"First-year applicants must take either the SAT or ACT."

SELECTIVITY	
Admissions Rating	**88**
# of applicants	601
% of applicants accepted	51
% of acceptees attending	37

FRESHMAN PROFILE	
Range SAT Critical Reading	500–610
Range SAT Math	490–620
Range SAT Writing	520–670
Range ACT Composite	21–28
Minimum paper TOEFL	550
Minimum computer TOEFL	213

DEADLINES	
Early Decision	
Deadline	11/15
Notification	12/15
Regular	
Priority	1/15
Deadline	8/1
Notification	rolling
Nonfall registration?	yes

AND SOMETIMES PREFER
Agnes Scott College
Emory University
University of Georgia

FINANCIAL FACTS	
Financial Aid Rating	**84**
Annual tuition	$17,500
Room and board	$8,000
Books and supplies	$1,000
% frosh rec. need-based scholarship or grant aid	66
% UG rec. need-based scholarship or grant aid	57
% frosh rec. non-need-based scholarship or grant aid	29
% UG rec. non-need-based scholarship or grant aid	24
% frosh rec. need-based self-help aid	43
% UG rec. need-based self-help aid	47
% frosh rec. any financial aid	83
% UG rec. any financial aid	81
% UG borrow to pay for school	58
Average cumulative indebtedness	$20,896

WESLEYAN UNIVERSITY

STEWART M. REID HOUSE, 70 WYLLYS AVENUE, MIDDLETOWN, CT 06459-0265 • ADMISSIONS: 860-685-3000 • FAX: 860-685-3001

CAMPUS LIFE
Quality of Life Rating	83
Fire Safety Rating	85
Green Rating	92
Type of school	private
Environment	town

STUDENTS
Total undergrad enrollment	2,748
% male/female	51/49
% from out of state	92
% from public high school	57
% live on campus	99
% in (# of) fraternities	2 (9)
% in (# of) sororities	NR (4)
% African American	7
% Asian	10
% Caucasian	59
% Hispanic	8
% international	7
# of countries represented	48

SURVEY SAYS . . .
Lots of liberal students
No one cheats
Great library
Athletic facilities are great
Students are friendly
Students aren't religious
Students are happy
Political activism is popular

ACADEMICS
Academic Rating	97
Calendar	semester
Student/faculty ratio	9:1
Profs interesting rating	89
Profs accessible rating	83
Most common reg class size	10–19 students
Most common lab size	20–29 students

MOST POPULAR MAJORS
English language and literature
political science and government
psychology

STUDENTS SAY ". . ."

Academics

Students at Wesleyan University relish "the immense amount of freedom the school gives you," both in terms of class choices ("because of the lack of core curriculum, you can mold each semester however you want: lots of lecture, lots of discussion, a mix") and in extracurricular life (in other words, "Public Safety rarely bothers the students"). This may sound like a recipe for a nonstop party, but that's hardly the case at Wesleyan. Students here don't see the school as a 24/7 kegger, but rather as "a playground for the most opinionated and social-norm-destroying students of our generation to debate issues that really matter to them." If that suggests a school entirely focused on humanities and social sciences, guess again; Wes "has one of the strongest science programs [of] any of the top liberal arts school[s]. One-quarter of the students major in a science. Since we're in a university, but have very few graduate students, there are tons of opportunities for students to get involved in research. As a sophomore, I was highly involved in a $5 million NIH grant. That's pretty unique and amazing." In all disciplines, "professors are incredible. They are all as available as they could be to us and more willing to help than I ever expected college professors to be." Those who teach "upper level courses are ridiculously passionate about what they teach, and are usually doing research that is very relevant to their field. At Wesleyan, I always get the sense I am surrounded by many brilliant minds." A "very active student body…frequently tries to make changes in the way the school is run," and "the administration does a good job [of] working with students to ensure we all have the most positive experience possible."

Life

The Wesleyan campus is a busy one, replete with club and intercollegiate athletics, frat and house parties, and lots of performances and lectures. One student explains, "The Wes social scene is very much what you want to make it. Want to party? We do have frats (though they're a super-small part of campus life) and house parties. Don't want to party? Go to a play, concert, movie, or just hang out. Not everyone here is partying." Indeed, "there is plenty to keep you occupied" at Wesleyan, including campus politics, as "on this campus there is always some issue being fought or demonstrated against." Students take a strong hand in driving campus life, as "everything is mostly student-run." "If a Wes student wants something that doesn't exist on campus, [he or she] make[s] it happen." Hometown Middletown, while "clearly lacking the resources of a large city," "has lots of opportunities to get involved and feel like a member of the community for four years." A junior reports, "Main Street in Middletown has changed tremendously just in the three years I have been here. Lots of new restaurants, bars, and art galleries have opened."

Student Body

"Passionate" is a word that pops up frequently when Wesleyan undergrads describe their peers, as does "intelligent." In fact, Wesleyan is a magnet for kids who value intellect, not only as a means to good grades and a career, but also as an instrument of self-development. "Everyone is excited about something," undergrads report. Students here are engaged in campus life, meaning "a lot of things on campus are student-run and a lot of learning takes place outside the classroom due to casual interaction between peers." Demographically speaking, there are "two main molds of a Wesleyan student: the preppy New England kid and the kid…who [is] some kind of mix between a hipster and a hippie. Outside of that it's an extremely diverse group of kids who come from all over and have a wide range of interests." Most students here "are liberal and 'alternative.'"

FINANCIAL AID: 860-685-2800 • E-MAIL: ADMISS@WESLEYAN.EDU • WEBSITE: WWW.WESLEYAN.EDU

THE PRINCETON REVIEW SAYS

Admissions

Very important factors considered include: rigor of secondary school record, *Important factors considered include:* Class rank, application essay, academic GPA, recommendation(s), standardized test scores, character/personal qualities, first generation, racial/ethnic status, talent/ability. *Other factors considered include:* alumni/ae relation, extracurricular activities, geographical residence, interview, volunteer work, work experience. SAT and SAT Subject Tests or ACT required; ACT with Writing component recommended. TOEFL required of all international applicants. High school diploma is required and GED is accepted. *Academic units recommended:* 4 English, 4 mathematics, 4 science, (3 science labs), 4 foreign language, 4 social studies, 4 history.

Financial Aid

Students should submit: FAFSA, CSS/Financial Aid PROFILE, state aid form, noncustodial PROFILE Regular filing deadline is 2/15. The Princeton Review suggests that all financial aid forms be submitted as soon as possible after 1/1. *Need-based scholarships/grants offered:* Federal Pell, SEOG, state scholarships/grants, private scholarships, the school's own gift aid. *Loan aid offered:* FFEL Subsidized Stafford, FFEL Unsubsidized Stafford, FFEL PLUS, Federal Perkins, college/university loans from institutional funds. Applicants will be notified of awards on or about 4/1. Federal Work-Study Program available. Institutional employment available. Off-campus job opportunities are good.

The Inside Word

You want the inside word on Wesleyan admissions? Read *The Gatekeepers: Inside the Admissions Process at a Premier College*, by Jacques Steinberg. The author spent an entire admissions season at the Wesleyan admissions office. His book is a wonderfully detailed description of the Wesleyan admissions process (which is quite similar to processes at other private, highly selective colleges and universities).

THE SCHOOL SAYS "..."

From The Admissions Office

"Wesleyan faculty believe in an education that is flexible and affords individual freedom and that a strong liberal arts education is the best foundation for success in any endeavor. The broad curriculum focuses on essential communication skills and analytical abilities through course content and teaching methodology, allowing students to pursue their intellectual interests with passion while honing those capabilities. As a result, Wesleyan students achieve a very personalized but broad education. Wesleyan's Dean of Admission and Financial Aid, Nancy Hargrave Meislahn, describes the qualities Wesleyan seeks in its students: 'Our very holistic process seeks to identify academically accomplished and intellectually curious students who can thrive in Wesleyan's rigorous and vibrant academic environment; we look for personal strengths, accomplishments, and potential for real contribution to our diverse community.'

"Applicants will meet standardized testing requirements one of two ways: by taking the SAT plus two SAT Subject Tests of the student's choice or by taking the ACT (Writing component recommended)."

SELECTIVITY

Admissions Rating	97
# of applicants	8,250
% of applicants accepted	27
% of acceptees attending	32
# accepting a place on wait list	700
% admitted from wait list	3
# of early decision applicants	650
% accepted early decision	46

FRESHMAN PROFILE

Range SAT Critical Reading	640–740
Range SAT Math	660–740
Range SAT Writing	640–740
Range ACT Composite	30–32
Minimum paper TOEFL	600
Minimum computer TOEFL	250
Minimum web-based TOEFL	100
Average HS GPA	3.95
% graduated top 10% of class	65
% graduated top 25% of class	91
% graduated top 50% of class	99

DEADLINES

Early Decision	
Deadline	11/15
Notification	12/15
Regular	
Deadline	1/1
Notification	4/1
Nonfall registration?	no

APPLICANTS ALSO LOOK AT

AND OFTEN PREFER
Harvard College, Stanford University
Yale University, Brown University

AND SOMETIMES PREFER
Swarthmore College, Amherst College

AND RARELY PREFER
Oberlin College, Vassar College
Tufts University

FINANCIAL FACTS

Financial Aid Rating	96
Annual tuition	$38,364
Room and board	$10,636
Required fees	$570
% frosh rec. need-based scholarship or grant aid	40
% UG rec. need-based scholarship or grant aid	43
% frosh rec. non-need-based scholarship or grant aid	1
% frosh rec. need-based self-help aid	45
% UG rec. need-based self-help aid	47
% frosh rec. any financial aid	43
% UG rec. any financial aid	44
% UG borrow to pay for school	43
Average cumulative indebtedness	$27,402

WEST VIRGINIA UNIVERSITY

ADMISSIONS OFFICE, PO BOX 6009, MORGANTOWN, WV 26506-6009 • ADMISSIONS: 304-293-2121 • FAX: 304-293-3080

CAMPUS LIFE
Quality of Life Rating	86
Fire Safety Rating	84
Green Rating	89
Type of school	public
Environment	town

STUDENTS
Total undergrad enrollment	21,930
% male/female	55/45
% from out of state	46
% live on campus	25
% in (# of) fraternities	7 (17)
% in (# of) sororities	8 (9)
% African American	3
% Asian	2
% Caucasian	89
% Hispanic	2
% international	2
# of countries represented	66

SURVEY SAYS . . .
Athletic facilities are great
Students are friendly
Everyone loves the Mountaineers
Student publications are popular
Lots of beer drinking
Hard liquor is popular

ACADEMICS
Academic Rating	69
Calendar	semester
Student/faculty ratio	23:1
Profs interesting rating	66
Profs accessible rating	69
Most common reg class size	fewer than 10 students
Most common lab size	20–29 students

MOST POPULAR MAJORS
business/commerce
engineering
health professions and related
clinical sciences

STUDENTS SAY ". . ."

Academics
Set in the "heart of the mountains of West Virginia," West Virginia University combines pastoral charm with an emphasis on providing a strong academic tradition to a large student body. With a strident regional appeal, West Virginia University couples "affordable" tuition with the resources of "a large university." "Close to home" for many, in-state students are quick to note the school's alluring trio of "proximity, money, and opportunity." "The journalism school is well-accepted," as is the advertising and communications programs. "If you apply yourself, the opportunities at WVU are endless." Though "every professor is different," "most professors are available and willing to provide extra help outside of the classrooms." Like most large universities, "with a variety of majors," "life at WVU is what you make of it…If you're able to handle making a commitment to your work, you can have a great time doing both!" West Virginia's academic curriculum excels in numerous areas, including engineering, premedicine, journalism, psychology, forensics, advertising, music, and athletic training. It also offers a rigorous intellectual program through its elite Honors College. "Professors are usually great. I love it here overall; it's a large university in a small state."

Life
West Virginia University is "very school spirited," legendary for its "good football team" and "a fun, relaxing atmosphere to learn." Full of "genuine people" who enjoy "working hard in the classroom," life on campus involves "meeting lots of people, getting involved," and occasionally "letting the good times roll." In a word, it's all about "unity." Students tell us that "when you go to a football game you'll feel it." An average week involves "going bowling or to dinner with friends for fun." Many take advantage of the surrounding mountains and rugged setting of a university "hidden away in the hills of West Virginia" and enjoy participating in outdoor activities and sporting events. Others are quick to comment on Morgantown's status as one of the best small cities in the country, noting that it "is one of the fastest growing cities in the nation." On the weekend, "people either go to WVU sporting events, party, go to bars/clubs, or spend time at the rec center," which is state-of-the-art and draws rave reviews. Though many note the abundance of "athletics and partying," "a typical student goes to class, makes time to study and get work done, and definitely finds time to go out and enjoy [himself]."

Student Body
Though many affectionately tout the "cheers, beers, and mountaineers" slogan, "most students are at WVU to learn." "Easygoing, kind, good people," "the typical student is an outgoing person that likes to have fun and can multitask and balance an abundant social life." Always "ready to succeed and have fun," "there are a few typical students that include 'the party animals,' 'the religious kids,' and the 'very academically focused kids.'" Students assure us that "everyone fits in if they try." Reflective of the school's regional appeal coupled with its nationally recognized journalism and honors program, array of majors and quality academics, "there are a lot of down-home, WV country boys. But then again, there are a lot of people from New Jersey as well." Overall, life at West Virginia University is "about growing socially, academically, and personally," and students are "kind and polite."

FINANCIAL AID: 304-293-5242 • E-MAIL: WVUADMISSIONS@ARC.WVU.EDU • WEBSITE: WWW.WVU.EDU

THE PRINCETON REVIEW SAYS

Admissions

Very important factors considered include: academic GPA, standardized test scores, *Important factors considered include:* rigor of secondary school record, level of applicant's interest, state residency. *Other factors considered include:* recommendation(s), extracurricular activities, talent/ability, volunteer work, SAT or ACT required; TOEFL required of all international applicants. High school diploma is required and GED is accepted. *Academic units required:* 4 English, 4 mathematics, 3 science, (3 science labs), 2 foreign language, 3 social studies, 1 visual/performing arts.

Financial Aid

Students should submit: FAFSA, state aid form Regular filing deadline is 3/1. The Princeton Review suggests that all financial aid forms be submitted as soon as possible after 1/1. *Need-based scholarships/grants offered:* Federal Pell, SEOG, state scholarships/grants, private scholarships, the school's own gift aid. *Loan aid offered:* Direct Subsidized Stafford, Direct Unsubsidized Stafford, Direct PLUS, Federal Perkins, college/university loans from institutional funds. Applicants will be notified of awards on a rolling basis beginning 3/15. Federal Work-Study Program available. Institutional employment available. Off-campus job opportunities are good.

The Inside Word

While standards for general admission to WVU are not especially rigorous, you'll find admission to its premier programs to be quite competitive. Admission to the College of Business and Economics, for example, requires a high school GPA of at least 3.75 and an SAT Math score of at least 610. Programs in computer science, education, engineering, fine arts, forensics, journalism, medicine, and nursing all require fairly impressive credentials. If you are not admitted to the program of your choice, you may be able to transfer to it later if your grades are good enough, but it won't be easy.

THE SCHOOL SAYS " . . ."

From The Admissions Office

"From quality academic programs and outstanding, caring faculty to incredible new facilities and a campus environment that focuses on students' needs, WVU is a place where dreams can come true. The university's tradition of academic excellence attracts some of the region's best high school seniors. WVU has produced 25 Rhodes Scholars, 32 Goldwater Scholars, 20 Truman Scholars, 5 members of *USA Today*'s All-U.S.A. College Academic First Team, and 2 Udall Scholarship winners. Whether your goal is to be an aerospace engineer, reporter, physicist, athletic trainer, opera singer, forensic investigator, pharmacist, or CEO, WVU's 186 degree choices can make it happen. Unique student-centered initiatives include Operation Jump Start, which helps students experience true education extending beyond the classroom. Resident Faculty Leaders live next to the residence halls to mentor students, and WVU Up All Night provides a way to relax and have fun with free food and activities nearly every weekend. The Mountaineer Parents' Club connects more than 13,000 WVU families, and a parents' helpline (800-WVU-0096) leads to a full-time parent advocate. A new Student Recreation Center includes athletic courts, pools, weight/fitness equipment, and a 50-foot indoor climbing wall. Also, a brand-new life sciences building and completely renovated library complex just opened. With programs for studying abroad, a Center for Black Culture and Research, an Office of Disability Services, and a student body that comes from every WV county, 50 states, and 99 different countries, WVU encourages and nurtures diversity. More than $150 million in annual grant funding makes WVU a major research institution where undergraduates can participate. All applicants are required to take the ACT Writing assessment as part of the ACT exam or take the SAT to be considered for admission."

SELECTIVITY

Admissions Rating	84
# of applicants	15,094
% of applicants accepted	88
% of acceptees attending	39

FRESHMAN PROFILE

Range SAT Critical Reading	470–560
Range SAT Math	480–580
Range ACT Composite	20–26
Minimum paper TOEFL	550
Minimum computer TOEFL	173
Average HS GPA	3.3
% graduated top 10% of class	19
% graduated top 25% of class	44
% graduated top 50% of class	77

DEADLINES

Regular	
Priority	2/1
Deadline	8/1
Notification	rolling
Nonfall registration?	yes

APPLICANTS ALSO LOOK AT

AND OFTEN PREFER
Virginia Tech
Penn State—University Park
University of Pittsburgh—Pittsburgh Campus

AND SOMETIMES PREFER
University of Maryland—College Park
Marshall University
The Ohio State University—Columbus
James Madison University

AND RARELY PREFER
University of Delaware
Fairmont State College
Shepherd University

FINANCIAL FACTS

Financial Aid Rating	77
Annual in-state tuition	$5,100
Annual out-of-state tuition	$15,770
Room and board	$7,434
Books and supplies	$1,160
% frosh rec. need-based scholarship or grant aid	35
% UG rec. need-based scholarship or grant aid	33
% frosh rec. non-need-based scholarship or grant aid	50
% UG rec. non-need-based scholarship or grant aid	35
% frosh rec. need-based self-help aid	33
% UG rec. need-based self-help aid	38
% frosh rec. athletic scholarships	1
% UG rec. athletic scholarships	1
% frosh rec. any financial aid	72
% UG rec. any financial aid	75

WESTMINSTER COLLEGE (PA)

319 SOUTH MARKET STREET, NEW WILMINGTON, PA 16172 • ADMISSIONS: 800-942-8033 • FAX: 724-946-7171

STUDENTS SAY ". . ."

Academics

Students choose Westminster College, a small Presbyterian-affiliated liberal arts school north of Pittsburgh, for its cozy atmosphere and well-regarded pre-professional programs. Undergrads describe Westminster as "an extremely small school where everyone pretty much knows each other," where "professors are dedicated to helping students on all levels. From [within] the classroom and outside of class in fact professors are known to call students on the weekends at home to discuss coursework." and The community is like "a family bound together with blue and white pride and a love for the people who are attending and those who have moved on." Indeed, "once you become a part of the Westminster tradition, it lasts for a lifetime!" The small class environment "creates opportunities above focused, by-rote study," facilitated by a "very hands-on" approach from both faculty and administrators. Premedical studies excel here. Students warn "being a biology major is much harder than some of the other majors, and even if you don't fail a class it is hard to graduate on time." However, this hard work pays off in Westminster's admit rate to medical schools, which is double the national average. Students also love the music, education, and public relations programs here. Other majors are "hit or miss…depending on the staff in the department." Where the school falls shortest, however, is in its facilities. Undergrads tell us that because Westminster is "a very old school that relies on alumni for donations, our building are terribly old and it shows." Westminster has spent $36 million on renovations in the last few years, however, and current renovations to McGill Library have just been completed.

Life

Westminster has "a very active Greek life in which the majority of our student population is involved." "Students have integrated Greek life as a positive force and influence in their school careers with many opportunities for leadership roles and future connections leading up to a week-long "Greek Week."" Weekends usually "involve going to the fraternities," which "gets old after a while," but since the school is located "in a very small town near an Amish community, there isn't much off campus to do besides go to fraternity houses." On-campus alternatives include "weekly events with a musician, comedian, etc. Also, there are two free movies offered each weekend." As one student warns, "If you're into the bar scene, clubs, or big-city life, don't go to Westminster. You'll be disappointed. If you like things more laid-back and prefer a slow-paced life, Westminster is probably going to fit you pretty well." Aesthetes will also find much to enjoy, as "the campus is the most beautiful [place]…There are so many wide open spaces with pastures, barns, acres of land and the trees are gorgeous in the fall." Among intercollegiate athletics, "Football is a big thing on campus as well as basketball. Many students come out to support their fellow teammates and friends."

Student Body

"Westminster does not have a lot of diversity," as "most students are local," meaning they tend to be "white and from a middle to upper middle class family." "Of course you have your various groups: the jocks, the gothic kids, the cheerleader types, the hippies that never bathe, etc., but the typical student here would have to be someone who is relatively laid back," explains one student. "They wear American Eagle jeans, vintage T-shirts, and flip-flops year round. They are moderately aware of the world around them, politically and environmentally. They play ultimate Frisbee and guitar, and have probably started or head some club on campus that is particular to their interests. In their free time they read poems, sing, practice an instrument, watch *Family Guy*, or catch up with some friends. Many on campus seem apathetic toward just about everything, but a surprising number actually take the responsibility and initiative to make a difference." Politically, the student body leans toward the "conservative."

FINANCIAL AID: 724-946-7102 • E-MAIL: ADMIS@WESTMINSTER.EDU • WEBSITE: WWW.WESTMINSTER.EDU

THE PRINCETON REVIEW SAYS

Admissions

Very important factors considered include: rigor of secondary school record, standardized test scores, interview, *Important factors considered include:* Class rank, application essay, recommendation(s), character/personal qualities. *Other factors considered include:* alumni/ae relation, extracurricular activities, racial/ethnic status, talent/ability, volunteer work, work experience. SAT or ACT required; TOEFL required of all international applicants. High school diploma is required and GED is accepted. *Academic units required:* 4 English, 3 mathematics, 2 science, (2 science labs), 2 foreign language, 2 social studies, 1 history, 3 academic electives.

Financial Aid

Students should submit: FAFSA, institution's own financial aid form. The Princeton Review suggests that all financial aid forms be submitted as soon as possible after 1/1. *Need-based scholarships/grants offered:* Federal Pell, SEOG, state scholarships/grants, private scholarships, the school's own gift aid. *Loan aid offered:* FFEL Subsidized Stafford, FFEL Unsubsidized Stafford, FFEL PLUS, Federal Perkins, Resource Loans. Applicants will be notified of awards on a rolling basis beginning 11/1.

The Inside Word

Westminster College has grown increasingly more selective throughout the decade, the result of a 200+ percent increase in its applicant pool (without any corresponding increase in the size of its freshman class). The school admits on a rolling basis. Apply early to improve your chances.

THE SCHOOL SAYS "..."

From The Admissions Office

"Since its founding, Westminster has been dedicated to a solid foundation in today's most crucial social, cultural, and ethical issues. Related to the Presbyterian Church (U.S.A.), Westminster is home to people of many faiths. Our students and faculty, tradition of campus, and small-town setting all contribute to an enlightening educational experience.

"For purposes of admission and merit scholarships Westminster College will evaluate applicants using the composite score of the Math and Critical Reading sections of the SAT or the composite score of the ACT. Westminster will collect new Writing section scores and compare with national percentiles for possible inclusion in admission and scholarship criteria for the future."

SELECTIVITY

Admissions Rating	81
# of applicants	2,945
% of applicants accepted	59
% of acceptees attending	32

FRESHMAN PROFILE

Range SAT Critical Reading	470–570
Range SAT Math	480–590
Range ACT Composite	20–25
Minimum paper TOEFL	550
Minimum computer TOEFL	213
Average HS GPA	3.4
% graduated top 10% of class	20
% graduated top 25% of class	55
% graduated top 50% of class	87

DEADLINES

Early action	
Deadline	11/15
Notification	11/15
Regular	
Deadline	4/15
Notification	rolling
Nonfall registration?	no

APPLICANTS ALSO LOOK AT
AND SOMETIMES PREFER
Duquesne University
AND RARELY PREFER
Washington & Jefferson College
Thiel College
Allegheny College

FINANCIAL FACTS

Financial Aid Rating	61
Annual tuition	$26,940
Room and board	$8,440
Required fees	$1,100
Books and supplies	$1,000
% frosh rec. need-based scholarship or grant aid	82
% UG rec. need-based scholarship or grant aid	80
% frosh rec. non-need-based scholarship or grant aid	83
% UG rec. non-need-based scholarship or grant aid	79
% frosh rec. need-based self-help aid	69
% UG rec. need-based self-help aid	66
% UG borrow to pay for school	76
Average cumulative indebtedness	$17,618

WESTMINSTER COLLEGE (UT)

1840 SOUTH 1300 EAST, SALT LAKE CITY, UT 84105 • ADMISSIONS: 801-832-2200 • FAX: 801-832-3101

CAMPUS LIFE
Quality of Life Rating	98
Fire Safety Rating	98
Green Rating	77
Type of school	private
Environment	metropolis

STUDENTS
Total undergrad enrollment	2,104
% male/female	44/56
% from out of state	21
% from public high school	77
% live on campus	27
% African American	1
% Asian	3
% Caucasian	76
% Hispanic	6
% international	1
# of countries represented	40

SURVEY SAYS . . .
Registration is a breeze
Athletic facilities are great
School is well run
Students get along with local
community
Campus feels safe
Students are happy
Frats and sororities are unpopular or
nonexistent

ACADEMICS
Academic Rating	89
Calendar	4/1/4
Student/faculty ratio	11:1
Profs interesting rating	97
Profs accessible rating	89
Most common reg class size	10–19 students
Most common lab size	fewer than 10 students

MOST POPULAR MAJORS
business/commerce
nursing/(bsn, msn)
psychology

STUDENTS SAY ". . ."

Academics

There is more than one Westminster College, so let's not get confused. This is the one in the heart of Salt Lake City that's "the only liberal arts college in Utah." "Small class sizes" and "personal attention" abound on this "beautiful campus." Pre-professional programs are strong, particularly in nursing, education, and business. Westminster also offers some of the coolest programs anywhere. During an intense May term, students take unique courses, such as "Chemistry and Biology of Brewing," or study off campus. You can study aviation in Alaska, for example, or traditional Indian culture—in India. "The May Term trips are a great opportunity" to "learn more about a different country," a junior writes. A semester-long program called Winter at Westminster offers backcountry touring, clinics in bobsledding and Nordic jumping, and camping in a yurt. Back on campus, Westminster's "easily accessible" professors facilitate "fun and interactive" discussions. "All the professors know you on a first-name basis," explains one happy student. "They practically beg you to come to their office hours for help." Views of the administration are mixed. Some students see Westminster as "a well-oiled machine" and its administrators as "genuinely interested in how the students are doing and making sure that any problems are solved as quickly as possible." Other students call the administration "disconnected." "Our science and lab facilities are substandard," a senior writes, but the school will complete a $30 million science center in early 2010, and has spent almost $2 million in the past two years for new, state-of-the-art equipment.

Life

At Westminster, "Life on campus is very dramatic." "Everyone knows everyone else," and "everyone is involved in everyone else's business." Fortunately, there are numerous reasons for undergrads to get out and about: "Many people are involved with extracurricular activities," and "leadership opportunities" are abundant. The ASWC (Associated Students of Westminster College) also sponsors "many activities each week," including stand-up comics and dances. In addition, "The Music and Theater Departments are very popular." Student opinion of the food ranges from "not great" to it "sucks"—"they fry everything." Off campus, "There is a lot to do" around the city and "the state of Utah." The college "is located in the heart of Sugarhouse," one of Salt Lake City's oldest neighborhoods. "Clothes stores, book stores, bars, and restaurants are all within walking distance." "For fun," students "go to a movie or out to dinner" or "bask in the aroma-rich atmospheres of the local coffee shops." While "many students go to clubs and bars for fun," "this isn't a real big party school." "There is a segment of the student body population that will not party for religious reasons," notes a junior. "Proximity to the beautiful mountains" means that "outdoor activities" abound here. Westminster is only "minutes away from some pretty awesome ski resorts," so skiers and snowboarders can "maximize their time on the slopes." "Utah has the greatest snow on earth," avows a junior.

Students

"Westminster is not religiously affiliated," and many students here "are not religious at all." At the same time, "a large portion" of the student body is "religious and wholesome." "We're in Utah," explains a junior. When asked to describe a typical student, Westminster undergrads offer: "White, middle-class, from Utah, [and] fresh out of high school." "Most of the students are traditional students," but "there are many people over age 25" as well. The "self-motivated" students here are "very active (and liberal) politically" and "pretty studious." They "tend to be kind of preppy, but you can find hippies." There are "the children of the very rich who are just mediocre and the children of the very poor who are brilliant." "There are not many minorities on campus," and Westminster is "less diverse than the average university" but "more diverse, generally, than the rest of the state." Students from ethnic minorities who are here "seem to integrate well into the social groups on a friendly level."

WESTMINSTER COLLEGE (UT)

FINANCIAL AID: 801-832-2500 • E-MAIL: ADMISSION@WESTMINSTERCOLLEGE.EDU • WEBSITE: WWW.WESTMINSTERCOLLEGE.EDU

THE PRINCETON REVIEW SAYS

Admissions

Very important factors considered include: academic GPA, rigor of secondary school record. *Important factors considered include:* Class rank, application essay, standardized test scores, interview. *Other factors considered include:* Recommendation(s), alumni/ae relation, character/personal qualities, extracurricular activities, geographical residence, talent/ability, SAT or ACT required; ACT with Writing component recommended. TOEFL required of all international applicants. High school diploma is required and GED is accepted. *Academic units required:* 4 English, 2 mathematics, 3 science, 2 foreign language, 2 social studies, 1 history, 2 academic electives. *Academic units recommended:* 4 English, 3 mathematics, 3 science, 3 foreign language, 2 social studies, 1 history, 3 academic electives.

Financial Aid

Students should submit: FAFSA. The Princeton Review suggests that all financial aid forms be submitted as soon as possible after 1/1. *Need-based scholarships/grants offered:* Federal Pell, SEOG, state scholarships/grants, private scholarships, the school's own gift aid, United Negro College Fund. *Loan aid offered:* FFEL Subsidized Stafford, FFEL Unsubsidized Stafford, FFEL PLUS, Federal Perkins. Applicants will be notified of awards on a rolling basis beginning 3/15. Federal Work-Study Program available. Institutional employment available. Off-campus job opportunities are excellent.

The Inside Word

It's not spectacularly difficult to gain admission to Westminster, particularly if you have solid grades and have taken a reasonably broad college-prep curriculum; your high school grades are probably the single biggest admissions factor here; essays are also important. Your standardized test scores, on the other hand, don't need to be out of this world. While almost every student at Westminster is on some kind of scholarship, you should pay special attention to every facet of the application if you are gunning for a lot of free money.

THE SCHOOL SAYS ". . ."

From The Admissions Office

"Founded in 1875, Westminster College is a private, comprehensive, liberal arts college dedicated to students and their learning, and offers one of the most unique learning environments in the country. Located where the Rocky Mountains meet the vibrant city of Salt Lake, Westminster blends classroom learning with experiences derived from its unique location to help students develop skills and attributes critical for success in a rapidly changing world. Impassioned teaching and active learning are the hallmarks of the Westminster experience.

"Each application is read and reviewed individually by an admissions committee who takes into account both level of challenge in course work and grades received. Either the SAT or ACT exam is accepted. Writing ability will be assessed through the Writing sections of the SAT, ACT, application essays, and in some cases, other writing samples such as graded papers.

"Westminster College has a rolling application deadline and will accept applications until the class is filled. To be eligible for the widest array of financial aid—and more than 97 percent of freshmen receive some financial aid—April 15 is the priority consideration deadline for fall semester, and May 15 is the deadline for on-campus housing applications."

SELECTIVITY

Admissions Rating	86
# of applicants	1,348
% of applicants accepted	81
% of acceptees attending	41

FRESHMAN PROFILE

Range SAT Critical Reading	500–610
Range SAT Math	505–625
Range ACT Composite	21–27
Minimum paper TOEFL	550
Minimum computer TOEFL	213
Average HS GPA	3.47
% graduated top 10% of class	26
% graduated top 25% of class	55
% graduated top 50% of class	86

DEADLINES

Regular	
Notification	rolling
Nonfall registration?	yes

APPLICANTS ALSO LOOK AT

AND OFTEN PREFER
Utah State University
University of Utah

AND SOMETIMES PREFER
Brigham Young University (UT)
University of Puget Sound
Colorado College
Gonzaga University

AND RARELY PREFER
Lewis & Clark College

FINANCIAL FACTS

Financial Aid Rating	70
Annual tuition	$23,790
Room and board	$6,672
Required fees	$390
Books and supplies	$1,200
% frosh rec. need-based scholarship or grant aid	54
% UG rec. need-based scholarship or grant aid	56
% frosh rec. non-need-based scholarship or grant aid	9
% UG rec. non-need-based scholarship or grant aid	6
% frosh rec. need-based self-help aid	42
% UG rec. need-based self-help aid	48
% frosh rec. athletic scholarships	1
% UG rec. athletic scholarships	1
% frosh rec. any financial aid	97
% UG rec. any financial aid	86
% UG borrow to pay for school	66
Average cumulative indebtedness	$18,548

WHEATON COLLEGE (IL)

501 COLLEGE AVENUE, WHEATON, IL 60187 • ADMISSIONS: 630-752-5005 • FAX: 630-752-5285

CAMPUS LIFE

Quality of Life Rating	95
Fire Safety Rating	86
Green Rating	83
Type of school	private
Environment	town

STUDENTS

Total undergrad enrollment	2,344
% male/female	50/50
% from out of state	78
% from public high school	59
% live on campus	90
% African American	3
% Asian	8
% Caucasian	83
% Hispanic	4
% international	1
# of countries represented	18

SURVEY SAYS . . .

Students are very religious
Students get along with local community
Great food on campus
Frats and sororities are unpopular or nonexistent
Very little beer drinking
Very little drug use

ACADEMICS

Academic Rating	88
Calendar	semester
Student/faculty ratio	12:1
Profs interesting rating	87
Profs accessible rating	87
Most common reg class size	10–19 students
Most common lab size	10–19 students

MOST POPULAR MAJORS

business/managerial economics
English language and literature
psychology

STUDENTS SAY ". . ."

Academics

"As cheesy as it sounds, [Wheaton] really is about the integration of faith and learning," students assert, telling us that the school "is a close community of students with the same values and beliefs doing their best to learn and grow closer to each other and to God." With a "great theology program," "excellent ministry programs," and business and economics departments led by professors with "real-life experience [bringing] many real-life situations into the classroom," Wheaton "is probably the top Evangelical college in the nation," according to its undergraduates. They support their claim by describing the "many internship opportunities" available here and by pointing out that "in terms of resumes and formal instruction from professors, [Wheaton] students are well prepared for the business world or some of the best grad schools in the nation." Wheaton's "liberal arts focus causes [students] not to specialize completely but to be interested in everything and draw connections between completely different things," creating an environment in which "Wheaton students are very good at engaging with everything we are exposed to. We love to delight in and enjoy what is good and beautiful, whether that means the wonderful idioms of a spoken language, the counterintuitive nuances of quantum mechanics, or the pattern made by the icicles hanging from Williston [Hall]'s dormer windows." Although "the academics at Wheaton are superb," some departments suffer from under-funding. "Our science building, our music building, and our Internet capabilities are all extremely sub-par," students complain.

Life

Wheaton is located just west of Chicago, so "students have the entire world of Chicago open to them, which has everything you could want in a city," and because "there is a train station right on campus," the city is extremely accessible. Making matters even better, The area surrounding the campus has a ton of little stores to explore and things to do." Wheaton's "rigorous course load" means that "school work consumes a large portion of [our time]," but students still make opportunities to "do very unusual things for fun, especially in winter when it is too cold to be outside, like pool, ping pong, darts, watching *The Office*, playing piano, movies (DVDs mainly), and when weather permits, Frisbee, volleyball, football, soccer, running, relaxing in the sun, and in general just talking with each other." What they don't do is "drink, smoke, or do drugs. Period. (Except for the occasional 21st birthday, and even then they don't get smashed.)" Whatever they're doing, "Whether it's playing games on the dorm floor, going into Chicago with friends, or getting involved in campus or church groups," "life at Wheaton revolves around community." As one student explains, "The Christian stance makes for a feeling of community that permeates almost all of the events and even the classes. We're all like one big family, and the general congeniality of the students and the ease with which we can communicate with our teachers reinforces that feeling."

Student Body

The typical Wheaton undergrad "comes from a middle-class family, [and]a strong Christian home, excelled in their high school, and scored highly on the SAT." Students tend to be "perfectionists...everyone wants to do the 'right' thing, so people stress a lot about grades, appearance, even making sure they have the right balance in their lives." Atypical students "probably [make up] 15 percent" of the student body; they include "those who are either here for athletic reasons or because their parents made them, and they don't follow the rules as much." Two conspicuous subpopulations here are the "conservies" (students of the conservatory) and homeschoolers, "The stereotype for these students is that they are socially awkward and are always practicing their instrument (conservies) or doing homework (homeschoolers)....The conservies all have each other...they hang out at the conservatory and talk about music. The homeschoolers eventually learn how to make friends and interact with people on a daily basis," although they are initially "socially awkward."

FINANCIAL AID: 630-752-5021 • E-MAIL: ADMISSIONS@WHEATON.EDU • WEBSITE: WWW.WHEATON.EDU

THE PRINCETON REVIEW SAYS

Admissions

Very important factors considered include: Application essay, academic GPA, recommendation(s), rigor of secondary school record, standardized test scores, character/personal qualities, interview, religious affiliation/commitment, *Important factors considered include:* extracurricular activities, talent/ability, volunteer work, work experience. *Other factors considered include:* Class rank, alumni/ae relation, first generation, geographical residence, level of applicant's interest, racial/ethnic status, state residency, SAT or ACT required; ACT with Writing component required. TOEFL required of all international applicants. High school diploma is required and GED is accepted. *Academic units recommended:* 4 English.

Financial Aid

Students should submit: FAFSA, institution's own financial aid form. The Princeton Review suggests that all financial aid forms be submitted as soon as possible after 1/1. *Need-based scholarships/grants offered:* Federal Pell, SEOG, state scholarships/grants, the school's own gift aid. *Loan aid offered:* FFEL Subsidized Stafford, FFEL Unsubsidized Stafford, FFEL PLUS, Federal Perkins. Applicants will be notified of awards on a rolling basis beginning 3/1. Federal Work-Study Program available. Institutional employment available. Off-campus job opportunities are excellent.

The Inside Word

Admissions at Wheaton are highly competitive. Applicants must demonstrate strong academic skills and aptitude through schoolwork and testing. The applicant pool is small enough for admissions officers to consider each candidate very closely to ensure a good match between school and student. A sincere profession of faith, along with a letter of recommendation from a pastor, Bible study leader, or church official, is an essential part of any application.

THE SCHOOL SAYS "..."

From The Admissions Office

"At Wheaton, we're commited to being a community that fearlessly pursues truth, upholds an academically rigorous curriculum, and promotes virtue. The college takes seriously its impact on society. The influence of Wheaton is seen in fields ranging from government (the former speaker of the house) to sports (two NBA coaches) to business (the CEO of John Deere) to music (Metropolitan Opera National Competition winners) to education (over 40 college presidents) to global ministry (Billy Graham). Wheaton seeks students who want to make a difference and are passionate about their Christian faith and rigorous academic pursuit.

"Applicants are required to submit results from the SAT or the ACT with Writing section. Wheaton will use the highest of these scores from either test in evaluating a student's application."

SELECTIVITY

Admissions Rating	99
# of applicants	2,083
% of applicants accepted	62
% of acceptees attending	45
# accepting a place on wait list	164
% admitted from wait list	91

FRESHMAN PROFILE

Range SAT Critical Reading	600–700
Range SAT Math	610–690
Range SAT Writing	600–710
Range ACT Composite	27–31
Minimum paper TOEFL	550
Minimum computer TOEFL	213
Average HS GPA	3.73
% graduated top 10% of class	59
% graduated top 25% of class	85
% graduated top 50% of class	98

DEADLINES

Early action	
Deadline	11/1
Notification	12/31
Regular	
Deadline	1/10
Notification	4/1
Nonfall registration?	no

APPLICANTS ALSO LOOK AT

AND SOMETIMES PREFER
Taylor University

AND RARELY PREFER
Grove City College
Gordon College
Bethel University (MN)
Calvin College
Cedarville University
Indiana Wesleyan University
Westmont College

FINANCIAL FACTS

Financial Aid Rating	77
Annual tuition	$25,500
Room and board	$7,618
Books and supplies	$782
% frosh rec. need-based scholarship or grant aid	50
% UG rec. need-based scholarship or grant aid	46
% frosh rec. non-need-based scholarship or grant aid	16
% UG rec. non-need-based scholarship or grant aid	17
% frosh rec. need-based self-help aid	52
% UG rec. need-based self-help aid	47
% frosh rec. any financial aid	69.8
% UG rec. any financial aid	67.8
% UG borrow to pay for school	57
Average cumulative indebtedness	$21,549

WHEATON COLLEGE (MA)

OFFICE OF ADMISSION, NORTON, MA 02766 • ADMISSIONS: 508-286-8251 • FAX: 508-286-8271

CAMPUS LIFE

Quality of Life Rating	67
Fire Safety Rating	83
Green Rating	86
Type of school	private
Environment	village

STUDENTS

Total undergrad enrollment	1,655
% male/female	39/61
% from out of state	67
% from public high school	63
% live on campus	91
% African American	5
% Asian	3
% Caucasian	78
% Hispanic	3
% international	4
# of countries represented	36

SURVEY SAYS . . .

Frats and sororities are unpopular or nonexistent
Student government is popular
Lots of beer drinking
Hard liquor is popular

ACADEMICS

Academic Rating	94
Calendar	semester
Student/faculty ratio	10:1
Profs interesting rating	88
Profs accessible rating	87
Most common reg class size	10–19 students
Most common lab size	10–19 students

MOST POPULAR MAJORS

literature
psychology
history
English

STUDENTS SAY " . . ."

Academics

A "small liberal arts school trying to break through and compete with the 'small Ivies' (Williams, Amherst, Colby etc.)," Wheaton College is "a true liberal arts college: People study what they are interested in for the sake of learning it and because it fascinates them". The school caters to students with eclectic interests through its Foundations requirements (which require at least one course in non-Western civilization) and its Connections curriculum (which requires students to take either two sets of two related courses or one set of three related courses across academic categories), leading students to crow that "Wheaton's curriculum is based on providing students with global awareness. It focuses on trying to get students to understand the dynamics of their own personal actions alongside that of those around the world." Undergrads also love the personal attention, "You can't get lost here. There's always someone you can talk to—your own age or a professor or administrator—if you're having problems. It's a really supportive and safe environment." And students love the "many opportunities to apply classroom knowledge outside of the class (whether through internships, research projects, fellowships, study abroad, etc.)." Many praise the school's new "absolutely amazing" Kollett Center, which houses "peer mentors, peer tutors for every subject, the academic advising office, and internship/career/job search," "the most useful college center on the face of the planet…because they help with you in writing resumes, finding internships, and preparing for life after college." Wheaton students also benefit from "a really active" alumni network "willing to help in any way."

Life

"From Monday through Wednesday, people are reserved and very focused" on the Wheaton campus. Thursday "usually starts the weekend where upperclassmen will head to the bars," while on "Friday and Saturday, most of the school will socialize by drinking at one of the on-campus houses or in groups in the dorms." Students explain that "because there are no frats, parties are held in houses (either on or off campus) or in dorm rooms." One student says, "It's actually a bit pathetic that that's the best they can do." There are also "college dances, which sometimes have free beer for those over 21," but many feel that "The dances are reminiscent of high school and usually suck except for the free beer." There are also "tons of musical and theatrical performances, club events, lectures, and other great things going on" around campus. Even so, students concede that the campus "gets a little boring at times." Hometown Norton "is very, very, very (did I say very yet?) small," the sort of place where "the biggest decision is whether you want to walk to Walgreens or CVS," so students seeking off-campus diversion must travel farther. That's why "A lot of students will go into Boston or Providence for a day on the weekends. Also, there are always home games or away games on the weekends, so many students attend one or the other."

Student Body

Wheaton "is made up of reasonably familiar subgroups. We have our jocks, and our über-nerds, slackers, and artists. There is, however, a large gray area, and most people don't limit themselves to one group." The predominant vibe is "a little bit preppy with a portion of hippie," with "the popped collar and pearls set" coexisting with "plenty of free spirits…Whether they choose to wear boat-shoes or Birks, they've got a place" here. Most students "are well-balanced…academically serious, but school is not the only activity in their lives." They "seem to generally be liberal, but everyone is so apathetic toward current events that it is difficult to inspire student activism." Undergrads estimate that "23 percent of us are varsity athletes;" and more than a few of the remaining 77 percent "do not like [the athletes] and feel like they get preferential treatment just because they are athletes."

FINANCIAL AID: 508-286-8232 • E-MAIL: ADMISSION@WHEATONCOLLEGE.EDU • WEBSITE: WWW.WHEATONCOLLEGE.EDU

THE PRINCETON REVIEW SAYS

Admissions

Very important factors considered include: Application essay, academic GPA, rigor of secondary school record, character/personal qualities, extracurricular activities, first generation, talent/ability, *Important factors considered include:* Class rank, recommendation(s), alumni/ae relation, interview, volunteer work, work experience. *Other factors considered include:* Geographical residence, level of applicant's interest, racial/ethnic status, state residency, TOEFL required of all international applicants. High school diploma is required and GED is accepted. *Academic units recommended:* 4 English, 4 mathematics, 3 science, (2 science labs), 4 foreign language, 3 social studies, 2 history.

Financial Aid

Students should submit: FAFSA, CSS/Financial Aid PROFILE, noncustodial PROFILE, business/farm supplement. Parent and Student Federal Tax Returns and W-2s. Regular filing deadline is 2/1. The Princeton Review suggests that all financial aid forms be submitted as soon as possible after 1/1. *Need-based scholarships/grants offered:* Federal Pell, SEOG, state scholarships/grants, private scholarships, the school's own gift aid. *Loan aid offered:* FFEL Subsidized Stafford, FFEL Unsubsidized Stafford, FFEL PLUS, Federal Perkins. Applicants will be notified of awards on or about 4/1. Federal Work-Study Program available. Institutional employment available. Off-campus job opportunities are good.

The Inside Word

Wheaton gives applicants the option of not submitting standardized test scores. The school also invites applicants to submit optional personal academic portfolios, collections of completed schoolwork that demonstrates talents the applicant wants to highlight. All applicants should seriously consider this option; for those who do not submit test scores, an academic portfolio is practically imperative, both as an indicator of the applicant's seriousness about Wheaton and as evidence of academic excellence (evidence that standardized test scores might otherwise provide).

THE SCHOOL SAYS "..."

From The Admissions Office

"What makes for a 'best college'? Is it merely the hard-to-define notions of prestige or image? We don't think so. We think what makes college 'best' and best for you is a school that will make you a first-rate thinker and writer, a pragmatic professional in your work, and an ethical practitioner in your life. To get you to all these places, Wheaton takes advantage of its great combinations: a beautiful, secluded New England campus combined with access to Boston and Providence; a high quality, classic liberal arts and sciences curriculum combined with award-winning internship, job, and community-service programs; and a campus that respects your individuality in the context of the larger community. What's the 'best' outcome of a Wheaton education? A start on life that combines meaningful work, significant relationships, and a commitment to your local and global community. Far more than for what they've studied or for what they've gone on to do for a living, we're most proud of Wheaton graduates for who they become.

"Wheaton does not require students to submit the results of any standardized testing. The only exception is the TOEFL for students for whom English is a second language. Students who choose to submit standardized testing may use results from the SAT or the ACT."

SELECTIVITY

Admissions Rating	93
# of applicants	3,832
% of applicants accepted	43
% of acceptees attending	25
# accepting a place on wait list	237
% admitted from wait list	27
# of early decision applicants	195
% accepted early decision	86

FRESHMAN PROFILE

Range SAT Critical Reading	580–680
Range SAT Math	580–670
Range ACT Composite	26–29
Minimum paper TOEFL	580
Minimum computer TOEFL	243
Average HS GPA	3.5
% graduated top 10% of class	56
% graduated top 25% of class	72
% graduated top 50% of class	86

DEADLINES

Early Decision	
Deadline	11/15
Notification	12/15
Regular	
Deadline	1/15
Notification	4/1
Nonfall registration?	yes

APPLICANTS ALSO LOOK AT

AND OFTEN PREFER
Connecticut College
Bates College

AND SOMETIMES PREFER
Hamilton College
University of Vermont
Skidmore College

AND RARELY PREFER
Brandeis University
Clark University
Boston University

FINANCIAL FACTS

Financial Aid Rating	90
Annual tuition	$39,565
Room and board	$9,590
Required fees	$285
Books and supplies	$940
% frosh rec. need-based scholarship or grant aid	51
% UG rec. need-based scholarship or grant aid	47
% frosh rec. non-need-based scholarship or grant aid	13
% UG rec. non-need-based scholarship or grant aid	13
% frosh rec. need-based self-help aid	55
% UG rec. need-based self-help aid	50
% frosh rec. any financial aid	70
% UG rec. any financial aid	65
% UG borrow to pay for school	48
Average cumulative indebtedness	$24,428

WHITMAN COLLEGE

345 BOYER AVENUE, WALLA WALLA, WA 99362-2083 • ADMISSIONS: 509-527-5176 • FAX: 509-527-4967

CAMPUS LIFE

Quality of Life Rating	98
Fire Safety Rating	60*
Green Rating	91
Type of school	private
Environment	town

STUDENTS

Total undergrad enrollment	1,430
% male/female	45/55
% from out of state	60
% from public high school	75
% live on campus	62
% in (# of) fraternities	34 (4)
% in (# of) sororities	29 (3)
% African American	2
% Asian	10
% Caucasian	66
% Hispanic	6
% Native American	1
% international	3
# of countries represented	32

SURVEY SAYS . . .

Athletic facilities are great
School is well run
Students are friendly
Dorms are like palaces
Intramural sports are popular
Musical organizations are popular

ACADEMICS

Academic Rating	98
Calendar	semester
Student/faculty ratio	9:1
Profs interesting rating	98
Profs accessible rating	97
Most common reg class size	10–19 students
Most common lab size	10–19 students

MOST POPULAR MAJORS

biology/biological sciences
history
political science and government

STUDENTS SAY ". . ."

Academics

If learning can be both rigorous and laid-back at the same time, it happens at Whitman College in Walla Walla, WA. The "challenging" academics here are coupled with a "relaxed attitude" in order to give students "the best education possible without sacrificing all the fun one expects of college." Populated mainly by "intelligent, ambitious liberals with far-reaching goals," this somewhat idealistic school seeks to build critical thinking skills through "an earnest discourse about 'life, the universe, and everything.'" So no one starts off with a blank slate, all first-year students are required to take a course referred to as "Core" which offers a survey of Western thought, starting with *The Odyssey*, working through Socrates, Plato, Augustine, up through Marx, Voltaire, and other thinkers who shaped modern thought. Distribution requirements ensure that all students get a breadth of courses, and a lack of TAs ensures that they get all the attention they need. Although there's always a dud or two in the mix, professors are "genuinely brilliant and interesting people" and "love to spend time with students outside of class," whether it be for academic help or just conversation. "It is not uncommon to have potlucks, classes, or movie night over at your professor's house with your class," says one student.

On the administrative side of things, bureaucracy and red tape are kept to a minimum in this chill environment through "effortless use of the 'system.'" and the administration gets raves all around for its devotion to "maintaining quality student life," which is something of a rarity. "I have never heard of ANY college being as supportive as this place has been to me in just the past two years," says a student. "Whitman's president gave me a ride to campus one semester after I met him at the airport," says another. As one can imagine, all these things come together to form a student body that's "happy, well-balanced, and well-cared-for."

Life

Most people stay on campus for their fun, "especially first-years," and throughout this "bubble" the "sense of closeness and comradeship is very evident through attendance at student-run concerts, art shows, etc." Everything is within ten minutes' walking distance. Academics take precedence for almost everyone, but "most students find time to party on the weekends" at the frats, due to a "lenient and fair" alcohol policy. Thanks to the campus activities board, "there's almost always something fun going on, whether or not a person chooses to drink," such as Drive-In Movie Night and Casino Night. With "four beautiful seasons," outdoor activities are also very popular, thanks to "a great gear rental program that gets people outside hiking, biking, kayaking, and rock climbing," and "Frisbees are everywhere when it's warm." In fact, there's so much going on "if someone says they are bored, students laugh and wish they could relate."

Student Body

It's a sociable bunch at Whitman, where most students "are interested in trying new things and meeting new people" and "everyone seems to have a weird interest or talent or passion." The quirky Whitties "usually have a strong opinion about SOMETHING," and one freshman refers to her classmates as ""cool nerds." As with many Northwestern schools, diversity here is pretty low, but the school at least puts up a fight for getting more than the typical "mid- to upperclass and white" contingent. Everyone here is pretty outdoorsy and environmentally aware ("to the point where you almost feel guilty for printing an assignment"), and leans far enough to the left to tip over; there's also not much of a religious quotient to the student body, and who that are find themselves "subtly looked down upon."

FINANCIAL AID: 509-527-5178 • E-MAIL: ADMISSION@WHITMAN.EDU • WEBSITE: WWW.WHITMAN.EDU

THE PRINCETON REVIEW SAYS

Admissions

Very important factors considered include: Application essay, academic GPA, rigor of secondary school record, character/personal qualities, *Important factors considered include:* Recommendation(s), standardized test scores, extracurricular activities, racial/ethnic status, talent/ability. *Other factors considered include:* Class rank, alumni/ae relation, first generation, geographical residence, interview, level of applicant's interest, state residency, volunteer work, work experience. SAT or ACT required; ACT with Writing component required. TOEFL required of all international applicants. High school diploma is required and GED is accepted. *Academic units recommended:* 4 English, 4 mathematics, 3 science, (2 science labs), 2 foreign language, 2 social studies, 2 history, 1 Arts.

Financial Aid

Students should submit: FAFSA, CSS/Financial Aid PROFILE. Regular filing deadline is 2/1. The Princeton Review suggests that all financial aid forms be submitted as soon as possible after 1/1. *Need-based scholarships/grants offered:* Federal Pell, SEOG, state scholarships/grants, private scholarships, the school's own gift aid. *Loan aid offered:* FFEL Subsidized Stafford, FFEL Unsubsidized Stafford, FFEL PLUS, Federal Perkins, state loans, alternative student loans. Applicants will be notified of awards on a rolling basis beginning 12/20. Federal Work-Study Program available. Institutional employment available. Off-campus job opportunities are good.

The Inside Word

Whitman's admissions committee emphasizes essays and extracurriculars more than SAT scores. The college cares much more about who you are and what you have to offer if you enroll than it does about what your numbers will do for the freshman academic profile. Whitman is a mega-sleeper. Educators all over the country know it as an excellent institution, and the college's alums support it at one of the highest rates of giving at any college in the nation. Students seeking a top-quality liberal arts college owe it to themselves to take a look.

THE SCHOOL SAYS "..."

From The Admissions Office

"Whitman is a place that encourages you to explore past the boundaries of disciplines because learning and living don't always fall neatly into tidy little compartments. Many students choose Whitman specifically because they're interested in a particular career such as business or engineering but want the well-rounded preparation that only a liberal arts education provides. Signatures of Whitman include Core (first-year program), senior exams, semester in the West, and Fellowships.

"Applicants are required to take the SAT or ACT with Writing section. For students who take the SAT or ACT more than once, Whitman will combine the best sub scores."

SELECTIVITY

Admissions Rating	99
# of applicants	3,096
% of applicants accepted	46
% of acceptees attending	28
# accepting a place on wait list	188
% admitted from wait list	13
# of early decision applicants	145
% accepted early decision	74

FRESHMAN PROFILE

Range SAT Critical Reading	630–730
Range SAT Math	610–700
Range SAT Writing	620–710
Range ACT Composite	28–32
Minimum paper TOEFL	560
Minimum computer TOEFL	220
Average HS GPA	3.81
% graduated top 10% of class	71
% graduated top 25% of class	94
% graduated top 50% of class	99

DEADLINES

Early Decision	
Deadline	11/15
Notification	12/21
Regular	
Priority	11/15
Deadline	1/15
Notification	4/1
Nonfall registration?	yes

APPLICANTS ALSO LOOK AT

AND OFTEN PREFER
Pomona College
Carleton College
Stanford University

AND SOMETIMES PREFER
Macalester College
Colorado College

AND RARELY PREFER
Lewis & Clark College
University of Puget Sound

FINANCIAL FACTS

Financial Aid Rating	71
Annual tuition	$34,880
Room and board	$8,820
Required fees	$312
Books and supplies	$1,400
% frosh rec. need-based scholarship or grant aid	48
% UG rec. need-based scholarship or grant aid	45
% frosh rec. non-need-based scholarship or grant aid	21
% UG rec. non-need-based scholarship or grant aid	12
% frosh rec. need-based self-help aid	37
% UG rec. need-based self-help aid	38
% frosh rec. any financial aid	81
% UG rec. any financial aid	76
% UG borrow to pay for school	49
Average cumulative indebtedness	$16,684

WHITTIER COLLEGE

13406 PHILADELPHIA STREET, PO BOX 634, WHITTIER, CA 90608 • ADMISSIONS: 562-907-4238 • FAX: 562-907-4870

CAMPUS LIFE

Quality of Life Rating	**69**
Fire Safety Rating	**82**
Green Rating	**83**
Type of school	private
Environment	city

STUDENTS

Total undergrad enrollment	1,257
% male/female	45/55
% from out of state	27
% live on campus	60
% in (# of) fraternities	14 (4)
% in (# of) sororities	20 (5)
% African American	3
% Asian	8
% Caucasian	46
% Hispanic	30
% Native American	1
% international	2
# of countries represented	17

SURVEY SAYS . . .

Great library
Diverse student types on campus
Different types of students interact
Great off-campus food
Student publications are popular
Lots of beer drinking
Hard liquor is popular

ACADEMICS

Academic Rating	**85**
Calendar	4/1/4
Student/faculty ratio	13:1
Profs interesting rating	87
Profs accessible rating	92
Most common reg class size	10–19 students
Most common lab size	10–19 students

MOST POPULAR MAJORS

biology/biological sciences
business/commerce
psychology

STUDENTS SAY ". . ."

Academics

Whittier College in California provides the quintessential liberal arts education by placing a strong focus on writing and maintaining a wide breadth and depth of knowledge within the humanities. With just 1,300 students enrolled, Whittier offers a small school experience, meaning "there aren't always a ton of choices, but the sense of community and the personal attention mostly makes up for it." "The academic experience all depends on how much work you put in," says a student, and the potential for greatness is there for those who want it. Higher up, students say that the school's administration "leaves much to be desired," alluding to a lack of communication between different divisions and uneven distribution of resources between different areas of campus life. However, one would be hard pressed to find better professors. They're here "because they love to teach and it shows"; all do most of the teaching themselves rather than "foisting it off onto a TA," which means that teachers and students have the opportunity to be peers and "defy typical 'college classroom' norms." Most classes are very small and are structured around discussion rather than straight lectures, and the instructors "keep the busywork to a minimum, basing your grade on a handful of papers, a midterm, and a final." "Really, the professors MAKE Whittier College," sums up a senior.

Life

The location of the campus is favorable due to the ease with which one is able to "travel to the posh LA scene, the beach, or to relax in Orange County." Uptown Whittier isn't really a college town, but it does offer a "number of different restaurants," as well as a movie theater, street fairs, and coffee shops. A brand-new student center that opened in August of 2008 includes new dining facilities, a bookstore, student office space, and a recreation room. Residential halls have also been updated in recent years, and the new housing and dining options should help alleviate complaints from prior years about "ancient facilities" and "poor...meal plan options." The college provides "a variety of dances, movie nights, athletic events, theatrical events, and guest entertainers/speakers to keep students moderately occupied," and students organizations and clubs help pass the rest of the time. "Even in January, there are days when we can lay out and sunbathe outside the dorms," says a junior. Though a lot of in-staters choose to go home on weekends, there is a "large chunk" of the school population involved in societies (Whittier's version of sororities or fraternities), and after class, "almost everyone is constantly in party mode." Many students "get the impression that people become bored easily here," and resort to drinking and marijuana, both of which are very prevalent at Whittier.

Student Body

Diversity is the name of the game at Whittier, and nearly a third of the campus is Hispanic, often the first generation in their family to attend college. International students are also well-represented, as are those hailing from Hawaii. Such a mixed pot makes for a lot of melting, and most students don't have any problems finding a niche, choosing to "stay with their clubs, majors, sports teams, and other such groupings," though mingling between defined groups is somewhat rare. Many students are here because of financial aid or scholarship, which makes some sad that their classmates "look forward to a night out at the nearby Radisson hotel for 'thirsty Thursdays' rather than an awesome discussion" in their class." It's a small campus, so by the time you're a senior, "you know pretty much everyone on campus," which most think is "a fabulous thing."

FINANCIAL AID: 562-907-4285 • E-MAIL: ADMISSION@WHITTIER.EDU • WEBSITE: WWW.WHITTIER.EDU

THE PRINCETON REVIEW SAYS

Admissions

Very important factors considered include: Application essay, rigor of secondary school record. *Important factors considered include:* Academic GPA, recommendation(s), standardized test scores, character/personal qualities, extracurricular activities, interview, talent/ability, volunteer work. *Other factors considered include:* Class rank, alumni/ae relation, first generation, geographical residence, racial/ethnic status, state residency, work experience. SAT or ACT required; ACT with Writing component required. TOEFL required of all international applicants. High school diploma is required and GED is accepted. *Academic units required:* 3 English, 2 mathematics, 1 science, (1 science labs), 2 foreign language, 1 social studies. *Academic units recommended:* 4 English, 3 mathematics, 2 science, 3 foreign language, 2 social studies.

Financial Aid

Students should submit: FAFSA, Whittier College Basic Asset Data Sheet. Regular filing deadline is 6/30. The Princeton Review suggests that all financial aid forms be submitted as soon as possible after 1/1. *Need-based scholarships/grants offered:* Federal Pell, SEOG, state scholarships/grants, private scholarships, the school's own gift aid. *Loan aid offered:* Direct PLUS, FFEL Subsidized Stafford, FFEL Unsubsidized Stafford, FFEL PLUS, Federal Perkins, alternative financing loans. Applicants will be notified of awards on a rolling basis beginning 2/15. Federal Work-Study Program available. Off-campus job opportunities are good.

The Inside Word

While the relatively high admissions rate for a private college may indicate otherwise, the Admissions Committee at Whittier subjects each candidate to very close scrutiny and their interest in making good solid matches between candidates and the college is paramount. If Whittier is high on your list, make sure you put forth a serious effort to demonstrate what you want out of the college and what you'll bring to the table in return.

THE SCHOOL SAYS "..."

From The Admissions Office

"Faculty and students at Whittier share a love of learning and delight in the life of the mind. They join in understanding the value of the intellectual quest, the use of reason, and a respect for values. They seek knowledge of their own culture and the informed appreciation of other traditions, and they explore the interrelatedness of knowledge and the connections among disciplines. An extraordinary community emerges from teachers and students representing a variety of academic pursuits, individuals who have come together at Whittier in the belief that study within the liberal arts forms the best foundation for rewarding endeavor throughout a lifetime.

"Whittier College is a vibrant, residential, four-year liberal arts institution where intellectual inquiry and experiential learning are fostered in a community that promotes respect for diversity of thought and culture. A Whittier College education produces enthusiastic, independent thinkers who flourish in graduate studies, the evolving global workplace, and life."

SELECTIVITY
Admissions Rating	84
# of applicants	2,196
% of applicants accepted	67
% of acceptees attending	20

FRESHMAN PROFILE
Range SAT Critical Reading	480–600
Range SAT Math	480–602
Range SAT Writing	480–590
Range ACT Composite	20–27
Minimum paper TOEFL	550
Minimum computer TOEFL	230
Average HS GPA	3.11
% graduated top 10% of class	34
% graduated top 25% of class	45
% graduated top 50% of class	89

DEADLINES
Early action	
Deadline	12/1
Notification	12/30
Regular	
Priority	2/1
Notification	rolling
Nonfall registration?	yes

APPLICANTS ALSO LOOK AT
AND OFTEN PREFER
University of Redlands
Occidental College
AND RARELY PREFER
Chapman University

FINANCIAL FACTS
Financial Aid Rating	85
Annual tuition	$31,950
Room and board	$9,050
Required fees	$520
Books and supplies	$1,566
% frosh rec. need-based scholarship or grant aid	54
% UG rec. need-based scholarship or grant aid	55
% frosh rec. non-need-based scholarship or grant aid	39
% UG rec. non-need-based scholarship or grant aid	45
% frosh rec. need-based self-help aid	59
% UG rec. need-based self-help aid	64
% frosh rec. any financial aid	92
% UG rec. any financial aid	89
% UG borrow to pay for school	73
Average cumulative indebtedness	$31,179

WILLAMETTE UNIVERSITY

900 STATE STREET, SALEM, OR 97301 • ADMISSIONS: 503-370-6303 • FAX: 503-375-5363

CAMPUS LIFE
Quality of Life Rating	78
Fire Safety Rating	81
Green Rating	88
Type of school	private
Affiliation	Methodist
Environment	city

STUDENTS
Total undergrad enrollment	1,821
% male/female	45/55
% from out of state	69
% from public high school	80
% live on campus	68
% in (# of) fraternities	20 (4)
% in (# of) sororities	27 (3)
% African American	4
% Asian	6
% Caucasian	57
% Hispanic	4
% international	1
# of countries represented	16

SURVEY SAYS . . .
No one cheats
Lab facilities are great
Great library
Students are friendly
Musical organizations are popular

ACADEMICS
Academic Rating	93
Calendar	semester
Student/faculty ratio	11:1
Profs interesting rating	87
Profs accessible rating	87
Most common reg class size	10–19 students

MOST POPULAR MAJORS
biology/biological sciences
economics
psychology

STUDENTS SAY ". . ."

Academics

Willamette University is an "academically rigorous," intimate, and "seriously gorgeous" liberal arts school in Oregon. "Outstanding" academic programs include the sciences, a "great focus" on the arts, a popular Japanese studies program, and "a highly acclaimed political science program." Across the board, undergrads report "a lot of school work" which includes a first-year seminar and a senior project. On the plus side, "small class sizes allow lots of discussion and personal attention," and undergraduate research opportunities allow students to work with faculty members on the kinds of projects reserved for grad students at most other schools. Willamette is also "very accommodating for double majors." Professors are, "for the most part, super interesting and exciting." "The really good professors make every single class really enjoyable," are "very involved with students' lives," and are "very responsive to the needs of students." A politics major beams: "I'm only a freshman and I've already had dinner at a professor's house, just like the 'spiel' said." Administrators "seem to slack off in a lot of ways" but, ultimately, they "will help you out with whatever you'd like to pursue." "If you want to start something on campus, there is usually a way."

Life

"The overall ambience" at Willamette is "relaxed and inviting." Students here describe their school as "an oasis of enlightenment" surrounded by a "sketchy" "cultural wasteland" (Salem, OR). Intercollegiate and intramural sports are hugely popular, and the "incredibly strong" track and cross-country programs are especially noteworthy. Quite often "you'll see students reading or relaxing on campus by the stream, or in the [quad]." "Some of the most fun I have is just hanging out with people at random places on campus," adds a sophomore. Willamette does, however, "gear up every now and again for campus activities like our music festival or for a sit-in," explains an anthropology major. While "there are several events that are sponsored by Greeks," frats don't dominate. "If you're in one and know people in them, they're great. If you aren't, then you don't really care." A junior takes a more concerned position: "One of the biggest drawbacks to our school is the party scene is not very good. The administration is very restrictive with Greek parties, off-campus parties, and other sorts of parties that students try to have." By all accounts, however, "access to outdoor activities" is fantastic. Willamette is "two hours from the coast" and "two hours from the mountains." Also, "it's only a 45-minute drive over to Portland" and "a ton of cultural stuff."

Student Body

Undergrads report "a lot of rich kids" at Willamette, and portray "the typical student" as "white," suburban, and "from the Northwest, most likely Oregon." Many students, however, receive "sweet" financial aid packages, and an excellent scholarship program "attracts students from a huge variety of backgrounds." Still, "there are not that many ethnic minorities." Asian students make up the largest minority here, and a fair number hail from Japan "as Willamette has a program with the Tokyo International University." Students at Willamette rate their "interesting, intelligent, genuine, [and] community-oriented" peers as "pretty hard workers" and say "there's a social group for almost everyone—jocks, preps, partiers, nerds; you name it." There are also "outdoorsy" types and "a lot of musicians" here. Conflict between groups is very minimal. "Everyone is accepting…so it's not intimidating to meet random people." Politically, Willamette is "extremely liberal." There are plenty of "politically left-wing people who love granola and Howard Dean," though, interestingly, few "real hippies."

FINANCIAL AID: 503-370-6273 • E-MAIL: LIBARTS@WILLAMETTE.EDU • WEBSITE: WWW.WILLAMETTE.EDU

THE PRINCETON REVIEW SAYS

Admissions

Very important factors considered include: Class rank, application essay, academic GPA, rigor of secondary school record, standardized test scores, *Important factors considered include:* recommendation(s), alumni/ae relation, character/personal qualities, interview. *Other factors considered include:* extracurricular activities, first generation, geographical residence, racial/ethnic status, talent/ability, volunteer work, work experience. SAT or ACT required; ACT with Writing component required. TOEFL required of all international applicants. High school diploma is required and GED is accepted. *Academic units recommended:* 4 English, 4 mathematics, 3 science, (3 science labs), 3 foreign language, 1 social studies, 2 history.

Financial Aid

Students should submit: FAFSA, CSS/Financial Aid PROFILE only required for Early Action applicants (to be filed by 12/01). Regular filing deadline is 2/1. The Princeton Review suggests that all financial aid forms be submitted as soon as possible after 1/1. *Need-based scholarships/grants offered:* Federal Pell, SEOG, state scholarships/grants, private scholarships, the school's own gift aid. *Loan aid offered:* FFEL Subsidized Stafford, FFEL Unsubsidized Stafford, FFEL PLUS, Federal Perkins, state loans, Private loans. Applicants will be notified of awards on or about 4/1. Federal Work-Study Program available. Institutional employment available. Off-campus job opportunities are excellent.

The Inside Word

Willamette is a bit of safety school for the Northwest. Although almost 50 percent of the students here graduated in the top 10 percent of their high school classes, test scores are within range for a lot of applicants. The admissions process is pretty standard for a small liberal arts college. Extracurriculars, recommendations, and essays are helpful but, more than likely, your grades will determine your fate.

THE SCHOOL SAYS "..."

From The Admissions Office

"The interactions between great teachers and great students are at the heart of the Willamette University experience. Considering that eight of the past 16 Oregon Professors of the Year (selected by the Council for Advancement and Support of Education) come from our campus, it is no surprise that student surveys overwhelmingly praise 'the quality of education' and 'interactions with faculty' as satisfying attributes of the Willamette experience. To further enhance the strength of the faculty and the opportunities for student-faculty interaction, Willamette is adding 25 new faculty positions over the next five years.

"The accomplishments of Willamette graduates help put the quality of the education in perspective. In the past decade, nearly 90 of our students have been awarded competitive, national scholarships and fellowships, including Trumans, Fulbrights, Goldwaters and Watsons. With 20 Peace Corps volunteers currently serving, Willamette ranks in the top 10 for small colleges and universities with the most alumni volunteers.

"Recent on-campus developments include the opening of Kaneko Commons, the first of four residential commons that will transform campus living organizations. Kaneko, much anticipated by the Campus Sustainability Council, was our first LEED-certified 'green' building."

SELECTIVITY

Admissions Rating	97
# of applicants	2,983
% of applicants accepted	77
% of acceptees attending	19
# accepting a place on wait list	136
% admitted from wait list	9

FRESHMAN PROFILE

Range SAT Critical Reading	570–690
Range SAT Math	550–660
Range SAT Writing	550–660
Range ACT Composite	25–29
Minimum paper TOEFL	550
Minimum computer TOEFL	213
Average HS GPA	3.68
% graduated top 10% of class	47
% graduated top 25% of class	76
% graduated top 50% of class	96

DEADLINES

Early action	
Deadline	12/1
Notification	1/15
Regular	
Priority	2/1
Notification	4/1
Nonfall registration?	yes

APPLICANTS ALSO LOOK AT

AND OFTEN PREFER
Whitman College

AND SOMETIMES PREFER
Occidental College
Lewis & Clark College
University of Puget Sound
University of Washington
Santa Clara University
Colorado College

AND RARELY PREFER
University of Oregon

FINANCIAL FACTS

Financial Aid Rating	85
Annual tuition	$28,416
Room and board	$7,000
Required fees	$170
Books and supplies	$800
% frosh rec. need-based scholarship or grant aid	66
% UG rec. need-based scholarship or grant aid	62
% frosh rec. non-need-based scholarship or grant aid	27
% UG rec. non-need-based scholarship or grant aid	15
% frosh rec. need-based self-help aid	57
% UG rec. need-based self-help aid	56
% frosh rec. any financial aid	92
% UG rec. any financial aid	92
% UG borrow to pay for school	79
Average cumulative indebtedness	$18,756

WILLIAM JEWELL COLLEGE

500 COLLEGE HILL, LIBERTY, MO 64068 • ADMISSIONS: 816-415-7511 • FAX: 816-415-5040

CAMPUS LIFE

Quality of Life Rating	**89**
Fire Safety Rating	**80**
Green Rating	**65**
Type of school	private
Environment	town

STUDENTS

Total undergrad enrollment	1,210
% male/female	40/60
% from out of state	30
% from public high school	90
% live on campus	69
% in (# of) fraternities	37 (4)
% in (# of) sororities	36 (4)
% African American	4
% Asian	1
% Caucasian	65
% Hispanic	2
% Native American	1
# of countries represented	5

SURVEY SAYS . . .

No one cheats
Career services are great
Students are friendly
Students get along with local community
Students love Liberty, MO
Great off-campus food
Students are happy
Frats and sororities dominate social scene
Musical organizations are popular
Student publications are popular
Very little drug use

ACADEMICS

Academic Rating	**87**
Calendar	semester
Student/faculty ratio	10:1
Profs interesting rating	90
Profs accessible rating	86
Most common reg class size	fewer than 10 students
Most common lab size	30–39 students

MOST POPULAR MAJORS

business/commerce
nursing/registered nurse
(rn, asn, bsn, msn)
psychology

STUDENTS SAY ". . ."

Academics

William Jewell College is a private, predominantly Christian liberal arts college with a solidly pre-professional bent that offers "strong academics, a personal atmosphere, and a close-knit community." "I love the one-on-one interaction with professors," beams a business major. "I love the small class sizes." Nursing, music, and education are among the notable programs here. A broad core curriculum includes lots of hands-on learning. The "extremely intense" Oxbridge Honors Program subjects students to English tutorial-style instruction and a year of study in England. There are study abroad opportunities in more than 30 other far-flung places as well. Some students call the professors "hit or miss." Others say the faculty is "a generally gifted bunch." Professors are "demanding" but "invested in their students' success and always there to help." The administration "has its moments of idiocy" but gets high marks for accessibility: Administrators are "always asking for our opinion and I think take it to heart," says a nursing major. "The President even eats daily in the cafeteria and enjoys it when students sit down with him."

Life

A new Sorority Complex should improve campus housing options, but students say "the school isn't known for fancy dorm rooms." And although recent technology upgrades have reportedly improved the speed of the campus internet connection, "Jewell's technology is way behind." "The actual college life is wonderful," though. "Everyone here is involved in a lot of activities." "The Greek system is our greatest strength," says a proud frat member. "Going Greek on this campus really helps a first-year get into college life in a healthy, safe way." Independent students aren't as thrilled by the frat scene and mention that relations between Greeks and everyone else is "a tense, frustrating thing." Whatever the case, the fraternities and sororities largely dominate social life, and William Jewell is "not a good place to go if you want to have a social life but don't want to be Greek." Also, unlike at other schools, the Greeks here don't really party on the weekends, or any other time. In fact, "there usually aren't parties" at all. "It is evident that William Jewell is a religious school," imparts a senior. "The worst thing you can find on our campus is a can of beer." Students frequently head to nearby Kansas City to shop and occasionally hit the bars and dance clubs. Also, the nationally recognized Harriman-Jewell Series arranges student tickets to a sweeping array of performing arts events in Kansas City.

Student Body

Jewell's population is largely "from the Midwest" and "middle class" (though a significant portion of students are certainly "well-to-do"). They are mostly "studious, hard workers who have an interest in their education." "There are very few atypical students" but, at the same time, "there are a lot of odd kids here." People of all types "are welcomed and fit in." "The social setup is no different than high school. There are the preppy kids, the jocks, the drama freaks, the band geeks, nerds, punks, etc.," observes a senior. "The only real difference is that they all get along and work together much better at college." You'll find some secular liberals here but the majority of Jewell's students range from "Christian and conservative" to "moderately religious Christian." "There are days when I would like to be somewhere else because of the lack of diversity," ponders a senior. "The school is taking drastic steps to bring in minorities," swears a sophomore. In the meantime, declares one student, "it is exhausting hearing about all the ways that Jewell is not diverse and all the ways Jewell is trying to become more diverse."

FINANCIAL AID: 888-2-JEWELL • E-MAIL: ADMISSION@WILLIAM.JEWELL.EDU • WEBSITE: WWW.JEWELL.EDU

THE PRINCETON REVIEW SAYS

Admissions

Very important factors considered include: rigor of secondary school record, *Important factors considered include:* Class rank, academic GPA, recommendation(s), standardized test scores. *Other factors considered include:* Application essay, alumni/ae relation, character/personal qualities, extracurricular activities, first generation, interview, talent/ability, volunteer work, work experience. SAT or ACT required; ACT with Writing component recommended. TOEFL required of all international applicants. High school diploma is required and GED is accepted. *Academic units required:* 4 English, 3 mathematics, 3 science, (1 lab science), 2 foreign language, 3 social studies. *Academic units recommended:* 4 English, 4 mathematics, 3 science, (1 lab science), 3 foreign language, 3 social studies, 2 academic electives.

Financial Aid

Students should submit: FAFSA. The Princeton Review suggests that all financial aid forms be submitted as soon as possible after 1/1. *Need-based scholarships/grants offered:* Federal Pell, SEOG, state scholarships/grants, the school's own gift aid. *Loan aid offered:* FFEL Subsidized Stafford, FFEL Unsubsidized Stafford, FFEL PLUS, Federal Perkins, Federal Nursing, Non-Federal Private Loans. Applicants will be notified of awards on a rolling basis beginning 2/15. Federal Work-Study Program available. Institutional employment available. Off-campus job opportunities are excellent.

The Inside Word

Admission to William Jewell requires the usual suspects: solid grades and test scores. The college is competitive, but admission is not out of reach for the average student. Once admitted, undergrads benefit from William Jewell's leading efforts in experiential learning.

THE SCHOOL SAYS "..."

From The Admissions Office

"William Jewell College is committed to bringing together talented students and gifted faculty mentors within a vibrant community sparked by a rigorous and intentional liberal arts curriculum. A full range of personal and professional development experiences are presented by the selective national liberal arts college's location within the Kansas City metroplex of more than 1.5 million. The William Jewell College experience focuses on enhancing the student's ability to apply learning to complex ethical, scientific and cultural problems. The College places a high value on experiential learning and gives students the opportunity to "live what they learn." By completing the College's 38-hour liberal arts core plus three applied learning experiences, Jewell students can receive a second major in Applied Critical Thought and Inquiry. This means that all students can graduate with double majors and some with triple majors. The internationally recognized Oxbridge Honors Program combines British tutorial methods of instruction with opportunities for a year of study in Oxford or Cambridge. It is the only program of its kind in the nation. Jewell's undergraduate Nonprofit Leadership major is one of only 13 nationwide and ranks among the top three in academic rigor. The Pryor Leadership Studies Program includes course work, community service projects and internships that help students enhance their leadership skills in a variety of settings. William Jewell students graduate equipped with deep content knowledge in their major(s), a host of social and real-world experiences, personal maturity and the intellectual habits of mind for success in a world of change and challenge."

SELECTIVITY

Admissions Rating	87
# of applicants	1,585
% of applicants accepted	63
% of acceptees attending	27

FRESHMAN PROFILE

Range SAT Critical Reading	540–660
Range SAT Math	500–610
Range ACT Composite	23–29
Minimum paper TOEFL	550
Minimum computer TOEFL	213
Minimum web-based TOEFL	80
Average HS GPA	3.68
% graduated top 10% of class	33
% graduated top 25% of class	60
% graduated top 50% of class	90

DEADLINES

Regular	
Priority	12/1
Deadline	8/15
Notification	rolling
Nonfall registration?	yes

APPLICANTS ALSO LOOK AT

AND OFTEN PREFER
University of Missouri—Columbia
Truman State University

AND SOMETIMES PREFER
Rockhurst University

AND RARELY PREFER
Northwest Missouri State University

FINANCIAL FACTS

Financial Aid Rating	79
Annual tuition	$24,300
Room and board	$6,700
Required fees	$300
Books and supplies	$1,100
% frosh rec. need-based scholarship or grant aid	75
% UG rec. need-based scholarship or grant aid	66
% frosh rec. non-need-based scholarship or grant aid	75
% UG rec. non-need-based scholarship or grant aid	66
% frosh rec. need-based self-help aid	52
% UG rec. need-based self-help aid	50
% frosh rec. athletic scholarships	7
% UG rec. athletic scholarships	11
% frosh rec. any financial aid	99
% UG rec. any financial aid	96
% UG borrow to pay for school	73
Average cumulative indebtedness	$22,123

WILLIAMS COLLEGE

33 STETSON COURT, WILLIAMSTOWN, MA 01267 • ADMISSIONS: 413-597-2211 • FAX: 413-597-4052

CAMPUS LIFE
Quality of Life Rating	91
Fire Safety Rating	60*
Green Rating	93
Type of school	private
Environment	village

STUDENTS
Total undergrad enrollment	1,970
% male/female	50/50
% from out of state	86
% from public high school	55
% live on campus	94
% African American	10
% Asian	11
% Caucasian	62
% Hispanic	9
% Native American	1
% international	7
# of countries represented	61

SURVEY SAYS . . .
Lab facilities are great
School is well run
Dorms are like palaces
Campus feels safe
Everyone loves the Ephs
Frats and sororities are unpopular or nonexistent

ACADEMICS
Academic Rating	99
Calendar	4/1/4
Student/faculty ratio	7:1
Profs interesting rating	94
Profs accessible rating	99
Most common reg class size	fewer than 10 students
Most common lab size	10–19 students

MOST POPULAR MAJORS
economics
English language and literature/letters
visual/performing arts

STUDENTS SAY ". . ."

Academics

Williams College is a small bastion of the liberal arts "with a fantastic academic reputation." Administrators sometimes "ignore student consensus in their misguided efforts to improve campus life," but they are "incredibly compassionate and accessible" and red tape is virtually unheard of. Financial aid is outrageous. Absolute, "full-ride" assistance with no loans is available to any student who needs it. "Williams students tend to spend a lot of time complaining about how much work they have" but they say the academic experience is "absolutely incomparable." Classes are "small" and "intense." "The facilities are absolutely top-notch in almost everything." Research opportunities are plentiful. A one-month January term offers study-abroad programs and a host of short pass/fail courses that are "a college student's dream come true." "The hard science departments are incredible." Economics, art history, and English are equally outstanding. Despite the occasional professor "who should not even be teaching at the high school level," the faculty at Williams is one of the best. Most professors "jump at every opportunity to help you love their subject." "They're here because they want to interact with undergrads." "If you complain about a Williams education then you would complain about education anywhere," wagers an economics major.

Life

Students at Williams enjoy a "stunning campus." "The Berkshire mountains are in the background every day as you walk to class" and opportunities for outdoor activity are numerous. The location is in "the boonies," though, and the surrounding "one-horse college town" is "quaint" at best. "There is no nearby place to buy necessities that is not ridiculously overpriced." Student life happens almost exclusively on campus. Dorm rooms are "large" and "well above par" but the housing system is "very weird." While some students like it, there is a general consensus that its creators "should be slapped and sent back to Amherst." Entertainment options include "lots of" performances, plays, and lectures. Some students are "obsessed with a capella groups." Intramurals are popular, especially broomball ("a sacred tradition involving a hockey rink, sneakers, a rubber ball, and paddles"). Intercollegiate sports are "a huge part of the social scene." For many students, the various varsity teams "are the basic social blocks at Williams." "Everyone for the most part gets along, but the sports teams seem to band together," explains a sophomore. Booze-laden parties" "and general disorder on weekends" are common. "A lot of people spend their lives between homework and practice and then just get completely smashed on weekends." Nothing gets out of hand, though. "We know how to unwind without being stupid," says a sophomore.

Student Body

The student population at Williams is not the most humble. They describe themselves as "interesting and beautiful" "geniuses of varying interests." They're "quirky, passionate, zany, and fun." They're "athletically awesome." They're "freakishly unique" and at the same time "cookie-cutter amazing." Ethnic diversity is stellar and you'll find all kinds of different students including "the goth students," "nerdier students," "a ladle of environmentally conscious pseudo-vegetarians," and a few "west coast hippies." However, "a typical student looks like a rich white kid" who grew up "playing field hockey just outside Boston" and spends summers "vacationing on the Cape." Sporty students abound. "There definitely is segregation between the artsy kids and the athlete types but there is also a significant amount of crossover." "Williams is a place where normal social labels tend not to apply," reports a junior. "Everyone here got in for a reason. So that football player in your theater class has amazing insight on Chekhov and that outspoken environmental activist also specializes in improv comedy."

FINANCIAL AID: 413-597-4181 • E-MAIL: ADMISSION@WILLIAMS.EDU • WEBSITE: WWW.WILLIAMS.EDU

THE PRINCETON REVIEW SAYS

Admissions

Very important factors considered include: Application essay, academic GPA, recommendation(s), rigor of secondary school record, standardized test scores, *Important factors considered include:* Class rank, extracurricular activities, talent/ability. *Other factors considered include:* alumni/ae relation, character/personal qualities, first generation, geographical residence, racial/ethnic status, volunteer work, work experience. SAT or ACT required; SAT and SAT Subject Tests or ACT required; ACT with Writing component required. High school diploma or equivalent is not required. *Academic units recommended:* 4 English, 4 mathematics, 3 science, (3 science labs), 4 foreign language, 3 social studies.

Financial Aid

Students should submit: FAFSA, CSS/Financial Aid PROFILE, noncustodial PROFILE, business/farm supplement. Parent and Student federal taxes and W-2s. Regular filing deadline is 2/1. The Princeton Review suggests that all financial aid forms be submitted as soon as possible after 1/1. *Need-based scholarships/grants offered:* Federal Pell, SEOG, state scholarships/grants, private scholarships, the school's own gift aid. *Loan aid offered:* Direct Subsidized Stafford, Direct Unsubsidized Stafford, Direct PLUS, Federal Perkins, college/university loans from institutional funds. Applicants will be notified of awards on or about 4/1. Federal Work-Study Program available. Institutional employment available.

The Inside Word

As is typical of highly selective colleges, at Williams high grades and test scores work more as qualifiers than to determine admissibility. Beyond a strong record of achievement, evidence of intellectual curiosity, noteworthy non-academic talents, and a non-college family background are some aspects of a candidate's application that might make for an offer of admission. But there are no guarantees—the evaluation process here is rigorous. The admissions committee (the entire admissions staff) discusses each candidate in comparison to the entire applicant pool. The pool is divided alphabetically for individual reading; after weak candidates are eliminated, those who remain undergo additional evaluations by different members of the staff. Admission decisions must be confirmed by the agreement of a plurality of the committee. Such close scrutiny demands a well-prepared candidate and application.

THE SCHOOL SAYS "..."

From The Admissions Office

"Special course offerings at Williams include Oxford-style tutorials, where students (in teams of two) research and defend ideas, engaging in weekly debate with a faculty tutor. Annually 30 Williams students devote a full year to the tutorial method of study at Oxford; half of Williams students pursue overseas education. Four weeks of winter study each January provide time for individualized projects, research, and novel fields of study. Students compete in 32 Division III athletic teams, perform in 25 musical groups, stage 10 theatrical productions, and volunteer in 30 service organizations. The college receives several million dollars annually for undergraduate science research and equipment. The town offers two distinguished art museums, and 2,200 forest acres—complete with a treetop canopy walkway—for environmental research and recreation.

"Students are required to submit either the SAT or the ACT including the optional Writing section. Applicants should also submit scores from any two SAT Subject Tests."

SELECTIVITY
Admissions Rating	99
# of applicants	7,552
% of applicants accepted	17
% of acceptees attending	42
# accepting a place on wait list	438
% admitted from wait list	10
# of early decision applicants	605
% accepted early decision	37

FRESHMAN PROFILE
Range SAT Critical Reading	660–760
Range SAT Math	660–760
Range ACT Composite	29–33
% graduated top 10% of class	87
% graduated top 25% of class	99
% graduated top 50% of class	100

DEADLINES
Early Decision	
Deadline	11/10
Notification	12/15
Regular	
Deadline	1/1
Notification	4/1
Nonfall registration?	no

APPLICANTS ALSO LOOK AT
AND OFTEN PREFER
Harvard College
Yale University
AND RARELY PREFER
Amherst College

FINANCIAL FACTS
Financial Aid Rating	99
Annual tuition	$37,400
Room and board	$9,890
Required fees	$240
Books and supplies	$800
% frosh rec. need-based scholarship or grant aid	50
% UG rec. need-based scholarship or grant aid	49
% frosh rec. need-based self-help aid	50
% UG rec. need-based self-help aid	49
% frosh rec. any financial aid	50
% UG rec. any financial aid	49
% UG borrow to pay for school	46
Average cumulative indebtedness	$9,214

WITTENBERG UNIVERSITY

PO Box 720, Springfield, OH 45501 • Admissions: 800-677-7558 • Fax: 937-327-6379

CAMPUS LIFE

Quality of Life Rating	78
Fire Safety Rating	96
Green Rating	70
Type of school	private
Affiliation	Lutheran
Environment	town

STUDENTS

Total undergrad enrollment	1,811
% male/female	44/56
% from out of state	24
% live on campus	88
% in (# of) fraternities	27 (6)
% in (# of) sororities	36 (6)
% African American	4
% Asian	1
% Caucasian	81
% Hispanic	1
% international	2
# of countries represented	26

SURVEY SAYS . . .

Students are friendly
Students are happy
Everyone loves the Tigers
Intramural sports are popular
Frats and sororities dominate social scene
Student government is popular

ACADEMICS

Academic Rating	92
Calendar	semester
Student/faculty ratio	12:1
Profs interesting rating	95
Profs accessible rating	91
Most common reg class size	10–19 students
Most common lab size	10–19 students

MOST POPULAR MAJORS

biology/biological sciences
business/commerce
education

STUDENTS SAY " . . ."

Academics

A little liberal arts school located in Springfield, OH, this "quaint college campus that values traditions" has multiple students talking about "discovering your own personal light" and spreading it to others (echoing the sentiment of Wittenberg's motto). The "small community atmosphere" means nothing much goes unnoticed, so it's a good thing students are pretty happy here. Teachers at Wittenberg are warmly revered, with students applauding their availability and their attitude toward understanding "how students learn and tailoring their lessons to each individual student." "They want to know about you as a person, your goals, and then they help you achieve them. "If one day, I do not speak in class discussion, my professor will pull me aside after class and ask if everything is going OK in my life, and ask if I need to talk about anything," says a senior. "I often find myself calling my family and friends to recite the amazing stories a professor just told in class," says another senior. Though a few students complain about the facilities needing to be updated, the school offers plenty of resources, such as the writing center, math workshop, and language center. As far as the administration goes, the majority of students are happy with what they've got, but a couple of feel "there is a disconnect when talking about student life and what actually goes on around campus. As far as drinking, partying, and social issues/needs," those in charge are neutralizing the social aspects of the school. The "engaging" president is so tied into the students "he even lived in a residence hall when he first became president to get a view of 'true' college life."

Life

Most students stay on campus on the weekends, but trips to Columbus or Dayton offer quick escapes. The on-campus weekend fun quite often involves "successful athletics" and/or drinking. "House parties are common," and "typically you can walk down the street and go into five or so houses, no questions asked." For those who prefer to stay dry, "you do not have to party to have fun because there are so many other things always going on" in terms of campus activities (such as "movies in the hollow, concert series, academic speakers, and philanthropy events") and student organizations. In fact, there are so many extracurriculars offered that "it's a must to get involved." The food on campus "can not be worse," which is a problem as "it's hard to get off campus to get food if you do not have a car."

Student Body

Naturally, there are "plenty of students from Ohio and the Midwest" who are "white, New-England-like, athletic or active, outgoing, and fun." Quite a few people mention they wouldn't mind seeing the student body diversified through out-of-state and international recruiting. Though "there aren't a lot of atypical students," the school "has embraced diversity so the minority students fit right in." The cozy atmosphere means "everyone generally ends up knowing each other," which lends itself to an overall amiability, and "it seems that most students can strike up a conversation with anyone and are very welcoming." Most people don't seclude themselves to one group of friends, and "although there are cliques, there's a lot of meshing between them."

FINANCIAL AID: 800-677-7558 • E-MAIL: ADMISSION@WITTENBERG.EDU • WEBSITE: WWW.WITTENBERG.EDU

THE PRINCETON REVIEW SAYS

Admissions

Very important factors considered include: Class rank, academic GPA, rigor of secondary school record, *Important factors considered include:* Application essay, recommendation(s), character/personal qualities, extracurricular activities, talent/ability, volunteer work. *Other factors considered include:* standardized test scores, alumni/ae relation, first generation, interview, work experience. TOEFL required of all international applicants. High school diploma is required and GED is accepted. *Academic units required:* 4 English, 3 mathematics, 3 science, (2 science labs), 2 foreign language, 2 history. *Academic units recommended:* 4 English, 4 mathematics, 5 science, (2 science labs), 3 foreign language, 3 history.

Financial Aid

Students should submit: FAFSA. The Princeton Review suggests that all financial aid forms be submitted as soon as possible after 1/1. *Need-based scholarships/grants offered:* Federal Pell, SEOG, state scholarships/grants, private scholarships, the school's own gift aid. *Loan aid offered:* FFEL Subsidized Stafford, FFEL Unsubsidized Stafford, FFEL PLUS, Federal Perkins, college/university loans from institutional funds, private "alternative" loans. Applicants will be notified of awards on a rolling basis beginning 3/1. Federal Work-Study Program available. Institutional employment available. Off-campus job opportunities are excellent.

The Inside Word

Wittenberg's applicant pool is small but quite solid coming off of a couple of strong years. Students who haven't successfully reached an above-average academic level in high school will meet with little success in the admissions process. Candidate evaluation is thorough and personal; applicants should devote serious attention to all aspects of their candidacy.

THE SCHOOL SAYS "..."

From The Admissions Office

"At Wittenberg, we believe that helping you to achieve symmetry demands a special environment, a setting where you can refine your definition of self yet gain exposure to the varied kinds of knowledge, people, views, activities, options, and ideas that add richness to our lives. Wittenberg is a university where students are able to thrive in a small campus environment with many opportunities for intellectual and personal growth in and out of the classroom. Campus life is as diverse as the interests of our students. Wittenberg attracts students from all over the United States and from many other countries. Historically, the university has been committed to geographical, educational, cultural, and religious diversity. With their varied backgrounds and interests, Wittenberg students have helped initiate many of the more than 125 student organizations that are active on campus. The students will be the first to tell you there's never a lack of things to do on or near the campus any day of the week, if you're willing to get involved.

"Wittenberg University requires freshman applicants to submit SAT scores. Students may also choose to submit scores from the ACT (with or without the Writing component) in lieu of the SAT."

SELECTIVITY

Admissions Rating	87
# of applicants	3,344
% of applicants accepted	69
% of acceptees attending	22
# of early decision applicants	51
% accepted early decision	61

FRESHMAN PROFILE

Range SAT Critical Reading	520–640
Range SAT Math	540–590
Range ACT Composite	23–29
Minimum paper TOEFL	550
Minimum computer TOEFL	213
Average HS GPA	3.46
% graduated top 10% of class	33
% graduated top 25% of class	61
% graduated top 50% of class	89

DEADLINES

Early Decision	
Deadline	11/15
Notification	12/15
Early action	
Deadline	12/1
Notification	1/1
Regular	
Priority	3/15
Notification	rolling
Nonfall registration?	yes

APPLICANTS ALSO LOOK AT

AND OFTEN PREFER

The College of Wooster
Denison University
Ohio University—Athens
Ohio Wesleyan University
Miami University
The Ohio State University—Columbus

AND SOMETIMES PREFER

Ohio Northern University
Capital University

FINANCIAL FACTS

Financial Aid Rating	85
Annual tuition	$33,890
Room and board	$8,772
Required fees	$300
Books and supplies	$1,000
% frosh rec. need-based scholarship or grant aid	68
% UG rec. need-based scholarship or grant aid	71
% frosh rec. need-based self-help aid	65
% UG rec. need-based self-help aid	68
% frosh rec. any financial aid	99
% UG rec. any financial aid	99

WOFFORD COLLEGE

429 NORTH CHURCH STREET, SPARTANBURG, SC 29303-3663 • ADMISSIONS: 864-597-4130 • FAX: 864-597-4147

CAMPUS LIFE

Quality of Life Rating	89
Fire Safety Rating	73
Green Rating	84
Type of school	private
Affiliation	Methodist
Environment	city

STUDENTS

Total undergrad enrollment	1,377
% male/female	52/48
% from out of state	40
% from public high school	61
% live on campus	96
% in (# of) fraternities	45 (8)
% in (# of) sororities	57 (4)
% African American	6
% Asian	3
% Caucasian	85
% Hispanic	2
% international	1
# of countries represented	6

SURVEY SAYS . . .

Lab facilities are great
School is well run
Low cost of living
Frats and sororities dominate social scene
(Almost) no one smokes

ACADEMICS

Academic Rating	93
Calendar	4/1/4
Student/faculty ratio	11:1
Profs interesting rating	98
Profs accessible rating	95
Most common reg class size	10–19 students
Most common lab size	20–29 students

MOST POPULAR MAJORS

biology/biological sciences
business/managerial economics
English language and literature

STUDENTS SAY ". . ."

Academics

Students agree Wofford is "an extremely challenging institution with a strong local and increasing national reputation." Undergrads are quick to heap praise on their professors stating they, "genuinely care about their students and...are willing to do everything it takes for each student to succeed." Perhaps even more importantly, Wofford profs "clearly love to teach," which "creates a fun and interesting academic environment." In turn, as one junior shares, this frequently fosters a "desire to continue learning about the course material." Additionally, professors encourage students to explore their own passions. However, slackers be warned, "You cannot come to Wofford, play around and still make an A. You need to work." Undergrads are also quite pleased with the folks who keep the college running smoothly. Indeed, administrators "are very nice and [always] willing to hear student opinion." And one sophomore boasts that "deans go out of their way to assist the students." The highly visible administration can often be seen "eating lunch on the Quad, at football games and other athletic events, and [at] various academic and extracurricular functions on campus." Perhaps Wofford can be summed up best by this junior who simply states it's "an educational dream."

Life

Students at Wofford are academically oriented and tend to put "their education first." That means weekdays are generally reserved for classes and studying. However, when Friday rolls around, these Terriers are ready to let loose. "A very high Greek population" typically means many students will flock to "fraternity row" on the weekends. Luckily, "all students are welcome" regardless of affiliation. Fortunately, "the student activities council ensures that plenty of non-Greek events are planned each semester also." Activities can range from "movies" and "paintball and ice skating" to "the occasional hot air balloon ride or bull riding." Additionally, with rampant school spirit, it's not surprising "football games...are very popular." Indeed, these "games are a big event where girls wear dresses and guys wear a coat, tie, and croakies." With all these options, it's no surprise an excited freshman shares, "There are so many activities on campus that you don't want to leave!" However, when undergrads do want to venture off campus, hometown "Spartanburg always has festivals and community gatherings, and there are plenty of restaurants to choose from." Students looking for additional adventure can easily escape to Greenville, a city about 30 minutes away, or the always entertaining Asheville, which is roughly an hour trip by car.

Student Body

Easily characterized with their "polo and pearls," Wofford undergrads admit the typical student is "Southern, Protestant, rich" and heavily "involved in Greek life." However, fret not if you don't find any of those adjectives applicable. A junior assures us "everyone interacts together, and there are no exclusive groups on campus." Indeed, most people are "friendly...and outgoing," and even atypical students will find it "easy to fit in...and get involved." Regardless of background, Wofford undergrads are an intellectual and curious lot. By and large, they tend to be academically "driven...and hard-working" and "motivated to do well" both in and out of the classroom. A few students bemoan the fact that Wofford seems to lack diversity, citing that most of their peers are "Caucasian" and "conservative." While others concede to this fact, they are quick to highlight this is slowly changing. As one experienced senior shares, "Despite the largely homogenous campus, diversity is growing rapidly." And this sentiment is echoed by a hopeful sophomore who confidently states, "Each year the number of students who defies this 'Wofford stereotype' is rising."

FINANCIAL AID: 864-597-4160 • E-MAIL: ADMISSIONS@WOFFORD.EDU • WEBSITE: WWW.WOFFORD.EDU

THE PRINCETON REVIEW SAYS

Admissions

Very important factors considered include: academic GPA, rigor of secondary school record, *Important factors considered include:* Class rank, application essay, standardized test scores, character/personal qualities, extracurricular activities, racial/ethnic status, talent/ability, volunteer work. *Other factors considered include:* recommendation(s), alumni/ae relation, first generation, geographical residence, interview, work experience. SAT or ACT required; ACT with Writing component required. TOEFL required of all international applicants. High school diploma is required and GED is accepted. *Academic units recommended:* 4 English, 4 mathematics, 3 science, (3 science labs), 3 foreign language, 2 social studies, 1 visual/performing arts, 1 computer science, 1 academic electives.

Financial Aid

Students should submit: FAFSA. The Princeton Review suggests that all financial aid forms be submitted as soon as possible after 1/1. *Need-based scholarships/grants offered:* Federal Pell, SEOG, state scholarships/grants, the school's own gift aid. *Loan aid offered:* FFEL Subsidized Stafford, FFEL Unsubsidized Stafford, FFEL PLUS, Federal Perkins. Applicants will be notified of awards on or about 3/31. Federal Work-Study Program available. Institutional employment available. Off-campus job opportunities are good.

The Inside Word

Wofford College distinguishes itself by providing its students with an extremely supportive environment. This concern extends to the applications it receives, each of which is given careful consideration. Students who have earned decent grades in challenging courses should find themselves with an opportunity to attend a school that is a gaining a reputation as one of the South's premier liberal arts colleges.

THE SCHOOL SAYS "..."

From The Admissions Office

"Approaching the end of his first year in office years ago, Wofford President Benjamin Dunlap (a Rhodes scholar and Harvard PhD) asked the faculty, 'If you had the assurance of sufficient time and institutional support to teach the sort of course you've always dreamed of, what would you do?' In response, using grants from the Andrew Mellon and National Science Foundations, Wofford faculty created approximately 50 new courses and almost a dozen new interdisciplinary course sequences. Some of the new courses are 'learning communities,' the prototype for which was fashioned by a biologist and an English professor on 'the nature and culture of water.' A Spanish language course is taught in conjunction with a Latin American and Caribbean history course and a sociology course featuring fieldwork in the local Hispanic community. Handsomely appointed rooms suitable for meetings, meals, and seminars have been included in an ongoing series of major building projects and renovations to forge even closer relationships between faculty and students. Blessed with a Phi Beta Kappa academic tradition, a nationally ranked program of studies abroad, and an economy of scale that encourages innovation and collaboration among faculty and students, Wofford is positioning itself among the national leaders in redefining the liberal arts. More importantly, however, the college community is vigorously pursuing a goal of educating young leaders who can make connections, cross boundaries, and negotiate a world no longer neatly divided into categories of endeavor.

"Wofford College requires freshman applicants to submit scores from either the SAT or the ACT."

SELECTIVITY

Admissions Rating	93
# of applicants	2,278
% of applicants accepted	59
% of acceptees attending	31
# accepting a place on wait list	11
% admitted from wait list	27
# of early decision applicants	587
% accepted early decision	64

FRESHMAN PROFILE

Range SAT Critical Reading	560–660
Range SAT Math	570–680
Range SAT Writing	560–660
Range ACT Composite	22–27
Minimum paper TOEFL	550
Minimum computer TOEFL	213
Average HS GPA	3.49
% graduated top 10% of class	56
% graduated top 25% of class	77
% graduated top 50% of class	98

DEADLINES

Early Decision	
Deadline	11/15
Notification	12/5
Regular	
Deadline	2/1
Notification	3/15
Nonfall registration?	yes

APPLICANTS ALSO LOOK AT

AND OFTEN PREFER
Wake Forest University

AND SOMETIMES PREFER
Furman University

AND RARELY PREFER
University of South Carolina—Columbia
Clemson University

FINANCIAL FACTS

Financial Aid Rating	88
Annual tuition	$29,465
Room and board	$8,190
Books and supplies	$1,050
% frosh rec. need-based scholarship or grant aid	45
% UG rec. need-based scholarship or grant aid	48
% frosh rec. non-need-based scholarship or grant aid	19
% UG rec. non-need-based scholarship or grant aid	19
% frosh rec. need-based self-help aid	29
% UG rec. need-based self-help aid	27
% frosh rec. athletic scholarships	10
% UG rec. athletic scholarships	13
% UG borrow to pay for school	50
Average cumulative indebtedness	$17,831

WORCESTER POLYTECHNIC INSTITUTE

100 INSTITUTE ROAD, WORCESTER, MA 01609 • ADMISSIONS: 508-831-5286 • FAX: 508-831-5875

CAMPUS LIFE

Quality of Life Rating	86
Fire Safety Rating	82
Green Rating	89
Type of school	private
Environment	city

STUDENTS

Total undergrad enrollment	3,160
% male/female	74/26
% from out of state	45
% from public high school	66
% live on campus	50
% in (# of) fraternities	28 (11)
% in (# of) sororities	32 (3)
% African American	3
% Asian	6
% Caucasian	75
% Hispanic	5
% international	8
# of countries represented	81

SURVEY SAYS . . .

Lab facilities are great
Career services are great
School is well run
Dorms are like palaces
Students are happy
Frats and sororities dominate social scene
Student government is popular

ACADEMICS

Academic Rating	91
Calendar	semester
Student/faculty ratio	14.1:1
Profs interesting rating	76
Profs accessible rating	89
Most common reg class size	fewer than 10 students
Most common lab size	20–29 students

MOST POPULAR MAJORS

computer science
electrical, electronics and communications engineering
mechanical engineering

STUDENTS SAY ". . ."

Academics

Worcester Polytechnic Institute, students boast, "is revolutionary with its approach to teaching," employing a "project-based curriculum that stresses the importance of both theory and practice." Students here must complete two projects, "one relating to the impact of technology on society, and a final senior project" that is typically a "group project done in cooperation with industry; i.e., not an 'academic' project." The Project Enhanced Curriculum ensures that students get "real-world industry experience before getting into the real world by applying what you learn in the classroom into projects." Students typically travel abroad to complete at least one of their projects, allowing them to "help another community on the other side of the world." As yet another added bonus, "the projects program looks excellent on your resume." Students also love WPI's quarterly academic calendar. One writes, "If I don't like a class but have to get through it, it's only seven weeks. If I love the material, I can get out in seven weeks and jump onto the next class!" Students warn that "the terms are pretty intense and go by so quickly that there is little room for error" but add that "it is very easy to get in touch with the professors after class, and they are very willing to help." A lenient grading system—"You can only receive an A, B, C, or an NR"—reduces the pressure somewhat, although it does little to mitigate the "immense workload." Independent students are especially well suited to WPI, which "fosters a can-do attitude that allows students to pave their own ways, create their own degree programs, and arrange their own degree requirement projects."

Life

"During the week [at WPI], most of the attention is focused on school activities, whether it's homework, clubs, or other extracurriculars," while "on the weekends, people try to relax after the week that has just ended and prepare themselves for the upcoming week." The campus enjoys "a strong sense of community, probably because of the campus set-up. The campus is on a hill, so we are separate from the city, and we are our own community with its own issues, and we deal with issues as a whole." Students tell us that "the Greek life on campus holds a big presence, and it is hard to find other activities to occupy your free time without at least socializing with members of the Greek community." Of the intercollegiate sports, "Basketball is big. The men's team made it to the NCAA Division III national tournament in the last five years." Though in the past students have noted that "Worcester isn't the greatest town this may be changing—it was named the 9th most liveable city in the US by Forbes.com." Students tend to stick close to campus for fun, although "we also make trips to Boston and other better cities," including Hartford and Providence.

Student Body

The WPI student body spans two extremes, from "the students who do not come out of their room and are very nerdy" to those who "are very involved and meet everyone and fit in." One student writes, "WPI is an experiment in social interactions the likes of which the world rarely sees. For every typical frat guy and girl, there's a computer nerd or D&D guru who could write this entire response in COBOL coding for you." Nearly everyone here was "an atypical high school student" who "did very well in high school" while also being "really good in X (where X is a sport, club president, highly active student)." Finally, the "one thing that binds everyone at WPI is their love for technology. Within that major division of technology-loving people, the campus is filled with diverse students."

WORCESTER POLYTECHNIC INSTITUTE

FINANCIAL AID: 508-831-5469 • E-MAIL: ADMISSIONS@WPI.EDU • WEBSITE: WWW.WPI.EDU

THE PRINCETON REVIEW SAYS

Admissions

Very important factors considered include: academic GPA, rigor of secondary school record, *Important factors considered include:* Class rank, application essay, recommendation(s), standardized test scores, character/personal qualities, extracurricular activities. *Other factors considered include:* alumni/ae relation, first generation, geographical residence, interview, level of applicant's interest, racial/ethnic status, talent/ability, volunteer work, work experience. TOEFL required of all international applicants. High school diploma is required and GED is accepted. *Academic units required:* 4 English, 4 mathematics, 2 science, (2 science labs), *Academic units recommended:* 4 science, 2 foreign language, 2 social studies, 1 history, 1 computer science.

Financial Aid

Students should submit: FAFSA, CSS/Financial Aid PROFILE, noncustodial PROFILE, Copy of parents' and student's prior year federal income tax return and W-2 statements. Regular filing deadline is 2/1. The Princeton Review suggests that all financial aid forms be submitted as soon as possible after 1/1. *Need-based scholarships/grants offered:* Federal Pell, SEOG, state scholarships/grants, private scholarships, the school's own gift aid. *Loan aid offered:* FFEL Subsidized Stafford, FFEL Unsubsidized Stafford, FFEL PLUS, Federal Perkins, state loans, college/university loans from institutional funds. Applicants will be notified of awards on or about 4/1. Federal Work-Study Program available. Institutional employment available. Off-campus job opportunities are good.

The Inside Word

WPI's high admission rate is the result of a self-selecting applicant pool; very few people bother to apply here if they don't think they have a good chance of getting in. The relatively low rate of acceptees attending tells you that WPI is a 'safety' or backup choice for students hoping to get into MIT, CalTech, Cornell, John Hopkins, Carnegie Mellon and other top tech schools.

THE SCHOOL SAYS " . . ."

From The Admissions Office

"Projects and research enrich WPI's academic program. WPI believes that in these times simply passing courses and accumulating theoretical knowledge is not enough to truly educate tomorrow's leaders. Tomorrow's professionals ought to be involved in project work that prepares them today for future challenges. Projects at WPI come as close to professional experience as a college program can possibly achieve. In fact, WPI works with more than 200 companies, government agencies, and private organizations each year. These groups provide opportunities where students get a chance to work in real, professional settings. Students gain invaluable experience in planning, coordinating team efforts, meeting deadlines, writing proposals and reports, making oral presentations, doing cost analyses, and making decisions.

"Applicants are required to take either the SAT or the ACT (the Writing section is optional). We will use the student's best scores from either test. Science and Math SAT Subject Tests are recommended."

SELECTIVITY	
Admissions Rating	97
# of applicants	5,706
% of applicants accepted	67
% of acceptees attending	24
# accepting a place on wait list	237
% admitted from wait list	17

FRESHMAN PROFILE	
Range SAT Critical Reading	550–660
Range SAT Math	630–720
Range SAT Writing	550–650
Range ACT Composite	25–30
Minimum paper TOEFL	550
Minimum computer TOEFL	213
Minimum web-based TOEFL	79
Average HS GPA	3.7
% graduated top 10% of class	53
% graduated top 25% of class	88
% graduated top 50% of class	99

DEADLINES	
Early action	
Deadline	11/10
Notification	12/20
Regular	
Deadline	2/1
Notification	4/1
Nonfall registration?	yes

APPLICANTS ALSO LOOK AT
AND OFTEN PREFER
Cornell University
Massachusetts Institute of Technology
Carnegie Mellon University

AND SOMETIMES PREFER
Lehigh University, Boston University
Tufts University
Rensselaer Polytechnic Institute

AND RARELY PREFER
Northeastern University
University of Connecticut
University of Massachusetts—Amherst
Clarkson University
Rochester Institute of Technology

FINANCIAL FACTS	
Financial Aid Rating	78
Annual tuition	$36,390
Room and board	$10,880
Required fees	$540
Books and supplies	$1,000
% frosh rec. need-based scholarship or grant aid	73
% UG rec. need-based scholarship or grant aid	66
% frosh rec. non-need-based scholarship or grant aid	21
% UG rec. non-need-based scholarship or grant aid	16
% frosh rec. need-based self-help aid	52
% UG rec. need-based self-help aid	55
% frosh rec. any financial aid	99
% UG rec. any financial aid	95
% UG borrow to pay for school	66
Average cumulative indebtedness	$37,032

XAVIER UNIVERSITY OF LOUISIANA

ONE DREXEL DRIVE, BOX 132, NEW ORLEANS, LA 70125-1098 • ADMISSIONS: 504-520-7388 • FAX: 504-520-7941

CAMPUS LIFE
Quality of Life Rating	**65**
Fire Safety Rating	**60***
Green Rating	**60***
Type of school	private
Affiliation	Roman Catholic
Environment	metropolis

STUDENTS
Total undergrad enrollment	2,435
% male/female	28/72
% from out of state	44
% from public high school	81
% live on campus	43
% in (# of) fraternities	1 (4)
% in (# of) sororities	1 (4)
% African American	76
% Asian	8
% Caucasian	2
% Hispanic	1
% international	2
# of countries represented	8

SURVEY SAYS . . .
Lab facilities are great
Students get along with local community
Great off-campus food
Frats and sororities dominate social scene
Student government is popular
Very little drug use

ACADEMICS
Academic Rating	**76**
Calendar	semester
Student/faculty ratio	15:1
Profs interesting rating	81
Profs accessible rating	83
Most common reg class size	20–29 students
Most common lab size	20–29 students

MOST POPULAR MAJORS
pre-medicine/pre-medical studies
pre-pharmacy studies
psychology

Academics

Located in New Orleans, LA, "Xavier University is a historically black, Catholic University that promotes learning, leadership, and service." On a national level, "Xavier's strength are its life sciences and pharmacy programs," and the school holds the claim-to-fame of being "number one in placing African Americans into medical school." However, "what people don't know is that every academic program is great" at Xavier. A freshman attests, "Being a History major, I know first-hand the liberal arts professors are the best you can find." No matter what your discipline, XU professors are intimately involved in the learning experience, and "if a student shows that they are in a classroom to learn, professors will go out of their way to make sure that he or she understands the material." On top of that, there are plenty of resources to help the struggling student, and "Xavier takes good care of their science majors by providing tutoring centers for each area, and requiring we attend drill sessions every week." The downside to the XU college experience is "Xavier focuses so much on academics that it is easy to get stressed." However, students agree the rigorous coursework is well worth the investment. A current student shares, "The course load is difficult so, while your final grade may not be one that you like, if you put in the time and worked hard, you finish knowing the material."

Life

While they are an outgoing and friendly bunch, Xavier students say there isn't much time for goofing off or going out at their serious school. A sophomore explains, "There are things on campus, but it is definitely not a party school. I think that most students appreciate this aspect though, because that's what they expected when they chose Xavier." Socializing can actually be a bit academic at times, as participation in study groups is "heavily promoted by the school." In addition to being academically prudent, study groups can be "a good way to meet other students." On campus, "the University Center is also an area where many students can be found inbetween classes and where most activities occur. Because the school is so small, it is not hard to meet people and most have the same interests." Despite the demands of coursework, students say it is possible to achieve a balanced lifestyle. A senior tells us, "It is hard to juggle school, work, and play, but with some discipline it can be done." When it comes to social activities, "Greek life is extremely popular and many students strive to be a part of different groups." However, students admit the administrative rules on campus—such as the nightly curfew in the dorms and strict alcohol policy—can be a bit "old-fashioned." As a result, many students look for their entertainment off campus. "Many people go to the movies, clubs, or house parties," and, thanks to the school's New Orleans location, "Bourbon Street is also a major attraction for the college students."

Student Body

United by a common desire for success, Xavier students describe their classmates as "very focused and goal-oriented." Fortunately, their interest in success does not translate into competitiveness, as most Xaverites are also "friendly and easy to get along with." When it comes to demographics, students explain, "Because Xavier is a historically black university, the majority of the student body is African-American. The student population is about 75 percent Black, nine percent white and Asian, and 16 percent other races (roughly)." As is the trend at universities nationwide, the school is majority female, at about 72 percent of the undergraduates are women. Xavier is Catholic-affiliated; however, a wide range of religions are represented in the campus community, and "less than half of the school's population is Catholic." Generally speaking, XU students make a good mix, and life at Xavier "seems like a huge community of all different kinds of people working together." Socially, students admit "everyone has their cliques." However, on the whole, "acceptance and equality permeates throughout the entire student, faculty, and staff population."

FINANCIAL AID: 504-520-7517 • E-MAIL: APPLY@XULA.EDU • WEBSITE: WWW.XULA.EDU

THE PRINCETON REVIEW SAYS

Admissions

Very important factors considered include: academic GPA, recommendation(s), rigor of secondary school record, standardized test scores, *Important factors considered include:* Class rank, application essay. *Other factors considered include:* alumni/ae relation, character/personal qualities, extracurricular activities, interview, talent/ability, volunteer work, work experience. SAT or ACT required; TOEFL required of all international applicants. High school diploma is required and GED is accepted. *Academic units required:* 4 English, 2 mathematics, 1 science, 1 social studies, 8 academic electives. *Academic units recommended:* 4 mathematics, 3 science, 1 foreign language, 1 history.

Financial Aid

Students should submit: FAFSA. The Princeton Review suggests that all financial aid forms be submitted as soon as possible after 1/1. *Need-based scholarships/grants offered:* Federal Pell, SEOG, state scholarships/grants, private scholarships, the school's own gift aid, United Negro College Fund. *Loan aid offered:* Direct Subsidized Stafford, Direct Unsubsidized Stafford, Direct PLUS, FFEL Subsidized Stafford, FFEL Unsubsidized Stafford, FFEL PLUS, Federal Perkins. Applicants will be notified of awards on a rolling basis beginning 4/1. Federal Work-Study Program available. Institutional employment available. Off-campus job opportunities are good.

Inside Word

This school is a prestigious pipeline for those committed to a career in both natural and hard sciences. Xavier is best known for its identity as a Catholic institution with a predominantly African American student body and its reputation as a great pre-med school.

THE SCHOOL SAYS "..."

From The Admissions Office

A Message FROM THE SGA president:

"It is my pleasure to invite you to a college experience that will change and enhance your life. Xavier alumni are known for being exceptional doctors, lawyers, educators, business leaders, journalists, and the like.

"As a graduating biology major, I know Xavier has prepared me for my career in medicine while nurturing me academically and socially.

" With hardship often comes an opportunity to rise to greater heights. In its own way, Hurricane Katrina in 2005 may have added to the character of our people and enhanced the very principles upon which this university was founded.

"St. Katharine Drexel clearly understood when she founded Xavier, the necessity to provide minority students with a quality education and the skills needed to become leaders in their communities. Her vision was to help build a more just and humane society. What better time than now to become a part of the rebuilding of one of America's most unique cities, New Orleans.

"Higher education is not only about gaining intellectual knowledge, but acquiring social and community skills as well. At Xavier we offer a wide array of clubs, organizations and teams to suit the needs and interests of the student body."

SELECTIVITY
Admissions Rating	**76**
# of applicants	3,516
% of applicants accepted	66
% of acceptees attending	34

FRESHMAN PROFILE
Range SAT Critical Reading	410–530
Range SAT Math	400–520
Range SAT Writing	510–520
Range ACT Composite	18–23
Minimum paper TOEFL	550
Average HS GPA	3.14
% graduated top 10% of class	18
% graduated top 25% of class	18
% graduated top 50% of class	29

DEADLINES
Early action	
Deadline	1/15
Notification	2/15
Regular	
Priority	3/1
Deadline	7/1
Notification	10/15
Nonfall registration?	yes

FINANCIAL FACTS
Financial Aid Rating	**70**
Annual tuition	$14,500
Room and board	$6,800
Required fees	$1,000
Books and supplies	$1,200
% frosh rec. need-based scholarship or grant aid	67
% UG rec. need-based scholarship or grant aid	55
% frosh rec. non-need-based scholarship or grant aid	62
% UG rec. non-need-based scholarship or grant aid	43
% frosh rec. need-based self-help aid	69
% UG rec. need-based self-help aid	57
% frosh rec. athletic scholarships	2
% UG rec. athletic scholarships	3
% frosh rec. any financial aid	84
% UG rec. any financial aid	87
% UG borrow to pay for school	70
Average cumulative indebtedness	$25,227

XAVIER UNIVERSITY (OH)

3800 VICTORY PARKWAY, CINCINNATI, OH 45207-5311 • ADMISSIONS: 513-745-3301 • FAX: 513-745-4319

CAMPUS LIFE

Quality of Life Rating	**85**
Fire Safety Rating	**72**
Green Rating	**78**
Type of school	private
Affiliation	Roman Catholic/Jesuit
Environment	metropolis

STUDENTS

Total undergrad enrollment	3,780
% male/female	44/56
% from out of state	39
% from public high school	49.3
% live on campus	45
% African American	12
% Asian	2
% Caucasian	79
% Hispanic	3
% international	2
# of countries represented	53

SURVEY SAYS . . .

School is well run
Students are friendly
Dorms are like palaces
Everyone loves the Musketeers
Frats and sororities are unpopular or
nonexistent
Student government is popular

ACADEMICS

Academic Rating	**80**
Calendar	semester
Student/faculty ratio	12:1
Profs interesting rating	80
Profs accessible rating	86
Most common	
reg class size	20–29 students
Most common	
lab size	10–19 students

MOST POPULAR MAJORS

liberal arts and sciences/liberal
studies
marketing/marketing management
nursing/registered nurse
(rn, asn, bsn, msn)

STUDENTS SAY ". . ."

Academics

Xavier University, a medium-sized Jesuit institution "in the heart of Cincinnati," instills "a real sense of community and social conscience" while still "giving students the needed skills to succeed in all of their life endeavors." Xavier even tosses in a broad liberal arts education for good measure, courtesy of a core curriculum and distribution requirements that include lots of theology, philosophy, English, history, and foreign language. But it's business that many students—one in four, to be more precise—major in here. Undergrads tout the "great entrepreneurship program" and XU's "great record" for placing accounting students in graduate schools. XU's nursing program is also "very strong," with "an excellent" "pass rate on the NCLEX," and the education program earns similar plaudits. In all areas, XU offers "relatively small" classes, "which can make it hard when it's time for registration, but when you're in class it's great." Academics are "challenging, but the teachers and administration help make the transition [from high school] smooth and are there whenever you need their help." "Academically, it is nearly impossible to fail," a freshman adds. "There are always tutoring centers and help [is] available for any subject, whenever you need it." The school also "excels at real-world placement. If you want an internship, just ask. There's even a team of people here whose only job is to find internships and co-ops for students." Undergrads also appreciate their classmates' low-key approach; they "care, but are very laid-back in classes."

Life

"Xavier University has a little bit of everything—service projects, strong academics, social events, religious events, weekend trips, and lots of other activities to get involved in." A good number of the aforementioned activities "are put on by [the] Student Activities Council and by student government." Many Xavier students "go to the sporting events," with a heavy focus on the men's basketball team, which "is obviously a huge deal here" (the team was the 2005–2006 Atlantic 10 champion). Students say XU parties "usually don't get too out of control. I've never really heard or experienced any...of the typical bad college party experiences," a sophomore reports. They also tell us "there are few bars around (mainly only one, for upper classmen) so people generally party at houses." Big-city living lures some students off campus. Cincinnati "is a great city to go out in—there are areas such as Mt. Adams and Newport that provide entertainment and dining for both college-aged students and young professionals."

Student Body

"I'd say 95 percent of the students at this school are friendly and always willing to meet new people or help you if you have a problem," writes one student, expressing a commonly held perception of Xavier undergrads. Students "spend a lot of time with varieties of people—not just a "clique" or single group of people—[so] it is fairly easy to get to know a large percentage of your classmates, especially the peers in your graduating class." In terms of demographics, "Lots of kids come from suburban areas and went to Catholic schools, so there is a large population of wealthy, religious students." Adding some ethnic diversity are "significant populations of minority students (black, Asian, international, etc.) who each have [a] strong voice on campus." Alternative culture is hardly found here, one student notes, "It's rare to find a kid with a mohawk unless the rugby team shaved his head. Most kids are clean-cut." An accounting and finance major adds, "There are no real emo/goth kids at this school (thank God)." However, a weekend degree program and night classes draw a substantial nontraditional population to the school.

FINANCIAL AID: 513-745-3142 • E-MAIL: XUADMIT@XAVIER.EDU • WEBSITE: WWW.XAVIER.EDU

THE PRINCETON REVIEW SAYS

Admissions

Very important factors considered include: rigor of secondary school record, *Important factors considered include:* Class rank, application essay, academic GPA, recommendation(s), standardized test scores, character/personal qualities. *Other factors considered include:* alumni/ae relation, extracurricular activities, first generation, level of applicant's interest, talent/ability, volunteer work, work experience. SAT or ACT required; TOEFL required of all international applicants. High school diploma is required and GED is accepted. *Academic units recommended:* 4 English, 3 mathematics, 3 science, 2 foreign language, 3 social studies, 5 academic electives, 1 health/physical education.

Financial Aid

Students should submit: FAFSA. The Princeton Review suggests that all financial aid forms be submitted as soon as possible after 1/1. *Need-based scholarships/grants offered:* Federal Pell, SEOG, state scholarships/grants, private scholarships, the school's own gift aid. *Loan aid offered:* FFEL Subsidized Stafford, FFEL Unsubsidized Stafford, FFEL PLUS, Federal Perkins. Applicants will be notified of awards on a rolling basis beginning 2/15. Federal Work-Study Program available. Institutional employment available. Off-campus job opportunities are excellent.

The Inside Word

Above-average students should encounter little difficulty in gaining admission to Xavier. Others may be able to finagle their way in with some elbow grease, credible demonstrations of commitment to academics and Jesuit ideals of service, and a Catholic approach to academics.

THE SCHOOL SAYS "..."

From The Admissions Office

"Founded in 1831, Xavier University is the fourth oldest of the 28 Jesuit colleges and universities in the United States. The Jesuit tradition is evident in the university's core curriculum, degree programs and involvement opportunities. Xavier is home to 6,600 total students; 3,800 degree-seeking undergraduates. The student population represents more than 34 states and 50 foreign countries. Xavier offers 69 academic majors and concentrations and 42 minors in the Colleges of Arts and Sciences; Business; and Social Sciences, Health, and Education. Most popular majors include business, communication arts, education, psychology, biology, sport management/marketing, and pre-professional study. Other programs of note include University Scholars; Honors AB; Philosophy, Politics, and the Public; Army ROTC, study abroad, academic service-learning, and service fellowship. There are more than 100 academic clubs, social and service organizations, and recreational sports activities on campus. Students participate in groups such as student government, campus ministry, performing arts, and intramural sports. Xavier is a member of the Division I Atlantic 10 Conference and fields teams in men's and women's basketball, cross-country, track, golf, soccer, swimming, and tennis, as well as men's baseball and women's volleyball.

"Xavier is situated on more than 148 acres in a residential area of Cincinnati, Ohio. The face of Xavier has continued to change with the planned addition of a technology-based learning commons, renovated library and classroom buildings, a new building for the Williams College of Business, a new retail and residential complex, and a new student recreation facility. The additions are part of a $200 million capital campaign and will begin being built in 2008.

"Applicants must submit results from the SAT or ACT. The student's best score(s) from either test will be used. The Writing portion of the SAT/ACT is not required and will not be used in admission and scholarship decisions."

SELECTIVITY

Admissions Rating	88
# of applicants	6,151
% of applicants accepted	76
% of acceptees attending	18
# accepting a place on wait list	43
% admitted from wait list	60

FRESHMAN PROFILE

Range SAT Critical Reading	500–610
Range SAT Math	500–610
Range SAT Writing	500–600
Range ACT Composite	22–28
Minimum paper TOEFL	530
Minimum computer TOEFL	197
Minimum web-based TOEFL	71
Average HS GPA	3.51
% graduated top 10% of class	27
% graduated top 25% of class	60
% graduated top 50% of class	84

DEADLINES

Regular	
Deadline	2/1
Notification	rolling
Nonfall registration?	yes

APPLICANTS ALSO LOOK AT

AND OFTEN PREFER
University of Notre Dame

AND SOMETIMES PREFER
University of Dayton
Miami University
The Ohio State University—Columbus

AND RARELY PREFER
University of Cincinnati
Ohio University—Athens

FINANCIAL FACTS

Financial Aid Rating	76
Annual tuition	$27,900
Room and board	$10,050
Required fees	$670
Books and supplies	$1,000
% frosh rec. need-based scholarship or grant aid	60
% UG rec. need-based scholarship or grant aid	51
% frosh rec. non-need-based scholarship or grant aid	13
% UG rec. non-need-based scholarship or grant aid	8
% frosh rec. need-based self-help aid	46
% UG rec. need-based self-help aid	42
% frosh rec. athletic scholarships	4
% UG rec. athletic scholarships	5
% frosh rec. any financial aid	98
% UG rec. any financial aid	85
% UG borrow to pay for school	68
Average cumulative indebtedness	$22,879

YALE UNIVERSITY

PO Box 208234, New Haven, CT 06520-8234 • Admissions: 203-432-9316 • Fax: 203-432-9392

CAMPUS LIFE

Quality of Life Rating	**95**
Fire Safety Rating	**60***
Green Rating	**99**
Type of school	private
Environment	city

STUDENTS

Total undergrad enrollment	5,256
% male/female	50/50
% from out of state	94
% from public high school	55
% live on campus	87
% African American	9
% Asian	14
% Caucasian	45
% Hispanic	9
% Native American	1
% international	9
# of countries represented	108

SURVEY SAYS . . .

School is well run
Musical organizations are popular
Theater is popular
Student publications are popular
Political activism is popular

ACADEMICS

Academic Rating	**95**
Calendar	semester
Student/faculty ratio	6:1
Profs interesting rating	83
Profs accessible rating	83
% classes taught by TAs	3
Most common	
reg class size	10–19 students

MOST POPULAR MAJORS

economics
history
political science and government

STUDENTS SAY ". . ."

Academics

Listening to Yale students wax rhapsodic about their school, one can be forgiven for wondering whether they aren't actually describing the Platonic form of the university. By their own account, students here benefit not only from "amazing academics and extensive resources" that provide "phenomenal in- and out-of-class education," but also from participation in "a student body that is committed to learning and to each other." Unlike some other prestigious, prominent research universities, Yale "places unparalleled focus on undergraduate education," requiring all professors to teach at least one undergraduate course each year. "So [you know] the professors actually love teaching, because if they just wanted to do their research, they could have easily gone elsewhere." A residential college system further personalizes the experience. Each residential college "has a Dean and a Master, each of which is only responsible for 300 to 500 students, so administrative attention is highly specialized and widely available." Students further enjoy access to "a seemingly never-ending supply of resources (they really just love throwing money at us)" that includes "the 12 million volumes in our libraries." In short, "The opportunities are truly endless." "The experiences you have here and the people that you meet will change your life and strengthen your dreams," says ones student. Looking for the flip side to all this? "If the weather were a bit nicer, that would be excellent," one student offers. Guess that will have to do.

Life

Yale is, of course, extremely challenging academically, but students assure us that "Aside from the stress of midterms and finals, life at Yale is relatively carefree." Work doesn't keep undergrads from participating in "a huge variety of activities for fun. There are more than 300 student groups, including singing, dancing, juggling fire, theater…the list goes on. Because of all of these groups, there are shows on-campus all the time, which are a lot of fun and usually free or less than $5. On top of that, there are parties and events on campus and off campus, as well as many subsidized trips to New York City and Boston." Many here "are politically active (or at least politically aware)" and "a very large number of students either volunteer or try to get involved in some sort of organization to make a difference in the world." When the weekend comes around, "there are always parties to go to, whether at the frats or in rooms, but there's definitely no pressure to drink if you don't want to. A good friend of mine pledged a frat without drinking and that's definitely not unheard of (but still not common)." The relationship between Yale and the city of New Haven "sometimes leaves a little to be desired, but overall it's a great place to be for four years."

Student Body

A typical Yalie is "tough to define because so much of what makes Yale special is the unique convergence of different students to form one cohesive entity. Nonetheless, the one common characteristic of Yale students is passion—each Yalie is driven and dedicated to what he or she loves most, and it creates a palpable atmosphere of enthusiasm on campus." True enough, the student body represents a wide variety of ethnic, religious, economic, and academic backgrounds, but they all "thrive on learning, whether in a class, from a book, or from a conversation with a new friend." Students here also "tend to do a lot." "Everyone has many activities that they are a part of, which in turn fosters the closely connected feel of the campus." Undergrads tend to lean to the left politically, but for "those whose political views aren't as liberal as the rest of the campus…there are several campus organizations that cater to them."

FINANCIAL AID: 203-432-2700 • E-MAIL: UNDERGRADUATE.ADMISSIONS@YALE.EDU • WEBSITE: WWW.YALE.EDU/ADMIT

THE PRINCETON REVIEW SAYS

Admissions

Very important factors considered include: Class rank, application essay, academic GPA, recommendation(s), rigor of secondary school record, standardized test scores, character/personal qualities, extracurricular activities, talent/ability. *Other factors considered include:* alumni/ae relation, first generation, geographical residence, interview, level of applicant's interest, racial/ethnic status, state residency, volunteer work, work experience. SAT and SAT Subject Tests or ACT required; ACT with Writing component required. TOEFL required of all international applicants. High school diploma or equivalent is not required.

Financial Aid

Students should submit: FAFSA, CSS/Financial Aid PROFILE, noncustodial PROFILE, business/farm supplement. Parent Tax returns. Regular filing deadline is 3/1. The Princeton Review suggests that all financial aid forms be submitted as soon as possible after 1/1. *Need-based scholarships/grants offered:* Federal Pell, SEOG, state scholarships/grants, private scholarships, the school's own gift aid, United Negro College Fund. *Loan aid offered:* FFEL Subsidized Stafford, FFEL Unsubsidized Stafford, FFEL PLUS, Federal Perkins, state loans, college/university loans from institutional funds. Applicants will be notified of awards on or about 4/1.

The Inside Word

Yale estimates that over three-quarters of all its applicants are qualified to attend the university, but less than ten percent get in. That adds up to a lot of broken hearts among kids who, if admitted, could probably handle the academic program. With so many qualified applicants to choose from, Yale can winnow to build an incoming class that is balanced in terms of income level, racial/ethnic background, geographic origin, and academic interest. For all but the most qualified, getting in typically hinges on offering just what an admissions officer is looking for to fill a specific slot. Legacies (descendents of Yale grads) gain some advantage—they're admitted at a 30 percent rate.

THE SCHOOL SAYS "..."

From The Admissions Office

"The most important questions the admissions committee must resolve are 'Who is likely to make the most of Yale's resources?' and 'Who will contribute significantly to the Yale community?' These questions suggest an approach to evaluating applicants that is more complex than whether Yale would rather admit well-rounded people or those with specialized talents. In selecting a class of 1,300 from more than 22,000 applicants, the admissions committee looks for academic ability and achievement combined with such personal characteristics as motivation, curiosity, energy, and leadership ability. The nature of these qualities is such that there is no simple profile of grades, scores, interests, and activities that will assure admission. Diversity within the student population is important, and the admissions committee selects a class of able and contributing individuals from a variety of backgrounds and with a broad range of interests and skills.

"Applicants for the entering class will be required to take the two SAT Subject Tests of their choice. Applicants may take the ACT, with the Writing component, as an alternative to the SAT and SAT Subject Tests."

SELECTIVITY

Admissions Rating	99
# of applicants	22,817
% of applicants accepted	9
% of acceptees attending	68
# accepting a place on wait list	815
% admitted from wait list	7

FRESHMAN PROFILE

Range SAT Critical Reading	700–800
Range SAT Math	700–790
Range SAT Writing	700–790
Range ACT Composite	30–34
Minimum paper TOEFL	600
Minimum computer TOEFL	250
Minimum web-based TOEFL	100
% graduated top 10% of class	97
% graduated top 25% of class	100
% graduated top 50% of class	100

DEADLINES

Early action	
Deadline	11/1
Notification	12/15
Regular	
Deadline	12/31
Notification	4/1
Nonfall registration?	no

FINANCIAL FACTS

Financial Aid Rating	97
Annual tuition	$35,300
Room and board	$10,700
Books and supplies	$950
% frosh rec. need-based scholarship or grant aid	46
% UG rec. need-based scholarship or grant aid	42
% frosh rec. need-based self-help aid	36
% UG rec. need-based self-help aid	37
% UG borrow to pay for school	34
Average cumulative indebtedness	$12,237

PART 4

"COW TIPPING IS DEFINITELY PASSÉ HERE."

Our survey has seven questions that allow students to answer in narrative form. We tell students that we don't care *what* they write: If it is "witty, informative, or accurate," we try to get it into this book. We use all the informative and accurate essays to write the "Students Speak Out" sections; below are excerpts from the wittiest, pithiest, and most outrageous narrative responses to our open-ended questions.

FOOD...

"When students first arrive, they call the Observatory Hill Dining Facility 'O-Hill.' They soon learn to call it 'O-Hell,' because the food here is beyond revolting."

— Greg F.,
University of Virginia

"If I had known that I'd be rooming with roaches and poisoned by the cafeteria staff I would have gone to Wayne State. I really can't complain, though, because I have met my husband here, like my mom did 20 years before."

— M.L.P., Fisk University

"You should mention Lil', the lady who has worked in the dining hall for 50 years and who everyone loves. She plays the spoons all the time and runs around."

— Aaron R., Tufts University

HOMETOWN...

"In my experience New York is a place that allows people to be anyone they want to be. You can wear a zebra-striped bikini in the middle of winter on a snow-covered street here, and people would hardly look twice"

—Sophomore, Barnard College

"Change the name of UC—Irvine to UC—Newport Beach and we would have more girls."

— Pat M., UC—Irvine

"Connecticut is a cute state. It's a great place to go to school, but I wouldn't want to live here."

— Claire S., NJ native,
Fairfield University

"Socially, the surrounding area is so dead that the Denny's closes at night."

— Thomas R., UC—Riverside

"The local liquor stores and towing companies make a lot of money."

— Katherine R.,
University of Rhode Island

"It is definitely important to have a car, as the population of Canton frequently matches our winter temperature. 'Canton gray,' our perennial sky color, is one Crayola missed."

— Daniel R., St. Lawrence University

"Montreal is the sh*@!"

—Elizabeth R., McGill University

"Fredericksburg is boring if one is not amused by the simple pleasures of existence such as breathing, sleep, and other things."

—Rich W., Mary Washington College

SECURITY...

"Campus security is made up of a bunch of midget high school dropouts with Napoleonic complexes who can spot a beer can from a mile away."

—Anonymous, UC—San Diego

"Public safety here is a joke. The public safety officers are like the Keystone Kops on Thorazine."

—Anonymous, Bryn Mawr College

CLASSMATES...

"If you're thinking of applying to MIT, go ahead. Because, believe it or not, most people here are at least as stupid as you are."

—Patrick L., MIT

"The typical student is mostly an easygoing, skirt-wearing, intelligent, procrastinating kid. Although, there [are] of course, many many many variations on this. Not all kids wear skirts. Not all the boys in skirts are straight. Not all the girls in skirts are straight. 'Everybody here looks like Jesus!' was a pretty accurate description from an outsider."

—Amy P., New College of Florida

"Students here mostly get along, and since it is a business school we all have a common goal of being rich."

—Female Sophomore, Babson College

"People who go to school here are all pretty good looking, especially the women. It should be renamed UKB, the University of Ken and Barbie."

—Tony H., Arizona State University

"Wesleyan is not only the 'diversity university' but also the 'controversy university,' the 'fight adversity university,' and the 'if we keep trying we might have some unity' university. We satisfy all types."

—John P., Wesleyan University

"Mt. Holyoke students are friendly and respectful with the exception of the occasions when the entire campus gets PMS."

—Abigail K., Mount Holyoke College

"My roommate's a complete jerk so I spend most of my nights sleeping in the backseat of my truck."

—Ronald G., Arizona State University

"Girls over 5'8", watch out—for some reason, guys here have munchkin blood in them or something."

—Robyn A., Tufts University

"A school can be defined by its graffiti and its level of cleverness. Three-quarters of our school graffiti is pro- or anti- a specific fraternity, with the other one-quarter devoted to homophobic or misogynist theories."

—Matthew E., College of William & Mary

"This is a great university if you're not studying sciences involving animal research, politics, teacher education (certification), or anything that offends any long-haired leftist who's a vegetarian."

—Brock M., University of Oregon

"Most of my peers are narrow-minded morons who seem to live in the '50s. Because of this constant annoyance, the rest of us have a camaraderie that allows us to see how the other half lives."

—Gary A., Louisiana State University

"Everyone here is too smart for their own good. As one upper-level executive in the Houston area put it, 'The students at Rice know how to make it rain, but they don't know to come in out of it.'"

—John B., Rice University

"Bates is so diverse! Yesterday I met somebody from Connecticut!"

—Ellen H., Bates College

"Most are either Bible-thumping, goodie-goodie, White, stuck-up, right-wing, straight-A losers or work-hard, play-harder and party-hardy, willing-to-try-anything cool people."

—Male Sophomore,
Colorado School of Mines

"We have this typical student stereotype we call 'Wendy Wellesley.' Wendy takes copious notes, is a devoted member of 10 organizations, always has an internship, goes over the page limit on every assignment, takes six classes, goes to all the office hours, triple majors, and is basically diligent, overcommitted, extroverted, overachieving, and energetic (but without a sense of humor or ability to relax)."

—R.D., Wellesley College

"I am constantly impressed with the creativity of hell-raisers on campus. One day I walked past the Manor House to find a dozen plastic babies climbing all over the roof! Right before Parents' Weekend, some people hung up signs saying 'Princeton Review reports: "LC students ignore herpes on a regular basis." Please visit the health clinic!'"

—Anonymous, Lewis & Clark College

"Diversity in the female population means different shades of hair color . . . we often joke that Burberry is SMU Sorority Camouflage."

—Male Senior,
Southern Methodist University

ADMINISTRATION...

"Despite the best efforts of the administration to provide TCNJ students with an inefficient, cold-hearted, red-tape-infested, snafu-riddled Soviet-style administrative bureaucracy, The College of New Jersey is a pretty decent place to go for a fairly reasonable amount of money."

—Anonymous,
The College of New Jersey

"Administration is like the stock market, you invest time and money, sometimes you get a return, other times you don't."

—J.W.R., Albertson College of Idaho

"Columbia is like a fruit truck. It picks up varied and exotic fruits and deposits them rotten at their destination."

—Paul L., Columbia University

"The University of Minnesota is a huge black hole of knowledge. It sucks things into it from far and wide, compressing to the essence. Unfortunately, it is very hard to get anything out of a black hole. What I have managed to eke out has been both rewarding and depressing."

—James McDonald,
University of Minnesota

"The strangest incident I've ever had in class was when one of my journalism profs burnt our tests in the microwave. But he decided to give everyone in the class an A, instead of retesting."

—Ashlea K., Ohio University

"Going to Northwestern is like having a beautiful girlfriend who treats you like crap."

—Jonathan J. G., Northwestern University

"Life at school is an oxymoron."

—Dave G., UC—Davis

"Vassar is like a sexual disease: Once you've accepted it, it's great, but when you realize you've got another three years to put up with it, you go see a medical adviser immediately."

—Henry R., Vassar College

"Getting an education from MIT is like getting a drink from a firehose."

—Juan G., MIT

"Intro classes have the consistency of Cheez Whiz: They go down easy, they taste horrible, and they are not good for you."

—Pat T., University of Vermont

SEX, DRUGS, ROCK & ROLL...

"Beam, Bud, beer, babes—the four essential B's."

—"Jim Beam," Wittenberg University

"Yeah, there aren't any guys, but who doesn't like doing homework on a Saturday night?"

—Nicole C., Wellesley College

"The dances here are a riot because I love watching nerds and intellectuals dance."

—Male Senior, Columbia University

"Any campus attempt to provide drug-free entertainment shuts down at 10:20 P.M. to allow plenty of time to be drunk. The general campus motto is 'If you weren't wasted, the night was.'"

—Junior, Lehigh University

"Drug use here is extremely prevalent. People smoke pot everywhere, even outdoors."

—Freshman, New College of Florida

SCHOOL VS. THE "REAL WORLD"...

"College is the best time of your life. Never again will you be surrounded by people the same age as you, free from grown-ups and the threat of working in the real world. Your parents give you money when you ask for it, and all you have to do is learn!"

—Jennifer F., Syracuse University

"Real-life experience in such concepts—alienation, depression, suppression, isolationism, edge of racial tension, apathy, etc.—before the 'real world.'"

—Anonymous, NYU

IN CASE YOU WERE WONDERING...

Drexel = (Content[good] - Schedule[finals] - Tuition)^[sum(geeks)/sum(jocks)] + [avg[i,j](sqrt[(geekPos[i] - jockPos[j]).x^2 + (geekPos[i] - jockPos[j]).y^2]) - 200ft] = 8.5/10

—Male Junior, Drexel University

"I am a hermit who enjoys Ramen noodles and skin flicks. In the winter, I sit in a yoga position by a patch of ice on the sidewalk and mock people as they fall. I often bend spoons with my mind."

—Junior, Indiana University of Pennsylvania

"When I'm not trying to free Mumia, experience non-gender orgasm/transgender interpretive dance, contracting any number of venereal diseases, or trying to be hopelessly unique, I obsess to no end in trying to reconcile my existentialist beliefs with paying $30,000 a year to attend this socially legitimizing institution."

—Katherine S., Bard College

"Those who oppose the Dark Lord will be crushed, but those who are its friend will receive rewards beyond the dreams of avarice."

—Anonymous, Sarah Lawrence College

"There is a real problem with moles on this campus; no one is willing to talk about them."

—Alexander D., Bates College

CONFUSED PEOPLE...

"A crust of bread is better than nothing. Nothing is better than true love. Therefore, by the transitive property, a crust of bread is better than true love."

—Jason G., Gettysburg College

"Bentley College has fulfilled all and more of my expectations than I ever imagined."

— Dawn T., Bentley College

On the academics/administration: "They think they know a lot but they actually don't know anything, but some of them know that, so they know everything."

—Male Junior, College of the Atlantic

PART 5

INDEXES

There are currently two professional organizations for independent counselors that require professional credential review: Independent Educational Consultants Association (IECA) and National Association for College Admission Counseling (NACAC). Counselors affiliated with both groups provide varied and detailed services to students and families exploring future educational opportunities. Should you consider seeking the services of an independent counselor, I encourage you to visit both the IECA and NACAC websites for up-to-date information and listings.

Sincerely,

Robert Franek

Lead Author, *The Best 371 Colleges*

VP—Publisher

The Princeton Review

IECA—The Independent Educational Consultants Association is a national non-profit professional association of independent consultants.

www.iecaonline.com

NACAC—The National Association for College Admission Counseling is an organization of 9,000 global professionals dedicated to serving students as they make choices in pursuing postsecondary education.

www.nacacnet.org

THE PRINCETON REVIEW NATIONAL COLLEGE COUNSELOR ADVISORY BOARD, 2009

We'd like to thank the following for their careful and considered input on our products and services during the year:

Lee Bierer, Counselor, College Admissions Strategies, Charlotte, NC

Carolyn Cuttler, Chairperson Guidance, Long Beach High School, NY

Cheryl Dennis, Counseling Dept. Chair, Redmond High School, WA

Mary Ann Doll, College Advisor, Palisades Charter High School, CA

Judy Fairfull, Director of Guidance, Doherty Memorial HS, MA

Ann R. Harris, Ph.D., Director of College Guidance, Parish Episcopal School, TX

Darnell Heywood, Director of College Counseling, Columbus School for Girls, OH

William Hirt, College Counselor, Professional Children's School, New York

Marilyn J. Kaufman, M.Ed., President, College Admission Consultants, TX

Geri Kellogg, Counselor, LPC, J.J. Pearce High School, TX

Donna Landreth, Counselor, Plano West Senior High, TX

Joanne Levy-Prewitt, College Admissions Adviser, CA

Marianna P. Marchese, Ed.D., Director of Pupil Personnel Services, West Morris Mendham High School, NJ

Susan S. Marrs, Director, College Counseling, Seven Hills School, OH

Alicia Moretti, private tutor, CA

Bruce Richardson, Director of Guidance, Plano Sr. High School, TX

Kim Rose, Director of Counseling and Guidance, Highland Park ISD, NJ

Dr. Kitty Scott, Head of Guidance, Glen Rock High School, NJ

Martha Sharp, M.Ed., CHHS Guidance Counselor, TX

Kim Simpson, Educational Consultant, Collegiate Admissions Counseling Services, LA

Theresa Urist, Director of College Counseling, Prospect Hill Academy Charter School, MA

Scott White, Director of Guidance Montclair High School, NJ

Michael Wilner, Principal, Wilner Education, VT

INDEX OF SCHOOLS

INDEX OF SCHOOLS BY LOCATION

UNITED STATES

Price categories are based on current tuition (out-of-state tuition for public schools) and do not include fees, room, board, transportation, or other expenses.

LESS THAN $15,000

University of Vermont	714–715
University of Virginia	716–717
University of Washington	718–719
University of Wisconsin—Madison	720–721
University of Wyoming	722–723
Virginia Tech	734–735
Washington State University	748–749
Webb Institute	752–753
West Virginia University	762–763
Xavier University of Louisiana	788–789

$15,000–$30,000

Agnes Scott College	52–53
Albion College	54–55
Alfred University	56–57
Baylor University	78–79
Bellarmine University	80–81
Berea College	88–89
Bradley University	98–99
Bryant University	106–107
Calvin College	116–117
Catawba College	124–125
Centenary College of Louisiana	128–129
Coe College	150–151
College of Idaho, The	162–163
Cornell College	182–183
Creighton University	186–187
DePaul University	196–197
Drexel University	204–205
Duquesne University	208–209
Elon University	212–213
Emerson College	214–215
Fisk University	224–225
Florida Southern College	228–229
Gonzaga University	250–251
Green Mountain College	254–255
Guilford College	260–261
Gustavus Adolphus College	262–263
Hampden-Sydney College	266–267
Hanover College	272–273
Hendrix College	280–281
Hillsdale College	282–283
Hiram College	284–285
Hofstra University	288–289
Hollins University	290–291
Illinois Institute of Technology	294–295
Loyola University—New Orleans	338–339
Loyola University—Chicago	334–335
Lynchburg College	340–341
Marist College	346–347
Marquette University	350–351
Mercer University	358–359
Millsaps College	370–371
Monmouth University (NJ)	374–375
Nazareth College	384–385
Oglethorpe University	404–405
Randolph College	432–433
Rice University	440–441
Rider University	442–443
Ripon College	444–445
Rochester Institute of Technology	446–447
Sacred Heart University	454–455
Samford University	466–467
Seattle University	474–475
Seton Hall University	476–477

Siena College	480–481
Southwestern University	494–495
St. Anselm College	456–457
St. Bonaventure University	498–499
St. John's University	504–505
Suffolk University	530–531
Sweet Briar College	536–537
Texas Christian University	544–545
Thomas Aquinas College	546–547
Transylvania University	548–549
Trinity University	552–553
Tuskegee University	560–561
University of Charleston	598–599
University of Dallas	608–609
University of Dayton	610–611
University of Tulsa, The	710–711
Valparaiso University	726–727
Wabash College	736–737
Warren Wilson College	742–743
Wells College	756–757
Wesleyan College	758–759
Westminster College (PA)	764–765
Westminster College of Salt Lake City	766–767
Wheaton College (IL)	768–769
Willamette University	776–777
William Jewell College	778–779
Wofford College	784–785
Xavier University (OH)	790–791

MORE THAN $30,000

Allegheny College	58–59
American University	60–61
Amherst College	62–63
Babson College	70–71
Bard College	72–73
Barnard College	74–75
Bates College	76–77
Beloit College	82–83
Bennington College	84–85
Bentley University	86–87
Boston College	92–93
Boston University	94–95
Bowdoin College	96–97
Brandeis University	100–101
Brown University	104–105
Bryn Mawr College	108–109
Bucknell University	110–111
California Institute of Technology	112–113
Carleton College	118–119
Carnegie Mellon University	120–121
Case Western Reserve University	122–123
Catholic University of America	126–127
Centre College	130–131
Chapman University	132–133
Claremont McKenna College	142–143
Clark University	144–145
Clarkson University	146–147
Colby College	152–153
Colgate University	154–155
College of the Atlantic	156–157
College of the Holy Cross	160–161
College of Wooster, The	170–171
Colorado College	172–173
Columbia University	176–177
Connecticut College	178–179

Robert Franek is a graduate of Drew University and vice president and publisher for The Princeton Review. He has proudly been a part of the company since 1999. Robert comes to The Princeton Review with an extensive admissions background. In addition, he owns a walking tour business, leading historically driven, yet not boring, walking tours of his favorite town, New York City!

Tom Meltzer is a graduate of Columbia University. He has taught for The Princeton Review since 1986 and is the author or coauthor of seven Princeton Review titles, the most recent of which is *Illustrated Word Smart*, which Tom cowrote with his wife, Lisa. He is also a professional musician and songwriter. A native of Baltimore, Tom now lives in Hillsborough, North Carolina.

Christopher Maier is a graduate of Dickinson College. During the past five years, he's lived variously in New York City, coastal Maine, western Oregon, central Pennsylvania, and eastern England. Now he's at an oasis somewhere in the Midwestern cornfields—the University of Illinois—where he's earning his MFA in fiction. Aside from writing for magazines, newspapers, and The Princeton Review, he's worked as a radio disc jockey, a helping hand in a bakery, and a laborer on a highway construction crew. He's trying to avoid highway construction these days.

Carson Brown graduated from Stanford University in 1998, and after getting paid too much for working for various Internet companies for several years, sold her BMW and moved to Mexico. She has now overstayed her welcome south of the border and is returning to San Francisco to be responsible and further her career working as a writer and editor.

Julie Doherty is a freelance writer, web designer, and preschool teacher. She lives in Mexico City.

Andrew Friedman graduated in 2003 from Stanford University, where he was a President's Scholar. He lives in New York City.

Paying For College 101

If you're reading this book, you've already made an investment in your education. You may have shelled out some cold hard cash for this book, and you've definitely invested time in reading it. It's probably even safe to say that this is one of the smaller investments you've made in your future so far. You put in the hours and hard work needed to keep up your GPA. You've paid test fees and applications fees, perhaps even travel expenses. You have probably committed time and effort to a host of extracurricular activities to make sure colleges know that you're a well-rounded student.

But after you get in, there's one more issue to think about: How do you pay for college?

Let's be honest, college is not cheap. The average tuition for a private four-year college is about $25,000 a year. The average tuition of a four-year public school is about $6,500 a year. And the cost is rising. Every year the sticker price of college education bumps up about 6 percent.

Like many of us, your family may not have 25 grand sitting around in a shoebox. With such a hefty price tag, you might be wondering: "Is a college education really worth it? The short answer: Yes! No question about it. A 2007 survey by the College Board showed that people with a college degree earn 60 percent more than people who enter the workforce with only a high school diploma. Despite its steep price tag, a college education ultimately pays for itself.

Still, the cost of college is no joke.

Here's the good news. Even in the wake of the current financial crisis, financial aid is available to almost any student who wants it. There is an estimated $143 billion—that's right, billion!—in financial aid offered to students annually. This comes in the form of federal grants, scholarships, state financed aid, loans, and other programs. Furthermore, the 2009 stimulus package made it easier to qualify for government aid, and lowered the interest rates on government loans.

We know that financial aid can seem like an overwhelmingly complex issue, but the introductory information in this chapter should help you grasp what's available and get you started in your search.

You'll find detailed and up-to-date information on financial aid, saving for college and getting education loans in our annual guidebook, Paying for College Without Going Broke, which is published each October. Authored by Kalman Chany, one of the the nation's most quoted experts in college funding, it's the only annual guide with a sample copy of the forthcoming year's FAFSA form all aid applicants must complete, plus line-by-line strategies on completing the form to one's best advantage.

HOW MUCH DOES COLLEGE REALLY COST?

When most people think about the price of a college education, they think of one thing and one thing alone: tuition. It's time to get that notion out of your head. While tuition is a significant portion of the cost of a college education, you need to think of all the other things that factor into the final price tag.

Let's break it down.

- Tuition and fees
- Room and board
- Books and supplies
- Personal expenses
- Travel expenses

Collectively, these things contribute to your total Cost of Attendance (COA) for one year at a college or university.

Understanding the distinction between tuition and COA is crucial because it will help you understand this simple equation:

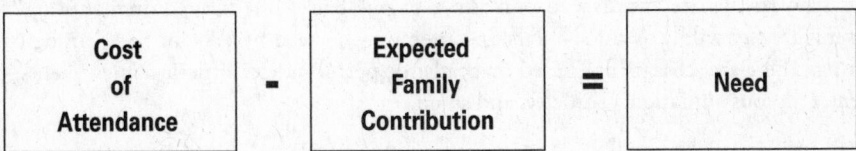

When you begin the financial aid process, you will see this equation again and again. We've already talked about the COA, so let's talk about the Estimated Family Contribution, or EFC. The EFC simply means, "How much you and your family can afford to pay for college." Sounds obvious right?

Here's the catch: What you think you can afford to pay for college, what the government thinks you can afford to pay for college, and what a college or university thinks you can afford to pay for college are, unfortunately, three different things. Keep that in mind as we discuss financing options later on.

The final term in the equation is self-explanatory. Anything that's left after what you and your family have contributed, still needs to be covered. That's where financial aid packages come in.

WHATS IN A FINANCIAL AID PACKAGE?

A typical financial aid package contains money—from the school, federal government, or state—in various forms: grants, scholarships, work-study programs, and loans.

Let's look at the non-loan options first. Non-loan options include grants, scholarships, and work-study programs. The crucial thing about them is that they involve monetary assistance that you won't be asked to pay back. They are as close as you'll get to "free money."

Grants

Grants are basically gifts. They are funds given to you by the federal government, state agencies, or individual colleges. They are usually need-based, and you are not required to pay them back.

One of the most important grants is the Pell Grant. Pell Grants are provided by the federal government but administered through individual schools. Under the 2009 stimulus package, the maximum award one can receive through the Pell Grant is $5,350 dollars a year.

You apply for a Pell Grant by filling out the Free Application for Federal Student Aid (FAFSA). Remember that acronym because you'll be seeing it again. Completing the FAFSA is the first step in applying for any federal aid. The FAFSA can be found online at www.fafsa.ed.gov.

There are several other major federal grant programs that hand out grants ranging from $100 to $4,000 dollars annually. Some of these grants are given to students entering a specific field of study and others are need-based, but all of them amount to money that you never have to pay back. Check out the FAFSA website for complete information about qualifying and applying for government grants.

The federal government isn't the only source of grant money. State governments and specific schools also offer grants. Use the Internet, your guidance counselor, and your library to see what non-federal grants you might be eligible for.

Scholarships

Like grants, scholarships are awards you don't have to pay back. But the requirements and terms of a scholarship might vary wildly. Most scholarships are merit- or need-based, but they can be based on almost anything. There are scholarships based on academic performance, athletic achievements, musical or artistic talent, religious affiliation, ethnicity, and so on.

When hunting for scholarships, one great place to start is the Department of Education's free "Scholarship Search," available at https://studentaid2.ed.gov/getmoney/scholarship. This database asks you a handful of questions about your academic history, interests, and future plans. It then uses this data to report on scholarships that you might be interested in pursuing. It's a free service and a great resource.

There is one important caveat about taking scholarship money. Some, but not all, schools think of scholarship money as income and will reduce the amount of aid they offer you accordingly. Know your school's policy on scholarship awards.

Federal Work-Study (FWS)

One of the ways Uncle Sam disperses aid money is by subsidizing part-time jobs, usually on campus, for students who need financial aid. Because your school will administer the money, they get to decide what your work-study job will be. Work-study participants are paid by the hour, and federal law requires that they cannot be paid less than the federal minimum wage.

One of the benefits of a work-study program is that you get a paycheck just like you would at a normal job. The money is intended to go towards school expenses, but there are no controls over exactly how you spend it.

Colleges and universities determine how to administer work-study programs on their own campuses, so you must apply for a FWS at your school's financial aid office.

LOANS

Most likely, your entire COA won't be covered by scholarships, grants, and work-study income. The next step in gathering the necessary funds is securing a loan. Broadly speaking, there are two routes to go: federal loans and private loans. Once upon a time, which route to choose might be open for debate. But these days the choice is clear: Always try to secure federal loans first. Almost without exception, federal loans provide unbeatable low fixed-interest rates; they come with generous repayment terms; and, although they have lending limits, these limits are quite generous and will take you a long way toward your goal. We'll talk about the benefits of private loans later, but they really can't measure up to what the government can provide.

Stafford Loans

The Stafford loan is the primary form of federal student loan. There are two kinds of Stafford loans: direct Stafford loans, which are administered by the Department of Education; and Federal Family Education Loans (FFEL), which are administered by a private lender bound by the terms the government sets for Stafford loans (FFEL loans are sometimes referred to as indirect Stafford loans, as well). Both direct and FFEL loans can be subsidized or unsubsidized. Students with demonstrated financial need may qualify for subsidized loans. This means that the government pays interest accumulated during the time the student is in school. Students with unsubsidized Stafford loans are responsible for the interest accumulated while in school. You can qualify for a subsidized Stafford loan, an unsubsidized Stafford loan, or a mixture of the two.

Stafford loans are available to all full-time students and most part-time students. Though the terms of the loan are based on demonstrated financial need, lack of need is not considered grounds for rejection. No payment is expected while the student is attending school. The interest rate on your Stafford loan will depend on when your first disbursement is. The chart below shows the fixed rates set by the government.

First disbursement made on or after	Interest rate on unpaid balance
July 1, 2008 to July 1, 2009	6.0 percent
July 1, 2009 to July 1, 2010	5.6 percent
July 1, 2010 to July 1, 2011	4.5 percent
July 1, 2011 to July 1, 2012	3.4 percent

Finally, depending on the amount owed and the payment plan agreed upon by the borrower and lender, students have between 10 and 25 years to pay off their loan.

As with grants, you must start by completing the Free Application for Federal Student Aid (FAFSA) to apply for a Stafford loan.

PLUS Loans

Another important federal loan is the PLUS loan. This loan is designed to help parents and guardians put dependent students through college. Like the Stafford loan, a PLUS loan might be a direct loan from the government, administered by your school's financial aid office, or it might be administered by a private lender who is bound to federal guidelines. Unlike the Stafford loan, the PLUS has no fixed limits or fixed interest rates. The annual limit on a PLUS loan is equal to your COA minus any other financial aid you are already receiving. It may be used on top of a Stafford loan. The interest rates on PLUS loans are variable though often comparable to, or even lower than, the interest rates on Stafford loans. Borrowers can choose when they will start paying the loan back: starting either 60 days from the first disbursement or six months after the dependent student has finished school.

To apply for a PLUS loan, your parents (or guardians) must apply to the financial aid office of your school or with a FFEL private lender.

Perkins Loan

A third and final federal loan you should be aware of is the Perkins loan. Intended to help out students in extreme need, the Perkins loan is a government-subsidized loan that is administered only through college and university financial aid offices. Under the terms of a Perkins loan, you may borrow up to $5,500 a year of undergraduate study, up to $27,500. The Perkins loan has a fixed interest rate of just 5 percent. Payments against the loan don't start until nine months after you graduate. Apply for Perkins loans through your school's financial aid office.

Private Lenders

We said it before, and we'll say it again: DO NOT get a private loan until you've exhausted all other options.

Before the crisis, many private lenders could offer competitive interest rates and relatively generous qualification standards. Now, for the most part, that's no longer the case. Private lenders are growing increasing selective of the borrowers they lend to, and the average interest rate for private loans hovers around 13 percent.

Still, there are some benefits to securing a private loan. First off, many students find that non-loan and federal loan options don't end up covering the entire bill. If that's the case, then private lenders might just save the day. Second, loans from private sources generally offer you greater flexibility with how you use the funds. Third, private loans can be taken out at anytime during your academic career. Unlike most non-loan and government-backed financial options, you can turn to private lenders whenever you need them.

All private lenders are not the same! As the old song says, "You better shop around." Every lender is going to offer you a different package of terms. What you need to do is find the package that best fits your needs and plans. Aside from low interest rates, which are crucially important, there other terms and conditions you will want to look out for.

Low origination fees

Origination fees are fees that lenders charge you for taking out a loan. Usually the fee is simply deducted automatically from your loan checks. Obviously, the lower the origination fee, the better.

Minimal guaranty fees

A guaranty fee is an amount you pay to a third-party who agrees to insure your loan. That way, if the borrower—that is you—can't pay the loan back, the guarantor steps in and pays the difference. Again, if you can minimize or eliminate this fee, all the better.

Interest rate reductions

Some lenders will reduce your interest rates if you're reliable with your payments. Some will even agree to knock a little off the interest rate if you agree to pay your loans through a direct deposit system. When shopping for the best loan, pay careful attention to factors that might help you curb your interest rates.

Flexible payment plans

One of the great things about most federal loans is the fact that you don't have to start paying them off until you leave school. In order to compete, many private lenders have been forced to adopt similarly flexible payment plans. Before saying yes to a private loan, make sure that it comes with a payment timetable you can live with.

WHERE THERE'S A WILL THERE'S A WAY

No matter what the state of the economy, going to college will always make good financial sense. This is especially true today, with the wealth of low-interest federal assistance programs available to you. There are plenty of excellent financing options out there. With a little effort (and a lot of form-filling!) you'll be able to pay your way through school without breaking the bank.

The Tools
You Need to Get In

The College App Map is the perfect companion to guide you through all of the challenges of applying (and getting accepted) to your top schools. Complete with checklists, charts, and trusted advice from *The Princeton Review*, this journal helps you de-stress and decode the college process, while getting you organized and motivated about your exciting journey ahead.

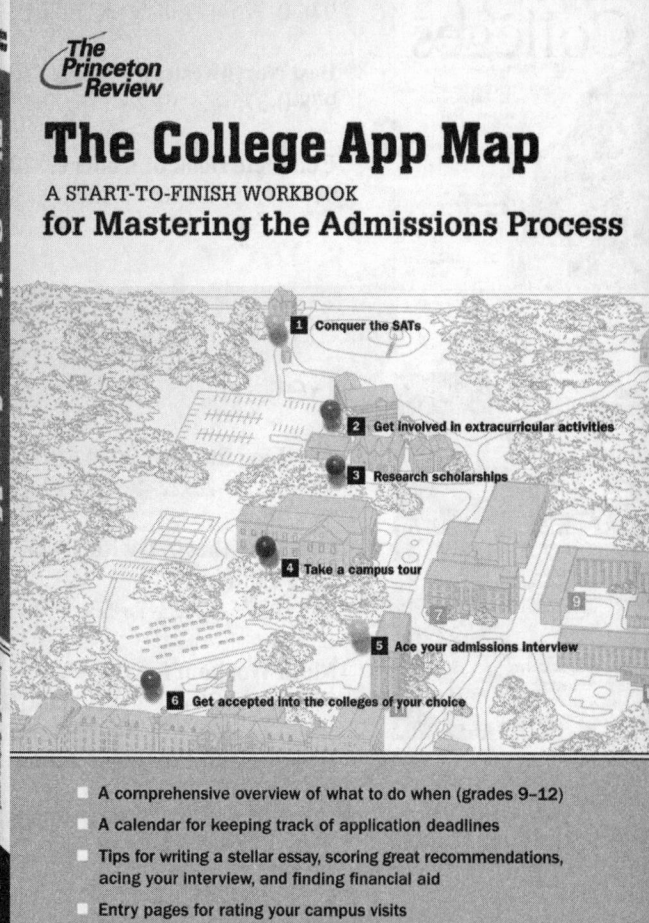

The Princeton Review

The College App Map

A START-TO-FINISH WORKBOOK
for Mastering the Admissions Process

1. Conquer the SATs
2. Get involved in extracurricular activities
3. Research scholarships
4. Take a campus tour
5. Ace your admissions interview
6. Get accepted into the colleges of your choice

- A comprehensive overview of what to do when (grades 9–12)
- A calendar for keeping track of application deadlines
- Tips for writing a stellar essay, scoring great recommendations, acing your interview, and finding financial aid
- Entry pages for rating your campus visits

Joyce E. Suber and The Princeton Review

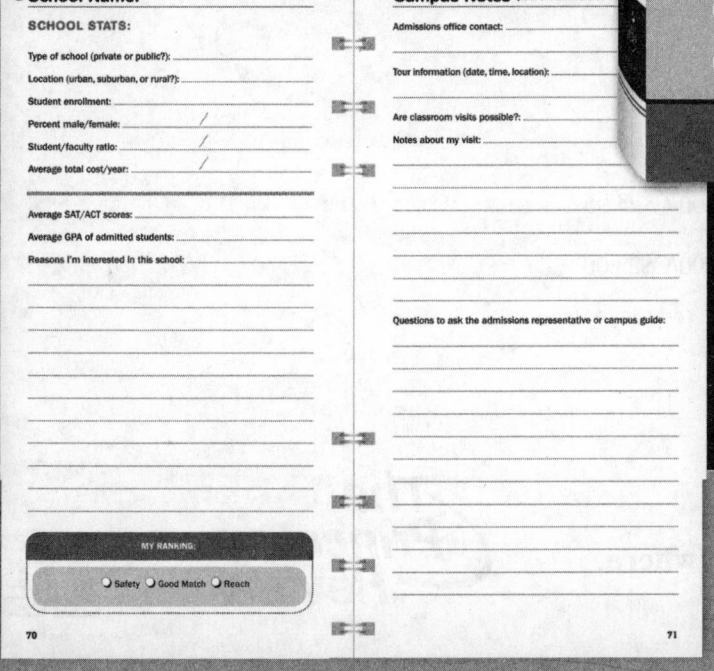

The College App Map
978-0-307-45312-9
$16.95 (Canada $19.95)

Available July 28, 2009
Potter Style
www.potterstyle.com

Our Books Help You Navigate the College Admissions Process

Find the Right School

Best 371 Colleges, 2010 Edition
978-0-375-42938-5 • $22.99/C$27.99

Best Northwestern Colleges, 2010 Edition
978-0-375-42939-2 • $16.99/C$21.99

Complete Book of Colleges, 2010 Edition
978-0-375-42940-8 • $26.99/C$33.99

College Navigator
978-0-375-76583-4 • $12.95/C$16.00

America's Best Value Colleges, 2008 Edition
978-0-375-76601-5 • $18.95/C$24.95

Guide to College Visits
978-0-375-76600-8 • $20.00/C$25.00

Get In

Cracking the SAT, 2010 Edition
978-0-375-42922-4 • $21.99/C$26.99

Cracking the SAT with DVD, 2010 Edition
978-0-375-42923-1 • $34.99/C$42.99

Math Workout for the SAT
978-0-375-76433-2 • $16.00/C$23.00

Reading and Writing Workout for the SAT
978-0-375-76431-8 • $16.00/C$23.00

11 Practice Tests for the SAT and PSAT, 2010 Edition
978-0-375-42934-7 • $22.99/C$27.99

Cracking the ACT, 2009 Edition
978-0-375-42899-9 • $19.95/C$22.95

Cracking the ACT with DVD, 2009 Edition
978-0-375-42900-2 • $31.95/C$35.95

Crash Course for the ACT, 3rd Edition
978-0-375-76587-2 • $9.95/C$12.95

Fund It

Paying for College Without Going Broke, 2010 Edition
978-0-375-42942-2 • $20.00/C$24.95
Previous Edition:
978-0-375-42883-8 • $20.00/C$23.00

Available online and in bookstores everywhere.
PrincetonReview.com

AP Exams

Cracking the AP Biology Exam, 2010 Edition
978-0-375-42914-9 • $18.99/C$23.99

Cracking the AP Calculus AB & BC Exams, 2010 Edition
978-0-375-42915-6 • $19.99/C $24.99

Cracking the AP Chemistry Exam, 2010 Edition
978-0-375-42916-3 • $18.00/C $22.00

Cracking the AP Computer Science A & AB Exams, 2006–2007 Edition
978-0-375-76528-5 • $19.00/C$27.00

Cracking the AP Economics Macro & Micro Exams, 2010 Edition
978-0-375-42917-0 • $18.00/C $22.00

Cracking the AP English Language & Composition Exam, 2010 Edition
978-0-375-42918-7 • $18.00 /C$22.00

Cracking the AP English Literature & Composition Exam, 2010 Edition
978-0-375-42943-9 • 18.00/C$22.00

Cracking the AP Environmental Science Exam, 2010 Edition
978-0-375-42944-6 • $18.00/C $22.00

Cracking the AP European History Exam, 2010 Edition
978-0-375-42945-3 • $18.99/C $23.99

Cracking the AP U.S. Government & Politics Exam, 2010 Edition
978-0-375-42951-4 • $18.99/C $23.99

Cracking the AP Human Geography Exam, 2010 Edition
978-0-375-42919-4 • $18.00/C $22.00

Cracking the AP Physics B Exam, 2010 Edition
978-0-375-42946-0 • $18.00/C $22.00

Cracking the AP Physics C Exam, 2010 Edition
978-0-375-42947-7 • $18.00/C $22.00

Cracking the AP Psychology Exam, 2010 Edition
978-0-375-42948-4 • $18.00/C $22.00

Cracking the AP Spanish Exam with Audio CD, 2010 Edition
978-0-375-42949-1 • $24.99/C $29.99

Cracking the AP Statistics Exam, 2010 Edition
978-0-375-42950-7 • $19.99/C $24.99

Cracking the AP U.S. History Exam, 2010 Edition
978-0-375-42952-1 • $18.99/C $23.99

Cracking the AP World History Exam, 2010 Edition
978-0-375-42953-8 • $18.00/C $22.00

SAT Subject Tests

Cracking the SAT Biology E/M Subject Test, 2009–2010 Edition
978-0-375-42905-7 • $19.00/C$22.00

Cracking the SAT Chemistry Subject Test, 2009–2010 Edition
978-0-375-42906-4 • $19.00/C$22.00

Cracking the SAT French Subject Test, 2009–2010 Edition
978-0-375-42907-1 • $19.00/C$22.00

Cracking the SAT U.S. & World History Subject Tests, 2009–2010 Edition
978-0-375-42908-8 • $19.00/C$22.00

Cracking the SAT Literature Subject Test, 2009–2010 Edition
978-0-375-42909-5 • $19.00/C$22.00

Cracking the SAT Math 1 & 2 Subject Tests, 2009–2010 Edition
978-0-375-42910-1 • $19.00/C$22.00

Cracking the SAT Physics Subject Test, 2009–2010 Edition
978-0-375-42911-8 • $19.00/C$22.00

Cracking the SAT Spanish Subject Test, 2009–2010 Edition
978-0-375-42912-5 • $19.00/C$22.00

WE KNOW APPLYING TO COLLEGES IS STRESSFUL.
Why Not Win $1,000 for It?

Participate in our 2010 "College Hopes & Worries Survey."

You might win our college scholarship prize.

The Princeton Review has conducted this survey of high school students applying to colleges and parents of applicants since 2002. Why? We're curious to know what concerns you the most about your application experiences and what your dream college would be.

Our survey has just 10 questions – way shorter than any college app. You can zip through it in less than three minutes. Plus, in addition to our $1,000 scholarship prize we'll give to one lucky participant chosen at random, we'll give another 25 participants (also chosen at random) a free copy of one of our college-related guidebooks. They can chose from either our *Paying for College without Going Broke*, our *Guide to College Majors*, or our *Parents' Guide to College Life*. In March, about the time you'll (hopefully) be receiving those college acceptance and financial aid award letters, we'll post the findings on our site and inform the scholarship winner and book winners. For more information, see "OFFICIAL RULES" below.

We know how exciting and how stressful college applications can be. We hope the college info on our site and in our books helps you find (and get in to!) the college best for you. We wish you great success in your applications and your college years ahead.

Official Rules:

Princeton Review 2010 "College Hopes & Worries Survey" Prize Sweepstakes

NO PURCHASE NECESSARY. OPEN TO RESIDENTS OF THE 50 UNITED STATES (AND D.C.) 13 YEARS OF AGE AND OLDER ONLY

1. HOW TO ENTER: To enter via the Internet, visit www.princetonreview.com/go/survey. You may also fax your completed questionnaire to: Robert Franek, 212-874-0775. LIMIT ONE ENTRY PER PERSON, EMAIL ADDRESS OR PHONE/FAX NUMBER. All on-line or faxed entries must be received by 11:59 p.m. EDT on March 7, 2010. To enter without Internet access or answering the questionnaire, handwrite your name, complete address and phone number on a postcard and mail to: The Princeton Review, 2010 College Hopes & Worries Survey c/o Robert Franek, 2315 Broadway, New York NY, 10024-4332. Mail-in entries must be received by March 14, 2009. Not responsible for lost, late or misdirected mail.

2. ELIGIBILITY: Open to residents of the 50 United States and D.C., 13 years of age and older, except for employees of The Princeton Review, Inc. ("Sponsor"), its affiliates, subsidiaries and agencies (collectively "Promotion Parties"), and members of their immediate family or persons living in the same household. Void where prohibited.

3. RANDOM DRAWINGS: A random drawing will be held on or about March 31, 2010. Odds of winning will depend upon the number of eligible entries received. Winner will be notified by e-mail/mail and/or telephone, at Sponsor's option and will be required to sign and return any required Affidavit of Eligibility, Release of Liability and Publicity Release within seven (7) days of attempted delivery or prize will be forfeited and an alternate winner may be selected. The return of any prize or prize notification as undeliverable may result in disqualification and an alternate winner may be selected.

4. PRIZES: One (1) Grand Prize: $1,000.00 Scholarship, awarded as a check. Twenty-Five (25) First Prizes: winners choice of one of the following Princeton Review books: Paying for College without Going Broke, Guide to College Majors, or Parents' Guide to College Life. Approximate Retail Value: $19.00. Total prize value: $1475.00. Limit one prize per family/household. All prizes will be awarded.

5. GENERAL RULES: All income taxes resulting from acceptance of prize are the responsibility of winner. By entering sweepstakes, entrant accepts and agrees to these Official Rules and the decisions of Sponsor, which shall be final in all matters. By accepting prize, winner agrees to hold Promotion Parties, their affiliates, directors, officers, employees and assigns harmless against any and all claims and liability arising out of use of prize. Acceptance also constitutes permission to the Promotion Parties to use winner's name and likeness for marketing purposes without further compensation or right of approval, unless prohibited by law. Promotion Parties are not responsible for lost or late mail, or for technical, hardware or software malfunctions, lost or unavailable network connections, or failed, incorrect, inaccurate, incomplete, garbled or delayed electronic communications whether caused by the sender or by any of the equipment or programming associated with or utilized in this sweepstakes, or by any human error which may occur in the processing of the entries in this sweepstakes. If, in the Sponsor's opinion, there is any suspected evidence of tampering with any portion of the promotion, or if technical difficulties compromise the integrity of the promotion, the Sponsor reserves the right to modify or terminate the sweepstakes in a manner deemed reasonable by the Sponsor, at the Sponsor's sole discretion. In the event a dispute arises as to the identity of a potentially winning online entrant, entries made by internet will be declared made by the name on the online entry form. All federal and state laws apply.

6. WINNERS LIST: For the names of the winners, available after May 1, 2010 send a self-addressed, stamped (#10) envelope to: The Princeton Review, 2010 College Hopes & Worries Survey Contest Winners, c/o Robert Franek, 2315 Broadway, New York, NY, 10024-4332

SPONSOR: The Princeton Review, Inc., New York, NY 10024.

College Hopes & Worries Survey 2010

www.PrincetonReview.com

Snail mail to Robert Franek, The Princeton Review, 2315 Broadway, New York, NY 10024
or fax to Robert Franek, 212-874-1754 or fill out online at PrincetonReview.com/go/survey

Name _____

Address (optional) _____

City / State / Zip _____

Daytime phone _____

E-mail address _____

I am ____ a parent of a student ____ a student applying to attend college beginning in

____ Spring or Fall 2010 ____ Spring or Fall 2011 ____ Later (indicate year:_____).

1 What would be your "dream" college? What college would you most like to attend (or see your child attend) if chance of being accepted or cost were not an issue?"

_____

2 How many colleges will you (your child) apply to?

____ 1 to 4

____ 5 to 8

____ 9 to 12

____ 13 or more

3 How would you rate the information and support you've received from your (your child's) school guidance counselor to help you through your (your child's) college application experience? (Choose one.)

____ Outstanding

____ Very good

____ Adequate

____ Fair

____ Poor

4 What has been, or do you think will be the toughest part of your (your child's) college application experience? (Choose one.)

____ Researching colleges and winnowing a list of schools to apply to

____ Taking admission and placement tests – the SAT, ACT, or APs

____ Completing the applications and getting everything in on time

____ Waiting for the acceptance/aid award letters and deciding which college to attend

5 What do you estimate your (or your child's) college degree will cost, including four years of tuition, room & board, fees, books and other expenses? (Choose one.)

____ More than $100,000

____ $75,000 to $100,000

____ $50,000 to $75,000

____ $25,000 to $50,000

____ Up to $25,000

6 How necessary will financial aid (education loans, scholarships or grants) be to pay for your (your child's) college education? (Choose one.)

____ Extremely

____ Very

____ Somewhat

____ Not at all

7 What's your biggest concern about applying to or attending college? (Choose one.)

____ Won't get into first-choice college

____ Will get into first-choice college, but won't have sufficient funds/financial aid to attend

____ Will attend a college I am (my child is) happy about, but will take on major loan debt to afford it

____ Will attend a college I (my child) may not be happy about

8 How would you gauge your stress level about the college application process? (Choose one.)

____ Very High

____ High

____ Average

____ Low

____ Very Low

9 Ideally, how far from home would you like the college you (your child) attends to be? (Choose one.)

____ 0 to 250 miles

____ 250 to 500 miles

____ 500 to 1,000 miles

____ 1,000 miles or more

10 When it comes to choosing which college you (or your child) will attend, which of the following do you think it is most likely to be? (Choose one.)

____ College with best academic reputation

____ College with best program for my (my child's) career interests

____ College that will be the most affordable

____ College that will be the best overall fit

11 If you (your child) had a way to compare colleges based on their commitment to environmental issues (from academic offerings to practices concerning energy use, recycling, etc.), how much would this contribute to your (your child's) decision to apply to or attend a school?

____ Strongly

____ Very much

____ Somewhat

____ Not much

____ Not at all

12 Has the economic downturn affected your (your child's) decisions about applying to or attending college? (Choose one)

____ Yes: Extremely

____ Yes: Very Much

____ Yes: Somewhat

____ No: Not at all

13 If your answer to the previous question was one of the three "Yes" choices, how would you describe the *major way* the economic downturn has affected your (your child's) college application decisions. (Choose one.)

____ Am applying to colleges with lower "sticker" prices.

____ Am applying to more 'financial aid safety' schools.

____ Am applying to colleges closer to home to save on travel costs.

Optional: What advice would you give to college applicants or parents of applicants going through this experience next year?

_____

_____

_____

_____

_____

_____

_____

_____

SAT® Vocab Challenge

for iPhone™ and iPod touch®

$4.99

Brought to you by the experts at The Princeton Review and Modality, Inc.

◀ From the home screen you can easily see your mastered words add up!

Swipe & flick ▶ through hundreds of words in just minutes

Available now in the Apple® App Store

250
need-to-know SAT vocab terms

4
fast-paced games to test your knowledge and build your skills

$4.99
A small price to pay for true vocab mastery

SAT mark is owned by the College Board. iPhone, iPod and Apple marks are owned by Apple, Inc. The Princeton Review is not affiliated with Princeton University.

www.PrincetonReview.com   **STUDY ANYWHERE**   www.modality.com